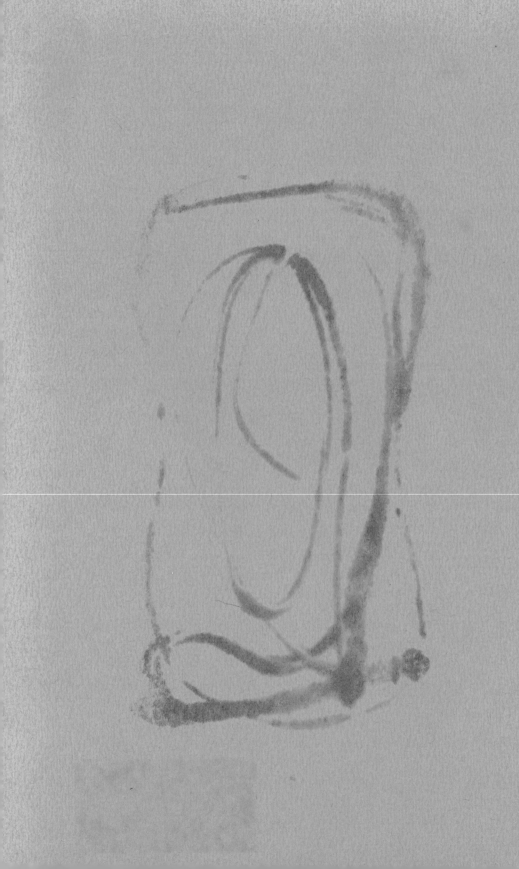

The
Poetical Works
of
Shelley

THE CAMBRIDGE EDITIONS

The Poetical Works of Elizabeth Barrett Browning
The Poetical Works of Robert Browning
The Poetical Works of Burns
The Poetical Works of Byron
The Poetical Works of Dryden
The Poetical Works of Oliver Wendell Holmes
The Poetical Works of Keats
The Poetical Works of Longfellow
The Poetical Works of Amy Lowell
The Poetical Works of Shelley
The Poetical Works of Tennyson
The Selected Works of Thoreau
The Poetical Works of Whittier
The Poetical Works of Wordsworth

The
Poetical Works
of
Shelley

Cambridge Edition

Edited by Newell F. Ford

Houghton Mifflin Company Boston

c 10 9 8 7 6 5 4 3 2

Library of Congress Cataloging in Publication Data

Shelley, Percy Bysshe, 1792–1822.
   The poetical works of Percy Bysshe Shelley.

   I. Ford, Newell F., 1912–   ed.
PR5402   1974c   821'.7   74-11133
ISBN 0-395-18461-4

Printed in the United States of America

EDITOR'S NOTE

The text of the poems is drawn from the Centenary Edition of Shelley, *The Complete Poetical Works*, edited by G. E. Woodberry in four volumes (1892), reduced to one volume in the Cambridge Edition (1901). A special feature of the new Cambridge Edition is the inclusion of five selections from Shelley's prose: *The Necessity of Atheism*, "Essay on Christianity," "On Love," "Una Favola," and "A Defence of Poetry." The text of the prose follows that of volumes 5–7 of *The Complete Works of Percy Bysshe Shelley*, edited by Roger Ingpen and Walter E. Peck (1926–1930). The Headnotes to the poems were prepared by Woodberry, who quotes liberally from Mrs. Shelley's indispensable Notes to the Poems (as found in her edition of *The Poetical Works* in four volumes, 1839). The Notes and Illustrations at the end of the volume are by Woodberry unless otherwise indicated. The present collection could be entitled The Complete Poetical Works were it not for the omission of some of the poems in the *Esdaile Notebook*, a collection of juvenile poems that has only recently come to light in its entirety. The full text of the *Notebook* is now available in two generously annotated editions.

NEWELL F. FORD

CONTENTS

CONTENTS

CONTENTS

NOTE ON BIOGRAPHY

The Introduction that follows is intended to be biographical, historical, and interpretative. It is a mental biography rather than a narration of outward events. For the clearest and fullest revelation of Shelley's mind and values, the reader is referred to his Letters and to Mrs. Shelley's Notes on the Poems. If he seeks a full-dress biography, the two volumes by Edward Dowden (1886) and the two volumes by Newman I. White (1940, revised in 1947) are notable for completeness, balance, and readability. There is also a one-volume condensation of Dowden's and of White's biographies. Edmund Blunden's *Shelley: A Life Story* (1946) is of comparable length and readability. George E. Woodberry's Biographical Sketch included in all earlier printings of the Cambridge Shelley condenses the life story into thirty attractively written pages.

All biographers draw upon the Letters, Mrs. Shelley's Notes, and several early biographies and reminiscences by Shelley's friends. Of these the briefest and probably the most balanced is the *Memoir* by Thomas L. Peacock (1855–1860). Whether Peacock's essential dryness of mind was the best vehicle for transmitting Shelley's intensity, idealism, and lyricism will always be debated. Thomas J. Hogg's *Life of Shelley* (1858) is a lively, anecdotally rich account of Shelley at Oxford, his expulsion from Oxford, and the years of his marriage with Harriet Westbrook. Unfortunately Hogg could not resist a tone of irony, almost of caricature, in his discussions of Shelley's idealism and unworldliness. Edward J. Trelawny knew Shelley and Byron during Shelley's last year of life in Italy and was in charge of the cremation after the drowning. His *Recollections of the Last Days of Shelley and Byron* (1858) is a vivid, sympathetic, and moving narrative. Sympathetic toward Shelley, that is; Trelawny saw less to admire in Byron. Both portraits seem "done from the life," and that will be enough for most readers. Those who seek a lifelike but comic treatment of Shelley's, Byron's, and Coleridge's life and ideals should turn to Peacock's delightful spoof of the Gothic novel, *Nightmare Abbey*.

NEWELL F. FORD

INTRODUCTION

Shelley's ashes lie in the quiet Protestant cemetery in Rome, a few paces from the simple grave of Keats. *Cor Cordium* is inscribed on his modest gravestone. The words were suggested by his friend Leigh Hunt. Trelawny added some verses from *The Tempest:*

> Nothing of him that doth fade,
> But doth suffer a sea-change
> Into something rich and strange.

Shelley was twenty-nine when he drowned in the sea off Leghorn in 1822. Keats was twenty-five when he died of consumption in Rome in 1821. Keats died fearing that his name "was writ on water." He could not know that Shelley's beautiful elegy, *Adonais,* would change the erasure of water to "a scroll of crystal, blazoning the name / Of Adonais!"

Regarding Keats, like himself, as an exiled victim of persecution, Shelley "in another's fate now wept his own" (*Adonais,* xxxiv). It was almost a prophecy that his own name would be "writ on water," literally not figuratively. His death came suddenly during a brief storm that swept down on a calm, glassy sea, sinking the sailing craft in which he and Edward Williams, his companion, had so delighted. He had evidently been reading Keats's last volume of poems when the storm struck, for the book was found doubled back in his pocket when his body was recovered ten days later. It looked as if he had hastily thrust the book into his pocket (there was a copy of Sophocles in the other pocket) when he awoke to the reality of the storm. Shelley had always loved boating, but he was not a very skillful or attentive sailor, and it was typical of him to be so absorbed in a book that he forgot outward circumstances.

Shelley had little fear of death. He did not swim, but he loved water and sailing. He and Williams had once capsized on the Arno River, and in a storm on Lake Geneva in 1816 when Byron had taken off his coat, preparing to swim for his life, Shelley, the nonswimmer, quietly grasped the locker rings, determined not to allow Byron to risk his life in saving Shelley's. Trelawny recounts an incident when he "was bathing one day in a deep pool in the Arno [River], and astonished the poet by performing a series of acquatic gymnastics."

On my coming out, whilst dressing, Shelley said mournfully: "Why can't I swim, it seems so very easy?" . . . He doffed his jacket and trousers, kicked off his shoes and socks, and plunged in, and there he lay stretched out on the bottom like a conger eel, not making the least effort or struggle to save himself. He would have been drowned if I had not instantly fished him out. When he recovered his breath, he said: "I always find the bottom of the well, and they say Truth lies there. In another minute I should have found it, and you would have found an empty shell."

In keeping with this is a story given in the second version of Trelawny's biography (*Records* . . . , 1878): On a calm evening he rowed his skiff, with Jane Williams and her two babies, far out on the Bay of Spezia. He was brooding and silent. Suddenly he brightened and exclaimed: "Now let us together solve the great mystery." Not a very imaginative or contemplative person, Jane dissuaded him: "No, thank you, not now; I should like my dinner first, and so would the children."

In a letter written shortly after Shelley's death, Leigh Hunt said: "Our dear friend was passionately fond of the sea, and has been heard to say that he would like it to be his death-bed."

There was no one to write an *Adonais* for Shelley. Leigh Hunt, his good friend who had been present with Byron and Trelawny at Shelley's cremation, wrote a brief account for English newspapers, calling him "the friend of the Universe," and a journal in Paris honored him as "a friend of the universe." The more powerful Tory press, long horrified by Shelley's views in religion and politics, called this "nauseating nonsense" and quoted passages from *Queen Mab* on the poet's views of God and monarchs. "Mr. Shelley is unfortunately but too well known for his infamous novels and poems. He openly professed himself an atheist," intoned *The Gentleman's Magazine*. *The Courier* gloated: "Shelley, the writer of some infidel poetry, has been drowned; *now* he knows whether there is a God or no." Leigh Hunt sought to answer *The Courier:* "the writer has the satisfaction of thinking the Divine Being will burn Mr. Shelley in everlasting flames for holding the same opinions as Spinoza and Bacon."

The New Monthly Magazine reminded its readers that Shelley's opinions "were opposed to a strong party in politics, which had he ranked on its side would have made the freedom and openness of those opinions the proof of virtuous honesty . . . Mr. Shelley has never been fairly treated as a poet; his works are full of wild beauties and original ideas . . . they display a richness of language and imagination rarely surpassed." *The Paris Monthly Review* had earlier protested that Shelley "has never had fair play . . . never was there a name associated with more black, poisonous, and bitter calumny than his . . . he had the misfortune to entertain, from his very earliest youth, opinions, both in religion and politics, diametrically opposed to established systems; and conceiving the happiness of mankind unattainable under the present forms of society, he set about the promulgation of his own theories with all the zeal and conviction of an apostle . . . the example of this audacity, in a youth of birth and fortune, not only aggravated the wrath of his theoretical opponents, but afforded them a butt against which they might securely launch their envenomed shafts . . . some invented gross libels upon his private character, . . . others . . . circulated atrocious innuendoes . . ."

The article went on to explain Shelley's perhaps too enthusiastic commitment to "the consummation of a political and moral Millennium" but insisted on "the benevolence of his heart." The penultimate paragraph justly balances Shelley's character and ideals against the fables and calumnies that beset his name — fables that even in the twentieth century have shown an attraction to minds that prefer caricature to truth:

> His pen, even when it was directed against his revilers, seemed to be guided by the hand of Love, and acrimonious expressions rarely fell from his lips. Could the reader, who has perhaps seen him held up in the pages of the *Quarterly Review* as a demon, have transported himself to the beautiful Bay of Lerici in the Gulf of Spezia, and beheld a fragile youth moving about upon the earth like a gentle spirit, imagining incessant plans for promoting

the welfare of the great circle of mankind, while he formed the happiness of the little one in which he moved, and recreating himself with music, literature, and poetic reveries while he floated . . . upon the blue waves of the Mediterranean — how little would he dream that he was gazing upon the traduced and calumniated Percy Bysshe Shelley ! . . .

To this we should add the words of Leigh Hunt in *The Liberal*, a journal sponsored by Byron and Hunt in Italy: "[Shelley was] one of the noblest of human beings, . . . who had more religion in his very differences with religion, than thousands of your church-and-state men . . ."

The truth of Hunt's assertion that Shelley was at heart a yearningly religious person, striving to supplant eighteenth-century scepticism with a transcendental explanation of man's place in the universe, has had to wait more than a hundred years for anything like full recognition. The recognition has come as the fierceness of sectarianism has subsided, enabling sober scholars of the twentieth century to perceive the deepest bent of Shelley's mind. Ironically, the recognition has come in a century more notable for the absence than the presence of deep religious conviction.

Was Shelley's personal character and behavior as "immoral" and infamous as the conservative journals would have their readers believe? And as prurient tourists, training their spyglasses on Byron and Shelley in Switzerland, thrilled to believe? Late in the century these fables were still capable of infecting Victorian minds, among them Matthew Arnold and Kingsley. Surprisingly, Mark Twain felt impelled to write a fervent defence of Shelley's first wife. W. S. Landor's account of his own error in succumbing to such tales is instructive. In 1828 he confessed:

Innocent and careless as a boy, [Shelley] possessed all the delicate feelings of a gentleman, all the discrimination of a scholar, and united, in just degrees, the ardour of the poet with the patience and forbearance of the philosopher. His generosity and charity went far beyond those of any man (I believe) at present in existence. He was never known to speak evil of any enemy, unless that enemy had done some grievous injustice to another; and he divided his income of only one thousand pounds, with the fallen and afflicted. This is the man against whom such clamours have been raised by the religious à la mode, and by those who live and lap under their tables: this is the man whom, from one false story about his former wife, I refused to visit at Pisa. I blush in anguish at my prejudice and injustice . . . He occupies the third place among the poets of our present age . . . for no other age since that of Sophocles has produced on the whole earth so many of such merit . . . and is incomparably the most elegant, graceful, and harmonious of prose-writers . . .

To this we may add two of Byron's descriptions. Not notable for generosity, Byron paid tribute to the selflessness and gentleness that all who knew Shelley agreed upon. First, in a letter to Murray in England in 1822: "You were all brutally mistaken about Shelley, who was without exception the best and least selfish man I ever knew. I never knew one that was not a beast in comparison." And in the next year, 1823, to Lady Blessington:

He was the most gentle, most amiable, and least worldly-minded person I ever met; full of delicacy, disinterested beyond all other men, and possessing a degree of genius, joined to a simplicity, as rare as it is admirable. He had formed to himself a *beau idéal* of all that is fine, high-minded, and noble, and he acted up to this ideal even to the very letter . . . I have seen nothing like him, and never shall again, I am certain.

As the century moved on, those who could "see Shelley plain" (Browning's phrase) slowly began to be heard. A group of Cambridge students sought to enlighten their contemporaries at Oxford in a debate in 1829. But the Oxford debaters complacently insisted that "if Shelley had been a great poet, we should have read him . . . ; but we have none of us done so." Some sixty years later their prejudice was still strong; they voted against a guinea subscription to the newly formed Shelley Society.

In the early 1830s the youthful Browning became a fervent disciple, hailing Shelley as the "Sun-treader — life and light be thine for ever; / . . . other bards arise, / But none like thee . . . / The air seems bright with thy past presence yet / . . . thou wert a star to men —" (*Pauline*). Tennyson, fresh from Cambridge, wrote in 1834: "Such writers as Byron and Shelley, however mistaken they may be, did yet give the world another heart and new pulses . . ." In 1837 William Bell Scott wrote to G. H. Lewes: "We both agree in loving Shelley." Many years later Tennyson said of his first discovery of Shelley: "*Alastor* was the first poem of his I read. I said 'This is what I want!' — and I still like it the best . . ." In his later years he grew more critical but still conceded: "as a writer of blank verse he was perhaps the most skillful of the moderns."

Despite the strictures on Shelley's ideas, his poetry, and his personal life by such eminent Victorians as Carlyle, Arnold, Kingsley, and Leslie Stephen, and despite the crudely violent attack by Jeaffreson in 1885, in 1870 W. M. Rossetti's *Memoir* began with unabashed praise: "To write the life of Shelley is (if I may trust my own belief) to write the life of the greatest English poet since Milton, or possibly since Shakespeare . . . To be a Shelley enthusiast has been the privilege of many a man in his youth, and he may esteem himself happy who cherishes the same feeling unblunted into the regions of middle or advanced age." In 1869 Swinburne, though valuing Shelley's devotion to liberty, saw his supreme gift as lyricism. He is "the master-singer of our modern poets." He "outsang all poets on record but some two or three throughout all time." Many years later, in an exhaustive three volume study of prosody (1910), George Saintsbury refused to allow his Tory politics to interfere with his judgment of Shelley's lyric achievement in *Prometheus:* "In all the long procession and pageantry of English poetry . . . , nothing has ever presented itself, and nothing, I think, will present itself in such a combination of prosodic beauty and variety as this" (III, 108–11).

Some gauge of the growing interest in Shelley may be seen in the fact that the middle and late Victorian age, undeterred by the disparagements and the attacks, "produced more than a dozen biographies, scores of editions, and hundreds of critical essays" (White, II, 411). In the twentieth century the work went steadily onward, though there was an onslaught from a new quarter: T. E. Hulme, T. S. Eliot, F. R. Leavis, and the "New Critics." Several new editions of the poems, the letters, and the prose appeared, one of them comprising ten volumes. To these were added new biographies and countless studies of Shelley's thought, symbolism, and imagery. The student new to Shelley will be surprised to discover that there are at least two books devoted solely to the interpretation of *Prometheus* and two editions of this poem with full *apparatus criticus*, still unsatisfying to many scholars. One study, devoted solely to Shelley's Platonism, runs to 671 pages. Two complete editions of the juvenile poems in the *Esdaile Notebook*, carefully annotated, appeared in the 1960s. Meanwhile the Carl Pforzheimer Library, with great expense and exemplary thoroughness, is giving us a series of elegant and capacious volumes of Shelleyana in *The Shelley Circle*.

*

To go back now to the main cause of the attacks on Shelley He was always a champion of the oppressed, and a staunch but nonviolent proponent of liberty. It is this "revolutionary" aspect of his thought that, with scattered exceptions, has been the chief source of his aspersion. When he wrote the ardent defence of the aspersed Keats in *Adonais*, he was conforming to a pattern easy to discern throughout his life and writings: that he repeatedly came to the aid of victims of persecution. It was largely for this reason that he married Harriet Westbrook when she threw herself on his mercies. When he wrote "Epipsychidion" in 1821, a few months before he composed *Adonais*, he was moved by the plight of Emilia Viviani, condemned to her convent-prison by parental autocracy. His warmly generous and sympathetic nature, coupled with his own repeated experiences of intolerance, abuse, and persecution, made him keenly susceptible to such appeals.

Keats had been attacked for his reputed esthetic sins and for his association with Leigh Hunt, Shelley's friend who was anathema to the conservatives because his newspaper, *The Examiner*, supported the liberal (to the Tories, radical) and reform movements of the day. Keats was not considered dangerous, however. Shelley was. Had he not shown himself to be unalterably opposed to monarchy, aristocracy, Christianity in its institutionalized form, priestarchy, and all forms of privilege, the marital institution itself, and "custom" in general? In the aftermath of the French Revolut ion, an era of fear and repression in England, Shelley's crusade against privilege, social and economic injustice, and all forms of intolerance, embodied in language far more impassioned (at least in the early *Queen Mab*) than Godwin's *Political Justice* (1793), beckoned to the deprived masses and threatened the comfort and security of the enjoyers of power and privilege.

The horror at Shelley's "atheism" (agnosticism would be a more accurate term, but the word did not then exist) and radicalism has not disappeared in the twentieth century. In the 1930s T. S. Eliot, declared royalist, classicist, and Anglo-Catholic, spoke of Shelley's "adolescent," "shabby," and "repellent" ideas. Other critics of conservative political and religious persuasion have found it difficult to give Shelley a fair hearing. Their strictures have been, it should be noted, part of a campaign to derogate nineteenth-century poetry and all poetry beginning with Milton, while exalting the "Metaphysical" poetry of the seventeenth century along with French Symbolist poetry of the late nineteenth century. One of their favorite whipping boys has been Shelley. As Edmund Wilson wrote in 1931, "It is as much as one's life is worth nowadays, among young people, to say an approving word for Shelley or a dubious one about Donne." I. A. Richards' insight was little heeded when in 1934 he wrote: "Our 'Neo-Classic' age is repeating those feats of its predecessor which we least applaud. It is showing a fascinating versatility in travesty. And the poets of the 'Romantic' period provide for it . . . effigies to be shot at because what they represent is no longer understood."

Though in 1972 Oxford invited students to a summer conference on Shelley, it is worth remembering that in the 1870s the headmaster of Eton, Shelley's school, declined to receive a bust of Shelley for the school. In the 1880s the president of Harvard University hesitated to accept the manuscript of Shelley's "The Cloud," though that poem has no political or religious overtones. In the 1930s a group of prisoners in a Milwaukee jail were reported to be reading *Queen Mab* aloud in order to convert fellow prisoners to Communism. In 1945 *The Shelley Legend*, a book-length attack, revived many of the old fictions about Shelley's reprehensible personal life as well as his opinions, requiring another book in 1951 by three noted Shelley scholars to expose its errors (*An Examination of the Shelley Legend*).

In recent years, it may be hoped, the need to impugn the personal lives of and to be outraged by the opinions of those who dissent in politics or religion has declined. Yet for more than a century it was unthinkable that Shelley should be buried in the Poets' Corner in Westminster Abbey, or even that a memorial tablet might be placed there. Byron was specifically interdicted as late as 1924. In the late 1960s, however, plaques were quietly installed for Shelley, Keats, and Byron. Several of Shelley's most treasured Notebooks have come to rest in the Bodleian Library at Oxford, the university which summarily expelled him for his authorship (or coauthorship) of *The Necessity of Atheism* in 1811.

The manuscript of *The Necessity of Atheism* now reposes in an American University library, at a cost of $9300 — not without an outcry, too late, from the legislators. In the new edition of *The Oxford Book of Religious Verse* Shelley, like Thomas Hardy, has found a place. If one considers how many poems and passages in Shelley, even in *Queen Mab* (see the rapt apostrophe to "Necessity! thou mother of the world!" — IV, 197 ff., 146 ff.) are hymns, prayers, and adorations, one wonders why sectarianism has been so persistently hostile to Shelley's devotional and worshipful form of imaginative religion.

Can it be said that Shelley's poetry has been instrumental in twentieth-century man's gradual emergence from intolerance in the area of religion and politics? *Post hoc ergo propter hoc?* No one knew better than Shelley, steeped as he was in eighteenth-century sceptical examinations of the concept of causality and in the problematicalness of all knowledge, that for visionaries and reformers the wish is often father to the thought. Nevertheless it was one of Shelley's deepest faiths that the "Pythian enthusiasm" of poetry would spread enlightenment and tolerance and charity, filling "the Universe with glorious beams, and kill[ing] / Error, the worm, with many a sun-like arrow / Of its reverberated lightning" ("Epipsychidion," 162 ff.). Error, the worm, was the Pythian monster slain by Apollo, and Shelley (especially when in sanguine mood) viewed the poet as a sunlike radiance dispersing "the contagion of the world's slow stain" (*Adonais*, 356).

Yet in the Victorian period Kingsley accused Shelley of preaching "the worship of uncleanness." Matthew Arnold, horrified by Shelley's two marriages and by Mary's and Shelley's failure to show moral indignation over the presence of Claire Clairmont in their household (she was Mary's half-sister and Byron's mistress, and was then with child by Byron), could find no word except "the French word, *sale*" to express his disgust. At one point Carlyle exclaimed that Shelley "was just a scoundrel, and ought to have been hanged."

Faced with hostilities and "righteous" misconstructions such as these, one wonders how Shelley could have gone on hoping that poetry might reconstitute society, advance the cause of enlightenment, spread the gospel of love, and alter individual human conduct. Are poets, as his *Defence of Poetry* and *Philosophical View of Reform* grandly claim, "the unacknowledged legislators of the world"? Are poets "creative evolutionists," to borrow a phrase from Shaw?

We know the advice that Keats offered Shelley on this subject. Disbelieving in perfectibility (and perhaps even in melioration), Keats advised Shelley to give up his passion for humanitarian causes and devote himself to beauty: "You might curb your magnanimity, and load every rift of your subject with ore." As Keats had written earlier: "with a great poet the sense of Beauty overcomes every other considera- tion . . ." (72). Keats wanted the poet to be the "camelion-poet" [sic], striving like Shakespeare for dramatic empathy and personal detachment. He could have joined Shelley in writing, "Didactic poetry is my abhorrence" (Preface to *Frometheus Un- bound*). But the meaning would have been different — Keats felt that the poet should stay free of efforts to alter governments or religions or opinion.

Shelley, on the contrary, confessed that he had "a passion for reforming the world" (Preface to *Frometheus*), and by abhorring didacticism he meant that his poetry did not offer "a reasoned system" and was not aimed at "the direct enforcement of reform," but at the presentation of "beautiful idealisms of moral excellence; aware that *until the mind can love, and admire, and trust, and hope, and endure, reasoned principles* of moral conduct are seeds cast upon the highway of life which the unconscious passenger tram- ples into dust . . ." (*ibid.* — italics added). Not a few twentieth-century minds, some of them psychotherapists, have come to similar conclusions.

It should be emphasized that Shelley was always opposed to anger, hatred, revenge, and violence in effecting reform. In the juvenile *Queen Mab*, it is true, he did not, as was his wont elsewhere, specifically warn against hatred of monarchs and other oppres- sors. He soon came to see, however, that the eradication of kings and institutions would not suddenly usher in the Golden Age. Reform could only come *gradually*, as society was leavened by the slow spread of enlightenment from "the most refined imaginations" (Preface to *Prometheus*). But the establishment did not so read him. Unable to deny Shelley's genius, their fear redoubled as they imagined the revolutionary influence of his doctrines.

Were they wrong? *Queen Mab* became the virtual Bible of the Owenites, making their first experiments in pacific socialism. It had a strong appeal to the working classes and made its contribution to the massive Chartist movement in the 1830s. Friedrich Engels, friend and collaborator of Karl Marx, is reported to have begun a translation of *Queen Mab*. At the end of the century, Shaw confessed how much his own socialism owed to Shelley and deliberately taunted the respectable Victorian members of the newly formed Shelley Society for their hypocrisy in honoring Shelley the lyric poet and ignoring Shelley the reformer. Meanwhile, Edward Dowden's excellent biography (1886) chose not to emphasize Shelley's central concern with reform. In 1940 Newman I. White wrote: "He was perhaps the greatest radical voice in poetry since Lucretius."

"Until the mind can love, and admire, and trust . . . ," Shelley had written in the Preface to *Frometheus*, "reasoned principles" have little efficacy in inducing men to better action. Like Wordsworth and Coleridge, Shelley discerned that our motivations are bound up with our feelings and can therefore only be reached by some appeal to those feelings. "I know no book," wrote Wordsworth, "or system of moral philosophy written with sufficient power to melt into our affections, to incorporate itself with the blood and vital juices of our minds, and thence to have an influence worth our notice" on ethical action (fragmentary Moral Essay). Shelley hoped to kindle the imagination and activate man's capacity for disinterested love and compassion. One cannot read poems like "Alastor," the "Hymn to Intellectual Beauty," and *Prometheus* without such kindling. Rational appeals to man's moral sense, like the exhortations in sermons and homilies, had been tried for centuries, but had had little effect on human conduct. It is not "for want of admirable doctrines that men hate, and despise, and censure, and deceive, and subjugate one another," as Shelley declared in *The Defence of Poetry*.

The passage continues: "Poetry acts in another and diviner manner. . . . The great secret of morals is love; or a going out of our own nature, and an identification of ourselves with the beautiful which exists in thought, action, or person, not our own. A man, to be greatly good, must imagine intensely and comprehensively; . . . the pains and pleasures of his species must become his own. The great instrument of moral good is the imagination; and poetry administers to the effect by acting upon the cause." Thus Love and Imagination become all but synonymous terms for Shelley; both are outgoing, sympathetic, empathetic. Both are creative. The passage from "Epipsychidion" previously quoted says the same thing in more resplendent imagery — imagery drawn from the Apollo-myth and from Newton's analysis of light: Love acts "like thy light, / Imagination! . . . [it] . . . kills Error, the worm, with many a sunlike arrow / Of its reverberated lightning" (162–69).

We find the heart of Shelley's message and mission in any of the three sentences quoted, from the Preface to *Prometheus*, from *The Defence of Poetry*, and from "Epipsychidion." It should be remembered, however, that he wrote all these Credos when in hopeful and confident mood. Perhaps no poet was given to wider swings of the emotional pendulum. When we recall his exile and ceaseless persecution and vilification, we understand his fear that *Prometheus*, "the best thing I ever wrote," might sell no more than twenty copies. "Epipsychidion," accordingly, was intended only "for the esoteric few."

When we come upon the reference in *Prometheus* to "evil, the immedicable plague" (II, iv, 101), when we recall the painful vision of humanity chained to and ground down by the Car of Life in "The Triumph of Life," the visions of the void in "Alastor" and "Lift not the painted veil . . . ," the despairing final stanza of the "Ode to Liberty," and the two stanzas of somber pessimism in the radiantly prophetic chorus concluding *Hellas*, we understand the deep sadness and discouragement that shadowed Shelley's most sanguine hopes for mankind. We understand the piercing sadness of many of his lyrics, and why in his last letter to Trelawny, not long before his death, he wrote, "I should regard it as a great kindness if you could procure me a small quantity" of prussic acid. "I would give any price for this medicine, . . . I confess it would be a great comfort to me to hold in my possession that golden key to the chamber of perpetual rest. I need not tell you," he added, "I have no intention of suicide at present." (June 18, 1822).

Though Shelley has been accused of "fall[ing] upon the thorns of life" too self-pityingly, it would be truer to recognize his generalizing of the immemorial sadness of the human race, to remember that his nerves were "formed sensitive to an unexampled degree" (Mary Shelley), and that the description of the Maniac in "Julian and Maddalo" is no less true of the poet himself: "*Me* — who am as a nerve o'er which do creep / The else unfelt oppressions of this earth" (449–50). As the oracular Moneta said to Keats when he began to feel guilty for devoting himself to the poetry of romance and bliss: "None can usurp this height . . . / But those to whom the miseries of the world / Are misery, and will not let them rest" ("The Fall of Hyperion," I, 147–49).

Not less important to remember is Shelley's Promethean courage and strength. True, at the grave of Keats he imagined himself as a "companionless" and "frail Form"

(*Adonais*, xxxi). But the next stanza reminds us of his inner core of strength: "A pard-like Spirit beautiful and swift — / A Love in desolation masked . . ." Love is the reality, "a *Power*" girt round "with weakness." The weakness and the desolation are "veils" and "masks" only, destined to dissolve in time.

The "weight of the superincumbent hour" took its emotional toll of this poet of dedication. At times he felt like "a splendour among shadows" ("Lift not . . ."). It was better to be "deluded by [a] generous error" and a "sacred thirst of doubtful knowledge" than to be one of "those meaner spirits that dare to abjure [the] dominion" of "that Power which strikes the luminaries of the world with . . . too exquisite a perception of its influences" (Preface to "Alastor"). For "man is a being of high aspirations . . . whose 'thoughts wander through eternity.' . . . Whatever may be his true and final destination, there is a spirit within him at enmity with nothingness and dissolution" (Essay "On Life"). At enmity also with lovelessness and intolerance and injustice, he might have added. Idealists and humanitarians must take the risk. Shelley never shrank from the risk or compromised. It must have been this resilient, Promethean spirit within him which prompted his remark to Trelawny: "I always go on until I am stopped, and I never am stopped."

We have spoken of the wide swings of the emotional pendulum between hope and discouragement. Some of the discouragement derived not from the entrenched power of the establishment or from the drag of human inertia, but from Shelley's own intellectual honesty. Few poets have been so keenly aware of the nature of mind and reality and illusion as this poet-philosopher. Witness his prose essays on the subject, and such poems as "Alastor," the "Hymn to Intellectual Beauty," "Mont Blanc," and *Prometheus*. Indeed, as Mary Shelley tells us, "Shelley possessed two remarkable qualities of intellect — a brilliant imagination and a logical exactness of reason. His inclinations led him . . . almost alike to poetry and metaphysical discussions . . . he said that he deliberated at one time whether he should dedicate himself to poetry or metaphysics . . ." (Note on *The Revolt of Islam*).

Few poets have been so deeply interested in the problem of knowledge or so ceaselessly inquisitive as to the origin and end of consciousness and the nature of life itself. "Death is the veil which those who live call life" is one of his most memorable formulations of the mystery that human mentality is powerless to resolve (*Prometheus* III, iii, 13). If we strive to lift the veil that screens our mortal vision from ultimate reality, we may discover a world of Platonic ideality or we may discover a sheer vacancy into which mind projects both its hopes and fears: "behind [the veil], lurk Fear / And Hope, twin Destinies; who ever weave / Their shadows, o'er the chasm, sightless and drear" ("Lift not . . ."). When Hope overcomes Fear we may discover, or seem to discover, the world of "the One" — radiant, immaterial, and timeless, "the abode where the Eternal are." But this abode, Shelley well knew, might be figurative and fictional only — a spatial hypostatization of what ought to be, not what is.

Shelley was "a natural Platonist," and he translated several of Plato's dialogues. But he was also a Humeian sceptic and empiricist. He yearned for the absolute, and in *Prometheus* the oracular voice of Demogorgon comes near to establishing Love as a cosmic absolute: "What to bid speak / Fate, Time, Occasion, Chance, and Change? To these / All things are subject but eternal Love." Yet the same oracular voice had a moment before said that "the deep truth is imageless" (II, iv, 114–20). Most commentators have felt that "imageless" suggests "unknowable," not merely nonimageable. Asia herself, to whom these answers are given, concludes: "of such truths / Each to itself must be the oracle" (122–23).

Speaking epistemologically, the problem is unsolvable. Vision and hope may overleap the chasm of the unknowable, or may people it with "cold hopes [that] swarm like worms within our living clay" (*Adonais*, 351). Language itself is part of the problem. Whether we persuade ourselves that all things are subject to eternal Love or to Intellectual Beauty or to "that Light whose smile kindles the Universe, / That Beauty in which all things work and move, / That Benediction which the eclipsing Curse / Of birth can quench not, that sustaining Love . . ." (*Adonais*, 478 ff.), language is deceptive, hope and imagination are deceptive as well as creative — or miscreative. Words, especially our "metaphysical" words, are "frail spells — whose uttered charm might not avail to sever, / From all we hear and all we see, / Doubt, chance, and mutability" ("Hymn . . . ," 29–31).

Impelled by a yearning for a realm of changeless perfection, Shelley knew that he might be indulging "the desire of the moth for the star." Even in his most ecstatic flights he remained poignantly aware of the limits of human cognition, the problem of causality, the indeterminable power of the will, and the intricacy and mystery of mind itself. "The mind [is] a wilderness of intricate paths, wide as the universe . . . ," he wrote in his notebook (quoted in Mary Shelley's Note to *Prometheus*). In his "Speculations on Metaphysics" he takes up the subject again and reminds us that the mind is a labyrinth within a cavern, or a ceaselessly flowing river, incapable of apprehending ultimate reality:

> But thought can with difficulty visit the intricate and winding chambers which it inhabits. It is like a river whose rapid and perpetual stream flows outwards; . . . The caverns of the mind are obscure, and shadowy; or pervaded with a lustre, beautifully bright indeed, but shining not beyond their portals.

The cave-cavern-labyrinth image is a recurring symbol in Shelley's poetry, as is the river of the mind and the stream of experience (see especially "Alastor," "Mont Blanc," *Prometheus*, and "The Witch of Atlas"). Sometimes the caves are "fountain-lighted" or "pervaded with lustre," but darkness and incertitude shadow their most radiant constructions, in language or in vision.

Thus he could write a hymn that is also a prayer to Intellectual Beauty, "O awful Loveliness"; he could pray to the West Wind, a kind of *Animus Mundi*, to make him its inspired lyre; he might exclaim in exalted moments that eternal Love or the One is the supreme Power in the universe, setting Doubt and Chance and Mutability at nought. In sadder moments he concedes that "Nought may endure but Mutability." Words are "frail spells," nets to catch the wind. Reality, whether infinite or finite, forever eludes them, stays or flows beyond their reach. "The winged words on which my soul would pierce / Into the height of Love's rare Universe, / Are chains of lead around its flight of fire" ("Epipsychidion," 588–90). More simply, in the language of prose:

> How vain is it to think that words can penetrate the mystery of our being. Rightly used they may make evident our ignorance to ourselves, and this is much. For what are we? Whence do we come? and whither do we go? Is birth the commencement, is death the conclusion of our being? (Essay "On Life")

In the same vein, but more pessimistically, the Poet in "Alastor" reflects upon a rivulet that symbolizes the course of human life from birth to death. The source of the river is a "searchless fountain" and is "inaccessibly profound." Dark or gleaming, the river images his life, says the Poet, but it offers no answer to "where these living thoughts reside" when the mortal span is ended. The rivulet becomes a river, enters a "wintry" ravine beneath "barren pinnacles," and at last plunges over a precipice into an "immeasurable void" (494–514, 569). Eventually the Poet dies "at peace, and faintly smiling" in the embrace of Nature. But his cold body has "no sense, no motion, no divinity." The "bright stream" of consciousness is "quenched for ever" (645, 659–71).

If one turns to Shelley's prose essay, "On a Future State," he finds a sober weighing of the evidence for and against personal immortality, with a sceptical conclusion: "if there is a future life, it lies beyond the experience of the human understanding." The source of such a faith is emotional: the "desire to be for ever as we are; the reluctance to a violent and unexperienced change . . ." The arguments supporting futurity "persuade . . . only those who desire to be persuaded."

If one part of Shelley's mind could see clearly the source of an illusion sustained through many centuries, another part of his spirit longed to be persuaded otherwise. His early letters are deeply concerned with the question, the "Hymn to Intellectual Beauty" includes a fervent prayer that this Spirit "depart not — lest the grave should be, / Like life and fear, a dark reality" (47–48). *Adonais*, with its lofty apotheosis of the dead Keats, is taken by many readers as an assurance of something like a resurrection. The problem is whether the apotheosis (xlii–lv) is literal or figurative, what ought to be rather than what is. "He wakes or sleeps with the enduring dead," the poem says simply. In *Prometheus*, as we have seen, the unsolvable enigma is beautifully stated: "Death is the veil which those who live call life; / They sleep and it is lifted." (Cf. the sonnet, "Lift not the painted veil . . .") Readers who know their Shelley do not make the mistake of construing this lifted veil as the promise of an entrance into a new state of consciousness. Shelley never forgets that such questions are "searchless," "secret," "mysterious," "unfathomable."

The Platonist and the sceptic were forever at war in this poet, and he was too honest to silence the sceptic. Meanwhile he could not still his yearning for "the white radiance of eternity," where the phenomenal world of the many and the mutable should yield to the transcendent and changeless world of "the One." That is why in his essay "On Life" the pendulum swings from the confession of the illusoriness of words and the answerlessness of the ultimate questions to a declaration of Promethean bravery: "man is a being of high aspirations, 'looking before and after,' whose 'thoughts wander through eternity,' disclaiming alliance with transience and decay . . . Whatever may be his true and final destination, there is a spirit within him at enmity with nothingness and dissolution." It is better, idealists must believe, to be "deluded by [a] generous error" and "a sacred thirst" than to be "morally dead, . . . selfish, blind, torpid" (Preface to "Alastor").

In the same way it is better, especially if one is a poet with a strong devotional bent, to be an apologist for poetry than a disparager of it. That is why Shelley wrote his ardent *Defence of Poetry* when Peacock lightly and wittily laughed at the anomaly and uselessness of poetry in an age of science and reason (*The Four Ages of Poetry*). Shelley always defended victims of aspersion or persecution and perhaps, as in his splendid exaltation of Keats in *Adonais*, he overstated the claims of poetry in order to counteract Peacock's aspersion. "Julian is rather serious," Shelley once wrote of himself (Preface to "Julian and Maddalo"). He took a serious and high view of poetry. It was anything but the toy and idle recreation that Peacock had described. Indeed, it might serve mankind, in a time when the old religion and the old morality were losing ground, as a surrogate for religion and an incitement to virtue. Poetry is the gift of Apollo, the original light-giver. It is the vessel of the true Promethean fire:

> What were virtue, love, patriotism, friendship, — what were the scenery of this beautiful universe which we inhabit; what were our consolations on this side of the grave — and what were our aspirations beyond it, if poetry did not ascend to bring light and fire from those eternal regions where the owl-winged faculty of calculation dare not ever soar? (*Defence of Poetry*)

Then comes the celebrated simile of the original creative moment:

> . . . for the mind in creation is as a fading coal, which some invisible influence, like an inconstant wind, awakens to transitory brightness; this power arises from within, like the colour of a flower which fades and changes as it is developed, and the conscious portions of our nature are unprophetic either of its approach or its departure. Could this influence be durable in its original purity and force, it is impossible to predict the greatness of the results; but when composition begins, inspiration is already on the decline, and the most glorious poetry that has ever been communicated to the world is probably a feeble shadow of the original conceptions of the poet.

It may be objected that not all poets create in this way. Few venture to hold such high claims for poetry. But Shelley is clearly speaking from his own experience. Notice that he does not say that poetry has a divine or empyreal origin, though he would like to believe this, and suggests it, at least figuratively, in other passages. He says that the invisible influence, the original creative impulse, "arises from within." Poetry is thus "our consolation on this side of the grave."

It is this constant tension between hope and fear, faith and doubt — man's "twin Destinies" — along with Shelley's unwavering intellectual honesty, that should commend him to readers in the twentieth century. If fear and hope are our twin Destinies, they are also our tormenting, Jupiterian Furies and our reassuring Promethean "subtle and fair spirits / Whose homes are the dim caves of human thought, . . . they behold / Beyond that twilight realm, as in a glass, / The future" (*Prometheus* I, 658 ff.).

More pessimistically, Hope and Fear are our *Alastors*, our evil geniuses or avenging furies. We are cursed as well as blessed with Hope. It "strikes the luminaries of the world with sudden darkness and extinction, by awakening them to too exquisite a perception of its influences" (Preface to "Alastor"). Is there any escape from the internecine conflict, the "grievous feud" as Keats called it? In the millennium perhaps, or in some postmortal or transmortal realm of ideality, but more likely in death. In death Adonais found release from "that unrest which men miscall delight" (354), from "the contagion of the world's slow stain" (356). It is death that finally releases the Poet in "Alastor" from the "twin Destinies" of Hope and Fear: "Hope and despair, / The torturers, slept; . . . till he lay breathing there / At peace, and faintly smiling" (639–45).

*

Having said this much about Shelley's mental world, it may be well to look at a few aspects of the twentieth century that make it difficult for some persons to read Shelley with sympathy and understanding. The poetry of prophetic vision is not in vogue today. Nor is it usual to hold that poets can be "creative evolutionists" or "unacknowledged legislators of the world." Our experience of war and its aftermath in the twentieth century has resulted in a literature of wastelands and futilitarianism, or a retreat into traditional religion, or a limitation of poetry to subjects without political or philosophical implications. In many quarters the faith ushered in by the scientific method and the early discoveries of nature's laws, the hope emerging from the age of the Enlightenment, has been replaced by an emphasis on human debility, neurosis, and Original Sin. In these quarters any form of idealism or faith in progress is looked upon with suspicion.

We have been told that we are Hollow Men dwelling in a Wasteland of the spirit, from which the intervention of divine grace is the only solution possible. It could be argued that Shelley was vividly aware of the wastelands of the human spirit (cf. "Alastor," "Lift not the painted veil . . . ," "The Masque of Anarchy," "The Triumph of Life," and other poems registering doubt and discouragement). But Shelley did not seek refuge in a traditional or outworn creed. Despite this he found a gospel of his own to share with his fellowmen — a gospel in many respects comparable to the gospel of Christ. Witness *Prometheus*, the "Essay on Christianity," and his continual urging of the value of disinterested love.

Shelley declined to assume that all men are ineradicably tainted with Original Sin, rescuable only by divine grace. Grace must come, if at all, out of the wheel of burning fire, out of the "crag-like agony" of the human heart (*Prometheus* IV, 557 ff.). In this respect his Prometheus bears not a few resemblances to Christ, even to the crucifixion — a resemblance of which Shelley was fully aware.

> Love, from its awful throne of patient power
> In the wise heart, from the last giddy hour
>   Of dread endurance, from the slippery, steep,
> And narrow verge of crag-like agony, springs
> And folds over the world its healing wings.
>   (*Prometheus* IV, 557 ff.)

It had taken Prometheus (or humanity) centuries of patient suffering to reach this pain-earned wisdom and compassion. External "thrones," the passage reminds us, no longer exist. The human heart is the throne of love in this slowly won victory over hatred, revenge, defiance, envy, suspicion, lovelessness, and all the other impulses urging hostility and aggression, self-hatred, self-distrust, fear, and futilitarianism. These "Jupiterian" impulses are also internal, ascending "thrones" of their own when we allow them to prevail, either in the individual or in society.

Modern psychotherapy will confirm many of Shelley's insights into the complex nature of the ego. Nevertheless the form in which Shelley presents his gospel may make some persons uncomfortable, for it invites them to feel guilty about their too tame surrender to the powers that govern them, both within and without. It keeps reminding them that human wills and human ideals are not impotent. As Shaw rightly discerned, Shelley "is still forcing us to make up our minds" on all crucial questions. If we accept that challenge we may lose our peace of mind.

We are not accustomed in the twentieth century to give ourselves easily to new gospels. All scientific and philosophical ideals may be, as William James once said, "altars to unknown gods" ("The Dilemma of Determinism"). But altar-building is not popular in our disparate, desperate, discordant, strident, arhythmic, often ugly and dreary age of technology. Such an age seems strangely out of key with Shelleyan vision and Shelleyan language. What poet today dares to be a seer, especially an optimistic one? What poet today dares to be a missionary, or to write in an incantatory style?

If we take a longer perspective, we know that fashions in language and in tone change from age to age. Likewise, estimates of the power of the human will, of love, of imagination vary from age to age and individual to individual. Despite a second World War, defeatism has ceased to be the dominant tone in our society or in our literature. Witness the dedicated conservationists and ecologists, the movement for civil rights and for the eradication of racism and of discrimination between the sexes. How many of the proponents of civil rights have read Shelley's soberly reasoned and temperate prose tract, "The Philosophical View of Reform" (not published until 1920, and little known today except to specialists, though it ought to be known to all)? How many of the proponents of women's liberation are familiar with Shelley's prevision of women "kind, *free*, and sincere," *the equals of men*, women "frank, beautiful, and kind . . . / From custom's evil taint exempt and pure; . . . / *Looking emotions once they feared to feel, / And changed to all which once they dared not be*" (*Prometheus* III, iv, 46–50, 131–63 — italics added)?

The faith that human effort and willed commitment can do something to meliorate man's condition, the belief that values and ideals can affect human conduct have not vanished from the world of the twentieth century. We have mentioned the efforts of conservationists and liberationists, and we could add the long, agonized protest against the war in Vietnam, the resolve "to hope till Hope creates / From its own wreck the thing it contemplates" (*Prometheus* IV, 573–74).

Ideals today are seen as dwelling not in the empyrean but within the human psyche, potentials waiting to be actualized, like Shelley's "subtle and fair spirits, / Whose homes are the dim caves of human thought / . . . they behold / . . . as in a glass, / The future." In *Prometheus* these "subtle and fair spirits" of human thought slowly but surely deprive the hating, destructive Furies, dwelling in the same caves of human thought, of their power (I, 444–663).

It is possible that the Furies will regain that power. Shelley the historical realist foresaw that possibility. The Furies are but variant forms of the oppressive Jupiter — or of the Freudian, subrationalist id — who is ceaselessly opposed by the Prometheus who has evolved from defiance to disinterested love and compassion. Should the Prometheus in humanity be subjugated once again by the Jupiter within (and without), the recipe for dethroning Jupiter is written out in the closing lines of Act IV of *Prometheus* (554 ff.). The recipe is not a prophecy of a final and lasting victory. Shelley the student of history is aware that history moves in cycles, that eras of liberation and enlightenment are followed by darker eras in which man slips back into the pit (see "The Philosophical View of Reform" or the "Ode to Liberty" or "Hellas").

The climbing out of the pit (the returning from exile, as it were, exile from man's better self) will not be easy. It will not be accomplished by a Messiah, earthly or divine. It will not come from a divine bestowal of "grace." It will be accomplished by the steadfast devotion of mortal men, "costing not less than everything" (T. S. Eliot, "Little Gidding").

The cost will be the "crag-like agony" of the human heart (*Prometheus* IV, 560). That metaphor (Prometheus was chained to an icy crag in the Caucasus) incarnates the whole of the Promethean and Shelleyan ideal and ordeal. It is a symbol of what man can accomplish for himself and his fellows — if he is strong, patient, enduring, and has learned the great mystery of disinterested love. He must be, like Shelley's Prometheus and Tennyson's Ulysses, "firm in will / To strive, to seek, to find, and not to yield." He must be willing

> To suffer woes which Hope thinks infinite;
> To forgive wrongs darker than death or night;
>   To defy Power, which seems omnipotent;
> To love and bear; to hope till Hope creates
> From its own wreck the thing it contemplates;
>   Neither to change, nor falter, nor repent;
> This, like thy glory, Titan, is to be
> Good, great and joyous, beautiful and free;
> This is alone Life, Joy, Empire, and Victory.
>   (*Prometheus* IV, 570–78)

If mankind, or "the sacred few" (*Triumph of Life*, 128), prove equal to this challenge, then it is not an exaggeration to hold that poets are, or may be, "the mirrors of the gigantic shadows which futurity casts upon the present" (*Defence of Poetry*).

Though it is tempting to end on this brave note and to regard Shelley as a kind of Isaiah of the modern world, we should remember that Shelley was many Shelleys. His "passion for reforming the world" was often uppermost and led to some of his most splendid visions of human possibility — the close of the "Ode to the West Wind" or the *Defence of Poetry*, for example. But what makes this reform-minded and visionary poet fascinating, especially to readers in the twentieth century, is that unlike most reformers he was not single-minded. He was not a zealot. He was temperate and good humored in listening to opposing opinion. As Peacock, a man of rational and satiric bent who did not share Shelley's sanguine views of human capability (he once called Shelley a "transcendental eleutherarch"), reported: "Indeed, one of the great charms of intercourse with him was the perfect good humour and openness to conviction with which he responded to opinions opposed to his own."

In fact Shelley was his own most searching opponent. His awareness of the limitations of human cognition, of the possible illusoriness of all knowledge, of the role that hope and desire and imagination play in determining our knowledge and our faiths, was openly confessed both in his verse and in his prose. It is this ceaseless intellectual honesty that produces the tension seldom absent from his poetry, the tension between the sacred commitment to ideal ends and the recognition that ideals may not be destined to prevail in our world (see, for example, the concluding chorus of *Hellas*, 1096–1101).

Nevertheless his courage in the face of these uncertainties, his refusal to compromise or surrender, his lifelong devotion to all that is good and generous and compassionate, his modesty and gentleness and selflessness, continue to stir and kindle all those who, putting prejudice aside, are willing to enter the "fountain-lighted caves" of his mental world. How can one fail to be stirred by his exalted metaphors for the power of mind and will? In the "Ode to Liberty" the will is likened to the Acropolis of fifth-century Athens, perdurable symbol of man's highest intellectual and artistic achievements:

> Athens, diviner yet,
> Gleamed with its crest of columns, on the will
> Of man, as on a mount of diamond, set;   (69–71)

Compare a similar tribute to the power of thought in *Hellas:*

> But Greece and her foundations are
> Built below the tide of war,
> Based on the crystalline sea
> Of thought and its eternity;
> Her citizens, imperial spirits,
>   Rule the present from the past.   (696–701)

To sum up, several instincts were united in Shelley — the instincts of the reformer and the instincts of the philosopher, the singer, and the seer. He was a supreme lyrist at the same time that he was a subtle metaphysician. An empiricist and a sceptic with, paradoxically, a yearning for the Absolute. An enthusiastic supporter of scientific discovery with an inclination to mysticism. A clear-eyed logician with an incandescent imagination. A visionary and a meliorist who was solidly grounded in the parliamentary reform movement. A revolutionary who counseled gradualism and nonviolence. A foe of governmental and ecclesiastical oppression who loved his fellow men. A decrier of marriage who exalted love. A rationalist who was also a rhapsode.

Can we say which was the essential Shelley? Was he Christ the apostle of Love, or Christ blasphemed and crucified? Was he the ardent revolutionary feeling the weight of the superincumbent hour, or the rapt prophet compelling the hours of the future to transform the condition of the present? Was he the desolate Solitary or the committed lover of his fellow men (kings and priests excepted)? Was he blinded by the many-colored veil or by the white radiance of eternity? Was he the moon pale with weariness and loneliness or the sunlike radiance filling the universe with glorious beams? Was he the eagle rising invincibly into the light of dawn or the swan plunging lifeless into the whelming sea? Was he the shattered lamp or the spirit tameless and swift and proud? Was he the herd-abandoned deer or the pardlike spirit going on until he is stopped yet never stopped? Was he the tired child or the trumpet of a prophecy, the cursed and outcast Cain or the lonely ensanguined Christ?

Whether one views these Shelleys within Shelley as phases, cycles, moods, or forces locked within him in ceaseless combat, it seems safe to predict that he will continue to compel the imagination of readers until the future disclaims alliance with the past.

NEWELL F. FORD

QUEEN MAB

A PHILOSOPHICAL POEM

WITH NOTES

ECRASEZ L'INFAME!
Corréspondance de Voltaire.

Avia Pieridum peragro loca, nullius ante
Trita solo, juvat integros accedere fonteis;
Atque haurire: juvatque novos decerpere flores.
. . . .
Unde prius nulli velarint tempora Musæ.
Primum quod magnis doceo de rebus; et arctis
Religionum animos exsolvere pergo.
LUCRETIUS, lib. iv.

Δὸς ποῦ στῶ, καὶ κόσμον κινήσω.
ARCHIMEDES.

'During my existence I have incessantly speculated, thought and read.' So Shelley wrote when he was yet not quite twenty years old; and the statement fairly represents the history of his boyhood and youth. *Queen Mab* was composed in 1812–13, in its present form, and issued during the summer of the latter year, when Shelley was just twenty-one. It embodies substantially the contents of his mind at that period, especially those speculative, religious and philanthropic opinions to the expression of which his 'passion for reforming the world' was the incentive; and, poetically, it is his first work of importance. Much of its subject-matter had been previously treated by him. The figure of Ahasuerus, which was a permanent imaginative motive for him, had been the centre of a juvenile poem, *The Wandering Jew*, in which Medwin claims to have collaborated with him, as early as 1809–10; and youthful verse written before 1812 is clearly incorporated in *Queen Mab*. It may fairly be regarded, poetically and intellectually, as the result of the three preceding years, from the eighteenth to the twenty-first of the poet's life.

The poem owes much to Shelley's studies in the Latin and French authors. The limitations of his poetical training and taste in English verse are justly stated by Mrs. Shelley, in her note:

'Our earlier English poetry was almost unknown to him. The love and knowledge of nature developed by Wordsworth — the lofty melody and mysterious beauty of Coleridge's poetry — and the wild fantastic machinery and gorgeous scenery adopted by Southey, composed his favorite reading. The rhythm of *Queen Mab* was founded on that of *Thalaba*, and the first few lines bear a striking resemblance in spirit, though not in idea, to the opening of that poem. His fertile imagination, and ear tuned to the finest sense of harmony, preserved him from imitation. Another of his favorite books was the poem of *Gebir*, by Walter Savage Landor.'

Queen Mab is, in form, what would be expected from such preferences. His own *Notes* indicate the prose sources of his thought. He dissented from all that was established in society, for the most part very radically, and was a believer in the perfectibility of man by moral means. Here, again, Mrs. Shelley's note is most just:

'He was animated to greater zeal by compassion for his fellow-creatures. His sympathy was excited by the misery with which the world is bursting. He witnessed the sufferings of the poor, and was aware of the evils of ignorance. He desired to induce every rich man to despoil himself of superfluity, and to create a brotherhood of property and service, and was ready to be the first to lay down the advantages of his birth. He was of too uncompromising a disposition to join any party.

He did not in his youth look forward to gradual improvement: nay, in those days of intolerance, now almost forgotten, it seemed as easy to look forward to the sort of millennium of freedom and brotherhood, which he thought the proper state of mankind, as to the present reign of moderation and improvement. Ill health made him believe that his race would soon be run; that a year or two was all he had of life. He desired that these years should be useful and illustrious. He saw, in a fervent call on his fellow-creatures to share alike the blessings of the creation, to love and serve each other, the noblest work that life and time permitted him. In this spirit he composed *Queen Mab.*

Shelley's own opinion of the poem changed in later years. He always referred to it as written in his nineteenth year, when it was apparently begun, though its final form at any rate dates from the next year. In 1817 he wrote of it as follows:

. . . 'Full of those errors which belong to youth, as far as imagery and language and a connected plan is concerned. But it was a sincere overflowing of the heart and mind, and that at a period when they are most uncorrupted and pure. It is the author's boast, and it constitutes no small portion of his happiness, that, after six years [this period supports the date 1811] of added experience and reflection, the doctrine of equality, and liberty, and disinterestedness, and entire unbelief in religion of any sort, to which this poem is devoted, have gained rather than lost that beauty and that grandeur which first determined him to devote his life to the investigation and inculcation of them.'

In 1821, when the poem was printed by W. Clark, Shelley, in a letter of protest to the editor of the *Examiner*, describes it in a different strain:

'A poem, entitled *Queen Mab*, was written by me, at the age of eighteen, I dare say in a sufficiently intemperate spirit — but even then was not intended for publication, and a few copies only were struck off, to be distributed among my personal friends. I have not seen this production for several years; I doubt not but that it is perfectly worthless in point of literary composition; and that in all that concerns moral and political speculation, as well as in the subtler discriminations of metaphysical and religious doctrine, it is still more crude and immature. I am a devoted enemy to religious, political, and domestic oppression; and I regret this publication not so much from literary vanity, as because I fear it is better fitted to injure than to serve the sacred cause of freedom.'

Queen Mab, as Shelley here states, was privately issued. The name of the printer was cut out of nearly all copies, for fear of prosecution. The edition was of two hundred and fifty copies, of which about seventy were put in circulation by gift. Many pirated editions were issued after Shelley's death both in England and America, and the poem was especially popular with the Owenites. By it Shelley was long most widely known, and it remains one of the most striking of his works in popular apprehension. Though at last he abandoned it, because of its crudities, he had felt interest in it after its first issue and had partly recast it, and included a portion of this revision in his next volume, *Alastor*, 1816, as the *Dæmon of the World*. The radical character of *Queen Mab*, which was made a part of the evidence against his character, on the occasion of the trial which resulted in his being deprived of the custody of his children by Lord Eldon, was a main element in the contemporary obloquy in which his name was involved in England, though very few persons could ever have read the poem then; but it may be doubted whether in the end it did not help his fame by the fascination it exercises over a certain class of minds in the first stages of social and intellectual revolt or angry unrest so widespread in this century.

The dedication *To Harriet* ***** is to his first wife.

TO HARRIET *****

Whose is the love that, gleaming through the world,
Wards off the poisonous arrow of its scorn?
　Whose is the warm and partial praise,
　Virtue's most sweet reward?

Beneath whose looks did my reviving soul
Riper in truth and virtuous daring grow?
　Whose eyes have I gazed fondly on,
　And loved mankind the more?

Harriet! on thine: — thou wert my purer mind;
Thou wert the inspiration of my song;
　Thine are these early wilding flowers,
　Though garlanded by me.

Then press into thy breast this pledge of love;
And know, though time may change and years may roll,
　Each floweret gathered in my heart
　It consecrates to thine.

I

How wonderful is Death,
Death, and his brother Sleep !
One, pale as yonder waning moon
    With lips of lurid blue ;
The other, rosy as the morn
When throned on ocean's wave
        It blushes o'er the world ;
Yet both so passing wonderful !

Hath then the gloomy Power
Whose reign is in the tainted sepulchres 10
    Seized on her sinless soul ?
    Must then that peerless form
Which love and admiration cannot view
Without a beating heart, those azure veins
Which steal like streams along a field of
        snow,
    That lovely outline which is fair
    As breathing marble, perish ?
    Must putrefaction's breath
Leave nothing of this heavenly sight
    But loathsomeness and ruin ?   20
Spare nothing but a gloomy theme,
On which the lightest heart might moral-
        ize?
    Or is it only a sweet slumber
    Stealing o'er sensation,
Which the breath of roseate morning
        Chaseth into darkness ?
    Will Ianthe wake again,
And give that faithful bosom joy
Whose sleepless spirit waits to catch
Light, life and rapture, from her smile ?

    Yes ! she will wake again,   31
Although her glowing limbs are motionless,
    And silent those sweet lips,
    Once breathing eloquence
That might have soothed a tiger's rage
Or thawed the cold heart of a conqueror.
    Her dewy eyes are closed,
And on their lids, whose texture fine
Scarce hides the dark blue orbs beneath,
    The baby Sleep is pillowed ;   40
    Her golden tresses shade
    The bosom's stainless pride,
Curling like tendrils of the parasite
    Around a marble column.

    Hark ! whence that rushing sound ?
    'T is like the wondrous strain
That round a lonely ruin swells,
Which, wandering on the echoing shore,
    The enthusiast hears at evening ;

'T is softer than the west wind's sigh ;
'T is wilder than the unmeasured notes
Of that strange lyre whose strings   52
The genii of the breezes sweep ;
    Those lines of rainbow light
Are like the moonbeams when they
        fall
Through some cathedral window, but the
        tints
    Are such as may not find
    Comparison on earth.

Behold the chariot of the Fairy Queen !
Celestial coursers paw the unyielding
        air;   60
Their filmy pennons at her word they
        furl,
And stop obedient to the reins of light ;
    These the Queen of Spells drew in ;
    She spread a charm around the spot,
And, leaning graceful from the ethereal
        car,
    Long did she gaze, and silently,
        Upon the slumbering maid.

Oh ! not the visioned poet in his dreams,
When silvery clouds float through the wil-
        dered brain,
When every sight of lovely, wild and
        grand   70
    Astonishes, enraptures, elevates,
    When fancy at a glance combines
    The wondrous and the beautiful, —
So bright, so fair, so wild a shape
        Hath ever yet beheld,
As that which reined the coursers of the
        air
And poured the magic of her gaze
        Upon the maiden's sleep.

    The broad and yellow moon
    Shone dimly through her form —   80
That form of faultless symmetry;
The pearly and pellucid car
    Moved not the moonlight's line.
'T was not an earthly pageant.
Those, who had looked upon the sight
    Passing all human glory,
    Saw not the yellow moon,
    Saw not the mortal scene,
    Heard not the night-wind's rush,
    Heard not an earthly sound,   90
    Saw but the fairy pageant,
    Heard but the heavenly strains
That filled the lonely dwelling.

The Fairy's frame was slight — yon fibrous
    cloud,
That catches but the palest tinge of even,
And which the straining eye can hardly
    seize
When melting into eastern twilight's shad-
    ow,
Were scarce so thin, so slight ; but the fair
    star
That gems the glittering coronet of morn,
Sheds not a light so mild, so powerful,   100
As that which, bursting from the Fairy's
    form,
Spread a purpureal halo round the scene,
    Yet with an undulating motion,
    Swayed to her outline gracefully.

    From her celestial car
    The Fairy Queen descended,
    And thrice she waved her wand
    Circled with wreaths of amaranth;
    Her thin and misty form
    Moved with the moving air,   110
    And the clear silver tones,
    As thus she spoke, were such
As are unheard by all but gifted ear.

        FAIRY

' Stars ! your balmiest influence shed !
Elements ! your wrath suspend !
Sleep, Ocean, in the rocky bounds
    That circle thy domain !
Let not a breath be seen to stir
Around yon grass-grown ruin's height !
    Let even the restless gossamer   120
    Sleep on the moveless air !
    Soul of Ianthe ! thou,
Judged alone worthy of the envied boon
That waits the good and the sincere ; that
    waits
Those who have struggled, and with reso-
    lute will
Vanquished earth's pride and meanness,
    burst the chains,
The icy chains of custom, and have shone
The day - stars of their age; — Soul of
    Ianthe !
    Awake ! arise ! '

    Sudden arose   130
    Ianthe's Soul; it stood
    All beautiful in naked purity,
The perfect semblance of its bodily frame;
Instinct with inexpressible beauty and
    grace —

    Each stain of earthliness
    Had passed away — it reassumed
    Its native dignity and stood
    Immortal amid ruin.

    Upon the couch the body lay,
    Wrapt in the depth of slumber;   140
Its features were fixed and meaningless,
    Yet animal life was there,
    And every organ yet performed
    Its natural functions; 'twas a sight
Of wonder to behold the body and the soul.
    The self-same lineaments, the same
    Marks of identity were there;
Yet, oh, how different ! One aspires to
    Heaven,
Pants for its sempiternal heritage,
And, ever changing, ever rising still,   150
    Wantons in endless being:
The other, for a time the unwilling sport
Of circumstance and passion, struggles on;
Fleets through its sad duration rapidly;
Then like an useless and worn-out machine,
    Rots, perishes, and passes.

        FAIRY

    ' Spirit ! who hast dived so deep;
    Spirit ! who hast soared so high;
    Thou the fearless, thou the mild,
Accept the boon thy worth hath earned,
    Ascend the car with me ! '   161

        SPIRIT

    ' Do I dream ? Is this new feeling
    But a visioned ghost of slumber ?
      If indeed I am a soul,
    A free, a disembodied soul,
      Speak again to me.'

        FAIRY

' I am the Fairy MAB: to me 'tis given
The wonders of the human world to keep;
The secrets of the immeasurable past,
In the unfailing consciences of men,   170
Those stern, unflattering chroniclers, I
    find;
The future, from the causes which arise
In each event, I gather; not the sting
Which retributive memory implants
In the hard bosom of the selfish man,
Nor that ecstatic and exulting throb
Which virtue's votary feels when he
    sums up
The thoughts and actions of a well-spent
    day,

Are unforeseen, unregistered by me;
And it is yet permitted me to rend   180
The veil of mortal frailty, that the spirit,
Clothed in its changeless purity, may
  know
How soonest to accomplish the great
  end
For which it hath its being, and may
  taste
That peace which in the end all life will
  share.
This is the meed of virtue; happy Soul,
Ascend the car with me!'

The chains of earth's immurement
  Fell from Ianthe's spirit;
They shrank and brake like bandages of
  straw   190
Beneath a wakened giant's strength.
  She knew her glorious change,
And felt in apprehension uncontrolled
  New raptures opening round;
Each day-dream of her mortal life,
Each frenzied vision of the slumbers
  That closed each well-spent day,
Seemed now to meet reality.
The Fairy and the Soul proceeded;
  The silver clouds disparted;   200
And as the car of magic they ascended,
  Again the speechless music swelled,
  Again the coursers of the air
Unfurled their azure pennons, and the
  Queen,
  Shaking the beamy reins,
  Bade them pursue their way.

The magic car moved on.
  The night was fair, and countless stars
Studded heaven's dark blue vault;
  Just o'er the eastern wave   210
Peeped the first faint smile of morn.
  The magic car moved on —
  From the celestial hoofs
The atmosphere in flaming sparkles flew,
  And where the burning wheels
Eddied above the mountain's loftiest peak,
  Was traced a line of lightning.
Now it flew far above a rock,
  The utmost verge of earth,   219
The rival of the Andes, whose dark brow
Lowered o'er the silver sea.

Far, far below the chariot's path,
  Calm as a slumbering babe,
  Tremendous Ocean lay.

The mirror of its stillness showed
  The pale and waning stars,
  The chariot's fiery track,
  And the gray light of morn
  Tinging those fleecy clouds
That canopied the dawn.   230

Seemed it that the chariot's way
Lay through the midst of an immense con-
  cave
Radiant with million constellations, tinged
  With shades of infinite color,
  And semicircled with a belt
  Flashing incessant meteors.

The magic car moved on.
  As they approached their goal,   238
  The coursers seemed to gather speed;
The sea no longer was distinguished; earth
  Appeared a vast and shadowy sphere;
  The sun's unclouded orb
  Rolled through the black concave;
  Its rays of rapid light
Parted around the chariot's swifter course,
  And fell, like ocean's feathery spray
  Dashed from the boiling surge
  Before a vessel's prow.

The magic car moved on.
  Earth's distant orb appeared   250
The smallest light that twinkles in the
  heaven;
  Whilst round the chariot's way
  Innumerable systems rolled
  And countless spheres diffused
  An ever-varying glory.
It was a sight of wonder: some
  Were hornèd like the crescent moon;
  Some shed a mild and silver beam
Like Hesperus o'er the western sea;   259
Some dashed athwart with trains of flame,
  Like worlds to death and ruin driven;
Some shone like suns, and as the chariot
  passed,
  Eclipsed all other light.

  Spirit of Nature! here —
In this interminable wilderness
Of worlds, at whose immensity
  Even soaring fancy staggers,
  Here is thy fitting temple!
  Yet not the lightest leaf   269
That quivers to the passing breeze
  Is less instinct with thee;
  Yet not the meanest worm

That lurks in graves and fattens on the
    dead,
  Less shares thy eternal breath!
  Spirit of Nature! thou,
  Imperishable as this scene —
  Here is thy fitting temple!

II

If solitude hath ever led thy steps
  To the wild ocean's echoing shore,
  And thou hast lingered there,
Until the sun's broad orb
Seemed resting on the burnished wave,
  Thou must have marked the lines
Of purple gold that motionless
  Hung o'er the sinking sphere;
Thou must have marked the billowy
    clouds,
  Edged with intolerable radiancy,   10
  Towering like rocks of jet
  Crowned with a diamond wreath;
  And yet there is a moment,
  When the sun's highest point
Peeps like a star o'er ocean's western edge,
When those far clouds of feathery gold,
  Shaded with deepest purple, gleam
Like islands on a dark blue sea;
Then has thy fancy soared above the earth
  And furled its wearied wing   20
  Within the Fairy's fane.

Yet not the golden islands
Gleaming in yon flood of light,
  Nor the feathery curtains
Stretching o'er the sun's bright couch,
  Nor the burnished ocean-waves
  Paving that gorgeous dome,
So fair, so wonderful a sight
As Mab's ethereal palace could afford.   29
Yet likest evening's vault, that faëry Hall!
As Heaven, low resting on the wave, it
    spread
  Its floors of flashing light,
  Its vast and azure dome,
  Its fertile golden islands
  Floating on a silver sea;
Whilst suns their mingling beamings darted
Through clouds of circumambient darkness,
  And pearly battlements around
Looked o'er the immense of Heaven.

The magic car no longer moved.   40
  The Fairy and the Spirit
  Entered the Hall of Spells.
  Those golden clouds

That rolled in glittering billows
  Beneath the azure canopy,
With the ethereal footsteps trembled not;
  The light and crimson mists,
Floating to strains of thrilling melody
  Through that unearthly dwelling,
Yielded to every movement of the will;   50
Upon their passive swell the Spirit leaned,
And, for the varied bliss that pressed
    around,
  Used not the glorious privilege
  Of virtue and of wisdom.

'Spirit!' the Fairy said,
And pointed to the gorgeous dome,
  'This is a wondrous sight
  And mocks all human grandeur;
But, were it virtue's only meed to dwell
In a celestial palace, all resigned   60
To pleasurable impulses, immured
Within the prison of itself, the will
Of changeless Nature would be unfulfilled.
Learn to make others happy. Spirit, come!
This is thine high reward: — the past shall
    rise;
Thou shalt behold the present; I will teach
  The secrets of the future.'

The Fairy and the Spirit
Approached the overhanging battlement.
  Below lay stretched the universe!   70
  There, far as the remotest line
  That bounds imagination's flight,
  Countless and unending orbs
  In mazy motion intermingled,
  Yet still fulfilled immutably
  Eternal Nature's law.
  Above, below, around,
  The circling systems formed
  A wilderness of harmony;
  Each with undeviating aim,   80
In eloquent silence, through the depths of
    space
  Pursued its wondrous way.

There was a little light
That twinkled in the misty distance.
  None but a spirit's eye
  Might ken that rolling orb.
  None but a spirit's eye,
  And in no other place
But that celestial dwelling, might behold
Each action of this earth's inhabitants. 90
  But matter, space, and time,
In those aërial mansions cease to act;

And all-prevailing wisdom, when it reaps
The harvest of its excellence, o'erbounds
Those obstacles of which an earthly soul
    Fears to attempt the conquest.

    The Fairy pointed to the earth.
    The Spirit's intellectual eye
    Its kindred beings recognized.   99
The thronging thousands, to a passing view,
Seemed like an ant-hill's citizens.
    How wonderful! that even
The passions, prejudices, interests,
That sway the meanest being — the weak touch
    That moves the finest nerve
    And in one human brain
Causes the faintest thought, becomes a link
    In the great chain of Nature!

   'Behold,' the Fairy cried,
   'Palmyra's ruined palaces!   110
   Behold where grandeur frowned!
   Behold where pleasure smiled!
What now remains? — the memory
   Of senselessness and shame.
   What is immortal there?
   Nothing — it stands to tell
   A melancholy tale, to give
   An awful warning; soon
Oblivion will steal silently
   The remnant of its fame.   120
Monarchs and conquerors there
Proud o'er prostrate millions trod —
The earthquakes of the human race;
   Like them, forgotten when the ruin
   That marks their shock is past.

   'Beside the eternal Nile
   The Pyramids have risen.
Nile shall pursue his changeless way;
   Those Pyramids shall fall.
Yea! not a stone shall stand to tell   130
   The spot whereon they stood;
Their very site shall be forgotten,
   As is their builder's name!

   'Behold yon sterile spot,
Where now the wandering Arab's tent
   Flaps in the desert blast!
There once old Salem's haughty fane
Reared high to heaven its thousand golden domes,
   And in the blushing face of day
   Exposed its shameful glory.   140
Oh! many a widow, many an orphan cursed

The building of that fane; and many a father,
Worn out with toil and slavery, implored
The poor man's God to sweep it from the earth
And spare his children the detested task
Of piling stone on stone and poisoning
   The choicest days of life
   To soothe a dotard's vanity.
There an inhuman and uncultured race   149
Howled hideous praises to their Demon-God;
They rushed to war, tore from the mother's womb
The unborn child — old age and infancy
Promiscuous perished; their victorious arms
Left not a soul to breathe. Oh! they were fiends!
But what was he who taught them that the God
Of Nature and benevolence had given
A special sanction to the trade of blood?
His name and theirs are fading, and the tales
Of this barbarian nation, which imposture
Recites till terror credits, are pursuing   160
   Itself into forgetfulness.

   'Where Athens, Rome, and Sparta stood,
There is a moral desert now.
The mean and miserable huts,
The yet more wretched palaces,
Contrasted with those ancient fanes
Now crumbling to oblivion, —
The long and lonely colonnades
Through which the ghost of Freedom stalks, —
   Seem like a well-known tune,   170
Which in some dear scene we have loved to hear,
   Remembered now in sadness.
   But, oh! how much more changed,
   How gloomier is the contrast
   Of human nature there!
Where Socrates expired, a tyrant's slave,
A coward and a fool, spreads death around —
   Then, shuddering, meets his own.
Where Cicero and Antoninus lived,
A cowled and hypocritical monk   180
   Prays, curses and deceives.

   'Spirit! ten thousand years
   Have scarcely passed away,

Since in the waste, where now the savage
   drinks
His enemy's blood, and, aping Europe's
   sons,
   Wakes the unholy song of war,
     Arose a stately city,
Metropolis of the western continent.
  There, now, the mossy column-stone,
Indented by time's unrelaxing grasp,   190
  Which once appeared to brave
All, save its country's ruin, —
  There the wide forest scene,
Rude in the uncultivated loveliness
  Of gardens long run wild, —
Seems, to the unwilling sojourner whose steps
Chance in that desert has delayed,
Thus to have stood since earth was what
   it is.
  Yet once it was the busiest haunt,   199
Whither, as to a common centre, flocked
  Strangers, and ships, and merchandise ;
  Once peace and freedom blest
  The cultivated plain;
  But wealth, that curse of man,
Blighted the bud of its prosperity;
Virtue and wisdom, truth and liberty,
Fled, to return not, until man shall know
  That they alone can give the bliss
    Worthy a soul that claims
    Its kindred with eternity.   210

' There 's not one atom of yon earth
  But once was living man;
Nor the minutest drop of rain,
That hangeth in its thinnest cloud,
  But flowed in human veins;
  And from the burning plains
  Where Libyan monsters yell,
  From the most gloomy glens
  Of Greenland's sunless clime,
  To where the golden fields   220
  Of fertile England spread
  Their harvest to the day,
  Thou canst not find one spot
  Whereon no city stood.

' How strange is human pride !
I tell thee that those living things,
To whom the fragile blade of grass
  That springeth in the morn
  And perisheth ere noon,
  Is an unbounded world;   230
I tell thee that those viewless beings,
Whose mansion is the smallest particle
Of the impassive atmosphere,

Think, feel and live like man;
That their affections and antipathies,
  Like his, produce the laws
  Ruling their moral state;
  And the minutest throb
That through their frame diffuses
  The slightest, faintest motion,   240
  Is fixed and indispensable
  As the majestic laws
  That rule yon rolling orbs.'

  The Fairy paused. The Spirit,
In ecstasy of admiration, felt
All knowledge of the past revived; the
   events
Of old and wondrous times,
Which dim tradition interruptedly
Teaches the credulous vulgar, were un-
   folded
  In just perspective to the view;   250
  Yet dim from their infinitude.
  The Spirit seemed to stand
High on an isolated pinnacle;
The flood of ages combating below,
The depth of the unbounded universe
  Above, and all around
Nature's unchanging harmony.

III

  ' Fairy !' the Spirit said,
  And on the Queen of Spells
  Fixed her ethereal eyes,
  ' I thank thee. Thou hast given
A boon which I will not resign, and taught
A lesson not to be unlearned. I know
The past, and thence I will essay to glean
A warning for the future, so that man
May profit by his errors and derive
  Experience from his folly;   10
For, when the power of imparting joy
Is equal to the will, the human soul
Requires no other heaven.'

MAB

' Turn thee, surpassing Spirit !
  Much yet remains unscanned.
  Thou knowest how great is man,
  Thou knowest his imbecility;
  Yet learn thou what he is;
  Yet learn the lofty destiny
  Which restless Time prepares   20
  For every living soul.

' Behold a gorgeous palace that amid
Yon populous city rears its thousand towers

And seems itself a city. Gloomy troops
Of sentinels in stern and silent ranks
Encompass it around; the dweller there
Cannot be free and happy; hearest thou
not
The curses of the fatherless, the groans
Of those who have no friend? He passes
on —
The King, the wearer of a gilded chain 30
That binds his soul to abjectness, the fool
Whom courtiers nickname monarch, whilst
a slave
Even to the basest appetites — that man
Heeds not the shriek of penury; he smiles
At the deep curses which the destitute
Mutter in secret, and a sullen joy
Pervades his bloodless heart when thou-
sands groan
But for those morsels which his wantonness
Wastes in unjoyous revelry, to save
All that they love from famine ; when he
hears 40
The tale of horror, to some ready-made
face
Of hypocritical assent he turns,
Smothering the glow of shame, that, spite
of him,
Flushes his bloated cheek.

Now to the meal
Of silence, grandeur and excess he drags
His palled unwilling appetite. If gold,
Gleaming around, and numerous viands
culled
From every clime could force the loathing
sense
To overcome satiety, — if wealth
The spring it draws from poisons not, — or
vice, 50
Unfeeling, stubborn vice, converteth not
Its food to deadliest venom ; then that king
Is happy ; and the peasant who fulfils
His unforced task, when he returns at even
And by the blazing fagot meets again
Her welcome for whom all his toil is sped,
Tastes not a sweeter meal.

Behold him now
Stretched on the gorgeous couch ; his fe-
vered brain
Reels dizzily awhile ; but ah ! too soon
The slumber of intemperance subsides, 60
And conscience, that undying serpent, calls
Her venomous brood to their nocturnal
task.

Listen ! he speaks ! oh ! mark that frenzied
eye —
Oh ! mark that deadly visage ! '

KING

'No cessation !
Oh ! must this last forever ! Awful death,
I wish, yet fear to clasp thee ! — Not one
moment
Of dreamless sleep ! O dear and blessèd
Peace,
Why dost thou shroud thy vestal purity
In penury and dungeons ? Wherefore
lurkest
With danger, death, and solitude ; yet
shun'st 70
The palace I have built thee ? Sacred
Peace !
Oh, visit me but once, — but pitying shed
One drop of balm upon my withered soul ! '

THE FAIRY

'Vain man ! that palace is the virtuous
heart,
And Peace defileth not her snowy robes
In such a shed as thine. Hark ! yet he
mutters ;
His slumbers are but varied agonies ;
They prey like scorpions on the springs of
life.
There needeth not the hell that bigots
frame
To punish those who err ; earth in itself 80
Contains at once the evil and the cure ;
And all-sufficing Nature can chastise
Those who transgress her law ; she only
knows
How justly to proportion to the fault
The punishment it merits.

Is it strange
That this poor wretch should pride him in
his woe ?
Take pleasure in his abjectness, and hug
The scorpion that consumes him ? Is it
strange
That, placed on a conspicuous throne of
thorns,
Grasping an iron sceptre, and immured 90
Within a splendid prison whose stern
bounds
Shut him from all that's good or dear on
earth,
His soul asserts not its humanity ?
That man's mild nature rises not in war

Against a king's employ? No — 'tis not
  strange.
He, like the vulgar, thinks, feels, acts, and
  lives
Just as his father did ; the unconquered
  powers
Of precedent and custom interpose
Between a *king* and virtue. Stranger yet,
To those who know not Nature nor de-
  duce   100
The future from the present, it may seem,
That not one slave, who suffers from the
  crimes
Of this unnatural being, not one wretch,
Whose children famish and whose nuptial
  bed
Is earth's unpitying bosom, rears an arm
To dash him from his throne !

                        Those gilded flies
That, basking in the sunshine of a court,
Fatten on its corruption ! what are they ? —
The drones of the community ; they feed
On the mechanic's labor ; the starved
  hind   110
For them compels the stubborn glebe to
  yield
Its unshared harvests ; and yon squalid
  form,
Leaner than fleshless misery, that wastes
A sunless life in the unwholesome mine,
Drags out in labor a protracted death
To glut their grandeur ; many faint with
  toil
That few may know the cares and woe of
  sloth.

Whence, thinkest thou, kings and parasites
  arose ?
Whence that unnatural line of drones who
  heap
Toil and unvanquishable penury   120
On those who build their palaces and bring
Their daily bread ? — From vice, black
  loathsome vice ;
From rapine, madness, treachery, and
  wrong ;
From all that genders misery, and makes
Of earth this thorny wilderness ; from lust,
Revenge, and murder. — And when reason's
  voice,
Loud as the voice of Nature, shall have
  waked
The nations ; and mankind perceive that
  vice

Is discord, war and misery ; that virtue
Is peace and happiness and harmony ;   130
When man's maturer nature shall disdain
The playthings of its childhood ; — kingly
  glare
Will lose its power to dazzle ; its authority
Will silently pass by ; the gorgeous throne
Shall stand unnoticed in the regal hall,
Fast falling to decay ; whilst falsehood's
  trade
Shall be as hateful and unprofitable
As that of truth is now.

                        Where is the fame
Which the vain-glorious mighty of the earth
Seek to eternize ? Oh ! the faintest
  sound   140
From time's light footfall, the minutest
  wave
That swells the flood of ages, whelms in
  nothing
The unsubstantial bubble. Ay ! to-day
Stern is the tyrant's mandate, red the gaze
That flashes desolation, strong the arm
That scatters multitudes. To - morrow
  comes !
That mandate is a thunder-peal that died
In ages past ; that gaze, a transient flash
On which the midnight closed ; and on that
  arm   149
The worm has made his meal.
                        The virtuous man,
Who, great in his humility as kings
Are little in their grandeur; he who leads
Invincibly a life of resolute good
And stands amid the silent dungeon-depths
More free and fearless than the trembling
  judge
Who, clothed in venal power, vainly strove
To bind the impassive spirit; — when he
  falls,
His mild eye beams benevolence no more;
Withered the hand outstretched but to re-
  lieve;   159
Sunk reason's simple eloquence that rolled
But to appall the guilty. Yes! the grave
Hath quenched that eye and death's relent-
  less frost
Withered that arm; but the unfading fame
Which virtue hangs upon its votary's tomb,
The deathless memory of that man whom
  kings
Call to their minds and tremble, the re-
  membrance
With which the happy spirit contemplates

Its well-spent pilgrimage on earth,
Shall never pass away.   169

' Nature rejects the monarch, not the man;
The subject, not the citizen; for kings
And subjects, mutual foes, forever play
A losing game into each other's hands,
Whose stakes are vice and misery.   The man
Of virtuous soul commands not, nor obeys.
Power, like a desolating pestilence,
Pollutes whate'er it touches; and obedience,
Bane of all genius, virtue, freedom, truth,
Makes slaves of men, and of the human
            frame   179
A mechanized automaton.

                        When Nero
High over flaming Rome with savage joy
Lowered like a fiend, drank with enrap-
    tured ear
The shrieks of agonizing death, beheld
The frightful desolation spread, and felt
A new-created sense within his soul
Thrill to the sight and vibrate to the
    sound, —
Thinkest thou his grandeur had not over-
    come
The force of human kindness?   And when
    Rome
With one stern blow hurled not the tyrant
    down,
Crushed not the arm red with her dearest
    blood,   190
Had not submissive abjectness destroyed
Nature's suggestions?

                        Look on yonder earth:
The golden harvests spring; the unfailing
    sun
Sheds light and life; the fruits, the flowers,
    the trees,
Arise in due succession; all things speak
Peace, harmony and love.   The universe,
In Nature's silent eloquence, declares
That all fulfil the works of love and joy, —
All but the outcast, Man.   He fabricates
The sword which stabs his peace; he
    cherisheth   200
The snakes that gnaw his heart; he raiseth
    up
The tyrant whose delight is in his woe,
Whose sport is in his agony.   Yon sun,
Lights it the great alone?   Yon silver
    beams,
Sleep they less sweetly on the cottage thatch

Than on the dome of kings?   Is mother
    earth
A step-dame to her numerous sons who earn
Her unshared gifts with unremitting toil;
A mother only to those puling babes   209
Who, nursed in ease and luxury, make men
The playthings of their babyhood and mar
In self-important childishness that peace
Which men alone appreciate?

        ' Spirit of Nature, no!
The pure diffusion of thy essence throbs
    Alike in every human heart.
        Thou aye erectest there
    Thy throne of power unappealable;
    Thou art the judge beneath whose nod
Man's brief and frail authority   220
        Is powerless as the wind
        That passeth idly by;
    Thine the tribunal which surpasseth
        The show of human justice
        As God surpasses man!

        ' Spirit of Nature! thou
Life of interminable multitudes;
    Soul of those mighty spheres
Whose changeless paths through Heaven's
        deep silence lie;
    Soul of that smallest being,   230
        The dwelling of whose life
    Is one faint April sun-gleam; —
        Man, like these passive things,
Thy will unconsciously fulfilleth;
    Like theirs, his age of endless peace,
        Which time is fast maturing,
        Will swiftly, surely, come;
And the unbounded frame which thou per-
        vadest,
        Will be without a flaw
    Marring its perfect symmetry!   240

                    IV

' How beautiful this night! the balmiest
        sigh,
Which vernal zephyrs breathe in evening's
        ear,
Were discord to the speaking quietude
That wraps this moveless scene.   Heaven's
    ebon vault,
Studded with stars unutterably bright,
Through which the moon's unclouded gran-
    deur rolls,
Seems like a canopy which love had spread
To curtain her sleeping world.   Yon gentle
    hills,

Robed in a garment of untrodden snow; 9
Yon darksome rocks, whence icicles depend
So stainless that their white and glittering
   spires
Tinge not the moon's pure beam ; yon
   castled steep
Whose banner hangeth o'er the time-worn
   tower
So idly that rapt fancy deemeth it
A metaphor of peace; — all form a scene
Where musing solitude might love to lift
Her soul above this sphere of earthliness;
Where silence undisturbed might watch
   alone —
So cold, so bright, so still.

               The orb of day
In southern climes o'er ocean's waveless
   field   20
Sinks sweetly smiling ; not the faintest
   breath
Steals o'er the unruffled deep ; the clouds
   of eve
Reflect unmoved the lingering beam of day;
And Vesper's image on the western main
Is beautifully still. To-morrow comes:
Cloud upon cloud, in dark and deepening
   mass,
Roll o'er the blackened waters; the deep
   roar
Of distant thunder mutters awfully;
Tempest unfolds its pinion o'er the gloom
That shrouds the boiling surge; the pitiless
   fiend,   30
With all his winds and lightnings, tracks
   his prey;
The torn deep yawns, — the vessel finds a
   grave
Beneath its jagged gulf.

              Ah ! whence yon glare
That fires the arch of heaven ? that dark
   red smoke
Blotting the silver moon ? The stars are
   quenched
In darkness, and the pure and spangling
   snow
Gleams faintly through the gloom that
   gathers round.
Hark to that roar whose swift and deafening peals
In countless echoes through the mountains
   ring,
Startling pale Midnight on her starry
   throne !   40

Now swells the intermingling din; the jar
Frequent and frightful of the bursting
   bomb;
The falling beam, the shriek, the groan,
   the shout,
The ceaseless clangor, and the rush of men
Inebriate with rage: — loud and more loud
The discord grows; till pale Death shuts
   the scene
And o'er the conqueror and the conquered
   draws
His cold and bloody shroud. — Of all the
   men
Whom day's departing beam saw blooming
   there
In proud and vigorous health; of all the
   hearts   50
That beat with anxious life at sunset there;
How few survive, how few are beating
   now !
All is deep silence, like the fearful calm
That slumbers in the storm's portentous
   pause;
Save when the frantic wail of widowed love
Comes shuddering on the blast, or the faint
   moan
With which some soul bursts from the
   frame of clay
Wrapt round its struggling powers.

               The gray morn
Dawns on the mournful scene; the sulphur-
   ous smoke
Before the icy wind slow rolls away,   60
And the bright beams of frosty morning
   dance
Along the spangling snow. There tracks
   of blood
Even to the forest's depth, and scattered
   arms,
And lifeless warriors, whose hard linea-
   ments
Death's self could change not, mark the
   dreadful path
Of the outsallying victors; far behind
Black ashes note where their proud city
   stood.
Within yon forest is a gloomy glen —
Each tree which guards its darkness from
   the day,   69
Waves o'er a warrior's tomb.

               I see thee shrink,
Surpassing Spirit ! — wert thou human
   else ?

I see a shade of doubt and horror fleet
Across thy stainless features; yet fear not;
This is no unconnected misery,
Nor stands uncaused and irretrievable.
Man's evil nature, that apology
Which kings who rule, and cowards who
    crouch, set up
For their unnumbered crimes, sheds not
    the blood
Which desolates the discord-wasted land.
From kings and priests and statesmen war
    arose,   80
Whose safety is man's deep unbettered
    woe,
Whose grandeur his debasement. Let the
    axe
Strike at the root, the poison-tree will fall;
And where its venomed exhalations spread
Ruin, and death, and woe, where millions
    lay
Quenching the serpent's famine, and their
    bones
Bleaching unburied in the putrid blast,
A garden shall arise, in loveliness
Surpassing fabled Eden.

                    Hath Nature's soul, —
That formed this world so beautiful, that
    spread   90
Earth's lap with plenty, and life's smallest
    chord
Strung to unchanging unison, that gave
The happy birds ·their dwelling in the
    grove,
That yielded to the wanderers of the deep
The lovely silence of the unfathomed main,
And filled the meanest worm that crawls in
    dust
With spirit, thought and love, — on Man
    alone,
Partial in causeless malice, wantonly
Heaped ruin, vice, and slavery; his soul 99
Blasted with withering curses; placed afar
The meteor-happiness, that shuns his grasp,
But serving on the frightful gulf to glare
Rent wide beneath his footsteps?

                    Nature ! — no !
Kings, priests and statesmen blast the hu-
    man flower
Even in its tender bud; their influence
    darts
Like subtle poison through the bloodless
    veins
Of desolate society. The child,

Ere he can lisp his mother's sacred name,
Swells with the unnatural pride of crime,
    and lifts
His baby-sword even in a hero's mood. 110
This infant arm becomes the bloodiest
    scourge
Of devastated earth; whilst specious names,
Learnt in soft childhood's unsuspecting
    hour,
Serve as the sophisms with which manhood
    dims
Bright reason's ray and sanctifies the sword
Upraised to shed a brother's innocent
    blood.
Let priest-led slaves cease to proclaim that
    man
Inherits vice and misery, when force
And falsehood hang even o'er the cradled
    babe,   119
Stifling with rudest grasp all natural good.

'Ah ! to the stranger-soul, when first it
    peeps
From its new tenement and looks abroad
For happiness and sympathy, how stern·
And desolate a tract is this wide world !
How withered all the buds of natural good !
No shade, no shelter from the sweeping
    storms
Of pitiless power ! On its wretched frame
Poisoned, perchance, by the disease and
    woe
Heaped on the wretched parent whence it
    sprung   129
By morals, law and custom, the pure winds
Of heaven, that renovate the insect tribes,
May breathe not. The untainting light of
    day
May visit not its longings. It is bound
Ere it has life; yea, all the chains are
    forged
Long ere its being; all liberty and love
And peace is torn from its defencelessness;
Cursed from its birth, even from its cradle
    doomed
To abjectness and bondage !

'Throughout this varied and eternal world
Soul is the only element, the block 140
That for uncounted ages has remained.
The moveless pillar of a mountain's weight
Is active living spirit. Every grain
Is sentient both in unity and part,
And the minutest atom comprehends
A world of loves and hatreds; these beget

Evil and good; hence truth and falsehood
   spring;
Hence will and thought and action, all the
   germs
Of pain or pleasure, sympathy or hate,
That variegate the eternal universe.   150
Soul is not more polluted than the beams
Of heaven's pure orb ere round their rapid
   lines
The taint of earth-born atmospheres arise.

' Man is of soul and body, formed for deeds
Of high resolve; on fancy's boldest wing
To soar unwearied, fearlessly to turn
The keenest pangs to peacefulness, and
   taste
The joys which mingled sense and spirit
   yield;
Or he is formed for abjectness and woe,
To grovel on the dunghill of his fears,   160
To shrink at every sound, to quench the
   flame
Of natural love in sensualism, to know
That hour as blest when on his worthless
   days
The frozen hand of death shall set its seal,
Yet fear the cure, though hating the disease.
The one is man that shall hereafter be;
The other, man as vice has made him now.

' War is the statesman's game, the priest's
   delight,
The lawyer's jest, the hired assassin's trade,
And to those royal murderers whose mean
   thrones   170
Are bought by crimes of treachery and gore,
The bread they eat, the staff on which they
   lean.
Guards, garbed in blood-red livery, sur-
   round
Their palaces, participate the crimes
That force defends and from a nation's rage
Secures the crown, which all the curses
   reach
That famine, frenzy, woe and penury
   breathe.
These are the hired bravos who defend
The tyrant's throne—the bullies of his fear;
These are the sinks and channels of worst
   vice,   180
The refuse of society, the dregs
Of all that is most vile; their cold hearts
   blend
Deceit with sternness, ignorance with pride,
All that is mean and villainous with rage

Which hopelessness of good and self-con-
   tempt
Alone might kindle; they are decked in
   wealth,
Honor and power, then are sent abroad
To do their work.   The pestilence that
   stalks
In gloomy triumph through some eastern
   land   189
Is less destroying.   They cajole with gold
And promises of fame the thoughtless youth
Already crushed with servitude; he knows
His wretchedness too late, and cherishes
Repentance for his ruin, when his doom
Is sealed in gold and blood !
Those too the tyrant serve, who, skilled to
   snare
The feet of justice in the toils of law,
Stand ready to oppress the weaker still,
And right or wrong will vindicate for gold,
Sneering at public virtue, which beneath
Their pitiless tread lies torn and trampled
   where   201
Honor sits smiling at the sale of truth.

' Then grave and hoary-headed hypocrites,
Without a hope, a passion or a love,
Who through a life of luxury and lies
Have crept by flattery to the seats of power,
Support the system whence their honors
   flow.
They have three words — well tyrants know
   their use,
Well pay them for the loan with usury
Torn from a bleeding world ! — God, Hell
   and Heaven: 210
A vengeful, pitiless, and almighty fiend,
Whose mercy is a nickname for the rage
Of tameless tigers hungering for blood;
Hell, a red gulf of everlasting fire,
Where poisonous and undying worms pro-
   long
Eternal misery to those hapless slaves
Whose life has been a penance for its
   crimes;
And Heaven, a meed for those who dare
   belie
Their human nature, quake, believe and
   cringe
Before the mockeries of earthly power.   220

' These tools the tyrant tempers to his
   work,
Wields in his wrath, and as he wills destroys,

Omnipotent in wickedness; the while
Youth springs, age moulders, manhood tamely does
His bidding, bribed by short-lived joys to lend
Force to the weakness of his trembling arm.
They rise, they fall; one generation comes
Yielding its harvest to destruction's scythe.
It fades, another blossoms; yet behold!
Red glows the tyrant's stamp-mark on its bloom,   230
Withering and cankering deep its passive prime.
He has invented lying words and modes,
Empty and vain as his own coreless heart;
Evasive meanings, nothings of much sound,
To lure the heedless victim to the toils
Spread round the valley of its paradise.

'Look to thyself, priest, conqueror or prince!
Whether thy trade is falsehood, and thy lusts
Deep wallow in the earnings of the poor,
With whom thy master was; or thou delight'st   240
In numbering o'er the myriads of thy slain,
All misery weighing nothing in the scale
Against thy short-lived fame; or thou dost load
With cowardice and crime the groaning land,
A pomp-fed king. Look to thy wretched self!
Ay, art thou not the veriest slave that e'er
Crawled on the loathing earth? Are not thy days
Days of unsatisfying listlessness?
Dost thou not cry, ere night's long rack is o'er,
"When will the morning come?" Is not thy youth   250
A vain and feverish dream of sensualism?
Thy manhood blighted with unripe disease?
Are not thy views of unregretted death
Drear, comfortless and horrible? Thy mind,
Is it not morbid as thy nerveless frame,
Incapable of judgment, hope or love?
And dost thou wish the errors to survive,
That bar thee from all sympathies of good,
After the miserable interest
Thou hold'st in their protraction? When the grave   260

Has swallowed up thy memory and thyself,
Dost thou desire the bane that poisons earth
To twine its roots around thy coffined clay,
Spring from thy bones, and blossom on thy tomb,
That of its fruit thy babes may eat and die?

V

'Thus do the generations of the earth
Go to the grave and issue from the womb,
Surviving still the imperishable change
That renovates the world; even as the leaves
Which the keen frost-wind of the waning year
Has scattered on the forest-soil and heaped
For many seasons there — though long they choke,
Loading with loathsome rottenness the land,
All germs of promise, yet when the tall trees
From which they fell, shorn of their lovely shapes,   10
Lie level with the earth to moulder there,
They fertilize the land they long deformed;
Till from the breathing lawn a forest springs
Of youth, integrity and loveliness,
Like that which gave it life, to spring and die.
Thus suicidal selfishness, that blights
The fairest feelings of the opening heart,
Is destined to decay, whilst from the soil
Shall spring all virtue, all delight, all love,
And judgment cease to wage unnatural war   20
With passion's unsubduable array.
Twin-sister of Religion, Selfishness!
Rival in crime and falsehood, aping all
The wanton horrors of her bloody play;
Yet frozen, unimpassioned, spiritless,
Shunning the light, and owning not its name,
Compelled by its deformity to screen
With flimsy veil of justice and of right
Its unattractive lineaments that scare
All save the brood of ignorance; at once   30
The cause and the effect of tyranny;
Unblushing, hardened, sensual and vile;
Dead to all love but of its abjectness;
With heart impassive by more noble powers
Than unshared pleasure, sordid gain, or fame;

Despising its own miserable being,
Which still it longs, yet fears, to disen-
   thrall.

'Hence commerce springs, the venal inter-
   change
Of all that human art or Nature yield ;
Which wealth should purchase not, but
   want demand,   40
And natural kindness hasten to supply
From the full fountain of its boundless
   love,
Forever stifled, drained and tainted now.
Commerce ! beneath whose poison-breath-
   ing shade
No solitary virtue dares to spring,
But poverty and wealth with equal hand
Scatter their withering curses, and unfold
The doors of premature and violent death
To pining famine and full-fed disease,
To all that shares the lot of human life, 50
Which, poisoned body and soul, scarce
   drags the chain
That lengthens as it goes and clanks be-
   hind.

'Commerce has set the mark of selfishness,
The signet of its all-enslaving power,
Upon a shining ore, and called it gold ;
Before whose image bow the vulgar great,
The vainly rich, the miserable proud,
The mob of peasants, nobles, priests and
   kings,
And with blind feelings reverence the
   power
That grinds them to the dust of misery. 60
But in the temple of their hireling hearts
Gold is a living god and rules in scorn
All earthly things but virtue.

'Since tyrants by the sale of human life
Heap luxuries to their sensualism, and
   fame
To their wide-wasting and insatiate pride,
Success has sanctioned to a credulous world
The ruin, the disgrace, the woe of war.
His hosts of blind and unresisting dupes
The despot numbers ; from his cabinet 70
These puppets of his schemes he moves at
   will,
Even as the slaves by force or famine
   driven,
Beneath a vulgar master, to perform
A task of cold and brutal drudgery ; —
Hardened to hope, insensible to fear,

Scarce living pulleys of a dead machine,
Mere wheels of work and articles of trade,
That grace the proud and noisy pomp of
   wealth !

'The harmony and happiness of man
Yields to the wealth of nations; that which
   lifts   80
His nature to the heaven of its pride,
Is bartered for the poison of his soul;
The weight that drags to earth his tower-
   ing hopes,
Blighting all prospect but of selfish gain,
Withering all passion but of slavish fear,
Extinguishing all free and generous love
Of enterprise and daring, even the pulse
That fancy kindles in the beating heart
To mingle with sensation, it destroys, —
Leaves nothing but the sordid lust of
   self,   90
The grovelling hope of interest and gold,
Unqualified, unmingled, unredeemed
Even by hypocrisy.

             And statesmen boast
Of wealth ! The wordy eloquence that
   lives
After the ruin of their hearts, can gild
The bitter poison of a nation's woe;
Can turn the worship of the servile mob
To their corrupt and glaring idol, fame,
From virtue, trampled by its iron tread, —
Although its dazzling pedestal be raised 100
Amid the horrors of a limb-strewn field,
With desolated dwellings smoking round.
The man of ease, who, by his warm fire-
   side,
To deeds of charitable intercourse
And bare fulfilment of the common laws
Of decency and prejudice confines
The struggling nature of his human heart,
Is duped by their cold sophistry; he sheds
A passing tear perchance upon the wreck
Of earthly peace, when near his dwelling's
   door   110
The frightful waves are driven, — when his
   son
Is murdered by the tyrant, or religion
Drives his wife raving mad. But the poor
   man
Whose life is misery, and fear and care;
Whom the morn wakens but to fruitless
   toil;
Who ever hears his famished offspring's
   scream;

Whom their pale mother's uncomplaining
    gaze
Forever meets, and the proud rich man's
    eye
Flashing command, and the heart-breaking
    scene
Of thousands like himself ; — he little heeds
The rhetoric of tyranny ; his hate   121
Is quenchless as his wrongs ; he laughs to
    scorn
The vain and bitter mockery of words,
Feeling the horror of the tyrant's deeds,
And unrestrained but by the arm of power,
That knows and dreads his enmity.

' The iron rod of penury still compels
Her wretched slave to bow the knee to
    wealth,
And poison, with unprofitable toil,
A life too void of solace to confirm   130
The very chains that bind him to his doom.
Nature, impartial in munificence,
Has gifted man with all-subduing will.
Matter, with all its transitory shapes,
Lies subjected and plastic at his feet,
That, weak from bondage, tremble as they
    tread.
How many a rustic Milton has passed by,
Stifling the speechless longings of his heart,
In unremitting drudgery and care !
How many a vulgar Cato has compelled   140
His energies, no longer tameless then,
To mould a pin or fabricate a nail !
How many a Newton, to whose passive ken
Those mighty spheres that gem infinity
Were only specks of tinsel fixed in heaven
To light the midnights of his native town !

' Yet every heart contains perfection's
    germ.
The wisest of the sages of the earth,
That ever from the stores of reason drew
Science and truth, and virtue's dreadless
    tone,   150
Were but a weak and inexperienced boy,
Proud, sensual, unimpassioned, unimbued
With pure desire and universal love,
Compared to that high being, of cloudless
    brain,
Untainted passion, elevated will,
Which death (who even would linger long
    in awe
Within his noble presence and beneath
His changeless eye-beam) might alone sub-
    due.

Him, every slave now dragging through
    the filth
Of some corrupted city his sad life,   160
Pining with famine, swoln with luxury,
Blunting the keenness of his spiritual sense
With narrow schemings and unworthy
    cares,
Or madly rushing through all violent crime
To move the deep stagnation of his soul, —
Might imitate and equal.

                     But mean lust
Has bound its chains so tight about the
    earth
That all within it but the virtuous man
Is venal ; gold or fame will surely reach
The price prefixed by Selfishness to all   170
But him of resolute and unchanging will ;
Whom nor the plaudits of a servile crowd,
Nor the vile joys of tainting luxury,
Can bribe to yield his elevated soul
To Tyranny or Falsehood, though they
    wield
With blood-red hand the sceptre of the
    world.

' All things are sold : the very light of
    heaven
Is venal ; earth's unsparing gifts of love,
The smallest and most despicable things
That lurk in the abysses of the deep,   180
All objects of our life, even life itself,
And the poor pittance which the laws al-
    low
Of liberty, the fellowship of man,
Those duties which his heart of human love
Should urge him to perform instinctively,
Are bought and sold as in a public mart
Of undisguising Selfishness, that sets
On each its price, the stamp-mark of her
    reign.
Even love is sold ; the solace of all woe
Is turned to deadliest agony, old age   190
Shivers in selfish beauty's loathing arms,
And youth's corrupted impulses prepare
A life of horror from the blighting bane
Of commerce ; whilst the pestilence that
    springs
From unenjoying sensualism, has filled
All human life with hydra-headed woes.

' Falsehood demands but gold to pay the
    pangs
Of outraged conscience ; for the slavish
    priest

Sets no great value on his hireling faith ;
A little passing pomp, some servile
    souls,   200
Whom cowardice itself might safely chain
Or the spare mite of avarice could bribe
To deck the triumph of their languid zeal,
Can make him minister to tyranny.
More daring crime requires a loftier meed.
Without a shudder the slave-soldier lends
His arm to murderous deeds, and steels his
    heart,
When the dread eloquence of dying men,
Low mingling on the lonely field of fame,
Assails that nature whose applause he
    sells   210
For the gross blessings of the patriot mob,
For the vile gratitude of heartless kings,
And for a cold world's good word, — viler
    still !

' There is a nobler glory which survives
Until our being fades, and, solacing
All human care, accompanies its change;
Deserts not virtue in the dungeon's gloom,
And in the precincts of the palace guides
Its footsteps through that labyrinth of
    crime ;
Imbues his lineaments with dauntless-
    ness,   220
Even when from power's avenging hand he
    takes
Its sweetest, last and noblest title — death ;
— The consciousness of good, which neither
    gold,
Nor sordid fame, nor hope of heavenly
    bliss,
Can purchase ; but a life of resolute good,
Unalterable will, quenchless desire
Of universal happiness, the heart
That beats with it in unison, the brain
Whose ever-wakeful wisdom toils to change
Reason's rich stores for its eternal weal. 230

' This commerce of sincerest virtue needs
No meditative signs of selfishness,
No jealous intercourse of wretched gain,
No balancings of prudence, cold and long ;
In just and equal measure all is weighed,
One scale contains the sum of human weal,
And one, the good man's heart.

             How vainly seek
The selfish for that happiness denied
To aught but virtue !   Blind and hardened,
    they,

Who hope for peace amid the storms of
    care,   240
Who covet power they know not how to
    use,
And sigh for pleasure they refuse to give, —
Madly they frustrate still their own de-
    signs;
And, where they hope that quiet to en-
    joy
Which virtue pictures, bitterness of soul,
Pining regrets, and vain repentances,
Disease, disgust and lassitude pervade
Their valueless and miserable lives.

' But hoary-headed selfishness has felt
Its death-blow and is tottering to the
    grave;   250
A brighter morn awaits the human day,
When every transfer of earth's natural
    gifts
Shall be a commerce of good words and
    works;
When poverty and wealth, the thirst of
    fame,
The fear of infamy, disease and woe,
War with its million horrors, and fierce
    hell,
Shall live but in the memory of time,
Who, like a penitent libertine, shall start,
Look back, and shudder at his younger
    years.'

              VI
     All touch, all eye, all ear,
The Spirit felt the Fairy's burning speech.
    O'er the thin texture of its frame
The varying periods painted changing
    glows,
     As on a summer even,
When soul-enfolding music floats around,
    The stainless mirror of the lake
    Re-images the eastern gloom,
Mingling convulsively its purple hues
     With sunset's burnished gold.   10
     Then thus the Spirit spoke :
' It is a wild and miserable world !
    Thorny, and full of care,
Which every fiend can make his prey at
    will !
    O Fairy ! in the lapse of years,
     Is there no hope in store ?
    Will yon vast suns roll on
Interminably, still illuming
The night of so many wretched souls,
    And see no hope for them ?   20

Will not the universal Spirit e'er
Revivify this withered limb of Heaven?'

  The Fairy calmly smiled
In comfort, and a kindling gleam of hope
Suffused the Spirit's lineaments.
'Oh! rest thee tranquil; chase those fear-
  ful doubts
Which ne'er could rack an everlasting soul
That sees the chains which bind it to its
  doom.
Yes! crime and misery are in yonder earth,
  Falsehood, mistake and lust; 30
  But the eternal world
Contains at once the evil and the cure.
Some eminent in virtue shall start up,
  Even in perversest time;
The truths of their pure lips, that never
  die,
Shall bind the scorpion falsehood with a
  wreath
  Of ever-living flame,
Until the monster sting itself to death.

  'How sweet a scene will earth become!
Of purest spirits a pure dwelling-place, 40
Symphonious with the planetary spheres;
When man, with changeless Nature coa-
  lescing,
Will undertake regeneration's work,
When its ungenial poles no longer point
  To the red and baleful sun
  That faintly twinkles there!

  'Spirit, on yonder earth,
Falsehood now triumphs; deadly power
Has fixed its seal upon the lip of truth!
  Madness and misery are there! 50
The happiest is most wretched! Yet con-
  fide
Until pure health-drops from the cup of
  joy
Fall like a dew of balm upon the world.
Now, to the scene I show, in silence turn,
And read the blood-stained charter of all
  woe,
Which Nature soon with recreating hand
Will blot in mercy from the book of earth.
How bold the flight of passion's wandering
  wing,
How swift the step of reason's firmer tread,
How calm and sweet the victories of life,
How terrorless the triumph of the grave!
How powerless were the mightiest mon-
  arch's arm, 62

Vain his loud threat, and impotent his
  frown!
How ludicrous the priest's dogmatic roar!
The weight of his exterminating curse
How light! and his affected charity,
To suit the pressure of the changing times,
What palpable deceit! — but for thy aid,
Religion! but for thee, prolific fiend,
Who peoplest earth with demons, hell with
  men, 70
And heaven with slaves!

  'Thou taintest all thou lookest upon! —
  the stars,
Which on thy cradle beamed so brightly
  sweet,
Were gods to the distempered playfulness
Of thy untutored infancy; the trees,
The grass, the clouds, the mountains and the
  sea,
All living things that walk, swim, creep or
  fly,
Were gods; the sun had homage, and the
  moon
Her worshipper. Then thou becamest, a
  boy, 79
More daring in thy frenzies; every shape,
Monstrous or vast, or beautifully wild,
Which from sensation's relics fancy culls;
The spirits of the air, the shuddering ghost,
The genii of the elements, the powers
That give a shape to Nature's varied
  works,
Had life and place in the corrupt belief
Of thy blind heart; yet still thy youthful
  hands
Were pure of human blood. Then man-
  hood gave
Its strength and ardor to thy frenzied
  brain;
Thine eager gaze scanned the stupendous
  scene, 90
Whose wonders mocked the knowledge of
  thy pride;
Their everlasting and unchanging laws
Reproached thine ignorance. Awhile thou
  stood'st
Baffled and gloomy; then thou didst sum
  up
The elements of all that thou didst know;
The changing seasons, winter's leafless
  reign,
The budding of the heaven-breathing trees,
The eternal orbs that beautify the night,
The sunrise, and the setting of the moon,

Earthquakes and wars, and poisons and
  disease,   100
And all their causes, to an abstract point
Converging thou didst bend, and called it
  God !
The self-sufficing, the omnipotent,
The merciful, and the avenging God !
Who, prototype of human misrule, sits
High in heaven's realm, upon a golden
  throne,
Even like an earthly king; and whose dread
  work,
Hell, gapes forever for the unhappy slaves
Of fate, whom he created in his sport
To triumph in their torments when they
  fell !   110
Earth heard the name; earth trembled as
  the smoke
Of his revenge ascended up to heaven,
Blotting the constellations; and the cries
Of millions butchered in sweet confidence
And unsuspecting peace, even when the
  bonds
Of safety were confirmed by wordy oaths
Sworn in his dreadful name, rung through
  the land;
Whilst innocent babes writhed on thy stub-
  born spear,
And thou didst laugh to hear the mother's
  shriek
Of maniac gladness, as the sacred steel 120
Felt cold in her torn entrails !

' Religion ! thou wert then in manhood's
  prime;
But age crept on; one God would not suf-
  fice
For senile puerility; thou framedst
A tale to suit thy dotage and to glut
Thy misery-thirsting soul, that the mad
  fiend
Thy wickedness had pictured might afford
A plea for sating the unnatural thirst
For murder, rapine, violence and crime, 129
That still consumed thy being, even when
Thou heard'st the step of fate; that flames
  might light
Thy funeral scene; and the shrill horrent
  shrieks
Of parents dying on the pile that burned
To light their children to thy paths, the roar
Of the encircling flames, the exulting cries
Of thine apostles loud commingling there,
    Might sate thine hungry ear
    Even on the bed of death !

' But now contempt is mocking thy gray
  hairs;
Thou art descending to the darksome
  grave,   140
Unhonored and unpitied but by those
Whose pride is passing by like thine, and
  sheds,
Like thine, a glare that fades before the
  sun
Of truth, and shines but in the dreadful
  night
That long has lowered above the ruined
  world.

' Throughout these infinite orbs of mingling
  light
Of which yon earth is one, is wide diffused
A Spirit of activity and life,
That knows no term, cessation or decay;
That fades not when the lamp of earthly
  life,   150
Extinguished in the dampness of the grave,
Awhile there slumbers, more than when
  the babe
In the dim newness of its being feels
The impulses of sublunary things,
And all is wonder to unpractised sense;
But, active, steadfast and eternal, still
Guides the fierce whirlwind, in the tempest
  roars,
Cheers in the day, breathes in the balmy
  groves,
Strengthens in health, and poisons in dis-
  ease;
And in the storm of change, that cease-
  lessly   160
Rolls round the eternal universe and shakes
Its undecaying battlement, presides,
Apportioning with irresistible law
The place each spring of its machine shall
  fill;
So that, when waves on waves tumultuous
  heap
Confusion to the clouds, and fiercely driven
Heaven's lightnings scorch the uprooted
  ocean-fords —
Whilst, to the eye of shipwrecked mariner,
Lone sitting on the bare and shuddering
  rock,
All seems unlinked contingency and
  chance —   170
No atom of this turbulence fulfils
A vague and unnecessitated task
Or acts but as it must and ought to act.
Even the minutest molecule of light,

That in an April sunbeam's fleeting glow
Fulfils its destined though invisible work,
The universal Spirit guides; nor less
When merciless ambition, or mad zeal,
Has led two hosts of dupes to battle-field,
That, blind, they there may dig each other's
    graves   180
And call the sad work glory, does it rule
All passions; not a thought, a will, an
    act,
No working of the tyrant's moody mind,
Nor one misgiving of the slaves who boast
Their servitude to hide the shame they
    feel,
Nor the events enchaining every will,
That from the depths of unrecorded time
Have drawn all-influencing virtue, pass
Unrecognized or unforeseen by thee,
Soul of the Universe! eternal spring   190
Of life and death, of happiness and woe,
Of all that chequers the phantasmal scene
That floats before our eyes in wavering
    light,
Which gleams but on the darkness of our
    prison
    Whose chains and massy walls
    We feel but cannot see.

'Spirit of Nature! all-sufficing Power,
Necessity! thou mother of the world!
Unlike the God of human error, thou
Requirest no prayers or praises; the ca-
    price   200
Of man's weak will belongs no more to
    thee
Than do the changeful passions of his
    breast
To thy unvarying harmony; the slave,
Whose horrible lusts spread misery o'er
    the world,
And the good man, who lifts with virtuous
    pride
His being in the sight of happiness
That springs from his own works; the
    poison-tree,
Beneath whose shade all life is withered
    up,
And the fair oak, whose leafy dome affords
A temple where the vows of happy love   210
Are registered, are equal in thy sight;
No love, no hate thou cherishest; revenge
And favoritism, and worst desire of fame
Thou knowest not; all that the wide world
    contains
Are but thy passive instruments, and thou

Regard'st them all with an impartial eye,
Whose joy or pain thy nature cannot feel,
    Because thou hast not human sense,
    Because thou art not human mind.

'Yes! when the sweeping storm of
    time   220
Has sung its death-dirge o'er the ruined
    fanes
And broken altars of the almighty fiend,
Whose name usurps thy honors, and the
    blood
Through centuries clotted there has floated
    down
The tainted flood of ages, shalt thou live
Unchangeable! A shrine is raised to thee,
    Which nor the tempest breath of time,
    Nor the interminable flood
    Over earth's slight pageant rolling,
    Availeth to destroy, —   230
The sensitive extension of the world;
    That wondrous and eternal fane,
Where pain and pleasure, good and evil
    join,
To do the will of strong necessity,
    And life, in multitudinous shapes,
Still pressing forward where no term can be,
    Like hungry and unresting flame
Curls round the eternal columns of its
    strength.'

VII

SPIRIT

'I was an infant when my mother went
To see an atheist burned. She took me
    there.
The dark-robed priests were met around
    the pile;
The multitude was gazing silently;
And as the culprit passed with dauntless
    mien,
Tempered disdain in his unaltering eye,
Mixed with a quiet smile, shone calmly
    forth;
The thirsty fire crept round his manly
    limbs;
His resolute eyes were scorched to blind-
    ness soon;
His death-pang rent my heart! the insen-
    sate mob   10
Uttered a cry of triumph, and I wept.
"Weep not, child!" cried my mother, "for
    that man
Has said, There is no God."'

FAIRY
                                'There is no God!
Nature confirms the faith his death-groan
    sealed.
Let heaven and earth, let man's revolving
    race,
His ceaseless generations, tell their tale;
Let every part depending on the chain
That links it to the whole, point to the
    hand
That grasps its term! Let every seed that
    falls
In silent eloquence unfold its store   20
Of argument; infinity within,
Infinity without, belie creation;
The exterminable spirit it contains
Is Nature's only God; but human pride
Is skilful to invent most serious names
To hide its ignorance.

                            ' The name of God
Has fenced about all crime with holiness,
Himself the creature of his worshippers,
Whose names and attributes and passions
    change,   29
Seeva, Buddh, Foh, Jehovah, God, or Lord,
Even with the human dupes who build his
    shrines,
Still serving o'er the war-polluted world
For desolation's watchword; whether hosts
Stain his death-blushing chariot-wheels, as
    on
Triumphantly they roll, whilst Brahmins
    raise
A sacred hymn to mingle with the groans;
Or countless partners of his power divide
His tyranny to weakness; or the smoke
Of burning towns, the cries of female help-
    lessness,   39
Unarmed old age, and youth, and infancy,
Horribly massacred, ascend to heaven
In honor of his name; or, last and worst,
Earth groans beneath religion's iron age,
And priests dare babble of a God of peace,
Even whilst their hands are red with guilt-
    less blood,
Murdering the while, uprooting every germ
Of truth, exterminating, spoiling all,
Making the earth a slaughter-house!

                ' O Spirit! through the sense
By which thy inner nature was apprised 50
    Of outward shows, vague dreams have
        rolled,
    And varied reminiscences have waked

Tablets that never fade;
All things have been imprinted there,
The stars, the sea, the earth, the sky,
Even the unshapeliest lineaments
    Of wild and fleeting visions
        Have left a record there
        To testify of earth.

' These are my empire, for to me is given 60
The wonders of the human world to keep,
And fancy's thin creations to endow
With manner, being and reality;
Therefore a wondrous phantom from the
    dreams
Of human error's dense and purblind faith
I will evoke, to meet thy questioning.
        Ahasuerus, rise!'

        A strange and woe-worn wight
        Arose beside the battlement,
            And stood unmoving there.   70
His inessential figure cast no shade
        Upon the golden floor;
His port and mien bore mark of many
    years,
And chronicles of untold ancientness
Were legible within his beamless eye;
    Yet his cheek bore the mark of youth;
Freshness and vigor knit his manly frame;
The wisdom of old age was mingled there
        With youth's primeval dauntlessness;
        And inexpressible woe,   80
Chastened by fearless resignation, gave
An awful grace to his all-speaking brow.

SPIRIT
' Is there a God ? '

AHASUERUS
' Is there a God! — ay, an almighty God,
And vengeful as almighty! Once his voice
Was heard on earth; earth shuddered at
    the sound;
The fiery-visaged firmament expressed
Abhorrence, and the grave of Nature
    yawned
To swallow all the dauntless and the good
That dared to hurl defiance at his throne,
Girt as it was with power. None but
    slaves   91
Survived, — cold-blooded slaves, who did
    the work
Of tyrannous omnipotence; whose souls
No honest indignation ever urged
To elevated daring, to one deed

Which gross and sensual self did not pol-
    lute.
These slaves built temples for the omnipo-
    tent fiend,
Gorgeous and vast; the costly altars smoked
With human blood, and hideous pæans rung
Through all the long-drawn aisles. A mur-
    derer heard   100
His voice in Egypt, one whose gifts and arts
Had raised him to his eminence in power,
Accomplice of omnipotence in crime
And confidant of the all-knowing one.
    These were Jehovah's words.

'"From an eternity of idleness
I, God, awoke ; in seven days' toil made
    earth
From nothing; rested, and created man;
I placed him in a paradise, and there
Planted the tree of evil, so that he   110
Might eat and perish, and my soul procure
Wherewith to sate its malice and to turn,
Even like a heartless conqueror of the
    earth,
All misery to my fame. The race of men,
Chosen to my honor, with impunity
May sate the lusts I planted in their heart.
Here I command thee hence to lead them
    on,
Until with hardened feet their conquering
    troops
Wade on the promised soil through wo-
    man's blood,
And make my name be dreaded through
    the land.   120
Yet ever-burning flame and ceaseless woe
Shall be the doom of their eternal souls,
With every soul on this ungrateful earth,
Virtuous or vicious, weak or strong, —
    even all
Shall perish, to fulfil the blind revenge
(Which you, to men, call justice) of their
    God."

            'The murderer's brow
Quivered with horror.

            '"God omnipotent,
Is there no mercy? must our punishment
Be endless? will long ages roll away,   130
And see no term? Oh! wherefore hast
    thou made
In mockery and wrath this evil earth?
Mercy becomes the powerful — be but just !
O God! repent and save!"

'"One way remains:
I will beget a son and he shall bear
The sins of all the world; he shall arise
In an unnoticed corner of the earth,
And there shall die upon a cross, and purge
The universal crime; so that the few
On whom my grace descends, those who are
    marked   140
As vessels to the honor of their God,
May credit this strange sacrifice and save
Their souls alive. Millions shall live and
    die,
Who ne'er shall call upon their Saviour's
    name,
But, unredeemed, go to the gaping grave,
Thousands shall deem it an old woman's
    tale,
Such as the nurses frighten babes withal;
These in a gulf of anguish and of flame
Shall curse their reprobation endlessly,
Yet tenfold pangs shall force them to
    avow,   150
Even on their beds of torment where they
    howl,
My honor and the justice of their doom.
What then avail their virtuous deeds, their
    thoughts
Of purity, with radiant genius bright
Or lit with human reason's earthly ray ?
Many are called, but few will I elect.
Do thou my bidding, Moses !"

            'Even the murderer's cheek
Was blanched with horror, and his quiver-
    ing lips
Scarce faintly uttered — "O almighty one,
I tremble and obey !"   160

'O Spirit ! centuries have set their seal
On this heart of many wounds, and loaded
    brain,
Since the Incarnate came ; humbly he came,
Veiling his horrible Godhead in the shape
Of man, scorned by the world, his name
    unheard
Save by the rabble of his native town,
Even as a parish demagogue. He led
The crowd ; he taught them justice, truth
    and peace,
In semblance ; but he lit within their souls
The quenchless flames of zeal, and blessed
    the sword   170
He brought on earth to satiate with the
    blood
Of truth and freedom his malignant soul.

At length his mortal frame was led to
    death.
I stood beside him; on the torturing cross
No pain assailed his unterrestrial sense;
And yet he groaned. Indignantly I summed
The massacres and miseries which his name
Had sanctioned in my country, and I cried,
"Go ! go !" in mockery.
A smile of godlike malice reillumined 180
His fading lineaments. "I go," he cried,
"But thou shalt wander o'er the unquiet
    earth
Eternally." The dampness of the grave
Bathed my imperishable front. I fell,
And long lay tranced upon the charmèd
    soil.
When I awoke hell burned within my brain
Which staggered on its seat; for all around
The mouldering relics of my kindred lay,
Even as the Almighty's ire arrested them,
And in their various attitudes of death 190
My murdered children's mute and eyeless
    skulls
Glared ghastily upon me.

                   But my soul,
From sight and sense of the polluting woe
Of tyranny, had long learned to prefer
Hell's freedom to the servitude of heaven.
Therefore I rose, and dauntlessly began
My lonely and unending pilgrimage,
Resolved to wage unweariable war
With my almighty tyrant and to hurl
Defiance at his impotence to harm 200
Beyond the curse I bore. The very hand,
That barred my passage to the peaceful
    grave,
Has crushed the earth to misery, and given
Its empire to the chosen of his slaves.
These I have seen, even from the earliest
    dawn
Of weak, unstable and precarious power,
Then preaching peace, as now they practise
    war;
So, when they turned but from the mas-
    sacre
Of unoffending infidels to quench
Their thirst for ruin in the very blood 210
That flowed in their own veins, and pitiless
    zeal
Froze every human feeling as the wife
Sheathed in her husband's heart the sacred
    steel,
Even whilst its hopes were dreaming of her
    love;

And friends to friends, brothers to brothers
    stood
Opposed in bloodiest battle-field, and war,
Scarce satiable by fate's last death-draught,
    waged,
Drunk from the wine-press of the Al-
    mighty's wrath;
Whilst the red cross, in mockery of peace,
Pointed to victory! When the fray was
    done, 220
No remnant of the exterminated faith
Survived to tell its ruin, but the flesh,
With putrid smoke poisoning the atmo-
    sphere,
That rotted on the half-extinguished pile.

'Yes ! I have seen God's worshippers un-
    sheathe
The sword of his revenge, when grace de-
    scended,
Confirming all unnatural impulses,
To sanctify their desolating deeds;
And frantic priests waved the ill-omened
    cross
O'er the unhappy earth ; then shone the
    sun 230
On showers of gore from the upflashing
    steel
Of safe assassination, and all crime
Made stingless by the spirits of the Lord,
And blood-red rainbows canopied the land.

'Spirit! no year of my eventful being
Has passed unstained by crime and misery,
Which flows from God's own faith. I've
    marked his slaves
With tongues, whose lies are venomous,
    beguile
The insensate mob, and, whilst one hand
    was red 239
With murder, feign to stretch the other out
For brotherhood and peace; and that they
    now
Babble of love and mercy, whilst their deeds
Are marked with all the narrowness and
    crime
That freedom's young arm dare not yet
    chastise,
Reason may claim our gratitude, who now,
Establishing the imperishable throne
Of truth and stubborn virtue, maketh vain
The unprevailing malice of my foe,
Whose bootless rage heaps torments for the
    brave,
Adds impotent eternities to pain, 250

Whilst keenest disappointment racks his
    breast
To see the smiles of peace around them
    play,
To frustrate or to sanctify their doom.

'Thus have I stood, — through a wild waste
    of years
Struggling with whirlwinds of mad agony,
Yet peaceful, and serene, and self-en-
    shrined,
Mocking my powerless tyrant's horrible
    curse
With stubborn and unalterable will,
Even as a giant oak, which heaven's fierce
    flame
Had scathèd in the wilderness, to stand 260
A monument of fadeless ruin there;
Yet peacefully and movelessly it braves
The midnight conflict of the wintry storm,
  As in the sunlight's calm it spreads
  Its worn and withered arms on high
To meet the quiet of a summer's noon.'

  The Fairy waved her wand;
  Ahasuerus fled
Fast as the shapes of mingled shade and
    mist, 269
That lurk in the glens of a twilight grove,
  Flee from the morning beam; —
  The matter of which dreams are made
  Not more endowed with actual life
  Than this phantasmal portraiture
  Of wandering human thought.

VIII

THE FAIRY

'The present and the past thou hast beheld.
It was a desolate sight. Now, Spirit, learn,
  The secrets of the future. — Time!
Unfold the brooding pinion of thy gloom,
Render thou up thy half-devoured babes,
And from the cradles of eternity,
Where millions lie lulled to their portioned
    sleep
By the deep murmuring stream of passing
    things,
Tear thou that gloomy shroud. — Spirit,
    behold
  Thy glorious destiny!' 10

  Joy to the Spirit came.
Through the wide rent in Time's eternal
    veil,

Hope was seen beaming through the mists
    of fear;
  Earth was no longer hell;
  Love, freedom, health had given
Their ripeness to the manhood of its prime,
  And all its pulses beat
Symphonious to the planetary spheres;
  Then dulcet music swelled 19
Concordant with the life-strings of the soul;
It throbbed in sweet and languid beatings
    there,
Catching new life from transitory death;
Like the vague sighings of a wind at even
That wakes the wavelets of the slumbering
    sea
And dies on the creation of its breath,
And sinks and rises, falls and swells by
    fits,
  Was the pure stream of feeling
  That sprung from these sweet notes,
And o'er the Spirit's human sympathies 29
With mild and gentle motion calmly flowed.

  Joy to the Spirit came, —
  Such joy as when a lover sees
The chosen of his soul in happiness
  And witnesses her peace
Whose woe to him were bitterer than death;
  Sees her unfaded cheek
Glow mantling in first luxury of health,
  Thrills with her lovely eyes,
Which like two stars amid the heaving
    main
  Sparkle through liquid bliss. 40

Then in her triumph spoke the Fairy Queen:
'I will not call the ghost of ages gone
To unfold the frightful secrets of its
    lore;
  The present now is past,
And those events that desolate the earth
Have faded from the memory of Time,
Who dares not give reality to that
Whose being I annul. To me is given
The wonders of the human world to keep,
Space, matter, time and mind. Futurity 50
Exposes now its treasure; let the sight
Renew and strengthen all thy failing hope.
O human Spirit! spur thee to the goal
Where virtue fixes universal peace,
And, 'midst the ebb and flow of human
    things,
Show somewhat stable, somewhat certain
    still,
A light-house o'er the wild of dreary waves.

'The habitable earth is full of bliss;
Those wastes of frozen billows that were
    hurled
By everlasting snow-storms round the
    poles,   60
Where matter dared not vegetate or live,
But ceaseless frost round the vast solitude
Bound its broad zone of stillness, are un-
    loosed;
And fragrant zephyrs there from spicy
    isles
Ruffle the placid ocean-deep, that rolls
Its broad, bright surges to the sloping sand,
Whose roar is wakened into echoings sweet
To murmur through the heaven-breathing
    groves
And melodize with man's blest nature
    there.

'Those deserts of immeasurable sand,   70
Whose age-collected fervors scarce allowed
A bird to live, a blade of grass to spring,
Where the shrill chirp of the green lizard's
    love
Broke on the sultry silentness alone,
Now teem with countless rills and shady
    woods,
Cornfields and pastures and white cottages;
And where the startled wilderness beheld
A savage conqueror stained in kindred
    blood,
A tigress sating with the flesh of lambs
The unnatural famine of her toothless
    cubs,   80
Whilst shouts and howlings through the
    desert rang, —
Sloping and smooth the daisy-spangled
    lawn,
Offering sweet incense to the sunrise, smiles
To see a babe before his mother's door,
    Sharing his morning's meal
  With the green and golden basilisk
  That comes to lick his feet.

'Those trackless deeps, where many a weary
    sail
Has seen above the illimitable plain
Morning on night and night on morning
    rise,   90
Whilst still no land to greet the wanderer
    spread
Its shadowy mountains on the sun-bright
    sea,
Where the loud roarings of the tempest-
    waves

So long have mingled with the gusty wind
In melancholy loneliness, and swept
The desert of those ocean solitudes
But vocal to the sea-bird's harrowing shriek,
The bellowing monster, and the rushing
    storm;
Now to the sweet and many-mingling
    sounds
Of kindliest human impulses respond. 100
Those lonely realms bright garden-isles
    begem,
With lightsome clouds and shining seas
    between,
And fertile valleys, resonant with bliss,
Whilst green woods overcanopy the wave,
Which like a toil-worn laborer leaps to
    shore
To meet the kisses of the flowrets there.

'All things are recreated, and the flame
Of consentaneous love inspires all life.
The fertile bosom of the earth gives suck
To myriads, who still grow beneath her
    care,   110
Rewarding her with their pure perfectness;
The balmy breathings of the wind inhale
Her virtues and diffuse them all abroad;
Health floats amid the gentle atmosphere,
Glows in the fruits and mantles on the
    stream;
No storms deform the beaming brow of
    heaven,
Nor scatter in the freshness of its pride
The foliage of the ever-verdant trees;
But fruits are ever ripe, flowers ever fair,
And autumn proudly bears her matron
    grace,   120
Kindling a flush on the fair cheek of spring,
Whose virgin bloom beneath the ruddy
    fruit
Reflects its tint and blushes into love.

'The lion now forgets to thirst for blood;
There might you see him sporting in the
    sun
Beside the dreadless kid; his claws are
    sheathed,
His teeth are harmless, custom's force has
    made
His nature as the nature of a lamb.
Like passion's fruit, the nightshade's tempt-
    ing bane
Poisons no more the pleasure it be-
    stows;   130
All bitterness is past; the cup of joy

Unmingled mantles to the goblet's brim
And courts the thirsty lips it fled before.

' But chief, ambiguous man, he that can
 know
More misery, and dream more joy than
 all;
Whose keen sensations thrill within his
 breast
To mingle with a loftier instinct there,
Lending their power to pleasure and to
 pain,
Yet raising, sharpening, and refining each;
Who stands amid the ever-varying world,
The burden or the glory of the earth; 141
He chief perceives the change; his being
 notes
The gradual renovation and defines
Each movement of its progress on his
 mind.

' Man, where the gloom of the long polar
 night
Lowers o'er the snow - clad rocks and
 frozen soil,
Where scarce the hardiest herb that braves
 the frost
Basks in the moonlight's ineffectual glow,
Shrank with the plants, and darkened with
 the night;
His chilled and narrow energies, his
 heart 150
Insensible to courage, truth or love,
His stunted stature and imbecile frame,
Marked him for some abortion of the earth,
Fit compeer of the bears that roamed
 around,
Whose habits and enjoyments were his
 own;
His life a feverish dream of stagnant woe,
Whose meagre wants, but scantily ful-
 filled,
Apprised him ever of the joyless length
Which his short being's wretchedness had
 reached;
His death a pang which famine, cold and
 toil 160
Long on the mind, whilst yet the vital
 spark
Clung to the body stubbornly, had brought:
All was inflicted here that earth's revenge
Could wreak on the infringers of her law;
One curse alone was spared — the name of
 God.

' Nor, where the tropics bound the realms
 of day
With a broad belt of mingling cloud and
 flame,
Where blue mists through the unmoving
 atmosphere
Scattered the seeds of pestilence and fed
Unnatural vegetation, where the land 170
Teemed with all earthquake, tempest and
 disease,
Was man a nobler being; slavery
Had crushed him to his country's blood-
 stained dust;
Or he was bartered for the fame of power,
Which, all internal impulses destroying,
Makes human will an article of trade;
Or he was changed with Christians for their
 gold
And dragged to distant isles, where to the
 sound
Of the flesh-mangling scourge he does the
 work
Of all-polluting luxury and wealth, 180
Which doubly visits on the tyrants' heads
The long-protracted fulness of their woe;
Or he was led to legal butchery,
To turn to worms beneath that burning sun
Where kings first leagued against the rights
 of men
And priests first traded with the name of
 God.

' Even where the milder zone afforded man
A seeming shelter, yet contagion there,
Blighting his being with unnumbered ills,
Spread like a quenchless fire; nor truth till
 late 190
Availed to arrest its progress or create
That peace which first in bloodless victory
 waved
Her snowy standard o'er this favored clime;
There man was long the train-bearer of
 slaves,
The mimic of surrounding misery,
The jackal of ambition's lion-rage,
The bloodhound of religion's hungry zeal.

' Here now the human being stands adorning
This loveliest earth with taintless body and
 mind;
Blest from his birth with all bland impulses, 200
Which gently in his noble bosom wake

All kindly passions and all pure desires.
Him, still from hope to hope the bliss pur-
 suing
Which from the exhaustless store of human
 weal
Draws on the virtuous mind, the thoughts
 that rise
In time-destroying infiniteness gift
With self-enshrined eternity, that mocks
The unprevailing hoariness of age;
And man, once fleeting o'er the transient
 scene
Swift as an unremembered vision, stands 210
Immortal upon earth; no longer now
He slays the lamb that looks him in the
 face,
And horribly devours his mangled flesh,
Which, still avenging Nature's broken
 law,
Kindled all putrid humors in his frame,
All evil passions and all vain belief,
Hatred, despair and loathing in his mind,
The germs of misery, death, disease and
 crime.
No longer now the wingèd habitants,
That in the woods their sweet lives sing
 away,   220
Flee from the form of man ; but gather
 round,
And prune their sunny feathers on the
 hands
Which little children stretch in friendly
 sport
Towards these dreadless partners of their
 play.
All things are void of terror; man has
 lost
His terrible prerogative, and stands
An equal amidst equals; happiness
And science dawn, though late, upon the
 earth;
Peace cheers the mind, health renovates
 the frame;   229
Disease and pleasure cease to mingle here,
Reason and passion cease to combat there;
Whilst each unfettered o'er the earth ex-
 tend
Their all-subduing energies, and wield
The sceptre of a vast dominion there;
Whilst every shape and mode of matter
 lends
Its force to the omnipotence of mind,
Which from its dark mine drags the gem
 of truth
To decorate its paradise of peace.'

IX

'O happy Earth, reality of Heaven!
To which those restless souls that cease-
 lessly
Throng through the human universe, aspire!
Thou consummation of all mortal hope!
Thou glorious prize of blindly working will,
Whose rays, diffused throughout all space
 and time,
Verge to one point and blend forever there!
Of purest spirits thou pure dwelling-place
Where care and sorrow, impotence and
 crime,
Languor, disease and ignorance dare not
 come!   10
O happy Earth, reality of Heaven!

'Genius has seen thee in her passionate
 dreams;
And dim forebodings of thy loveliness,
Haunting the human heart, have there en-
 twined
Those rooted hopes of some sweet place of
 bliss,
Where friends and lovers meet to part no
 more.
Thou art the end of all desire and will,
The product of all action; and the souls,
That by the paths of an aspiring change 19
Have reached thy haven of perpetual peace,
There rest from the eternity of toil
That framed the fabric of thy perfectness.

'Even Time, the conqueror, fled thee in his
 fear;
That hoary giant, who in lonely pride
So long had ruled the world that nations
 fell
Beneath his silent footstep. Pyramids,
That for millenniums had withstood the tide
Of human things, his storm-breath drove in
 sand
Across that desert where their stones sur-
 vived
The name of him whose pride had heaped
 them there.   30
Yon monarch, in his solitary pomp,
Was but the mushroom of a summer day,
That his light-wingèd footstep pressed to
 dust;
Time was the king of earth; all things gave
 way
Before him but the fixed and virtuous will,
The sacred sympathies of soul and sense,
That mocked his fury and prepared his fall.

'Yet slow and gradual dawned the morn of
love;
Long lay the clouds of darkness o'er the
scene,
Till from its native heaven they rolled
away: 40
First, crime triumphant o'er all hope ca-
reered
Unblushing, undisguising, bold and strong,
Whilst falsehood, tricked in virtue's attri-
butes,
Long sanctified all deeds of vice and woe,
Till, done by her own venomous sting to
death,
She left the moral world without a law,
No longer fettering passion's fearless wing,
Nor searing reason with the brand of God.
Then steadily the happy ferment worked;
Reason was free; and wild though passion
went 50
Through tangled glens and wood-embos-
omed meads,
Gathering a garland of the strangest flow-
ers,
Yet, like the bee returning to her queen,
She bound the sweetest on her sister's brow,
Who meek and sober kissed the sportive
child,
No longer trembling at the broken rod.

' Mild was the slow necessity of death.
The tranquil spirit failed beneath its grasp,
Without a groan, almost without a fear,
Calm as a voyager to some distant land, 60
And full of wonder, full of hope as he.
The deadly germs of languor and disease
Died in the human frame, and purity
Blessed with all gifts her earthly worship-
pers.
How vigorous 'then the athletic form of
age !
How clear its open and unwrinkled brow !
Where neither avarice, cunning, pride or
care
Had stamped the seal of gray deformity
On all the mingling lineaments of time.
How lovely the intrepid front of youth, 70
Which meek-eyed courage decked with
freshest grace;
Courage of soul, that dreaded not a name,
And elevated will, that journeyed on
Through life's phantasmal scene in fear-
lessness,
With virtue, love and pleasure, hand in
hand !

' Then, that sweet bondage which is free-
dom's self,
And rivets with sensation's softest tie
The kindred sympathies of human souls,
Needed no fetters of tyrannic law.
Those delicate and timid impulses 80
In Nature's primal modesty arose,
And with undoubting confidence disclosed
The growing longings of its dawning love,
Unchecked by dull and selfish chastity,
That virtue of the cheaply virtuous,
Who pride themselves in senselessness and
frost.
No longer prostitution's venomed bane
Poisoned the springs of happiness and
life;
Woman and man, in confidence and love,
Equal and free and pure together trod 90
The mountain - paths of virtue, which no
more
Were stained with blood from many a pil-
grim's feet.

' Then, where, through distant ages, long
in pride
The palace of the monarch - slave had
mocked
Famine's faint groan and penury's silent
tear,
A heap of crumbling ruins stood, and
threw
Year after year their stones upon the field,
Wakening a lonely echo; and the leaves
Of the old thorn, that on the topmost tower
Usurped the royal ensign's grandeur, shook
In the stern storm that swayed the topmost
tower, 101
And whispered strange tales in the whirl-
wind's ear.

' Low through the lone cathedral's roofless
aisles
The melancholy winds a death-dirge sung.
It were a sight of awfulness to see
The works of faith and slavery, so vast,
So sumptuous, yet so perishing withal,
Even as the corpse that rests beneath its
wall !
A thousand mourners deck the pomp of
death 109
To-day, the breathing marble glows above
To decorate its memory, and tongues
Are busy of its life; to-morrow, worms
In silence and in darkness seize their
prey.

'Within the massy prison's mouldering
    courts,
Fearless and free the ruddy children played,
Weaving gay chaplets for their innocent
    brows
With the green ivy and the red wall-flower
That mock the dungeon's unavailing gloom;
The ponderous chains and gratings of
    strong iron   119
There rusted amid heaps of broken stone
That mingled slowly with their native
    earth;
There the broad beam of day, which feebly
    once
Lighted the cheek of lean captivity
With a pale and sickly glare, then freely
    shone
On the pure smiles of infant playfulness;
No more the shuddering voice of hoarse
    despair
Pealed through the echoing vaults, but
    soothing notes
Of ivy-fingered winds and gladsome birds
And merriment were resonant around.   129

'These ruins soon left not a wreck behind;
Their elements, wide-scattered o'er the
    globe,
To happier shapes were moulded, and be-
    came
Ministrant to all blissful impulses;
Thus human things were perfected, and
    earth,
Even as a child beneath its mother's love,
Was strengthened in all excellence, and
    grew
Fairer and nobler with each passing year.

'Now Time his dusky pennons o'er the
    scene
Closes in steadfast darkness, and the past
Fades from our charmèd sight. My task
    is done;   140
Thy lore is learned. Earth's wonders are
    thine own
With all the fear and all the hope they
    bring.
My spells are passed; the present now re-
    curs.
Ah me! a pathless wilderness remains
Yet unsubdued by man's reclaiming hand.

'Yet, human Spirit! bravely hold thy
    course;
Let virtue teach thee firmly to pursue

The gradual paths of an aspiring change;
For birth and life and death, and that
    strange state   149
Before the naked soul has found its home,
All tend to perfect happiness, and urge
The restless wheels of being on their
    way,
Whose flashing spokes, instinct with infi-
    nite life,
Bicker and burn to gain their destined
    goal;
For birth but wakes the spirit to the sense
Of outward shows, whose unexperienced
    shape
New modes of passion to its frame may
    lend;
Life is its state of action, and the store
Of all events is aggregated there
That variegate the eternal universe;   160
Death is a gate of dreariness and gloom,
That leads to azure isles and beaming
    skies
And happy regions of eternal hope.
Therefore, O Spirit! fearlessly bear on.
Though storms may break the primrose on
    its stalk,
Though frosts may blight the freshness of
    its bloom,
Yet spring's awakening breath will woo
    the earth
To feed with kindliest dews its favorite
    flower,
That blooms in mossy bank and darksome
    glens,
Lighting the greenwood with its sunny
    smile.   170

'Fear not then, Spirit, death's disrobing
    hand,
So welcome when the tyrant is awake,
So welcome when the bigot's hell-torch
    burns;
'T is but the voyage of a darksome hour,
The transient gulf-dream of a startling
    sleep.
Death is no foe to virtue; earth has seen
Love's brightest roses on the scaffold bloom,
Mingling with freedom's fadeless laurels
    there,
And presaging the truth of visioned bliss.
Are there not hopes within thee, which this
    scene   180
Of linked and gradual being has confirmed?
Whose stingings bade thy heart look further
    still,

When, to the moonlight walk by Henry led,
Sweetly and sadly thou didst talk of death ?
And wilt thou rudely tear them from thy
    breast,
Listening supinely to a bigot's creed,
Or tamely crouching to the tyrant's rod,
Whose iron thongs are red with human
    gore ?
Never : but bravely bearing on, thy will
Is destined an eternal war to wage   190
With tyranny and falsehood, and uproot
The germs of misery from the human heart.
Thine is the hand whose piety would soothe
The thorny pillow of unhappy crime,
Whose impotence an easy pardon gains,
Watching its wanderings as a friend's dis-
    ease ;
Thine is the brow whose mildness would
    defy
Its fiercest rage, and brave its sternest
    will,
When fenced by power and master of the
    world.
Thou art sincere and good ; of resolute
    mind,   200
Free from heart-withering custom's cold
    control,
Of passion lofty, pure and unsubdued.
Earth's pride and meanness could not van-
    quish thee,
And therefore art thou worthy of the boon
Which thou hast now received; virtue shall
    keep
Thy footsteps in the path that thou hast
    trod,
And many days of beaming hope shall bless
Thy spotless life of sweet and sacred love.
Go, happy one, and give that bosom joy,
  Whose sleepless spirit waits to catch 210
  Light, life and rapture from thy smile !'

  The Fairy waves her wand of charm.
Speechless with bliss the Spirit mounts the
    car,
That rolled beside the battlement,
Bending her beamy eyes in thankfulness.
  Again the enchanted steeds were yoked ;
  Again the burning wheels inflame
The steep descent of heaven's untrodden
    way.
  Fast and far the chariot flew;
  The vast and fiery globes that rolled 220
  Around the Fairy's palace-gate
Lessened by slow degrees, and soon ap-
    peared
Such tiny twinklers as the planet orbs
That there attendant on the solar power
With borrowed light pursued their nar-
    rower way.

  Earth floated then below;
  The chariot paused a moment there;
  The Spirit then descended;
The restless coursers pawed the ungenial
    soil,
Snuffed the gross air, and then, their errand
    done,   230
Unfurled their pinions to the winds of
    heaven.

The Body and the Soul united then.
A gentle start convulsed Ianthe's frame;
Her veiny eyelids quietly unclosed;
Moveless awhile the dark blue orbs re-
    mained.
She looked around in wonder, and beheld
Henry, who kneeled in silence by her couch,
Watching her sleep with looks of speech-
    less love,
  And the bright beaming stars
  That through the casement shone. 240

ALASTOR

OR

THE SPIRIT OF SOLITUDE

Nondum amabam, et amare amabam,
quærebam quid amarem, amans amare.
Confess. St. August.

Alastor was published nearly three years after the issue of *Queen Mab*, in 1816, in a thin volume with a few other poems. It is strongly opposed to the earlier poem, and begins that series of ideal portraits, — in the main, incarnations of Shelley's own aspiring and melancholy spirit, — which contain his personal charm and shadow forth his own history of isolation in the world ; they are interpretations of the hero rather than pronunciamentos of the cause,

and are free from the entanglements of political and social reform and religious strife. The poetical antecedents of *Alastor* are Wordsworth and Coleridge. The deepening of the poet's self-consciousness is evident in every line, and the growth of his genius in grace and strength, in the element of expression, is so marked as to give a different cadence to his verse. He composed the poem in the autumn of 1815, when he was twenty-three years old and after the earlier misfortunes of his life had befallen him. Mrs. Shelley's account of the poem is the best, and nothing has since been added to it:

'*Alastor* is written in a very different tone from *Queen Mab*. In the latter, Shelley poured out all the cherished speculations of his youth — all the irrepressible emotions of sympathy, censure, and hope, to which the present suffering, and what he considers the proper destiny of his fellow - creatures, gave birth. *Alastor*, on the contrary, contains an individual interest only. A very few years, with their attendant events, had checked the ardor of Shelley's hopes, though he still thought them well-grounded, and that to advance their fulfilment was the noblest task man could achieve.

'This is neither the time nor place to speak of the misfortunes that checkered his life. It will be sufficient to say, that in all he did, he at the time of doing it believed himself justified to his own conscience; while the various ills of poverty and loss of friends brought home to him the sad realities of life. Physical suffering had also considerable influence in causing him to turn his eyes inward; inclining him rather to brood over the thoughts and emotions of his own soul, than to glance abroad, and to make, as in *Queen Mab*, the whole universe the object and subject of his song. In the spring of 1815, an eminent physician pronounced that he was dying rapidly of a consumption; abscesses were formed on his lungs, and he suffered acute spasms. Suddenly a complete change took place; and though through life he was a martyr to pain and debility, every symptom of pulmonary disease vanished. His nerves, which nature had formed sensitive to an unexampled degree, were rendered still more susceptible by the state of his health.

'As soon as the peace of 1814 had opened the Continent, he went abroad. He visited some of the more magnificent scenes of Switzerland, and returned to England from Lucerne by the Reuss and the Rhine. This river-navigation enchanted him. In his favorite poem of *Thalaba* his imagination had been excited by a description of such a voyage. In the summer of 1815, after a tour along the southern coast of Devonshire and a visit to Clifton, he rented a house on Bishopgate Heath, on the borders of Windsor Forest, where he enjoyed several months of comparative health and tranquil happiness. The later summer months were warm and dry. Accompanied by a few friends, he visited the source of the Thames, making a voyage in a wherry from Windsor to Crichlade. His beautiful stanzas in the churchyard of Lechlade were written on that occasion. *Alastor* was composed on his return. He spent his days under the oak-shades of Windsor Great Park; and the magnificent wood ___d was a fitting study to inspire the various descriptions of forest scenery we find in the poem.

'None of Shelley's poems is more characteristic than this. The solemn spirit that reigns throughout, the worship of the majesty of nature, the broodings of a poet's heart in solitude — the mingling of the exulting joy which the various aspect of the visible universe inspires, with the sad and struggling pangs which human passion imparts, give a touching interest to the whole. The death which he had often contemplated during the last months as certain and near, he here represented in such colors as had, in his lonely musings, soothed his soul to peace. The versification sustains the solemn spirit which breathes throughout: it is peculiarly melodious. The poem ought rather to be considered didactic than narrative: it was the outpouring of his own emotions, embodied in the purest form he could conceive, painted in the ideal hues which his brilliant imagination inspired, and softened by the recent anticipation of death.'

Peacock explains the title: 'At this time Shelley wrote his *Alastor*. He was at a loss for a title, and I proposed that which he adopted: *Alastor; or, the Spirit of Solitude*. The Greek word, 'Αλάστωρ, is an evil genius, κακοδαίμων, though the sense of the two words is somewhat different, as in the Φανεὶς 'Αλάστωρ ἢ κακὸς δαίμων πόθεν of Æschylus. The poem treated the spirit of solitude as a spirit of evil. I mention the true meaning of the word because many have supposed *Alastor* to be the name of the hero of the poem.'

In his *Preface* Shelley thus describes the main character, and draws its moral:

'The poem entitled *Alastor* may be considered as allegorical of one of the most interesting situations of the human mind. It represents a youth of uncorrupted feelings and adventurous genius led forth by an imagination inflamed and purified through familiarity with all that is excellent and majestic to the contemplation of the universe. He drinks deep of the fountains of knowledge and is still insatiate. The magnificence and beauty of the external world sinks profoundly into the frame of his conceptions and affords to their modifications a variety not to be exhausted. So long as it is possible for his desires to point towards objects thus infinite and unmeasured, he is joyous and tranquil and self-possessed. But the period arrives when these objects cease to suffice. His mind is at length suddenly awakened and thirsts for intercourse with an intelligence similar to itself. He images to himself the Being whom he loves. Conversant with speculations of the sublimest and most perfect natures, the vision in which he embodies his own imaginations unites all of wonderful or wise or beautiful, which the poet, the philosopher or the lover could depicture. The intellectual faculties, the imagination, the functions of sense have their respective requisitions on the sympathy of corresponding powers in other human beings. The Poet is represented as uniting these requisitions and attaching them to a single image. He seeks in vain for a prototype of his conception. Blasted by his disappointment, he descends to an untimely grave.

'The picture is not barren of instruction to actual men. The Poet's self-centred seclusion was avenged by the furies of an irresistible passion pursuing him to speedy ruin. But that Power, which strikes the luminaries of the world with sudden darkness and extinction by awakening them to too exquisite a perception of its influences, dooms to a slow and poisonous decay those meaner spirits that dare to abjure its dominion. Their destiny is more abject and inglorious as their delinquency is more contemptible and pernicious. They who, deluded by no generous error, instigated by no sacred thirst of doubtful knowledge, duped by no illustrious superstition, loving nothing on this earth, and cherishing no hopes beyond, yet keep aloof from sympathies with their kind, rejoicing neither in human joy nor mourning with human grief; these, and such as they, have their apportioned curse. They languish, because none feel with them their common nature. They are morally dead. They are neither friends, nor lovers, nor fathers, nor citizens of the world, nor benefactors of their country. Among those who attempt to exist without human sympathy, the pure and tender-hearted perish through the intensity and passion of their search after its communities, when the vacancy of their spirit suddenly makes itself felt. All else, selfish, blind and torpid, are those unforeseeing multitudes who constitute, together with their own, the lasting misery and loneliness of the world. Those who love not their fellow-beings live unfruitful lives and prepare for their old age a miserable grave.

'The good die first,
And those whose hearts are dry as summer dust
Burn to the socket!
'*December* 14, 1815.'

EARTH, Ocean, Air, belovèd brotherhood!
If our great Mother has imbued my soul
With aught of natural piety to feel
Your love, and recompense the boon with mine;
If dewy morn, and odorous noon, and even,
With sunset and its gorgeous ministers,
And solemn midnight's tingling silentness;
If Autumn's hollow sighs in the sere wood,
And Winter robing with pure snow and crowns
Of starry ice the gray grass and bare boughs;   10
If Spring's voluptuous pantings when she breathes
Her first sweet kisses, — have been dear to me;
If no bright bird, insect, or gentle beast
I consciously have injured, but still loved
And cherished these my kindred; then forgive
This boast, belovèd brethren, and withdraw
No portion of your wonted favor now!

Mother of this unfathomable world!
Favor my solemn song, for I have loved 19
Thee ever, and thee only; I have watched
Thy shadow, and the darkness of thy steps,
And my heart ever gazes on the depth
Of thy deep mysteries. I have made my bed
In charnels and on coffins, where black death
Keeps record of the trophies won from thee,
Hoping to still these obstinate questionings
Of thee and thine, by forcing some lone ghost,
Thy messenger, to render up the tale
Of what we are. In lone and silent hours,
When night makes a weird sound of its own stillness,   30
Like an inspired and desperate alchemist
Staking his very life on some dark hope,
Have I mixed awful talk and asking looks
With my most innocent love, until strange tears,
Uniting with those breathless kisses, made
Such magic as compels the charmèd night

To render up thy charge; and, though
    ne'er yet
Thou hast unveiled thy inmost sanctuary,
Enough from incommunicable dream,
And twilight phantasms, and deep noonday
    thought,   40
Has shone within me, that serenely now
And moveless, as a long-forgotten lyre
Suspended in the solitary dome
Of some mysterious and deserted fane,
I wait thy breath, Great Parent, that my
    strain
May modulate with murmurs of the air,
And motions of the forests and the sea,
And voice of living beings, and woven
    hymns
Of night and day, and the deep heart of
    man.   49

    There was a Poet whose untimely tomb
No human hands with pious reverence
    reared,
But the charmed eddies of autumnal winds
Built o'er his mouldering bones a pyra-
    mid
Of mouldering leaves in the waste wilder-
    ness :
A lovely youth, — no mourning maiden
    decked
With weeping flowers, or votive cypress
    wreath,
The lone couch of his everlasting sleep :
Gentle, and brave, and generous, — no lorn
    bard
Breathed o'er his dark fate one melodious
    sigh :
He lived, he died, he sung in solitude. 60
Strangers have wept to hear his passionate
    notes,
And virgins, as unknown he passed, have
    pined
And wasted for fond love of his wild eyes.
The fire of those soft orbs has ceased to
    burn,
And Silence, too enamoured of that voice,
Locks its mute music in her rugged cell.

    By solemn vision and bright silver dream
His infancy was nurtured. Every sight
And sound from the vast earth and ambient
    air
Sent to his heart its choicest impulses. 70
The fountains of divine philosophy
Fled not his thirsting lips, and all of great,
Or good, or lovely, which the sacred past

In truth or fable consecrates, he felt
And knew. When early youth had passed,
    he left
His cold fireside and alienated home
To seek strange truths in undiscovered
    lands.
Many a wide waste and tangled wilder-
    ness
Has lured his fearless steps; and he has
    bought
With his sweet voice and eyes, from savage
    men,   80
His rest and food. Nature's most secret
    steps
He like her shadow has pursued, where'er
The red volcano overcanopies
Its fields of snow and pinnacles of ice
With burning smoke, or where bitumen
    lakes
On black bare pointed islets ever beat
With sluggish surge, or where the secret
    caves,
Rugged and dark, winding among the
    springs
Of fire and poison, inaccessible
To avarice or pride, their starry domes 90
Of diamond and of gold expand above
Numberless and immeasurable halls,
Frequent with crystal column, and clear
    shrines
Of pearl, and thrones radiant with chryso-
    lite.
Nor had that scene of ampler majesty
Than gems or gold, the varying roof of
    heaven
And the green earth, lost in his heart its
    claims
To love and wonder; he would linger long
In lonesome vales, making the wild his
    home,
Until the doves and squirrels would par-
    take   100
From his innocuous hand his bloodless food,
Lured by the gentle meaning of his looks,
And the wild antelope, that starts when-
    e'er
The dry leaf rustles in the brake, suspend
Her timid steps, to gaze upon a form
More graceful than her own.

                  His wandering step,
Obedient to high thoughts, has visited
The awful ruins of the days of old :
Athens, and Tyre, and Balbec, and the
    waste   109

Where stood Jerusalem, the fallen towers
Of Babylon, the eternal pyramids,
Memphis and Thebes, and whatsoe'er of
    strange,
Sculptured on alabaster obelisk
Or jasper tomb or mutilated sphinx,
Dark Æthiopia in her desert hills
Conceals. Among the ruined temples
    there,
Stupendous columns, and wild images
Of more than man, where marble daemons
    watch
The Zodiac's brazen mystery, and dead
    men
Hang their mute thoughts on the mute
    walls around,   120
He lingered, poring on memorials
Of the world's youth: through the long
    burning day
Gazed on those speechless shapes; nor,
    when the moon
Filled the mysterious halls with floating
    shades
Suspended he that task, but ever gazed
ɪnd gazed, till meaning on his vacant
    mind
Flashed like strong inspiration, and he saw
The thrilling secrets of the birth of time.

Meanwhile an Arab maiden brought his
    food,   129
Her daily portion, from her father's tent,
And spread her matting for his couch, and
    stole
From duties and repose to tend his steps,
Enamoured, yet not daring for deep awe
To speak her love, and watched his nightly
    sleep,
Sleepless herself, to gaze upon his lips
Parted in slumber, whence the regular
    breath
Of innocent dreams arose; then, when red
    morn
Made paler the pale moon, to her cold
    home
Wildered, and wan, and panting, she re-
    turned.

The Poet, wandering on, through Ara-
    bie,   140
And Persia, and the wild Carmanian waste,
And o'er the aërial mountains which pour
    down
Indus and Oxus from their icy caves,
In joy and exultation held his way;

Till in the vale of Cashmire, far within
Its loneliest dell, where odorous plants en-
    twine
Beneath the hollow rocks a natural bower,
Beside a sparkling rivulet he stretched
His languid limbs. A vision on his sleep
There came, a dream of hopes that never
    yet   150
Had flushed his cheek. He dreamed a
    veilèd maid
Sate near him, talking in low solemn tones.
Her voice was like the voice of his own
    soul
Heard in the calm of thought; its music
    long,
Like woven sounds of streams and breezes,
    held
His inmost sense suspended in its web
Of many-colored woof and shifting hues.
Knowledge and truth and virtue were her
    theme,
And lofty hopes of divine liberty,   159
Thoughts the most dear to him, and poesy,
Herself a poet. Soon the solemn mood
Of her pure mind kindled through all her
    frame
A permeating fire; wild numbers then
She raised, with voice stifled in tremulous
    sobs
Subdued by its own pathos; her fair hands
Were bare alone, sweeping from some
    strange harp
Strange symphony, and in their branching
    veins
The eloquent blood told an ineffable tale.
The beating of her heart was heard to fill
The pauses of her music, and her breath
Tumultuously accorded with those fits   171
Of intermitted song. Sudden she rose,
As if her heart impatiently endured
Its bursting burden; at the sound he turned,
And saw by the warm light of their own
    life
Her glowing limbs beneath the sinuous veil
Of woven wind, her outspread arms now
    bare,
Her dark locks floating in the breath of
    night,
Her beamy bending eyes, her parted lips
Outstretched, and pale, and quivering
    eagerly.   180
His strong heart sunk and sickened with
    excess
Of love. He reared his shuddering limbs,
    and quelled

His gasping breath, and spread his arms to
    meet
Her panting bosom : — she drew back
    awhile,
Then, yielding to the irresistible joy,
With frantic gesture and short breathless
    cry
Folded his frame in her dissolving arms.
Now blackness veiled his dizzy eyes, and
    night
Involved and swallowed up the vision;
    sleep,   189
Like a dark flood suspended in its course,
Rolled back its impulse on his vacant brain.

Roused by the shock, he started from his
    trance —
The cold white light of morning, the blue
    moon
Low in the west, the clear and garish hills,
The distinct valley and the vacant woods,
Spread round him where he stood. Whither
    have fled
The hues of heaven that canopied his
    bower
Of yesternight ? The sounds that soothed
    his sleep,
The mystery and the majesty of Earth,
The joy, the exultation ? His wan eyes 200
Gaze on the empty scene as vacantly
As ocean's moon looks on the moon in
    heaven.
The spirit of sweet human love has sent
A vision to the sleep of him who spurned
Her choicest gifts. He eagerly pursues
Beyond the realms of dream that fleeting
    shade;
He overleaps the bounds. Alas ! alas !
Were limbs and breath and being inter-
    twined
Thus treacherously ? Lost, lost, forever
    lost   209
In the wide pathless desert of dim sleep,
That beautiful shape ! Does the dark gate
    of death
Conduct to thy mysterious paradise,
O Sleep ? Does the bright arch of rain-
    bow clouds
And pendent mountains seen in the calm
    lake
Lead only to a black and watery depth,
While death's blue vault with loathliest
    vapors hung,
Where every shade which the foul grave
    exhales

Hides its dead eye from the detested day,
Conducts, O Sleep, to thy delightful realms?
This doubt with sudden tide flowed on his
    heart;   220
The insatiate hope which it awakened
    stung
His brain even like despair.

                        While daylight held
The sky, the Poet kept mute conference
With his still soul. At night the passion
    came,
Like the fierce fiend of a distempered
    dream,
And shook him from his rest, and led him
    forth
Into the darkness. As an eagle, grasped
In folds of the green serpent, feels her
    breast
Burn with the poison, and precipitates
Through night and day, tempest, and calm,
    and cloud,   230
Frantic with dizzying anguish, her blind
    flight
O'er the wide aëry wilderness: thus driven
By the bright shadow of that lovely dream,
Beneath the cold glare of the desolate
    night,
Through tangled swamps and deep preci-
    pitous dells,
Startling with careless step the moon-light
    snake,
He fled. Red morning dawned upon his
    flight,
Shedding the mockery of its vital hues
Upon his cheek of death. He wandered
    on   239
Till vast Aornos seen from Petra's steep
Hung o'er the low horizon like a cloud;
Through Balk, and where the desolated
    tombs
Of Parthian kings scatter to every wind
Their wasting dust, wildly he wandered on,
Day after day, a weary waste of hours,
Bearing within his life the brooding care
That ever fed on its decaying flame.
And now his limbs were lean; his scattered
    hair,
Sered by the autumn of strange suffering,
Sung dirges in the wind; his listless hand
Hung like dead bone within its withered
    skin;   251
Life, and the lustre that consumed it,
    shone,
As in a furnace burning secretly,

From his dark eyes alone. The cottagers,
Who ministered with human charity
His human wants, beheld with wondering
    awe
Their fleeting visitant. The mountaineer,
Encountering on some dizzy precipice
That spectral form, deemed that the Spirit
    of Wind,
With lightning eyes, and eager breath, and
    feet   260
Disturbing not the drifted snow, had paused
In its career; the infant would conceal
His troubled visage in his mother's robe
In terror at the glare of those wild eyes,
To remember their strange light in many a
    dream
Of after times ; but youthful maidens,
    taught
By nature, would interpret half the woe
That wasted him, would call him with false
    names
Brother and friend, would press his pallid
    hand
At parting, and watch, dim through tears,
    the path   270
Of his departure from their father's door.

At length upon the lone Chorasmian shore
He paused, a wide and melancholy waste
Of putrid marshes. A strong impulse urged
His steps to the sea-shore. A swan was
    there,
Beside a sluggish stream among the reeds.
It rose as he approached, and, with strong
    wings
Scaling the upward sky, bent its bright
    course
High over the immeasurable main.
His eyes pursued its flight: — 'Thou hast a
    home,   280
Beautiful bird ! thou voyagest to thine
    home,
Where thy sweet mate will twine her downy
    neck
With thine, and welcome thy return with
    eyes
Bright in the lustre of their own fond joy.
And what am I that I should linger here,
With voice far sweeter than thy dying
    notes,
Spirit more vast than thine, frame more
    attuned
To beauty, wasting these surpassing powers
In the deaf air, to the blind earth, and
    heaven

That echoes not my thoughts ? ' A gloomy
    smile   290
Of desperate hope wrinkled his quivering
    lips.
For sleep, he knew, kept most relentlessly
Its precious charge, and silent death ex-
    posed,
Faithless perhaps as sleep, a shadowy lure,
With doubtful smile mocking its own
    strange charms.

Startled by his own thoughts, he looked
    around.
There was no fair fiend near him, not a
    sight
Or sound of awe but in his own deep mind.
A little shallop floating near the shore
Caught the impatient wandering of his
    gaze.   300
It had been long abandoned, for its sides
Gaped wide with many a rift, and its frail
    joints
Swayed with the undulations of the tide.
A restless impulse urged him to embark
And meet lone Death on the drear ocean's
    waste;
For well he knew that mighty Shadow
    loves
The slimy caverns of the populous deep.

The day was fair and sunny; sea and sky
Drank its inspiring radiance, and the wind
Swept strongly from the shore, blackening
    the waves.   310
Following his eager soul, the wanderer
Leaped in the boat ; he spread his cloak
    aloft
On the bare mast, and took his lonely seat,
And felt the boat speed o'er the tranquil
    sea
Like a torn cloud before the hurricane.

As one that in a silver vision floats
Obedient to the sweep of odorous winds
Upon resplendent clouds, so rapidly
Along the dark and ruffled waters fled
The straining boat. A whirlwind swept it
    on,   320
With fierce gusts and precipitating force,
Through the white ridges of the chafèd sea.
The waves arose. Higher and higher still
Their fierce necks writhed beneath the
    tempest's scourge
Like serpents struggling in a vulture's
    grasp.

Calm and rejoicing in the fearful war
Of wave ruining on wave, and blast on blast
Descending, and black flood on whirlpool
    driven
With dark obliterating course, he sate:
As if their genii were the ministers   330
Appointed to conduct him to the light
Of those belovèd eyes, the Poet sate,
Holding the steady helm.   Evening came
    on;
The beams of sunset hung their rainbow
    hues
High 'mid the shifting domes of sheeted
    spray
That canopied his path o'er the waste deep;
Twilight, ascending slowly from the east,
Entwined in duskier wreaths her braided
    locks
O'er the fair front and radiant eyes of Day;
Night followed, clad with stars.   On every
    side   340
More horribly the multitudinous streams
Of ocean's mountainous waste to mutual
    war
Rushed in dark tumult thundering, as to
    mock
The calm and spangled sky.   The little
    boat
Still fled before the storm; still fled, like
    foam
Down the steep cataract of a wintry river;
Now pausing on the edge of the riven wave;
Now leaving far behind the bursting mass
That fell, convulsing ocean; safely fled — 350
As if that frail and wasted human form
Had been an elemental god.

                          At midnight
The moon arose; and lo! the ethereal cliffs
Of Caucasus, whose icy summits shone
Among the stars like sunlight, and around
Whose caverned base the whirlpools and
    the waves
Bursting and eddying irresistibly
Rage and resound forever. — Who shall
    save ? —
The boat fled on, — the boiling torrent
    drove, —
The crags closed round with black and
    jagged arms,   359
The shattered mountain overhung the sea,
And faster still, beyond all human speed,
Suspended on the sweep of the smooth
    wave,
The little boat was driven.   A cavern there

Yawned, and amid its slant and winding
    depths
Ingulfed the rushing sea.   The boat fled on
With unrelaxing speed. — ' Vision and
    Love ! '
The Poet cried aloud, ' I have beheld
The path of thy departure.   Sleep and
    death
Shall not divide us long.'

                          The boat pursued
The windings of the cavern.   Daylight
    shone   370
At length upon that gloomy river's flow;
Now, where the fiercest war among the
    waves
Is calm, on the unfathomable stream
The boat moved slowly.   Where the moun-
    tain, riven,
Exposed those black depths to the azure
    sky,
Ere yet the flood's enormous volume fell
Even to the base of Caucasus, with sound
That shook the everlasting rocks, the mass
Filled with one whirlpool all that ample
    chasm;   379
Stair above stair the eddying waters rose,
Circling immeasurably fast, and laved
With alternating dash the gnarlèd roots
Of mighty trees, that stretched their giant
    arms
In darkness over it.   I' the midst was left,
Reflecting yet distorting every cloud,
A pool of treacherous and tremendous
    calm.
Seized by the sway of the ascending stream,
With dizzy swiftness, round and round and
    round,
Ridge after ridge the straining boat arose,
Till on the verge of the extremest curve,
Where through an opening of the rocky
    bank   391
The waters overflow, and a smooth spot
Of glassy quiet 'mid those battling tides
Is left, the boat paused shuddering. —
    Shall it sink
Down the abyss?   Shall the reverting
    stress
Of that resistless gulf embosom it ?
Now shall it fall ? — A wandering stream
    of wind
Breathed from the west, has caught the
    expanded sail,
And, lo ! with gentle motion between banks
Of mossy slope, and on a placid stream, 400

Beneath a woven grove, it sails, and, hark !
The ghastly torrent mingles its far roar
With the breeze murmuring in the musical
    woods.
Where the embowering trees recede, and
    leave
A little space of green expanse, the cove
Is closed by meeting banks, whose yellow
    flowers
Forever gaze on their own drooping eyes,
Reflected in the crystal calm.   The wave
Of the boat's motion marred their pensive
    task,
Which naught but vagrant bird, or wanton
    wind,   410
Or falling spear-grass, or their own decay
Had e'er disturbed before.   The Poet
    longed
To deck with their bright hues his withered
    hair,
But on his heart its solitude returned,
And he forbore.   Not the strong impulse
    hid
In those flushed cheeks, bent eyes, and
    shadowy frame,
Had yet performed its ministry; it hung
Upon his life, as lightning in a cloud
Gleams, hovering ere it vanish, ere the
    floods   419
Of night close over it.

                        The noonday sun
Now shone upon the forest, one vast mass
Of mingling shade, whose brown magnifi-
    cence
A narrow vale embosoms.   There, huge
    caves,
Scooped in the dark base of their aëry
    rocks,
Mocking its moans, respond and roar for-
    ever.
The meeting boughs and implicated leaves
Wove twilight o'er the Poet's path, as, led
By love, or dream, or god, or mightier
    Death,
He sought in Nature's dearest haunt some
    bank,   429
Her cradle and his sepulchre.   More dark
And dark the shades accumulate.   The oak,
Expanding its immense and knotty arms,
Embraces the light beech.   The pyramids
Of the tall cedar overarching frame
Most solemn domes within, and far below,
Like clouds suspended in an emerald sky,
The ash and the acacia floating hang

Tremulous and pale.   Like restless ser-
    pents, clothed
In rainbow and in fire, the parasites,
Starred with ten thousand blossoms, flow
    around   440
The gray trunks, and, as gamesome infants'
    eyes,
With gentle meanings, and most innocent
    wiles,
Fold their beams round the hearts of those
    that love,
These twine their tendrils with the wedded
    boughs,
Uniting their close union; the woven leaves
Make network of the dark blue light of day
And the night's noontide clearness, mutable
As shapes in the weird clouds.   Soft mossy
    lawns
Beneath these canopies extend their swells,
Fragrant with perfumed herbs, and eyed
    with blooms   450
Minute yet beautiful.   One darkest glen
Sends from its woods of musk-rose twined
    with jasmine
A soul-dissolving odor to invite
To some more lovely mystery.   Through
    the dell
Silence and Twilight here, twin-sisters,
    keep
Their noonday watch, and sail among the
    shades,
Like vaporous shapes half-seen; beyond, a
    well,
Dark, gleaming, and of most translucent
    wave,
Images all the woven boughs above,   459
And each depending leaf, and every speck
Of azure sky darting between their chasms;
Nor aught else in the liquid mirror laves
Its portraiture, but some inconstant star,
Between one foliaged lattice twinkling fair,
Or painted bird, sleeping beneath the moon,
Or gorgeous insect floating motionless,
Unconscious of the day, ere yet his wings
Have spread their glories to the gaze of
    noon.

Hither the Poet came.   His eyes beheld
Their own wan light through the reflected
    lines   470
Of his thin hair, distinct in the dark depth
Of that still fountain; as the human heart,
Gazing in dreams over the gloomy grave,
Sees its own treacherous likeness there.   He
    heard

The motion of the leaves — the grass that
    sprung
Startled and glanced and trembled even to
    feel
An unaccustomed presence — and the sound
Of the sweet brook that from the secret
    springs
Of that dark fountain rose. A Spirit
    seemed
To stand beside him — clothed in no bright
    robes   480
Of shadowy silver or enshrining light,
Borrowed from aught the visible world
    affords
Of grace, or majesty, or mystery;
But undulating woods, and silent well,
And leaping rivulet, and evening gloom
Now deepening the dark shades, for speech
    assuming,
Held commune with him, as if he and it
Were all that was; only — when his regard
Was raised by intense pensiveness — two
    eyes,
Two starry eyes, hung in the gloom of
    thought,   490
And seemed with their serene and azure
    smiles
To beckon him.

          Obedient to the light
That shone within his soul, he went, pur-
    suing
The windings of the dell. The rivulet,
Wanton and wild, through many a green
    ravine
Beneath the forest flowed. Sometimes it
    fell
Among the moss with hollow harmony
Dark and profound. Now on the polished
    stones
It danced, like childhood laughing as it
    went ;
Then, through the plain in tranquil wan-
    derings crept,   500
Reflecting every herb and drooping bud
That overhung its quietness. — ' O stream !
Whose source is inaccessibly profound,
Whither do thy mysterious waters tend ?
Thou imagest my life. Thy darksome still-
    ness,
Thy dazzling waves, thy loud and hollow
    gulfs,
Thy searchless fountain and invisible course,
Have each their type in me ; and the wide
    sky

And measureless ocean may declare as soon
What oozy cavern or what wandering
    cloud   510
Contains thy waters, as the universe
Tell where these living thoughts reside,
    when stretched
Upon thy flowers my bloodless limbs shall
    waste
I' the passing wind !'

          Beside the grassy shore
Of the small stream he went ; he did im-
    press
On the green moss his tremulous step, that
    caught
Strong shuddering from his burning limbs.
    As one
Roused by some joyous madness from the
    couch
Of fever, he did move ; yet not like him
Forgetful of the grave, where, when the
    flame   520
Of his frail exultation shall be spent,
He must descend. With rapid steps he
    went
Beneath the shade of trees, beside the flow
Of the wild babbling rivulet ; and now
The forest's solemn canopies were changed
For the uniform and lightsome evening sky.
Gray rocks did peep from the spare moss,
    and stemmed
The struggling brook ; tall spires of win-
    dlestrae
Threw their thin shadows down the rugged
    slope,
And nought but gnarlèd roots of ancient
    pines   530
Branchless and blasted, clenched with
    grasping roots
The unwilling soil. A gradual change was
    here
Yet ghastly. For, as fast years flow away,
The smooth brow gathers, and the hair
    grows thin
And white, and where irradiate dewy eyes
Had shone, gleam stony orbs : — so from
    his steps
Bright flowers departed, and the beautiful
    shade
Of the green groves, with all their odorous
    winds
And musical motions. Calm he still pur-
    sued
The stream, that with a larger volume
    now   540

Rolled through the labyrinthine dell ; and there
Fretted a path through its descending curves
With its wintry speed. On every side now rose
Rocks, which, in unimaginable forms,
Lifted their black and barren pinnacles
In the light of evening, and its precipice
Obscuring the ravine, disclosed above,
'Mid toppling stones, black gulfs and yawning caves,
Whose windings gave ten thousand various tongues
To the loud stream. Lo ! where the pass expands   550
Its stony jaws, the abrupt mountain breaks,
And seems with its accumulated crags
To overhang the world ; for wide expand
Beneath the wan stars and descending moon
Islanded seas, blue mountains, mighty streams,
Dim tracts and vast, robed in the lustrous gloom
Of leaden-colored even, and fiery hills
Mingling their flames with twilight, on the verge
Of the remote horizon. The near scene,
In naked and severe simplicity,   560
Made contrast with the universe. A pine,
Rock-rooted, stretched athwart the vacancy
Its swinging boughs, to each inconstant blast
Yielding one only response at each pause
In most familiar cadence, with the howl,
The thunder and the hiss of homeless streams
Mingling its solemn song, whilst the broad river
Foaming and hurrying o'er its rugged path,
Fell into that immeasurable void,
Scattering its waters to the passing winds.   570

Yet the gray precipice and solemn pine
And torrent were not all ; — one silent nook
Was there. Even on the edge of that vast mountain,
Upheld by knotty roots and fallen rocks,
It overlooked in its serenity
The dark earth and the bending vault of stars.
It was a tranquil spot that seemed to smile
Even in the lap of horror. Ivy clasped
The fissured stones with its entwining arms,

And did embower with leaves forever green   580
And berries dark the smooth and even space
Of its inviolated floor ; and here
The children of the autumnal whirlwind bore
In wanton sport those bright leaves whose decay,
Red, yellow, or ethereally pale,
Rivals the pride of summer. 'T is the haunt
Of every gentle wind whose breath can teach
The wilds to love tranquillity. One step,
One human step alone, has ever broken
The stillness of its solitude ; one voice   590
Alone inspired its echoes ; — even that voice
Which hither came, floating among the winds,
And led the loveliest among human forms
To make their wild haunts the depository
Of all the grace and beauty that endued
Its motions, render up its majesty,
Scatter its music on the unfeeling storm,
And to the damp leaves and blue cavern mould,
Nurses of rainbow flowers and branching moss,
Commit the colors of that varying cheek,   600
That snowy breast, those dark and drooping eyes.

The dim and hornèd moon hung low, and poured
A sea of lustre on the horizon's verge
That overflowed its mountains. Yellow mist
Filled the unbounded atmosphere, and drank
Wan moonlight even to fulness ; not a star
Shone, not a sound was heard ; the very winds,
Danger's grim playmates, on that precipice
Slept, clasped in his embrace. — O storm of death,
Whose sightless speed divides this sullen night !   610
And thou, colossal Skeleton, that, still
Guiding its irresistible career
In thy devastating omnipotence,
Art king of this frail world ! from the red field
Of slaughter, from the reeking hospital,
The patriot's sacred couch, the snowy bed
Of innocence, the scaffold and the throne,

A mighty voice invokes thee ! Ruin calls
His brother Death ! A rare and regal prey
He hath prepared, prowling around the
    world;   620
Glutted with which thou mayst repose, and
    men
Go to their graves like flowers or creeping
    worms,
Nor ever more offer at thy dark shrine
The unheeded tribute of a broken heart.

    When on the threshold of the green
      recess
The wanderer's footsteps fell, he knew that
    death
Was on him. Yet a little, ere it fled,
Did he resign his high and holy soul
To images of the majestic past,   629
That paused within his passive being now,
Like winds that bear sweet music, when
    they breathe
Through some dim latticed chamber. He
    did place
His pale lean hand upon the rugged trunk
Of the old pine; upon an ivied stone
Reclined his languid head; his limbs did
    rest,
Diffused and motionless, on the smooth
    brink
Of that obscurest chasm; — and thus he
    lay,
Surrendering to their final impulses
The hovering powers of life. Hope and
    Despair,
The torturers, slept; no mortal pain or
    fear   640
Marred his repose; the influxes of sense
And his own being, unalloyed by pain,
Yet feebler and more feeble, calmly fed
The stream of thought, till he lay breath-
    ing there
At peace, and faintly smiling. His last
    sight
Was the great moon, which o'er the western
    line
Of the wide world her mighty horn sus-
    pended,
With whose dun beams inwoven darkness
    seemed
To mingle. Now upon the jagged hills
It rests; and still as the divided frame 650
Of the vast meteor sunk, the Poet's blood,
That ever beat in mystic sympathy
With Nature's ebb and flow, grew feebler
    still;

And when two lessening points of light
    alone
Gleamed through the darkness, the alter-
    nate gasp
Of his faint respiration scarce did stir
The stagnate night : — till the minutest ray
Was quenched, the pulse yet lingered in
    his heart.
It paused — it fluttered. But when hea-
    ven remained   659
Utterly black, the murky shades involved
An image silent, cold, and motionless,
As their own voiceless earth and vacant
    air.
Even as a vapor fed with golden beams
That ministered on sunlight, ere the west
Eclipses it, was now that wondrous frame —
No sense, no motion, no divinity —
A fragile lute, on whose harmonious strings
The breath of heaven did wander — a bright
    stream
Once fed with many-voicèd waves — a
    dream
Of youth, which night and time have
    quenched forever —   670
Still, dark, and dry, and unremembered
    now.

    Oh, for Medea's wondrous alchemy,
Which wheresoe'er it fell made the earth
    gleam
With bright flowers, and the wintry boughs
    exhale
From vernal blooms fresh fragrance ! Oh,
    that God,
Profuse of poisons, would concede the
    chalice
Which but one living man has drained, who
    now,
Vessel of deathless wrath, a slave that feels
No proud exemption in the blighting curse
He bears, over the world wanders for-
    ever,   680
Lone as incarnate death ! Oh, that the
    dream
Of dark magician in his visioned cave,
Raking the cinders of a crucible
For life and power, even when his feeble
    hand
Shakes in its last decay, were the true law
Of this so lovely world ! But thou art fled,
Like some frail exhalation, which the dawn
Robes in its golden beams, — ah ! thou
    hast fled !
The brave, the gentle and the beautiful,

The child of grace and genius. Heartless
    things   690
Are done and said i' the world, and many
    worms
And beasts and men live on, and mighty
    Earth
From sea and mountain, city and wilder-
    ness,
In vesper low or joyous orison,
Lifts still its solemn voice : — but thou art
    fled —
Thou canst no longer know or love the
    shapes
Of this phantasmal scene, who have to thee
Been purest ministers, who are, alas !
Now thou art not ! Upon those pallid lips
So sweet even in their silence, on those
    eyes   700
That image sleep in death, upon that form
Yet safe from the worm's outrage, let no
    tear
Be shed — not even in thought. Nor, when
    those hues
Are gone, and those divinest lineaments,
Worn by the senseless wind, shall live alone

In the frail pauses of this simple strain,
Let not high verse, mourning the memory
Of that which is no more, or painting's
    woe
Or sculpture, speak in feeble imagery
Their own cold powers. Art and elo-
    quence,   710
And all the shows o' the world, are frail
    and vain
To weep a loss that turns their lights to
    shade.
It is a woe "too deep for tears," when
    all
Is reft at once, when some surpassing
    Spirit,
Whose light adorned the world around it,
    leaves
Those who remain behind, not sobs or
    groans,
The passionate tumult of a clinging hope;
But pale despair and cold tranquillity,
Nature's vast frame, the web of human
    things,
Birth and the grave, that are not as they
    were.   720

THE REVOLT OF ISLAM

A POEM

IN TWELVE CANTOS

ΟΣΑΙΣ ΔΕ ΒΡΟΤΟΝ ΕΘΝΟΣ ΑΓΛΑΙΑΙΣ ΑΠΤΟΜΕΣΘΑ,
    ΠΕΡΑΙΝΕΙ ΠΡΟΣ ΕΣΧΑΤΟΝ
ΠΛΟΟΝ· ΝΑΥΣΙ Δ' ΟΥΤΕ ΠΕΖΟΣ ΙΩΝ ΑΝ ΕΥΡΟΙΣ
ΕΣ ΥΠΕΡΒΟΡΕΩΝ ΑΓΩΝΑ ΘΑΥΜΑΤΑΝ ΟΔΟΝ.
                    PINDAR, *Pyth.* X.

The Revolt of Islam is a return to the social
and political propaganda of *Queen Mab*, though
the narrative element is stronger and the ideal
characterization is along the more human lines
of *Alastor*. It belongs distinctly in the class
of reform poems and obeys a didactic motive
in the same way as does the *Faerie Queene*, in
the stanza of which it is written. It was composed in the spring and summer of 1817, and
embodies the opinions of Shelley nearly as
completely as *Queen Mab* had done, five years
earlier. It was printed under the title *Laon
and Cythna; or, The Revolution of the Golden
City: A Vision of the Nineteenth Century;* a
few copies only were issued, when the publisher refused to proceed with the work unless
radical alterations were made in the text.
Shelley reluctantly consented to this, and made
the required changes. The title was altered,

and the work published. The circumstances
under which the poem was written are told by
Mrs. Shelley, with a word upon the main
characters :
    ' He chose for his hero a youth nourished in
dreams of liberty, some of whose actions are
in direct opposition to the opinions of the
world, but who is animated throughout by an
ardent love of virtue, and a resolution to confer
the boons of political and intellectual freedom
on his fellow-creatures. He created for this
youth a woman such as he delighted to imagine
— full of enthusiasm for the same objects;
and they both, with will unvanquished and the
deepest sense of the justice of their cause, met
adversity and death. There exists in this poem
a memorial of a friend of his youth. The
character of the old man who liberates Laon
from his tower prison, and tends on him in

sickness, is founded on that of Doctor Lind, who, when Shelley was at Eton, had often stood by to befriend and support him, and whose name he never mentioned without love and veneration.

'During the year 1817 we were established at Marlow, in Buckinghamshire. Shelley's choice of abode was fixed chiefly by this town being at no great distance from London, and its neighborhood to the Thames. The poem was written in his boat, as it floated under the beech groves of Bisham, or during wanderings in the neighboring country, which is distinguished for peculiar beauty. The chalk hills break into cliffs that overhang the Thames, or form valleys clothed with beech; the wilder portion of the country is rendered beautiful by exuberant vegetation; and the cultivated part is peculiarly fertile. With all this wealth of nature which, either in the form of gentlemen's parks or soil dedicated to agriculture, flourishes around, Marlow was inhabited (I hope it is altered now) by a very poor population. The women are lacemakers, and lose their health by sedentary labor, for which they were very ill paid. The poor-laws ground to the dust not only the paupers, but those who had risen just above that state, and were obliged to pay poor-rates. The changes produced by peace following a long war, and a bad harvest, brought with them the most heart-rending evils to the poor. Shelley afforded what alleviation he could. In the winter, while bringing out his poem, he had a severe attack of ophthalmia, caught while visiting the poor cottages. I mention these things, — for this minute and active sympathy with his fellow-creatures gives a thousand-fold interest to his speculations, and stamps with reality his pleadings for the human race.'

Shelley himself gave two accounts of the poem, of which the most interesting occurs in a letter to Godwin, December 11, 1817:

'The Poem was produced by a series of thoughts which filled my mind with unbounded and sustained enthusiasm. I felt the precariousness of my life, and I engaged in this task, resolved to leave some record of myself. Much of what the volume contains was written with the same feeling, as real, though not so prophetic, as the communications of a dying man. I never presumed indeed to consider it anything approaching to faultless; but when I consider contemporary productions of the same apparent pretensions, I own I was filled with confidence. I felt that it was in many respects a genuine picture of my own mind. I felt that the sentiments were true, not assumed. And in this have I long believed that my power consists; in sympathy and that part of the imagination which relates to sentiment and contemplation. I am formed, if for anything not in common with the herd of mankind, to apprehend minute and remote distinctions of feeling, whether relative to external nature or the living beings which surround us, and to communicate the conceptions which result from considering either the moral or the material universe as a whole. Of course, I believe these faculties, which perhaps comprehend all that is sublime in man, to exist very imperfectly in my own mind.'

The second is contained in an earlier letter to a publisher, October 13, 1817:

'The whole poem, with the exception of the first canto and part of the last, is a mere human story without the smallest intermixture of supernatural interference. The first canto is, indeed, in some measure a distinct poem, though very necessary to the wholeness of the work. I say this because, if it were all written in the manner of the first canto, I could not expect that it would be interesting to any great number of people. I have attempted in the progress of my work to speak to the common elementary emotions of the human heart, so that, though it is the story of violence and revolution, it is relieved by milder pictures of friendship and love and natural affections. The scene is supposed to be laid in Constantinople and modern Greece, but without much attempt at minute delineation of Mahometan manners. It is, in fact, a tale illustrative of such a revolution as might be supposed to take place in an European nation, acted upon by the opinions of what has been called (erroneously, as I think) the modern philosophy, and contending with ancient notions and the supposed advantage derived from them to those who support them. It is a Revolution of this kind that is the *beau idéal*, as it were, of the French Revolution, but produced by the influence of individual genius and out of general knowledge.'

Peacock supplements Mrs. Shelley's note, with some details of the revision:

'In the summer of 1817 he wrote *The Revolt of Islam*, chiefly on a seat on a high prominence in Bisham Wood where he passed whole mornings with a blank book and a pencil. This work when completed was printed under the title of *Laon and Cythna*. In this poem he had carried the expression of his opinions, moral, political, and theological, beyond the bounds of discretion. The terror which, in those days of persecution of the press, the perusal of the book inspired in Mr. Ollier, the publisher, induced him to solicit the alteration of many passages which he had marked. Shelley was for some time inflexible; but Mr. Ollier's refusal to publish the poem as it was, backed by the advice of all his friends, induced him to submit to the required changes.'

Shelley subsequently revised the poem still more, in expectation of a second edition, but the changes so made are now unknown.

PREFACE

The Poem which I now present to the world is an attempt from which I scarcely dare to expect success, and in which a writer of established fame might fail without disgrace. It is an experiment on the temper of the public mind as to how far a thirst for a happier condition of moral and political society survives, among the enlightened and refined, the tempests which have shaken the age in which we live. I have sought to enlist the harmony of metrical language, the ethereal combinations of the fancy, the rapid and subtle transitions of human passion, all those elements which essentially compose a poem, in the cause of a liberal and comprehensive morality; and in the view of kindling within the bosoms of my readers a virtuous enthusiasm for those doctrines of liberty and justice, that faith and hope in something good, which neither violence, nor misrepresentation, nor prejudice, can ever totally extinguish among mankind.

For this purpose I have chosen a story of human passion in its most universal character, diversified with moving and romantic adventures, and appealing, in contempt of all artificial opinions or institutions, to the common sympathies of every human breast. I have made no attempt to recommend the motives which I would substitute for those at present governing mankind, by methodical and systematic argument. I would only awaken the feelings, so that the reader should see the beauty of true virtue, and be incited to those inquiries which have led to my moral and political creed, and that of some of the sublimest intellects in the world. The Poem therefore (with the exception of the first Canto, which is purely introductory) is narrative, not didactic. It is a succession of pictures illustrating the growth and progress of individual mind aspiring after excellence and devoted to the love of mankind; its influence in refining and making pure the most daring and uncommon impulses of the imagination, the understanding, and the senses; its impatience at 'all the oppressions which are done under the sun;' its tendency to awaken public hope and to enlighten and improve mankind; the rapid effects of the application of that tendency; the awakening of an immense nation from their slavery and degradation to a true sense of moral dignity and freedom; the bloodless dethronement of their oppressors and the unveiling of the reli-

gious frauds by which they had been deluded into submission; the tranquillity of successful patriotism and the universal toleration and benevolence of true philanthropy; the treachery and barbarity of hired soldiers; vice not the object of punishment and hatred, but kindness and pity; the faithlessness of tyrants; the confederacy of the Rulers of the World and the restoration of the expelled Dynasty by foreign arms; the massacre and extermination of the Patriots and the victory of established power; the consequences of legitimate despotism, — civil war, famine, plague, superstition, and an utter extinction of the domestic affections; the judicial murder of the advocates of liberty; the temporary triumph of oppression, that secure earnest of its final and inevitable fall; the transient nature of ignorance and error and the eternity of genius and virtue. Such is the series of delineations of which the Poem consists. And if the lofty passions with which it has been my scope to distinguish this story shall not excite in the reader a generous impulse, an ardent thirst for excellence, an interest profound and strong, such as belongs to no meaner desires, let not the failure be imputed to a natural unfitness for human sympathy in these sublime and animating themes. It is the business of the poet to communicate to others the pleasure and the enthusiasm arising out of those images and feelings in the vivid presence of which within his own mind consists at once his inspiration and his reward.

The panic which, like an epidemic transport, seized upon all classes of men during the excesses consequent upon the French Revolution, is gradually giving place to sanity. It has ceased to be believed that whole generations of mankind ought to consign themselves to a hopeless inheritance of ignorance and misery because a nation of men who had been dupes and slaves for centuries were incapable of conducting themselves with the wisdom and tranquillity of freemen so soon as some of their fetters were partially loosened. That their conduct could not have been marked by any other characters than ferocity and thoughtlessness is the historical fact from which liberty derives all its recommendations, and falsehood the worst features of its deformity. There is a reflux in the tide of human things which bears the shipwrecked hopes of men into a secure haven after the storms are past. Methinks those who now live have survived an age of despair.

The French Revolution may be considered as one of those manifestations of a general state of feeling among civilized mankind, produced by a defect of correspondence between the knowledge existing in society and the improvement or gradual abolition of political institutions. The year 1788 may be assumed as the epoch of one of the most important crises produced by this feeling. The sympathies connected with that event extended to every bosom. The most generous and amiable natures were those which participated the most extensively in these sympathies. But such a degree of unmingled good was expected as it was impossible to realize. If the Revolution had been in every respect prosperous, then misrule and superstition would lose' half their claims to our abhorrence, as fetters which the captive can unlock with the slightest motion of his fingers, and which do not eat with poisonous rust into the soul. The revulsion occasioned by the atrocities of the demagogues and the reëstablishment of successive tyrannies in France was terrible, and felt in the remotest corner of the civilized world. Could they listen to the plea of reason who had groaned under the calamities of a social state, according to the provisions of which one man riots in luxury whilst another famishes for want of bread ? Can he who the day before was a trampled slave suddenly become liberal-minded, forbearing, and independent ? This is the consequence of the habits of a state of society to be produced by resolute perseverance and indefatigable hope, and long-suffering and long-believing courage, and the systematic efforts of generations of men of intellect and virtue. Such is the lesson which experience teaches now. But on the first reverses of hope in the progress of French liberty, the sanguine eagerness for good overleapt the solution of these questions, and for a time extinguished itself in the unexpectedness of their result. Thus many of the most ardent and tender-hearted of the worshippers of public good have been morally ruined by what a partial glimpse of the events they deplored appeared to show as the melancholy desolation of all their cherished hopes. Hence gloom and misanthropy have become the characteristics of the age in which we live, the solace of a disappointment that unconsciously finds relief only in the wilful exaggeration of its own despair. This influence has tainted the literature of the age with the hopelessness of the minds from which it flows. Metaphysics,[1] and inquiries into moral and political science, have become little else than vain attempts to revive exploded superstitions, or sophisms like those [2] of Mr. Malthus, calculated to lull the oppressors of mankind into a

security of everlasting triumph. Our works of fiction and poetry have been overshadowed by the same infectious gloom. But mankind appear to me to be emerging from their trance. I am aware, methinks, of a slow, gradual, silent change. In that belief I have composed the following Poem.

I do not presume to enter into competition with our greatest contemporary poets. Yet I am unwilling to tread in the footsteps of any who have preceded me. I have sought to avoid the imitation of any style of language or versification peculiar to the original minds of which it is the character, designing that even if what I have produced be worthless, it should still be properly my own. Nor have I permitted any system relating to mere words to divert the attention of the reader from whatever interest I may have succeeded in creating, to my own ingenuity in contriving to disgust them according to the rules of criticism. I have simply clothed my thoughts in what appeared to me the most obvious and appropriate language. A person familiar with Nature, and with the most celebrated productions of the human mind, can scarcely err in following the instinct, with respect to selection of language, produced by that familiarity.

There is an education peculiarly fitted for ɩ poet, without which genius and sensibility can hardly fill the circle of their capacities. No education indeed can entitle to this appellation a dull and unobservant mind, or one, though neither dull nor unobservant, in which the channels of communication between thought and expression have been obstructed or closed. How far it is my fortune to belong to either of the latter classes I cannot know. I aspire to be something better. The circumstances of my accidental education have been favorable to this ambition. I have been familiar from boyhood with mountains and lakes, and the sea, and the solitude of forests ; Danger which sports upon the brink of precipices has been my playmate. I have trodden the glaciers of the Alps, and lived under the eye of Mont Blanc. I have been a wanderer among distant fields. I have sailed down mighty rivers, and seen the sun rise and set, and the stars come forth, whilst I have sailed night and day down a rapid stream among mountains. I have seen populous cities, and have watched the passions which rise and spread, and sink and change, amongst assembled multitudes of men. I have seen the theatre of the more visible ravages of tyranny and

---

[1] I ought to except Sir W. Drummond's *Academical Questions ;* a volume of very acute and powerful metaphysical criticism.

[2] It is remarkable, as a symptom of the revival of public hope, that Mr. Malthus has assigned, in the later editions of his work, an indefinite dominion to moral

restraint over the principle of population. This concession answers all the inferences from his doctrine unfavorable to human improvement, and reduces the *Essay on Population* to a commentary illustrative of the unanswerableness of *Political Justice*.

war, cities and villages reduced to scattered groups of black and roofless houses, and the naked inhabitants sitting famished upon their desolate thresholds. I have conversed with living men of genius. The poetry of ancient Greece and Rome, and modern Italy, and our own country, has been to me like external nature, a passion and an enjoyment. Such are the sources from which the materials for the imagery of my Poem have been drawn. I have considered poetry in its most comprehensive sense, and have read the poets and the historians, and the metaphysicians [1] whose writings have been accessible to me, and have looked upon the beautiful and majestic scenery of the earth, as common sources of those elements which it is the province of the poet to embody and combine. Yet the experience and the feelings to which I refer do not in themselves constitute men poets, but only prepares them to be the auditors of those who are. How far I shall be found to possess that more essential attribute of poetry, the power of awakening in others sensations like those which animate my own bosom, is that which, to speak sincerely, I know not; and which, with an acquiescent and contented spirit, I expect to be taught by the effect which I shall produce pon those whom I now address.

I have avoided, as I have said before, the imitation of any contemporary style. But there must be a resemblance, which does not depend upon their own will, between all the writers of any particular age. They cannot escape from subjection to a common influence which arises out of an infinite combination of circumstances belonging to the times in which they live, though each is in a degree the author of the very influence by which his being is thus pervaded. Thus, the tragic poets of the age of Pericles; the Italian revivers of ancient learning; those mighty intellects of our own country that succeeded the Reformation, the translators of the Bible, Shakespeare, Spenser, the Dramatists of the reign of Elizabeth, and Lord Bacon; [2] the colder spirits of the interval that succeeded; — all resemble each other, and differ from every other in their several classes. In this view of things, Ford can no more be called the imitator of Shakespeare than Shakespeare the imitator of Ford. There were perhaps few other points of resemblance between these two men than that which the universal and inevitable influence of their age produced. And this is an influence which neither the meanest scribbler nor the sublimest genius of any

era can escape; and which I have not attempted to escape.

I have adopted the stanza of Spenser (a measure inexpressibly beautiful) not because I consider it a finer model of poetical harmony than the blank verse of Shakespeare and Milton, but because in the latter there is no shelter for mediocrity; you must either succeed or fail. This perhaps an aspiring spirit should desire. But I was enticed also by the brilliancy and magnificence of sound which a mind that has been nourished upon musical thoughts can produce by a just and harmonious arrangement of the pauses of this measure. Yet there will be found some instances where I have completely failed in this attempt, and one, which I here request the reader to consider as an erratum, where there is left most inadvertently an alexandrine in the middle of a stanza.

But in this, as in every other respect, I have written fearlessly. It is the misfortune of this age that its writers, too thoughtless of immortality, are exquisitely sensible to temporary praise or blame. They write with the fear of Reviews before their eyes. This system of criticism sprang up in that torpid interval when poetry was not. Poetry and the art which professes to regulate and limit its powers cannot subsist together. Longinus could not have been the contemporary of Homer, nor Boileau of Horace. Yet this species of criticism never presumed to assert an understanding of its own; it has always, unlike true science, followed, not preceded the opinion of mankind, and would even now bribe with worthless adulation some of our greatest poets to impose gratuitous fetters on their own imaginations and become unconscious accomplices in the daily murder of all genius either not so aspiring or not so fortunate as their own. I have sought therefore to write, as I believe that Homer, Shakespeare, and Milton wrote, with an utter disregard of anonymous censure. I am certain that calumny and misrepresentation, though it may move me to compassion, cannot disturb my peace. I shall understand the expressive silence of those sagacious enemies who dare not trust themselves to speak. I shall endeavor to extract from the midst of insult and contempt and maledictions those admonitions which may tend to correct whatever imperfections such censurers may discover in this my first serious appeal to the public. If certain critics were as clearsighted as they are malignant, how great would be the benefit to be derived from their virulent

---

[1] In this sense there may be such a thing as perfectibility in works of fiction, notwithstanding the concession often made by the advocates of human improvement, that perfectibility is a term applicable only to science.

[2] Milton stands alone in the age which he illumined.

writings! As it is, I fear I shall be malicious enough to be amused with their paltry tricks and lame invectives. Should the public judge that my composition is worthless, I shall indeed bow before the tribunal from which Milton received his crown of immortality, and shall seek to gather, if I live, strength from that defeat, which may nerve me to some new enterprise of thought which may *not* be worthless. I cannot conceive that Lucretius, when he meditated that poem whose doctrines are yet the basis of our metaphysical knowledge and whose eloquence has been the wonder of mankind, wrote in awe of such censure as the hired sophists of the impure and superstitious noblemen of Rome might affix to what he should produce. It was at the period when Greece was led captive and Asia made tributary to the Republic, fast verging itself to slavery and ruin, that a multitude of Syrian captives, bigoted to the worship of their obscene Ashtaroth, and the unworthy successors of Socrates and Zeno, found there a precarious subsistence by administering, under the name of freedmen, to the vices and vanities of the great. These wretched men were skilled to plead, with a superficial but plausible set of sophisms, in favor of that contempt for virtue which is the portion of slaves, and that faith in portents, the most fatal substitute for benevolence in the imaginations of men, which arising from the enslaved communities of the East then first began to overwhelm the western nations in its stream. Were these the kind of men whose disapprobation the wise and loftyminded Lucretius should have regarded with a salutary awe? The latest and perhaps the meanest of those who follow in his footsteps would disdain to hold life on such conditions.

The Poem now presented to the public occupied little more than six months in the composition. That period has been devoted to the task with unremitting ardor and enthusiasm. I have exercised a watchful and earnest criticism on my work as it grew under my hands. I would willingly have sent it forth to the world with that perfection which long labor and revision is said to bestow. But I found that if I should gain something in exactness by this method, I might lose much of the newness and energy of imagery and language as it flowed fresh from my mind. And although the mere composition occupied no more than six months, the thoughts thus arranged were slowly gathered in as many years.

I trust that the reader will carefully distinguish between those opinions which have a dramatic propriety in reference to the characters which they are designed to elucidate, and such as are properly my own. The erroneous and degrading idea which men have conceived of a Supreme Being, for instance, is spoken against, but not the Supreme Being itself. The belief which some superstitious persons whom I have brought upon the stage entertain of the Deity, as injurious to the character of his benevolence, is widely different from my own. In recommending also a great and important change in the spirit which animates the social institutions of mankind, I have avoided all flattery to those violent and malignant passions of our nature which are ever on the watch to mingle with and to alloy the most beneficial innovations. There is no quarter given to revenge, or envy, or prejudice. Love is celebrated everywhere as the sole law which should govern the moral world.

In *Laon and Cythna* the following passage was added, in conclusion:

In the personal conduct of my hero and heroine, there is one circumstance which was intended to startle the reader from the trance of ordinary life. It was my object to break through the crust of those outworn opinions on which established institutions depend. I have appealed therefore to the most universal of all feelings, and have endeavored to strengthen the moral sense by forbidding it to waste its energies in seeking to avoid actions which are only crimes of convention. It is because there is so great a multitude of artificial vices that there are so few real virtues. Those feelings alone which are benevolent or malevolent are essentially good or bad. The circumstance of which I speak was introduced, however, merely to accustom men to that charity and toleration which the exhibition of a practice widely differing from their own has a tendency to promote.[1] Nothing indeed can be more mischievous than many actions innocent in themselves which might bring down upon individuals the bigoted contempt and rage of the multitude.

[1] The sentiments connected with and characteristic of this circumstance have no personal reference to the writer.

DEDICATION

There is no danger to a man that knows
What life and death is: there's not any law
Exceeds his knowledge; neither is it lawful
That he should stoop to any other law.
CHAPMAN.

TO MARY —— ——

I

So now my summer-task is ended, Mary,
And I return to thee, mine own heart's
home;
As to his Queen some victor Knight of
Faëry,
Earning bright spoils for her enchanted
dome;
Nor thou disdain, that ere my fame be-
come
A star among the stars of mortal night,
If it indeed may cleave its natal gloom,
Its doubtful promise thus I would unite
With thy belovèd name, thou Child of love
and light.

II

The toil which stole from thee so many
an hour,
Is ended, — and the fruit is at thy feet!
No longer where the woods to frame a
bower
With interlacèd branches mix and meet,
Or where, with sound like many voices
sweet,
Water-falls leap among wild islands
green,
Which framed for my lone boat a lone
retreat
Of moss-grown trees and weeds, shall I
be seen;
But beside thee, where still my heart has
ever been.

III

Thoughts of great deeds were mine, dear
Friend, when first
The clouds which wrap this world from
youth did pass.
I do remember well the hour which burst
My spirit's sleep. A fresh May-dawn it
was,
When I walked forth upon the glittering
grass,
And wept, I knew not why; until there
rose
From the near school-room voices that,
alas!
Were but one echo from a world of
woes —
The harsh and grating strife of tyrants and
of foes.

IV

And then I clasped my hands and looked
around,
But none was near to mock my streaming
eyes,
Which poured their warm drops on the
sunny ground —
So without shame I spake: — 'I will be
wise,
And just, and free, and mild, if in me
lies
Such power, for I grow weary to behold
The selfish and the strong still tyrannize
Without reproach or check.' I then con-
trolled
My tears, my heart grew calm, and I was
meek and bold.

V

And from that hour did I with earnest
thought
Heap knowledge from forbidden mines of
lore;
Yet nothing that my tyrants knew or
taught
I cared to learn, but from that secret
store
Wrought linkèd armor for my soul, before
It might walk forth to war among mankind;
Thus power and hope were strengthened
more and more
Within me, till there came upon my
mind
A sense of loneliness, a thirst with which I
pined.

VI

Alas, that love should be a blight and
snare
To those who seek all sympathies in one!
Such once I sought in vain; then black
despair,
The shadow of a starless night, was
thrown
Over the world in which I moved alone: —
Yet never found I one not false to me,
Hard hearts, and cold, like weights of icy
stone
Which crushed and withered mine, that
could not be
Aught but a lifeless clog, until revived by
thee.

VII

Thou Friend, whose presence on my win-
　try heart
Fell, like bright Spring upon some herb-
　less plain;
How beautiful and calm and free thou
　wert
In thy young wisdom, when the mortal
　chain
Of Custom thou didst burst and rend in
　twain,
And walked as free as light the clouds
　among,
Which many an envious slave then
　breathed in vain
From his dim dungeon, and my spirit
　sprung
To meet thee from the woes which had
　begirt it long !

VIII

No more alone through the world's wil-
　derness,
Although I trod the paths of high intent,
I journeyed now; no more companion-
　less,
Where solitude is like despair, I went.
There is the wisdom of a stern content
When Poverty can blight the just and
　good,
When Infamy dares mock the innocent,
And cherished friends turn with the mul-
　titude
To trample: this was ours, and we un-
　shaken stood !

IX

Now has descended a serener hour,
And with inconstant fortune, friends re-
　turn;
Though suffering leaves the knowledge
　and the power
Which says, — Let scorn be not repaid
　with scorn.
And from thy side two gentle babes are
　born
To fill our home with smiles, and thus
　are we
Most fortunate beneath life's beaming
　morn;
And these delights, and thou, have been
　to me
The parents of the Song I consecrate to
　thee.

X

Is it that now my inexperienced fingers
But strike the prelude of a loftier strain?
Or must the lyre on which my spirit lin-
　gers
Soon pause in silence, ne'er to sound
　again,
Though it might shake the Anarch Cus-
　tom's reign,
And charm the minds of men to Truth's
　own sway,
Holier than was Amphion's ?   I would
　fain
Reply in hope — but I am worn away,
And Death and Love are yet contending
　for their prey.

XI

And what art thou ?   I know, but dare
　not speak:
Time may interpret to his silent years.
Yet in the paleness of thy thoughtful
　cheek,
And in the light thine ample forehead
　wears,
And in thy sweetest smiles, and in thy
　tears,
And in thy gentle speech, a prophecy
Is whispered to subdue my fondest fears;
And, through thine eyes, even in thy soul
　I see
A lamp of vestal fire burning internally.

XII

They say that thou wert lovely from thy
　birth,
Of glorious parents thou aspiring Child !
I wonder not — for One then left this
　earth
Whose life was like a setting planet
　mild,
Which clothed thee in the radiance unde-
　filed
Of its departing glory; still her fame
Shines on thee, through the tempests
　dark and wild
Which shake these latter days; and thou
　canst claim
The shelter, from thy Sire, of an immortal
　name.

XIII

One voice came forth from many a
　mighty spirit,

Which was the echo of three thousand
    years;
And the tumultuous world stood mute to
    hear it,
As some lone man who in a desert hears
The music of his home : — unwonted
    fears
Fell on the pale oppressors of our race,
And Faith, and Custom, and low-
    thoughted cares,
Like thunder-stricken dragons, for a
    space
Left the torn human heart, their food and
    dwelling-place.

XIV

Truth's deathless voice pauses among
    mankind!
If there must be no response to my
    cry —
If men must rise and stamp with fury
    blind
On his pure name who loves them, —
    thou and I,
Sweet Friend! can look from our tran-
    quillity
Like lamps into the world's tempestuous
    night, —
Two tranquil stars, while clouds are
    passing by
Which wrap them from the foundering
    seaman's sight,
That burn from year to year with unextin-
    guished light.

CANTO FIRST

I

WHEN the last hope of trampled France
    had failed
Like a brief dream of unremaining glory,
From visions of despair I rose, and
    scaled
The peak of an aërial promontory,
Whose caverned base with the vexed
    surge was hoary;
And saw the golden dawn break forth,
    and waken
Each cloud and every wave: — but tran-
    sitory
The calm; for sudden, the firm earth
    was shaken,
As if by the last wreck its frame were over-
    taken.

II

So as I stood, one blast of muttering
    thunder
Burst in far peals along the waveless deep,
When, gathering fast, around, above
    and under,
Long trains of tremulous mist began to
    creep,
Until their complicating lines did steep
The orient sun in shadow: — not a sound
Was heard; one horrible repose did keep
The forests and the floods, and all around
Darkness more dread than. night was
    poured upon the ground.

III

Hark ! 't is the rushing of a wind that
    sweeps
Earth and the ocean. See! the light-
    nings yawn,
Deluging Heaven with fire, and the
    lashed deeps
Glitter and boil beneath! it rages on,
One mighty stream, whirlwind and waves
    upthrown,
Lightning, and hail, and darkness eddy-
    ing by!
There is a pause — the sea-birds, that
    were gone
Into their caves to shriek, come forth to
    spy
What calm has fall'n on earth, what light
    is in the sky.

IV

For, where the irresistible storm had
    cloven
That fearful darkness, the blue sky was
    seen,
Fretted with many a fair cloud inter-
    woven
Most delicately, and the ocean green,
Beneath that opening spot of blue serene,
Quivered like burning emerald; calm
    was spread
On all below; but far on high, between
Earth and the upper air, the vast clouds
    fled,
Countless and swift as leaves on autumn's
    tempest shed.

V

For ever as the war became more fierce
Between the whirlwinds and the rack on
    high,

That spot grew more serene; blue light
   did pierce
The woof of those white clouds, which
   seemed to lie
Far, deep and motionless; while through
   the sky
The pallid semicircle of the moon
Passed on, in slow and moving majesty;
Its upper horn arrayed in mists, which
   soon,
But slowly, fled, like dew beneath the
   beams of noon.

VI

I could not choose but gaze; a fascina-
   tion
Dwelt in that moon, and sky, and clouds,
   which drew
My fancy thither, and in expectation
Of what I knew not, I remained. The
   hue
Of the white moon, amid that heaven so
   blue
Suddenly stained with shadow did ap-
   pear;
A speck, a cloud, a shape, approaching
   grew,
Like a great ship in the sun's sinking
   sphere
Beheld afar at sea, and swift it came anear.

VII

Even like a bark, which from a chasm of
   mountains,
Dark, vast and overhanging, on a river
Which there collects the strength of all
   its fountains,
Comes forth, whilst with the speed its
   frame doth quiver,
Sails, oars and stream, tending to one
   endeavor;
So, from that chasm of light a wingèd
   Form
On all the winds of heaven approaching
   ever
Floated, dilating as it came; the storm
Pursued it with fierce blasts, and light-
   nings swift and warm.

VIII

A course precipitous, of dizzy speed,
Suspending thought and breath; a mon-
   strous sight!
For in the air do I behold indeed

An Eagle and a Serpent wreathed in
   fight : —
And now, relaxing its impetuous flight,
Before the aërial rock on which I stood,
The Eagle, hovering, wheeled to left and
   right,
And hung with lingering wings over the
   flood,
And startled with its yells the wide air's
   solitude.

IX

A shaft of light upon its wings de-
   scended,
And every golden feather gleamed
   therein —
Feather and scale inextricably blended.
The Serpent's mailed and many-colored
   skin
Shone through the plumes its coils were
   twined within
By many a swollen and knotted fold,
   and high
And far, the neck receding lithe and
   thin,
Sustained a crested head, which warily
Shifted and glanced before the Eagle's
   steadfast eye.

X

Around, around, in ceaseless circles
   wheeling
With clang of wings and scream, the
   Eagle sailed
Incessantly — sometimes on high con-
   cealing
Its lessening orbs, sometimes as if it
   failed,
Drooped through the air; and still it
   shrieked and wailed,
And casting back its eager head, with
   beak
And talon unremittingly assailed
The wreathèd Serpent, who did ever seek
Upon his enemy's heart a mortal wound to
   wreak.

XI

What life, what power, was kindled and
   arose
Within the sphere of that appalling fray!
For, from the encounter of those won-
   drous foes,
A vapor like the sea's suspended spray

Hung gathered ; in the void air, far
    away,
Floated the shattered plumes ; bright
    scales did leap,
Where'er the Eagle's talons made their
    way,
Like sparks into the darkness; — as they
    sweep,
Blood stains the snowy foam of the tumul-
    tuous deep.

XII

Swift chances in that combat — many a
    check,
And many a change, a dark and wild
    turmoil!
Sometimes the Snake around his enemy's
    neck
Locked in stiff rings his adamantine
    coil,
Until the Eagle, faint with pain and
    toil,
Remitted his strong flight, and near the
    sea
Languidly fluttered, hopeless so to foil
His adversary, who then reared on high
His red and burning crest, radiant with
    victory.

XIII

Then on the white edge of the bursting
    surge,
Where they had sunk together, would
    the Snake
Relax his suffocating grasp, and scourge
The wind with his wild writhings; for,
    to break
That chain of torment, the vast bird would
    shake
The strength of his unconquerable wings
As in despair, and with his sinewy neck
Dissolve in sudden shock those linkèd
    rings —
Then soar, as swift as smoke from a vol-
    cano springs.

XIV

Wile baffled wile, and strength encoun-
    tered strength,
Thus long, but unprevailing. The event
Of that portentous fight appeared at
    length.
Until the lamp of day was almost spent
It had endured, when lifeless, stark and
    rent,

Hung high that mighty Serpent, and at
    last
Fell to the sea, while o'er the continent
With clang of wings and scream the
    Eagle passed,
Heavily borne away on the exhausted blast.

XV

And with it fled the tempest, so that
    ocean
And earth and sky shone through the
    atmosphere;
Only, 't was strange to see the red com-
    motion
Of waves like mountains o'er the sinking
    sphere
Of sunset sweep, and their fierce roar to
    hear
Amid the calm ; down the steep path I
    wound
To the sea-shore — the evening was most
    clear
And beautiful, and there the sea I found
Calm as a cradled child in dreamless slum-
    ber bound.

XVI

There was a Woman, beautiful as morn-
    ing,
Sitting beneath the rocks upon the sand
Of the waste sea — fair as one flower
    adorning
An icy wilderness; each delicate hand
Lay crossed upon her bosom, and the
    band
Of her dark hair had fall'n, and so she
    sate
Looking upon the waves ; on the bare
    strand
Upon the sea-mark a small boat did wait,
Fair as herself, like Love by Hope left
    desolate.

XVII

It seemed that this fair Shape had looked
    upon
That unimaginable fight, and now
That her sweet eyes were weary of the
    sun,
As brightly it illustrated her woe;
For in the tears, which silently to flow
Paused not, its lustre hung: she, watch-
    ing aye
The foam-wreaths which the faint tide
    wove below

Upon the spangled sands, groaned heavily,
And after every groan looked up over the
sea.

XVIII

And when she saw the wounded Serpent
make
His path between the waves, her lips
grew pale,
Parted and quivered; the tears ceased to
break
From her immovable eyes; no voice of
wail
Escaped her; but she rose, and on the
gale
Loosening her star-bright robe and
shadowy hair,
Poured forth her voice; the caverns of
the vale
That opened to the ocean, caught it there,
And filled with silver sounds the overflowing air.

XIX

She spake in language whose strange
melody
Might not belong to earth. I heard alone
What made its music more melodious
be,
The pity and the love of every tone;
But to the Snake those accents sweet
were known
His native tongue and hers; nor did he
beat
The hoar spray idly then, but winding on
Through the green shadows of the waves
that meet
Near to the shore, did pause beside her
snowy feet.

XX

Then on the sands the Woman sate
again,
And wept and clasped her hands, and, all
between,
Renewed the unintelligible strain
Of her melodious voice and eloquent
mien;
And she unveiled her bosom, and the
green
And glancing shadows of the sea did
play
O'er its marmoreal depth — one moment
seen,

For ere the next, the Serpent did obey
Her voice, and, coiled in rest, in her embrace it lay.

XXI

Then she arose, and smiled on me with
eyes
Serene yet sorrowing, like that planet
fair,
While yet the daylight lingereth in the
skies,
Which cleaves with arrowy beams the
dark-red air,
And said: 'To grieve is wise, but the despair
Was weak and vain which led thee here
from sleep.
This shalt thou know, and more, if thou
dost dare
With me and with this Serpent, o'er the
deep,
A voyage divine and strange, companionship to keep.'

XXII

Her voice was like the wildest, saddest
tone,
Yet sweet, of some loved voice heard
long ago.
I wept. Shall this fair woman all alone
Over the sea with that fierce Serpent go?
His head is on her heart, and who can
know
How soon he may devour his feeble
prey? —
Such were my thoughts, when the tide
'gan to flow;
And that strange boat like the moon's
shade did sway
Amid reflected stars that in the waters lay.

XXIII

A boat of rare device, which had no
sail
But its own curvèd prow of thin moonstone,
Wrought like a web of texture fine and
frail,
To catch those gentlest winds which are
not known
To breathe, but by the steady speed alone
With which it cleaves the sparkling sea;
and now
We are embarked — the mountains hang
and frown

Over the starry deep that gleams below
A vast and dim expanse, as o'er the waves
   we go.

XXIV

And as we sailed, a strange and awful tale
That Woman told, like such mysterious
   dream
As makes the slumberer's cheek with
   wonder pale!
'T was midnight, and around, a shoreless
   stream,
Wide ocean rolled, when that majestic
   theme
Shrined in her heart found utterance, and
   she bent
Her looks on mine; those eyes a kin-
   dling beam
Of love divine into my spirit sent,
And, ere her lips could move, made the air
   eloquent.

XXV

'Speak not to me, but hear! much shalt
   thou learn,
Much must remain unthought, and more
   untold,
In the dark Future's ever-flowing urn.
Know then that from the depth of ages
   old
Two Powers o'er mortal things dominion
   hold,
Ruling the world with a divided lot,
Immortal, all-pervading, manifold,
Twin Genii, equal Gods — when life and
   thought
Sprang forth, they burst the womb of in-
   essential Nought.

XXVI

'The earliest dweller of the world alone
Stood on the verge of chaos. Lo! afar
O'er the wide wild abyss two meteors
   shone,
Sprung from the depth of its tempestu-
   ous jar —
A blood-red Comet and the Morning Star
Mingling their beams in combat. As he
   stood
All thoughts within his mind waged mu-
   tual war
In dreadful sympathy — when to the
   flood
That fair Star fell, he turned and shed his
   brother's blood.

XXVII

'Thus Evil triumphed, and the Spirit of
   Evil,
One Power of many shapes which none
   may know,
One Shape of many names; the Fiend
   did revel
In victory, reigning o'er a world of woe,
For the new race of man went to and fro,
Famished and homeless, loathed and
   loathing, wild,
And hating good — for his immortal foe,
He changed from starry shape, beauteous
   and mild,
To a dire Snake, with man and beast un-
   reconciled.

XXVIII

'The darkness lingering o'er the dawn of
   things
Was Evil's breath and life; this made
   him strong
To soar aloft with overshadowing wings;
And the great Spirit of Good did creep
   among
The nations of mankind, and every tongue
Cursed and blasphemed him as he passed;
   for none
Knew good from evil, though their names
   were hung
In mockery o'er the fane where many a
   groan,
As King, and Lord, and God, the conquer-
   ing Fiend did own.

XXIX

'The Fiend, whose name was Legion:
   Death, Decay,
Earthquake and Blight, and Want, and
   Madness pale,
Wingèd and wan diseases, an array
Numerous as leaves that strew the au-
   tumnal gale;
Poison, a snake in flowers, beneath the
   veil
Of food and mirth, hiding his mortal
   head;
And, without whom all these might
   nought avail,
Fear, Hatred, Faith and Tyranny, who
   spread
Those subtle nets which snare the living
   and the dead.

XXX

'His spirit is their power, and they his
    slaves
In air, and light, and thought, and lan-
    guage dwell;
And keep their state from palaces to
    graves,
In all resorts of men — invisible,
But when, in ebon mirror, Nightmare fell,
To tyrant or impostor bids them rise,
Black wingèd demon - forms — whom,
    from the hell,
His reign and dwelling beneath nether
    skies,
He loosens to their dark and blasting min-
    istries.

XXXI

'In the world's youth his empire was as
    firm
As its foundations. Soon the Spirit of
    Good,
Though in the likeness of a loathsome
    worm,
Sprang from the billows of the formless
    flood,
Which shrank and fled; and with that
    Fiend of blood
Renewed the doubtful war.   Thrones
    then first shook,
And earth's immense and trampled mul-
    titude
In hope on their own powers began to
    look,
And Fear, the demon pale, his sanguine
    shrine forsook.

XXXII

'Then Greece arose, and to its bards and
    sages,
In dream, the golden - pinioned Genii
    came,
Even where they slept amid the night
    of ages,
Steeping their hearts in the divinest flame
Which thy breath kindled, Power of
    holiest name!
And oft in cycles since, when darkness
    gave
New weapons to thy foe, their sunlike
    fame
Upon the combat shone — a light to save,
Like Paradise spread forth beyond the
    shadowy grave.

XXXIII

'Such is this conflict — when mankind
    doth strive
With its oppressors in a strife of blood,
Or when free thoughts, like lightnings,
    are alive,
And in each bosom of the multitude
Justice and truth with custom's hydra
    brood
Wage silent war; when priests and
    kings dissemble
In smiles or frowns their fierce disqui-
    etude,
When round pure hearts a host of hopes
    assemble,
The Snake and Eagle meet — the world's
    foundations tremble!

XXXIV

'Thou hast beheld that fight — when to
    thy home
Thou dost return, steep not its hearth
    in tears;
Though thou mayst hear that earth is
    now become
The tyrant's garbage, which to his com-
    peers,
The vile reward of their dishonored
    years,
He will dividing give.   The victor
    Fiend
Omnipotent of yore, now quails, and
    fears
His triumph dearly won, which soon will
    lend
An impulse swift and sure to his approach-
    ing end.

XXXV

'List, stranger, list! mine is an human
    form
Like that thou wearest — touch me —
    shrink not now!
My hand thou feel'st is not a ghost's,
    but warm
With human blood. 'T was many years
    ago,
Since first my thirsting soul aspired to
    know
The secrets of this wondrous world,
    when deep
My heart was pierced with sympathy for
    woe

Which could not be mine own, and
　　thought did keep
In dream unnatural watch beside an in-
　　fant's sleep.

XXXVI

' Woe could not be mine own, since far
　　from men
I dwelt, a free and happy orphan child,
By the sea-shore, in a deep mountain glen;
And near the waves and through the for-
　　ests wild
I roamed, to storm and darkness recon-
　　ciled;
For I was calm while tempest shook the
　　sky,
But when the breathless heavens in
　　beauty smiled,
I wept sweet tears, yet too tumultuously
For peace, and clasped my hands aloft in
　　ecstasy.

XXXVII

' These were forebodings of my fate. Be-
　　fore
A woman's heart beat in my virgin
　　breast,
It had been nurtured in divinest lore;
A dying poet gave me books, and blessed
With wild but holy talk the sweet unrest
In which I watched him as he died away;
A youth with hoary hair, a fleeting guest
Of our lone mountains; and this lore did
　　sway
My spirit like a storm, contending there
　　alway.

XXXVIII

' Thus the dark tale which history doth
　　unfold
I knew, but not, methinks, as others
　　know,
For they weep not; and Wisdom had
　　unrolled
The clouds which hide the gulf of mortal
　　woe;
To few can she that warning vision show;
For I loved all things with intense devo-
　　tion,
So that when Hope's deep source in full-
　　est flow,
Like earthquake did uplift the stagnant
　　ocean
Of human thoughts, mine shook beneath
　　the wide emotion.

XXXIX

' When first the living blood through all
　　these veins
Kindled a thought in sense, great France
　　sprang forth,
And seized, as if to break, the ponderous
　　chains
Which bind in woe the nations of the
　. earth.
I saw, and started from my cottage
　　hearth;
And to the clouds and waves in tameless
　　gladness
Shrieked, till they caught immeasurable
　　mirth,
And laughed in light and music: soon
　　sweet madness
Was poured upon my heart, a soft and
　　thrilling sadness.

XL

' Deep slumber fell on me: — my dreams
　　were fire,
Soft and delightful thoughts did rest and
　　hover
Like shadows o'er my brain; and strange
　　desire,
The tempest of a passion, raging over
My tranquil soul, its depths with light
　　did cover,
Which passed; and calm, and darkness,
　　sweeter far,
Came — then I loved; but not a human
　　lover !
For when I rose from sleep, the Morning
　　Star
Shone through the woodbine wreaths which
　　round my casement were.

XLI

' 'T was like an eye which seemed to smile
　　on me.
I watched, till by the sun made pale it
　　sank
Under the billows of the heaving sea;
But from its beams deep love my spirit
　　drank,
And to my brain the boundless world
　　now shrank
Into one thought — one image — yes,
　　forever!
Even like the dayspring, poured on va-
　　pors dank,

The beams of that one Star did shoot
          and quiver
Through my benighted mind — and were
          extinguished never.

XLII

'The day passed thus. At night, me-
          thought, in dream
A shape of speechless beauty did ap-
          pear;
It stood like light on a careering stream
Of golden clouds which shook the atmo-
          sphere;
A wingèd youth, his radiant brow did
          wear
The Morning Star; a wild dissolving
          bliss
Over my frame he breathed, approach-
          ing near,
And bent his eyes of kindling tender-
          ness
Near mine, and on my lips impressed a
          lingering kiss,

XLIII

'And said: "A Spirit loves thee, mortal
          maiden;
How wilt thou prove thy worth?" Then
          joy and sleep
Together fled; my soul was deeply
          laden,
And to the shore I went to muse and
          weep;
But as I moved, over my heart did creep
A joy less soft, but more profound and
          strong
Than my sweet dream; and it forbade to
          keep
The path of the sea-shore; that Spirit's
          tongue
Seemed whispering in my heart, and bore
          my steps along.

XLIV

'How, to that vast and peopled city led,
Which was a field of holy warfare
          then,
I walked among the dying and the dead,
And shared in fearless deeds with evil
          men,
Calm as an angel in the dragon's den;
How I braved death for liberty and
          truth,
And spurned at peace, and power, and
          fame; and when

Those hopes had lost the glory of their
          youth,
How sadly I returned — might move the
          hearer's ruth.

XLV

'Warm tears throng fast! the tale may
          not be said.
Know then that, when this grief had
          been subdued,
I was not left, like others, cold and dead;
The Spirit whom I loved in solitude
Sustained his child; the tempest-shaken
          wood,
The waves, the fountains, and the hush
          of night —
These were his voice, and well I under-
          stood
His smile divine, when the calm sea was
          bright
With silent stars, and Heaven was breath-
          less with delight.

XLVI

'In lonely glens, amid the roar of rivers,
When the dim nights were moonless,
          have I known
Joys which no tongue can tell; my pale
          lip quivers
When thought revisits them: — know
          thou alone,
That, after many wondrous years were
          flown,
I was awakened by a shriek of woe;
And over me a mystic robe was thrown
By viewless hands, and a bright Star did
          glow
Before my steps — the Snake then met his
          mortal foe.'

XLVII

'Thou fearest not then the Serpent on thy
          heart?'
'Fear it!' she said, with brief and pas-
          sionate cry,
And spake no more. That silence made
          me start —
I looked, and we were sailing pleasantly,
Swift as a cloud between the sea and sky,
Beneath the rising moon seen far away;
Mountains of ice, like sapphire, piled on
          high,
Hemming the horizon round, in silence lay
On the still waters — these we did ap-
          proach alway.

XLVIII

And swift and swifter grew the vessel's
    motion,
So that a dizzy trance fell on my brain, —
Wild music woke me; we had passed the
    ocean
Which girds the pole, Nature's remotest
    reign;
And we glode fast o'er a pellucid plain
Of waters, azure with the noontide day.
Ethereal mountains shone around; a
    Fane
Stood in the midst, girt by green isles
    which lay
On the blue sunny deep, resplendent far
    away.

XLIX

It was a Temple, such as mortal hand
Has never built, nor ecstasy, nor dream
Reared in the cities of enchanted land;
'T was likest Heaven, ere yet day's purple
    stream
Ebbs o'er the western forest, while the
    gleam
Of the unrisen moon among the clouds
Is gathering — when with many a golden
    beam
The thronging constellations rush in
    crowds,
Paving with fire the sky and the marmo-
    real floods.

L

Like what may be conceived of this vast
    dome,
When from the depths which thought
    can seldom pierce
Genius beholds it rise, his native home,
Girt by the deserts of the Universe;
Yet, nor in painting's light, or mightier
    verse,
Or sculpture's marble language can in-
    vest
That shape to mortal sense — such
    glooms immerse
That incommunicable sight, and rest
Upon the laboring brain and over-burdened
    breast.

LI

Winding among the lawny islands fair,
Whose blosmy forests starred the shad-
    owy deep,
The wingless boat paused where an ivory
    stair
Its fretwork in the crystal sea did steep,
Encircling that vast Fane's aërial heap.
We disembarked, and through a portal
    wide
We passed, whose roof of moonstone
    carved did keep
A glimmering o'er the forms on every
    side,
Sculptures like life and thought, immovable,
    deep-eyed.

LII

We came to a vast hall, whose glorious
    roof
Was diamond which had drunk the
    lightning's sheen
In darkness and now poured it through
    the woof
Of spell-inwoven clouds hung there to
    screen
Its blinding splendor — through such veil
    was seen
That work of subtlest power, divine and
    rare;
Orb above orb, with starry shapes be-
    tween,
And hornèd moons, and meteors strange
    and fair,
On night-black columns poised — one hol-
    low hemisphere!

LIII

Ten thousand columns in that quivering
    light
Distinct, between whose shafts wound far
    away
The long and labyrinthine aisles, more
    bright
With their own radiance than the Heaven
    of Day;
And on the jasper walls around there lay
Paintings, the poesy of mightiest thought,
Which did the Spirit's history display;
A tale of passionate change, divinely
    taught,
Which, in their wingèd dance, unconscious
    Genii wrought.

LIV

Beneath there sate on many a sapphire
    throne
The Great who had departed from man-
    kind,
A mighty Senate; — some, whose white
    hair shone

Like mountain snow, mild, beautiful and
blind;
Some, female forms, whose gestures
beamed with mind;
And ardent youths, and children bright
and fair;
And some had lyres whose strings were
intertwined
With pale and clinging flames, which
ever there
Waked faint yet thrilling sounds that
pierced the crystal air.

LV

One seat was vacant in the midst, a throne,
Reared on a pyramid like sculptured
flame,
Distinct with circling steps which rested
on
Their own deep fire. Soon as the Woman
came
Into that hall, she shrieked the Spirit's
name
And fell; and vanished slowly from the
sight.
Darkness arose from her dissolving
frame, —
Which, gathering, filled that dome of
woven light,
Blotting its spherèd stars with supernatural
night.

LVI

Then first two glittering lights were seen
to glide
In circles on the amethystine floor,
Small serpent eyes trailing from side to
side,
Like meteors on a river's grassy shore;
They round each other rolled, dilating
more
And more — then rose, commingling into
one,
One clear and mighty planet hanging
o'er
A cloud of deepest shadow which was
thrown
Athwart the glowing steps and the crystal-
line throne.

LVII

The cloud which rested on that cone of
flame
Was cloven; beneath the planet sate a
Form,

Fairer than tongue can speak or thought
may frame,
The radiance of whose limbs rose-like
and warm
Flowed forth, and did with softest light
inform
The shadowy dome, the sculptures and
the state
Of those assembled shapes — with clinging charm
Sinking upon their hearts and mine. He
sate
Majestic yet most mild, calm yet compassionate.

LVIII

Wonder and joy a passing faintness threw
Over my brow — a hand supported me,
Whose touch was magic strength; an eye
of blue
Looked into mine, like moonlight, sooth-
ingly;
And a voice said, ' Thou must a listener be
This day; two mighty Spirits now return,
Like birds of calm, from the world's
raging sea;
They pour fresh light from Hope's im-
mortal urn;
A tale of human power — despair not —
list and learn!

LIX

I looked, and lo! one stood forth eloquently.
His eyes were dark and deep, and the
clear brow
Which shadowed them was like the
morning sky,
The cloudless Heaven of Spring, when
in their flow
Through the bright air the soft winds as
they blow
Wake the green world ; his gestures did
obey
The oracular mind that made his features glow,
And where his curvèd lips half open lay,
Passion's divinest stream had made impetuous way.

LX

Beneath the darkness of his outspread
hair
He stood thus beautiful; but there was
One

Who sate beside him like his shadow there,
And held his hand — far lovelier; she was known
To be thus fair by the few lines alone
Which through her floating locks and gathered cloke,
Glances of soul-dissolving glory, shone;
None else beheld her eyes — in him they woke
Memories which found a tongue, as thus he silence broke.

CANTO SECOND

I

THE star-light smile of children, the sweet looks
Of women, the fair breast from which I fed,
The murmur of the unreposing brooks,
And the green light which, shifting overhead,
Some tangled bower of vines around me shed,
The shells on the sea-sand, and the wild flowers,
The lamp - light through the rafters cheerly spread
And on the twining flax — in life's young hours
These sights and sounds did nurse my spirit's folded powers.

II

In Argolis, beside the echoing sea,
Such impulses within my mortal frame
Arose, and they were dear to memory,
Like tokens of the dead; but others came
Soon, in another shape — the wondrous fame
Of the past world, the vital words and deeds
Of minds whom neither time nor change can tame,
Traditions dark and old whence evil creeds
Start forth and whose dim shade a stream of poison feeds.

III

I heard, as all have heard, the various story
Of human life, and wept unwilling tears.

Feeble historians of its shame and glory,
False disputants on all its hopes and fears,
Victims who worshipped ruin, chroniclers
Of daily scorn, and slaves who loathed their state,
Yet, flattering Power, had given its ministers
A throne of judgment in the grave —
't was fate,
That among such as these my youth should seek its mate.

IV

The land in which I lived by a fell bane
Was withered up. Tyrants dwelt side by side,
And stabled in our homes, until the chain
Stifled the captive's cry, and to abide
That blasting curse men had no shame. All vied
In evil, slave and despot; fear with lust
Strange fellowship through mutual hate had tied,
Like two dark serpents tangled in the dust,
Which on the paths of men their mingling poison thrust.

V

Earth, our bright home, its mountains and its waters,
And the ethereal shapes which are suspended
Over its green expanse, and those fair daughters,
The clouds, of Sun and Ocean, who have blended
The colors of the air since first extended
It cradled the young world, none wandered forth
To see or feel; a darkness had descended
On every heart; the light which shows its worth
Must among gentle thoughts and fearless take its birth.

VI

This vital world, this home of happy spirits,
Was as a dungeon to my blasted kind;
All that despair from murdered hope inherits

They sought, and, in their helpless misery
    blind,
A deeper prison and heavier chains did
    find,
And stronger tyrants: — a dark gulf
    before,
The realm of a stern Ruler, yawned;
    behind,
Terror and Time conflicting drove, and
    bore
On their tempestuous flood the shrieking
    wretch from shore.

VII

Out of that Ocean's wrecks had Guilt
    and Woe
Framed a dark dwelling for their home-
    less thought,
And, starting at the ghosts which to and
    fro
Glide o'er its dim and gloomy strand, had
    brought
The worship thence which they each
    other taught.
Well might men loathe their life! well
    might they turn
Even to the ills again from which they
    sought
Such refuge after death! — well might
    they learn
To gaze on this fair world with hopeless un-
    concern!

VIII

For they all pined in bondage; body and
    soul,
Tyrant and slave, victim and torturer,
    bent
Before one Power, to which supreme
    control
Over their will by their own weakness
    lent
Made all its many names omnipotent;
All symbols of things evil, all divine;
And hymns of blood or mockery, which
    rent
The air from all its fanes, did intertwine
Imposture's impious toils round each dis-
    cordant shrine.

IX

I heard, as all have heard, life's various
    story,
And in no careless heart transcribed the
    tale;

But, from the sneers of men who had
    grown hoary
In shame and scorn, from groans of
    crowds made pale
By famine, from a mother's desolate wail
O'er her polluted child, from innocent
    blood
Poured on the earth, and brows anxious
    and pale
With the heart's warfare, did I gather
    food
To feed my many thoughts — a tameless
    multitude!

X

I wandered through the wrecks of days
    departed
Far by the desolated shore, when even
O'er the still sea and jagged islets darted
The light of moonrise ; in the northern
    Heaven,
Among the clouds near the horizon
    driven,
The mountains lay beneath one planet
    pale;
Around me broken tombs and columns
    riven
Looked vast in twilight, and the sorrow-
    ing gale
Waked in those ruins gray its everlasting
    wail!

XI

I knew not who had framed these won-
    ders then,
Nor had I heard the story of their deeds;
But dwellings of a race of mightier
    men,
And monuments of less ungentle creeds,
Tell their own tale to him who wisely
    heeds
The language which they speak; and
    now, to me,
The moonlight making pale the blooming
    weeds,
The bright stars shining in the breathless
    sea,
Interpreted those scrolls of mortal mys-
    tery.

XII

Such man has been, and such may yet
    become!
Ay, wiser, greater, gentler even than
    they

Who on the fragments of yon shattered
    dome
Have stamped the sign of power! I felt
    the sway
Of the vast stream of ages bear away
My floating thoughts — my heart beat
    loud and fast —
Even as a storm let loose beneath the
    ray
Of the still moon, my spirit onward
    passed
Beneath truth's steady beams upon its tu-
    mult cast.

XIII

It shall be thus no more! too long, too
    long,
Sons of the glorious dead, have ye lain
    bound
In darkness and in ruin! Hope is strong,
Justice and Truth their wingèd child
    have found!
Awake! arise! until the mighty sound
Of your career shall scatter in its gust
The thrones of the oppressor, and the
    ground
Hide the last altar's unregarded dust,
Whose Idol has so long betrayed your im-
    pious trust.

XIV

It must be so — I will arise and waken
The multitude, and like a sulphurous
    hill,
Which on a sudden from its snows has
    shaken
The swoon of ages, it shall burst, and fill
The world with cleansing fire; it must, it
    will —
It may not be restrained ! — and who
    shall stand
Amid the rocking earthquake steadfast
    still
But Laon ? on high Freedom's desert
    land
A tower whose marble walls the leaguèd
    storms withstand!

XV

One summer night, in commune with the
    hope
Thus deeply fed, amid those ruins gray
I watched beneath the dark sky's starry
    cope;
And ever from that hour upon me lay

The burden of this hope, and night or
    day,
In vision or in dream, clove to my breast;
Among mankind, or when gone far away
To the lone shores and mountains, 't was
    a guest
Which followed where I fled, and watched
    when I did rest.

XVI

These hopes found words through which
    my spirit sought
To weave a bondage of such sympathy
As might create some response to the
    thought
Which ruled me now — and as the vapors
    lie
Bright in the outspread morning's radi-
    ancy,
So were these thoughts invested with the
    light
Of language; and all bosoms made reply
On which its lustre streamed, whene'er
    it might
Through darkness wide and deep those
    trancèd spirits smite.

XVII

Yes, many an eye with dizzy tears was
    dim,
And oft I thought to clasp my own heart's
    brother,
When I could feel the listener's senses
    swim,
And hear his breath its own swift gasp-
    ings smother
Even as my words evoked them — and
    another,
And yet another, I did fondly deem,
Felt that we all were sons of one great
    mother;
And the cold truth such sad reverse did
    seem
As to awake in grief from some delightful
    dream.

XVIII

Yes, oft beside the ruined labyrinth
Which skirts the hoary caves of the
    green deep
Did Laon and his friend on one gray
    plinth,
Round whose worn base the wild waves
    hiss and leap,
Resting at eve, a lofty converse keep;

And that this friend was false may now
  be said
Calmly — that he like other men could
  weep
Tears which are lies, and could betray
  and spread
Snares for that guileless heart which for
  his own had bled.

XIX

Then, had no great aim recompensed my
  sorrow,
I must have sought dark respite from its
  stress
In dreamless rest, in sleep that sees no
  morrow —
For to tread life's dismaying wilderness
Without one smile to cheer, one voice to
  bless,
Amid the snares and scoffs of human-
  kind,
Is hard — but I betrayed it not, nor less
With love that scorned return sought to
  unbind
The interwoven clouds which make its
  wisdom blind.

XX

With deathless minds, which leave where
  they have passed
A path of light, my soul communion
  knew,
Till from that glorious intercourse, at
  last,
As from a mine of magic store, I drew
Words which were weapons; round my
  heart there grew
The adamantine armor of their power;
And from my fancy wings of golden hue
Sprang forth — yet not alone from wis-
  dom's tower,
A minister of truth, these plumes young
  Laon bore.

XXI

An orphan with my parents lived, whose
  eyes
Were lodestars of delight, which drew
  me home
When I might wander forth; nor did I
  prize
Aught human thing beneath Heaven's
  mighty dome
Beyond this child; so when sad hours
  were come,

And baffled hope like ice still clung to
  me,
Since kin were cold, and friends had now
  become
Heartless and false, I turned from all
  to be,
Cythna, the only source of tears and smiles
  to thee.

XXII

What wert thou then ? A child most
  infantine,
Yet wandering far beyond that innocent
  age
In all but its sweet looks and mien divine;
Even then, methought, with the world's
  tyrant rage
A patient warfare thy young heart did
  wage,
When those soft eyes of scarcely conscious thought
Some tale or thine own fancies would
  engage
To overflow with tears, or converse
  fraught
With passion o'er their depths its fleeting
  light had wrought.

XXIII

She moved upon this earth a shape of
  brightness,
A power, that from its objects scarcely
  drew
One impulse of her being — in her lightness
Most like some radiant cloud of morning
  dew
Which wanders through the waste air's
  pathless blue
To nourish some far desert; she did
  seem
Beside me, gathering beauty as she grew,
Like the bright shade of some immortal
  dream
Which walks, when tempest sleeps, the
  wave of life's dark stream.

XXIV

As mine own shadow was this child
  to me,
A second self, far dearer and more fair,
Which clothed in undissolving radiancy
All those steep paths which languor and
  despair

Of human things had made so dark and
    bare,
But which I trod alone — nor, till be-
    reft
Of friends, and overcome by lonely care,
Knew I what solace for that loss was
    left,
Though by a bitter wound my trusting
    heart was cleft.

XXV

Once she was dear, now she was all I
    had
To love in human life — this playmate
    sweet,
This child of twelve years old. So she
    was made
My sole associate, and her willing feet
Wandered with mine where Earth and
    Ocean meet,
Beyond the aërial mountains whose vast
    cells
The unreposing billows ever beat,
Through forests wild and old, and lawny
    dells
Where boughs of incense droop over the
    emerald wells.

XXVI

And warm and light I felt her clasping
    hand
When twined in mine; she followed
    where I went,
Through the lone paths of our immortal
    land.
It had no waste but some memorial lent
Which strung me to my toil — some
    monument
Vital with mind; then Cythna by my
    side,
Until the bright and beaming day were
    spent,
Would rest, with looks entreating to
    abide,
Too earnest and too sweet ever to be de-
    nied.

XXVII

And soon I could not have refused her.
    Thus
Forever, day and night, we two were
    ne'er
Parted but when brief sleep divided us;
And, when the pauses of the lulling air
Of noon beside the sea had made a lair

For her soothed senses, in my arms she
    slept,
And I kept watch over her slumbers
    there,
While, as the shifting visions over her
    swept,
Amid her innocent rest by turns she smiled
    and wept.

XXVIII

And in the murmur of her dreams was
    heard
Sometimes the name of Laon. Suddenly
She would arise, and, like the secret bird
Whom sunset wakens, fill the shore and
    sky
With her sweet accents, a wild mel-
    ody, —
Hymns which my soul had woven to
    Freedom, strong
The source of passion whence they rose
    to be;
Triumphant strains which, like a spirit's
    tongue,
To the enchanted waves that child of glory
    sung —

XXIX

Her white arms lifted through the shad-
    owy stream
Of her loose hair. Oh, excellently great
Seemed to me then my purpose, the vast
    theme
Of those impassioned songs, when Cythna
    sate
Amid the calm which rapture doth cre-
    ate
After its tumult, her heart vibrating,
Her spirit o'er the Ocean's floating state
From her deep eyes far wandering, on
    the wing
Of visions that were mine, beyond its ut-
    most spring !

XXX

For, before Cythna loved it, had my song
Peopled with thoughts the boundless uni-
    verse,
A mighty congregation, which were
    strong,
Where'er they trod the darkness, to dis-
    perse
The cloud of that unutterable curse
Which clings upon mankind; all things
    became

Slaves to my holy and heroic verse,
Earth, sea and sky, the planets, life and
    fame
And fate, or whate'er else binds the world's
    wondrous frame.

XXXI

And this belovèd child thus felt the sway
Of my conceptions, gathering like a
    cloud
The very wind on which it rolls away;
Hers too were all my thoughts, ere yet
    endowed
With music and with light their foun-
    tains flowed
In poesy; and her still and earnest face,
Pallid with feelings which intensely
    glowed
Within, was turned on mine with speech-
    less grace,
Watching the hopes which there her heart
    had learned to trace.

XXXII

In me, communion with this purest being
Kindled intenser zeal, and made me wise
In knowledge, which in hers mine own
    mind seeing
Left in the human world few mysteries.
How without fear of evil or disguise
Was Cythna! what a spirit strong and
    mild,
Which death or pain or peril could de-
    spise,
Yet melt in tenderness! what genius
    wild,
Yet mighty, was enclosed within one simple
    child!

XXXIII

New lore was this. Old age with its gray
    hair,
And wrinkled legends of unworthy
    things,
And icy sneers, is nought: it cannot dare
To burst the chains which life forever
    flings
On the entangled soul's aspiring wings;
So is it cold and cruel, and is made
The careless slave of that dark Power
    which brings
Evil, like blight, on man, who, still be-
    trayed,
Laughs o'er the grave in which his living
    hopes are laid.

XXXIV

Nor are the strong and the severe to keep
The empire of the world. Thus Cythna
    taught
Even in the visions of her eloquent sleep,
Unconscious of the power through which
    she wrought
The woof of such intelligible thought,
As from the tranquil strength which
    cradled lay
In her smile-peopled rest my spirit
    sought
Why the deceiver and the slave has sway
O'er heralds so divine of truth's arising
    day.

XXXV

Within that fairest form the female mind,
Untainted by the poison clouds which
    rest
On the dark world, a sacred home did
    find;
But else from the wide earth's maternal
    breast
Victorious Evil, which had dispossessed
All native power, had those fair children
    torn,
And made them slaves to soothe his vile
    unrest,
And minister to lust its joys forlorn,
Till they had learned to breathe the atmo-
    sphere of scorn.

XXXVI

This misery was but coldly felt, till she
Became my only friend, who had endued
My purpose with a wider sympathy.
Thus Cythna mourned with me the servi-
    tude
In which the half of humankind were
    mewed,
Victims of lust and hate, the slaves of
    slaves;
She mourned that grace and power were
    thrown as food
To the hyena Lust, who, among graves,
Over his loathèd meal, laughing in agony,
    raves.

XXXVII

And I, still gazing on that glorious child,
Even as these thoughts flushed o'er her:
    — 'Cythna sweet,
Well with the world art thou unrecon-
    ciled;

Never will peace and human nature meet
Till free and equal man and woman greet
Domestic peace; and ere this power can
    make
In human hearts its calm and holy seat,
This slavery must be broken ' — as I
    spake,
From Cythna's eyes a light of exultation
    brake.

XXXVIII

She replied earnestly: — ' It shall be
    mine,
This task, — mine, Laon ! thou hast much
    to gain;
Nor wilt thou at poor Cythna's pride re-
    pine,
If she should lead a happy female train
To meet thee over the rejoicing plain,
When myriads at thy call shall throng
    around
The Golden City.' — Then the child did
    strain
My arm upon her tremulous heart, and
    wound
Her own about my neck, till some reply
    she found.

XXXIX

I smiled, and spake not. — ' Wherefore
    dost thou smile
At what I say ? Laon, I am not weak,
And, though my cheek might become pale
    the while,
With thee, if thou desirest, will I seek
Through their array of banded slaves to
    wreak
Ruin upon the tyrants. I had thought
It was more hard to turn my unpractised
    cheek
To scorn and shame, and this belovèd
    spot
And thee, O dearest friend, to leave and
    murmur not.

XL

' Whence came I what I am ? Thou, Laon,
    knowest
How a young child should thus undaunted
    be;
Methinks it is a power which thou be-
    stowest,
Through which I seek, by most resem-
    bling thee,

So to become most good, and great, and
    free;
Yet, far beyond this Ocean's utmost roar,
In towers and huts are many like to
    me,
Who, could they see thine eyes, or feel
    such lore
As I have learnt from them, like me would
    fear no more.

XLI

' Think'st thou that I shall speak unskil-
    fully,
And none will heed me ? I remember
    now
How once a slave in tortures doomed to
    die
Was saved because in accents sweet and
    low
He sung a song his judge loved long
    ago,
As he was led to death. All shall relent
Who hear me; tears as mine have flowed,
    shall flow,
Hearts beat as mine now beats, with such
    intent
As renovates the world; a will omnipotent!

XLII

' Yes, I will tread Pride's golden palaces,
Through Penury's roofless huts and
    squalid cells
Will I descend, where'er in abjectness
Woman with some vile slave her tyrant
    dwells;
There with the music of thine own sweet
    spells
Will disenchant the captives, and will
    pour
For the despairing, from the crystal wells
Of thy deep spirit, reason's mighty lore,
And power shall then abound, and hope
    arise once more.

XLIII

' Can man be free if woman be a slave ?
Chain one who lives, and breathes this
    boundless air,
To the corruption of a closèd grave!
Can they, whose mates are beasts con-
    demned to bear
Scorn heavier far than toil or anguish,
    dare
To trample their oppressors ? In their
    home,

Among their babes, thou knowest a curse
would wear
The shape of woman — hoary Crime
would come
Behind, and Fraud rebuild Religion's tottering dome.

XLIV

'I am a child: — I would not yet de-
part.
When I go forth alone, bearing the lamp
Aloft which thou hast kindled in my
heart,
Millions of slaves from many a dungeon
damp
Shall leap in joy, as the benumbing
cramp
Of ages leaves their limbs. No ill may
harm
Thy Cythna ever. Truth its radiant
stamp
Has fixed, as an invulnerable charm,
Upon her children's brow, dark Falsehood
to disarm.

XLV

'Wait yet awhile for the appointed day.
Thou wilt depart, and I with tears shall
stand
Watching thy dim sail skirt the ocean
gray;
Amid the dwellers of this lonely land
I shall remain alone — and thy command
Shall then dissolve the world's unquiet
trance,
And, multitudinous as the desert sand
Borne on the storm, its millions shall ad-
vance,
Thronging round thee, the light of their
deliverance.

XLVI

'Then, like the forests of some pathless
mountain
Which from remotest glens two warring
winds
Involve in fire which not the loosened
fountain
Of broadest floods might quench, shall
all the kinds
Of evil catch from our uniting minds
The spark which must consume them; —
Cythna then
Will have cast off the impotence that
binds

Her childhood now, and through the
paths of men
Will pass, as the charmed bird that haunts
the serpent's den.

XLVII

'We part! — O Laon, I must dare, nor
tremble,
To meet those looks no more! — Oh,
heavy stroke!
Sweet brother of my soul! can I dis-
semble
The agony of this thought?' — As thus
she spoke
The gathered sobs her quivering accents
broke,
And in my arms she hid her beating
breast.
I remained still for tears — sudden she
woke
As one awakes from sleep, and wildly
pressed
My bosom, her whole frame impetuously
possessed.

XLVIII

'We part to meet again — but yon blue
waste,
Yon desert wide and deep, holds no recess
Within whose happy silence, thus em-
braced,
We might survive all ills in one caress;
Nor doth the grave — I fear 't is passion-
less —
Nor yon cold vacant Heaven: — we meet
again
Within the minds of men, whose lips
shall bless
Our memory, and whose hopes its light
retain
When these dissevered bones are trodden
in the plain.'

XLIX

I could not speak, though she had ceased,
for now
The fountains of her feeling, swift and
deep,
Seemed to suspend the tumult of their
flow.
So we arose, and by the star-light steep
Went homeward — neither did we speak
nor weep,
But, pale, were calm with passion. Thus
subdued,

Like evening shades that o'er the moun-
    tains creep,
We moved towards our home; where, in
    this mood,
Each from the other sought refuge in soli-
    tude.

CANTO THIRD

I

WHAT thoughts had sway o'er Cythna's
    lonely slumber
That night, I know not; but my own did
    seem
As if they might ten thousand years out-
    number
Of waking life, the visions of a dream
Which hid in one dim gulf the troubled
    stream
Of mind; a boundless chaos wild and
    vast,
Whose limits yet were never memory's
    theme;
And I lay struggling as its whirlwinds
    passed,
Sometimes for rapture sick, sometimes for
    pain aghast.

II

Two hours, whose mighty circle did em-
    brace
More time than might make gray the in-
    fant world,
Rolled thus, a weary and tumultuous
    space;
When the third came, like mist on
    breezes curled,
From my dim sleep a shadow was un-
    furled;
Methought, upon the threshold of a cave
I sate with Cythna; drooping briony,
    pearled
With dew from the wild streamlet's
    shattered wave,
Hung, where we sate to taste the joys which
    Nature gave.

III

We lived a day as we were wont to live,
But Nature had a robe of glory on,
And the bright air o'er every shape did
    weave
Intenser hues, so that the herbless stone,
The leafless bough among the leaves
    alone,

Had being clearer than its own could be;
And Cythna's pure and radiant self was
    shown,
In this strange vision, so divine to me,
That if I loved before, now love was agony.

IV

Morn fled, noon came, evening, then
    night, descended,
And we prolonged calm talk beneath the
    sphere
Of the calm moon — when suddenly was
    blended
With our repose a nameless sense of
    fear;
And from the cave behind I seemed to
    hear
Sounds gathering upwards — accents in-
    complete,
And stifled shrieks, — and now, more
    near and near,
A tumult and a rush of thronging feet
The cavern's secret depths beneath the
    earth did beat.

V

The scene was changed, and away, away,
    away!
Through the air and over the sea we
    sped,
And Cythna in my sheltering bosom lay,
And the winds bore me; through the
    darkness spread
Around, the gaping earth then vomited
Legions of foul and ghastly shapes,
    which hung
Upon my flight; and ever as we fled
They plucked at Cythna; soon to me
    then clung
A sense of actual things those monstrous
    dreams among.

VI

And I lay struggling in the impotence
Of sleep, while outward life had burst
    its bound,
Though, still deluded, strove the tor-
    tured sense
To its dire wanderings to adapt the
    sound
Which in the light of morn was poured
    around
Our dwelling; breathless, pale and una-
    ware
I rose, and all the cottage crowded found

With armèd men, whose glittering swords
were bare,
And whose degraded limbs the Tyrant's
garb did wear.

VII

And ere with rapid lips and gathered
brow
I could demand the cause, a feeble
shriek —
It was a feeble shriek, faint, far and
low —
Arrested me; my mien grew calm and
meek,
And grasping a small knife I went to
seek
That voice among the crowd — 't was
Cythna's cry!
Beneath most calm resolve did agony
wreak
Its whirlwind rage: — so I passed quietly
Till I beheld where bound that dearest
child did lie.

VIII

I started to behold her, for delight
And exultation, and a joyance free,
Solemn, serene and lofty, filled the
light
Of the calm smile with which she looked
on me;
So that I feared some brainless ecstasy,
Wrought from that bitter woe, had wil-
dered her.
'Farewell! farewell!' she said, as I drew
nigh;
'At first my peace was marred by this
strange stir,
Now I am calm as truth — its chosen min-
ister.

IX

'Look not so, Laon — say farewell in
hope;
These bloody men are but the slaves who
bear
Their mistress to her task; it was my
scope
The slavery where they drag me now to
share,
And among captives willing chains to
wear
Awhile — the rest thou knowest. Return,
dear friend!
Let our first triumph trample the despair

Which would ensnare us now, for, in the
end,
In victory or in death our hopes and fears
must blend.'

X

These words had fallen on my unheed-
ing ear,
Whilst I had watched the motions of the
crew
With seeming careless glance; not many
were
Around her, for their comrades just
withdrew
To guard some other victim; so I drew
My knife, and with one impulse, sud-
denly,
All unaware three of their number slew,
And grasped a fourth by the throat, and
with loud cry
My countrymen invoked to death or lib-
erty.

XI

What followed then I know not, for a
stroke,
On my raised arm and naked head came
down,
Filling my eyes with blood. — When I
awoke,
I felt that they had bound me in my
swoon,
And up a rock which overhangs the town
By the steep path were bearing me;
below
The plain was filled with slaughter, —
overthrown
The vineyards and the harvests, and the
glow
Of blazing roofs shone far o'er the white
Ocean's flow.

XII

Upon that rock a mighty column stood,
Whose capital seemed sculptured in the
sky,
Which to the wanderers o'er the solitude
Of distant seas, from ages long gone
by,
Had made a landmark; o'er its height to
fly
Scarcely the cloud, the vulture or the
blast
Has power, and when the shades of even-
ing lie

On Earth and Ocean, its carved summits cast
The sunken daylight far through the aërial waste.

XIII

They bore me to a cavern in the hill
Beneath that column, and unbound me there;
And one did strip me stark; and one did fill
A vessel from the putrid pool; one bare
A lighted torch, and four with friendless care
Guided my steps the cavern-paths along;
Then up a steep and dark and narrow stair
We wound, until the torch's fiery tongue
Amid the gushing day beamless and pallid hung.

XIV

They raised me to the platform of the pile,
That column's dizzy height; the grate of brass,
Through which they thrust me, open stood the while,
As to its ponderous and suspended mass,
With chains which eat into the flesh, alas!
With brazen links, my naked limbs they bound;
The grate, as they departed to repass,
With horrid clangor fell, and the far sound
Of their retiring steps in the dense gloom was drowned.

XV

The noon was calm and bright: — around that column
The overhanging sky and circling sea,
Spread forth in silentness profound and solemn,
The darkness of brief frenzy cast on me,
So that I knew not my own misery;
The islands and the mountains in the day
Like clouds reposed afar; and I could see
The town among the woods below that lay,
And the dark rocks which bound the bright and glassy bay.

XVI

It was so calm, that scarce the feathery weed
Sown by some eagle on the topmost stone
Swayed in the air: — so bright, that noon did breed
No shadow in the sky beside mine own —
Mine, and the shadow of my chain alone.
Below, the smoke of roofs involved in flame
Rested like night; all else was clearly shown
In that broad glare; yet sound to me none came,
But of the living blood that ran within my frame.

XVII

The peace of madness fled, and ah, too soon!
A ship was lying on the sunny main;
Its sails were flagging in the breathless noon;
Its shadow lay beyond. That sight again
Waked with its presence in my trancèd brain
The stings of a known sorrow, keen and cold;
I knew that ship bore Cythna o'er the plain
Of waters, to her blighting slavery sold,
And watched it with such thoughts as must remain untold.

XVIII

I watched until the shades of evening wrapped
Earth like an exhalation; then the bark
Moved, for that calm was by the sunset snapped.
It moved a speck upon the Ocean dark;
Soon the wan stars came forth, and I could mark
Its path no more! I sought to close mine eyes,
But, like the balls, their lids were stiff and stark;
I would have risen, but ere that I could rise
My parchèd skin was split with piercing agonies.

XIX

I gnawed my brazen chain, and sought to sever

Its adamantine links, that I might die.
O Liberty! forgive the base endeavor,
Forgive me, if, reserved for victory,
The Champion of thy faith e'er sought
　　to fly!
That starry night, with its clear silence,
　　sent
Tameless resolve which laughed at misery
Into my soul — linkèd remembrance lent
To that such power, to me such a severe
　　content.

XX

To breathe, to be, to hope, or to despair
And die, I questioned not; nor, though
　　the Sun,
Its shafts of agony kindling through the
　　air,
Moved over me, nor though in evening
　　dun,
Or when the stars their visible courses
　　run,
Or morning, the wide universe was
　　spread
In dreary calmness round me, did I shun
Its presence, nor seek refuge with the
　　dead
From one faint hope whose flower a drop-
　　ping poison shed.

XXI

Two days thus passed — I neither raved
　　nor died;
Thirst raged within me, like a scorpion's
　　nest
Built in mine entrails; I had spurned
　　aside
The water-vessel, while despair pos-
　　sessed
My thoughts, and now no drop remained.
　　The uprest
Of the third sun brought hunger — but
　　the crust
Which had been left was to my craving
　　breast
Fuel, not food. I chewed the bitter dust,
And bit my bloodless arm, and licked the
　　brazen rust.

XXII

My brain began to fail when the fourth
　　morn
Burst o'er the golden isles. A fearful
　　sleep,

Which through the caverns dreary and
　　forlorn
Of the riven soul sent its foul dreams to
　　sweep
With whirlwind swiftness — a fall far
　　and deep —
A gulf, a void, a sense of senselessness —
These things dwelt in me, even as shadows
　　keep
Their watch in some dim charnel's lone-
　　liness, —
A shoreless sea, a sky sunless and planet-
　　less!

XXIII

The forms which peopled this terrific
　　trance
I well remember. Like a choir of devils,
Around me they involved a giddy dance;
Legions seemed gathering from the misty
　　levels
Of Ocean, to supply those ceaseless
　　revels, —
Foul, ceaseless shadows; thought could
　　not divide
The actual world from these entangling
　　evils,
Which so bemocked themselves that I
　　descried
All shapes like mine own self hideously
　　multiplied.

XXIV

The sense of day and night, of false and
　　true,
Was dead within me. Yet two visions
　　burst
That darkness; one, as since that hour I
　　knew,
Was not a phantom of the realms ac-
　　cursed,
Where then my spirit dwelt — but of the
　　first
I know not yet, was it a dream or no;
But both, though not distincter, were
　　immersed
In hues which, when through memory's
　　waste they flow,
Make their divided streams more bright
　　and rapid now.

XXV

Methought that grate was lifted, and the
　　seven,

Who brought me thither, four stiff
    corpses bare,
And from the frieze to the four winds of
    Heaven
Hung them on high by the entangled
    hair;
Swarthy were three — the fourth was
    very fair;
As they retired, the golden moon up-
    sprung,
And eagerly, out in the giddy air,
Leaning that I might eat, I stretched
    and clung
Over the shapeless depth in which those
    corpses hung.

XXVI

A woman's shape, now lank and cold and
    blue,
The dwelling of the many-colored worm,
Hung there; the white and hollow cheek
    I drew
To my dry lips — What radiance did
    inform
Those horny eyes? whose was that with-
    ered form?
Alas, alas! it seemed that Cythna's ghost
Laughed in those looks, and that the
    flesh was warm
Within my teeth! — a whirlwind keen
    as frost
Then in its sinking gulfs my sickening spirit
    tossed.

XXVII

Then seemed it that a tameless hurricane
Arose, and bore me in its dark career
Beyond the sun, beyond the stars that
    wane
On the verge of formless space — it lan-
    guished there,
And, dying, left a silence lone and drear,
More horrible than famine. In the deep
The shape of an old man did then ap-
    pear,
Stately and beautiful; that dreadful sleep
His heavenly smiles dispersed, and I could
    wake and weep.

XXVIII

And, when the blinding tears had fallen,
    I saw
That column, and those corpses, and the
    moon,

And felt the poisonous tooth of hunger
    gnaw
My vitals; I rejoiced, as if the boon
Of senseless death would be accorded
    soon,
When from that stony gloom a voice
    arose,
Solemn and sweet as when low winds
    attune
The midnight pines; the grate did then
    unclose,
And on that reverend form the moonlight
    did repose.

XXIX

He struck my chains, and gently spake
    and smiled;
As they were loosened by that Hermit
    old,
Mine eyes were of their madness half
    beguiled
To answer those kind looks; he did en-
    fold
His giant arms around me to uphold
My wretched frame; my scorchèd limbs
    he wound
In linen moist and balmy, and as cold
As dew to drooping leaves; the chain,
    with sound
Like earthquake, through the chasm of
    that steep stair did bound,

XXX

As, lifting me, it fell! — What next I
    heard
Were billows leaping on the harbor bar,
And the shrill sea-wind whose breath
    idly stirred
My hair; I looked abroad, and saw a
    star
Shining beside a sail, and distant far
That mountain and its column, the known
    mark
Of those who in the wide deep wander-
    ing are, —
So that I feared some Spirit, fell and
    dark,
In trance had lain me thus within a fiend-
    ish bark.

XXXI

For now, indeed, over the salt sea billow
I sailed; yet dared not look upon the
    shape

Of him who ruled the helm, although
  the pillow
For my light head was hollowed in his
  lap,
And my bare limbs his mantle did en-
  wrap, —
Fearing it was a fiend; at last, he bent
O'er me his aged face; as if to snap
Those dreadful thoughts, the gentle
  grandsire bent,
And to my inmost soul his soothing looks
  he sent.

XXXII

A soft and healing potion to my lips
At intervals he raised — now looked on
  high
To mark if yet the starry giant dips
His zone in the dim sea — now cheer-
  ingly,
Though he said little, did he speak to me.
' It is a friend beside thee — take good
  cheer
Poor victim, thou art now at liberty!'
I joyed as those a human tone to hear
Who in cells deep and lone have languished
  many a year.

XXXIII

A dim and feeble joy, whose glimpses oft
Were quenched in a relapse of wildering
  dreams;
Yet still methought we sailed, until aloft
The stars of night grew pallid, and the
  beams
Of morn descended on the ocean-streams;
And still that aged man, so grand and
  mild,
Tended me, even as some sick mother
  seems
To hang in hope over a dying child,
Till in the azure East darkness again was
  piled.

XXXIV

And then the night-wind, steaming from
  the shore,
Sent odors dying sweet across the sea,
And the swift boat the little waves which
  bore,
Were cut by its keen keel, though slant-
  ingly;
Soon I could hear the leaves sigh, and
  could see

The myrtle-blossoms starring the dim
  grove,
As past the pebbly beach the boat did
  flee
On sidelong wing into a silent cove
Where ebon pines a shade under the starlight wove.

CANTO FOURTH

I

THE old man took the oars, and soon the
  bark
Smote on the beach beside a tower of
  stone.
It was a crumbling heap whose portal
  dark
With blooming ivy-trails was overgrown;
Upon whose floor the spangling sands
  were strown,
And rarest sea-shells, which the eternal
  flood,
Slave to the mother of the months, had
  thrown
Within the walls of that gray tower,
  which stood
A changeling of man's art nursed amid
  Nature's brood.

II

When the old man his boat had anchorèd,
He wound me in his arms with tender
  care,
And very few but kindly words he said,
And bore me through the tower adown a
  stair,
Whose smooth descent some ceaseless
  step to wear
For many a year had fallen. We came
  at last
To a small chamber which with mosses
  rare
Was tapestried, where me his soft hands
  placed
Upon a couch of grass and oak-leaves in-
  terlaced.

III

The moon was darting through the lat-
  tices
Its yellow light, warm as the beams of
  day —
So warm that to admit the dewy breeze

The old man opened them; the moonlight
lay
Upon a lake whose waters wove their
play
Even to the threshold of that lonely
home;
Within was seen in the dim wavering
ray
The antique sculptured roof, and many a
tome
Whose lore had made that sage all that he
had become.

IV

The rock-built barrier of the sea was
passed
And I was on the margin of a lake,
A lonely lake, amid the forests vast
And snowy mountains. Did my spirit
wake
From sleep as many-colored as the snake
That girds eternity? in life and truth
Might not my heart its cravings ever
slake?
Was Cythna then a dream, and all my
youth,
And all its hopes and fears, and all its joy
and ruth?

V

Thus madness came again, — a milder
madness,
Which darkened nought but time's un-
quiet flow
With supernatural shades of clinging
sadness;
That gentle Hermit, in my helpless woe,
By my sick couch was busy to and fro,
Like a strong spirit ministrant of good;
When I was healed, he led me forth to
show
The wonders of his sylvan solitude,
And we together sate by that isle-fretted
flood.

VI

He knew his soothing words to weave
with skill
From all my madness told; like mine
own heart,
Of Cythna would he question me, until
That thrilling name had ceased to make
me start,
From his familiar lips; it was not art,

Of wisdom and of justice when he
spoke —
When 'mid soft looks of pity, there would
dart
A glance as keen as is the lightning's
stroke
When it doth rive the knots of some ancestral oak.

VII

Thus slowly from my brain the darkness
rolled;
My thoughts their due array did reas-
sume
Through the enchantments of that Hermit
old.
Then I bethought me of the glorious
doom
Of those who sternly struggle to relume
The lamp of Hope o'er man's bewildered
lot;
And, sitting by the waters, in the gloom
Of eve, to that friend's heart I told my
thought —
That heart which had grown old, but had
corrupted not.

VIII

That hoary man had spent his livelong
age
In converse with the dead who leave the
stamp
Of ever-burning thoughts on many a
page,
When they are gone into the senseless
damp
Of graves; his spirit thus became a lamp
Of splendor, like to those on which it
fed;
Through peopled haunts, the City and
the Camp,
Deep thirst for knowledge had his footsteps led,
And all the ways of men among mankind
he read.

IX

But custom maketh blind and obdurate
The loftiest hearts; he had beheld the
woe
In which mankind was bound, but
deemed that fate
Which made them abject would preserve them so;

And in such faith, some steadfast joy to
　　know,
He sought this cell; but when fame went
　　abroad
That one in Argolis did undergo
Torture for liberty, and that the crowd
High truths from gifted lips had heard and
　　understood,

X

And that the multitude was gathering
　　wide, —
His spirit leaped within his aged frame;
In lonely peace he could no more abide,
But to the land on which the victor's
　　flame
Had fed, my native land, the Hermit
　　came;
Each heart was there a shield, and every
　　tongue
Was as a sword of truth — young Laon's
　　name
Rallied their secret hopes, though tyrants
　　sung
Hymns of triumphant joy our scattered
　　tribes among.

XI

He came to the lone column on the rock,
And with his sweet and mighty elo-
　　quence
The hearts of those who watched it did
　　unlock,
And made them melt in tears of peni-
　　tence.
They gave him entrance free to bear me
　　thence.
'Since this,' the old man said, 'seven
　　years are spent,
While slowly truth on thy benighted
　　sense
Has crept; the hope which wildered it
　　has lent,
Meanwhile, to me the power of a sublime
　　intent.

XII

'Yes, from the records of my youthful
　　state,
And from the lore of bards and sages
　　old,
From whatsoe'er my wakened thoughts
　　create
Out of the hopes of thine aspirings bold,
Have I collected language to unfold

Truth to my countrymen; from shore to
　　shore
Doctrines of human power my words
　　have told;
They have been heard, and men aspire
　　to more
Than they have ever gained or ever lost
　　of yore.

XIII

'In secret chambers parents read, and
　　weep,
My writings to their babes, no longer
　　blind;
And young men gather when their ty-
　　rants sleep,
And vows of faith each to the other
　　bind;
And marriageable maidens, who have
　　pined
With love till life seemed melting
　　through their look,
A warmer zeal, a nobler hope, now find;
And every bosom thus is rapt and shook,
Like autumn's myriad leaves in one swoln
　　mountain brook.

XIV

'The tyrants of the Golden City tremble
At voices which are heard about the
　　streets;
The ministers of fraud can scarce dis-
　　semble
The lies of their own heart, but when
　　one meets
Another at the shrine, he inly weets,
Though he says nothing, that the truth
　　is known;
Murderers are pale upon the judgment-
　　seats,
And gold grows vile even to the wealthy
　　crone,
And laughter fills the Fane, and curses
　　shake the Throne.

XV

'Kind thoughts, and mighty hopes, and
　　gentle deeds
Abound; for fearless love, and the pure
　　law
Of mild equality and peace, succeeds
To faiths which long have held the world
　　in awe,
Bloody, and false, and cold.　As whirl-
　　pools draw

All wrecks of Ocean to their chasm, the
    sway
Of thy strong genius, Laon, which fore-
    saw
This hope, compels all spirits to obey,
Which round thy secret strength now
    throng in wide array.

XVI

'For I have been thy passive instru-
    ment'—
(As thus the old man spake, his counte-
    nance
Gleamed on me like a spirit's) — 'thou
    hast lent
To me, to all, the power to advance
Towards this unforeseen deliverance
From our ancestral chains — ay, thou
    didst rear
That lamp of hope on high, which time
    nor chance
Nor change may not extinguish, and my
    share
Of good was o'er the world its gathered
    beams to bear.

XVII

'But I, alas! am both unknown and old,
And though the woof of wisdom I know
    well
To dye in hues of language, I am cold
In seeming, and the hopes which inly
    dwell
My manners note that I did long repel;
But Laon's name to the tumultuous
    throng
Were like the star whose beams the
    waves compel
And tempests, and his soul - subduing
    tongue
Were as a lance to quell the mailèd crest
    of wrong.

XVIII

'Perchance blood need not flow; if thou
    at length
Wouldst rise, perchance the very slaves
    would spare
Their brethren and themselves; great is
    the strength
Of words — for lately did a maiden fair,
Who from her childhood has been
    taught to bear
The Tyrant's heaviest yoke, arise, and
    make

Her sex the law of truth and freedom
    hear,
And with these quiet words — "for thine
    own sake
I prithee spare me,"—did with ruth so
    take

XIX

'All hearts that even the torturer, who
    had bound
Her meek calm frame, ere it was yet
    impaled,
Loosened her weeping then; nor could
    be found
One human hand to harm her. Unas-
    sailed
Therefore she walks through the great
    City, veiled
In virtue's adamantine eloquence,
'Gainst scorn and death and pain thus
    trebly mailed,
And blending in the smiles of that de-
    fence
The serpent and the dove, wisdom and
    innocence.

XX

'The wild-eyed women throng around her
    path;
From their luxurious dungeons, from the
    dust
Of meaner thralls, from the oppressor's
    wrath,
Or the caresses of his sated lust,
They congregate; in her they put their
    trust.
The tyrants send their armèd slaves to
    quell
Her power; they, even like a thunder-
    gust
Caught by some forest, bend beneath the
    spell
Of that young maiden's speech, and to their
    chiefs rebel.

XXI

'Thus she doth equal laws and justice
    teach
To woman, outraged and polluted long;
Gathering the sweetest fruit in human
    reach
For those fair hands now free, while
    armèd wrong
Trembles before her look, though it be
    strong;

Thousands thus dwell beside her, virgins
    bright
And matrons with their babes, a stately
    throng !
Lovers renew the vows which they did
    plight
In early faith, and hearts long parted now
    unite;

XXII

' And homeless orphans find a home near
    her,
And those poor victims of the proud, no
    less,
Fair wrecks, on whom the smiling world
    with stir
Thrusts the redemption of its wicked-
    ness.
In squalid huts, and in its palaces,
Sits Lust alone, while o'er the land is
    borne
Her voice, whose awful sweetness doth
    repress
All evil; and her foes relenting turn,
And cast the vote of love in hope's aban-
    doned urn.

XXIII

' So in the populous City, a young maiden
Has baffled Havoc of the prey which he
Marks as his own, whene'er with chains
    o'erladen
Men make them arms to hurl down ty-
    ranny, —
False arbiter between the bound and free;
And o'er the land, in hamlets and in
    towns
The multitudes collect tumultuously,
And throng in arms; but tyranny dis-
    owns
Their claim, and gathers strength around
    its trembling thrones.

XXIV

' Blood soon, although unwillingly, to shed
The free cannot forbear. The Queen of
    Slaves, ·
The hood-winked Angel of the blind and
    dead,
Custom, with iron mace points to the
    graves
Where her own standard desolately waves
Over the dust of Prophets and of Kings.
Many yet stand in her array — " she
    paves

Her path with human hearts," and o'er it
    flings
The wildering gloom of her immeasurable
    wings.

XXV

' There is a plain beneath the City's wall,
Bounded by misty mountains, wide and
    vast;
Millions there lift at Freedom's thrilling
    call
Ten thousand standards wide; they load
    the blast
Which bears one sound of many voices
    past,
And startles on his throne their sceptred
    foe;
He sits amid his idle pomp aghast,
And that his power hath passed away,
    doth know —
Why pause the victor swords to seal his
    overthrow ?

XXVI

' The Tyrant's guards resistance yet main-
    tain,
Fearless, and fierce, and hard as beasts
    of blood;
They stand a speck amid the peopled
    plain;
Carnage and ruin have been made their
    food
From infancy; ill has become their good,
And for its hateful sake their will has
    wove
The chains which eat their hearts. The
    multitude,
Surrounding them, with words of human
    love
Seek from their own decay their stubborn
    minds to move.

XXVII

' Over the land is felt a sudden pause,
As night and day those ruthless bands
    around
The watch of love is kept — a trance
    which awes
The thoughts of men with hope; as when
    the sound
Of whirlwind, whose fierce blasts the
    waves and clouds confound,
Dies suddenly, the mariner in fear
Feels silence sink upon his heart — thus
    bound

The conquerors pause; and oh! may free-
    men ne'er
Clasp the relentless knees of Dread, the
    murderer!

XXVIII

'If blood be shed, 't is but a change and
    choice
Of bonds — from slavery to cowardice, —
A wretched fall! Uplift thy charmèd
    voice,
Pour on those evil men the love that
    lies
Hovering within those spirit-soothing
    eyes!
Arise, my friend, farewell!' — As thus
    he spake,
From the green earth lightly I did arise,
As one out of dim dreams that doth
    awake,
And looked upon the depth of that reposing
    lake.

XXIX

I saw my countenance reflected there; —
And then my youth fell on me like a
    wind
Descending on still waters. My thin hair
Was prematurely gray; my face was
    lined
With channels, such as suffering leaves
    behind,
Not age; my brow was pale, but in my
    cheek
And lips a flush of gnawing fire did find
Their food and dwelling; though mine
    eyes might speak
A subtle mind and strong within a frame
    thus weak.

XXX

And though their lustre now was spent
    and faded,
Yet in my hollow looks and withered
    mien
The likeness of a shape for which was
    braided
The brightest woof of genius still was
    seen —
One who, methought, had gone from the
    world's scene,
And left it vacant — 't was her lover's
    face —
It might resemble her — it once had
    been

The mirror of her thoughts, and still the
    grace
Which her mind's shadow cast left there a
    lingering trace.

XXXI

What then was I? She slumbered with
    the dead.
Glory and joy and peace had come and
    gone.
Doth the cloud perish when the beams
    are fled
Which steeped its skirts in gold? or,
    dark and lone,
Doth it not through the paths of night
    unknown,
On outspread wings of its own wind up-
    borne,
Pour rain upon the earth? the stars are
    shown,
When the cold moon sharpens her silver
    horn
Under the sea, and make the wide night
    not forlorn.

XXXII

Strengthened in heart, yet sad, that aged
    man
I left, with interchange of looks and tears
And lingering speech, and to the Camp
    began
My way. O'er many a mountain-chain
    which rears
Its hundred crests aloft my spirit bears
My frame, o'er many a dale and many a
    moor;
And gayly now meseems serene earth
    wears
The blosmy spring's star-bright investi-
    ture, —
A vision which aught sad from sadness
    might allure.

XXXIII

My powers revived within me, and I
    went,
As one whom winds waft o'er the bend-
    ing grass,
Through many a vale of that broad con-
    tinent.
At night when I reposed, fair dreams did
    pass
Before my pillow; my own Cythna was,
Not like a child of death, among them
    ever;

When I arose from rest, a woful mass
That gentlest sleep seemed from my life
    to sever,
As if the light of youth were not withdrawn
    forever.

XXXIV

Aye as I went, that maiden who had
    reared
The torch of Truth afar, of whose high
    deeds
The Hermit in his pilgrimage had heard,
Haunted my thoughts. Ah, Hope its
    sickness feeds
With whatsoe'er it finds, or flowers or
    weeds!
Could she be Cythna? Was that corpse
    a shade
Such as self-torturing thought from mad-
    ness breeds?
Why was this hope not torture? Yet it
    made
A light around my steps which would not
    ever fade.

CANTO FIFTH

I

OVER the utmost hill at length I sped,
A snowy steep: — the moon was hanging
    low
Over the Asian mountains, and, out-
    spread
The plain, the City, and the Camp be-
    low,
Skirted the midnight Ocean's glimmer-
    ing flow;
The City's moon-lit spires and myriad
    lamps
Like stars in a sublunar sky did glow,
And fires blazed far amid the scattered
    camps,
Like springs of flame which burst where'er
    swift Earthquake stamps.

II

All slept but those in watchful arms who
    stood,
And those who sate tending the beacon's
    light;
And the few sounds from that vast mul-
    titude
Made silence more profound. Oh, what
    a might

Of human thought was cradled in that
    night!
How many hearts impenetrably veiled
Beat underneath its shade! what secret
    fight
Evil and Good, in woven passions mailed,
Waged through that silent throng — a war
    that never failed!

III

And now the Power of Good held victory.
So, through the labyrinth of many a tent,
Among the silent millions who did lie
In innocent sleep, exultingly I went.
The moon had left Heaven desert now,
    but lent
From eastern morn the first faint lustre
    showed
An armèd youth; over his spear he bent
His downward face : — 'A friend!' I
    cried aloud,
And quickly common hopes made freemen
    understood.

IV

I sate beside him while the morning
    beam
Crept slowly over Heaven, and talked
    with him
Of those immortal hopes, a glorious
    theme,
Which led us forth, until the stars grew
    dim;
And all the while methought his voice
    did swim,
As if it drownèd in remembrance were
Of thoughts which make the moist eyes
    overbrim;
At last, when daylight 'gan to fill the air,
He looked on me, and cried in wonder,
    ' Thou art here!'

V

Then, suddenly, I knew it was the youth
In whom its earliest hopes my spirit
    found;
But envious tongues had stained his
    spotless truth,
And thoughtless pride his love in silence
    bound,
And shame and sorrow mine in toils had
    wound,
Whilst he was innocent, and I deluded;
The truth now came upon me — on the
    ground

Tears of repenting joy, which fast in-
truded,
Fell fast — and o'er its peace our mingling
spirits brooded.

VI

Thus, while with rapid lips and earnest
eyes
We talked, a sound of sweeping conflict,
spread
As from the earth, did suddenly arise.
From every tent, roused by that clamor
dread,
Our bands outsprung and seized their
arms; we sped
Towards the sound; our tribes were
gathering far.
Those sanguine slaves, amid ten thousand
dead
Stabbed in their sleep, trampled in
treacherous war
The gentle hearts whose power their lives
had sought to spare.

VII

Like rabid snakes that sting some gentle
child
Who brings them food when winter false
and fair
Allures them forth with its cold smiles,
so wild
They rage among the camp; they overbear
The patriot hosts — confusion, then despair,
Descends like night — when 'Laon!'
one did cry;
Like a bright ghost from Heaven that
shout did scare
The slaves, and, widening through the
vaulted sky,
Seemed sent from Earth to Heaven in sign
of victory.

VIII

In sudden panic those false murderers
fled,
Like insect tribes before the northern
gale;
But swifter still our hosts encompassèd
Their shattered ranks, and in a craggy
vale,
Where even their fierce despair might
nought avail,

Hemmed them around! — and then re-
venge and fear
Made the high virtue of the patriots fail;
One pointed on his foe the mortal spear —
I rushed before its point, and cried ' For-
bear, forbear!'

IX

The spear transfixed my arm that was
uplifted
In swift expostulation, and the blood
Gushed round its point; I smiled, and —
' Oh! thou gifted
With eloquence which shall not be with-
stood,
Flow thus!' I cried in joy, ' thou vital
flood,
Until my heart be dry, ere thus the cause
For which thou wert aught worthy be
subdued! —
Ah, ye are pale — ye weep — your pas-
sions pause —
'T is well! ye feel the truth of love's be-
nignant laws.

X

' Soldiers, our brethren and our friends
are slain;
Ye murdered them, I think, as they did
sleep!
Alas, what have ye done ? The slightest
pain
Which ye might suffer, there were eyes
to weep,
But ye have quenched them — there
were smiles to steep
Your hearts in balm, but they are lost in
woe;
And those whom love did set his watch
to keep
Around your tents truth's freedom to
bestow,
Ye stabbed as they did sleep — but they
forgive ye now.

XI

' Oh, wherefore should ill ever flow from
ill,
And pain still keener pain forever breed ?
We all are brethren — even the slaves
who kill
For hire are men; and to avenge misdeed
On the misdoer doth but Misery feed
With her own broken heart! O Earth,
O Heaven!

And thou, dread Nature, which to every
    deed
And all that lives, or is, to be hath given,
Even as to thee have these done ill, and are
    forgiven.

XII

'Join then your hands and hearts, and let
    the past
Be as a grave which gives not up its dead
To evil thoughts.' — A film then over-
    cast
My sense with dimness, for the wound,
    which bled
Freshly, swift shadows o'er mine eyes
    had shed.
When I awoke, I lay 'mid friends and
    foes,
And earnest countenances on me shed
The light of questioning looks, whilst
    one did close
My wound with balmiest herbs, and soothed
    me to repose;

XIII

And one, whose spear had pierced me,
    leaned beside
With quivering lips and humid eyes; and
    all
Seemed like some brothers on a journey
    wide
Gone forth, whom now strange meeting
    did befall
In a strange land round one whom they
    might call
Their friend, their chief, their father, for
    assay
Of peril, which had saved them from the
    thrall
Of death, now suffering. Thus the vast
    array
Of those fraternal bands were reconciled
    that day.

XIV

Lifting the thunder of their acclamation,
Towards the City then the multitude,
And I among them, went in joy — a
    nation
Made free by love; a mighty brother-
    hood
Linked by a jealous interchange of good;
A glorious pageant, more magnificent
Than kingly slaves arrayed in gold and
    blood,

When they return from carnage, and are
    sent
In triumph bright beneath the populous
    battlement.

XV

Afar, the City walls were thronged on
    high,
And myriads on each giddy turret clung,
And to each spire far lessening in the
    sky
Bright pennons on the idle winds were
    hung;
As we approached, a shout of joyance
    sprung
At once from all the crowd, as if the
    vast
And peopled Earth its boundless skies
    among
The sudden clamor of delight had cast,
When from before its face some general
    wreck had passed.

XVI

Our armies through the City's hundred
    gates
Were poured, like brooks which to the
    rocky lair
Of some deep lake, whose silence them
    awaits,
Throng from the mountains when the
    storms are there;
And, as we passed through the calm
    sunny air,
A thousand flower-inwoven crowns were
    shed,
The token-flowers of truth and freedom
    fair,
And fairest hands bound them on many
    a head,
Those angels of love's heaven that over all
    was spread.

XVII

I trod as one tranced in some rapturous
    vision;
Those bloody bands so lately reconciled,
Were ever, as they went, by the contri-
    tion
Of anger turned to love, from ill be-
    guiled,
And every one on them more gently
    smiled
Because they had done evil; the sweet
    awe

Of such mild looks made their own hearts
    grow mild,
And did with soft attraction ever draw
Their spirits to the love of freedom's equal
    law.

XVIII

And they, and all, in one loud symphony
My name with Liberty commingling
    lifted —
' The friend and the preserver of the free!
The parent of this joy!' and fair eyes,
    gifted
With feelings caught from one who had
    uplifted
The light of a great spirit, round me
    shone;
And all the shapes of this grand scenery
    shifted
Like restless clouds before the steadfast
    sun.
Where was that Maid ? I asked, but it was
    known of none.

XIX

Laone was the name her love had chosen,
For she was nameless, and her birth
    none knew.
Where was Laone now ? — The words
    were frozen
Within my lips with fear; but to sub-
    due
Such dreadful hope to my great task was
    due,
And when at length one brought reply
    that she
To-morrow would appear, I then with-
    drew
To judge what need for that great throng
    might be,
For now the stars came thick over the twi-
    light sea.

XX

Yet need was none for rest or food to
    care,
Even though that multitude was passing
    great,
Since each one for the other did prepare
All kindly succor. Therefore to the
    gate
Of the Imperial House, now desolate,
I passed, and there was found aghast,
    alone,
The fallen Tyrant! — silently he sate
Upon the footstool of his golden throne,
Which, starred with sunny gems, in its own
    lustre shone.

XXI

Alone, but for one child who led before
    him
A graceful dance — the only living
    thing,
Of all the crowd, which thither to adore
    him
Flocked yesterday, who solace sought to
    bring
In his abandonment; she knew the King
Had praised her dance of yore, and now
    she wove
Its circles, aye weeping and murmur-
    ing,
'Mid her sad task of unregarded love,
That to no smiles it might his speechless
    sadness move.

XXII

She fled to him, and wildly clasped his
    feet
When human steps were heard; he
    moved nor spoke,
Nor changed his hue, nor raised his looks
    to meet
The gaze of strangers. Our loud en-
    trance woke
The echoes of the hall, which circling
    broke
The calm of its recesses; like a tomb
Its sculptured walls vacantly to the
    stroke
Of footfalls answered, and the twilight's
    gloom
Lay like a charnel's mist within the radiant
    dome.

XXIII

The little child stood up when we came
    nigh;
Her lips and cheeks seemed very pale
    and wan,
But on her forehead and within her eye
Lay beauty which makes hearts that feed
    thereon
Sick with excess of sweetness; on the
    throne
She leaned; the King, with gathered
    brow and lips
Wreathed by long scorn, did inly sneer
    and frown,

With hue like that when some great
    painter dips
His pencil in the gloom of earthquake and
    eclipse.

XXIV

She stood beside him like a rainbow
    braided
Within some storm, when scarce its
    shadows vast
From the blue paths of the swift sun
    have faded;
A sweet and solemn smile, like Cythna's,
    cast
One moment's light, which made my
    heart beat fast,
O'er that child's parted lips — a gleam
    of bliss,
A shade of vanished days; as the tears
    passed
Which wrapped it, even as with a father's
    kiss
I pressed those softest eyes in trembling
    tenderness.

XXV

The sceptred wretch then from that soli-
    tude
I drew, and, of his change compassion-
    ate,
With words of sadness soothed his rugged
    mood.
But he, while pride and fear held deep
    debate,
With sullen guile of ill-dissembled hate
Glared on me as a toothless snake might
    glare;
Pity, not scorn, I felt, though desolate
The desolator now, and unaware
The curses which he mocked had caught
    him by the hair.

XXVI

I led him forth from that which now
    might seem
A gorgeous grave; through portals sculp-
    tured deep
With imagery beautiful as dream
We went, and left the shades which tend
    on sleep
Over its unregarded gold to keep
Their silent watch. The child trod
    faintingly,
And as she went, the tears which she did
    weep

Glanced in the star-light; wilderèd
    seemed she,
And, when I spake, for sobs she could not
    answer me.

XXVII

At last the Tyrant cried, 'She hungers,
    slave!
Stab her, or give her bread!' — It was a
    tone
Such as sick fancies in a new-made grave
Might hear. I trembled, for the truth
    was known, —
He with this child had thus been left
    alone,
And neither had gone forth for food, but
    he
In mingled pride and awe cowered near
    his throne,
And she, a nursling of captivity,
Knew nought beyond those walls, nor what
    such change might be.

XXVIII

And he was troubled at a charm with-
    drawn
Thus suddenly — that sceptres ruled no
    more,
That even from gold the dreadful strength
    was gone
Which once made all things subject to its
    power;
Such wonder seized him as if hour by
    hour
The past had come again; and the swift
    fall
Of one so great and terrible of yore
To desolateness, in the hearts of all
Like wonder stirred who saw such awful
    change befall.

XXIX

A mighty crowd, such as the wide land
    pours
Once in a thousand years, now gathered
    round
The fallen Tyrant; like the rush of
    showers
Of hail in spring, pattering along the
    ground,
Their many footsteps fell — else came no
    sound
From the wide multitude; that lonely
    man
Then knew the burden of his change,
    and found,

Concealing in the dust his visage wan,
Refuge from the keen looks which through
his bosom ran.

XXX

And he was faint withal. I sate beside
him
Upon the earth, and took that child so fair
From his weak arms, that ill might none
betide him
Or her; when food was brought to them,
her share
To his averted lips the child did bear,
But, when she saw he had enough, she
ate,
And wept the while; the lonely man's de-
spair
Hunger then overcame, and, of his state
Forgetful, on the dust as in a trance he sate.

XXXI

Slowly the silence of the multitudes
Passed, as when far is heard in some lone
dell
The gathering of a wind among the
woods:
' And he is fallen!' they cry, 'he who did
dwell
Like famine or the plague, or aught more
fell,
Among our homes, is fallen! the mur-
derer
Who slaked his thirsting soul, as from a
well
Of blood and tears, with ruin! he is here!
Sunk in a gulf of scorn from which none
may him rear!'

XXXII

Then was heard — 'He who judged, let
him be brought
To judgment! blood for blood cries from
the soil
On which his crimes have deep pollution
wrought!
Shall Othman only unavenged despoil?
Shall they, who by the stress of grinding
toil
Wrest from the unwilling earth his lux-
uries,
Perish for crime, while his foul blood
may boil
Or creep within his veins at will? Arise!
And to high Justice make her chosen sacri-
fice!'

XXXIII

' What do ye seek ? what fear ye ? ' then
I cried,
Suddenly starting forth, 'that ye should
shed
The blood of Othman? if your hearts are
tried
In the true love of freedom, cease to
dread
This one poor lonely man ; beneath
Heaven spread
In purest light above us all, through
Earth —
Maternal Earth, who doth her sweet
smiles shed
For all — let him go free, until the worth
Of human nature win from these a second
birth.

XXXIV

' What call ye *justice*? Is there one who
ne'er
In secret thought has wished another's
ill?
Are ye all pure? Let those stand forth
who hear
And tremble not. Shall they insult and
kill,
If such they be? their mild eyes can they
fill
With the false anger of the hypocrite?
Alas, such were not pure! The chastened
will
Of virtue sees that justice is the light
Of love, and not revenge and terror and
despite.'

XXXV

The murmur of the people, slowly dying,
Paused as I spake; then those who near
me were
Cast gentle looks where the lone man
was lying
Shrouding his head, which now that infant fair
Clasped on her lap in silence; through
the air
Sobs were then heard, and many kissed
my feet
In pity's madness, and to the despair
Of him whom late they cursed a solace
sweet
His very victims brought — soft looks and
speeches meet.

XXXVI

Then to a home for his repose assigned,
Accompanied by the still throng, he went
In silence, where to soothe his rankling
    mind
Some likeness of his ancient state was
    lent;
And if his heart could have been inno-
    cent
As those who pardoned him, he might
    have ended
His days in peace; but his straight lips
    were bent,
Men said, into a smile which guile por-
    tended, —
A sight with which that child, like hope
    with fear, was blended.

XXXVII

'T was midnight now, the eve of that
    great day
Whereon the many nations, at whose
    call
The chains of earth like mist melted
    away,
Decreed to hold a sacred Festival,
A rite to attest the equality of all
Who live. So to their homes, to dream
    or wake,
All went. The sleepless silence did re-
    call
Laone to my thoughts, with hopes that
    make
The flood recede from which their thirst
    they seek to slake.

XXXVIII

The dawn flowed forth, and from its
    purple fountains
I drank those hopes which make the spirit
    quail,
As to the plain between the misty moun-
    tains
And the great City, with a countenance
    pale,
I went. It was a sight which might avail
To make men weep exulting tears, for
    whom
Now first from human power the rev-
    erend veil
Was torn, to see Earth from her general
    womb
Pour forth her swarming sons to a fraternal
    doom:

XXXIX

To see, far glancing in the misty morn-
    ing,
The signs of that innumerable host;
To hear one sound of many made, the
    warning
Of Earth to Heaven from its free chil-
    dren tossed;
While the eternal hills, and the sea lost
In wavering light, and, starring the blue
    sky,
The City's myriad spires of gold, almost
With human joy made mute society —
Its witnesses with men who must hereafter
    be:

XL

To see, like some vast island from the
    Ocean,
The Altar of the Federation rear
Its pile i' the midst — a work which the
    devotion
Of millions in one night created there,
Sudden as when the moonrise makes ap-
    pear
Strange clouds in the east — a marble
    pyramid
Distinct with steps ; — that mighty shape
    did wear
The light of genius; its still shadow hid
Far ships; to know its height the morning
    mists forbid! —

XLI

To hear the restless multitudes forever
Around the base of that great Altar
    flow,
As on some mountain islet burst and
    shiver
Atlantic waves; and, solemnly and slow,
As the wind bore that tumult to and fro,
To feel the dreamlike music, which did
    swim
Like beams through floating clouds on
    waves below,
Falling in pauses, from that Altar dim,
As silver-sounding tongues breathed an
    aërial hymn.

XLII

To hear, to see, to live, was on that
    morn
Lethean joy! so that all those assembled
Cast off their memories of the past out-
    worn;

Two only bosoms with their own life
  trembled,
And mine was one, — and we had both
  dissembled;
So with a beating heart I went, and one,
Who having much, covets yet more, resembled, —
A lost and dear possession, which not
  won,
He walks in lonely gloom beneath the noonday sun.

XLIII

To the great Pyramid I came; its stair
With female choirs was thronged, the
  loveliest
Among the free, grouped with its sculp-
  tures rare.
As I approached, the morning's golden
  mist,
Which now the wonder-stricken breezes
  kissed
With their cold lips, fled, and the sum-
  mit shone
Like Athos seen from Samothracia,
  dressed
In earliest light, by vintagers; and One
Sate there, a female Shape upon an ivory
  throne: —

XLIV

A Form most like the imagined habitant
Of silver exhalations sprung from dawn,
By winds which feed on sunrise woven,
  to enchant
The faiths of men. All mortal eyes were
  drawn —
As famished mariners through strange
  seas gone
Gaze on a burning watch-tower — by the
  light
Of those divinest lineaments. Alone,
With thoughts which none could share,
  from that fair sight
I turned in sickness, for a veil shrouded
  her countenance bright.

XLV

And neither did I hear the acclamations,
Which from brief silence bursting filled
  the air
With her strange name and mine, from
  all the nations
Which we, they said, in strength had
  gathered there

From the sleep of bondage; nor the
  vision fair
Of that bright pageantry beheld; but
  blind
And silent, as a breathing corpse, did fare,
Leaning upon my friend, till like a wind
To fevered cheeks a voice flowed o'er my
  troubled mind.

XLVI

Like music of some minstrel heavenly
  gifted,
To one whom fiends enthrall, this voice
  to me;
Scarce did I wish her veil to be uplifted,
I was so calm and joyous. I could see
The platform where we stood, the statues
  three
Which kept their marble watch on that
  high shrine,
The multitudes, the mountains, and the
  sea, —
As, when eclipse hath passed, things sud-
  den shine
To men's astonished eyes most clear and
  crystalline.

XLVII

At first Laone spoke most tremulously;
But soon her voice the calmness which it
  shed
Gathered, and — 'Thou art whom I
  sought to see,
And thou art our first votary here,' she
  said;
'I had a dear friend once, but he is dead!
And, of all those on the wide earth who
  breathe,
Thou dost resemble him alone. I spread
This veil between us two that thou be-
  neath
Shouldst image one who may have been
  long lost in death.

XLVIII

'For this wilt thou not henceforth pardon
  me?
Yes, but those joys which silence well
  requite
Forbid reply. Why men have chosen me
To be the Priestess of this holiest rite
I scarcely know, but that the floods of
  light
Which flow over the world have borne
  me hither

To meet thee, long most dear. And now
  unite
Thine hand with mine, and may all comfort wither
From both the hearts whose pulse in joy
  now beat together,

XLIX

' If our own will as others' law we bind,
If the foul worship trampled here we fear,
If as ourselves we cease to love our
  kind !' —
She paused, and pointed upwards —
  sculptured there
Three shapes around her ivory throne
  appear.
One was a Giant, like a child asleep
On a loose rock, whose grasp crushed, as
  it were
In dream, sceptres and crowns; and one
  did keep
Its watchful eyes in doubt whether to
  smile or weep —

L

A Woman sitting on the sculptured disk
Of the broad earth, and feeding from
  one breast
A human babe and a young basilisk;
Her looks were sweet as Heaven's when
  loveliest
In Autumn eves. The third Image was
  dressed
In white wings swift as clouds in winter
  skies;
Beneath his feet, 'mongst ghastliest
  forms, repressed
Lay Faith, an obscene worm, who sought
  to rise, —
While calmly on the Sun he turned his dia-
  mond eyes.

LI

Beside that Image then I sate, while she
Stood 'mid the throngs which ever ebbed
  and flowed,
Like light amid the shadows of the sea
Cast from one cloudless star, and on the
  crowd
That touch which none who feels forgets
  bestowed;
And whilst the sun returned the steadfast
  gaze
Of the great Image, as o'er Heaven it
  glode,

That rite had place; it ceased when sunset's blaze
Burned o'er the isles; all stood in joy and
  deep amaze —
When in the silence of all spirits there
Laone's voice was felt, and through the
  air
Her thrilling gestures spoke, most eloquently fair.

I

' Calm art thou as yon sunset! swift and
  strong
As new-fledged Eagles beautiful and young,
That float among the blinding beams of
  morning;
And underneath thy feet writhe Faith and
  Folly,
Custom and Hell and mortal Melancholy.
Hark! the Earth starts to hear the mighty
  warning
  Of thy voice sublime and holy;
  Its free spirits here assembled
See thee, feel thee, know thee now;
To thy voice their hearts have trembled,
Like ten thousand clouds which flow
With one wide wind as it flies!
Wisdom! thy irresistible children rise
To hail thee; and the elements they chain,
And their own will, to swell the glory of
  thy train!

2

' O Spirit vast and deep as Night and
  Heaven,
Mother and soul of all to which is given
The light of life, the loveliness of being!
Lo! thou dost reascend the human heart,
Thy throne of power, almighty as thou
  wert
In dreams of Poets old grown pale by see-
  ing
  The shade of thee; — now millions start
  To feel thy lightnings through them
  burning!
  Nature, or God, or Love, or Pleasure,
  Or Sympathy, the sad tears turning
  To mutual smiles, a drainless treasure,
  Descends amidst us! Scorn and Hate,
Revenge and Selfishness, are desolate!
A hundred nations swear that there shall
  be
Pity and Peace and Love among the good
  and free!

3

'Eldest of things, divine Equality!
Wisdom and Love are but the slaves of
  thee,
The angels of thy sway, who pour around
  thee
Treasures from all the cells of human
  thought
And from the Stars and from the Ocean
  brought,
And the last living heart whose beatings
  bound thee.
  The powerful and the wise had sought
Thy coming; thou, in light descending
O'er the wide land which is thine own,
Like the spring whose breath is blending
All blasts of fragrance into one,
Comest upon the paths of men!
Earth bares her general bosom to thy ken,
And all her children here in glory meet
To feed upon thy smiles, and clasp thy
  sacred feet.

4

'My brethren, we are free! the plains and
  mountains,
The gray sea-shore, the forests and the
  fountains,
Are haunts of happiest dwellers; man and
  woman,
Their common bondage burst, may freely
  borrow
From lawless love a solace for their sorrow;
For oft we still must weep, since we are
  human.
  A stormy night's serenest morrow,
Whose showers are pity's gentle tears,
Whose clouds are smiles of those that die
Like infants without hopes or fears,
And whose beams are joys that lie
In blended hearts, now holds dominion, —
The dawn of mind, which, upwards on a
  pinion
Borne, swift as sunrise, far illumines space,
And clasps this barren world in its own
  bright embrace!

5

'My brethren, we are free! the fruits are
  glowing
Beneath the stars, and the night-winds are
  flowing
O'er the ripe corn, the birds and beasts are
  dreaming.

Never again may blood of bird or beast
Stain with its venomous stream a human
  feast,
To the pure skies in accusation steaming!
  Avenging poisons shall have ceased
To feed disease and fear and madness;
The dwellers of the earth and air
Shall throng around our steps in gladness,
Seeking their food or refuge there.
Our toil from thought all glorious forms
  shall cull,
To make this earth, our home, more beau-
  tiful,
And Science, and her sister Poesy,
Shall clothe in light the fields and cities of
  the free!

6

'Victory, Victory to the prostrate nations!
Bear witness, Night, and ye mute Constel-
  lations
Who gaze on us from your crystalline cars!
Thoughts have gone forth whose powers
  can sleep no more!
Victory! Victory! Earth's remotest shore,
Regions which groan beneath the Antarctic
  stars,
  The green lands cradled in the roar
Of western waves, and wildernesses
Peopled and vast which skirt the oceans,
Where Morning dyes her golden tresses,
Shall soon partake our high emotions.
Kings shall turn pale! Almighty Fear,
The Fiend-God, when our charmèd name
  he hear,
Shall fade like shadow from his thousand
  fanes,
While Truth with Joy enthroned o'er his
  lost empire reigns!'

LII

Ere she had ceased, the mists of night
  entwining
Their dim woof floated o'er the infinite
  throng;
She, like a spirit through the darkness
  shining,
In tones whose sweetness silence did prolong
As if to lingering winds they did belong,
Poured forth her inmost soul: a passionate speech
With wild and thrilling pauses woven
  among,

Which whoso heard was mute, for it
    could teach
To rapture like her own all listening hearts
    to reach.

LIII

Her voice was as a mountain stream
    which sweeps
The withered leaves of autumn to the
    lake,
And in some deep and narrow bay then
    sleeps
In the shadow of the shores; as dead
    leaves wake,
Under the wave, in flowers and herbs
    which make
Those green depths beautiful when skies
    are blue,
The multitude so moveless did par-
    take
Such living change, and kindling mur-
    murs flew
As o'er that speechless calm delight and
    wonder grew.

LIV

Over the plain the throngs were scattered
    then
In groups around the fires, which from
    the sea
Even to the gorge of the first mountain
    glen
Blazed wide and far; the banquet of the
    free
Was spread beneath many a dark cypress
    tree,
Beneath whose spires, which swayed in
    the red flame,
Reclining as they ate, of Liberty
And Hope and Justice and Laone's name
Earth's children did a woof of happy con-
    verse frame.

LV

Their feast was such as Earth, the gen-
    eral mother,
Pours from her fairest bosom, when she
    smiles
In the embrace of Autumn; to each
    other
As when some parent fondly reconciles
Her warring children — she their wrath
    beguiles
With her own sustenance, they relenting
    weep —

Such was this Festival, which from their
    isles
And continents and winds and oceans
    deep
All shapes might throng to share that fly
    or walk or creep;

LVI

Might share in peace and innocence, for
    gore
Or poison none this festal did pollute,
But, piled on high, an overflowing store
Of pomegranates and citrons, fairest
    fruit,
Melons, and dates, and figs, and many a
    root
Sweet and sustaining, and bright grapes
    ere yet
Accursed fire their mild juice could trans-
    mute
Into a mortal· bane, and brown corn
    set
In baskets; with pure streams their thirst-
    ing lips they wet.

LVII

Laone had descended from the shrine,
And every deepest look and holiest mind
Fed on her form, though now those tones
    divine
Were silent as she passed; she did un-
    wind
Her veil, as with the crowds of her own
    kind
She mixed; some impulse made my heart
    refrain
From seeking her that night, so I re-
    clined
Amidst a group, where on the utmost
    plain
A festal watch-fire burned beside the dusky
    main.

LVIII

And joyous was our feast; pathetic talk,
And wit, and harmony of choral strains,
While far Orion o'er the waves did
    walk
That flow among the isles, held us in
    chains
Of sweet captivity which none disdains
Who feels; but, when his zone grew dim
    in mist
Which clothes the Ocean's bosom, o'er
    the plains

The multitudes went homeward to their rest,
Which that delightful day with its own shadow blest.

CANTO SIXTH

I

BESIDE the dimness of the glimmering sea,
Weaving swift language from impassioned themes,
With that dear friend I lingered, who to me
So late had been restored, beneath the gleams
Of the silver stars; and ever in soft dreams
Of future love and peace sweet converse lapped
Our willing fancies, till the pallid beams
Of the last watch-fire fell, and darkness wrapped
The waves, and each bright chain of floating fire was snapped,

II

And till we came even to the City's wall
And the great gate. Then, none knew whence or why,
Disquiet on the multitudes did fall;
And first, one pale and breathless passed us by,
And stared and spoke not; then with piercing cry
A troop of wild-eyed women — by the shrieks
Of their own terror driven, tumultuously
Hither and thither hurrying with pale cheeks —
Each one from fear unknown a sudden refuge seeks

III

Then, rallying cries of treason and of danger
Resounded, and — 'They come! to arms! to arms!
The Tyrant is amongst us, and the stranger
Comes to enslave us in his name! to arms!'
In vain: for Panic, the pale fiend who charms

Strength to forswear her right, those millions swept
Like waves before the tempest. These alarms
Came to me, as to know their cause I leapt
On the gate's turret, and in rage and grief and scorn I wept!

IV

For to the north I saw the town on fire,
And its red light made morning pallid now,
Which burst over wide Asia; — louder, higher,
The yells of victory and the screams of woe
I heard approach, and saw the throng below
Stream through the gates like foam-wrought waterfalls
Fed from a thousand storms — the fearful glow
Of bombs flares overhead — at intervals
The red artillery's bolt mangling among them falls.

V

And now the horsemen come — and all was done
Swifter than I have spoken — I beheld
Their red swords flash in the unrisen sun.
I rushed among the rout to have repelled
That miserable flight — one moment quelled
By voice, and looks, and eloquent despair,
As if reproach from their own hearts withheld
Their steps, they stood; but soon came pouring there
New multitudes, and did those rallied bands o'erbear.

VI

I strove, as drifted on some cataract
By irresistible streams some wretch might strive
Who hears its fatal roar; the files compact
Whelmed me, and from the gate availed to drive
With quickening impulse, as each bolt did rive
Their ranks with bloodier chasm; into the plain

Disgorged at length the dead and the
   alive
In one dread mass were parted, and the
   stain
Of blood from mortal steel fell o'er the
   fields like rain.

VII

For now the despot's bloodhounds with
   their prey,
Unarmed and unaware, were gorging
   deep
Their gluttony of death ; the loose array
Of horsemen o'er the wide fields murdering sweep,
And with loud laughter for their Tyrant
   reap
A harvest sown with other hopes; the
   while,
Far overhead, ships from Propontis keep
A killing rain of fire.   When the waves
   smile
As sudden earthquakes light many a volcano isle,

VIII

Thus sudden, unexpected feast was
   spread
For the carrion fowls of Heaven. I saw
   the sight —
I moved — I lived — as o'er the heaps of
   dead,
Whose stony eyes glared in the morning
   light,
I trod; to me there came no thought of
   flight,
But with loud cries of scorn, which
   whoso heard
That dreaded death felt in his veins the
   might
Of virtuous shame return, the crowd I
   stirred,
And desperation's hope in many hearts re-
   curred.

IX

A band of brothers gathering round me
   made,
Although unarmed, a steadfast front, and,
   still
Retreating, with stern looks beneath the
   shade
Of gathered eyebrows, did the victors
   fill

With doubt even in success; deliberate
   will
Inspired our growing troop; not overthrown,
It gained the shelter of a grassy hill, —
And ever still our comrades were hewn
   down,
And their defenceless limbs beneath our
   footsteps strown.

X

Immovably we stood; in joy I found
Beside me then, firm as a giant pine
Among the mountain vapors driven
   around,
The old man whom I loved; his eyes
   divine
With a mild look of courage answered
   mine,
And my young friend was near, and
   ardently
His hand grasped mine a moment; now
   the line
Of war extended, to our rallying cry
As myriads flocked in love and brotherhood
   to die.

XI

For ever while the sun was climbing
   Heaven
The horseman hewed our unarmed
   myriads down
Safely, though when by thirst of carnage
   driven
Too near, those slaves were swiftly over-
   thrown
By hundreds leaping on them; flesh and
   bone
Soon made our ghastly ramparts; then
   the shaft
Of the artillery from the sea was thrown
More fast and fiery, and the conquerors
   laughed
In pride to hear the wind our screams of
   torment waft.

XII

For on one side alone the hill gave shelter,
So vast that phalanx of unconquered
   men,
And there the living in the blood did
   welter
Of the dead and dying, which in that
   green glen,

Like stifled torrents, made a plashy
    fen
Under the feet. Thus was the butchery
    waged
While the sun clomb Heaven's eastern
    steep; but, when
It 'gan to sink, a fiercer combat raged,
For in more doubtful strife the armies were
    engaged.

XIII

Within a cave upon the hill were found
A bundle of rude pikes, the instrument
Of those who war but on their native
    ground
For natural rights; a shout of joyance,
    sent
Even from our hearts, the wide air
    pierced and rent,
As those few arms the bravest and the
    best
Seized, and each sixth, thus armed, did
    now present
A line which covered and sustained the
    rest,
A confident phalanx which the foes on
    every side invest.

XIV

That onset turned the foes to flight al-
    most;
But soon they saw their present strength,
    and knew
That coming night would to our resolute
    host
Bring victory; so, dismounting, close they
    drew
Their glittering files, and then the com-
    bat grew
Unequal but most horrible; and ever
Our myriads, whom the swift bolt over-
    threw,
Or the red sword, failed like a mountain
    river
Which rushes forth in foam to sink in
    sands forever.

XV

Sorrow and shame, to see with their own
    kind
Our human brethren mix, like beasts of
    blood,
To mutual ruin armed by one behind
Who sits and scoffs! — that friend so
    mild and good,

Who like its shadow near my youth had
    stood,
Was stabbed! — my old preserver's
    hoary hair,
With the flesh clinging to its roots, was
    strewed
Under my feet! I lost all sense or care,
And like the rest I grew desperate and
    unaware.

XVI

The battle became ghastlier; in the
    midst
I paused, and saw how ugly and how fell,
O Hate! thou art, even when thy life
    thou shedd'st
For love. The ground in many a little
    dell
Was broken, up and down whose steeps
    befell
Alternate victory and defeat; and there
The combatants with rage most horrible
Strove, and their eyes started with crack-
    ing stare,
And impotent their tongues they lolled
    into the air,

XVII

Flaccid and foamy, like a mad dog's
    hanging.
Want, and Moon-madness, and the pest's
    swift Bane,
When its shafts smite — while yet its
    bow is twanging —
Have each their mark and sign, some
    ghastly stain;
And this was thine, O War! of hate and
    pain
Thou loathèd slave! I saw all shapes of
    death,
And ministered to many, o'er the plain
While carnage in the sunbeam's warmth
    did seethe,
Till Twilight o'er the east wove her seren-
    est wreath.

XVIII

The few who yet survived, resolute and
    firm,
Around me fought. At the decline of
    day,
Winding above the mountain's snowy
    term,
New banners shone; they quivered in
    the ray

Of the sun's unseen orb; ere night the
array
Of fresh troops hemmed us in — of those
brave bands
I soon survived alone — and now I lay
Vanquished and faint, the grasp of
bloody hands
I felt, and saw on high the glare of falling
brands,

XIX

When on my foes a sudden terror
came,
And they fled, scattering. — Lo ! with
reinless speed
A black Tartarian horse of giant frame,
Comes trampling over the dead; the
living bleed
Beneath the hoofs of that tremendous
steed,
On which, like to an Angel, robed in
white,
Sate one waving a sword; the hosts recede
And fly, as through their ranks, with
awful might
Sweeps in the shadow of eve that Phantom
swift and bright;

XX

And its path made a solitude.   I rose
And marked its coming; it relaxed its
course
As it approached me, and the wind that
flows
Through night bore accents to mine ear
whose force
Might create smiles in death.   The Tar-
tar horse
Paused, and I saw the shape its might
which swayed,
And heard her musical pants, like the
sweet source
Of waters in the desert, as she said,
'Mount with me, Laon, now' — I rapidly
obeyed.

XXI

Then, 'Away ! away !' she cried, and
stretched her sword
As 't were a scourge over the courser's
head,
And lightly shook the reins.   We spake
no word,
But like the vapor of the tempest fled

Over the plain; her dark hair was
dispread
Like the pine's locks upon the lingering
blast;
Over mine eyes its shadowy strings it
spread
Fitfully, and the hills and streams fled
fast,
As o'er their glimmering forms the steed's
broad shadow passed.

XXII

And his hoofs ground the rocks to fire
and dust,
His strong sides made the torrents rise
in spray,
And turbulence, as of a whirlwind's gust,
Surrounded us; — and still away, away,
Through the desert night we sped, while
she alway
Gazed on a mountain which we neared,
whose crest,
Crowned with a marble ruin, in the ray
Of the obscure stars gleamed; its rugged
breast
The steed strained up, and then his impulse
did arrest.

XXIII

A rocky hill which overhung the
Ocean: —
From that lone ruin, when the steed that
panted
Paused, might be heard the murmur of
the motion
Of waters, as in spots forever haunted
By the choicest winds of Heaven which
are enchanted
To music by the wand of Solitude,
That wizard wild, — and the far tents
implanted
Upon the plain, be seen by those who
stood
Thence marking the dark shore of Ocean's
curvèd flood.

XXIV

One moment these were heard and seen
— another
Passed; and the two who stood beneath
that night
Each only heard or saw or felt the other.
As from the lofty steed she did alight,
Cythna (for, from the eyes whose deepest
light

Of love and sadness made my lips feel
pale
With influence strange of mournfullest
delight,
My own sweet Cythna looked) with joy
did quail,
And felt her strength in tears of human
weakness fail.

XXV

And for a space in my embrace she
rested,
Her head on my unquiet heart reposing,
While my faint arms her languid frame
invested;
At length she looked on me, and, half
unclosing
Her tremulous lips, said, 'Friend, thy
bands were losing
The battle, as I stood before the King
In bonds. I burst them then, and, swiftly
choosing
The time, did seize a Tartar's sword,
and spring
Upon his horse, and swift as on the whirl-
wind's wing

XXVI

' Have thou and I been borne beyond pursuer,
And we are here.' Then, turning to the
steed,
She pressed the white moon on his front
with pure
And rose-like lips, and many a fragrant
weed
From the green ruin plucked that he
might feed;
But I to a stone seat that Maiden led,
And, kissing her fair eyes, said, 'Thou
hast need
Of rest,' and I heaped up the courser's
bed
In a green mossy nook, with mountain
flowers dispread.

XXVII

Within that ruin, where a shattered
portal
Looks to the eastern stars — abandoned
now
By man to be the home of things immortal,
Memories, like awful ghosts which come
and go,

And must inherit all he builds below
When he is gone — a hall stood; o'er
whose roof
Fair clinging weeds with ivy pale did
grow,
Clasping its gray rents with a verdurous
woof,
A hanging dome of leaves, a canopy moon-
proof.

XXVIII

The autumnal winds, as if spell-bound,
had made
A natural couch of leaves in that recess,
Which seasons none disturbed; but, in
the shade
Of flowering parasites, did Spring love
to dress
With their sweet blooms the wintry lone-
liness
Of those dead leaves, shedding their
stars whene'er
The wandering wind her nurslings might
caress;
Whose intertwining fingers ever there
Made music wild and soft that filled the
listening air.

XXIX

We know not where we go, or what
sweet dream
May pilot us through caverns strange
and fair
Of far and pathless passion, while the
stream
Of life our bark doth on its whirlpools
bear,
Spreading swift wings as sails to the dim
air;
Nor should we seek to know, so the de-
votion
Of love and gentle thoughts be heard
still there
Louder and louder from the utmost
Ocean
Of universal life, attuning its commotion.

XXX

To the pure all things are pure! Oblivion
wrapped
Our spirits, and the fearful overthrow
Of public hope was from our being
snapped,
Though linkèd years had bound it there;
for now

A power, a thirst, a knowledge, which
    below
All thoughts, like light beyond the at-
    mosphere
Clothing its clouds with grace, doth ever
    flow,
Came on us, as we sate in silence there,
Beneath the golden stars of the clear azure
    air; —

XXXI

In silence which doth follow talk that
    causes
The baffled heart to speak with sighs
    and tears,
When wildering passion swalloweth up
    the pauses
Of inexpressive speech; — the youthful
    years
Which we together passed, their hopes
    and fears,
The blood itself which ran within our
    frames,
That likeness of the features which en-
    dears
The thoughts expressed by them, our
    very names,
And all the wingèd hours which speechless
    memory claims,

XXXII

Had found a voice; and ere that voice
    did pass,
The night grew damp and dim, and,
    through a rent
Of the ruin where we sate, from the
    morass
A wandering Meteor by some wild wind
    sent
Hung high in the green dome, to which
    it lent
A faint and pallid lustre; while the
    song
Of blasts, in which its blue hair quiver-
    ing bent,
Strewed strangest sounds the moving
    leaves among;
A wondrous light, the sound as of a spirit's
    tongue.

XXXIII

The Meteor showed the leaves on which
    we sate,
And Cythna's glowing arms, and the
    thick ties

Of her soft hair which bent with gath-
    ered weight
My neck near hers; her dark and deep-
    ening eyes,
Which, as twin phantoms of one star
    that lies
O'er a dim well move though the star
    reposes,
Swam in our mute and liquid ecstasies;
Her marble brow, and eager lips, like
    roses,
With their own fragrance pale, which
    Spring but half uncloses.

XXXIV

The Meteor to its far morass returned.
The beating of our veins one interval
Made still; and then I felt the blood that
    burned
Within her frame mingle with mine, and
    fall
Around my heart like fire; and over
    all
A mist was spread, the sickness of a
    deep
And speechless swoon of joy, as might
    befall
Two disunited spirits when they leap
In union from this earth's obscure and
    fading sleep.

XXXV

Was it one moment that confounded
    thus
All thought, all sense, all feeling, into
    one
Unutterable power, which shielded us
Even from our own cold looks, when we
    had gone
Into a wide and wild oblivion
Of tumult and of tenderness? or now
Had ages, such as make the moon and
    sun,
The seasons, and mankind their changes
    know,
Left fear and time unfelt by us alone be-
    low?

XXXVI

I know not. What are kisses whose fire
    clasps
The failing heart in languishment, or
    limb
Twined within limb? or the quick dying
    gasps

Of the life meeting, when the faint eyes
    swim
Through tears of a wide mist boundless
    and dim,
In one caress? What is the strong con-
    trol
Which leads the heart that dizzy steep
    to climb
Where far over the world those vapors
    roll
Which blend two restless frames in one re-
    posing soul?

XXXVII

It is the shadow which doth float unseen,
But not unfelt, o'er blind mortality,
Whose divine darkness fled not from
    that green
And lone recess, where lapped in peace
    did lie
Our linkèd frames, till, from the chan-
    ging sky
That night and still another day had
    fled;
And then I saw and felt. The moon was
    high,
And clouds, as of a coming storm, were
    spread
Under its orb, — loud winds were gather-
    ing overhead.

XXXVIII

Cythna's sweet lips seemed lurid in the
    moon,
Her fairest limbs with the night wind
    were chill,
And her dark tresses were all loosely
    strewn
O'er her pale bosom; all within was still,
And the sweet peace of joy did almost
    fill
The depth of her unfathomable look;
And we sate calmly, though that rocky
    hill
The waves contending in its caverns
    strook,
For they foreknew the storm, and the gray
    ruin shook.

XXXIX

There we unheeding sate in the com-
    munion
Of interchangèd vows, which, with a rite
Of faith most sweet and sacred, stamped
    our union.

Few were the living hearts which could
    unite
Like ours, or celebrate a bridal night
With such close sympathies, for they
    had sprung
From linkèd youth, and from the gentle
    might
Of earliest love, delayed and cherished
    long,
Which common hopes and fears made, like
    a tempest, strong.

XL

And such is Nature's law divine that
    those
Who grow together cannot choose but
    love,
If faith or custom do not interpose,
Or common slavery mar what else might
    move
All gentlest thoughts. As in the sacred
    grove
Which shades the springs of Æthiopian
    Nile,
That living tree which, if the arrowy
    dove
Strike with her shadow, shrinks in fear
    awhile,
But its own kindred leaves clasps while the
    sunbeams smile,

XLI

And clings to them when darkness may
    dissever
The close caresses of all duller plants
Which bloom on the wide earth; — thus
    we forever
Were linked, for love had nursed us in
    the haunts
Where knowledge from its secret source
    enchants
Young hearts with the fresh music of its
    springing,
Ere yet its gathered flood feeds human
    wants
As the great Nile feeds Egypt, — ever
    flinging
Light on the woven boughs which o'er its
    waves are swinging.

XLII

The tones of Cythna's voice like echoes
    were
Of those far murmuring streams; they
    rose and fell,

Mixed with mine own in the tempestuous
   air;
And so we sate, until our talk befell
Of the late ruin, swift and horrible,
And how those seeds of hope might yet
   be sown,
Whose fruit is Evil's mortal poison.
   Well,
For us, this ruin made a watch-tower
   lone,
But Cythna's eyes looked faint, and now
   two days were gone

XLIII

Since she had food. Therefore I did
   awaken
The Tartar steed, who, from his ebon
   mane
Soon as the clinging slumbers he had
   shaken,
Bent his thin head to seek the brazen
   rein,
Following me obediently. With pain
Of heart so deep and dread that one
   caress,
When lips and heart refuse to part again
Till they have told their fill, could scarce
   express
The anguish of her mute and fearful ten-
   derness,

XLIV

Cythna beheld me part, as I bestrode
That willing steed. The tempest and the
   night,
Which gave my path its safety as I rode
Down the ravine of rocks, did soon unite
The darkness and the tumult of their
   might
Borne on all winds. — Far through the
   streaming rain
Floating, at intervals the garments white
Of Cythna gleamed, and her voice once
   again
Came to me on the gust, and soon I reached
   the plain.

XLV

I dreaded not the tempest, nor did he
Who bore me, but his eyeballs wide and
   red
Turned on the lightning's cleft exultingly;
And when the earth beneath his tameless tread

Shook with the sullen thunder, he would
   spread
His nostrils to the blast, and joyously
Mock the fierce peal with neighings; —
   thus we sped
O'er the lit plain, and soon I could de-
   scry
Where Death and Fire had gorged the
   spoil of victory.

XLVI

There was a desolate village in a wood,
Whose bloom-inwoven leaves now scattering fed
The hungry storm; it was a place of
   blood,
A heap of heartless walls; — the flames
   were dead
Within those dwellings now, — the life
   had fled
From all those corpses now, — but the
   wide sky
Flooded with lightning was ribbed overhead
By the black rafters, and around did
   lie
Women and babes and men, slaughtered
   confusedly.

XLVII

Beside the fountain in the market-place
Dismounting, I beheld those corpses
   stare
With horny eyes upon each other's face,
And on the earth, and on the vacant
   air,
And upon me, close to the waters where
I stooped to slake my thirst; — I shrank
   to taste,
For the salt bitterness of blood was
   there!
But tied the steed beside, and sought in
   haste
If any yet survived amid that ghastly waste.

XLVIII

No living thing was there beside one
   woman
Whom I found wandering in the streets,
   and she
Was withered from a likeness of aught
   human
Into a fiend, by some strange misery;
Soon as she heard my steps she leaped
   on me,

And glued her burning lips to mine, and
    laughed
With a loud, long and frantic laugh of
    glee,
And cried, 'Now, mortal, thou hast
    deeply quaffed
The Plague's blue kisses — soon millions
    shall pledge the draught!

XLIX

'My name is Pestilence; this bosom dry
Once fed two babes — a sister and a
    brother;
When I came home, one in the blood did
    lie
Of three death-wounds — the flames had
    ate the other!
Since then I have no longer been a
    mother,
But I am Pestilence; hither and thither
I flit about, that I may slay and smother;
All lips which I have kissed must surely
    wither,
But Death's — if thou art he, we 'll go to
    work together!

L

'What seek'st thou here? the moonlight
    comes in flashes;
The dew is rising dankly from the dell;
'T will moisten her! and thou shalt see
    the gashes
In my sweet boy, now full of worms. But
    tell
First what thou seek'st.' — 'I seek for
    food.' — ''T is well,
Thou shalt have food. Famine, my par-
    amour,
Waits for us at the feast — cruel and fell
Is Famine, but he drives not from his
    door
Those whom these lips have kissed, alone.
    No more, no more!'

LI

As thus she spake, she grasped me with
    the strength
Of madness, and by many a ruined
    hearth
She led, and over many a corpse. At
    length
We came to a lone hut, where on the
    earth
Which made its floor she in her ghastly
    mirth,

Gathering from all those homes now
    desolate,
Had piled three heaps of loaves, making
    a dearth
Among the dead — round which she set
    in state
A ring of cold, stiff babes; silent and stark
    they sate.

LII

She leaped upon a pile, and lifted high
Her mad looks to the lightning, and
    cried, 'Eat!
Share the great feast — to-morrow we
    must die!'
And then she spurned the loaves with
    her pale feet
Towards her bloodless guests; — that
    sight to meet,
Mine eyes and my heart ached, and but
    that she
Who loved me did with absent looks
    defeat
Despair, I might have raved in sympa-
    thy;
But now I took the food that woman of-
    fered me;

LIII

And vainly having with her madness
    striven
If I might win her to return with me,
Departed. In the eastern beams of
    Heaven
The lightning now grew pallid, rapidly
As by the shore of the tempestuous sea
The dark steed bore me; and the moun-
    tain gray
Soon echoed to his hoofs, and I could
    see
Cythna among the rocks, where she al-
    way
Had sate with anxious eyes fixed on the
    lingering day.

LIV

And joy was ours to meet. She was
    most pale,
Famished and wet and weary; so I cast
My arms around her, lest her steps
    should fail
As to our home we went, — and, thus
    embraced,
Her full heart seemed a deeper joy to
    taste

Than e'er the prosperous know; the
　　steed behind
Trod peacefully along the mountain
　　waste;
We reached our home ere morning could
　　unbind
Night's latest veil, and on our bridal couch
　　reclined.

LV

Her chilled heart having cherished in
　　my bosom,
And sweetest kisses past, we two did
　　share
Our peaceful meal; as an autumnal blos-
　　som,
Which spreads its shrunk leaves in the
　　sunny air
After cold showers, like rainbows woven
　　there,
Thus in her lips and cheeks the vital
　　spirit
Mantled, and in her eyes an atmosphere
Of health and hope; and sorrow lan-
　　guished near it,
And fear, and all that dark despondence
　　doth inherit.

CANTO SEVENTH

I

So we sate joyous as the morning ray
Which fed upon the wrecks of night and
　　storm
Now lingering on the winds; light airs
　　did play
Among the dewy weeds, the sun was
　　warm,
And we sate linked in the inwoven charm
Of converse and caresses sweet and
　　deep —
Speechless caresses, talk that might dis-
　　arm
Time, though he wield the darts of
　　death and sleep,
And those thrice mortal barbs in his own
　　poison steep.

II

I told her of my sufferings and my mad-
　　ness,
And how, awakened from that dreamy
　　mood
By Liberty's uprise, the strength of
　　gladness

Came to my spirit in my solitude,
And all that now I was, while tears pur-
　　sued
Each other down her fair and listening
　　cheek
Fast as the thoughts which fed them,
　　like a flood
From sunbright dales; and when I ceased
　　to speak,
Her accents soft and sweet the pausing air
　　did wake.

III

She told me a strange tale of strange
　　endurance,
Like broken memories of many a heart
Woven into one; to which no firm assur-
　　ance,
So wild were they, could her own faith
　　impart.
She said that not a tear did dare to start
From the swoln brain, and that her
　　thoughts were firm,
When from all mortal hope she did de-
　　part,
Borne by those slaves across the Ocean's
　　term,
And that she reached the port without one
　　fear infirm.

IV

One was she among many there, the
　　thralls
Of the cold Tyrant's cruel lust; and they
Laughed mournfully in those polluted
　　halls;
But she was calm and sad, musing alway
On loftiest enterprise, till on a day
The Tyrant heard her singing to her
　　lute
A wild and sad and spirit-thrilling lay,
Like winds that die in wastes — one mo-
　　ment mute
The evil thoughts it made which did his
　　breast pollute.

V

Even when he saw her wondrous loveli-
　　ness,
One moment to great Nature's sacred
　　power
He bent, and was no longer passionless;
But when he bade her to his secret bower
Be borne, a loveless victim, and she
　　tore

Her locks in agony, and her words of
flame
And mightier looks availed not, then he
bore
Again his load of slavery, and became
A king, a heartless beast, a pageant and a
name.

VI

She told me what a loathsome agony
Is that when selfishness mocks love's
delight,
Foul as in dreams, most fearful imagery,
To dally with the mowing dead; that
night
All torture, fear, or horror made seem
light
Which the soul dreams or knows, and
when the day
Shone on her awful frenzy, from the
sight,
Where like a Spirit in fleshly chains she
lay
Struggling, aghast and pale the Tyrant fled
away.

VII

Her madness was a beam of light, a
power
Which dawned through the rent soul;
and words it gave,
Gestures and looks, such as in whirlwinds bore
(Which might not be withstood, whence
none could save)
All who approached their sphere, like
some calm wave
Vexed into whirlpools by the chasms beneath;
And sympathy made each attendant slave
Fearless and free, and they began to
breathe
Deep curses, like the voice of flames far
underneath.

VIII

The King felt pale upon his noon-day
throne.
At night two slaves he to her chamber
sent;
One was a green and wrinkled eunuch,
grown
From human shape into an instrument
Of all things ill — distorted, bowed and
bent;

The other was a wretch from infancy
Made dumb by poison; who nought knew
or meant
But to obey; from the fire isles came he,
A diver lean and strong, of Oman's coral
sea.

IX

They bore her to a bark, and the swift
stroke
Of silent rowers clove the blue moonlight
seas,
Until upon their path the morning broke;
They anchored then, where, be there
calm or breeze,
The gloomiest of the drear Symplegades
Shakes with the sleepless surge; the
Æthiop there
Wound his long arms around her, and
with knees
Like iron clasped her feet, and plunged
with her
Among the closing waves out of the bound-
less air.

X

'Swift as an eagle stooping from the plain
Of morning light into some shadowy
wood,
He plunged through the green silence of
the main,
Through many a cavern which the eternal flood
Had scooped as dark lairs for its monster
brood;
And among mighty shapes which fled in
wonder,
And among mightier shadows which pursued
His heels, he wound; until the dark rocks
under
He touched a golden chain — a sound arose
like thunder,

XI

'A stunning clang of massive bolts re-
doubling
Beneath the deep — a burst of waters
driven
As from the roots of the sea, raging and
bubbling:
And in that roof of crags a space was
riven
Through which there shone the emerald
beams of heaven,

Shot through the lines of many waves
    inwoven,
Like sunlight through acacia woods at
    even,
Through which his way the diver having
    cloven
Passed like a spark sent up out of a burn-
    ing oven.

XII

' And then,' she said, ' he laid me in a cave
Above the waters, by that chasm of sea,
A fountain round and vast, in which the
    wave
Imprisoned, boiled and leaped perpet-
    ually,
Down which, one moment resting, he did
    flee,
Winning the adverse depth; that spacious
    cell
Like an hupaithric temple wide and high,
Whose aëry dome is inaccessible,
Was pierced with one round cleft through
    which the sunbeams fell.

XIII

' Below, the fountain's brink was richly
    paven
With the deep's wealth, coral, and pearl,
    and sand
Like spangling gold, and purple shells
    engraven
With mystic legends by no mortal hand,
Left there when, thronging to the moon's
    command,
The gathering waves rent the Hesperian
    gate
Of mountains; and on such bright floor
    did stand
Columns, and shapes like statues, and
    the state
Of kingless thrones, which Earth did in her
    heart create.

XIV

' The fiend of madness which had made
    its prey
Of my poor heart was lulled to sleep
    awhile.
There was an interval of many a day;
And a sea-eagle brought me food the
    while,
Whose nest was built in that untrodden
    isle,
And who to be the jailer had been taught

Of that strange dungeon; as a friend
    whose smile
Like light and rest at morn and even is
    sought
That wild bird was to me, till madness
    misery brought: —

XV

' The misery of a madness slow and creep-
    ing,
Which made the earth seem fire, the sea
    seem air,
And the white clouds of noon which oft
    were sleeping
In the blue heaven so beautiful and fair,
Like hosts of ghastly shadows hovering
    there;
And the sea-eagle looked a fiend who
    bore
Thy mangled limbs for food ! — thus all
    things were
Transformed into the agony which I
    wore
Even as a poisoned robe around my bosom's
    core.

XVI

' Again I knew the day and night fast
    fleeing,
The eagle and the fountain and the air;
Another frenzy came — there seemed a
    being
Within me — a strange load my heart
    did bear,
As if some living thing had made its lair
Even in the fountains of my life; — a
    long
And wondrous vision wrought from my
    despair,
Then grew, like sweet reality among
Dim visionary woes, an unreposing throng.

XVII

' Methought I was about to be a mother.
Month after month went by, and still I
    dreamed
That we should soon be all to one another,
I and my child; and still new pulses
    seemed
To beat beside my heart, and still I
    deemed
There was a babe within — and when the
    rain
Of winter through the rifted cavern
    streamed,

Methought, after a lapse of lingering
    pain,
I saw that lovely shape which near my
    heart had lain.

XVIII

'It was a babe, beautiful from its birth, —
It was like thee, dear love! its eyes were
    thine,
Its brow, its lips, and so upon the earth
It laid its fingers as now rest on mine
Thine own, belovèd! — 't was a dream
    divine;
Even to remember how it fled, how swift,
How utterly, might make the heart re-
    pine, —
Though 't was a dream.' — Then Cythna
    did uplift
Her looks on mine, as if some doubt she
    sought to shift —

XIX

A doubt which would not flee, a tender-
    ness
Of questioning grief, a source of throng-
    ing tears;
Which having passed, as one whom sobs
    oppress
She spoke: 'Yes, in the wilderness of
    years
Her memory aye like a green home ap-
    pears.
She sucked her fill even at this breast,
    sweet love,
For many months. I had no mortal
    fears;
Methought I felt her lips and breath ap-
    prove
It was a human thing which to my bosom
    clove.

XX

'I watched the dawn of her first smiles;
    and soon
When zenith stars were trembling on the
    wave,
Or when the beams of the invisible moon
Or sun from many a prism within the
    cave
Their gem-born shadows to the water
    gave,
Her looks would hunt them, and with
    outspread hand,
From the swift lights which might that
    fountain pave,

She would mark one, and laugh when,
    that command
Slighting, it lingered there, and could not
    understand.

XXI

'Methought her looks began to talk with
    me;
And no articulate sounds, but something
    sweet
Her lips would frame, — so sweet it
    could not be
That it was meaningless; her touch would
    meet
Mine, and our pulses calmly flow and
    beat
In response while we slept; and, on a day
When I was happiest in that strange re-
    treat,
With heaps of golden shells we two did
    play —
Both infants, weaving wings for time's per-
    petual way.

XXII

'Ere night, methought, her waning eyes
    were grown
Weary with joy — and, tired with our
    delight,
We, on the earth, like sister twins lay
    down
On one fair mother's bosom: — from that
    night
She fled, — like those illusions clear and
    bright,
Which dwell in lakes, when the red moon
    on high
Pause ere it wakens tempest; and her
    flight,
Though 't was the death of brainless fan-
    tasy,
Yet smote my lonesome heart more than
    all misery.

XXIII

'It seemed that in the dreary night the
    diver
Who brought me thither came again,
    and bore
My child away. I saw the waters quiver,
When he so swiftly sunk, as once before;
Then morning came — it shone even as
    of yore,
But I was changed — the very life was
    gone

Out of my heart—I wasted more and
   more,
Day after day, and, sitting there alone,
Vexed the inconstant waves with my perpetual moan.

XXIV

'I was no longer mad, and yet methought
   My breasts were swoln and changed:—
      in every vein
   The blood stood still one moment, while
      that thought
   Was passing—with a gush of sickening
      pain
   It ebbed even to its withered springs
      again;
   When my wan eyes in stern resolve I
      turned
   From that most strange delusion, which
      would fain
   Have waked the dream for which my
      spirit yearned
With more than human love,—then left it
   unreturned.

XXV

'So now my reason was restored to me
   I struggled with that dream, which like
      a beast
   Most fierce and beauteous in my mem-
      ory
   Had made its lair, and on my heart did
      feast;
   But all that cave and all its shapes, pos-
      sessed
   By thoughts which could not fade, re-
      newed each one
   Some smile, some look, some gesture
      which had blessed
   Me heretofore; I, sitting there alone,
Vexed the inconstant waves with my per-
   petual moan.

XXVI

'Time passed, I know not whether months
   or years;
   For day, nor night, nor change of seasons
      made
   Its note, but thoughts and unavailing
      tears;
   And I became at last even as a shade,
   A smoke, a cloud on which the winds
      have preyed,
   Till it be thin as air; until, one even,
   A Nautilus upon the fountain played,

Spreading his azure sail where breath of
   heaven
Descended not, among the waves and
   whirlpools driven.

XXVII

'And when the Eagle came, that lovely
   thing,
   Oaring with rosy feet its silver boat,
   Fled near me as for shelter; on slow
      wing
   The Eagle hovering o'er his prey did
      float;
   But when he saw that I with fear did
      note
   His purpose, proffering my own food to
      him,
   The eager plumes subsided on his
      throat—
   He came where that bright child of sea
      did swim,
And o'er it cast in peace his shadow broad
   and dim.

XXVIII

'This wakened me, it gave me human
   strength;
   And hope, I know not whence or where-
      fore, rose,
   But I resumed my ancient powers at
      length;
   My spirit felt again like one of those,
   Like thine, whose fate it is to make the
      woes
   Of humankind their prey. What was
      this cave?
   Its deep foundation no firm purpose
      knows
   Immutable, resistless, strong to save,
Like mind while yet it mocks the all-de-
   vouring grave.

XXIX

'And where was Laon? might my heart
   be dead,
   While that far dearer heart could move
      and be?
   Or whilst over the earth the pall was
      spread
   Which I had sworn to rend? I might
      be free,
   Could I but win that friendly bird to me
   To bring me ropes; and long in vain I
      sought
   By intercourse of mutual imagery

Of objects if such aid he could be taught;
But fruit and flowers and boughs, yet never
   ropes he brought.

XXX

'We live in our own world, and mine was
   made
From glorious fantasies of hope departed;
Aye we are darkened with their floating
   shade,
Or cast a lustre on them; time imparted
Such power to me — I became fearless-
   hearted,
My eye and voice grew firm, calm was
   my mind,
And piercing, like the morn, now it has
   darted
Its lustre on all hidden things behind
Yon dim and fading clouds which load the
   weary wind.

XXXI

'My mind became the book through which
   I grew
Wise in all human wisdom, and its cave,
Which like a mine I rifled through and
   through,
To me the keeping of its secrets gave —
One mind, the type of all, the moveless
   wave
Whose calm reflects all moving things
   that are,
Necessity, and love, and life, the grave,
And sympathy, fountains of hope and
   fear,
Justice, and truth, and time, and the world's
   natural sphere.

XXXII

'And on the sand would I make signs to
   range
These woofs, as they were woven, of my
   thought;
Clear elemental shapes, whose smallest
   change
A subtler language within language
   wrought —
The key of truths which once were dimly
   taught
In old Crotona; and sweet melodies
Of love in that lorn solitude I caught
From mine own voice in dream, when
   thy dear eyes
Shone through my sleep, and did that utter-
   ance harmonize.

XXXIII

'Thy songs were winds whereon I fled at
   will,
As in a wingèd chariot, o'er the plain
Of crystal youth; and thou wert there to
   fill
My heart with joy, and there we sate
   again
On the gray margin of the glimmering
   main,
Happy as then but wiser far, for we
Smiled on the flowery grave in which
   were lain
Fear, Faith and Slavery: and mankind
   was free,
Equal, and pure, and wise, in Wisdom's
   prophecy.

XXXIV

'For to my will my fancies were as slaves
To do their sweet and subtle minis-
   tries;
And oft from that bright fountain's
   shadowy waves
They would make human throngs gather
   and rise
To combat with my overflowing eyes
And voice made deep with passion; —
   thus I grew
Familiar with the shock and the sur-
   prise
And war of earthly minds, from which I
   drew
The power which has been mine to frame
   their thoughts anew.

XXXV

'And thus my prison was the populous
   earth,
Where I saw — even as misery dreams
   of morn
Before the east has given its glory
   birth —
Religion's pomp made desolate by the
   scorn
Of Wisdom's faintest smile, and thrones
   uptorn,
And dwellings of mild people interspersed
With undivided fields of ripening corn,
And love made free — a hope which we
   have nursed
Even with our blood and tears, — until its
   glory burst.

XXXVI

'All is not lost! There is some recompense
For hope whose fountain can be thus profound, —
Even thronèd Evil's splendid impotence
Girt by its hell of power, the secret sound
Of hymns to truth and freedom, the dread bound
Of life and death passed fearlessly and well,
Dungeons wherein the high resolve is found,
Racks which degraded woman's greatness tell,
And what may else be good and irresistible.

XXXVII

'Such are the thoughts which, like the fires that flare
In storm-encompassed isles, we cherish yet
In this dark ruin — such were mine even there;
As in its sleep some odorous violet,
While yet its leaves with nightly dews are wet,
Breathes in prophetic dreams of day's uprise,
Or as, ere Scythian frost in fear has met
Spring's messengers descending from the skies,
The buds foreknow their life — this hope must ever rise.

XXXVIII

'So years had passed, when sudden earthquake rent
The depth of Ocean, and the cavern cracked
With sound, as if the world's wide continent
Had fallen in universal ruin wracked,
And through the cleft streamed in one cataract
The stifling waters: — when I woke, the flood
Whose banded waves that crystal cave had sacked
Was ebbing round me, and my bright abode
Before me yawned — a chasm desert, and bare, and broad.

XXXIX

'Above me was the sky, beneath the sea;
I stood upon a point of shattered stone,
And heard loose rocks rushing tumultuously
With splash and shock into the deep — anon
All ceased, and there was silence wide and lone.
I felt that I was free! The Ocean spray
Quivered beneath my feet, the broad Heaven shone
Around, and in my hair the winds did play
Lingering as they pursued their unimpeded way.

XL

'My spirit moved upon the sea like wind
Which round some thymy cape will lag and hover,
Though it can wake the still cloud, and unbind
The strength of tempest. Day was almost over,
When through the fading light I could discover
A ship approaching — its white sails were fed
With the north wind — its moving shade did cover
The twilight deep; the mariners in dread
Cast anchor when they saw new rocks around them spread.

XLI

'And when they saw one sitting on a crag,
They sent a boat to me; the sailors rowed
In awe through many a new and fearful jag
Of overhanging rock, through which there flowed
The foam of streams that cannot make abode.
They came and questioned me, but when they heard
My voice, they became silent, and they stood
And moved as men in whom new love had stirred
Deep thoughts; so to the ship we passed without a word.

CANTO EIGHTH

I

' I SATE beside the steersman then, and
  gazing
Upon the west cried, " Spread the sails !
  behold !
The sinking moon is like a watch-tower
  blazing
Over the mountains yet; the City of
  Gold
Yon Cape alone does from the sight with-
  hold;
The stream is fleet — the north breathes
  steadily
Beneath the stars; they tremble with the
  cold !
Ye cannot rest upon the dreary sea ! —
Haste, haste to the warm home of happier
  destiny ! "

II

' The Mariners obeyed; the Captain stood
Aloof, and whispering to the Pilot said,
" Alas, alas ! I fear we are pursued
By wicked ghosts; a Phantom of the
  Dead,
The night before we sailed, came to my
  bed
In dream, like that ! " The Pilot then
  replied,
" It cannot be — she is a human maid —
Her low voice makes you weep — she is
  some bride,
Or daughter of high birth — she can be
  nought beside."

III

' We passed the islets, borne by wind and
  stream,
And as we sailed the Mariners came near
And thronged around to listen; in the
  gleam
Of the pale moon I stood, as one whom
  fear
May not attaint, and my calm voice did
  rear:
" Ye are all human — yon broad moon
  gives light
To millions who the self-same likeness
  wear,
Even while I speak — beneath this very
  night,
Their thoughts flow on like ours, in sadness
  or delight.

IV

' " What dream ye ? Your own hands have
  built an home
Even for yourselves on a belovèd shore;
For some, fond eyes are pining till they
  come —
How they will greet him when his toils
  are o'er,
And laughing babes rush from the well-
  known door!
Is this your care ? ye toil for your own
  good —
Ye feel and think — has some immortal
  power
Such purposes ? or in a human mood
Dream ye some Power thus builds for man
  in solitude?

V

' " What is that Power ? Ye mock your-
  selves, and give
A human heart to what ye cannot know:
As if the cause of life could think and
  live!
'T were as if man's own works should
  feel, and show
The hopes and fears and thoughts from
  which they flow,
And he be like to them. Lo ! Plague is
  free
To waste, Blight, Poison, Earthquake,
  Hail, and Snow,
Disease, and Want, and worse Necessity
Of hate and ill, and Pride, and Fear, and
  Tyranny.

VI

' " What is that Power ? Some moon-
  struck sophist stood,
Watching the shade from his own soul
  upthrown
Fill Heaven and darken Earth, and in
  such mood
The Form he saw and worshipped was
  his own,
His likeness in the world's vast mirror
  shown;
And 't were an innocent dream, but that
  a faith
Nursed by fear's dew of poison grows
  thereon,
And that men say that Power has chosen
  Death
On all who scorn its laws to wreak immortal
  wrath.

VII

' " Men say that they themselves have heard
    and seen,
Or known from others who have known
    such things,
A Shade, a Form, which Earth and
    Heaven between
Wields an invisible rod — that Priests
    and Kings,
Custom, domestic sway, ay, all that
    brings
Man's free-born soul beneath the op-
    pressor's heel,
Are his strong ministers, and that the
    stings
Of death will make the wise his ven-
    geance feel,
Though truth and virtue arm their hearts
    with tenfold steel.

VIII

' " And it is said this Power will punish
    wrong;
Yes, add despair to crime, and pain to
    pain !
And deepest hell, and deathless snakes
    among,
Will bind the wretch on whom is fixed a
    stain,
Which, like a plague, a burden, and a
    bane,
Clung to him while he lived; for love
    and hate,
Virtue and vice, they say, are difference
    vain —
The will of strength is right. This hu-
    man state
Tyrants, that they may rule, with lies thus
    desolate.

IX

' " Alas, what strength ? Opinion is more
    frail
Than yon dim cloud now fading on the
    moon
Even while we gaze, though it awhile
    avail
To hide the orb of truth — and every
    throne
Of Earth or Heaven, though shadow,
    rests thereon,
One shape of many names: — for this ye
    plough
The barren waves of Ocean — hence
    each one

Is slave or tyrant; all betray and bow,
Command, or kill, or fear, or wreak or
    suffer woe.

X

' " Its names are each a sign which mak-
    eth holy
All power — ay, the ghost, the dream,
    the shade
Of power — lust, falsehood, hate, and
    pride, and folly;
The pattern whence all fraud and wrong
    is made,
A law to which mankind has been be-
    trayed;
And human love is as the name well
    known
Of a dear mother whom the murderer
    laid
In bloody grave, and, into darkness
    thrown,
Gathered her wildered babes around him
    as his own.

XI

' " O Love, who to the hearts of wander-
    ing men
Art as the calm to Ocean's weary waves !
Justice, or Truth, or Joy ! those only can
From slavery and religion's labyrinth-
    caves
Guide us, as one clear star the seaman
    saves.
To give to all an equal share of good,
To track the steps of Freedom, though
    through graves
She pass, to suffer all in patient mood,
To weep for crime though stained with
    thy friend's dearest blood,

XII

' " To feel the peace of self-contentment's
    lot,
To own all sympathies, and outrage none,
And in the inmost bowers of sense and
    thought,
Until life's sunny day is quite gone down,
To sit and smile with Joy, or, not alone,
To kiss salt tears from the worn cheek
    of Woe;
To live as if to love and live were one, —
This is not faith or law, nor those who
    bow
To thrones on Heaven or Earth such destiny
    may know.

XIII

' " But children near their parents tremble
now,
Because they must obey; one rules
another,
And, as one Power rules both high and
low,
So man is made the captive of his brother,
And Hate is throned on high with Fear
his mother
Above the Highest; and those fountain-
cells,
Whence love yet flowed when faith had
choked all other,
Are darkened — Woman as the bond-
slave dwells
Of man, a slave; and life is poisoned in its
wells.

XIV

' " Man seeks for gold in mines that he
may weave
A lasting chain for his own slavery;
In fear and restless care that he may live
He toils for others who must ever be
The joyless thralls of like captivity;
He murders, for his chiefs delight in ruin;
He builds the altar that its idol's fee
May be his very blood; he is pursuing —
Oh, blind and willing wretch ! — his own
obscure undoing.

XV

' " Woman ! — she is his slave, she has
become
A thing I weep to speak — the child of
scorn,
The outcast of a desolated home;
Falsehood, and fear, and toil, like waves
have worn
Channels upon her cheek, which smiles
adorn
As calm decks the false Ocean: — well
ye know
What Woman is, for none of Woman born
Can choose but drain the bitter dregs of
woe,
Which ever from the oppressed to the op-
pressors flow.

XVI

' " This need not be; ye might arise, and
will
That gold should lose its power, and
thrones their glory;

That love, which none may bind, be free
to fill
The world, like light; and evil faith,
grown hoary
With crime, be quenched and die. —
Yon promontory
Even now eclipses the descending
moon ! —
Dungeons and palaces are transitory —
High temples fade like vapor — Man
alone
Remains, whose will has power when all
beside is gone.

XVII

' " Let all be free and equal ! — from
your hearts
I feel an echo; through my inmost frame
Like sweetest sound, seeking its mate,
it darts.
Whence come ye, friends ?   Alas, I can-
not name
All that I read of sorrow, toil and shame
On your worn faces; as in legends old
Which make immortal the disastrous
fame
Of conquerors and impostors false and
bold,
The discord of your hearts I in your looks
behold.

XVIII

' " Whence come ye, friends ? from pouring human blood
Forth on the earth ? or bring ye steel
and gold,
That kings may dupe and slay the multitude ?
Or from the famished poor, pale, weak
and cold,
Bear ye the earnings of their toil ? unfold !
Speak ! are your hands in slaughter's
sanguine hue
Stained freshly ? have your hearts in
guile grown old ?
Know yourselves thus ! ye shall be pure
as dew,
And I will be a friend and sister unto you.

XIX

' " Disguise it not — we have one human
heart —
All mortal thoughts confess a common
home;

Blush not for what may to thyself impart
Stains of inevitable crime; the doom
Is this, which has, or may, or must, be-
come
Thine, and all humankind's. Ye are
the spoil
Which Time thus marks for the devour-
ing tomb —
Thou and thy thoughts, and they, and all
the toil
Wherewith ye twine the rings of life's per-
petual coil.

XX

' " Disguise it not — ye blush for what ye
hate,
And Enmity is sister unto Shame;
Look on your mind — it is the book of
fate —
Ah! it is dark with many a blazoned
name
Of misery — all are mirrors of the same;
But the dark fiend who with his iron pen,
Dipped in scorn's fiery poison, makes
his fame
Enduring there, would o'er the heads of
men
Pass harmless, if they scorned to make
their hearts his den.

XXI

' " Yes, it is Hate, that shapeless fiendly
thing
Of many names, all evil, some divine,
Whom self-contempt arms with a mortal
sting;
Which, when the heart its snaky folds
entwine,
Is wasted quite, and when it doth repine
To gorge such bitter prey, on all beside
It turns with ninefold rage, as with its
twine
When Amphisbæna some fair bird has
tied,
Soon o'er the putrid mass he threats on
every side.

XXII

' " Reproach not thine own soul, but know
thyself,
Nor hate another's crime, nor loathe thine
own.
It is the dark idolatry of self,
Which, when our thoughts and actions
once are gone,

Demands that man should weep, and
bleed, and groan;
Oh, vacant expiation ! be at rest !
The past is Death's, the future is thine
own;
And love and joy can make the foulest
breast
A paradise of flowers, where peace might
build her nest.

XXIII

' " Speak thou ! whence come ye ? " —
A youth made reply, —
" Wearily, wearily o'er the boundless
deep
We sail; thou readest well the misery
Told in these faded eyes, but much doth
sleep
Within, which there the poor heart loves
to keep,
Or dare not write on the dishonored
brow;
Even from our childhood have we learned
to steep
The bread of slavery in the tears of woe,
And never dreamed of hope or refuge un-
til now.

XXIV

' " Yes — I must speak — my secret should
have perished
Even with the heart it wasted, as a
brand
Fades in the dying flame whose life it
cherished,
But that no human bosom can withstand
Thee, wondrous Lady, and the mild
command
Of thy keen eyes: — yes, we are wretched
slaves,
Who from their wonted loves and native
land
Are reft, and bear o'er the dividing waves
The unregarded prey of calm and happy
graves.

XXV

' " We drag afar from pastoral vales the
fairest
Among the daughters of those mountains
lone;
We drag them there where all things
best and rarest
Are stained and trampled; years have
come and gone

Since, like the ship which bears me, I
    have known
No thought; but now the eyes of one
    dear maid
On mine with light of mutual love have
    shone —
She is my life — I am but as the shade
Of her — a smoke sent up from ashes, soon
    to fade! —

XXVI

' " For she must perish in the Tyrant's
    hall —
Alas, alas! " — He ceased, and by the
    sail
Sat cowering — but his sobs were heard
    by all,
And still before the Ocean and the gale
The ship fled fast till the stars 'gan to
    fail;
And, round me gathered with mute
    countenance,
The Seamen gazed, the Pilot, worn and
    pale
With toil, the Captain with gray locks
    whose glance
Met mine in restless awe — they stood as
    in a trance.

XXVII

' " Recede not! pause not now! thou art
    grown old,
But Hope will make thee young, for
    Hope and Youth
Are children of one mother, even Love
    — behold!
The eternal stars gaze on us! — is the
    truth
Within your soul? care for your own,
    or ruth
For others' sufferings? do ye thirst to
    bear
A heart which not the serpent Custom's
    tooth
May violate? — be free! and even here,
Swear to be firm till death! " — they cried,
    " We swear! we swear! "

XXVIII

' The very darkness shook, as with a blast
Of subterranean thunder, at the cry;
The hollow shore its thousand echoes
    cast
Into the night, as if the sea and sky
And earth rejoiced with new-born liberty,

For in that name they swore! Bolts
    were undrawn,
And on the deck with unaccustomed eye
The captives gazing stood, and every
    one
Shrank as the inconstant torch upon her
    countenance shone.

XXIX

' They were earth's purest children,
    young and fair,
With eyes the shrines of unawakened
    thought,
And brows as bright as spring or morn-
    ing, ere
Dark time had there its evil legend
    wrought
In characters of cloud which wither not.
The change was like a dream to them;
    but soon
They knew the glory of their altered
    lot —
In the bright wisdom of youth's breath-
    less noon,
Sweet talk and smiles and sighs all bosoms
    did attune.

XXX

' But one was mute; her cheeks and lips
    most fair,
Changing their hue like lilies newly
    blown
Beneath a bright acacia's shadowy hair
Waved by the wind amid the sunny noon,
Showed that her soul was quivering; and
    full soon
That youth arose, and breathlessly did
    look
On her and me, as for some speechless
    boon;
I smiled, and both their hands in mine I
    took,
And felt a soft delight from what their
    spirits shook.

CANTO NINTH

I

' THAT night we anchored in a woody bay,
And sleep no more around us dared to
    hover
Than, when all doubt and fear has passed
    away,
It shades the couch of some unresting
    lover

Whose heart is now at rest; thus night
  passed over
In mutual joy; around, a forest grew
Of poplars and dark oaks, whose shade
  did cover
The waning stars pranked in the waters
  blue,
And trembled in the wind which from the
  morning flew.

II

'The joyous mariners and each free maiden
Now brought from the deep forest many
  a bough,
With woodland spoil most innocently
  laden;
Soon wreaths of budding foliage seemed
  to flow
Over the mast and sails; the stern and
  prow
Were canopied with blooming boughs;
  the while
On the slant sun's path o'er the waves
  we go
Rejoicing, like the dwellers of an isle
Doomed to pursue those waves that cannot
  cease to smile.

III

'The many ships spotting the dark blue
  deep
With snowy sails, fled fast as ours came
  nigh,
In fear and wonder; and on every steep
Thousands did gaze. They heard the
  startling cry,
Like earth's own voice lifted unconquer-
  ably
To all her children, the unbounded mirth,
The glorious joy of thy name — Liberty !
They heard ! — As o'er the mountains
  of the earth
From peak to peak leap on the beams of
  morning's birth,

IV

'So from that cry over the boundless
  hills
Sudden was caught one universal sound,
Like a volcano's voice whose thunder
  fills
Remotest skies, — such glorious madness
  found
A path through human hearts with
  stream which drowned

Its struggling fears and cares, dark Custom's brood;
They knew not whence it came, but felt
  around
A wide contagion poured — they called
  aloud
On Liberty — that name lived on the sunny
  flood.

V

'We reached the port. Alas ! from many
  spirits
The wisdom which had waked that cry
  was fled,
Like the brief glory which dark Heaven
  inherits
From the false dawn, which fades ere it
  is spread,
Upon the night's devouring darkness
  shed;
Yet soon bright day will burst — even
  like a chasm
Of fire, to burn the shrouds outworn and
  dead
Which wrap the world; a wide enthusiasm,
To cleanse the fevered world as with an
  earthquake's spasm !

VI

'I walked through the great City then,
  but free
From shame or fear; those toil-worn
  mariners
And happy maidens did encompass me;
And like a subterranean wind that
  stirs
Some forest among caves, the hopes and
  fears
From every human soul a murmur
  strange
Made as I passed; and many wept with
  tears
Of joy and awe, and wingèd thoughts did
  range,
And half-extinguished words which prophesied of change.

VII

'For with strong speech I tore the veil
  that hid
Nature, and Truth, and Liberty, and
  Love, —
As one who from some mountain's pyra-
  mid

Points to the unrisen sun ! the shades
approve
His truth, and flee from every stream
and grove.
Thus, gentle thoughts did many a bosom
fill,
Wisdom the mail of tried affections wove
For many a heart, and tameless scorn of
ill
Thrice steeped in molten steel the unconquerable will.

VIII

'Some said I was a maniac wild and
lost;
Some, that I scarce had risen from the
grave
The Prophet's virgin bride, a heavenly
ghost;
Some said I was a fiend from my weird
cave,
Who had stolen human shape, and o'er
the wave,
The forest, and the mountain, came;
some said
I was the child of God, sent down to save
Woman from bonds and death, and on
my head
The burden of their sins would frightfully
be laid.

IX

'But soon my human words found sympa-
thy
In human hearts; the purest and the best,
As friend with friend, made common
cause with me,
And they were few, but resolute; the
rest,
Ere yet success the enterprise had
blessed,
Leagued with me in their hearts; their
meals, their slumber,
Their hourly occupations, were possessed
By hopes which I had armed to over-
number
Those hosts of meaner cares which life's
strong wings encumber.

X

'But chiefly women, whom my voice did
waken
From their cold, careless, willing slavery,
Sought me; one truth their dreary prison
has shaken,

They looked around, and lo! they became free !
Their many tyrants, sitting desolately
In slave-deserted halls, could none re-
strain;
For wrath's red fire had withered in the
eye
Whose lightning once was death, — nor
fear nor gain
Could tempt one captive now to lock another's chain.

XI

'Those who were sent to bind me wept,
and felt
Their minds outsoar the bonds which
clasped them round,
Even as a waxen shape may waste and
melt
In the white furnace; and a visioned
swound,
A pause of hope and awe, the City bound,
Which, like the silence of a tempest's
birth,
When in its awful shadow it has wound
The sun, the wind, the ocean, and the
earth,
Hung terrible, ere yet the lightnings have
leaped forth.

XII

'Like clouds inwoven in the silent sky
By winds from distant regions meeting
there,
In the high name of Truth and Liberty
Around the City millions gathered were
By hopes which sprang from many a
hidden lair, —
Words which the lore of truth in hues of
grace
Arrayed, thine own wild songs which in
the air
Like homeless odors floated, and the
name
Of thee, and many a tongue which thou
hadst dipped in flame.

XIII

'The Tyrant knew his power was gone,
but Fear,
The nurse of Vengeance, bade him wait
the event —
That perfidy and custom, gold and
prayer,
And whatsoe'er, when Force is impotent,

To Fraud the sceptre of the world has
   lent,
Might, as he judged, confirm his failing
   sway.
Therefore throughout the streets, the
   Priests he sent
To curse the rebels. To their gods did
   they
For Earthquake, Plague and Want, kneel
   in the public way.

XIV

' And grave and hoary men were bribed to
   tell,
From seats where law is made the slave
   of wrong,
How glorious Athens in her splendor fell,
Because her sons were free, — and that
   among
Mankind, the many to the few belong
By Heaven, and Nature, and Necessity.
They said, that age was truth, and that
   the young
Marred with wild hopes the peace of
   slavery,
With which old times and men had quelled
   the vain and free.

XV

' And with the falsehood of their poisonous
   lips
They breathed on the enduring memory
Of sages and of bards a brief eclipse.
There was one teacher, who necessity
Had armed with strength and wrong
   against mankind,
His slave and his avenger aye to be;
That we were weak and sinful, frail and
   blind,
And that the will of one was peace, and
   we
Should seek for nought on earth but toil
   and misery —

XVI

' " For thus we might avoid the hell hereafter."
So spake the hypocrites, who cursed and
   lied.
Alas, their sway was passed, and tears
   and laughter
Clung to their hoary hair, withering the
   pride
Which in their hollow hearts dared still
   abide;

And yet obscener slaves with smoother
   brow,
And sneers on their strait lips, thin, blue
   and wide,
Said that the rule of men was over now,
And hence the subject world to woman's
   will must bow.

XVII

' And gold was scattered through the
   streets, and wine
Flowed at a hundred feasts within the
   wall.
In vain ! the steady towers in Heaven
   did shine
As they were wont, nor at the priestly call
Left Plague her banquet in the Æthiop's
   hall,
Nor Famine from the rich man's portal
   came,
Where at her ease she ever preys on all
Who throng to kneel for food; nor fear,
   nor shame,
Nor faith, nor discord, dimmed hope's newly
   kindled flame.

XVIII

' For gold was as a god whose faith be-
   gan
To fade, so that its worshippers were
   few;
And Faith itself, which in the heart of
   man
Gives shape, voice, name, to spectral
   Terror, knew
Its downfall, as the altars lonelier grew,
Till the Priests stood alone within the
   fane;
The shafts of falsehood unpolluting flew,
And the cold sneers of calumny were vain
The union of the free with discord's brand
   to stain.

XIX

' The rest thou knowest. — Lo ! we two
   are here —
We have survived a ruin wide and deep —
Strange thoughts are mine.   I cannot
   grieve or fear.
Sitting with thee upon this lonely steep
I smile, though human love should make
   me weep.
We have survived a joy that knows no
   sorrow,
And I do feel a mighty calmness creep

Over my heart, which can no longer
    borrow
Its hues from chance or change, dark chil-
    dren of to-morrow.

XX

'We know not what will come. Yet, Laon,
    dearest,
Cythna shall be the prophetess of Love;
Her lips shall rob thee of the grace thou
    wearest,
To hide thy heart, and clothe the shapes
    which rove
Within the homeless Future's wintry
    grove;
For I now, sitting thus beside thee,
    seem
Even with thy breath and blood to live
    and move,
And violence and wrong are as a dream
Which rolls from steadfast truth, — an un-
    returning stream.

XXI

'The blasts of Autumn drive the wingèd
    seeds
Over the earth; next come the snows,
    and rain,
And frosts, and storms, which dreary
    Winter leads
Out of his Scythian cave, a savage train.
Behold! Spring sweeps over the world
    again,
Shedding soft dews from her ethereal
    wings;
Flowers on the mountains, fruits over
    the plain,
And music on the waves and woods she
    flings,
And love on all that lives, and calm on life-
    less things.

XXII

'O Spring, of hope and love and youth and
    gladness
Wind-wingèd emblem! brightest, best
    and fairest!
Whence comest thou, when, with dark
    Winter's sadness
The tears that fade in sunny smiles thou
    sharest?
Sister of joy! thou art the child who
    wearest
Thy mother's dying smile, tender and
    sweet;

Thy mother Autumn, for whose grave
    thou bearest
Fresh flowers, and beams like flowers,
    with gentle feet,
Disturbing not the leaves which are her
    winding sheet.

XXIII

'Virtue and Hope and Love, like light
    and Heaven,
Surround the world. We are their chosen
    slaves.
Has not the whirlwind of our spirit driven
Truth's deathless germs to thought's re-
    motest caves?
Lo, Winter comes! — the grief of many
    graves,
The frost of death, the tempest of the
    sword,
The flood of tyranny, whose sanguine
    waves
Stagnate like ice at Faith the enchanter's
    word,
And bind all human hearts in its repose
    abhorred.

XXIV

'The seeds are sleeping in the soil. Mean-
    while
The Tyrant peoples dungeons with his
    prey;
Pale victims on the guarded scaffold
    smile
Because they cannot speak; and, day by
    day,
The moon of wasting Science wanes
    away
Among her stars, and in that darkness
    vast
The sons of earth to their foul idols pray,
And gray Priests triumph, and like
    blight or blast
A shade of selfish care o'er human looks is
    cast.

XXV

'This is the Winter of the world; and
    here
We die, even as the winds of Autumn
    fade,
Expiring in the frore and foggy air.
Behold! Spring comes, though we must
    pass who made
The promise of its birth, — even as the
    shade

Which from our death, as from a mountain, flings
The future, a broad sunrise; thus arrayed
As with the plumes of overshadowing wings,
From its dark gulf of chains Earth like an eagle springs.

XXVI

' O dearest love! we shall be dead and cold
Before this morn may on the world arise.
Wouldst thou the glory of its dawn behold?
Alas! gaze not on me, but turn thine eyes
On thine own heart — it is a Paradise
Which everlasting spring has made its own,
And while drear winter fills the naked skies,
Sweet streams of sunny thought, and flowers fresh blown,
Are there, and weave their sounds and odors into one.

XXVII

' In their own hearts the earnest of the hope
Which made them great the good will ever find;
And though some envious shade may interlope
Between the effect and it, One comes behind,
Who aye the future to the past will bind —
Necessity, whose sightless strength forever
Evil with evil, good with good, must wind
In bands of union, which no power may sever;
They must bring forth their kind, and be divided never!

XXVIII

' The good and mighty of departed ages
Are in their graves, the innocent and free,
Heroes, and Poets, and prevailing Sages,
Who leave the vesture of their majesty
To adorn and clothe this naked world;
— and we

Are like to them — such perish, but they leave
All hope, or love, or truth, or liberty,
Whose forms their mighty spirits could conceive,
To be a rule and law to ages that survive.

XXIX

' So be the turf heaped over our remains
Even in our happy youth, and that strange lot,
Whate'er it be, when in these mingling veins
The blood is still, be ours; let sense and thought
Pass from our being, or be numbered not
Among the things that are; let those who come
Behind, for whom our steadfast will has bought
A calm inheritance, a glorious doom,
Insult with careless tread our undivided tomb.

XXX

' Our many thoughts and deeds, our life and love,
Our happiness, and all that we have been,
Immortally must live and burn and move
When we shall be no more; — the world has seen
A type of peace; and as some most serene
And lovely spot to a poor maniac's eye —
After long years some sweet and moving scene
Of youthful hope returning suddenly —
Quells his long madness, thus Man shall remember thee.

XXXI

' And Calumny meanwhile shall feed on us
As worms devour the dead, and near the throne
And at the altar most accepted thus
Shall sneers and curses be; — what we have done
None shall dare vouch, though it be truly known;
That record shall remain when they must pass
Who built their pride on its oblivion,

And fame, in human hope which sculptured was,
Survive the perished scrolls of unenduring
brass.

XXXII

'The while we two, belovèd, must depart,
And Sense and Reason, those enchanters
fair,
Whose wand of power is hope, would
bid the heart
That gazed beyond the wormy grave
despair ;
These eyes, these lips, this blood, seems
darkly there
To fade in hideous ruin ; no calm sleep,
Peopling with golden dreams the stagnant
air,
Seems our obscure and rotting eyes to
steep
In joy; — but senseless death — a ruin
dark and deep !

XXXIII

'These are blind fancies. Reason cannot
know
What sense can neither feel nor thought
conceive;
There is delusion in the world — and
woe,
And fear, and pain — we know not
whence we live,
Or why, or how, or what mute Power
may give
Their being to each plant, and star, and
beast,
Or even these thoughts. — Come near
me ! I do weave
A chain I cannot break — I am possessed
With thoughts too swift and strong for one
lone human breast.

XXXIV

'Yes, yes — thy kiss is sweet, thy lips
are warm —
Oh, willingly, belovèd, would these eyes
Might they no more drink being from
thy form,
Even as to sleep whence we again arise,
Close their faint orbs in death. I fear
nor prize
Aught that can now betide, unshared by
thee.
Yes, Love when Wisdom fails makes
Cythna wise;

Darkness and death, if death be true,
must be
Dearer than life and hope if unenjoyed
with thee.

XXXV

'Alas! our thoughts flow on with stream
whose waters
Return not to their fountain; Earth and
Heaven,
The Ocean and the Sun, the clouds their
daughters,
Winter, and Spring, and Morn, and
Noon, and Even —
All that we are or know, is darkly driven
Towards one gulf. — Lo! what a change
is come
Since I first spake — but time shall be for-
given,
Though it change all but thee !' She
ceased — night's gloom
Meanwhile had fallen on earth from the
sky's sunless dome.

XXXVI

Though she had ceased, her countenance
uplifted
To Heaven still spake with solemn glory
bright;
Her dark deep eyes, her lips, whose motions gifted
The air they breathed with love, her
locks undight;
'Fair star of life and love,' I cried, 'my
soul's delight,
Why lookest thou on the crystalline
skies?
Oh, that my spirit were yon Heaven of
night,
Which gazes on thee with its thousand
eyes !'
She turned to me and smiled — that smile
was Paradise !

CANTO TENTH

I

WAS there a human spirit in the steed
That thus with his proud voice, ere night
was gone,
He broke our linkèd rest ? or do indeed
All living things a common nature own,
And thought erect an universal throne,
Where many shapes one tribute ever
bear ?

And Earth, their mutual mother, does
  she groan
To see her sons contend ? and makes she
  bare
Her breast that all in peace its drainless
  stores may share ?

II

I have heard friendly sounds from many
  a tongue
Which was not human; the lone nightingale
Has answered me with her most soothing
  song,
Out of her ivy bower, when I sate pale
With grief, and sighed beneath; from
  many a dale
The antelopes who flocked for food have
  spoken
With happy sounds and motions that
  avail
Like man's own speech; and such was
  now the token
Of waning night, whose calm by that proud
  neigh was broken.

III

Each night that mighty steed bore me
  abroad,
And I returned with food to our retreat,
And dark intelligence; the blood which
  flowed
Over the fields had stained the courser's
  feet;
Soon the dust drinks that bitter dew, —
  then meet
The vulture, and the wild-dog, and the
  snake,
The wolf, and the hyena gray, and eat
The dead in horrid truce; their throngs
  did make
Behind the steed a chasm like waves in a
  ship's wake.

IV

For from the utmost realms of earth
  came pouring
The banded slaves whom every despot
  sent
At that throned traitor's summons; like
  the roaring
Of fire, whose floods the wild deer cir-
  cumvent
In the scorched pastures of the south, so
  bent

The armies of the leaguèd kings around
Their files of steel and flame; the conti-
  nent
Trembled, as with a zone of ruin bound,
Beneath their feet — the sea shook with
  their Navies' sound.

V

From every nation of the earth they
  came,
The multitude of moving heartless things,
Whom slaves call men; obediently they
  came,
Like sheep whom from the fold the shep-
  herd brings
To the stall, red with blood; their many
  kings
Led them, thus erring, from their native
  land —
Tartar and Frank, and millions whom
  the wings
Of Indian breezes lull; and many a band
The Arctic Anarch sent, and Idumea's sand

VI

Fertile in prodigies and lies. So there
Strange natures made a brotherhood of
  ill.
The desert savage ceased to grasp in fear
His Asian shield and bow when, at the
  will
Of Europe's subtler son, the bolt would
  kill
Some shepherd sitting on a rock secure;
But smiles of wondering joy his face
  would fill,
And savage sympathy; those slaves im-
  pure
Each one the other thus from ill to ill did
  lure.

VII

For traitorously did that foul Tyrant
  robe
His countenance in lies; even at the hour
When he was snatched from death, then
  o'er the globe,
With secret signs from many a mountain tower,
With smoke by day, and fire by night,
  the power
Of Kings and Priests, those dark con-
  spirators,
He called; they knew his cause their
  own, and swore

Like wolves and serpents to their mu-
tual wars
Strange truce, with many a rite which
Earth and Heaven abhors.

VIII

Myriads had come — millions were on
their way;
The Tyrant passed, surrounded by the
steel
Of hired assassins, through the public
way,
Choked with his country's dead; his footsteps reel
On the fresh blood — he smiles. 'Ay,
now I feel
I am a King in truth!' he said, and took
His royal seat, and bade the torturing
wheel
Be brought, and fire, and pincers, and
the hook,
And scorpions, that his soul on its revenge
might look.

IX

' But first, go slay the rebels — why return
The victor bands?' he said, 'millions
yet live,
Of whom the weakest with one word
might turn
The scales of victory yet; let none sur-
vive
But those within the walls — each fifth
shall give
The expiation for his brethren here.
Go forth, and waste and kill!' — 'O
king, forgive
My speech,' a soldier answered, 'but we
fear
The spirits of the night, and morn is draw-
ing near;

X

' For we were slaying still without remorse,
And now that dreadful chief beneath my
hand
Defenceless lay, when on a hell-black
horse
An Angel bright as day, waving a brand
Which flashed among the stars, passed.'
— ' Dost thou stand
Parleying with me, thou wretch?' the
king replied;
'Slaves, bind him to the wheel; and of
this band

Whoso will drag that woman to his side
That scared him thus may burn his dearest
foe beside;

XI

'And gold and glory shall be his. Go
forth !'
They rushed into the plain. Loud was
the roar
Of their career; the horsemen shook the
earth;
The wheeled artillery's speed the pavement tore;
The infantry, file after file, did pour
Their clouds on the utmost hills. Five
days they slew
Among the wasted fields; the sixth saw
gore
Stream through the City; on the seventh
the dew
Of slaughter became stiff, and there was
peace anew:

XII

Peace in the desert fields and villages,
Between the glutted beasts and mangled
dead !
Peace in the silent streets ! save when
the cries
Of victims, to their fiery judgment led,
Made pale their voiceless lips who seemed
to dread,
Even in their dearest kindred, lest some
tongue
Be faithless to the fear yet unbetrayed;
Peace in the Tyrant's palace, where the
throng
Waste the triumphal hours in festival and
song !

XIII

Day after day the burning Sun rolled on
Over the death-polluted land. It came
Out of the east like fire, and fiercely
shone
A lamp of autumn, ripening with its
flame
The few lone ears of corn; the sky be-
came
Stagnate with heat, so that each cloud
and blast
Languished and died; the thirsting air
did claim
All moisture, and a rotting vapor passed
From the unburied dead, invisible and fast.

XIV

First Want, then Plague, came on the
    beasts; their food
Failed, and they drew the breath of its
    decay.
Millions on millions, whom the scent of
    blood
Had lured, or who from regions far
    away
Had tracked the hosts in festival array,
From their dark deserts, gaunt and
    wasting now
Stalked like fell shades among their
    perished prey;
In their green eyes a strange disease did
    glow —
They sank in hideous spasm, or pains severe
    and slow.

XV

The fish were poisoned in the streams;
    the birds
In the green woods perished; the insect
    race
Was withered up; the scattered flocks
    and herds
Who had survived the wild beasts' hun-
    gry chase
Died moaning, each upon the other's face
In helpless agony gazing; round the
    City
All night, the lean hyenas their sad
    case
Like starving infants wailed — a woful
    ditty;
And many a mother wept, pierced with
    unnatural pity.

XVI

Amid the aërial minarets on high
The Æthiopian vultures fluttering fell
From their long line of brethren in the
    sky,
Startling the concourse of mankind.
    Too well
These signs the coming mischief did
    foretell.
Strange panic first, a deep and sickening
    dread,
Within each heart, like ice, did sink and
    dwell,
A voiceless thought of evil, which did
    spread
With the quick glance of eyes, like wither-
    ing lightnings shed.

XVII

Day after day, when the year wanes, the
    frosts
Strip its green crown of leaves till all is
    bare;
So on those strange and congregated
    hosts
Came Famine, a swift shadow, and the
    air
Groaned with the burden of a new de-
    spair;
Famine, than whom Misrule no deadlier
    daughter
Feeds from her thousand breasts, though
    sleeping there
With lidless eyes lie Faith and Plague
    and Slaughter —
A ghastly brood conceived of Lethe's sullen
    water.

XVIII

There was no food; the corn was tram-
    pled down,
The flocks and herds had perished; on
    the shore
The dead and putrid fish were ever
    thrown;
The deeps were foodless, and the winds
    no more
Creaked with the weight of birds, but as
    before
Those wingèd things sprang forth, were
    void of shade;
The vines and orchards, autumn's golden
    store,
Were burned; so that the meanest food
    was weighed
With gold, and avarice died before the god
    it made.

XIX

There was no corn — in the wide market-
    place
All loathliest things, even human flesh,
    was sold;
They weighed it in small scales — and
    many a face
Was fixed in eager horror then. His
    gold
The miser brought; the tender maid,
    grown bold
Through hunger, bared her scornèd
    charms in vain;
The mother brought her eldest born,
    controlled

By instinct blind as love, but turned again
And bade her infant suck, and died in
   silent pain.

XX

Then fell blue Plague upon the race of
   man.
'Oh, for the sheathèd steel, so late which
   gave
Oblivion to the dead when the streets ran
With brothers' blood! Oh, that the
   earthquake's grave
Would gape, or Ocean lift its stifling
   wave!'
Vain cries — throughout the streets thou-
   sands pursued
Each by his fiery torture howl and rave
Or sit in frenzy's unimagined mood
Upon fresh heaps of dead — a ghastly
   multitude.

XXI

It was not hunger now, but thirst.
   . Each well
Was choked with rotting corpses, and
   became
A caldron of green mist made visible
At sunrise. Thither still the myriads
   came,
Seeking to quench the agony of the flame
Which raged like poison through their
   bursting veins;
Naked they were from torture, without
   shame,
Spotted with nameless scars and lurid
   blains —
Childhood, and youth, and age, writhing in
   savage pains.

XXII

It was not thirst, but madness! Many
   saw
Their own lean image everywhere — it
   went
A ghastlier self beside them, till the awe
Of that dread sight to self-destruction
   sent
Those shrieking victims; some, ere life
   was spent,
Sought, with a horrid sympathy, to shed
Contagion on the sound; and others rent
Their matted hair, and cried aloud, 'We
   tread
On fire! the avenging Power his hell on
   earth has spread.'

XXIII

Sometimes the living by the dead were
   hid.
Near the great fountain in the public
   square,
Where corpses made a crumbling pyra-
   mid
Under the sun, was heard one stifled
   prayer
For life, in the hot silence of the air;
And strange 't was 'mid that hideous
   heap to see
Some shrouded in their long and golden
   hair,
As if not dead, but slumbering quietly,
Like forms which sculptors carve, then
   love to agony.

XXIV

Famine had spared the palace of the
   King;
He rioted in festival the while,
He and his guards and Priests; but
   Plague did fling
One shadow upon all. Famine can smile
On him who brings it food, and pass,
   with guile
Of thankful falsehood, like a courtier
   gray,
The house-dog of the throne; but many
   a mile
Comes Plague, a wingèd wolf, who
   loathes alway
The garbage and the scum that strangers
   make her prey.

XXV

So, near the throne, amid the gorgeous
   feast,
Sheathed in resplendent arms, or loosely
   dight
To luxury, ere the mockery yet had
   ceased
That lingered on his lips, the warrior's
   might
Was loosened, and a new and ghastlier
   night
In dreams of frenzy lapped his eyes; he
   fell
Headlong, or with stiff eyeballs sate up-
   right
Among the guests, or raving mad did
   tell
Strange truths — a dying seer of dark oppression's hell.

XXVI

The Princes and the Priests were pale
  with terror;
That monstrous faith wherewith they
  ruled mankind
Fell, like a shaft loosed by the bowman's
  error,
On their own hearts; they sought and
  they could find
No refuge — 't was the blind who led the
  blind !
So, through the desolate streets to the
  high fane,
The many-tongued and endless armies
  wind
In sad procession; each among the train
To his own idol lifts his supplications
  vain.

XXVII

'O God !' they cried, 'we know our secret
  pride
Has scorned thee, and thy worship, and
  thy name;
Secure in human power, we have defied
Thy fearful might; we bend in fear and
  shame
Before thy presence; with the dust we
  claim
Kindred; be merciful, O King of Heaven!
Most justly have we suffered for thy
  fame
Made dim, but be at length our sins for-
  given,
Ere to despair and death thy worshippers
  be driven !

XXVIII

'O King of Glory ! Thou alone hast
  power !
Who can resist thy will? who can re-
  strain
Thy wrath when on the guilty thou dost
  shower
The shafts of thy revenge, a blistering
  rain ?
Greatest and best, be merciful again !
Have we not stabbed thine enemies, and
  made
The Earth an altar, and the Heavens a
  fane,
Where thou wert worshipped with their
  blood, and laid
Those hearts in dust which would thy
  searchless works have weighed ?

XXIX

'Well didst thou loosen on this impious
  City
Thine angels of revenge ! recall them
  now;
Thy worshippers abased here kneel for
  pity,
And bind their souls by an immortal
  vow.
We swear by thee — and to our oath do
  thou
Give sanction from thine hell of fiends
  and flame —
That we will kill with fire and torments
  slow
The last of those who mocked thy holy
  name
And scorned the sacred laws thy prophets
  did proclaim.'

XXX

Thus they with trembling limbs and
  pallid lips
Worshipped their own hearts' image,
  dim and vast,
Scared by the shade wherewith they
  would eclipse
The light of other minds; troubled they
  passed
From the great Temple; fiercely still
  and fast
The arrows of the plague among them
  fell,
And they on one another gazed aghast,
And through the hosts contention wild
  befell,
As each of his own god the wondrous works
  did tell.

XXXI

And Oromaze, Joshua, and Mahomet,
Moses, and Buddh, Zerdusht, and Brahm,
  and Foh,
A tumult of strange names, which never
  met
Before, as watchwords of a single woe,
Arose; each raging votary 'gan to throw
Aloft his armèd hands, and each did
  howl
'Our God alone is God !' and slaughter
  now
Would have gone forth, when from be-
  neath a cowl
A voice came forth which pierced like ice
  through every soul.

XXXII

'T was an Iberian Priest from whom it
    came,
A zealous man, who led the legioned
    West,
With words which faith and pride had
    steeped in flame,
To quell the unbelievers; a dire guest
Even to his friends was he, for in his
    breast
Did hate and guile lie watchful, inter-
    twined,
Twin serpents in one deep and winding
    nest;
He loathed all faith beside his own, and
    pined
To wreak his fear of Heaven in vengeance
    on mankind.

XXXIII

But more he loathed and hated the clear
    light
Of wisdom and free thought, and more
    did fear,
Lest, kindled once, its beams might
    pierce the night,
Even where his Idol stood; for far and
    near
Did many a heart in Europe leap to hear
That faith and tyranny were trampled
    down, —
Many a pale victim, doomed for truth to
    share
The murderer's cell, or see with helpless
    groan
The Priests his children drag for slaves to
    serve their own.

XXXIV

He dared not kill the infidels with fire
Or steel, in Europe; the slow agonies
Of legal torture mocked his keen desire;
So he made truce with those who did de-
    spise
The expiation and the sacrifice,
That, though detested, Islam's kindred
    creed
Might crush for him those deadlier ene-
    mies;
For fear of God did in his bosom breed
A jealous hate of man, an unreposing need.

XXXV

'Peace ! Peace !' he cried, 'when we are
    dead, the Day

Of Judgment comes, and all shall surely
    know
Whose God is God; each fearfully shall
    pay
The errors of his faith in endless woe !
But there is sent a mortal vengeance
    now
On earth, because an impious race had
    spurned
Him whom we all adore, — a subtle foe,
By whom for ye this dread reward was
    earned,
And kingly thrones, which rest on faith,
    nigh overturned.

XXXVI

'Think ye, because ye weep and kneel
    and pray,
That God will lull the pestilence ? It
    rose
Even from beneath his throne, where,
    many a day,
His mercy soothed it to a dark repose;
It walks upon the earth to judge his foes,
And what art thou and I, that he should
    deign
To curb his ghastly minister, or close
The gates of death, ere they receive the
    twain
Who shook with mortal spells his unde-
    fended reign ?

XXXVII

' Ay, there is famine in the gulf of hell,
Its giant worms of fire forever yawn, —
Their lurid eyes are on us! those who fell
By the swift shafts of pestilence ere
    dawn
Are in their jaws ! they hunger for the
    spawn
Of Satan, their own brethren, who were
    sent
To make our souls their spoil. See, see !
    they fawn
Like dogs, and they will sleep, with lux-
    ury spent,
When those detested hearts their iron fangs
    have rent !

XXXVIII

' Our God may then lull Pestilence to
    sleep.
Pile high the pyre of expiation now !
A forest's spoil of boughs; and on the
    heap

Pour venomous gums, which sullenly and
  slow,
When touched by flame, shall burn, and
  melt, and flow,
A stream of clinging fire, — and fix on
  high
A net of iron, and spread forth below
A couch of snakes, and scorpions, and
  the fry
Of centipedes and worms, earth's hellish
  progeny !

XXXIX

'Let Laon and Laone on that pyre,
Linked tight with burning brass, perish!
  — then pray
That with this sacrifice the withering ire
Of Heaven may be appeased.' He ceased,
  and they
A space stood silent, as far, far away
The echoes of his voice among them
  died;
And he knelt down upon the dust, alway
Muttering the curses of his speechless
  pride,
Whilst shame, and fear, and awe, the armies
  did divide.

XL

His voice was like a blast that burst the
  portal
Of fabled hell; and as he spake, each
  one
Saw gape beneath the chasms of fire im-
  mortal,
And Heaven above seemed cloven, where,
  on a throne
Girt round with storms and shadows, sate
  alone
Their King and Judge. Fear killed in
  every breast
All natural pity then, a fear unknown
Before, and with an inward fire possessed
They raged like homeless beasts whom
  burning woods invest.

XLI

'T was morn. — At noon the public crier
  went forth,
Proclaiming through the living and the
  dead, —
'The Monarch saith that his great em-
  pire's worth
Is set on Laon and Laone's head;
He who but one yet living here can lead,

Or who the life from both their hearts
  can wring,
Shall be the kingdom's heir — a glorious
  meed !
But he who both alive can hither bring
The Princess shall espouse, and reign an
  equal King.'

XLII

Ere night the pyre was piled, the net of
  iron
Was spread above, the fearful couch below;
It overtopped the towers that did environ
That spacious square; for Fear is never
  slow
To build the thrones of Hate, her mate
  and foe;
So she scourged forth the maniac multitude
To rear this pyramid — tottering and
  slow,
Plague-stricken, foodless, like lean herds
  pursued
By gadflies, they have piled the heath and
  gums and wood.

XLIII

Night came, a starless and a moonless
  gloom.
Until the dawn, those hosts of many a
  nation
Stood round that pile, as near one lover's
  tomb
Two gentle sisters mourn their desola-
  tion;
And in the silence of that expectation
Was heard on high the reptiles' hiss and
  crawl —
It was so deep, save when the devastation
Of the swift pest with fearful interval,
Marking its path with shrieks, among the
  crowd would fall.

XLIV

Morn came. — Among those sleepless
  multitudes,
Madness, and Fear, and Plague, and
  Famine, still
Heaped corpse on corpse, as in autumnal
  woods
The frosts of many a wind with dead
  leaves fill
Earth's cold and sullen brooks; in silence
  still,

The pale survivors stood; ere noon the
    fear
Of Hell became a panic, which did kill
Like hunger or disease, with whispers
    drear,
As 'Hush! hark! come they yet? — Just
    Heaven, thine hour is near!'

XLV

And Priests rushed through their ranks,
    some counterfeiting
The rage they did inspire, some mad in-
    deed
With their own lies. They said their
    god was waiting
To see his enemies writhe, and burn, and
    bleed, —
And that, till then, the snakes of Hell had
    need
Of human souls; three hundred furnaces
Soon blazed through the wide City,
    where, with speed,
Men brought their infidel kindred to ap-
    pease
God's wrath, and, while they burned, knelt
    round on quivering knees.

XLVI

The noontide sun was darkened with that
    smoke;
The winds of eve dispersed those ashes
    gray.
The madness, which these rites had lulled,
    awoke
Again at sunset. Who shall dare to say
The deeds which night and fear brought
    forth, or weigh
In balance just the good and evil there?
He might man's deep and searchless
    heart display,
And cast a light on those dim labyrinths
    where
Hope near imagined chasms is struggling
    with despair.

XLVII

'T is said a mother dragged three chil-
    dren then
To those fierce flames which roast the
    eyes in the head,
And laughed, and died; and that unholy
    men,
Feasting like fiends upon the infidel dead,
Looked from their meal, and saw an
    angel tread

The visible floor of Heaven, and it was
    she!
And, on that night, one without doubt or
    dread
Came to the fire, and said, 'Stop, I am
    he!
Kill me!' — They burned them both with
    hellish mockery.

XLVIII

And, one by one, that night, young
    maidens came,
Beauteous and calm, like shapes of living
    stone
Clothed in the light of dreams, and by
    the flame,
Which shrank as overgorged, they laid
    them down,
And sung a low sweet song, of which
    alone
One word was heard, and that was
    Liberty;
And that some kissed their marble feet,
    with moan
Like love, and died, and then that they
    did die
With happy smiles, which sunk in white
    tranquillity.

CANTO ELEVENTH

I

SHE saw me not — she heard me not —
    alone
Upon the mountain's dizzy brink she
    stood;
She spake not, breathed not, moved not
    — there was thrown
Over her look the shadow of a mood
Which only clothes the heart in solitude,
A thought of voiceless depth; — she
    stood alone —
Above, the Heavens were spread — be-
    low, the flood
Was murmuring in its caves — the wind
    had blown
Her hair apart, through which her eyes
    and forehead shone.

II

A cloud was hanging o'er the western
    mountains;
Before its blue and moveless depth were
    flying

Gray mists poured forth from the unresting fountains
Of darkness in the North; the day was
dying;
Sudden, the sun shone forth — its beams
were lying
Like boiling gold on Ocean, strange to
see,
And on the shattered vapors which,
defying
The power of light in vain, tossed restlessly
In the red Heaven, like wrecks in a tempestuous sea.

III

It was a stream of living beams, whose
bank
On either side by the cloud's cleft was
made;
And where its chasms that flood of glory
drank,
Its waves gushed forth like fire, and as
if swayed
By some mute tempest, rolled on *her;*
the shade
Of her bright image floated on the river
Of liquid light, which then did end and
fade —
Her radiant shape upon its verge did
shiver;
Aloft, her flowing hair like strings of flame
did quiver.

IV

I stood beside her, but she saw me not —
She looked upon the sea, and skies, and
earth.
Rapture and love and admiration wrought
A passion deeper far than tears, or mirth,
Or speech, or gesture, or whate'er has
birth
From common joy; which with the
speechless feeling
That led her there united, and shot forth
From her far eyes a light of deep re-
vealing,
All but her dearest self from my regard
concealing.

V

Her lips were parted, and the measured
breath
Was now heard there; her dark and intricate eyes,

Orb within orb, deeper than sleep or
death,
Absorbed the glories of the burning
skies,
Which, mingling with her heart's deep
ecstasies,
Burst from her looks and gestures; and
a light
Of liquid tenderness, like love, did rise
From her whole frame — an atmosphere
which quite
Arrayed her in its beams, tremulous and
soft and bright.

VI

She would have clasped me to her glowing frame;
Those warm and odorous lips might soon
have shed
On mine the fragrance and the invisible
flame
Which now the cold winds stole; she
would have laid
Upon my languid heart her dearest head;
I might have heard her voice, tender and
sweet;
Her eyes, mingling with mine, might
soon have fed
My soul with their own joy. — One moment yet
I gazed — we parted then, never again to
meet !

VII

Never but once to meet on earth again !
She heard me as I fled — her eager tone
Sunk on my heart, and almost wove a
chain
Around my will to link it with her own,
So that my stern resolve was almost
gone.
' I cannot reach thee ! whither dost thou
fly ?
My steps are faint. — Come back, thou
dearest one —
Return, ah me ! return ! ' — the wind
passed by
On which those accents died, faint, far, and
lingeringly.

VIII

Woe ! woe ! that moonless midnight !
Want and Pest
Were horrible, but one more fell doth
rear,

As in a hydra's swarming lair, its crest
Eminent among those victims — even the
    Fear
Of Hell; each girt by the hot atmosphere
Of his blind agony, like a scorpion stung
By his own rage upon his burning bier
Of circling coals of fire. But still there
    clung
One hope, like a keen sword on starting
    threads uphung: —

IX

Not death — death was no more refuge
    or rest;
Not life — it was despair to be ! — not
    sleep,
For fiends and chasms of fire had dis-
    possessed
All natural dreams; to wake was not to
    weep,
But to gaze, mad and pallid, at the leap
To which the Future, like a snaky
    scourge,
Or like some tyrant's eye which aye doth
    keep
Its withering beam upon his slaves, did
    urge
Their steps; they heard the roar of Hell's
    sulphureous surge.

X

Each of that multitude, alone and lost
To sense of outward things, one hope
    yet knew;
As on a foam-girt crag some seaman
    tossed
Stares at the rising tide, or like the crew
Whilst now the ship is splitting through
    and through;
Each, if the tramp of a far steed was
    heard,
Started from sick despair, or if there
    flew .
One murmur on the wind, or if some
    word
Which none can gather yet the distant
    crowd has stirred.

XI

Why became cheeks, wan with the kiss
    of death,
Paler from hope ? they had sustained
    despair.
Why watched those myriads with sus-
    pended breath

Sleepless a second night ? they are not
    here,
The victims — and hour by hour, a vision
    drear,
Warm corpses fall upon the clay-cold
    dead;
And even in death their lips are wreathed
    with fear.
The crowd is mute and moveless — over-
    head
Silent Arcturus shines — ha ! hear'st thou
    not the tread

XII

Of rushing feet ? laughter ? the shout,
    the scream
Of triumph not to be contained ? See !
    hark !
They come, they come ! give way ! Alas,
    ye deem
Falsely — 't is but a crowd of maniacs
    stark
Driven, like a troop of spectres, through
    the dark
From the choked well, whence a bright
    death-fire sprung,
A lurid earth-star, which dropped many
    a spark
From its blue train, and, spreading
    widely, clung
To their wild hair, like mist the topmost
    pines among.

XIII

And many, from the crowd collected
    there,
Joined that strange dance in fearful
    sympathies;
There was the silence of a long despair,
When the last echo of those terrible cries
Came from a distant street, like agonies
Stifled afar. — Before the Tyrant's
    throne
All night his agèd Senate sate, their
    eyes
In stony expectation fixed; when one
Sudden before them stood, a Stranger and
    alone.

XIV

Dark Priests and haughty Warriors
    gazed on him
With baffled wonder, for a hermit's vest
Concealed his face; but when he spake,
    his tone

Ere yet the matter did their thoughts
　　arrest —
Earnest, benignant, calm, as from a
　　breast
Void of all hate or terror — made them
　　start;
For as with gentle accents he addressed
His speech to them, on each unwilling
　　heart
Unusual awe did fall — a spirit-quelling
　　dart.

XV

' Ye Princes of the Earth, ye sit aghast
　　Amid the ruin which yourselves have
　　made;
Yes, Desolation heard your trumpet's
　　blast,
And sprang from sleep ! — dark Terror
　　has obeyed
Your bidding. Oh, that I, whom ye have
　　made
Your foe, could set my dearest enemy
　　free
From pain and fear ! but evil casts a
　　shade
Which cannot pass so soon, and Hate
　　must be
The nurse and parent still of an ill progeny.

XVI

' Ye turn to Heaven for aid in your dis-
　　tress;
Alas, that ye, the mighty and the wise,
Who, if ye dared, might not aspire to
　　less
Than ye conceive of power, should fear
　　the lies
Which thou, and thou, didst frame for
　　mysteries
To blind your slaves ! consider your own
　　thought —
An empty and a cruel sacrifice
Ye now prepare for a vain idol wrought
Out of the fears and hate which vain de-
　　sires have brought.

XVII

' Ye seek for happiness — alas the day !
Ye find it not in luxury nor in gold,
Nor in the fame, nor in the envied sway
For which, O willing slaves to Custom
　　old,
Severe task - mistress, ye your hearts
　　have sold.

Ye seek for peace, and, when ye die, to
　　dream
No evil dreams; — all mortal things are
　　cold
And senseless then; if aught survive, I
　　deem
It must be love and joy, for they immortal
　　seem.

XVIII

' Fear not the future, weep not for the
　　past.
Oh, could I win your ears to dare be now
Glorious, and great, and calm ! that ye
　　would cast
Into the dust those symbols of your woe,
Purple, and gold, and steel ! that ye
　　would go
Proclaiming to the nations whence ye
　　came
That Want and Plague and Fear from
　　slavery flow;
And that mankind is free, and that the
　　shame
Of royalty and faith is lost in freedom's
　　fame !

XIX

' If thus 't is well — if not, I come to say
That Laon — ' While the Stranger
　　spoke, among
The Council sudden tumult and affray
Arose, for many of those warriors young
Had on his eloquent accents fed and
　　hung
Like bees on mountain-flowers; they
　　knew the truth,
And from their thrones in vindication
　　sprung;
The men of faith and law then without
　　ruth
Drew forth their secret steel, and stabbed
　　each ardent youth.

XX

They stabbed them in the back and
　　sneered — a slave,
Who stood behind the throne, those
　　corpses drew
Each to its bloody, dark and secret
　　grave;
And one more daring raised his steel
　　anew
To pierce the Stranger: ' What hast
　　thou to do

With me, poor wretch?' — Calm, sol-
emn and severe,
That voice unstrung his sinews, and he
threw
His dagger on the ground, and, pale with
fear,
Sate silently — his voice then did the
Stranger rear.

XXI

'It doth avail not that I weep for ye —
Ye cannot change, since ye are old and
gray,
And ye have chosen your lot — your
fame must be
A book of blood, whence in a milder day
Men shall learn truth, when ye are
wrapped in clay;
Now ye shall triumph. I am Laon's
friend,
And him to your revenge will I betray,
So ye concede one easy boon. Attend!
For now I speak of things which ye can
apprehend.

XXII

'There is a People mighty in its youth,
A land beyond the Oceans of the West,
Where, though with rudest rites, Free-
dom and Truth
Are worshipped; from a glorious Mo-
ther's breast,
Who, since high Athens fell, among the
rest
Sate like the Queen of Nations, but in
woe,
By inbred monsters outraged and op-
pressed,
Turns to her chainless child for succor
now,
It draws the milk of Power in Wisdom's
fullest flow.

XXIII

'That land is like an Eagle, whose young
gaze
Feeds on the noontide beam, whose
golden plume
Floats moveless on the storm, and in the
blaze
Of sunrise gleams when earth is wrapped
in gloom;
An epitaph of glory for the tomb
Of murdered Europe may thy fame be
made,

Great People! as the sands shalt thou
become;
Thy growth is swift as morn when night
must fade;
The multitudinous Earth shall sleep beneath thy shade.

XXIV

'Yes, in the desert there is built a home
For Freedom. Genius is made strong
to rear
The monuments of man beneath the
dome
Of a new Heaven; myriads assemble
there,
Whom the proud lords of man, in rage
or fear,
Drive from their wasted homes. The
boon I pray
Is this — that Cythna shall be convoyed
there, —
Nay, start not at the name — America!
And then to you this night Laon will I
betray.

XXV

'With me do what ye will. I am your
foe!'
The light of such a joy as makes the
stare
Of hungry snakes like living emeralds
glow
Shone in a hundred human eyes. —
'Where, where
Is Laon? haste! fly! drag him swiftly
here!
We grant thy boon.' — 'I put no trust
in ye,
Swear by the Power ye dread.' — 'We
swear, we swear!'
The Stranger threw his vest back sud-
denly,
And smiled in gentle pride, and said, 'Lo!
I am he!'

CANTO TWELFTH

I

THE transport of a fierce and monstrous
gladness
Spread through the multitudinous streets,
fast flying
Upon the winds of fear; from his dull
madness

The starveling waked, and died in joy;
   the dying,
Among the corpses in stark agony lying,
Just heard the happy tidings, and in
   hope
Closed their faint eyes; from house to
   house replying
With loud acclaim, the living shook
   Heaven's cope,
And filled the startled Earth with echoes.
   Morn did ope

II

Its pale eyes then; and lo! the long
   array
Of guards in golden arms, and Priests
   beside,
Singing their bloody hymns, whose garbs
   betray
The blackness of the faith it seems to
   hide;
And see the Tyrant's gem-wrought
   chariot glide
Among the gloomy cowls and glittering
   spears —
A Shape of light is sitting by his side,
A child most beautiful. I' the midst
   appears
Laon — exempt alone from mortal hopes
   and fears.

III

His head and feet are bare, his hands
   are bound
Behind with heavy chains, yet none do
   wreak
Their scoffs on him, though myriads
   throng around;
There are no sneers upon his lip which
   speak
That scorn or hate has made him bold;
   his cheek
Resolve has not turned pale; his eyes are
   mild
And calm, and, like the morn about to
   break,
Smile on mankind; his heart seems reconciled
To all things and itself, like a reposing
   child.

IV

Tumult was in the soul of all beside,
Ill joy, or doubt, or fear; but those who
   saw

Their tranquil victim pass felt wonder
   glide
Into their brain, and became calm with
   awe. —
See, the slow pageant near the pile doth
   draw.
A thousand torches in the spacious
   square,
Borne by the ready slaves of ruthless law,
Await the signal round; the morning fair
Is changed to a dim night by that unnat-
   ural glare.

V

And see! beneath a sun-bright canopy,
Upon a platform level with the pile,
The anxious Tyrant sit, enthroned on
   high,
Girt by the chieftains of the host; all
   smile
In expectation but one child: the while
I, Laon, led by mutes, ascend my bier
Of fire, and look around; — each distant
   isle
Is dark in the bright dawn; towers far
   and near
Pierce like reposing flames the tremulous
   atmosphere.

VI

There was such silence through the host
   as when
An earthquake, trampling on some populous town,
Has crushed ten thousand with one tread,
   and men
Expect the second; all were mute but
   one,
That fairest child, who, bold with love,
   alone
Stood up before the king, without avail,
Pleading for Laon's life — her stifled
   groan
Was heard — she trembled like one aspen
   pale
Among the gloomy pines of a Norwegian
   vale.

VII

What were his thoughts linked in the
   morning sun,
Among those reptiles, stingless with
   delay,
Even like a tyrant's wrath? — the sig-
   nal-gun

Roared — hark, again ! in that dread
   pause he lay
As in a quiet dream — the slaves obey —
A thousand torches drop, — and hark,
   the last
Bursts on that awful silence; far away
Millions, with hearts that beat both loud
   and fast,
Watch for the springing flame expectant
   and aghast.

VIII

They fly — the torches fall — a cry of
   fear
Has startled the triumphant ! — they
   recede !
For, ere the cannon's roar has died, they
   hear
The tramp of hoofs like earthquake, and
   a steed
Dark and gigantic, with the tempest's
   speed,
Bursts through their ranks; a woman
   sits thereon,
Fairer it seems than aught that earth
   can breed,
Calm, radiant, like the phantom of the
   dawn,
A spirit from the caves of daylight wandering gone.

IX

All thought it was God's Angel come to
   sweep
The lingering guilty to their fiery grave;
The Tyrant from his throne in dread did
   leap, —
Her innocence his child from fear did
   save;
Scared by the faith they feigned, each
   priestly slave
Knelt for His mercy whom they served
   with blood,
And, like the refluence of a mighty
   wave
Sucked into the loud sea, the multitude
With crushing panic fled in terror's altered
   mood.

X

They pause, they blush, they gaze; a
   gathering shout
Bursts like one sound from the ten thousand streams
Of a tempestuous sea; that sudden rout

One checked who never in his mildest
   dreams
Felt awe from grace or loveliness, the
   seams
Of his rent heart so hard and cold a creed
Had seared with blistering ice; but he
   misdeems
That he is wise whose wounds do only
   bleed
Inly for self, — thus thought the Iberian
   Priest indeed,

XI

And others, too, thought he was wise to
   see
In pain, and fear, and hate, something
   divine —
In love and beauty, no divinity.
Now with a bitter smile, whose light did
   shine
Like a fiend's hope upon his lips and
   eyne,
He said, and the persuasion of that sneer
Rallied his trembling comrades — ' Is it
   mine
To stand alone, when kings and soldiers
   fear
A woman ? Heaven has sent its other
   victim here.'

XII

' Were it not impious,' said the King, ' to
   break
Our holy oath ? ' — ' Impious to keep it,
   say !'
Shrieked the exulting Priest : — ' Slaves,
   to the stake
Bind her, and on my head the burden lay
Of her just torments; at the Judgment
   Day
Will I stand up before the golden throne
Of Heaven, and cry, — " To Thee did I
   betray
An infidel ! but for me she would have
   known
Another moment's joy !" the glory be
   thine own.'

XIII

They trembled, but replied not, nor
   obeyed,
Pausing in breathless silence. Cythna
   sprung
From her gigantic steed, who, like a
   shade

Chased by the winds, those vacant streets
among
Fled tameless, as the brazen rein she
flung
Upon his neck, and kissed his moonèd
brow.
A piteous sight, that one so fair and
young
The clasp of such a fearful death should
woo
With smiles of tender joy as beamed from
Cythna now.

XIV

The warm tears burst in spite of faith
and fear
From many a tremulous eye, but, like
soft dews
Which feed spring's earliest buds, hung
gathered there,
Frozen by doubt, — alas ! they could not
choose
But weep; for, when her faint limbs did
refuse
To climb the pyre, upon the mutes she
smiled;
And with her eloquent gestures, and the
hues
Of her quick lips, even as a weary child
Wins sleep from some fond nurse with its
caresses mild,

XV

She won them, though unwilling, her to
bind
Near me, among the snakes. When then
had fled
One soft reproach that was most thrilling
kind,
She smiled on me, and nothing then we
said,
But each upon the other's countenance
fed
Looks of insatiate love; the mighty veil
Which doth divide the living and the
dead
Was almost rent, the world grew dim
and pale —
All light in Heaven or Earth beside our
love did fail.

XVI

Yet — yet — one brief relapse, like the
last beam
Of dying flames, the stainless air around

Hung silent and serene — a blood-red
gleam
Burst upwards, hurling fiercely from the
ground
The globèd smoke; I heard the mighty
sound
Of its uprise, like a tempestuous ocean;
And, through its chasms I saw, as in a
swound,
The Tyrant's child fall without life or
motion
Before his throne, subdued by some unseen
emotion. —

XVII

And is this death ? — The pyre has dis-
appeared,
The Pestilence, the Tyrant, and the
throng;
The flames grow silent — slowly there is
heard
The music of a breath-suspending song,
Which, like the kiss of love when life is
young,
Steeps the faint eyes in darkness sweet
and deep;
With ever-changing notes it floats along,
Till on my passive soul there seemed to
creep
A melody, like waves on wrinkled sands
that leap.

XVIII

The warm touch of a soft and tremulous
hand
Wakened me then; lo, Cythna sate re-
clined
Beside me, on the waved and golden sand
Of a clear pool, upon a bank o'ertwined
With strange and star-bright flowers
which to the wind
Breathed divine odor; high above was
spread
The emerald heaven of trees of unknown
kind,
Whose moonlike blooms and bright fruit
overhead
A shadow, which was light, upon the waters
shed.

XIX

And round about sloped many a lawny
mountain
With incense-bearing forests and vast
caves

Of marble radiance, to that mighty foun-
    tain;
And, where the flood its own bright mar-
    gin laves,
Their echoes talk with its eternal waves,
Which from the depths whose jagged
    caverns breed
Their unreposing strife it lifts and heaves,
Till through a chasm of hills they roll,
    and feed
A river deep, which flies with smooth but
    arrowy speed.

XX

As we sate gazing in a trance of wonder,
A boat approached, borne by the musical
    air
Along the waves which sung and sparkled
    under
Its rapid keel. A wingèd Shape sate
    there,
A child with silver-shining wings, so
    fair
That, as her bark did through the waters
    glide,
The shadow of the lingering waves did
    wear
Light, as from starry beams; from side
    to side
While veering to the wind her plumes the
    bark did guide.

XXI

The boat was one curved shell of hollow
    pearl,
Almost translucent with the light divine
Of her within; the prow and stern did
    curl,
Hornèd on high, like the young moon
    supine,
When o'er dim twilight mountains dark
    with pine
It floats upon the sunset's sea of beams,
Whose golden waves in many a purple
    line
Fade fast, till, borne on sunlight's ebbing
    streams,
Dilating, on earth's verge the sunken me-
    teor gleams.

XXII

Its keel has struck the sands beside our
    feet.
Then Cythna turned to me, and from her
    eyes,

Which swam with unshed tears, a look
    more sweet
Than happy love, a wild and glad sur-
    prise,
Glanced as she spake: ' Ay, this is Para-
    dise
And not a dream, and we are all united !
Lo, that is mine own child, who in the
    guise
Of madness came, like day to one be-
    nighted
In lonesome woods; my heart is now too
    well requited ! '

XXIII

And then she wept aloud, and in her arms
Clasped that bright Shape, less marvel-
    lously fair
Than her own human hues and living
    charms,
Which, as she leaned in passion's silence
    there,
Breathed warmth on the cold bosom of
    the air,
Which seemed to blush and tremble with
    delight;
The glossy darkness of her streaming hair
Fell o'er that snowy child, and wrapped
    from sight
The fond and long embrace which did their
    hearts unite.

XXIV

Then the bright child, the plumèd
    Seraph, came,
And fixed its blue and beaming eyes on
    mine,
And said, ' I was disturbed by tremulous
    shame
When once we met, yet knew that I was
    thine
From the same hour in which thy lips
    divine
Kindled a clinging dream within my
    brain,
Which ever waked when I might sleep,
    to twine
Thine image with *her* memory dear;
    again
We meet, exempted now from mortal fear
    or pain.

XXV

' When the consuming flames had wrapped
    ye round,

The hope which I had cherished went
  away;
I fell in agony on the senseless ground,
And hid mine eyes in dust, and far astray
My mind was gone, when bright, like
  dawning day,
The Spectre of the Plague before me flew,
And breathed upon my lips, and seemed
  to say,
" They wait for thee, belovèd ! " — then
  I knew
The death-mark on my breast, and became
  calm anew.

XXVI

' It was the calm of love — for I was
  dying.
I saw the black and half-extinguished
  pyre
In its own gray and shrunken ashes
  lying;
The pitchy smoke of the departed fire
Still hung in many a hollow dome and
  spire
Above the towers, like night, — beneath
  whose shade,
Awed by the ending of their own desire,
The armies stood; a vacancy was made
In expectation's depth, and so they stood
  dismayed.

XXVII

' The frightful silence of that altered mood
The tortures of the dying clove alone,
Till one uprose among the multitude,
And said — " The flood of time is rolling
  on;
We stand upon its brink, whilst *they* are
  gone
To glide in peace down death's myste-
  rious stream.
Have ye done well ? they moulder, flesh
  and bone,
Who might have made this life's enven-
  omed dream
A sweeter draught than ye will ever taste,
  I deem.

XXVIII

' " These perish as the good and great of
  yore
Have perished, and their murderers will
  repent;
Yes, vain and barren tears shall flow
  before

Yon smoke has faded from the firma-
  ment,
Even for this cause, that ye, who must
  lament
The death of those that made this world
  so fair,
Cannot recall them now; but then is lent
To man the wisdom of a high despair,
When such can die, and he live on and
  linger here.

XXIX

' " Ay, ye may fear not now the Pestilence,
From fabled hell as by a charm with-
  drawn;
All power and faith must pass, since
  calmly hence
In pain and fire have unbelievers gone;
And ye must sadly turn away, and moan
In secret, to his home each one returning;
And to long ages shall this hour be
  known,
And slowly shall its memory, ever burn-
  ing,
Fill this dark night of things with an
  eternal morning.

XXX

' " For me that world is grown too void
  and cold,
Since hope pursues immortal destiny
With steps thus slow — therefore shall
  ye behold
How those who love, yet fear not, dare
  to die;
Tell to your children this ! " then suddenly
He sheathed a dagger in his heart, and
  fell;
My brain grew dark in death, and yet to
  me
There came a murmur from the crowd
  to tell
Of deep and mighty change which suddenly
  befell.

XXXI

" Then suddenly I stood, a wingèd Thought,
Before the immortal Senate, and the seat
Of that star-shining Spirit, whence is
  wrought
The strength of its dominion, good and
  great,
The Better Genius of this world's estate.
His realm around one mighty Fane is
  spread,

Elysian islands bright and fortunate,
Calm dwellings of the free and happy
    dead,
Where I am sent to lead !' These wingèd
    words she said,

XXXII

And with the silence of her eloquent
    smile,
Bade us embark in her divine canoe;
Then at the helm we took our seat, the
    while
Above her head those plumes of dazzling
    hue
Into the winds' invisible stream she
    threw,
Sitting beside the prow; like gossamer
On the swift breath of morn the vessel
    flew
O'er the bright whirlpools of that foun-
    tain fair,
Whose shores receded fast while we seemed
    lingering there;

XXXIII

Till down that mighty stream dark, calm
    and fleet,
Between a chasm of cedarn mountains
    riven,
Chased by the thronging winds whose
    viewless feet,
As swift as twinkling beams, had under
    Heaven
From woods and waves wild sounds and
    odors driven,
The boat fled visibly; three nights and
    days,
Borne like a cloud through morn, and
    noon, and even,
We sailed along the winding watery ways
Of the vast stream, a long and labyrinthine
    maze.

XXXIV

A scene of joy and wonder to behold, —
That river's shapes and shadows chang-
    ing ever,
Where the broad sunrise filled with
    deepening gold
Its whirlpools where all hues did spread
    and quiver;
And where melodious falls did burst and
    shiver
Among rocks clad with flowers, the foam
    and spray

Sparkled like stars upon the sunny river;
Or, when the moonlight poured a holier
    day,
One vast and glittering lake around green
    islands lay.

XXXV

Morn, noon and even, that boat of pearl
    outran
The streams which bore it, like the
    arrowy cloud
Of tempest, or the speedier thought of
    man,
Which flieth forth and cannot make
    abode;
Sometimes through forests, deep like
    night, we glode,
Between the walls of mighty mountains
    crowned
With Cyclopean piles, whose turrets
    proud,
The homes of the departed, dimly
    frowned
O'er the bright waves which girt their dark
    foundations round.

XXXVI

Sometimes between the wide and flow-
    ering meadows
Mile after mile we sailed, and 't was
    delight
To see far off the sunbeams chase the
    shadows
Over the grass; sometimes beneath the
    night
Of wide and vaulted caves, whose roofs
    were bright
With starry gems, we fled, whilst from
    their deep
And dark green chasms shades beautiful
    and white,
Amid sweet sounds across our path would
    sweep,
Like swift and lovely dreams that walk the
    waves of sleep.

XXXVII

And ever as we sailed, our minds were
    full
Of love and wisdom, which would over-
    flow
In converse wild, and sweet, and won-
    derful;
And in quick smiles whose light would
    come and go,

Like music o'er wide waves, and in the
flow
Of sudden tears, and in the mute caress;
For a deep shade was cleft, and we did
know,
That virtue, though obscured on Earth,
not less
Survives all mortal change in lasting loveliness.

XXXVIII

Three days and nights we sailed, as
thought and feeling
Number delightful hours — for through
the sky
The spherèd lamps of day and night, revealing
New changes and new glories, rolled on
high,
Sun, Moon and moonlike lamps, the
progeny
Of a diviner Heaven, serene and fair;
On the fourth day, wild as a wind-
wrought sea
The stream became, and fast and faster
bare
The spirit-wingèd boat, steadily speeding
there.

XXXIX

Steady and swift, where the waves rolled
like mountains
Within the vast ravine, whose rifts did
pour
Tumultuous floods from their ten thousand fountains,
The thunder of whose earth-uplifting
roar
Made the air sweep in whirlwinds from
the shore,

Calm as a shade, the boat of that fair
child
Securely fled that rapid stress before,
Amid the topmost spray and sunbows
wild
Wreathed in the silver mist; in joy and
pride we smiled.

XL

The torrent of that wide and raging river
Is passed, and our aërial speed suspended.
We look behind; a golden mist did quiver
When its wild surges with the lake were
blended;
Our bark hung there, as on a line sus-
pended
Between two heavens, — that windless,
waveless lake,
Which four great cataracts from four
vales, attended
By mists, aye feed; from rocks and
clouds they break,
And of that azure sea a silent refuge make.

XLI

Motionless resting on the lake awhile,
I saw its marge of snow-bright moun-
tains rear
Their peaks aloft; I saw each radiant
isle;
And in the midst, afar, even like a sphere
Hung in one hollow sky, did there ap-
pear
The Temple of the Spirit; on the sound
Which issued thence drawn nearer and
more near
Like the swift moon this glorious earth
around,
The charmèd boat approached, and there
its haven found.

ROSALIND AND HELEN

A MODERN ECLOGUE

Rosalind and Helen was begun at Marlow as
early as the summer of 1817, and was sufficiently far advanced to lead Shelley to send
copy to the publisher just before leaving
England in March, 1818; it was finished in
August, at the Baths of Lucca, and published
in the spring of 1819. Shelley's original *Advertisement* to the volume, dated Naples, December 20, 1818, opens with the following:
'The story of *Rosalind and Helen* is, undoubtedly, not an attempt in the highest style
of poetry. It is in no degree calculated to
excite profound meditation; and if, by interesting the affections and amusing the imagination, it awaken a certain ideal melancholy
favorable to the reception of more important
impressions, it will produce in the reader all
that the writer experienced in the composition.
I resigned myself, as I wrote, to the impulse
of the feelings which moulded the conception

of the story; and this impulse determined the pauses of a measure, which only pretends to be regular inasmuch as it corresponds with, and expresses, the irregularity of the imaginations which inspired it.'

The feelings here spoken of ' which moulded the conception of the story' were suggested, in part, by the relation of Mrs. Shelley with a friend of her girlhood, Isabel Baxter, who fell away from her early attachment in consequence of Mrs. Shelley's flight with Shelley in July, 1814, and was afterward reconciled with her. (Dowden, *Life*, ii. 130, 131.) Forman (Type Facsimile of the original edition, Shelley Society's Publications, Second Series, No. 17, Introduction) discusses the matter at length, together with the reflection of political events in England possibly to be detected in the poem. Shelley wrote to Peacock, 'I lay no stress on it one way or the other.' Mrs. Shelley's note develops the reason for this indifference:

' *Rosalind and Helen* was begun at Marlow, and thrown aside, till I found it; and, at my request, it was completed. Shelley had no care for any of his poems that did not emanate from the depths of his mind, and develop some high or abstruse truth. When he does touch on human life and the human heart, no pictures can be more faithful, more delicate, more subtle, or more pathetic. He never mentioned Love, but he shed a grace, borrowed from his own nature, that scarcely any other poet has bestowed on that passion. When he spoke of it as the law of life, which inasmuch as we rebel against, we err and injure ourselves and others, he promulgated that which he considered an irrefragable truth. In his eyes it was the essence of our being, and all woe and pain arose from the war made against it by selfishness, or insensibility, or mistake. By reverting in his mind to this first principle, he discovered the source of many emotions, and could disclose the secrets of all hearts, and his delineations of passion and emotion touch the finest chords in our nature. *Rosalind and Helen* was finished during the summer of 1818, while we were at the Baths of Lucca.'

ROSALIND AND HELEN

Rosalind, Helen, *and her Child.*

Scene. *The Shore of the Lake of Como.*

HELEN

Come hither, my sweet Rosalind.
'T is long since thou and I have met;
And yet methinks it were unkind
Those moments to forget.
Come, sit by me. I see thee stand
By this lone lake, in this far land,
Thy loose hair in the light wind flying,
Thy sweet voice to each tone of even
United, and thine eyes replying
To the hues of yon fair heaven.   10
Come, gentle friend! wilt sit by me?
And be as thou wert wont to be
Ere we were disunited?
None doth behold us now; the power
That led us forth at this lone hour
Will be but ill requited
If thou depart in scorn. Oh, come,
And talk of our abandoned home!
Remember, this is Italy,
And we are exiles. Talk with me   20
Of that our land, whose wilds and floods,
Barren and dark although they be,
Were dearer than these chestnut woods;
Those heathy paths, that inland stream,
And the blue mountains, shapes which seem
Like wrecks of childhood's sunny dream;

Which that we have abandoned now,
Weighs on the heart like that remorse
Which altered friendship leaves. I seek
No more our youthful intercourse.   30
That cannot be! Rosalind, speak,
Speak to me! Leave me not! When morn
    did come,
When evening fell upon our common home,
When for one hour we parted,—do not
    frown;
I would not chide thee, though thy faith is
    broken;
But turn to me. Oh! by this cherished
    token
Of woven hair, which thou wilt not disown,
Turn, as 't were but the memory of me,
And not my scornèd self who prayed to thee!

ROSALIND

Is it a dream, or do I see   40
And hear frail Helen? I would flee
Thy tainting touch; but former years
Arise, and bring forbidden tears;
And my o'erburdened memory
Seeks yet its lost repose in thee.
I share thy crime. I cannot choose
But weep for thee; mine own strange grief
But seldom stoops to such relief;
Nor ever did I love thee less,
Though mourning o'er thy wickedness   50
Even with a sister's woe. I knew
What to the evil world is due,

And therefore sternly did refuse
To link me with the infamy
Of one so lost as Helen. Now,
Bewildered by my dire despair,
Wondering I blush, and weep that thou
Shouldst love me still — thou only ! —
    There,
Let us sit on that gray stone
Till our mournful talk be done.   60

HELEN

Alas ! not there; I cannot bear
The murmur of this lake to hear.
A sound from there, Rosalind dear,
Which never yet I heard elsewhere
But in our native land, recurs,
Even here where now we meet. It stirs
Too much of suffocating sorrow !
In the dell of yon dark chestnut wood
Is a stone seat, a solitude
Less like our own. The ghost of peace 70
Will not desert this spot. To-morrow,
If thy kind feelings should not cease,
We may sit here.

ROSALIND

                Thou lead, my sweet,
And I will follow.

HENRY

                'T is Fenici's seat
Where you are going ? This is not the
    way,
Mamma; it leads behind those trees that
    grow
Close to the little river.

HELEN

                Yes, I know;
I was bewildered. Kiss me and be gay,
Dear boy; why do you sob ?

HENRY

                I do not know;
But it might break any one's heart to see 80
You and the lady cry so bitterly.

HELEN

It is a gentle child, my friend. Go home,
Henry, and play with Lilla till I come.
We only cried with joy to see each other;
We are quite merry now. Good night.

                The boy
Lifted a sudden look upon his mother,

And, in the gleam of forced and hollow
    joy
Which lightened o'er her face, laughed with
    the glee
Of light and unsuspecting infancy,
And whispered in her ear, 'Bring home
    with you   90
That sweet strange lady-friend.' Then off
    he flew,
But stopped, and beckoned with a meaning
    smile,
Where the road turned. Pale Rosalind
    the while,
Hiding her face, stood weeping silently.

In silence then they took the way
Beneath the forest's solitude.
It was a vast and antique wood,
Through which they took their way;
And the gray shades of evening
O'er that green wilderness did fling   100
Still deeper solitude.
Pursuing still the path that wound
The vast and knotted trees around,
Through which slow shades were wander-
    ing,
To a deep lawny dell they came,
To a stone seat beside a spring,
O'er which the columned wood did frame
A roofless temple, like the fane
Where, ere new creeds could faith ob-
    tain,
Man's early race once knelt beneath   110
The overhanging deity.
O'er this fair fountain hung the sky,
Now spangled with rare stars. The snake,
The pale snake, that with eager breath
Creeps here his noontide thirst to slake,
Is beaming with many a mingled hue,
Shed from yon dome's eternal blue,
When he floats on that dark and lucid
    flood
In the light of his own loveliness;
And the birds, that in the fountain dip 120
Their plumes, with fearless fellowship
Above and round him wheel and hover.
The fitful wind is heard to stir
One solitary leaf on high;
The chirping of the grasshopper
Fills every pause. There is emotion
In all that dwells at noontide here;
Then through the intricate wild wood
A maze of life and light and motion
Is woven. But there is stillness now — 130
Gloom, and the trance of Nature now.

The snake is in his cave asleep;
The birds are on the branches dreaming;
Only the shadows creep;
Only the glow-worm is gleaming;
Only the owls and the nightingales
Wake in this dell when daylight fails,
And gray shades gather in the woods;
And the owls have all fled far away
In a merrier glen to hoot and play, 140
For the moon is veiled and sleeping now.
The accustomed nightingale still broods
On her accustomed bough,
But she is mute; for her false mate
Has fled and left her desolate.

This silent spot tradition old
Had peopled with the spectral dead.
For the roots of the speaker's hair felt cold
And stiff, as with tremulous lips he told
That a hellish shape at midnight led 150
The ghost of a youth with hoary hair,
And sate on the seat beside him there,
Till a naked child came wandering by,
When the fiend would change to a lady
fair !
A fearful tale ! the truth was worse;
For here a sister and a brother
Had solemnized a monstrous curse,
Meeting in this fair solitude;
For beneath yon very sky,
Had they resigned to one another 160
Body and soul. The multitude,
Tracking them to the secret wood,
Tore limb from limb their innocent child,
And stabbed and trampled on its mother;
But the youth, for God's most holy grace,
A priest saved to burn in the market-place.

Duly at evening Helen came
To this lone silent spot,
From the wrecks of a tale of wilder sorrow
So much of sympathy to borrow 170
As soothed her own dark lot.
Duly each evening from her home,
With her fair child would Helen come
To sit upon that antique seat,
While the hues of day were pale;
And the bright boy beside her feet
Now lay, lifting at intervals
His broad blue eyes on her;
Now, where some sudden impulse calls,
Following. He was a gentle boy 180
And in all gentle sports took joy.
Oft in a dry leaf for a boat,
With a small feather for a sail,

His fancy on that spring would float,
If some invisible breeze might stir
Its marble calm; and Helen smiled
Through tears of awe on the gay child,
To think that a boy as fair as he,
In years which never more may be,
By that same fount, in that same wood, 190
The like sweet fancies had pursued;
And that a mother, lost like her,
Had mournfully sate watching him.
Then all the scene was wont to swim
Through the mist of a burning tear.
For many months had Helen known
This scene; and now she thither turned
Her footsteps, not alone.
The friend whose falsehood she had
mourned
Sate with her on that seat of stone. 200
Silent they sate; for evening,
And the power its glimpses bring,
Had with one awful shadow quelled
The passion of their grief. They sate
With linkèd hands, for unrepelled
Had Helen taken Rosalind's.
Like the autumn wind, when it unbinds
The tangled locks of the nightshade's hair
Which is twined in the sultry summer air
Round the walls of an outworn sepulchre,
Did the voice of Helen, sad and sweet, 211
And the sound of her heart that ever beat
As with sighs and words she breathed on
her,
Unbind the knots of her friend's despair,
Till her thoughts were free to float and flow;
And from her laboring bosom now,
Like the bursting of a prisoned flame,
The voice of a long-pent sorrow came.

ROSALIND

I saw the dark earth fall upon
The coffin; and I saw the stone 220
Laid over him whom this cold breast
Had pillowed to his nightly rest !
Thou knowest not, thou canst not know
My agony. Oh ! I could not weep.
The sources whence such blessings flow
Were not to be approached by me !
But I could smile, and I could sleep,
Though with a self-accusing heart.
In morning's light, in evening's gloom,
I watched — and would not thence de-
part — 230
My husband's unlamented tomb.
My children knew their sire was gone;
But when I told them, 'He is dead,'

They laughed aloud in frantic glee,
They clapped their hands and leaped about,
Answering each other's ecstasy
With many a prank and merry shout.
But I sate silent and alone,
Wrapped in the mock of mourning weed.

They laughed, for he was dead; but I   240
Sate with a hard and tearless eye,
And with a heart which would deny
The secret joy it could not quell,
Low muttering o'er his loathèd name;
Till from that self-contention came
Remorse where sin was none; a hell
Which in pure spirits should not dwell.

I 'll tell thee truth. He was a man
Hard, selfish, loving only gold,
Yet full of guile; his pale eyes ran   250
With tears which each some falsehood told,
And oft his smooth and bridled tongue
Would give the lie to his flushing cheek;
He was a coward to the strong;
He was a tyrant to the weak,
On whom his vengeance he would wreak;
For scorn, whose arrows search the heart,
From many a stranger's eye would dart,
And on his memory cling, and follow
His soul to its home so cold and hollow. 260
He was a tyrant to the weak,
And we were such, alas the day !
Oft, when my little ones at play
Were in youth's natural lightness gay,
Or if they listened to some tale
Of travellers, or of fairyland,
When the light from the wood-fire's dying
     brand
Flashed on their faces, — if they heard
Or thought they heard upon the stair
His footstep, the suspended word   270
Died on my lips; we all grew pale;
The babe at my bosom was hushed with
     fear
If it thought it heard its father near;
And my two wild boys would near my knee
Cling, cowed and cowering fearfully.

I 'll tell thee truth: I loved another.
His name in my ear was ever ringing,
His form to my brain was ever clinging;
Yet, if some stranger breathed that name,
My lips turned white, and my heart beat
     fast.   280
My nights were once haunted by dreams of
     flame,

My days were dim in the shadow cast
By the memory of the same !
Day and night, day and night,
He was my breath and life and light,
For three short years, which soon were
     passed.
On the fourth, my gentle mother
Led me to the shrine, to be
His sworn bride eternally.
And now we stood on the altar stair,   290
When my father came from a distant land,
And with a loud and fearful cry
Rushed between us suddenly.
I saw the stream of his thin gray hair,
I saw his lean and lifted hand,
And heard his words — and live ! O God !
Wherefore do I live ? — ' Hold, hold !'
He cried, ' I tell thee 't is her brother !
Thy mother, boy, beneath the sod
Of yon churchyard rests in her shroud so
     cold;   300
I am now weak, and pale, and old;
We were once dear to one another,
I and that corpse !   Thou art our child !'
Then with a laugh both long and wild
The youth upon the pavement fell.
They found him dead !   All looked on
     me,
The spasms of my despair to see;
But I was calm.   I went away;
I was clammy-cold like clay.
I did not weep; I did not speak;   310
But day by day, week after week,
I walked about like a corpse alive.
Alas ! sweet friend, you must believe
This heart is stone — it did not break.

My father lived a little while,
But all might see that he was dying,
He smiled with such a woful smile.
When he was in the churchyard lying
Among the worms, we grew quite poor,
So that no one would give us bread;   320
My mother looked at me, and said
Faint words of cheer, which only meant
That she could die and be content;
So I went forth from the same church door
To another husband's bed.
And this was he who died at last,
When weeks and months and years had
     passed,
Through which I firmly did fulfil
My duties, a devoted wife,
With the stern step of vanquished will   330
Walking beneath the night of life,

Whose hours extinguished, like slow rain
Falling forever, pain by pain,
The very hope of death's dear rest;
Which, since the heart within my breast
Of natural life was dispossessed,
Its strange sustainer there had been.

When flowers were dead, and grass was
    green
Upon my mother's grave — that mother
Whom to outlive, and cheer, and make 340
My wan eyes glitter for her sake,
Was my vowed task, the single care
Which once gave life to my despair —
When she was a thing that did not stir,
And the crawling worms were cradling her
To a sleep more deep and so more sweet
Than a baby's rocked on its nurse's knee,
I lived; a living pulse then beat
Beneath my heart that awakened me.
What was this pulse so warm and free ? 350
Alas ! I knew it could not be
My own dull blood. 'T was like a thought
Of liquid love, that spread and wrought
Under my bosom and in my brain,
And crept with the blood through every
    vein,
And hour by hour, day after day,
The wonder could not charm away
But laid in sleep my wakeful pain,
Until I knew it was a child,
And then I wept. For long, long years 360
These frozen eyes had shed no tears;
But now — 't was the season fair and mild
When April has wept itself to May;
I sate through the sweet sunny day
By my window bowered round with leaves,
And down my cheeks the quick tears ran
Like twinkling rain-drops from the eaves,
When warm spring showers are passing
    o'er.
O Helen, none can ever tell
The joy it was to weep once more ! 370

I wept to think how hard it were
To kill my babe, and take from it
The sense of light, and the warm air,
And my own fond and tender care,
And love and smiles; ere I knew yet
That these for it might, as for me,
Be the masks of a grinning mockery.
And haply, I would dream, 't were sweet
To feed it from my faded breast,
Or mark my own heart's restless beat 380
Rock it to its untroubled rest,

And watch the growing soul beneath
Dawn in faint smiles; and hear its breath,
Half interrupted by calm sighs,
And search the depth of its fair eyes
For long departed memories !
And so I lived till that sweet load
Was lightened.   Darkly forward flowed
The stream of years, and on it bore
Two shapes of gladness to my sight; 390
Two other babes, delightful more,
In my lost soul's abandoned night,
Than their own country ships may be
Sailing towards wrecked mariners
Who cling to the rock of a wintry sea.
For each, as it came, brought soothing
    tears;
And a loosening warmth, as each one lay
Sucking the sullen milk away,
About my frozen heart did play,
And weaned it, oh, how painfully — 400
As they themselves were weaned each one
From that sweet food — even from the
    thirst
Of death, and nothingness, and rest,
Strange inmate of a living breast,
Which all that I had undergone
Of grief and shame, since she who first
The gates of that dark refuge closed
Came to my sight, and almost burst
The seal of that Lethean spring —
But these fair shadows interposed. 410
For all delights are shadows now !
And from my brain to my dull brow
The heavy tears gather and flow.
I cannot speak — oh, let me weep !

The tears which fell from her wan eyes
Glimmered among the moonlight dew.
Her deep hard sobs and heavy sighs
Their echoes in the darkness threw.
When she grew calm, she thus did keep
The tenor of her tale: —

                  He died; 420
I know not how; he was not old,
If age be numbered by its years;
But he was bowed and bent with fears,
Pale with the quenchless thirst of gold,
Which, like fierce fever, left him weak;
And his strait lip and bloated cheek
Were warped in spasms by hollow sneers;
And selfish cares with barren plough,
Not age, had lined his narrow brow,
And foul and cruel thoughts, which feed 430
Upon the withering life within,

Like vipers on some poisonous weed.
Whether his ill were death or sin
None knew, until he died indeed,
And then men owned they were the same.

Seven days within my chamber lay
That corse, and my babes made holiday.
At last, I told them what is death.
The eldest, with a kind of shame,
Came to my knees with silent breath,   440
And sate awe-stricken at my feet;
And soon the others left their play,
And sate there too.   It is unmeet
To shed on the brief flower of youth
The withering knowledge of the grave.
From me remorse then wrung that truth.
I could not bear the joy which gave
Too just a response to mine own.
In vain.   I dared not feign a groan;
And in their artless looks I saw,   450
Between the mists of fear and awe,
That my own thought was theirs; and they
Expressed it not in words, but said,
Each in its heart, how every day
Will pass in happy work and play,
Now he is dead and gone away !

After the funeral all our kin
Assembled, and the will was read.
My friend, I tell thee, even the dead
Have strength, their putrid shrouds within,
To blast and torture.   Those who live   461
Still fear the living, but a corse
Is merciless, and Power doth give
To such pale tyrants half the spoil
He rends from those who groan and toil,
Because they blush not with remorse
Among their crawling worms.   Behold,
I have no child ! my tale grows old
With grief, and staggers; let it reach
The limits of my feeble speech,   470
And languidly at length recline
On the brink of its own grave and mine.

Thou knowest what a thing is Poverty
Among the fallen on evil days.
'T is Crime, and Fear, and Infamy,
And houseless Want in frozen ways
Wandering ungarmented, and Pain,
And, worse than all, that inward stain,
Foul Self-contempt, which drowns in sneers
Youth's starlight smile, and makes its
       tears   480
First like hot gall, then dry forever !
And well thou knowest a mother never

Could doom her children to this ill,
And well he knew the same.   The will
Imported that, if e'er again
I sought my children to behold,
Or in my birthplace did remain
Beyond three days, whose hours were told,
They should inherit nought; and he,
To whom next came their patrimony,   490
A sallow lawyer, cruel and cold,
Aye watched me, as the will was read,
With eyes askance, which sought to see
The secrets of my agony;
And with close lips and anxious brow
Stood canvassing still to and fro
The chance of my resolve, and all
The dead man's caution just did call;
For in that killing lie 't was said —
' She is adulterous, and doth hold   500
In secret that the Christian creed
Is false, and therefore is much need
That I should have a care to save
My children from eternal fire.'
Friend, he was sheltered by the grave,
And therefore dared to be a liar !
In truth, the Indian on the pyre
Of her dead husband, half consumed,
As well might there be false as I
To those abhorred embraces doomed,   510
Far worse than fire's brief agony.
As to the Christian creed, if true
Or false, I never questioned it;
I took it as the vulgar do;
Nor my vexed soul had leisure yet
To doubt the things men say, or deem
That they are other than they seem.

All present who those crimes did hear,
In feigned or actual scorn and fear,
Men, women, children, slunk away,   520
Whispering with self-contented pride
Which half suspects its own base lie.
I spoke to none, nor did abide,
But silently I went my way,
Nor noticed I where joyously
Sate my two younger babes at play
In the courtyard through which I passed;
But went with footsteps firm and fast
Till I came to the brink of the ocean
       green,
And there, a woman with gray hairs,   530
Who had my mother's servant been,
Kneeling, with many tears and prayers,
Made me accept a purse of gold,
Half of the earnings she had kept
To refuge her when weak and old.

With woe, which never sleeps or slept,
I wander now. 'T is a vain thought —
But on yon Alp, whose snowy head
'Mid the azure air is islanded,
(We see it — o'er the flood of cloud,   540
Which sunrise from its eastern caves
Drives, wrinkling into golden waves,
Hung with its precipices proud —
From that gray stone where first we met)
There — now who knows the dead feel
     nought ? —
Should be my grave; for he who yet
Is my soul's soul once said: ' 'T were sweet
'Mid stars and lightnings to abide,
And winds, and lulling snows that beat
With their soft flakes the mountain wide,
Where weary meteor lamps repose,   551
And languid storms their pinions close,
And all things strong and bright and pure,
And ever during, aye endure.
Who knows, if one were buried there,
But these things might our spirits make,
Amid the all-surrounding air,
Their own eternity partake ? '
Then 't was a wild and playful saying
At which I laughed or seemed to laugh. 560
They were his words — now heed my pray-
     ing,
And let them be my epitaph.
Thy memory for a term may be
My monument. Wilt remember me ?
I know thou wilt; and canst forgive,
Whilst in this erring world to live
My soul disdained not, that I thought
Its lying forms were worthy aught,
And much less thee.

HELEN

          Oh, speak not so !
But come to me and pour thy woe   570
Into this heart, full though it be,
Aye overflowing with its own.
I thought that grief had severed me
From all beside who weep and groan,
Its likeness upon earth to be —
Its express image; but thou art
More wretched. Sweet, we will not part
Henceforth, if death be not division;
If so, the dead feel no contrition.
But wilt thou hear, since last we parted, 580
All that has left me broken-hearted ?

ROSALIND

Yes, speak. The faintest stars are scarcely
     shorn

Of their thin beams by that delusive morn
Which sinks again in darkness, like the
     light
Of early love, soon lost in total night.

HELEN

Alas ! Italian winds are mild,
But my bosom is cold — wintry cold;
When the warm air weaves, among the
     fresh leaves,
Soft music, my poor brain is wild,
And I am weak like a nursling child,   590
Though my soul with grief is gray and
     old.

ROSALIND

Weep not at thine own words, though they
     must make
Me weep. What is thy tale ?

HELEN

          I fear 't will shake
Thy gentle heart with tears. Thou well
Rememberest when we met no more;
And, though I dwelt with Lionel,
That friendless caution pierced me sore
With grief; a wound my spirit bore
Indignantly — but when he died,
With him lay dead both hope and pride.

Alas ! all hope is buried now.   601
But then men dreamed the aged earth
Was laboring in that mighty birth
Which many a poet and a sage
Has aye foreseen — the happy age
When truth and love shall dwell below
Among the works and ways of men;
Which on this world not power but will
Even now is wanting to fulfil.

Among mankind what thence befell   610
Of strife, how vain, is known too well;
When Liberty's dear pæan fell
'Mid murderous howls. To Lionel,
Though of great wealth and lineage high,
Yet through those dungeon walls there
     came
Thy thrilling light, O Liberty !
And as the meteor's midnight flame
Startles the dreamer, sun-like truth
Flashed on his visionary youth,
And filled him, not with love, but faith, 620
And hope, and courage mute in death;
For love and life in him were twins,
Born at one birth. In every other

First life, then love, its course begins,
Though they be children of one mother;
And so through this dark world they fleet
Divided, till in death they meet;
But he loved all things ever. Then
He passed amid the strife of men,
And stood at the throne of armèd power
Pleading for a world of woe.   631
Secure as one on a rock-built tower
O'er the wrecks which the surge trails to
     and fro,
'Mid the passions wild of humankind
He stood, like a spirit calming them;
For, it was said, his words could bind
Like music the lulled crowd, and stem
That torrent of unquiet dream
Which mortals truth and reason deem,
But is revenge and fear and pride.   640
Joyous he was; and hope and peace
On all who heard him did abide,
Raining like dew from his sweet talk,
As where the evening star may walk
Along the brink of the gloomy seas,
Liquid mists of splendor quiver.
His very gestures touched to tears
The unpersuaded tyrant, never
So moved before; his presence stung
The torturers with their victim's pain,   650
And none knew how; and through their
     ears
The subtle witchcraft of his tongue
Unlocked the hearts of those who keep
Gold, the world's bond of slavery.
Men wondered, and some sneered to see
One sow what he could never reap;
For he is rich, they said, and young,
And might drink from the depths of luxury.
If he seeks fame, fame never crowned
The champion of a trampled creed;   660
If he seeks power, power is enthroned
'Mid ancient rights and wrongs, to feed
Which hungry wolves with praise and spoil
Those who would sit near power must toil;
And such, there sitting, all may see.
What seeks he ?   All that others seek
He casts away, like a vile weed
Which the sea casts unreturningly.
That poor and hungry men should break
The laws which wreak them toil and scorn
We understand; but Lionel,   671
We know, is rich and nobly born.
So wondered they; yet all men loved
Young Lionel, though few approved;
All but the priests, whose hatred fell
Like the unseen blight of a smiling day,

The withering honey-dew which clings
Under the bright green buds of May
Whilst they unfold their emerald wings;
For he made verses wild and queer   680
On the strange creeds priests hold so dear
Because they bring them land and gold.
Of devils and saints and all such gear
He made tales which whoso heard or read
Would laugh till he were almost dead.
So this grew a proverb: ' Don't get old
Till Lionel's *Banquet in Hell* you hear,
And then you will laugh yourself young
     again.'
So the priests hated him, and he
Repaid their hate with cheerful glee.   690

Ah, smiles and joyance quickly died,
For public hope grew pale and dim
In an altered time and tide,
And in its wasting withered him,
As a summer flower that blows too soon
Droops in the smile of the waning moon,
When it scatters through an April night
The frozen dews of wrinkling blight.
None now hoped more.   Gray Power was
     seated
Safely on her ancestral throne;   700
And Faith, the Python, undefeated
Even to its blood-stained steps dragged on
Her foul and wounded train; and men
Were trampled and deceived again,
And words and shows again could bind
The wailing tribes of humankind
In scorn and famine.   Fire and blood
Raged round the raging multitude,
To fields remote by tyrants sent
To be the scornèd instrument   710
With which they drag from mines of gore
The chains their slaves yet ever wore;
And in the streets men met each other,
And by old altars and in halls,
And smiled again at festivals.
But each man found in his heart's brother
Cold cheer; for all, though half deceived,
The outworn creeds again believed,
And the same round anew began
Which the weary world yet ever ran.   720

Many then wept, not tears, but gall,
Within their hearts, like drops which fall
Wasting the fountain-stone away.
And in that dark and evil day
Did all desires and thoughts that claim
Men's care — ambition, friendship, fame,
Love, hope, though hope was now despair —

Indue the colors of this change,
As from the all-surrounding air   729
The earth takes hues obscure and strange,
When storm and earthquake linger there.

And so, my friend, it then befell
To many, — most to Lionel,
Whose hope was like the life of youth
Within him, and when dead became
A spirit of unresting flame,
Which goaded him in his distress
Over the world's vast wilderness.
Three years he left his native land,
And on the fourth, when he returned,   740
None knew him; he was stricken deep
With some disease of mind, and turned
Into aught unlike Lionel.
On him — on whom, did he pause in sleep,
Serenest smiles were wont to keep,
And, did he wake, a wingèd band
Of bright Persuasions, which had fed
On his sweet lips and liquid eyes,
Kept their swift pinions half outspread
To do on men his least command —   750
On him, whom once 't was paradise
Even to behold, now misery lay.
In his own heart 't was merciless —
To all things else none may express
Its innocence and tenderness.

'T was said that he had refuge sought
In love from his unquiet thought
In distant lands, and been deceived
By some strange show; for there were found,
Blotted with tears — as those relieved   760
By their own words are wont to do —
These mournful verses on the ground,
By all who read them blotted too.

'How am I changed! my hopes were once
   like fire;
   I loved, and I believed that life was love.
How am I lost! on wings of swift desire
   Among Heaven's winds my spirit once
   did move.
I slept, and silver dreams did aye inspire
   My liquid sleep; I woke, and did approve
All Nature to my heart, and thought to
   make   770
A paradise of earth for one sweet sake.

'I love, but I believe in love no more.
   I feel desire, but hope not. Oh, from
   sleep

Most vainly must my weary brain implore
   Its long lost flattery now! I wake to
   weep,
And sit through the long day gnawing the
   core
   Of my bitter heart, and, like a miser,
   keep —
Since none in what I feel take pain or
   pleasure —
To my own soul its self-consuming treasure.'

He dwelt beside me near the sea;   780
And oft in evening did we meet,
When the waves, beneath the starlight,
   flee
O'er the yellow sands with silver feet,
And talked. Our talk was sad and sweet,
Till slowly from his mien there passed
The desolation which it spoke;
And smiles — as when the lightning's blast
Has parched some heaven-delighting oak,
The next spring shows leaves pale and
   rare,
But like flowers delicate and fair,   790
On its rent boughs — again arrayed
His countenance in tender light;
His words grew subtle fire, which made
The air his hearers breathed delight;
His motions, like the winds, were free,
Which bend the bright grass gracefully,
Then fade away in circlets faint;
And wingèd Hope — on which upborne
His soul seemed hovering in his eyes,
Like some bright spirit newly born   800
Floating amid the sunny skies —
Sprang forth from his rent heart anew.
Yet o'er his talk, and looks, and mien,
Tempering their loveliness too keen,
Past woe its shadow backward threw;
Till, like an exhalation spread
From flowers half drunk with evening dew,
They did become infectious — sweet
And subtle mists of sense and thought,
Which wrapped us soon, when we might
   meet,   810
Almost from our own looks and aught
The wild world holds. And so his mind
Was healed, while mine grew sick with
   fear;
For ever now his health declined,
Like some frail bark which cannot bear
The impulse of an altered wind,
Though prosperous; and my heart grew
   full,

'Mid its new joy, of a new care;
For his cheek became, not pale, but fair,
As rose-o'ershadowed lilies are;   820
And soon his deep and sunny hair,
In this alone less beautiful,
Like grass in tombs grew wild and rare.
The blood in his translucent veins
Beat, not like animal life, but love
Seemed now its sullen springs to move,
When life had failed, and all its pains;
And sudden sleep would seize him oft
Like death, so calm, — but that a tear,
His pointed eye-lashes between,   830
Would gather in the light serene
Of smiles whose lustre bright and soft
Beneath lay undulating there.
His breath was like inconstant flame
As eagerly it went and came;
And I hung o'er him in his sleep,
Till, like an image in the lake
Which rains disturb, my tears would break
The shadow of that slumber deep.
Then he would bid me not to weep,   840
And say, with flattery false yet sweet,
That death and he could never meet,
If I would never part with him.
And so we loved, and did unite
All that in us was yet divided;
For when he said, that many a rite,
By men to bind but once provided,
Could not be shared by him and me,
Or they would kill him in their glee,
I shuddered, and then laughing said —
'We will have rites our faith to bind,   851
But our church shall be the starry night,
Our altar the grassy earth outspread,
And our priest the muttering wind.'

'T was sunset as I spoke.   One star
Had scarce burst forth, when from afar
The ministers of misrule sent
Seized upon Lionel, and bore
His chained limbs to a dreary tower,
In the midst of a city vast and wide.   860
For he, they said, from his mind had
    bent
Against their gods keen blasphemy,
For which, though his soul must roasted
    be
In hell's red lakes immortally,
Yet even on earth must he abide
The vengeance of their slaves: a trial,
I think, men call it.   What avail
Are prayers and tears, which chase de-
    nial

From the fierce savage nursed in hate ?
What the knit soul that pleading and
    pale   870
Makes wan the quivering cheek which
    late
It painted with its own delight ?
We were divided.   As I could,
I stilled the tingling of my blood,
And followed him in their despite,
As a widow follows, pale and wild,
The murderers and corse of her only child;
And when we came to the prison door,
And I prayed to share his dungeon floor
With prayers which rarely have been
    spurned,   880
And when men drove me forth, and I
Stared with blank frenzy on the sky, —
A farewell look of love he turned,
Half calming me; then gazed awhile,
As if through that black and massy pile,
And through the crowd around him there,
And through the dense and murky air,
And the thronged streets, he did espy
What poets know and prophesy;
And said, with voice that made them
    shiver   890
And clung like music in my brain,
And which the mute walls spoke again
Prolonging it with deepened strain —
'Fear not the tyrants shall rule forever,
Or the priests of the bloody faith;
They stand on the brink of that mighty
    river,
Whose waves they have tainted with death;
It is fed from the depths of a thousand
    dells,
Around them it foams, and rages, and
    swells,
And their swords and their sceptres I float-
    ing see,   900
Like wrecks, in the surge of eternity.'

I dwelt beside the prison gate;
And the strange crowd that out and in
Passed, some, no doubt, with nine own
    fate,
Might have fretted me with its ceaseless
    din,
But the fever of care was louder within.
Soon but too late, in penitence
Or fear, his foes released him thence.
I saw his thin and languid form,
As leaning on the jailor's arm,   910
Whose hardened eyes grew moist the while
To meet his mute and faded smile

And hear his words of kind farewell,
He tottered forth from his damp cell.
Many had never wept before,
From whom fast tears then gushed and
    fell;
Many will relent no more,
Who sobbed like infants then; ay, all
Who thronged the prison's stony hall,
The rulers or the slaves of law,   920
Felt with a new surprise and awe
That they were human, till strong shame
Made them again become the same.
The prison bloodhounds, huge and grim,
From human looks the infection caught,
And fondly crouched and fawned on him;
And men have heard the prisoners say,
Who in their rotting dungeons lay,
That from that hour, throughout one
    day,
The fierce despair and hate which kept 930
Their trampled bosoms almost slept,
Where, like twin vultures, they hung feed-
    ing
On each heart's wound, wide torn and
    bleeding, —
Because their jailors' rule, they thought,
Grew merciful, like a parent's sway.

I know not how, but we were free;
And Lionel sate alone with me,
As the carriage drove through the streets
    apace;
And we looked upon each other's face;
And the blood in our fingers intertwined 940
Ran like the thoughts of a single mind,
As the swift emotions went and came
Through the veins of each united frame.
So through the long, long streets we passed
Of the million-peopled City vast;
Which is that desert, where each one
Seeks his mate yet is alone,
Beloved and sought and mourned of none;
Until the clear blue sky was seen,
And the grassy meadows bright and
    green.   950
And then I sunk in his embrace
Enclosing there a mighty space
Of love; and so we travelled on
By woods, and fields of yellow flowers,
And towns, and villages, and towers,
Day after day of happy hours.
It was the azure time of June,
When the skies are deep in the stainless
    noon,
And the warm and fitful breezes shake

The fresh green leaves of the hedge-row
    briar;   960
And there were odors then to make
The very breath we did respire
A liquid element, whereon
Our spirits, like delighted things
That walk the air on subtle wings,
Floated and mingled far away
'Mid the warm winds of the sunny day.
And when the evening star came forth
Above the curve of the new bent moon,
And light and sound ebbed from the
    earth,   970
Like the tide of the full and the weary
    sea
To the depths of its own tranquillity,
Our natures to its own repose
Did the earth's breathless sleep attune;
Like flowers, which on each other close
Their languid leaves when daylight's gone,
We lay, till new emotions came,
Which seemed to make each mortal frame
One soul of interwoven flame,
A life in life, a second birth   980
In worlds diviner far than earth; —
Which, like two strains of harmony
That mingle in the silent sky,
Then slowly disunite, passed by
And left the tenderness of tears,
A soft oblivion of all fears,
A sweet sleep: — so we travelled on
Till we came to the home of Lionel,
Among the mountains wild and lone,
Beside the hoary western sea,   990
Which near the verge of the echoing shore
The massy forest shadowed o'er.

The ancient steward with hair all hoar,
As we alighted, wept to see
His master changed so fearfully;
And the old man's sobs did waken me
From my dream of unremaining gladness;
The truth flashed o'er me like quick mad-
    ness
When I looked, and saw that there was
    death
On Lionel. Yet day by day   1000
He lived, till fear grew hope and faith,
And in my soul I dared to say,
Nothing so bright can pass away;
Death is dark, and foul, and dull,
But he is — oh, how beautiful!
Yet day by day he grew more weak,
And his sweet voice, when he might
    speak,

Which ne'er was loud, became more low;
And the light which flashed through his
    waxen cheek
Grew faint, as the rose-like hues which
    flow   1010
From sunset o'er the Alpine snow;
And death seemed not like death in him,
For the spirit of life o'er every limb
Lingered, a mist of sense and thought.
When the summer wind faint odors
    brought
From mountain flowers, even as it passed,
His cheek would change, as the noonday
    sea
Which the dying breeze sweeps fitfully.
If but a cloud the sky o'ercast,   1019
You might see his color come and go,
And the softest strain of music made
Sweet smiles, yet sad, arise and fade
Amid the dew of his tender eyes;
And the breath, with intermitting flow,
Made his pale lips quiver and part.
You might hear the beatings of his heart,
Quick but not strong; and with my
    tresses
When oft he playfully would bind
In the bowers of mossy lonelinesses
His neck, and win me so to mingle   1030
In the sweet depth of woven caresses,
And our faint limbs were intertwined, —
Alas! the unquiet life did tingle
From mine own heart through every
    vein,
Like a captive in dreams of liberty,
Who beats the walls of his stony cell.
But his, it seemed already free,
Like the shadow of fire surrounding me!
On my faint eyes and limbs did dwell
That spirit as it passed, till soon —   1040
As a frail cloud wandering o'er the moon,
Beneath its light invisible,
Is seen when it folds its gray wings
    again
To alight on midnight's dusky plain —
I lived and saw, and the gathering soul
Passed from beneath that strong control,
And I fell on a life which was sick with
    fear
Of all the woe that now I bear.

Amid a bloomless myrtle wood,
On a green and sea-girt promontory   1050
Not far from where we dwelt, there
    stood,
In record of a sweet sad story,

An altar and a temple bright
Circled by steps, and o'er the gate
Was sculptured, ' To Fidelity; '
And in the shrine an image sate
All veiled; but there was seen the light
Of smiles which faintly could express
A mingled pain and tenderness
Through that ethereal drapery.   1060
The left hand held the head, the right —
Beyond the veil, beneath the skin,
You might see the nerves quivering
    within —
Was forcing the point of a barbèd dart
Into its side-convulsing heart.
An unskilled hand, yet one informed
With genius, had the marble warmed
With that pathetic life.   This tale
It told: A dog had from the sea,
When the tide was raging fearfully,   1070
Dragged Lionel's mother, weak and pale,
Then died beside her on the sand,
And she that temple thence had planned;
But it was Lionel's own hand
Had wrought the image.   Each new moon
That lady did, in this lone fane,
The rites of a religion sweet
Whose god was in her heart and brain.
The seasons' loveliest flowers were strewn
On the marble floor beneath her feet,   1080
And she brought crowns of sea-buds
    white
Whose odor is so sweet and faint,
And weeds, like branching chrysolite,
Woven in devices fine and quaint;
And tears from her brown eyes did stain
The altar; need but look upon
That dying statue, fair and wan,
If tears should cease, to weep again;
And rare Arabian odors came,
Through the myrtle copses, steaming
    thence   1090
From the hissing frankincense,
Whose smoke, wool-white as ocean foam,
Hung in dense flocks beneath the dome —
That ivory dome, whose azure night
With golden stars, like heaven, was bright
O'er the split cedar's pointed flame;
And the lady's harp would kindle there
The melody of an old air,
Softer than sleep; the villagers
Mixed their religion up with hers,   1100
And, as they listened round, shed tears.

One eve he led me to this fane.
Daylight on its last purple cloud

Was lingering gray, and soon her strain
The nightingale began; now loud,
Climbing in circles the windless sky,
Now dying music; suddenly
'T is scattered in a thousand notes;
And now to the hushed ear it floats
Like field-smells known in infancy,   1110
Then, failing, soothes the air again.
We sate within that temple lone,
Pavilioned round with Parian stone;
His mother's harp stood near, and oft
I had awakened music soft
Amid its wires; the nightingale
Was pausing in her heaven-taught tale.
' Now drain the cup,' said Lionel,
' Which the poet-bird has crowned so
    well
With the wine of her bright and liquid
    song !   1120
Heard'st thou not sweet words among
That heaven-resounding minstrelsy ?
Heard'st thou not that those who die
Awake in a world of ecstasy ?
That love, when limbs are interwoven,
And sleep, when the night of life is cloven,
And thought, to the world's dim bound-
    aries clinging,
And music, when one beloved is singing,
Is death ?   Let us drain right joyously
The cup which the sweet bird fills for
    me.'   1130
He paused, and to my lips he bent
His own; like spirit his words went
Through all my limbs with the speed of
    fire;
And his keen eyes, glittering through
    mine,
Filled me with the flame divine
Which in their orbs was burning far,
Like the light of an unmeasured star
In the sky of midnight dark and deep;
Yes, 't was his soul that did inspire   1139
Sounds which my skill could ne'er awaken;
And first, I felt my fingers sweep
The harp, and a long quivering cry
Burst from my lips in symphony;
The dusk and solid air was shaken,
As swift and swifter the notes came
From my touch, that wandered like quick
    flame,
And from my bosom, laboring
With some unutterable thing.
The awful sound of my own voice made
My faint lips tremble; in some mood   1150
Of wordless thought Lionel stood

So pale, that even beside his cheek
The snowy column from its shade
Caught whiteness; yet his countenance,
Raised upward, burned with radiance
Of spirit-piercing joy whose light,
Like the moon struggling through the night
Of whirlwind-rifted clouds, did break
With beams that might not be confined.
I paused, but soon his gestures kindled
New power, as by the moving wind   1161
The waves are lifted; and my song
To low soft notes now changed and dwin-
    dled,
And, from the twinkling wires among,
My languid fingers drew and flung
Circles of life-dissolving sound,
Yet faint; in aëry rings they bound
My Lionel, who, as every strain
Grew fainter but more sweet, his mien
Sunk with the sound relaxedly;   1170
And slowly now he turned to me,
As slowly faded from his face
That awful joy; with look serene
He was soon drawn to my embrace,
And my wild song then died away
In murmurs; words I dare not say
We mixed, and on his lips mine fed
Till they methought felt still and cold.
' What is it with thee, love ? '   I said;
No word, no look, no motion ! yes,   1180
There was a change, but spare to guess,
Nor let that moment's hope be told.
I looked, — and knew that he was dead;
And fell, as the eagle on the plain
Falls when life deserts her brain,
And the mortal lightning is veiled again.

Oh, that I were now dead ! but such —
Did they not, love, demand too much,
Those dying murmurs ? — he forbade.
Oh, that I once again were mad !   1190
And yet, dear Rosalind, not so,
For I would live to share thy woe.
Sweet boy ! did I forget thee too ?
Alas, we know not what we do
When we speak words.

                        No memory more
Is in my mind of that sea-shore.
Madness came on me, and a troop
Of misty shapes did seem to sit
Beside me, on a vessel's poop,   1199
And the clear north wind was driving it.
Then I heard strange tongues, and saw
    strange flowers,

And the stars methought grew unlike ours,
And the azure sky and the stormless sea
Made me believe that I had died
And waked in a world which was to me
Drear hell, though heaven to all beside.
Then a dead sleep fell on my mind,
Whilst animal life many long years
Had rescued from a chasm of tears;
And, when I woke, I wept to find   1210
That the same lady, bright and wise,
With silver locks and quick brown eyes,
The mother of my Lionel,
Had tended me in my distress,
And died some months before.   Nor less
Wonder, but far more peace and joy,
Brought in that hour my lovely boy.
For through that trance my soul had well
The impress of thy being kept;
And if I waked or if I slept,   1220
No doubt, though memory faithless be,
Thy image ever dwelt on me;
And thus, O Lionel, like thee
Is our sweet child.   'T is sure most strange
I knew not of so great a change
As that which gave him birth, who now
Is all the solace of my woe.

That Lionel great wealth had left
By will to me, and that of all
The ready lies of law bereft   1230
My child and me, — might well befall.
But let me think not of the scorn
Which from the meanest I have borne,
When, for my child's belovèd sake,
I mixed with slaves, to vindicate
The very laws themselves do make;
Let me not say scorn is my fate,
Lest I be proud, suffering the same
With those who live in deathless fame.

She ceased. — 'Lo, where red morning
        through the woods   1240
Is burning o'er the dew!' said Rosalind.
And with these words they rose, and
        towards the flood
Of the blue lake, beneath the leaves, now
        wind
With equal steps and fingers intertwined.
Thence to a lonely dwelling, where the
        shore
Is shadowed with steep rocks, and cypresses
Cleave with their dark green cones the
        silent skies
And with their shadows the clear depths
        below,

And where a little terrace from its bowers
Of blooming myrtle and faint lemon
        flowers   1250
Scatters its sense-dissolving fragrance o'er
The liquid marble of the windless lake;
And where the aged forest's limbs look
        hoar
Under the leaves which their green gar-
        ments make,
They come.   'T is Helen's home, and clean
        and white,
Like one which tyrants spare on our own
        land
In some such solitude; its casements bright
Shone through their vine-leaves in the
        morning sun,
And even within 't was scarce like Italy.
And when she saw how all things there
        were planned   1260
As in an English home, dim memory
Disturbed poor Rosalind; she stood as one
Whose mind is where his body cannot
        be,
Till Helen led her where her child yet
        slept,
And said, ' Observe, that brow was Lionel's,
Those lips were his, and so he ever kept
One arm in sleep, pillowing his head with
        it.
You cannot see his eyes — they are two
        wells
Of liquid love.   Let us not wake him yet.'
But Rosalind could bear no more, and
        wept   1270
A shower of burning tears which fell upon
His face, and so his opening lashes shone
With tears unlike his own, as he did leap
In sudden wonder from his innocent sleep.

So Rosalind and Helen lived together
Thenceforth — changed in all else, yet
        friends again,
Such as they were, when o'er the mountain
        heather
They wandered in their youth through sun
        and rain.
And after many years, for human things
Change even like the ocean and the wind,
Her daughter was restored to Rosalind, 1281
And in their circle thence some visitings
Of joy 'mid their new calm would inter-
        vene.
A lovely child she was, of looks serene,
And motions which o'er things indifferent
        shed

The grace and gentleness from whence
    they came.
And Helen's boy grew with her, and they
    fed
From the same flowers of thought, until
    each mind
Like springs which mingle in one flood
    became;   1289
And in their union soon their parents saw
The shadow of the peace denied to them.
And Rosalind — for when the living stem
Is cankered in its heart, the tree must
    fall.—
Died ere her time; and with deep grief and
    awe
The pale survivors followed her remains
Beyond the region of dissolving rains,
Up the cold mountain she was wont to
    call
Her tomb; and on Chiavenna's precipice
They raised a pyramid of lasting ice,
Whose polished sides, ere day had yet
    begun,   1300
Caught the first glow of the unrisen sun,
The last, when it had sunk; and through
    the night

The charioteers of Arctos wheelèd round
Its glittering point, as seen from Helen's
    home,
Whose sad inhabitants each year would
    come,
With willing steps climbing that rugged
    height,
And hang long locks of hair, and garlands
    bound
With amaranth flowers, which, in the
    clime's despite,
Filled the frore air with unaccustomed
    light;
Such flowers as in the wintry memory
    bloom   1310
Of one friend left adorned that frozen
    tomb.

Helen, whose spirit was of softer mould,
Whose sufferings too were less, death slow-
    lier led
Into the peace of his dominion cold.
She died among her kindred, being old.
And know, that if love die not in the dead
As in the living, none of mortal kind
Are blessed as now Helen and Rosalind.

JULIAN AND MADDALO

A CONVERSATION

The meadows with fresh streams, the bees with thyme,
The goats with the green leaves of budding Spring,
Are saturated not — nor Love with tears.
                         VIRGIL'S *Gallus.*

Julian and Maddalo is the fruit of Shelley's first visit to Venice in 1818, where he found Byron, and the poem is a reflection of their companionship, *Julian* standing for Shelley, *Maddalo* for Byron, and the child being Byron's daughter, Allegra. It was written in the fall, at Este, and received its last revision in May, 1819, but was not published, notwithstanding some efforts of Shelley to bring it out, until after his death, when it was included in the *Posthumous Poems*, 1824. Shelley had it in mind to write three other similar poems, laying the scenes at Rome, Florence and Naples, but he did not carry out the plan. He once refers to the tale, or 'conversation' as among 'his saddest verses;' but his important comment on it is contained in a letter to Hunt, August 15, 1819:

'I send you a little poem to give to Ollier for publication, but *without my name.* Peacock will correct the proofs. I wrote it with the idea of offering it to the *Examiner*, but I find it is too long. It was composed last year at Este; two of the characters you will recognize; and the third is also in some degree a painting from nature, but, with respect to time and place, ideal. You will find the little piece, I think, in some degree consistent with your own ideas of the manner in which poetry ought to be written. I have employed a certain familiar style of language to express the actual way in which people talk with each other, whom education and a certain refinement of sentiment have placed above the use of vulgar idioms. I use the word *vulgar* in its most extensive sense. The vulgarity of rank and fashion is as gross in its way as that of poverty, and its cant terms equally expressive of base conceptions, and, therefore, equally unfit for poetry. Not that the familiar style is to be admitted in the treatment of a subject wholly ideal, or in that part of any subject which relates to common life, where the passion, exceeding a certain limit, touches the boundaries of that which is ideal. Strong passion expresses itself in metaphor, borrowed from objects alike remote or near, and casts over all the shadow of its own greatness. But what am I about? If my grandmother sucks eggs, was it I who taught her?

'If *you* would really correct the proof, I need not trouble Peacock, who, I suppose, has enough. Can you take it as a compliment that I prefer to trouble you?

'I do not particularly wish this poem to be known as mine; but, at all events, I would not put my name to it. I leave you to judge whether it is best to throw it into the fire, or to publish it. So much for self — *self*, that burr that will stick to one.'

PREFACE

COUNT MADDALO is a Venetian nobleman of ancient family and of great fortune, who, without mixing much in the society of his countrymen, resides chiefly at his magnificent palace in that city. He is a person of the most consummate genius, and capable, if he would direct his energies to such an end, of becoming the redeemer of his degraded country. But it is his weakness to be proud. He derives, from a comparison of his own extraordinary mind with the dwarfish intellects that surround him, an intense apprehension of the nothingness of human life. His passions and his powers are incomparably greater than those of other men; and, instead of the latter having been employed in curbing the former, they have mutually lent each other strength. His ambition preys upon itself, for want of objects which it can consider worthy of exertion. I say that Maddalo is proud, because I can find no other word to express the concentred and impatient feelings which consume him; but it is on his own hopes and affections only that he seems to trample, for in social life no human being can be more gentle, patient and unassuming than Maddalo. He is cheerful, frank and witty. His more serious conversation is a sort of intoxication; men are held by it as by a spell. He has travelled much; and there is an inexpressible charm in his relation of his adventures in different countries.

Julian is an Englishman of good family, passionately attached to those philosophical notions which assert the power of man over his own mind, and the immense improvements of which. by the extinction of certain moral superstitions, human society may be yet susceptible. Without concealing the evil in the world he is forever speculating how good may be made superior. He is a complete infidel and a scoffer at all things reputed holy; and Maddalo takes a wicked pleasure in drawing out his taunts against religion. What Maddalo thinks on these matters is not exactly known. Julian, in spite of his heterodox opinions, is conjectured by his friends to possess some good qualities. How far this is possible the pious reader will determine. Julian is rather serious.

Of the Maniac I can give no information. He seems, by his own account, to have been disappointed in love. He was evidently a very cultivated and amiable person when in his right senses. His story, told at length, might be like many other stories of the same kind. The unconnected exclamations of his agony will perhaps be found a sufficient comment for the text of every heart.

I RODE one evening with Count Maddalo
Upon the bank of land which breaks the flow
Of Adria towards Venice. A bare strand
Of hillocks, heaped from ever-shifting sand,
Matted with thistles and amphibious weeds,
Such as from earth's embrace the salt ooze breeds,
Is this; an uninhabited sea-side,
Which the lone fisher, when his nets are dried,
Abandons; and no other object breaks
The waste but one dwarf tree and some few stakes   10
Broken and unrepaired, and the tide makes
A narrow space of level sand thereon,
Where 't was our wont to ride while day went down.

This ride was my delight. I love all waste
And solitary places; where we taste
The pleasure of believing what we see
Is boundless, as we wish our souls to be;
And such was this wide ocean, and this shore
More barren than its billows; and yet more
Than all, with a remembered friend I love   20
To ride as then I rode; — for the winds drove
The living spray along the sunny air
Into our faces; the blue heavens were bare,
Stripped to their depths by the awakening north;
And from the waves sound like delight broke forth
Harmonizing with solitude, and sent
Into our hearts aërial merriment.

So, as we rode, we talked; and the swift
    thought,
Winging itself with laughter, lingered not,
But flew from brain to brain, — such glee
    was ours,   30
Charged with light memories of remem-
    bered hours,
None slow enough for sadness; till we came
Homeward, which always makes the spirit
    tame.
This day had been cheerful but cold, and
    now
The sun was sinking, and the wind also.
Our talk grew somewhat serious, as may be
Talk interrupted with such raillery
As mocks itself, because it cannot scorn
The thoughts it would extinguish. 'T was
    forlorn,
Yet pleasing; such as once, so poets tell, 40
The devils held within the dales of Hell,
Concerning God, freewill and destiny;
Of all that earth has been, or yet may be,
All that vain men imagine or believe,
Or hope can paint, or suffering may achieve,
We descanted; and I (for ever still
Is it not wise to make the best of ill ?)
Argued against despondency, but pride
Made my companion take the darker side.
The sense that he was greater than his
    kind   50
Had struck, methinks, his eagle spirit blind
By gazing on its own exceeding light.
Meanwhile the sun paused ere it should
    alight,
Over the horizon of the mountains. Oh,
How beautiful is sunset, when the glow
Of Heaven descends upon a land like thee,
Thou Paradise of exiles, Italy !
Thy mountains, seas and vineyards and the
    towers
Of cities they encircle ! — It was ours
To stand on thee, beholding it; and then, 60
Just where we had dismounted, the Count's
    men
Were waiting for us with the gondola.
As those who pause on some delightful way
Though bent on pleasant pilgrimage, we
    stood
Looking upon the evening, and the flood,
Which lay between the city and the shore,
Paved with the image of the sky. The
    hoar
And aëry Alps towards the north appeared,
Through mist, an heaven-sustaining bul-
    wark reared

Between the east and west; and half the
    sky   70
Was roofed with clouds of rich emblazonry,
Dark purple at the zenith, which still grew
Down the steep west into a wondrous hue
Brighter than burning gold, even to the rent
Where the swift sun yet paused in his
    descent
Among the many-folded hills. They were
Those famous Euganean hills, which bear,
As seen from Lido through the harbor piles,
The likeness of a clump of peakèd isles; 79
And then, as if the earth and sea had been
Dissolved into one lake of fire, were seen
Those mountains towering as from waves
    of flame
Around the vaporous sun, from which there
    came
The inmost purple spirit of light, and made
Their very peaks transparent. 'Ere it
    fade,'
Said my companion, 'I will show you soon
A better station.' So, o'er the lagune
We glided; and from that funereal bark
I leaned, and saw the city, and could mark
How from their many isles, in evening's
    gleam,   90
Its temples and its palaces did seem
Like fabrics of enchantment piled to
    Heaven.
I was about to speak, when — 'We are
    even
Now at the point I meant,' said Maddalo,
And bade the gondolieri cease to row.
'Look, Julian, on the west, and listen well
If you hear not a deep and heavy bell.'
I looked, and saw between us and the sun
A building on an island, — such a one
As age to age might add, for uses vile, 100
A windowless, deformed and dreary pile;
And on the top an open tower, where hung
A bell, which in the radiance swayed and
    swung;
We could just hear its hoarse and iron
    tongue;
The broad sun sunk behind it, and it tolled
In strong and black relief. 'What we
    behold
Shall be the madhouse and its belfry
    tower,'
Said Maddalo; 'and ever at this hour
Those who may cross the water hear that
    bell,
Which calls the maniacs each one from his
    cell   110

To vespers.' — 'As much skill as need to
    pray
In thanks or hope for their dark lot have
    they
To their stern Maker,' I replied. ' O ho !
You talk as in years past,' said Maddalo.
' 'T is strange men change not. You were
    ever still
Among Christ's flock a perilous infidel,
A wolf for the meek lambs — if you can't
    swim,
Beware of Providence.' I looked on him,
But the gay smile had faded in his eye, —
' And such,' he cried, 'is our mortality; 120
And this must be the emblem and the sign
Of what should be eternal and divine !
And, like that black and dreary bell, the
    soul,
Hung in a heaven-illumined tower, must
    toll
Our thoughts and our desires to meet below
Round the rent heart and pray — as mad-
    men do
For what ? they know not, till the night of
    death,
As sunset that strange vision, severeth 128
Our memory from itself, and us from all
We sought, and yet were baffled.' I recall
The sense of what he said, although I mar
The force of his expressions. The broad
    star
Of day meanwhile had sunk behind the hill,
And the black bell became invisible,
And the red tower looked gray, and all
    between,
The churches, ships and palaces were seen
Huddled in gloom; into the purple sea
The orange hues of heaven sunk silently.
We hardly spoke, and soon the gondola
Conveyed me to my lodgings by the way.
    The following morn was rainy, cold, and
    dim.   141
Ere Maddalo arose, I called on him,
And whilst I waited, with his child I played.
A lovelier toy sweet Nature never made;
A serious, subtle, wild, yet gentle being,
Graceful without design, and unforeseeing,
With eyes — oh, speak not of her eyes ! —
    which seem
Twin mirrors of Italian heaven, yet gleam
With such deep meaning as we never see
But in the human countenance. With me
She was a special favorite; I had nursed
Her fine and feeble limbs when she came
    first   152

To this bleak world; and she yet seemed
    to know
On second sight her ancient playfellow,
Less changed than she was by six months or
    so;
For, after her first shyness was worn out,
We sate there, rolling billiard balls about,
When the Count entered. Salutations
    past —
' The words you spoke last night might well
    have cast
A darkness on my spirit. If man be   160
The passive thing you say, I should not see
Much harm in the religions and old saws,
(Though I may never own such leaden
    laws)
Which break a teachless nature to the
    yoke.
Mine is another faith.' Thus much I spoke,
And noting he replied not, added: 'See
This lovely child, blithe, innocent and free;
She spends a happy time with little care,
While we to such sick thoughts subjected
    are   169
As came on you last night. It is our will
That thus enchains us to permitted ill.
We might be otherwise; we might be all
We dream of happy, high, majestical.
Where is the love, beauty and truth we
    seek,
But in our mind ? and if we were not weak,
Should we be less in deed than in desire ? '
'Ay, if we were not weak — and we aspire
How vainly to be strong ! ' said Maddalo;
' You talk Utopia.' ' It remains to know,'
I then rejoined, 'and those who try may
    find   180
How strong the chains are which our spirit
    bind;
Brittle perchance as straw. We are assured
Much may be conquered, much may be
    endured
Of what degrades and crushes us. We
    know
That we have power over ourselves to do
And suffer — what, we know not till we try;
But something nobler than to live and die.
So taught those kings of old philosophy,
Who reigned before religion made men
    blind;
And those who suffer with their suffering
    kind   190
Yet feel this faith religion.' ' My dear
    friend,'
Said Maddalo, ' my judgment will not bend

To your opinion, though I think you might
Make such a system refutation-tight
As far as words go. I knew one like you,
Who to this city came some months ago,
With whom I argued in this sort, and he
Is now gone mad, — and so he answered
    me, —
Poor fellow! but if you would like to go,
We 'll visit him, and his wild talk will
    show   200
How vain are such aspiring theories.'
'I hope to prove the induction otherwise,
And that a want of that true theory still,
Which seeks " a soul of goodness " in things
    ill,
Or in himself or others, has thus bowed
His being. There are some by nature
    proud,
Who patient in all else demand but this —
To love and be beloved with gentleness;
And, being scorned, what wonder if they die
Some living death? this is not destiny   210
But man's own wilful ill.'

              As thus I spoke,
Servants announced the gondola, and we
Through the fast-falling rain and high-
    wrought sea
Sailed to the island where the madhouse
    stands.
We disembarked. The clap of tortured
    hands,
Fierce yells and howlings and lamentings
    keen,
And laughter where complaint had merrier
    been,
Moans, shrieks, and curses, and blasphem-
    ing prayers,   218
Accosted us. We climbed the oozy stairs
Into an old courtyard. I heard on high,
Then, fragments of most touching melody,
But looking up saw not the singer there.
Through the black bars in the tempestuous
    air
I saw, like weeds on a wrecked palace
    growing,
Long tangled locks flung wildly forth, and
    flowing,
Of those who on a sudden were beguiled
Into strange silence, and looked forth and
    smiled
Hearing sweet sounds. Then I: 'Methinks
    there were
A cure of these with patience and kind
    care,'   229

If music can thus move. But what is he,
Whom we seek here?' 'Of his sad history
I know but this,' said Maddalo: 'he came
To Venice a dejected man, and fame
Said he was wealthy, or he had been so.
Some thought the loss of fortune wrought
    him woe;
But he was ever talking in such sort
As you do — far more sadly; he seemed
    hurt,
Even as a man with his peculiar wrong,
To hear but of the oppression of the strong,
Or those absurd deceits (I think with you
In some respects, you know) which carry
    through   241
The excellent impostors of this earth
When they outface detection. He had
    worth,
Poor fellow! but a humorist in his way.'
'Alas, what drove him mad?' 'I cannot
    say;
A lady came with him from France, and
    when
She left him and returned, he wandered
    then
About yon lonely isles of desert sand
Till he grew wild. He had no cash or land
Remaining; the police had brought him
    here;   250
Some fancy took him and he would not bear
Removal; so I fitted up for him
Those rooms beside the sea, to please his
    whim,
And sent him busts and books and urns for
    flowers,
Which had adorned his life in happier
    hours,
And instruments of music. You may guess
A stranger could do little more or less
For one so gentle and unfortunate;
And those are his sweet strains which
    charm the weight
From madmen's chains, and make this Hell
    appear   260
A heaven of sacred silence, hushed to hear.'
'Nay, this was kind of you; he had no
    claim,
As the world says.' 'None — but the very
    same
Which I on all mankind, were I as he
Fallen to such deep reverse. His melody
Is interrupted; now we hear the din
Of madmen, shriek on shriek, again begin.
Let us now visit him; after this strain
He ever communes with himself again,

And sees nor hears not any.' Having said
These words, we called the keeper, and he
    led   271
To an apartment opening on the sea.
There the poor wretch was sitting mourn-
    fully
Near a piano, his pale fingers twined
One with the other, and the ooze and wind
Rushed through an open casement, and did
    sway
His hair, and starred it with the brackish
    spray;
His head was leaning on a music-book,
And he was muttering, and his lean limbs
    shook;   279
His lips were pressed against a folded leaf,
In hue too beautiful for health, and grief
Smiled in their motions as they lay apart.
As one who wrought from his own fervid
    heart
The eloquence of passion, soon he raised
His sad meek face, and eyes lustrous and
    glazed,
And spoke — sometimes as one who wrote,
    and thought
His words might move some heart that
    heeded not,
If sent to distant lands; and then as one
Reproaching deeds never to be undone
With wondering self-compassion; then his
    speech   290
Was lost in grief, and then his words came
    each
Unmodulated, cold, expressionless,
But that from one jarred accent you might
    guess
It was despair made them so uniform;
And all the while the loud and gusty storm
Hissed through the window, and we stood
    behind
Stealing his accents from the envious wind
Unseen. I yet remember what he said
Distinctly; such impression his words made.

'Month after month,' he cried, 'to bear
    this load,   300
And, as a jade urged by the whip and goad,
To drag life on — which like a heavy chain
Lengthens behind with many a link of
    pain ! —
And not to speak my grief — oh, not to dare
To give a human voice to my despair,
But live, and move, and, wretched thing !
    smile on
As if I never went aside to groan;

And wear this mask of falsehood even to
    those
Who are most dear — not for my own re-
    pose —
Alas, no scorn or pain or hate could be 310
So heavy as that falsehood is to me !
But that I cannot bear more altered faces
Than needs must be, more changed and
    cold embraces,
More misery, disappointment and mistrust
To own me for their father. Would the
    dust
Were covered in upon my body now !
That the life ceased to toil within my brow !
And then these thoughts would at the least
    be fled;
Let us not fear such pain can vex the dead.

'What Power delights to torture us ? I
    know   320
That to myself I do not wholly owe
What now I suffer, though in part I may.
Alas ! none strewed sweet flowers upon the
    way
Where, wandering heedlessly, I met pale
    Pain,
My shadow, which will leave me not
    again.
If I have erred, there was no joy in error,
But pain and insult and unrest and terror;
I have not, as some do, bought penitence
With pleasure, and a dark yet sweet of-
    fence;
For then — if love and tenderness and
    truth   330
Had overlived hope's momentary youth,
My creed should have redeemed me from
    repenting;
But loathèd scorn and outrage unrelenting
Met love excited by far other seeming
Until the end was gained; as one from
    dreaming
Of sweetest peace, I woke, and found my
    state
Such as it is —

             'O Thou my spirit's mate !
Who, for thou art compassionate and wise,
Wouldst pity me from thy most gentle eyes
If this sad writing thou shouldst ever
    see —   340
My secret groans must be unheard by thee;
Thou wouldst weep tears bitter as blood to
    know
Thy lost friend's incommunicable woe.

'Ye few by whom my nature has been
 weighed
In friendship, let me not that name de-
 grade
By placing on your hearts the secret load
Which crushes mine to dust. There is one
 road
To peace, and that is truth, which follow
 ye !
Love sometimes leads astray to misery.
Yet think not, though subdued — and I may
 well 350
Say that I am subdued — that the full
 hell
Within me would infect the untainted
 breast
Of sacred Nature with its own unrest;
As some perverted beings think to find
In scorn or hate a medicine for the mind
Which scorn or hate have wounded — oh,
 how vain !
The dagger heals not, but may rend again !
Believe that I am ever still the same
In creed as in resolve; and what may tame
My heart must leave the understanding
 free, 360
Or all would sink in this keen agony;
Nor dream that I will join the vulgar cry;
Or with my silence sanction tyranny;
Or seek a moment's shelter from my pain
In any madness which the world calls gain,
Ambition or revenge or thoughts as stern
As those which make me what I am; or
 turn
To avarice or misanthropy or lust.
Heap on me soon, O grave, thy welcome
 dust !
Till then the dungeon may demand its
 prey, 370
And Poverty and Shame may meet and
 say,
Halting beside me on the public way,
"That love-devoted youth is ours; let's sit
Beside him; he may live some six months
 yet."
Or the red scaffold, as our country bends,
May ask some willing victim; or ye, friends,
May fall under some sorrow, which this
 heart
Or hand may share or vanquish or avert;
I am prepared — in truth, with no proud
 joy,
To do or suffer aught, as when a boy 380
I did devote to justice and to love
My nature, worthless now ! —

 ' I must remove
A veil from my pent mind. 'T is torn
 aside !
O pallid as Death's dedicated bride,
Thou mockery which art sitting by my
 side,
Am I not wan like thee ? at the grave's
 call
I haste, invited to thy wedding-ball,
To greet the ghastly paramour for whom
Thou hast deserted me — and made the
 tomb
Thy bridal bed — but I beside your feet 390
Will lie and watch ye from my winding-
 sheet —
Thus — wide-awake though dead — yet
 stay, oh, stay !
Go not so soon — I know not what I say —
Hear but my reasons — I am mad, I fear,
My fancy is o'erwrought — thou art not
 here;
Pale art thou, 't is most true — but thou
 art gone,
Thy work is finished — I am left alone.
.   .   .   .
'Nay, was it I who wooed thee to this
 breast,
Which like a serpent thou envenomest
As in repayment of the warmth it lent ? 400
Didst thou not seek me for thine own con-
 tent ?
Did not thy love awaken mine ? I thought
That thou wert she who said "You kiss me
 not
Ever; I fear you do not love me now " —
In truth I loved even to my overthrow
Her who would fain forget these words;
 but they
Cling to her mind, and cannot pass away.
.   .   .   .
'You say that I am proud — that when I
 speak
My lip is tortured with the wrongs which
 break
The spirit it expresses. — Never one 410
Humbled himself before, as I have done !
Even the instinctive worm on which we
 tread
Turns, though it wound not — then with
 prostrate head
Sinks in the dust and writhes like me —
 and dies ?
No: wears a living death of agonies !
As the slow shadows of the pointed grass
Mark the eternal periods, his pangs pass,

Slow, ever-moving, making moments be
As mine seem, — each an immortality !

'That you had never seen me — never
   heard   420
My voice, and more than ,all had ne'er en-
   dured
The deep pollution of my loathed em-
   brace —
That your eyes ne'er had lied love in my
   face —
That, like some maniac monk, I had torn out
The nerves of manhood by their bleeding
   root
With mine own quivering fingers, so that
   ne'er
Our hearts had for a moment mingled there
To disunite in horror — these were not
With thee like some suppressed and hideous
   thought
Which flits athwart our musings but can
   find   430
No rest within a pure and gentle mind;
Thou sealedst them with many a bare
   broad word,   .
And sear'dst my memory o'er them, — for
   I heard
And can forget not; — they were ministered
One after one, those curses.   Mix them up
Like self-destroying poisons in one cup,
And they will make one blessing, which
   thou ne'er
Didst imprecate for on me, — death.

                        'It were
A cruel punishment for one most cruel,
If such can love, to make that love the
   fuel   440
Of the mind's hell — hate, scorn, remorse,
   despair;
But *me*, whose heart a stranger's tear might
   wear
As water-drops the sandy fountain-stone,
Who loved and pitied all things, and could
   moan
For woes which others hear not, and could
   see
The absent with the glance of fantasy,
And with the poor and trampled sit and
   weep,
Following the captive to his dungeon deep;
Me — who am as a nerve o'er which do
   creep   449
The else unfelt oppressions of this earth,
And was to thee the flame upon thy hearth,

When all beside was cold: — that thou on me
Shouldst rain these plagues of blistering
   agony !
Such curses are from lips once eloquent
With love's too partial praise ! Let none
   relent
Who intend deeds too dreadful for a name
Henceforth, if an example for the same
They seek: — for thou on me look'dst so,
   and so —
And didst speak thus — and thus.   I live
   to show   459
How much men bear and die not !

                 'Thou wilt tell
With the grimace of hate how horrible
It was to meet my love when thine grew
   less;
Thou wilt admire how I could e'er address
Such features to love's work.   This taunt,
   though true,
(For indeed Nature nor in form nor hue
Bestowed on me her choicest workmanship)
Shall not be thy defence; for since thy lip
Met mine first, years long past, — since
   thine eye kindled
With soft fire under mine, — I have not
   dwindled,
Nor changed in mind or body, or in aught
But as love changes what it loveth not   471
After long years and many trials.

                   'How vain
Are words !   I thought never to speak
   again,
Not even in secret, not to mine own heart;
But from my lips the unwilling accents
   start,
And from my pen the words flow as I write,
Dazzling my eyes with scalding tears ; my
   sight
Is dim to see that charactered in vain
On this unfeeling leaf, which burns the
   brain
And eats into it, blotting all things fair 480
And wise and good which time had written
   there.

Those who inflict must suffer, for they see
The work of their own hearts, and this
   must be
Our chastisement   or recompense. — O
   child !
I would that thine were like to be more
   mild

For both our wretched sakes, — for thine
    the most
Who feelest already all that thou hast lost
Without the power to wish it thine again;
And as slow years pass, a funereal train,
Each with the ghost of some lost hope or
    friend   490
Following it like its shadow, wilt thou bend
No thought on my dead memory ?
· · · · · · · · ·
                    ' Alas, love !
Fear me not — against thee I would not
    move
A finger in despite.   Do I not live
That thou mayst have less bitter cause to
    grieve ?
I give thee tears for scorn, and love for
    hate;
And that thy lot may be less desolate
Than his on whom thou tramplest, I refrain
From that sweet sleep which medicines all
    pain.   499
Then, when thou speakest of me, never say
" He could forgive not." Here I cast away
All human passions, all revenge, all pride;
I think, speak, act no ill; I do but hide
Under these words, like embers, every
    spark
Of that which has consumed me. Quick
    and dark
The grave is yawning — as its roof shall
    cover
My limbs with dust and worms under and
    over,
So let Oblivion hide this grief — the air
Closes upon my accents as despair   509
Upon my heart — let death upon despair ! '

He ceased, and overcome leant back
    awhile;
Then rising, with a melancholy smile,
Went to a sofa, and lay down, and slept
A heavy sleep, and in his dreams he wept,
And muttered some familiar name, and we
Wept without shame in his society.
I think I never was impressed so much;
The man who were not must have lacked a
    touch   518
Of human nature. — Then we lingered not,
Although our argument was quite forgot;
But, calling the attendants, went to dine
At Maddalo's; yet neither cheer nor wine
Could give us spirits, for we talked of him
And nothing else, till daylight made stars
    dim;

And we agreed his was some dreadful ill
Wrought on him boldly, yet unspeakable,
By a dear friend; some deadly change in
    love
Of one vowed deeply, which he dreamed
    not of;
For whose sake he, it seemed, had fixed a
    blot
Of falsehood on his mind which flourished
    not   530
But in the light of all-beholding truth;
And having stamped this canker on his
    youth
She had abandoned him — and how much
    more
Might be his woe, we guessed not; he had
    store
Of friends and fortune once, as we could
    guess
From his nice habits and his gentleness;
These were now lost — it were a grief
    indeed
If he had changed one unsustaining reed
For all that such a man might else adorn.
The colors of his mind seemed yet unworn;
For the wild language of his grief was
    high —   541
Such as in measure were called poetry.
And I remember one remark which then
Maddalo made. He said — ' Most wretched
    men
Are cradled into poetry by wrong;
They learn in suffering what they teach in
    song.'

If I had been an unconnected man,
I, from this moment, should have formed
    some plan
Never to leave sweet Venice, — for to me
It was delight to ride by the lone sea; 550
And then the town is silent — one may
    write
Or read in gondolas by day or night,
Having the little brazen lamp alight,
Unseen, uninterrupted; books are there,
Pictures, and casts from all those statues
    fair
Which were twin-born with poetry, and all
We seek in towns, with little to recall
Regrets for the green country. I might sit
In Maddalo's great palace, and his wit
And subtle talk would cheer the winter
    night   560
And make me know myself, and the fire-
    light

Would flash upon our faces, till the day
Might dawn and make me wonder at my
    stay.
But I had friends in London too. The
    chief
Attraction here was that I sought relief
From the deep tenderness that maniac
    wrought
Within me — 't was perhaps an idle thought,
But I imagined that if day by day   568
I watched him, and but seldom went away,
And studied all the beatings of his heart
With zeal, as men study some stubborn art
For their own good, and could by patience
    find
An entrance to the caverns of his mind,
I might reclaim him from this dark estate.
In friendships I had been most fortunate,
Yet never saw I one whom I would call
More willingly my friend; and this was all
Accomplished not; such dreams of baseless
    good
Oft come and go in crowds and solitude
And leave no trace, — but what I now de-
    signed   580
Made, for long years, impression on my
    mind.
The following morning, urged by my
    affairs,
I left bright Venice.

                    After many years,
And many changes, I returned; the name
Of Venice, and its aspect, was the same;
But Maddalo was travelling far away
Among the mountains of Armenia.
His dog was dead. His child had now be-
    come   588
A woman; such as it has been my doom
To meet with few, a wonder of this earth,
Where there is little of transcendent worth,

Like one of Shakespeare's women. Kindly
    she,
And with a manner beyond courtesy,
Received her father's friend; and, when I
    asked
Of the lorn maniac, she her memory tasked,
And told, as she had heard, the mournful
    tale:
' That the poor sufferer's health began to
    fail
Two years from my departure, but that
    then
The lady, who had left him, came again.
Her mien had been imperious, but she now
Looked meek — perhaps remorse had
    brought her low.   601
Her coming made him better, and they
    stayed
Together at my father's — for I played
As I remember with the lady's shawl;
I might be six years old — but after all
She left him.' ' Why, her heart must have
    been tough.
How did it end ? ' ' And was not this
    enough ?
They met — they parted.' ' Child, is there
    no more ? '
' Something within that interval which bore
The stamp of *why* they parted, *how* they
    met;   610
Yet if thine aged eyes disdain to wet
Those wrinkled cheeks with youth's re-
    membered tears,
Ask me no more, but let the silent years
Be closed and cered over their memory,
As yon mute marble where their corpses
    lie.'
I urged and questioned still; she told me
    how
All happened — but the cold world shall
    not know.

PROMETHEUS UNBOUND

A LYRICAL DRAMA

IN FOUR ACTS

AUDISNE HÆC, AMPHIARÆ, SUB TERRAM ABDITE ?

Prometheus Unbound best combines the various elements of Shelley's genius in their most
complete expression, and unites harmoniously
his lyrically creative power of imagination and
his ' passion for reforming the world.' It is
the fruit of an outburst of poetic energy under the double stimulus of his enthusiastic
Greek studies, begun under Peacock's influ-

ence, and of his delight in the beauty of Italy, whither he had removed for health and rest. It marks his full mastery of his powers. It is, not less than *Queen Mab* and *The Revolt of Islam*, a poem of the moral perfection of man; and, not less than *Alastor* and *Epipsychidion*, a poem of spiritual ideality. He was himself in love with it: 'a poem of a higher character than anything I have yet attempted and perhaps less an imitation of anything that has gone before it,' he writes to Ollier; and again, 'a poem in my best style, whatever that may amount to, . . . the most perfect of my productions,' and 'the best thing I ever wrote;' and finally he says, '*Prometheus Unbound*, I must tell you, is my favorite poem; I charge you, therefore, especially to pet him and feed him with fine ink and good paper. . . . I think, if I can judge by its merits, the *Prometheus* cannot sell beyond twenty copies.' Nor did he lose his affection for it. Trelawny records him as saying, 'If that is not durable poetry, tried by the severest test, I do not know what is. It is a lofty subject, not inadequately treated, and should not perish with me.' . . . 'My friends say my *Prometheus* is too wild, ideal, and perplexed with imagery. It may be so. It has no resemblance to the Greek drama. It is original; and cost me severe mental labor. Authors, like mothers, prefer the children who have given them most trouble.'

The drama was begun in the summer-house of his garden at Este about September, 1818, and the first Act had been finished as early as October 8; it was apparently laid aside, and again taken up at Rome in the spring of 1819, where, under the circumstances described in the preface, the second and third Acts were added, and the work, in its first form, was thus completed by April 6. The fourth Act was an afterthought, and was composed at Florence toward the end of the year. The whole was published, with other poems, in the summer of 1820.

The following extracts from Mrs. Shelley's long and admirable note show the progress of the poem during its composition, the atmosphere of its creation, and its general scheme:

'The first aspect of Italy enchanted Shelley; it seemed a garden of delight placed beneath a clearer and brighter heaven than any he had lived under before. He wrote long descriptive letters during the first year of his residence in Italy, which, as compositions, are the most beautiful in the world, and show how truly he appreciated and studied the wonders of nature and art in that divine land.

'The poetical spirit within him speedily revived with all the power and with more than all the beauty of his first attempts. He meditated three subjects as the groundwork for lyrical Dramas. One was the story of Tasso: of this a slight fragment of a song of Tasso remains. The other was one founded on the book of Job, which he never abandoned in idea, but of which no trace remains among his papers. The third was the *Prometheus Unbound*. The Greek tragedians were now his most familiar companions in his wanderings, and the sublime majesty of Æschylus filled him with wonder and delight. The father of Greek tragedy does not possess the pathos of Sophocles, nor the variety and tenderness of Euripides; the interest on which he founds his dramas is often elevated above human vicissitudes into the mighty passions and throes of gods and demigods — such fascinated the abstract imagination of Shelley.

'We spent a month at Milan, visiting the Lake of Como during that interval. Thence we passed in succession to Pisa, Leghorn, the Baths of Lucca, Venice, Este, Rome, Naples, and back again to Rome, whither we returned early in March, 1819. During all this time Shelley meditated the subject of his drama, and wrote portions of it. Other poems were composed during this interval, and while at the Bagni di Lucca he translated Plato's *Symposium*. But though he diversified his studies, his thoughts centred in the *Prometheus*. At last, when at Rome, during a bright and beautiful spring, he gave up his whole time to the composition. The spot selected for his study was, as he mentions in his preface, the mountainous ruins of the Baths of Caracalla. These are little known to the ordinary visitor at Rome. He describes them in a letter, with that poetry, and delicacy, and truth of description, which rendered his narrated impressions of scenery of unequalled beauty and interest.

'At first he completed the drama in three acts. It was not till several months after, when at Florence, that he conceived that a fourth act, a sort of hymn of rejoicing in the fulfilment of the prophecies with regard to Prometheus, ought to be added to complete the composition.

'The prominent feature of Shelley's theory of the destiny of the human species was, that evil is not inherent in the system of the creation, but an accident that might be expelled. This also forms a portion of Christianity; God made earth and man perfect, till he, by his fall,

'"Brought death into the world and all our woe."

Shelley believed that mankind had only to will that there should be no evil, and there would be none. It is not my part in these notes to notice the arguments that have been urged against this opinion, but to mention the fact that he entertained it, and was indeed attached to it with fervent enthusiasm. That man could be so perfectionized as to be able to expel evil from his own nature, and from the greater part of the creation, was the cardinal point of his system. And the subject he loved best to dwell on, was the image of One warring with the Evil Principle, oppressed not only by it, but by all, even the good, who were deluded into considering evil a necessary portion of humanity; a victim full of fortitude and hope, and the spirit of triumph emanating from a reliance in the ultimate omnipotence of good. Such he had depicted in his last poem, when he made Laon the enemy and the victim of tyrants. He now took a more idealized image of the same subject. He followed certain classical authorities in figuring Saturn as the good principle, Jupiter the usurping evil one, and Prometheus as the regenerator, who, unable to bring mankind back to primitive innocence, used knowledge as a weapon to defeat evil, by leading mankind beyond the state wherein they are sinless through ignorance, to that in which they are virtuous through wisdom. Jupiter punished the temerity of the Titan by chaining him to a rock of Caucasus, and causing a vulture to devour his still-renewed heart. There was a prophecy afloat in heaven portending the fall of Jove, the secret of averting which was known only to Prometheus; and the god offered freedom from torture on condition of its being communicated to him. According to the mythological story, this referred to the offspring of Thetis, who was destined to be greater than his father. Prometheus at last bought pardon for his crime of enriching mankind with his gifts, by revealing the prophecy. Hercules killed the vulture and set him free, and Thetis was married to Peleus the father of Achilles.

‘Shelley adapted the catastrophe of this story to his peculiar views. The son, greater than his father, born of the nuptials of Jupiter and Thetis, was to dethrone Evil and bring back a happier reign than that of Saturn. Prometheus defies the power of his enemy, and endures centuries of torture, till the hour arrives when Jove, blind to the real event, but darkly guessing that some great good to himself will flow, espouses Thetis. At the moment, the Primal Power of the world drives him from his usurped throne, and Strength, in the person of Hercules, liberates Humanity, typified in Prometheus, from the tortures generated by evil done or suffered. Asia, one of the Oceanides, is the wife of Prometheus — she was, according to other mythological interpretations, the same as Venus and Nature. When the Benefactor of Mankind is liberated, Nature resumes the beauty of her prime, and is united to her husband, the emblem of the human race, in perfect and happy union. In the

fourth Act, the poet gives further scope to his imagination, and idealizes the forms of creation, such as we know them, instead of such as they appeared to the Greeks. Maternal Earth, the mighty Parent, is superseded by the Spirit of the Earth — the guide of our planet through the realms of sky — while his fair and weaker companion and attendant, the Spirit of the Moon, receives bliss from the annihilation of Evil in the superior sphere.

‘Shelley develops, more particularly in the lyrics of this drama, his abstruse and imaginative theories with regard to the Creation. It requires a mind as subtle and penetrating as his own to understand the mystic meanings scattered throughout the poem. They elude the ordinary reader by their abstraction and delicacy of distinction, but they are far from vague. It was his design to write prose metaphysical essays on the nature of Man, which would have served to explain much of what is obscure in his poetry; a few scattered fragments of observations and remarks alone remain. He considered these philosophical views of mind and nature to be instinct with the intensest spirit of poetry.

‘More popular poets clothe the ideal with familiar and sensible imagery. Shelley loved to idealize the real — to gift the mechanism of the material universe with a soul and a voice, and to bestow such also on the most delicate and abstract emotions and thoughts of the mind. . . .

‘Through the whole Poem there reigns a sort of calm and holy spirit of love; it soothes the tortured, and is hope to the expectant, till the prophecy is fulfilled, and Love, untainted by any evil, becomes the law of the world. . . .

‘The charm of the Roman climate helped to clothe his thoughts in greater beauty than they had ever worn before; and as he wandered among the ruins, made one with nature in their decay, or gazed on the Praxitelean shapes that throng the Vatican, the Capitol, and the palaces of Rome, his soul imbibed forms of loveliness which became a portion of itself. There are many passages in the *Prometheus* which show the intense delight he received from such studies, and give back the impression with a beauty of poetical description peculiarly his own.’

PREFACE

The Greek tragic writers, in selecting as their subject any portion of their national history or mythology, employed in their treatment of it a certain arbitrary discretion. They by no means conceived themselves bound to adhere to the common interpretation or to imitate in story as in title their rivals and predecessors.

Such a system would have amounted to a resignation of those claims to preference over their competitors which incited the composition. The Agamemnonian story was exhibited on the Athenian theatre with as many variations as dramas.

I have presumed to employ a similar license. The *Prometheus Unbound* of Æschylus supposed the reconciliation of Jupiter with his victim as the price of the disclosure of the danger threatened to his empire by the consummation of his marriage with Thetis. Thetis, according to this view of the subject, was given in marriage to Peleus, and Prometheus, by the permission of Jupiter, delivered from his captivity by Hercules. Had I framed my story on this model, I should have done no more than have attempted to restore the lost drama of Æschylus; an ambition which, if my preference to this mode of treating the subject had incited me to cherish, the recollection of the high comparison such an attempt would challenge might well abate. But, in truth, I was averse from a catastrophe so feeble as that of reconciling the Champion with the Oppressor of mankind. The moral interest of the fable, which is so powerfully sustained by the sufferings and endurance of Prometheus, would be annihilated if we could conceive of him as unsaying his high language and quailing before his successful and perfidious adversary. The only imaginary being, resembling in any degree Prometheus, is Satan; and Prometheus is, in my judgment, a more poetical character than Satan, because, in addition to courage, and majesty, and firm and patient opposition to omnipotent force, he is susceptible of being described as exempt from the taints of ambition, envy, revenge, and a desire for personal aggrandizement, which, in the hero of *Paradise Lost*, interfere with the interest. The character of Satan engenders in the mind a pernicious casuistry which leads us to weigh his faults with his wrongs, and to excuse the former because the latter exceed all measure. In the minds of those who consider that magnificent fiction with a religious feeling it engenders something worse. But Prometheus is, as it were, the type of the highest perfection of moral and intellectual nature impelled by the purest and the truest motives to the best and noblest ends.

This Poem was chiefly written upon the mountainous ruins of the Baths of Caracalla, among the flowery glades and thickets of odoriferous blossoming trees, which are extended in ever winding labyrinths upon its immense platforms and dizzy arches suspended in the air. The bright blue sky of Rome, and the effect of the vigorous awakening spring in that divinest climate, and the new life with which it drenches the spirits even to intoxication, were the inspiration of this drama.

The imagery which I have employed will be found, in many instances, to have been drawn from the operations of the human mind, or from those external actions by which they are expressed. This is unusual in modern poetry, although Dante and Shakespeare are full of instances of the same kind; Dante indeed more than any other poet, and with greater success. But the Greek poets, as writers to whom no resource of awakening the sympathy of their contemporaries was unknown, were in the habitual use of this power; and it is the study of their works (since a higher merit would probably be denied me) to which I am willing that my readers should impute this singularity.

One word is due in candor to the degree in which the study of contemporary writings may have tinged my composition, for such has been a topic of censure with regard to poems far more popular, and indeed more deservedly popular, than mine. It is impossible that any one, who inhabits the same age with such writers as those who stand in the foremost ranks of our own, can conscientiously assure himself that his language and tone of thought may not have been modified by the study of the productions of those extraordinary intellects. It is true that, not the spirit of their genius, but the forms in which it has manifested itself, are due less to the peculiarities of their own minds than to the peculiarity of the moral and intellectual condition of the minds among which they have been produced. Thus a number of writers possess the form, whilst they want the spirit of those whom, it is alleged, they imitate; because the former is the endowment of the age in which they live, and the latter must be the uncommunicated lightning of their own mind.

The peculiar style of intense and comprehensive imagery which distinguishes the modern literature of England has not been, as a general power, the product of the imitation of any particular writer. The mass of capabilities remains at every period materially the same; the circumstances which awaken it to action perpetually change. If England were divided into forty republics, each equal in population and extent to Athens, there is no reason to suppose but that, under institutions not more perfect than those of Athens, each would produce philosophers and poets equal to those who (if we except Shakespeare) have never been surpassed. We owe the great writers of the golden age of our literature to that fervid awakening of the public mind which shook to dust the oldest and most oppressive form of the Christian religion. We owe Milton to the progress and development of the same spirit: the sacred Milton was, let it ever be remembered, a republican and a bold inquirer into morals and religion. The great writers of our own age are, we have reason to suppose, the companions and forerunners of some unimagined change in our social condition or the opinions which cement it. The cloud of mind is discharging its collected lightning, and the equilibrium between institutions and opinions is now restoring or is about to be restored.

As to imitation, poetry is a mimetic art. It creates, but it creates by combination and representation. Poetical abstractions are beautiful and new, not because the portions of which they are composed had no previous existence in the mind of man or in Nature, but because the whole produced by their combination has some intelligible and beautiful analogy with those sources of emotion and thought and with the contemporary condition of them. One great poet is a masterpiece of Nature which another not only ought to study but must study. He might as wisely and as easily determine that his mind should no longer be the mirror of all that is lovely in the visible universe as exclude from his contemplation the beautiful which exists in the writings of a great contemporary. The pretence of doing it would be a presumption in any but the greatest; the effect, even in him, would be strained, unnatural and ineffectual. A poet is the combined product of such internal powers as modify the nature of others, and of such external influences as excite and sustain these powers; he is not one, but both. Every man's mind is, in this respect, modified by all the objects of Nature and art; by every word and every suggestion which he ever admitted to act upon his consciousness; it is the mirror upon which all forms are reflected and in which they compose one form. Poets, not otherwise than philosophers, painters, sculptors and musicians, are, in one sense, the creators, and, in another, the creations, of their age. From this subjection the loftiest do not escape. There is a similarity between Homer and Hesiod, between Æschylus and Euripides, between Virgil and Horace, between Dante and Petrarch, between Shakespeare and Fletcher, between Dryden

and Pope; each has a generic resemblance under which their specific distinctions are arranged. If this similarity be the result of imitation, I am willing to confess that I have imitated.

Let this opportunity be conceded to me of acknowledging that I have what a Scotch philosopher characteristically terms a ' passion for reforming the world: ' what passion incited him to write and publish his book he omits to explain. For my part I had rather be damned with Plato and Lord Bacon than go to Heaven with Paley and Malthus. But it is a mistake to suppose that I dedicate my poetical compositions solely to the direct enforcement of reform, or that I consider them in any degree as containing a reasoned system on the theory of human life. Didactic poetry is my abhorrence; nothing can be equally well expressed in prose that is not tedious and supererogatory in verse. My purpose has hitherto been simply to familiarize the highly refined imagination of the more select classes of poetical readers with beautiful idealisms of moral excellence; aware that, until the mind can love, and admire, and trust, and hope, and endure, reasoned principles of moral conduct are seeds cast upon the highway of life which the unconscious passenger tramples into dust, although they would bear the harvest of his happiness. Should I live to accomplish what I purpose, that is, produce a systematical history of what appear to me to be the genuine elements of human society, let not the advocates of injustice and superstition flatter themselves that I should take Æschylus rather than Plato as my model.

The having spoken of myself with unaffected freedom will need little apology with the candid; and let the uncandid consider that they injure me less than their own hearts and minds by misrepresentation. Whatever talents a person may possess to amuse and instruct others, be they ever so inconsiderable, he is yet bound to exert them: if his attempt be ineffectual, let the punishment of an unaccomplished purpose have been sufficient; let none trouble themselves to heap the dust of oblivion upon his efforts; the pile they raise will betray his grave which might otherwise have been unknown.

PROMETHEUS UNBOUND

DRAMATIS PERSONÆ

PROMETHEUS.
DEMOGORGON.
JUPITER.
THE EARTH.
OCEAN.
APOLLO.
MERCURY.
HERCULES.

ASIA
PANTHEA } Oceanides.
IONE
THE PHANTASM OF JUPITER.
THE SPIRIT OF THE EARTH.
THE SPIRIT OF THE MOON.
SPIRITS OF THE HOURS.
SPIRITS. ECHOES. FAUNS.
FURIES.

ACT I

SCENE, *a Ravine of Icy Rocks in the Indian Caucasus.* PROMETHEUS *is discovered bound to the Precipice.* PANTHEA *and* IONE *are seated at his feet. Time, Night. During the Scene morning slowly breaks.*

PROMETHEUS

MONARCH of Gods and Dæmons, and all Spirits
But One, who throng those bright and rolling worlds
Which Thou and I alone of living things
Behold with sleepless eyes! regard this Earth
Made multitudinous with thy slaves, whom thou
Requitest for knee-worship, prayer, and praise,
And toil, and hecatombs of broken hearts,
With fear and self-contempt and barren hope;
Whilst me, who am thy foe, eyeless in hate,
Hast thou made reign and triumph, to thy scorn,   10
O'er mine own misery and thy vain revenge.
Three thousand years of sleep-unsheltered hours,
And moments aye divided by keen pangs
Till they seemed years, torture and solitude,
Scorn and despair — these are mine empire:
More glorious far than that which thou surveyest
From thine unenvied throne, O Mighty God!
Almighty, had I deigned to share the shame
Of thine ill tyranny, and hung not here
Nailed to this wall of eagle-baffling mountain,   20

Black, wintry, dead, unmeasured; without herb,
Insect, or beast, or shape or sound of life.
Ah me! alas, pain, pain ever, forever!

No change, no pause, no hope! Yet I endure.
I ask the Earth, have not the mountains felt?
I ask yon Heaven, the all-beholding Sun,
Has it not seen? The Sea, in storm or calm,
Heaven's ever-changing shadow, spread below,
Have its deaf waves not heard my agony?
Ah me! alas, pain, pain ever, forever!   30

The crawling glaciers pierce me with the spears
Of their moon-freezing crystals; the bright chains
Eat with their burning cold into my bones.
Heaven's wingèd hound, polluting from thy lips
His beak in poison not his own, tears up
My heart; and shapeless sights come wandering by,
The ghastly people of the realm of dream,
Mocking me; and the Earthquake-fiends are charged
To wrench the rivets from my quivering wounds
When the rocks split and close again behind;   40
While from their loud abysses howling throng
The genii of the storm, urging the rage
Of whirlwind, and afflict me with keen hail.
And yet to me welcome is day and night,
Whether one breaks the hoar-frost of the morn,
Or starry, dim, and slow, the other climbs
The leaden-colored east; for then they lead
The wingless, crawling hours, one among whom —
As some dark Priest hales the reluctant victim —
Shall drag thee, cruel King, to kiss the blood   50
From these pale feet, which then might trample thee
If they disdained not such a prostrate slave.

Disdain! Ah, no! I pity thee. What ruin
Will hunt thee undefended through the
     wide Heaven!
How will thy soul, cloven to its depth with
     terror,
Gape like a hell within! I speak in grief,
Not exultation, for I hate no more,
As then ere misery made me wise. The
     curse
Once breathed on thee I would recall. Ye
     Mountains,
Whose many-voicèd Echoes, through the
     mist   60
Of cataracts, flung the thunder of that
     spell!
Ye icy Springs, stagnant with wrinkling
     frost,
Which vibrated to hear me, and then crept
Shuddering through India! Thou serenest
     Air
Through which the Sun walks burning
     without beams!
And ye swift Whirlwinds, who on poisèd
     wings
Hung mute and moveless o'er yon hushed
     abyss,
As thunder, louder than your own, made
     rock
The orbèd world! If then my words had
     power,
Though I am changed so that aught evil
     wish   70
Is dead within; although no memory be
Of what is hate, let them not lose it now!
What was that curse? for ye all heard me
     speak.

FIRST VOICE: *from the Mountains*

Thrice three hundred thousand years
     O'er the earthquake's couch we stood;
Oft, as men convulsed with fears,
     We trembled in our multitude.

SECOND VOICE: *from the Springs*

Thunderbolts had parched our water,
     We had been stained with bitter blood,
And had run mute, 'mid shrieks of
     slaughter   80
     Through a city and a solitude.

THIRD VOICE: *from the Air*

I had clothed, since Earth uprose,
     Its wastes in colors not their own,
And oft had my serene repose
     Been cloven by many a rending groan.

FOURTH VOICE: *from the Whirlwinds*

We had soared beneath these mountains
     Unresting ages; nor had thunder,
Nor yon volcano's flaming fountains,
     Nor any power above or under.
Ever made us mute with wonder.   90

FIRST VOICE

But never bowed our snowy crest
As at the voice of thine unrest.

SECOND VOICE

Never such a sound before
To the Indian waves we bore.
A pilot asleep on the howling sea
Leaped up from the deck in agony,
And heard, and cried, 'Ah, woe is me!'
And died as mad as the wild waves be.

THIRD VOICE

By such dread words from Earth to Heaven
My still realm was never riven;   100
When its wound was closed, there stood
Darkness o'er the day like blood.

FOURTH VOICE

And we shrank back: for dreams of ruin
To frozen caves our flight pursuing
Made us keep silence — thus — and thus —
Though silence is a hell to us.

THE EARTH

The tongueless caverns of the craggy hills
Cried, 'Misery!' then; the hollow Heaven
     replied,
'Misery!' And the Ocean's purple waves,
Climbing the land, howled to the lashing
     winds,   110
And the pale nations heard it, 'Misery!'

PROMETHEUS

I hear a sound of voices; not the voice
Which I gave forth. Mother, thy sons and
     thou
Scorn him, without whose all-enduring will
Beneath the fierce omnipotence of Jove,
Both they and thou had vanished, like thin
     mist
Unrolled on the morning wind. Know ye
     not me,
The Titan? He who made his agony
The barrier to your else all-conquering foe?
O rock-embosomed lawns and snow-fed
     streams,   120
Now seen athwart frore vapors, deep below,

Through whose o'ershadowing woods I
    wandered once
With Asia, drinking life from her loved
    eyes;
Why scorns the spirit, which informs ye,
    now
To commune with me? me alone who
    checked,
As one who checks a fiend-drawn charioteer,
The falsehood and the force of him who
    reigns
Supreme, and with the groans of pining
    slaves
Fills your dim glens and liquid wildernesses:
Why answer ye not, still?   Brethren!

THE EARTH
            They dare not. 130

PROMETHEUS
Who dares? for I would hear that curse
    again.
Ha, what an awful whisper rises up!
'T is scarce like sound; it tingles through
    the frame
As lightning tingles, hovering ere it strike.
Speak, Spirit! from thine inorganic voice
I only know that thou art moving near
And love. How cursed I him?

THE EARTH
           How canst thou hear
Who knowest not the language of the dead?

PROMETHEUS
Thou art a living spirit; speak as they.

THE EARTH
I dare not speak like life, lest Heaven's
    fell King   140
Should hear, and link me to some wheel of
    pain
More torturing than the one whereon I roll.
Subtle thou art and good; and though the
    Gods
Hear not this voice, yet thou art more than
    God,
Being wise and kind: earnestly hearken
    now.

PROMETHEUS
Obscurely through my brain, like shadows
    dim,
Sweep awful thoughts, rapid and thick.
    I feel

Faint, like one mingled in entwining love;
Yet 't is not pleasure.

THE EARTH
           No, thou canst not hear;
Thou art immortal, and this tongue is
    known   150
Only to those who die.

PROMETHEUS
           And what art thou,
O melancholy Voice?

THE EARTH
           I am the Earth,
Thy mother; she within whose stony veins,
To the last fibre of the loftiest tree
Whose thin leaves trembled in the frozen
    air,
Joy ran, as blood within a living frame,
When thou didst from her bosom, like a
    cloud
Of glory, arise, a spirit of keen joy!
And at thy voice her pining sons uplifted
Their prostrate brows from the polluting
    dust,   160
And our almighty Tyrant with fierce dread
Grew pale, until his thunder chained thee
    here.
Then — see those million worlds which burn
    and roll
Around us — their inhabitants beheld
My spherèd light wane in wide Heaven;
    the sea
Was lifted by strange tempest, and new fire
From earthquake-rifted mountains of
    bright snow
Shook its portentous hair beneath Heaven's
    frown;
Lightning and Inundation vexed the plains;
Blue thistles bloomed in cities; foodless
    toads   170
Within voluptuous chambers panting
    crawled.
When Plague had fallen on man and beast
    and worm,
And Famine; and black blight on herb and
    tree;
And in the corn, and vines, and meadow-
    grass,
Teemed ineradicable poisonous weeds
Draining their growth, for my wan breast
    was dry
With grief, and the thin air, my breath,
    was stained

With the contagion of a mother's hate
Breathed on her child's destroyer; ay, I
   heard
Thy curse, the which, if thou rememberest
   not,   180
Yet my innumerable seas and streams,
Mountains, and caves, and winds, and yon
   wide air,
And the inarticulate people of the dead,
Preserve, a treasured spell. We meditate
In secret joy and hope those dreadful
   words,
But dare not speak them.

PROMETHEUS

          Venerable mother !
All else who live and suffer take from thee
Some comfort; flowers, and fruits, and
   happy sounds,
And love, though fleeting; these may not
   be mine.
But mine own words, I pray, deny me
   not.   190

THE EARTH

They shall be told. Ere Babylon was dust,
The Magus Zoroaster, my dead child,
Met his own image walking in the gar-
   den.
That apparition, sole of men, he saw.
For know there are two worlds of life and
   death:
One that which thou beholdest; but the
   other
Is underneath the grave, where do inhabit
The shadows of all forms that think and
   live,
Till death unite them and they part no
   more;   199
Dreams and the light imaginings of men,
And all that faith creates or love desires,
Terrible, strange, sublime and beauteous
   shapes.
There thou art, and dost hang, a writhing
   shade,
'Mid whirlwind-peopled mountains; all the
   gods
Are there, and all the powers of nameless
   worlds,
Vast, sceptred phantoms; heroes, men, and
   beasts;
And Demogorgon, a tremendous gloom;
And he, the supreme Tyrant, on his throne
Of burning gold. Son, one of these shall
   utter

The curse which all remember. Call at
   will   210
Thine own ghost, or the ghost of Jupiter,
Hades or Typhon, or what mightier Gods
From all-prolific Evil, since thy ruin,
Have sprung, and trampled on my prostrate
   sons.
Ask, and they must reply: so the revenge
Of the Supreme may sweep through vacant
   shades,
As rainy wind through the abandoned gate
Of a fallen palace.

PROMETHEUS

         Mother, let not aught
Of that which may be evil pass again
My lips, or those of aught resembling me.
Phantasm of Jupiter, arise, appear !   221

IONE

My wings are folded o'er mine ears;
   My wings are crossèd o'er mine eyes;
Yet through their silver shade appears,
   And through their lulling plumes arise,
A Shape, a throng of sounds.
   May it be no ill to thee
O thou of many wounds !
Near whom, for our sweet sister's sake,
Ever thus we watch and wake.   230

PANTHEA

The sound is of whirlwind underground,
   Earthquake, and fire, and mountains
      cloven;
The shape is awful, like the sound,
   Clothed in dark purple, star-inwoven.
A sceptre of pale gold,
   To stay steps proud, o'er the slow
      cloud,
His veinèd hand doth hold.
Cruel he looks, but calm and strong,
Like one who does, not suffers wrong.

PHANTASM OF JUPITER

Why have the secret powers of this strange
   world   240
Driven me, a frail and empty phantom,
   hither
On direst storms ? What unaccustomed
   sounds
Are hovering on my lips, unlike the voice
With which our pallid race hold ghastly
   talk
In darkness ? And, proud sufferer, who
   art thou ?

PROMETHEUS

Tremendous Image ! as thou art must be
He whom thou shadowest forth. I am his
    foe,
The Titan. Speak the words which I would
    hear,
Although no thought inform thine empty
    voice.

THE EARTH

Listen ! And though your echoes must be
    mute, 250
Gray mountains, and old woods, and
    haunted springs,
Prophetic caves, and isle - surrounding
    streams,
Rejoice to hear what yet ye cannot speak.

PHANTASM

A spirit seizes me and speaks within;
It tears me as fire tears a thunder-cloud.

PANTHEA

See how he lifts his mighty looks ! the
    Heaven
Darkens above.

IONE

He speaks ! Oh, shelter me !

PROMETHEUS

I see the curse on gestures proud and cold,
And looks of firm defiance, and calm hate,
And such despair as mocks itself with
    smiles, 260
Written as on a scroll: yet speak ! Oh,
    speak !

PHANTASM

Fiend, I defy thee ! with a calm, fixed
    mind,
    All that thou canst inflict I bid thee
    do;
Foul tyrant both of Gods and human-
    kind,
    One only being shalt thou not sub-
    due.
    Rain then thy plagues upon me here,
    Ghastly disease, and frenzying fear ;
    And let alternate frost and fire
    Eat into me, and be thine ire
Lightning, and cutting hail, and legioned
    forms 270
Of furies, driving by upon the wounding
    storms.

Ay, do thy worst ! Thou art omnipotent.
    O'er all things but thyself I gave thee
    power,
And my own will. Be thy swift mis-
    chiefs sent
    To blast mankind, from yon ethereal
    tower.
    Let thy malignant spirit move
    In darkness over those I love;
    On me and mine I imprecate
    The utmost torture of thy hate;
And thus devote to sleepless agony, 280
This undeclining head while thou must
    reign on high.

But thou, who art the God and Lord: O
    thou
    Who fillest with thy soul this world of
    woe,
    To whom all things of Earth and Heaven
    do bow
    In fear and worship — all-prevailing
    foe !
    I curse thee ! let a sufferer's curse
    Clasp thee, his torturer, like remorse;
    Till thine Infinity shall be
    A robe of envenomed agony; 289
And thine Omnipotence a crown of pain,
To cling like burning gold round thy dis-
    solving brain !

Heap on thy soul, by virtue of this Curse,
    Ill deeds; then be thou damned, be-
    holding good;
Both infinite as is the universe,
    And thou, and thy self-torturing soli-
    tude.
    An awful image of calm power
    Though now thou sittest, let the hour
    Come, when thou must appear to be
    That which thou art internally;
And after many a false and fruitless
    crime, 300
Scorn track thy lagging fall through
    boundless space and time !

PROMETHEUS

Were these my words, O Parent ?

THE EARTH

They were thine.

PROMETHEUS

It doth repent me; words are quick and
    vain;

Grief for awhile is blind, and so was mine.
I wish no living thing to suffer pain.

THE EARTH

Misery, oh, misery to me,
That Jove at length should vanquish
    thee !
Wail, howl aloud, Land and Sea,   308
The Earth's rent heart shall answer ye !
Howl, Spirits of the living and the dead,
Your refuge, your defence, lies fallen and
    vanquishèd !

FIRST ECHO

Lies fallen and vanquishèd !

SECOND ECHO

    Fallen and vanquishèd !

IONE

Fear not: 't is but some passing spasm,
    The Titan is unvanquished still.
But see, where through the azure chasm
    Of yon forked and snowy hill,
Trampling the slant winds on high
    With golden-sandalled feet, that glow
        Under plumes of purple dye,   320
        Like rose-ensanguined ivory,
    A Shape comes now,
Stretching on high from his right hand
    A serpent-cinctured wand.

PANTHEA

'T is Jove's world-wandering herald, Mer-
    cury.

IONE

And who are those with hydra tresses
    And iron wings, that climb the wind,
Whom the frowning God represses, —
    Like vapors steaming up behind,
Clanging loud, an endless crowd ?   330

PANTHEA

These are Jove's tempest-walking
    hounds,
Whom he gluts with groans and blood,
When charioted on sulphurous cloud
    He bursts Heaven's bounds.

IONE

Are they now led from the thin dead
    On new pangs to be fed ?

PANTHEA

The Titan looks as ever, firm, not proud.

FIRST FURY

Ha ! I scent life !

SECOND FURY

    Let me but look into his eyes !

THIRD FURY

The hope of torturing him smells like a
    heap
Of corpses to a death-bird after battle. 340

FIRST FURY

Darest thou delay, O Herald ! take cheer,
    Hounds
Of Hell: what if the Son of Maia soon
Should make us food and sport — who can
    please long
The Omnipotent ?

MERCURY

        Back to your towers of iron,
And gnash, beside the streams of fire and
    wail,
Your foodless teeth. Geryon, arise ! and
    Gorgon,
Chimæra, and thou Sphinx, subtlest of
    fiends,
Who ministered to Thebes Heaven's poi-
    soned wine,   348
Unnatural love, and more unnatural hate:
These shall perform your task.

FIRST FURY

    Oh, mercy ! mercy !
We die with our desire ! drive us not back !

MERCURY

Crouch then in silence.
        Awful Sufferer !
To thee unwilling, most unwillingly
I come, by the great Father's will driven
    down,
To execute a doom of new revenge.
Alas ! I pity thee, and hate myself
That I can do no more; aye from thy sight
Returning, for a season, Heaven seems
    Hell,
So thy worn form pursues me night and day,
Smiling reproach. Wise art thou, firm and
    good,   360

But vainly wouldst stand forth alone in
    strife
Against the Omnipotent; as yon clear
    lamps,
That measure and divide the weary years
From which there is no refuge, long have
    taught
And long must teach. Even now thy Tor-
    turer arms
With the strange might of unimagined
    pains
The powers who scheme slow agonies in
    Hell,
And my commission is to lead them here,
Or what more subtle, foul, or savage fiends
People the abyss, and leave them to their
    task.   370
Be it not so ! there is a secret known
To thee, and to none else of living things,
Which may transfer the sceptre of wide
    Heaven,
The fear of which perplexes the Supreme.
Clothe it in words, and bid it clasp his
    throne
In intercession; bend thy soul in prayer,
And like a suppliant in some gorgeous fane,
Let the will kneel within thy haughty
    heart,
For benefits and meek submission tame
The fiercest and the mightiest.

PROMETHEUS

                 Evil minds
Change good to their own nature. I gave
    all   381
He has; and in return he chains me here
Years, ages, night and day; whether the
    Sun
Split my parched skin, or in the moony
    night
The crystal-wingèd snow cling round my
    hair;
Whilst my belovèd race is trampled down
By his thought-executing ministers.
Such is the tyrant's recompense. 'T is just.
He who is evil can receive no good;
And for a world bestowed, or a friend
    lost,
He can feel hate, fear, shame; not grati-
    tude.   391
He but requites me for his own misdeed.
Kindness to such is keen reproach, which
    breaks
With bitter stings the light sleep of Re-
    venge.

Submission thou dost know I cannot try.
For what submission but that fatal word,
The death-seal of mankind's captivity,
Like the Sicilian's hair-suspended sword,
Which trembles o'er his crown, would he
    accept,
Or could I yield ? Which yet I will not
    yield.   400
Let others flatter Crime where it sits
    throned
In brief Omnipotence; secure are they;
For Justice, when triumphant, will weep
    down
Pity, not punishment, on her own wrongs,
Too much avenged by those who err. I
    wait,
Enduring thus, the retributive hour
Which since we spake is even nearer
    now.
But hark, the hell-hounds clamor: fear
    delay:
Behold ! Heaven lowers under thy Father's
    frown.   409

MERCURY

Oh, that we might be spared; I to inflict,
And thou to suffer ! Once more answer
    me.
Thou knowest not the period of Jove's
    power ?

PROMETHEUS

I know but this, that it must come.

MERCURY

                     Alas !
Thou canst not count thy years to come of
    pain !

PROMETHEUS

They last while Jove must reign; nor
    more, nor less
Do I desire or fear.

MERCURY

             Yet pause, and plunge
Into Eternity, where recorded time,
Even all that we imagine, age on age,
Seems but a point, and the reluctant mind
Flags wearily in its unending flight,   420
Till it sink, dizzy, blind, lost, shelterless;
Perchance it has not numbered the slow
    years
Which thou must spend in torture, unre-
    prieved ?

PROMETHEUS

Perchance no thought can count them, yet
they pass.

MERCURY

If thou mightst dwell among the Gods the
while,
Lapped in voluptuous joy ?

PROMETHEUS

              I would not quit
This bleak ravine, these unrepentant pains.

MERCURY

Alas ! I wonder at, yet pity thee.

PROMETHEUS

Pity the self-despising slaves of Heaven,
Not me, within whose mind sits peace
    serene,   430
As light in the sun, throned. How vain is
    talk !
Call up the fiends.

IONE

           Oh, sister, look ! White fire
Has cloven to the roots yon huge snow-
    loaded cedar;
How fearfully God's thunder howls be-
    hind !

MERCURY

I must obey his words and thine.   Alas !
Most heavily remorse hangs at my heart !

PANTHEA

See where the child of Heaven, with wingèd
    feet,
Runs down the slanted sunlight of the
    dawn.

IONE

Dear sister, close thy plumes over thine
    eyes
Lest thou behold and die; they come —
    they come —   440
Blackening the birth of day with countless
    wings,
And hollow underneath, like death.

FIRST FURY

               Prometheus !

SECOND FURY

Immortal Titan !

THIRD FURY

Champion of Heaven's slaves !

PROMETHEUS

He whom some dreadful voice invokes is
    here,
Prometheus, the chained Titan.   Horrible
    forms,
What and who are ye ?   Never yet there
    came
Phantasms so foul through monster-teeming
    Hell
From the all-miscreative brain of Jove.
Whilst I behold such execrable shapes,
Methinks I grow like what I contemplate,
And laugh and stare in loathsome sym-
    pathy.   451

FIRST FURY

We are the ministers of pain, and fear,
And disappointment, and mistrust, and
    hate,
And clinging crime; and as lean dogs pur-
    sue
Through wood and lake some struck and
    sobbing fawn,
We track all things that weep, and bleed,
    and live,
When the great King betrays them to our
    will.

PROMETHEUS

O many fearful natures in one name,
I know ye; and these lakes and echoes
    know
The darkness and the clangor of your
    wings !   460
But why more hideous than your loathèd
    selves
Gather ye up in legions from the deep ?

SECOND FURY

We knew not that.   Sisters, rejoice, re-
    joice !

PROMETHEUS

Can aught exult in its deformity ?

SECOND FURY

The beauty of delight makes lovers glad,
Gazing on one another: so are we.
As from the rose which the pale priestess
    kneels
To gather for her festal crown of flowers
The aërial crimson falls, flushing her cheek,

So from our victim's destined agony   470
The shade which is our form invests us
   round;
Else we are shapeless as our mother Night.

PROMETHEUS

I laugh your power, and his who sent you
   here,
To lowest scorn. Pour forth the cup of
   pain.

FIRST FURY

Thou thinkest we will rend thee bone from
   bone
And nerve from nerve, working like fire
   within ?

PROMETHEUS

Pain is my element, as hate is thine;
Ye rend me now; I care not.

SECOND FURY

              Dost imagine
We will but laugh into thy lidless eyes ?

PROMETHEUS

I weigh not what ye do, but what ye
   suffer,
Being evil. Cruel was the power which
   called   481
You, or aught else so wretched, into light.

THIRD FURY

Thou think'st we will live through thee,
   one by one,
Like animal life, and though we can obscure
   not
The soul which burns within, that we will
   dwell
Beside it, like a vain loud multitude,
Vexing the self-content of wisest men;
That we will be dread thought beneath thy
   brain,
And foul desire round thine astonished
   heart,
And blood within thy labyrinthine veins 490
Crawling like agony ?

PROMETHEUS

            Why, ye are thus now;
Yet am I king over myself, and rule
The torturing and conflicting throngs
   within,
As Jove rules you when Hell grows muti-
   nous.

CHORUS OF FURIES

From the ends of the earth, from the ends
   of the earth,
Where the night has its grave and the
   morning its birth,
       Come, come, come !
O ye who shake hills with the scream of
   your mirth
When cities sink howling in ruin; and ye
Who with wingless footsteps trample the
   sea,   500
And close upon Shipwreck and Famine's
   track
Sit chattering with joy on the foodless
   wreck;
       Come, come, come !
   Leave the bed, low, cold, and red,
   Strewed beneath a nation dead;
   Leave the hatred, as in ashes
     Fire is left for future burning;
   It will burst in bloodier flashes
     When ye stir it, soon returning;
   Leave the self-contempt implanted   510
   In young spirits, sense-enchanted,
     Misery's yet unkindled fuel;
   Leave Hell's secrets half unchanted
     To the maniac dreamer; cruel
More than ye can be with hate
     Is he with fear.
       Come, come, come !
We are steaming up from Hell's wide gate
And we burden the blasts of the atmo-
   sphere,
But vainly we toil till ye come here.   520

IONE

Sister, I hear the thunder of new wings.

PANTHEA

These solid mountains quiver with the sound
Even as the tremulous air; their shadows
   make
The space within my plumes more black
   than night.

FIRST FURY

Your call was as a wingèd car,
Driven on whirlwinds fast and far;
It rapt us from red gulfs of war.

SECOND FURY

From wide cities, famine-wasted;

THIRD FURY

Groans half heard, and blood untasted;

FOURTH FURY

Kingly conclaves stern and cold, 530
Where blood with gold is bought and sold;

FIFTH FURY

From the furnace, white and hot,
In which —

A FURY

Speak not; whisper not;
I know all that ye would tell,
But to speak might break the spell
Which must bend the Invincible,
The stern of thought;
He yet defies the deepest power of Hell.

FURY

Tear the veil!

ANOTHER FURY

It is torn.

CHORUS

The pale stars of the morn
Shine on a misery, dire to be borne. 540
Dost thou faint, mighty Titan? We
laugh thee to scorn.
Dost thou boast the clear knowledge thou
waken'dst for man?
Then was kindled within him a thirst
which outran
Those perishing waters; a thirst of fierce
fever,
Hope, love, doubt, desire, which consume
him forever.
One came forth of gentle worth,
Smiling on the sanguine earth;
His words outlived him, like swift poison
Withering up truth, peace, and pity.
Look! where round the wide horizon 550
Many a million-peopled city
Vomits smoke in the bright air!
Mark that outcry of despair!
'T is his mild and gentle ghost
Wailing for the faith he kindled.
Look again! the flames almost
To a glow-worm's lamp have dwindled;
The survivors round the embers
Gather in dread.
Joy, joy, joy! 560
Past ages crowd on thee, but each one re-
members,
And the future is dark, and the present is
spread

Like a pillow of thorns for thy slumberless
head.

SEMICHORUS I

Drops of bloody agony flow
From his white and quivering brow.
Grant a little respite now.
See! a disenchanted nation
Springs like day from desolation;
To Truth its state is dedicate,
And Freedom leads it forth, her mate;
A legioned band of linkèd brothers, 571
Whom Love calls children —

SEMICHORUS II

'T is another's.
See how kindred murder kin!
'T is the vintage-time for Death and Sin;
Blood, like new wine, bubbles within;
Till Despair smothers
The struggling world, which slaves and
tyrants win.

[All the FURIES vanish, except one.

IONE

Hark, sister! what a low yet dreadful groan
Quite unsuppressed is tearing up the heart
Of the good Titan, as storms tear the deep,
And beasts hear the sea moan in inland
caves. 581
Darest thou observe how the fiends torture
him?

PANTHEA

Alas! I looked forth twice, but will no
more.

IONE

What didst thou see?

PANTHEA

A woful sight: a youth
With patient looks nailed to a crucifix.

IONE

What next?

PANTHEA

The heaven around, the earth below,
Was peopled with thick shapes of human
death,
All horrible, and wrought by human hands;
And some appeared the work of human
hearts, 589

For men were slowly killed by frowns and
    smiles;
And other sights too foul to speak and live
Were wandering by. Let us not tempt
    worse fear
By looking forth; those groans are grief
    enough.

FURY

Behold an emblem: those who do endure
Deep wrongs for man, and scorn, and chains,
    but heap
Thousand-fold torment on themselves and
    him.

PROMETHEUS

Remit the anguish of that lighted stare;
Close those wan lips; let that thorn-wounded
    brow
Stream not with blood; it mingles with
    thy tears !
Fix, fix those tortured orbs in peace and
    death,   600
So thy sick throes shake not that crucifix,
So those pale fingers play not with thy
    gore.
Oh, horrible ! Thy name I will not speak —
It hath become a curse. I see, I see
The wise, the mild, the lofty, and the just,
Whom thy slaves hate for being like to
    thee,
Some hunted by foul lies from their heart's
    home,
An early-chosen, late-lamented home,
As hooded ounces cling to the driven hind;
Some linked to corpses in unwholesome
    cells;   610
Some — hear I not the multitude laugh
    loud ? —
Impaled in lingering fire; and mighty
    realms
Float by my feet, like sea-uprooted isles,
Whose sons are kneaded down in common
    blood
By the red light of their own burning
    homes.

FURY

Blood thou canst see, and fire; and canst
    hear groans:
Worse things unheard, unseen, remain be-
    hind.

PROMETHEUS

Worse ?

FURY

In each human heart terror survives
The ruin it has gorged: the loftiest fear
All that they would disdain to think were
    true.   620
Hypocrisy and custom make their minds
The fanes of many a worship, now outworn.
They dare not devise good for man's es-
    tate,
And yet they know not that they do not
    dare.
The good want power, but to weep barren
    tears.
The powerful goodness want; worse need
    for them.
The wise want love; and those who love
    want wisdom;
And all best things are thus confused to
    ill.
Many are strong and rich, and would be
    just,   629
But live among their suffering fellow-men
As if none felt; they know not what they
    do.

PROMETHEUS

Thy words are like a cloud of wingèd
    snakes;
And yet I pity those they torture not.

FURY

Thou pitiest them ? I speak no more !
                                    [Vanishes.

PROMETHEUS

                            Ah woe !
Ah woe ! Alas ! pain, pain ever, forever !
I close my tearless eyes, but see more clear
Thy works within my woe-illumèd mind,
Thou subtle tyrant ! Peace is in the
    grave.
The grave hides all things beautiful and
    good.
I am a God and cannot find it there,   640
Nor would I seek it ; for, though dread
    revenge,
This is defeat, fierce king, not victory.
The sights with which thou torturest gird
    my soul
With new endurance, till the hour arrives
When they shall be no types of things
    which are.

PANTHEA

Alas ! what sawest thou ?

PROMETHEUS

There are two woes —
To speak and to behold; thou spare me
   one.
Names are there, Nature's sacred watch-
   words, they
Were borne aloft in bright emblazonry;
The nations thronged around, and cried
   aloud,   650
As with one voice, Truth, Liberty, and
   Love !
Suddenly fierce confusion fell from heaven
Among them; there was strife, deceit, and
   fear;
Tyrants rushed in, and did divide the spoil.
This was the shadow of the truth I saw.

THE EARTH

I felt thy torture, son, with such mixed
   joy
As pain and virtue give. To cheer thy
   state
I bid ascend those subtle and fair spirits,
Whose homes are the dim caves of human
   thought,   659
And who inhabit, as birds wing the wind,
Its world-surrounding ether; they behold
Beyond that twilight realm, as in a glass,
The future; may they speak comfort to
   thee !

PANTHEA

Look, sister, where a troop of spirits gather,
Like flocks of clouds in spring's delightful
   weather,
Thronging in the blue air !

IONE

           And see ! more come,
Like fountain-vapors when the winds are
   dumb,
That climb up the ravine in scattered lines.
And hark ! is it the music of the pines ?
Is it the lake ? Is it the waterfall ?   670

PANTHEA

'T is something sadder, sweeter far than
   all.

CHORUS OF SPIRITS

From unremembered ages we
Gentle guides and guardians be
Of heaven-oppressed mortality;

And we breathe, and sicken not,
The atmosphere of human thought:
Be it dim, and dank, and gray,
Like a storm-extinguished day,
Travelled o'er by dying gleams;
  Be it bright as all between   680
Cloudless skies and windless streams,
  Silent, liquid, and serene ;
As the birds within the wind,
  As the fish within the wave,
As the thoughts of man's own mind
  Float through all above the grave;
We make there our liquid lair,
Voyaging cloudlike and unpent
Through the boundless element:
Thence we bear the prophecy   690
Which begins and ends in thee !

IONE

More yet come, one by one; the air around
   them
Looks radiant as the air around a star.

FIRST SPIRIT

On a battle-trumpet's blast
I fled hither, fast, fast, fast,
'Mid the darkness upward cast.
From the dust of creeds outworn,
From the tyrant's banner torn,
Gathering round me, onward borne,
There was mingled many a cry —   700
Freedom ! Hope ! Death ! Victory !
Till they faded through the sky;
And one sound above, around,
One sound beneath, around, above,
Was moving; 't was the soul of love;
'T was the hope, the prophecy,
Which begins and ends in thee.

SECOND SPIRIT

A rainbow's arch stood on the sea,
Which rocked beneath, immovably;
And the triumphant storm did flee,   710
Like a conqueror, swift and proud,
Begirt with many a captive cloud,
A shapeless, dark and rapid crowd,
Each by lightning riven in half.
I heard the thunder hoarsely laugh.
Mighty fleets were strewn like chaff
And spread beneath a hell of death
O'er the white waters. I alit
On a great ship lightning-split,
And speeded hither on the sigh   720
Of one who gave an enemy
His plank, then plunged aside to die.

THIRD SPIRIT

I sat beside a sage's bed,
And the lamp was burning red
Near the book where he had fed,
When a Dream with plumes of flame
To his pillow hovering came,
And I knew it was the same
Which had kindled long ago
Pity, eloquence, and woe;   730
And the world awhile below
Wore the shade its lustre made.
It has borne me here as fleet
As Desire's lightning feet;
I must ride it back ere morrow,
Or the sage will wake in sorrow.

FOURTH SPIRIT

On a poet's lips I slept
Dreaming like a love-adept
In the sound his breathing kept;
Nor seeks nor finds he mortal blisses,   740
But feeds on the aërial kisses
Of shapes that haunt thought's wilder-
    nesses.
He will watch from dawn to gloom
The lake-reflected sun illume
The yellow bees in the ivy-bloom,
Nor heed nor see what things they be;
But from these create he can
Forms more real than living man,
Nurslings of immortality!
One of these awakened me,   750
And I sped to succor thee.

IONE

Behold'st thou not two shapes from the
    east and west
Come, as two doves to one belovèd nest,
Twin nurslings of the all-sustaining air,
On swift still wings glide down the at-
    mosphere?
And, hark! their sweet sad voices! 't is
    despair
Mingled with love and then dissolved in
    sound.

PANTHEA

Canst thou speak, sister? all my words are
    drowned.

IONE

Their beauty gives me voice. See how
    they float
On their sustaining wings of skyey grain,   760

Orange and azure deepening into gold!
Their soft smiles light the air like a star's
    fire.

CHORUS OF SPIRITS

Hast thou beheld the form of Love?

FIFTH SPIRIT

         As over wide dominions
I sped, like some swift cloud that wings
    the wide air's wildernesses,
That planet-crested Shape swept by on
    lightning-braided pinions,
Scattering the liquid joy of life from his
    ambrosial tresses.
His footsteps paved the world with light;
    but as I passed 't was fading,
And hollow Ruin yawned behind; great
    sages bound in madness,
And headless patriots, and pale youths who
    perished, unupbraiding,
Gleamed in the night. I wandered o'er,
    till thou, O King of sadness,   770
Turned by thy smile the worst I saw to
    recollected gladness.

SIXTH SPIRIT

Ah, sister! Desolation is a delicate thing:
It walks not on the earth, it floats not on
    the air,
But treads with killing footstep, and fans
    with silent wing
The tender hopes which in their hearts the
    best and gentlest bear;
Who, soothed to false repose by the fan-
    ning plumes above
And the music-stirring motion of its soft
    and busy feet,
Dream visions of aërial joy, and call the
    monster, Love,
And wake, and find the shadow Pain, as
    he whom now we greet.

CHORUS

Though Ruin now Love's shadow be,   780
Following him, destroyingly,
   On Death's white and wingèd steed,
Which the fleetest cannot flee,
   Trampling down both flower and weed,
Man and beast, and foul and fair,
Like a tempest through the air;
Thou shalt quell this horseman grim,
Woundless though in heart or limb.

PROMETHEUS

Spirits ! how know ye this shall be ?

CHORUS

In the atmosphere we breathe,   790
As buds grow red, when the snow-storms
     flee,
From spring gathering up beneath,
Whose mild winds shake the elder-brake,
And the wandering herdsmen know
That the white-thorn soon will blow:
Wisdom, Justice, Love, and Peace,
When they struggle to increase,
Are to us as soft winds be
To shepherd boys, the prophecy
Which begins and ends in thee.   800

IONE

Where are the Spirits fled ?

PANTHEA

          Only a sense
Remains of them, like the omnipotence
Of music, when the inspired voice and lute
Languish, ere yet the responses are mute,
Which through the deep and labyrinthine
     soul,
Like echoes through long caverns, wind
     and roll.

PROMETHEUS

How fair these air-born shapes ! and yet I
     feel
Most vain all hope but love; and thou art
     far,
Asia ! who, when my being overflowed,   809
Wert like a golden chalice to bright wine
Which else had sunk into the thirsty dust.
All things are still.   Alas ! how heavily
This quiet morning weighs upon my heart;
Though I should dream I could even
     sleep with grief,
If slumber were denied not.   I would fain
Be what it is my destiny to be,
The saviour and the strength of suffering
     man,
Or sink into the original gulf of things.
There is no agony, and no solace left;
Earth can console, Heaven can torment no
     more.   820

PANTHEA

Hast thou forgotten one who watches thee
The cold dark night, and never sleeps but
     when
The shadow of thy spirit falls on her ?

PROMETHEUS

I said all hope was vain but love; thou
     lovest.

PANTHEA

Deeply in truth; but the eastern star looks
     white,
And Asia waits in that far Indian vale,
The scene of her sad exile; rugged once
And desolate and frozen, like this ravine;
But now invested with fair flowers and
     herbs,
And haunted by sweet airs and sounds,
     which flow   830
Among the woods and waters, from the
     ether
Of her transforming presence, which would
     fade
If it were mingled not with thine.   Fare-
     well !

ACT II

SCENE I. — *Morning. A lovely Vale in the
Indian Caucasus.* ASIA, *alone.*

ASIA

FROM all the blasts of heaven thou hast
     descended;
Yes, like a spirit, like a thought, which
     makes
Unwonted tears throng to the horny eyes,
And beatings haunt the desolated heart,
Which should have learned repose; thou
     hast descended
Cradled in tempests; thou dost wake, O
     Spring !
O child of many winds !   As suddenly
Thou comest as the memory of a dream,
Which now is sad because it hath been
     sweet;
Like genius, or like joy which riseth up   10
As from the earth, clothing with golden
     clouds
The desert of our life.
This is the season, this the day, the hour;
At sunrise thou shouldst come, sweet sister
     mine,
Too long desired, too long delaying, come !
How like death-worms the wingless mo-
     ments crawl !
The point of one white star is quivering
     still
Deep in the orange light of widening morn
Beyond the purple mountains; through a
     chasm

Of wind-divided mist the darker lake   20
Reflects it; now it wanes; it gleams again
As the waves fade, and as the burning
     threads
Of woven cloud unravel in pale air;
'T is lost ! and through yon peaks of cloud-
     like snow
The roseate sunlight quivers; hear I not
The Æolian music of her sea-green plumes
Winnowing the crimson dawn ?

PANTHEA *enters*
                              I feel, I see
Those eyes which burn through smiles that
     fade in tears,
Like stars half-quenched in mists of silver
     dew.   29
Belovèd and most beautiful, who wearest
The shadow of that soul by which I live,
How late thou art ! the spherèd sun had
     climbed
The sea; my heart was sick with hope,
     before
The printless air felt thy belated plumes.

PANTHEA
Pardon, great Sister ! but my wings were
     faint
With the delight of a remembered dream,
As are the noontide plumes of summer
     winds
Satiate with sweet flowers. I was wont to
     sleep
Peacefully, and awake refreshed and calm,
Before the sacred Titan's fall and thy   40
Unhappy love had made, through use and
     pity,
Both love and woe familiar to my heart
As they had grown to thine: erewhile I
     slept
Under the glaucous caverns of old Ocean
Within dim bowers of green and purple
     moss,
Our young Ione's soft and milky arms
Locked then, as now, behind my dark,
     moist hair,
While my shut eyes and cheek were pressed
     within
The folded depth of her life-breathing
     bosom: 49
But not as now, since I am made the
     wind
Which fails beneath the music that I bear
Of thy most wordless converse; since dis-
     solved

Into the sense with which love talks, my
     rest
Was troubled and yet sweet; my waking
     hours
Too full of care and pain.

ASIA
                              Lift up thine eyes,
And let me read thy dream.

PANTHEA
                              As I have said,
With our sea-sister at his feet I slept.
The mountain mists, condensing at our
     voice
Under the moon, had spread their snowy
     flakes,
From the keen ice shielding our linkèd
     sleep.   60
Then two dreams came. One I remember
     not.
But in the other his pale wound-worn limbs
Fell from Prometheus, and the azure night
Grew radiant with the glory of that form
Which lives unchanged within, and his
     voice fell
Like music which makes giddy the dim
     brain,
Faint with intoxication of keen joy:
' Sister of her whose footsteps pave the
     world
With loveliness — more fair than aught
     but her,
Whose shadow thou art — lift thine eyes
     on me.'   70
I lifted them; the overpowering light
Of that immortal shape was shadowed o'er
By love; which, from his soft and flowing
     limbs,
And passion-parted lips, and keen, faint
     eyes,
Steamed forth like vaporous fire; an at-
     mosphere
Which wrapped me in its all-dissolving
     power,
As the warm ether of the morning sun
Wraps ere it drinks some cloud of wander-
     ing dew.
I saw not, heard not, moved not, only felt
His presence flow and mingle through my
     blood   80
Till it became his life, and his grew mine,
And I was thus absorbed, until it passed,
And like the vapors when the sun sinks
     down,

Gathering again in drops upon the pines,
And tremulous as they, in the deep night
My being was condensed; and as the rays
Of thought were slowly gathered, I could
      hear
His voice, whose accents lingered ere they
      died
Like footsteps of weak melody; thy name
Among the many sounds alone I heard   90
Of what might be articulate; though still
I listened through the night when sound
      was none.
Ione wakened then, and said to me:
'Canst thou divine what troubles me to-
      night?
I always knew what I desired before,
Nor ever found delight to wish in vain.
But now I cannot tell thee what I seek;
I know not; something sweet, since it is
      sweet
Even to desire ; it is thy sport, false sis-
      ter;
Thou hast discovered some enchantment
      old,   100
Whose spells have stolen my spirit as I
      slept
And mingled it with thine; for when just
      now
We kissed, I felt within thy parted lips
The sweet air that sustained me; and the
      warmth
Of the life-blood, for loss of which I
      faint,
Quivered between our intertwining arms.'
I answered not, for the Eastern star grew
      pale,
But fled to thee.

ASIA
            Thou speakest, but thy words
Are as the air; I feel them not.   Oh, lift
Thine eyes, that I may read his written
      soul!   110

PANTHEA
I lift them, though they droop beneath the
      load
Of that they would express; what canst
      thou see
But thine own fairest shadow imaged there ?

ASIA
Thine eyes are like the deep, blue, bound-
      less heaven
Contracted to two circles underneath

Their long, fine lashes; dark, far, measure-
      less,
Orb within orb, and line through line in-
      woven.

PANTHEA
Why lookest thou as if a spirit passed ?

ASIA
There is a change; beyond their inmost
      depth
I see a shade, a shape: 't is He, arrayed 120
In the soft light of his own smiles, which
      spread
Like radiance from the cloud-surrounded
      moon.
Prometheus, it is thine ! depart not yet !
Say not those smiles that we shall meet
      again
Within that bright pavilion which their
      beams
Shall build on the waste world ? The dream
      is told.
What shape is that between us ? Its rude
      hair
Roughens the wind that lifts it, its regard
Is wild and quick, yet 't is a thing of air,
For through its gray robe gleams the golden
      dew   130
Whose stars the noon has quenched not.

DREAM
            Follow ! Follow !

PANTHEA
It is mine other dream.

ASIA
            It disappears.

PANTHEA
It passes now into my mind.   Methought
As we sate here, the flower-infolding buds
Burst on yon lightning - blasted almond
      tree;
When swift from the white Scythian wil-
      derness
A wind swept forth wrinkling the Earth
      with frost;
I looked, and all the blossoms were blown
      down;
But on each leaf was stamped, as the blue
      bells
Of Hyacinth tell Apollo's written grief, 140
OH, FOLLOW, FOLLOW !

ASIA

As you speak, your words
Fill, pause by pause, my own forgotten
   sleep
With shapes. Methought among the lawns
   together
We wandered, underneath the young gray
   dawn,
And multitudes of dense white fleecy clouds
Were wandering in thick flocks along the
   mountains,
Shepherded by the slow, unwilling wind;
And the white dew on the new-bladed
   grass,
Just piercing the dark earth, hung silently;
And there was more which I remember
   not;   150
But on the shadows of the morning clouds,
Athwart the purple mountain slope, was
   written
FOLLOW, OH, FOLLOW! as they vanished
   by;
And on each herb, from which Heaven's
   dew had fallen,
The like was stamped, as with a withering
   fire;
A wind arose among the pines; it shook
The clinging music from their boughs, and
   then
Low, sweet, faint sounds, like the farewell
   of ghosts,
Were heard: OH, FOLLOW, FOLLOW, FOLLOW
   ME !
And then I said, 'Panthea, look on me.' 160
But in the depth of those belovèd eyes
Still I saw, FOLLOW, FOLLOW !

ECHO

Follow, follow !

PANTHEA

The crags, this clear spring morning, mock
   our voices,
As they were spirit-tongued.

ASIA

It is some being
Around the crags. What fine clear sounds!
Oh, list!

ECHOES, *unseen*

Echoes we: listen !
  We cannot stay:
As dew-stars glisten
  Then fade away —
    Child of Ocean !   170

ASIA

Hark ! Spirits speak. The liquid responses
Of their aërial tongues yet sound.

PANTHEA

I hear.

ECHOES

Oh, follow, follow,
  As our voice recedeth
Through the caverns hollow,
  Where the forest spreadeth;
    (*More distant*)
Oh, follow, follow !
Through the caverns hollow,
As the song floats thou pursue,
Where the wild bee never flew,   180
Through the noontide darkness deep,
By the odor-breathing sleep
Of faint night-flowers, and the waves
At the fountain-lighted caves,
While our music, wild and sweet,
Mocks thy gently falling feet,
    Child of Ocean !

ASIA

Shall we pursue the sound ? It grows
   more faint
And distant.

PANTHEA

List ! the strain floats nearer now.

ECHOES

In the world unknown   190
  Sleeps a voice unspoken;
By thy step alone
  Can its rest be broken;
    Child of Ocean !

ASIA

How the notes sink upon the ebbing wind !

ECHOES

Oh, follow, follow !
Through the caverns hollow,
As the song floats thou pursue,
By the woodland noontide dew;
By the forests, lakes, and fountains, 200
Through the many-folded mountains;
To the rents, and gulfs, and chasms,
Where the Earth reposed from spasms,
On the day when He and thou
Parted, to commingle now;
    Child of Ocean !

ASIA

Come, sweet Panthea, link thy hand in
   mine,
And follow, ere the voices fade away.

SCENE II. — *A Forest intermingled with Rocks
and Caverns.* ASIA *and* PANTHEA *pass into
it. Two young Fauns are sitting on a Rock,
listening.*

SEMICHORUS I OF SPIRITS

The path through which that lovely twain
  Have passed, by cedar, pine, and yew,
  And each dark tree that ever grew,
  Is curtained out from Heaven's wide
    blue;
Nor sun, nor moon, nor wind, nor rain,
   Can pierce its interwoven bowers,
  Nor aught, save where some cloud of
    dew,
Drifted along the earth-creeping breeze
Between the trunks of the hoar trees,   9
   Hangs each a pearl in the pale flowers
  Of the green laurel blown anew,
And bends, and then fades silently,
One frail and fair anemone;
Or when some star of many a one
That climbs and wanders through steep
   night,
Has found the cleft through which alone
Beams fall from high those depths upon, —
Ere it is borne away, away,
By the swift Heavens that cannot stay,
It scatters drops of golden light,   20
Like lines of rain that ne'er unite;
And the gloom divine is all around;
And underneath is the mossy ground.

SEMICHORUS II

There the voluptuous nightingales,
  Are awake through all the broad noon-
   day:
When one with bliss or sadness fails,
  And through the windless ivy-boughs,
Sick with sweet love, droops dying away
On its mate's music-panting bosom;
Another from the swinging blossom,   30
   Watching to catch the languid close
Of the last strain, then lifts on high
The wings of the weak melody,
Till some new strain of feeling bear
  The song, and all the woods are mute;
When there is heard through the dim air
The rush of wings, and rising there,
  Like many a lake-surrounded flute,

Sounds overflow the listener's brain
So sweet, that joy is almost pain.   40

SEMICHORUS I

There those enchanted eddies play
  Of echoes, music-tongued, which draw,
  By Demogorgon's mighty law,
  With melting rapture, or sweet awe,
All spirits on that secret way,
   As inland boats are driven to Ocean
Down streams made strong with mountain-
   thaw;
And first there comes a gentle sound
To those in talk or slumber bound,
  And wakes the destined; soft emo-
   tion   50
Attracts, impels them; those who saw
Say from the breathing earth behind
There steams a plume-uplifting wind
Which drives them on their path, while
   they
Believe their own swift wings and feet
The sweet desires within obey;
And so they float upon their way,
  Until, still sweet, but loud and strong,
  The storm of sound is driven along,
  Sucked up and hurrying; as they fleet 60
  Behind, its gathering billows meet
And to the fatal mountain bear
Like clouds amid the yielding air.

FIRST FAUN

Canst thou imagine where those spirits
   live
Which make such delicate music in the
   woods ?
We haunt within the least frequented caves
And closest coverts, and we know these
   wilds,
Yet never meet them, though we hear
   them oft:
Where may they hide themselves ?

SECOND FAUN

             'T is hard to tell;
I have heard those more skilled in spirits
   say,   70
The bubbles, which the enchantment of the
   sun
Sucks from the pale faint water-flowers
   that pave
The oozy bottom of clear lakes and pools,
Are the pavilions where such dwell and
   float
Under the green and golden atmosphere

Which noontide kindles through the woven
leaves;
And when these burst, and the thin fiery
air,
The which they breathed within those lucent domes,
Ascends to flow like meteors through the
night,
They ride on them, and rein their headlong
speed,   80
And bow their burning crests, and glide in
fire
Under the waters of the earth again.

FIRST FAUN

If such live thus, have others other lives,
Under pink blossoms or within the bells
Of meadow flowers or folded violets deep,
Or on their dying odors, when they die,
Or in the sunlight of the spherèd dew ?

SECOND FAUN

Ay, many more which we may well divine.
But should we stay to speak, noontide
would come,
And thwart Silenus find his goats un-
drawn,   90
And grudge to sing those wise and lovely
songs
Of Fate, and Chance, and God, and Chaos
old,
And Love and the chained Titan's woful
doom,
And how he shall be loosed, and make the
earth
One brotherhood; delightful strains which
cheer
Our solitary twilights, and which charm
To silence the unenvying nightingales.

SCENE III. — *A Pinnacle of Rock among
Mountains.* ASIA *and* PANTHEA.

PANTHEA

Hither the sound has borne us — to the
realm
Of Demogorgon, and the mighty portal,
Like a volcano's meteor-breathing chasm,
Whence the oracular vapor is hurled up
Which lonely men drink wandering in their
youth,
And call truth, virtue, love, genius, or joy,
That maddening wine of life, whose dregs
they drain

To deep intoxication; and uplift,
Like Mænads who cry loud, Evoe ! Evoe!
The voice which is contagion to the
world.   10

ASIA

Fit throne for such a Power! Magnifi-
cent !
How glorious art thou, Earth ! and if thou
be
The shadow of some spirit lovelier still,
Though evil stain its work, and it should
be
Like its creation, weak yet beautiful,
I could fall down and worship that and
thee.
Even now my heart adoreth.   Wonderful !
Look, sister, ere the vapor dim thy brain:
Beneath is a wide plain of billowy mist,
As a lake, paving in the morning sky,   20
With azure waves which burst in silver
light,
Some Indian vale.   Behold it, rolling on
Under the curdling winds, and islanding
The peak whereon we stand, midway,
around,
Encinctured by the dark and blooming
forests,
Dim twilight-lawns, and stream-illumined
caves,
And wind-enchanted shapes of wandering
mist;
And far on high the keen sky-cleaving
mountains
From icy spires of sunlike radiance fling 29
The dawn, as lifted Ocean's dazzling spray,
From some Atlantic islet scattered up,
Spangles the wind with lamp-like water-
drops.
The vale is girdled with their walls, a
howl
Of cataracts from their thaw-cloven ra-
vines
Satiates the listening wind, continuous, vast,
Awful as silence.   Hark ! the rushing
snow !
The sun-awakened avalanche ! whose mass,
Thrice sifted by the storm, had gathered
there
Flake after flake, in heaven-defying minds
As thought by thought is piled, till some
great truth   40
Is loosened, and the nations echo round,
Shaken to their roots, as do the mountains
now.

PANTHEA

Look how the gusty sea of mist is breaking
In crimson foam, even at our feet ! it rises
As Ocean at the enchantment of the moon
Round foodless men wrecked on some oozy
    isle.

ASIA

The fragments of the cloud are scattered
    up;
The wind that lifts them disentwines my
    hair;
Its billows now sweep o'er mine eyes; my
    brain   49
Grows dizzy; I see shapes within the mist.

PANTHEA

A countenance with beckoning smiles;
    there burns
An azure fire within its golden locks !
Another and another: hark ! they speak !

SONG OF SPIRITS

To the deep, to the deep,
    Down, down !
Through the shade of sleep,
Through the cloudy strife
Of Death and of Life;
Through the veil and the bar
Of things which seem and are,   60
Even to the steps of the remotest throne,
    Down, down !

While the sound whirls around,
    Down, down !
As the fawn draws the hound,
As the lightning the vapor,
As a weak moth the taper;
Death, despair; love, sorrow;
Time, both; to-day, to-morrow;
As steel obeys the spirit of the stone,   70
    Down, down !

Through the gray, void abysm,
    Down, down !
Where the air is no prism,
And the moon and stars are not,
And the cavern-crags wear not
The radiance of Heaven,
Nor the gloom to Earth given,
Where there is one pervading, one alone,
    Down, down !   80

In the depth of the deep
    Down, down !

Like veiled lightning asleep,
Like the spark nursed in embers,
The last look Love remembers,
Like a diamond, which shines
On the dark wealth of mines,
A spell is treasured but for thee alone.
    Down, down !

We have bound thee, we guide thee; 90
    Down, down !
With the bright form beside thee;
    Resist not the weakness,
Such strength is in meekness
That the Eternal, the Immortal,
Must unloose through life's portal
The snake-like Doom coiled underneath
    his throne
    By that alone.

SCENE IV. — *The Cave of* DEMOGORGON.
ASIA *and* PANTHEA.

PANTHEA

What veilèd form sits on that ebon throne ?

ASIA

The veil has fallen.

PANTHEA

        I see a mighty darkness
Filling the seat of power, and rays of gloom
Dart round, as light from the meridian sun,
Ungazed upon and shapeless; neither limb,
Nor form, nor outline; yet we feel it is
A living Spirit.

DEMOGORGON

    Ask what thou wouldst know.

ASIA

What canst thou tell ?

DEMOGORGON

    All things thou dar'st demand.

ASIA

Who made the living world ?

DEMOGORGON

        God.

ASIA

        Who made all
That it contains ? thought, passion, reason,
    will,   10
Imagination ?

DEMOGORGON
God : Almighty God.

ASIA

Who made that sense which, when the
   winds of spring
In rarest visitation, or the voice
Of one belovèd heard in youth alone,
Fills the faint eyes with falling tears which
   dim
The radiant looks of unbewailing flowers,
And leaves this peopled earth a solitude
When it returns no more ?

DEMOGORGON
Merciful God.

ASIA

And who made terror, madness, crime, re-
   morse,
Which from the links of the great chain of
   things   20
To every thought within the mind of man
Sway and drag heavily, and each one reels
Under the load towards the pit of death ;
Abandoned hope, and love that turns to
   hate;
And self-contempt, bitterer to drink than
   blood;
Pain, whose unheeded and familiar speech
Is howling, and keen shrieks, day after
   day;
And Hell, or the sharp fear of Hell ?

DEMOGORGON
He reigns.

ASIA

Utter his name ; a world pining in pain
Asks but his name; curses shall drag him
   down.   30

DEMOGORGON
He reigns.

ASIA
I feel, I know it: who ?

DEMOGORGON
He reigns.

ASIA

Who reigns ?   There was the Heaven and
   Earth at first,
And Light and Love; then Saturn, from
   whose throne
Time fell, an envious shadow; such the
   state
Of the earth's primal spirits beneath his
   sway,
As the calm joy of flowers and living
   leaves
Before the wind or sun has withered them
And semivital worms ; but he refused
The birthright of their being, knowledge,
   power,
The skill which wields the elements, the
   thought   40
Which pierces this dim universe like light,
Self-empire, and the majesty of love;
For thirst of which they fainted.   Then
   Prometheus
Gave wisdom, which is strength, to Jupiter,
And with this law alone, 'Let man be
   free,'
Clothed him with the dominion of wide
   Heaven.
To know nor faith, nor love, nor law, to be
Omnipotent but friendless, is to reign;
And Jove now reigned; for on the race of
   man
First famine, and then toil, and then dis-
   ease,   50
Strife, wounds, and ghastly death unseen
   before,
Fell; and the unseasonable seasons drove,
With alternating shafts of frost and fire,
Their shelterless, pale tribes to mountain
   caves;
And in their desert hearts fierce wants he
   sent,
And mad disquietudes, and shadows idle
Of unreal good, which levied mutual war,
So ruining the lair wherein they raged.
Prometheus saw, and waked the legioned
   hopes   59
Which sleep within folded Elysian flowers,
Nepenthe, Moly, Amaranth, fadeless
   blooms,
That they might hide with thin and rain-
   bow wings
The shape of Death; and Love he sent to
   bind
The disunited tendrils of that vine
Which bears the wine of life, the human
   heart;
And he tamed fire which, like some beast
   of prey,
Most terrible, but lovely, played beneath

The frown of man; and tortured to his
    will
Iron and gold, the slaves and signs of
    power,
And gems and poisons, and all subtlest
    forms   70
Hidden beneath the mountains and the
    waves.
He gave man speech, and speech created
    thought,
Which is the measure of the universe;
And Science struck the thrones of earth
    and heaven,
Which shook, but fell not; and the har-
    monious mind
Poured itself forth in all-prophetic song;
And music lifted up the listening spirit
Until it walked, exempt from mortal care,
Godlike, o'er the clear billows of sweet
    sound;
And human hands first mimicked and then
    mocked,   80
With moulded limbs more lovely than its
    own,
The human form, till marble grew divine;
And mothers, gazing, drank the love men
    see
Reflected in their race, behold, and perish.
He told the hidden power of herbs and
    springs,
And Disease drank and slept. Death grew
    like sleep.
He taught the implicated orbits woven
Of the wide-wandering stars; and how the
    sun
Changes his lair, and by what secret spell
The pale moon is transformed, when her
    broad eye   90
Gazes not on the interlunar sea.
He taught to rule, as life directs the limbs,
The tempest-wingèd chariots of the Ocean,
And the Celt knew the Indian. Cities then
Were built, and through their snow-like
    columns flowed
The warm winds, and the azure ether shone,
And the blue sea and shadowy hills were
    seen.
Such, the alleviations of his state,
Prometheus gave to man, for which he
    hangs
Withering in destined pain; but who rains
    down   100
Evil, the immedicable plague, which, while
Man looks on his creation like a god
And sees that it is glorious, drives him on,

The wreck of his own will, the scorn of
    earth,
The outcast, the abandoned, the alone ?
Not Jove: while yet his frown shook heaven
    ay, when
His adversary from adamantine chains
Cursed him, he trembled like a slave. De-
    clare
Who is his master ? Is he too a slave ?

DEMOGORGON

All spirits are enslaved which serve things
    evil: 110
Thou knowest if Jupiter be such or no.

ASIA

Whom called'st thou God ?

DEMOGORGON

            I spoke but as ye speak,
For Jove is the supreme of living things.

ASIA

Who is the master of the slave ?

DEMOGORGON

                If the abysm
Could vomit forth its secrets — but a voice
Is wanting, the deep truth is imageless;
For what would it avail to bid thee gaze
On the revolving world ? What to bid
    speak
Fate, Time, Occasion, Chance and Change ?
    To these
All things are subject but eternal Love. 120

ASIA

So much I asked before, and my heart gave
The response thou hast given; and of such
    truths
Each to itself must be the oracle.
One more demand; and do thou answer me
As my own soul would answer, did it know
That which I ask. Prometheus shall arise
Henceforth the sun of this rejoicing world:
When shall the destined hour arrive ?

DEMOGORGON

                    Behold !

ASIA

The rocks are cloven, and through the pur-
    ple night
I see cars drawn by rainbow - wingèd
    steeds   130

Which trample the dim winds; in each there
    stands
A wild-eyed charioteer urging their flight.
Some look behind, as fiends pursued them
    there,
And yet I see no shapes but the keen stars;
Others, with burning eyes, lean forth, and
    drink
With eager lips the wind of their own
    speed,
As if the thing they loved fled on before,
And now, even now, they clasped it. Their
    bright locks
Stream like a comet's flashing hair; they
    all   139
Sweep onward.

DEMOGORGON

        These are the immortal Hours,
Of whom thou didst demand. One waits
    for thee.

ASIA

A Spirit with a dreadful countenance
Checks its dark chariot by the craggy gulf.
Unlike thy brethren, ghastly Charioteer,
Who art thou? Whither wouldst thou
    bear me? Speak!

SPIRIT

I am the Shadow of a destiny
More dread than is my aspect; ere yon
    planet
Has set, the darkness which ascends with
    me
Shall wrap in lasting night heaven's kingless
    throne.   149

ASIA

What meanest thou?

PANTHEA

        That terrible Shadow floats
Up from its throne, as may the lurid smoke
Of earthquake-ruined cities o'er the sea.
Lo! it ascends the car; the coursers fly
Terrified; watch its path among the stars
Blackening the night!

ASIA

        Thus I am answered: strange!

PANTHEA

See, near the verge, another chariot stays;
An ivory shell inlaid with crimson fire,

Which comes and goes within its sculptured
    rim
Of delicate strange tracery; the young
    Spirit
That guides it has the dove-like eyes of
    hope;   160
How its soft smiles attract the soul! as
    light
Lures wingèd insects through the lampless
    air.

SPIRIT

My coursers are fed with the lightning,
    They drink of the whirlwind's stream,
And when the red morning is bright'ning
    They bathe in the fresh sunbeam.
    They have strength for their swiftness I
        deem;
Then ascend with me, daughter of Ocean.

I desire — and their speed makes night
    kindle;
    I fear — they outstrip the typhoon;   170
Ere the cloud piled on Atlas can dwindle
    We encircle the earth and the moon.
    We shall rest from long labors at noon;
Then ascend with me, daughter of Ocean.

SCENE V. — *The Car pauses within a Cloud on
the Top of a snowy Mountain.* ASIA, PAN-
THEA, *and the* SPIRIT OF THE HOUR.

SPIRIT

On the brink of the night and the morning
    My coursers are wont to respire;
But the Earth has just whispered a warn-
        ing
    That their flight must be swifter than
        fire;
    They shall drink the hot speed of desire!

ASIA

Thou breathest on their nostrils, but my
    breath
Would give them swifter speed.

SPIRIT

        Alas! it could not.

PANTHEA

O Spirit! pause, and tell whence is the
    light
Which fills the cloud? the sun is yet un-
    risen.   9

SPIRIT

The sun will rise not until noon. Apollo
Is held in heaven by wonder; and the light
Which fills this vapor, as the aërial hue
Of fountain-gazing roses fills the water,
Flows from thy mighty sister.

PANTHEA

Yes, I feel —

ASIA

What is it with thee, sister ? Thou art
    pale.

PANTHEA

How thou art changed ! I dare not look
    on thee;
I feel but see thee not. I scarce endure
The radiance of thy beauty. Some good
    change
Is working in the elements, which suffer
Thy presence thus unveiled. The Nereids
    tell   20
That on the day when the clear hyaline
Was cloven at thy uprise, and thou didst
    stand
Within a veinèd shell, which floated on
Over the calm floor of the crystal sea,
Among the Ægean isles, and by the shores
Which bear thy name, — love, like the at-
    mosphere
Of the sun's fire filling the living world,
Burst from thee, and illumined earth and
    heaven
And the deep ocean and the sunless caves
And all that dwells within them; till grief
    cast   30
Eclipse upon the soul from which it came.
Such art thou now; nor is it I alone,
Thy sister, thy companion, thine own chosen
    one,
But the whole world which seeks thy sym-
    pathy.
Hearest thou not sounds i' the air which
    speak the love
Of all articulate beings ? Feelest thou not
The inanimate winds enamoured of thee ?
    List !   [Music.

ASIA

Thy words are sweeter than aught else but
    his
Whose echoes they are; yet all love is
    sweet,
Given or returned. Common as light is
    love,   40

And its familiar voice wearies not ever.
Like the wide heaven, the all-sustaining air,
It makes the reptile equal to the God;
They who inspire it most are fortunate,
As I am now; but those who feel it most
Are happier still, after long sufferings,
As I shall soon become.

PANTHEA

List ! Spirits speak.

VOICE in the air, singing

Life of Life, thy lips enkindle
    With their love the breath between them;
And thy smiles before they dwindle   50
    Make the cold air fire; then screen them
In those looks, where whoso gazes
Faints, entangled in their mazes.

Child of Light ! thy limbs are burning
    Through the vest which seems to hide
        them;
As the radiant lines of morning
    Through the clouds, ere they divide
        them;
And this atmosphere divinest
Shrouds thee wheresoe'er thou shinest.

Fair are others; none beholds thee,   60
    But thy voice sounds low and tender
Like the fairest, for it folds thee
    From the sight, that liquid splendor,
And all feel, yet see thee never,
As I feel now, lost forever !

Lamp of Earth ! where'er thou movest
    Its dim shapes are clad with brightness,
And the souls of whom thou lovest
    Walk upon the winds with lightness,
Till they fail, as I am failing,   70
Dizzy, lost, yet unbewailing !

ASIA

My soul is an enchanted boat,
    Which, like a sleeping swan, doth float
Upon the silver waves of thy sweet sing-
    ing;
    And thine doth like an angel sit
    Beside a helm conducting it,
Whilst all the winds with melody are ring-
    ing.
    It seems to float ever, forever,
    Upon that many-winding river,
Between mountains, woods, abysses,   80
A paradise of wildernesses !

Till, like one in slumber bound,
Borne to the ocean, I float down, around,
Into a sea profound of ever-spreading
    sound.

Meanwhile thy spirit lifts its pinions
  In music's most serene dominions;
Catching the winds that fan that happy
    heaven.
  And we sail on, away, afar,
  Without a course, without a star,
But, by the instinct of sweet music
    driven;   90
Till through Elysian garden islets
  By thee most beautiful of pilots,
Where never mortal pinnace glided,
  The boat of my desire is guided;
Realms where the air we breathe is love,
Which in the winds on the waves doth
    move,
Harmonizing this earth with what we feel
    above.

  We have passed Age's icy caves,
  And Manhood's dark and tossing waves,
And Youth's smooth ocean, smiling to
    betray;   100
  Beyond the glassy gulfs we flee
  Of shadow-peopled Infancy,
Through Death and Birth, to a diviner day;
  A paradise of vaulted bowers
  Lit by downward-gazing flowers,
  And watery paths that wind between
Wildernesses calm and green,
Peopled by shapes too bright to see,
And rest, having beheld; somewhat like
    thee;
Which walk upon the sea, and chant melo-
    diously!   110

ACT III

SCENE I. — *Heaven.* JUPITER *on his Throne;*
THETIS *and the other Deities assembled.*

JUPITER

YE congregated powers of heaven, who
    share
The glory and the strength of him ye
    serve,
Rejoice! henceforth I am omnipotent.
All else had been subdued to me; alone
The soul of man, like unextinguished fire,
Yet burns towards heaven with fierce re-
    proach, and doubt,

And lamentation, and reluctant prayer,
Hurling up insurrection, which might
    make
Our antique empire insecure, though built
On eldest faith, and hell's coeval, fear; 10
And though my curses through the pendu-
    lous air,
Like snow on herbless peaks, fall flake by
    flake,
And cling to it; though under my wrath's
    night
It climb the crags of life, step after step,
Which wound it, as ice wounds unsandalled
    feet,
It yet remains supreme o'er misery,
Aspiring, unrepressed, yet soon to fall;
Even now have I begotten a strange won-
    der,
That fatal child, the terror of the earth,
Who waits but till the destined hour ar-
    rive,   20
Bearing from Demogorgon's vacant throne
The dreadful might of ever-living limbs
Which clothed that awful spirit unbeheld,
To redescend, and trample out the spark.

Pour forth heaven's wine, Idæan Gany-
    mede,
And let it fill the dædal cups like fire,
And from the flower-inwoven soil divine,
Ye all-triumphant harmonies, arise,
As dew from earth under the twilight
    stars.
Drink! be the nectar circling through your
    veins   30
The soul of joy, ye ever-living Gods,
Till exultation burst in one wide voice
Like music from Elysian winds.
                    And thou
Ascend beside me, veilèd in the light
Of the desire which makes thee one with
    me,
Thetis, bright image of eternity!
When thou didst cry, 'Insufferable might!
God! spare me! I sustain not the quick
    .flames,
The penetrating presence; all my being,
Like him whom the Numidian seps did
    thaw   40
Into a dew with poison, is dissolved,
Sinking through its foundations,' — even
    then
Two mighty spirits, mingling, made a
    third
Mightier than either, which, unbodied now,

Between us floats, felt, although unbeheld,
Waiting the incarnation, which ascends,
(Hear ye the thunder of the fiery wheels
Griding the winds?) from Demogorgon's
    throne.
Victory! victory! Feel'st thou not, O
    world,
The earthquake of his chariot thundering
    up   50
Olympus?

> [*The Car of the* HOUR *arrives.* DEMO-
> GORGON *descends and moves towards the
> Throne of* JUPITER.

Awful shape, what art thou? Speak!

DEMOGORGON

Eternity. Demand no direr name.
Descend, and follow me down the abyss.
I am thy child, as thou wert Saturn's
    child;
Mightier than thee; and we must dwell to-
    gether
Henceforth in darkness. Lift thy light-
    nings not.
The tyranny of heaven none may retain,
Or reassume, or hold, succeeding thee;
Yet if thou wilt, as 't is the destiny
Of trodden worms to writhe till they are
    dead,   60
Put forth thy might.

JUPITER
                    Detested prodigy!
Even thus beneath the deep Titanian
    prisons
I trample thee! Thou lingerest?
                    Mercy! mercy!
No pity, no release, no respite! Oh,
That thou wouldst make mine enemy my
    judge,
Even where he hangs, seared by my long
    revenge,
On Caucasus! he would not doom me
    thus.
Gentle, and just, and dreadless, is he not
The monarch of the world? What then
    art thou?   69
No refuge! no appeal!
                    Sink with me then,
We two will sink on the wide waves of
    ruin,
Even as a vulture and a snake outspent
Drop, twisted in inextricable fight,
Into a shoreless sea! Let hell unlock

Its mounded oceans of tempestuous fire,
And whelm on them into the bottomless
    void
This desolated world, and thee, and me,
The conqueror and the conquered, and the
    wreck
Of that for which they combated!
                                    Ai, Ai!
The elements obey me not. I sink   80
Dizzily down, ever, forever, down.
And, like a cloud, mine enemy above
Darkens my fall with victory! Ai, Ai!

SCENE II. — *The Mouth of a great River in the
    Island Atlantis.* OCEAN *is discovered reclin-
    ing near the shore;* APOLLO *stands beside
    him.*

OCEAN

He fell, thou sayest, beneath his conquer-
    or's frown?

APOLLO

Ay, when the strife was ended which made
    dim
The orb I rule, and shook the solid stars,
The terrors of his eye illumined heaven
With sanguine light, through the thick
    ragged skirts
Of the victorious darkness, as he fell;
Like the last glare of day's red agony,
Which, from a rent among the fiery clouds,
Burns far along the tempest-wrinkled deep.

OCEAN

He sunk to the abyss? to the dark
    void?   10

APOLLO

An eagle so caught in some bursting cloud
On Caucasus, his thunder-baffled wings
Entangled in the whirlwind, and his eyes,
Which gazed on the undazzling sun, now
    blinded
By the white lightning, while the ponder-
    ous hail
Beats on his struggling form, which sinks
    at length
Prone, and the aërial ice clings over it.

OCEAN

Henceforth the fields of Heaven-reflecting
    sea
Which are my realm, will heave, unstained
    with blood,

Beneath the uplifting winds, like plains of
   corn   20
Swayed by the summer air; my streams
   will flow
Round many-peopled continents, and round
Fortunate isles; and from their glassy
   thrones
Blue Proteus and his humid nymphs shall
   mark
The shadow of fair ships, as mortals see
The floating bark of the light-laden moon
With that white star, its sightless pilot's
   crest,
Borne down the rapid sunset's ebbing sea ;
Tracking their path no more by blood and
   groans,
And desolation, and the mingled voice   30
Of slavery and command; but by the light
Of wave-reflected flowers, and floating
   odors,
And music soft, and mild, free, gentle
   voices,
That sweetest music, such as spirits love.

APOLLO

And I shall gaze not on the deeds which
   make
My mind obscure with sorrow, as eclipse
Darkens the sphere I guide. But list, I hear
The small, clear, silver lute of the young
   Spirit
That sits i' the morning star.

OCEAN
                   Thou must away ;
Thy steeds will pause at even, till when
   farewell.   40
The loud deep calls me home even now to
   feed it
With azure calm out of the emerald urns
Which stand forever full beside my throne.
Behold the Nereids under the green sea,
Their wavering limbs borne on the wind-
   like stream,
Their white arms lifted o'er their stream-
   ing hair,
With garlands pied and starry sea-flower
   crowns,
Hastening to grace their mighty sister's joy.
            [A sound of waves is heard.
It is the unpastured sea hungering for calm.
Peace, monster; I come now.   Farewell.

APOLLO
                  Farewell.   50

SCENE III. — *Caucasus.* PROMETHEUS, HER-
CULES, IONE, *the* EARTH, SPIRITS, ASIA, *and*
PANTHEA, *borne in the Car with the* SPIRIT
OF THE HOUR. HERCULES *unbinds* PRO-
METHEUS, *who descends.*

HERCULES

Most glorious among spirits ! thus doth
   strength
To wisdom, courage, and long-suffering
   love,
And thee, who art the form they animate,
Minister like a slave.

PROMETHEUS
               Thy gentle words
Are sweeter even than freedom long de-
   sired
And long delayed.

               Asia, thou light of life,
Shadow of beauty unbeheld; and ye,
Fair sister nymphs, who made long years
   of pain
Sweet to remember, through your love and
   care;
Henceforth we will not part. There is a
   cave,   10
All overgrown with trailing odorous plants,
Which curtain out the day with leaves and
   flowers,
And paved with veinèd emerald; and a
   fountain
Leaps in the midst with an awakening
   sound.
From its curved roof the mountain's frozen
   tears,
Like snow, or silver, or long diamond spires,
Hang downward, raining forth a doubtful
   light;
And there is heard the ever-moving air
Whispering without from tree to tree, and
   birds,
And bees; and all around are mossy
   seats,   20
And the rough walls are clothed with long
   soft grass;
A simple dwelling, which shall be our
   own ;
Where we will sit and talk of time and
   change,
As the world ebbs and flows, ourselves un-
   changed.
What can hide man from mutability ?
And if ye sigh, then I will smile; and thou,

Ione, shalt chant fragments of sea-music,
Until I weep, when ye shall smile away
The tears she brought, which yet were
    sweet to shed.
We will entangle buds and flowers and
    beams   30
Which twinkle on the fountain's brim, and
    make
Strange combinations out of common
    things,
Like human babes in their brief innocence;
And we will search, with looks and words
    of love,
For hidden thoughts, each lovelier than the
    last,
Our unexhausted spirits; and, like lutes
Touched by the skill of the enamoured wind,
Weave harmonies divine, yet ever new,
From difference sweet where discord can-
    not be;
And hither come, sped on the charmèd
    winds,   40
Which meet from all the points of heaven
    — as bees
From every flower aërial Enna feeds
At their known island-homes in Himera —
The echoes of the human world, which
    tell
Of the low voice of love, almost unheard,
And dove-eyed pity's murmured pain, and
    music,
Itself the echo of the heart, and all
That tempers or improves man's life, now
    free;
And lovely apparitions, — dim at first,
Then radiant, as the mind arising bright   50
From the embrace of beauty (whence the
    forms
Of which these are the phantoms) casts on
    them
The gathered rays which are reality —
Shall visit us, the progeny immortal
Of Painting, Sculpture, and rapt Poesy,
And arts, though unimagined, yet to be;
The wandering voices and the shadows
    these
Of all that man becomes, the mediators
Of that best worship, love, by him and us
Given and returned; swift shapes and
    sounds, which grow   60
More fair and soft as man grows wise and
    kind,
And, veil by veil, evil and error fall.
Such virtue has the cave and place around.
    [*Turning to the* SPIRIT OF THE HOUR.

For thee, fair Spirit, one toil remains.
    Ione,
Give her that curvèd shell, which Proteus
    old
Made Asia's nuptial boon, breathing within
    it
A voice to be accomplished, and which thou
Didst hide in grass under the hollow rock.

IONE

Thou most desired Hour, more loved and
    lovely
Than all thy sisters, this is the mystic
    shell.   70
See the pale azure fading into silver
Lining it with a soft yet glowing light.
Looks it not like lulled music sleeping
    there ?

SPIRIT

It seems in truth the fairest shell of Ocean:
Its sound must be at once both sweet and
    strange.

PROMETHEUS

Go, borne over the cities of mankind
On whirlwind-footed coursers; once again
Outspeed the sun around the orbèd world;
And as thy chariot cleaves the kindling air,
Thou breathe into the many-folded shell,
Loosening its mighty music; it shall be   81
As thunder mingled with clear echoes; then
Return; and thou shalt dwell beside our
    cave.

And thou, O Mother Earth ! —

THE EARTH

               I hear, I feel;
Thy lips are on me, and thy touch runs
    down
Even to the adamantine central gloom
Along these marble nerves; 't is life, 't is
    joy,
And, through my withered, old, and icy
    frame
The warmth of an immortal youth shoots
    down
Circling. Henceforth the many children
    fair   90
Folded in my sustaining arms; all plants,
And creeping forms, and insects rainbow-
    winged,
And birds, and beasts, and fish, and human
    shapes,

Which drew disease and pain from my
  wan bosom,
Draining the poison of despair, shall take
And interchange sweet nutriment; to me
Shall they become like sister-antelopes
By one fair dam, snow-white, and swift as
  wind,
Nursed among lilies near a brimming
  stream.
The dew-mists of my sunless sleep shall
  float   100
Under the stars like balm; night-folded
  flowers
Shall suck unwithering hues in their repose;
And men and beasts in happy dreams shall
  gather
Strength for the coming day, and all its
  joy,
And death shall be the last embrace of her
Who takes the life she gave, even as a mo-
  ther,
Folding her child, says, 'Leave me not
  again.'

ASIA

Oh, mother ! wherefore speak the name of
  death ?
Cease they to love, and move, and breathe,
  and speak,
Who die ?

THE EARTH

          It would avail not to reply; 110
Thou art immortal and this tongue is known
But to the uncommunicating dead.
Death is the veil which those who live call
  life;
They sleep, and it is lifted; and meanwhile
In mild variety the seasons mild
With rainbow-skirted showers, and odorous
  winds,
And long blue meteors cleansing the dull
  night,
And the life-kindling shafts of the keen
  sun's
All-piercing bow, and the dew-mingled rain
Of the calm moonbeams, a soft influence
  mild,   120
Shall clothe the forests and the fields, ay,
  even
The crag-built deserts of the barren deep,
With ever-living leaves, and fruits, and
  flowers.
And thou ! there is a cavern where my
  spirit

Was panted forth in anguish whilst thy
  pain
Made my heart mad, and those who did
  inhale it
Became mad too, and built a temple there,
And spoke, and were oracular, and lured
The erring nations round to mutual war,
And faithless faith, such as Jove kept with
  thee;   130
Which breath now rises as amongst tall
  weeds
A violet's exhalation, and it fills
With a serener light and crimson air
Intense, yet soft, the rocks and woods
  around;
It feeds the quick growth of the serpent
  vine,
And the dark linkèd ivy tangling wild,
And budding, blown, or odor-faded blooms
Which star the winds with points of col-
  ored light
As they rain through them, and bright
  golden globes
Of fruit suspended in their own green hea-
  ven,   140
And through their veinèd leaves and amber
  stems
The flowers whose purple and translucid
  bowls
Stand ever mantling with aërial dew,
The drink of spirits; and it circles round,
Like the soft waving wings of noonday
  dreams,
Inspiring calm and happy thoughts, like
  mine,
Now thou art thus restored.   This cave is
  thine.
Arise !   Appear !
    [A SPIRIT rises in the likeness of a winged
    child.
                This is my torch-bearer;
Who let his lamp out in old time with gazing
On eyes from which he kindled it anew 150
With love, which is as fire, sweet daughter
  mine,
For such is that within thine own.   Run,
  wayward,
And guide this company beyond the peak
Of Bacchic Nysa, Mænad-haunted moun-
  tain,
And beyond Indus and its tribute rivers,
Trampling the torrent streams and glassy
  lakes
With feet unwet, unwearied, undelaying,
And up the green ravine, across the vale,

Beside the windless and crystalline pool,
Where ever lies, on unerasing waves,   160
The image of a temple, built above,
Distinct with column, arch, and architrave,
And palm-like capital, and overwrought,
And populous most with living imagery,
Praxitelean shapes, whose marble smiles
Fill the hushed air with everlasting love.
It is deserted now, but once it bore
Thy name, Prometheus; there the emulous
      youths
Bore to thy honor through the divine
      gloom
The lamp which was thine emblem; even
      as those   170
Who bear the untransmitted torch of hope
Into the grave, across the night of life,
As thou hast borne it most triumphantly
To this far goal of Time. Depart, fare-
      well !
Beside that temple is the destined cave.

SCENE IV. — *A Forest. In the background a
   Cave.* PROMETHEUS, ASIA, PANTHEA, IONE,
   and the SPIRIT OF THE EARTH.

IONE

Sister, it is not earthly; how it glides
Under the leaves ! how on its head there
      burns
A light, like a green star, whose emerald
      beams
Are twined with its fair hair ! how, as it
      moves,
The splendor drops in flakes upon the
      grass !
Knowest thou it ?

PANTHEA

                  It is the delicate spirit
That guides the earth through heaven.
      From afar
The populous constellations call that light
The loveliest of the planets; and sometimes
It floats along the spray of the salt sea,   10
Or makes its chariot of a foggy cloud,
Or walks through fields or cities while men
      sleep,
Or o'er the mountain tops, or down the
      rivers,
Or through the green waste wilderness, as
      now,
Wondering at all it sees. Before Jove
      reigned
It loved our sister Asia, and it came

Each leisure hour to drink the liquid light
Out of her eyes, for which it said it thirsted
As one bit by a dipsas, and with her
It made its childish confidence, and told
      her   20
All it had known or seen, for it saw much,
Yet idly reasoned what it saw; and called
      her,
For whence it sprung it knew not, nor
      do I,
Mother, dear mother.

THE SPIRIT OF THE EARTH, *running to* ASIA
                  Mother, dearest mother !
May I then talk with thee as I was wont ?
May I then hide my eyes in thy soft arms,
After thy looks have made them tired of
      joy ?
May I then play beside thee the long
      noons,
When work is none in the bright silent
      air ?   29

ASIA

I love thee, gentlest being, and henceforth
Can cherish thee unenvied. Speak, I
      pray;
Thy simple talk once solaced, now de-
      lights.

SPIRIT OF THE EARTH

Mother, I am grown wiser, though a child
Cannot be wise like thee, within this day;
And happier too; happier and wiser both.
Thou knowest that toads, and snakes, and
      loathly worms,
And venomous and malicious beasts, and
      boughs
That bore ill berries in the woods, were
      ever
An hindrance to my walks o'er the green
      world;
And that, among the haunts of human-
      kind,   40
Hard-featured men, or with proud, angry
      looks,
Or cold, staid gait, or false and hollow
      smiles,
Or the dull sneer of self-loved ignorance,
Or other such foul masks, with which ill
      thoughts
Hide. that fair being whom we spirits call
      man;
And women too, ugliest of all things evil,
(Though fair, even in a world where thou
      art fair,

When good and kind, free and sincere like
    thee)
When false or frowning made me sick at
    heart
To pass them, though they slept, and I un-
    seen.   50
Well, my path lately lay through a great
    city
Into the woody hills surrounding it;
A sentinel was sleeping at the gate;
When there was heard a sound, so loud, it
    shook
The towers amid the moonlight, yet more
    sweet
Than any voice but thine, sweetest of all;
A long, long sound, as it would never end;
And all the inhabitants leapt suddenly
Out of their rest, and gathered in the
    streets,
Looking in wonder up to Heaven, while
    yet   60
The music pealed along. I hid myself
Within a fountain in the public square,
Where I lay like the reflex of the moon
Seen in a wave under green leaves; and
    soon
Those ugly human shapes and visages
Of which I spoke as having wrought me
    pain,
Passed floating through the air, and fading
    still
Into the winds that scattered them; and
    those
From whom they passed seemed mild and
    lovely forms
After some foul disguise had fallen, and
    all   70
Were somewhat changed, and after brief
    surprise
And greetings of delighted wonder, all
Went to their sleep again; and when the
    dawn
Came, wouldst thou think that toads, and
    snakes, and efts,
Could e'er be beautiful ? yet so they were,
And that with little change of shape or
    hue;
All things had put their evil nature off;
I cannot tell my joy, when o'er a lake,
Upon a drooping bough with nightshade
    twined,
I saw two azure halcyons clinging down-
    ward   80
And thinning one bright bunch of amber
    berries,

With quick long beaks, and in the deep
    there lay
Those lovely forms imaged as in a sky;
So with my thoughts full of these happy
    changes,
We meet again, the happiest change of all.

ASIA

And never will we part, till thy chaste
    sister,
Who guides the frozen and inconstant
    moon,
Will look on thy more warm and equal
    light
Till her heart thaw like flakes of April
    snow,   89
And love thee.

SPIRIT OF THE EARTH

What ! as Asia loves Prometheus ?

ASIA

Peace, wanton ! thou art yet not old
    enough.
Think ye by gazing on each other's eyes
To multiply your lovely selves, and fill
With sphered fires the interlunar air ?

SPIRIT OF THE EARTH

Nay, mother, while my sister trims her
    lamp
'T is hard I should go darkling.

ASIA

                            Listen; look !

The SPIRIT OF THE HOUR *enters*

PROMETHEUS

We feel what thou hast heard and seen;
    yet speak.

SPIRIT OF THE HOUR

Soon as the sound had ceased whose thunder
    filled
The abysses of the sky and the wide earth,
There was a change; the impalpable thin
    air   100
And the all-circling sunlight were trans-
    formed,
As if the sense of love, dissolved in them,
Had folded itself round the sphered world.
My vision then grew clear, and I could see
Into the mysteries of the universe.
Dizzy as with delight I floated down;

Winnowing the lightsome air with languid
   plumes,
My coursers sought their birthplace in the
   sun,
Where they henceforth will live exempt
   from toil,
Pasturing flowers of vegetable fire,   110
And where my moonlike car will stand
   within
A temple, gazed upon by Phidian forms
Of thee, and Asia, and the Earth, and me,
And you, fair nymphs, looking the love we
   feel, —
In memory of the tidings it has borne, —
Beneath a dome fretted with graven
   flowers,
Poised on twelve columns of resplendent
   stone,
And open to the bright and liquid sky.
Yoked to it by an amphisbenic snake
The likeness of those wingèd steeds will
   mock   120
The flight from which they find repose.
   Alas,
Whither has wandered now my partial
   tongue
When all remains untold which ye would
   hear?
As I have said, I floated to the earth;
It was, as it is still, the pain of bliss
To move, to breathe, to be. I wandering
   went
Among the haunts and dwellings of man-
   kind,
And first was disappointed not to see
Such mighty change as I had felt within
Expressed in outward things; but soon I
   looked,   130
And behold, thrones were kingless, and men
   walked
One with the other even as spirits do —
None fawned, none trampled; hate, dis-
   dain, or fear,
Self-love or self-contempt, on human brows
No more inscribed, as o'er the gate of hell,
' All hope abandon, ye who enter here.'
None frowned, none trembled, none with
   eager fear
Gazed on another's eye of cold command,
Until the subject of a tyrant's will   139
Became, worse fate, the abject of his own,
Which spurred him, like an outspent horse,
   to death.
None wrought his lips in truth-entangling
   lines

Which smiled the lie his tongue disdained
   to speak.
None, with firm sneer, trod out in his own
   heart
The sparks of love and hope till there re-
   mained
Those bitter ashes, a soul self-consumed,
And the wretch crept a vampire among
   men,
Infecting all with his own hideous ill.
None talked that common, false, cold, hol-
   low talk
Which makes the heart deny the *yes* it
   breathes,   150
Yet question that unmeant hypocrisy
With such a self-mistrust as has no name.
And women, too, frank, beautiful, and kind,
As the free heaven which rains fresh light
   and dew
On the wide earth, passed; gentle, radiant
   forms,
From custom's evil taint exempt and pure;
Speaking the wisdom once they could not
   think,
Looking emotions once they feared to feel,
And changed to all which once they dared
   not be,
Yet being now, made earth like heaven;
   nor pride,   160
Nor jealousy, nor envy, nor ill shame,
The bitterest of those drops of treasured
   gall,
Spoiled the sweet taste of the nepenthe,
   love.

Thrones, altars, judgment-seats, and pris-
   ons, wherein,
And beside which, by wretched men were
   borne
Sceptres, tiaras, swords, and chains, and
   tomes
Of reasoned wrong, glozed on by ignorance,
Were like those monstrous and barbaric
   shapes,
The ghosts of a no-more-remembered fame
Which from their unworn obelisks, look
   forth   170
In triumph o'er the palaces and tombs
Of those who were their conquerors; mould-
   ering round,
Those imaged to the pride of kings and
   priests
A dark yet mighty faith, a power as wide
As is the world it wasted, and are now
But an astonishment; even so the tools

And emblems of its last captivity,
Amid the dwellings of the peopled earth,
Stand, not o'erthrown, but unregarded now.
And those foul shapes, — abhorred by god
    and man,   180
Which, under many a name and many a
    form
Strange, savage, ghastly, dark, and ex-
    ecrable,
Were Jupiter, the tyrant of the world,
And which the nations, panic-stricken,
    served
With blood, and hearts broken by long
    hope, and love
Dragged to his altars soiled and garland-
    less,
And slain among men's unreclaiming tears,
Flattering the thing they feared, which fear
    was hate, —
Frown, mouldering fast, o'er their aban-
    doned shrines.
The painted veil, by those who were, called
    life,   190
Which mimicked, as with colors idly spread,
All men believed and hoped, is torn aside;
The loathsome mask has fallen, the man
    remains
Sceptreless, free, uncircumscribed, but man
Equal, unclassed, tribeless, and nationless,
Exempt from awe, worship, degree, the
    king
Over himself; just, gentle, wise; but man
Passionless — no, yet free from guilt or pain,
Which were, for his will made or suffered
    them;
Nor yet exempt, though ruling them like
    slaves,   200
From chance, and death, and mutability,
The clogs of that which else might over-
    soar
The loftiest star of unascended heaven,
Pinnacled dim in the intense inane.

ACT IV

SCENE — *A part of the Forest near the Cave
of* PROMETHEUS. PANTHEA *and* IONE *are
sleeping: they awaken gradually during the
first Song.*

VOICE OF UNSEEN SPIRITS

THE pale stars are gone !
For the sun, their swift shepherd
To their folds them compelling,
In the depths of the dawn,

Hastes, in meteor-eclipsing array, and they
    flee
  Beyond his blue dwelling,
  As fawns flee the leopard,
    But where are ye ?

*A Train of dark Forms and Shadows passes by
confusedly, singing.*

  Here, oh, here !
  We bear the bier   10
Of the father of many a cancelled year !
  Spectres we
  Of the dead Hours be;
We bear Time to his tomb in eternity.

  Strew, oh, strew
  Hair, not yew !
Wet the dusty pall with tears, not dew !
  Be the faded flowers
  Of Death's bare bowers
Spread on the corpse of the King of
  Hours !   20

  Haste, oh, haste !
  As shades are chased,
Trembling, by day, from heaven's blue
  waste,
  We melt away,
  Like dissolving spray,
From the children of a diviner day,
  With the lullaby
  Of winds that die
On the bosom of their own harmony !

IONE

What dark forms were they ?   30

PANTHEA

The past Hours weak and gray,
With the spoil which their toil
  Raked together
From the conquest but One could foil.

IONE

Have they passed ?

PANTHEA

          They have passed;
They outspeeded the blast,
While 't is said, they are fled !

IONE

Whither, oh, whither ?

PANTHEA

To the dark, to the past, to the dead.

VOICE OF UNSEEN SPIRITS

Bright clouds float in heaven,   40
Dew-stars gleam on earth,
Waves assemble on ocean,
They are gathered and driven
By the storm of delight, by the panic of
          glee !
They shake with emotion,
They dance in their mirth.
          But where are ye ?

The pine boughs are singing
Old songs with new gladness,
The billows and fountains   50
Fresh music are flinging,
Like the notes of a spirit from land and
          from sea;
The storms mock the mountains
With the thunder of gladness,
          But where are ye ?

IONE

What charioteers are these ?

PANTHEA

          Where are their chariots ?

SEMICHORUS OF HOURS

The voice of the Spirits of Air and of
          Earth
Has drawn back the figured curtain of
          sleep,
Which covered our being and darkened
          our birth   59
In the deep.

A VOICE

In the deep ?

SEMICHORUS II

          Oh ! below the deep.

SEMICHORUS I

An hundred ages we had been kept
Cradled in visions of hate and care,
And each one who waked as his brother
          slept
Found the truth —

SEMICHORUS II

Worse than his visions were !

SEMICHORUS I

We have heard the lute of Hope in sleep;

We have known the voice of Love in
          dreams ;
We have felt the wand of Power, and
          leap —

SEMICHORUS II

As the billows leap in the morning beams !

CHORUS

Weave the dance on the floor of the breeze,
Pierce with song heaven's silent light,   70
Enchant the day that too swiftly flees,
To check its flight ere the cave of night.

Once the hungry Hours were hounds
Which chased the day like a bleeding
          deer,
And it limped and stumbled with many
          wounds
Through the nightly dells of the desert
          year.

But now, oh, weave the mystic measure
Of music, and dance, and shapes of light,
Let the Hours, and the Spirits of might
          and pleasure,   79
Like the clouds and sunbeams, unite —

A VOICE

          Unite !

PANTHEA

See, where the Spirits of the human mind,
Wrapped in sweet sounds, as in bright veils,
          approach.

CHORUS OF SPIRITS

We join the throng
Of the dance and the song,
By the whirlwind of gladness borne along;
As the flying-fish leap
From the Indian deep
And mix with the sea-birds half-asleep.

CHORUS OF HOURS

Whence come ye, so wild and so fleet,   89
For sandals of lightning are on your feet,
And your wings are soft and swift as
          thought,
And your eyes are as love which is veilèd
          not ?

CHORUS OF SPIRITS

We come from the mind
Of humankind,

Which was late so dusk, and obscene, and
    blind ;
    Now 't is an ocean
    Of clear emotion,
A heaven of serene and mighty motion.

    From that deep abyss
    Of wonder and bliss,   100
Whose caverns are crystal palaces;
    From those skyey towers
    Where Thought's crowned powers
Sit watching your dance, ye happy Hours !

    From the dim recesses
    Of woven caresses,
Where lovers catch ye by your loose tresses;
    From the azure isles,
    Where sweet Wisdom smiles,   109
Delaying your ships with her siren wiles.

    From the temples high
    Of Man's ear and eye,
Roofed over Sculpture and Poesy;
    From the murmurings
    Of the unsealed springs,
Where Science bedews his dædal wings.

    Years after years,
    Through blood, and tears,
And a thick hell of hatreds, and hopes, and
    fears,
    We waded and flew,   120
    And the islets were few
Where the bud-blighted flowers of happi-
    ness grew.

    Our feet now, every palm,
    Are sandalled with calm,
And the dew of our wings is a rain of
    balm;
    And, beyond our eyes,
    The human love lies,
Which makes all it gazes on Paradise.

CHORUS OF SPIRITS AND HOURS

Then weave the web of the mystic mea-
    sure;
    From the depths of the sky and the ends
      of the earth,   130
Come, swift Spirits of might and of plea-
    sure,
    Fill the dance and the music of mirth,
As the waves of a thousand streams rush
    by
To an ocean of splendor and harmony !

CHORUS OF SPIRITS
    Our spoil is won,
    Our task is done,
We are free to dive, or soar, or run;
    Beyond and around,
    Or within the bound   139
Which clips the world with darkness round.

    We 'll pass the eyes
    Of the starry skies
Into the hoar deep to colonize;
    Death, Chaos and Night,
    From the sound of our flight,
Shall flee, like mist from a tempest's might.

    And Earth, Air and Light,
    And the Spirit of Might,
Which drives round the stars in their fiery
    flight;
    And Love, Thought and Breath,   150
    The powers that quell Death,
Wherever we soar shall assemble beneath.

    And our singing shall build
    In the void's loose field
A world for the Spirit of Wisdom to wield;
    We will take our plan
    From the new world of man,
And our work shall be called the Prome-
    thean.

CHORUS OF HOURS

Break the dance, and scatter the song;
    Let some depart, and some remain; 160

SEMICHORUS I

We, beyond heaven, are driven along;

SEMICHORUS II

Us the enchantments of earth retain;

SEMICHORUS I

Ceaseless, and rapid, and fierce, and free,
With the Spirits which build a new earth
    and sea,
And a heaven where yet heaven could never
    be;

SEMICHORUS II

Solemn, and slow, and serene, and bright,
Leading the Day, and outspeeding the
    Night,
With the powers of a world of perfect
    light;

SEMICHORUS I

We whirl, singing loud, round the gathering sphere,
Till the trees, and the beasts, and the clouds
appear   170
From its chaos made calm by love, not
fear;

SEMICHORUS II

We encircle the ocean and mountains of
earth,
And the happy forms of its death and birth
Change to the music of our sweet mirth.

CHORUS OF HOURS AND SPIRITS

Break the dance, and scatter the song;
Let some depart, and some remain;
Wherever we fly we lead along
In leashes, like star-beams, soft yet strong,
The clouds that are heavy with love's
sweet rain.   179

PANTHEA

Ha! they are gone!

IONE

               Yet feel you no delight
From the past sweetness?

PANTHEA

               As the bare green hill,
When some soft cloud vanishes into rain,
Laughs with a thousand drops of sunny
water
To the unpavilioned sky!

IONE

               Even whilst we speak
New notes arise. What is that awful
sound?

PANTHEA

'T is the deep music of the rolling world,
Kindling within the strings of the waved
air
Æolian modulations.

IONE

               Listen too,
How every pause is filled with under-notes,
Clear, silver, icy, keen awakening tones,
Which pierce the sense, and live within the
soul,   191
As the sharp stars pierce winter's crystal
air
And gaze upon themselves within the sea.

PANTHEA

But see where, through two openings in
the forest
Which hanging branches overcanopy,
And where two runnels of a rivulet,
Between the close moss violet-inwoven,
Have made their path of melody, like sis-
ters
Who part with sighs that they may meet
in smiles,
Turning their dear disunion to an isle   200
Of lovely grief, a wood of sweet sad
thoughts;
Two visions of strange radiance float upon
The ocean-like enchantment of strong
sound,
Which flows intenser, keener, deeper yet,
Under the ground and through the wind-
less air.

IONE

I see a chariot like that thinnest boat
In which the mother of the months is borne
By ebbing night into her western cave,
When she upsprings from interlunar
dreams;   209
O'er which is curved an orb-like canopy
Of gentle darkness, and the hills and woods,
Distinctly seen through that dusk airy veil,
Regard like shapes in an enchanter's glass;
Its wheels are solid clouds, azure and gold,
Such as the genii of the thunder-storm
Pile on the floor of the illumined sea
When the sun rushes under it; they roll
And move and grow as with an inward
wind;
Within it sits a wingèd infant — white
Its countenance, like the whiteness of bright
snow,   220
Its plumes are as feathers of sunny frost,
Its limbs gleam white, through the wind-
flowing folds
Of its white robe, woof of ethereal pearl,
Its hair is white, the brightness of white
light
Scattered in strings; yet its two eyes are
heavens
Of liquid darkness, which the Deity
Within seems pouring, as a storm is poured
From jagged clouds, out of their arrowy
lashes,
Tempering the cold and radiant air around
With fire that is not brightness; in its hand
It sways a quivering moonbeam, from whose
point   231

A guiding power directs the chariot's prow
Over its wheelèd clouds, which as they roll
Over the grass, and flowers, and waves,
　　wake sounds,
Sweet as a singing rain of silver dew.

PANTHEA

And from the other opening in the wood
Rushes, with loud and whirlwind harmony,
A sphere, which is as many thousand
　　spheres;
Solid as crystal, yet through all its mass
Flow, as through empty space, music and
　　light;　　　　　　　　　　240
Ten thousand orbs involving and involved,
Purple and azure, white, green and golden,
Sphere within sphere; and every space
　　between'
Peopled with unimaginable shapes,
Such as ghosts dream dwell in the lampless
　　deep;
Yet each inter-transpicuous; and they whirl
Over each other with a thousand motions,
Upon a thousand sightless axles spinning,
And with the force of self-destroying swift-
　　ness,
Intensely, slowly, solemnly, roll on,　　250
Kindling with mingled sounds, and many
　　tones,
Intelligible words and music wild.
With mighty whirl the multitudinous orb
Grinds the bright brook into an azure mist
Of elemental subtlety, like light;
And the wild odor of the forest flowers,
The music of the living grass and air,
The emerald light of leaf-entangled beams,
Round its intense yet self-conflicting speed
Seem kneaded into one aërial mass　　260
Which drowns the sense. Within the orb
　　itself,
Pillowed upon its alabaster arms,
Like to a child o'erwearied with sweet toil,
On its own folded wings and wavy hair
The Spirit of the Earth is laid asleep,
And you can see its little lips are moving,
Amid the changing light of their own smiles,
Like one who talks of what he loves in
　　dream.

IONE

'T is only mocking the orb's harmony.

PANTHEA

And from a star upon its forehead shoot,　270
Like swords of azure fire or golden spears

With tyrant-quelling myrtle overtwined,
Embleming heaven and earth united now,
Vast beams like spokes of some invisible
　　wheel
Which whirl as the orb whirls, swifter than
　　thought,
Filling the abyss with sun-like lightnings,
And perpendicular now, and now transverse,
Pierce the dark soil, and as they pierce and
　　pass
Make bare the secrets of the earth's deep
　　heart;
Infinite mine of adamant and gold,　　280
Valueless stones, and unimagined gems,
And caverns on crystalline columns poised
With vegetable silver overspread;
Wells of unfathomed fire, and water-springs
Whence the great sea even as a child is fed,
Whose vapors clothe earth's monarch
　　mountain-tops
With kingly, ermine snow. The beams
　　flash on
And make appear the melancholy ruins
Of cancelled cycles; anchors, beaks of
　　ships;
Planks turned to marble; quivers, helms,
　　and spears,　　　　　　　　290
And gorgon-headed targes, and the wheels
Of scythèd chariots, and the emblazonry
Of trophies, standards, and armorial beasts,
Round which death laughed, sepulchred
　　emblems
Of dead destruction, ruin within ruin !
The wrecks beside of many a city vast,
Whose population which the earth grew
　　over
Was mortal, but not human; see, they lie,
Their monstrous works, and uncouth skele-
　　tons,
Their statues, homes and fanes; prodigious
　　shapes　　　　　　　　　　300
Huddled in gray annihilation, split,
Jammed in the hard, black deep; and over
　　these,
The anatomies of unknown wingèd things,
And fishes which were isles of living scale,
And serpents, bony chains, twisted around
The iron crags, or within heaps of dust
To which the tortuous strength of their last
　　pangs
Had crushed the iron crags; and over these
The jagged alligator, and the might　　309
Of earth-convulsing behemoth, which once
Were monarch beasts, and on the slimy
　　shores,

And weed-overgrown continents of earth,
Increased and multiplied like summer
    worms
On an abandoned corpse, till the blue globe
Wrapped deluge round it like a cloke, and
    they
Yelled, gasped, and were abolished; or
    some God,
Whose throne was in a comet, passed, and
    cried,
Be not ! and like my words they were no
    more.

THE EARTH

The joy, the triumph, the delight, the mad-
    ness !
The boundless, overflowing, bursting glad-
    ness,   320
The vaporous exultation not to be confined !
Ha ! ha ! the animation of delight
Which wraps me, like an atmosphere of
    light,
And bears me as a cloud is borne by its
    own wind.

THE MOON

Brother mine, calm wanderer,
Happy globe of land and air,
Some Spirit is darted like a beam from
    thee,
Which penetrates my frozen frame,
And passes with the warmth of flame,
With love, and odor, and deep melody   330
    Through me, through me !

THE EARTH

Ha ! ha ! the caverns of my hollow moun-
    tains,
My cloven fire-crags, sound-exulting
    fountains,
Laugh with a vast and inextinguishable
    laughter.
The oceans, and the deserts, and the
    abysses,
And the deep air's unmeasured wilder-
    nesses,
Answer from all their clouds and billows,
    echoing after.

They cry aloud as I do.   Sceptred curse,
Who all our green and azure universe
Threatenedst to muffle round with black
    destruction, sending   340
A solid cloud to rain hot thunder-stones
And splinter and knead down my chil-
    dren's bones,

All I bring forth, to one void mass batter-
    ing and blending,

Until each crag-like tower, and storied
    column,
Palace, and obelisk, and temple solemn,
My imperial mountains crowned with cloud,
    and snow, and fire,
My sea-like forests, every blade and
    blossom
Which finds a grave or cradle in my
    bosom,
Were stamped by thy strong hate into a
    lifeless mire:

How art thou sunk, withdrawn, covered,
    drunk up   350
By thirsty nothing, as the brackish cup
Drained by a desert-troop, a little drop for
    all;
And from beneath, around, within, above,
Filling thy void annihilation, love
Bursts in like light on caves cloven by the
    thunder-ball !

THE MOON

The snow upon my lifeless mountains
Is loosened into living fountains,
My solid oceans flow, and sing and shine;
A spirit from my heart bursts forth,
It clothes with unexpected birth   360
My cold bare bosom.   Oh, it must be thine
    On mine, on mine !

Gazing on thee I feel, I know,
Green stalks burst forth, and bright
    flowers grow,
And living shapes upon my bosom move;
Music is in the sea and air,
Wingèd clouds soar here and there
Dark with the rain new buds are dream-
    ing of:
    'T is love, all love !

THE EARTH

It interpenetrates my granite mass,   370
Through tangled roots and trodden clay
    doth pass
Into the utmost leaves and delicatest flow-
    ers;
Upon the winds, among the clouds 't is
    spread,
It wakes a life in the forgotten dead, —
They breathe a spirit up from their obscur-
    est bowers;

And like a storm bursting its cloudy
    prison
With thunder, and with whirlwind, has
    arisen
Out of the lampless caves of unimagined
    being;
With earthquake shock and swiftness
    making shiver
Thought's stagnant chaos, unremoved
    forever,   380
Till hate, and fear, and pain, light-van-
    quished shadows, fleeing,

Leave Man, who was a many-sided mir-
    ror
Which could distort to many a shape of
    error
This true fair world of things, a sea re-
    flecting love;
Which over all his kind, as the sun's hea-
    ven
Gliding o'er ocean, smooth, serene, and
    even,
Darting from starry depths radiance and
    life doth move:

Leave Man even as a leprous child is
    left,
Who follows a sick beast to some warm
    cleft
Of rocks, through which the might of heal-
    ing springs is poured;   390
Then when it wanders home with rosy
    smile,
Unconscious, and its mother fears awhile
It is a spirit, then weeps on her child re-
    stored:

Man, oh, not men! a chain of linkèd
    thought,
Of love and might to be divided not,
Compelling the elements with 'adamantine
    stress;
As the sun rules even with a tyrant's
    gaze
The unquiet republic of the maze
Of planets, struggling fierce towards hea-
    ven's free wilderness:

Man, one harmonious soul of many a
    soul,   400
Whose nature is its own divine control,
Where all things flow to all, as rivers to the
    sea;
Familiar acts are beautiful through love;

Labor, and pain, and grief, in life's green
    grove
Sport like tame beasts; none knew how
    gentle they could be !

His will, with all mean passions, bad
    delights,
And selfish cares, its trembling satellites,
A spirit ill to guide, but mighty to obey,
Is as a tempest-wingèd ship, whose helm
Love rules, through waves which dare
    not overwhelm,   410
Forcing life's wildest shores to own its sov-
    ereign sway.

All things confess his strength. Through
    the cold mass
Of marble and of color his dreams
    pass —
Bright threads whence mothers weave the
    robes their children wear;
Language is a perpetual Orphic song,
Which rules with dædal harmony a
    throng
Of thoughts and forms, which else senseless
    and shapeless were.

The lightning is his slave; heaven's ut-
    most deep
Gives up her stars, and like a flock of
    sheep
They pass before his eye, are numbered,
    and roll on !   420
The tempest is his steed, he strides the
    air;
And the abyss shouts from her depth
    laid bare,
'Heaven, hast thou secrets ? Man unveils
    me; I have none.'

THE MOON

The shadow of white death has passed
From my path in heaven at last,
A clinging shroud of solid frost and sleep;
And through my newly woven bowers,
Wander happy paramours,
Less mighty, but as mild as those who
    keep
    Thy vales more deep.   430

THE EARTH

As the dissolving warmth of dawn may
    fold
A half unfrozen dew-globe, green, and
    gold,

And crystalline, till it becomes a wingèd
    mist,
And wanders up the vault of the blue
    day,
Outlives the noon, and on the sun's last
    ray
Hangs o'er the sea, a fleece of fire and
    amethyst.

THE MOON

Thou art folded, thou art lying
In the light which is undying
Of thine own joy, and heaven's smile
    divine;
All suns and constellations shower 440
On thee a light, a life, a power,
Which doth array thy sphere; thou pour-
    est thine
        On mine, on mine !

THE EARTH

I spin beneath my pyramid of night
Which points into the heavens, dreaming
    delight,
Murmuring victorious joy in my enchanted
    sleep;
As a youth lulled in love-dreams faintly
    sighing,
Under the shadow of his beauty lying,
Which round his rest a watch of light and
    warmth doth keep.

THE MOON

As in the soft and sweet eclipse,   450
When soul meets soul on lovers' lips,
High hearts are calm, and brightest eyes
    are dull;
So when thy shadow falls on me,
Then am I mute and still, by thee
Covered; of thy love, Orb most beautiful,
    Full, oh, too full !

Thou art speeding round the sun,
Brightest world of many a one;
Green and azure sphere which shinest
With a light which is divinest   460
Among all the lamps of Heaven
To whom life and light is given;
I, thy crystal paramour,
Borne beside thee by a power
Like the polar Paradise,
Magnet-like, of lovers' eyes;
I, a most enamoured maiden,
Whose weak brain is overladen

With the pleasure of her love,
Maniac-like around thee move,   470
Gazing, an insatiate bride,
On thy form from every side,
Like a Mænad round the cup
Which Agave lifted up
In the weird Cadmean forest.
Brother, wheresoe'er thou soarest
I must hurry, whirl and follow
Through the heavens wide and hollow,
Sheltered by the warm embrace
Of thy soul from hungry space,   480
Drinking from thy sense and sight
Beauty, majesty and might,
As a lover or a chameleon
Grows like what it looks upon,
As a violet's gentle eye
Gazes on the azure sky
Until its hue grows like what it beholds,
As a gray and watery mist
Glows like solid amethyst
Athwart the western mountain it en-
    folds,   490
When the sunset sleeps
    Upon its snow.

THE EARTH

And the weak day weeps
    That it should be so.
O gentle Moon, the voice of thy delight
Falls on me like thy clear and tender light
Soothing the seaman borne the summer
    night
    Through isles forever calm;
O gentle Moon, thy crystal accents pierce
The caverns of my pride's deep universe, 500
Charming the tiger joy, whose tramplings
    fierce
Made wounds which need thy balm.

PANTHEA

I rise as from a bath of sparkling water,
A bath of azure light, among dark rocks,
Out of the stream of sound.

IONE

        Ah me ! sweet sister,
The stream of sound has ebbed away from
    us,
And you pretend to rise out of its wave,
Because your words fall like the clear soft
    dew
Shaken from a bathing wood-nymph's limbs
    and hair.

PANTHEA

Peace, peace ! a mighty Power, which is as
    darkness,   510
Is rising out of Earth, and from the sky
Is showered like night, and from within
    the air
Bursts, like eclipse which had been gathered
    up
Into the pores of sunlight; the bright
    visions,
Wherein the singing Spirits rode and shone,
Gleam like pale meteors through a watery
    night.

IONE

There is a sense of words upon mine ear.

PANTHEA

An universal sound like words: Oh, list !

DEMOGORGON

Thou, Earth, calm empire of a happy soul,
    Sphere of divinest shapes and harmo-
    nies,   520
Beautiful orb ! gathering as thou dost roll
    The love which paves thy path along the
    skies:

THE EARTH

I hear: I am as a drop of dew that dies.

DEMOGORGON

Thou, Moon, which gazest on the nightly
    Earth
    With wonder, as it gazes upon thee;
Whilst each to men, and beasts, and the
    swift birth
Of birds, is beauty, love, calm, harmony:

THE MOON

I hear: I am a leaf shaken by thee.

DEMOGORGON

Ye kings of suns and stars, Dæmons and
    Gods,
    Ethereal Dominations, who possess   530
Elysian, windless, fortunate abodes
    Beyond Heaven's constellated wilder-
    ness:

A VOICE (*from above*)

Our great Republic hears: we are blessed,
    and bless.

DEMOGORGON

Ye happy dead, whom beams of brightest
    verse

Are clouds to hide, not colors to portray,
Whether your nature is that universe
    Which once ye saw and suffered —

A VOICE FROM BENEATH

                            Or, as they
Whom we have left, we change and pass
    away.

DEMOGORGON

Ye elemental Genii, who have homes
    From man's high mind even to the cen-
    tral stone   540
Of sullen lead; from Heaven's star-fretted
    domes
To the dull weed some sea-worm battens
    on:

A CONFUSED VOICE

We hear: thy words waken Oblivion.

DEMOGORGON

Spirits, whose homes are flesh; ye beasts
    and birds,
    Ye worms and fish; ye living leaves and
    buds;
Lightning and wind; and ye untamable
    herds,
    Meteors and mists, which throng air's
    solitudes:

A VOICE

Thy voice to us is wind among still woods.

DEMOGORGON

Man, who wert once a despot and a slave,
    A dupe and a deceiver, a decay,   550
A traveller from the cradle to the grave
    Through the dim night of this immortal
    day:

ALL

Speak: thy strong words may never pass
    away.

DEMOGORGON

This is the day which down the void abysm
At the Earth-born's spell yawns for Hea-
    ven's despotism,
    And Conquest is dragged captive through
    the deep;
Love, from its awful throne of patient
    power
    In the wise heart, from the last giddy hour
Of dread endurance, from the slippery,
    steep,

And narrow verge of crag-like agony,
   springs   560
And folds over the world its healing wings.

Gentleness, Virtue, Wisdom, and Endur-
   ance —
These are the seals of that most firm assur-
   ance
Which bars the pit over Destruction's
   strength;
And if, with infirm hand, Eternity,
Mother of many acts and hours, should
   free
   The serpent that would clasp her with
      his length,

These are the spells by which to reassume
An empire o'er the disentangled doom. 569

To suffer woes which Hope thinks infinite;
To forgive wrongs darker than death or
   night;
To defy Power, which seems omnipotent;
To love, and bear; to hope till Hope creates
From its own wreck the thing it contem-
   plates;
Neither to change, nor falter, nor repent;
This, like thy glory, Titan, is to be
Good, great and joyous, beautiful and free;
This is alone Life, Joy, Empire, and Vic-
   tory !

THE CENCI

A TRAGEDY

IN FIVE ACTS

The Cenci was Shelley's first attempt at writing drama, a form of composition for which he had conceived himself to have no talent. It was executed with greater rapidity than any of his earlier works, being begun at Rome by May 14, and finished at Leghorn, August 8, 1819, though as usual Shelley continued to revise it till it left his hands. He printed two hundred and fifty copies at an Italian press, and these were issued in the spring of 1820, at London, as the first edition. A second edition was published the following year. Shelley desired that the play should be put upon the stage, and had it offered at Covent Garden by Peacock, but it was declined on account of the subject. He thought it was written in a way to make it popular, and that the repulsive element in the story had been eliminated by the delicacy of his treatment. His interest in it lessened after its refusal by the managers; but their judgment was supported by the unfavorable impression made by it when it was privately played for the first time under the auspices of the Shelley Society, at London, in 1886.

Mrs. Shelley's note, as usual, gives nearly all that is essential to the history of the poem and of Shelley's interest in it:

'When in Rome, in 1819, a friend put into our hands the old manuscript account of the story of *The Cenci.* We visited the Colonna and Doria palaces, where the portraits of Beatrice were to be found; and her beauty cast the reflection of its own grace over her appalling story. Shelley's imagination became strongly excited, and he urged the subject to me as one fitted for a tragedy. More than ever I felt my incompetence; but I entreated him to write it instead; and he began and proceeded swiftly, urged on by intense sympathy with the sufferings of the human beings whose passions, so long cold in the tomb, he revived, and gifted with poetic language. This tragedy is the only one of his works that he communicated to me during its progress. We talked over the arrangement of the scenes together. . . .

' We suffered a severe affliction in Rome by the loss of our eldest child, who was of such beauty and promise as to cause him deservedly to be the idol of our hearts. We left the capital of the world, anxious for a time to escape a spot associated too intimately with his presence and loss. Some friends of ours were residing in the neighborhood of Leghorn, and we took a small house, Villa Valsovano, about half-way between the town and Monte Nero, where we remained during the summer. Our villa was situated in the midst of a *podere;* the peasants sang as they worked beneath our windows, during the heats of a very hot season, and at night the water-wheel creaked as the process of irrigation went on, and the fireflies flashed from among the myrtle hedges: — nature was bright, sunshiny, and cheerful, or diversified by storms of a majestic terror, such as we had never before witnessed.

' At the top of the house there was a sort of terrace. There is often such in Italy, generally roofed. This one was very small, yet not only roofed but glazed; this Shelley made his study; it looked out on a wide prospect of fertile country, and commanded a view of the near sea. The storms that sometimes varied our day showed themselves most picturesquely as they were driven across the ocean; sometimes the dark lurid clouds dipped towards the waves, and became water spouts, that churned up the waters beneath, as they were chased onward, and scattered by the tempest. At other times the dazzling sunlight and heat made it almost intolerable to every other; but Shelley basked in both, and his health and spirits revived under their influence. In this airy cell he wrote the principal part of *The Cenci*. He was making a study of Calderon at the time, reading his best tragedies with an accomplished lady [Mrs. Gisborne] living near us, to whom his letter from Leghorn was addressed during the following year. He admired Calderon, both for his poetry and his dramatic genius; but it shows his judgment and originality, that, though greatly struck by his first acquaintance with the Spanish poet, none of his peculiarities crept into the composition of *The Cenci;* and there is no trace of his new studies, except in that passage to which he himself alludes, as suggested by one in *El Purgatorio de San Patricio.*

'Shelley wished *The Cenci* to be acted. He was not a play-goer, being of such fastidious taste that he was easily disgusted by the bad filling up of the inferior parts. While preparing for our departure from England, however, he saw Miss O'Neil several times; she was then in the zenith of her glory, and Shelley was deeply moved by her impersonation of several parts, and by the graceful sweetness, the intense pathos, and sublime vehemence of passion she displayed. She was often in his thoughts as he wrote, and when he had finished, he became anxious that his tragedy should be acted, and receive the advantage of having this accomplished actress to fill the part of the heroine. With this view he wrote the following letter to a friend [Peacock, July, 1819] in London: —

' " The object of the present letter is to ask a favor of you. I have written a tragedy on the subject of a story well known in Italy, and, in my conception, eminently dramatic. I have taken some pains to make my play fit for representation, and those who have already seen it judge favorably. It is written without any of the peculiar feelings and opinions which characterize my other compositions; I having attended simply to the impartial development of such characters as it is probable the persons represented really were, together with the greatest degree of popular effect to be produced by such a development. I send you a translation of the Italian MS. on which my play is founded; the chief subject of which I have touched very delicately; for my principal doubt as to whether it would succeed, as an acting play, hangs entirely on the question, as to whether such a thing as incest in this shape, however treated, would be admitted on the stage. I think, however, it will form no objection, considering, first, that the facts are matter of history and, secondly, the peculiar delicacy with which I have treated it.

' " I am exceedingly interested in the question of whether this attempt of mine will succeed or no. I am strongly inclined to the affirmative at present; founding my hopes on this, that as a composition it is certainly not inferior to any of the modern plays that have been acted, with the exception of *Remorse;* that the interest of its plot is incredibly greater and more real, and that there is nothing beyond what the multitude are contented to believe that they can understand, either in imagery, opinion, or sentiment. I wish to preserve a complete incognito, and can trust to you that, whatever else you do, you will at least favor me on this point. Indeed this is essential, deeply essential to its success. After it had been acted, and successfully (could I hope such a thing), I would own it if I pleased, and use the celebrity it might acquire, to my own purposes.

' " What I want you to do, is to procure for me its presentation at Covent Garden. The principal character, Beatrice, is precisely fitted for Miss O'Neil, and it might even seem written for her, (God forbid that I should ever see her play it — it would tear my nerves to pieces,) and in all respects it is fitted only for Covent Garden. The chief male character I confess I should be very unwilling that any one but Kean should play — that is impossible, and I must be contented with an inferior actor."

' The play was accordingly sent to Mr. Harris. He pronounced the subject to be so objectionable that he could not even submit the part to Miss O'Neil for perusal, but expressed his desire that the author would write a tragedy on some other subject, which he would gladly accept. Shelley printed a small edition at Leghorn, to insure its correctness; as he was much annoyed by the many mistakes that crept into his text, when distance prevented him from correcting the press.

' Universal approbation soon stamped *The Cenci* as the best tragedy of modern times. Writing concerning it, Shelley said : " I have been cautious to avoid the introducing faults of youthful composition; diffuseness, a profusion of inapplicable imagery, vagueness, generality, and, as Hamlet says, *words, words.*"

There is nothing that is not purely dramatic throughout; and the character of Beatrice, proceeding from vehement struggle to horror, to deadly resolution, and lastly, to the elevated dignity of calm suffering, joined to passionate tenderness and pathos, is touched with hues so vivid and so beautiful, that the poet seems to have read intimately the secrets of the noble heart imaged in the lovely countenance of the unfortunate girl. The Fifth Act is a masterpiece. It is the finest thing he ever wrote, and may claim proud comparison not only with any contemporary, but preceding poet. The varying feelings of Beatrice are expressed with passionate, heart-reaching eloquence. Every character has a voice that echoes truth in its tones. It is curious, to one acquainted with the written story, to mark the success with which the poet has inwoven the real incidents of the tragedy into his scenes, and yet, through the power of poetry, has obliterated all that would otherwise have shown too harsh or too hideous in the picture. His success was a double triumph; and often after he was earnestly entreated to write again in a style that commanded popular favor, while it was not less instinct with truth and genius. But the bent of his mind went the other way; and even when employed on subjects whose interest depended on character and incident, he would start off in another direction, and leave the delineations of human passion, which he could depict in so able a manner, for fantastic creations of his fancy, or the expression of those opinions and sentiments with regard to human nature and its destiny, a desire to diffuse which was the master passion of his soul.'

Though Shelley's references to the drama, in his correspondence, are many, they are rather concerned with the stage-production and publication of it than with criticism. While still warm with its composition he wrote to Peacock, ' My work on *The Cenci*, which was done in two months, was a fine antidote to nervous medicines and kept up, I think, the pain in my side as sticks do a fire. Since then I have materially improved;' and in offering the dedication to Leigh Hunt, he says, — ' I have written something and finished it, different from anything else, and a new attempt for me; and I mean to dedicate it to you. I should not have done so without your approbation, but I asked your picture last night, and it smiled assent. If I did not think it in some degree worthy of you, I would not make you a public offering of it. I expect to have to write to you soon about it. If Ollier is not turned Christian, Jew, or become infected with *the Murrain*, he will publish it. Don't let him be frightened, for it is nothing which by any courtesy of language can be termed either moral or immoral.'

In letters to Ollier he describes it as ' calculated to produce a very popular effect,' ' expressly written for theatrical exhibition,' and ' written for the multitude.' He doubtless had in mind, while using these phrases, its restraint of style, in which it is unique among his longer works, and its freedom from abstract thought and the peculiar imagery in which he delighted. Its failure disappointed him, as it is the only one of his works from which he seems to have expected contemporary and popular success. ' *The Cenci* ought to have been popular,' he writes again to Ollier; and the effect of continued neglect of his writings, in depressing his spirits, is shown in a letter the preceding day to Peacock, — ' Nothing is more difficult and unwelcome than to write without a confidence of finding readers; and if my play of *The Cenci* found none or few, I despair of ever producing anything that shall merit them.' Byron was ' loud in censure,' and Keats was critical, in the very point where criticism was perhaps least needed; he wrote, acknowledging a gift copy, — ' You, I am sure, will forgive me for sincerely remarking that you might curb your magnanimity, and be more of an artist, and load every rift of your subject with ore. The thought of such discipline must fall like cold chains upon you, who perhaps never sat with your wings furled for six months together. And is not this extraordinary talk for the writer of *Endymion*, whose mind was like a pack of scattered cards?' Trelawny records Shelley's last, and most condensed judgment: ' In writing *The Cenci* my object was to see how I could succeed in describing passions I have never felt, and to tell the most dreadful story in pure and refined language. The image of Beatrice haunted me after seeing her portrait. The story is well authenticated, and the details far more horrible than I have painted them. *The Cenci* is a work of art; it is not colored by my feelings nor obscured by my metaphysics. I don't think much of it. It gave me less trouble than anything I have written of the same length.'

DEDICATION

TO LEIGH HUNT, ESQ.

MY DEAR FRIEND, — I inscribe with your name, from a distant country, and after an absence whose months have seemed years, this the latest of my literary efforts.

Those writings which I have hitherto published have been little else than visions which impersonate my own apprehensions of the beautiful and the just. I can also perceive in them the literary defects incidental to youth and impatience; they are dreams of what ought to be or may be. The drama which I now present to you is a sad reality. I lay aside the presumptuous attitude of an instructor and am content to paint, with such colors as my own heart furnishes, that which has been.

Had I known a person more highly endowed than yourself with all that it becomes a man to possess, I had solicited for this work the ornament of his name. One more gentle, honorable, innocent and brave; one of more exalted toleration for all who do and think evil, and yet himself more free from evil; one who knows better how to receive and how to confer a benefit, though he must ever confer far more than he can receive; one of simpler, and, in the highest sense of the word, of purer life and manners, I never knew; and I had already been fortunate in friendships when your name was added to the list.

In that patient and irreconcilable enmity with domestic and political tyranny and imposture which the tenor of your life has illustrated, and which, had I health and talents, should illustrate mine, let us, comforting each other in our task, live and die.

All happiness attend you!

Your affectionate friend,

PERCY B. SHELLEY.

ROME, *May* 29, 1819.

PREFACE

A MANUSCRIPT was communicated to me during my travels in Italy, which was copied from the archives of the Cenci Palace at Rome and contains a detailed account of the horrors which ended in the extinction of one of the noblest and richest families of that city, during the Pontificate of Clement VIII., in the year 1599. The story is that an old man, having spent his life in debauchery and wickedness, conceived at length an implacable hatred towards his children; which showed itself towards one daughter under the form of an incestuous passion, aggravated by every circumstance of cruelty and violence. This daughter, after long and vain attempts to escape from what she considered a perpetual contamination both of body and mind, at length plotted with her mother-in-law and brother to murder their common tyrant. The young maiden who was urged to this tremendous deed by an impulse which overpowered its horror was evidently a most gentle and amiable being, a creature formed to adorn and be admired, and thus violently thwarted from her nature by the necessity of circumstance and opinion. The deed was quickly discovered, and, in spite of the most earnest prayers made to the Pope by the highest persons in Rome, the criminals were put to death. The old man had during his life repeatedly bought his pardon from the Pope for capital crimes of the most enormous and unspeakable kind at the price of a hundred thousand crowns; the death therefore of his victims can scarcely be accounted for by the love of justice. The Pope, among other motives for severity, probably felt that whoever killed the Count Cenci deprived his treasury of a certain and copious source of revenue.[1] Such a story, if told so as to present to the reader all the feelings of those who once acted it, their hopes and fears, their confidences and misgivings, their various interests, passions and opinions, acting upon and with each other yet all conspiring to one tremendous end, would be as a light to make apparent some of the most dark and secret caverns of the human heart.

On my arrival at Rome I found that the story of the Cenci was a subject not to be mentioned in Italian society without awakening a deep and breathless interest; and that the feelings of the company never failed to incline to a romantic pity for the wrongs and a passionate exculpation of the horrible deed to which they urged her who has been mingled two centuries with the common dust. All ranks of people knew the outlines of this history and participated in the overwhelming interest which it seems to have the magic of exciting in the human heart. I had a copy of Guido's picture of Beatrice which is preserved in the Colonna Palace, and my servant instantly recognized it as the portrait of *La Cenci*.

This national and universal interest which the story produces and has produced for two centuries and among all ranks of people in a great City, where the imagination is kept forever active and awake, first suggested to me the conception of its fitness for a dramatic purpose. In fact it is a tragedy which has already received, from its capacity of awakening and sustaining the sympathy of men, approbation and success. Nothing remained as I imagined but to clothe it to the apprehensions of my countrymen in such language and action as would bring it home to their hearts. The deepest and the sublimest tragic compositions, King Lear and the two plays in which the tale of Œdipus is told, were stories which already existed in tradition, as matters of popular belief and interest, before Shakespeare and Sophocles made them familiar to the sympathy of all succeeding generations of mankind.

This story of the Cenci is indeed eminently

[1] The Papal Government formerly took the most extraordinary precautions against the publicity of facts which offer so tragical a demonstration of its own wickedness and weakness; so that the communication of the MS. had become, until very lately, a matter of some difficulty.

fearful and monstrous; anything like a dry exhibition of it on the stage would be insupportable. The person who would treat such a subject must increase the ideal and diminish the actual horror of the events, so that the pleasure which arises from the poetry which exists in these tempestuous sufferings and crimes may mitigate the pain of the contemplation of the moral deformity from which they spring. There must also be nothing attempted to make the exhibition subservient to what is vulgarly termed a moral purpose. The highest moral purpose aimed at in the highest species of the drama is the teaching the human heart, through its sympathies and antipathies, the knowledge of itself; in proportion to the possession of which knowledge every human being is wise, just, sincere, tolerant and kind. If dogmas can do more, it is well: but a drama is no fit place for the enforcement of them. Undoubtedly no person can be truly dishonored by the act of another; and the fit return to make to the most enormous injuries is kindness and forbearance and a resolution to convert the injurer from his dark passions by peace and love. Revenge, retaliation, atonement, are pernicious mistakes. If Beatrice had thought in this manner she would have been wiser and better; but she would never have been a tragic character. The few whom such an exhibition would have interested could never have been sufficiently interested for a dramatic purpose, from the want of finding sympathy in their interest among the mass who surround them. It is in the restless and anatomizing casuistry with which men seek the justification of Beatrice, yet feel that she has done what needs justification; it is in the superstitious horror with which they contemplate alike her wrongs and their revenge, — that the dramatic character of what she did and suffered, consists.

I have endeavored as nearly as possible to represent the characters as they probably were, and have sought to avoid the error of making them actuated by my own conceptions of right or wrong, false or true: thus under a thin veil converting names and actions of the sixteenth century into cold impersonations of my own mind. They are represented as Catholics, and as Catholics deeply tinged with religion. To a Protestant apprehension there will appear something unnatural in the earnest and perpetual sentiment of the relations between God and men which pervade the tragedy of the Cenci. It will especially be startled at the combination of an undoubting persuasion of the truth of the popular religion with a cool and determined perseverance in enormous guilt. But religion in Italy is not, as in Protestant countries, a cloak to be worn on particular

days; or a passport which those who do not wish to be railed at carry with them to exhibit; or a gloomy passion for penetrating the impenetrable mysteries of our being, which terrifies its possessor at the darkness of the abyss to the brink of which it has conducted him. Religion coexists, as it were, in the mind of an Italian Catholic, with a faith in that of which all men have the most certain knowledge. It is interwoven with the whole fabric of life. It is adoration, faith, submission, penitence, blind admiration; not a rule for moral conduct. It has no necessary connection with any one virtue. The most atrocious villain may be rigidly devout, and without any shock to established faith confess himself to be so. Religion pervades intensely the whole frame of society, and is, according to the temper of the mind which it inhabits, a passion, a persuasion, an excuse, a refuge; never a check. Cenci himself built a chapel in the court of his Palace, and dedicated it to St. Thomas the Apostle, and established masses for the peace of his soul. Thus in the first scene of the fourth act Lucretia's design in exposing herself to the consequences of an expostulation with Cenci after having administered the opiate was to induce him by a feigned tale to confess himself before death, this being esteemed by Catholics as essential to salvation; and she only relinquishes her purpose when she perceives that her perseverance would expose Beatrice to new outrages.

I have avoided with great care in writing this play the introduction of what is commonly called mere poetry, and I imagine there will scarcely be found a detached simile or a single isolated description, unless Beatrice's description of the chasm appointed for her father's murder should be judged to be of that nature.[1]

In a dramatic composition the imagery and the passion should interpenetrate one another, the former being reserved simply for the full development and illustration of the latter. Imagination is as the immortal God which should assume flesh for the redemption of mortal passion. It is thus that the most remote and the most familiar imagery may alike be fit for dramatic purposes when employed in the illustration of strong feeling, which raises what is low and levels to the apprehension that which is lofty, casting over all the shadow of its own greatness. In other respects I have written more carelessly; that is, without an overfastidious and learned choice of words. In this respect I entirely agree with those modern critics who assert that in order to move men to true sympathy we must use the

---

[1] An idea in this speech was suggested by a most sublime passage in *El Purgatorio de San Patricio* of Calderon; the only plagiarism which I have intentionally committed in the whole piece.

familiar language of men, and that our great
ancestors the ancient English poets are the
writers, a study of whom might incite us to do
that for our own age which they have done for
theirs. But it must be the real language of
men in general and not that of any particular
class to whose society the writer happens to
belong. So much for what I have attempted;
I need not be assured that success is a very
different matter; particularly for one whose
attention has but newly been awakened to the
study of dramatic literature.

I endeavored whilst at Rome to observe such
monuments of this story as might be accessible
to a stranger. The portrait of Beatrice at the
Colonna Palace is admirable as a work of art;
it was taken by Guido during her confinement
in prison. But it is most interesting as a just
representation of one of the loveliest specimens
of the workmanship of Nature. There is a
fixed and pale composure upon the features;
she seems sad and stricken down in spirit, yet
the despair thus expressed is lightened by the
patience of gentleness. Her head is bound
with folds of white drapery from which the
yellow strings of her golden hair escape and
fall about her neck. The moulding of her
face is exquisitely delicate; the eyebrows are
distinct and arched; the lips have that permanent meaning of imagination and sensibility
which suffering has not repressed and which it
seems as if death scarcely could extinguish.
Her forehead is large and clear; her eyes,
which we are told were remarkable for their
vivacity, are swollen with weeping and lustre-

less, but beautifully tender and serene. In
the whole mien there is a simplicity and dignity
which, united with her exquisite loveliness and
deep sorrow, are inexpressibly pathetic. Beatrice Cenci appears to have been one of those
rare persons in whom energy and gentleness
dwell together without destroying one another;
her nature was simple and profound. The
crimes and miseries in which she was an actor
and a sufferer are as the mask and the mantle
in which circumstances clothed her for her
impersonation on the scene of the world.

The Cenci Palace is of great extent; and,
though in part modernized, there yet remains
a vast and gloomy pile of feudal architecture
in the same state as during the dreadful scenes
which are the subject of this tragedy. The
Palace is situated in an obscure corner of
Rome, near the quarter of the Jews, and from
the upper windows you see the immense ruins
of Mount Palatine half hidden under their
profuse overgrowth of trees. There is a court
in one part of the Palace (perhaps that in
which Cenci built the Chapel to St. Thomas),
supported by granite columns and adorned with
antique friezes of fine workmanship, and built
up, according to the ancient Italian fashion,
with balcony over balcony of openwork. One
of the gates of the Palace formed of immense
stones and leading through a passage, dark
and lofty and opening into gloomy subterranean chambers, struck me particularly.

Of the Castle of Petrella, I could obtain no
further information than that which is to be
found in the manuscript.

THE CENCI

DRAMATIS PERSONÆ

Count Francesco Cenci.
Giacomo, } his Sons.
Bernardo, }
Cardinal Camillo.
Prince Colonna.
Orsino, a Prelate.
Savella, the Pope's Legate.
Olimpio, } Assassins.
Marzio, }

Andrea, Servant to Cenci.
Nobles. Judges.
Guards. Servants.
Lucretia, Wife of Cenci and Stepmo-
ther of his children.
Beatrice, his Daugh-
ter.

The Scene lies principally in Rome, but changes dur-
ing the fourth Act to Pretrella, a castle among the
Apulian Apennines.
Time. During the Pontificate of Clement VIII.

ACT I

Scene I. — *An Apartment in the* Cenci *Palace.*
Enter Count Cenci *and* Cardinal Camillo.

CAMILLO

That matter of the murder is hushed up
If you consent to yield his Holiness

Your fief that lies beyond the Pincian gate.
It needed all my interest in the conclave
To bend him to this point; he said that you
Bought perilous impunity with your gold;
That crimes like yours if once or twice
        compounded
Enriched the Church, and respited from hell
An erring soul which might repent and live;
But that the glory and the interest   10
Of the high throne he fills little consist
With making it a daily mart of guilt
As manifold and hideous as the deeds
Which you scarce hide from men's re-
        volted eyes.

CENCI

The third of my possessions — let it go!
Ay, I once heard the nephew of the Pope
Had sent his architect to view the ground,
Meaning to build a villa on my vines
The next time I compounded with his uncle.
I little thought he should outwit me so! 20

Henceforth no witness — not the lamp —
   shall see
That which the vassal threatened to divulge,
Whose throat is choked with dust for his
   reward.
The deed he saw could not have rated
   higher
Than his most worthless life — it angers
   me!
Respited me from Hell! So may the
   Devil
Respite their souls from Heaven! No
   doubt Pope Clement,
And his most charitable nephews, pray
That the Apostle Peter and the saints
Will grant for their sake that I long
   enjoy   30
Strength, wealth, and pride, and lust, and
   length of days
Wherein to act the deeds which are the
   stewards
Of their revenue. — But much yet remains
To which they show no title.

CAMILLO

                   Oh, Count Cenci!
So much that thou mightst honorably live
And reconcile thyself with thine own heart
And with thy God and with the offended
   world.
How hideously look deeds of lust and blood
Through those snow-white and venerable
   hairs!
Your children should be sitting round you
   now   40
But that you fear to read upon their looks
The shame and misery you have written
   there.
Where is your wife? Where is your gentle
   daughter?
Methinks her sweet looks, which make all
   things else
Beauteous and glad, might kill the fiend
   within you.
Why is she barred from all society
But her own strange and uncomplaining
   wrongs?
Talk with me, Count, — you know I mean
   you well.
I stood beside your dark and fiery youth,
Watching its bold and bad career, as men   50
Watch meteors, but it vanished not; I
   marked
Your desperate and remorseless manhood;
   now

Do I behold you in dishonored age
Charged with a thousand unrepented
   crimes.
Yet I have ever hoped you would amend,
And in that hope have saved your life three
   times.

CENCI

For which Aldobrandino owes you now
My fief beyond the Pincian. Cardinal,
One thing, I pray you, recollect henceforth,
And so we shall converse with less re-
   straint.   60
A man you knew spoke of my wife and
   daughter;
He was accustomed to frequent my house;
So the next day *his* wife and daughter came
And asked if I had seen him; and I smiled.
I think they never saw him any more.

CAMILLO

Thou execrable man, beware!

CENCI

                     Of thee?
Nay, this is idle. We should know each
   other.
As to my character for what men call crime,
Seeing I please my senses as I list,
And vindicate that right with force or
   guile,   70
It is a public matter, and I care not
If I discuss it with you. I may speak
Alike to you and my own conscious heart,
For you give out that you have half re-
   formed me;
Therefore strong vanity will keep you
   silent,
If fear should not; both will, I do not
   doubt.
All men delight in sensual luxury;
All men enjoy revenge, and most exult
Over the tortures they can never feel,
Flattering their secret peace with others'
   pain.   80
But I delight in nothing else. I love
The sight of agony, and the sense of joy,
When this shall be another's and that mine;
And I have no remorse and little fear,
Which are, I think, the checks of other
   men.
This mood has grown upon me, until now
Any design my captious fancy makes
The picture of its wish — and it forms
   none

But such as men like you would start to
    know —
Is as my natural food and rest debarred   90
Until it be accomplished.

CAMILLO

              Art thou not
Most miserable?

CENCI

              Why miserable?
No. I am what your theologians call
Hardened; which they must be in impu-
    dence,
So to revile a man's peculiar taste.
True, I was happier than I am, while yet
Manhood remained to act the thing I
    thought, —
While lust was sweeter than revenge; and
    now
Invention palls. Ay, we must all grow old.
And but that there remains a deed to act
Whose horror might make sharp an appe-
    tite   101
Duller than mine — I 'd do, — I know not
    what.
When I was young I thought of nothing
    else
But pleasure; and I fed on honey sweets.
Men, by St. Thomas! cannot live like
    bees, —
And I grew tired; yet, till I killed a foe,
And heard his groans, and heard his chil-
    dren's groans,
Knew I not what delight was else on
    earth, —
Which now delights me little. I the rather
Look on such pangs as terror ill conceals —
The dry, fixed eyeball, the pale, quivering
    lip,   111
Which tell me that the spirit weeps within
Tears bitterer than the bloody sweat of
    Christ.
I rarely kill the body, which preserves,
Like a strong prison, the soul within my
    power,
Wherein I feed it with the breath of fear
For hourly pain.

CAMILLO

              Hell's most abandoned fiend
Did never, in the drunkenness of guilt,
Speak to his heart as now you speak to
    me.
I thank my God that I believe you not.   120

Enter ANDREA

ANDREA

My Lord, a gentleman from Salamanca
Would speak with you.

CENCI

              Bid him attend me
In the grand saloon.

              [*Exit* ANDREA.

CAMILLO

              Farewell; and I will pray
Almighty God that thy false, impious words
Tempt not his spirit to abandon thee.

              [*Exit* CAMILLO.

CENCI

The third of my possessions! I must use
Close husbandry, or gold, the old man's
    sword,
Falls from my withered hand. But yester-
    day
There came an order from the Pope to make
Fourfold provision for my cursèd sons,   130
Whom I had sent from Rome to Salamanca,
Hoping some accident might cut them off,
And meaning, if I could, to starve them
    there.
I pray thee, God, send some quick death
    upon them!
Bernardo and my wife could not be worse
If dead and damned. Then, as to Bea-
    trice —

    [*Looking around him suspiciously.*
I think they cannot hear me at that door.
What if they should? And yet I need not
    speak,
Though the heart triumphs with itself in
    words.   139
O thou most silent air, that shalt not hear
What now I think! Thou pavement which
    I tread
Towards her chamber, — let your echoes
    talk
Of my imperious step, scorning surprise,
But not of my intent! — Andrea!

Enter ANDREA

ANDREA

              My Lord?

CENCI

Bid Beatrice attend me in her chamber
This evening: — no, at midnight and alone.

              [*Exeunt.*

SCENE II. — *A Garden of the Cenci Palace.*
Enter BEATRICE *and* ORSINO, *as in conversation.*

BEATRICE

Pervert not truth,
Orsino. You remember where we held
That conversation; nay, we see the spot
Even from this cypress; two long years are
passed
Since, on an April midnight, underneath
The moonlight ruins of Mount Palatine,
I did confess to you my secret mind.

ORSINO

You said you loved me then.

BEATRICE

You are a priest.
Speak to me not of love.

ORSINO

I may obtain
The dispensation of the Pope to marry. 10
Because I am a priest do you believe
Your image, as the hunter some struck
deer,
Follows me not whether I wake or sleep ?

BEATRICE

As I have said, speak to me not of love;
Had you a dispensation, I have not;
Nor will I leave this home of misery
Whilst my poor Bernard, and that gentle
lady
To whom I owe life and these virtuous
thoughts,
Must suffer what I still have strength to
share.
Alas, Orsino !   All the love that once   20
I felt for you is turned to bitter pain.
Ours was a youthful contract, which you
first
Broke by assuming vows no Pope will
loose.
And thus I love you still, but holily,
Even as a sister or a spirit might;
And so I swear a cold fidelity.
And it is well perhaps we shall not marry.
You have a sly, equivocating vein
That suits me not. — Ah, wretched that I
am !
Where shall I turn ?   Even now you look
on me   30
As you were not my friend, and as if you

Discovered that I thought so, with false
smiles
Making my true suspicion seem your wrong.
Ah, no, forgive me; sorrow makes me seem
Sterner than else my nature might have
been;
I have a weight of melancholy thoughts,
And they forebode, — but what can they
forebode
Worse than I now endure ?

ORSINO

All will be well.
Is the petition yet prepared ?   You know
My zeal for all you wish, sweet Beatrice; 40
Doubt not but I will use my utmost skill
So that the Pope attend to your complaint.

BEATRICE

Your zeal for all I wish.   Ah me, you are
cold !
Your utmost skill — speak but one word —
(*Aside*)   Alas !
Weak and deserted creature that I am,
Here I stand bickering with my only friend !

(*To* ORSINO)

This night my father gives a sumptuous
feast,
Orsino; he has heard some happy news
From Salamanca, from my brothers there,
And with this outward show of love he
mocks   50
His inward hate.   'T is bold hypocrisy,
For he would gladlier celebrate their deaths,
Which I have heard him pray for on his
knees.
Great God ! that such a father should be
mine !
But there is mighty preparation made,
And all our kin, the Cenci, will be there,
And all the chief nobility of Rome.
And he has bidden me and my pale mother
Attire ourselves in festival array.   59
Poor lady ! she expects some happy change
In his dark spirit from this act; I none.
At supper I will give you the petition;
Till when — farewell.

ORSINO

Farewell.
[*Exit* BEATRICE.
I know the Pope
Will ne'er absolve me from my priestly vow
But by absolving me from the revenue

Of many a wealthy see; and, Beatrice,
I think to win thee at an easier rate.
Nor shall he read her eloquent petition.
He might bestow her on some poor relation
Of his sixth cousin, as he did her sister, 70
And I should be debarred from all access.
Then as to what she suffers from her
    father,
In all this there is much exaggeration.
Old men are testy, and will have their way.
A man may stab his enemy, or his vassal,
And live a free life as to wine or women,
And with a peevish temper may return
To a dull home, and rate his wife and chil-
    dren;
Daughters and wives call this foul tyranny.
I shall be well content if on my conscience
There rest no heavier sin than what they
    suffer   81
From the devices of my love — a net
From which she shall escape not.   Yet I
    fear
Her subtle mind, her awe-inspiring gaze,
Whose beams anatomize me, nerve by
    nerve,
And lay me bare, and make me blush to
    see
My hidden thoughts. — Ah, no ! a friend-
    less girl
Who clings to me, as to her only hope !
I were a fool, not less than if a panther 89
Were panic-stricken by the antelope's eye,
If she escape me.
                                        [*Exit.*

SCENE III. — *A magnificent Hall in the Cenci
    Palace.   A Banquet.   Enter* CENCI, LU-
    CRETIA, BEATRICE, ORSINO, CAMILLO, NO-
    BLES.

CENCI

Welcome, my friends and kinsmen; wel-
    come ye,
Princes and Cardinals, pillars of the church,
Whose presence honors our festivity.
I have too long lived like an anchorite,
And in my absence from your merry meet-
    ings
An evil word is gone abroad of me;
But I do hope that you, my noble friends,
When you have shared the entertainment
    here,
And heard the pious cause for which 't is
    given,
And we have pledged a health or two to-
    gether,   10

Will think me flesh and blood as well as
    you;
Sinful indeed, for Adam made all so,
But tender-hearted, meek and pitiful.

FIRST GUEST

In truth, my Lord, you seem too light of
    heart,
Too sprightly and companionable a man,
To act the deeds that rumor pins on you.
                          [*To his companion.*
I never saw such blithe and open cheer
In any eye !

SECOND GUEST

                 Some most desired event,
In which we all demand a common joy,
Has brought us hither; let us hear it,
    Count.   20

CENCI

It is indeed a most desired event.
If when a parent from a parent's heart
Lifts from this earth to the great Father of
    all
A prayer, both when he lays him down to
    sleep,
And when he rises up from dreaming it;
One supplication, one desire, one hope,
That he would grant a wish for his two
    sons,
Even all that he demands in their regard,
And suddenly beyond his dearest hope 29
It is accomplished, he should then rejoice,
And call his friends and kinsmen to a feast,
And task their love to grace his merri-
    ment, —
Then honor me thus far, for I am he.

BEATRICE (*to* LUCRETIA) .

Great God ! How horrible ! some dreadful
    ill
Must have befallen my brothers.

LUCRETIA

                          Fear not, child,
He speaks too frankly.

BEATRICE

                 Ah ! My blood runs cold.
I fear that wicked laughter round his
    eye,
Which wrinkles up the skin even to the
    hair.

CENCI

Here are the letters brought from Salamanca.
Beatrice, read them to your mother. God![39]
I thank thee! In one night didst thou perform,
By ways inscrutable, the thing I sought.
My disobedient and rebellious sons
Are dead! — Why, dead! — What means this change of cheer?
You hear me not — I tell you they are dead;
And they will need no food or raiment more;
The tapers that did light them the dark way
Are their last cost. The Pope, I think, will not
Expect I should maintain them in their coffins.
Rejoice with me — my heart is wondrous glad. [50]

BEATRICE (LUCRETIA *sinks, half fainting;* BEATRICE *supports her*)

It is not true! — Dear Lady, pray look up.
Had it been true — there is a God in Heaven —
He would not live to boast of such a boon.
Unnatural man, thou knowest that it is false.

CENCI

Ay, as the word of God; whom here I call
To witness that I speak the sober truth;
And whose most favoring providence was shown
Even in the manner of their deaths. For Rocco
Was kneeling at the mass, with sixteen others,
When the church fell and crushed him to a mummy; [60]
The rest escaped unhurt. Cristofano
Was stabbed in error by a jealous man,
Whilst she he loved was sleeping with his rival,
All in the self-same hour of the same night;
Which shows that Heaven has special care of me.
I beg those friends who love me that they mark
The day a feast upon their calendars.
It was the twenty-seventh of December.
Ay, read the letters if you doubt my oath.

[*The assembly appears confused; several of the guests rise.*

FIRST GUEST

Oh, horrible! I will depart.

SECOND GUEST

And I.

THIRD GUEST

No, stay!
I do believe it is some jest; though, faith!
'T is mocking us somewhat too solemnly. [72]
I think his son has married the Infanta,
Or found a mine of gold in El Dorado.
'T is but to season some such news; stay, stay!
I see 't is only raillery by his smile.

CENCI (*filling a bowl of wine, and lifting it up*)

O thou bright wine, whose purple splendor leaps
And bubbles gayly in this golden bowl
Under the lamp-light, as my spirits do,
To hear the death of my accursèd sons! [80]
Could I believe thou wert their mingled blood,
Then would I taste thee like a sacrament,
And pledge with thee the mighty Devil in Hell,
Who, if a father's curses, as men say,
Climb with swift wings after their children's souls,
And drag them from the very throne of Heaven,
Now triumphs in my triumph! — But thou art
Superfluous; I have drunken deep of joy,
And I will taste no other wine to-night.
Here, Andrea! Bear the bowl around. [90]

A GUEST (*rising*)

Thou wretch!
Will none among this noble company
Check the abandoned villain?

CAMILLO

For God's sake,
Let me dismiss the guests! You are insane.
Some ill will come of this.

SECOND GUEST

Seize, silence him!

FIRST GUEST

I will !

THIRD GUEST

And I !

CENCI (*addressing those who rise with a threatening gesture*)

Who moves ? Who speaks ?
[*Turning to the company.*
'T is nothing,
Enjoy yourselves. — Beware ! for my revenge
Is as the sealed commission of a king,
That kills, and none dare name the murderer.
[*The Banquet is broken up; several of the Guests are departing.*

BEATRICE

I do entreat you, go not, noble guests; 99
What although tyranny and impious hate
Stand sheltered by a father's hoary hair ?
What if 't is he who clothed us in these limbs
Who tortures them, and triumphs ? What, if we,
The desolate and the dead, were his own flesh,
His children and his wife, whom he is bound
To love and shelter ? Shall we therefore find
No refuge in this merciless wide world ?
Oh, think what deep wrongs must have blotted out
First love, then reverence, in a child's prone mind,
Till it thus vanquish shame and fear ! Oh, think ! 110
I have borne much, and kissed the sacred hand
Which crushed us to the earth, and thought its stroke
Was perhaps some paternal chastisement !
Have excused much, doubted; and when no doubt
Remained, have sought by patience, love and tears
To soften him; and when this could not be,
I have knelt down through the long sleepless nights,
And lifted up to God, the father of all,
Passionate prayers; and when these were not heard, 119
I have still borne, — until I meet you here,

Princes and kinsmen, at this hideous feast
Given at my brothers' deaths. Two yet remain;
His wife remains and I, whom if ye save not,
Ye may soon share such merriment again
As fathers make over their children's graves.
Oh ! Prince Colonna, thou art our near kinsman;
Cardinal, thou art the Pope's chamberlain;
Camillo, thou art chief justiciary;
Take us away !

CENCI (*he has been conversing with* CAMILLO *during the first part of* BEATRICE'S *speech; he hears the conclusion, and now advances*)

I hope my good friends here
Will think of their own daughters — or perhaps 130
Of their own throats — before they lend an ear
To this wild girl.

BEATRICE (*not noticing the words of* CENCI)

Dare no one look on me ?
None answer ?   Can one tyrant overbear
The sense of many best and wisest men ?
Or is it that I sue not in some form
Of scrupulous law that ye deny my suit ?
Oh, God ! that I were buried with my brothers !
And that the flowers of this departed spring
Were fading on my grave ! and that my father
Were celebrating now one feast for all ! 140

CAMILLO

A bitter wish for one so young and gentle.
Can we do nothing ? —

COLONNA

Nothing that I see.
Count Cenci were a dangerous enemy;
Yet I would second any one.

A CARDINAL

And I.

CENCI

Retire to your chamber, insolent girl !

BEATRICE

Retire thou, impious man ! Ay, hide thyself
Where never eye can look upon thee more !

Wouldst thou have honor and obedience,
Who art a torturer? Father, never dream,
Though thou mayst overbear this com-
    pany, 150
But ill must come of ill. Frown not on
    me!
Haste, hide thyself, lest with avenging
    looks
My brothers' ghosts should hunt thee from
    thy seat!
Cover thy face from every living eye,
And start if thou but hear a human step;
Seek out some dark and silent corner —
    there
Bow thy white head before offended God,
And we will kneel around, and fervently
Pray that he pity both ourselves and thee.

CENCI

My friends, I do lament this insane girl 160
Has spoiled the mirth of our festivity.
Good night, farewell; I will not make you
    longer
Spectators of our dull domestic quarrels.
Another time. —
      [*Exeunt all but* CENCI *and* BEATRICE.
        My brain is swimming round.
Give me a bowl of wine!

      (*To* BEATRICE)
            Thou painted viper!
Beast that thou art! Fair and yet terri-
    ble!
I know a charm shall make thee meek and
    tame,
Now get thee from my sight!
            [*Exit* BEATRICE.
          Here, Andrea,
Fill up this goblet with Greek wine. I
    said
I would not drink this evening, but I
    must; 170
For, strange to say, I feel my spirits fail
With thinking what I have decreed to
    do.
           (*Drinking the wine*)
Be thou the resolution of quick youth
Within my veins, and manhood's purpose
    stern,
And age's firm, cold, subtle villainy;
As if thou wert indeed my children's blood
Which I did thirst to drink! The charm
    works well.
It must be done; it shall be done, I swear!
               [*Exit.*

ACT II

SCENE I. — *An Apartment in the Cenci Palace.*
    Enter LUCRETIA *and* BERNARDO.

LUCRETIA

WEEP not, my gentle boy; he struck but
    me,
Who have borne deeper wrongs. In truth,
    if he
Had killed me, he had done a kinder deed.
O God Almighty, do thou look upon us,
We have no other friend but only thee!
Yet weep not; though I love you as my
    own,
I am not your true mother.

BERNARDO
             Oh, more, more
Than ever mother was to any child,
That have you been to me! Had he not
    been
My father, do you think that I should
    weep? 10

LUCRETIA

Alas! poor boy, what else couldst thou have
    done!

      Enter BEATRICE

BEATRICE (*in a hurried voice*)
Did he pass this way? Have you seen him,
    brother?
Ah, no! that is his step upon the stairs;
'T is nearer now; his hand is on the door;
Mother, if I to thee have ever been
A duteous child, now save me! Thou,
    great God,
Whose image upon earth a father is,
Dost thou indeed abandon me? He
    comes;
The door is opening now; I see his face; 19
He frowns on others, but he smiles on me,
Even as he did after the feast last night.

      Enter a Servant

Almighty God, how merciful thou art!
'T is but Orsino's servant. — Well, what
    news?

SERVANT

My master bids me say the Holy Father
Has sent back your petition thus unopened.
           (*Giving a paper*)

And he demands at what hour 't were
    secure
To visit you again ?

LUCRETIA

    At the Ave Mary.
              [*Exit Servant.*
So, daughter, our last hope has failed.
    Ah me,
How pale you look ! you tremble, and you
    stand
Wrapped in some fixed and fearful medita-
    tion,   30
As if one thought were overstrong for you;
Your eyes have a chill glare; oh, dearest
    child !
Are you gone mad ?   If not, pray speak to
    me.

BEATRICE

You see I am not mad; I speak to you.

LUCRETIA

You talked of something that your father
    did
After that dreadful feast ?   Could it be
    worse
Than when he smiled, and cried, ' My sons
    are dead ! '
And every one looked in his neighbor's face
To see if others were as white as he ?   39
At the first word he spoke I felt the blood
Rush to my heart, and fell into a trance;
And when it passed I sat all weak and
    wild;
Whilst you alone stood up, and with strong
    words
Checked his unnatural pride; and I could
    see
The devil was rebuked that lives in him.
Until this hour thus you have ever stood
Between us and your father's moody wrath
Like a protecting presence; your firm mind
Has been our only refuge and defence.
What can have thus subdued it ?   What
    can now   50
Have given you that cold melancholy look,
Succeeding to your unaccustomed fear ?

BEATRICE

What is it that you say ?   I was just think-
    ing
'T were better not to struggle any more.
Men, like my father, have been dark and
    bloody;

Yet never — oh ! before worse comes of it,
'T were wise to die; it ends in that at last.

LUCRETIA

Oh, talk not so, dear child !   Tell me at
    once
What did your father do or say to you ?
He stayed not after that accursèd feast   60
One moment in your chamber. — Speak to
    me.

BERNARDO

Oh, sister, sister, prithee, speak to us !

BEATRICE (*speaking very slowly, with a forced
    calmness*)
It was one word, mother, one little word;
One look, one smile.
                (*Wildly*)
           Oh ! he has trampled me
Under his feet, and made the blood stream
    down
My pallid cheeks.   And he has given us
    all
Ditch-water, and the fever-stricken flesh
Of buffaloes, and bade us eat or starve,
And we have eaten.   He has made me look
On my beloved Bernardo, when the rust   70
Of heavy chains has gangrened his sweet
    limbs;
And I have never yet despaired — but
    now !
What would I say?
            (*Recovering herself*)
           Ah, no ! 't is nothing new.
The sufferings we all share have made me
    wild;
He only struck and cursed me as he
    passed;
He said, he looked, he did, — nothing at
    all
Beyond his wont, yet it disordered me.
Alas ! I am forgetful of my duty;
I should preserve my senses for your sake.

LUCRETIA

Nay, Beatrice; have courage, my sweet
    girl.   80
If any one despairs it should be I,
Who loved him once, and now must live
    with him
Till God in pity call for him or me.
For you may, like your sister, find some
    husband,
And smile, years hence, with children round
    your knees;

Whilst I, then dead, and all this hideous
    coil,
Shall be remembered only as a dream.

BEATRICE

Talk not to me, dear Lady, of a husband.
Did you not nurse me when my mother
    died ?
Did you not shield me and that dearest
    boy ?   90
And had we any other friend but you
In infancy, with gentle words and looks,
To win our father not to murder us ?
And shall I now desert you ? May the
    ghost
Of my dead mother plead against my soul,
If I abandon her who filled the place
She left, with more, even, than a mother's
    love !

BERNARDO

And I am of my sister's mind. Indeed
I would not leave you in this wretched-
    ness,
Even though the Pope should make me
    free to live   100
In some blithe place, like others of my
    age,
With sports, and delicate food, and the
    fresh air.
Oh, never think that I will leave you, mo-
    ther !

LUCRETIA

My dear, dear children !

Enter CENCI, *suddenly*

CENCI

                What ! Beatrice here !
Come hither !
    [*She shrinks back, and covers her face.*
          Nay, hide not your face, 't is fair;
Look up ! Why, yesternight you dared to
    look
With disobedient insolence upon me,
Bending a stern and an inquiring brow
On what I meant; whilst I then sought to
    hide
That which I came to tell you — but in
    vain.   110

BEATRICE (*wildly staggering towards the door*)

Oh, that the earth would gape ! Hide me,
    O God !

CENCI

Then it was I whose inarticulate words
Fell from my lips, and who with tottering
    steps
Fled from your presence, as you now from
    mine.
Stay, I command you ! From this day and
    hour
Never again, I think, with fearless eye,
And brow superior, and unaltered cheek,
And that lip made for tenderness or scorn,
Shalt thou strike dumb the meanest of
    mankind;
Me least of all. Now get thee to thy
    chamber !   120
Thou too, loathed image of thy cursèd
    mother,

(*To* BERNARDO)

Thy milky, meek face makes me sick with
    hate !

    [*Exeunt* BEATRICE *and* BERNARDO.
(*Aside*) So much has passed between us
    as must make
Me bold, her fearful. — 'T is an awful
    thing
To touch such mischief as I now conceive;
So men sit shivering on the dewy bank
And try the chill stream with their feet;
    once in —
How the delighted spirit pants for joy !

LUCRETIA (*advancing timidly towards him*)

O husband ! pray forgive poor Beatrice.
She meant not any ill.

CENCI

                Nor you perhaps ?
Nor that young imp, whom you have taught
    by rote   131
Parricide with his alphabet ? nor Giacomo?
Nor those two most unnatural sons who
    stirred
Enmity up against me with the Pope ?
Whom in one night merciful God cut off.
Innocent lambs! They thought not any
    ill.
You were not here conspiring ? you said
    nothing
Of how I might be dungeoned as a mad-
    man;
Or be condemned to death for some offence,
And you would be the witnesses ? This
    failing,   140

How just it were to hire assassins, or
Put sudden poison in my evening drink ?
Or smother me when overcome by wine ?
Seeing we had no other judge but God,
And he had sentenced me, and there were
   none
But you to be the executioners
Of his decree enregistered in heaven ?
Oh, no ! You said not this ?

LUCRETIA

          So help me God,
I never thought the things you charge me
   with !   149

CENCI

If you dare to speak that wicked lie again,
I 'll kill you. What ! it was not by your
   counsel
That Beatrice disturbed the feast last
   night ?
You did not hope to stir some enemies
Against me, and escape, and laugh to scorn
What every nerve of you now trembles at ?
You judged that men were bolder than
   they are ;
Few dare to stand between their grave and
   me.

LUCRETIA

Look not so dreadfully ! By my salvation
I knew not aught that Beatrice designed ;
Nor do I think she designed anything   160
Until she heard you talk of her dead bro-
   thers.

CENCI

Blaspheming liar ! you are damned for
   this !
But I will take you where you may per-
   suade
The stones you tread on to deliver you ;
For men shall there be none but those who
   dare
All things — not question that which I
   command.
On Wednesday next I shall set out ; you
   know
That savage rock, the Castle of Petrella ;
'T is safely walled, and moated round
   about ;
Its dungeons under ground and its thick
   towers   170
Never told tales ; though they have heard
   and seen

What might make dumb things speak.
   Why do you linger ?
Make speediest preparation for the jour-
   ney !
                   [*Exit* LUCRETIA.
The all-beholding sun yet shines ; I hear
A busy stir of men about the streets ;
I see the bright sky through the window
   panes.
It is a garish, broad, and peering day ;
Loud, light, suspicious, full of eyes and
   ears ;
And every little corner, nook, and hole,
Is penetrated with the insolent light.   180
Come, darkness ! Yet, what is the day to
   me ?
And wherefore should I wish for night,
   who do
A deed which shall confound both night
   and day ?
'T is she shall grope through a bewildering
   mist
Of horror ; if there be a sun in heaven,
She shall not dare to look upon its beams ;
Nor feel its warmth. Let her, then, wish
   for night ;
The act I think shall soon extinguish all
For me ; I bear a darker, deadlier gloom
Than the earth's shade, or interlunar air,
Or constellations quenched in murkiest
   cloud,   191
In which I walk secure and unbeheld
Towards my purpose. — Would that it were
   done !
                       [*Exit.*

SCENE II. — *A Chamber in the Vatican. Enter*
   CAMILLO *and* GIACOMO, *in conversation.*

CAMILLO

There is an obsolete and doubtful law
By which you might obtain a bare provision
Of food and clothing.

GIACOMO

             Nothing more ? Alas !
Bare must be the provision which strict
   law
Awards, and aged sullen avarice pays.
Why did my father not apprentice me
To some mechanic trade ? I should have
   then
Been trained in no highborn necessities
Which I could meet not by my daily toil.
The eldest son of a rich nobleman   10

Is heir to all his incapacities;
He has wide wants, and narrow powers.
  If you,
Cardinal Camillo, were reduced at once
From thrice-driven beds of down, and deli-
  cate food,
An hundred servants, and six palaces,
To that which nature doth indeed re-
  quire ? —

CAMILLO

Nay, there is reason in your plea; 't were
  hard.

GIACOMO

'T is hard for a firm man to bear; but I
Have a dear wife, a lady of high birth,
Whose dowry in ill hour I lent my father,
Without a bond or witness to the deed; 21
And children, who inherit her fine senses,
The fairest creatures in this breathing
  world;
And she and they reproach me not.   Cardi-
  nal,
Do you not think the Pope will interpose
And stretch authority beyond the law ?

CAMILLO

Though your peculiar case is hard, I know
The Pope will not divert the course of law.
After that impious feast the other night
I spoke with him, and urged him then to
  check   30
Your father's cruel hand; he frowned and
  said,
' Children are disobedient, and they sting
Their fathers' hearts to madness and de-
  spair,
Requiting years of care with contumely.
I pity the Count Cenci from my heart;
His outraged love perhaps awakened hate,
And thus he is exasperated to ill.
In the great war between the old and young,
I, who have white hairs and a tottering
  body,
Will keep at least blameless neutrality.' 40

Enter ORSINO

You, my good lord Orsino, heard those
  words.

ORSINO

What words ?

GIACOMO

                 Alas, repeat them not again !
There then is no redress for me; at least

None but that which I may achieve myself,
Since I am driven to the brink. — But, say,
My innocent sister and my only brother
Are dying underneath my father's eye.
The memorable torturers of this land,
Galeaz Visconti, Borgia, Ezzelin,
Never inflicted on their meanest slave   50
What these endure; shall they have no
  protection ?

CAMILLO

Why, if they would petition to the Pope,
I see not how he could refuse it; yet
He holds it of most dangerous example
In aught to weaken the paternal power,
Being, as 't were, the shadow of his own.
I pray you now excuse me.   I have busi-
  ness
That will not bear delay.
                         [*Exit* CAMILLO.

GIACOMO

                     But you, Orsino,
Have the petition; wherefore not present it ?

ORSINO

I have presented it, and backed it with 60
My earnest prayers and urgent interest;
It was returned unanswered.   I doubt not
But that the strange and execrable deeds
Alleged in it — in truth they might well
  baffle
Any belief — have turned the Pope's dis-
  pleasure
Upon the accusers from the criminal.
So I should guess from what Camillo said.

GIACOMO

My friend, that palace-walking devil, Gold,
Has whispered silence to His Holiness;
And we are left, as scorpions ringed with
  fire.   70
What should we do but strike ourselves to
  death ?
For he who is our murderous persecutor
Is shielded by a father's holy name,
Or I would —
                     [*Stops abruptly.*

ORSINO

   What ?   Fear not to speak your thought.
Words are but holy as the deeds they cover;
A priest who has forsworn the God he
  serves,
A judge who makes Truth weep at his de-
  cree,

A friend who should weave counsel, as I
  now,
But as the mantle of some selfish guile,
A father who is all a tyrant seems, —   80
Were the profaner for his sacred name.

ORSINO — GIACOMO
GIACOMO

Ask me not what I think; the unwilling
  brain
Feigns often what it would not; and we
  trust
Imagination with such fantasies
As the tongue dares not fashion into words —
Which have no words, their horror makes
  them dim
To the mind's eye.   My heart denies itself
To think what you demand.

ORSINO

                    But a friend's bosom
Is as the inmost cave of our own mind,
Where we sit shut from the wide gaze of
  day   90
And from the all-communicating air.
You look what I suspected —

GIACOMO

                    Spare me now!
I am as one lost in a midnight wood,
Who dares not ask some harmless passen-
  ger
The path across the wilderness, lest he,
As my thoughts are, should be — a mur-
  derer.
I know you are my friend, and all I dare
Speak to my soul that will I trust with
  thee.
But now my heart is heavy, and would take
Lone counsel from a night of sleepless
  care.   100
Pardon me that I say farewell — farewell!
I would that to my own suspected self
I could address a word so full of peace.

ORSINO

Farewell! — Be your thoughts better or
  more bold.
                              [Exit GIACOMO.
I had disposed the Cardinal Camillo
To feed his hope with cold encouragement.
It fortunately serves my close designs
That 't is a trick of this same family
To analyze their own and other minds.
Such self-anatomy shall teach the will   110

Dangerous secrets; for it tempts our
  powers,
Knowing what must be thought, and may
  be done,
Into the depth of darkest purposes.
So Cenci fell into the pit; even I,
Since Beatrice unveiled me to myself,
And made me shrink from what I cannot
  shun,
Show a poor figure to my own esteem,
To which I grow half reconciled.   I 'll do
As little mischief as I can; that thought
Shall fee the accuser conscience.
                              (After a pause)
                    Now what harm
If Cenci should be murdered? — Yet, if
  murdered,   121
Wherefore by me?   And what if I could
  take
The profit, yet omit the sin and peril
In such an action?   Of all earthly things
I fear a man whose blows outspeed his
  words;
And such is Cenci; and, while Cenci lives,
His daughter's dowry were a secret grave
If a priest wins her. — O fair Beatrice!
Would that I loved thee not, or, loving
  thee,
Could but despise danger and gold and
  all   130
That frowns between my wish and its
  effect,
Or smiles beyond it!   There is no escape;
Her bright form kneels beside me at the
  altar,
And follows me to the resort of men,
And fills my slumber with tumultuous
  dreams,
So when I wake my blood seems liquid
  fire;
And if I strike my damp and dizzy head,
My hot palm scorches it; her very name,
But spoken by a stranger, makes my heart
Sicken and pant; and thus unprofitably   140
I clasp the phantom of unfelt delights
Till weak imagination half possesses
The self-created shadow.   Yet much longer
Will I not nurse this life of feverous hours.
From the unravelled hopes of Giacomo
I must work out my own dear purposes.
I see, as from a tower, the end of all:
Her father dead; her brother bound to
  me
By a dark secret, surer than the grave;
Her mother scared and unexpostulating 150

From the dread manner of her wish
    achieved;
And she ! — Once more take courage, my
    faint heart;
What dares a friendless maiden matched
    with thee ?
I have such foresight as assures success.
Some unbeheld divinity doth ever,
When dread events are near, stir up men's
    minds
To black suggestions; and he prospers
    best,
Not who becomes the instrument of ill,
But who can flatter the dark spirit that
    makes
Its empire and its prey of other hearts 160
Till it become his slave — as I will do.
                      [*Exit.*

ACT III

SCENE I. — *An Apartment in the Cenci Palace.*
  LUCRETIA ; *to her enter* BEATRICE.

BEATRICE (*she enters staggering and speaks
        wildly*)

REACH me that handkerchief ! — My brain
    is hurt;
My eyes are full of blood; just wipe them
    for me —
I see but indistinctly.

LUCRETIA
                My sweet child,
You have no wound; 't is only a cold dew
That starts from your dear brow. — Alas,
    alas !
What has befallen ?

BEATRICE
           How comes this hair undone ?
Its wandering strings must be what blind
    me so,
And yet I tied it fast. — Oh, horrible !
The pavement sinks under my feet ! The
    walls
Spin round ! I see a woman weeping
    there,   10
And standing calm and motionless, whilst I
Slide giddily as the world reels. — My
    God !
The beautiful blue heaven is flecked with
    blood !
The sunshine on the floor is black ! The
    air

Is changed to vapors such as the dead
    breathe
In charnel-pits ! Pah ! I am choked !
    There creeps
A clinging, black, contaminating mist
About me — 't is substantial, heavy, thick;
I cannot pluck it from me, for it glues
My fingers and my limbs to one another, 20
And eats into my sinews, and dissolves
My flesh to a pollution, poisoning
The subtle, pure, and inmost spirit of life !
My God ! I never knew what the mad felt
Before; for I am mad beyond all doubt !
                (*More wildly*)
No, I am dead ! These putrefying limbs
Shut round and sepulchre the panting soul
Which would burst forth into the wander-
    ing air !
                  (*A pause*)
What hideous thought was that I had even
    now ?   29
'T is gone; and yet its burden remains here
O'er these dull eyes — upon this weary
    heart !
O world ! O life ! O day! O misery !

LUCRETIA

What ails thee, my poor child ? She an-
    swers not.
Her spirit apprehends the sense of pain,
But not its cause; suffering has dried away
The source from which it sprung.

BEATRICE (*frantically*)
                   Like Parricide —
Misery has killed its father; yet its father
Never like mine — O God ! what thing
    am I ?

LUCRETIA

My dearest child, what has your father
    done ?

BEATRICE (*doubtfully*)
Who art thou, questioner ? I have no
    father.   40
                        [*Aside.*
She is the madhouse nurse who tends on
    me,
It is a piteous office.

(*To* LUCRETIA, *in a slow, subdued voice*)
                   Do you know,
I thought I was that wretched Beatrice
Men speak of, whom her father sometimes
    hales

From hall to hall by the entangled hair;
At others, pens up naked in damp cells
Where scaly reptiles crawl, and starves her
   there
Till she will eat strange flesh. This woful
   story
So did I overact in my sick dreams
That I imagined — no, it cannot be !   50
Horrible things have been in this wild
   world,
Prodigious mixtures, and confusions strange
Of good and ill; and worse have been con-
   ceived
Than ever there was found a heart to do.
But never fancy imaged such a deed
As —

(Pauses, suddenly recollecting herself)

Who art thou ? Swear to me, ere I die
With fearful expectation, that indeed
Thou art not what thou seemest — Mother !

LUCRETIA

Oh !

My sweet child, know you —

BEATRICE

Yet speak it not;
For then if this be truth, that other too 60
Must be a truth, a firm enduring truth,
Linked with each lasting circumstance of
   life,
Never to change, never to pass away.
Why so it is. This is the Cenci Palace;
Thou art Lucretia; I am Beatrice.
I have talked some wild words, but will
   no more.
Mother, come near me; from this point of
   time,
I am —

(Her voice dies away faintly)

LUCRETIA

Alas ! what has befallen thee, child ?
What has thy father done ?

BEATRICE

What have I done ?
Am I not innocent ? Is it my crime 70
That one with white hair and imperious brow,
Who tortured me from my forgotten years
As parents only dare, should call himself
My father, yet should be ! — Oh, what am I ?
What name, what place, what memory
   shall be mine ?
What retrospects, outliving even despair ?

LUCRETIA

He is a violent tyrant, surely, child;
We know that death alone can make us
   free;
His death or ours. But what can he have
   done
Of deadlier outrage or worse injury ? 80
Thou art unlike thyself; thine eyes shoot
   forth
A wandering and strange spirit. Speak to
   me,
Unlock those pallid hands whose fingers
   twine
With one another.

BEATRICE

'T is the restless life
Tortured within them. If I try to speak,
I shall go mad. Ay, something must be
   done;
What, yet I know not — something which
   shall make
The thing that I have suffered but a shadow
In the dread lightning which avenges it;
Brief, rapid, irreversible, destroying 90
The consequence of what it cannot cure.
Some such thing is to be endured or done;
When I know what, I shall be still and
   calm,
And never anything will move me more.
But now ! — O blood, which art my father's
   blood,
Circling through these contaminated veins,
If thou, poured forth on the polluted earth,
Could wash away the crime and punish-
   ment
By which I suffer — no, that cannot be ! 99
Many might doubt there were a God above
Who sees and permits evil, and so die;
That faith no agony shall obscure in me.

LUCRETIA

It must indeed have been some bitter wrong;
Yet what, I dare not guess. Oh, my lost
   child,
Hide not in proud impenetrable grief
Thy sufferings from my fear.

BEATRICE

I hide them not.
What are the words which you would have
   me speak ?
I, who can feign no image in my mind
Of that which has transformed me; I,
   whose thought

Is like a ghost shrouded and folded up 110
In its own formless horror — of all words,
That minister to mortal intercourse,
Which wouldst thou hear ? for there is
   none to tell
My misery; if another ever knew
Aught like to it, she died as I will die,
And left it, as I must, without a name.
Death, death ! our law and our religion
   call thee
A punishment and a reward; oh, which
Have I deserved ?

LUCRETIA

      The peace of innocence,
Till in your season you be called to heaven.
Whate'er you may have suffered, you have
   done 121
No evil. Death must be the punishment
Of crime, or the reward of trampling down
The thorns which God has strewed upon
   the path
Which leads to immortality.

BEATRICE

          Ay, death —
The punishment of crime. I pray thee,
   God,
Let me not be bewildered while I judge.
If I must live day after day, and keep
These limbs, the unworthy temple of thy
   spirit,
As a foul den from which what thou abhor-
   rest 130
May mock thee unavenged — it shall not
   be !
Self-murder — no, that might be no escape,
For thy decree yawns like a Hell between
Our will and it. — Oh ! in this mortal
   world
There is no vindication and no law,
Which can adjudge and execute the doom
Of that through which I suffer.

Enter ORSINO
(*She approaches him solemnly*)
          Welcome, friend !
I have to tell you that, since last we met,
I have endured a wrong so great and
   strange
That neither life nor death can give me
   rest. 140
Ask me not what it is, for there are deeds
Which have no form, sufferings which have
   no tongue.

ORSINO

And what is he who has thus injured you ?

BEATRICE

The man they call my father; a dread
   name.

ORSINO

It cannot be —

BEATRICE

        What it can be, or not,
Forbear to think. It is, and it has been;
Advise me how it shall not be again.
I thought to die; but a religious awe
Restrains me, and the dread lest death
   itself 149
Might be no refuge from the consciousness
Of what is yet unexpiated. Oh, speak !

ORSINO

Accuse him of the deed, and let the law
Avenge thee.

BEATRICE

       Oh, ice-hearted counsellor !
If I could find a word that might make
   known
The crime of my destroyer; and that done,
My tongue should like a knife tear out the
   secret
Which cankers my heart's core; ay, lay all
   bare,
So that my unpolluted fame should be
With vilest gossips a stale mouthèd story;
A mock, a byword, an astonishment: — 160
If this were done, which never shall be
   done,
Think of the offender's gold, his dreaded
   hate,
And the strange horror of the accuser's
   tale,
Baffling belief, and overpowering speech;
Scarce whispered, unimaginable, wrapped
In hideous hints — Oh, most assured re-
   dress !

ORSINO

You will endure it then ?

BEATRICE

         Endure ! — Orsino,
It seems your counsel is small profit.
   (*Turns from him, and speaks half to herself*)
                  Ay,
All must be suddenly resolved and done.

What is this undistinguishable mist   170
Of thoughts, which rise, like shadow after
    shadow,
Darkening each other ?

ORSINO
         Should the offender live ?
Triumph in his misdeed ? and make, by
    use,
His crime, whate'er it is, dreadful no
    doubt,
Thine element; until thou mayest become
Utterly lost; subdued even to the hue
Of that which thou permittest ?

BEATRICE (to herself)
         Mighty death !
Thou double-visaged shadow ! only judge !
Rightfullest arbiter !
    (She retires, absorbed in thought)

LUCRETIA
         If the lightning
Of God has e'er descended to avenge —

ORSINO
Blaspheme not ! His high Providence
    commits   181
Its glory on this earth and their own
    wrongs
Into the hands of men; if they neglect
To punish crime —

LUCRETIA
         But if one, like this wretch,
Should mock with gold opinion, law and
    power ?
If there be no appeal to that which makes
The guiltiest tremble ? if, because our
    wrongs,
For that they are unnatural, strange and
    monstrous,
Exceed all measure of belief ? Oh, God !
If, for the very reasons which should make
Redress most swift and sure, our injurer
    triumphs ?   191
And we, the victims, bear worse punish-
    ment
Than that appointed for their torturer ?

ORSINO
         Think not
But that there is redress where there is
    wrong,
So we be bold enough to seize it.

LUCRETIA
         How ?
If there were any way to make all sure,
I know not — but I think it might be good
To —

ORSINO
         Why, his late outrage to Beatrice —
For it is such, as I but faintly guess,   199
As makes remorse dishonor, and leaves
    her
Only one duty, how she may avenge;
You, but one refuge from ills ill endured;
Me, but one counsel —

LUCRETIA
         For we cannot hope
That aid, or retribution, or resource
Will arise thence, where every other one
Might find them with less need.
    [BEATRICE advances.

ORSINO
         Then —

BEATRICE
         Peace, Orsino !
And, honored Lady, while I speak, I pray
That you put off, as garments overworn,
Forbearance and respect, remorse and fear,
And all the fit restraints of daily life,   210
Which have been borne from childhood,
    but which now
Would be a mockery to my holier plea.
As I have said, I have endured a wrong,
Which, though it be expressionless, is such
As asks atonement, both for what is passed,
And lest I be reserved, day after day,
To load with crimes an overburdened soul,
And be — what ye can dream not. I have
    prayed
To God, and I have talked with my own
    heart,
And have unravelled my entangled will, 220
And have at length determined what is
    right.
Art thou my friend, Orsino ? False or
    true ?
Pledge thy salvation ere I speak.

ORSINO
         I swear
To dedicate my cunning, and my strength,
My silence, and whatever else is mine,
To thy commands.

LUCRETIA

　　　　You think we should devise
His death?

BEATRICE

　　　　And execute what is devised,
And suddenly. We must be brief and
　　bold.

ORSINO

And yet most cautious.

LUCRETIA

　　　　For the jealous laws
Would punish us with death and infamy　230
For that which it became themselves to do.

BEATRICE

Be cautious as ye may, but prompt. Or-
　sino,
What are the means?

ORSINO

　　　　I know two dull, fierce outlaws,
Who think man's spirit as a worm's, and
　they
Would trample out, for any slight caprice,
The meanest or the noblest life. This
　mood
Is marketable here in Rome. They sell
What we now want.

LUCRETIA

　　　　To-morrow, before dawn,
Cenci will take us to that lonely rock,
Petrella, in the Apulian Apennines.　240
If he arrive there —

BEATRICE

　　　　He must not arrive.

ORSINO

Will it be dark before you reach the
　tower?

LUCRETIA

The sun will scarce be set.

BEATRICE

　　　　But I remember
Two miles on this side of the fort the road
Crosses a deep ravine; 't is rough and nar-
　row,
And winds with short turns down the pre-
　cipice;

And in its depth there is a mighty rock,
Which has, from unimaginable years,
Sustained itself with terror and with toil
Over a gulf, and with the agony　250
With which it clings seems slowly coming
　down;
Even as a wretched soul hour after hour
Clings to the mass of life; yet, clinging,
　leans;
And, leaning, makes more dark the dread
　abyss
In which it fears to fall; beneath this
　crag
Huge as despair, as if in weariness,
The melancholy mountain yawns; below,
You hear but see not an impetuous torrent
Raging among the caverns, and a bridge
Crosses the chasm; and high above there
　grow,　260
With intersecting trunks, from crag to
　crag,
Cedars, and yews, and pines; whose tan-
　gled hair
Is matted in one solid roof of shade
By the dark ivy's twine. At noonday here
'T is twilight, and at sunset blackest night.

ORSINO

Before you reach that bridge make some
　excuse
For spurring on your mules, or loitering
Until —

BEATRICE

　　　　What sound is that?

LUCRETIA

Hark! No, it cannot be a servant's step;
It must be Cenci, unexpectedly　270
Returned — make some excuse for being
　here.

BEATRICE (*to* ORSINO *as she goes out*)

That step we hear approach must never
　pass
The bridge of which we spoke.
　　　　[*Exeunt* LUCRETIA *and* BEATRICE.

ORSINO

　　　　What shall I do?
Cenci must find me here, and I must bear
The imperious inquisition of his looks
As to what brought me hither; let me
　mask
Mine own in some inane and vacant smile.

Enter GIACOMO, *in a hurried manner*

How ! have you ventured hither ? know
    you then   278
That Cenci is from home ?

GIACOMO

        I sought him here;
And now must wait till he returns.

ORSINO

        Great God !
Weigh you the danger of this rashness ?

GIACOMO

        Ay !
Does my destroyer know his danger ?   We
Are now no more, as once, parent and
    child,
But man to man; the oppressor to the op-
    pressed,
The slanderer to the slandered; foe to foe.
He has cast Nature off, which was his
    shield,
And Nature casts him off, who is her
    shame;
And I spurn both. Is it a father's throat
Which I will shake, and say, I ask not
    gold;
I ask not happy years; nor memories   290
Of tranquil childhood; nor home-sheltered
    love;
Though all these hast thou torn from me,
    and more;
But only my fair fame; only one hoard
Of peace, which I thought hidden from thy
    hate
Under the penury heaped on me by thee;
Or I will — God can understand and pardon,
Why should I speak with man ?

ORSINO

        Be calm, dear friend.

GIACOMO

Well, I will calmly tell you what he did.
This old Francesco Cenci, as you know,
Borrowed the dowry of my wife from me,
And then denied the loan; and left me so
In poverty, the which I sought to mend
By holding a poor office in the state.   303
It had been promised to me, and already
I bought new clothing for my ragged babes,
And my wife smiled; and my heart knew
    repose;
When Cenci's intercession, as I found,

Conferred this office on a wretch, whom
    thus
He paid for vilest service. I returned
With this ill news, and we sate sad to-
    gether   310
Solacing our despondency with tears
Of such affection and unbroken faith
As temper life's worst bitterness; when he,
As he is wont, came to upbraid and curse,
Mocking our poverty, and telling us
Such was God's scourge for disobedient
    sons.
And then, that I might strike him dumb
    with shame,
I spoke of my wife's dowry; but he coined
A brief yet specious tale, how I had wasted
The sum in secret riot; and he saw   320
My wife was touched, and he went smiling
    forth.
And when I knew the impression he had
    made,
And felt my wife insult with silent scorn
My ardent truth, and look averse and cold,
I went forth too; but soon returned again;
Yet not so soon but that my wife had taught
My children her harsh thoughts, and they
    all cried,
'Give us clothes, father ! Give us better
    food !
What you in one night squander were
    enough
For months !' I looked, and saw that
    home was hell.   330
And to that hell will I return no more,
Until mine enemy has rendered up
Atonement, or, as he gave life to me,
I will, reversing Nature's law —

ORSINO

        Trust me,
The compensation which thou seekest here
Will be denied.

GIACOMO

        Then — Are you not my friend ?
Did you not hint at the alternative,
Upon the brink of which you see I stand,
The other day when we conversed together ?
My wrongs were then less. That word,
    parricide,   340
Although I am resolved, haunts me like
    fear.

ORSINO

It must be fear itself, for the bare word
Is hollow mockery. Mark how wisest God

Draws to one point the threads of a just
doom,
So sanctifying it; what you devise
Is, as it were, accomplished.

GIACOMO

Is he dead ?

ORSINO

His grave is ready. Know that since we
met
Cenci has done an outrage to his daughter.

GIACOMO

What outrage ?

ORSINO

That she speaks not, but you may
Conceive such half conjectures as I do   350
From her fixed paleness, and the lofty
grief
Of her stern brow, bent on the idle air,
And her severe unmodulated voice,
Drowning both tenderness and dread; and
last
From this; that whilst her step-mother and I,
Bewildered in our horror, talked together
With obscure hints, both self-misunder-
stood,
And darkly guessing, stumbling, in our talk,
Over the truth and yet to its revenge,
She interrupted us, and with a look   360
Which told, before she spoke it, he must
die —

GIACOMO

It is enough. My doubts are well appeased;
There is a higher reason for the act
Than mine; there is a holier judge than
me,
A more unblamed avenger. Beatrice,
Who in the gentleness of thy sweet youth
Hast never trodden on a worm, or bruised
A living flower, but thou hast pitied it
With needless tears ! fair sister, thou in
whom
Men wondered how such loveliness and wis-
dom   370
Did not destroy each other ! is there made
Ravage of thee ? O heart, I ask no more
Justification ! Shall I wait, Orsino,
Till he return, and stab him at the door ?

ORSINO

Not so; some accident might interpose
To rescue him from what is now most sure;

And you are unprovided where to fly,
How to excuse or to conceal. Nay, listen;
All is contrived; success is so assured
That —

Enter BEATRICE

BEATRICE

'T is my brother's voice ! You know me
not ?   380

GIACOMO

My sister, my lost sister !

BEATRICE

Lost indeed !
I see Orsino has talked with you, and
That you conjecture things too horrible
To speak, yet far less than the truth. Now
stay not,
He might return; yet kiss me; I shall
know
That then thou hast consented to his death.
Farewell, farewell ! Let piety to God,
Brotherly love, justice and clemency,
And all things that make tender hardest
hearts,
Make thine hard, brother. Answer not —
farewell.   390
[*Exeunt severally.*

SCENE II. — *A mean Apartment in* GIACOMO'S
House. GIACOMO *alone.*

GIACOMO

'T is midnight, and Orsino comes not yet.
(*Thunder, and the sound of a storm*)
What ! can the everlasting elements
Feel with a worm like man ? If so, the
shaft
Of mercy-wingèd lightning would not fall
On stones and trees. My wife and children
sleep;
They are now living in unmeaning dreams;
But I must wake, still doubting if that
deed
Be just which was most necessary. Oh,
Thou unreplenished lamp, whose narrow
fire
Is shaken by the wind, and on whose edge   9
Devouring darkness hovers ! thou small
flame,
Which, as a dying pulse rises and falls,
Still flickerest up and down, how very
soon,
Did I not feed thee, wouldst thou fail and be

As thou hadst never been !   So wastes and
    sinks
Even now, perhaps, the life that kindled
    mine;
But that no power can fill with vital oil, —
That broken lamp of flesh.   Ha ! 't is the
    blood
Which fed these veins that ebbs till all is
    cold;
It is the form that moulded mine that
    sinks   20
Into the white and yellow spasms of death;
It is the soul by which mine was arrayed
In God's immortal likeness which now
    stands
Naked before Heaven's judgment-seat !
                 (*A bell strikes*)
                 One ! Two !
The hours crawl on; and, when my hairs
    are white,
My son will then perhaps be waiting thus,
Tortured between just hate and vain re-
    morse;
Chiding the tardy messenger of news
Like those which I expect.   I almost wish
He be not dead, although my wrongs are
    great;   30
Yet — 't is Orsino's step.

         Enter ORSINO
            Speak !

       ORSINO
                 I am come
To say he has escaped.

       GIACOMO
           Escaped !

       ORSINO
                 And safe
Within Petrella.   He passed by the spot
Appointed for the deed an hour too soon.

       GIACOMO
Are we the fools of such contingencies ?
And do we waste in blind misgivings thus
The hours when we should act ?   Then
    wind and thunder,
Which seemed to howl his knell, is the
    loud laughter
With which Heaven mocks our weakness !
    I henceforth
Will ne'er repent of aught designed or
    done,   40
But my repentance.

       ORSINO
          See, the lamp is out.

       GIACOMO
If no remorse is ours when the dim air
Has drunk this innocent flame, why should
    we quail
When Cenci's life, that light by which ill
    spirits
See the worst deeds they prompt, shall sink
    forever ?
No, I am hardened.

       ORSINO
          Why, what need of this ?
Who feared the pale intrusion of remorse
In a just deed ?   Although our first plan
    failed,
Doubt not but he will soon be laid to rest.
But light the lamp; let us not talk i' the
    dark.   50

     GIACOMO (*lighting the lamp*)
And yet, once quenched, I cannot thus re-
    lume
My father's life; do you not think his
    ghost
Might plead that argument with God ?

       ORSINO
                 Once gone,
You cannot now recall your sister's peace;
Your own extinguished years of youth and
    hope;
Nor your wife's bitter words; nor all the
    taunts
Which, from the prosperous, weak misfor-
    tune takes;
Nor your dead mother; nor —

       GIACOMO
            Oh, speak no more !
I am resolved, although this very hand
Must quench the life that animated it.   60

       ORSINO
There is no need of that.   Listen; you
    know
Olimpio, the castellan of Petrella
In old Colonna's time; him whom your
    father
Degraded from his post ?   And Marzio,
That desperate wretch, whom he deprived
    last year
Of a reward of blood, well earned and due ?

GIACOMO

I knew Olimpio; and they say he hated
Old Cenci so, that in his silent rage
His lips grew white only to see him pass.
Of Marzio I know nothing.

ORSINO

Marzio's hate
Matches Olimpio's.   I have sent these men,
But in your name, and as at your request,
To talk with Beatrice and Lucretia.   73

GIACOMO

Only to talk?

ORSINO

The moments which even now
Pass onward to to-morrow's midnight hour
May memorize their flight with death; ere
then
They must have talked, and may perhaps
have done,
And made an end.

GIACOMO

Listen!   What sound is that?

ORSINO

The house-dog moans, and the beams
crack; nought else.

GIACOMO

It is my wife complaining in her sleep;   80
I doubt not she is saying bitter things
Of me; and all my children round her
dreaming
That I deny them sustenance.

ORSINO

Whilst he
Who truly took it from them, and who
fills
Their hungry rest with bitterness, now
sleeps
Lapped in bad pleasures, and triumphantly
Mocks thee in visions of successful hate
Too like the truth of day.

GIACOMO

If e'er he wakes
Again, I will not trust to hireling hands —

ORSINO

Why, that were well.   I must be gone;
good night!   90
When next we meet, may all be done!

GIACOMO

And all
Forgotten!   Oh, that I had never been!
[Exeunt.

ACT IV

SCENE I. — *An Apartment in the Castle of Petrella.   Enter* CENCI.

CENCI

SHE comes not; yet I left her even now
Vanquished and faint.   She knows the
penalty
Of her delay; yet what if threats are vain?
Am I not now within Petrella's moat?
Or fear I still the eyes and ears of Rome?
Might I not drag her by the golden hair?
Stamp on her?   keep her sleepless till her
brain
Be overworn?   tame her with chains and
famine?
Less would suffice.   Yet so to leave un-
done
What I most seek!   No, 't is her stubborn
will,   10
Which, by its own consent, shall stoop as
low
As that which drags it down.

Enter LUCRETIA

Thou loathèd wretch!
Hide thee from my abhorrence; fly, be-
gone!
Yet stay!   Bid Beatrice come hither.

LUCRETIA

Oh,
Husband!   I pray, for thine own wretched
sake,
Heed what thou dost.   A man who walks
like thee
Through crimes, and through the danger
of his crimes,
Each hour may stumble o'er a sudden
grave.
And thou art old; thy hairs are hoary gray;
As thou wouldst save thyself from death
and hell,   20
Pity thy daughter; give her to some friend
In marriage; so that she may tempt thee
not
To hatred, or worse thoughts, if worse
there be.

CENCI

What ! like her sister, who has found a
   home
To mock my hate from with prosperity ?
Strange ruin shall destroy both her and
   thee,
And all that yet remain. My death may
   be
Rapid, her destiny outspeeds it. Go,
Bid her come hither, and before my mood
Be changed, lest I should drag her by the
   hair.   30

LUCRETIA

She sent me to thee, husband. At thy pre-
   sence
She fell, as thou dost know, into a trance;
And in that trance she heard a voice which
   said,
' Cenci must die ! Let him confess him-
   self !
Even now the accusing Angel waits to
   hear
If God, to punish his enormous crimes,
Harden his dying heart ! '

CENCI

         Why — such things are.
No doubt divine revealings may be made.
'T is plain I have been favored from above,
For when I cursed my sons, they died. —
Ay — so.   40
As to the right or wrong, that 's talk. Re-
   pentance ?
Repentance is an easy moment's work,
And more depends on God than me. Well
   — well —
I must give up the greater point, which was
To poison and corrupt her soul.

(*A pause;* LUCRETIA *approaches anxiously,
and then shrinks back as he speaks*)

         One, two;
Ay — Rocco and Cristofano my curse
Strangled; and Giacomo, I think, will find
Life a worse Hell than that beyond the
   grave;
Beatrice shall, if there be skill in hate,   49
Die in despair, blaspheming; to Bernardo,
He is so innocent, I will bequeathe
The memory of these deeds, and make his
   youth
The sepulchre of hope, where evil thoughts
Shall grow like weeds on a neglected tomb.
When all is done, out in the wide Cam-
   pagna

I will pile up my silver and my gold;
My costly robes, paintings, and tapestries;
My parchments, and all records of my
   wealth;
And make a bonfire in my joy, and leave
Of my possessions nothing but my name; 60
Which shall be an inheritance to strip
Its wearer bare as infamy. That done,
My soul, which is a scourge, will I resign
Into the hands of Him who wielded it;
Be it for its own punishment or theirs,
He will not ask it of me till the lash
Be broken in its last and deepest wound;
Until its hate be all inflicted. Yet,
Lest death outspeed my purpose, let me
   make   69
Short work and sure.
               [*Going.*

LUCRETIA (*stops him*)
         Oh, stay ! it was a feint;
She had no vision, and she heard no voice.
I said it but to awe thee.

CENCI

            That is well.
Vile palterer with the sacred truth of God,
Be thy soul choked with that blaspheming
   lie !
For Beatrice worse terrors are in store
To bend her to my will.

LUCRETIA

         Oh, to what will ?
What cruel sufferings more than she has
   known
Canst thou inflict ?

CENCI

        Andrea ! go, call my daughter
And if she comes not, tell her that I come.

(*To* LUCRETIA)

What sufferings ? I will drag her, step by
   step,   80
Through infamies unheard of among men;
She shall stand shelterless in the broad
   noon
Of public scorn, for acts blazoned abroad,
One among which shall be — what ? canst
   thou guess ?
She shall become (for what she most abhors
Shall have a fascination to entrap
Her loathing will) to her own conscious self
All she appears to others; and when dead,
As she shall die unshrived and unforgiven,

A rebel to her father and her God,   90
Her corpse shall be abandoned to the
    hounds;
Her name shall be the terror of the earth;
Her spirit shall approach the throne of
    God
Plague-spotted with my curses. I will
    make
Body and soul a monstrous lump of ruin.

Enter ANDREA

ANDREA

The Lady Beatrice —

CENCI

                    Speak, pale slave ! what
Said she ?

ANDREA

   My Lord, 't was what she looked; she
       said,
'Go tell my father that I see the gulf
Of Hell between us two, which he may
    pass;   99
I will not.'
                                [*Exit* ANDREA.

CENCI

             Go thou quick, Lucretia,
Tell her to come; yet let her understand
Her coming is consent; and say, moreover,
That if she come not I will curse her.
                             [*Exit* LUCRETIA.

                                        Ha !
With what but with a father's curse doth
    God
Panic-strike armèd victory, and make pale
Cities in their prosperity ? The world's
    Father
Must grant a parent's prayer against his
    child,
Be he who asks even what men call me.
Will not the deaths of her rebellious
    brothers
Awe her before I speak ? for I on them 110
Did imprecate quick ruin, and it came.

Enter LUCRETIA

Well; what ?   Speak, wretch !

LUCRETIA

              She said, 'I cannot come;
Go tell my father that I see a torrent
Of his own blood raging between us.'

CENCI (*kneeling*)
                                        God,
Hear me ! If this most specious mass of
    flesh,
Which thou hast made my daughter; this
    my blood,
This particle of my divided being;
Or rather, this my bane and my disease,
Whose sight infects and poisons me; this
    devil,
Which sprung from me as from a hell, was
    meant   120
To aught good use; if her bright loveliness
Was kindled to illumine this dark world;
If, nursed by thy selectest dew of love,
Such virtues blossom in her as should make
The peace of life, I pray thee for my sake,
As thou the common God and Father art
Of her, and me, and all; reverse that doom !
Earth, in the name of God, let her food be
Poison, until she be encrusted round
With leprous stains !   Heaven, rain upon
    her head   130
The blistering drops of the Maremma's
    dew
Till she be speckled like a toad; parch up
Those love-enkindled lips, warp those fine
    limbs
To loathèd lameness !   All-beholding sun,
Strike in thine envy those life-darting eyes
With thine own blinding beams !

LUCRETIA
                         Peace, peace !
For thine own sake unsay those dreadful
    words.
When high God grants, he punishes such
    prayers.   138

CENCI (*leaping up, and throwing his right hand
    towards Heaven*)

He does his will, I mine !   This in addition,
That if she have a child —

LUCRETIA
                     Horrible thought !

CENCI

That if she ever have a child — and thou,
Quick Nature ! I adjure thee by thy God,
That thou be fruitful in her, and increase
And multiply, fulfilling his command,
And my deep imprecation ! — may it be
A hideous likeness of herself; that as
From a distorting mirror she may see

Her image mixed with what she most ab-
hors,
Smiling upon her from her nursing breast !
And that the child may from its infancy
Grow, day by day, more wicked and de-
formed,   151
Turning her mother's love to misery !
And that both she and it may live until
It shall repay her care and pain with hate,
Or what may else be more unnatural;
So he may hunt her through the clamorous
scoffs
Of the loud world to a dishonored grave !
Shall I revoke this curse ? Go, bid her
come,
Before my words are chronicled in heaven.
    [*Exit* LUCRETIA.
I do not feel as if I were a man,   160
But like a fiend appointed to chastise
The offences of some unremembered world.
My blood is running up and down my veins;
A fearful pleasure makes it prick and tin-
gle;
I feel a giddy sickness of strange awe;
My heart is beating with an expectation
Of horrid joy.

Enter LUCRETIA
    What ? Speak !

LUCRETIA
          She bids thee curse;
And if thy curses, as they cannot do,
Could kill her soul —

CENCI
        She would not come. 'T is well,
I can do both; first take what I demand,
And then extort concession. To thy
chamber !   171
Fly ere I spurn thee; and beware this night
That thou cross not my footsteps. It were
safer
To come between the tiger and his prey.
    [*Exit* LUCRETIA.
It must be late; mine eyes grow weary dim
With unaccustomed heaviness of sleep.
Conscience ! O thou most insolent of lies !
They say that sleep, that healing dew of
heaven,
Steeps not in balm the foldings of the brain
Which thinks thee an impostor. I will go,
First to belie thee with an hour of rest, 181
Which will be deep and calm, I feel; and
then —

O multitudinous Hell, the fiends will shake
Thine arches with the laughter of their joy !
There shall be lamentation heard in Hea-
ven
As o'er an angel fallen; and upon Earth
All good shall droop and sicken, and ill
things
Shall, with a spirit of unnatural life,
Stir and be quickened — even as I am now.
    [*Exit*.

SCENE II. — *Before the Castle of Petrella.
Enter* BEATRICE *and* LUCRETIA *above on the
ramparts.*

BEATRICE
They come not yet.

LUCRETIA
        'T is scarce midnight.

BEATRICE
           How slow
Behind the course of thought, even sick
with speed,
Lags leaden-footed Time !

LUCRETIA
          The minutes pass.
If he should wake before the deed is done ?

BEATRICE
O mother ! he must never wake again.
What thou hast said persuades me that our
act
Will but dislodge a spirit of deep hell
Out of a human form.

LUCRETIA
         'T is true he spoke
Of death and judgment with strange con-
fidence
For one so wicked; as a man believing   10
In God, yet recking not of good or ill.
And yet to die without confession ! —

BEATRICE
            Oh !
Believe that Heaven is merciful and just,
And will not add our dread necessity
To the amount of his offences.

Enter OLIMPIO *and* MARZIO *below*

LUCRETIA
          See,
They come.

BEATRICE

All mortal things must hasten thus
To their dark end.   Let us go down.
[*Exeunt* LUCRETIA *and* BEATRICE *from above.*

OLIMPIO

How feel you to this work ?

MARZIO

As one who thinks
A thousand crowns excellent market price
For an old murderer's life.   Your cheeks
    are pale.   20

OLIMPIO

It is the white reflection of your own,
Which you call pale.

MARZIO

Is that their natural hue ?

OLIMPIO

Or 't is my hate, and the deferred desire
To wreak it, which extinguishes their blood.

MARZIO

You are inclined then to this business ?

OLIMPIO

Ay,
If one should bribe me with a thousand
    crowns
To kill a serpent which had stung my
    child,
I could not be more willing.

Enter BEATRICE *and* LUCRETIA *below*
Noble ladies !

BEATRICE

Are ye resolved ?

OLIMPIO

Is he asleep ?

MARZIO

Is all
Quiet ?

LUCRETIA

I mixed an opiate with his drink;
He sleeps so soundly —

BEATRICE

That his death will be
But as a change of sin-chastising dreams, 32
A dark continuance of the hell within him,

Which God extinguish !   But ye are re-
    solved ?
Ye know it is a high and holy deed ?

OLIMPIO

We are resolved.

MARZIO

As to the how this act
Be warranted, it rests with you.

BEATRICE

Well, follow !

OLIMPIO

Hush !   Hark !   what noise is that ?

MARZIO

Ha !   some one comes !

BEATRICE

Ye conscience-stricken cravens, rock to
    rest
Your baby hearts.   It is the iron gate,   40
Which ye left open, swinging to the
    wind,
That enters whistling as in scorn.   Come,
    follow !
And be your steps like mine, light, quick
    and bold.
[*Exeunt.*

SCENE III. — *An Apartment in the Castle.*
Enter BEATRICE *and* LUCRETIA.

LUCRETIA

They are about it now.

BEATRICE

Nay, it is done.

LUCRETIA

I have not heard him groan.

BEATRICE

He will not groan.

LUCRETIA

What sound is that ?

BEATRICE

List !   't is the tread of feet
About his bed.

LUCRETIA

My God !
If he be now a cold, stiff corpse —

BEATRICE
Oh, fear not
What may be done, but what is left un-
done;
The act seals all.

Enter OLIMPIO *and* MARZIO
Is it accomplished ?

MARZIO
What ?

OLIMPIO
Did you not call ?

BEATRICE
When ?

OLIMPIO
Now.

BEATRICE
I ask if all is over ?

OLIMPIO
We dare not kill an old and sleeping man;
His thin gray hair, his stern and reverent
brow,   10
His veinèd hands crossed on his heaving
breast,
And the calm innocent sleep in which he
lay,
Quelled me. Indeed, indeed, I cannot do
it.

MARZIO
But I was bolder; for I chid Olimpio,
And bade him bear his wrongs to his own
grave,
And leave me the reward. And now my
knife
Touched the loose wrinkled throat, when
the old man
Stirred in his sleep, and said, ' God ! hear,
oh, hear
A father's curse ! What, art thou not our
father ? '
And then he laughed. I knew it was the
ghost   20
Of my dead father speaking through his
lips,
And could not kill him.

BEATRICE
Miserable slaves !
Where, if ye dare not kill a sleeping man,
Found ye the boldness to return to me

With such a deed undone ? Base palter-
ers !
Cowards and traitors ! Why, the very
conscience
Which ye would sell for gold and for re-
venge
Is an equivocation; it sleeps over
A thousand daily acts disgracing men;
And when a deed, where mercy insults hea-
ven —   30
Why do I talk ?
(*Snatching a dagger from one of them, and
raising it*)
Hadst thou a tongue to say,
She murdered her own father, I must do
it !
But never dream ye shall outlive him long !

OLIMPIO
Stop, for God's sake !

MARZIO
I will go back and kill him.

OLIMPIO
Give me the weapon, we must do thy will.

BEATRICE
Take it ! Depart ! Return !
[*Exeunt* OLIMPIO *and* MARZIO.
How pale thou art !
We do but that which 't were a deadly
crime
To leave undone.

LUCRETIA
Would it were done !

BEATRICE
Even whilst
That doubt is passing through your mind,
the world
Is conscious of a change. Darkness and
hell   40
Have swallowed up the vapor they sent
forth
To blacken the sweet light of life. My
breath
Comes, methinks, lighter, and the jellied
blood
Runs freely through my veins. Hark !

Enter OLIMPIO *and* MARZIO
He is —

OLIMPIO
Dead !

MARZIO

We strangled him, that there might be no
　blood;
And then we threw his heavy corpse i' the
　garden
Under the balcony; 't will seem it fell.

BEATRICE (*giving them a bag of coin*)

Here take this gold and hasten to your
　homes.
And, Marzio, because thou wast only awed
By that which made me tremble, wear thou
　this !   50
　　(*Clothes him in a rich mantle*)
It was the mantle which my grandfather
Wore in his high prosperity, and men
Envied his state; so may they envy thine.
Thou wert a weapon in the hand of God
To a just use. Live long and thrive ! And,
　mark,
If thou hast crimes, repent; this deed is
　none.
　　　　　　　(*A horn is sounded*)

LUCRETIA

Hark, 't is the castle horn: my God ! it
　sounds
Like the last trump.

BEATRICE

　　　　　Some tedious guest is coming.

LUCRETIA

The drawbridge is let down; there is a
　tramp
Of horses in the court; fly, hide your-
　selves !   60
　　[*Exeunt* OLIMPIO *and* MARZIO.

BEATRICE

Let us retire to counterfeit deep rest;
I scarcely need to counterfeit it now;
The spirit which doth reign within these
　limbs
Seems strangely undisturbed. I could even
　sleep
Fearless and calm; all ill is surely past.
　　　　　　　　　　　　　[*Exeunt.*

SCENE IV. — *Another Apartment in the Castle.
Enter on one side the Legate* SAVELLA, *intro-
duced by a Servant, and on the other* LUCRE-
TIA *and* BERNARDO.

SAVELLA

Lady, my duty to his Holiness
Be my excuse that thus unseasonably

I break upon your rest. I must speak
　with
Count Cenci; doth he sleep ?

LUCRETIA (*in a hurried and confused manner*)
　　　　　　　　　　I think he sleeps;
Yet, wake him not, I pray, spare me
　awhile.
He is a wicked and a wrathful man;
Should he be roused out of his sleep to-
　night,
Which is, I know, a hell of angry dreams,
It were not well; indeed it were not
　well.
Wait till day break.
　　　　(*Aside*) Oh, I am deadly sick !

SAVELLA

I grieve thus to distress you, but the
　Count   11
Must answer charges of the gravest im-
　port,
And suddenly; such my commission is.

LUCRETIA (*with increased agitation*)

I dare not rouse him, I know none who
　dare;
'T were perilous; you might as safely
　waken
A serpent, or a corpse in which some fiend
Were laid to sleep.

SAVELLA

　　　　　Lady, my moments here
Are counted. I must rouse him from his
　sleep,   18
Since none else dare.

LUCRETIA (*aside*)
　　　　　Oh, terror ! oh, despair !

(*To* BERNARDO)

Bernardo, conduct you the Lord Legate to
Your father's chamber.
　　[*Exeunt* SAVELLA *and* BERNARDO.

Enter BEATRICE

BEATRICE
　　　　　'T is a messenger
Come to arrest the culprit who now stands
Before the throne of unappealable God.
Both Earth and Heaven, consenting arbi-
　ters,
Acquit our deed.

LUCRETIA

Oh, agony of fear !
Would that he yet might live ! Even now
I heard
The Legate's followers whisper as they
passed
They had a warrant for his instant death.
All was prepared by unforbidden means,
Which we must pay so dearly, having done.
Even now they search the tower, and find
the body; 31
Now they suspect the truth; now they
consult
Before they come to tax us with the fact.
Oh, horrible, 't is all discovered !

BEATRICE

Mother,
What is done wisely is done well. Be bold
As thou art just. 'T is like a truant child,
To fear that others know what thou hast
done,
Even from thine own strong consciousness,
and thus
Write on unsteady eyes and altered cheeks
All thou wouldst hide. Be faithful to thy-
self, 40
And fear no other witness but thy fear.
For if, as cannot be, some circumstance
Should rise in accusation, we can blind
Suspicion with such cheap astonishment,
Or overbear it with such guiltless pride,
As murderers cannot feign. The deed is
done,
And what may follow now regards not me.
I am as universal as the light;
Free as the earth-surrounding air; as firm
As the world's centre. Consequence, to
me, 50
Is as the wind which strikes the solid rock,
But shakes it not.
(A cry within and tumult)

VOICES

Murder ! Murder ! Murder !

Enter BERNARDO and SAVELLA

SAVELLA (to his followers)

Go, search the castle round; sound the
alarm;
Look to the gates, that none escape !

BEATRICE

What now ?

BERNARDO

I know not what to say — my father 's
dead.

BEATRICE

How, dead ! he only sleeps; you mistake,
brother.
His sleep is very calm, very like death;
'T is wonderful how well a tyrant sleeps.
He is not dead ?

BERNARDO

Dead; murdered !

LUCRETIA (with extreme agitation)

Oh, no, no !
He is not murdered, though he may be
dead; 60
I have alone the keys of those apartments.

SAVELLA

Ha ! is it so ?

BEATRICE

My Lord, I pray excuse us;
We will retire; my mother is not well;
She seems quite overcome with this strange
horror.
[Exeunt LUCRETIA and BEATRICE.

SAVELLA

Can you suspect who may have murdered
him ?

BERNARDO

I know not what to think.

SAVELLA

Can you name any
Who had an interest in his death ?

BERNARDO

Alas !
I can name none who had not, and those
most
Who most lament that such a deed is done;
My mother, and my sister, and myself. 70

SAVELLA

'T is strange ! There were clear marks of
violence.
I found the old man's body in the moonlight,
Hanging beneath the window of his chamber
Among the branches of a pine; he could
not

Have fallen there, for all his limbs lay
  heaped
And effortless; 't is true there was no blood.
Favor me, sir — it much imports your
  house
That all should be made clear — to tell the
  ladies
That I request their presence.

  [*Exit* BERNARDO.

Enter Guards, bringing in MARZIO

GUARD

                            We have one.

OFFICER

My Lord, we found this ruffian and another
Lurking among the rocks; there is no
  doubt   81
But that they are the murderers of Count
  Cenci;
Each had a bag of coin; this fellow wore
A gold-inwoven robe, which, shining bright
Under the dark rocks to the glimmering
  moon,
Betrayed them to our notice; the other fell
Desperately fighting.

SAVELLA

              What does he confess?

OFFICER

He keeps firm silence; but these lines found
  on him   88
May speak.

SAVELLA

      Their language is at least sincere.

                                      (*Reads*)

"TO THE LADY BEATRICE.

  That the atonement of what my nature
sickens to conjecture may soon arrive, I
send thee, at thy brother's desire, those
who will speak and do more than I dare
write.
              Thy devoted servant,
                            ORSINO."

Enter LUCRETIA, BEATRICE, *and* BERNARDO
Knowest thou this writing, lady?

BEATRICE

                  No.

SAVELLA

                            Nor thou?

LUCRETIA (*her conduct throughout the scene is
  marked by extreme agitation*)
Where was it found? What is it? It
  should be
Orsino's hand! It speaks of that strange
  horror
Which never yet found utterance, but
  which made
Between that hapless child and her dead
  father
A gulf of obscure hatred.

SAVELLA

                      Is it so,   100
Is it true, Lady, that thy father did
Such outrages as to awaken in thee
Unfilial hate?

BEATRICE

        Not hate, 't was more than hate;
This is most true, yet wherefore question
  me?

SAVELLA

There is a deed demanding question done;
Thou hast a secret which will answer not.

BEATRICE

What sayest? My Lord, your words are
  bold and rash.

SAVELLA

I do arrest all present in the name
Of the Pope's Holiness. You must to
  Rome.   109

LUCRETIA

Oh, not to Rome! indeed we are not guilty.

BEATRICE

Guilty! who dares talk of guilt? My
  Lord,
I am more innocent of parricide
Than is a child born fatherless. Dear
  mother,
Your gentleness and patience are no shield
For this keen-judging world, this two-
  edged lie,
Which seems, but is not. What! will hu-
  man laws,
Rather will ye who are their ministers,
Bar all access to retribution first,
And then, when Heaven doth interpose to do
What ye neglect, arming familiar things   120
To the redress of an unwonted crime,
Make ye the victims who demanded it

Culprits ? 'T is ye are culprits ! That
    poor wretch
Who stands so pale, and trembling, and
    amazed,
If it be true he murdered Cenci, was
A sword in the right hand of justest God.
Wherefore should I have wielded it ? un-
    less
The crimes which mortal tongue dare never
    name   128
God therefore scruples to avenge.

SAVELLA

                      You own
That you desired his death ?

BEATRICE

              It would have been
A crime no less than his, if for one moment
That fierce desire had faded in my heart.
'T is true I did believe, and hope, and
    pray,
Ay, I even knew — for God is wise and
    just —
That some strange sudden death hung over
    him.
'T is true that this did happen, and most
    true
There was no other rest for me on earth,
No other hope in Heaven. Now what of
    this ?

SAVELLA

Strange thoughts beget strange deeds; and
    here are both;   139
I judge thee not.

BEATRICE

           And yet, if you arrest me,
You are the judge and executioner
Of that which is the life of life; the breath
Of accusation kills an innocent name,
And leaves for lame acquittal the poor life
Which is a mask without it. 'T is most
    false
That I am guilty of foul parricide;
Although I must rejoice, for justest cause,
That other hands have sent my father's
    soul
To ask the mercy he denied to me.   149
Now leave us free; stain not a noble house
With vague surmises of rejected crime;
Add to our sufferings and your own neglect
No heavier sum; let them have been enough;
Leave us the wreck we have.

SAVELLA

                I dare not, Lady.
I pray that you prepare yourselves for
    Rome.
There the Pope's further pleasure will be
    known.

LUCRETIA

Oh, not to Rome ! Oh, take us not to Rome !

BEATRICE

Why not to Rome, dear mother ? There
    as here
Our innocence is as an armèd heel   159
To trample accusation. God is there,
As here, and with his shadow ever clothes
The innocent, the injured, and the weak;
And such are we. Cheer up, dear Lady !
    lean
On me; collect your wandering thoughts.
    My Lord,
As soon as you have taken some refresh-
    ment,
And had all such examinations made
Upon the spot as may be necessary
To the full understanding of this matter,
We shall be ready. Mother, will you come ?

LUCRETIA

Ha ! they will bind us to the rack, and
    wrest   170
Self-accusation from our agony !
Will Giacomo be there ? Orsino ? Marzio ?
All present; all confronted; all demanding
Each from the other's countenance the
    thing
Which is in every heart ! Oh, misery !
             (She faints, and is borne out)

SAVELLA

She faints; an ill appearance this.

BEATRICE

                   My Lord,
She knows not yet the uses of the world.
She fears that power is as a beast which
    grasps
And loosens not; a snake whose look trans-
    mutes   179
All things to guilt which is its nutriment.
She cannot know how well the supine slaves
Of blind authority read the truth of things
When written on a brow of guilelessness;
She sees not yet triumphant Innocence
Stand at the judgment-seat of mortal man,

A judge and an accuser of the wrong
Which drags it there.   Prepare yourself,
   my Lord.
Our suite will join yours in the court below.
                                    [*Exeunt.*

ACT V

SCENE I. — *An Apartment in* ORSINO'S *Palace.*
   Enter ORSINO *and* GIACOMO.

GIACOMO

Do evil deeds thus quickly come to end ?
Oh, that the vain remorse which must chas-
   tise
Crimes done had but as loud a voice to warn
As its keen sting is mortal to avenge !
Oh, that the hour when present had cast off
The mantle of its mystery, and shown
The ghastly form with which it now returns
When its scared game is roused, cheering
   the hounds
Of conscience to their prey !   Alas, alas !
It was a wicked thought, a piteous deed,   10
To kill an old and hoary-headed father.

ORSINO

It has turned out unluckily, in truth.

GIACOMO

To violate the sacred doors of sleep;
To cheat kind nature of the placid death
Which she prepares for overwearied age;
To drag from Heaven an unrepentant soul,
Which might have quenched in reconciling
   prayers
A life of burning crimes —

ORSINO

                              You cannot say
I urged you to the deed.

GIACOMO

                        Oh, had I never
Found in thy smooth and ready counte-
   nance   20
The mirror of my darkest thoughts; hadst
   thou
Never with hints and questions made me
   look
Upon the monster of my thought, until
It grew familiar to desire —

ORSINO

                        'T is thus
Men cast the blame of their unprosperous
   acts

Upon the abettors of their own resolve;
Or anything but their weak, guilty selves.
And yet, confess the truth, it is the peril
In which you stand that gives you this pale
   sickness
Of penitence; confess 't is fear disguised   30
From its own shame that takes the mantle
   now
Of thin remorse.   What if we yet were
   safe ?

GIACOMO

How can that be ?   Already Beatrice,
Lucretia and the murderer are in prison.
I doubt not officers are, whilst we speak,
Sent to arrest us.

ORSINO

                  I have all prepared
For instant flight.   We can escape even
   now,
So we take fleet occasion by the hair.

GIACOMO

Rather expire in tortures, as I may.
What ! will you cast by self-accusing
   flight   40
Assured conviction upon Beatrice ?
She who alone, in this unnatural work
Stands like God's angel ministered upon
By fiends ; avenging such a nameless
   wrong
As turns black parricide to piety;
Whilst we for basest ends — I fear, Or-
   sino,
While I consider all your words and looks,
Comparing them with your proposal now,
That you must be a villain.   For what end
Could you engage in such a perilous
   crime,   50
Training me on with hints, and signs, and
   smiles,
Even to this gulf ?   Thou art no liar ?
   No,   .
Thou art a lie !   Traitor and murderer !
Coward and slave !   But no — defend thy-
   self;
                              (*Drawing*)
Let the sword speak what the indignant
   tongue
Disdains to brand thee with.

ORSINO

                        Put up your weapon.
Is it the desperation of your fear

Makes you thus rash and sudden with a
    friend,
Now ruined for your sake? If honest
    anger
Have moved you, know, that what I just
    proposed   60
Was but to try you. As for me, I think
Thankless affection led me to this point,
From which, if my firm temper could re-
    pent,
I cannot now recede. Even whilst we
    speak,
The ministers of justice wait below;
They grant me these brief moments. Now,
    if you
Have any word of melancholy comfort
To speak to your pale wife, 't were best to
    pass
Out at the postern, and avoid them so.

GIACOMO

O generous friend! how canst thou pardon
    me?   70
Would that my life could purchase thine!

ORSINO

               That wish
Now comes a day too late. Haste; fare
    thee well!
Hear'st thou not steps along the corridor?
            [Exit GIACOMO.
I 'm sorry for it; but the guards are wait-
    ing
At his own gate, and such was my contriv-
    ance
That I might rid me both of him and
    them.
I thought to act a solemn comedy
Upon the painted scene of this new world,
And to attain my own peculiar ends
By some such plot of mingled good and
    ill   80
As others weave; but there arose a Power
Which grasped and snapped the threads of
    my device,
And turned it to a net of ruin — Ha!
            (A shout is heard)
Is that my name I hear proclaimed abroad?
But I will pass, wrapped in a vile disguise,
Rags on my back and a false innocence
Upon my face, through the misdeeming
    crowd,
Which judges by what seems. 'T is easy
    then,
For a new name and for a country new,

And a new life fashioned on old desires, 90
To change the honors of abandoned Rome.
And these must be the masks of that
    within,
Which must remain unaltered. — Oh, I
    fear
That what is past will never let me rest!
Why, when none else is conscious, but
    myself,
Of my misdeeds, should my own heart's
    contempt
Trouble me? Have I not the power to
    fly
My own reproaches? Shall I be the
    slave
Of — what? A word? which those of
    this false world
Employ against each other, not them-
    selves,   100
As men wear daggers not for self-offence.
But if I am mistaken, where shall I
Find the disguise to hide me from myself,
As now I skulk from every other eye?
                 [Exit.

SCENE II. — A Hall of Justice. CAMILLO,
    JUDGES, etc., are discovered seated; MARZIO
    is led in.

FIRST JUDGE

Accused, do you persist in your denial?
I ask you, are you innocent, or guilty?
I demand who were the participators
In your offence. Speak truth, and the
    whole truth.

MARZIO

My God! I did not kill him; I know no-
    thing;
Olimpio sold the robe to me from which
You would infer my guilt.

SECOND JUDGE

               Away with him!

FIRST JUDGE

Dare you, with lips yet white from the
    rack's kiss,
Speak false? Is it so soft a questioner   9
That you would bandy lover's talk with it,
Till it wind out your life and soul? Away!

MARZIO

Spare me! Oh, spare! I will confess.

FIRST JUDGE

               Then speak.

MARZIO

I strangled him in his sleep.

FIRST JUDGE

Who urged you to it ?

MARZIO

His own son Giacomo and the young pre-
late
Orsino sent me to Petrella; there
The ladies Beatrice and Lucretia
Tempted me with a thousand crowns,
and I
And my companion forthwith murdered
him. 18
Now let me die.

FIRST JUDGE

This sounds as bad as truth.
Guards, there, lead forth the prisoners.

Enter LUCRETIA, BEATRICE, *and* GIACOMO,
guarded

Look upon this man;
When did you see him last ?

BEATRICE

We never saw him.

MARZIO

You know me too well, Lady Beatrice.

BEATRICE

I know thee ! how ? where ? when ?

MARZIO

You know 't was I
Whom you did urge with menaces and
bribes
To kill your father. When the thing was
done,
You clothed me in a robe of woven gold,
And bade me thrive; how I have thriven,
you see.
You, my Lord Giacomo, Lady Lucretia,
You know that what I speak is true.

[BEATRICE *advances towards him; he
covers his face, and shrinks back.*

Oh, dart
The terrible resentment of those eyes 30
On the dead earth ! Turn them away from
me !
They wound; 't was torture forced the
truth. My Lords,
Having said this, let me be led to death.

BEATRICE

Poor wretch, I pity thee; yet stay awhile.

CAMILLO

Guards, lead him not away.

BEATRICE

Cardinal Camillo,
You have a good repute for gentleness
And wisdom; can it be that you sit here
To countenance a wicked farce like this ?
When some obscure and trembling slave is
dragged
From sufferings which might shake the
sternest heart 40
And bade to answer, not as he believes,
But as those may suspect or do desire
Whose questions thence suggest their own
reply;
And that in peril of such hideous tor-
ments
As merciful God spares even the damned.
Speak now
The thing you surely know, which is, that
you,
If your fine frame were stretched upon
that wheel,
And you were told, 'Confess that you did
poison
Your little nephew; that fair blue-eyed
child
Who was the lodestar of your life;' and
though 50
All see, since his most swift and piteous
death,
That day and night, and heaven and earth,
and time,
And all the things hoped for or done
therein,
Are changed to you, through your exceed-
ing grief,
Yet you would say, 'I confess anything,'
And beg from your tormentors, like that
slave,
The refuge of dishonorable death.
I pray thee, Cardinal, that thou assert
My innocence.

CAMILLO (*much moved*)

What shall we think, my Lords ?
Shame on these tears ! I thought the heart
was frozen 60
Which is their fountain. I would pledge
my soul
That she is guiltless.

JUDGE

Yet she must be tortured.

CAMILLO

I would as soon have tortured mine own
   nephew
(If he now lived, he would be just her age;
His hair, too, was her color, and his eyes
Like hers in shape, but blue and not so
   deep)
As that most perfect image of God's love
That ever came sorrowing upon the earth.
She is as pure as speechless infancy !

JUDGE

Well, be her purity on your head, my
   Lord,   70
If you forbid the rack. His Holiness
Enjoined us to pursue this monstrous crime
By the severest forms of law; nay, even
To stretch a point against the criminals.
The prisoners stand accused of parricide
Upon such evidence as justifies
Torture.

BEATRICE

What evidence ? This man's ?

JUDGE

Even so.

BEATRICE (to MARZIO)

Come near. And who art thou, thus chosen
   forth
Out of the multitude of living men,
To kill the innocent ?

MARZIO

I am Marzio,   80
Thy father's vassal.

BEATRICE

Fix thine eyes on mine;
Answer to what I ask.
           (Turning to the Judges)
           I prithee mark
His countenance; unlike bold calumny,
Which sometimes dares not speak the thing
   it looks,
He dares not look the thing he speaks, but
   bends
His gaze on the blind earth.

(To MARZIO)

What ! wilt thou say
That I did murder my own father ?

MARZIO

Oh !
Spare me ! My brain swims round — I
   cannot speak —
It was that horrid torture forced the truth.
Take me away ! Let her not look on me !
I am a guilty miserable wretch !   91
I have said all I know; now, let me die !

BEATRICE

My Lords, if by my nature I had been
So stern as to have planned the crime
   alleged,
Which your suspicions dictate to this slave
And the rack makes him utter, do you
   think
I should have left this two-edged instru-
   ment
Of my misdeed; this man, this bloody
   knife,
With my own name engraven on the heft,
Lying unsheathed amid a world of foes,
For my own death ? that with such horri-
   ble need   101
For deepest silence I should have neglected
So trivial a precaution as the making
His tomb the keeper of a secret written
On a thief's memory ? What is his poor
   life ?
What are a thousand lives ? A parricide
Had trampled them like dust; and see, he
   lives !
(Turning to MARZIO)
And thou —

MARZIO

Oh, spare me ! Speak to me no more !
That stern yet piteous look, those solemn
   tones,   109
Wound worse than torture.

(To the Judges)
I have told it all;
For pity's sake lead me away to death.

CAMILLO

Guards, lead him nearer the Lady Beatrice;
He shrinks from her regard like autumn's
   leaf
From the keen breath of the serenest north.

BEATRICE

O thou who tremblest on the giddy verge
Of life and death, pause ere thou answerest
   me;

So mayst thou answer God with less dis-
may.
What evil have we done thee ?   I, alas !
Have lived but on this earth a few sad
years,   119
And so my lot was ordered that a father
First turned the moments of awakening life
To drops, each poisoning youth's sweet
hope; and then
Stabbed with one blow my everlasting soul,
And my untainted fame; and even that
peace
Which sleeps within the core of the heart's
heart.
But the wound was not mortal; so my hate
Became the only worship I could lift
To our great Father, who in pity and love
Armed thee, as thou dost say, to cut him
off;   129
And thus his wrong becomes my accusa-
tion.
And art thou the accuser ? If thou hopest
Mercy in heaven, show justice upon earth;
Worse than a bloody hand is a hard heart.
If thou hast done murders, made thy life's
path
Over the trampled laws of God and man,
Rush not before thy Judge, and say: ' My
Maker,
I have done this and more; for there was
one
Who was most pure and innocent on earth;
And because she endured what never any,
Guilty or innocent, endured before,   140
Because her wrongs could not be told, nor
thought,
Because thy hand at length did rescue her,
I with my words killed her and all her
kin.'
Think, I adjure you, what it is to slay
The reverence living in the minds of men
Towards our ancient house and stainless
fame !
Think what it is to strangle infant pity,
Cradled in the belief of guileless looks,
Till it become a crime to suffer.   Think
What 't is to blot with infamy and blood
All that which shows like innocence, and
is —   151
Hear me, great God ! — I swear, most in-
nocent;
So that the world lose all discrimination
Between the sly, fierce, wild regard of
guilt,
And that which now compels thee to reply

To what I ask: Am I, or am I not
A parricide ?

MARZIO

Thou art not !

JUDGE

What is this ?

MARZIO

I here declare those whom I did accuse
Are innocent.   'T is I alone am guilty.   159

JUDGE

Drag him away to torments; let them be
Subtle and long drawn out, to tear the
folds
Of the heart's inmost cell.   Unbind him
not
Till he confess.

MARZIO

Torture me as ye will;
A keener pang has wrung a higher truth
From my last breath.   She is most inno-
cent !
Bloodhounds, not men, glut yourselves well
with me !
I will not give you that fine piece of nature
To rend and ruin.

[Exit MARZIO, guarded.

CAMILLO

What say ye now, my Lords ?

JUDGE

Let tortures strain the truth till it be
white   169
As snow thrice-sifted by the frozen wind.

CAMILLO

Yet stained with blood.

JUDGE (to BEATRICE)

Know you this paper, Lady ?

BEATRICE

Entrap me not with questions. Who stands
here
As my accuser ? Ha ! wilt thou be he,
Who art my judge ?   Accuser, witness,
judge,
What, all in one ? Here is Orsino's name;
Where is Orsino ? Let his eye meet mine.
What means this scrawl ? Alas ! ye know
not what,

And therefore on the chance that it may be
Some evil, will ye kill us ?

Enter an Officer

OFFICER
                    Marzio 's dead.

JUDGE
What did he say ?

OFFICER
                    Nothing. As soon as we
Had bound him on the wheel, he smiled on
    us,   181
As one who baffles a deep adversary;
And holding his breath died.

JUDGE
                    There remains nothing
But to apply the question to those prisoners
Who yet remain stubborn.

CAMILLO
                    I overrule
Further proceedings, and in the behalf
Of these most innocent and noble persons
Will use my interest with the Holy Father.

JUDGE
Let the Pope's pleasure then be done.
    Meanwhile
Conduct these culprits each to separate
    cells;   190
And be the engines ready; for this night,
If the Pope's resolution be as grave,
Pious, and just as once, I 'll wring the
    truth
Out of those nerves and sinews, groan by
    groan.
                                        [*Exeunt.*

SCENE III. — *The Cell of a Prison.* BEATRICE
is discovered asleep on a couch.

Enter BERNARDO

BERNARDO
How gently slumber rests upon her face,
Like the last thoughts of some day sweetly
    spent,
Closing in night and dreams, and so pro-
    longed.
After such torments as she bore last night,
How light and soft her breathing comes.
    Ay me !

Methinks that I shall never sleep again.
But I must shake the heavenly dew of rest
From this sweet folded flower, thus —
    wake, awake !
What, sister, canst thou sleep ?

BEATRICE (*awaking*)
                    I was just dreaming
That we were all in Paradise. Thou
    knowest   10
This cell seems like a kind of Paradise
After our father's presence.

BERNARDO
                    Dear, dear sister,
Would that thy dream were not a dream !
    Oh, God,
How shall I tell ?

BEATRICE
What wouldst thou tell, sweet brother ?

BERNARDO
Look not so calm and happy, or even whilst
I stand considering what I have to say,
My heart will break.

BEATRICE
                    See now, thou mak'st me weep;
How very friendless thou wouldst be, dear
    child,
If I were dead. Say what thou hast to
    say.

BERNARDO
They have confessed; they could endure no
    more   20
The tortures —

BEATRICE
                    Ha ! what was there to confess ?
They must have told some weak and wicked
    lie
To flatter their tormentors. Have they
    said
That they were guilty ? O white innocence,
That thou shouldst wear the mask of guilt
    to hide
Thine awful and serenest countenance
From those who know thee not !

Enter JUDGE, *with* LUCRETIA *and* GIACOMO,
    guarded

                    Ignoble hearts !
For some brief spasms of pain, which are
    at least

As mortal as the limbs through which they
   pass,
Are centuries of high splendor laid in
   dust?   30
And that eternal honor, which should live
Sunlike, above the reek of mortal fame,
Changed to a mockery and a byword?
   What!
Will you give up these bodies to be
   dragged
At horses' heels, so that our hair should
   sweep
The footsteps of the vain and senseless
   crowd,
Who, that they may make our calamity
Their worship and their spectacle, will
   leave
The churches and the theatres as void
As their own hearts? Shall the light
   multitude   40
Fling, at their choice, curses or faded pity,
Sad funeral flowers to deck a living corpse,
Upon us as we pass to pass away,
And leave — what memory of our having
   been?
Infamy, blood, terror, despair? O thou
Who wert a mother to the parentless,
Kill not thy child! let not her wrongs kill
   thee!
Brother, lie down with me upon the rack,
And let us each be silent as a corpse;
It soon will be as soft as any grave.   50
'T is but the falsehood it can wring from
   fear
Makes the rack cruel.

GIACOMO

        They will tear the truth
Even from thee at last, those cruel pains;
For pity's sake say thou art guilty now.

LUCRETIA

Oh, speak the truth! Let us all quickly
   die;
And after death, God is our judge, not
   they;
He will have mercy on us.

BERNARDO

           If indeed
It can be true, say so, dear sister mine;   58
And then the Pope will surely pardon
   you,
And all be well.

JUDGE

         Confess, or I will warp
Your limbs with such keen tortures —

BEATRICE

            Tortures! Turn
The rack henceforth into a spinning-wheel!
Torture your dog, that he may tell when
   last
He lapped the blood his master shed —
   not me!
My pangs are of the mind, and of the heart,
And of the soul; ay, of the inmost soul,
Which weeps within tears as of burning
   gall
To see, in this ill world where none are
   true,
My kindred false to their deserted selves;
And with considering all the wretched life
Which I have lived, and its now wretched
   end;   71
And the small justice shown by Heaven
   and Earth
To me or mine; and what a tyrant thou
   art,
And what slaves these; and what a world
   we make,
The oppressor and the oppressed — such
   pangs compel
My answer. What is it thou wouldst with
   me?

JUDGE

Art thou not guilty of thy father's death?

BEATRICE

Or wilt thou rather tax high-judging God
That he permitted such an act as that
Which I have suffered, and which he be-
   held;   80
Made it unutterable, and took from it
All refuge, all revenge, all consequence,
But that which thou hast called my father's
   death?
Which is or is not what men call a crime,
Which either I have done, or have not done;
Say what ye will. I shall deny no more.
If ye desire it thus, thus let it be,
And so an end of all. Now do your will;
No other pains shall force another word.

JUDGE

She is convicted, but has not confessed. 90
Be it enough. Until their final sentence

Let none have converse with them. You,
  young Lord,
Linger not here !

BEATRICE

Oh, tear him not away !

JUDGE

Guards ! do your duty.

BERNARDO (*embracing* BEATRICE)
                Oh ! would ye divide
Body from soul ?

OFFICER

That is the headsman's business.

[*Exeunt all but* LUCRETIA, BEATRICE, *and*
  GIACOMO.

GIACOMO

Have I confessed ? Is it all over now ?
No hope ! no refuge ! O weak, wicked
  tongue,
Which hast destroyed me, would that thou
  hadst been
Cut out and thrown to dogs first ! To
  have killed
My father first, and then betrayed my
  sister —   100
Ay, thee ! the one thing innocent and pure
In this black, guilty world — to that
  which I
So well deserve ! My wife ! my little
  ones !
Destitute, helpless; and I — Father ! God !
Canst thou forgive even the unforgiving,
When their full hearts break thus, thus ?
        (*Covers his face and weeps*)

LUCRETIA

                O my child !
To what a dreadful end are we all come !
Why did I yield ? Why did I not sustain
Those torments ? Oh, that I were all dis-
  solved
Into these fast and unavailing tears,   110
Which flow and feel not !

BEATRICE

          What 't was weak to do,
'T is weaker to lament, once being done;
Take cheer ! The God who knew my
  wrong, and made
Our speedy act the angel of his wrath,
Seems, and but seems, to have abandoned
  us.

Let us not think that we shall die for this.
Brother, sit near me; give me your firm
  hand,
You had a manly heart. Bear up ! bear
  up !
O dearest Lady, put your gentle head
Upon my lap, and try to sleep awhile;   120
Your eyes look pale, hollow, and overworn,
With heaviness of watching and slow grief.
Come, I will sing you some low, sleepy
  tune,
Not cheerful, nor yet sad; some dull old
  thing,
Some outworn and unused monotony,
Such as our country gossips sing and spin,
Till they almost forget they live. Lie
  down —
So, that will do. Have I forgot the words ?
Faith ! they are sadder than I thought they
  were.

SONG

False friend, wilt thou smile or weep   130
When my life is laid asleep ?
Little cares for a smile or a tear,
The clay-cold corpse upon the bier !
  Farewell ! Heigh-ho !
  What is this whispers low ?
There is a snake in thy smile, my dear;
And bitter poison within thy tear.

Sweet sleep ! were death like to thee,
Or if thou couldst mortal be,
I would close these eyes of pain;   140
When to wake ? Never again.
  O World ! farewell !
  Listen to the passing bell !
It says, thou and I must part,
With a light and a heavy heart.
        (*The scene closes*)

SCENE IV. — *A Hall of the Prison. Enter*
  CAMILLO *and* BERNARDO.

CAMILLO

The Pope is stern; not to be moved or
  bent.
He looked as calm and keen as is the en-
  gine
Which tortures and which kills, exempt it-
  self
From aught that it inflicts; a marble form,
A rite, a law, a custom; not a man.
He frowned, as if to frown had been the
  trick

Of his machinery, on the advocates
Presenting the defences, which he tore
And threw behind, muttering with hoarse,
　　　harsh voice —
'Which among ye defended their old fa-
　　　ther　　　　　　　　　　　　　　10
Killed in his sleep ?' then to another —
' Thou
Dost this in virtue of thy place; 't is well.'
He turned to me then, looking depreca-
　　　tion,
And said these three words, coldly — 'They
　　　must die.'

BERNARDO

And yet you left him not ?

CAMILLO

　　　　　　　　　　I urged him still;
Pleading, as I could guess, the devilish
　　　wrong
Which prompted your unnatural parent's
　　　death.
And he replied — 'Paolo Santa Croce
Murdered his mother yester evening,
And he is fled.　Parricide grows so rife, 20
That soon, for some just cause no doubt,
　　　the young
Will strangle us all, dozing in our chairs.
Authority, and power, and hoary hair
Are grown crimes capital.　You are my
　　　nephew,
You come to ask their pardon; stay a mo-
　　　ment;
Here is their sentence; never see me more
Till, to the letter, it be all fulfilled.'

BERNARDO

Oh, God, not so !　I did believe indeed
That all you said was but sad prepara-
　　　tion
For happy news.　Oh, there are words and
　　　looks　　　　　　　　　　　　　30
To bend the sternest purpose !　Once I
　　　knew them,
Now I forget them at my dearest need.
What think you if I seek him out, and
　　　bathe
His feet and robe with hot and bitter
　　　tears ?
Importune him with prayers, vexing his
　　　brain
With my perpetual cries, until in rage
He strike me with his pastoral cross, and
　　　trample

Upon my prostrate head, so that my blood
May stain the senseless dust on which he
　　　treads,
And remorse waken mercy ?　I will do it ! 39
Oh, wait till I return !

　　　　　　　　　　　　　[Rushes out.

CAMILLO

　　　　　　　　　　Alas, poor boy !
A wreck-devoted seaman thus might pray
To the deaf sea.

Enter LUCRETIA, BEATRICE, and GIACOMO,
　　　guarded

BEATRICE

　　　　　　　　　　I hardly dare to fear
That thou bring'st other news than a just
　　　pardon.

CAMILLO

May God in heaven be less inexorable
To the Pope's prayers than he has been to
　　　mine.
Here is the sentence and the warrant.

BEATRICE (wildly)

　　　　　　　　　　　　　　　　Oh,
My God !　Can it be possible I have
To die so suddenly ? so young to go
Under the obscure, cold, rotting, wormy
　　　ground !　　　　　　　　　　　50
To be nailed down into a narrow place;
To see no more sweet sunshine; hear no
　　　more
Blithe voice of living thing; muse not
　　　again
Upon familiar thoughts, sad, yet thus lost !
How fearful ! to be nothing !　Or to be —
What ?　Oh, where am I ?　Let me not
　　　go mad !
Sweet Heaven, forgive weak thoughts !
　　　If there should be
No God, no Heaven, no Earth in the void
　　　world —
The wide, gray, lampless, deep, unpeopled
　　　world !
If all things then should be — my father's
　　　spirit,　　　　　　　　　　　60
His eye, his voice, his touch surrounding
　　　me;
The atmosphere and breath of my dead
　　　life !
If sometimes, as a shape more like him-
　　　self,
Even the form which tortured me on earth,

Masked in gray hairs and wrinkles, he
    should come,
And wind me in his hellish arms, and fix
His eyes on mine, and drag me down,
    down, down !
For was he not alone omnipotent
On Earth, and ever present ? even though
    dead,   69
Does not his spirit live in all that breathe,
And work for me and mine still the same
    ruin,
Scorn, pain, despair ? Who ever yet re-
    turned
To teach the laws of death's untrodden
    realm ?
Unjust perhaps as those which drive us
    now,
Oh, whither, whither ?

LUCRETIA

            Trust in God's sweet love,
The tender promises of Christ; ere night,
Think we shall be in Paradise.

BEATRICE

               'T is past !
Whatever comes, my heart shall sink no
    more.
And yet, I know not why, your words
    strike chill;
How tedious, false, and cold seem all
    things ! I   80
Have met with much injustice in this
    world;
No difference has been made by God or
    man,
Or any power moulding my wretched lot,
'Twixt good or evil, as regarded me.
I am cut off from the only world I know,
From light, and life, and love, in youth's
    sweet prime.
You do well telling me to trust in God;
I hope I do trust in him. In whom else
Can any trust ? And yet my heart is
    cold.

    (*During the latter speeches* GIACOMO *has re-
    tired conversing with* CAMILLO, *who now
    goes out ;* GIACOMO *advances*)

GIACOMO

Know you not, mother — sister, know you
    not ?   90
Bernardo even now is gone to implore
The Pope to grant our pardon.

LUCRETIA

             Child, perhaps
It will be granted. We may all then live
To make these woes a tale for distant years.
Oh, what a thought ! It gushes to my
    heart
Like the warm blood.

BEATRICE

            Yet both will soon be cold.
Oh, trample out that thought ! Worse than
    despair,
Worse than the bitterness of death, is hope;
It is the only ill which can find place   99
Upon the giddy, sharp, and narrow hour
Tottering beneath us. Plead with the swift
    frost
That it should spare the eldest flower of
    spring;
Plead with awakening earthquake, o'er
    whose couch
Even now a city stands, strong, fair, and
    free;
Now stench and blackness yawn, like death.
    Oh, plead
With famine, or wind-walking pestilence,
Blind lightning, or the deaf sea, not with
    man —
Cruel, cold, formal man; righteous in
    words,
In deeds a Cain. No, mother, we must die;
Since such is the reward of innocent lives,
Such the alleviation of worst wrongs.   111
And whilst our murderers live, and hard,
    cold men,
Smiling and slow, walk through a world of
    tears
To death as to life's sleep; 't were just the
    grave
Were some strange joy for us. Come, ob-
    scure Death,
And wind me in thine all-embracing arms !
Like a fond mother hide me in thy bosom,
And rock me to the sleep from which none
    wake.
Live ye, who live, subject to one another
As we were once, who now —

BERNARDO *rushes in*

BERNARDO

               Oh, horrible !
That tears, that looks, that hope poured
    forth in prayer,   121
Even till the heart is vacant and despairs,

Should all be vain ! The ministers of death
Are waiting round the doors. I thought I saw
Blood on the face of one — what if 't were fancy ?
Soon the heart's blood of all I love on earth
Will sprinkle him, and he will wipe it off
As if 't were only rain. O life ! O world !
Cover me ! let me be no more ! To see
That perfect mirror of pure innocence   130
Wherein I gazed, and grew happy and good,
Shivered to dust ! To see thee, Beatrice,
Who made all lovely thou didst look upon —
Thee, light of life — dead, dark ! while I say, sister,
To hear I have no sister; and thou, mother,
Whose love was as a bond to all our loves —
Dead ! the sweet bond broken !

Enter CAMILLO *and Guards*
     They come ! Let me
Kiss those warm lips before their crimson leaves
Are blighted — white — cold. Say farewell, before
Death chokes that gentle voice ! Oh, let me hear   140
You speak !

    BEATRICE
 Farewell, my tender brother. Think
Of our sad fate with gentleness, as now;
And let mild, pitying thoughts lighten for thee
Thy sorrow's load. Err not in harsh despair,

But tears and patience. One thing more, my child;
For thine own sake be constant to the love
Thou bearest us; and to the faith that I,
Though wrapped in a strange cloud of crime and shame,
Lived ever holy and unstained. And though
Ill tongues shall wound me, and our common name   150
Be as a mark stamped on thine innocent brow
For men to point at as they pass, do thou
Forbear, and never think a thought unkind
Of those who perhaps love thee in their graves.
So mayest thou die as I do; fear and pain
Being subdued. Farewell ! Farewell ! Farewell !

    BERNARDO
I cannot say farewell !

    CAMILLO
    O Lady Beatrice !

    BEATRICE
Give yourself no unnecessary pain,
My dear Lord Cardinal. Here, mother, tie
My girdle for me, and bind up this hair   160
In any simple knot; ay, that does well.
And yours I see is coming down. How often
Have we done this for one another; now
We shall not do it any more. My Lord,
We are quite ready. Well — 't is very well.

THE MASK OF ANARCHY

WRITTEN ON THE OCCASION OF THE MASSACRE AT MANCHESTER

The Mask of Anarchy was composed in the fall of 1819, soon after the Manchester riot of that summer. The Manchester or ' Peterloo Massacre,' as it was called, was occasioned by an attempt to hold a mass meeting on August 9, 1819, at St. Peter's Field, Manchester, in behalf of parliamentary reform. It was declared illegal and forbidden by the magistrates, and was in consequence postponed. It was held August 16, and attended by several thousands. The chief constable was ordered to arrest the ringleaders, and in particular the chairman, Henry Hunt, an agitator unconnected with Leigh Hunt. He asked

military aid, and went accompanied by forty cavalrymen; on the failure of the officer and his escort to penetrate the crowd which surrounded them, orders were given three hundred hussars to disperse the people; in the charge six persons were killed, twenty or thirty received sabre wounds, and fifty or more were injured in other ways. Eldon was Lord High Chancellor, Sidmouth, Home Secretary, and Castlereagh, Foreign Secretary; the government supported the authorities and publicly approved their conduct. News of these events reached Shelley while still residing at the Villa Valsovano, near Leghorn, and employed in revising *The Cenci*, and 'roused in him,' says Mrs. Shelley, 'violent emotions of indignation and compassion.' The nature of these emotions is shown in the letter he wrote to Ollier, from whom he heard of the affair: 'The same day that your letter came, came the news of the Manchester work, and the torrent of my indignation has not yet done boiling in my veins. I wait anxiously to hear how the country will express its sense of this bloody, murderous oppression of its destroyers. "Something must be done. What, yet I know not."' In a similar vein he addressed Peacock, who had forwarded newspaper accounts: 'Many thanks for your attention in sending the papers which contain the terrible and important news of Manchester. These are, as it were, the distant thunders of the terrible storm which is approaching. The tyrants here, as in the French Revolution, have first shed blood. May their execrable lessons not be learned with equal docility! I still think there will be no coming to close quarters until financial affairs bring the oppressors and the oppressed together. Pray let me have the *earliest* political news which you consider of importance at this crisis.'

Shelley sent the poem to Leigh Hunt to be published in *The Examiner*, but it did not appear. He wrote to Hunt on the subject in November.

'You do not tell me whether you have received my lines on the Manchester affair. They are of the exoteric species, and are meant, not for the *Indicator*, but the *Examiner*. . . . The great thing to do is to hold the balance between popular impatience and tyrannical obstinacy; to inculcate with fervor both the right of resistance and the duty of forbearance. You know my principles incite me to take all the good I can get in politics, forever aspiring to something more. I am one of those whom nothing will fully satisfy, but who are ready to be partially satisfied by all that is practicable. We shall see.'

The poem was at last issued, under Hunt's editorship, in 1832. He assigns, in his preface, as the reason for his failure to publish it when it was written, his own belief that 'the public at large had not become sufficiently discerning to do justice to the sincerity and kindheartedness of his spirit, that walked in the flaming robe of verse.'

I

As I lay asleep in Italy,
There came a voice from over the sea,
And with great power it forth led me
To walk in the visions of Poesy.

II

I met Murder on the way —
He had a mask like Castlereagh;
Very smooth he looked, yet grim;
Seven bloodhounds followed him.

III

All were fat; and well they might
Be in admirable plight,
For one by one, and two by two,
He tossed them human hearts to chew,
Which from his wide cloak he drew.

IV

Next came Fraud, and he had on,
Like Eldon, an ermined gown;
His big tears, for he wept well,
Turned to mill-stones as they fell;

V

And the little children, who
Round his feet played to and fro,
Thinking every tear a gem,
Had their brains knocked out by them.

VI

Clothed with the Bible as with light,
And the shadows of the night, ·
Like Sidmouth, next Hypocrisy
On a crocodile rode by.

VII

And many more Destructions played
In this ghastly masquerade,
All disguised, even to the eyes,
Like bishops, lawyers, peers or spies.

VIII

Last came Anarchy; he rode
On a white horse splashed with blood;
He was pale even to the lips,
Like Death in the Apocalypse.

IX

And he wore a kingly crown;
In his grasp a sceptre shone;
On his brow this mark I saw —
'I AM GOD, AND KING, AND LAW !'

X

With a pace stately and fast,
Over English land he passed,
Trampling to a mire of blood
The adoring multitude.

XI

And a mighty troop around
With their trampling shook the ground,
Waving each a bloody sword
For the service of their Lord.

XII

And, with glorious triumph, they
Rode through England, proud and gay,
Drunk as with intoxication
Of the wine of desolation.

XIII

O'er fields and towns, from sea to sea,
Passed that Pageant swift and free,
Tearing up, and trampling down,
Till they came to London town.

XIV

And each dweller, panic-stricken,
Felt his heart with terror sicken,
Hearing the tempestuous cry
Of the triumph of Anarchy.

XV

For with pomp to meet him came,
Clothed in arms like blood and flame,
The hired murderers who did sing,
'Thou art God, and Law, and King.

XVI

'We have waited, weak and lone,
For thy coming, Mighty One !
Our purses are empty, our swords are
    cold,
Give us glory, and blood, and gold.'

XVII

Lawyers and priests, a motley crowd,
To the earth their pale brows bowed;
Like a bad prayer not over loud,
Whispering — ' Thou art Law and God !'

XVIII

Then all cried with one accord,
' Thou art King, and God, and Lord;
Anarchy, to thee we bow,
Be thy name made holy now !'

XIX

And Anarchy, the Skeleton,
Bowed and grinned to every one,
As well as if his education
Had cost ten millions to the nation.

XX

For he knew the palaces
Of our kings were rightly his;
His the sceptre, crown, and globe,
And the gold-inwoven robe.

XXI

So he sent his slaves before
To seize upon the Bank and Tower,
And was proceeding with intent
To meet his pensioned parliament,

XXII

When one fled past, a maniac maid,
And her name was Hope, she said;
But she looked more like Despair,
And she cried out in the air:

XXIII

' My father Time is weak and gray
With waiting for a better day;
See how idiot-like he stands,
Fumbling with his palsied hands !

XXIV

' He has had child after child,
And the dust of death is piled
Over every one but me.
Misery ! oh, misery ! '

XXV

Then she lay down in the street,
Right before the horses' feet,
Expecting with a patient eye
Murder, Fraud, and Anarchy;

XXVI

When between her and her foes
A mist, a light, an image rose, —
Small at first, and weak, and frail,
Like the vapor of a vale;

XXVII

Till as clouds grow on the blast,
Like tower-crowned giants striding fast,
And glare with lightnings as they fly,
And speak in thunder to the sky,

XXVIII

It grew — a Shape arrayed in mail
Brighter than the viper's scale,
And upborne on wings whose grain
Was as the light of sunny rain.

XXIX

On its helm, seen far away,
A planet, like the Morning's, lay;
And those plumes its light rained through,
Like a shower of crimson dew.

XXX

With step as soft as wind it passed
O'er the heads of men — so fast
That they knew the presence there,
And looked — but all was empty air.

XXXI

As flowers beneath May's footstep waken,
As stars from Night's loose hair are
    shaken,
As waves arise when loud winds call,
Thoughts sprung where'er that step did fall.

XXXII

And the prostrate multitude
Looked — and ankle-deep in blood,
Hope, that maiden most serene,
Was walking with a quiet mien;

XXXIII

And Anarchy, the ghastly birth,
Lay dead earth upon the earth;
The Horse of Death, tameless as wind
Fled, and with his hoofs did grind
To dust the murderers thronged behind.

XXXIV

A rushing light of clouds and splendor,
A sense, awakening and yet tender,
Was heard and felt — and at its close
These words of joy and fear arose,

XXXV

As if their own indignant earth,
Which gave the sons of England birth,
Had felt their blood upon her brow,
And shuddering with a mother's throe

XXXVI

Had turned every drop of blood,
By which her face had been bedewed,
To an accent unwithstood,
As if her heart cried out aloud:

XXXVII

' Men of England, heirs of glory,
Heroes of unwritten story,
Nurslings of one mighty Mother,
Hopes of her, and one another:

XXXVIII

' Rise like lions after slumber,
In unvanquishable number;
Shake your chains to earth like dew
Which in sleep had fallen on you —
Ye are many, they are few.

XXXIX

' What is Freedom ? — Ye can tell
That which Slavery is too well,
For its very name has grown
To an echo of your own.

XL

' 'T is to work, and have such pay
As just keeps life from day to day
In your limbs, as in a cell,
For the tyrants' use to dwell,

XLI

' So that ye for them are made
Loom, and plough, and sword, and spade —
With or without your own will bent
To their defence and nourishment.

XLII

' 'T is to see your children weak
With their mothers pine and peak,
When the winter winds are bleak —
They are dying whilst I speak.

XLIII

' 'T is to hunger for such diet,
As the rich man in his riot
Casts to the fat dogs that lie
Surfeiting beneath his eye.

XLIV

' 'T is to let the Ghost of Gold
Take from toil a thousand-fold
More than e'er its substance could
In the tyrannies of old ;

XLV

' Paper coin — that forgery
Of the title deeds which ye
Hold to something of the worth
Of the inheritance of Earth.

XLVI

' 'T is to be a slave in soul,
And to hold no strong control
Over your own will, but be
All that others make of ye.

XLVII

' And at length when ye complain
With a murmur weak and vain,
'T is to see the Tyrant's crew
Ride over your wives and you —
Blood is on the grass like dew !

XLVIII

' Then it is to feel revenge,
Fiercely thirsting to exchange
Blood for blood — and wrong for wrong :
Do not thus when ye are strong !

XLIX

' Birds find rest in narrow nest,
When weary of their wingèd quest,
Beasts find fare in woody lair,
When storm and snow are in the air.

L

' Horses, oxen, have a home,
When from daily toil they come ;
Household dogs, when the wind roars,
Find a home within warm doors.

LI

' Asses, swine, have litter spread,
And with fitting food are fed ;
All things have a home but one —
Thou, O Englishman, hast none !

LII

' This is Slavery; savage men,
Or wild beasts within a den,
Would endure not as ye do —
But such ills they never knew.

LIII

' What art thou, Freedom ?   Oh, could
          slaves
Answer from their living graves
This demand, tyrants would flee
Like a dream's dim imagery.

LIV

' Thou art not, as impostors say,
A shadow soon to pass away
A superstition and a name
Echoing from the cave of Fame.

LV

' For the laborer thou art bread
And a comely table spread,
From his daily labor come
In a neat and happy home.

LVI

' Thou art clothes, and fire, and food,
For the trampled multitude;
No — in countries that are free
Such starvation cannot be
As in England now we see.

LVII

' To the rich thou art a check;
When his foot is on the neck
Of his victim, thou dost make
That he treads upon a snake.

LVIII

' Thou art Justice — ne'er for gold
May thy righteous laws be sold,
As laws are in England; thou
Shield'st alike both high and low.

LIX

' Thou art Wisdom — freemen never
Dream that God will damn forever
All who think those things untrue
Of which priests make such ado.

LX

' Thou art Peace — never by thee
Would blood and treasure wasted be,
As tyrants wasted them, when all
Leagued to quench thy flame in Gaul.

LXI

' What if English toil and blood
Was poured forth, even as a flood ?
It availed, O Liberty !
To dim, but not extinguish thee.

LXII

' Thou art Love — the rich have kissed
Thy feet, and, like him following Christ,
Give their substance to the free
And through the rough world follow thee;

LXIII

' Or turn their wealth to arms, and make
War for thy belovèd sake
On wealth and war and fraud, whence
          they
Drew the power which is their prey.

LXIV

' Science, Poetry and Thought
Are thy lamps; they make the lot
Of the dwellers in a cot
Such they curse their maker not.

LXV

'Spirit, Patience, Gentleness,
All that can adorn and bless,
Art thou — let deeds, not words, express
Thine exceeding loveliness.

LXVI

'Let a great Assembly be
Of the fearless and the free
On some spot of English ground,
Where the plains stretch wide around.

LXVII

'Let the blue sky overhead,
The green earth on which ye tread,
All that must eternal be,
Witness the solemnity.

LXVIII

'From the corners uttermost
Of the bounds of English coast;
From every hut, village and town,
Where those, who live and suffer, moan
For others' misery or their own;

LXIX

'From the workhouse and the prison,
Where pale as corpses newly risen,
Women, children, young and old,
Groan for pain, and weep for cold;

LXX

'From the haunts of daily life,
Where is waged the daily strife
With common wants and common cares,
Which sows the human heart with tares;

LXXI

'Lastly, from the palaces
Where the murmur of distress
Echoes, like the distant sound
Of a wind alive, around

LXXII

'Those prison-halls of wealth and fashion,
Where some few feel such compassion
For those who groan, and toil, and wail,
As must make their brethren pale; —

LXXIII

'Ye who suffer woes untold,
Or to feel or to behold
Your lost country bought and sold
With a price of blood and gold:

LXXIV

'Let a vast assembly be,
And with great solemnity
Declare with measured words that ye
Are, as God has made ye, free !

LXXV

'Be your strong and simple words
Keen to wound as sharpened swords;
And wide as targes let them be,
With their shade to cover ye.

LXXVI

'Let the tyrants pour around
With a quick and startling sound,
Like the loosening of a sea,
Troops of armed emblazonry.

LXXVII

'Let the charged artillery drive
Till the dead air seems alive
With the clash of clanging wheels
And the tramp of horses' heels.

LXXVIII

'Let the fixèd bayonet
Gleam with sharp desire to wet
Its bright point in English blood,
Looking keen as one for food.

LXXIX

'Let the horsemen's scimitars
Wheel and flash, like sphereless stars
Thirsting to eclipse their burning
In a sea of death and mourning.

LXXX

'Stand ye calm and resolute,
Like a forest close and mute,
With folded arms, and looks which are
Weapons of unvanquished war.

LXXXI

'And let Panic, who outspeeds
The career of armèd steeds,
Pass, a disregarded shade,
Through your phalanx undismayed.

LXXXII

'Let the laws of your own land,
Good or ill, between ye stand,
Hand to hand, and foot to foot,
Arbiters of the dispute: —

LXXXIII

'The old laws of England — they
Whose reverend heads with age are gray,
Children of a wiser day;
And whose solemn voice must be
Thine own echo — Liberty !

LXXXIV

'On those who first should violate
Such sacred heralds in their state
Rest the blood that must ensue;
And it will not rest on you.

LXXXV

'And if then the tyrants dare,
Let them ride among you there,
Slash, and stab, and maim, and hew;
What they like, that let them do.

LXXXVI

'With folded arms and steady eyes,
And little fear, and less surprise,
Look upon them as they slay,
Till their rage has died away.

LXXXVII

'Then they will return with shame
To the place from which they came;
And the blood thus shed will speak
In hot blushes on their cheek.

LXXXVIII

'Every woman in the land
Will point at them as they stand;
They will hardly dare to greet
Their acquaintance in the street.

LXXXIX

'And the bold true warriors,
Who have hugged Danger in wars,
Will turn to those who would be free,
Ashamed of such base company.

XC

'And that slaughter to the Nation
Shall steam up like inspiration,
Eloquent, oracular;
A volcano heard afar.

XCI

'And these words shall then become
Like oppression's thundered doom,
Ringing through each heart and brain,
Heard again — again — again !

XCII

'Rise like lions after slumber
In unvanquishable number !
Shake your chains to earth, like dew
Which in sleep had fallen on you —
Ye are many, they are few !'

PETER BELL THE THIRD

BY MICHING MALLECHO, ESQ.

Is it a party in a parlor,
Crammed just as they on earth were crammed,
Some sipping punch — some sipping tea ;
But, as you by their faces see,
All silent, and all —— damned !
        Peter Bell, by W. WORDSWORTH.

Ophelia.— What means this, my lord ?
Hamlet. — Marry, this is Miching Mallecho; it means mischief.
                        SHAKESPEARE.

Peter Bell the Third was suggested by some reviews, in *The Examiner*, of Wordsworth's *Peter Bell* and of John Hamilton Reynolds's satire on Wordsworth of the same title. They amused Shelley, and he wrote the present poem in that vein of fun which seldom appeared in his verse, though it was a characteristic trait of his private life. 'I think *Peter* not bad in his way,' wrote Shelley to Ollier, 'but perhaps no one will believe in anything in the shape of a joke from me.' Shelley's satire is meant pleasantly enough, as his admiration for Wordsworth's poetic powers is evident in many ways, and he was careful to change the name *Emma* to *Betty*, having inadvertently used the former, — 'Emma, I recollect, is the real name of the sister of a great poet who might be mistaken for *Peter*.' Mrs. Shelley in her note states the case frankly and fairly:
'A critique on Wordsworth's *Peter Bell* reached us at Leghorn, which amused Shelley exceedingly and suggested this poem. I need

scarcely observe that nothing personal to the Author of *Peter Bell* is intended in this poem. No man ever admired Wordsworth's poetry more; — he read it perpetually, and taught others to appreciate its beauties. This poem is, like all others written by Shelley, ideal. He conceived the idealism of a poet — a man of lofty and creative genius — quitting the glorious calling of discovering and announcing the beautiful and good, to support and propagate ignorant prejudices and pernicious errors; imparting to the unenlightened, not that ardor for truth and spirit of toleration which Shelley looked on as the sources of the moral improvement and happiness of mankind; but false and injurious opinions, that evil was good, and that ignorance and force were the best allies of purity and virtue. His idea was that a man gifted even as transcendently as the Author of *Peter Bell*, with the highest qualities of genius, must, if he fostered such errors, be infected with dulness. This poem was written, as a warning — not as a narration of the reality. He was unacquainted personally with Wordsworth or with Coleridge (to whom he alludes in the fifth part of the poem), and therefore, I repeat, his poem is purely ideal; — it contains something of criticism on the compositions of these great poets, but nothing injurious to the men themselves.

' No poem contains more of Shelley's peculiar views, with regard to the errors into which many of the wisest have fallen, and of the pernicious effects of certain opinions on society. Much of it is beautifully written — and though, like the burlesque drama of Swellfoot, it must be looked on as a plaything, it has so much merit and poetry — so much of *himself* in it, that it cannot fail to interest greatly, and by right belongs to the world for whose instruction and benefit it was written.'

Shelley's own account of the burlesque is given in a letter to Hunt:

' Now, I only send you a *very heroic* poem, which I wish you to give to Ollier, and desire him to print and publish immediately, you being kind enough to take upon yourself the correction of the press — not, however, with my name; and you must tell Ollier that the author is to be kept a secret, and that I confide in him for this object as I would confide in a physician or lawyer, or any other man whose professional situation renders the betraying of what is entrusted a dishonor. My motive in this is solely not to prejudge myself in the present moment, as I have only expended a few days in this party squib, and, of course, taken little pains. The verses and language I have let come as they would, and I am about to publish more serious things this winter; afterwards, that is next year, if the thing should be remembered

so long, I have no objection to the author being known, but *not now*. I should like well enough that it should both go to press and be printed very quickly; as more serious things are on the eve of engaging both the public attention and mine.'

The poem was written at Florence, in the latter part of October, 1819, and sent forward to Hunt at once for publication. It did not appear, however, until twenty years after, when it was included in Mrs. Shelley's second edition of the collected poems, 1839.

DEDICATION

TO THOMAS BROWN, ESQ., THE YOUNGER, H. F.

DEAR TOM, — Allow me to request you to introduce Mr. Peter Bell to the respectable family of the Fudges. Although he may fall short of those very considerable personages in the more active properties which characterize the Rat and the Apostate, I suspect that even you, their historian, will confess that he surpasses them in the more peculiarly legitimate qualification of intolerable dulness.

You know Mr. Examiner Hunt; well — it was he who presented me to two of the Mr. Bells. My intimacy with the younger Mr. Bell naturally sprung from this introduction to his brothers. And in presenting him to you I have the satisfaction of being able to assure you that he is considerably the dullest of the three.

There is this particular advantage in an acquaintance with any one of the Peter Bells that, if you know one Peter Bell, you know three Peter Bells; they are not one, but three; not three, but one. An awful mystery, which, after having caused torrents of blood and having been hymned by groans enough to deafen the music of the spheres, is at length illustrated to the satisfaction of all parties in the theological world by the nature of Mr. Peter Bell.

Peter is a polyhedric Peter, or a Peter with many sides. He changes colors like a chameleon and his coat like a snake. He is a Proteus of a Peter. He was at first sublime, pathetic, impressive, profound; then dull; then prosy and dull; and now dull — oh, so very dull! it is an ultra-legitimate dulness.

You will perceive that it is not necessary to consider Hell and the Devil as supernatural machinery. The whole scene of my epic is in ' this world which is ' — so Peter informed us before his conversion to *White Obi* —

The world of all of us, *and where*
We find our happiness, or not at all.

Let me observe that I have spent six or seven days in composing this sublime piece;

the orb of my moon-like genius has made the fourth part of its revolution round the dull earth which you inhabit, driving you mad, while it has retained its calmness and its splendor, and I have been fitting this its last phase 'to occupy a permanent station in the literature of my country.'

Your works, indeed, dear Tom, sell better; but mine are far superior. The public is no judge; posterity sets all to rights.

Allow me to observe that so much has been written of Peter Bell that the present history can be considered only, like the Iliad, as a continuation of that series of cyclic poems which have already been candidates for bestowing immortality upon, at the same time that they receive it from, his character and adventures. In this point of view I have violated no rule of syntax in beginning my composition with a conjunction; the full stop, which closes the poem continued by me, being, like the full stops at the end of the Iliad and Odyssey, a full stop of a very qualified import.

Hoping that the immortality which you have given to the Fudges, you will receive from them; and in the firm expectation that when London shall be an habitation of bitterns, when St. Paul's and Westminster Abbey shall stand, shapeless and nameless ruins, in the midst of an unpeopled marsh; when the piers of Waterloo Bridge shall become the nuclei of islets of reeds and osiers, and cast the jagged shadows of their broken arches on the solitary stream, some transatlantic commentator will be weighing in the scales of some new and now unimagined system of criticism the respective merits of the Bells and the Fudges and their historians,

I remain, dear Tom,
Yours sincerely,
December 1, 1819.   MICHING MALLECHO.

P. S. — Pray excuse the date of place; so soon as the profits of the publication come in, I mean to hire lodgings in a more respectable street.

PROLOGUE

PETER BELLS, one, two and three,
O'er the wide world wandering be.
First, the antenatal Peter,
Wrapped in weeds of the same metre,
The so long predestined raiment,
Clothed in which to walk his way meant
The second Peter; whose ambition
Is to link the proposition,
As the mean of two extremes,
(This was learned from Aldrich's themes),
Shielding from the guilt of schism
The orthodoxal syllogism;
The First Peter — he who was
Like the shadow in the glass
Of the second, yet unripe,
His substantial antitype.
Then came Peter Bell the Second,
Who henceforward must be reckoned
The body of a double soul,
And that portion of the whole
Without which the rest would seem
Ends of a disjointed dream.
And the Third is he who has
O'er the grave been forced to pass
To the other side, which is —
Go and try else — just like this.
Peter Bell the First was Peter
Smugger, milder, softer, neater,
Like the soul before it is
Born from *that* world into *this*.
The next Peter Bell was he,

Predevote, like you and me,
To good or evil, as may come;
His was the severer doom, —
For he was an evil Cotter,
And a polygamic Potter.
And the last is Peter Bell,
Damned since our first parents fell,
Damned eternally to Hell —
Surely he deserves it well!

PART THE FIRST

DEATH

I

AND Peter Bell, when he had been
   With fresh-imported Hell-fire warmed,
Grew serious — from his dress and mien
'T was very plainly to be seen
   Peter was quite reformed.

II

His eyes turned up, his mouth turned down;
He's accent caught a nasal twang;
He oiled his hair; there might be heard
The grace of God in every word
   Which Peter said or sang.

III

But Peter now grew old, and had
   An ill no doctor could unravel;

His torments almost drove him mad;
Some said it was a fever bad;
   Some swore it was the gravel.

IV

His holy friends then came about,
   And with long preaching and persuasion
Convinced the patient that without
The smallest shadow of a doubt
   He was predestined to damnation.

V

They said — 'Thy name is Peter Bell;
   Thy skin is of a brimstone hue;
Alive or dead — ay, sick or well —
The one God made to rhyme with hell;
   The other, I think, rhymes with you.'

VI

Then Peter set up such a yell !
   The nurse, who with some water gruel
Was climbing up the stairs, as well
As her old legs could climb them — fell,
   And broke them both — the fall was
      cruel.

VII

The Parson from the casement leapt
   Into the lake of Windermere;
And many an eel — though no adept
In God's right reason for it — kept
   Gnawing his kidneys half a year.

VIII

And all the rest rushed through the door,
   And tumbled over one another,
And broke their skulls. — Upon the floor
Meanwhile sat Peter Bell, and swore,
   And cursed his father and his mother;

IX

And raved of God, and sin, and death,
   Blaspheming like an infidel;
And said that with his clenchèd teeth
He 'd seize the earth from underneath
   And drag it with him down to hell.

X

As he was speaking came a spasm
   And wrenched his gnashing teeth asun-
      der;
Like one who sees a strange phantasm
He lay, — there was a silent chasm
   Betwixt his upper jaw and under.

XI

And yellow death lay on his face;
   And a fixed smile that was not human
Told, as I understand the case,
That he was gone to the wrong place.
   I heard all this from the old woman.

XII

Then there came down from Langdale
      Pike
   A cloud, with lightning, wind and hail;
It swept over the mountains like
An ocean, — and I heard it strike
   The woods and crags of Grasmere vale.

XIII

And I saw the black storm come
   Nearer, minute after minute;
Its thunder made the cataracts dumb;
With hiss, and clash, and hollow hum,
   It neared as if the Devil was in it.

XIV

The Devil *was* in it; he had bought
   Peter for half-a-crown; and when
The storm which bore him vanished,
      nought
That in the house that storm had caught
   Was ever seen again.

XV

The gaping neighbors came next day;
   They found all vanished from the shore;
The Bible, whence he used to pray,
Half scorched under a hen-coop lay;
   Smashed glass — and nothing more !

PART THE SECOND

THE DEVIL

I

THE Devil, I safely can aver,
   Has neither hoof, nor tail, nor sting;
Nor is he, as some sages swear,
A spirit, neither here nor there,
   In nothing — yet in everything.

II

He is — what we are; for sometimes
   The Devil is a gentleman;
At others a bard bartering rhymes
For sack; a statesman spinning crimes;
   A swindler, living as he can;

III

A thief, who cometh in the night,
  With whole boots and net pantaloons,
Like some one whom it were not right
To mention, — or the luckless wight,
  From whom he steals nine silver spoons.

IV

But in this case he did appear
  Like a slop-merchant from Wapping,
And with smug face and eye severe
On every side did perk and peer
  Till he saw Peter dead or napping.

V

He had on an upper Benjamin
  (For he was of the driving schism)
In the which he wrapped his skin
From the storm he travelled in,
  For fear of rheumatism.

VI

He called the ghost out of the corse, —
  It was exceedingly like Peter,
Only its voice was hollow and hoarse;
It had a queerish look, of course;
  Its dress too was a little neater.

VII

The Devil knew not his name and lot;
  Peter knew not that he was Bell ;
Each had an upper stream of thought,
Which made all seem as it was not,
  Fitting itself to all things well.

VIII

Peter thought he had parents dear,
  Brothers, sisters, cousins, cronies,
In the fens of Lincolnshire;
He perhaps had found them there
  Had he gone and boldly shown his

IX

Solemn phiz in his own village,
  Where he thought oft when a boy
He 'd clomb the orchard walls to pillage
The produce of his neighbor's tillage,
  With marvellous pride and joy.

X

And the Devil thought he had,
  'Mid the misery and confusion
Of an unjust war, just made
A fortune by the gainful trade
Of giving soldiers rations bad —
  The world is full of strange delusion;

XI

That he had a mansion planned
  In a square like Grosvenor-square,
That he was aping fashion, and
That he now came to Westmoreland
  To see what was romantic there.

XII

And all this, though quite ideal,
  Ready at a breath to vanish,
Was a state not more unreal
Than the peace he could not feel,
  Or the care he could not banish.

XIII

After a little conversation,
  The Devil told Peter, if he chose,
He 'd bring him to the world of fashion
By giving him a situation
  In his own service — and new clothes.

XIV

And Peter bowed, quite pleased and proud,
  And after waiting some few days
For a new livery — dirty yellow
Turned up with black — the wretched
    fellow
  Was bowled to Hell in the Devil's
    chaise.

PART THE THIRD

HELL

I

HELL is a city much like London —
  A populous and a smoky city;
There are all sorts of people undone,
And there is little or no fun done;
  Small justice shown, and still less pity.

II

There is a Castles, and a Canning,
  A Cobbett, and a Castlereagh;
All sorts of caitiff corpses planning
All sorts of cozening for trepanning
  Corpses less corrupt than they.

III

There is a ——, who has lost
  His wits, or sold them, none knows which;

He walks about a double ghost,
And, though as thin as Fraud almost,
  Ever grows more grim and rich.

IV

There is a Chancery Court; a King;
  A manufacturing mob; a set
Of thieves who by themselves are sent
Similar thieves to represent;
  An army; and a public debt.

V

Which last is a scheme of paper money,
  And means — being interpreted —
' Bees, keep your wax — give us the honey,
And we will plant, while skies are sunny,
  Flowers, which in winter serve instead.'

VI

There is great talk of revolution —
  And a great chance of despotism —
German soldiers — camps — confusion —
Tumults — lotteries — rage — delusion —
  Gin — suicide — and methodism;

VII

Taxes too, on wine and bread,
  And meat, and beer, and tea, and cheese,
From which those patriots pure are fed,
Who gorge before they reel to bed,
  The tenfold essence of all these.

VIII

There are mincing women, mewing
  (Like cats, who *amant miserè*)
Of their own virtue, and pursuing
Their gentler sisters to that ruin
  Without which — what were chastity ?

IX

Lawyers — judges — old hobnobbers
  Are there — bailiffs — chancellors —
Bishops — great and little robbers —
Rhymesters — pamphleteers — stock-job-
    bers —
  Men of glory in the wars;

X

Things whose trade is, over ladies
  To lean, and flirt, and stare, and sim-
    per,
Till all that is divine in woman
Grows cruel, courteous, smooth, inhuman,
  Crucified 'twixt a smile and whimper;

XI

Thrusting, toiling, wailing, moiling,
  Frowning, preaching — such a riot !
Each with never-ceasing labor,
Whilst he thinks he cheats his neighbor,
  Cheating his own heart of quiet.

XII

And all these meet at levees;
  Dinners convivial and political;
Suppers of epic poets; teas,
Where small talk dies in agonies;
  Breakfasts professional and critical;

XIII

Lunches and snacks so aldermanic
  That one would furnish forth ten din-
    ners,
Where reigns a Cretan-tonguèd panic,
Lest news Russ, Dutch, or Alemannic
  Should make some losers, and some
    winners;

XIV

At conversazioni — balls —
  Conventicles — and drawing-rooms —
Courts of law — committees — calls
Of a morning — clubs — book-stalls —
  Churches — masquerades — and tombs.

XV

And this is Hell — and in this smother
  Are all damnable and damned;
Each one, damning, damns the other;
They are damned by one another,
  By none other are they damned.

XVI

'T is a lie to say, ' God damns ! '
  Where was Heaven's Attorney-General
When they first gave out such flams ?
Let there be an end of shams;
  They are mines of poisonous mineral.

XVII

Statesmen damn themselves to be
  Cursed; and lawyers damn their souls
To the auction of a fee;
Churchmen damn themselves to see
  God's sweet love in burning coals.

XVIII

The rich are damned, beyond all cure,
  To taunt, and starve, and trample on

The weak and wretched; and the poor
Damn their broken hearts to endure
  Stripe on stripe, with groan on groan.

XIX

Sometimes the poor are damned indeed
  To take, not means for being blessed,
But Cobbett's snuff, revenge; that weed
From which the worms that it doth feed
  Squeeze less than they before pos-
    sessed.

XX

And some few, like we know who,
  Damned — but God alone knows why —
To believe their minds are given
To make this ugly Hell a Heaven;
  In which faith they live and die.

XXI

Thus, as in a town, plague-stricken,
  Each man, be he sound or no,
Must indifferently sicken;
As when day begins to thicken,
  None knows a pigeon from a crow;

XXII

So good and bad, sane and mad,
  The oppressor and the oppressed;
Those who weep to see what others
Smile to inflict upon their brothers;
  Lovers, haters, worst and best;

XXIII

All are damned — they breathe an air,
  Thick, infected, joy-dispelling;
Each pursues what seems most fair,
Mining, like moles, through mind, and
    there
Scoop palace-caverns vast, where Care
  In thronèd state is ever dwelling.

PART THE FOURTH

SIN

I

Lo, Peter in Hell's Grosvenor-square,
  A footman in the Devil's service!
And the misjudging world would swear
That every man in service there
  To virtue would prefer vice.

II

But Peter, though now damned, was not
  What Peter was before damnation.
Men oftentimes prepare a lot
Which, ere it finds them, is not what
  Suits with their genuine station.

III

All things that Peter saw and felt
  Had a peculiar aspect to him;
And when they came within the belt
Of his own nature, seemed to melt,
  Like cloud to cloud, into him.

IV

And so the outward world uniting
  To that within him, he became
Considerably uninviting
To those, who meditation slighting,
  Were moulded in a different frame.

V

And he scorned them, and they scorned
    him;
  And he scorned all they did; and they
Did all that men of their own trim
Are wont to do to please their whim —
  Drinking, lying, swearing, play.

VI

Such were his fellow-servants; thus
  His virtue, like our own, was built
Too much on that indignant fuss
Hypocrite Pride stirs up in us
  To bully one another's guilt.

VII

He had a mind which was somehow
  At once circumference and centre
Of all he might or feel or know;
Nothing went ever out, although
  Something did ever enter.

VIII

He had as much imagination
  As a pint-pot; — he never could
Fancy another situation,
From which to dart his contemplation,
  Than that wherein he stood.

IX

Yet his was individual mind,
  And new-created all he saw
In a new manner, and refined

Those new creations, and combined
  Them, by a master-spirit's law

X

Thus — though unimaginative —
  An apprehension clear, intense,
Of his mind's work, had made alive
The things it wrought on; I believe
  Wakening a sort of thought in sense.

XI

But from the first 't was Peter's drift
  To be a kind of moral eunuch;
He touched the hem of Nature's shift,
Felt faint — and never dared uplift
  The closest, all-concealing tunic.

XII

She laughed the while, with an arch
    smile,
  And kissed him with a sister's kiss,
And said — ' My best Diogenes,
I love you well — but, if you please,
  Tempt not again my deepest bliss.

XIII

' 'T is you are cold — for I, not coy,
  Yield love for love, frank, warm and
    true;
And Burns, a Scottish peasant boy —
His errors prove it — knew my joy
  More, learnèd friend, than you.

XIV

' *Bocca bacciata non perde ventura*
  Anzi rinnuova come fa la luna : —
So thought Boccaccio, whose sweet words
    might cure a
Male prude, like you, from what you now
    endure, a
  Low-tide in soul, like a stagnant laguna.'

XV

Then Peter rubbed his eyes severe,
  And smoothed his spacious forehead
    down,
With his broad palm; 'twixt love and
    fear,
He looked, as he no doubt felt, queer,
  And in his dream sate down.

XVI

The Devil was no uncommon creature;
  A leaden-witted thief — just huddled
Out of the dross and scum of nature;

A toad-like lump of limb and feature,
  With mind, and heart, and fancy mud-
    dled.

XVII

He was that heavy, dull, cold thing,
  The spirit of evil well may be;
A drone too base to have a sting;
Who gluts, and grimes his lazy wing,
  And calls lust luxury.

XVIII

Now he was quite the kind of wight
  Round whom collect, at a fixed era,
Venison, turtle, hock, and claret, —
Good cheer — and those who come to share
    it —
  And best East Indian madeira !

XIX

It was his fancy to invite
  Men of science, wit, and learning,
Who came to lend each other light;
He proudly thought that his gold's might
  Had set those spirits burning.

XX

And men of learning, science, wit,
  Considered him as you and I
Think of some rotten tree, and sit
Lounging and dining under it,
  Exposed to the wide sky.

XXI

And all the while, with loose fat smile,
  The willing wretch sat winking there,
Believing 't was his power that made
That jovial scene — and that all paid
  Homage to his unnoticed chair;

XXII

Though to be sure this place was Hell;
  He was the Devil — and all they —
What though the claret circled well,
And wit, like ocean, rose and fell ? —
  Were damned eternally.

PART THE FIFTH

GRACE

I

AMONG the guests who often stayed
  Till the Devil's petits-soupers,

A man there came, fair as a maid,
And Peter noted what he said,
  Standing behind his master's chair.

II

He was a mighty poet — and
  A subtle-souled psychologist;
All things he seemed to understand,
Of old or new — of sea or land —
  But his own mind — which was a mist.

III

This was a man who might have turned
  Hell into Heaven — and so in gladness
A Heaven unto himself have earned;
But he in shadows undiscerned
  Trusted, — and damned himself to madness.

IV

He spoke of poetry, and how
  ' Divine it was — a light — a love —
A spirit which like wind doth blow
As it listeth, to and fro;
  A dew rained down from God above;

V

' A power which comes and goes like dream,
  And which none can ever trace —
Heaven's light on earth — Truth's brightest beam.'
And when he ceased there lay the gleam
  Of those words upon his face.

VI

Now Peter, when he heard such talk,
  Would, heedless of a broken pate,
Stand like a man asleep, or balk
Some wishing guest of knife or fork,
  Or drop and break his master's plate.

VII

At night he oft would start and wake
  Like a lover, and began
In a wild measure songs to make
On moor, and glen, and rocky lake,
  And on the heart of man, —

VIII

And on the universal sky,
  And the wide earth's bosom green,
And the sweet, strange mystery
Of what beyond these things may lie,
  And yet remain unseen.

IX

For in his thought he visited
  The spots in which, ere dead and damned,
He his wayward life had led;
Yet knew not whence the thoughts were fed,
  Which thus his fancy crammed.

X

And these obscure remembrances
  Stirred such harmony in Peter,
That whensoever he should please,
He could speak of rocks and trees
  In poetic metre.

XI

For though it was without a sense
  Of memory, yet he remembered well
Many a ditch and quick-set fence;
Of lakes he had intelligence;
  He knew something of heath and fell.

XII

He had also dim recollections
  Of pedlers tramping on their rounds;
Milk-pans and pails; and odd collections
Of saws and proverbs; and reflections
  Old parsons make in burying-grounds.

XIII

But Peter's verse was clear, and came
  Announcing from the frozen hearth
Of a cold age, that none might tame
The soul of that diviner flame
  It augured to the Earth;

XIV

Like gentle rains, on the dry plains,
  Making that green which late was gray,
Or like the sudden moon, that stains
Some gloomy chamber's window panes
  With a broad light like day.

XV

For language was in Peter's hand
  Like clay while he was yet a potter;
And he made songs for all the land,
Sweet, both to feel and understand,
  As pipkins late to mountain cotter.

XVI

And Mr. ——, the bookseller,
  Gave twenty pounds for some; — then scorning

A footman's yellow coat to wear,
Peter, too proud of heart, I fear,
  Instantly gave the Devil warning.

XVII

Whereat the Devil took offence,
  And swore in his soul a great oath
    then,
' That for his damned impertinence,
He 'd bring him to a proper sense
  Of what was dùe to gentlemen ! '

PART THE SIXTH

DAMNATION

I

' O THAT mine enemy had written
  A book ! ' — cried Job; a fearful curse,
If to the Arab, as the Briton,
'T was galling to be critic-bitten;
  The Devil to Peter wished no worse.

II

When Peter's next new book found vent,
  The Devil to all the first Reviews
A copy of it slyly sent,
With five-pound note as compliment,
  And this short notice — ' Pray abuse.'

III

Then *seriatim*, month and quarter,
  Appeared such mad tirades. One said, —
' Peter seduced Mrs. Foy's daughter,
Then drowned the mother in Ullswater
  The last thing as he went to bed.'

IV

Another — ' Let him shave his head !
  Where 's Dr. Willis ? — Or is he jok-
    ing ?
What does the rascal mean or hope,
No longer imitating Pope,
  In that barbarian Shakespeare poking ? '

V

One more, ' Is incest not enough,
  And must there be adultery too ?
Grace after meat ?   Miscreant and Liar !
Thief ! Blackguard ! Scoundrel ! Fool !
    Hell-fire
  Is twenty times too good for you.

VI

' By that last book of yours WE think
  You 've double damned yourself to
    scorn;
We warned you whilst yet on the brink
You stood. From your black name will
    shrink
  The babe that is unborn.'

VII

All these Reviews the Devil made
Up in a parcel, which he had
Safely to Peter's house conveyed.
For carriage, tenpence Peter paid —
  Untied them — read them — went half-
    mad.

VIII

' What ! ' cried he, ' this is my reward
  For nights of thought, and days of
    toil ?
Do poets, but to be abhorred
By men of whom they never heard,
  Consume their spirits' oil ?

IX

' What have I done to them ? — and
    who
  Is Mrs. Foy ?   'T is very cruel
To speak of me and Betty so !
Adultery ! God defend me ! Oh !
  I 've half a mind to fight a duel.

X

' Or,' cried he, a grave look collecting,
  ' Is it my genius, like the moon,
Sets those who stand her face inspecting,
That face within their brain reflecting,
  Like a crazed bell-chime, out of tune ? '

XI

For Peter did not know the town,
  But thought, as country readers do,
For half a guinea or a crown
He bought oblivion or renown
  From God's own voice in a Review.

XII

All Peter did on this occasion
  Was writing some sad stuff in prose.
It is a dangerous invasion
When poets criticise; their station
  Is to delight, not pose.

XIII

The Devil then sent to Leipsic fair,
  For Born's translation of Kant's book;
A world of words, tail foremost, where
Right, wrong, false, true, and foul, and
    . fair
  As in a lottery-wheel are shook;

XIV

Five thousand crammed octavo pages
  Of German psychologics, — he
Who his *furor verborum* assuages
Thereon deserves just seven months' wages
  More than will e'er be due to me.

XV

I looked on them nine several days,
  And then I saw that they were bad;
A friend, too, spoke in their dispraise, —
He never read them; with amaze
  I found Sir William Drummond had.

XVI

When the book came, the Devil sent
  It to P. Verbovale, Esquire,
With a brief note of compliment,
By that night's Carlisle mail. It went,
  And set his soul on fire —

XVII

Fire, which *ex luce præbens fumum*,
  Made him beyond the bottom see
Of truth's clear well — when I and you,
    Ma'am,
Go, as we shall do, *subter humum*,
  We may know more than he.

XVIII

Now Peter ran to seed in soul
  Into a walking paradox;
For he was neither part nor whole,
Nor good, nor bad, nor knave nor fool, —
  Among the woods and rocks.

XIX

Furious he rode, where late he ran,
  Lashing and spurring his tame hobby;
Turned to a formal puritan,
A solemn and unsexual man, —
  He half believed *White Obi*.

XX

This steed in vision he would ride,
  High trotting over nine-inch bridges,
With Flibbertigibbet, imp of pride,
Mocking and mowing by his side —
  A mad-brained goblin for a guide —
  Over cornfields, gates and hedges.

XXI

After these ghastly rides, he came
  Home to his heart, and found from
    thence
Much stolen of its accustomed flame;
His thoughts grew weak, drowsy, and lame
  Of their intelligence.

XXII

To Peter's view, all seemed one hue;
  He was no whig, he was no tory;
No Deist and no Christian he;
He got so subtle that to be
  Nothing was all his glory.

XXIII

One single point in his belief
  From his organization sprung,
The heart-enrooted faith, the chief
Ear in his doctrines' blighted sheaf,
  That 'happiness is wrong.'

XXIV

So thought Calvin and Dominic;
  So think their fierce successors, who
Even now would neither stint nor stick
Our flesh from off our bones to pick,
  If they might 'do their do.'

XXV

His morals thus were undermined;
  The old Peter — the hard, old Potter
Was born anew within his mind;
He grew dull, harsh, sly, unrefined,
  As when he tramped beside the Otter.

XXVI

In the death hues of agony
  Lambently flashing from a fish,
Now Peter felt amused to see
Shades like a rainbow's rise and flee,
  Mixed with a certain hungry wish.

XXVII

So in his Country's dying face
  He looked — and lovely as she lay,
Seeking in vain his last embrace,
Wailing her own abandoned case,
  With hardened sneer he turned away;

XXVIII

And coolly to his own soul said, —
    ' Do you not think that we might make
A poem on her when she 's dead;
Or, no — a thought is in my head —
    Her shroud for a new sheet I 'll take;

XXIX

' My wife wants one. Let who will bury
    This mangled corpse ! And I and you,
My dearest Soul, will then make merry,
As the Prince Regent did with Sherry, —
    Ay — and at last desert me too.'

XXX

And so his soul would not be gay,
    But moaned within him; like a fawn
Moaning within a cave, it lay
Wounded and wasting, day by day,
    Till all its life of life was gone.

XXXI

As troubled skies stain waters clear,
    The storm in Peter's heart and mind
Now made his verses dark and queer;
They were the ghosts of what they were,
    Shaking dim grave clothes in the wind.

XXXII

For he now raved enormous folly,
    Of   Baptisms,   Sunday-schools,   and
        Graves;
'T would make George Colman melancholy
To have heard him, like a male Molly,
    Chanting those stupid staves.

XXXIII

Yet the Reviews, who heaped abuse
    On Peter while he wrote for freedom,
So soon as in his song they spy
The folly which soothes tyranny,
    Praise him, for those who feed 'em.

XXXIV

' He was a man, too great to scan;
    A planet lost in truth's keen rays;
His virtue, awful and prodigious;
He was the most sublime, religious,
    Pure-minded Poet of these days.'

XXXV

As soon as he read that, cried Peter,
    ' Eureka ! I have found the way
To make a better thing of metre

Than e'er was made by living creature
    Up to this blessèd day.'

XXXVI

Then Peter wrote odes to the Devil,
    In one of which he meekly said:
' May Carnage and Slaughter,
Thy niece and thy daughter,
May Rapine and Famine,
Thy gorge ever cramming,
    Glut thee with living and dead !

XXXVII

' May death and damnation,
    And consternation,
Flit up from hell with pure intent !
    Slash them at Manchester,
    Glasgow, Leeds and Chester;
Drench all with blood from Avon to Trent.

XXXVIII

' Let thy body-guard yeomen
    Hew down babes and women
And laugh with bold triumph till Heaven
    be rent !
    When Moloch in Jewry
    Munched children with fury,
It was thou, Devil, dining with pure in-
    tent.'

PART THE SEVENTH

DOUBLE DAMNATION

I

The Devil now knew his proper cue.
    Soon as he read the ode, he drove
To his friend Lord MacMurderchouse's,
A man of interest in both houses,
    And said: — ' For money or for love,

II

' Pray find some cure or sinecure;
    To feed from the superfluous taxes,
A friend of ours — a poet; fewer
Have fluttered tamer to the lure
    Than he.' His lordship stands and racks
    his

III

Stupid brains, while one might count
    As many beads as he had boroughs, —

At length replies, from his mean front,
Like one who rubs out an account,
  Smoothing away the unmeaning fur-
    rows:

IV

' It happens fortunately, dear Sir,
  I can. I hope I need require
No pledge from you that he will stir
In our affairs; — like Oliver,
  That he 'll be worthy of his hire.'

V

These words exchanged, the news sent off
  To Peter, home the Devil hied, —
Took to his bed; he had no cough,
No doctor, — meat and drink enough, —
  Yet that same night he died.

VI

The Devil's corpse was leaded down;
  His decent heirs enjoyed his pelf;
Mourning-coaches, many a one,
Followed his hearse along the town; —
  Where was the Devil himself?

VII

When Peter heard of his promotion,
  His eyes grew like two stars for bliss;
There was a bow of sleek devotion,
Engendering in his back; each motion
  Seemed a Lord's shoe to kiss.

VIII

He hired a house, bought plate, and made
  A genteel drive up to his door,
With sifted gravel neatly laid,
As if defying all who said,
  Peter was ever poor.

IX

But a disease soon struck into
  The very life and soul of Peter;
He walked about — slept — had the hue
Of health upon his cheeks — and few
  Dug better — none a heartier eater.

X

And yet a strange and horrid curse
  Clung upon Peter, night and day;
Month after month the thing grew worse,
And deadlier than in this my verse
  I can find strength to say.

XI

Peter was dull — he was at first
  Dull — oh, so dull — so very dull!
Whether he talked, wrote, or rehearsed —
Still with this dulness was he cursed —
  Dull — beyond all conception — dull.

XII

No one could read his books — no mortal,
  But a few natural friends, would hear
    him;
The parson came not near his portal;
His state was like that of the immortal
  Described by Swift — no man could bear
    him.

XIII

His sister, wife, and children yawned,
  With a long, slow, and drear ennui,
All human patience far beyond;
Their hopes of Heaven each would have
    pawned
  Anywhere else to be.

XIV

But in his verse, and in his prose,
  The essence of his dulness was
Concentred and compressed so close,
'T would have made Guatimozin doze
  On his red gridiron of brass.

XV

A printer's boy, folding those pages,
  Fell slumbrously upon one side,
Like those famed seven who slept three
    ages;
To wakeful frenzy's vigil rages,
  As opiates, were the same applied.

XVI

Even the Reviewers who were hired
  To do the work of his reviewing,
With adamantine nerves, grew tired;
Gaping and torpid they retired
  To dream of what they should be do-
    ing.

XVII

And worse and worse the drowsy curse
  Yawned in him, till it grew a pest —
A wide contagious atmosphere
Creeping like cold through all things
    near,
  A power to infect and to infest.

XVIII

His servant-maids and dogs grew dull;
　His kitten, late a sportive elf;
The woods and lakes, so beautiful,
Of dim stupidity were full;
　All grew dull as Peter's self.

XIX

The earth under his feet — the springs
　Which lived within it a quick life,
The air, the winds of many wings
That fan it with new murmurings,
　Were dead to their harmonious strife.

XX

The birds and beasts within the wood,
　The insects, and each creeping thing,
Were now a silent multitude;
Love's work was left unwrought — no
　　brood
　Near Peter's house took wing.

XXI

And every neighboring cottager
　Stupidly yawned upon the other;

No jackass brayed; no little cur
Cocked up his ears; no man would stir
　To save a dying mother.

XXII

Yet all from that charmed district went
　But some half-idiot and half-knave,
Who rather than pay any rent
Would live with marvellous content
　Over his father's grave.

XXIII

No bailiff dared within that space,
　For fear of the dull charm, to enter;
A man would bear upon his face,
For fifteen months in any case,
　The yawn of such a venture.

XXIV

Seven miles above — below — around —
　This pest of dulness holds its sway;
A ghastly life without a sound;
To Peter's soul the spell is bound —
　How should it ever pass away?

THE WITCH OF ATLAS

The Witch of Atlas was conceived during a solitary walk from the Baths of San Giuliano, near Pisa, to the top of Monte San Pellegrino, August 12, 1820, and was written August 14, 15, and 16. It was sent to Ollier to be published with Shelley's name, but was first issued in Mrs. Shelley's edition of the *Posthumous Poems*, 1824. Her own note gives all our information concerning it, except Shelley's characteristic sigh 'if its merit be measured by the labor which it cost, [it] is worth nothing.' Mrs. Shelley writes :

' We spent the summer at the Baths of San Giuliano, four miles from Pisa. These baths were of great use to Shelley in soothing his nervous irritability. We made several excursions in the neighborhood. The country around is fertile, and diversified and rendered picturesque by ranges of near hills and more distant mountains. The peasantry are a handsome, intelligent race, and there was a gladsome sunny heaven spread over us, that rendered home and every scene we visited cheerful and bright. During some of the hottest days of August, Shelley made a solitary journey on foot to the summit of Monte San Pelegrino — a mountain of some height, on the top of which

there is a chapel, the object, during certain days in the year, of many pilgrimages. The excursion delighted him while it lasted, though he exerted himself too much, and the effect was considerable lassitude and weakness on his return. During the expedition he conceived the idea and wrote, in the three days immediately succeeding to his return, *The Witch of Atlas*. This poem is peculiarly characteristic of his tastes — wildly fanciful, full of brilliant imagery, and discarding human interest and passion, to revel in the fantastic ideas that his imagination suggested.

' The surpassing excellence of *The Cenci* had made me greatly desire that Shelley should increase his popularity, by adopting subjects that would more suit the popular taste than a poem conceived in the abstract and dreamy spirit of *The Witch of Atlas*. It was not only that I wished him to acquire popularity as redounding to his fame ; but I believed that he would obtain a greater mastery over his own powers, and greater happiness in his mind, if public applause crowned his endeavors. The few stanzas that precede the poem were addressed to me on my representing these ideas to him. Even now I believe that I was in the right.

Shelley did not expect sympathy and approbation from the public; but the want of it took away a portion of the ardor that ought to have sustained him while writing. He was thrown on his own resources and on the inspiration of his own soul, and wrote because his mind overflowed, without the hope of being appreciated. I had not the most distant wish that he should truckle in opinion, or submit his lofty aspirations for the human race to the low ambition and pride of the many, but I felt sure that if his poems were more addressed to the common feelings of men, his proper rank among the writers of the day would be acknowledged; and that popularity as a poet would enable his countrymen to do justice to his character and virtues; which, in those days, it was the mode to attack with the most flagitious calumnies and insulting abuse. That he felt these things deeply cannot be doubted, though he armed himself with the consciousness of acting from a lofty and heroic sense of right. The truth burst from his heart sometimes in solitude, and he would write a few unfinished verses that showed that he felt the sting. . . .

'I believed that all this morbid feeling would vanish, if the chord of sympathy between him and his countrymen were touched. But my persuasions were vain; the mind could not be bent from its natural inclination. Shelley shrunk instinctively from portraying human passion, with its mixture of good and evil, of disappointment and disquiet. Such opened again the wounds of his own heart, and he loved to shelter himself rather in the airiest flights of fancy, forgetting love and hate and regret and lost hope, in such imaginations as borrowed their hues from sunrise or sunset, from the yellow moonshine or paly twilight, from the aspect of the far ocean or the shadows of the woods; which celebrated the singing of the winds among the pines, the flow of a murmuring stream, and the thousand harmonious sounds which nature creates in her solitudes. These are the materials which form *The Witch of Atlas;* it is a brilliant congregation of ideas, such as his senses gathered, and his fancy colored, during his rambles in the sunny land he so much loved.'

TO MARY

ON HER OBJECTING TO THE FOLLOWING POEM UPON THE SCORE OF ITS CONTAINING NO HUMAN INTEREST

I

How, my dear Mary, are you critic-bitten
  (For vipers kill, though dead) by some review,
That you condemn these verses I have written,
  Because they tell no story, false or true!
What, though no mice are caught by a young kitten,
  May it not leap and play as grown cats do,
Till its claws come? Prithee, for this one time,
Content thee with a visionary rhyme.

II

What hand would crush the silken-winged fly,
  The youngest of inconstant April's minions,
Because it cannot climb the purest sky,
  Where the swan sings, amid the sun's dominions?
Not thine. Thou knowest 't is its doom to die,

When day shall hide within her twilight pinions
The lucent eyes, and the eternal smile,
Serene as thine, which lent it life awhile.

III

To thy fair feet a wingèd Vision came,
  Whose date should have been longer than a day,
And o'er thy head did beat its wings for fame,
  And in thy sight its fading plumes display;
The watery bow burned in the evening flame,
  But the shower fell, the swift sun went his way —
And that is dead. Oh, let me not believe
That anything of mine is fit to live!

IV

Wordsworth informs us he was nineteen years
  Considering and retouching Peter Bell;
Watering his laurels with the killing tears
  Of slow, dull care, so that their roots to hell
Might pierce, and their wide branches blot the spheres
  Of heaven, with dewy leaves and flowers; this well

May be, for Heaven and Earth conspire to
    foil
The over-busy gardener's blundering toil.

V

My Witch indeed is not so sweet a creature
    As Ruth or Lucy, whom his graceful
    praise
Clothes for our grandsons — but she
    matches Peter,
    Though he took nineteen years, and she
    three days,
In dressing. Light the vest of flowing
    metre
    She wears; he, proud as dandy with his
    stays,
Has hung upon his wiry limbs a dress
Like King Lear's 'looped and windowed
    raggedness.'

VI

If you strip Peter, you will see a fellow
    Scorched by Hell's hyperequatorial cli-
    mate
Into a kind of a sulphureous yellow:
    A lean mark, hardly fit to fling a rhyme
    at;
In shape a Scaramouch, in hue Othello.
    If you unveil my Witch, no priest nor
    primate
Can shrive you of that sin, — if sin there be
In love, when it becomes idolatry.

I

BEFORE those cruel Twins, whom at one
    birth
    Incestuous Change bore to her father
    Time,
Error and Truth, had hunted from the
    earth
    All those bright natures which adorned
    its prime,
And left us nothing to believe in, worth
    The pains of putting into learnèd rhyme,
A Lady-Witch there lived on Atlas' moun-
    tain
Within a cavern by a secret fountain.

II

Her mother was one of the Atlantides;
    The all-beholding Sun had ne'er beholden
In his wide voyage o'er continents and seas
    So fair a creature, as she lay enfolden
In the warm shadow of her loveliness;

He kissed her with his beams, and made
    all golden
The chamber of gray rock in which she lay;
She, in that dream of joy, dissolved away.

III

'T is said, she first was changed into a va-
    por,
    And then into a cloud, such clouds as flit,
Like splendor-wingèd moths about a taper,
    Round the red west when the sun dies
    in it;
And then into a meteor, such as caper
    On hill-tops when the moon is in a fit;
Then, into one of those mysterious stars
Which hide themselves between the Earth
    and Mars.

IV

Ten times the Mother of the Months had
    bent
    Her bow beside the folding-star, and
    bidden
With that bright sign the billows to in-
    dent
    The sea-deserted sand — like children
    chidden,
At her command they ever came and went—
    Since in that cave a dewy splendor hid-
    den
Took shape and motion; with the living
    form
Of this embodied Power the cave grew
    warm.

V

A lovely lady garmented in light
    From her own beauty; deep her eyes as
    are
Two openings of unfathomable night
    Seen through a temple's cloven roof; her
    hair
Dark; the dim brain whirls dizzy with de-
    light,
    Picturing her form; her soft smiles shone
    afar,
And her low voice was heard like love, and
    drew
All living things towards this wonder new.

VI

And first the spotted camelopard came,
    And then the wise and fearless elephant;
Then the sly serpent, in the golden flame

Of his own volumes intervolved. All
    gaunt
And sanguine beasts her gentle looks made
    tame;
    They drank before her at her sacred
      fount;
And every beast of beating heart grew bold,
Such gentleness and power even to behold.

VII

The brinded lioness led forth her young,
    That she might teach them how they
      should forego
Their inborn thirst of death; the pard un-
    strung
    His sinews at her feet, and sought to
      know,
With looks whose motions spoke without a
    tongue,
    How he might be as gentle as the doe.
The magic circle of her voice and eyes
All savage natures did imparadise.

VIII

And old Silenus, shaking a green stick
    Of lilies, and the wood-gods in a crew
Came, blithe, as in the olive copses thick
    Cicadæ are, drunk with the noonday dew;
And Dryope and Faunus followed quick,
    Teasing the god to sing them something
      new;
Till in this cave they found the Lady lone,
Sitting upon a seat of emerald stone.

IX

And universal Pan, 't is said, was there;
    And — though none saw him — through
      the adamant
Of the deep mountains, through the track-
    less air
    And through those living spirits, like a
      want,
He passed out of his everlasting lair
    Where the quick heart of the great
      world doth pant,
And felt that wondrous Lady all alone, —
And she felt him upon her emerald throne.

X

And every nymph of stream and spreading
    tree,
    And every shepherdess of Ocean's flocks,
Who drives her white waves over the green
    sea,

And Ocean, with the brine on his gray
    locks,
And quaint Priapus with his company,
    All came, much wondering how the en-
      wombèd rocks
Could have brought forth so beautiful a
    birth;
Her love subdued their wonder and their
    mirth.

XI

The herdsman and the mountain maidens
    came,
    And the rude kings of pastoral Garamant;
Their spirits shook within them, as a flame
    Stirred by the air under a cavern gaunt;
Pygmies, and Polyphemes, by many a name,
    Centaurs and Satyrs, and such shapes as
      haunt
Wet clefts, and lumps neither alive nor
    dead,
Dog-headed, bosom-eyed, and bird-footed.

XII

For she was beautiful; her beauty made
    The bright world dim, and everything
      beside
Seemed like the fleeting image of a shade;
    No thought of living spirit could abide,
Which to her looks had ever been betrayed,
    On any object in the world so wide,
On any hope within the circling skies,
But on her form, and in her inmost eyes.

XIII

Which when the Lady knew, she took her
    spindle
    And twined three threads of fleecy mist,
      and three
Long lines of light, such as the dawn may
    kindle
    The clouds and waves and mountains
      with; and she
As many star-beams, ere their lamps could
    dwindle
    In the belated moon, wound skilfully;
And with these threads a subtle veil she
    wove —
A shadow for the splendor of her love.

XIV

The deep recesses of her odorous dwelling
    Were stored with magic treasures —
      sounds of air

Which had the power all spirits of com-
pelling,
　Folded in cells of crystal silence there;
Such as we hear in youth, and think the
feeling
　Will never die — yet ere we are aware,
The feeling and the sound are fled and
gone,
And the regret they leave remains alone.

XV

And there lay Visions swift, and sweet, and
quaint,
　Each in its thin sheath like a chrysalis;
Some eager to burst forth, some weak and
faint
　With the soft burden of intensest bliss
It is its work to bear to many a saint
　Whose heart adores the shrine which
holiest is,
Even Love's; and others white, green, gray,
and black,
And of all shapes — and each was at her
beck.

XVI

And odors in a kind of aviary
　Of ever-blooming Eden-trees she kept,
Clipped in a floating net a love-sick Fairy
　Had woven from dew-beams while the
moon yet slept;
As bats at the wired window of a dairy,
　They beat their vans; and each was an
adept,
When loosed and missioned, making wings
of winds,
To stir sweet thoughts or sad, in destined
minds.

XVII

And liquors clear and sweet, whose health-
ful might
　Could medicine the sick soul to happy
sleep,
And change eternal death into a night
　Of glorious dreams — or, if eyes needs
must weep,
Could make their tears all wonder and de-
light —
　She in her crystal vials did closely
keep;
If men could drink of those clear vials, 't is
said,
The living were not envied of the dead.

XVIII

Her cave was stored with scrolls of strange
device,
　The works of some Saturnian Archi-
mage,
Which taught the expiations at whose price
　Men from the gods might win that happy
age
Too lightly lost, redeeming native vice;
　And which might quench the earth-con-
suming rage
Of gold and blood, till men should live and
move
Harmonious as the sacred stars above;

XIX

And how all things that seem untamable,
　Not to be checked and not to be confined,
Obey the spells of wisdom's wizard skill;
　Time, earth and fire, the ocean and the
wind,
And all their shapes, and man's imperial
will;
　And other scrolls whose writings did un-
bind
The inmost lore of Love — let the profane
Tremble to ask what secrets they contain.

XX

And wondrous works of substances un-
known,
　To which the enchantment of her father's
power
Had changed those ragged blocks of savage
stone,
　Were heaped in the recesses of her bower;
Carved lamps and chalices, and vials which
shone
　In their own golden beams — each like a
flower
Out of whose depth a fire-fly shakes his
light
Under a cypress in a starless night.

XXI

At first she lived alone in this wild home,
　And her own thoughts were each a min-
ister,
Clothing themselves or with the ocean-foam,
　Or with the wind, or with the speed of
fire,
To work whatever purposes might come
　Into her mind; such power her mighty
Sire

Had girt them with, whether to fly or run,
Through all the regions which he shines
    upon.

XXII

The Ocean-nymphs and Hamadryades,
    Oreads and Naiads with long weedy locks,
Offered to do her bidding through the seas,
    Under the earth, and in the hollow rocks,
And far beneath the matted roots of trees,
    And in the gnarlèd heart of stubborn oaks,
So they might live forever in the light
Of her sweet presence — each a satellite.

XXIII

' This may not be,' the Wizard Maid re-
    plied;
    ' The fountains where the Naiades bedew
Their shining hair, at length are drained
    and dried;
The solid oaks forget their strength, and
    strew
Their latest leaf upon the mountains wide;
    The boundless ocean, like a drop of dew,
Will be consumed — the stubborn centre
    must
Be scattered, like a cloud of summer dust;

XXIV

' And ye with them will perish one by one.
    If I must sigh to think that this shall be,
If I must weep when the surviving Sun
    Shall smile on your decay, oh, ask not me
To love you till your little race is run;
    I cannot die as ye must — over me
Your leaves shall glance — the streams in
    which ye dwell
Shall be my paths henceforth, and so —
    farewell ! '

XXV

She spoke and wept; the dark and azure
    well
    Sparkled beneath the shower of her
    bright tears,
And every little circlet where they fell
    Flung to the cavern-roof inconstant
    spheres
And intertangled lines of light; a knell
    Of sobbing voices came upon her ears
From those departing Forms, o'er the se-
    rene
Of the white streams and of the forest
    green.

XXVI

All day the Wizard Lady sate aloof,
    Spelling out scrolls of dread antiquity,
Under the cavern's fountain-lighted roof;
    Or broidering the pictured poesy
Of some high tale upon her growing woof,
    Which the sweet splendor of her smiles
    could dye
In hues outshining Heaven — and ever she
Added some grace to the wrought poesy.

XXVII

While on her hearth lay blazing many a
    piece
    Of sandal-wood, rare gums and cinnamon;
Men scarcely know how beautiful fire is;
    Each flame of it is as a precious stone
Dissolved in ever-moving light, and this
    Belongs to each and all who gaze upon;
The Witch beheld it not, for in her hand
She held a woof that dimmed the burning
    brand.

XXVIII

This Lady never slept, but lay in trance
    All night within the fountain, as in sleep.
Its emerald crags glowed in her beauty's
    glance;
    Through the green splendor of the water
    deep
She saw the constellations reel and dance
    Like fire-flies, and withal did ever keep
The tenor of her contemplations calm,
With open eyes, closed feet, and folded
    palm.

XXIX

And when the whirlwinds and the clouds
    descended
    From the white pinnacles of that cold
    hill,
She passed at dewfall to a space extended,
    Where, in a lawn of flowering asphodel
Amid a wood of pines and cedars blended,
    There yawned an inextinguishable well
Of crimson fire, full even to the brim,
And overflowing all the margin trim;

XXX

Within the which she lay when the fierce
    war
    Of wintry winds shook that innocuous
    liquor
In many a mimic moon and bearded star,

O'er woods and lawns; the serpent heard
  it flicker
In sleep, and, dreaming still, he crept afar;
  And when the windless snow descended
    thicker
Than autumn leaves, she watched it as it
  came
Melt on the surface of the level flame.

XXXI

She had a boat which some say Vulcan
  wrought
  For Venus, as the chariot of her star;
But it was found too feeble to be fraught
  With all the ardors in that sphere which
    are,
And so she sold it, and Apollo bought
  And gave it to this daughter; from a car
Changed to the fairest and the lightest boat
Which ever upon mortal stream did float.

XXXII

And others say, that, when but three hours
  old,
  The first-born Love out of his cradle
    leapt,
And clove dun Chaos with his wings of gold,
  And like a horticultural adept,
Stole a strange seed, and wrapped it up in
  mould,
  And sowed it in his mother's star, and
    kept
Watering it all the summer with sweet
  dew,
And with his wings fanning it as it grew.

XXXIII

The plant grew strong and green; the
  snowy flower
  Fell, and the long and gourd-like fruit
    began
To turn the light and dew by inward power
  To its own substance; woven tracery ran
Of light firm texture, ribbed and branch-
  ing, o'er
  The solid rind, like a leaf's veinèd fan,
Of which Love scooped this boat, and with
  soft motion
Piloted it round the circumfluous ocean.

XXXIV

This boat she moored upon her fount, and
  lit
  A living spirit within all its frame,
Breathing the soul of swiftness into it.

Couched on the fountain, like a panther
  tame —
One of the twain at Evan's feet that sit —
  Or as on Vesta's sceptre a swift flame,
Or on blind Homer's heart a wingèd
  thought, —
In joyous expectation lay the boat.

XXXV

Then by strange art she kneaded fire and
  snow
Together, tempering the repugnant mass
With liquid love — all things together grow
  Through which the harmony of love can
    pass:
And a fair Shape out of her hands did flow,
  A living Image, which did far surpass
In beauty that bright shape of vital stone
Which drew the heart out of Pygmalion.

XXXVI

A sexless thing it was, and in its growth
  It seemed to have developed no defect
Of either sex, yet all the grace of both;
  In gentleness and strength its limbs were
    decked;
The bosom lightly swelled with its full
  youth,
  The countenance was such as might select
Some artist that his skill should never die,
Imaging forth such perfect purity.

XXXVII

From its smooth shoulders hung two rapid
  wings,
  Fit to have borne it to the seventh sphere,
Tipped with the speed of liquid lightnings,
  Dyed in the ardors of the atmosphere.
She led her creature to the boiling springs
  Where the light boat was moored, and
    said, ' Sit here ! '
And pointed to the prow and took her seat
Beside the rudder with opposing feet.

XXXVIII

And down the streams which clove those
  mountains vast,
  Around their inland islets, and amid
The panther-peopled forests, whose shade
  cast
Darkness and odors, and a pleasure hid
In melancholy gloom, the pinnace passed;
  By many a star-surrounded pyramid
Of icy crag cleaving the purple sky,
And caverns yawning round unfathomably.

XXXIX

The silver noon into that winding dell,
  With slanted gleam athwart the forest
    tops,
Tempered like golden evening, feebly
    fell;
  A green and glowing light, like that
    which drops
From folded lilies in which glow-worms
    dwell,
  When earth over her face night's mantle
    wraps;
Between the severed mountains lay on
    high,
Over the stream, a narrow rift of sky.

XL

And ever as she went, the Image lay
  With folded wings and unawakened eyes;
And o'er its gentle countenance did play
  The busy dreams, as thick as summer
    flies,
Chasing the rapid smiles that would not
    stay,
  And drinking the warm tears, and the
    sweet sighs
Inhaling, which, with busy murmur vain,
They had aroused from that full heart and
    brain.

XLI

And ever down the prone vale, like a cloud
  Upon a stream of wind, the pinnace went;
Now lingering on the pools, in which abode
  The calm and darkness of the deep con-
    tent
In which they paused; now o'er the shallow
    road
  Of white and dancing waters, all besprent
With sand and polished pebbles: mortal
    boat
In such a shallow rapid could not float.

XLII

And down the earthquaking cataracts,
    which shiver
  Their snow-like waters into golden air,
Or under chasms unfathomable ever
  Sepulchre them, till in their rage they
    tear
A subterranean portal for the river,
  It fled — the circling sunbows did upbear
Its fall down the hoar precipice of spray,
Lighting it far upon its lampless way.

XLIII

And when the Wizard Lady would ascend
  The labyrinths of some many-winding
    vale,
Which to the inmost mountain upward
    tend,
  She called 'Hermaphroditus!' and the
    pale
And heavy hue which slumber could extend
  Over its lips and eyes, as on the gale
A rapid shadow from a slope of grass,
Into the darkness of the stream did pass.

XLIV

And it unfurled its heaven-colored pinions,
  With stars of fire spotting the stream
    below,
And from above into the Sun's dominions
  Flinging a glory, like the golden glow
In which Spring clothes her emerald-wingèd
    minions,
  All interwoven with fine feathery snow
And moonlight splendor of intensest rime
With which frost paints the pines in winter
    time;

XLV

And then it winnowed the Elysian air,
  Which ever hung about that lady bright,
With its ethereal vans; and speeding
    there,
  Like a star up the torrent of the night,
Or a swift eagle in the morning glare
  Breasting the whirlwind with impetuous
    flight,
The pinnace, oared by those enchanted
    wings,
Clove the fierce streams towards their up-
    per springs.

XLVI

The water flashed, like sunlight by the prow
  Of a noon-wandering meteor flung to
    Heaven;
The still air seemed as if its waves did
    flow
  In tempest down the mountains; loosely
    driven
The lady's radiant hair streamed to and
    fro;
  Beneath, the billows, having vainly
    striven
Indignant and impetuous, roared to feel
The swift and steady motion of the keel.

XLVII

Or, when the weary moon was in the wane,
  Or in the noon of interlunar night,
The Lady-Witch in visions could not chain
  Her spirit; but sailed forth under the
    light
Of shooting stars, and bade extend amain
  Its storm-outspeeding wings the Herma-
    phrodite;
She to the Austral waters took her way,
Beyond the fabulous Thamandocana,

XLVIII

Where, like a meadow which no scythe has
    shaven,
  Which rain could never bend, or whirl-
    blast shake,
With the Antarctic constellations paven,
  Canopus and his crew, lay the Austral
    lake;
There she would build herself a windless
    haven
  Out of the clouds whose moving turrets
    make
The bastions of the storm, when through
    the sky
The spirits of the tempest thundered by;

XLIX

A haven, beneath whose translucent floor
  The tremulous stars sparkled unfathom-
    ably,
And around which the solid vapors hoar,
  Based on the level waters, to the sky
Lifted their dreadful crags, and, like a
    shore
  Of wintry mountains, inaccessibly
Hemmed in, with rifts and precipices gray
And hanging crags, many a cove and bay.

L

And whilst the outer lake beneath the lash
  Of the wind's scourge foamed like a
    wounded thing,
And the incessant hail with stony clash
  Ploughed up the waters, and the flagging
    wing
Of the roused cormorant in the lightning
    flash
  Looked like the wreck of some wind-
    wandering
Fragment of inky thunder-smoke — this
    haven
Was as a gem to copy Heaven engraven;

LI

On which that Lady played her many
    pranks,
  Circling the image of a shooting star,
Even as a tiger on Hydaspes' banks
  Outspeeds the antelopes which speediest
    are,
In her light boat; and many quips and
    cranks
  She played upon the water; till the car
Of the late moon, like a sick matron wan,
To journey from the misty east began.

LII

And then she called out of the hollow tur-
    rets
  Of those high clouds, white, golden and
    vermilion,
The armies of her ministering spirits;
  In mighty legions, million after million,
They came, each troop emblazoning its
    merits
  On meteor flags; and many a proud pa-
    vilion
Of the intertexture of the atmosphere
They pitched upon the plain of the calm
    mere.

LIII

They framed the imperial tent of their
    great Queen
  Of woven exhalations, underlaid
With lambent lightning-fire, as may be seen
  A dome of thin and open ivory inlaid
With crimson silk; cressets from the serene
  Hung there, and on the water for her
    tread
A tapestry of fleece-like mist was strewn,
Dyed in the beams of the ascending moon.

LIV

And on a throne o'erlaid with starlight,
    caught
  Upon those wandering isles of aëry dew
Which highest shoals of mountain ship-
    wreck not,
  She sate, and heard all that had hap-
    pened new
Between the earth and moon since they
    had brought
  The last intelligence; and now she grew
Pale as that moon lost in the watery night,
And now she wept, and now she laughed
    outright.

LV

These were tame pleasures. She would
    often climb
  The steepest ladder of the crudded rack
Up to some beakèd cape of cloud sublime,
  And like Arion on the dolphin's back
Ride singing through the shoreless air;
    oft-time
  Following the serpent lightning's winding
    track,
She ran upon the platforms of the wind,
And laughed to hear the fire-balls roar be-
    hind.

LVI

And sometimes to those streams of upper
    air,
  Which whirl the earth in its diurnal
    round,
She would ascend, and win the spirits
    there
  To let her join their chorus. Mortals
    found
That on those days the sky was calm and
    fair,
  And mystic snatches of harmonious sound
Wandered upon the earth where'er she
    passed,
And happy thoughts of hope, too sweet to
    last.

LVII

But her choice sport was, in the hours of
    sleep,
  To glide adown old Nilus, where he
    threads
Egypt and Æthiopia, from the steep
  Of utmost Axumé, until he spreads,
Like a calm flock of silver-fleecèd sheep,
  His waters on the plain, — and crested
    heads
Of cities and proud temples gleam amid,
And many a vapor-belted pyramid;

LVIII

By Mœris and the Mareotid lakes,
  Strewn with faint blooms, like bridal-
    chamber floors,
Where naked boys bridling tame water-
    snakes,
  Or charioteering ghastly alligators,
Had left on the sweet waters mighty wakes
  Of those huge forms — within the brazen
    doors

Of the great Labyrinth slept both boy and
    beast
Tired with the pomp of their Osirian feast;

LIX

And where within the surface of the river
  The shadows of the massy temples lie,
And never are erased — but tremble ever
  Like things which every cloud can doom
    to die;
Through lotus-paven canals, and whereso-
    ever
  The works of man pierced that serenest
    sky
With tombs, and towers, and fanes, — 't was
    her delight
To wander in the shadow of the night.

LX

With motion like the spirit of that wind
  Whose soft step deepens slumber, her
    light feet
Passed through the peopled haunts of hu-
    mankind,
  Scattering sweet visions from her pre-
    sence sweet;
Through fane and palace-court and laby-
    rinth mined
  With many a dark and subterranean
    street
Under the Nile, through chambers high and
    deep
She passed, observing mortals in their sleep.

LXI

A pleasure sweet doubtless it was to see
  Mortals subdued in all the shapes of
    sleep.
Here lay two sister-twins in infancy;
  There a lone youth who in his dreams
    did weep;
Within, two lovers linkèd innocently
  In their loose locks which over both did
    creep
Like ivy from one stem; and there lay calm
Old age with snow-bright hair and folded
    palm.

LXII

But other troubled forms of sleep she saw,
  Not to be mirrored in a holy song;
Distortions foul of supernatural awe,
  And pale imaginings of visioned wrong,
And all the code of custom's lawless law

Written upon the brows of old and young;
'This,' said the Wizard Maiden, 'is the
    strife
Which stirs the liquid surface of man's life.'

LXIII

And little did the sight disturb her soul.
  We, the weak mariners of that wide lake,
Where'er its shores extend or billows roll,
  Our course unpiloted and starless make
O'er its wild surface to an unknown goal;
    But she in the calm depths her way could
      take
Where in bright bowers immortal forms
    abide,
Beneath the weltering of the restless tide.

LXIV

And she saw princes couched under the
    glow
  Of sun-like gems; and round each tem-
    ple-court
In dormitories ranged, row after row,
  She saw the priests asleep, all of one sort,
For all were educated to be so.
    The peasants in their huts, and in the
      port
The sailors she saw cradled on the waves,
And the dead lulled within their dreamless
    graves.

LXV

And all the forms in which those spirits lay
  Were to her sight like the diaphanous
Veils in which those sweet ladies oft array
  Their delicate limbs, who would conceal
    from us
Only their scorn of all concealment; they
  Move in the light of their own beauty
    thus.
But these and all now lay with sleep upon
    them,
And little thought a Witch was looking on
    them.

LXVI

She all those human figures breathing there
  Beheld as living spirits; to her eyes
The naked beauty of the soul lay bare;
  And often through a rude and worn dis-
    guise
She saw the inner form most bright and
    fair;
  And then she had a charm of strange
    device,

Which, murmured on mute lips with tender
    tone,
Could make that spirit mingle with her
    own.

LXVII

Alas, Aurora ! what wouldst thou have
    given
  For such a charm, when Tithon became
    gray ?
Or how much, Venus, of thy silver Heaven
  Wouldst thou have yielded, ere Proser-
    pina
Had half (oh ! why not all ?) the debt for-
    given
  Which dear Adonis had been doomed to
    pay,
To any witch who would have taught you
    it ?
The Heliad doth not know its value yet.

LXVIII

'T is said in after times her spirit free
  Knew what love was, and felt itself
    alone;
But holy Dian could not chaster be
  Before she stooped to kiss Endymion,
Than now this lady — like a sexless bee
  Tasting all blossoms and confined to none;
Among those mortal forms the Wizard-
    Maiden
Passed with an eye serene and heart un-
    laden.

LXIX

To those she saw most beautiful, she gave
  Strange panacea in a crystal bowl;
They drank in their deep sleep of that
    sweet wave,
  And lived thenceforward as if some con-
    trol,
Mightier than life, were in them; and the
    grave
  Of such, when death oppressed the weary
    soul,
Was as a green and over-arching bower
Lit by the gems of many a starry flower.

LXX

For on the night when they were buried,
    she
  Restored the embalmers' ruining and
    shook
The light out of the funeral lamps, to be
  A mimic day within that deathy nook;

And she unwound the woven imagery
  Of second childhood's swaddling bands,
    and took
The coffin, its last cradle, from its niche,
And threw it with contempt into a ditch.

LXXI

And there the body lay, age after age,
  Mute, breathing, beating, warm, and
    undecaying,
Like one asleep in a green hermitage,
  With gentle smiles about its eyelids
    playing,
And living in its dreams beyond the rage
  Of death or life, while they were still
    arraying
In liveries ever new the rapid, blind,
And fleeting generations of mankind.

LXXII

And she would write strange dreams upon
  the brain
  Of those who were less beautiful, and
    make
All harsh and crooked purposes more vain
  Than in the desert is the serpent's wake
Which the sand covers; all his evil gain
  The miser in such dreams would rise and
    shake
Into a beggar's lap; the lying scribe
Would his own lies betray without a bribe.

LXXIII

The priests would write an explanation
  full,
  Translating hieroglyphics into Greek,
How the god Apis really was a bull,
  And nothing more; and bid the herald
    stick
The same against the temple doors, and
  pull
  The old cant down; they licensed all to
    speak
Whate'er they thought of hawks, and cats,
  and geese,
By pastoral letters to each diocese.

LXXIV

The king would dress an ape up in his
  crown
  And robes, and seat him on his glorious
    seat,
And on the right hand of the sun-like throne
  Would place a gaudy mock-bird to re-
    peat

The chatterings of the monkey. Every
  one
  Of the prone courtiers crawled to kiss
    the feet
Of their great emperor when the morning
  came,
And kissed — alas, how many kiss the
  same !

LXXV

The soldiers dreamed that they were black-
  smiths, and
  Walked out of quarters in somnambu-
    lism;
Round the red anvils you might see them
  stand,
  Like Cyclopses in Vulcan's sooty abysm,
Beating their swords to ploughshares; in a
  band
  The gaolers sent those of the liberal
    schism
Free through the streets of Memphis, —
  much, I wis,
To the annoyance of king Amasis.

LXXVI

And timid lovers who had been so coy
  They hardly knew whether they loved or
    not,
Would rise out of their rest, and take sweet
  joy,
  To the fulfilment of their inmost thought;
And when next day the maiden and the
  boy
  Met one another, both, like sinners
    caught,
Blushed at the thing which each believed
  was done
Only in fancy — till the tenth moon shone;

LXXVII

And then the Witch would let them take
  no ill;
  Of many thousand schemes which lovers
    find
The Witch found one, — and so they took
  their fill
  Of happiness in marriage warm and
    kind.
Friends who, by practice of some envious
  skill,
  Were torn apart — a wide wound, mind
    from mind —
She did unite again with visions clear
Of deep affection and of truth sincere.

LXXVIII

These were the pranks she played among
the cities
Of mortal men, and what she did to
sprites
And Gods, entangling them in her sweet
ditties

To do her will, and show their subtle
slights,
I will declare another time; for it is
A tale more fit for the weird winter
nights
Than for these garish summer days, when
we
Scarcely believe much more than we can see.

ŒDIPUS TYRANNUS OR SWELLFOOT THE TYRANT

A TRAGEDY

IN TWO ACTS

TRANSLATED FROM THE ORIGINAL DORIC

———— Choose Reform or Civil War,
When through thy streets, instead of hare with dogs,
A CONSORT-QUEEN shall hunt a KING with hogs,
Riding on the IONIAN MINOTAUR.

Œdipus Tyrannus, a piece of drollery like *Peter Bell*, was begun, under the circumstances described in Mrs. Shelley's Note, August 24, 1819, at the Baths of San Giuliano, near Pisa. It was sent to Horace Smith, who had it published as a pamphlet without Shelley's name. It was threatened with prosecution by citizens of the ward, and some steps thereto seem to have been taken; but at the suggestion of Alderman Rothwell the publisher gave up the whole edition, except seven copies, which had been sold, and also told the name of his employer. The secret of the authorship was kept by Horace Smith, who said only that the work had been sent to him from Pisa. The drama was suggested by the affair of Queen Caroline. Of the characters Purganax stands for Lord Castlereagh, Dakry for Lord Eldon, and Laoctonos for the Duke of Wellington. Mrs. Shelley's Note completes the history of the poem:

' In the brief journal I kept in those days, I find recorded in August [24], 1820, "Shelley begins *Swellfoot the Tyrant*, suggested by the pigs at the fair of San Giuliano." This was the period of Queen Caroline's landing in England, and the struggles made by George IV. to get rid of her claims; which failing, Lord Castlereagh placed the "Green Bag" on the table of the House of Commons, demanding, in the King's name, that an inquiry should be instituted into his wife's conduct. These circumstances were the theme of all conversation among the English. We were then at the Baths of San Giuliano; a friend [Mrs. Mason]

came to visit us on the day when a fair was held in the square, beneath our windows. Shelley read to us his *Ode to Liberty*; and was riotously accompanied by the grunting of a quantity of pigs brought for sale to the fair. He compared it to the "chorus of frogs" in the satiric drama of Aristophanes; and it being an hour of merriment, and one ludicrous association suggesting another, he imagined a political satirical drama on the circumstances of the day, to which the pigs would serve as chorus — and *Swellfoot* was begun. When finished, it was transmitted to England, printed and published anonymously; but stifled at the very dawn of its existence by the "Society for the Suppression of Vice," who threatened to prosecute it, if not immediately withdrawn. The friend who had taken the trouble of bringing it out, of course did not think it worth the annoyance and expense of a contest, and it was laid aside.

' Hesitation of whether it would do honor to Shelley prevented my publishing it at first; but I cannot bring myself to keep back anything he ever wrote, for each word is fraught with the peculiar views and sentiments which he believed to be beneficial to the human race, and the bright light of poetry irradiates every thought. The world has a right to the entire compositions of such a man; for it does not live and thrive by the outworn lesson of the dullard or the hypocrite, but by the original free thoughts of men of genius, who aspire to pluck bright truth

' " from the pale-faced moon;
Or dive into the bottom of the deep,
Where fathom-line could never touch the ground,
And pluck up drowned "

truth. Even those who may dissent from his
opinions will consider that he was a man of
genius, and that the world will take more
interest in his slightest word, than from the
waters of Lethe, which are so eagerly prescribed as medicinal for all its wrongs and woes.
This drama, however, must not be judged for
more than was meant. It is a mere plaything
of the imagination, which even may not excite
smiles among many, who will not see wit in
those combinations of thought which were full
of the ridiculous to the author. But, like
everything he wrote, it breathes that deep
sympathy for the sorrows of humanity, and
indignation against its oppressors, which make
it worthy of his name.'

ADVERTISEMENT

THIS Tragedy is one of a triad or system of
three Plays (an arrangement according to which
the Greeks were accustomed to connect their

ŒDIPUS TYRANNUS

DRAMATIS PERSONÆ

TYRANT SWELLFOOT, King of Thebes.	The GADFLY.
	The LEECH.
IONA TAURINA, his Queen.	The RAT.
	The MINOTAUR.
MAMMON, Arch-Priest of Famine.	MOSES, the Sow-gelder.
	SOLOMON, the Porkman.
PURGANAX } Wizards,	ZEPHANIAH, Pig-butcher.
DAKRY } Ministers	
LAOCTONOS } of SWELL-FOOT.	

Chorus of the Swinish Multitude.
GUARDS, ATTENDANTS, PRIESTS, etc., etc.

SCENE. Thebes.

ACT I

SCENE — *A magnificent Temple, built of thigh-
bones and death's-heads, and tiled with scalps.
Over the Altar the statue of Famine, veiled;
a number of boars, sows and sucking-pigs,
crowned with thistle, shamrock and oak, sitting
on the steps and clinging round the Altar of
the Temple.*

Enter SWELLFOOT, *in his royal robes, without
perceiving the Pigs.*

SWELLFOOT

THOU supreme goddess! by whose power
divine

dramatic representations) elucidating the wonderful and appalling fortunes of the Swellfoot
dynasty. It was evidently written by some
learned Theban; and, from its characteristic
dulness, apparently before the duties on the
importation of *Attic salt* had been repealed by
the Bœotarchs. The tenderness with which
he treats the Pigs proves him to have been a
sus Bœotiæ; possibly *Epicuri de grege porcus;*
for, as the poet observes,

' A fellow feeling makes us wondrous kind.'

No liberty has been taken with the translation of this remarkable piece of antiquity
except the suppressing a seditious and blas-
phemous Chorus of the Pigs and Bulls at the
last act. The word Hoydipouse (or more
properly Œdipus), has been rendered literally
Swellfoot without its having been conceived
necessary to determine whether a swelling of
the hind or the fore feet of the Swinish monarch is particularly indicated.

Should the remaining portions of this Tragedy be found, entitled *Swellfoot in Angaria* and
Charité, the Translator might be tempted to
give them to the reading Public.

These graceful limbs are clothed in proud
array
[*He contemplates himself with satisfaction.*
Of gold and purple, and this kingly paunch
Swells like a sail before a favoring breeze,
And these most sacred nether promontories
Lie satisfied with layers of fat; and these
Bœotian cheeks, like Egypt's pyramid,
(Nor with less toil were their foundations
laid)
Sustain the cone of my untroubled brain,
That point, the emblem of a pointless
nothing!   10
Thou to whom Kings and laurelled Em-
perors,
Radical-butchers, Paper-money-millers,
Bishops and deacons, and the entire army
Of those fat martyrs to the persecution
Of stifling turtle-soup and brandy-devils,
Offer their secret vows! thou plenteous
Ceres
Of their Eleusis, hail!

SWINE

Eigh! eigh! eigh! eigh!

SWELLFOOT

Ha! what are ye,
Who, crowned with leaves devoted to the
Furies,
Cling round this sacred shrine?

SWINE

Aigh! aigh! aigh!

SWELLFOOT

                    What! ye that are
The very beasts that, offered at her altar 20
With blood and groans, salt-cake, and fat,
    and inwards,
Ever propitiate her reluctant will
When taxes are withheld?

SWINE

Ugh! ugh! ugh!

SWELLFOOT

                    What! ye who grub
With filthy snouts my red potatoes up
In Allan's rushy bog? who eat the oats
Up, from my cavalry in the Hebrides?
Who swill the hog-wash soup my cooks
    digest
From bones, and rags, and scraps of shoe-
    leather,
Which should be given to cleaner Pigs
    than you?

SEMICHORUS I OF SWINE

The same, alas! the same;   30
Though only now the name
    Of Pig remains to me.

SEMICHORUS II OF SWINE

If 't were your kingly will
Us wretched Swine to kill,
    What should we yield to thee?

SWELLFOOT

Why, skin and bones, and some few hairs
    for mortar.

CHORUS OF SWINE

I have heard your Laureate sing
That pity was a royal thing;
Under your mighty ancestors we Pigs
Were blessed as nightingales on myrtle
    sprigs   40
Or grasshoppers that live on noonday
    dew,
And sung, old annals tell, as sweetly too;
But now our sties are fallen in, we catch
    The murrain and the mange, the scab
    and itch;
Sometimes your royal dogs tear down our
    thatch,
    And then we seek the shelter of a ditch;

Hog-wash or grains, or rutabaga, none
Has yet been ours since your reign begun.

FIRST SOW

My Pigs, 't is in vain to tug.

SECOND SOW

I could almost eat my litter.   50

FIRST PIG

I suck, but no milk will come from the
    dug.

SECOND PIG

Our skin and our bones would be bit-
    ter.

BOARS

We fight for this rag of greasy rug,
    Though a trough of wash would be fit-
    ter.

SEMICHORUS

Happier Swine were they than we,
Drowned in the Gadarean sea!
I wish that pity would drive out the devils
Which in your royal bosom hold their
    revels,
And sink us in the waves of thy compas-
    sion!
Alas, the Pigs are an unhappy nation!   60
Now if your Majesty would have our bris-
    tles
    To bind your mortar with, or fill our
    colons
With rich blood, or make brawn out of our
    gristles,
    In policy — ask else your royal Solons —
You ought to give us hog-wash and clean
    straw,
And sties well thatched; besides, it is the
    law!

SWELLFOOT

This is sedition, and rank blasphemy!
Ho! there, my guards!

Enter a GUARD

GUARD

                    Your sacred Majesty.

SWELLFOOT

Call in the Jews, Solomon the court Porkman,

Moses the Sow-gelder, and Zephaniah   70
The Hog-butcher.

GUARD
They are in waiting, Sire.

Enter SOLOMON, MOSES, *and* ZEPHANIAH

SWELLFOOT
Out with your knife, old Moses, and spay
  those Sows
     [*The Pigs run about in consternation.*
That load the earth with Pigs; cut close
  and deep.
Moral restraint I see has no effect,
Nor prostitution, nor our own example,
Starvation, typhus-fever, war, nor prison.
This was the art which the arch-priest of
  Famine
Hinted at in his charge to the Theban
  clergy.
Cut close and deep, good Moses.

MOSES
               Let your Majesty
Keep the Boars quiet, else —

SWELLFOOT
              Zephaniah, cut   80
That fat Hog's throat, the brute seems
  overfed;
Seditious hunks! to whine for want of
  grains!

ZEPHANIAH
Your sacred Majesty, he has the dropsy.
We shall find pints of hydatids in 's liver;
He has not half an inch of wholesome fat
Upon his carious ribs —

SWELLFOOT
             'T is all the same.
He 'll serve instead of riot-money, when
Our murmuring troops bivouac in Thebes'
  streets;
And January winds, after a day
Of butchering, will make them relish car-
  rion.   90
Now, Solomon, I 'll sell you in a lump
The whole kit of them.

SOLOMON
            Why, your Majesty,
I could not give —

SWELLFOOT
          Kill them out of the way —
That shall be price enough; and let me
  hear
Their everlasting grunts and whines no
  more!
       [*Exeunt, driving in the Swine.*

Enter MAMMON, *the Arch-Priest; and* PUR-
GANAX, *Chief of the Council of Wizards*

PURGANAX
The future looks as black as death; a cloud,
Dark as the frown of Hell, hangs over it.
The troops grow mutinous, the revenue
  fails,
There 's something rotten in us; for the
  level   99
Of the state slopes, its very bases topple;
The boldest turn their backs upon them-
  selves!

MAMMON
Why, what 's the matter, my dear fellow,
  now?
Do the troops mutiny? — decimate some
  regiments.
Does money fail? — come to my mint —
  coin paper,
Till gold be at a discount, and, ashamed
To show his bilious face, go purge himself,
In emulation of her vestal whiteness.

PURGANAX
Oh, would that this were all! The oracle!!

MAMMON
Why it was I who spoke that oracle,   109
And whether I was dead-drunk or inspired
I cannot well remember; nor, in truth,
The oracle itself!

PURGANAX
            The words went thus:
' Bœotia, choose reform or civil war,
When through thy streets, instead of hare
  with dogs,
A Consort-Queen shall hunt a King with
  hogs,
Riding on the Ionian Minotaur.'

MAMMON
Now if the oracle had ne'er foretold
This sad alternative, it must arrive,

Or not, and so it must now that it has;
And whether I was urged by grace divine
Or Lesbian liquor to declare these words,
Which must, as all words must, be false
     or true,   122
It matters not; for the same power made
     all,
Oracle, wine, and me and you — or none —
'T is the same thing. If you knew as much
Of oracles as I do —

PURGANAX
             You arch-priests
Believe in nothing; if you were to dream
Of a particular number in the lottery,
You would not buy the ticket !

MAMMON
             Yet our tickets
Are seldom blanks. But what steps have
     you taken ?   130
For prophecies, when once they get abroad,
Like liars who tell the truth to serve their
     ends,
Or hypocrites, who, from assuming virtue,
Do the same actions that the virtuous do,
Contrive their own fulfilment. This Iona —
Well — you know what the chaste Pasiphaë
     did,
Wife to that most religious King of Crete,
And still how popular the tale is here;
And these dull Swine of Thebes boast their
     descent
From the free Minotaur. You know they
     still   140
Call themselves Bulls, though thus degen-
     erate;
And everything relating to a Bull
Is popular and respectable in Thebes;
Their arms are seven Bulls in a field gules;
They think their strength consists in eating
     beef;
Now there were danger in the precedent
If Queen Iona —

PURGANAX
             I have taken good care
That shall not be. I struck the crust o'
     the earth
With this enchanted rod, and Hell lay
     bare !
And from a cavern full of ugly shapes, 150
I chose a Leech, a Gadfly, and a Rat.
The gadfly was the same which Juno sent
To agitate Io, and which Ezekiel mentions

That the Lord whistled for out of the
     mountains
Of utmost Æthiopia to torment
Mesopotamian Babylon. The beast
Has a loud trumpet like the Scarabee;
His crookèd tail is barbed with many
     stings,
Each able to make a thousand wounds, and
     each
Immedicable; from his convex eyes   160
He sees fair things in many hideous shapes,
And trumpets all his falsehood to the
     world.
Like other beetles he is fed on dung;
He has eleven feet with which he crawls,
Trailing a blistering slime; and this foul
     beast
Has tracked Iona from the Theban limits,
From isle to isle, from city unto city,
Urging her flight from the far Chersonese
To fabulous Solyma and the Ætnean Isle,
Ortygia, Melite, and Calypso's Rock,   170
And the swart tribes of Garamant and Fez,
Æolia and Elysium, and thy shores,
Parthenope, which now, alas ! are free !
And through the fortunate Saturnian land
Into the darkness of the West.

MAMMON
             But if
This Gadfly should drive Iona hither ?

PURGANAX
Gods ! what an *if!* but there is my gray
     Rat,
So thin with want he can crawl in and out
Of any narrow chink and filthy hole,   179
And he shall creep into her dressing-room,
And —

MAMMON
My dear friend, where are your wits ?
     as if
She does not always toast a piece of cheese,
And bait the trap ? and rats, when lean
     enough
To crawl through *such* chinks —

PURGANAX
             But my Leech — a leech
Fit to suck blood, with lubricous round
     rings,
Capaciously expatiative, which make
His little body like a red balloon,
As full of blood as that of hydrogen,

Sucked from men's hearts; insatiably he
  sucks
And clings and pulls — a horse-leech whose
  deep maw   190
The plethoric King Swellfoot could not
  fill,
And who, till full, will cling forever.

MAMMON

                       This
For Queen Iona might suffice, and less;
But 't is the Swinish multitude I fear,
And in that fear I have —

PURGANAX

           Done what?

MAMMON

                Disinherited
My eldest son Chrysaor, because he
Attended public meetings, and would al-
  ways
Stand prating there of commerce, public
  faith,
Economy, and unadulterate coin,
And other topics, ultra-radical;   200
And have entailed my estate, called the
  Fool's Paradise,
And funds in fairy-money, bonds, and bills,
Upon my accomplished daughter Bankno-
  tina,
And married her to the Gallows.

PURGANAX

           A good match!

MAMMON

A high connection, Purganax. The bride-
  groom
Is of a very ancient family,
Of Hounslow Heath, Tyburn, and the New
  Drop,
And has great influence in both Houses. Oh,
He makes the fondest husband; nay, *too*
  fond —
New married people should not kiss in
  public;   210
But the poor souls love one another so!
And then my little grandchildren, the
  Gibbets,
Promising children as you ever saw, —
The young playing at hanging, the elder
  learning

How to hold radicals. They are well
  taught too,
For every Gibbet says its catechism,
And reads a select chapter in the Bible
Before it goes to play.

    (*A most tremendous humming is heard*)

PURGANAX

        Ha! what do I hear?

Enter the GADFLY

MAMMON

Your Gadfly, as it seems, is tired of gad-
  ding.

GADFLY

Hum, hum, hum!   220
From the lakes of the Alps and the cold
  gray scalps
    Of the mountains, I come!
Hum, hum, hum!
From Morocco and Fez, and the high
  palaces
    Of golden Byzantium;
From the temples divine of old Palestine,
    From Athens and Rome,
    With a ha! and a hum!
    I come, I come!

All inn-doors and windows   230
    Were open to me;
    I saw all that sin does,
    Which lamps hardly see
That burn in the night by the curtained
  bed —
The impudent lamps! for they blushed not
  red.
    Dinging and singing,
    From slumber I rung her,
    Loud as the clank of an ironmon-
      ger;
    Hum, hum, hum!

Far, far, far,   240
With the trump of my lips and the sting
  at my hips,
    I drove her — afar!
    Far, far, far,
From city to city, abandoned of pity,
  A ship without needle or star;
Homeless she passed, like a cloud on the
  blast,
    Seeking peace, finding war;
    She is here in her car,

From afar, and afar.
   Hum, hum !   250

I have stung her and wrung her !
   The venom is working;
And if you had hung her
   With canting and quirking,
She could not be deader than she will be
   soon;
I have driven her close to you, under the
   moon,
   Night and day, hum, hum, ha !
I have hummed her and drummed her
From place to place, till at last I have
   dumbed her,
   Hum, hum, hum !   260

Enter the LEECH *and the* RAT

LEECH

I will suck
   Blood or muck !
The disease of the state is a plethory,
Who so fit to reduce it as I ?

RAT

I 'll slyly seize and
   Let blood from her weasand, —
Creeping through crevice, and chink, and
   cranny,
With my snaky tail, and my sides so
   scranny.

PURGANAX

Aroint ye, thou unprofitable worm :
       (*To the* LEECH)
And thou, dull beetle, get thee back to
   hell,   270
       (*To the* GADFLY)
To sting the ghosts of Babylonian kings,
And the ox-headed Io.

SWINE (*within*)
           Ugh, ugh, ugh !
Hail, Iona the divine !
We will be no longer Swine,
But Bulls with horns and dewlaps.

RAT
            For,
You know, my lord, the Minotaur —

PURGANAX (*fiercely*)
Be silent ! get to hell ! or I will call

The cat out of the kitchen.   Well, Lord
   Mammon,
This is a pretty business !
           [*Exit the* RAT.

MAMMON
           I will go
And spell some scheme to make it ugly
   then.   280
           [*Exit.*

Enter SWELLFOOT

SWELLFOOT

She is returned ! Taurina is in Thebes
When Swellfoot wishes that she were in
   hell !
O Hymen ! clothed in yellow jealousy
And waving o'er the couch of wedded
   kings
The torch of Discord with its fiery hair —
This is thy work, thou patron saint of
   queens !
Swellfoot is wived ! though parted by the
   sea,
The very name of wife had conjugal rights;
Her cursed image ate, drank, slept with
   me,
And in the arms of Adiposa oft   290
Her memory has received a husband's —

(*A loud tumult, and cries of* 'IONA FOREVER !
     — NO SWELLFOOT !')

SWELLFOOT
           Hark !
How the Swine cry Iona Taurina !
I suffer the real presence.   Purganax,
Off with her head !

PURGANAX
         But I must first impanel
A jury of the Pigs.

SWELLFOOT
         Pack them then.

PURGANAX

Or fattening some few in two separate sties,
And giving them clean straw, tying some
   bits
Of ribbon round their legs — giving their
   Sows
Some tawdry lace and bits of lustre glass,
And their young Boars white and red rags,
   and tails   300

Of cows, and jay feathers, and sticking
        cauliflowers
Between the ears of the old ones; and when
They are persuaded that, by the inherent
        virtue
Of these things, they are all imperial Pigs,
Good Lord ! they 'd rip each other's bellies
        up,
Not to say help us in destroying her.

SWELLFOOT

This plan might be tried too.   Where 's
        General
Laoctonos ?

Enter LAOCTONOS
                It is my royal pleasure
That you, Lord General, bring the head
        and body,
If separate it would please me better,
        hither   310
Of Queen Iona.

LAOCTONOS
                        That pleasure I well knew,
And made a charge with those battalions
        bold,
Called, from their dress and grin, the
        Royal Apes,
Upon the Swine, who in a hollow square
Enclosed her, and received the first attack
Like so many rhinoceroses, and then
Retreating in good order, with bare tusks
And wrinkled snouts presented to the foe,
Bore her in triumph to the public sty.
What is still worse, some Sows upon the
        ground   320
Have given the Ape-guards apples, nuts
        and gin,
And they all whisk their tails aloft, and
        cry,
'Long live Iona ! down with Swellfoot !'

PURGANAX
                                        Hark.

THE SWINE (*without*)
Long live Iona ! down with Swellfoot !

Enter DAKRY

DAKRY

Went to the garret of the Swineherd's
        tower,

Which overlooks the sty, and made a long
Harangue (all words) to the assembled
        Swine,
Of delicacy, mercy, judgment, law,
Morals, and precedents, and purity,
Adultery, destitution, and divorce,   330
Piety, faith, and state necessity,
And how I loved the Queen ! — and then
        I wept
With the pathos of my own eloquence,
And every tear turned to a millstone
        which
Brained many a gaping Pig, and there was
        made
A slough of blood and brains upon the
        place,
Greased with the pounded bacon; round
        and round
The millstones rolled, ploughing the pave-
        ment up,
And hurling sucking Pigs into the air,
With dust and stones.

Enter MAMMON

MAMMON
                I wonder that gray wizards
Like you should be so beardless in their
        schemes;   341
It had been but a point of policy
To keep Iona and the Swine apart.
Divide and rule ! but ye have made a junc-
        tion
Between two parties who will govern you,
But for my art. — Behold this Bag ! it is
The poison Bag of that Green Spider huge,
On which our spies skulked in ovation
        through
The streets of Thebes, when they were
        paved with dead: 349
A bane so much the deadlier fills it now
As calumny is worse than death; for here
The Gadfly's venom, fifty times distilled,
Is mingled with the vomit of the Leech,
In due proportion, and black ratsbane,
        which
That very Rat, who, like the Pontic ty-
        rant,
Nurtures himself on poison, dare not touch.
All is sealed up with the broad seal of
        Fraud,
Who is the Devil's Lord High Chancellor,
And over it the Primate of all Hell
Murmured this pious baptism: — 'Be thou
        called   360

The Green Bag; and this power and grace
   be thine:
That thy contents, on whomsoever poured,
Turn innocence to guilt, and gentlest looks
To savage, foul, and fierce deformity;
Let all baptized by thy infernal dew
Be called adulterer, drunkard, liar, wretch !
No name left out which orthodoxy loves,
Court Journal or legitimate Review !
Be they called tyrant, beast, fool, glutton,
   lover
Of other wives and husbands than their
   own —   370
The heaviest sin on this side of the Alps !
Wither they to a ghastly caricature
Of what was human ! — let not man or
   beast
Behold their face with unaverted eyes,
Or hear their names with ears that tingle
   not
With blood of indignation, rage, and
   shame !'
This is a perilous liquor, good my Lords.
[SWELLFOOT *approaches to touch the Green Bag.*
Beware ! for God's sake, beware ! — if you
   should break
The seal, and touch the fatal liquor —

PURGANAX
                      There,
Give it to me. I have been used to handle
All sorts of poisons. His dread Majesty
Only desires to see the color of it.   382

MAMMON
Now, with a little common sense, my
   Lords,
Only undoing all that has been done,
(Yet so as it may seem we but confirm it)
Our victory is assured. We must entice
Her Majesty from the sty, and make the
   Pigs
Believe that the contents of the Green
   Bag
Are the true test of guilt or innocence;
And that, if she be guilty, 't will transform
   her   390
To manifest deformity like guilt;
If innocent, she will become transfigured
Into an angel, such as they say she is;
And they will see her flying through the
   air,
So bright that she will dim the noonday
   sun,

Showering down blessings in the shape of
   comfits.
This, trust a priest, is just the sort of
   thing
Swine will believe. I 'll wager you will
   see them
Climbing upon the thatch of their low sties,
With pieces of smoked glass, to watch her
   sail   400
Among the clouds, and some will hold the
   flaps
Of one another's ears between their teeth,
To catch the coming hail of comfits in.
You, Purganax, who have the gift o' the
   gab,
Make them a solemn speech to this effect.
I go to put in readiness the feast
Kept to the honor of our goddess Famine,
Where, for more glory, let the ceremony
Take place of the uglification of the Queen.

DAKRY (*to* SWELLFOOT)
I, as the keeper of your sacred conscience,
Humbly remind your Majesty that the
   care   411
Of your high office, as Man-milliner
Te red Bellona, should not be deferred.

PURGANAX
All part, in happier plight to meet again.
                    [*Exeunt.*

ACT II

SCENE I.— *The Public Sty. The Boars in full
   Assembly.*

Enter PURGANAX

PURGANAX
GRANT me your patience, Gentlemen and
   Boars,
Ye, by whose patience under public bur-
   dens
The glorious constitution of these sties
Subsists, and shall subsist. The Lean-Pig
   rates
Grow with the growing populace of Swine;
The taxes, that true source of Piggishness,
(How can I find a more appropriate term
To include religion, morals, peace and
   plenty,
And all that fit Bœotia as a nation
To teach the other nations how to live ?) 10

Increase with Piggishness itself; and still
Does the revenue, that great spring of all
The patronage, and pensions, and by-pay-
    ments,
Which free-born Pigs regard with jealous
    eyes,
Diminish, till at length, by glorious steps,
All the land's produce will be merged in
    taxes,
And the revenue will amount to —— no-
    thing !
The failure of a foreign market for
Sausages, bristles, and blood-puddings,
And such home manufactures, is but par-
    tial;   20
And, that the population of the Pigs,
Instead of hog-wash, has been fed on straw
And water, is a fact which is — you
    know —
That is — it is a state necessity —
Temporary, of course. Those impious
    Pigs,
Who, by frequent squeaks, have dared im-
    pugn
The settled Swellfoot system, or to make
Irreverent mockery of the genuflexions
Inculcated by the arch-priest, have been
    whipped
Into a loyal and an orthodox whine.   30
Things being in this happy state, the Queen
Iona ——

    (A loud cry from the Pigs)
    She is innocent, most innocent !

PURGANAX

That is the very thing that I was saying,
Gentlemen Swine; the Queen Iona being
Most innocent, no doubt, returns to Thebes,
And the lean Sows and Boars collect about
    her,
Wishing to make her think that *we* believe
(I mean those more substantial Pigs who
    swill
Rich hog-wash, while the others mouth
    damp straw)
That she is guilty; thus, the Lean-Pig fac-
    tion   40
Seeks to obtain that hog-wash, which has
    been
Your immemorial right, and which I will
Maintain you in to the last drop of —

    A BOAR *(interrupting him)*
                      What
Does any one accuse her of ?

PURGANAX
                    Why, no one
Makes *any* positive accusation; but
There were hints dropped, and so the privy
    wizards
Conceived that it became them to advise
His Majesty to investigate their truth;
Not for his own sake; he could be content
To let his wife play any pranks she pleased,
If, by that sufferance, *he* could please the
    Pigs;   51
But then he fears the morals of the Swine,
The Sows especially, and what effect
It might produce upon the purity and
Religion of the rising generation
Of sucking Pigs, if it could be suspected
That Queen Iona —

                      (A pause)

    FIRST BOAR
           Well, go on; we long
To hear what she can possibly have done.

PURGANAX

Why, it is hinted, that a certain Bull —
Thus much is *known :* — the milk-white
    Bulls that feed   60
Beside Clitumnus and the crystal lakes
Of the Cisalpine mountains, in fresh dews
Of lotus-grass and blossoming asphodel
Sleeking their silken hair, and with sweet
    breath
Loading the morning winds until they
    faint
With living fragrance, are so beautiful !
Well, *I* say nothing; but Europa rode
On such a one from Asia into Crete,
And the enamoured sea grew calm be-
    neath
His gliding beauty. And Pasiphaë,   70
Iona's grandmother, —— but *she* is inno-
    cent !
And that both you and I, and all assert.

    FIRST BOAR
Most innocent !

    PURGANAX
          Behold this Bag; a Bag —

    SECOND BOAR
Oh ! no Green Bags ! ! Jealousy's eyes
    are green,
Scorpions are green, and water-snakes,
    and efts,
And verdigris, and —

PURGANAX

          Honorable Swine,
In Piggish souls can prepossessions reign ?
Allow me to remind you, grass is green —
All flesh is grass; no bacon but is flesh —
Ye are but bacon. This divining Bag   80
(Which is not green, but only bacon color)
Is filled with liquor, which if sprinkled o'er
A woman guilty of — we all know what —
Makes her so hideous, till she finds one
    blind
She never can commit the like again;
If innocent, she will turn into an angel
And rain down blessings in the shape of
    comfits
As she flies up to heaven. Now, my pro-
    posal
Is to convert her sacred Majesty   89
Into an angel (as I am sure we shall do)
By pouring on her head this mystic water.
            [*Showing the Bag.*
I know that she is innocent; I wish
Only to prove her so to all the world.

FIRST BOAR

Excellent, just, and noble Purganax !

SECOND BOAR

How glorious it will be to see her Majesty
Flying above our heads, her petticoats
Streaming like — like — like —

THIRD BOAR

          Anything.

PURGANAX

          Oh, no !
But like a standard of an admiral's ship,
Or like the banner of a conquering host,
Or like a cloud dyed in the dying day,   100
Unravelled on the blast from a white
    mountain;
Or like a meteor, or a war-steed's mane,
Or waterfall from a dizzy precipice
Scattered upon the wind.

FIRST BOAR

          Or a cow's tail, —

SECOND BOAR

Or *anything*, as the learned Boar observed.

PURGANAX

Gentlemen Boars, I move a resolution,
That her most sacred Majesty should be

Invited to attend the feast of Famine,
And to receive upon her chaste white
    body
Dews of apotheosis from this Bag.   110

[*A great confusion is heard, of the Pigs out of
Doors, which communicates itself to those
within. During the first strophe, the doors
of the sty are staved in, and a number of exceedingly lean Pigs and Sows and Boars
rush in.*

SEMICHORUS I

No ! Yes !

SEMICHORUS II

Yes ! No !

SEMICHORUS I

A law !

SEMICHORUS II

A flaw !

SEMICHORUS I

Porkers, we shall lose our wash,
Or must share it with the Lean-Pigs !

FIRST BOAR

Order ! order ! be not rash !
Was there ever such a scene, Pigs !

AN OLD SOW (*rushing in*)

I never saw so fine a dash
Since I first began to wean Pigs.   120

SECOND BOAR (*solemnly*)

The Queen will be an angel time enough.
I vote, in form of an amendment, that
Purganax rub a little of that stuff
Upon his face —

PURGANAX (*his heart is seen to beat through his
waistcoat*)

        Gods ! What would ye be at ?

SEMICHORUS I

Purganax has plainly shown a
Cloven foot and jackdaw feather.

SEMICHORUS II

I vote Swellfoot and Iona
Try the magic test together;
Whenever royal spouses bicker,
Both should try the magic liquor.   130

AN OLD BOAR (*aside*)

A miserable state is that of Pigs,
For if their drivers would tear caps and
    wigs,
The Swine must bite each other's ear there-
    for.

AN OLD SOW (*aside*)

A wretched lot Jove has assigned to
    Swine,
Squabbling makes Pig-herds hungry, and
    they dine
On bacon, and whip sucking Pigs the more.

CHORUS

Hog-wash has been ta'en away;
    If the Bull-Queen is divested,
We shall be in every way
    Hunted, stripped, exposed, molested;
Let us do whate'er we may,   141
    That she shall not be arrested.
Queen, we entrench you with walls of
    brawn,
    And palisades of tusks, sharp as a bayo-
    net.
Place your most Sacred Person here. We
    pawn
    Our lives that none a finger dare to lay
    on it.
Those who wrong you, wrong us;
Those who hate you, hate us;
Those who sting you, sting us;
Those who bait you, bait us;   150
The *oracle* is now about to be
Fulfilled by circumvolving destiny,
Which says: 'Thebes, choose reform or
    civil war,
When through your streets, instead of
    hare with dogs,
A Consort-Queen shall hunt a King with
    hogs,
Riding upon the Ionian Minotaur.'

Enter IONA TAURINA

IONA TAURINA (*coming forward*)

Gentlemen Swine, and gentle Lady-Pigs,
The tender heart of every Boar acquits
Their Queen of any act incongruous   159
With native Piggishness, and she reposing
With confidence upon the grunting nation,
Has thrown herself, her cause, her life, her
    all,
Her innocence, into their Hoggish arms;
Nor has the expectation been deceived

Of finding shelter there.   Yet know, great
    Boars,
(For such whoever lives among you finds
    you,
And so do I) the innocent are proud !
I have accepted your protection only
In compliment of your kind love and care,
Not for necessity.   The innocent   170
Are safest there where trials and dangers
    . wait;
Innocent queens o'er white-hot plough-
    shares tread
Unsinged; and ladies, Erin's laureate sings
    it,
Decked with rare gems, and beauty rarer
    still,
Walked from Killarney to the Giant's
    Causeway
Through rebels, smugglers, troops of yeo-
    manry,
White-boys, and Orange-boys, and consta-
    bles,
Tithe-proctors, and excise people, unin-
    jured !
Thus I ! —
Lord Purganax, I do commit myself   180
Into your custody, and am prepared
To stand the test, whatever it may be !

PURGANAX

This magnanimity in your sacred Majesty
Must please the Pigs. You cannot fail of
    being
A heavenly angel. Smoke your bits of
    glass,
Ye loyal Swine, or her transfiguration
Will blind your wondering eyes.

AN OLD BOAR (*aside*)

                    Take care, my Lord,
They do not smoke you first.

PURGANAX

                    At the approaching feast
Of Famine let the expiation be.

SWINE

Content   content !

IONA TAURINA (*aside*)

            I, most content of all,   190
Know that my foes even thus prepare their
    fall !

                    [*Exeunt omnes.*

SCENE II. — *The interior of the Temple of Famine. The statue of the Goddess, a skeleton clothed in party-colored rags, seated upon a heap of skulls and loaves intermingled. A number of exceedingly fat Priests in black garments arrayed on each side, with marrow-bones and cleavers in their hands. A flourish of trumpets.*

Enter MAMMON *as Arch-priest*, SWELLFOOT, DAKRY, PURGANAX, LAOCTONOS, *followed by* IONA TAURINA *guarded. On the other side enter the Swine.*

CHORUS OF PRIESTS (*accompanied by the Court Porkman on marrow-bones and cleavers*)

Goddess bare, and gaunt, and pale,
Empress of the world, all hail !
What though Cretans old called thee
City-crested Cybele ?
We call thee Famine !
Goddess of fasts and feasts, starving and
    cramming;
Through thee, for emperors, kings and
    priests and lords,
Who rule by viziers, sceptres, bank-notes,
    words,
    The earth pours forth its plenteous fruits,
    Corn, wool, linen, flesh, and roots.   10
Those who consume these fruits through
    thee grow fat,
Those who produce these fruits through
    thee grow lean,
Whatever change takes place, oh, stick to
    that,
    And let things be as they have ever
    been;
    At least while we remain thy priests,
    And proclaim thy fasts and feasts !
Through thee the sacred Swellfoot dynasty
Is based upon a rock amid that sea
Whose waves are Swine — so let it ever be !

[SWELLFOOT, *etc., seat themselves at a table, magnificently covered, at the upper end of the temple. Attendants pass over the stage with hog-wash in pails. A number of Pigs, exceedingly lean, follow them, licking up the wash.*

MAMMON

I fear your sacred Majesty has lost   20
The appetite which you were used to have.
Allow me now to recommend this dish —
A simple kickshaw by your Persian cook,
Such as is served at the great King's second
    table.

The price and pains which its ingredients
    cost
Might have maintained some dozen families
A winter or two — not more — so plain a
    dish
Could scarcely disagree.

SWELLFOOT

             After the trial,
And these fastidious Pigs are gone, perhaps
I may recover my lost appetite.   30
I feel the gout flying about my stomach;
Give me a glass of Maraschino punch.

PURGANAX (*filling his glass, and standing up*)
The glorious constitution of the Pigs !

ALL

A toast ! a toast ! stand up, and three
    times three !

DAKRY

No heel-taps — darken day-lights !

LAOCTONOS

             Claret, somehow,
Puts me in mind of blood, and blood of
    claret !

SWELLFOOT

Laoctonos is fishing for a compliment;
But 't is his due. Yes, you have drunk
    more wine,
And shed more blood, than any man in
    Thebes.

(*To* PURGANAX)

For God's sake stop the grunting of those
    Pigs !   40

PURGANAX

We dare not, Sire ! 't is Famine's privi-
    lege.

CHORUS OF SWINE

Hail to thee, hail to thee, Famine !
    Thy throne is on blood, and thy robe is
        of rags;
Thou devil which livest on damning;
    Saint of new churches and cant, and
        Green Bags;
Till in pity and terror thou risest,
Confounding the schemes of the wisest;
When thou liftest thy skeleton form,
    When the loaves and the skulls roll
        about,

We will greet thee — the voice of a storm
Would be lost in our terrible shout !   51

Then hail to thee, hail to thee, Famine !
Hail to thee, Empress of Earth !
When thou risest, dividing possessions,
When thou risest, uprooting oppressions,
In the pride of thy ghastly mirth;
Over palaces, temples, and graves
   We will rush as thy minister-slaves,
   Trampling behind in thy train,
   Till all be made level again !   60

MAMMON

I hear a crackling of the giant bones
Of the dread image, and in the black pits
Which once were eyes, I see two livid
   flames.
These prodigies are oracular, and show
The presence of the unseen Deity.
Mighty events are hastening to their doom !

SWELLFOOT

I only hear the lean and mutinous Swine
Grunting about the temple.

DAKRY

           In a crisis
Of such exceeding delicacy, I think   69
We ought to put her Majesty, the Queen,
Upon her trial without delay.

MAMMON

                The Bag
Is here.

PURGANAX

      I have rehearsed the entire scene
With an ox-bladder and some ditch-water,
On Lady P——; it cannot fail.

> [*Taking up the Bag.*
         Your Majesty

     (*To* SWELLFOOT)
In such a filthy business had better
Stand on one side, lest it should sprinkle you.
A spot or two on me would do no harm;
Nay, it might hide the blood, which the sad
     genius
Of the Green Isle has fixed, as by a spell,
Upon my brow — which would stain all its
     seas,   80
But which those seas could never wash
     away !

IONA TAURINA

My Lord, I am ready — nay, I am impatient,
To undergo the test.

[*A graceful figure in a semi-transparent veil
passes unnoticed through the Temple ; the word
LIBERTY is seen through the veil, as if it were
written in fire upon its forehead. Its words
are almost drowned in the furious grunting of
the Pigs, and the business of the trial. She
kneels on the steps of the Altar, and speaks in
tones at first faint and low, but which ever become louder and louder.*

LIBERTY

Mighty Empress, Death's white wife,
   Ghastly mother-in-law of life !
By the God who made thee such,
By the magic of thy touch,
By the starving and the cramming
Of fasts and feasts ! — by thy dread self,
   O Famine !
I charge thee, when thou wake the multi-
   tude,   90
Thou lead them not upon the paths of
   blood.
The earth did never mean her foison
For those who crown life's cup with poison
Of fanatic rage and meaningless revenge;
   But for those radiant spirits, who are
     still
The standard-bearers in the van of Change.
   Be they th' appointed stewards, to fill
The lap of Pain, and Toil, and Age !
Remit, O Queen ! thy accustomed rage !
Be what thou art not ! In voice faint and
   low   100
Freedom calls Famine, her eternal foe,
To brief alliance, hollow truce. — Rise
   now !

[*Whilst the veiled figure has been chanting the
strophe, MAMMON, DAKRY, LAOCTONOS, and
SWELLFOOT have surrounded IONA TAURINA,
who, with her hands folded on her breast and
her eyes lifted to Heaven, stands, as with
saint-like resignation, to wait the issue of the
business in perfect confidence of her innocence.
PURGANAX, after unsealing the Green Bag, is
gravely about to pour the liquor upon her head,
when suddenly the whole expression of her
figure and countenance changes ; she snatches
it from his hand with a loud laugh of triumph,
and empties it over SWELLFOOT and his whole
Court, who are instantly changed into a number*

of filthy and ugly animals, and rush out of the Temple. The image of Famine then arises with a tremendous sound, the Pigs begin scrambling for the loaves, and are tripped up by the skulls; all those who eat the loaves are turned into Bulls, and arrange themselves quietly behind the altar. The image of Famine sinks through a chasm in the earth, and a MINOTAUR rises.

MINOTAUR

I am the Ionian Minotaur, the mightiest
Of all Europa's taurine progeny;
I am the old traditional Man-Bull;
And from my ancestors having been Ionian
I am called Ion, which, by interpretation,
Is John; in plain Theban, that is to say,
My name's John Bull; I am a famous hunter,
And can leap any gate in all Bœotia,   110
Even the palings of the royal park
Or double ditch about the new enclosures;
And if your Majesty will deign to mount me,
At least till you have hunted down your game,
I will not throw you.

IONA TAURINA

[During this speech she has been putting on boots and spurs and a hunting-cap, buckishly cocked on one side; and, tucking up her hair, she leaps nimbly on his back.

Hoa, hoa! tally-ho! tally-ho! ho! ho!
Come, let us hunt these ugly badgers down,

These stinking foxes, these devouring otters,
These hares, these wolves, these anything but men.
Hey, for a whipper-in! my loyal Pigs,   120
Now let your noses be as keen as beagles',
Your steps as swift as greyhounds', and your cries
More dulcet and symphonious than the bells
Of village-towers, on sunshine holiday;
Wake all the dewy woods with jangling music.
Give them no law (are they not beasts of blood?)
But such as they gave you. Tally-ho! ho!
Through forest, furze and bog, and den and desert,
Pursue the ugly beasts! Tally-ho! ho!

FULL CHORUS OF IONA AND THE SWINE
Tally-ho! tally-ho!   130
Through rain, hail, and snow,
Through brake, gorse, and briar,
Through fen, flood, and mire,
We go, we go!

Tally-ho! tally-ho!
Through pond, ditch, and slough,
Wind them, and find them,
Like the Devil behind them!
Tally-ho, tally-ho!

[Exeunt, in full cry; IONA driving on the Swine, with the empty Green Bag.

EPIPSYCHIDION

VERSES ADDRESSED TO THE NOBLE AND UNFORTUNATE LADY

EMILIA V———

NOW IMPRISONED IN THE CONVENT OF ———

L' anima amante si slancia fuori del creato, e si crea nell' infinito un mondo tutto per essa, diverso assai da questo oscuro e pauroso baratro.

HER OWN WORDS.

The noble and unfortunate lady, Emilia V———, who inspired *Epipsychidion* was Teresa Emilia Viviani, eldest daughter of Count Viviani, a nobleman of Pisa. She had been placed by her family in the neighboring Convent of St. Anna, and there Shelley met her at the be-

ginning of December, 1820, and interested himself in her fortunes. The episode, which is too long for narration in a note, is best described in Mrs. Marshall's *Life of Mary Wollstonecraft Shelley*. Its personal incidents are unimportant, since they do not enter into the substance of the poem, which is 'an idealized history' of Shelley's spirit. The lady, to whom the verses are addressed, soon lost the enchantment which Shelley's imagination and sympathy had woven about her, and she ceased to interest him except as an object of compassion.

Shelley was fully aware of the mystical nature of the poem, which shows the most spiritual elements of his genius at their point of highest intensity of passion. He wrote to Gisborne: 'The *Epipsychidion* is a mystery; as to real flesh and blood, you know that I do not deal in those articles; you might as well go to a gin-shop for a leg of mutton, as expect anything human or earthly from me;' and again, 'The *Epipsychidion* I cannot look at; the person whom it celebrates was a cloud instead of a Juno, and poor Ixion starts from the centaur that was the offspring of his own embrace. If you are curious, however, to hear what I am and have been, it will tell you something thereof. It is an idealized history of my life and feelings. I think one is always in love with something or other; the error, and I confess it is not easy for spirits cased in flesh and blood to avoid it, consists in seeking in a mortal image the likeness of what is, perhaps, eternal.'

In sending it for publication to Ollier, he says: 'I send you . . . and a longer piece, entitled *Epipsychidion*. . . . The longer poem, I desire, should not be considered as my own; indeed, in a certain sense, it is a production of a portion of me already dead; and in this sense the advertisement is no fiction. It is to be published simply for the esoteric few; and I make its author a secret, to avoid the malignity of those who turn sweet food into poison, transforming all they touch into the corruption of their own natures. My wish with respect to it is that it should be printed immediately in the simplest form, and merely one hundred copies: those who are capable of judging and feeling rightly with respect to a composition of so abstruse a nature, certainly do not arrive at that number — among those, at least, who would ever be excited to read an obscure and anonymous production; and it would give me no pleasure that the vulgar should read it. If you have any book-selling reason against publishing so small a number as a hundred, merely, distribute copies among those to whom you think the poetry would afford any pleasure,

and send me, as soon as you can, a copy by the post.'

The poem was composed at Pisa during the first weeks of 1821, and an edition of one hundred copies was published at London the following summer. The title means, as Dr. Stopford Brooke points out, 'this soul out of my soul.'

ADVERTISEMENT

THE writer of the following lines died at Florence, as he was preparing for a voyage to one of the wildest of the Sporades, which he had bought and where he had fitted up the ruins of an old building, and where it was his hope to have realized a scheme of life, suited perhaps to that happier and better world of which he is now an inhabitant, but hardly practicable in this. His life was singular; less on account of the romantic vicissitudes which diversified it than the ideal tinge which it received from his own character and feelings. The present Poem, like the *Vita Nuova* of Dante, is sufficiently intelligible to a certain class of readers without a matter-of-fact history of the circumstances to which it relates; and to a certain other class it must ever remain incomprehensible from a defect of a common organ of perception for the ideas of which it treats. Not but that, *gran vergogna sarebbe a colui, che rimasse cosa sotto veste di figura o di colore rettorico: e domandato non sapesse denudare le sue parole da cotal veste, in guisa che avessero verace intendimento.*

The present poem appears to have been intended by the writer as the dedication to some longer one. The stanza on the opposite page [below] is almost a literal translation from Dante's famous Canzone

Voi, ch' intendendo, il terzo ciel movete, etc.

The presumptuous application of the concluding lines to his own composition will raise a smile at the expense of my unfortunate friend: be it a smile not of contempt, but pity.

My Song, I fear that thou wilt find but few
Who fitly shall conceive thy reasoning,
Of such hard matter dost thou entertain;
Whence, if by misadventure chance should bring
Thee to base company (as chance may do)
Quite unaware of what thou dost contain,
I prithee, comfort thy sweet self again,
My last delight! tell them that they are dull,
And bid them own that thou art beautiful.

SWEET Spirit! sister of that orphan one,
Whose empire is the name thou weepest on,
In my heart's temple I suspend to thee
These votive wreaths of withered memory.

Poor captive bird! who from thy narrow cage
Pourest such music that it might assuage
The rugged hearts of those who prisoned thee,

Were they not deaf to all sweet melody, —
This song shall be thy rose; its petals pale
Are dead, indeed, my adored nightingale !
But soft and fragrant is the faded blos-
    som,
And it has no thorn left to wound thy
    bosom.   12

  High, spirit-wingèd Heart ! who dost
    forever
Beat thine unfeeling bars with vain en-
    deavor,
Till those bright plumes of thought, in
    which arrayed
It over-soared this low and worldly shade,
Lie shattered; and thy panting wounded
    breast
Stains with dear blood its unmaternal nest !
I weep vain tears; blood would less bitter
    be,
Yet poured forth gladlier, could it profit
    thee.   20

  Seraph of Heaven ! too gentle to be
    human,
Veiling beneath that radiant form of Wo-
    man
All that is insupportable in thee
Of light, and love, and immortality !
Sweet Benediction in the eternal Curse !
Veiled glory of this lampless Universe !
Thou Moon beyond the clouds ! thou living
    Form
Among the Dead ! thou Star above the
    Storm !
Thou Wonder, and thou Beauty, and thou
    Terror !
Thou Harmony of Nature's art ! thou Mir-
    ror   30
In whom, as in the splendor of the Sun,
All shapes look glorious which thou gazest
    on !
Ay, even the dim words which obscure thee
    now
Flash, lightning-like, with unaccustomed
    glow;
I pray thee that thou blot from this sad
    song
All of its much mortality and wrong,
With those clear drops, which start like
    sacred dew
From the twin lights thy sweet soul dark-
    ens through,
Weeping, till sorrow becomes ecstasy —
Then smile on it, so that it may not die. 40

  I never thought before my death to see
Youth's vision thus made perfect. Emily,
I love thee; though the world by no thin
    name
Will hide that love from its unvalued
    shame.
Would we two had been twins of the same
    mother !
Or that the name my heart lent to another
Could be a sister's bond for her and thee,
Blending two beams of one eternity !
Yet were one lawful and the other true,
These names, though dear, could paint not,
    as is due,   50
How beyond refuge I am thine. Ah me !
I am not thine — I am a part of *thee.*

  Sweet Lamp ! my moth-like Muse has
    burned its wings;
Or, like a dying swan who soars and sings,
Young Love should teach Time, in his own
    gray style,
All that thou art. Art thou not void of
    guile,
A lovely soul formed to be blessed and
    bless ?
A well of sealed and secret happiness,
Whose waters like blithe light and music
    are,
Vanquishing dissonance and gloom ? a
    star   60
Which moves not in the moving Heavens,
    alone ?
A smile amid dark frowns ? a gentle tone
Amid rude voices ? a belovèd light ?
A solitude, a refuge, a delight ?
A lute, which those whom love has taught to
    play
Make music on, to soothe the roughest day
And lull fond grief asleep ? a buried trea-
    sure ?
A cradle of young thoughts of wingless
    pleasure ?
A violet-shrouded grave of woe ? — I mea-
    sure
The world of fancies, seeking one like thee,
And find — alas ! mine own infirmity.   71

  She met me, Stranger, upon life's rough
    way,
And lured me towards sweet death; as
    Night by Day,
Winter by Spring, or Sorrow by swift
    Hope,
Led into light, life, peace. An antelope,

In the suspended impulse of its lightness,
Were less ethereally light; the brightness
Of her divinest presence trembles through
Her limbs, as underneath a cloud of dew 79
Embodied in the windless heaven of June,
Amid the splendor-wingèd stars, the Moon
Burns, inextinguishably beautiful;
And from her lips, as from a hyacinth full
Of honey-dew, a liquid murmur drops,
Killing the sense with passion, sweet as stops
Of planetary music heard in trance.
In her mild lights the starry spirits dance,
The sunbeams of those wells which ever leap
Under the lightnings of the soul — too deep
For the brief fathom-line of thought or sense. 90
The glory of her being, issuing thence,
Stains the dead, blank, cold air with a warm shade
Of unentangled intermixture, made
By Love, of light and motion; one intense
Diffusion, one serene Omnipresence,
Whose flowing outlines mingle in their flowing,
Around her cheeks and utmost fingers glowing,
With the unintermitted blood, which there
Quivers (as in a fleece of snow-like air
The crimson pulse of living morning quiver) 100
Continuously prolonged, and ending never
Till they are lost, and in that Beauty furled
Which penetrates, and clasps and fills the world;
Scarce visible from extreme loveliness.
Warm fragrance seems to fall from her light dress,
And her loose hair; and where some heavy tress
The air of her own speed has disentwined,
The sweetness seems to satiate the faint wind;
And in the soul a wild odor is felt,
Beyond the sense, like fiery dews that melt
Into the bosom of a frozen bud. 111
See where she stands! a mortal shape indued
With love and life and light and deity,
And motion which may change but cannot die;
An image of some bright Eternity;

A shadow of some golden dream; a Splendor
Leaving the third sphere pilotless; a tender
Reflection of the eternal Moon of Love,
Under whose motions life's dull billows move;
A metaphor of Spring and Youth and Morning; 120
A vision like incarnate April, warning,
With smiles and tears, Frost the Anatomy
Into his summer grave.

　　　　　　　　　Ah! woe is me!
What have I dared? where am I lifted? how
Shall I descend, and perish not? I know
That Love makes all things equal; I have heard
By mine own heart this joyous truth averred:
The spirit of the worm beneath the sod,
In love and worship, blends itself with God.

Spouse! Sister! Angel! Pilot of the Fate 130
Whose course has been so starless! Oh, too late
Belovèd! Oh, too soon adored, by me!
For in the fields of immortality
My spirit should at first have worshipped thine,
A divine presence in a place divine;
Or should have moved beside it on this earth,
A shadow of that substance, from its birth;
But not as now. I love thee; yes, I feel
That on the fountain of my heart a seal
Is set, to keep its waters pure and bright
For thee, since in those *tears* thou hast delight. 141
We — are we not formed, as notes of music are,
For one another, though dissimilar;
Such difference without discord as can make
Those sweetest sounds, in which all spirits shake
As trembling leaves in a continuous air?

　Thy wisdom speaks in me, and bids me dare
Beacon the rocks on which high hearts are wrecked.

I never was attached to that great sect,
Whose doctrine is, that each one should
    select   150
Out of the crowd a mistress or a friend,
And all the rest, though fair and wise,
    commend
To cold oblivion, though 't is in the code
Of modern morals, and the beaten road
Which those poor slaves with weary foot-
    steps tread
Who travel to their home among the dead
By the broad highway of the world, and so
With one chained friend, perhaps a jealous
    foe,
The dreariest and the longest journey go.

True Love in this differs from gold and
    clay,   160
That to divide is not to take away.
Love is like 'understanding that grows
    bright
Gazing on many truths; 't is like thy light,
Imagination! which, from earth and sky,
And from the depths of human fantasy,
As from a thousand prisms and mirrors,
    fills
The Universe with glorious beams, and
    kills
Error, the worm, with many a sun-like
    arrow
Of its reverberated lightning. Narrow
The heart that loves, the brain that con-
    templates,   170
The life that wears, the spirit that creates
One object, and one form, and builds
    thereby
A sepulchre for its eternity.

Mind from its object differs most in this;
Evil from good; misery from happiness;
The baser from the nobler; the impure
And frail, from what is clear and must
    endure:
If you divide suffering and dross, you
    may
Diminish till it is consumed away;
If you divide pleasure and love and thought,
Each part exceeds the whole; and we know
    not   181
How much, while any yet remains unshared,
Of pleasure may be gained, of sorrow
    spared.
This truth is that deep well, whence sages
    draw
The unenvied light of hope; the eternal law

By which those live, to whom this world of
    life
Is as a garden ravaged, and whose strife
Tills for the promise of a later birth
The wilderness of this Elysian earth.   189

There was a Being whom my spirit oft
Met on its visioned wanderings, far aloft,
In the clear golden prime of my youth's
    dawn,
Upon the fairy isles of sunny lawn,
Amid the enchanted mountains, and the
    caves
Of divine sleep, and on the air-like waves
Of wonder-level dream, whose tremulous
    floor
Paved her light steps. On an imagined
    shore,
Under the gray beak of some promontory
She met me, robed in such exceeding glory
That I beheld her not. In solitudes   200
Her voice came to me through the whis-
    pering woods,
And from the fountains and the odors deep
Of flowers, which, like lips murmuring in
    their sleep
Of the sweet kisses which had lulled them
    there,
Breathed but of *her* to the enamoured air;
And from the breezes whether low or loud,
And from the rain of every passing cloud,
And from the singing of the summer-birds,
And from all sounds, all silence. In the
    words
Of antique verse and high romance, in
    form,   210
Sound, color, in whatever checks that Storm
Which with the shattered present chokes
    the past,
And in that best philosophy, whose taste
Makes this cold common hell, our life, a
    doom
As glorious as a fiery martyrdom —
Her Spirit was the harmony of truth.

Then from the caverns of my dreamy
    youth
I sprang, as one sandalled with plumes of
    fire,
And towards the lodestar of my one desire
I flitted, like a dizzy moth, whose flight 220
Is as a dead leaf's in the owlet light,
When it would seek in Hesper's setting
    sphere
A radiant death, a fiery sepulchre,

As if it were a lamp of earthly flame.
But She, whom prayers or tears then could
    not tame,
Passed, like a god throned on a wingèd
    planet,
Whose burning plumes to tenfold swiftness
    fan it,
Into the dreary cone of our life's shade;
And as a man with mighty loss dismayed,
I would have followed, though the grave
    between   230
Yawned like a gulf whose spectres are un-
    seen;
When a voice said: — 'O Thou of hearts
    the weakest,
The phantom is beside thee whom thou
    seekest.'
Then I — 'Where?' the world's echo an-
    swered 'Where?'
And in that silence, and in my despair,
I questioned every tongueless wind that
    flew
Over my tower of mourning, if it knew
Whither 't was fled, this soul out of my
    soul;
And murmured names and spells which
    have control
Over the sightless tyrants of our fate;   240
But neither prayer nor verse could dissipate
The night which closed on her; nor uncreate
That world within this Chaos, mine and
    me,
Of which she was the veiled Divinity, —
The world I say of thoughts that wor-
    shipped her;
And therefore I went forth, with hope and
    fear
And every gentle passion sick to death,
Feeding my course with expectation's
    breath,
Into the wintry forest of our life;
And struggling through its error with vain
    strife,   250
And stumbling in my weakness and my
    haste,
And half bewildered by new forms, I
    passed
Seeking among those untaught foresters
If I could find one form resembling hers,
In which she might have masked herself
    from me.
There, — One whose voice was venomed
    melody
Sate by a well, under blue night-shade
    bowers;

The breath of her false mouth was like
    faint flowers;
Her touch was as electric poison, — flame
Out of her looks into my vitals came,   260
And from her living cheeks and bosom flew
A killing air, which pierced like honey-dew
Into the core of my green heart, and lay
Upon its leaves; until, as hair grown gray
O'er a young brow, they hid its unblown
    prime
With ruins of unseasonable time.

In many mortal forms I rashly sought
The shadow of that idol of my thought.
And some were fair — but beauty dies
    away;
Others were wise — but honeyed words
    betray;   270
And one was true — oh! why not true to
    me?
Then, as a hunted deer that could not flee,
I turned upon my thoughts, and stood at
    bay,
Wounded and weak and panting; the cold
    day
Trembled, for pity of my strife and pain,
When, like a noonday dawn, there shone
    again
Deliverance. One stood on my path who
    seemed
As like the glorious shape, which I had
    dreamed,
As is the Moon, whose changes ever run
Into themselves, to the eternal Sun;   280
The cold chaste Moon, the Queen of Hea-
    ven's bright isles,
Who makes all beautiful on which she
    smiles;
That wandering shrine of soft yet icy flame,
Which ever is transformed, yet still the
    same,
And warms not but illumines. Young and
    fair
As the descended Spirit of that sphere,
She hid me, as the Moon may hide the
    night
From its own darkness, until all was bright
Between the Heaven and Earth of my
    calm mind,
And, as a cloud charioted by the wind,   290
She led me to a cave in that wild place,
And sate beside me, with her downward
    face
Illumining my slumbers, like the Moon
Waxing and waning o'er Endymion.

And I was laid asleep, spirit and limb,
And all my being became bright or dim
As the Moon's image in a summer sea,
According as she smiled or frowned on me;
And there I lay, within a chaste cold bed.
Alas, I then was nor alive nor dead;　300
For at her silver voice came Death and Life,
Unmindful each of their accustomed strife,
Masked like twin babes, a sister and a brother,
The wandering hopes of one abandoned mother,
And through the cavern without wings they flew,
And cried, 'Away ! he is not of our crew.'
I wept, and though it be a dream, I weep.

What storms then shook the ocean of my sleep,
Blotting that Moon, whose pale and waning lips　309
Then shrank as in the sickness of eclipse;
And how my soul was as a lampless sea,
And who was then its Tempest: and when She,
The Planet of that hour, was quenched, what frost
Crept o'er those waters, till from coast to coast
The moving billows of my being fell
Into a death of ice, immovable;
And then what earthquakes made it gape and split,
The white Moon smiling all the while on it ; —
These words conceal; if not, each word would be
The key of stanchless tears. Weep not for me !　320

At length, into the obscure forest came
The Vision I had sought through grief and shame.
Athwart that wintry wilderness of thorns
Flashed from her motion splendor like the Morn's,
And from her presence life was radiated
Through the gray earth and branches bare and dead;
So that her way was paved and roofed above
With flowers as soft as thoughts of budding love;
And music from her respiration spread

Like light, — all other sounds were penetrated　330
By the small, still, sweet spirit of that sound,
So that the savage winds hung mute around;
And odors warm and fresh fell from her hair
Dissolving the dull cold in the frore air.
Soft as an Incarnation of the Sun,
When light is changed to love, this glorious One
Floated into the cavern where I lay,
And called my Spirit, and the dreaming clay
Was lifted by the thing that dreamed below　339
As smoke by fire, and in her beauty's glow
I stood, and felt the dawn of my long night
Was penetrating me with living light;
I knew it was the Vision veiled from me
So many years — that it was Emily.

Twin Spheres of light who rule this passive Earth,
This world of love, this *me ;* and into birth
Awaken all its fruits and flowers, and dart
Magnetic might into its central heart;
And lift its billows and its mists, and guide
By everlasting laws each wind and tide　350
To its fit cloud, and its appointed cave;
And lull its storms, each in the craggy grave
Which was its cradle, luring to faint bowers
The armies of the rainbow-wingèd showers;
And, as those married lights, which from the towers
Of Heaven look forth and fold the wandering globe
In liquid sleep and splendor, as a robe;
And all their many-mingled influence blend,
If equal, yet unlike, to one sweet end; —
So ye, bright regents, with alternate sway,
Govern my sphere of being, night and day !
Thou, not disdaining even a borrowed might;　362
Thou, not eclipsing a remoter light;
And, through the shadow of the seasons three,
From Spring to Autumn's sere maturity,
Light it into the Winter of the tomb,
Where it may ripen to a brighter bloom.
Thou too, O Comet, beautiful and fierce,
Who drew the heart of this frail Universe

Towards thine own; till, wrecked in that
   convulsion,   370
Alternating attraction and repulsion,
Thine went astray, and that was rent in
   twain;
Oh, float into our azure heaven again !
Be there love's folding-star at thy return;
The living Sun will feed thee from its urn
Of golden fire; the Moon will veil her horn
In thy last smiles; adoring Even and Morn
Will worship thee with incense of calm
   breath
And lights and shadows, as the star of
   Death
And Birth is worshipped by those sisters
   wild   380
Called Hope and Fear — upon the heart
   are piled
Their offerings, — of this sacrifice divine
A World shall be the altar.

                         Lady mine,
Scorn not these flowers of thought, the
   fading birth,
Which from its heart of hearts that plant
   puts forth,
Whose fruit, made perfect by thy sunny
   eyes,
Will be as of the trees of Paradise.

  The day is come, and thou wilt fly with
   me.
To whatsoe'er of dull mortality
Is mine remain a vestal sister still;   390
To the intense, the deep, the imperishable,
Not mine, but me, henceforth be thou
   united
Even as a bride, delighting and delighted.
The hour is come — the destined Star has
   risen
Which shall descend upon a vacant prison.
The walls are high, the gates are strong,
   thick set
The sentinels — but true love never yet
Was thus constrained; it overleaps all
   fence;
Like lightning, with invisible violence
Piercing its continents; like Heaven's free
   breath,   400
Which he who grasps can hold not; liker
   Death,
Who rides upon a thought, and makes his
   way
Through temple, tower, and palace, and the
   array

Of arms; more strength has Love than he
   or they;
For it can burst his charnel, and make free
The limbs in chains, the heart in agony,
The soul in dust and chaos.

                      Emily,
A ship is floating in the harbor now,
A wind is hovering o'er the mountain's
   brow;
There is a path on the sea's azure floor —
No keel has ever ploughed that path be-
   fore;   411
The halcyons brood around the foamless
   isles;
The treacherous Ocean has forsworn its
   wiles;
The merry mariners are bold and free:
Say, my heart's sister, wilt thou sail with
   me ?
Our bark is as an albatross, whose nest
Is a far Eden of the purple East;
And we between her wings will sit, while
   Night,
And Day, and Storm, and Calm, pursue
   their flight,
Our ministers, along the boundless Sea, 420
Treading each other's heels, unheededly.
It is an isle under Ionian skies,
Beautiful as a wreck of Paradise,
And, for the harbors are not safe and good,
This land would have remained a solitude
But for some pastoral people native there,
Who from the Elysian, clear, and golden
   air
Draw the last spirit of the age of gold,
Simple and spirited, innocent and bold.
The blue Ægean girds this chosen home 430
With ever-changing sound and light and
   foam
Kissing the sifted sands and caverns hoar;
And all the winds wandering along the
   shore
Undulate with the undulating tide;
There are thick woods where sylvan forms
   abide,
And many a fountain, rivulet, and pond,
As clear as elemental diamond,
Or serene morning air; and far beyond,
The mossy tracks made by the goats and
   deer
(Which the rough shepherd treads but once
   a year)   440
Pierce into glades, caverns, and bowers,
   and halls

Built round with ivy, which the waterfalls
Illumining, with sound that never fails
Accompany the noonday nightingales;
And all the place is peopled with sweet airs;
The light clear element which the isle
      wears
Is heavy with the scent of lemon-flowers,
Which floats like mist laden with unseen
      showers,
And falls upon the eyelids like faint sleep;
And from the moss violets and jonquils
      peep,   450
And dart their arrowy odor through the
      brain
Till you might faint with that delicious pain.
And every motion, odor, beam, and tone,
With that deep music is in unison,
Which is a soul within the soul; they seem
Like echoes of an antenatal dream.
It is an isle 'twixt Heaven, Air, Earth, and
      Sea,
Cradled and hung in clear tranquillity;
Bright as that wandering Eden, Lucifer,
Washed by the soft blue Oceans of young
      air.   460
It is a favored place. Famine or Blight,
Pestilence, War, and Earthquake, never
      light
Upon its mountain-peaks; blind vultures,
      they
Sail onward far upon their fatal way;
The wingèd storms, chanting their thunder-
      psalm
To other lands, leave azure chasms of calm
Over this isle, or weep themselves in dew,
From which its fields and woods ever renew
Their green and golden immortality.
And from the sea there rise, and from the
      sky   470
There fall, clear exhalations, soft and
      bright,
Veil after veil, each hiding some delight,
Which Sun or Moon or zephyr draw aside,
Till the isle's beauty, like a naked bride
Glowing at once with love and loveliness,
Blushes and trembles at its own excess;
Yet, like a buried lamp, a Soul no less
Burns in the heart of this delicious isle,
An atom of the Eternal, whose own smile
Unfolds itself, and may be felt, not seen, 480
O'er the gray rocks, blue waves, and forests
      green,
Filling their bare and void interstices.
But the chief marvel of the wilderness
Is a lone dwelling, built by whom or how

None of the rustic island-people know;
'T is not a tower of strength, though with
      its height
It overtops the woods; but, for delight,
Some wise and tender Ocean-King, ere
      crime
Had been invented, in the world's young
      prime,
Reared it, a wonder of that simple time, 490
And envy of the isles, a pleasure-house
Made sacred to his sister and his spouse.
It scarce seems now a wreck of human art,
But, as it were, Titanic, in the heart
Of Earth having assumed its form, then
      grown
Out of the mountains, from the living stone,
Lifting itself in caverns light and high;
For all the antique and learned imagery
Has been erased, and in the place of it
The ivy and the wild vine interknit   500
The volumes of their many-twining stems;
Parasite flowers illume with dewy gems
The lampless halls, and, when they fade,
      the sky
Peeps through their winter-woof of tracery
With moonlight patches, or star-atoms keen,
Or fragments of the day's intense serene,
Working mosaic on their Parian floors.
And, day and night, aloof, from the high
      towers
And terraces, the Earth and Ocean seem
To sleep in one another's arms, and dream
Of waves, flowers, clouds, woods, rocks,
      and all that we   511
Read in their smiles, and call reality.

This isle and house are mine, and I have
      vowed
Thee to be lady of the solitude.
And I have fitted up some chambers there
Looking towards the golden Eastern air,
And level with the living winds, which flow
Like waves above the living waves below.
I have sent books and music there, and all
Those instruments with which high spirits
      call   520
The future from its cradle, and the past
Out of its grave, and make the present last
In thoughts and joys which sleep, but can-
      not die,
Folded within their own eternity.
Our simple life wants little, and true taste
Hires not the pale drudge Luxury to waste
The scene it would adorn, and therefore still
Nature with all her children haunts the hill.

The ring-dove, in the embowering ivy, yet
Keeps up her love-lament, and the owls flit
Round the evening tower, and the young
    stars glance   531
Between the quick bats in their twilight
    dance;
The spotted deer bask in the fresh moon-
    light
Before our gate, and the slow silent night
Is measured by the pants of their calm
    sleep.
Be this our home in life, and when years
    heap
Their withered hours, like leaves, on our
    decay,
Let us become the overhanging day,
The living soul of this Elysian isle,   539
Conscious, inseparable, one.   Meanwhile
We two will rise, and sit, and walk together
Under the roof of blue Ionian weather,
And wander in the meadows, or ascend
The mossy mountains, where the blue hea-
    vens bend
With lightest winds, to touch their para-
    mour;
Or linger, where the pebble-paven shore,
Under the quick faint kisses of the sea
Trembles and sparkles as with ecstasy, —
Possessing and possessed by all that is   549
Within that calm circumference of bliss,
And by each other, till to love and live
Be one; or, at the noontide hour, arrive
Where some old cavern hoar seems yet to
    keep
The moonlight of the expired night asleep,
Through which the awakened day can never
    peep;
A veil for our seclusion, close as Night's,
Where secure sleep may kill thine innocent
    lights;
Sleep, the fresh dew of languid love, the rain
Whose drops quench kisses till they burn
    again.   559
And we will talk, until thought's melody
Become too sweet for utterance, and it die
In words, to live again in looks, which dart
With thrilling tone into the voiceless heart,
Harmonizing silence without a sound.
Our breath shall intermix, our bosoms
    bound,
And our veins beat together; and our lips,
With other eloquence than words, eclipse
The soul that burns between them; and the
    wells
Which boil under our being's inmost cells,

The fountains of our deepest life, shall be
Confused in passion's golden purity,   571
As mountain-springs under the morning
    Sun.
We shall become the same, we shall be one
Spirit within two frames, oh! wherefore
    two?
One passion in twin-hearts, which grows
    and grew,
Till like two meteors of expanding flame
Those spheres instinct with it become the
    same,
Touch, mingle, are transfigured; ever still
Burning, yet ever inconsumable;
In one another's substance finding food, 580
Like flames too pure and light and unim-
    bued
To nourish their bright lives with baser
    prey,
Which point to Heaven and cannot pass
    away;
One hope within two wills, one will beneath
Two overshadowing minds, one life, one
    death,
One Heaven, one Hell, one immortality,
And one annihilation.   Woe is me!
The wingèd words on which my soul would
    pierce
Into the height of love's rare Universe,
Are chains of lead around its flight of fire.
I pant, I sink, I tremble, I expire!   591

———

Weak Verses, go, kneel at your Sover-
    eign's feet,
And say: — 'We are the masters of thy
    slave,
What wouldest thou with us and ours and
    thine?'
Then call your sisters from Oblivion's cave,
All singing loud: 'Love's very pain is
    sweet,
But its reward is in the world divine,
Which, if not here, it builds beyond the
    grave.'
So shall ye live when I am there.   Then
    haste
Over the hearts of men, until ye meet   600
Marina, Vanna, Primus, and the rest,
And bid them love each other and be
    blessed;
And leave the troop which errs, and which
    reproves,
And come and be my guest, — for I am
    Love's.

ADONAIS

AN ELEGY ON THE DEATH OF JOHN KEATS

'Αστὴρ πρὶν μὲν ἔλαμπες ἐνὶ ζώοισιν ἑῶος.
Νῦν δὲ θανὼν, λάμπεις ἕσπερος ἐν φθιμένοις.
PLATO.

Adonais, perhaps the most widely read of the longer poems of Shelley, owes something of its charm to the fact noted by Mrs. Shelley that much in it ' seems now more applicable to Shelley himself than to the young and gifted poet whom he mourned.' The elegy has contributed much to the feeling that links these two poets in one memory, though in life they were rather pleasant than intimate friends. Keats died at Rome, February 23, 1821; and Shelley composed the poem between the late days of May and June 11, or at the latest, June 16; it was printed at Pisa, under his own care, by July 13, and copies sent to London for issue there by his publisher. During the period of composition he felt that he was succeeding, and wrote of it as ' a highly wrought *piece of art*, and perhaps better, in point of composition, than anything I have written ; ' and after its completion, he says, ' The *Adonais*, in spite of its mysticism, is the least imperfect of my compositions, and, as the image of my regret and honor for poor Keats, I wish it to be so.' He continued to indulge hopes of its success, as in the case of *The Cenci*, though on a different plane, and wrote to Ollier, ' I am especially curious to hear the fate of *Adonais*. I confess I should be surprised if *that* poem were born to an immortality of oblivion ; ' and, shortly after this, to Hunt, — ' Pray tell me what effect was produced by *Adonais*. My faculties are shaken to atoms, and torpid. I can write nothing ; and if *Adonais* had no success and excited no interest, what incentive can I have to write ? ' A month or two later he writes to Gisborne, still strong in his faith in the poem, — ' I know what to think of *Adonais*, but what to think of those who confound it with the many bad poems of the day, I know not. . . . It is absurd in any Review to criticise *Adonais*, and still more to pretend that the verses are bad.' His friends praised it, except Byron, who kept silence, perhaps, Shelley says, because he was mentioned in it.' Shelley's letter to Severn has a peculiar interest : —

' I send you the Elegy on poor Keats — and I wish it were better worth your acceptance. You will see, by the preface, that it was written before I could obtain any particular account of his last moments ; all that I still know, was communicated to me by a friend who had derived his information from Colonel Finch ; I have ventured to express, as I felt, the respect and admiration which *your* conduct towards him demands.

' In spite of his transcendent genius, Keats never was, nor ever will be, a popular poet; and the total neglect and obscurity in which the astonishing remnants of his mind still lie, was hardly to be dissipated by a writer, who, however he may differ from Keats in more important qualities, at least resembles him in that accidental one, a want of popularity.

' I have little hope, therefore, that the poem I send you will excite any attention, nor do I feel assured that a critical notice of his writings would find a single reader. But for these considerations, it had been my intention to have collected the remnants of his compositions, and to have published them with a Life and Criticism. Has he left any poems or writings of whatsoever kind, and in whose possession are they ? Perhaps you would oblige me by information on this point.'

PREFACE

Φάρμακον ἦλθε, Βίων, ποτὶ σὸν στόμα, φάρμακον εἶδες.
Τοιούτοις χείλεσσι ποτέδραμε, κοὐκ ἐγλυκάνθη ;
Τίς δὲ βροτὸς τοσσοῦτον ἀνάμερος, ἢ κεράσαι τοι
Ἡ δοῦναι χατέοντι τὸ φάρμακον ἔκφυγεν ἀδάν ;
MOSCHUS, EPITAPH. BION.

IT is my intention to subjoin to the London edition of this poem a criticism upon the claims of its lamented object to be classed among the writers of the highest genius who have adorned our age. My known repugnance to the narrow principles of taste on which several of his earlier compositions were modelled prove, at least, that I am an impartial judge. I consider the fragment of Hyperion as second to nothing that was ever produced by a writer of the same years.

John Keats died at Rome of a consumption, in his twenty-fourth year, on the —— of —— 1821 ; and was buried in the romantic and lonely cemetery of the Protestants in that city, under the pyramid which is the tomb of Cestius and the massy walls and towers, now mouldering and desolate, which formed the circuit of ancient Rome. The cemetery is an open space among the ruins, covered in winter with violets and daisies. It might make one in love with death to think that one should be buried in so sweet a place.

The genius of the lamented person to whose memory I have dedicated these unworthy verses was not less delicate and fragile than it was beautiful; and where cankerworms abound what wonder if its young flower was blighted in the bud? The savage criticism on his *Endymion*, which appeared in the *Quarterly Review*, produced the most violent effect on his susceptible mind; the agitation thus originated ended in the rupture of a blood-vessel in the lungs; a rapid consumption ensued, and the succeeding acknowledgments from more candid critics of the true greatness of his powers were ineffectual to heal the wound thus wantonly inflicted.

It may be well said that these wretched men know not what they do. They scatter their insults and their slanders without heed as to whether the poisoned shaft lights on a heart made callous by many blows, or one like Keats's composed of more penetrable stuff. One of their associates is, to my knowledge, a most base and unprincipled calumniator. As to *Endymion*, was it a poem, whatever might be its defects, to be treated contemptuously by those who had celebrated with various degrees of complacency and panegyric *Paris* and *Woman* and a *Syrian Tale*, and Mrs. Lefanu and Mr. Barrett and Mr. Howard Payne and a long list of the illustrious obscure? Are these the men who in their venal good nature presumed to draw a parallel between the Rev. Mr. Milman and Lord Byron? What gnat did they strain at here after having swallowed all those camels? Against what woman taken in adultery dares the foremost of these literary prostitutes to cast his opprobrious stone? Miserable man! you, one of the meanest, have wantonly defaced one of the noblest specimens of the workmanship of God. Nor shall it be your excuse that, murderer as you are, you have spoken daggers but used none.

The circumstances of the closing scene of poor Keats's life were not made known to me until the *Elegy* was ready for the press. I am given to understand that the wound which his sensitive spirit had received from the criticism of *Endymion* was exasperated by the bitter sense of unrequited benefits; the poor fellow seems to have been hooted from the stage of life no less by those on whom he had wasted the promise of his genius than those on whom he had lavished his fortune and his care. He was accompanied to Rome and attended in his last illness by Mr. Severn, a young artist of the highest promise, who, I have been informed, 'almost risked his own life, and sacrificed every prospect to unwearied attendance upon his dying friend.' Had I known these circumstances before the completion of my poem, I should have been tempted to add my feeble tribute of applause to the more solid recompense which the virtuous man finds in the recollection of his own motives. Mr. Severn can dispense with a reward from 'such stuff as dreams are made of.' His conduct is a golden augury of the success of his future career — may the unextinguished Spirit of his illustrious friend animate the creations of his pencil, and plead against Oblivion for his name!

I

I WEEP for Adonais — he is dead!
Oh, weep for Adonais! though our tears
Thaw not the frost which binds so dear a
      head!
And thou, sad Hour, selected from all
      years
To mourn our loss, rouse thy obscure
      compeers,
And teach them thine own sorrow! Say:
      'With me
Died Adonais; till the Future dares
Forget the Past, his fate and fame shall be
An echo and a light unto eternity!'

II

Where wert thou, mighty Mother, when
      he lay,
When thy Son lay, pierced by the shaft
      which flies
In darkness? where was lorn Urania
When Adonais died? With veilèd eyes,
'Mid listening Echoes, in her Paradise
She sate, while one, with soft enamoured
      breath,
Rekindled all the fading melodies,
With which, like flowers that mock the
      corse beneath,
He had adorned and hid the coming bulk
      of death.

III

Oh, weep for Adonais — he is dead!
Wake, melancholy Mother, wake and
      weep!
Yet wherefore? Quench within their
      burning bed
Thy fiery tears, and let thy loud heart
      keep
Like his a mute and uncomplaining
      sleep;

For he is gone where all things wise and fair
Descend.   Oh, dream not that the amorous Deep
Will yet restore him to the vital air;
Death feeds on his mute voice, and laughs at our despair.

IV

Most musical of mourners, weep again !
Lament anew, Urania ! — He died,
Who was the sire of an immortal strain,
Blind, old, and lonely, when his country's pride
The priest, the slave, and the liberticide
Trampled and mocked with many a loathèd rite
Of lust and blood; he went, unterrified,
Into the gulf of death; but his clear Sprite
Yet reigns o'er earth, the third among the sons of light.

V

Most musical of mourners, weep anew !
Not all to that bright station dared to climb;
And happier they their happiness who knew,
Whose tapers yet burn through that night of time
In which suns perished; others more sublime,
Struck by the envious wrath of man or God,
Have sunk, extinct in their refulgent prime;
And some yet live, treading the thorny road,
Which leads, through toil and hate, to Fame's serene abode.

VI

But now, thy youngest, dearest one has perished,
The nursling of thy widowhood, who grew,
Like a pale flower by some sad maiden cherished
And fed with true-love tears instead of dew;
Most musical of mourners, weep anew !
Thy extreme hope, the loveliest and the last,

The bloom, whose petals, nipped before they blew,
Died on the promise of the fruit, is waste;
The broken lily lies — the storm is overpast.

VII

To that high Capital, where kingly Death
Keeps his pale court in beauty and decay,
He came; and bought, with price of purest breath,
A grave among the eternal. — Come away !
Haste, while the vault of blue Italian day
Is yet his fitting charnel-roof ! while still
He lies, as if in dewy sleep he lay;
Awake him not ! surely he takes his fill
Of deep and liquid rest, forgetful of all ill.

VIII

He will awake no more, oh, never more !
Within the twilight chamber spreads apace
The shadow of white Death, and at the door
Invisible Corruption waits to trace
His extreme way to her dim dwelling-place;
The eternal Hunger sits, but pity and awe
Soothe her pale rage, nor dares she to deface
So fair a prey, till darkness and the law
Of change shall o'er his sleep the mortal curtain draw.

IX

Oh, weep for Adonais ! — The quick Dreams,
The passion-wingèd ministers of thought,
Who were his flocks, whom near the living streams
Of his young spirit he fed, and whom he taught
The love which was its music, wander not, —
Wander no more, from kindling brain to brain,
But droop there, whence they sprung; and mourn their lot
Round the cold heart, where, after their sweet pain,
They ne'er will gather strength, or find a home again.

X

And one with trembling hand clasps his
  cold head,
And fans him with her moonlight wings,
  and cries,
'Our love, our hope, our sorrow, is not
  dead;
See, on the silken fringe of his faint eyes,
Like dew upon a sleeping flower, there
  lies
A tear some Dream has loosened from
  his brain.'
Lost Angel of a ruined Paradise !
She knew not 't was her own; as with no
  stain
She faded, like a cloud which had outwept
  its rain.

XI

One from a lucid urn of starry dew
Washed his light limbs, as if embalming
  them;
Another clipped her profuse locks, and
  threw
The wreath upon him, like an anadem,
Which frozen tears instead of pearls be-
  gem;
Another in her wilful grief would break
Her bow and wingèd reeds, as if to stem
A greater loss with one which was more
  weak;
And dull the barbèd fire against his frozen
  cheek.

XII

Another Splendor on his mouth alit,
That mouth whence it was wont to draw
  the breath
Which gave it strength to pierce the
  guarded wit,
And pass into the panting heart beneath
With lightning and with music; the
  damp death
Quenched its caress upon his icy lips;
And, as a dying meteor stains a wreath
Of moonlight vapor, which the cold night
  clips,
It flushed through his pale limbs, and
  passed to its eclipse.

XIII

And others came — Desires and Adora-
  tions,
Wingèd Persuasions and veiled Desti-
  nies,
Splendors, and Glooms, and glimmering
  Incarnations
Of hopes and fears, and twilight Fanta-
  sies;
And Sorrow, with her family of Sighs,
And Pleasure, blind with tears, led by
  the gleam
Of her own dying smile instead of eyes,
Came in slow pomp; — the moving pomp
  might seem
Like pageantry of mist on an autumnal
  stream.

XIV

All he had loved, and moulded into
  thought
From shape, and hue, and odor, and sweet
  sound,
Lamented Adonais.   Morning sought
Her eastern watch tower, and her hair
  unbound,
Wet with the tears which should adorn
  the ground,
Dimmed the aërial eyes that kindle day;
Afar the melancholy thunder moaned,
Pale Ocean in unquiet slumber lay,
And the wild winds flew round, sobbing in
  their dismay.

XV

Lost Echo sits amid the voiceless mountains,
And feeds her grief with his remembered lay,
And will no more reply to winds or
  fountains,
Or amorous birds perched on the young
  green spray,
Or herdsman's horn, or bell at closing
  day;
Since she can mimic not his lips, more
  dear
Than those for whose disdain she pined
  away
Into a shadow of all sounds: — a drear
Murmur, between their songs, is all the
  woodmen hear.

XVI

Grief made the young Spring wild, and
  she threw down
Her kindling buds, as if she Autumn
  were,
Or they dead leaves; since her delight is
  flown,

For whom should she have waked the sullen year?
To Phœbus was not Hyacinth so dear,
Nor to himself Narcissus, as to both
Thou, Adonais; wan they stand and sere
Amid the faint companions of their youth,
With dew all turned to tears; odor, to sighing ruth.

XVII

Thy spirit's sister, the lorn nightingale,
Mourns not her mate with such melodious pain;
Not so the eagle, who like thee could scale
Heaven, and could nourish in the sun's domain
Her mighty youth with morning, doth complain,
Soaring and screaming round her empty nest,
As Albion wails for thee: the curse of Cain
Light on his head who pierced thy innocent breast,
And scared the angel soul that was its earthly guest!

XVIII

Ah woe is me! Winter is come and gone,
But grief returns with the revolving year;
The airs and streams renew their joyous tone;
The ants, the bees, the swallows, reappear;
Fresh leaves and flowers deck the dead Seasons' bier;
The amorous birds now pair in every brake,
And build their mossy homes in field and brere;
And the green lizard and the golden snake,
Like unimprisoned flames, out of their trance awake.

XIX

Through wood and stream and field and hill and Ocean,
A quickening life from the Earth's heart has burst,
As it has ever done, with change and motion,
From the great morning of the world when first

God dawned on Chaos; in its stream immersed,
The lamps of Heaven flash with a softer light;
All baser things pant with life's sacred thirst,
Diffuse themselves, and spend in love's delight
The beauty and the joy of their renewèd might.

XX

The leprous corpse, touched by this spirit tender.
Exhales itself in flowers of gentle breath;
Like incarnations of the stars, when splendor
Is changed to fragrance, they illumine death
And mock the merry worm that wakes beneath.
Nought we know dies. Shall that alone which knows
Be as a sword consumed before the sheath
By sightless lightning? the intense atom glows
A moment, then is quenched in a most cold repose.

XXI

Alas! that all we loved of him should be,
But for our grief, as if it had not been,
And grief itself be mortal! Woe is me!
Whence are we, and why are we? of what scene
The actors or spectators? Great and mean
Meet massed in death, who lends what life must borrow.
As long as skies are blue and fields are green,
Evening must usher night, night urge the morrow,
Month follow month with woe, and year wake year to sorrow.

XXII

He will awake no more, oh, never more!
'Wake thou,' cried Misery, 'childless Mother, rise
Out of thy sleep, and slake, in thy heart's core,
A wound more fierce than his with tears and sighs.'

And all the Dreams that watched Urania's eyes,
And all the Echoes whom their sister's
song
Had held in holy silence, cried, ' Arise ! '
Swift as a Thought by the snake Memory stung,
From her ambrosial rest the fading Splendor sprung.

XXIII

She rose like an autumnal Night, that
springs
Out of the East, and follows wild and
drear
The golden Day, which, on eternal wings,
Even as a ghost abandoning a bier,
Had left the Earth a corpse; — sorrow
and fear
So struck, so roused, so rapt Urania;
So saddened round her like an atmo-
sphere
Of stormy mist; so swept her on her way
Even to the mournful place where Adonais
lay.

XXIV

Out of her secret Paradise she sped,
Through camps and cities rough with
stone, and steel,
And human hearts which, to her airy
tread
Yielding not, wounded the invisible
Palms of her tender feet where'er they
fell;
And barbèd tongues, and thoughts more
sharp than they,
Rent the soft Form they never could
repel,
Whose sacred blood, like the young tears
of May,
Paved with eternal flowers that undeserving
way.

XXV

In the death-chamber for a moment
Death,
Shamed by the presence of that living
Might,
Blushed to annihilation, and the breath
Revisited those lips, and life's pale light
Flashed through those limbs, so late her
dear delight.
' Leave me not wild and drear and com-
fortless,

As silent lightning leaves the starless
night !
Leave me not ! ' cried Urania; her distress
Roused Death; Death rose and smiled, and
met her vain caress.

XXVI

' Stay yet awhile ! speak to me once again;
Kiss me, so long but as a kiss may live;
And in my heartless breast and burning
brain
That word, that kiss, shall all thoughts
else survive,
With food of saddest memory kept
alive,
Now thou art dead, as if it were a part
Of thee, my Adonais ! I would give
All that I am to be as thou now art !
But I am chained to Time, and cannot
thence depart !

XXVII

' O gentle child, beautiful as thou wert,
Why didst thou leave the trodden paths
of men
Too soon, and with weak hands though
mighty heart
Dare the unpastured dragon in his den ?
Defenceless as thou wert, oh, where was
then
Wisdom the mirrored shield, or scorn
the spear ?
Or hadst thou waited the full cycle, when
Thy spirit should have filled its crescent
sphere,
The monsters of life's waste had fled from
thee like deer.

XXVIII

' The herded wolves, bold only to pursue;
The obscene ravens, clamorous o'er the
dead;
The vultures, to the conqueror's banner
true,
Who feed where Desolation first has
fed,
And whose wings rain contagion; — how
they fled,
When, like Apollo, from his golden bow
The Pythian of the age one arrow sped
And smiled ! — The spoilers tempt no
second blow,
They fawn on the proud feet that spurn
them lying low.

XXIX

'The sun comes forth, and many reptiles spawn;
He sets, and each ephemeral insect then
Is gathered into death without a dawn,
And the immortal stars awake again;
So is it in the world of living men:
A godlike mind soars forth, in its delight
Making earth bare and veiling heaven, and when
It sinks, the swarms that dimmed or shared its light
Leave to its kindred lamps the spirit's awful night.'

XXX

Thus ceased she; and the mountain shepherds came,
Their garlands sere, their magic mantles rent;
The Pilgrim of Eternity, whose fame
Over his living head like Heaven is bent,
An early but enduring monument,
Came, veiling all the lightnings of his song
In sorrow; from her wilds Ierne sent
The sweetest lyrist of her saddest wrong,
And love taught grief to fall like music from his tongue.

XXXI

'Midst others of less note, came one frail Form,
A phantom among men; companionless
As the last cloud of an expiring storm
Whose thunder is its knell; he, as I guess,
Had gazed on Nature's naked loveliness,
Actæon-like, and now he fled astray
With feeble steps o'er the world's wilderness,
And his own thoughts, along that rugged way,
Pursued, like raging hounds, their father and their prey.

XXXII

A pard-like Spirit beautiful and swift —
A love in desolation masked; — a Power
Girt round with weakness; — it can scarce uplift
The weight of the superincumbent hour;
It is a dying lamp, a falling shower,
A breaking billow; — even whilst we speak
Is it not broken? On the withering flower
The killing sun smiles brightly; on a cheek
The life can burn in blood, even while the heart may break.

XXXIII

His head was bound with pansies overblown,
And faded violets, white, and pied, and blue;
And a light spear topped with a cypress cone,
Round whose rude shaft dark ivy-tresses grew
Yet dripping with the forest's noonday dew,
Vibrated, as the ever-beating heart
Shook the weak hand that grasped it; of that crew
He came the last, neglected and apart;
A herd-abandoned deer struck by the hunter's dart.

XXXIV

All stood aloof, and at his partial moan
Smiled through their tears; well knew that gentle band
Who in another's fate now wept his own,
As in the accents of an unknown land
He sung new sorrow; sad Urania scanned
The Stranger's mien, and murmured: 'Who art thou?'
He answered not, but with a sudden hand
Made bare his branded and ensanguined brow,
Which was like Cain's or Christ's — oh! that it should be so!

XXXV

What softer voice is hushed over the dead?
Athwart what brow is that dark mantle thrown?
What form leans sadly o'er the white death-bed,
In mockery of monumental stone,
The heavy heart heaving without a moan?
If it be He, who, gentlest of the wise,
Taught, soothed, loved, honored the departed one,
Let me not vex with inharmonious sighs
The silence of that heart's accepted sacrifice.

XXXVI

Our Adonais has drunk poison — oh,
What deaf and viperous murderer could
  crown
Life's early cup with such a draught of
  woe ?
The nameless worm would now itself
  disown;
It felt, yet could escape the magic tone
Whose prelude held all envy, hate and
  wrong,
But what was howling in one breast
  alone,
Silent with expectation of the song,
Whose master's hand is cold, whose silver
  lyre unstrung.

XXXVII

Live thou, whose infamy is not thy
  fame !
Live ! fear no heavier chastisement from
  me,
Thou noteless blot on a remembered
  name !
But be thyself, and know thyself to
  be !
And ever at thy season be thou free
To spill the venom when thy fangs o'erflow;
Remorse and Self-contempt shall cling
  to thee;
Hot Shame shall burn upon thy secret
  brow,
And like a beaten hound tremble thou shalt
  — as now.

XXXVIII

Nor let us weep that our delight is
  fled
Far from these carrion kites that scream
  below;
He wakes or sleeps with the enduring
  dead;
Thou canst not soar where he is sitting
  now.
Dust to the dust ! but the pure spirit
  shall flow
Back to the burning fountain whence it
  came,
A portion of the Eternal, which must
  glow
Through time and change, unquenchably
  the same,
Whilst thy cold embers choke the sordid
  hearth of shame.

XXXIX

Peace, peace ! he is not dead, he doth
  not sleep —
He hath awakened from the dream of
  life —
'T is we, who, lost in stormy visions, keep
With phantoms an unprofitable strife,
And in mad trance strike with our spir-
  it's knife
Invulnerable nothings. *We* decay
Like corpses in a charnel; fear and grief
Convulse us and consume us day by
  day,
And cold hopes swarm like worms within
  our living clay.

XL

He has outsoared the shadow of our
  night;
Envy and calumny and hate and pain,
And that unrest which men miscall de-
  light,
Can touch him not and torture not again;
From the contagion of the world's slow
  stain
He is secure, and now can never mourn
A heart grown cold, a head grown gray
  in vain;
Nor, when the spirit's self has ceased to
  burn,
With sparkless ashes load an unlamented
  urn.

XLI

He lives, he wakes — 't is Death is dead,
  not he;
Mourn not for Adonais. — Thou young
  Dawn,
Turn all thy dew to splendor, for from
  thee
The spirit thou lamentest is not gone;
Ye caverns and ye forests, cease to moan !
Cease, ye faint flowers and fountains, and
  thou Air,
Which like a mourning veil thy scarf
  hadst thrown
O'er the abandoned Earth, now leave it
  bare
Even to the joyous stars which smile on its
  despair !

XLII

He is made one with Nature: there is
  heard
His voice in all her music, from the moan

Of thunder to the song of night's sweet
bird;
He is a presence to be felt and known
In darkness and in light, from herb and
stone,
Spreading itself where'er that Power
may move
Which has withdrawn his being to its own;
Which wields the world with never-wea-
ried love,
Sustains it from beneath, and kindles it
above.

XLIII

He is a portion of the loveliness
Which once he made more lovely; he
doth bear
His part, while the one Spirit's plastic
stress
Sweeps through the dull dense world,
compelling there
All new successions to the forms they
wear,
Torturing the unwilling dross that checks
its flight
To its own likeness, as each mass may
bear,
And bursting in its beauty and its might
From trees and beasts and men into the
Heaven's light.

XLIV

The splendors of the firmament of time
May be eclipsed, but are extinguished
not;
Like stars to their appointed height they
climb,
And death is a low mist which cannot
blot
The brightness it may veil. When lofty
thought
Lifts a young heart above its mortal
lair,
And love and life contend in it for what
Shall be its earthly doom, the dead live
there
And move like winds of light on dark and
stormy air.

XLV

The inheritors of unfulfilled renown
Rose from their thrones, built beyond
mortal thought,
Far in the Unapparent. Chatterton
Rose pale, — his solemn agony had not

Yet faded from him; Sidney, as he fought
And as he fell and as he lived and loved
Sublimely mild, a Spirit without spot,
Arose; and Lucan, by his death ap-
proved;
Oblivion as they rose shrank like a thing
reproved.

XLVI

And many more, whose names on earth
are dark
But whose transmitted effluence cannot
die
So long as fire outlives the parent spark,
Rose, robed in dazzling immortality.
'Thou art become as one of us,' they
cry;
'It was for thee yon kingless sphere has
long
Swung blind in unascended majesty,
Silent alone amid an Heaven of song.
Assume thy wingèd throne, thou Vesper of
our throng!'

XLVII

Who mourns for Adonais? Oh, come
forth,
Fond wretch! and know thyself and him
aright.
Clasp with thy panting soul the pendu-
lous Earth;
As from a centre, dart thy spirit's light
Beyond all worlds, until its spacious
might
Satiate the void circumference; then
shrink
Even to a point within our day and night;
And keep thy heart light lest it make
thee sink
When hope has kindled hope, and lured
thee to the brink.

XLVIII

Or go to Rome, which is the sepulchre,
Oh, not of him, but of our joy; 't is
nought
That ages, empires, and religions, there
Lie buried in the ravage they have
wrought;
For such as he can lend, — they borrow
not
Glory from those who made the world
their prey;
And he is gathered to the kings of
thought

Who waged contention with their time's
    decay,
And of the past are all that cannot pass
    away.

XLIX

Go thou to Rome, — at once the Para-
    dise,
The grave, the city, and the wilderness;
And where its wrecks like shattered
    mountains rise,
And flowering weeds and fragrant copses
    dress
The bones of Desolation's nakedness,
Pass, till the Spirit of the spot shall
    lead
Thy footsteps to a slope of green access,
Where, like an infant's smile, over the
    dead
A light of laughing flowers along the grass
    is spread;

L

And gray walls moulder round, on which
    dull Time
Feeds, like slow fire upon a hoary brand;
And one keen pyramid with wedge sub-
    lime,
Pavilioning the dust of him who planned
This refuge for his memory, doth stand
Like flame transformed to marble; and
    beneath,
A field is spread, on which a newer band
Have pitched in Heaven's smile their
    camp of death,
Welcoming him we lose with scarce extin-
    guished breath.

LI

Here pause: these graves are all too
    young as yet
To have outgrown the sorrow which con-
    signed
Its charge to each; and if the seal is
    set,
Here, on one fountain of a mourning
    mind,
Break it not thou ! too surely shalt thou
    find
Thine own well full, if thou returnest
    home,
Of tears and gall. From the world's
    bitter wind
Seek shelter in the shadow of the tomb.
What Adonais is, why fear we to become ?

LII

The One remains, the many change and
    pass;
Heaven's light forever shines, Earth's
    shadows fly;
Life, like a dome of many-colored glass,
Stains the white radiance of Eternity,
Until Death tramples it to fragments. —
    Die,
If thou wouldst be with that which thou
    dost seek !
Follow where all is fled ! — Rome's
    azure sky,
Flowers, ruins, statues, music, words, are
    weak
The glory they transfuse with fitting truth
    to speak.

LIII

Why linger, why turn back, why shrink,
    my Heart ?
Thy hopes are gone before; from all
    things here
They have departed; thou shouldst now
    depart !
A light is passed from the revolving
    year,
And man, and woman; and what still is
    dear
Attracts to crush, repels to make thee
    wither.
The soft sky smiles, — the low wind
    whispers near;
'T is Adonais calls ! oh, hasten thither,
No more let Life divide what Death can
    join together.

LIV

That Light whose smile kindles the Uni-
    verse,
That Beauty in which all things work
    and move,
That Benediction which the eclipsing
    Curse
Of birth can quench not, that sustaining
    Love
Which through the web of being blindly
    wove
By man and beast and earth and air and
    sea,
Burns bright or dim, as each are mirrors
    of
The fire for which all thirst, now beams
    on me,
Consuming the last clouds of cold mortality.

LV

The breath whose might I have invoked
  in song
Descends on me; my spirit's bark is
  driven
Far from the shore, far from the trembling throng
Whose sails were never to the tempest
  given;

The massy earth and spherèd skies are
  riven!
I am borne darkly, fearfully, afar;
Whilst, burning through the inmost veil
  of Heaven,
The soul of Adonais, like a star,
Beacons from the abode where the Eternal
  are.

HELLAS

A LYRICAL DRAMA

ΜΑΝΤΙΣ 'ΕΙΜ' 'ΕΣΘΛΩΝ 'ΑΓΩΝΩΝ
ŒDIP. COLON.

Hellas, the last of Shelley's political poems, was written at Pisa in the fall of 1821, and published the next spring at London by Ollier, who made some omissions in the notes and preface with Shelley's permission. Edward Williams suggested the title, and was much interested in the poem as it grew. Shelley describes it, during its composition, as 'a sort of imitation of the *Persæ* of Æschylus, full of lyrical poetry. I try to be what I might have been, but am not successful;' and in mentioning to Gisborne the accuracy of the proof-reading he says, — 'Am I to thank you for the revision of the press? or who acted as midwife to this last of my orphans, introducing it to oblivion, and me to my accustomed failure? May the cause it celebrates be more fortunate than either! Tell me how you like *Hellas*, and give me your opinion freely. It was written without much care, and in one of those few moments of enthusiasm which now seldom visit me, and which make me pay dear for their visits.'

Mrs. Shelley's note gives an excellent account of the circumstances amid which it was written, and of its spirit:

'The south of Europe was in a state of great political excitement at the beginning of the year 1821. The Spanish Revolution had been a signal to Italy — secret societies were formed — and when Naples rose to declare the Constitution, the call was responded to from Brundusium to the foot of the Alps. To crush these attempts to obtain liberty, early in 1821, the Austrians poured their armies into the Peninsula: at first their coming rather seemed to add energy and resolution to a people long enslaved. The Piedmontese asserted their freedom; Genoa threw off the yoke of the King of Sardinia; and, as if in playful imitation, the people of the little state of Massa and Carrara gave the *congé* to their sovereign and set up a republic.

'Tuscany alone was perfectly tranquil. It was said that the Austrian minister presented a list of sixty Carbonari to the grand-duke, urging their imprisonment; and the grand-duke replied, "I do not know whether these sixty men are Carbonari, but I know if I imprison them, I shall directly have sixty thousand start up." But though the Tuscans had no desire to disturb the paternal government, beneath whose shelter they slumbered, they regarded the progress of the various Italian revolutions with intense interest, and hatred for the Austrian was warm in every bosom. But they had slender hopes; they knew that the Neapolitans would offer no fit resistance to the regular German troops, and that the overthrow of the Constitution in Naples would act as a decisive blow against all struggles for liberty in Italy.

'We have seen the rise and progress of reform. But the Holy Alliance was alive and active in those days, and few could dream of the peaceful triumph of liberty. It seemed then that the armed assertion of freedom in the south of Europe was the only hope of the liberals, as, if it prevailed, the nations of the north would imitate the example. Happily the reverse has proved the fact. The countries accustomed to the exercise of the privileges of freemen, to a limited extent, have extended, and are extending these limits. Freedom and knowledge have now a chance of proceeding hand in hand; and if it continue thus, we may hope for the durability of both. Then, as I have said, in 1821, Shelley, as well as every other lover of liberty, looked upon the struggles in Spain and Italy as decisive of the destinies of the world, probably for centuries to come. The interest he took in the progress of affairs was intense. When Genoa declared itself free, his hopes were at their highest. Day after day, he read the bulletins of the Austrian army, and sought eagerly to gather tokens of its defeat. He heard of the revolt of Genoa with emotions of transport. His whole heart and soul were in the triumph of their cause. We were living at Pisa at that time; and several well-informed Italians, at the head of whom we may place the celebrated Vaccá, were accustomed to seek for sympathy in their hopes from Shelley: they did not find such for the despair they too generally experienced, founded on contempt for their southern countrymen.

' While the fate of the progress of the Austrian armies then invading Naples was yet in suspense, the news of another revolution filled him with exultation. We had formed the acquaintance at Pisa of several Constantinopolitan Greeks, of the family of Prince Caradja, formerly Hospodar of Wallachia, who, hearing that the bowstring, the accustomed finale of his viceroyalty, was on the road to him, escaped with his treasures, and took up his abode in Tuscany. Among these was the gentleman to whom the drama of *Hellas* is dedicated. Prince Mavrocordato was warmed by those aspirations for the independence of his country, which filled the hearts of many of his countrymen. He often intimated the possibility of an insurrection in Greece; but we had no idea of its being so near at hand, when, on the 1st of April, 1821, he called on Shelley; bringing the proclamation of his cousin, Prince Ipsilanti, and, radiant with exultation and delight, declared that henceforth Greece would be free.

' Shelley had hymned the dawn of liberty in Spain and Naples, in two odes, dictated by the warmest enthusiasm; — he felt himself naturally impelled to decorate with poetry the uprise of the descendants of that people, whose works he regarded with deep admiration; and to adopt the vaticinatory character in prophesying their success. *Hellas* was written in a moment of enthusiasm. It is curious to remark how well he overcomes the difficulty of forming a drama out of such scant materials. His prophecies, indeed, came true in their general, not their particular purport. He did not foresee the death of Lord Londonderry, which was to be the epoch of a change in English politics, particularly as regarded foreign affairs; nor that the navy of his country would fight for instead of against the Greeks: and by the battle of Navarino secure their enfranchisement from the Turks. Almost against reason, as it appeared to him, he resolved to believe that Greece would prove triumphant: and in this spirit, auguring ultimate good, yet

grieving over the vicissitudes to be endured in the interval, he composed his drama. . . .

' *Hellas* was among 'the last of his compositions, and is among the most beautiful. The choruses are singularly imaginative, and melodious in their versification. There are some stanzas that beautifully exemplify Shelley's peculiar style. . . .

' The conclusion of the last chorus is among the most beautiful of his lyrics; the imagery is distinct and majestic; the prophecy, such as poets love to dwell upon, the regeneration of mankind — and that regeneration reflecting back splendor on the foregone time, from which it inherits so much of intellectual wealth, and memory of past virtuous deeds, as must render the possession of happiness and peace of tenfold value.'

To

HIS EXCELLENCY

PRINCE ALEXANDER MAVROCORDATO

LATE SECRETARY FOR FOREIGN AFFAIRS
TO THE HOSPODAR OF WALLACHIA

THE DRAMA OF HELLAS

IS INSCRIBED

AS AN IMPERFECT TOKEN

OF THE ADMIRATION, SYMPATHY, AND FRIENDSHIP

OF

THE AUTHOR

PISA, *November* 1, 1821.

PREFACE

THE poem of *Hellas*, written at the suggestion of the events of the moment, is a mere improvise, and derives its interest (should it be found to possess any) solely from the intense sympathy which the Author feels with the cause he would celebrate.

The subject in its present state is insusceptible of being treated otherwise than lyrically, and if I have called this poem a drama from the circumstance of its being composed in dialogue, the license is not greater than that which has been assumed by other poets who have called their productions epics, only because they have been divided into twelve or twenty-four books.

The *Persæ* of Æschylus afforded me the first model of my conception, although the decision of the glorious contest now waging in Greece being yet suspended forbids a catastrophe parallel to the return of Xerxes and the desolation of the Persians. I have, therefore, contented myself with exhibiting a series of lyric pictures and with having wrought upon the curtain of futurity, which falls upon the unfinished scene, such figures of indistinct and visionary delineation as suggest the final triumph of the Greek cause as a portion of the cause of civilization and social improvement.

The drama (if drama it must be called) is, however, so inartificial that I doubt whether, if recited on the Thespian wagon to an Athenian village at the Dionysiaca, it would have obtained the prize of the goat. I shall bear with equanimity any punishment greater than the loss of such a reward which the Aristarchi of the hour may think fit to inflict.

The only *goat-song* which I have yet attempted has, I confess, in spite of the unfavorable nature of the subject, received a greater and a more valuable portion of applause than I expected or than it deserved.

Common fame is the only authority which I can allege for the details which form the basis of the poem, and I must trespass upon the forgiveness of my readers for the display of newspaper erudition to which I have been reduced. Undoubtedly, until the conclusion of the war, it will be impossible to obtain an account of it sufficiently authentic for historical materials; but poets have their privilege, and it is unquestionable that actions of the most exalted courage have been performed by the Greeks — that they have gained more than one naval victory, and that their defeat in Wallachia was signalized by circumstances of heroism more glorious even than victory.

The apathy of the rulers of the civilized world to the astonishing circumstance of the descendants of that nation to which they owe their civilization — rising as it were from the ashes of their ruin — is something perfectly inexplicable to a mere spectator of the shows of this mortal scene. We are all Greeks. Our laws, our literature, our religion, our arts, have their root in Greece. But for Greece, Rome, the instructor, the conqueror, or the metropolis of our ancestors, would have spread no illumination with her arms, and we might still have been savages and idolaters; or, what is worse, might have arrived at such a stagnant and miserable state of social institution as China and Japan possess.

The human form and the human mind attained to a perfection in Greece which has impressed its image on those faultless productions whose very fragments are the despair of modern art, and has propagated impulses which cannot cease, through a thousand channels of manifest or imperceptible operation, to ennoble and delight mankind until the extinction of the race.

The modern Greek is the descendant of those glorious beings whom the imagination almost refuses to figure to itself as belonging to our kind, and he inherits much of their sensibility, their rapidity of conception, their enthusiasm and their courage. If in many instances he is degraded by moral and political slavery to the practice of the basest vices it engenders — and that below the level of ordinary degradation — let us reflect that the corruption of the best produces the worst, and that habits which subsist only in relation to a peculiar state of social institution may be expected to cease so soon as that relation is dissolved. In fact, the Greeks, since the admirable novel of *Anastasius* could have been a faithful picture of their manners, have undergone most important changes; the flower of their youth returning to their country from the universities of Italy, Germany and France have communicated to their fellow-citizens the latest results of that social perfection of which their ancestors were the original source. The university of Chios contained before the breaking out of the revolution eight hundred students, and among them several Germans and Americans. The munificence and energy of many of the Greek princes and merchants, directed to the renovation of their country with a spirit and a wisdom which has few examples, is above all praise.

The English permit their own oppressors to act according to their natural sympathy with the Turkish tyrant and to brand upon their name the indelible blot of an alliance with the enemies of domestic happiness, of Christianity and civilization.

Russia desires to possess, not to liberate Greece; and is contented to see the Turks, its natural enemies, and the Greeks, its intended slaves, enfeeble each other until one or both fall into its net. The wise and generous policy of England would have consisted in establishing the independence of Greece and in maintaining it both against Russia and the Turk; — but when was the oppressor generous or just?

Should the English people ever become free, they will reflect upon the part which those who presume to represent their will have played in the great drama of the revival of liberty, with feelings which it would become them to anticipate. This is the age of the war of the oppressed against the oppressors, and every one of those ringleaders of the privileged gangs of murderers and swindlers, called sovereigns, look to each other for aid against the common enemy, and suspend their mutual jealousies in the presence of a mightier fear. Of this holy alliance all the despots of the earth are virtual members. But a new race has arisen throughout Europe, nursed in the abhorrence of the opinions which are its chains, and she will continue to produce fresh generations to accomplish that destiny which tyrants foresee and dread.

The Spanish Peninsula is already free. France is tranquil in the enjoyment of a partial exemption from the abuses which its unnatural and feeble government are vainly attempting to revive. The seed of blood and misery has been sown in Italy, and a more vigorous race is arising to go forth to the harvest. The world waits only the news of a revolution of Germany to see the tyrants who have pinna-

cled themselves on its supineness precipitated into the ruin from which they shall never arise. Well do these destroyers of mankind know their enemy, when they impute the insurrection in Greece to the same spirit before which they tremble throughout the rest of Europe, and that enemy well knows the power and the cunning of its opponents and watches the moment of their approaching weakness and inevitable division to wrest the bloody sceptres from their grasp.

HELLAS

DRAMATIS PERSONÆ

THE PROLOGUE : —
  HERALD OF ETERNITY.
  CHRIST.
  SATAN.
  MAHOMET.
  CHORUS.

THE DRAMA : —
  MAHMUD.
  HASSAN.
  DAOOD.
  AHASUERUS, a Jew.
  PHANTOM OF MAHOMET THE SECOND.
  CHORUS OF GREEK CAPTIVE WOMEN.
  MESSENGERS, SLAVES AND ATTENDANTS.

    SCENE. Constantinople.
    TIME. Sunset.

PROLOGUE : A FRAGMENT

HERALD OF ETERNITY

IT is the day when all the sons of God
Wait in the roofless senate-house, whose floor
Is Chaos, and the immovable abyss
Frozen by His steadfast word to hyaline
  .   .   .   .
The shadow of God, and delegate
Of that before whose breath the universe
Is as a print of dew.

                Hierarchs and kings
Who from your thrones pinnacled on the past
Sway the reluctant present, ye who sit
Pavilioned on the radiance or the gloom   10
Of mortal thought, which like an exhalation
Steaming from earth conceals the   of
  heaven
Which gave it birth,   assemble here
Before your Father's throne; the swift decree
Yet hovers, and the fiery incarnation

Is yet withheld, clothèd in which it shall
                annul
The fairest of those wandering isles that
  gem
The sapphire space of interstellar air,
That green and azure sphere, that earth
  enwrapped   20
Less in the beauty of its tender light
Than in an atmosphere of living spirit
Which interpenetrating all the . . .
       it rolls from realm to realm
And age to age, and in its ebb and flow
Impels the generations
To their appointed place,
Whilst the high Arbiter
Beholds the strife, and at the appointed
  time
Sends his decrees veiled in eternal . . .   30

Within the circuit of this pendant orb
There lies an antique region, on which fell
The dews of thought in the world's golden
  dawn
Earliest and most benign, and from it
  sprung
Temples and cities and immortal forms
And harmonies of wisdom and of song,
And thoughts, and deeds worthy of thoughts
  so fair.
And when the sun of its dominion failed,
And when the winter of its glory came,
The winds that stripped it bare blew on,
  and swept   40
That dew into the utmost wildernesses
In wandering clouds of sunny rain that
  thawed
The unmaternal bosom of the North.
Haste, sons of God,   for ye beheld,
Reluctant, or consenting, or astonished,
The stern decrees go forth, which heaped
  on Greece
Ruin and degradation and despair.
A fourth now waits : assemble, sons of
  God,

To speed, or to prevent, or to suspend,
If, as ye dream, such power be not with-
    held, 50
The unaccomplished destiny.

. . . .

CHORUS

The curtain of the Universe
Is rent and shattered,
The splendor-wingèd worlds disperse
Like wild doves scattered.

Space is roofless and bare,
And in the midst a cloudy shrine,
    Dark amid thrones of light.
In the blue glow of hyaline
Golden worlds revolve and shine. 60
    In   flight
From every point of the Infinite,
    Like a thousand dawns on a single night,
The splendors rise and spread;
And through thunder and darkness dread
Light and music are radiated,
And, in their pavilioned chariots led
By living wings high overhead,
    The giant Powers move, 69
Gloomy or bright as the thrones they fill.

. . . .

A chaos of light and motion
Upon that glassy ocean.

. . . .

The senate of the Gods is met,
Each in his rank and station set;
    There is silence in the spaces —
Lo ! Satan, Christ, and Mahomet
    Start from their places !

CHRIST
            Almighty Father !
Low-kneeling at the feet of Destiny

. . . .

There are two fountains in which spirits
        weep 80
When mortals err, Discord and Slavery
        named,
And with their bitter dew two Destinies
Filled each their irrevocable urns; the third,
Fiercest and mightiest, mingled both, and
        added
Chaos and Death, and slow Oblivion's lymph,
And hate and terror, and the poisoned rain

. . . .

The Aurora of the nations. By this brow
Whose pores wept tears of blood, by these
        wide wounds,

By this imperial crown of agony,
By infamy and solitude and death, 90
For this I underwent, and by the pain
Of pity for those who would   for me
The unremembered joy of a revenge,
For this I felt — by Plato's sacred light,
Of which my spirit was a burning morrow —
By Greece and all she cannot cease to be,
Her quenchless words, sparks of immortal
        truth,
Stars of all night — her harmonies and
        forms,
Echoes and shadows of what Love adores .
In thee, I do compel thee, send forth
        Fate, 100
Thy irrevocable child: let her descend
A seraph-wingèd victory [arrayed]
In tempest of the omnipotence of God
Which sweeps through all things.
From hollow leagues, from Tyranny which
        arms
Adverse miscreeds and emulous anarchies
To stamp, as on a wingèd serpent's seed,
Upon the name of Freedom; from the
        storm
Of faction, which like earthquake shakes
        and sickens
The solid heart of enterprise; from all 110
By which the holiest dreams of highest
        spirits
Are stars beneath the dawn . . .

                    She shall arise
Victorious as the world arose from Chaos !
And as the Heavens and the Earth arrayed
Their presence in the beauty and the light
Of thy first smile, O Father, as they gather
The spirit of thy love which paves for them
Their path o'er the abyss, till every sphere
Shall be one living Spirit, so shall Greece —

SATAN

Be as all things beneath the empyrean 120
Mine ! Art thou eyeless like old Destiny,
Thou mockery-king, crowned with a wreath
        of thorns ?
Whose sceptre is a reed, the broken reed
Which pierces thee ! whose throne a chair
        of scorn;
For seest thou not beneath this crystal floor
The innumerable worlds of golden light
Which are my empire, and the least of
        them
    which thou wouldst redeem from me ?
Know'st thou not them my portion ?

Or wouldst rekindle the   strife ?   130
Which our great Father then did arbitrate
When he assigned to his competing sons
Each his apportioned realm ?
                              Thou Destiny,
Thou who art mailed in the omnipotence
Of Him who sends thee forth, whate'er
     thy task,
Speed, spare not to accomplish, and be mine
Thy trophies, whether Greece again become
The fountain in the desert whence the
     earth
Shall drink of freedom, which shall give it
     strength
To suffer, or a gulf of hollow death   140
To swallow all delight, all life, all hope.
Go, thou Vicegerent of my will, no less
Than of the Father's; but lest thou shouldst
     faint,
The wingèd hounds, Famine and Pestilence,
Shall wait on thee, the hundred-forkèd
     snake,
Insatiate Superstition, still shall
The earth behind thy steps, and War shall
     hover
Above, and Fraud shall gape below, and
     Change
Shall flit before thee on her dragon wings,
Convulsing and consuming, and I add   150
Three vials of the tears which demons weep
When virtuous spirits through the gate of
     Death
Pass triumphing over the thorns of life,
Sceptres and crowns, mitres and swords and
     snares,
Trampling in scorn, like Him and Socrates.
The first is Anarchy; when Power and
     Pleasure,
Glory and science and security,
On Freedom hang like fruit on the green
     tree,
Then pour it forth, and men shall gather
     ashes.
The second Tyranny —

CHRIST

                    Obdurate spirit !
Thou seest but the Past in the To-come. 161
Pride is thy error and thy punishment.
Boast not thine empire, dream not that thy
     worlds
Are more than furnace-sparks or rainbow-
     drops
Before the Power that wields and kindles
     them.

True greatness asks not space, true excel-
     lence
Lives in the Spirit of all things that live,
Which lends it to the worlds thou callest
     thine.

MAHOMET

     Haste thou and fill the waning crescent
With beams as keen as those which pierced
     the shadow   170
Of Christian night rolled back upon the
     West
When the orient moon of Islam rode in
     triumph
From Tmolus to the Acroceraunian snow.

                    Wake, thou Word
Of God, and from the throne of Destiny
Even to the utmost limit of thy way
May Triumph

     Be thou a curse on them whose creed
Divides and multiplies the most high God.

HELLAS

SCENE — *A Terrace, on the Seraglio.* MAHMUD
(*sleeping*) ; *an Indian Slave sitting beside his
Couch.*

CHORUS OF GREEK CAPTIVE WOMEN

We strew these opiate flowers
     On thy restless pillow;
They were stripped from orient bowers,
     By the Indian billow.
          Be thy sleep
          Calm and deep,
Like theirs who fell — not ours who weep !

INDIAN

Away, unlovely dreams !
     Away, false shapes of sleep !
Be his, as Heaven seems,   10
     Clear, and bright, and deep !
Soft as love, and calm as death,
Sweet as a summer night without a breath.

CHORUS

Sleep, sleep ! our song is laden
     With the soul of slumber;
It was sung by a Samian maiden,

Whose lover was of the number
    Who now keep
    That calm sleep
Whence none may wake, where none shall
    weep.   20

INDIAN

I touch thy temples pale!
I breathe my soul on thee!
And could my prayers avail,
    All my joy should be
Dead, and I would live to weep,
So thou mightst win one hour of quiet
    sleep.

CHORUS

    Breathe low, low,
The spell of the mighty mistress now!
When Conscience lulls her sated snake,
And Tyrants sleep, let Freedom wake. 30
    Breathe low — low,
The words, which, like secret fire, shall
    flow
Through the veins of the frozen earth —
    low, low!

SEMICHORUS I

Life may change, but it may fly not;
Hope may vanish, but can die not;
Truth be veiled, but still it burneth;
Love repulsed, — but it returneth.

SEMICHORUS II

Yet were life a charnel, where
Hope lay coffined with Despair;
Yet were truth a sacred lie.   40
Love were lust —

SEMICHORUS I

        If Liberty
Lent not life its soul of light,
Hope its iris of delight,
Truth its prophet's robe to wear,
Love its power to give and bear.

CHORUS

In the great morning of the world,
The spirit of God with might unfurled
The flag of Freedom over Chaos,
    And all its banded anarchs fled,
Like vultures frighted from Imaus 50
    Before an earthquake's tread.
So from Time's tempestuous dawn
Freedom's splendor burst and shone;
Thermopylæ and Marathon

Caught, like mountains beacon-lighted,
    The springing Fire; the wingèd
    glory
On Philippi half-alighted,
    Like an eagle on a promontory.
Its unwearied wings could fan
The quenchless ashes of Milan.   60
From age to age, from man to man
    It lived; and lit from land to land
    Florence, Albion, Switzerland.

Then night fell; and, as from night,
Reassuming fiery flight,
From the West swift Freedom came,
    Against the course of heaven and
    doom,
A second sun arrayed in flame,
    To burn, to kindle, to illume.
From far Atlantis its young beams 70
Chased the shadows and the dreams.
France, with all her sanguine steams,
    Hid, but quenched it not; again
Through clouds its shafts of glory rain
From utmost Germany to Spain.

As an eagle fed with morning
Scorns the embattled tempest's warning,
When she seeks her aerie hanging
    In the mountain-cedar's hair,
And her brood expect the clanging   80
    Of her wings through the wild air,
Sick with famine; — Freedom so
To what of Greece remaineth now
Returns; her hoary ruins glow
Like orient mountains lost in day;
    Beneath the safety of her wings
Her renovated nurslings play,
    And in the naked lightnings
Of truth they purge their dazzled eyes.
Let Freedom leave, where'er she flies, 90
A desert, or a paradise;
    Let the beautiful and the brave
    Share her glory, or a grave.

SEMICHORUS I

With the gifts of gladness
    Greece did thy cradle strew;

SEMICHORUS II

With the tears of sadness
    Greece did thy shroud bedew;

SEMICHORUS I

With an orphan's affection
    She followed thy bier through time;

SEMICHORUS II

And at thy resurrection   100
  Reappeareth, like thou, sublime !

SEMICHORUS I

If Heaven should resume thee,
  To Heaven shall her spirit ascend;

SEMICHORUS II

If Hell should entomb thee,
  To Hell shall her high hearts bend.

SEMICHORUS I

If Annihilation —

SEMICHORUS II

Dust let her glories be;
And a name and a nation
  Be forgotten, Freedom, with thee !

INDIAN

His brow grows darker — breathe not —
    move not !   110
He starts — he shudders; ye that love not,
With your panting loud and fast
Have awakened him at last.

MAHMUD (*starting from his sleep*)

Man the Seraglio-guard ! make fast the
    gate.
What ! from a cannonade of three short
    hours ?
'T is false ! that breach towards the Bos-
    phorus
Cannot be practicable yet — who stirs ?
Stand to the match, that, when the foe pre-
    vails,
One spark may mix in reconciling ruin
The conqueror and the conquered ! Heave
    the tower   120
Into the gap — wrench off the roof.

Enter HASSAN

                              Ha ! what !
The truth of day lightens upon my dream,
And I am Mahmud still.

HASSAN

                    Your Sublime Highness
Is strangely moved.

MAHMUD

          The times do cast strange shadows
On those who watch and who must rule
    their course,

Lest they, being first in peril as in glory,
Be whelmed in the fierce ebb: — and these
    are of them.
Thrice has a gloomy vision hunted me
As thus from sleep into the troubled day;
It shakes me as the tempest shakes the
    sea,   130
Leaving no figure upon memory's glass.
Would that — no matter. Thou didst say
    thou knewest
A Jew, whose spirit is a chronicle
Of strange and secret and forgotten things.
I bade thee summon him; 't is said his tribe
Dream, and are wise interpreters of dreams.

HASSAN

The Jew of whom I spake is old, so old
He seems to have outlived a world's decay;
The hoary mountains and the wrinkled
    ocean
Seem younger still than he; his hair and
    beard   140
Are whiter than the tempest-sifted snow;
His cold pale limbs and pulseless arteries
Are like the fibres of a cloud instinct
With light, and to the soul that quickens
    them
Are as the atoms of the mountain-drift
To the winter wind; but from his eye
    looks forth
A life of unconsumèd thought which pierces
The present, and the past, and the to-
    come.
Some say that this is he whom the great
    prophet
Jesus, the son of Joseph, for his mockery,
Mocked with the curse of immortality. 151
Some feign that he is Enoch; others dream
He was pre-adamite, and has survived
Cycles of generation and of ruin.
The sage, in truth, by dreadful abstinence,
And conquering penance of the mutinous
    flesh,
Deep contemplation, and unwearied study,
In years outstretched beyond the date of
    man,
May have attained to sovereignty and sci-
    ence
Over those strong and secret things and
    thoughts   160
Which others fear and know not.

MAHMUD

                              I would talk
With this old Jew.

HASSAN

                        Thy will is even now
Made known to him, where he dwells in a
    sea-cavern
'Mid the Demonesi, less accessible
Than thou or God! He who would ques-
    tion him
Must sail alone at sunset, where the stream
Of Ocean sleeps around those foamless
    isles,
When the young moon is westering as now,
And evening airs wander upon the wave;
And when the pines of that bee-pasturing
    isle,   170
Green Erebinthus, quench the fiery shadow
Of its gilt prow within the sapphire water,
Then must the lonely helmsman cry aloud,
Ahasuerus! and the caverns round
Will answer, Ahasuerus! If his prayer
Be granted, a faint meteor will arise,
Lighting him over Marmora, and a wind
Will rush out of the sighing pine forest,
And with the wind a storm of harmony
Unutterably sweet, and pilot him   180
Through the soft twilight to the Bos-
    phorus:
Thence, at the hour and place and circum-
    stance
Fit for the matter of their conference,
The Jew appears. Few dare, and few who
    dare
Win the desired communion — but that
    shout
Bodes —
                              [*A shout within.*

MAHMUD

Evil, doubtless; like all human sounds.
Let me converse with spirits.

HASSAN

                        That shout again.

MAHMUD

This Jew whom thou hast summoned —

HASSAN

                        Will be here —

MAHMUD

When the omnipotent hour, to which are
    yoked
He, I, and all things, shall compel —
    enough.   190

Silence those mutineers — that drunken
    crew
That crowd about the pilot in the storm.
Ay! strike the foremost shorter by a head!
They weary me, and I have need of rest.
Kings are like stars — they rise and set,
    they have
The worship of the world, but no repose.
                              [*Exeunt severally.*

CHORUS

Worlds on worlds are rolling ever
    From creation to decay,
Like the bubbles on a river,
    Sparkling, bursting, borne away.   200
    But they are still immortal
    Who, through birth's orient portal
And death's dark chasm hurrying to and
    fro,
    Clothe their unceasing flight
    In the brief dust and light
Gathered around their chariots as they
    go;
    New shapes they still may weave,
    New gods, new laws receive,
Bright or dim are they, as the robes they
    last
On Death's bare ribs had cast.   210

A power from the unknown God,
    A Promethean conqueror, came;
Like a triumphal path he trod
    The thorns of death and shame.
    A mortal shape to him
    Was like the vapor dim
Which the orient planet animates with
    light;
    Hell, Sin and Slavery came,
    Like bloodhounds mild and tame,
Nor preyed until their lord had taken
    flight;   220
    The moon of Mahomet
    Arose, and it shall set;
While blazoned as on heaven's immortal
    noon
The cross leads generations on.

Swift as the radiant shapes of sleep
    From one, whose dreams are Paradise,
Fly, when the fond wretch wakes to
    weep,
    And day peers forth with her blank
    eyes;
    So fleet, so faint, so fair,
    The Powers of earth and air   230

Fled from the folding star of Bethlehem;
    Apollo, Pan, and Love,
    And even Olympian Jove,
Grew weak, for killing Truth had glared
        on them;
    Our hills and seas and streams,
    Dispeopled of their dreams,
Their waters turned to blood, their dew to
        tears,
    Wailed for the golden years.

Enter MAHMUD, HASSAN, DAOOD, *and others*

MAHMUD

More gold ? our ancestors bought gold with
    victory,   239
And shall I sell it for defeat ?

DAOOD

                        The Janizars
Clamor for pay.

MAHMUD

                    Go, bid them pay themselves
With Christian blood !   Are there no Gre-
    cian virgins
Whose shrieks and spasms and tears they
    may enjoy ?
No infidel children to impale on spears ?
No hoary priests after that Patriarch
Who bent the curse against his country's
    heart,
Which clove his own at last ?   Go ! bid
    them kill;
Blood is the seed of gold.

DAOOD

                    It has been sown,
And yet the harvest to the sickle-men   249
Is as a grain to each.

MAHMUD

                    Then take this signet.
Unlock the seventh chamber, in which lie
The treasures of victorious Solyman,
An empire's spoil stored for a day of ruin.
O spirit of my sires, is it not come ?
The prey-birds and the wolves are gorged
    and sleep;
But these, who spread their feast on the
    red earth,
Hunger for gold, which fills not. — See
    them fed;
Then lead them to the rivers of fresh death.
                                    [*Exit* DAOOD.

Oh, miserable dawn, after a night
More glorious than the day which it
    usurped !   260
O faith in God !   O power on earth !   O
    word
Of the great Prophet, whose o'ershadowing
    wings
Darkened the thrones and idols of the
    West,
Now bright ! — for thy sake cursèd be the
    hour,
Even as a father by an evil child,
When the orient moon of Islam rolled in
    triumph
From Caucasus to white Ceraunia !
Ruin above, and anarchy below;
Terror without, and treachery within;
The chalice of destruction full, and all   270
Thirsting to drink; and who among us
    dares
To dash it from his lips ? and where is
Hope ?

HASSAN

The lamp of our dominion still rides high;
One God is God — Mahomet is his Pro-
    phet.
Four hundred thousand Moslems, from the
    limits
Of utmost Asia, irresistibly
Throng, like full clouds at the Sirocco's cry,
But not like them to weep their strength
    in tears;
They bear destroying lightning, and their
    step
Wakes earthquake, to consume and over-
    whelm,   280
And reign in ruin.   Phrygian Olympus,
Tmolus, and Latmos, and Mycale, roughen
With horrent arms; and lofty ships, even
    now,
Like vapors anchored to a mountain's edge,
Freighted with fire and whirlwind, wait at
    Scala
The convoy of the ever-veering wind.
Samos is drunk with blood; the Greek has
    paid
Brief victory with swift loss and long de-
    spair.
The false Moldavian serfs fled fast and far
When the fierce shout of Allah-illa-Allah
Rose like the war-cry of the northern
    wind,   291
Which kills the sluggish clouds, and leaves
    a flock

Of wild swans struggling with the naked
    storm.
So were the lost Greeks on the Danube's
    day !
If night is mute, yet the returning sun
Kindles the voices of the morning birds;
Nor at thy bidding less exultingly
Than birds rejoicing in the golden day
The Anarchies of Africa unleash
Their tempest-wingèd cities of the sea,   300
To speak in thunder to the rebel world.
Like sulphurous clouds half-shattered by
    the storm,
They sweep the pale Ægean, while the
    Queen
Of Ocean, bound upon her island throne,
Far in the West, sits mourning that her
    sons,
Who frown on Freedom, spare a smile for
    thee.
Russia still hovers, as an eagle might
Within a cloud, near which a kite and
    crane
Hang tangled in inextricable fight,
To stoop upon the victor; for she fears 310
The name of Freedom, even as she hates
    thine.
But recreant Austria loves thee as the
    Grave
Loves Pestilence, and her slow dogs of war,
Fleshed with the chase, come up from
    Italy,
And howl upon their limits; for they see
The panther, Freedom, fled to her old
    cover,
Amid seas and mountains, and a mightier
    brood
Crouch round. What Anarch wears a
    crown or mitre,
Or bears the sword, or grasps the key of
    gold,
Whose friends are not thy friends, whose
    foes thy foes ?   320
Our arsenals and our armories are full;
Our forts defy assault; ten thousand can-
    non
Lie ranged upon the beach, and hour by
    hour
Their earth-convulsing wheels affright the
    city;
The galloping of fiery steeds makes pale
The Christian merchant; and the yellow
    Jew
Hides his hoard deeper in the faithless
    earth.

Like clouds, and like the shadows of the
    clouds,
Over the hills of Anatolia,
Swift in wide troops the Tartar chivalry 330
Sweep; the far-flashing of their starry
    lances
Reverberates the dying light of day.
We have one God, one King, one Hope,
    one Law;
But many-headed Insurrection stands
Divided in itself, and soon must fall.

MAHMUD

Proud words, when deeds come short, are
    seasonable.
Look, Hassan, on yon crescent moon, em-
    blazoned
Upon that shattered flag of fiery cloud
Which leads the rear of the departing
    day,
Wan emblem of an empire fading now   340
See how it trembles in the blood-red air,
And like a mighty lamp whose oil is spent,
Shrinks on the horizon's edge, while, from
    above,
One star with insolent and victorious light,
Hovers above its fall, and with keen beams
Like arrows through a fainting antelope,
Strikes its weak form to death.

HASSAN
                    Even as that moon
Renews itself —

MAHMUD
                Shall we be not renewed!
Far other bark than ours were needed now
To stem the torrent of descending time; 350
The spirit that lifts the slave before his
    lord
Stalks through the capitals of armèd kings,
And spreads his ensign in the wilderness;
Exults in chains; and, when the rebel
    falls,
Cries like the blood of Abel from the dust;
And the inheritors of the earth, like beasts
When earthquake is unleashed, with idiot
    fear
Cower in their kingly dens — as I do now.
What were Defeat, when Victory must
    appall ?
Or Danger, when Security looks pale ?   360
How said the messenger, who from the fort
Islanded in the Danube saw the battle
Of Bucharest ? that —

HASSAN

Ibrahim's scimitar
Drew with its gleam swift victory from
heaven
To burn before him in the night of battle —
A light and a destruction.

MAHMUD

Ay ! the day
Was ours; but how ?

HASSAN

The light Wallachians,
The Arnaut, Servian, and Albanian allies,
Fled from the glance of our artillery
Almost before the thunder-stone alit;   370
One half the Grecian army made a bridge
Of safe and slow retreat with Moslem
dead;
The other —

MAHMUD

Speak — tremble not.

HASSAN

Islanded
By victor myriads formed in hollow square
With rough and steadfast front, and thrice
flung back
The deluge of our foaming cavalry;
Thrice their keen wedge of battle pierced
our lines.
Our baffled army trembled like one man
Before a host, and gave them space; but
soon
From the surrounding hills the batteries
blazed,   380
Kneading them down with fire and iron
rain.
Yet none approached; till, like a field of
corn
Under the hook of the swart sickle-man,
The band, entrenched in mounds of Turk-
ish dead,
drew weak and few. Then said the Pacha,
' Slaves,
Render yourselves — they have abandoned
you —
What hope of refuge, or retreat, or aid ?
We grant your lives.' — ' Grant that which
is thine own ! '
Cried one, and fell upon his sword and
died !
Another — ' God, and man, and hope aban-
don me;   390

But I to them and to myself remain
Constant;' he bowed his head and his
heart burst.
A third exclaimed, ' There is a refuge,
tyrant,
Where thou darest not pursue; and canst
not harm,
Shouldst thou pursue; there we shall meet
again.'
Then held his breath, and, after a brief
spasm,
The indignant spirit cast its mortal garment
Among the slain — dead earth upon the
earth !
So these survivors, each by different ways,
Some strange, all sudden, none dishonor-
able,   400
Met in triumphant death; and, when our
army
Closed in, while yet wonder, and awe, and
shame
Held back the base hyenas of the battle
That feed upon the dead and fly the living,
One rose out of the chaos of the slain;
And if it were a corpse which some drea/
spirit
Of the old saviors of the land we rule
Had lifted in its anger, wandering by;
Or if there burned within the dying man
Unquenchable disdain of death, and faith
Creating what it feigned, — I cannot tell;
But he cried, ' Phantoms of the free, we
come !   412
Armies of the Eternal, ye who strike
To dust the citadels of sanguine kings,
And shake the souls throned on their stony
hearts,
And thaw their frost-work diadems like
dew;
O ye who float around this clime, and weave
The garment of the glory which it wears,
Whose fame, though earth betray the dust
it clasped,
Lies sepulchred in monumental thought; 420
Progenitors of all that yet is great,
Ascribe to your bright senate, oh, accept
In your high ministrations, us, your sons —
Us first, and the more glorious yet to
come !
And ye, weak conquerors ! giants, who look
pale
When the crushed worm rebels beneath
your tread —
The vultures, and the dogs, your pensioners
tame,

Are overgorged; but, like oppressors, still
They crave the relic of Destruction's feast.
The exhalations and the thirsty winds   430
Are sick with blood; the dew is foul with
    death;
Heaven's light is quenched in slaughter;
    thus where'er
Upon your camps, cities, or towers, or
    fleets,
The obscene birds the reeking remnants
    cast
Of these dead limbs, — upon your streams
    and mountains,
Upon your fields, your gardens, and your
    housetops, —
Where'er the winds shall creep, or the
    clouds fly,
Or the dews fall, or the angry sun look
    down
With poisoned light — Famine, and Pesti-
    lence,   439
And Panic, shall wage war upon our side!
Nature from all her boundaries is moved
Against ye; Time has found ye light as
    foam.
The Earth rebels; and Good and Evil stake
Their empire o'er the unborn world of men
On this one cast; but ere the die be thrown,
The renovated genius of our race,
Proud umpire of the impious game, de-
    scends,
A seraph-wingèd Victory, bestriding
The tempest of the Omnipotence of God,
Which sweeps all things to their appointed
    doom,   450
And you to oblivion!' — More he would
    have said,
But —

MAHMUD

Died — as thou shouldst ere thy lips had
    painted
Their ruin in the hues of our success.
A rebel's crime, gilt with a rebel's tongue!
Your heart is Greek, Hassan.

HASSAN

It may be so:
A spirit not my own wrenched me within,
And I have spoken words I fear and hate;
Yet would I die for —

MAHMUD

Live! oh, live! outlive
Me and this sinking empire. But the
    fleet —

HASSAN

Alas!

MAHMUD

The fleet which, like a flock of clouds
Chased by the wind, flies the insurgent
    banner!   461
Our wingèd castles from their merchant
    ships!
Our myriads before their weak pirate
    bands!
Our arms before their chains! our years of
    empire
Before their centuries of servile fear!
Death is awake! Repulse is on the wa-
    ters;
They own no more the thunder-bearing
    banner
Of Mahmud, but, like hounds of a base
    breed,
Gorge from a stranger's hand, and rend
    their master.

HASSAN

Latmos, and Ampelos, and Phanæ, saw   470
The wreck —

MAHMUD

The caves of the Icarian isles
Told each to the other in loud mockery,
And with the tongue as of a thousand
    echoes,
First of the sea-convulsing fight — and
    then —
Thou darest to speak — senseless are the
    mountains;
Interpret thou their voice!

HASSAN

My presence bore
A part in that day's shame. The Grecian
    fleet
Bore down at daybreak from the north, and
    hung
As multitudinous on the ocean line
As cranes upon the cloudless Thracian
    wind.   480
Our squadron, convoying ten thousand
    men,
Was stretching towards Nauplia when the
    battle
Was kindled.
First through the hail of our artillery
The agile Hydriote barks with press of sail
Dashed; ship to ship, cannon to cannon,
    man

To man, were grappled in the embrace of war,
Inextricable but by death or victory.
The tempest of the raging fight convulsed
To its crystalline depths that stainless sea,
And shook heaven's roof of golden morn-
   ing clouds   491
Poised on an hundred azure mountain isles.
In the brief trances of the artillery
One cry from the destroyed and the de-
   stroyer
Rose, and a cloud of desolation wrapped
The unforeseen event, till the north wind
Sprung from the sea, lifting the heavy veil
Of battle-smoke — then victory — victory !
For, as we thought, three frigates from
   Algiers
Bore down from Naxos to our aid, but soon
The abhorrèd cross glimmered behind, be-
   fore,   501
Among, around us; and that fatal sign
Dried with its beams the strength in Mos-
   lem hearts,
As the sun drinks the dew. — What more ?
   We fled !
Our noonday path over the sanguine foam
Was beaconed — and the glare struck the
   sun pale —
By our consuming transports; the fierce
   light
Made all the shadows of our sails blood-
   red,
And every countenance blank. Some ships
   lay feeding
The ravening fire even to the water's level:
Some were blown up; some, settling heav-
   ily,   511
Sunk; and the shrieks of our companions
   died
Upon the wind that bore us fast and far,
Even after they were dead.   Nine thousand
   perished !
We met the vultures legioned in the air,
Stemming the torrent of the tainted wind;
They, screaming from their cloudy moun-
   tain peaks,
Stooped through the sulphurous battle-
   smoke, and perched
Each on the weltering carcass that we
   loved,
Like its ill angel or its damnèd soul,   520
Riding upon the bosom of the sea.
We saw the dog-fish hastening to their
   feast.
Joy waked the voiceless people of the sea,

And ravening Famine left his ocean-cave
To dwell with War, with us, and with De-
   spair.
We met night three hours to the west of
   Patmos,
And with night, tempest —

MAHMUD
Cease !

Enter a Messenger

MESSENGER
             Your Sublime Highness,
That Christian hound, the Muscovite am-
   bassador,
Has left the city.   If the rebel fleet
Had anchored in the port, had victory   530
Crowned the Greek legions in the Hippo-
   drome,
Panic were tamer.   Obedience and Mutiny,
Like giants in contention planet-struck,
Stand gazing on each other.   There is peace
In Stamboul.

MAHMUD
          Is the grave not calmer still ?
Its ruins shall be mine.

HASSAN
            Fear not the Russian;
The tiger leagues not with the stag at bay
Against the hunter.   Cunning, base, and
   cruel,
He crouches, watching till the spoil be won,
And must be paid for his reserve in blood.
After the war is fought, yield the sleek
   Russian   541
That which thou canst not keep, his de-
   served portion
Of blood, which shall not flow through
   streets and fields,
Rivers and seas, like that which we may
   win,
But stagnate in the veins of Christian
   slaves !

Enter Second Messenger

SECOND MESSENGER
Nauplia, Tripolizza, Mothon, Athens,
Navarin, Artas, Monembasia,
Corinth and Thebes, are carried by as-
   sault;
And every Islamite who made his dogs
Fat with the flesh of Galilean slaves   550

Passed at the edge of the sword; the lust
of blood,
Which made our warriors drunk, is
quenched in death;
But like a fiery plague breaks out anew
In deeds which make the Christian cause
look pale
In its own light. The garrison of Patras
Has store but for ten days, nor is there
hope
But from the Briton; at once slave and
tyrant,
His wishes still are weaker than his fears,
Or he would sell what faith may yet re-
main
From the oaths broke in Genoa and in
Norway;   560
And if you buy him not, your treasury
Is empty even of promises — his own coin.
The freedman of a western poet chief
Holds Attica with seven thousand rebels,
And has beat back the Pacha of Negropont;
The aged Ali sits in Yanina,
A crownless metaphor of empire;
His name, that shadow of his withered
might,
Holds our besieging army like a spell
In prey to famine, pest, and mutiny;   570
He, bastioned in his citadel, looks forth
Joyless upon the sapphire lake that mirrors
The ruins of the city where he reigned,
Childless and sceptreless. The Greek has
reaped
The costly harvest his own blood matured,
Not the sower, Ali — who has bought a
truce
From Ypsilanti, with ten camel-loads
Of Indian gold.

Enter a Third Messenger

MAHMUD
What more?

THIRD MESSENGER
                    The Christian tribes
Of Lebanon and the Syrian wilderness
Are in revolt; Damascus, Hems, Aleppo, 580
Tremble; the Arab menaces Medina;
The Æthiop has entrenched himself in Sen-
naar,
And keeps the Egyptian rebel well em-
ployed,
Who denies homage, claims investiture
As price of tardy aid. Persia demands

The cities on the Tigris, and the Georgians
Refuse their living tribute. Crete and
Cyprus,
Like mountain-twins that from each other's
veins
Catch the volcano fire and earthquake
spasm,
Shake in the general fever. Through the
city,   590
Like birds before a storm, the Santons
shriek,
And prophesyings horrible and new
Are heard among the crowd; that sea of
men
Sleeps on the wrecks it made, breathless
and still.
A Dervise, learnèd in the Koran, preaches
That it is written how the sins of Islam
Must raise up a destroyer even now.
The Greeks expect a Saviour from the west,
Who shall not come, men say, in clouds
and glory,
But in the Omnipresence of that Spirit 600
In which all live and are. Ominous signs
Are blazoned broadly on the noonday sky;
One saw a red cross stamped upon the
sun;
It has rained blood; and monstrous births
declare
The secret wrath of Nature and her Lord.
The army encamped upon the Cydaris
Was roused last night by the alarm of bat-
tle,
And saw two hosts conflicting in the air, —
The shadows doubtless of the unborn time
Cast on the mirror of the night. While
yet   610
The fight hung balanced, there arose a
storm
Which swept the phantoms from among
the stars.
At the third watch the Spirit of the Plague
Was heard abroad flapping among the
tents;
Those who relieved watch found the senti-
nels dead.
The last news from the camp is that a
thousand
Have sickened, and —

Enter a Fourth Messenger

MAHMUD
          And thou, pale ghost, dim shadow
Of some untimely rumor, speak!

FOURTH MESSENGER

One comes
Fainting with toil, covered with foam and
blood;
He stood, he says, on Chelonites'   620
Promontory, which o'erlooks the isles that
groan
Under the Briton's frown, and all their wa-
ters
Then trembling in the splendor of the
moon;
When, as the wandering clouds unveiled or
hid
Her boundless light, he saw two adverse
fleets
Stalk through the night in the horizon's
glimmer,
Mingling fierce thunders and sulphureous
gleams,
And smoke which strangled every infant
wind
That soothed the silver clouds through the
deep air.
At length the battle slept, but the Sirocco
Awoke, and drove his flock of thunder-
clouds   631
Over the sea-horizon, blotting out
All objects — save that in the faint moon-
glimpse
He saw, or dreamed he saw, the Turkish
admiral
And two the loftiest of our ships of war
With the bright image of that Queen of
Heaven,
Who hid, perhaps, her face for grief, re-
versed;
And the abhorrèd cross —

Enter an Attendant

ATTENDANT

Your Sublime Highness,
The Jew, who —

MAHMUD

Could not come more seasonably.
Bid him attend. I'll hear no more! too
long   640
We gaze on danger through the mist of
fear,
And multiply upon our shattered hopes
The images of ruin. Come what will!
To-morrow and to-morrow are as lamps
Set in our path to light us to the edge

Through rough and smooth; nor can we
suffer aught
Which he inflicts not in whose hand we are.
[*Exeunt.*

SEMICHORUS I

Would I were the wingèd cloud
Of a tempest swift and loud!
I would scorn   650
The smile of morn,
And the wave where the moonrise is born!
I would leave
The spirits of eve
A shroud for the corpse of the day to weave
From other threads than mine!
Bask in the deep blue noon divine
Who would, not I.

SEMICHORUS II

Whither to fly?

SEMICHORUS I

Where the rocks that gird the Ægean   660
Echo to the battle pæan
Of the free,
I would flee,
A tempestuous herald of victory!
My golden rain
For the Grecian slain
Should mingle in tears with the bloody
main;
And my solemn thunder-knell
Should ring to the world the passing-bell
Of tyranny!   670

SEMICHORUS II

Ah king! wilt thou chain
The rack and the rain?
Wilt thou fetter the lightning and hurri-
cane?
The storms are free,
But we ——

CHORUS

O Slavery! thou frost of the world's prime,
Killing its flowers and leaving its thorns
bare!
Thy touch has stamped these limbs with
crime,
These brows thy branding garland bear;
But the free heart, the impassive soul,
Scorn thy control!   681

SEMICHORUS I

Let there be light! said Liberty;
And like sunrise from the sea

Athens arose ! — Around her born,
Shone like mountains in the morn
Glorious states; — and are they now
Ashes, wrecks, oblivion ?

SEMICHORUS II
Go
Where Thermæ and Asopus swallowed
Persia, as the sand does foam;
Deluge upon deluge followed,   690
Discord, Macedon, and Rome;
And, lastly, thou !

SEMICHORUS I
Temples and towers,
Citadels and marts, and they
Who live and die there, have been ours,
And may be thine, and must decay;
But Greece and her foundations are
Built below the tide of war,
Based on the crystalline sea
Of thought and its eternity;
Her citizens, imperial spirits,   700
Rule the present from the past;
On all this world of men inherits
Their seal is set.

SEMICHORUS II
Hear ye the blast,
Whose Orphic thunder thrilling calls
From ruin her Titanian walls ?
Whose spirit shakes the sapless bones
Of Slavery ? Argos, Corinth, Crete,
Hear, and from their mountain thrones
The dæmons and the nymphs repeat
The harmony.

SEMICHORUS I
I hear, I hear !   710

SEMICHORUS II
The world's eyeless charioteer,
Destiny, is hurrying by !
What faith is crushed, what empire
bleeds
Beneath her earthquake-footed steeds ?
What eagle-wingèd Victory sits
At her right hand ? what Shadow flits
Before ? what Splendor rolls behind ?
Ruin and Renovation cry,
Who but we ?

SEMICHORUS I
I hear, I hear !
The hiss as of a rushing wind,   720

The roar as of an ocean foaming,
The thunder as of earthquake coming.
I hear, I hear !
The crash as of an empire falling,
The shrieks as of a people calling
Mercy ! Mercy ! — How they thrill !
Then a shout of ' Kill, kill, kill ! '
And then a small still voice, thus —

SEMICHORUS II
For
Revenge and Wrong bring forth their kind;
The foul cubs like their parents are;   730
Their den is in the guilty mind,
And Conscience feeds them with despair;

SEMICHORUS I
In sacred Athens, near the fane
Of Wisdom, Pity's altar stood;
Serve not the unknown God in vain,
But pay that broken shrine again
Love for hate, and tears for blood.

Enter MAHMUD *and* AHASUERUS

MAHMUD
Thou art a man, thou sayest, even as we.

AHASUERUS
No more !

MAHMUD
But raised above thy fellow-men
By thought, as I by power.

AHASUERUS
Thou sayest so.

MAHMUD
Thou art an adept in the difficult lore   741
Of Greek and Frank philosophy; thou
numberest
The flowers, and thou measurest the stars;
Thou severest element from element;
Thy spirit is present in the past, and sees
The birth of this old world through all its
cycles
Of desolation and of loveliness,
And when man was not, and how man be-
came
The monarch and the slave of this low
sphere,
And all its narrow circles — it is much.   750
I honor thee, and would be what thou art
Were I not what I am; but the unborn
hour,

Cradled in fear and hope, conflicting storms,
Who shall unveil ? Nor thou, nor I, nor
 any
Mighty or wise. I apprehended not
What thou hast taught me, but I now per-
 ceive
That thou art no interpreter of dreams;
Thou dost not own that art, device, or God,
Can make the future present — let it come !
Moreover thou disdainest us and ours ! 760
Thou art as God, whom thou contemplatest.

AHASUERUS

Disdain thee ? — not the worm beneath
 thy feet !
The Fathomless has care for meaner things
Than thou canst dream, and has made
 pride for those
Who would be what they may not, or would
 seem
That which they are not. Sultan ! talk no
 more
Of thee and me, the future and the past;
But look on that which cannot change —
 the One,
The unborn and the undying. Earth and
 Ocean,
Space, and the isles of life or light that
 gem   770
The sapphire floods of interstellar air,
This firmament pavilioned upon chaos,
With all its cressets of immortal fire,
Whose outwall, bastionèd impregnably
Against the escape of boldest thoughts,
 repels them
As Calpe the Atlantic clouds — this Whole
Of suns, and worlds, and men, and beasts,
 and flowers,
With all the silent or tempestuous workings
By which they have been, are, or cease to
 be,
Is but a vision; all that it inherits 780
Are motes of a sick eye, bubbles, and
 dreams;
Thought is its cradle and its grave, nor less
The future and the past are idle shadows
Of thought's eternal flight — they have no
 being;
Nought is but that which feels itself to be.

MAHMUD

What meanest thou ? thy words stream
 like a tempest
Of dazzling mist within my brain — they
 shake

The earth on which I stand, and hang like
 night
On Heaven above me. What can they
 avail ?
They cast on all things, surest, brightest,
 best, —   790
Doubt, insecurity, astonishment.

AHASUERUS

Mistake me not ! All is contained in each.
Dodona's forest to an acorn's cup
Is that which has been or will be, to that
Which is — the absent to the present.
 Thought
Alone, and its quick elements, Will, Pas-
 sion,
Reason, Imagination, cannot die;
They are what that which they regard ap-
 pears,
The stuff whence mutability can weave
All that it hath dominion o'er — worlds,
 worms,   800
Empires, and superstitions. What has
 thought
To do with time, or place, or circumstance ?
Wouldst thou behold the future ? — ask
 and have !
Knock and it shall be opened — look, and
 lo !
The coming age is shadowed on the past
As on a glass.

MAHMUD

    Wild, wilder thoughts convulse
My spirit. Did not Mahomet the Second
Win Stamboul ?

AHASUERUS

    Thou wouldst ask that giant spirit
The written fortunes of thy house and
 faith.
Thou wouldst cite one out of the grave to
 tell   810
How what was born in blood must die.

MAHMUD

       Thy words
Have power on me ! I see —

AHASUERUS

    What hearest thou ?

MAHMUD

A far whisper —
    Terrible silence.

AHASUERUS

What succeeds ?

MAHMUD

The sound
As of the assault of an imperial city,
The hiss of inextinguishable fire,
The roar of giant cannon; the earth-quaking
Fall of vast bastions and precipitous towers,
The shock of crags shot from strange enginery,
The clash of wheels, and clang of armèd
hoofs   820
And crash of brazen mail, as of the wreck
Of adamantine mountains; the mad blast
Of trumpets, and the neigh of raging
steeds,
And shrieks of women whose thrill jars
the blood,
And one sweet laugh, most horrible to
hear,
As of a joyous infant waked, and playing
With its dead mother's breast; and now
more loud
The mingled battle-cry — ha ! hear I not
Ἐν τούτῳ νίκη. Allah-illah-Allah !

AHASUERUS

The sulphurous mist is raised — thou
seest —

MAHMUD

A chasm,
As of two mountains, in the wall of Stamboul;   831
And in that ghastly breach the Islamites,
Like giants on the ruins of a world,
Stand in the light of sunrise. In the dust
Glimmers a kingless diadem, and one
Of regal port has cast himself beneath
The stream of war. Another proudly clad
In golden arms spurs a Tartarian barb
Into the gap, and with his iron mace
Directs the torrent of that tide of men,   840
And seems — he is — Mahomet !

AHASUERUS

What thou seest
Is but the ghost of thy forgotten dream;
A dream itself, yet less, perhaps, than that
Thou call'st reality. Thou mayst behold
How cities, on which empire sleeps enthroned,
Bow their towered crests to mutability.

Poised by the flood, e'en on the height thou
holdest,
Thou mayst now learn how the full tide of
power
Ebbs to its depths. Inheritor of glory
Conceived in darkness, born in blood, and
nourished   850
With tears and toil, thou seest the mortal
throes
Of that whose birth was but the same.
The Past
Now stands before thee like an Incarnation
Of the To-come; yet wouldst thou commune
with
That portion of thyself which was ere thou
Didst start for this brief race whose crown
is death,
Dissolve with that strong faith and fervent
passion,
Which called it from the uncreated deep,
Yon cloud of war with its tempestuous
phantoms
Of raging death; and draw with mighty
will   860
The imperial shade hither.

[Exit AHASUERUS.

MAHMUD

Approach !

PHANTOM

I come
Thence whither thou must go ! The grave
is fitter
To take the living than give up the dead;
Yet has thy faith prevailed, and I am here.
The heavy fragments of the power which
fell
When I arose, like shapeless crags and
clouds,
Hang round my throne on the abyss, and
voices
Of strange lament soothe my supreme repose,
Wailing for glory never to return.
A later empire nods in its decay;   870
The autumn of a greener faith is come;
And wolfish change, like winter, howls to
strip
The foliage in which Fame, the eagle,
built
Her aerie, while Dominion whelped below.
The storm is in its branches, and the frost
Is on its leaves, and the blank deep expects
Oblivion on oblivion, spoil on spoil,

Ruin on ruin. Thou art slow, my son;
The Anarchs of the world of darkness keep
A throne for thee, round which thine em-
    pire lies   880
Boundless and mute; and for thy subjects
    thou,
Like us, shalt rule the ghosts of murdered
    life,
The phantoms of the powers who rule thee
    now —
Mutinous passions and conflicting fears,
And hopes that sate themselves on dust and
    die,
Stripped of their mortal strength, as thou
    of thine.
Islam must fall, but we will reign together
Over its ruins in the world of death;
And if the trunk be dry, yet shall the seed
Unfold itself even in the shape of that 890
Which gathers birth in its decay. Woe!
    Woe!
To the weak people tangled in the grasp
Of its last spasms !

MAHMUD
                    Spirit, woe to all ;
Woe to the wronged and the avenger!
    Woe
To the destroyer, woe to the destroyed !
Woe to the dupe, and woe to the deceiver !
Woe to the oppressed, and woe to the op-
    pressor !
Woe both to those that suffer and inflict;
Those who are born, and those who die !
    But say,
Imperial shadow of the thing I am,   900
When, how, by whom, Destruction must
    accomplish
Her consummation ?

PHANTOM
                    Ask the cold pale Hour,
Rich in reversion of impending death,
When *he* shall fall upon whose ripe gray
    hairs
Sit Care, and Sorrow, and Infirmity —
The weight which Crime, whose wings are
    plumed with years,
Leaves in his flight from ravaged heart to
    heart
Over the heads of men, under which bur-
    den
They bow themselves unto the grave.
    Fond wretch !
He leans upon his crutch, and talks of years

To come, and how in hours of youth re-
    newed   911
He will renew lost joys, and —

VOICE (*without*)
                    Victory ! victory !
                    [*The Phantom vanishes.*

MAHMUD
What sound of the importunate earth has
    broken
My mighty trance ?

VOICE (*without*)
                    Victory ! victory !

MAHMUD
Weak lightning before darkness ! poor
    faint smile
Of dying Islam ! Voice which art the re-
    sponse
Of hollow weakness ! Do I wake and
    live ?
Were there such things ? or may the un-
    quiet brain,
Vexed by the wise mad talk of the old
    Jew,
Have shaped itself these shadows of its
    fear ?   920
It matters not ! — for nought we see or
    dream,
Possess, or lose, or grasp at, can be worth
More than it gives or teaches. Come what
    may,
The future must become the past, and I
As they were, to whom once this present
    hour,
This gloomy crag of time to which I cling,
Seemed an Elysian isle of peace and joy
Never to be attained. — I must rebuke
This drunkenness of triumph ere it die,
And dying, bring despair. Victory ! poor
    slaves !   930
                    [*Exit* MAHMUD.

VOICE (*without*)
Shout in the jubilee of death ! the Greeks
Are as a brood of lions in the net
Round which the kingly hunters of the
    earth
Stand smiling. Anarchs, ye whose daily
    food
Are curses, groans, and gold, the fruit of
    death,
From Thule to the girdle of the world,

Come, feast ! the board groans with the
    flesh of men;
The cup is foaming with a nation's blood;
Famine and Thirst await ! eat, drink, and
    die !

SEMICHORUS I

Victorious Wrong, with vulture scream,
Salutes the risen sun, pursues the flying
    day !   941
I saw her ghastly as a tyrant's dream,
Perch on the trembling pyramid of night,
Beneath which earth and all her realms
    pavilioned lay
In visions of the dawning undelight.
      Who shall impede her flight ?
      Who rob her of her prey ?

VOICE (*without*)

Victory, victory ! Russia's famished eagles
Dare not to prey beneath the crescent's
    light.
Impale the remnant of the Greeks ! de-
    spoil !   950
Violate ! make their flesh cheaper than
    dust !

SEMICHORUS II

    Thou voice which art
The herald of the ill in splendor hid !
Thou echo of the hollow heart
Of monarchy, bear me to thine abode
When desolation flashes o'er a world de-
    stroyed.
Oh, bear me to those isles of jagged cloud
    Which float like mountains on the
      earthquake, mid   958
The momentary oceans of the lightning;
    Or to some toppling promontory proud
    Of solid tempest, whose black pyramid,
Riven, overhangs the founts intensely
    brightning
Of those dawn-tinted deluges of fire
Before their waves expire,
When heaven and earth are light, and only
    light
      In the thunder-night !

VOICE (*without*)

Victory, victory ! Austria, Russia, England,
And that tame serpent, that poor shadow,
    France,
Cry peace, and that means death when
    monarchs speak.
Ho, there ! bring torches, sharpen those
    red stakes !   970

These chains are light, fitter for slaves and
    poisoners
Than Greeks. Kill, plunder, burn ! let
    none remain.

SEMICHORUS I

    Alas for Liberty !
If numbers, wealth, or unfulfilling years,
    Or fate, can quell the free !
    Alas for Virtue ! when
Torments, or contumely, or the sneers
    Of erring judging men
Can break the heart where it abides !
Alas ! if Love, whose smile makes this ob-
    scure world splendid,   980
Can change, with its false times and tides,
    Like hope and terror —
    Alas for Love !
And Truth, who wanderest lone and unbe-
    friended,
If thou canst veil thy lie-consuming mir-
    ror
Before the dazzled eyes of Error,
Alas for thee ! Image of the Above !

SEMICHORUS II

Repulse, with plumes from conquest torn,
Led the ten thousand from the limits of
    the morn
Through many an hostile Anarchy !   990
At length they wept aloud and cried, 'the
    sea ! the sea !'
Through exile, persecution, and despair,
    Rome was, and young Atlantis shall
      become,
The wonder, or the terror, or the tomb,
Of all whose step wakes Power lulled in
    her savage lair.
But Greece was as a hermit child,
    Whose fairest thoughts and limbs were
      built .
To woman's growth by dreams so mild
She knew not pain or guilt;
And now, O Victory, blush ! and Empire,
    tremble,   1000
    When ye desert the free !
    If Greece must be
A wreck, yet shall its fragments reassem-
    ble,
And build themselves again impregnably
    In a diviner clime,
To Amphionic music, on some Cape sub-
    lime
Which frowns above the idle foam of
    time.

SEMICHORUS I

Let the tyrants rule the desert they have
     made;
   Let the free possess the paradise they
     claim;
Be the fortune of our fierce oppressors
     weighed   1010
   With our ruin, our resistance, and our
     name !

SEMICHORUS II

Our dead shall be the seed of their decay,
   Our survivors be the shadows of their
     pride,
Our adversity a dream to pass away, —
   Their dishonor a remembrance to abide !

VOICE (*without*)

Victory ! Victory ! the bought Briton sends
The keys of ocean to the Islamite.
Now shall the blazon of the cross be veiled,
And British skill, directing Othman might,
Thunder-strike rebel victory.   Oh, keep
     holy   1020
This jubilee of unrevengèd blood !
Kill, crush, despoil !   Let not a Greek es-
     cape !

SEMICHORUS I

Darkness has dawned in the East
   On the noon of time;
The death birds descend to their feast,
   From the hungry clime.
Let Freedom and Peace flee far
   To a sunnier strand,
And follow Love's folding star
   To the Evening land !   1030

SEMICHORUS II

   The young moon has fed
   Her exhausted horn
With the sunset's fire;
   The weak day is dead,
   But the night is not born;
And, like loveliness panting with wild de-
     sire,
   While it trembles with fear and delight,
Hesperus flies from awakening night,
And pants in its beauty and speed with light
   Fast-flashing, soft and bright.   1040
Thou beacon of love ! thou lamp of the free !
   Guide us far, far away,
To climes where now, veiled by the ardor
     of day,
   Thou art hidden

From waves on which weary Noon
Faints in her summer swoon,
Between kingless continents, sinless as
   Eden,
Around mountains and islands inviola-
   bly
Pranked on the sapphire sea.

SEMICHORUS I

   Through the sunset of hope,   1050
Like the shapes of a dream,
What Paradise islands of glory gleam !
   Beneath Heaven's cope,
Their shadows more clear float by;
The sound of their oceans, the light of
   their sky,
The music and fragrance their solitudes
   breathe,
Burst like morning on dream, or like Hea-
   ven on death,
   Through the walls of our prison;
And Greece, which was dead, is arisen !

CHORUS

The world's great age begins anew,   1060
   The golden years return,
The earth doth like a snake renew
   Her winter weeds outworn;
Heaven smiles, and faiths and empires
   gleam,
Like wrecks of a dissolving dream.

A brighter Hellas rears its mountains
   From waves serener far;
A new Peneus rolls his fountains
   Against the morning-star.
Where fairer Tempes bloom, there sleep
Young Cyclads on a sunnier deep.   1071

A loftier Argo cleaves the main,
   Fraught with a later prize;
Another Orpheus sings again,
   And loves, and weeps, and dies.
A new Ulysses leaves once more
Calypso for his native shore.

Oh, write no more the tale of Troy,
   If earth Death's scroll must be !
Nor mix with Laian rage the joy   1080
   Which dawns upon the free;
Although a subtler Sphinx renew
Riddles of death Thebes never knew.

Another Athens shall arise,
   And to remoter time

Bequeath, like sunset to the skies,
  The splendor of its prime;
And leave, if nought so bright may live,
All earth can take or Heaven can give.

Saturn and Love their long repose   1090
  Shall burst, more bright and good
Than all who fell, than One who rose,
  Than many unsubdued;

Not gold, not blood, their altar dowers,
But votive tears and symbol flowers.

Oh, cease ! must hate and death return ?
  Cease ! must men kill and die ?
Cease! drain not to its dregs the urn
  Of bitter prophecy.
The world is weary of the past,   1100
Oh, might it die or rest at last !

MISCELLANEOUS POEMS

EARLY POEMS

1813–1815

The *Miscellaneous Poems*, with some exceptions, were published either by Shelley, in his successive volumes, or by Mrs. Shelley, in *Posthumous Poems*, 1824, and the two editions of 1839. A few first appeared elsewhere and were included in the collected editions by Mrs. Shelley, and still others have from time to time found their way to the public. The original issue of each poem is here stated in the introductory note, and its history so far as known is given. By far the greater portion of Shelley's shorter poems is personal, and many of them are addressed to his friends and companions or those who made up the domestic circle in his wanderings ; even those which are most entirely poems of nature are, with few exceptions, charged with his moods, and governed by passing circumstances ; as a whole, therefore, they require, for full understanding, intimacy with the events of his private life, and the reader must be referred to the *Life* of the poet for such a narrative as could not be condensed intelligibly into brief introductory notes, with respect both to persons and facts. Mrs. Shelley's biographical notes, however, have been largely used to preface the poems of each year because of their extraordinary truth to the feeling and atmosphere of Shelley's Italian life. The few political poems are sufficiently explained by reference to current events ; in most of these Shelley owes the manner to Coleridge's example.

Tradition has established *Queen Mab* at the head of Shelley's mature work, and in accordance with it all poems earlier than *Queen Mab* are included under *Juvenilia*. A more just sense would have given this honor to *Alastor*, and have relegated the poems of 1815 to the period of immaturity, to which with all the events relating to them they together with *Queen Mab* belong. It is, however, not deemed wise to attempt to disturb the traditionary arrangement at so late a time.

The Early Poems mainly relate to Shelley's domestic history. A few only show his political interest. Mrs. Shelley describes the summer of 1815 as one of rest, but it was exceptional, as these years were the most troubled of his life. Her record begins with 1815.

' He never spent a season more tranquilly than the summer of 1815. He had just recovered from a severe pulmonary attack ; the weather was warm and pleasant. He lived near Windsor Forest, and his life was spent under its shades, or on the water ; meditating subjects for verse. Hitherto, he had chiefly aimed at extending his political doctrines ; and attempted so to do by appeals, in prose essays, to the people, exhorting them to claim their rights ; but he had now begun to feel that the time for action was not ripe in England, and that the pen was the only instrument wherewith to prepare the way for better things.'

EVENING

TO HARRIET

Composed at Bracknell, July 31, 1813, for the birthday (August 1) of Harriet, his first wife, on the completion of her eighteenth year. Published by Dowden, *Life of Shelley*, 1887.

O THOU bright Sun ! beneath the dark blue
    line
Of western distance that sublime descendest,
And, gleaming lovelier as thy beams decline,
Thy million hues to every vapor lendest,

And, over cobweb lawn and grove and
    stream
Sheddest the liquid magic of thy light,
Till calm Earth, with the parting splen-
    dor bright,
Shows like the vision of a beauteous
    dream;
What gazer now with astronomic eye
    Could coldly count the spots within thy
        sphere?
Such were thy lover, Harriet, could he fly
The thoughts of all that makes his passion
    dear,
    And, turning senseless from thy warm
        caress,
Pick flaws in our close-woven happiness.

TO IANTHE

Elizabeth Ianthe, Shelley's first child, was
born June, 1813. Published by Dowden, *Life
of Shelley*, 1887.

I LOVE thee, Baby! for thine own sweet
    sake;
    Those azure eyes, that faintly dimpled
        cheek,
    Thy tender frame, so eloquently weak,
Love in the sternest heart of hate might
    wake;
But more when o'er thy fitful slumber
    bending
    Thy mother folds thee to her wakeful
        heart,
    Whilst love and pity, in her glances
        blending,
All that thy passive eyes can feel im-
    part:
More, when some feeble lineaments of her,
    Who bore thy weight beneath her spot-
        less bosom,
    As with deep love I read thy face, re-
        cur, —
More dear art thou, O fair and fragile
    blossom;
    Dearest when most thy tender traits ex-
        press
The image of thy mother's loveliness.

THE TRIUMPH OF LIFE

The circumstances of this poem are described
by Mrs. Shelley in words that should always
accompany the verse because of the clearness
with which they render the scene of Shelley's
last composition: 'In the wild but beautiful
Bay of Spezzia the winds and waves which he
loved became his playmates. His days were
chiefly spent on the water; the management
of his boat, its alterations and improvements,
were his principal occupations. At night,
when the unclouded moon shone on the calm
sea, he often went alone in his little shallop to
the rocky caves that bordered it, and sitting
beneath their shelter wrote *The Triumph of
Life*, the last of his productions. The beauty
but strangeness of this lonely place, the refined
pleasure which he felt in the companionship of
a few selected friends, our entire sequestration
from the rest of the world, all contributed to
render this period of his life one of continued
enjoyment. I am convinced that the two
months we passed there were the happiest he
had ever known. . . .
'At first the fatal boat had not arrived, and
was expected with great impatience. On
Monday, May 12th, it came. Williams records
the long wished for fact in his journal:
"Cloudy and threatening weather. M. Mag-
lian called, and after dinner and while walking
with him on the terrace, we discovered a strange
sail coming round the point of Porto Venere,
which proved at length to be Shelley's boat.
She had left Genoa on Thursday last, but had
been driven back by the prevailing bad winds.
A Mr. Heslop and two English seamen brought
her round, and they speak most highly of her
performances. She does indeed excite my surprise and admiration. Shelley and I walked
to Lerici, and made a stretch off the land to
try her; and I find she fetches whatever she
looks at. In short, we have now a perfect
plaything for the summer." — It was thus
that short-sighted mortals welcomed death, he
having disguised his grim form in a pleasing
mask! The time of the friends was now spent
on the sea; the weather became fine, and our
whole party often passed the evenings on the
water, when the wind promised pleasant sailing. Shelley and Williams made longer excursions; they sailed several times to Massa;
they had engaged one of the seamen who
brought her round, a boy, by name Charles
Vivian; and they had not the slightest apprehension of danger. When the weather was
unfavorable, they employed themselves with
alterations in the rigging, and by building a
boat of canvas and reeds, as light as possible,

to have on board the other, for the convenience of landing in waters too shallow for the larger vessel. When Shelley was on board, he had his papers with him; and much of the *Triumph of Life* was written as he sailed or weltered on that sea which was soon to engulf him.'

The fragment was published by Mrs. Shelley, 1824; she describes it as 'in so unfinished a state that I arranged it in its present form with the greatest difficulty.'

SWIFT as a spirit hastening to his task
Of glory and of good, the Sun sprang forth
Rejoicing in his splendor, and the mask

Of darkness fell from the awakened Earth;
The smokeless altars of the mountain snows
Flamed above crimson clouds, and at the birth

Of light the Ocean's orison arose,
To which the birds tempered their matin lay.
All flowers in field or forest, which unclose

Their trembling eyelids to the kiss of day,   11
Swinging their censers in the element,
With orient incense lit by the new ray

Burned slow and inconsumably, and sent
Their odorous sighs up to the smiling air;
And, in succession due, did continent,

Isle, ocean, and all things that in them wear
The form and character of mortal mould,
Rise, as the Sun their father rose, to bear

Their portion of the toil which he of old
Took as his own and then imposed on them.   20
But I, whom thoughts which must remain untold

Had kept as wakeful as the stars that gem
The cone of night, now they were laid asleep
Stretched my faint limbs beneath the hoary stem

Which an old chestnut flung athwart the steep

Of a green Apennine. Before me fled
The night; behind me rose the day; the deep

Was at my feet, and Heaven above my head; —
When a strange trance over my fancy grew
Which was not slumber, for the shade it spread   30

Was so transparent that the scene came through,
As clear as when a veil of light is drawn
O'er evening hills they glimmer; and I knew

That I had felt the freshness of that dawn
Bathe in the same cold dew my brow and hair,
And sate as thus upon that slope of lawn

Under the self-same bough, and heard as there

The birds, the fountains and the ocean hold
Sweet talk in music through the enamoured air.   39
And then a vision on my brain was rolled.

As in that trance of wondrous thought I lay,
This was the tenor of my waking dream.
Methought I sate beside a public way

Thick strewn with summer dust; and a great stream
Of people there was hurrying to and fro,
Numerous as gnats upon the evening gleam, —

All hastening onward, yet none seemed to know
Whither he went, or whence he came, or why
He made one of the multitude, and so

Was borne amid the crowd, as through the sky   50
One of the million leaves of summer's bier.
Old age and youth, manhood and infancy,

Mixed in one mighty torrent did appear;
Some flying from the thing they feared, and some
Seeking the object of another's fear;

And others, as with steps towards the tomb,
Pored on the trodden worms that crawled
    beneath;
And others mournfully within the gloom

Of their own shadow walked, and called it
    death;
And some fled from it as it were a ghost,
Half fainting in the affliction of vain
    breath;   61

But more, with motions which each other
    crossed,
Pursued or shunned the shadows the clouds
    threw
Or birds within the noonday ether lost,

Upon that path where flowers never
    grew, —
And, weary with vain toil and faint for
    thirst,
Heard not the fountains whose melodious
    dew

Out of their mossy cells forever burst,
Nor felt the breeze which from the forest
    told
Of grassy paths and wood-lawns inter-
    spersed   70

With overarching elms, and caverns cold,
And violet banks where sweet dreams
    brood; but they
Pursued their serious folly as of old.

And, as I gazed, methought that in the way
The throng grew wilder, as the woods of
    June
When the south wind shakes the extin-
    guished day;

And a cold glare, intenser than the noon
But icy cold, obscured with blinding light
The sun, as he the stars. Like the young
    moon —

When on the sunlit limits of the night   80
Her white shell trembles amid crimson air,
And whilst the sleeping tempest gathers
    might —

Doth, as the herald of its coming, bear
The ghost of its dead mother, whose dim
    form
Bends in dark ether from her infant's
    chair; —

So came a chariot on the silent storm
Of its own rushing splendor; and a Shape
So sate within, as one whom years deform,

Beneath a dusky hood and double cape,
Crouching within the shadow of a tomb;   90
And o'er what seemed the head a cloud-
    like crape

Was bent, a dun and faint ethereal gloom
Tempering the light. Upon the chariot-
    beam
A Janus-visaged Shadow did assume

The guidance of that wonder-wingèd team;
The shapes which drew it in thick lightnings
Were lost — I heard alone on the air's soft
    stream

The music of their ever-moving wings.
All the four faces of that charioteer   99
Had their eyes banded; little profit brings

Speed in the van and blindness in the rear,
Nor then avail the beams that quench the
    sun, —
Or that with banded eyes could pierce the
    sphere

Of all that is, has been or will be done;
So ill was the car guided — but it passed
With solemn speed majestically on.

The crowd gave way, and I arose aghast,
Or seemed to rise, so mighty was the
    trance,
And saw, like clouds upon the thunder
    blast,

The million with fierce song and maniac
    dance   110
Raging around. Such seemed the jubilee
As when to greet some conqueror's ad-
    vance

Imperial Rome poured forth her living sea
From senate-house, and forum, and theatre,
When   upon the free

Had bound a yoke, which soon they stooped
    to bear.
Nor wanted here the just similitude
Of a triumphal pageant, for, where'er

The chariot rolled, a captive multitude
Was driven; — all those who had grown
    old in power   120
Or misery; all who had their age subdued

By action or by suffering, and whose hour
Was drained to its last sand in weal or woe,
So that the trunk survived both fruit and
    flower;

All those whose fame or infamy must grow
Till the great winter lay the form and
    name
Of this green earth with them forever low;

All but the sacred few who could not tame
Their spirits to the conquerors, but, as soon
As they had touched the world with living
    flame,   130

Fled back like eagles to their native
    noon, —
Or those who put aside the diadem
Of earthly thrones or gems . . .

Were there, of Athens or Jerusalem,
Were neither mid the mighty captives
    seen,
Nor mid the ribald crowd that followed
    them,

Nor those who went before fierce and ob-
    scene.
The wild dance maddens in the van; and
    those
Who lead it, fleet as shadows on the green,

Outspeed the chariot, and without repose
Mix with each other in tempestuous mea-
    sure   141
To savage music, wilder as it grows.

They, tortured by their agonizing pleasure,
Convulsed and on the rapid whirlwinds
    spun
Of that fierce spirit whose unholy leisure

Was soothed by mischief since the world
    begun,
Throw back their heads and loose their
    streaming hair;
And, in their dance round her who dims
    the sun,

Maidens and youths fling their wild arms
    in air
As their feet twinkle; they recede, and
    now,   150
Bending within each other's atmosphere,

Kindle invisibly, and, as they glow,
Like moths by light attracted and repelled,
Oft to their bright destruction come and
    go:

Till, like two clouds into one vale im-
    pelled
That shake the mountains when their light-
    nings mingle
And die in rain, the fiery band which held

Their natures, snaps, while the shock still
    may tingle; —
One falls and then another in the path
Senseless, nor is the desolation single,   160

Yet ere I can say where, the chariot hath
Passed over them — nor other trace I
    find
But as of foam after the ocean's wrath

Is spent upon the desert shore. Behind,
Old men and women foully disarrayed
Shake their gray hairs in the insulting
    wind

And follow in the dance, with limbs de-
    cayed,
Seeking to reach the light which leaves
    them still
Farther behind and deeper in the shade.

But not the less with impotence of will   170
They wheel, though ghastly shadows inter-
    pose
Round them and round each other, and
    fulfil

Their work, and in the dust from whence
    they rose
Sink, and corruption veils them as they
    lie,
And past in these performs what   in
    those.

Struck to the heart by this sad pageantry,
Half to myself I said — 'And what is
    this?
Whose shape is that within the car? And
    why' —

I would have added — 'is all here
    amiss?' —
But a voice answered — 'Life!' — I turned,
    and knew   180
(O Heaven, have mercy on such wretched-
    ness!)

That what I thought was an old root which
    grew
To strange distortion out of the hillside
Was indeed one of those deluded crew;

And that the grass, which methought hung
    so wide
And white, was but his thin discolored
    hair;
And that the holes he vainly sought to hide

Were or had been eyes: — 'If thou canst,
    forbear
To join the dance, which I had well for-
    borne!'
Said the grim Feature (of my thought
    aware).   190

'I will unfold that which to this deep scorn
Led me and my companions, and relate
The progress of the pageant since the
    morn.

'If thirst of knowledge shall not then abate,
Follow it thou even to the night; but I
Am weary.' — Then like one who with the
    weight

Of his own words is staggered, wearily
He paused; and ere he could resume, I
    cried:
'First, who art thou?' — 'Before thy mem-
    ory,

'I feared, loved, hated, suffered, did, and
    died,   200
And if the spark with which Heaven lit my
    spirit
Had been with purer nutriment supplied,

'Corruption would not now thus much in-
    herit
Of what was once Rousseau, — nor this
    disguise
Stain that which ought to have disdained
    to wear it;

'If I have been extinguished, yet there rise
A thousand beacons from the spark I
    bore' —
'And who are those chained to the car?'
    'The wise,

'The great, the unforgotten, — they who
    wore
Mitres and helms and crowns, or wreaths
    of light,   210
Signs of thought's empire over thought;
    their lore

'Taught them not this, to know themselves;
    their might
Could not repress the mystery within,
And, for the morn of truth they feigned,
    deep night

'Caught them ere evening.' 'Who is he
    with chin
Upon his breast, and hands crossed on his
    chain?'
'The child of a fierce hour; he sought to
    win

'The world, and lost all that it did contain
Of greatness, in its hope destroyed; and
    more
Of fame and peace than virtue's self can
    gain   220

'Without the opportunity which bore
Him on its eagle pinions to the peak
From which a thousand climbers have be-
    fore

'Fallen, as Napoleon fell.' — I felt my
    cheek
Alter, to see the shadow pass away,
Whose grasp had left the giant world so
    weak

That every pigmy kicked it as it lay;
And much I grieved to think how power
    and will
In opposition rule our mortal day,

And why God made irreconcilable   230
Good and the means of good; and for de-
    spair
I half disdained mine eyes' desire to fill

With the spent vision of the times that
were
And scarce have ceased to be. 'Dost thou
behold,'
Said my guide, 'those spoilers spoiled, Voltaire,

'Frederick, and Paul, Catherine, and Leo-
pold,
And hoary anarchs, demagogues, and
sage —
          names which the world thinks
          always old,   238

'For in the battle Life and they did wage,
She remained conqueror. I was overcome
By my own heart alone, which neither
age,

'Nor tears, nor infamy, nor now the tomb,
Could temper to its object.' — 'Let them
pass,'
I cried, 'the world and its mysterious
doom

'Is not so much more glorious than it was
That I desire to worship those who drew
New figures on its false and fragile glass

'As the old faded.' — 'Figures ever new
Rise on the bubble, paint them as you
may;
We have but thrown, as those before us
threw,   250

'Our shadows on it as it passed away.
But mark how chained to the triumphal
chair
The mighty phantoms of an elder day;

'All that is mortal of great Plato there
Expiates the joy and woe his Master knew
not;
The star that ruled his doom was far too
fair,

'And life, where long that flower of Heaven grew not,
Conquered that heart by love, which gold,
or pain,
Or age, or sloth, or slavery, could subdue
not.

'And near him walk the   twain, 260
The tutor and his pupil, whom Dominion
Followed as tame as vulture in a chain.

'The world was darkened beneath either
pinion
Of him whom from the flock of conquerors
Fame singled out for her thunder-bearing
minion;

'The other long outlived both woes and
wars,
Throned in the thoughts of men, and still
had kept
The jealous key of truth's eternal doors,

'If Bacon's eagle spirit had not leapt
Like lightning out of darkness — he com-
pelled   270
The Proteus shape of Nature, as it slept,

'To wake, and lead him to the caves that
held
The treasure of the secrets of its reign.
See the great bards of elder time, who
quelled

'The passions which they sung, as by their
strain
May well be known: their living melody
Tempers its own contagion to the vein

'Of those who are infected with it.   I
Have suffered what I wrote, or viler
pain!   279
And so my words have seeds of misery —
.   .   .   .
'Even as the deeds of others, not as theirs.'
And then he pointed to a company,

'Midst whom I quickly recognized the
heirs
Of Cæsar's crime, from him to Constantine;
The anarch chiefs, whose force and murderous snares

Had founded many a sceptre-bearing line,
And spread the plague of gold and blood
abroad;
And Gregory and John, and men divine,

Who rose like shadows between man and
God,
Till that eclipse, still hanging over heaven,
Was worshipped, by the world o'er which
they strode,   291

For the true sun it quenched. 'Their
power was given
But to destroy,' replied the leader: — 'I
Am one of those who have created, even

'If it be but a world of agony.'
'Whence camest thou? and whither goest
thou?
How did thy course begin?' I said, 'and
why?

'Mine eyes are sick of this perpetual
flow
Of people, and my heart sick of one sad
thought —
Speak!' — 'Whence I am, I partly seem
to know,   300

'And how and by what paths I have been
brought
To this dread pass, methinks even thou
mayst guess.
Why this should be, my mind can compass
not;

'Whither the conqueror hurries me, still
less.
But follow thou, and from spectator turn
Actor or victim in this wretchedness;

'And what thou wouldst be taught I then
may learn
From thee. Now listen: — In the April
prime,
When all the forest tips began to burn

'With kindling green, touched by the
azure clime   310
Of the young season, I was laid asleep
Under a mountain, which from unknown
time

'Had yawned into a cavern, high and deep;
And from it came a gentle rivulet,
Whose water, like clear air, in its calm
sweep

'Bent the soft grass, and kept forever
wet
The stems of the sweet flowers, and filled
the grove
With sounds which whoso hears must needs
forget

'All pleasure and all pain, all hate and
love,
Which they had known before that hour of
rest.   320
A sleeping mother then would dream not of

'Her only child who died upon the breast
At eventide; a king would mourn no more
The crown of which his brows were dispos-
sessed

'When the sun lingered o'er his ocean floor
To gild his rival's new prosperity;
Thou wouldst forget thus vainly to deplore

'Ills, which, if ills, can find no cure from
thee,
The thought of which no other sleep will
quell,
Nor other music blot from memory, —   330

'So sweet and deep is the oblivious spell;
And whether life had been before that
sleep
The heaven which I imagine, or a hell

'Like this harsh world in which I wake to
weep,
I know not. I arose, and for a space
The scene of woods and waters seemed to
keep,

'Though it was now broad day, a gentle
trace
Of light diviner than the common sun
Sheds on the common earth, and all the
place

'Was filled with magic sounds woven into
one   340
Oblivious melody, confusing sense
Amid the gliding waves and shadows dun;

'And, as I looked, the bright omnipresence
Of morning through the orient cavern
flowed,
And the sun's image radiantly intense

'Burned on the waters of the well that
glowed
Like gold, and threaded all the forest's
maze
With winding paths of emerald fire. There
stood

'Amid the sun, as he amid the blaze
Of his own glory, on the vibrating   350
Floor of the fountain, paved with flashing
    rays,

'A Shape all light, which with one hand
    did fling
Dew on the earth, as if she were the dawn,
And the invisible rain did ever sing

'A silver music on the mossy lawn;
And still before me on the dusky grass,
Iris her many-colored scarf had drawn:

'In her right hand she bore a crystal glass,
Mantling with bright nepenthe; the fierce
    splendor
Fell from her as she moved under the
    mass   360

'Of the deep cavern, and, with palms so
    tender
Their tread broke not the mirror of its
    billow,
Glided along the river, and did bend her

'Head under the dark boughs, till like a
    willow,
Her fair hair swept the bosom of the stream
That whispered with delight to be its pil-
    low.

'As one enamoured is upborne in dream
O'er lily-paven lakes mid silver mist,
To wondrous music, so this Shape might
    seem

'Partly to tread the waves with feet which
    kissed   370
The dancing foam; partly to glide along
The air which roughened the moist ame-
    thyst,

'Or the faint morning beams that fell
    among
The trees, or the soft shadows of the trees;
And her feet, ever to the ceaseless song

'Of leaves and winds and waves and birds
    and bees
And falling drops, moved in a measure new,
Yet sweet, as on the summer evening
    breeze

'Up from the lake a shape of golden dew
Between two rocks, athwart the rising
    moon,   380
Dances i' the wind, where never eagle flew;

'And still her feet, no less than the sweet
    tune
To which they moved, seemed as they
    moved to blot
The thoughts of him who gazed on them;
    and soon

'All that was seemed as if it had been not;
And all the gazer's mind was strewn be-
    neath
Her feet like embers; and she, thought by
    thought,

'Trampled its sparks into the dust of death,
As Day upon the threshold of the east
Treads out the lamps of night, until the
    breath   390

'Of darkness reillumine even the least
Of heaven's living eyes; like day she came,
Making the night a dream; and ere she
    ceased

'To move, as one between desire and
    shame
Suspended, I said — "If, as it doth seem,
Thou comest from the realm without a
    name,

' "Into this valley of perpetual dream,
Show whence I came, and where I am, and
    why —
Pass not away upon the passing stream."

' "Arise and quench thy thirst," was her
    reply.   400
And, as a shut lily stricken by the wand
Of dewy morning's vital alchemy,

'I rose; and, bending at her sweet com-
    mand,
Touched with faint lips the cup she raised,
And suddenly my brain became as sand

'Where the first wave had more than half
    erased
The track of deer on desert Labrador,
Whilst the wolf, from which they fled
    amazed,

'Leaves his stamp visibly upon the shore
Until the second bursts; — so on my sight
Burst a new Vision, never seen before,   411

'And the fair Shape waned in the coming
      light,
As veil by veil the silent splendor drops
From Lucifer, amid the chrysolite

'Of sunrise, ere it tinge the mountain tops;
And as the presence of that fairest planet,
Although unseen, is felt by one who hopes

'That his day's path may end, as he be-
      gan it,
In that star's smile whose light is like the
      scent   419
Of a jonquil when evening breezes fan it,

'Or the soft note in which his dear lament
The Brescian shepherd breathes, or the
      caress
That turned his weary slumber to con-
      tent, —

'So knew I in that light's severe excess
The presence of that Shape which on the
      stream
Moved, as I moved along the wilderness,

'More dimly than a day-appearing dream,
The ghost of a forgotten form of sleep,
A light of heaven whose half-extinguished
      beam

'Through the sick day, in which we wake
      to weep,   430
Glimmers, forever sought, forever lost;
So did that Shape its obscure tenor keep

'Beside my path, as silent as a ghost.
But the new Vision, and the cold bright car,
With solemn speed and stunning music,
      crossed

'The forest; and, as if from some dread
      war
Triumphantly returning, the loud million
Fiercely extolled the fortune of her star.

'A moving arch of victory, the vermilion
And green and azure plumes of Iris had   440
Built high over her wind-wingèd pavilion;

'And underneath ethereal glory clad
The wilderness; and far before her flew
The tempest of the splendor, which for-
      bade

'Shadow to fall from leaf and stone. The
      crew
Seemed in that light, like atomies to dance
Within a sunbeam. Some upon the new

'Embroidery of flowers, that did enhance
The grassy vesture of the desert, played,
Forgetful of the chariot's swift advance;   450

'Others stood grazing, till within the shade
Of the great mountain its light left them
      dim;
Others outspeeded it; and others made

'Circles around it, like the clouds that swim
Round the high moon in a bright sea of air;
And more did follow, with exulting hymn,

'The chariot and the captives fettered there;
But all like bubbles on an eddying flood
Fell into the same track at last, and were

'Borne onward. I among the multitude
Was swept. Me sweetest flowers delayed
      not long;   461
Me not the shadow nor the solitude;

'Me not that falling stream's Lethean
      song;
Me not the phantom of that early Form
Which moved upon its motion: but among

'The thickest billows of that living storm
I plunged, and bared my bosom to the
      clime
Of that cold light, whose airs too soon de-
      form.

'Before the chariot had begun to climb
The opposing steep of that mysterious dell,
Behold a wonder worthy of the rhyme   471

'Of him who from the lowest depths of hell,
Through every paradise and through all
      glory,
Love led serene, and who returned to tell

'The words of hate and awe, — the won-
      drous story

How all things are transfigured except
    Love;
For deaf as is a sea which wrath makes
    hoary,

'The world can hear not the sweet notes
    that move
The sphere whose light is melody to
    lovers, —
A wonder worthy of his rhyme. The grove

'Grew dense with shadows to the inmost
    covers;   481
The earth was gray with phantoms; and
    the air
Was peopled with dim forms, as when there
    hovers

'A flock of vampire-bats before the glare
Of the tropic sun, bringing, ere evening,
Strange night upon some Indian isle.
    Thus were

'Phantoms diffused around; and some did
    fling
Shadows of shadows, yet unlike themselves,
Behind them; some like eaglets on the
    wing

'Were lost in the white day; others like
    elves   490
Danced in a thousand unimagined shapes
Upon the sunny streams and grassy shelves;

'And others sate chattering like restless
    apes
On vulgar hands, . . .
Some made a cradle of the ermined capes

'Of kingly mantles; some across the tiar
Of pontiffs sate like vultures; others played
Under the crown which girt with empire

'A baby's or an idiot's brow, and made
Their nests in it. The old anatomies   500
Sate hatching their bare broods under the
    shade

'Of demon wings, and laughed from their
    dead eyes
To reassume the delegated power,
Arrayed in which those worms did mon-
    archize

'Who made this earth their charnel.
    Others more
Humble, like falcons, sate upon the fist
Of common men, and round their heads
    did soar;

'Or like small gnats and flies, as thick as
    mist
On evening marshes, thronged about the
    brow   509
Of lawyers, statesmen, priest and theorist;

'And others, like discolored flakes of
    snow,
On fairest bosoms and the sunniest hair,
Fell, and were melted by the youthful
    glow

'Which they extinguished; and, like tears,
    they were
A veil to those from whose faint lids they
    rained
In drops of sorrow. I became aware

'Of whence those forms proceeded which
    thus stained
The track in which we moved. After
    brief space,
From every form the beauty slowly waned;

'From every firmest limb and fairest face
The strength and freshness fell like dust,
    and left   521
The action and the shape without the grace

'Of life. The marble brow of youth was
    cleft
With care; and in those eyes where once
    hope shone,
Desire, like a lioness bereft

'Of her last cub, glared ere it died; each
    one
Of that great crowd sent forth incessantly
These shadows, numerous as the dead
    leaves blown

'In autumn evening from a poplar tree.   529
Each like himself and like each other were
At first; but some, distorted, seemed to be

'Obscure clouds, moulded by the casual
    air;

And of this stuff the car's creative ray
Wrought all the busy phantoms that were
    there,

'As the sun shapes the clouds. Thus on
    the way
Mask after mask fell from the countenance
And form of all; and, long before the day

'Was old, the joy, which waked like
    heaven's glance
The sleepers in the oblivious valley, died;
And some grew weary of the ghastly dance,

'And fell, as I have fallen, by the way-
    side; —   541
Those soonest from whose forms most
    shadows passed,
And least of strength and beauty did abide.'

'Then, what is life? I cried.' —

STANZA

WRITTEN AT BRACKNELL

The stanza apparently refers to Mrs. Boin-
ville, from whose house Shelley writes to Hogg,
March 16, 1814 : ' I have written nothing but
one stanza, which has no meaning, and that I
have only written in thought. This is the
vision of a delirious and distempered dream,
which passes away at the cold clear light of
morning. Its surpassing excellence and exquisite perfections have no more reality than
the color of an autumnal sunset.' Published
by Hogg, *Life of Shelley.* 1858.

THY dewy looks sink in my breast;
    Thy gentle words stir poison there;
Thou hast disturbed the only rest
    That was the portion of despair !

Subdued to Duty's hard control,
    I could have borne my wayward lot:
The chains that bind this ruined soul
    Had cankered then — but crushed it not.

TO ——

ΔΑΚΡΥΣΙ ΔΙΟΙΣΩ ΠΟΤΜΟΝ 'ΑΠΟΤΜΟΝ.

Mrs. Shelley states that Coleridge is the person addressed : ' The poem beginning " Oh,
there are spirits in the air " was addressed in
idea to Coleridge, whom he never knew ; and
at whose character he could only guess imperfectly, through his writings and accounts he
heard of him from some who knew him well.
He regarded his change of opinions as rather
an act of will than conviction, and believed
that in his inner heart he would be haunted by
what Shelley considered the better and holier
aspirations of his youth.' Dowden questions
' whether it was not rather addressed in a de-
spondent mood by Shelley to his own spirit.'
This suggestion was first advanced by Bertram
Dobell, in his reprint of *Alastor,* and supported
by the assent of Rossetti there given ; that it
is correct is reasonably certain. Published
with *Alastor,* 1816.

OH, there are spirits of the air,
    And genii of the evening breeze,
And gentle ghosts, with eyes as fair
As star-beams among twilight trees !
Such lovely ministers to meet
Oft hast thou turned from men thy lonely
    feet.

With mountain winds, and babbling
    springs,
    And moonlight seas, that are the voice
Of these inexplicable things,
    Thou didst hold commune, and rejoice
When they did answer thee; but they
Cast, like a worthless boon, thy love away.

And thou hast sought in starry eyes
    Beams that were never meant for
    thine,

Another's wealth; — tame sacrifice
  To a fond faith ! still dost thou pine ?
Still dost thou hope that greeting hands,
Voice, looks or lips, may answer thy de-
      mands ?

Ah, wherefore didst thou build thine hope
  On the false earth's inconstancy ?
Did thine own mind afford no scope
  Of love, or moving thoughts to thee,
That natural scenes or human smiles
Could steal the power to wind thee in their
      wiles ?

Yes, all the faithless smiles are fled
  Whose falsehood left thee broken-
      hearted;
The glory of the moon is dead;
  Night's ghost and dreams have now
      departed;
Thine own soul still is true to thee,
But changed to a foul fiend through misery.

This fiend, whose ghastly presence ever
  Beside thee like thy shadow hangs,
Dream not to chase; — the mad endeavor
  Would scourge thee to severer pangs.
Be as thou art.   Thy settled fate,
Dark as it is, all change would aggravate.

TO ——

This poem is placed conjecturally by Mrs.
Shelley with the poems of 1817 ; but Dowden
suggests that it was addressed to Mary Godwin
in June, 1814. Harriet answers as well or
better to the situation described. Published
by Mrs. Shelley, 2d ed., 1839.

YET look on me — take not thine eyes
    away,
  Which feed upon the love within mine
    own,
Which is indeed but the reflected ray
  Of thine own beauty from my spirit
    thrown.
Yet speak to me — thy voice is as the
    tone
Of my heart's echo, and I think I hear
  That thou yet lovest me; yet thou alone
Like one before a mirror, without care

Of aught but thine own features, imaged
    there;
And yet I wear out life in watching thee;
  A toil so sweet at times, and thou indeed
Art kind when I am sick, and pity me.

STANZAS.   APRIL, 1814

Described by Dowden as 'a fragment of
transmuted biography ;' he ascribes Shelley's
mood to his bidding farewell to the Boinvilles
on his return to his own home. The incident
that occasioned the verses has not been recorded. It was composed at Bracknell, and
published with *Alastor*, 1816.

AWAY ! the moor is dark beneath the moon,
  Rapid clouds have drunk the last pale
    beam of even.
Away ! the gathering winds will call the
    darkness soon,
  And profoundest midnight shroud the
    serene lights of heaven.
Pause not ! the time is past ! every voice
    cries, Away !
  Tempt not with one last tear thy friend's
    ungentle mood;
Thy lover's eye, so glazed and cold, dares
    not entreat thy stay;
  Duty and dereliction guide thee back to
    solitude.

Away, away ! to thy sad and silent home;
  Pour bitter tears on its desolated hearth;
Watch the dim shades as like ghosts they
    go and come,
  And complicate strange webs of melan-
    choly mirth.
The leaves of wasted autumn woods shall
    float around thine head;
  The blooms of dewy spring shall gleam
    beneath thy feet;
But thy soul or this world must fade in the
    frost that binds the dead,
  Ere midnight's frown and morning's
    smile, ere thou and peace, may meet.

The cloud-shadows of midnight possess
    their own repose,
  For the weary winds are silent, or the
    moon is in the deep;
Some respite to its turbulence unresting
    ocean knows;
  Whatever moves, or toils, or grieves,
    hath its appointed sleep.

Thou in the grave shalt rest — yet till the
   phantoms flee,
Which that house and heath and garden
   made dear to thee erewhile,
Thy remembrance, and repentance, and
   deep musings are not free
From the music of two voices, and the
   light of one sweet smile.

TO HARRIET

Dowden, who published the poem in *Life of
Shelley*, 1887, describes it as ' the first of a few
[five] short pieces added in Harriet's handwriting to the MS. collection of poems prepared for publication in the early days of the
preceding year.' It was composed in May,
1814.

THY look of love has power to calm
   The stormiest passion of my soul;
Thy gentle words are drops of balm
   In life's too bitter bowl;
No grief is mine, but that alone
These choicest blessings I have known.

Harriet ! if all who long to live
   In the warm sunshine of thine eye,
That price beyond all pain must give, —
   Beneath thy scorn to die;
Then hear thy chosen own too late
His heart most worthy of thy hate.

Be thou, then, one among mankind
   Whose heart is harder not for state,
Thou only virtuous, gentle, kind,
   Amid a world of hate;
And by a slight endurance seal
A fellow-being's lasting weal.

For pale with anguish is his cheek,
   His breath comes fast, his eyes are dim,
Thy name is struggling ere he speak,
   Weak is each trembling limb;
In mercy let him not endure
The misery of a fatal cure.

Oh, trust for once no erring guide !
   Bid the remorseless feeling flee;
'T is malice, 't is revenge, 't is pride,
   'T is anything but thee;
Oh, deign a nobler pride to prove,
And pity if thou canst not love.

TO MARY WOLLSTONECRAFT GODWIN·

Composed in June, 1814, and published by
Mrs. Shelley, *Posthumous Poems*, 1824.

I

MINE eyes were dim with tears unshed;
   Yes, I was firm — thus wert not thou;
My baffled looks did fear yet dread
   To meet thy looks — I could not know
How anxiously they sought to shine
With soothing pity upon mine.

II

To sit and curb the soul's mute rage
   Which preys upon itself alone;
To curse the life which is the cage
   Of fettered grief that dares not groan,
Hiding from many a careless eye
The scornèd load of agony;

III

Whilst thou alone, then not regarded,
   The   thou alone should be, —
To spend years thus, and be rewarded,
   As thou, sweet love, requited me
When none were near — Oh, I did wake
From torture for that moment's sake.

IV

Upon my heart thy accents sweet
   Of peace and pity fell like dew
On flowers half dead; thy lips did meet
   Mine tremblingly; thy dark eyes threw
Their soft persuasion on my brain,
Charming away its dream of pain.

V

We are not happy, sweet ! our state
   Is strange and full of doubt and fear;
More need of words that ills abate; —
   Reserve or censure come not near
Our sacred friendship, lest there be
No solace left for thee and me.

VI

Gentle and good and mild thou art,
   Nor can I live if thou appear
Aught but thyself, or turn thine heart
   Away from me, or stoop to wear
The mask of scorn, although it be
To hide the love thou feel'st for me.

MUTABILITY

Published with *Alastor*, 1816.

WE are as clouds that veil the midnight
   moon;
  How restlessly they speed, and gleam,
    and quiver,
Streaking the darkness radiantly! — yet
   soon
  Night closes round, and they are lost
   forever:

Or like forgotten lyres whose dissonant
   strings
  Give various response to each varying
   blast,
To whose frail frame no second motion
   brings
  One mood or modulation like the last.

We rest — a dream has power to poison
   sleep;
  We rise — one wandering thought pollutes the day;
We feel, conceive or reason, laugh or weep;
  Embrace fond woe, or cast our cares
   away:

It is the same! — for, be it joy or sorrow,
  The path of its departure still is free;
Man's yesterday may ne'er be like his
   morrow;
Nought may endure but Mutability.

ON DEATH

Published with *Alastor*, 1816. An earlier
version is among the Esdaile MSS. in the collection Shelley intended to issue with *Queen Mab*
in 1813, and the poem is the only one preserved
by him out of that collection.

There is no work, nor device, nor knowledge, nor
wisdom, in the grave, whither thou goest. — ECCLESI-
ASTES.

THE pale, the cold, and the moony smile
  Which the meteor beam of a starless
   night
Sheds on a lonely and sea-girt isle,
  Ere the dawning of morn's undoubted
   light,
Is the flame of life so fickle and wan
That flits round our steps till their strength
  is gone.

O man! hold thee on in courage of soul
  Through the stormy shades of thy
   worldly way,
And the billows of cloud that around thee
   roll
  Shall sleep in the light of a wondrous
   day,
Where hell and heaven shall leave thee
   free
To the universe of destiny.

This world is the nurse of all we know,
  This world is the mother of all we feel;
And the coming of death is a fearful blow
  To a brain unencompassed with nerves of
   steel,
When all that we know, or feel, or see,
Shall pass like an unreal mystery.

The secret things of the grave are there,
  Where all but this frame must surely be,
Though the fine-wrought eye and the won-
   drous ear
  No longer will live to hear or to see
All that is great and all that is strange
In the boundless realm of unending
   change.

Who telleth a tale of unspeaking death?
  Who lifteth the veil of what is to come?
Who painteth the shadows that are beneath
  The wide-winding caves of the peopled
   tomb?
Or uniteth the hopes of what shall be
With the fears and the love for that which
   we see?

A SUMMER EVENING CHURCH-YARD

LECHLADE, GLOUCESTERSHIRE

Composed September, 1815, while on a voyage up the Thames with Peacock. Published
with *Alastor*, 1816.

THE wind has swept from the wide atmosphere
  Each vapor that obscured the sunset's
   ray;
And pallid Evening twines its beaming
   hair
  In duskier braids around the languid
   eyes of Day.

Silence and Twilight, unbeloved of men,
Creep hand in hand from yon obscurest
glen.

They breathe their spells toward the departing day,
Encompassing the earth, air, stars and
sea;
Light, sound and motion own the potent
sway,
Responding to the charm with its own
mystery.
The winds are still, or the dry church-
tower grass
Knows not their gentle motions as they
pass.

Thou too, aërial Pile, whose pinnacles
Point from one shrine like pyramids of
fire,
Obeyest in silence their sweet solemn
spells,
Clothing in hues of heaven thy dim and
distant spire,
Around whose lessening and invisible
height
Gather among the stars the clouds of
night.

The dead are sleeping in their sepulchres;
And, mouldering as they sleep, a thrill-
ing sound,
Half sense, half thought, among the dark-
ness stirs,
Breathed from their wormy beds all liv-
ing things around;
And mingling with the still night and
mute sky
Its awful hush is felt inaudibly.

Thus solemnized and softened, death is
mild
And terrorless as this serenest night;
Here could I hope, like some inquiring child
Sporting on graves, that death did hide
from human sight
Sweet secrets, or beside its breathless sleep
That loveliest dreams perpetual watch did
keep.

TO WORDSWORTH

This poem reflects the contemporary feeling
of the radicals toward Wordsworth's conservative politics. Published with *Alastor*, 1816.

POET of Nature, thou hast wept to know
That things depart which never may re-
turn;
Childhood and youth, friendship and
love's first glow,
Have fled like sweet dreams, leaving thee
to mourn.
These common woes I feel. One loss is
mine,
Which thou too feel'st, yet I alone de-
plore;
Thou wert as a lone star whose light did
shine
On some frail bark in winter's midnight
roar;
Thou hast like to a rock-built refuge
stood
Above the blind and battling multitude;
In honored poverty thy voice did weave
Songs consecrate to truth and liberty; —
Deserting these, thou leavest me to
grieve,
Thus having been, that thou shouldst
cease to be.

FEELINGS OF A REPUBLICAN ON THE FALL OF BONAPARTE

Published with *Alastor*, 1816.

I HATED thee, fallen tyrant! I did groan
To think that a most unambitious slave,
Like thou, shouldst dance and revel on
the grave
Of Liberty. Thou mightst have built
thy throne
Where it had stood even now: thou didst
prefer
A frail and bloody pomp which time has
swept
In fragments towards oblivion. Massa-
cre,
For this I prayed, would on thy sleep
have crept,
Treason and Slavery, Rapine, Fear, and
Lust,
And stifled thee, their minister. I know
Too late, since thou and France are in
the dust,
That Virtue owns a more eternal foe
Than Force or Fraud: old Custom,
Legal Crime,
And bloody Faith, the foulest birth of
time.

LINES

This poem apparently refers to the death of Harriet, in November, 1816, and was published by Hunt in *The Literary Pocket-Book*, 1823.

THE cold earth slept below;
  Above the cold sky shone;
    And all around,
    With a chilling sound,
From caves of ice and fields of snow
The breath of night like death did flow
  Beneath the sinking moon.

The wintry hedge was black;
  The green grass was not seen;
    The birds did rest
    On the bare thorn's breast,
Whose roots, beside the pathway track,
Had bound their folds o'er many a crack
  Which the frost had made between.

Thine eyes glowed in the glare
  Of the moon's dying light;
    As a fen-fire's beam
    On a sluggish stream
Gleams dimly — so the moon shone there,
And it yellowed the strings of thy tangled hair,
  That shook in the wind of night.

The moon made thy lips pale, belovèd;
  The wind made thy bosom chill;
    The night did shed
    On thy dear head
Its frozen dew, and thou didst lie
Where the bitter breath of the naked sky
  Might visit thee at will.

POEMS WRITTEN IN 1816

THE SUNSET

This poem seems to contain elements of memory as well as of imagination. It was composed at Bishopsgate in the spring, and published in part by Hunt, *The Literary Pocket-Book*, 1823, and entire by Mrs. Shelley, *Posthumous Poems*, 1824.

THERE late was One within whose subtle being,
As light and wind within some delicate cloud

That fades amid the blue noon's burning sky,
Genius and death contended.   None may know
The sweetness of the joy which made his breath
Fail, like the trances of the summer air,
When, with the lady of his love, who then
First knew the unreserve of mingled being,
He walked along the pathway of a field,
Which to the east a hoar wood shadowed o'er,   10
But to the west was open to the sky.
There now the sun had sunk; but lines of gold
Hung on the ashen clouds, and on the points
Of the far level grass and nodding flowers,
And the old dandelion's hoary beard,
And, mingled with the shades of twilight, lay
On the brown massy woods; and in the east
The broad and burning moon lingeringly rose
Between the black trunks of the crowded trees,
While the faint stars were gathering over-head.   20
' Is it not strange, Isabel,' said the youth,
' I never saw the sun?   We will walk here
To-morrow; thou shalt look on it with me.'

That night the youth and lady mingled lay
In love and sleep; but when the morning came
The lady found her lover dead and cold.
Let none believe that God in mercy gave
That stroke.   The lady died not, nor grew wild,   28
But year by year lived on; in truth I think
Her gentleness and patience and sad smiles,
And that she did not die, but lived to tend
Her aged father, were a kind of madness,
If madness 't is to be unlike the world.
For but to see her were to read the tale
Woven by some subtlest bard to make hard hearts
Dissolve away in wisdom-working grief.
Her eyes were black and lustreless and wan,
Her eyelashes were worn away with tears,
Her lips and cheeks were like things dead — so pale;
Her hands were thin, and through their wandering veins   40

And weak articulations might be seen
Day's ruddy light. The tomb of thy dead
  self
Which one vexed ghost inhabits, night and
  day,
Is all, lost child, that now remains of
  thee !

'Inheritor of more than earth can give,
Passionless calm and silence unreproved, —
Whether the dead find, oh, not sleep, but
  rest,
And are the uncomplaining things they
  seem,
Or live, or drop in the deep sea of Love;
Oh, that, like thine, mine epitaph were —
  Peace !'   50
This was the only moan she ever made.

HYMN TO INTELLECTUAL BEAUTY

Composed in Switzerland, where Shelley
spent the summer, and conceived, Mrs. Shelley
says, during his voyage round the Lake of Geneva with Lord Byron. It was published by
Hunt, *The Examiner*, 1817.

I

THE awful shadow of some unseen Power
  Floats though unseen among us, visit-
    ing
  This various world with as inconstant
    wing
  As summer winds that creep from flower
    to flower;
Like moonbeams that behind some piny
    mountain shower,
  It visits with inconstant glance
  Each human heart and countenance;
Like hues and harmonies of evening,
  Like clouds in starlight widely spread,
  Like memory of music fled,
  Like aught that for its grace may
    be
Dear, and yet dearer for its mystery.

II

Spirit of Beauty, that dost consecrate
  With thine own hues all thou dost
    shine upon
  Of human thought or form, where art
    thou gone ?
Why dost thou pass away, and leave our
    state,

This dim vast vale of tears, vacant and
    desolate ? —
  Ask why the sunlight not forever
  Weaves rainbows o'er yon mountain
    river;
Why aught should fail and fade that
    once is shown;
  Why fear and dream and death and
    birth
  Cast on the daylight of this earth
  Such gloom; why man has such a
    scope
For love and hate, despondency and
    hope.

III

No voice from some sublimer world hath
    ever
  To sage or poet these responses given;
  Therefore the names of Demon, Ghost
    and Heaven,
Remain the records of their vain en-
    deavor —
Frail spells, whose uttered charm might
    not avail to sever,
  From all we hear and all we see,
  Doubt, chance and mutability.
Thy light alone, like mist o'er mountains
    driven,
  Or music by the night wind sent
  Through strings of some still instru-
    ment,
  Or moonlight on a midnight stream,
Gives grace and truth to life's unquiet
    dream.

IV

Love, Hope and Self-esteem, like clouds,
    depart,
  And come, for some uncertain mo-
    ments lent.
Man were immortal and omnipotent,
  Didst thou, unknown and awful as thou
    art,
Keep with thy glorious train firm state
    within his heart.
  Thou messenger of sympathies
  That wax and wane in lovers' eyes !
Thou, that to human thought art nourish-
    ment,
  Like darkness to a dying flame,
  Depart not as thy shadow came !
  Depart not, lest the grave should
    be,
Like life and fear, a dark reality !

V

While yet a boy I sought for ghosts, and
    sped
Through many a listening chamber,
    cave and ruin,
And starlight wood, with fearful steps
    pursuing
Hopes of high talk with the departed
    dead;
I called on poisonous names with which our
    youth is fed.
I was not heard — I saw them not —
When, musing deeply on the lot
Of life, at that sweet time when winds
    are wooing
All vital things that wake to bring
News of birds and blossoming, —
Sudden thy shadow fell on me;
I shrieked, and clasped my hands in
    ecstasy!

VI

I vowed that I would dedicate my
    powers
To thee and thine — have I not kept
    the vow?
With beating heart and streaming
    eyes, even now
I call the phantoms of a thousand hours
Each from his voiceless grave: they have
    in visioned bowers
Of studious zeal or love's delight
Outwatched with me the envious
    night —
They know that never joy illumed my
    brow
Unlinked with hope that thou wouldst
    free
This world from its dark slavery, —
That thou, O awful Loveliness,
Wouldst give whate'er these words can-
    not express.

VII

The day becomes more solemn and
    serene
When noon is past; there is a harmony
In autumn, and a lustre in its sky,
Which through the summer is not heard
    or seen,
As if it could not be, as if it had not been!
Thus let thy power, which like the
    truth
Of nature on my passive youth
Descended, to my onward life supply

Its calm, — to one who worships thee,
And every form containing thee,
Whom, Spirit fair, thy spells did bind
To fear himself, and love all humankind.

MONT BLANC

LINES WRITTEN IN THE VALE OF CHA-
MOUNI

'The poem,' Shelley writes, in his Preface to
History of a Six Weeks Tour, 1817, where it
appeared, 'was composed under the immediate
impression of the deep and powerful feelings
excited by the objects which it attempts to describe; and, as an undisciplined overflowing of
the soul, rests its claim to approbation on an
attempt to imitate the untamable wildness and
inaccessible solemnity from which those feelings sprang.'
The, 'objects' referred to, Mrs. Shelley
notes, were Mont Blanc and 'its surrounding
peaks and valleys, as he lingered on the Bridge
of Arve on his way through the Valley of
Chamouni.'

I

THE everlasting universe of things
Flows through the mind, and rolls its rapid
    waves,
Now dark, now glittering, now reflecting
    gloom,
Now lending splendor, where from secret
    springs
The source of human thought its tribute
    brings
Of waters, — with a sound but half its own,
Such as a feeble brook will oft assume
In the wild woods, among the mountains
    lone,
Where waterfalls around it leap forever,
Where woods and winds contend, and a
    vast river   10
Over its rocks ceaselessly bursts and raves.

II

Thus thou, Ravine of Arve — dark, deep
    Ravine —
Thou many-colored, many-voicèd vale,
Over whose pines, and crags, and caverns
    sail
Fast cloud-shadows, and sunbeams! awful
    scene,
Where Power in likeness of the Arve comes
    down
From the ice-gulfs that gird his secret throne,

Bursting through these dark mountains like
  the flame
Of lightning through the tempest! thou
  dost lie, —
Thy giant brood of pines around thee cling-
  ing,   20
Children of elder time, in whose devotion
The chainless winds still come and ever
  came
To drink their odors, and their mighty
  swinging
To hear — an old and solemn harmony;
Thine earthly rainbows stretched across the
  sweep
Of the ethereal waterfall, whose veil
Robes some unsculptured image; the
  strange sleep
Which when the voices of the desert fail
Wraps all in its own deep eternity;
Thy caverns echoing to the Arve's commo-
  tion —   30
A loud, lone sound no other sound can
  tame.
Thou art pervaded with that ceaseless mo-
  tion,
Thou art the path of that unresting sound,
Dizzy Ravine! and when I gaze on thee,
I seem as in a trance sublime and strange
To muse on my own separate fantasy,
My own, my human mind, which passively
Now renders and receives fast influencings,
Holding an unremitting interchange
With the clear universe of things around;
One legion of wild thoughts, whose wan-
  dering wings   41
Now float above thy darkness, and now
  rest,
Where that or thou art no unbidden guest,
In the still cave of the witch Poesy,
Seeking among the shadows that pass by —
Ghosts of all things that are — some shade
  of thee,
Some phantom, some faint image; till the
  breast
From which they fled recalls them, thou
  art there!

III

Some say that gleams of a remoter world
Visit the soul in sleep, — that death is
  slumber,   50
And that its shapes the busy thoughts outnumber
Of those who wake and live. I look on
  high;

Has some unknown Omnipotence unfurled
The veil of life and death? or do I lie
In dream, and does the mightier world of
  sleep
Spread far around and inaccessibly
Its circles? for the very spirit fails,
Driven like a homeless cloud from steep to
  steep
That vanishes among the viewless gales!
Far, far above, piercing the infinite sky, 60
Mont Blanc appears, — still, snowy and
  serene —
Its subject mountains their unearthly forms
Pile around it, ice and rock; broad vales
  between
Of frozen floods, unfathomable deeps,
Blue as the overhanging heaven, that spread
And wind among the accumulated steeps;
A desert peopled by the storms alone,
Save when the eagle brings some hunter's
  bone,
And the wolf tracks her there. How hid-
  eously
Its shapes are heaped around! rude, bare
  and high,   70
Ghastly, and scarred, and riven. — Is this
  the scene
Where the old Earthquake-dæmon taught
  her young
Ruin? Were these their toys? or did a
  sea
Of fire envelop once this silent snow?
None can reply — all seems eternal now.
The wilderness has a mysterious tongue
Which teaches awful doubt, or faith so
  mild,
So solemn, so serene, that man may be
But for such faith with Nature reconciled;
Thou hast a voice, great Mountain, to re-
  peal   80
Large codes of fraud and woe; not under-
  stood
By all, but which the wise, and great, and
  good,
Interpret, or make felt, or deeply feel.

IV

The fields, the lakes, the forests and the
  streams,
Ocean, and all the living things that dwell
Within the dædal earth, lightning, and
  rain,
Earthquake, and fiery flood, and hurricane,
The torpor of the year when feeble dreams
Visit the hidden buds or dreamless sleep

Holds every future leaf and flower, the bound   90
With which from that detested trance they leap,
The works and ways of man, their death and birth,
And that of him and all that his may be, —
All things that move and breathe with toil and sound
Are born and die, revolve, subside and swell;
Power dwells apart in its tranquillity,
Remote, serene, and inaccessible; —
And *this*, the naked countenance of earth
On which I gaze, even these primeval mountains,
Teach the adverting mind. The glaciers creep,   100
Like snakes that watch their prey, from their far fountains,
Slow rolling on; there many a precipice
Frost and the Sun in scorn of mortal power
Have piled — dome, pyramid and pinnacle,
A city of death, distinct with many a tower
And wall impregnable of beaming ice;
Yet not a city, but a flood of ruin
Is there, that from the boundaries of the sky
Rolls its perpetual stream; vast pines are strewing
Its destined path, or in the mangled soil
Branchless and shattered stand; the rocks, drawn down   111
From yon remotest waste, have overthrown
The limits of the dead and living world,
Never to be reclaimed. The dwelling-place
Of insects, beasts and birds, becomes its spoil,
Their food and their retreat forever gone;
So much of life and joy is lost. The race
Of man flies far in dread; his work and dwelling

Vanish, like smoke before the tempest's stream,
And their place is not known. Below, vast caves   120
Shine in the rushing torrents' restless gleam,
Which from those secret chasms in tumult welling
Meet in the Vale; and one majestic River,
The breath and blood of distant lands, forever
Rolls its loud waters to the ocean waves,
Breathes its swift vapors to the circling air.

V

Mont Blanc yet gleams on high: the power is there,
The still and solemn power of many sights
And many sounds, and much of life and death.
In the calm darkness of the moonless nights,   130
In the lone glare of day, the snows descend
Upon that Mountain; none beholds them there,
Nor when the flakes burn in the sinking sun,
Or the star-beams dart through them; winds contend
Silently there, and heap the snow, with breath
Rapid and strong, but silently ! Its home
The voiceless lightning in these solitudes
Keeps innocently, and like vapor broods
Over the snow. The secret strength of things,
Which governs thought, and to the infinite dome   140
Of heaven is as a law, inhabits thee !
And what were thou, and earth, and stars, and sea,
If to the human mind's imaginings
Silence and solitude were vacancy ?

POEMS WRITTEN IN 1817

Mrs. Shelley, in her note on the poems of this year, summarizes Shelley's life at the time: 'The very illness that oppressed, and the aspect of death which had approached so near Shelley, appears to have kindled to yet keener life the spirit of poetry in his heart. The restless thoughts kept awake by pain clothed themselves in verse. Much was composed during this year. *The Revolt of Islam*, written and printed, was a great effort — *Rosalind and*

Helen was begun — and the fragments and poems I can trace to the same period, show how full of passion and reflection were his solitary hours.

. . . .

'His readings this year were chiefly Greek. Besides the Hymns of Homer and the Iliad, he read the Dramas of Æschylus and Sophocles, the Symposium of Plato, and Arrian's Historia Indica. In Latin, Apuleius alone is named. In English, the Bible was his constant study ; he read a great portion of it aloud in the evening. Among these evening readings, I find also mentioned the Faëry Queen ; and other modern works, the production of his contemporaries, Coleridge, Wordsworth, Moore, and Byron.

' His life was now spent more in thought than action — he had lost the eager spirit which believed it could achieve what it projected for the benefit of mankind. And yet in the converse of daily life Shelley was far from being a melancholy man. He was eloquent when philosophy, or politics, or taste were the subjects of conversation. He was playful — and indulged in the wild spirit that mocked itself and others — not in bitterness, but in sport. The Author of *Nightmare Abbey* [Peacock] seized on some points of his character and some habits of his life when he painted *Scythrop*. He was not addicted to " port or madeira," but in youth he had read of " Illuminati and Eleutherarchs," and believed that he possessed the power of operating an immediate change in the minds of men and the state of society. These wild dreams had faded ; sorrow and adversity had struck home ; but he struggled with despondency as he did with physical pain. There are few who remember him sailing paper boats, and watching the navigation of his tiny craft with eagerness — or repeating with wild energy *The Ancient Mariner*, and Southey's *Old Woman of Berkeley* — but those who do, will recollect that it was in such, and in the creations of his own fancy, when that was most daring and ideal, that he sheltered himself from the storms and disappointments, the pain and sorrow, that beset his life.'

MARIANNE'S DREAM

The dream here put into verse was told Shelley by Mrs. Hunt, the ' Marianne ' of the poem. It was composed at Marlow, and published by Hunt, *The Literary Pocket-Book*, 1819.

I

A PALE dream came to a Lady fair,
  And said, ' A boon, a boon, I pray!
I know the secrets of the air;
  And things are lost in the glare of day,
Which I can make the sleeping see,
If they will put their trust in me.

II

' And thou shalt know of things unknown,
  If thou wilt let me rest between
The veiny lids whose fringe is thrown
  Over thine eyes so dark and sheen.'
And half in hope and half in fright
The Lady closed her eyes so bright.

III

At first all deadly shapes were driven
  Tumultuously across her sleep,
And o'er the vast cope of bending heaven
  All ghastly-visaged clouds did sweep;
And the Lady ever looked to spy
If the golden sun shone forth on high.

IV

And, as towards the east she turned,
  She saw aloft in the morning air,
Which now with hues of sunrise burned,
  A great black Anchor rising there;
And, wherever the Lady turned her eyes,
It hung before her in the skies.

V

The sky was blue as the summer sea,
  The depths were cloudless overhead,
The air was calm as it could be,
  There was no sight or sound of dread,
But that black Anchor floating still
Over the piny eastern hill.

VI

The Lady grew sick with a weight of fear
To see that Anchor ever hanging,
And veiled her eyes; she then did hear
  The sound as of a dim low clanging,
And looked abroad if she might know
Was it aught else, or but the flow
Of the blood in her own veins, to and fro.

VII

There was a mist in the sunless air,
  Which shook as it were with an earthquake's shock,
But the very weeds that blossomed there
  Were moveless, and each mighty rock
Stood on its basis steadfastly;
The Anchor was seen no more on high.

VIII

But piled around, with summits hid
  In lines of cloud at intervals,
Stood many a mountain pyramid,
  Among whose everlasting walls

Two mighty cities shone, and ever
Through the red mist their domes did
    quiver.

IX

On two dread mountains, from whose
    crest
  Might seem the eagle for her brood
Would ne'er have hung her dizzy nest,
  Those tower-encircled cities stood.
A vision strange such towers to see,
Sculptured and wrought so gorgeously,
Where human art could never be.

X

And columns framed of marble white,
  And giant fanes, dome over dome
Piled, and triumphant gates, all bright
  With workmanship, which could not come
From touch of mortal instrument,
Shot o'er the vales, or lustre lent
From its own shapes magnificent.

XI

But still the Lady heard that clang
  Filling the wide air far away;
And still the mist whose light did hang
  Among the mountains shook alway;
So that the Lady's heart beat fast,
As, half in joy and half aghast,
On those high domes her look she cast.

XII

Sudden from out that city sprung
  A light that made the earth grow red;
Two flames that each with quivering
    tongue
  Licked its high domes, and overhead
Among those mighty towers and fanes
Dropped fire, as a volcano rains
Its sulphurous ruin on the plains.

XIII

And hark ! a rush, as if the deep
  Had burst its bonds; she looked behind,
And saw over the western steep
  A raging flood descend, and wind
Through that wide vale; she felt no fear,
But said within herself, ' 'T is clear
These towers are Nature's own, and she
To save them has sent forth the sea.'

XIV

And now those raging billows came
  Where that fair Lady sate, and she

Was borne towards the showering flame
  By the wild waves heaped tumultuously;
And, on a little plank, the flow
Of the whirlpool bore her to and fro.

XV

The flames were fiercely vomited
  From every tower and every dome,
And dreary light did widely shed
  O'er that vast flood's suspended foam,
Beneath the smoke which hung its night
On the stained cope of heaven's light.

XVI

The plank whereon that Lady sate
  Was driven through the chasms, about
    and about,
Between the peaks so desolate
  Of the drowning mountains, in and out,
As the thistle-beard on a whirlwind sails —
While the flood was filling those hollow
    vales.

XVII

At last her plank an eddy crossed,
  And bore her to the city's wall,
Which now the flood had reached almost;
  It might the stoutest heart appall
To hear the fire roar and hiss
Through the domes of those mighty
    palaces.

XVIII

The eddy whirled her round and round
  Before a gorgeous gate, which stood
Piercing the clouds of smoke which bound
  Its aëry arch with light like blood;
She looked on that gate of marble clear
With wonder that extinguished fear;

XIX

For it was filled with sculptures rarest,
  Of forms most beautiful and strange,
Like nothing human, but the fairest
  Of wingèd shapes, whose legions range
Throughout the sleep of those that are,
Like this same Lady, good and fair.

XX

And as she looked, still lovelier grew
  Those marble forms; — the sculptor sure
Was a strong spirit, and the hue
  Of his own mind did there endure,
After the touch, whose power had braided
Such grace, was in some sad change faded.

XXI

She looked, — the flames were dim, the
    flood
Grew tranquil as a woodland river
Winding through hills in solitude;
    Those marble shapes then seemed to
       quiver,
And their fair limbs to float in motion,
Like weeds unfolding in the ocean;

XXII

And their lips moved; one seemed to
    speak,
    When suddenly the mountains cracked,
And through the chasm the flood did
    break
    With an earth-uplifting cataract;
The statues gave a joyous scream,
And on its wings the pale thin dream
Lifted the Lady from the stream.

XXIII

The dizzy flight of that phantom pale
    Waked the fair Lady from her sleep,
And she arose, while from the veil
    Of her dark eyes the dream did creep;
And she walked about as one who knew
That sleep has sights as clear and true
As any waking eyes can view.

TO CONSTANTIA

SINGING

This poem was addressed to Miss Clairmont,
and the name *Constantia* was probably due to
Shelley's admiration for the character of *Con-
stantia Dudley*, in Charles Brockden Brown's
Ormond. It was published by Mrs. Shelley,
Posthumous Poems, 1824.

I

THUS to be lost and thus to sink and die,
    Perchance were death indeed ! — Con-
       stantia, turn !
In thy dark eyes a power like light doth
    lie,
    Even though the sounds which were thy
       voice, which burn
Between thy lips, are laid to sleep;
    Within thy breath, and on thy hair, like
       odor it is yet,
And from thy touch like fire doth leap.
    Even while I write, my burning cheeks
       are wet —

Alas, that the torn heart can bleed, but
    not forget !

II

A breathless awe, like the swift change
    Unseen but felt in youthful slumbers,
Wild, sweet, but uncommunicably strange,
    Thou breathest now in fast ascending
       numbers.
The cope of heaven seems rent and cloven
    By the enchantment of thy strain;
And on my shoulders wings are woven
    To follow its sublime career
Beyond the mighty moons that wane
    Upon the verge of Nature's utmost
       sphere,
    Till the world's shadowy walls are passed
       and disappear.

III

Her voice is hovering o'er my soul — it
    lingers
    O'ershadowing it with soft and lulling
       wings;
The blood and life within those snowy
    fingers
    Teach witchcraft to the instrumental
       strings.
My brain is wild, my breath comes
    quick —
    The blood is listening in my frame,
And thronging shadows, fast and thick,
    Fall on my overflowing eyes;
My heart is quivering like a flame;
    As morning dew, that in the sunbeam
       dies,
    I am dissolved in these consuming
       ecstasies.

IV

I have no life, Constantia, now, but thee,
    Whilst, like the world-surrounding air,
       thy song
Flows on, and fills all things with mel-
    ody.
    Now is thy voice a tempest swift and
       strong,
On which, like one in trance upborne,
    Secure o'er rocks and waves I sweep,
Rejoicing like a cloud of morn;
    Now 't is the breath of summer night,
Which, when the starry waters sleep,
Round western isles, with incense-blossoms
    bright,
Lingering, suspends my soul in its voluptu-
    ous flight.

TO THE LORD CHANCELLOR

The decree which deprived Shelley of the custody of his children was pronounced in August. Mrs. Shelley writes: 'His heart, attuned to every kindly affection, was full of burning love for his offspring. No words can express the anguish he felt when his elder children were torn from him. In his first resentment against the Chancellor, on the passing of the decree, he had written a curse, in which there breathes, besides haughty indignation, all the tenderness of a father's love, which could imagine and fondly dwell upon its loss and the consequences.' It was published by Mrs. Shelley, in her first collected edition, 1839.

I

THY country's curse is on thee, darkest crest
  Of that foul, knotted, many-headed worm
Which rends our Mother's bosom! —
  Priestly Pest!
Masked Resurrection of a buried Form!

II

Thy country's curse is on thee! Justice sold,
  Truth trampled, Nature's landmarks overthrown,
And heaps of fraud-accumulated gold,
  Plead, loud as thunder, at Destruction's throne.

III

And, whilst that sure slow Angel, which aye stands
  Watching the beck of Mutability,
Delays to execute her high commands,
  And, though a nation weeps, spares thine and thee,

IV

Oh, let a father's curse be on thy soul,
  And let a daughter's hope be on thy tomb;
Be both, on thy gray head, a leaden cowl
  To weigh thee down to thine approaching doom!

V

I curse thee! By a parent's outraged love,
  By hopes long cherished and too lately lost, —

By gentle feelings thou couldst never prove,
  By griefs which thy stern nature never crossed;

VI

By those infantine smiles of happy light,
  Which were a fire within a stranger's hearth,
Quenched even when kindled, — in untimely night,
  Hiding the promise of a lovely birth;

VII

By those unpractised accents of young speech,
  Which he who is a father thought to frame
To gentlest lore, such as the wisest teach —
  Thou strike the lyre of mind! — oh, grief and shame!

VIII

By all the happy see in children's growth,
  That undeveloped flower of budding years —
Sweetness and sadness interwoven both,
  Source of the sweetest hopes and saddest fears —

IX

By all the days under an hireling's care,
  Of dull constraint and bitter heaviness, —
Oh, wretched ye if ever any were, —
  Sadder than orphans, yet not fatherless!

X

By the false cant which on their innocent lips
  Must hang like poison on an opening bloom,
By the dark creeds which cover with eclipse
  Their pathway from the cradle to the tomb —

XI

By thy most impious Hell, and all its terror;
  By all the grief, the madness, and the guilt
Of thine impostures, which must be their error —
  That sand on which thy crumbling Power is built —

XII

By thy complicity with lust and hate —
　Thy thirst for tears — thy hunger after
　　gold —
The ready frauds which ever on thee
　wait —
　The servile arts in which thou hast grown
　old —

XIII

By thy most killing sneer, and by thy
　smile —
　By all the arts and snares of thy black
　den,
And — for thou canst outweep the croco-
　dile —
　By thy false tears — those millstones
　braining men —

XIV

By all the hate which checks a father's
　love —
　By all the scorn which kills a father's
　care —
By those most impious hands which dared
　remove
　Nature's high bounds — by thee — and
　by despair —

XV

Yes, the despair which bids a father
　groan,
　And cry, 'My children are no longer
　mine —
The blood within those veins may be mine
　own,
　But, Tyrant, their polluted souls are
　thine;' —

XVI

I curse thee, though I hate thee not. — O
　slave !
　If thou couldst quench the earth-consum-
　ing Hell
Of which thou art a demon, on thy grave
　This curse should be a blessing.　Fare
　thee well !

TO WILLIAM SHELLEY

William Shelley was born at Bishopsgate,
January 24, 1816, baptized at St.-Giles-in-the-
Fields, March 9, 1818, died at Rome, June 7,
1819.　Mrs. Shelley notes : 'At one time, while
the question was still pending, the Chancellor
had said some words that seemed to intimate
that Shelley should not be permitted the care
of any of his children, and for a moment he
feared that our infant son would be torn from
us. He did not hesitate to resolve, if such
were menaced, to abandon country, fortune,
everything, and to escape with his child ; and
I find some unfinished stanzas addressed to this
son, whom afterwards we lost at Rome, written
under the idea that we might suddenly be
forced to cross the sea, so to preserve him.
This poem, as well as the one previously
quoted, were not written to exhibit the pangs
of distress to the public ; they were the spontaneous outbursts of a man who brooded over his
wrongs and woes, and was impelled to shed the
grace of his genius over the uncontrollable
emotions of his heart.'　The poem was published by Mrs. Shelley, in part, in her first collected edition, 1839, and entire, in the second, of
the same year.

I

THE billows on the beach are leaping
　around it,
　The bark is weak and frail,
The sea looks black, and the clouds that
　bound it
　Darkly strew the gale.
Come with me, thou delightful child,
Come with me — though the wave is wild,
And the winds are loose, we must not stay,
Or the slaves of the law may rend thee
　away.

II

They have taken thy brother and sister
　dear,
　They have made them unfit for thee;
They have withered the smile and dried
　the tear
　Which should have been sacred to me.
To a blighting faith and a cause of crime
They have bound them slaves in youthly
　prime,
And they will curse my name and thee
Because we are fearless and free.

III

Come thou, belovèd as thou art;
　Another sleepeth still
Near thy sweet mother's anxious heart,
　Which thou with joy shalt fill, —
With fairest smiles of wonder thrown
On that which is indeed our own,
And which in distant lands will be
The dearest playmate unto thee.

IV

Fear not the tyrants will rule forever,
  Or the priests of the evil faith;
They stand on the brink of that raging
    river
  Whose waves they have tainted with
    death.
It is fed from the depth of a thousand
    dells,
Around them it foams and rages and swells;
And their swords and their sceptres I float-
    ing see,
Like wrecks on the surge of eternity.

V

Rest, rest, and shriek not, thou gentle
    child !
  The rocking of the boat thou fearest,
And the cold spray and the clamor wild ? —
    There sit between us two, thou dear-
      est —
Me and thy mother — well we know
The storm at which thou tremblest so,
With all its dark and hungry graves,
Less cruel than the savage slaves
Who hunt us o'er these sheltering waves.

VI

This hour will in thy memory
  Be a dream of days forgotten long;
We soon shall dwell by the azure sea
Of serene and golden Italy,
  Or Greece, the Mother of the free;
  And I will teach thine infant tongue
To call upon those heroes old
In their own language, and will mould
Thy growing spirit in the flame
Of Grecian lore, that by such name
A patriot's birthright thou mayst claim !

ON FANNY GODWIN

Fanny Godwin, half-sister of Mary, committed suicide by taking laudanum, at an inn in
Swansea, October 9, 1816. Shelley had recently seen her in London. The poem was
published by Mrs. Shelley in her first collected edition, 1839.

HER voice did quiver as we parted,
  Yet knew I not that heart was broken
From which it came, and I departed
  Heeding not the words then spoken.
    Misery — O Misery,
    This world is all too wide for thee.

LINES

Composed November 5, and published by
Mrs. Shelley, *Posthumous Poems*, 1824.

I

THAT time is dead forever, child,
Drowned, frozen, dead forever !
  We look on the past,
  And stare aghast
At the spectres wailing, pale and ghast,
Of hopes which thou and I beguiled
  To death on life's dark river.

II

The stream we gazed on then, rolled by;
Its waves are unreturning;
  But we yet stand
  In a lone land,
Like tombs to mark the memory
Of hopes and fears, which fade and flee
  In the light of life's dim morning.

DEATH

Published by Mrs. Shelley, *Posthumous
Poems*, 1824.

THEY die — the dead return not. Misery
  Sits near an open grave and calls them
    over,
A Youth with hoary hair and haggard eye.
  They are the names of kindred, friend
    and lover,
Which he so feebly calls; they all are
    gone —
Fond wretch, all dead ! those vacant names
    alone,
  This most familiar scene, my pain,
  These tombs, — alone remain.

Misery, my sweetest friend, oh, weep no
    more !
  Thou wilt not be consoled — I wonder
    not !
For I have seen thee from thy dwelling's
    door
  Watch the calm sunset with them, and
    this spot
Was even as bright and calm, but transi-
    tory, —
And now thy hopes are gone, thy hair is
    hoary;
  This most familiar scene, my pain,
  These tombs, — alone remain.

SONNET. — OZYMANDIAS

Published by Hunt, *The Examiner*, 1818.

I MET a traveller from an antique land
Who said: 'Two vast and trunkless legs of
  stone
Stand in the desert. Near them, on the
  sand,
Half sunk, a shattered visage lies, whose
  frown,
And wrinkled lip, and sneer of cold com-
  mand,
Tell that its sculptor well those passions
  read
Which yet survive, stamped on these life-
  less things,
The hand that mocked them and the heart
  that fed.
And on the pedestal these words appear —
" My name is Ozymandias, king of kings:
Look on my works, ye Mighty, and de-
  spair ! "
Nothing beside remains. Round the de-
  cay
Of that colossal wreck, boundless and bare
The lone and level sands stretch far away.'

LINES TO A CRITIC

Published by Hunt, *The Liberal*, 1823.

I

HONEY from silkworms who can gather,
  Or silk from the yellow bee ?
The grass may grow in winter weather
  As soon as hate in me.

II

Hate men who cant, and men who pray,
  And men who rail like thee;
An equal passion to repay
  They are not coy like me.

III

Or seek some slave of power and gold,
  To be thy dear heart's mate;
Thy love will move that bigot cold
  Sooner than me thy hate.

IV

A passion like the one I prove
  Cannot divided be;
I hate thy want of truth and love —
  How should I then hate thee ?

POEMS WRITTEN IN 1818

Mrs. Shelley describes the scenes and character of this first year in Italy at length: 'I
Capuccini was a villa built on the site of a
Capuchin convent, demolished when the French
suppressed religious houses; it was situated on
the very overhanging brow of a low hill at the
foot of a range of higher ones. The house
was cheerful and pleasant; a vine-trellised
walk, a *pergola*, as it is called in Italian, led
from the hall door to a summer-house at the
end of the garden, which Shelley made his
study, and in which he began the *Prometheus;*
and here also, as he mentions in a letter, he
wrote *Julian and Maddalo ;* a slight ravine,
with a road in its depth, divided the garden
from the hill, on which stood the ruins of the
ancient castle of Este, whose dark massive wall
gave forth an echo, and from whose ruined
crevices, owls and bats flitted forth at night,
as the crescent moon sunk behind the black
and heavy battlements. We looked from the
garden over the wide plain of Lombardy,
bounded to the west by the far Apennines,
while to the east, the horizon was lost in misty
distance. After the picturesque but limited
view of mountain, ravine, and chestnut wood

at the baths of Lucca, there was something
infinitely gratifying to the eye in the wide
range of prospect commanded by our new
abode.

' Our first misfortune, of the kind from which
we soon suffered even more severely, happened
here. Our little girl, an infant in whose small
features I fancied that I traced great resemblance to her father, showed symptoms of suffering from the heat of the climate. Teething
increased her illness and danger. We were at
Este, and when we became alarmed, hastened
to Venice for the best advice. When we arrived at Fusina, we found that we had forgotten our passport, and the soldiers on duty
attempted to prevent our crossing the laguna;
but they could not resist Shelley's impetuosity
at such a moment. We had scarcely arrived
at Venice, before life fled from the little sufferer, and we returned to Este to weep her
loss.

' After a few weeks spent in this retreat,
which were interspersed by visits to Venice,
we proceeded southward. We often hear of
persons disappointed by a first visit to Italy.
This was not Shelley's case — the aspect of its

nature, its sunny sky, its majestic storms; of the luxuriant vegetation of the country, and the noble marble-built cities, enchanted him. The sight of the works of art was full [of] enjoyment and wonder; he had not studied pictures or statues before; he now did so with the eye of taste, that referred not to the rules of schools, but to those of nature and truth. The first entrance to Rome opened to him a scene of remains of antique grandeur that far surpassed his expectations; and the unspeakable beauty of Naples and its environs added to the impression he received of the transcendent and glorious beauty of Italy. As I have said, he wrote long letters during the first year of our residence in this country, and these, when published, will be the best testimonials of his appreciation of the harmonious and beautiful in art and nature, and his delicate taste in discerning and describing them.

'Our winter was spent at Naples. Here he wrote the fragments of *Marenghi* and *The Woodman and the Nightingale*, which he afterwards threw aside. At this time Shelley suffered greatly in health. He put himself under the care of a medical man, who promised great things, and made him endure severe bodily pain, without any good results. Constant and poignant physical suffering exhausted him; and though he preserved the appearance of cheerfulness, and often greatly enjoyed our wanderings in the environs of Naples, and our excursions on its sunny sea, yet many hours were passed when his thoughts, shadowed by illness, became gloomy, and then he escaped to solitude, and in verses, which he hid from fear of wounding me, poured forth morbid but too natural bursts of discontent and sadness. One looks back with unspeakable regret and gnawing remorse to such periods; fancying that had one been more alive to the nature of his feelings, and more attentive to soothe them, such would not have existed—and yet enjoying, as he appeared to do, every sight or influence of earth or sky, it was difficult to imagine that any melancholy he showed was aught but the effect of the constant pain to which he was a martyr.

'We lived in utter solitude—and such is often not the nurse of cheerfulness; for then, at least with those who have been exposed to adversity, the mind broods over its sorrows too intently; while the society of the enlightened, the witty, and the wise, enables us to forget ourselves by making us the sharers of the thoughts of others, which is a portion of the philosophy of happiness. Shelley never liked society in numbers, it harassed and wearied him; but neither did he like loneliness, and usually when alone sheltered himself against memory and reflection, in a book. But with one or two whom he loved, he gave way to wild and joyous spirits, or in more serious conversation expounded his opinions with vivacity and eloquence.'

SONNET: TO THE NILE

This is the sonnet composed in competition with Hunt and Keats, on the same subject February 4. It was published in the *St. James Magazine*, 1876.

MONTH after month the gathered rains descend
  Drenching yon secret Æthiopian dells;
  And from the desert's ice-girt pinnacles,
  Where Frost and Heat in strange embraces blend
On Atlas, fields of moist snow half depend;
  Girt there with blasts and meteors, Tempest dwells
  By Nile's aërial urn, with rapid spells
  Urging those waters to their mighty end.
O'er Egypt's land of Memory floods are level,
  And they are thine, O Nile!—and well thou knowest
That soul-sustaining airs and blasts of evil,
And fruits and poisons, spring where'er thou flowest.
  Beware, O Man! for knowledge must to thee
  Like the great flood to Egypt ever be.

PASSAGE OF THE APENNINES

Composed May 4, and published by Mrs. Shelley, *Posthumous Poems*, 1824.

LISTEN, listen, Mary mine,
To the whisper of the Apennine,
It bursts on the roof like the thunder's roar,
Or like the sea on a northern shore,
Heard in its raging ebb and flow
By the captives pent in the cave below.
The Apennine in the light of day
Is a mighty mountain dim and gray,
Which between the earth and sky doth lay;

But when night comes, a chaos dread
On the dim starlight then is spread,
And the Apennine walks abroad with the
   storm.

THE PAST

Published by Mrs. Shelley, *Posthumous
Poems*, 1824.

WILT thou forget the happy hours
Which we buried in Love's sweet bow-
   ers,
Heaping over their corpses cold
Blossoms and leaves instead of mould ?
   Blossoms which were the joys that fell,
     And leaves, the hopes that yet re-
     main.

Forget the dead, the past ?   Oh, yet
There are ghosts that may take revenge
   for it;
Memories that make the heart a tomb,
Regrets which glide through the spirit's
   gloom,
   And with ghastly whispers tell
   That joy, once lost, is pain.

ON A FADED VIOLET

Sent by Shelley, in a letter, to Miss Sophia
Stacey, March 7, 1820: ' I promised you what
I cannot perform : a song on singing : — there
are only two subjects remaining. I have a few
old stanzas on one which, though simple and
rude, look as if they were dictated by the
heart. — And so — if you tell no one *whose* they
are, you are welcome to them. Pardon these
dull verses from one who is dull — but who is
not the less, ever yours, P. B. S.' It was published by Hunt, *The Literary Pocket-Book,*
1821.

I

THE odor from the flower is gone,
   Which like thy kisses breathed on me;
The color from the flower is flown,
   Which glowed of thee, and only thee !

II

A shrivelled, lifeless, vacant form,
   It lies on my abandoned breast,
And mocks the heart, which yet is warm,
   With cold and silent rest.

III

I weep — my tears revive it not;
   I sigh — it breathes no more on me;
Its mute and uncomplaining lot
   Is such as mine should be.

LINES WRITTEN AMONG THE EUGANEAN HILLS

Composed at Este, in October, and possibly
revised at Naples the following month. The
passage on Byron was inserted after the poem
had gone to the printer. It was published
with *Rosalind and Helen*, 1819, and in the
Preface Shelley says it ' was written after a
day's excursion among those lovely mountains
which surround what was once the retreat, and
where is now the sepulchre, of Petrarch. If
any one is inclined to condemn the insertion of
the introductory lines, which image forth the
sudden relief of a state of deep despondency
by the radiant visions disclosed by the sudden
burst of an Italian sunrise in autumn, on the
highest peak of those delightful mountains, I
can only offer as my excuse, that they were
not erased at the request of a dear friend, with
whom added years of intercourse only add to
my apprehension of its value, and who would
have had more right than any one to complain,
that she has not been able to extinguish in me
the very power of delineating sadness.'

MANY a green isle needs must be
In the deep, wide sea of misery,
Or the mariner, worn and wan,
Never thus could voyage on
Day and night, and night and day,
Drifting on his dreary way,
With the solid darkness black
Closing round his vessel's track;
Whilst above, the sunless sky,
Big with clouds, hangs heavily,   10
And behind, the tempest fleet
Hurries on with lightning feet,
Riving sail, and cord, and plank,
Till the ship has almost drank
Death from the o'er-brimming deep,
And sinks down, down — like that sleep
When the dreamer seems to be
Weltering through eternity;
And the dim low line before
Of a dark and distant shore   20
Still recedes, as ever still,
Longing with divided will
But no power to seek or shun,
He is ever drifted on

O'er the unreposing wave
To the haven of the grave.
What, if there no friends will greet ?
What, if there no heart will meet
His with love's impatient beat ?
Wander wheresoe'er he may,   30
Can he dream before that day
To find refuge from distress
In friendship's smile, in love's caress ?
Then 't will wreak him little woe
Whether such there be or no.
Senseless is the breast, and cold,
Which relenting love would fold;
Bloodless are the veins, and chill,
Which the pulse of pain did fill;
Every little living nerve   40
That from bitter words did swerve
Round the tortured lips and brow,
Are like sapless leaflets now
Frozen upon December's bough.

On the beach of a northern sea
Which tempests shake eternally,
As once the wretch there lay to sleep,
Lies a solitary heap,
One white skull and seven dry bones,
On the margin of the stones,   50
Where a few gray rushes stand,
Boundaries of the sea and land:
Nor is heard one voice of wail
But the sea-mews, as they sail
O'er the billows of the gale;
Or the whirlwind up and down
Howling, like a slaughtered town
When a king in glory rides
Through the pomp of fratricides.
Those unburied bones around   60
There is many a mournful sound;
There is no lament for him,
Like a sunless vapor, dim,
Who once clothed with life and thought
What now moves nor murmurs not.

Ay, many flowering islands lie
In the waters of wide Agony.
To such a one this morn was led
My bark, by soft winds piloted.
Mid the mountains Euganean   70
I stood listening to the pæan
With which the legioned rooks did hail
The sun's uprise majestical;
Gathering round with wings all hoar,
Through the dewy mist they soar
Like gray shades, till the eastern heaven
Bursts, and then, as clouds of even,

Flecked with fire and azure, lie
In the unfathomable sky,
So their plumes of purple grain,   80
Starred with drops of golden rain,
Gleam above the sunlight woods,
As in silent multitudes
On the morning's fitful gale
Through the broken mist they sail,
And the vapors cloven and gleaming
Follow down the dark steep streaming,
Till all is bright, and clear, and still,
Round the solitary hill.

Beneath is spread like a green sea   90
The waveless plain of Lombardy,
Bounded by the vaporous air,
Islanded by cities fair;
Underneath day's azure eyes,
Ocean's nursling, Venice lies,
A peopled labyrinth of walls,
Amphitrite's destined halls,
Which her hoary sire now paves
With his blue and beaming waves.
Lo ! the sun upsprings behind,   100
Broad, red, radiant, half-reclined
On the level quivering line
Of the waters crystalline;
And before that chasm of light,
As within a furnace bright,
Column, tower, and dome and spire,
Shine like obelisks of fire,
Pointing with inconstant motion
From the altar of dark ocean
To the sapphire-tinted skies;   110
As the flames of sacrifice
From the marble shrines did rise
As to pierce the dome of gold
Where Apollo spoke of old.

Sun-girt City ! thou hast been
Ocean's child, and then his queen;
Now is come a darker day,
And thou soon must be his prey,
If the power that raised thee here
Hallow so thy watery bier.   120
A less drear ruin then than now,
With thy conquest-branded brow
Stooping to the slave of slaves
From thy throne among the waves,
Wilt thou be, when the sea-mew
Flies, as once before it flew,
O'er thine isles depopulate,
And all is in its ancient state,
Save where many a palace-gate
With green sea-flowers overgrown   130

Like a rock of ocean's own,
Topples o'er the abandoned sea
As the tides change sullenly.
The fisher on his watery way,
Wandering at the close of day,
Will spread his sail and seize his oar
Till he pass the gloomy shore,
Lest thy dead should, from their sleep
Bursting o'er the starlight deep,
Lead a rapid masque of death   140
O'er the waters of his path.

Those who alone thy towers behold
Quivering through aërial gold,
As I now behold them here,
Would imagine not they were
Sepulchres, where human forms,
Like pollution-nourished worms,
To the corpse of greatness cling,
Murdered, and now mouldering.
But if Freedom should awake   150
In her omnipotence, and shake
From the Celtic Anarch's hold
All the keys of dungeons cold,
Where a hundred cities lie
Chained like thee, ingloriously,
Thou and all thy sister band
Might adorn this sunny land,
Twining memories of old time
With new virtues more sublime.
If not, perish thou and they!—   160
Clouds which stain truth's rising day
By her sun consumed away—
Earth can spare ye; while like flowers,
In the waste of years and hours,
From your dust new nations spring
With more kindly blossoming.

Perish! let there only be
Floating o'er thy hearthless sea,
As the garment of thy sky
Clothes the world immortally,   170
One remembrance, more sublime
Than the tattered pall of time,
Which scarce hides thy visage wan;—
That a tempest-cleaving Swan
Of the songs of Albion,
Driven from his ancestral streams
By the might of evil dreams,
Found a nest in thee; and Ocean
Welcomed him with such emotion
That its joy grew his, and sprung   180
From his lips like music flung
O'er a mighty thunder-fit,

Chastening terror. What though yet
Poesy's unfailing River,
Which through Albion winds forever
Lashing with melodious wave
Many a sacred poet's grave,
Mourn its latest nursling fled?
What though thou with all thy dead
Scarce can for this fame repay   190
Aught thine own? oh, rather say
Though thy sins and slaveries foul
Overcloud a sun-like soul?
As the ghost of Homer clings
Round Scamander's wasting springs;
As divinest Shakespeare's might
Fills Avon and the world with light
Like omniscient power which he
Imaged 'mid mortality;
As the love from Petrarch's urn   200
Yet amid yon hills doth burn,
A quenchless lamp, by which the heart,
Sees things unearthly;— so thou art,
Mighty spirit! so shall be
The City that did refuge thee!

Lo, the sun floats up the sky,
Like thought-wingèd Liberty,
Till the universal light
Seems to level plain and height.
From the sea a mist has spread,   210
And the beams of morn lie dead
On the towers of Venice now,
Like its glory long ago.
By the skirts of that gray cloud
Many-domèd Padua proud
Stands, a peopled solitude,
Mid the harvest-shining plain,
Where the peasant heaps his grain
In the garner of his foe,
And the milk-white oxen slow   220
With the purple vintage strain,
Heaped upon the creaking wain,
That the brutal Celt may swill
Drunken sleep with savage will;
And the sickle to the sword
Lies unchanged, though many a lord,
Like a weed whose shade is poison,
Overgrows this region's foison,
Sheaves of whom are ripe to come
To destruction's harvest-home.   230
Men must reap the things they sow,
Force from force must ever flow,
Or worse; but 't is a bitter woe
That love or reason cannot change
The despot's rage, the slave's revenge.

Padua, thou within whose walls
Those mute guests at festivals,
Son and Mother, Death and Sin,
Played at dice for Ezzelin,
Till Death cried, 'I win, I win!'   240
And Sin cursed to lose the wager,
But Death promised, to assuage her,
That he would petition for
Her to be made Vice-Emperor,
When the destined years were o'er,
Over all between the Po
And the eastern Alpine snow,
Under the mighty Austrian.
Sin smiled so as Sin only can,
And since that time, ay, long before,   250
Both have ruled from shore to shore —
That incestuous pair, who follow
Tyrants as the sun the swallow,
As Repentance follows Crime,
And as changes follow Time.

In thine halls the lamp of learning,
Padua, now no more is burning;
Like a meteor whose wild way
Is lost over the grave of day,
It gleams betrayed and to betray.   260
Once remotest nations came
To adore that sacred flame,
When it lit not many a hearth
On this cold and gloomy earth;
Now new fires from antique light
Spring beneath the wide world's might;
But their spark lies dead in thee,
Trampled out by tyranny.
As the Norway woodman quells,
In the depth of piny dells,   270
One light flame among the brakes,
While the boundless forest shakes,
And its mighty trunks are torn
By the fire thus lowly born; —
The spark beneath his feet is dead,
He starts to see the flames it fed
Howling through the darkened sky
With myriad tongues victoriously,
And sinks down in fear; — so thou,
O Tyranny! beholdest now   280
Light around thee, and thou hearest
The loud flames ascend, and fearest.
Grovel on the earth! ay, hide
In the dust thy purple pride!

Noon descends around me now.
'T is the noon of autumn's glow,
When a soft and purple mist,
Like a vaporous amethyst,

Or an air-dissolvèd star
Mingling light and fragrance, far   290
From the curved horizon's bound
To the point of heaven's profound
Fills the overflowing sky.
And the plains that silent lie
Underneath; the leaves unsodden
Where the infant frost has trodden
With his morning-wingèd feet,
Whose bright print is gleaming yet;
And the red and golden vines,
Piercing with their trellised lines   300
The rough, dark-skirted wilderness;
The dun and bladed grass no less,
Pointing from this hoary tower
In the windless air; the flower
Glimmering at my feet; the line
Of the olive-sandalled Apennine
In the south dimly islanded;
And the Alps, whose snows are spread
High between the clouds and sun;
And of living things each one;   310
And my spirit, which so long
Darkened this swift stream of song, —
Interpenetrated lie
By the glory of the sky:
Be it love, light, harmony,
Odor, or the soul of all
Which from heaven like dew doth fall,
Or the mind which feeds this verse
Peopling the lone universe.

Noon descends, and after noon   320
Autumn's evening meets me soon,
Leading the infantine moon
And that one star, which to her
Almost seems to minister
Half the crimson light she brings
From the sunset's radiant springs;
And the soft dreams of the morn
(Which like wingèd winds had borne
To that silent isle, which lies
Mid remembered agonies,   330
The frail bark of this lone being)
Pass, to other sufferers fleeing,
And its ancient pilot, Pain,
Sits beside the helm again.

Other flowering isles must be
In the sea of life and agony;
Other spirits float and flee
O'er that gulf: even now, perhaps,
On some rock the wild wave wraps,
With folding wings they waiting sit   340
For my bark, to pilot it

To some calm and blooming cove,
Where for me, and those I love,
May a windless bower be built,
Far from passion, pain, and guilt,
In a dell mid lawny hills,
Which the wild sea-murmur fills,
And soft sunshine, and the sound
Of old forests echoing round,
And the light and smell divine   350
Of all flowers that breathe and shine.
We may live so happy there,
That the spirits of the air,
Envying us, may even entice
To our healing paradise
The polluting multitude;
But their rage would be subdued
By that clime divine and calm,
And the winds whose wings rain balm
On the uplifted soul, and leaves   360
Under which the bright sea heaves;
While each breathless interval
In their whisperings musical
The inspired soul supplies
With its own deep melodies,
And the love which heals all strife,
Circling, like the breath of life,
All things in that sweet abode
With its own mild brotherhood.
They, not it, would change; and soon   370
Every sprite beneath the moon
Would repent its envy vain,
And the earth grow young again.

INVOCATION TO MISERY

Published by Medwin, *The Athenæum*, 1832.
He wove about it a mystery of a lady who
followed Shelley to Naples and there died in
hopeless love for him. The tale has never been
substantiated, but his various biographers take
note of it, in connection with his depression at
Naples. The poem itself is purely ideal, and
such as he might have written at any time.

I

COME, be happy! — sit near me,
Shadow-vested Misery;
Coy, unwilling, silent bride,
Mourning in thy robe of pride,
Desolation — deified!

II

Come, be happy! — sit near me.
Sad as I may seem to thee,
I am happier far than thou,
Lady, whose imperial brow
Is endiademed with woe.

III

Misery! we have known each other,
Like a sister and a brother
Living in the same lone home,
Many years — we must live some
Hours or ages yet to come.

IV

'T is an evil lot, and yet
Let us make the best of it;
If love can live when pleasure dies,
We two will love, till in our eyes
This heart's Hell seem Paradise.

V

Come, be happy! — lie thee down
On the fresh grass newly mown,
Where the grasshopper doth sing
Merrily — one joyous thing
In a world of sorrowing.

VI

There our tent shall be the willow,
And mine arm shall be thy pillow;
Sounds and odors, sorrowful
Because they once were sweet, shall
        lull
Us to slumber, deep and dull.

VII

Ha! thy frozen pulses flutter
With a love thou darest not utter.
Thou art murmuring — thou art weep-
        ing —
Is thine icy bosom leaping
While my burning heart lies sleeping?

VIII

Kiss me; — oh! thy lips are cold;
Round my neck thine arms enfold —
They are soft, but chill and dead;
And thy tears upon my head
Burn like points of frozen lead.

IX

Hasten to the bridal bed —
Underneath the grave 't is spread:
In darkness may our love be hid,
Oblivion be our coverlid —
We may rest, and none forbid.

X

Clasp me, till our hearts be grown
Like two shadows into one;
Till this dreadful transport may
Like a vapor fade away
In the sleep that lasts alway.

XI

We may dream, in that long sleep,
That we are not those who weep;
E'en as Pleasure dreams of thee,
Life-deserting Misery,
Thou mayst dream of her with me.

XII

Let us laugh, and make our mirth,
At the shadows of the earth,
As dogs bay the moonlight clouds,
Which, like spectres wrapped in shrouds,
Pass o'er night in multitudes.

XIII

All the wide world beside us
Show like multitudinous
Puppets passing from a scene;
What but mockery can they mean,
Where I am — where thou hast been ?

STANZAS

WRITTEN IN DEJECTION, NEAR NAPLES

This poem, in the same mood as the preceding, was composed in December, and published by Mrs. Shelley, *Posthumous Poems*, 1824.

I

THE sun is warm, the sky is clear,
   The waves are dancing fast and bright;
Blue isles and snowy mountains wear
   The purple noon's transparent might;
   The breath of the moist earth is light
Around its unexpanded buds;
   Like many a voice of one delight,
The winds, the birds, the ocean floods,
The City's voice itself is soft like Solitude's.

II

I see the Deep's untrampled floor
   With green and purple sea-weeds strown;
I see the waves upon the shore,
   Like light dissolved in star-showers, thrown;

I sit upon the sands alone —
   The lightning of the noontide ocean
   Is flashing round me, and a tone
Arises from its measured motion,
How sweet ! did any heart now share in my emotion.

III

Alas ! I have nor hope nor health,
   Nor peace within nor calm around,
Nor that content surpassing wealth
   The sage in meditation found,
   And walked with inward glory crowned —
Nor fame, nor power, nor love, nor leisure.
   Others I see whom these surround —
Smiling they live, and call life pleasure; —
To me that cup has been dealt in another measure.

IV

Yet now despair itself is mild,
   Even as the winds and waters are;
I could lie down like a tired child,
   And weep away the life of care
   Which I have borne and yet must bear,
Till death like sleep might steal on me,
   And I might feel in the warm air
My cheek grow cold, and hear the sea
Breathe o'er my dying brain its last monotony.

V

Some might lament that I were cold,
   As I when this sweet day is gone,
Which my lost heart, too soon grown old,
   Insults with this untimely moan;
   They might lament — for I am one
Whom men love not, — and yet regret,
   Unlike this day, which, when the sun
Shall on its stainless glory set,
Will linger, though enjoyed, like joy in memory yet.

SONNET

Published by Mrs. Shelley, *Posthumous Poems*, 1824.

LIFT not the painted veil which those who live
Call Life; though unreal shapes be pictured there,

And it but mimic all we would believe
With colors idly spread, — behind, lurk
    Fear
And Hope, twin Destinies, who ever weave
Their shadows o'er the chasm sightless and
    drear.
I knew one who had lifted it — he sought,
For his lost heart was tender, things to
    love,

But found them not, alas! nor was there
    aught
The world contains the which he could ap-
    prove.
Through the unheeding many he did move,
A splendor among shadows, a bright blot
Upon this gloomy scene, a Spirit that strove
For truth, and like the Preacher found it
    not.

POEMS WRITTEN IN 1819

This was the year of the composition of *Prometheus Unbound, The Cenci, The Mask of Anarchy*, and *Peter Bell The Third*. Its his-tory has already been given with sufficient fulness under these titles, from Mrs. Shelley's notes.

LINES

WRITTEN DURING THE CASTLEREAGH ADMINISTRATION

Published by Medwin, *The Athenæum*, 1832.

I

CORPSES are cold in the tomb —
Stones on the pavement are dumb —
Abortions are dead in the womb,
And their mothers look pale, like the death-
    white shore
    Of Albion, free no more.

II

Her sons are as stones in the way —
They are masses of senseless clay —
They are trodden and move not
    away —
The abortion with which *she* travaileth
    Is Liberty, smitten to death.

III

Then trample and dance, thou Op-
    pressor!
For thy victim is no redresser —
Thou art sole lord and possessor
Of her corpses, and clods, and abortions
    — they pave
    Thy path to the grave.

IV

Hearest thou the festival din
Of Death and Destruction and Sin,
And Wealth crying, Havoc! within?
'Tis the Bacchanal triumph that makes
    truth dumb, —
    Thine Epithalamium.

V

Ay, marry thy ghastly wife!
Let Fear and Disquiet and Strife
Spread thy couch in the chamber of
    Life;
Marry Ruin, thou Tyrant! and Hell be thy
    guide
    To the bed of the bride!

SONG

TO THE MEN OF ENGLAND

This poem, like all the group, is to be ascribed to Shelley's renewed political excitement ow-ing to the Manchester Massacre. It was pub-lished by Mrs. Shelley, in her first collected edition, 1839.

I

MEN of England, wherefore plough
For the lords who lay ye low?
Wherefore weave with toil and care
The rich robes your tyrants wear?

II

Wherefore feed, and clothe, and save,
From the cradle to the grave,
Those ungrateful drones who would
Drain your sweat — nay, drink your
    blood?

III

Wherefore, Bees of England, forge
Many a weapon, chain, and scourge,
That these stingless drones may spoil
The forced produce of your toil?

IV

Have ye leisure, comfort, calm,
Shelter, food, love's gentle balm?
Or what is it ye buy so dear
With your pain and with your fear?

V

The seed ye sow, another reaps;
The wealth ye find, another keeps;
The robes ye weave, another wears;
The arms ye forge, another bears.

VI

Sow seed, — but let no tyrant reap;
Find wealth, — let no impostor heap;
Weave robes, — let not the idle wear;
Forge arms, — in your defence to bear.

VII

Shrink to your cellars, holes, and cells;
In halls ye deck, another dwells.
Why shake the chains ye wrought? Ye
    see
The steel ye tempered glance on ye.

VIII

With plough and spade, and hoe and
    loom,
Trace your grave, and build your tomb,
And weave your winding-sheet, till fair
England be your sepulchre.

TO SIDMOUTH AND CASTLE-REAGH

Published by Medwin, *The Athenœum*, 1832.

I

As from an ancestral oak
  Two empty ravens sound their clarion,
Yell by yell, and croak by croak,
When they scent the noonday smoke
  Of fresh human carrion: —

II

As two gibbering night-birds flit
  From their bowers of deadly yew
Through the night to frighten it,
When the moon is in a fit,
  And the stars are none, or few: —

III

As a shark and dog-fish wait,
  Under an Atlantic isle,
For the negro-ship, whose freight
Is the theme of their debate,
  Wrinkling their red gills the while —

IV

Are ye, two vultures sick for battle,
  Two scorpions under one wet stone,
Two bloodless wolves whose dry throats
    rattle,
Two crows perched on the murrained cat-
    tle,
  Two vipers tangled into one.

ENGLAND IN 1819

This sonnet was sent by Shelley to Hunt,
November 23, 1819, — 'I don't expect you to
publish it, but you may show it to whom you
please.' It was published by Mrs. Shelley, in
her first collected edition, 1839.

An old, mad, blind, despised and dying
    king;
Princes, the dregs of their dull race, who
    flow
Through public scorn — mud from a muddy
    spring;
Rulers, who neither see, nor feel, nor know,
But leech-like to their fainting country
    cling,
Till they drop, blind in blood, without a
    blow;
A people starved and stabbed in the un-
    tilled field;
An army which liberticide and prey
Makes as a two-edged sword to all who
    wield;
Golden and sanguine laws which tempt and
    slay;
Religion Christless, Godless — a book
    sealed;
A Senate — Time's worst statute unrepealed,
Are graves from which a glorious Phantom
    may
Burst to illumine our tempestuous day.

NATIONAL ANTHEM

Published by Mrs. Shelley in her second collected edition, 1839.

I

God prosper, speed, and save,
God raise from England's grave
  Her murdered Queen!

Pave with swift victory
The steps of Liberty,
Whom Britons own to be
Immortal Queen.

II

See, she comes throned on high,
On swift Eternity,
God save the Queen!
Millions on millions wait
Firm, rapid, and elate,
On her majestic state!
God save the Queen!

III

She is thine own pure soul
Moulding the mighty whole, —
God save the Queen!
She is thine own deep love
Rained down from heaven above, —
Wherever she rest or move,
God save our Queen!

IV

Wilder her enemies
In their own dark disguise, —
God save our Queen!
All earthly things that dare
Her sacred name to bear,
Strip them, as kings are, bare;
God save the Queen!

V

Be her eternal throne
Built in our hearts alone, —
God save the Queen!
Let the oppressor hold
Canopied seats of gold;
She sits enthroned of old
O'er our hearts Queen.

VI

Lips touched by seraphim
Breathe out the choral hymn, —
God save the Queen!
Sweet as if angels sang,
Loud as that trumpet's clang,
Wakening the world's dead gang, —
God save the Queen!

ODE TO HEAVEN

Composed as early as December, and published with *Prometheus Unbound*, 1820. Mrs.

Shelley writes as follows: 'Shelley was a disciple of the immaterial philosophy of Berkeley. This theory gave unity and grandeur to his ideas, while it opened a wide field for his imagination. The creation, such as it was perceived by his mind — a unit in immensity, was slight and narrow compared with the interminable forms of thought that might exist beyond, to be perceived perhaps hereafter by his own mind; all of which are perceptible to other minds that fill the universe, not of space in the material sense, but of infinity in the immaterial one. Such ideas are, in some degree, developed in his poem entitled *Heaven:* and when he makes one of the interlocutors exclaim,

"Peace! the abyss is wreathed in scorn
Of thy presumption, atom-born"

he expresses his despair of being able to conceive, far less express, all of variety, majesty, and beauty, which is veiled from our imperfect senses in the unknown realm, the mystery of which his poetic vision sought in vain to penetrate.'

CHORUS OF SPIRITS

FIRST SPIRIT

PALACE-ROOF of cloudless nights!
Paradise of golden lights!
Deep, immeasurable, vast,
Which art now, and which wert then,
Of the present and the past,
Of the eternal where and when,
Presence-chamber, temple, home,
Ever-canopying dome
Of acts and ages yet to come!

Glorious shapes have life in thee,
Earth, and all earth's company;
Living globes which ever throng
Thy deep chasms and wildernesses;
And green worlds that glide along;
And swift stars with flashing tresses;
And icy moons most cold and bright,
And mighty suns beyond the night,
Atoms of intensest light.

Even thy name is as a god,
Heaven! for thou art the abode
Of that power which is the glass
Wherein man his nature sees.
Generations as they pass
Worship thee with bended knees.
Their unremaining gods and they
Like a river roll away;
Thou remainest such alway.

SECOND SPIRIT

Thou art but the mind's first chamber,
Round which its young fancies clamber,
  Like weak insects in a cave,
Lighted up by stalactites;
  But the portal of the grave,
Where a world of new delights
  Will make thy best glories seem
  But a dim and noonday gleam
From the shadow of a dream!

THIRD SPIRIT

Peace! the abyss is wreathed with scorn
At your presumption, atom-born!
  What is heaven? and what are ye
Who its brief expanse inherit?
  What are suns and spheres which flee
With the instinct of that Spirit
  Of which ye are but a part?
Drops which Nature's mighty heart
Drives through thinnest veins. Depart!

What is heaven? a globe of dew,
Filling in the morning new
  Some eyed flower whose young leaves waken
On an unimagined world;
  Constellated suns unshaken,
Orbits measureless, are furled
  In that frail and fading sphere,
  With ten millions gathered there,
To tremble, gleam, and disappear.

AN EXHORTATION

Shelley writes to Mrs. Gisborne, May 8, 1820, concerning this poem: ' As an excuse for mine and Mary's incurable stupidity, I send a little thing about poets, which is itself a kind of excuse for Wordsworth.' It was published with *Prometheus Unbound*, 1820.

CHAMELEONS feed on light and air;
  Poets' food is love and fame;
If in this wide world of care
  Poets could but find the same
With as little toil as they,
  Would they ever change their hue
As the light chameleons do,
Suiting it to every ray
  Twenty times a day?

Poets are on this cold earth,
  As chameleons might be,
Hidden from their early birth
  In a cave beneath the sea.
Where light is, chameleons change;
  Where love is not, poets do;
  Fame is love disguised; if few
Find either, never think it strange
  That poets range.

Yet dare not stain with wealth or power
  A poet's free and heavenly mind.
If bright chameleons should devour
  Any food but beams and wind,
They would grow as earthly soon
  As their brother lizards are.
Children of a sunnier star,
Spirits from beyond the moon,
  Oh, refuse the boon!

ODE TO THE WEST WIND

Shelley describes in a note the circumstances under which this ode was composed: 'This poem was conceived and chiefly written in a wood that skirts the Arno, near Florence, and on a day when that tempestuous wind, whose temperature is at once mild and animating, was collecting the vapors which pour down the autumnal rains. They began, as I foresaw, at sunset with a violent tempest of hail and rain, attended by that magnificent thunder and lightning peculiar to the Cisalpine regions.
'The phenomenon alluded to at the conclusion of the third stanza is well known to naturalists. The vegetation at the bottom of the sea, of rivers, and of lakes, sympathizes with that of the land in the change of seasons, and is consequently influenced by the winds which announce it.' It was published with *Prometheus Unbound*, 1820.

I

O WILD West Wind, thou breath of Autumn's being,
Thou, from whose unseen presence the leaves dead
Are driven, like ghosts from an enchanter fleeing,

Yellow, and black, and pale, and hectic red
Pestilence-stricken multitudes: O thou,
Who chariotest to their dark wintry bed

The wingèd seeds, where they lie cold and low,
Each like a corpse within its grave, until
Thine azure sister of the Spring shall blow

Her clarion o'er the dreaming earth, and
    fill
(Driving sweet buds like flocks to feed in
    air)
With living hues and odors plain and hill :

Wild Spirit, which art moving everywhere ;
Destroyer and preserver; hear, oh, hear !

II

Thou on whose stream, mid the steep sky's
    commotion,
Loose clouds like earth's decaying leaves
    are shed,
Shook from the tangled boughs of Heaven
    and Ocean,

Angels of rain and lightning: there are
    spread
On the blue surface of thine airy surge,
Like the bright hair uplifted from the
    head

Of some fierce Mænad, even from the dim
    verge
Of the horizon to the zenith's height,
The locks of the approaching storm. Thou
    dirge

Of the dying year, to which this closing
    night
Will be the dome of a vast sepulchre,
Vaulted with all thy congregated might

Of vapors, from whose solid atmosphere
Black rain, and fire, and hail will burst:
    oh, hear !

III

Thou who didst waken from his summer
    dreams
The blue Mediterranean, where he lay,
Lulled by the coil of his crystalline
    streams,

Beside a pumice isle in Baiæ's bay,
And saw in sleep old palaces and towers
Quivering within the wave's intenser day,

All overgrown with azure moss and flow-
    ers
So sweet the sense faints picturing them !
    thou
For whose path the Atlantic's level pow-
    ers

Cleave themselves into chasms, while far
    below
The sea-blooms and the oozy woods which
    wear
The sapless foliage of the ocean know

Thy voice, and suddenly grow gray with
    fear,
And tremble and despoil themselves : oh,
    hear !

IV

If I were a dead leaf thou mightest bear;
If I were a swift cloud to fly with thee;
A wave to pant beneath thy power, and
    share

The impulse of thy strength, only less free
Than thou, O uncontrollable ! If even
I were as in my boyhood, and could be

The comrade of thy wanderings over
    heaven,
As then, when to outstrip thy skyey speed
Scarce seemed a vision; I would ne'er have
    striven

As thus with thee in prayer in my sore need.
Oh, lift me as a wave, a leaf, a cloud !
I fall upon the thorns of life ! I bleed !

A heavy weight of hours has chained and
    bowed
One too like thee: tameless, and swift, and
    proud.

V

Make me thy lyre, even as the forest is :
What if my leaves are falling like its own !
The tumult of thy mighty harmonies

Will take from both a deep, autumnal tone.
Sweet though in sadness. Be thou, Spirit
    fierce,
My spirit ! Be thou me, impetuous one !

Drive my dead thoughts over the universe
Like withered leaves to quicken a new
    birth !
And, by the incantation of this verse,

Scatter, as from an unextinguished hearth
Ashes and sparks, my words among man-
    kind !
Be through my lips to unawakened earth

The trumpet of a prophecy ! O Wind,
If Winter comes, can Spring be far be-
    hind ?

AN ODE

WRITTEN OCTOBER, 1819, BEFORE THE
SPANIARDS HAD RECOVERED THEIR
LIBERTY

Published with *Prometheus Unbound*, 1820.
Mrs. Shelley's note exhibits the state of Shelley's mind in his efforts to arouse and agitate
among the people : ' Shelley loved the people,
and respected them as often more virtuous, as
always more suffering, and, therefore, more de-
serving of sympathy, than the great. He believed that a clash between the two classes of
society was inevitable, and he eagerly ranged
himself on the people's side. He had an idea
of publishing a series of poems adapted expressly to commemorate their circumstances
and wrongs — he wrote a few, but in those
days of prosecution for libel they could not be
printed. They are not among the best of his
productions, a writer being always shackled
when he endeavors to write down to the comprehension of those who could not understand
or feel a highly imaginative style ; but they
show his earnestness, and with what heartfelt
compassion he went home to the direct point
of injury — that oppression is detestable, as
being the parent of starvation, nakedness, and
ignorance. Besides these outpourings of compassion and indignation, he had meant to adorn
the cause he loved with loftier poetry of glory
and triumph — such is the scope of the *Ode to
the Assertors of Liberty*. He sketched also a new
version of our national anthem, as addressed to
Liberty.'

ARISE, arise, arise !
There is blood on the earth that denies
    ye bread !
Be your wounds like eyes
To weep for the dead, the dead, the dead.
What other grief were it just to pay ?
Your sons, your wives, your brethren, were
    they !
Who said they were slain on the battle-
    day ?

Awaken, awaken, awaken !
The slave and the tyrant are twin-born
    foes.
Be the cold chains shaken
To the dust where your kindred repose,
    repose.

Their bones in the grave will start and
    move
When they hear the voices of those they
    love
Most loud in the holy combat above.

Wave, wave high the banner,
When Freedom is riding to conquest by!
    Though the slaves that fan her
Be Famine and Toil, giving sigh for
    sigh.
And ye who attend her imperial car,
Lift not your hands in the banded war
But in her defence whose children ye are.

Glory, glory, glory,
    To those who have greatly suffered and
    done !
Never name in story
Was greater than that which ye shall
    have won.
Conquerors have conquered their foes alone,
Whose revenge, pride, and power, they
    have overthrown.
Ride ye, more victorious, over your own.

Bind, bind every brow
With crownals of violet, ivy, and pine !
    Hide the blood-stains now
With hues which sweet nature has made
    divine —
Green strength, azure hope, and eternity;
But let not the pansy among them be —
Ye were injured, and that means memory.

ON THE MEDUSA OF LEO-NARDO DA VINCI

IN THE FLORENTINE GALLERY

Composed at Florence, in the latter part of
the year, and published by Mrs. Shelley, *Posthumous Poems*, 1824.

I

IT lieth, gazing on the midnight sky,
    Upon the cloudy mountain peak supine;
Below, far lands are seen tremblingly;
    Its horror and its beauty are divine.
Upon its lips and eyelids seems to lie
    Loveliness like a shadow, from which
    shine,
Fiery and lurid, struggling underneath,
The agonies of anguish and of death.

II

Yet it is less the horror than the grace
  Which turns the gazer's spirit into stone,
Whereon the lineaments of that dead face
  Are graven, till the characters be grown
Into itself, and thought no more can trace;
  'T is the melodious hue of beauty thrown
Athwart the darkness and the glare of
    pain,
Which humanize and harmonize the strain.

III

And from its head as from one body grow,
  As   grass out of a watery rock,
Hairs which are vipers, and they curl and
    flow
And their long tangles in each other
    lock,
And with unending involutions show
  Their mailèd radiance, as it were to
    mock
The torture and the death within, and saw
The solid air with many a ragged jaw.

IV

And, from a stone beside, a poisonous eft
  Peeps idly into those Gorgonian eyes;
Whilst in the air a ghastly bat, bereft
  Of sense, has flitted with a mad surprise
Out of the cave this hideous light had
    cleft,
  And he comes hastening like a moth that
    hies
After a taper; and the midnight sky
Flares, a light more dread than obscurity.

V

'T is the tempestuous loveliness of terror;
  For from the serpents gleams a brazen
    glare
Kindled by that inextricable error,
  Which makes a thrilling vapor of the air
Become a   and ever-shifting mirror
  Of all the beauty and the terror there —
A woman's countenance, with serpent
    locks,
Gazing in death on heaven from those wet
    rocks.

THE INDIAN SERENADE

This poem, erroneously said to have been
composed for Mrs. Williams and 'adapted to
the celebrated Persian air sung by the Knautch
girls, *Tazee be tazee no be no*,' was given to Miss
Sophia Stacey in 1819. Several versions of it
exist. Browning's account of deciphering one
of them is interesting: he writes to Hunt, October 6, 1857: ' Is it not strange that I should
have transcribed for the first time last night
the *Indian Serenade* that, together with some
verses of *Metastasio*, accompanied that book?
[the volume of Keats found in Shelley's pocket
and burned with his body] — that I should
have been reserved to tell the present possessor of them, to whom they were given by Captain Roberts, *what* the poem was, and *that it
had been published*? It is preserved religiously;
but the characters are all but illegible, and I
needed a good magnifying-glass to be quite
sure of such of them as remain. The end is
that I have rescued three or four variations in
the reading of that divine little poem — as one
reads it, at least, in the *Posthumous Poems*.'
It was published by Hunt, *The Liberal*, 1822.

I

I ARISE from dreams of thee
In the first sweet sleep of night,
When the winds are breathing low,
And the stars are shining bright;
I arise from dreams of thee,
And a spirit in my feet
Hath led me — who knows how?
To thy chamber window, sweet!

II

The wandering airs, they faint
On the dark, the silent stream;
The champak odors fail
Like sweet thoughts in a dream;
The nightingale's complaint,
It dies upon her heart,
As I must die on thine,
Oh, belovèd as thou art!

III

Oh, lift me from the grass!
I die! I faint! I fail!
Let thy love in kisses rain
On my lips and eyelids pale.
My cheek is cold and white, alas!
My heart beats loud and fast,
Oh! press it close to thine again,
Where it will break at last.

TO SOPHIA

Mrs. Shelley describes the lady to whom
these lines are addressed, in a letter to Mrs.

Gisborne, December 1, 1819: 'There are some ladies come to this house who knew Shelley's family: the younger one was *entousiasmée* to see him. . . . The younger lady was a ward of one of Shelley's uncles. She is lively and unaffected. She sings well for an English *débutante* and, if she would learn the scales, would sing exceedingly well, for she has a sweet voice.' Miss Sophia Stacey was a ward of Mr. Parker, of Bath, an uncle by marriage of Shelley. The poem was published by Rossetti, 1870.

I

THOU art fair, and few are fairer
  Of the nymphs of earth or ocean;
They are robes that fit the wearer —
  Those soft limbs of thine, whose motion
Ever falls and shifts and glances
As the life within them dances.

II

Thy deep eyes, a double Planet,
  Gaze the wisest into madness
With soft clear fire; the winds that fan
    it
  Are those thoughts of tender gladness
Which, like zephyrs on the billow,
Make thy gentle soul their pillow.

III

If, whatever face thou paintest
  In those eyes, grows pale with pleasure,
If the fainting soul is faintest
  When it hears thy harp's wild measure,

Wonder not that when thou speakest
Of the weak my heart is weakest.

IV

As dew beneath the wind of morning,
  As the sea which whirlwinds waken,
As the birds at thunder's warning,
  As aught mute yet deeply shaken,
As one who feels an unseen spirit, —
Is my heart when thine is near it.

LOVE'S PHILOSOPHY

Published by Hunt, *The Indicator*, 1819.

I

THE fountains mingle with the river,
  And the rivers with the ocean;
The winds of heaven mix forever
  With a sweet emotion;
Nothing in the world is single;
  All things by a law divine
In one another's being mingle:
  Why not I with thine ?

II

See the mountains kiss high heaven,
  And the waves clasp one another;
No sister flower would be forgiven
  If it disdained its brother;
And the sunlight clasps the earth,
  And the moonbeams kiss the sea:
What are all these kissings worth,
  If thou kiss not me ?

POEMS WRITTEN IN 1820

  Mrs. Shelley gives in brief passages the account of the various removals of this year, and of Shelley's general state : 'There was something in Florence that disagreed excessively with his health, and he suffered far more pain than usual ; so much so that we left it sooner than we intended, and removed to Pisa, where we had some friends, and, above all, where we could consult the celebrated Vaccà, as to the cause of Shelley's sufferings. He, like every other medical man, could only guess at that, and gave little hope of immediate relief ; he enjoined him to abstain from all physicians and medicine, and to leave his complaint to nature. As he had vainly consulted medical men of the highest repute in England, he was easily persuaded to adopt this advice. Pain and ill-health followed him to the end, but the residence at Pisa agreed with him better than any other, and there in consequence we remained. . . .
  'We spent the summer at the baths of San Giuliano, four miles from Pisa. These baths were of great use to Shelley in soothing his nervous irritability. We made several excursions in the neighborhood. The country around is fertile, and diversified and rendered picturesque by ranges of near hills and more distant mountains. The peasantry are a handsome, intelligent race, and there was a gladsome sunny heaven spread over us, that rendered home and every scene we visited cheerful and bright. . . .
  'We then removed to Pisa, and took up our abode there for the winter. The extreme mildness of the climate suited Shelley, and his solitude was enlivened by an intercourse with

several intimate friends. Chance cast us, strangely enough, on this quiet, half-unpeopled town; but its very peace suited Shelley, — its river, the near mountains, and not distant sea, added to its attractions, and were the objects of many delightful excursions. We feared the south of Italy, and a hotter climate, on account of our child; our former bereavement inspiring us with terror. We seemed to take root here, and moved little afterwards; often, indeed,

entertaining projects for visiting other parts of Italy, but still delaying. But for our fears on account of our child, I believe we should have wandered over the world, both being passionately fond of travelling. But human life, besides its great unalterable necessities, is ruled by a thousand Liliputian ties, that shackle at the time, although it is difficult to account afterwards for their influence over our destiny.'

THE SENSITIVE PLANT

Composed at Pisa, as early as March, and published with *Prometheus Unbound*, 1820. Shelley afterward identified Mrs. Williams as 'the exact antitype of the lady I described in *The Sensitive Plant*, though this must have been *a pure anticipated cognition*, as it was written a year before I knew her.'

PART FIRST

A SENSITIVE Plant in a garden grew,
And the young winds fed it with silver dew,
And it opened its fan-like leaves to the light,
And closed them beneath the kisses of Night.

And the Spring arose on the garden fair,
Like the Spirit of Love felt everywhere;
And each flower and herb on Earth's dark breast
Rose from the dreams of its wintry rest.

But none ever trembled and panted with bliss
In the garden, the field, or the wilderness,
Like a doe in the noontide with love's sweet want,   11
As the companionless Sensitive Plant.

The snowdrop, and then the violet,
Arose from the ground with warm rain wet,
And their breath was mixed with fresh odor, sent
From the turf, like the voice and the instrument.

Then the pied wind-flowers and the tulip tall,
And narcissi, the fairest among them all,

Who gaze on their eyes in the stream's recess
Till they die of their own dear loveliness;   20

And the Naiad-like lily of the vale,
Whom youth makes so fair, and passion so pale,
That the light of its tremulous bells is seen
Through their pavilions of tender green;

And the hyacinth purple, and white, and blue,
Which flung from its bells a sweet peal anew
Of music so delicate, soft, and intense,
It was felt like an odor within the sense;

And the rose like a nymph to the bath addressed,
Which unveiled the depth of her glowing breast,   30
Till, fold after fold, to the fainting air
The soul of her beauty and love lay bare;

And the wand-like lily, which lifted up,
As a Mænad, its moonlight-colored cup,
Till the fiery star, which is its eye,
Gazed through clear dew on the tender sky;

And the jessamine faint, and the sweet tube-rose,
The sweetest flower for scent that blows;
And all rare blossoms from every clime
Grew in that garden in perfect prime.   40

And on the stream whose inconstant bosom
Was pranked, under boughs of embowering blossom,
With golden and green light, slanting through
Their heaven of many a tangled hue,

Broad water-lilies lay tremulously,
And starry river-buds glimmered by,
And around them the soft stream did glide
    and dance
With a motion of sweet sound and radi-
    ance.

And the sinuous paths of lawn and of moss,
Which led through the garden along and
    across,   50
Some open at once to the sun and the
    breeze,
Some lost among bowers of blossoming
    trees, —

Were all paved with daisies and delicate
    bells,
As fair as the fabulous asphodels,
And flowrets which, drooping as day
    drooped too,
Fell into pavilions white, purple, and blue,
To roof the glowworm from the evening
    dew.

And from this undefiled Paradise
The flowers (as an infant's awakening eyes
Smile on its mother, whose singing sweet 60
Can first lull, and at last must awaken it)

When Heaven's blithe winds had unfolded
    them
As mine-lamps enkindle a hidden gem,
Shone smiling to Heaven, and every one
Shared joy in the light of the gentle sun;

For each one was interpenetrated
With the light and the odor its neighbor
    shed,
Like young lovers whom youth and love
    make dear,
Wrapped and filled by their mutual atmo-
    sphere.

But the Sensitive Plant, which could give
    small fruit   70
Of the love which it felt from the leaf to
    the root,
Received more than all, it loved more than
    ever,
Where none wanted but it, could belong to
    the giver;

For the Sensitive Plant has no bright
    flower;
Radiance and odor are not its dower;

It loves, even like Love, its deep heart is
    full,
It desires what it has not, the beautiful !

The light winds which from unsustaining
    wings
Shed the music of many murmurings;
The beams which dart from many a star 80
Of the flowers whose hues they bear afar;

The plumèd insects swift and free,
Like golden boats on a sunny sea,
Laden with light and odor, which pass
Over the gleam of the living grass;

The unseen clouds of the dew, which lie
Like fire in the flowers till the sun rides
    high,
Then wander like spirits among the
    spheres,
Each cloud faint with the fragance it
    bears;

The quivering vapors of dim noontide,   90
Which like a sea o'er the warm earth
    glide,
In which every sound, and odor, and beam,
Move, as reeds in a single stream; —

Each and all like ministering angels were
For the Sensitive Plant sweet joy to bear,
Whilst the lagging hours of the day went
    by
Like windless clouds o'er a tender sky.

And when evening descended from heaven
    above,
And the Earth was all rest, and the air was
    all love,
And delight, though less bright, was far
    more deep,   100
And the day's veil fell from the world of
    sleep,

And the beasts, and the birds, and the in-
    sects were drowned
In an ocean of dreams without a sound,
Whose waves never mark, though they
    ever impress
The light sand which paves it, conscious-
    ness;

(Only overhead the sweet nightingale
Ever sang more sweet as the day might
    fail,

And snatches of its Elysian chant
Were mixed with the dreams of the Sensi-
      tive Plant); —

The Sensitive Plant was the earliest   110
Upgathered into the bosom of rest;
A sweet child weary of its delight,
The feeblest and yet the favorite,
Cradled within the embrace of night.

PART SECOND

There was a Power in this sweet place,
An Eve in this Eden; a ruling grace
Which to the flowers, did they waken or
      dream,
Was as God is to the starry scheme.

A Lady, the wonder of her kind,
Whose form was upborne by a lovely mind
Which, dilating, had moulded her mien
      and motion
Like a sea-flower unfolded beneath the
      ocean,

Tended the garden from morn to even;
And the meteors of that sublunar heaven,
Like the lamps of the air when Night walks
      forth,   11
Laughed round her footsteps up from the
      Earth !

She had no companion of mortal race,
But her tremulous breath and her flushing
      face
Told, whilst the morn kissed the sleep from
      her eyes,
That her dreams were less slumber than
      Paradise :

As if some bright Spirit for her sweet
      sake
Had deserted heaven while the stars were
      awake,
As if yet around her he lingering were,
Though the veil of daylight concealed him
      from her.   20

Her step seemed to pity the grass it
      pressed;
You might hear, by the heaving of her
      breast,
That the coming and going of the wind
Brought pleasure there and left passion
      behind.

And wherever her airy footstep trod,
Her trailing hair from the grassy sod
Erased its light vestige, with shadowy
      sweep,
Like a sunny storm o'er the dark green
      deep.

I doubt not the flowers of that garden
      sweet
Rejoiced in the sound of her gentle feet; 30
I doubt not they felt the spirit that came
From her glowing fingers through all their
      frame.

She sprinkled bright water from the stream
On those that were faint with the sunny
      beam;
And out of the cups of the heavy flowers
She emptied the rain of the thunder
      showers. •

She lifted their heads with her tender
      hands,
And sustained them with rods and osier-
      bands;
If the flowers had been her own infants,
      she
Could never have nursed them more ten-
      derly.   40

And all killing insects and gnawing worms,
And things of obscene and unlovely forms,
She bore in a basket of Indian woof,
Into the rough woods far aloof, —

In a basket, of grasses and wild flowers
      full,
The freshest her gentle hands could pull
For the poor banished insects, whose in-
      tent,
Although they did ill, was innocent.

But the bee, and the beam-like ephemeris
Whose path is the lightning's, and soft
      moths that kiss   50
The sweet lips of the flowers, and harm not,
      did she
Make her attendant angels be.

And many an antenatal tomb,
Where butterflies dream of the life to
      come,
She left clinging round the smooth and
      dark
Edge of the odorous cedar bark.

This fairest creature from earliest spring
Thus moved through the garden minister-
ing
All the sweet season of summer tide,
And ere the first leaf looked brown — she
died!   60

PART THIRD

Three days the flowers of the garden fair,
Like stars when the moon is awakened,
were,
Or the waves of Baiæ, ere luminous
She floats up through the smoke of Vesu-
vius.

And on the fourth, the Sensitive Plant
Felt the sound of the funeral chant,
And the steps of the bearers, heavy and
slow,
And the sobs of the mourners, deep and
low;

The weary sound and the heavy breath,
And the silent motions of passing death, 10
And the smell, cold, oppressive, and dank,
Sent through the pores of the coffin plank.

The dark grass, and the flowers among the
grass,
Were bright with tears as the crowd did
pass;
From their sighs the wind caught a mournful tone,
And sate in the pines, and gave groan for
groan.

The garden, once fair, became cold and
foul,
Like the corpse of her who had been its
soul
Which at first was lovely as if in sleep,
Then slowly changed, till it grew a heap 20
To make men tremble who never weep.

Swift summer into the autumn flowed,
And frost in the mist of the morning rode,
Though the noonday sun looked clear and
bright,
Mocking the spoil of the secret night.

The rose leaves, like flakes of crimson
snow,
Paved the turf and the moss below.

The lilies were drooping, and white, and
wan,
Like the head and the skin of a dying man.

And Indian plants, of scent and hue   30
The sweetest that ever were fed on dew,
Leaf by leaf, day after day,
Were massed into the common clay.

And the leaves, brown, yellow, and gray,
and red,
And white with the whiteness of what is
dead,
Like troops of ghosts on the dry wind
passed;
Their whistling noise made the birds aghast.

And the gusty winds waked the wingèd
seeds
Out of their birthplace of ugly weeds,
Till they clung round many a sweet flower's
stem,   40
Which rotted into the earth with them.

The water-blooms under the rivulet
Fell from the stalks on which they were
set;
And the eddies drove them here and there,
As the winds did those of the upper air.

Then the rain came down, and the broken
stalks
Were bent and tangled across the walks;
And the leafless network of parasite bow-
ers
Massed into ruin, and all sweet flowers.

Between the time of the wind and the
snow   50
All loathliest weeds began to grow,
Whose coarse leaves were splashed with
many a speck,
Like the water-snake's belly and the toad's
back.

And thistles, and nettles, and darnels rank,
And the dock, and henbane, and hemlock
dank,
Stretched out its long and hollow shank,
And stifled the air till the dead wind stank.

And plants, at whose names the verse feels
loath,
Filled the place with a monstrous undergrowth,

Prickly, and pulpous, and blistering, and
    blue,   60
Livid, and starred with a lurid dew.

And agarics and fungi, with mildew and
    mould,
Started like mist from the wet ground
    cold;
Pale, fleshy, as if the decaying dead
With a spirit of growth had been animated !

Spawn, weeds, and filth, a leprous scum,
Made the running rivulet thick and dumb,
And at its outlet flags huge as stakes
Dammed it up with roots knotted like wa-
    ter-snakes.

And hour by hour, when the air was still, 70
The vapors arose which have strength to
    kill;
At morn they were seen, at noon they were
    felt,
At night they were darkness no star could
    melt.

And unctuous meteors from spray to spray
Crept and flitted in broad noonday
Unseen; every branch on which they alit
By a venomous blight was burned and
    bit.

The Sensitive Plant, like one forbid,
Wept, and the tears within each lid   79
Of its folded leaves, which together grew,
Were changed to a blight of frozen glue.

For the leaves soon fell, and the branches
    soon
By the heavy axe of the blast were hewn;
The sap shrank to the root through every
    pore,
As blood to a heart that will beat no more.

For Winter came; the wind was his whip;
One choppy finger was on his lip;
He had torn the cataracts from the hills
And they clanked at his girdle like mana-
    cles;

His breath was a chain which without a
    sound   90
The earth, and the air, and the water bound;
He came, fiercely driven, in his chariot-
    throne,
By the tenfold blasts of the Arctic zone.

Then the weeds which were forms of living
    death
Fled from the frost to the earth beneath.
Their decay and sudden flight from frost
Was but like the vanishing of a ghost !

And under the roots of the Sensitive Plant
The moles and the dormice died for want;
The birds dropped stiff from the frozen air
And were caught in the branches naked
    and bare.   101

First there came down a thawing rain,
And its dull drops froze on the boughs
    again;
Then there steamed up a freezing dew
Which to the drops of the thaw-rain grew;

And a northern whirlwind, wandering
    about
Like a wolf that had smelt a dead child
    out,
Shook the boughs thus laden and heavy and
    stiff,
And snapped them off with his rigid griff.

When Winter had gone and Spring came
    back,   110
The Sensitive Plant was a leafless wreck;
But the mandrakes, and toadstools, and
    docks, and darnels,
Rose like the dead from their ruined char-
    nels.

CONCLUSION

Whether the Sensitive Plant, or that
Which within its boughs like a spirit sat,
Ere its outward form had known decay,
Now felt this change, I cannot say.

Whether that lady's gentle mind,
No longer with the form combined
Which scattered love, as stars do light, 120
Found sadness where it left delight,

I dare not guess; but in this life
Of error, ignorance and strife,
Where nothing is, but all things seem,
And we the shadows of the dream,

It is a modest creed, and yet
Pleasant, if one considers it,
To own that death itself must be,
Like all the rest, a mockery.

That garden sweet, that lady fair,   130
And all sweet shapes and odors there,
In truth have never passed away :
'T is we, 't is ours, are changed; not they.

For love, and beauty, and delight,
There is no death nor change : their might
Exceeds our organs, which endure
No light, being themselves obscure.

A VISION OF THE SEA

Composed at Pisa as early as April, and published with *Prometheus Unbound*, 1820.

'T is the terror of tempest. The rags of
the sail
Are flickering in ribbons within the fierce
gale;
From the stark night of vapors the dim rain
is driven,
And, when lightning is loosed, like a deluge
from heaven,
She sees the black trunks of the water-
spouts spin
And bend, as if heaven was ruining in,
Which they seemed to sustain with their
terrible mass
As if ocean had sunk from beneath them;
they pass
To their graves in the deep with an earth-
quake of sound,
And the waves and the thunders, made
silent around,   10
Leave the wind to its echo. The vessel,
now tossed
Through the low trailing rack of the tem-
pest, is lost
In the skirts of the thundercloud; now
down the sweep
Of the wind-cloven wave to the chasm of
the deep
It sinks, and the walls of the watery vale
Whose depths of dread calm are unmoved
by the gale,
Dim mirrors of ruin, hang gleaming about;
While the surf, like a chaos of stars, like
a rout
Of death-flames, like whirlpools of fire-
flowing iron,
With splendor and terror the black ship
environ,   20
Or, like sulphur-flakes hurled from a mine
of pale fire,
In fountains spout o'er it. In many a spire

The pyramid-billows, with white points of
brine,
In the cope of the lightning inconstantly
shine,
As piercing the sky from the floor of the
sea.
The great ship seems splitting ! it cracks
as a tree,
While an earthquake is splintering its root,
ere the blast
Of the whirlwind that stripped it of
branches has passed.
The intense thunder-balls which are rain-
ing from heaven
Have shattered its mast, and it stands black
and riven.   30
The chinks suck destruction. The heavy
dead hulk
On the living sea rolls an inanimate bulk,
Like a corpse on the clay which is hunger-
ing to fold
Its corruption around it. Meanwhile, from
the hold,
One deck is burst up by the waters below,
And it splits like the ice when the thaw-
breezes blow
O'er the lakes of the desert ! Who sit on
the other ?
Is that all the crew that lie burying each
other,
Like the dead in a breach, round the fore-
mast ? Are those
Twin tigers who burst, when the waters
arose,   40
In the agony of terror, their chains in the
hold, —
(What now makes them tame is what then
made them bold)
Who crouch, side by side, and have driven,
like a crank,
The deep grip of their claws through the
vibrating plank, —
Are these all ? Nine weeks the tall vessel
had lain
On the windless expanse of the watery
plain,
Where the death-darting sun cast no shadow
at noon,
And there seemed to be fire in the beams
of the moon,
Till a lead-colored fog gathered up from
the deep,
Whose breath was quick pestilence; then,
the cold sleep   50

Crept, like blight through the ears of a
   thick field of corn,
O'er the populous vessel.   And even and
   morn,
With their hammocks for coffins, the sea-
   men aghast
Like dead men the dead limbs of their
   comrades cast
Down the deep, which closed on them above
   and around,
And the sharks and the dogfish their grave-
   clothes unbound,
And were glutted like Jews with this
   manna rained down
From God on their wilderness.   One after
   one
The mariners died; on the eve of this day,
When the tempest was gathering in cloudy
   array,   60
But seven remained.   Six the thunder has
   smitten,
And they lie black as mummies on which
   Time has written
His scorn of the embalmer; the seventh,
   from the deck
An oak-splinter pierced through his breast
   and his back,
And hung out to the tempest, a wreck on
   the wreck.
No more?   At the helm sits a woman
   more fair
Than heaven when, unbinding its star-
   braided hair,
It sinks with the sun on the earth and the
   sea.
She clasps a bright child on her upgathered
   knee;
It laughs at the lightning, it mocks the
   mixed thunder   70
Of the air and the sea; with desire and
   with wonder
It is beckoning the tigers to rise and come
   near;
It would play with those eyes where the
   radiance of fear
Is outshining the meteors; its bosom beats
   high,
The heart-fire of pleasure has kindled its eye,
Whilst its mother's is lustreless: 'Smile
   not, my child,
But sleep deeply and sweetly, and so be
   beguiled
Of the pang that awaits us, whatever that be,
So dreadful since thou must divide it with
   me !

Dream, sleep ! This pale bosom, thy cra-
   dle and bed,   80
Will it rock thee not, infant ?   'T is beat-
   ing with dread !
Alas ! what is life, what is death, what are
   we,
That when the ship sinks we no longer
   may be ?
What ! to see thee no more, and to feel
   thee no more ?
To be after life what we have been before ?
Not to touch those sweet hands, not to look
   on those eyes,
Those lips, and that hair, all that smiling
   disguise
Thou yet wearest, sweet spirit, which I,
   day by day,
Have so long called my child, but which
   now fades away
Like a rainbow, and I the fallen shower ?'
   Lo ! the ship   90
Is settling, it topples, the leeward ports dip;
The tigers leap up when they feel the slow
   brine
Crawling inch by inch on them; hair, ears,
   limbs, and eyne
Stand rigid with horror; a loud, long,
   hoarse cry
Bursts at once from their vitals tremen-
   dously,
And 't is borne down the mountainous vale
   of the wave,
Rebounding, like thunder, from crag to
   cave,
Mixed with the clash of the lashing rain,
Hurried on by the might of the hurricane.
The hurricane came from the west, and
   passed on   100
By the path of the gate of the eastern sun,
Transversely dividing the stream of the
   storm;
As an arrowy serpent, pursuing the form
Of an elephant, bursts through the brakes
   of the waste.
Black as a cormorant the screaming blast,
Between ocean and heaven, like an ocean,
   passed,
Till it came to the clouds on the verge of
   the world
Which, based on the sea and to heaven up-
   curled,
Like columns and walls did surround and
   sustain
The dome of the tempest; it rent them in
   twain,   110

As a flood rends its barriers of mountain-
ous crag;
And the dense clouds in many a ruin and
. rag,
Like the stones of a temple ere earthquake
has passed,
Like the dust of its fall, on the whirlwind
are cast;
They are scattered like foam on the tor-
rent; and where
The wind has burst out through the chasm,
from the air
Of clear morning the beams of the sunrise
flow in,
Unimpeded, keen, golden, and crystalline,
Banded armies of light and of air; at one
gate
They encounter, but interpenetrate.   120
And that breach in the tempest is widening
away,
And the caverns of cloud are torn up by
the day,
And the fierce winds are sinking with weary
wings,
Lulled by the motion and murmurings
And the long glassy heave of the rocking
sea,
And overhead glorious, but dreadful to
see,
The wrecks of the tempest, like vapors of
gold,
Are consuming in sunrise. The heaped
waves behold
The deep calm of blue heaven dilating
above,
And,ˈ like passions made still by the pre-
sence of Love,   130
Beneath the clear surface reflecting it slide
Tremulous with soft influence; extending
its tide
From the Andes to Atlas, round mountain
and isle,
Round sea-birds and wrecks, paved with
heaven's azure smile,
The wide world of waters is vibrating.
Where
Is the ship? On the verge of the wave
where it lay
One tiger is mingled in ghastly affray
With a sea-snake. The foam and the
smoke of the battle
Stain the clear air with sunbows. The jar,
and the rattle   139
Of solid bones crushed by the infinite stress
Of the snake's adamantine voluminousness;

And the hum of the hot blood that spouts
and rains
Where the gripe of the tiger has wounded
the veins,
Swollen with rage, strength, and effort; the
whirl and the splash
As of some hideous engine whose brazen
teeth smash
The thin winds and soft waves into thun-
der; the screams
And hissings, crawl fast o'er the smooth
ocean-streams,
Each sound like a centipede. Near this
commotion
A blue shark is hanging within the blue
ocean,
The fin-wingèd tomb of the victor. The
other   150
Is winning his way from the fate of his
brother,
To his own with the speed of despair. Lo!
a boat
Advances; twelve rowers with the impulse
of thought
Urge on the keen keel, — the brine foams.
At the stern
Three marksmen stand levelling. Hot
bullets burn
In the breast of the tiger, which yet bears
him on
To his refuge and ruin. One fragment
alone —
'T is dwindling and sinking, 't is now almost
gone —
Of the wreck of the vessel peers out of the
sea.
With her left hand she grasps it impetu-
ously,   160
With her right hand she sustains her fair
infant. Death, Fear,
Love, Beauty, are mixed in the atmo-
sphere,
Which trembles and burns with the fervor
of dread
Around her wild eyes, her bright hand,
and her head,
Like a meteor of light o'er the waters! her
child
Is yet smiling, and playing, and murmuring; so smiled
The false deep ere the storm. Like a sister and brother
The child and the ocean still smile on each
other,
Whilst ——

THE CLOUD

Published with *Prometheus Unbound*, 1820.

I BRING fresh showers for the thirsting
    flowers,
  From the seas and the streams;
I bear light shade for the leaves when laid
  In their noonday dreams.
From my wings are shaken the dews that
    waken
  The sweet buds every one,
When rocked to rest on their mother's
    breast,
  As she dances about the sun.
I wield the flail of the lashing hail,
  And whiten the green plains under,   10
And then again I dissolve it in rain,
  And laugh as I pass in thunder.

I sift the snow on the mountains below,
  And their great pines groan aghast;
And all the night 't is my pillow white,
  While I sleep in the arms of the blast.
Sublime on the towers of my skyey bow-
    ers,
  Lightning my pilot sits;
In a cavern under is fettered the thunder,
  It struggles and howls at fits;   20
Over earth and ocean with gentle motion,
  This pilot is guiding me,
Lured by the love of the genii that move
  In the depths of the purple sea;
Over the rills, and the crags, and the hills,
  Over the lakes and the plains,
Wherever he dream, under mountain or
    stream,
  The Spirit he loves remains;
And I all the while bask in heaven's blue
    smile,
  Whilst he is dissolving in rains.   30

The sanguine sunrise, with his meteor eyes,
  And his burning plumes outspread,
Leaps on the back of my sailing rack,
  When the morning star shines dead;
As on the jag of a mountain crag,
  Which an earthquake rocks and swings,
An eagle alit one moment may sit
  In the light of its golden wings.
And when sunset may breathe, from the
    lit sea beneath,
  Its ardors of rest and of love,   40
And the crimson pall of eve may fall
  From the depth of heaven above,

With wings folded I rest, on mine airy
    nest,
  As still as a brooding dove.

That orbèd maiden, with white fire laden,
  Whom mortals call the Moon,
Glides glimmering o'er my fleece-like floor,
  By the midnight breezes strewn;
And wherever the beat of her unseen feet,
  Which only the angels hear,   50
May have broken the woof of my tent's
    thin roof,
  The stars peep behind her and peer;
And I laugh to see them whirl and flee,
  Like a swarm of golden bees,
When I widen the rent in my wind-built
    tent,
  Till the calm rivers, lakes, and seas,
Like strips of the sky fallen through me
    on high,
  Are each paved with the moon and
    these.

I bind the sun's throne with a burning zone,
  And the moon's with a girdle of pearl;
The volcanoes are dim, and the stars reel
    and swim,   61
  When the whirlwinds my banner unfurl.
From cape to cape, with a bridge-like
    shape,
  Over a torrent sea,
Sunbeam-proof, I hang like a roof, —
  The mountains its columns be.
The triumphal arch, through which I
    march,
  With hurricane, fire, and snow,
When the powers of the air are chained to
    my chair,
  Is the million-colored bow;   70
The sphere-fire above its soft colors wove,
  While the moist earth was laughing
    below.

I am the daughter of earth and water,
  And the nursling of the sky;
I pass through the pores of the ocean and
    shores;
  I change, but I cannot die.
For after the rain, when with never a stain
  The pavilion of heaven is bare,
And the winds and sunbeams with their
    convex gleams
  Build up the blue dome of air,   80
I silently laugh at my own cenotaph,
  And out of the caverns of rain,

Like a child from the womb, like a ghost
    from the tomb,
I arise and unbuild it again.

TO A SKYLARK

Composed at Leghorn, and published with
Prometheus Unbound, 1820. The occasion is
described by Mrs. Shelley: ' In the spring we
spent a week or two near Leghorn, borrowing
the house of some friends, who were absent on
a journey to England. It was on a beautiful
summer evening while wandering among the
lanes, whose myrtle hedges were the bowers
of the fireflies, that we heard the carolling of
the skylark, which inspired one of the most
beautiful of his poems.'

  HAIL to thee, blithe Spirit !
    Bird thou never wert,
  That from Heaven, or near it,
    Pourest thy full heart
In profuse strains of unpremeditated art.

  Higher still and higher
    From the earth thou springest
  Like a cloud of fire;
    The blue deep thou wingest,
And singing still dost soar, and soaring
  ever singest.   10

  In the golden lightning
    Of the sunken sun,
  O'er which clouds are bright'ning,
    Thou dost float and run;
Like an unbodied joy whose race is just
  begun.

  The pale purple even
    Melts around thy flight;
  Like a star of heaven
    In the broad daylight
Thou art unseen, — but yet I hear thy shrill
  delight,   20

  Keen as are the arrows
    Of that silver sphere,
  Whose intense lamp narrows
    In the white dawn clear
Until we hardly see — we feel that it is
  there;

  All the earth and air
    With thy voice is loud,

  As when Night is bare
    From one lonely cloud
The moon rains out her beams, and Heaven
  is overflowed.   30

  What thou art we know not;
    What is most like thee ?
  From rainbow clouds there flow
    not
    Drops so bright to see
As from thy presence showers a rain of
  melody.

  Like a Poet hidden
    In the light of thought,
  Singing hymns unbidden
    Till the world is wrought
To sympathy with hopes and fears it heeded
  not :   40

  Like a high-born maiden
    In a palace tower,
  Soothing her love-laden
    Soul in secret hour
With music sweet as love, — which over-
  flows her bower :

  Like a glowworm golden
    In a dell of dew,
  Scattering unbeholden
    Its aërial hue
Among the flowers and grass which screen
  it from the view :   50

  Like a rose embowered
    In its own green leaves,
  By warm winds deflowered,
    Till the scent it gives
Makes faint with too much sweet those
  heavy wingèd thieves.

  Sound of vernal showers
    On the twinkling grass,
  Rain-awakened flowers,
    All that ever was
Joyous and clear and fresh, thy music doth
  surpass.   60

  Teach us, Sprite or Bird,
    What sweet thoughts are thine;
  I have never heard
    Praise of love or wine
That panted forth a flood of rapture so
  divine.

Chorus Hymeneal,
  Or triumphal chant,
Matched with thine, would be all
  But an empty vaunt,
A thing wherein we feel there is some
hidden want.   70

What objects are the fountains
  Of thy happy strain?
What fields or waves or mountains?
  What shapes of sky or plain?
What love of thine own kind? what igno-
rance of pain?

With thy clear keen joyance
  Languor cannot be;
Shadow of annoyance
  Never came near thee;
Thou lovest — but ne'er knew love's sad
satiety.   80

Waking or asleep
  Thou of death must deem
Things more true and deep
  Than we mortals dream —
Or how could thy notes flow in such a crys-
tal stream?

We look before and after,
  And pine for what is not;
Our sincerest laughter
  With some pain is fraught;
Our sweetest songs are those that tell of
saddest thought.   90

Yet if we could scorn
  Hate and pride and fear;
If we were things born
  Not to shed a tear,
I know not how thy joy we ever should
come near.

Better than all measures
  Of delightful sound,
Better than all treasures
  That in books are found,
Thy skill to poet were, thou scorner of the
ground!   100

Teach me half the gladness
  That thy brain must know,
Such harmonious madness
  From my lips would flow
The world should listen then — as I am
listening now.

ODE TO LIBERTY

Published with *Prometheus Unbound*, 1820.
Shelley sent it to Peacock with permission to
insert asterisks in stanzas fifteen and sixteen
in case his publisher objected to the expressions
there used.

Yet Freedom, yet, thy banner torn but flying
Streams like a thunder-storm against the wind.
                     BYRON.

I

A GLORIOUS people vibrated again
  The lightning of the Nations; Liberty,
From heart to heart, from tower to tower,
    o'er Spain,
  Scattering contagious fire into the sky,
Gleamed. My soul spurned the chains of
    its dismay,
    And in the rapid plumes of song
    Clothed itself, sublime and strong;
As a young eagle soars the morning clouds
    among,
  Hovering in verse o'er its accustomed
    prey;
    Till from its station in the Heaven of
    fame
  The Spirit's whirlwind rapt it, and the ray
    Of the remotest sphere of living flame
Which paves the void was from behind it
    flung,
  As foam from a ship's swiftness, when
    there came
A voice out of the deep: I will record the
    same.

II

The Sun and the serenest Moon sprang
    forth;
  The burning stars of the abyss were
    hurled
Into the depths of heaven. The dædal
    earth,
  That island in the ocean of the world,
Hung in its cloud of all-sustaining air;
    But this divinest universe
    Was yet a chaos and a curse,
For thou wert not; but power from worst
    producing worse,
  The spirit of the beasts was kindled there,
    And of the birds, and of the watery
    forms,
  And there was war among them, and
    despair
    Within them, raging without truce or
    terms.

The bosom of their violated nurse
  Groaned, for beasts warred on beasts,
    and worms on worms,
And men on men; each heart was as a hell
  of storms.

III

Man, the imperial shape, then multiplied
  His generations under the pavilion
Of the Sun's throne; palace and pyramid,
  Temple and prison, to many a swarming
    million
Were as to mountain wolves their ragged
  caves.
    This human living multitude
    Was savage, cunning, blind, and rude,
For thou wert not; but o'er the populous
  solitude,
  Like one fierce cloud over a waste of
    waves,
  Hung Tyranny; beneath, sate deified
The sister-pest, congregator of slaves;
  Into the shadow of her pinions wide
Anarchs and priests who feed on gold and
  blood
  Till with the stain their inmost souls are
    dyed,
  Drove the astonished herds of men from
    every side.

IV

The nodding promontories, and blue isles,
  And cloud-like mountains, and dividuous
    waves
Of Greece, basked glorious in the open
  smiles
  Of favoring heaven; from their en-
    chanted caves
Prophetic echoes flung dim melody.
    On the unapprehensive wild
    The vine, the corn, the olive mild,
Grew savage yet, to human use unrecon-
  ciled;
  And, like unfolded flowers beneath the sea,
  Like the man's thought dark in the in-
    fant's brain,
  Like aught that is which wraps what is
    to be,
    Art's deathless dreams lay veiled by
      many a vein
Of Parian stone; and, yet a speechless child,
  Verse murmured, and Philosophy did
    strain
Her lidless eyes for thee; when o'er the
  Ægean main

V

Athens arose; a city such as vision
  Builds from the purple crags and silver
    towers
Of battlemented cloud, as in derision
  Of kingliest masonry: the ocean floors
Pave it; the evening sky pavilions it;
    Its portals are inhabited
    By thunder-zonèd winds, each head
Within its cloudy wings with sun-fire gar-
  landed, —
  A divine work! Athens, diviner yet,
  Gleamed with its crest of columns, on
    the will
Of man, as on a mount of diamond,
  set;
  For thou wert, and thine all-creative
    skill
Peopled, with forms that mock the eternal
  dead
In marble immortality, that hill
Which was thine earliest throne and lat-
  est oracle.

VI

Within the surface of Time's fleeting river
  Its wrinkled image lies, as then it lay
Immovably unquiet, and forever
  It trembles, but it cannot pass away!
The voices of thy bards and sages thunder
    With an earth-awakening blast
    Through the caverns of the past;
Religion veils her eyes; Oppression shrinks
  aghast.
  A wingèd sound of joy, and love, and
    wonder,
  Which soars where Expectation never
    flew,
Rending the veil of space and time asun-
  der!
  One ocean feeds the clouds, and
    streams, and dew;
One sun illumines heaven; one spirit vast
  With life and love makes chaos ever new,
  As Athens doth the world with thy de-
    light renew.

VII

Then Rome was, and from thy deep bosom
  fairest,
  Like a wolf-cub from a Cadmean Mænad,
She drew the milk of greatness, though thy
  dearest
  From that Elysian food was yet un-
    weanèd;

And many a deed of terrible uprightness
    By thy sweet love was sanctified;
    And in thy smile, and by thy side,
Saintly Camillus lived, and firm Atilius died.
    But when tears stained thy robe of vestal
        whiteness,
        And gold profaned thy Capitolian
            throne,
    Thou didst desert, with spirit-wingèd
        lightness,
        The senate of the tyrants: they sunk
            prone
Slaves of one tyrant. Palatinus sighed
    Faint echoes of Ionian song; that tone
Thou didst delay to hear, lamenting to
    disown.

VIII

From what Hyrcanian glen or frozen hill,
    Or piny promontory of the Arctic main,
Or utmost islet inaccessible,
    Didst thou lament the ruin of thy reign,
Teaching the woods and waves, and desert
        rocks,
        And every Naiad's ice-cold urn,
        To talk in echoes sad and stern,
Of that sublimest lore which man had dared
        unlearn?
    For neither didst thou watch the wizard
        flocks
        Of the Scald's dreams, nor haunt the
            Druid's sleep.
    What if the tears rained through thy
        shattered locks
        Were quickly dried? for thou didst
            groan, not weep,
When from its sea of death, to kill and
        burn,
    The Galilean serpent forth did creep,
And made thy world an undistinguishable
    heap.

IX

A thousand years the Earth cried, Where
        art thou?
    And then the shadow of thy coming
        fell
On Saxon Alfred's olive-cinctured brow;
    And many a warrior-peopled citadel,
Like rocks which fire lifts out of the flat
        deep,
        Arose in sacred Italy,
        Frowning o'er the tempestuous sea
Of kings, and priests, and slaves, in tower-
    crowned majesty;

That multitudinous anarchy did sweep
    And burst around their walls, like idle
        foam,
Whilst from the human spirit's deepest
    deep,
    Strange melody with love and awe
        struck dumb
Dissonant arms; and Art, which cannot die,
    With divine wand traced on our earthly
        home
Fit imagery to pave heaven's everlasting
    dome.

X

Thou huntress swifter than the Moon!
        thou terror
    Of the world's wolves! thou bearer of
        the quiver,
Whose sun-like shafts pierce tempest-
        wingèd Error,
    As light may pierce the clouds when they
        dissever
In the calm regions of the orient day!
        Luther caught thy wakening glance;
        Like lightning, from his leaden lance
Reflected, it dissolved the visions of the
        trance
    In which, as in a tomb, the nations lay;
        And England's prophets hailed thee
            as their queen,
    In songs whose music cannot pass away,
        Though it must flow forever; not un-
            seen
Before the spirit-sighted countenance
    Of Milton didst thou pass, from the sad
        scene
    Beyond whose night he saw, with a de-
        jected mien.

XI

The eager hours and unreluctant years
    As on a dawn-illumined mountain stood,
Trampling to silence their loud hopes and
        fears,
    Darkening each other with their multi-
        tude,
And cried aloud, Liberty! Indignation
        Answered Pity from her cave;
        Death grew pale within the grave,
    And Desolation howled to the destroyer,
        Save!
    When, like heaven's sun girt by the ex-
        halation
        Of its own glorious light, thou didst
            arise,

Chasing thy foes from nation unto nation
  Like shadows: as if day had cloven
    the skies
At dreaming midnight o'er the western
    wave,
  Men started, staggering with a glad sur-
    prise,
  Under the lightnings of thine unfamiliar
    eyes.

XII

Thou heaven of earth! what spells could
    pall thee then,
  In ominous eclipse? a thousand years,
Bred from the slime of deep oppression's
    den,
  Dyed all thy liquid light with blood and
    tears,
Till thy sweet stars could weep the stain
    away;
    How like Bacchanals of blood
    Round France, the ghastly vintage,
      stood
Destruction's sceptred slaves, and Folly's
    mitred brood!
When one, like them, but mightier far
    than they,
    The Anarch of thine own bewildered
      powers,
  Rose; armies mingled in obscure array,
    Like clouds with clouds, darkening the
      sacred bowers
Of serene heaven. He, by the past pur-
    sued,
  Rests with those dead but unforgotten
    hours,
  Whose ghosts scare victor kings in their
    ancestral towers.

XIII

England yet sleeps: was she not called of
    old?
  Spain calls her now, as with its thrilling
    thunder
Vesuvius wakens Ætna, and the cold
  Snow-crags by its reply are cloven in
    sunder;
O'er the lit waves every Æolian isle
    From Pithecusa to Pelorus
    Howls, and leaps, and glares in
      chorus;
They cry, Be dim, ye lamps of heaven
    suspended o'er us!
  Her chains are threads of gold, she need
    but smile

And they dissolve; but Spain's were
    links of steel,
Till bit to dust by virtue's keenest file.
  Twins of a single destiny! appeal
To the eternal years enthroned before us
  In the dim West; impress us from a seal,
  All ye have thought and done! Time
    cannot dare conceal.

XIV

Tomb of Arminius! render up thy dead
  Till, like a standard from a watch-tower's
    staff,
His soul may stream over the tyrant's head;
  Thy victory shall be his epitaph,
Wild Bacchanal of truth's mysterious wine,
    King-deluded Germany,
    His dead spirit lives in thee.
Why do we fear or hope? thou art already
    free!
  And thou, lost Paradise of this divine
    And glorious world! thou flowery
      wilderness!
  Thou island of eternity! thou shrine
    Where desolation clothed with loveli-
      ness
Worships the thing thou wert! O Italy,
  Gather thy blood into thy heart; repress
  The beasts who make their dens thy
    sacred palaces.

XV

Oh, that the free would stamp the impious
    name
  Of King into the dust! or write it there,
So that this blot upon the page of fame
  Were as a serpent's path, which the light
    air
Erases, and the flat sands close behind!
    Ye the oracle have heard.
    Lift the victory-flashing sword,
And cut the snaky knots of this foul gor-
    dian word,
  Which, weak itself as stubble, yet can
    bind
  Into a mass, irrefragably firm,
  The axes and the rods which awe man-
    kind;
    The sound has poison in it, 't is the
      sperm
Of what makes life foul, cankerous, and
    abhorred;
  Disdain not thou, at thine appointed term,
  To set thine armèd heel on this reluctant
    worm.

XVI

Oh, that the wise from their bright minds
    would kindle
  Such lamps within the dome of this dim
    world,
That the pale name of Priest might shrink
    and dwindle
Into the hell from which it first was
    hurled,
A scoff of impious pride from fiends im-
    pure;
    Till human thoughts might kneel
      alone,
    Each before the judgment-throne
Of its own aweless soul, or of the power
    unknown !
  Oh, that the words which make the
    thoughts obscure
    From which they spring, as clouds of
      glimmering dew
From a white lake blot heaven's blue
    portraiture,
    Were stripped of their thin masks and
      various hue
And frowns and smiles and splendors not
    their own,
Till in the nakedness of false and true
They stand before their Lord, each to re-
    ceive its due.

XVII

He who taught man to vanquish whatsoever
Can be between the cradle and the grave
Crowned him the King of Life. Oh, vain
    endeavor !
If on his own high will, a willing slave,
He has enthroned the oppression and the
    oppressor.
    What if earth can clothe and feed
    Amplest millions at their need,
And power in thought be as the tree within
    the seed ?
Oh, what if Art, an ardent intercessor,
    Driving on fiery wings to Nature's
      throne,
    Checks the great mother stooping to ca-
      ress her
    And cries: 'Give me, thy child, domin-
      ion
Over all height and depth ? ' if Life can
    breed
    New wants, and wealth from those who
      toil and groan
    Rend of thy gifts and hers a thousand-
      fold for one.

XVIII

Come thou, but lead out of the inmost
    cave
  Of man's deep spirit, as the morning-
    star
Beckons the sun from the Eoan wave,
    Wisdom. I hear the pennons of her
      car
Self-moving, like cloud charioted by flame;
    Comes she not, and come ye not,
      Rulers of eternal thought,
To judge with solemn truth life's ill-appor-
    tioned lot ?
    Blind Love, and equal Justice, and the
    Fame
      Of what has been, the Hope of what
      will be ?
    O Liberty ! if such could be thy name
      Wert thou disjoined from these, or
      they from thee —
If thine or theirs were treasures to be
    bought
    By blood or tears, have not the wise and
    free
    Wept tears, and blood like tears ? — The
      solemn harmony

XIX

Paused, and the Spirit of that mighty sing-
    ing
  To its abyss was suddenly withdrawn;
Then as a wild swan, when sublimely wing-
    ing
  Its path athwart the thunder-smoke of
      dawn,
Sinks headlong through the aërial golden
    light
    On the heavy sounding plain,
      When the bolt has pierced its
      brain;
As summer clouds dissolve unburdened of
    their rain;
    As a far taper fades with fading
    night,
      As a brief insect dies with dying
      day, —
My song, its pinions disarrayed of might,
    Drooped; o'er it closed the echoes far
      away
Of the great voice which did its flight sus-
    tain,
    As waves which lately paved his watery
    way
    Hiss round a drowner's head in their
      tempestuous play.

TO ——

Published by Mrs. Shelley, *Posthumous Poems*, 1824.

I FEAR thy kisses, gentle maiden,
  Thou needest not fear mine;
My spirit is too deeply laden
  Ever to burden thine.

I fear thy mien, thy tones, thy motion,
  Thou needest not fear mine;
Innocent is the heart's devotion
  With which I worship thine.

ARETHUSA

Composed at Pisa, and published by Mrs. Shelley, *Posthumous Poems*, 1824.

I

ARETHUSA arose
  From her couch of snows
In the Acroceraunian mountains,
  From cloud and from crag,
  With many a jag,
Shepherding her bright fountains.
  She leapt down the rocks,
  With her rainbow locks
Streaming among the streams;
  Her steps paved with green
  The downward ravine
Which slopes to the western gleams;
  And gliding and springing,
  She went, ever singing,
In murmurs as soft as sleep;
  The Earth seemed to love her,
  And Heaven smiled above her,
As she lingered towards the deep.

II

Then Alpheus bold,
  On his glacier cold,
With his trident the mountains strook;
  And opened a chasm
  In the rocks — with the spasm
All Erymanthus shook.
  And the black south wind
  It concealed behind
The urns of the silent snow,
  And earthquake and thunder
  Did rend in sunder
The bars of the springs below.

The beard and the hair
  Of the River-god were
Seen through the torrent's sweep,
  As he followed the light
  Of the fleet nymph's flight
To the brink of the Dorian deep.

III

'Oh, save me! Oh, guide me,
  And bid the deep hide me,
For he grasps me now by the hair!'
  The loud Ocean heard,
  To its blue depth stirred,
And divided at her prayer;
  And under the water
  The Earth's white daughter
Fled like a sunny beam;
  Behind her descended
  Her billows, unblended
With the brackish Dorian stream.
  Like a gloomy stain
  On the emerald main
Alpheus rushed behind,
  As an eagle pursuing
  A dove to its ruin
Down the streams of the cloudy wind.

IV

Under the bowers
  Where the Ocean Powers
Sit on their pearlèd thrones;
  Through the coral woods
  Of the weltering floods,
Over heaps of unvalued stones;
  Through the dim beams
  Which amid the streams
Weave a network of colored light;
  And under the caves,
  Where the shadowy waves
Are as green as the forest's night;
  Outspeeding the shark,
  And the swordfish dark,
Under the ocean foam,
  And up through the rifts
  Of the mountain clifts
They passed to their Dorian home.

V

And now from their fountains
  In Enna's mountains,
Down one vale where the morning basks,
  Like friends once parted
  Grown single-hearted,
They ply their watery tasks.

At sunrise they leap
From their cradles steep
In the cave of the shelving hill;
At noontide they flow
Through the woods below
And the meadows of asphodel;
And at night they sleep
In the rocking deep
Beneath the Ortygian shore,
Like spirits that lie
In the azure sky
When they love but live no more.

SONG OF PROSERPINE

WHILE GATHERING FLOWERS ON THE PLAIN OF ENNA

Published by Mrs. Shelley, in her first collected edition, 1839.

SACRED Goddess, Mother Earth,
Thou from whose immortal bosom
Gods, and men, and beasts have birth,
Leaf and blade, and bud and blossom,
Breathe thine influence most divine
On thine own child, Proserpine.

If with mists of evening dew
Thou dost nourish these young flowers
Till they grow, in scent and hue,
Fairest children of the hours,
Breathe thine influence most divine
On thine own child, Proserpine.

HYMN OF APOLLO

This and the following poem were composed for insertion in a projected drama of Williams, *Midas*. It was published by Mrs. Shelley, *Posthumous Poems*, 1824.

I

THE sleepless Hours who watch me as I lie,
Curtained with star-inwoven tapestries
From the broad moonlight of the sky,
Fanning the busy dreams from my dim eyes,
Waken me when their Mother, the gray Dawn,
Tells them that dreams and that the moon is gone.

II

Then I arise, and climbing Heaven's blue dome,
I walk over the mountains and the waves,
Leaving my robe upon the ocean foam;
My footsteps pave the clouds with fire; the caves
Are filled with my bright presence, and the air
Leaves the green earth to my embraces bare.

III

The sunbeams are my shafts, with which I kill
Deceit, that loves the night and fears the day;
All men who do or even imagine ill
Fly me, and from the glory of my ray
Good minds and open actions take new might,
Until diminished by the reign of night.

IV

I feed the clouds, the rainbows and the flowers
With their ethereal colors; the moon's globe
And the pure stars in their eternal bowers
Are cinctured with my power as with a robe;
Whatever lamps on Earth or Heaven may shine
Are portions of one power, which is mine.

V

I stand at noon upon the peak of Heaven,
Then with unwilling steps I wander down
Into the clouds of the Atlantic even;
For grief that I depart they weep and frown.
What look is more delightful than the smile
With which I soothe them from the western isle ?

VI

I am the eye with which the Universe
Beholds itself, and knows itself divine;
All harmony of instrument or verse,
All prophecy, all medicine are mine,
All light of Art or Nature; — to my song
Victory and praise in their own right belong.

HYMN OF PAN

Published by Mrs. Shelley, *Posthumous Poems*, 1824.

I

FROM the forests and highlands
  We come, we come;
From the river-girt islands,
  Where loud waves are dumb
    Listening to my sweet pipings.
The wind in the reeds and the rushes,
  The bees on the bells of thyme,
The birds on the myrtle bushes,
  The cicale above in the lime,
And the lizards below in the grass,
Were as silent as ever old Tmolus was,
    Listening to my sweet pipings.

II

Liquid Peneus was flowing,
  And all dark Tempe lay
In Pelion's shadow, outgrowing
  The light of the dying day,
    Speeded by my sweet pipings.
The Sileni, and Sylvans, and Fauns,
  And the Nymphs of the woods and waves,
To the edge of the moist river-lawns,
  And the brink of the dewy caves,
And all that did then attend and follow,
Were silent with love, as you now, Apollo,
  With envy of my sweet pipings.

III

I sang of the dancing stars,
  I sang of the dædal Earth,
And of Heaven — and the giant wars,
  And Love, and Death, and Birth; —
    And then I changed my pipings,
Singing how down the vale of Mænalus
  I pursued a maiden and clasped a reed.
Gods and men, we are all deluded thus!
  It breaks in our bosom and then we bleed.
All wept, as I think both ye now would
If envy or age had not frozen your blood,
    At the sorrow of my sweet pipings.

THE QUESTION

Published by Hunt, *The Literary Pocket-Book*, 1822.

I

I DREAMED that, as I wandered by the way,
  Bare winter suddenly was changed to spring,
And gentle odors led my steps astray,
  Mixed with a sound of waters murmuring
Along a shelving bank of turf, which lay
  Under a copse, and hardly dared to fling
Its green arms round the bosom of the
    stream,
But kissed it and then fled, as thou might-
    est in dream.

II

There grew pied wind-flowers and violets,
  Daisies, those pearled Arcturi of the
    earth,
The constellated flower that never sets;
  Faint oxlips; tender bluebells, at whose
    birth
The sod scarce heaved; and that tall flower
    that wets —
(Like a child, half in tenderness and
    mirth)
Its mother's face with heaven - collected
    tears,
When the low wind, its playmate's voice,
    it hears.

III

And in the warm hedge grew lush eglan-
    tine,
  Green cowbind and the moonlight-colored
    May,
And cherry blossoms, and white cups,
    whose wine
Was the bright dew yet drained not by
    the day,
And wild roses, and ivy serpentine,
  With its dark buds and leaves, wander-
    ing astray;
And flowers azure, black, and streaked
    with gold,
Fairer than any wakened eyes behold.

IV

And nearer to the river's trembling edge
  There grew broad flag-flowers, purple
    pranked with white;
And starry river buds among the sedge;
  And floating water-lilies, broad and
    bright,
Which lit the oak that overhung the hedge
  With moonlight beams of their own
    watery light;
And bulrushes and reeds, of such deep
    green
As soothed the dazzled eye with sober
    sheen.

V

Methought that of these visionary flowers
  I made a nosegay, bound in such a way
That the same hues, which in their natural
    bowers
Were mingled or opposed, the like array
Kept these imprisoned children of the
    Hours
  Within my hand, — and then, elate and
    gay,
I hastened to the spot whence I had come,
That I might there present it ! — Oh, to
    whom ?

THE TWO SPIRITS

Published by Mrs. Shelley, *Posthumous Poems*, 1824.

AN ALLEGORY

FIRST SPIRIT

O THOU, who plumed with strong desire
  Wouldst float above the earth, beware !
A Shadow tracks thy flight of fire —
    Night is coming !
Bright are the regions of the air,
  And among the winds and beams
It were delight to wander there —
    Night is coming !

SECOND SPIRIT

The deathless stars are bright above;
  If I would cross the shade of night,
Within my heart is the lamp of love,
    And that is day !
And the moon will smile with gentle light
  On my golden plumes where'er they
    move;
The meteors will linger round my flight,
  And make night day.

FIRST SPIRIT

But if the whirlwinds of darkness waken
  Hail, and lightning, and stormy rain ?
See, the bounds of the air are shaken —
    Night is coming !
The red swift clouds of the hurricane
  Yon declining sun have overtaken;
The clash of the hail sweeps over the
    plain —
    Night is coming !

SECOND SPIRIT

I see the light, and I hear the sound;
  I 'll sail on the flood of the tempest dark,
With the calm within and the light around
    Which makes night day;
And thou, when the gloom is deep and
    stark,
Look from thy dull earth, slumber-
    bound;
My moon-like flight thou then mayst mark
    On high, far away.

Some say there is a precipice
  Where one vast pine is frozen to ruin
O'er piles of snow and chasms of ice
    Mid Alpine mountains;
And that the languid storm pursuing
  That wingèd shape forever flies
Round those hoar branches, aye renewing
    Its aëry fountains.

Some say when nights are dry and clear,
  And the death-dews sleep on the mo-
    rass,
Sweet whispers are heard by the travel-
    ler,
  Which make night day;
And a silver shape like his early love doth
    pass,
  Upborne by her wild and glittering hair,
And, when he awakes on the fragrant
    grass,
  He finds night day.

LETTER TO MARIA GISBORNE

This letter was written from the house of Mrs. Gisborne, where Shelley had turned the workshop of her son, Mr. Reveley, an engineer, into a study. 'Mrs. Gisborne,' writes Mrs. Shelley, 'had been a friend of my father in her younger days. She was a lady of great accomplishments, and charming from her frank and affectionate nature. She had the most intense love of knowledge, a delicate and trembling sensibility, and preserved freshness of mind after a life of considerable adversity. As a favorite friend of my father we had sought her with eagerness, and the most open and cordial friendship was established between us.' Shelley also describes her : 'Mrs. Gisborne is a sufficiently amiable and very accomplished woman ; [she is δημοκρατικη and αθεη — how far she may be φιλανθρωπη I don't know, for] she is the antipodes of enthusiasm.'

The poem was published by Mrs. Shelley, *Posthumous Poems*, 1824.

LEGHORN, *July* 1, 1820.
THE spider spreads her webs whether she be
In poet's tower, cellar, or barn, or tree;
The silkworm in the dark green mulberry
    leaves
His winding sheet and cradle ever weaves;
So I, a thing whom moralists call worm,
Sit spinning still round this decaying form,
From the fine threads of rare and subtle
    thought —
No net of words in garish colors wrought
To catch the idle buzzers of the day —
But a soft cell, where when that fades away
Memory may clothe in wings my living
    name   11
And feed it with the asphodels of fame,
Which in those hearts which must remem-
    ber me
Grow, making love-an immortality.

Whoever should behold me now, I wist,
Would think I were a mighty mechanist,
Bent with sublime Archimedean art
To breathe a soul into the iron heart
Of some machine portentous, or strange gin,
Which by the force of figured spells might
    win   20
Its way over the sea, and sport therein;
For round the walls are hung dread engines,
    such
As Vulcan never wrought for Jove to
    clutch
Ixion or the Titan, — or the quick
Wit of that man of God, St. Dominic,
To convince Atheist, Turk or Heretic,
Or those in philanthropic council met,
Who thought to pay some interest for the
    debt
They owed to Jesus Christ for their salva-
    tion,
By giving a faint foretaste of damnation 30
To Shakespeare, Sidney, Spenser and the
    rest
Who made our land an island of the blest,
When lamp-like Spain, who now relumes
    her fire
On Freedom's hearth, grew dim with Em-
    pire: —
With thumbscrews, wheels, with tooth and
    spike and jag,
Which fishers found under the utmost crag
Of Cornwall and the storm-encompassed
    isles,
Where to the sky the rude sea rarely
    smiles

Unless in treacherous wrath, as on the
    morn
When the exulting elements in scorn,   40
Satiated with destroyed destruction, lay
Sleeping in beauty on their mangled prey,
As panthers sleep; — and other strange
    and dread
Magical forms the brick floor overspread —
Proteus transformed to metal did not make
More figures, or more strange; nor did he
    take
Such shapes of unintelligible brass,
Or heap himself in such a horrid mass
Of tin and iron, not to be understood,
And forms of unimaginable wood   50
To puzzle Tubal Cain and all his brood;
Great screws, and cones, and wheels, and
    groovèd blocks, —
The elements of what will stand the shocks
Of wave and wind and time. Upon the
    table
More knacks and quips there be than I am
    able
To catalogize in this verse of mine : —
A pretty bowl of wood — not full of wine,
But quicksilver; that dew which the gnomes
    drink
When at their subterranean toil they swink,
Pledging the demons of the earthquake,
    who   60
Reply to them in lava — cry halloo !
And call out to the cities o'er their head, —
Roofs, towers and shrines, the dying and
    the dead,
Crash through the chinks of earth — and
    then all quaff
Another rouse, and hold their sides and
    laugh.
This quicksilver no gnome has drunk —
    within
The walnut bowl it lies, veinèd and thin,
In color like the wake of light that stains
The Tuscan deep, when from the moist
    moon rains
The inmost shower of its white fire — the
    breeze   70
Is still — blue heaven smiles over the pale
    seas.
And in this bowl of quicksilver — for I
Yield to the impulse of an infancy
Outlasting manhood — I have made to float
A rude idealism of a paper boat, —
A hollow screw with cogs — Henry will
    know
The thing I mean and laugh at me, if so

He fears not I should do more mischief.
　　Next
Lie bills and calculations much perplexed,
With steamboats, frigates, and machinery
　　quaint　　　　　　　　　　　　　　　80
Traced over them in blue and yellow paint.
Then comes a range of mathematical
Instruments, for plans nautical and stati-
　　cal;
A heap of rosin, a queer broken glass
With ink in it; a china cup that was
What it will never be again, I think,
A thing from which sweet lips were wont
　　to drink
The liquor doctors rail at — and which I
Will quaff in spite of them — and when we
　　die
We 'll toss up who died first of drinking tea,
And cry out, · heads or tails ? ' where'er we
　　be.　　　　　　　　　　　　　　　　91
Near that a dusty paint box, some odd
　　hooks,
A half-burnt match, an ivory block, three
　　books,
Where conic sections, spherics, logarithms,
To great Laplace from Saunderson and
　　Sims,
Lie heaped in their harmonious disarray
Of figures, — disentangle them who may.
Baron de Tott's Memoirs beside them lie,
And some odd volumes of old chemistry.
Near those a most inexplicable thing,　100
With lead in the middle — I 'm conjectur-
　　ing
How to make Henry understand; but no —
I 'll leave, as Spenser says, with many mo,
This secret in the pregnant womb of time,
Too vast a matter for so weak a rhyme.

　　And here like some weird Archimage
　　　sit I,
Plotting dark spells, and devilish enginery,
The self-impelling steam-wheels of the
　　mind
Which pump up oaths from clergymen,
　　and grind
The gentle spirit of our meek reviews　110
Into a powdery foam of salt abuse,
Ruffling the ocean of their self-content;
I sit — and smile or sigh as is my bent,
But not for them; Libeccio rushes round
With an inconstant and an idle sound —
I heed him more than them; the thunder-
　　smoke
Is gathering on the mountains, like a cloak

Folded athwart their shoulders broad and
　　bare;
The ripe corn under the undulating air
Undulates like an ocean; and the vines　120
Are trembling wide in all their trellised
　　lines.
The murmur of the awakening sea doth
　　fill
The empty pauses of the blast; the hill
Looks hoary through the white electric
　　rain,
And from the glens beyond, in sullen strain,
The interrupted thunder howls; above
One chasm of heaven smiles, like the eye
　　of Love
On the unquiet world; — while such things
　　are,
How could one worth your friendship heed
　　the war
Of worms ? the shriek of the world's car-
　　rion jays,　　　　　　　　　　　　130
Their censure, or their wonder, or their
　　praise ?

　　You are not here ! the quaint witch
　　　Memory sees
In vacant chairs your absent images,
And points where once you sat, and now
　　should be
But are not. I demand if ever we
Shall meet as then we met; and she re-
　　plies,
Veiling in awe her second-sighted eyes;
' I know the past alone — but summon
　　home
My sister Hope, — she speaks of all to
　　come.'
But I, an old diviner, who knew well　140
Every false verse of that sweet oracle,
Turned to the sad enchantress once again,
And sought a respite from my gentle pain,
In citing every passage o'er and o'er
Of our communion — how on the seashore
We watched the ocean and the sky to-
　　gether,
Under the roof of blue Italian weather;
How I ran home through last year's thun-
　　der-storm,
And felt the transverse lightning linger
　　warm　　　　　　　　　　　　　　149
Upon my cheek; and how we often made
Feasts for each other, where good-will out-
　　weighed
The frugal luxury of our country cheer,
As well it might, were it less firm and clear

Than ours must ever be; and how we
    spun
A shroud of talk to hide us from the sun
Of this familiar life which seems to be
But is not — or is but quaint mockery
Of all we would believe — and sadly blame
The jarring and inexplicable frame   159
Of this wrong world; and then anatomize
The purposes and thoughts of men whose
    eyes
Were closed in distant years; or widely
    guess
The issue of the earth's great business,
When we shall be as we no longer are, —
Like babbling gossips safe, who hear the
    war
Of winds, and sigh, but tremble not; — or
    how
You listened to some interrupted flow
Of visionary rhyme, — in joy and pain
Struck from the inmost fountains of my
    brain,   169
With little skill perhaps; or how we sought
Those deepest wells of passion or of thought
Wrought by wise poets in the waste of
    years,
Staining their sacred waters with our
    tears, —
Quenching a thirst ever to be renewed.
Or how I, wisest lady! then indued
The language of a land which now is
    free,
And, winged with thoughts of truth and
    majesty,
Flits round the tyrant's sceptre like a cloud,
And bursts the peopled prisons, and cries
    aloud,
'My name is Legion!' — that majestic
    tongue   180
Which Calderon over the desert flung
Of ages and of nations, — and which found
An echo in our hearts, — and with the
    sound
Startled oblivion; — thou wert then to me
As is a nurse — when inarticulately
A child would talk as its grown parents do.
If living winds the rapid clouds pursue,
If hawks chase doves through the ethereal
    way,
Huntsmen the innocent deer, and beasts
    their prey,
Why should not we rouse with the spirit's
    blast   190
Out of the forest of the pathless past
These recollected pleasures?

               You are now
In London, that great sea, whose ebb and
    flow
At once is deaf and loud, and on the shore
Vomits its wrecks, and still howls on for
    more.
Yet in its depth what treasures! You will
    see
That which was Godwin, — greater none
    than he
Though fallen — and fallen on evil times
    — to stand
Among the spirits of our age and land,
Before the dread tribunal of *to come*   200
The foremost, — while Rebuke cowers pale
    and dumb.
You will see Coleridge — he who sits ob-
    scure
In the exceeding lustre and the pure
Intense irradiation of a mind,
Which, with its own internal lightning
    blind,
Flags wearily through darkness and de-
    spair —
A cloud-encircled meteor of the air,
A hooded eagle among blinking owls.
You will see Hunt — one of those happy
    souls
Which are the salt of the earth, and with-
    out whom   210
This world would smell like what it is — a
    tomb;
Who is what others seem; his room no
    doubt
Is still adorned by many a cast from Shout,
With graceful flowers tastefully placed
    about,
And coronals of bay from ribbons hung,
And brighter wreaths in neat disorder
    flung, —
The gifts of the most learned among some
    dozens
Of female friends, sisters-in-law and cous-
    ins.
And there is he with his eternal puns,
Which beat the dullest brain for smiles,
    like duns   220
Thundering for money at a poet's door;
Alas! it is no use to say, 'I'm poor!'
Or oft in graver mood, when he will
    look
Things wiser than were ever read in book,
Except in Shakespeare's wisest tender-
    ness. —
You will see Hogg, — and I cannot express

His virtues, — though I know that they
    are great,
Because he locks, then barricades the gate
Within which they inhabit; of his wit
And wisdom you 'll cry out when you are
    bit.   230
He is a pearl within an oyster shell,
One of the richest of the deep. And there
Is English Peacock, with his mountain fair,
Turned into a Flamingo, — that shy bird
That gleams i' the Indian air; — have you
    not heard
When a man marries, dies, or turns Hindoo,
His best friends hear no more of him ? —
    but you
Will see him, and will like him too, I hope,
With the milk-white Snowdonian Antelope
Matched with this camelopard; his fine
    wit   240
Makes such a wound, the knife is lost in
    it;
A strain too learnèd for a shallow age,
Too wise for selfish bigots; let his page
Which charms the chosen spirits of the
    time,
Fold itself up for the serener clime
Of years to come, and find its recompense
In that just expectation. Wit and sense,
Virtue and human knowledge; all that
    might
Make this dull world a business of de-
    light, —
Are all combined in Horace Smith. And
    these,   250
With some exceptions, which I need not
    tease
Your patience by descanting on, are all
You and I know in London.

                    I recall
My thoughts, and bid you look upon the
    night.
As water does a sponge, so the moonlight
Fills the void, hollow, universal air.
What see you ? — unpavilioned heaven is
    fair
Whether the moon, into her chamber gone,
Leaves midnight to the golden stars, or wan
Climbs with diminished beams the azure
    steep;   260
Or whether clouds sail o'er the inverse
    deep,
Piloted by the many-wandering blast,
And the rare stars rush through them dim
    and fast: —

All this is beautiful in every land.
But what see you beside ? — a shabby stand
Of Hackney coaches — a brick house or
    wall
Fencing some lonely court, white with the
    scrawl
Of our unhappy politics; or worse —
A wretched woman reeling by, whose curse
Mixed with the watchman's, partner of her
    trade,   270
You must accept in place of serenade, —
Or yellow-haired Pollonia murmuring
To Henry, some unutterable thing.
I see a chaos of green leaves and fruit
Built round dark caverns, even to the root
Of the living stems that feed them — in
    whose bowers
There sleep in their dark dew the folded
    flowers;
Beyond, the surface of the unsickled corn
Trembles not in the slumbering air, and
    borne   279
In circles quaint and ever changing dance,
Like wingèd stars, the fireflies flash and
    glance,
Pale in the open moonshine, but each one
Under the dark trees seems a little sun,
A meteor tamed, a fixed star gone astray
From the silver regions of the milky way;
Afar the Contadino's song is heard,
Rude, but made sweet by distance — and a
    bird
Which cannot be the Nightingale, and yet
I know none else that sings so sweet as
    it
At this late hour; — and then all is still. —
Now Italy or London, which you will !   291

    Next winter you must pass with me; I 'll
    have
My house by that time turned into a grave
Of dead despondence and low-thoughted
    care,
And all the dreams which our tormentors
    are;
Oh ! that Hunt, Hogg, Peacock and Smith
    were there,
With every thing belonging to them fair ! —
We will have books, Spanish, Italian,
    Greek;
And ask one week to make another week
As like his father, as I 'm unlike mine,   300
Which is not his fault, as you may divine.
Though we eat little flesh and drink no
    wine,

Yet let 's be merry: we 'll have tea and
        toast;
Custards for supper, and an endless host
Of syllabubs and jellies and mince-pies,
And other such lady-like luxuries, —
Feasting on which we will philosophize !
And we 'll have fires out of the Grand
        Duke's wood,
To thaw the six weeks' winter in our blood.
And then we 'll talk; — what shall we talk
        about ?   310
Oh ! there are themes enough for many a
        bout
Of thought-entangled descant; — as to
        nerves —
With cones and parallelograms and curves
I 've sworn to strangle them if once they
        dare
To bother me — when you are with me
        there.
And they shall never more sip laudanum,
From Helicon or Himeros; — well, come,
And in despite of God and of the devil,
We 'll make our friendly philosophic revel
Outlast the leafless time; till buds and
        flowers   320
Warn the obscure inevitable hours
Sweet meeting by sad parting to renew; —
'To-morrow to fresh woods and pastures
        new.'

ODE TO NAPLES

The revolutionary uprisings of this year affected Shelley as powerfully as the Manchester
Riot of 1819, and this poem is the fruit of that
fleeting renascence of political hope so often
illustrated in his verse. He composed it at the
Baths of San Giuliano, August 17-25, and it
was published by Mrs. Shelley, *Posthumous
Poems*, 1824. Shelley added a note to the
poem, as follows : 'The author has connected
many recollections of his visit to Pompeii
and Baiæ with the enthusiasm excited by the
intelligence of the proclamation of a Constitu-
tional Government at Naples. This has given
a tinge of picturesque and descriptive imagery
to the introductory Epodes which depicture
these scenes, and some of the majestic feelings
permanently connected with the scene of the
animating event.'

EPODE I a
I STOOD within the city disinterred;
    And heard the autumnal leaves like
        light footfalls

Of spirits passing through the streets; and
        heard
    The Mountain's slumberous voice at
        intervals
    Thrill through those roofless halls;
The oracular thunder penetrating shook
    The listening soul in my suspended
        blood;
I felt that Earth out of her deep heart
        spoke —
    I felt, but heard not. Through white
        columns glowed
    The isle-sustaining Ocean-flood,   10
A plane of light between two Heavens of
        azure:
    Around me gleamed many a bright sep-
        ulchre
Of whose pure beauty, Time, as if his plea-
        sure
    Were to spare Death, had never made
        erasure;
    But every living lineament was clear
    As in the sculptor's thought; and
        there
The wreaths of stony myrtle, ivy and
        pine,
    Like winter leaves o'ergrown by moulded
        snow,
    Seemed only not to move and grow
    Because the crystal silence of the air 20
Weighed on their life; even as the Power
        divine,
    Which then lulled all things, brooded
        upon mine.

EPODE II a
    Then gentle winds arose,
    With many a mingled close
Of wild Æolian sound and mountain odor
        keen;
    And where the Baian ocean
    Welters with air-like motion,
Within, above, around its bowers of starry
        green,
    Moving the sea-flowers in those purple
        caves,   29
    Even as the ever stormless atmosphere
    Floats o'er the Elysian realm,
It bore me, like an angel, o'er the waves
    Of sunlight, whose swift pinnace of
        dewy air
    No storm can overwhelm.
    I sailed where ever flows
    Under the calm Serene
    A spirit of deep emotion

From the unknown graves
Of the dead kings of Melody.
Shadowy Aornus darkened o'er the helm 40
The horizontal ether ; heaven stripped
    bare
Its depths over Elysium, where the prow
Made the invisible water white as snow;
From that Typhæan mount, Inarimé,
    There streamed a sunlit vapor, like the
        standard
        Of some ethereal host;
        Whilst from all the coast,
    Louder and louder, gathering round,
        there wandered
Over the oracular woods and divine sea
Prophesyings which grew articulate — 50
They seize me — I must speak them — be
    they fate !

STROPHE α 1

Naples, thou Heart of men, which ever
    pantest
    Naked, beneath the lidless eye of hea-
        ven !
Elysian City, which to calm enchantest
    The mutinous air and sea ! they round
        thee, even
    As sleep round Love, are driven !
Metropolis of a ruined Paradise
    Long lost, late won, and yet but half re-
        gained !
Bright Altar of the bloodless sacrifice,
    Which armèd Victory offers up un-
        stained 60
    To Love, the flower-enchained !
Thou which wert once, and then didst cease
    to be,
Now art, and henceforth ever shalt be,
    free,
    If Hope, and Truth, and Justice can
        avail, —
        Hail, hail, all hail !

STROPHE β 2

    Thou youngest giant birth,
    Which from the groaning earth
Leap'st, clothed in armor of impenetrable
    scale !
    Last of the intercessors
    Who 'gainst the Crowned Trans-
        gressors 70
Pleadest before God's love ! Arrayed in
    Wisdom's mail,
    Wave thy lightning lance in mirth,
    Nor let thy high heart fail,

Though from their hundred gates the
    leagued Oppressors,
    With hurried legions move !
    Hail, hail, all hail !

ANTISTROPHE α 1

What though Cimmerian anarchs dare blas-
    pheme
    Freedom and thee ? thy shield is as a
        mirror
To make their blind slaves see, and with
    fierce gleam
To turn his hungry sword upon the
    wearer; 80
    A new Actæon's error
Shall theirs have been — devoured by their
    own hounds !
Be thou like the imperial Basilisk,
Killing thy foe with unapparent wounds !
Gaze on oppression, till, at that dread
    risk
Aghast, she pass from the Earth's
    disk;
Fear not, but gaze — for freemen mightier
    grow,
And slaves more feeble, gazing on their
    foe.
    If Hope, and Truth, and Justice may
        avail,
    Thou shalt be great. — All hail ! 90

ANTISTROPHE β 2

    From Freedom's form divine,
    From Nature's inmost shrine,
Strip every impious gaud, rend Error veil
    by veil;
    O'er Ruin desolate,
    O'er Falsehood's fallen state,
Sit thou sublime, unawed; be the Destroyer
    pale !
    And equal laws be thine,
    And wingèd words let sail,
Freighted with truth even from the throne
    of God;
    That wealth, surviving fate, 100
    Be thine. — All hail !

ANTISTROPHE α γ

Didst thou not start to hear Spain's thrill-
    ing pæan
    From land to land reëchoed solemnly,
Till silence became music ? From the
    Ææan
    To the cold Alps, eternal Italy
    Starts to hear thine ! The Sea

Which paves the desert streets of Venice
    laughs
In light and music ; widowed Genoa
    wan
By moonlight spells ancestral epitaphs,
    Murmuring, Where is Doria ? Fair Milan,
        Within whose veins long ran   111
The viper's palsying venom, lifts her heel
To bruise his head. The signal and the
    seal
    (If Hope, and Truth, and Justice can
        avail)
    Art thou of all these hopes. — O hail !

ANTISTROPHE β γ

Florence ! beneath the sun,
    Of cities fairest one,
Blushes within her bower for Freedom's
    expectation
    From eyes of quenchless hope
    Rome tears the priestly cope,   120
As ruling once by power, so now by ad-
    miration, —
    An athlete stripped to run
    From a remoter station
For the high prize lost on Philippi's
    shore : —
    As then Hope, Truth, and Justice did
        avail,
    So now may Fraud and Wrong ! O
        hail !

EPODE I β

Hear ye the march as of the Earth-born
    Forms
    Arrayed against the ever-living Gods ?
The crash and darkness of a thousand
    storms
    Bursting their inaccessible abodes   130
    Of crags and thunder-clouds ?
See ye the banners blazoned to the day,
    Inwrought with emblems of barbaric
        pride ?
Dissonant threats kill Silence far away,
    The serene Heaven which wraps our
        Eden wide
    With iron light is dyed,
The Anarchs of the North lead forth their
    legions
    Like Chaos o'er creation, uncreat-
        ing;
An hundred tribes nourished on strange re-
    ligions
And lawless slaveries, — down the aërial
    regions   140

Of the white Alps, desolating,
    Famished wolves that bide no wait-
        ing,
Blotting the glowing footsteps of old glory,
Trampling our columned cities into dust,
    Their dull and savage lust
    On Beauty's corse to sickness satiat-
        ing —
They come ! The fields they tread look
    black and hoary
With fire — from their red feet the streams
    run gory !

EPODE II β

Great Spirit, deepest Love !
    Which rulest and dost move   150
All things which live and are, within the
    Italian shore;
    Who spreadest heaven around it,
    Whose woods, rocks, waves, sur-
        round it;
Who sittest in thy star, o'er Ocean's west-
    ern floor;
    Spirit of beauty ! at whose soft com-
        mand
The sunbeams and the showers distil its
    foison
    From the Earth's bosom chill;
    Oh, bid those beams be each a blinding
        brand
Of lightning ! bid those showers be dews of
    poison !
    Bid the Earth's plenty kill !   160
    Bid thy bright Heaven above,
    Whilst light and darkness bound it,
    Be their tomb who planned
    To make it ours and thine !
Or with thine harmonizing ardors fill
And raise thy sons, as o'er the prone hori-
    zon
Thy lamp feeds every twilight wave with
    fire !
Be man's high hope and unextinct de-
    sire
The instrument to work thy will divine !
    Then clouds from sunbeams, antelopes
        from leopards,   170
    And frowns and fears from Thee,
    Would not more swiftly flee,
Than Celtic wolves from the Ausonian
    shepherds. —
Whatever, Spirit, from thy starry
    shrine
Thou yieldest or withholdest, oh, let be
This city of thy worship, ever free !

AUTUMN

A DIRGE

Published by Mrs. Shelley, *Posthumous Poems*, 1824.

THE warm sun is failing, the bleak wind is
　　wailing,
The bare boughs are sighing, the pale
　　flowers are dying,
　　　　And the year
On the earth, her death-bed, in a shroud of
　　leaves dead,
　　　　　Is lying.
　　　Come, Months, come away,
　　　From November to May,
　　　In your saddest array;
　　　Follow the bier
　　　Of the dead cold year,
And like dim shadows watch by her sepul-
　　chre.

The chill rain is falling, the nipped worm
　　is crawling,
The rivers are swelling, the thunder is
　　knelling
　　　　For the year;
The blithe swallows are flown, and the liz-
　　ards each gone
　　　　To his dwelling;
　　　Come, Months, come away,
　　　Put on white, black, and gray;
　　　Let your light sisters play —
　　　Ye, follow the bier
　　　Of the dead cold year,
And make her grave green with tear on
　　tear.

DEATH

Published by Mrs. Shelley, *Posthumous Poems*, 1824.

I

DEATH is here, and death is there,
Death is busy everywhere,
All around, within, beneath,
Above, is death — and we are death.

II

Death has set his mark and seal
On all we are and all we feel,
On all we know and all we fear,
　.　　.　　.　　.　　.　　.　　.　　.

III

First our pleasures die — and then
Our hopes, and then our fears — and when
These are dead, the debt is due,
Dust claims dust — and we die too.

IV

All things that we love and cherish,
Like ourselves, must fade and perish;
Such is our rude mortal lot —
Love itself would, did they not.

LIBERTY

Published by Mrs. Shelley, *Posthumous Poems*, 1824.

I

THE fiery mountains answer each other,
Their thunderings are echoed from zone to
　　zone;
The tempestuous oceans awake one another,
And the ice-rocks are shaken round Win-
　　ter's throne,
　　When the clarion of the Typhoon is
　　　blown.

II

From a single cloud the lightning flashes,
Whilst a thousand isles are illumined
　　around;
Earthquake is trampling one city to ashes,
An hundred are shuddering and tottering;
　　the sound
　　Is bellowing underground.

III

But keener thy gaze than the lightning's
　　glare,
And swifter thy step than the earthquake's
　　tramp;
Thou deafenest the rage of the ocean; thy
　　stare
Makes blind the volcanoes; the sun's
　　bright lamp
　　To thine is a fen-fire damp.

IV

From billow and mountain and exhalation
The sunlight is darted through vapor and
　　blast;
From spirit to spirit, from nation to nation,
From city to hamlet, thy dawning is cast, —
And tyrants and slaves are like shadows of
　　night
　　In the van of the morning light.

SUMMER AND WINTER

Published by Mrs. Shelley, *The Keepsake*, 1829.

It was a bright and cheerful afternoon
Towards the end of the sunny month of
    June,
When the north wind congregates in crowds
The floating mountains of the silver clouds
From the horizon — and the stainless sky
Opens beyond them like eternity.
All things rejoiced beneath the sun; the
    weeds,
The river, and the cornfields, and the
    reeds;
The willow leaves that glanced in the light
    breeze,
And the firm foliage of the larger trees.

It was a winter such as when birds die
In the deep forests; and the fishes lie
Stiffened in the translucent ice, which
    makes
Even the mud and slime of the warm lakes
A wrinkled clod as hard as brick; and
    when
Among their children comfortable men
Gather about great fires, and yet feel
    cold:
Alas, then, for the homeless beggar old!

THE TOWER OF FAMINE

Published by Mrs. Shelley, *The Keepsake*, 1829.

Amid the desolation of a city,
Which was the cradle and is now the grave
Of an extinguished people, — so that pity

Weeps o'er the shipwrecks of oblivion's
    wave,
There stands the Tower of Famine. It is
    built
Upon some prison-homes, whose dwellers
    rave

For bread, and gold, and blood; pain, linked
    to guilt,
Agitates the light flame of their hours,
Until its vital oil is spent or spilt.

There stands the pile, a tower amid the
    towers

And sacred domes, — each marble-ribbèd
    roof,
The brazen-gated temples and the bowers

Of solitary wealth; the tempest-proof
Pavilions of the dark Italian air
Are by its presence dimmed — they stand
    aloof,

And are withdrawn — so that the world is
    bare;
As if a spectre, wrapped in shapeless ter-
    ror,
Amid a company of ladies fair

Should glide and glow, till it became a
    mirror
Of all their beauty, — and their hair and
    hue,
The life of their sweet eyes, with all its
    error,
Should be absorbed, till they to marble
    grew.

AN ALLEGORY

Published by Mrs. Shelley, *Posthumous Poems*, 1824.

I

A portal as of shadowy adamant
    Stands yawning on the highway of the
      life
Which we all tread, a cavern huge and
    gaunt;
    Around it rages an unceasing strife
Of shadows, like the restless clouds that
    haunt
The gap of some cleft mountain, lifted
    high
Into the whirlwinds of the upper sky.

II

And many pass it by with careless tread,
    Not knowing that a shadowy . . .
Tracks every traveler even to where the
    dead
    Wait peacefully for their companion
      new;
But others, by more curious humor led,
    Pause to examine; these are very few,
And they learn little there, except to know
That shadows follow them where'er they
    go.

THE WORLD'S WANDERERS

Published by Mrs. Shelley, *Posthumous Poems*, 1824.

I

TELL me, thou star, whose wings of light
Speed thee in thy fiery flight,
In what cavern of the night
    Will thy pinions close now ?

II

Tell me, moon, thou pale and gray
Pilgrim of heaven's homeless way,
In what depth of night or day
    Seekest thou repose now ?

III

Weary wind, who wanderest
Like the world's rejected guest,
Hast thou still some secret nest
    On the tree or billow ?

SONNET

Published by Hunt, *The Literary Pocket-Book*, 1824.

YE hasten to the grave ! What seek ye
    there,
Ye restless thoughts and busy purposes
Of the idle brain, which the world's livery
    wear ?
O thou quick heart, which pantest to pos-
    sess
All that pale expectation feigneth fair !
Thou vainly curious mind which wouldest
    guess
Whence thou didst come, and whither thou
    must go,
And all that never yet was known would
    know, —
Oh, whither hasten ye, that thus ye
    press
With such swift feet life's green and plea-
    sant path,
Seeking alike from happiness and woe
A refuge in the cavern of gray death ?
O heart, and mind, and thoughts ! what
    thing do you
Hope to inherit in the grave below ?

LINES TO A REVIEWER

Published by Hunt, *The Literary Pocket-Book*, 1823.

ALAS ! good friend, what profit can you see
In hating such a hateless thing as me ?
There is no sport in hate when all the rage
Is on one side. In vain would you assuage
Your frowns upon an unresisting smile,
In which not even contempt lurks to beguile
Your heart by some faint sympathy of hate.
Oh, conquer what you cannot satiate !
For to your passion I am far more coy
Than ever yet was coldest maid or boy
In winter noon. Of your antipathy
If I am the Narcissus, you are free
To pine into a sound with hating me.

TIME LONG PAST

Published by Rossetti, 1870.

I

LIKE the ghost of a dear friend dead
    Is Time long past.
A tone which is now forever fled,
A hope which is now forever past,
    Was Time long past.

II

There were sweet dreams in the night
    Of Time long past.
And, was it sadness or delight,
Each day a shadow onward cast
Which made us wish it yet might last —
    That Time long past.

III

There is regret, almost remorse,
    For Time long past.
'T is like a child's belovèd corse
A father watches, till at last
Beauty is like remembrance cast
    From Time long past.

BUONA NOTTE

Published by Medwin, *The Angler in Wales*, 1834.

Medwin writes in his *Life of Shelley*: 'I often asked Shelley if he had never attempted to write, like Matthias, in Italian, and he showed me a sort of serenade which I give as a curiosity,—but proving that he had not made a profound study of the language, which, like Spanish, he had acquired without a grammar, — trusting to his fine ear and memory, rather than to rules.'

I

' BUONA notte, buona notte ! ' — Come mai
La notte sarà buona senza te ?
Non dirmi buona notte, — chè tu sai,
La notte sà star buona da per sè.

II

Solinga, scura, cupa, senza speme,
La notte quando Lilla m'abbandona;
Pei cuori chi si batton insieme
Ogni notte, senza dirla, sarà buona.

III

Come male buona notte si suona
Con sospiri e parole interrotte ! —
Il modo di aver la notte buona
E mai non di dir la buona notte.

GOOD-NIGHT

Published by Hunt, *The Literary Pocket-Book*, 1822.

I

GOOD-NIGHT ? ah, no ! the hour is ill
Which severs those it should unite;
Let us remain together still,
Then it will be *good night*.

II

How can I call the lone night good,
Though thy sweet wishes wing its flight ?
Be it not said, thought, understood,
Then it will be *good night*.

III

To hearts which near each other move
From evening close to morning light,
The night is good; because, my love,
They never *say* good-night.

POEMS WRITTEN IN 1821

Mrs. Shelley gives, as usual, the general scene and atmosphere of the year, which was spent at Pisa or the Baths of San Giuliano : ' We were not, as our wont had been, alone — friends had gathered round us. Nearly all are dead; and when memory recurs to the past, she wanders among tombs : the genius with all his blighting errors and mighty powers ; the companion of Shelley's ocean-wanderings, and the sharer of his fate, than whom no man ever existed more gentle, generous, and fearless; and others, who found in Shelley's society, and in his great knowledge and warm sympathy, delight, instruction and solace, have joined him beyond the grave. . . .

' Shelley's favorite taste was boating; when living near the Thames, or by the lake of Geneva, much of his life was spent on the water. On the shore of every lake, or stream, or sea, near which he dwelt, he had a boat moored. He had latterly enjoyed this pleasure again. There are no pleasure-boats on the Arno, and the shallowness of its waters, except in winter time, when the stream is too turbid and impetuous for boating, rendered it difficult to get any skiff light enough to float. Shelley, however, overcame the difficulty; he, together with a friend, contrived a boat such as the huntsmen carry about with them in the Maremma, to cross the sluggish but deep streams that intersect the forests, a boat of laths and pitched canvas; it held three persons, and he was often seen on the Arno in it, to the horror of the Italians, who remonstrated on the danger, and could not understand how any one could take pleasure in an exercise that risked life. " Ma va per la vita! " they exclaimed. I little thought how true their words would prove. He once ventured with a friend [Williams], on the glassy sea of a calm day, down the Arno and round the coast, to Leghorn, which by keeping close in shore was very practicable. They returned to Pisa by the canal, when, missing the direct cut, they got entangled among weeds, and the boat upset; a wetting was all the harm done except that the intense cold of his drenched clothes made Shelley faint. Once I went down with him to the mouth of the Arno, where the stream, then high and swift, met the tideless sea and disturbed its sluggish waters; it was a waste and dreary scene ; the desert sand stretched into a point surrounded by waves that broke idly though perpetually around; it was a scene very similar to Lido, of which he had said, —

' " I love all waste
And solitary places, where we taste
The pleasure of believing what we see
Is boundless, as we wish our souls to be;
And such was this wide ocean, and this shore
More barren than its billows."

'Our little boat was of greater use, unaccompanied by any danger, when we removed to the baths. Some friends [the Williamses] lived at the village of Pugnano, four miles off, and we went to and fro to see them, in our boat, by the canal, which, fed by the Serchio, was, though an artificial, a full and picturesque stream, making its way under verdant banks, sheltered by trees that dipped their boughs into the murmuring waters. By day, multitudes of ephemera darted to and fro on the surface; at night, the fireflies came out among the shrubs on the banks; the cicale at noonday kept up their hum; the aziola cooed in the quiet evening. It was a pleasant summer, bright in all but Shelley's health and inconstant spirits; yet he enjoyed himself greatly, and became more and more attached to the part of the country where chance appeared to cast us. Sometimes he projected taking a farm, situated on the height of one of the near hills, surrounded by chestnut and pine woods, and overlooking a wide extent of country; or of settling still further in the maritime Apennines, at Massa. Several of his slighter and unfinished poems were inspired by these scenes, and by the companions around us. It is the nature of that poetry, however, which overflows from the soul, oftener to express sorrow and regret than joy; for it is when oppressed by the weight of life, and away from those he loves, that the poet has recourse to the solace of expression in verse.

'Still Shelley's passion was the ocean; and he wished that our summers, instead of being passed among the hills near Pisa, should be spent on the shores of the sea. It was very difficult to find a spot. We shrank from Naples from a fear that the heats would disagree with Percy; Leghorn had lost its only attraction, since our friends who had resided there were returned to England; and Monte Nero being the resort of many English, we did not wish to find ourselves in the midst of a colony of chance travellers. No one then thought it possible to reside at Viareggio, which latterly has become a summer resort. The low lands and bad air of Maremma stretch the whole length of the western shores of the Mediterranean, till broken by the rocks and hills of Spezia. It was a vague idea; but Shelley suggested an excursion to Spezia, to see whether it would be feasible to spend a summer there. The beauty of the bay enchanted him — we saw no house to suit us — but the notion took root, and many circumstances, enchained as by fatality, occurred to urge him to execute it.'

DIRGE FOR THE YEAR

Composed January 1, and published by Mrs. Shelley, *Posthumous Poems*, 1824.

I

ORPHAN hours, the year is dead,
　Come and sigh, come and weep!
Merry hours, smile instead,
　For the year is but asleep.
See, it smiles as it is sleeping,
Mocking your untimely weeping.

II

As an earthquake rocks a corse
　In its coffin in the clay,
So White Winter, that rough nurse,
　Rocks the death-cold year to-day;
Solemn hours! wail aloud
For your mother in her shroud.

III

As the wild air stirs and sways
　The tree-swung cradle of a child,
So the breath of these rude days
　Rocks the year: — be calm and mild,
Trembling hours; she will arise
With new love within her eyes.

IV

January gray is here,
　Like a sexton by her grave;
February bears the bier,
　March with grief doth howl and rave,
And April weeps — but, O ye hours!
Follow with May's fairest flowers.

TIME

Published by Mrs. Shelley, *Posthumous Poems*, 1824.

UNFATHOMABLE Sea! whose waves are
　years,
Ocean of Time, whose waters of deep woe
Are brackish with the salt of human tears!
　Thou shoreless flood, which in thy ebb
　　and flow
Claspest the limits of mortality,
　And sick of prey, yet howling on for
　　more,
Vomitest thy wrecks on its inhospitable
　shore;
　Treacherous in calm, and terrible in
　　storm,
　　Who shall put forth on thee,
　　Unfathomable Sea?

FROM THE ARABIC

AN IMITATION

Published by Mrs. Shelley, *Posthumous Poems*, 1824.

I

My faint spirit was sitting in the light
  Of thy looks, my love;
It panted for thee like the hind at noon
  For the brooks, my love.
Thy barb, whose hoofs outspeed the tem-
    pest's flight,
  Bore thee far from me;
My heart, for my weak feet were weary
    soon,
  Did companion thee.

II

Ah ! fleeter far than fleetest storm or steed,
  Or the death they bear,
The heart which tender thought clothes
    like a dove
  With the wings of care;
In the battle, in the darkness, in the need,
  Shall mine cling to thee,
Nor claim one smile for all the comfort,
    love,
  It may bring to thee.

SONG

Published by Mrs. Shelley, *Posthumous Poems*, 1824.

I

Rarely, rarely, comest thou,
  Spirit of Delight !
Wherefore hast thou left me now
  Many a day and night ?
Many a weary night and day
'T is since thou art fled away.

II

How shall ever one like me
  Win thee back again ?
With the joyous and the free
  Thou wilt scoff at pain.
Spirit false ! thou hast forgot
All but those who need thee not.

III

As a lizard with the shade
  Of a trembling leaf,

Thou with sorrow art dismayed;
  Even the sighs of grief
Reproach thee, that thou art not near,
And reproach thou wilt not hear.

IV

Let me set my mournful ditty
  To a merry measure;
Thou wilt never come for pity,
  Thou wilt come for pleasure;
Pity then will cut away
Those cruel wings, and thou wilt stay.

V

I love all that thou lovest,
  Spirit of Delight !
The fresh Earth in new leaves dressed,
  And the starry night;
Autumn evening, and the morn
When the golden mists are born.

VI

I love snow, and all the forms
  Of the radiant frost;
I love waves, and winds, and storms,
  Everything almost
Which is Nature's, and may be
Untainted by man's misery.

VII

I love tranquil solitude,
  And such society
As is quiet, wise, and good;
  Between thee and me
What difference ? but thou dost possess
The things I seek, not love them less.

VIII

I love Love — though he has wings,
  And like light can flee,
But above all other things,
  Spirit, I love thee.
Thou art love and life ! Oh, come,
Make once more my heart thy home.

TO NIGHT

Published by Mrs. Shelley, *Posthumous Poems*, 1824.

I

Swiftly walk o'er the western wave,
  Spirit of Night !
Out of the misty eastern cave,
Where all the long and lone daylight

Thou wovest dreams of joy and fear,
Which make thee terrible and dear, —
    Swift be thy flight !

II

Wrap thy form in a mantle gray,
    Star-inwrought !
Blind with thine hair the eyes of Day;
Kiss her until she be wearied out;
Then wander o'er city, and sea, and land,
Touching all with thine opiate wand —
    Come, long-sought !

III

When I arose and saw the dawn,
    I sighed for thee;
When light rode high, and the dew was
    gone,
And noon lay heavy on flower and tree,
And the weary Day turned to his rest,
Lingering like an unloved guest,
    I sighed for thee.

IV

Thy brother Death came, and cried,
    Wouldst thou me ?
Thy sweet child Sleep, the filmy-eyed,
Murmured like a noontide bee,
Shall I nestle near thy side ?
Wouldst thou me ? — and I replied,
    No, not thee !

V

Death will come when thou art dead,
    Soon, too soon;
Sleep will come when thou art fled;
Of neither would I ask the boon
I ask of thee, belovèd Night, —
Swift be thine approaching flight,
    Come soon, soon !

TO ——

Published by Mrs. Shelley, *Posthumous Poems*, 1824.

Music, when soft voices die,
Vibrates in the memory;
Odors, when sweet violets sicken,
Live within the sense they quicken.

Rose leaves, when the rose is dead,
Are heaped for the belovèd's bed;
And so thy thoughts, when thou art gone,
Love itself shall slumber on.

TO ——

Published by Mrs. Shelley, *Posthumous Poems*, 1824.

I

When passion's trance is overpast,
If tenderness and truth could last,
Or live, whilst all wild feelings keep
Some mortal slumber, dark and deep,
I should not weep, I should not weep !

II

It were enough to feel, to see
Thy soft eyes gazing tenderly,
And dream the rest — and burn and be
The secret food of fires unseen,
Couldst thou but be as thou hast been.

III

After the slumber of the year
The woodland violets reappear;
All things revive in field or grove,
And sky and sea, but two, which move
And form all others, life and love.

MUTABILITY

Published by Mrs. Shelley, *Posthumous Poems*, 1824.

I

The flower that smiles to-day
    To-morrow dies;
All that we wish to stay,
    Tempts and then flies.
What is this world's delight?
Lightning that mocks the night,
    Brief even as bright.

II

Virtue, how frail it is !
    Friendship how rare !
Love, how it sells poor bliss
    For proud despair !
But we, though soon they fall,
Survive their joy and all
    Which ours we call.

III

Whilst skies are blue and bright,
    Whilst flowers are gay,
Whilst eyes that change ere night
    Make glad the day,

Whilst yet the calm hours creep,
Dream thou — and from thy sleep
Then wake to weep.

LINES

Published by Mrs. Shelley, *Posthumous
Poems*, 1824.

I

FAR, far away, O ye
Halcyons of Memory,
Seek some far calmer nest
Than this abandoned breast !
No news of your false spring
To my heart's winter bring;
Once having gone, in vain
    Ye come again.

II

Vultures, who build your bowers
High in the Future's towers,
Withered hopes on hopes are spread !
Dying joys, choked by the dead,
Will serve your beaks for prey
    Many a day.

THE FUGITIVES

Published by Mrs. Shelley, *Posthumous
Poems*, 1824.

I

THE waters are flashing,
The white hail is dashing,
The lightnings are glancing,
The hoar-spray is dancing —
    Away !

The whirlwind is rolling,
The thunder is tolling,
The forest is swinging,
The minster bells ringing —
    Come away !

The Earth is like Ocean,
Wreck-strewn and in motion;
Bird, beast, man and worm
Have crept out of the storm —
    Come away !

II

' Our boat has one sail,
And the helmsman is pale;

A bold pilot I trow,
Who should follow us now,' —
    Shouted he;

And she cried, ' Ply the oar;
Put off gayly from shore !' —
As she spoke, bolts of death
Mixed with hail specked their path
    O'er the sea.

And from isle, tower and rock,
The blue beacon cloud broke
And though dumb in the blast,
The red cannon flashed fast
    From the lee.

III

And fear'st thou, and fear'st thou ?
And see'st thou, and hear'st thou ?
And drive we not free
O'er the terrible sea,
    I and thou ? '

One boat-cloak did cover
The loved and the lover;
Their blood beats one measure,
They murmur proud pleasure
    Soft and low;

While around the lashed Ocean,
Like mountains in motion,
Is withdrawn and uplifted,
Sunk, shattered and shifted
    To and fro.

IV

In the court of the fortress
Beside the pale portress,
Like a bloodhound well beaten
The bridegroom stands, eaten
    By shame;

On the topmost watch-turret,
As a death-boding spirit,
Stands the gray tyrant father;
To his voice the mad weather
    Seems tame;

And with curses as wild
As e'er clung to child,
He devotes to the blast
The best, loveliest, and last
    Of his name !

LINES

WRITTEN ON HEARING THE NEWS OF THE
DEATH OF NAPOLEON

Published with *Hellas*, 1821.

WHAT ! alive and so bold, O Earth ?
Art, thou not over-bold ?
What ! leapest thou forth as of old
In the light of thy morning mirth,
The last of the flock of the starry fold ?
Ha ! leapest thou forth as of old ?
Are not the limbs still when the ghost is fled,
And canst thou move, Napoleon being dead ?

How ! is not thy quick heart cold ?
  What spark is alive on thy hearth?
  How ! is not *his* death-knell knolled ?
  And livest *thou* still, Mother Earth ?
Thou wert warming thy fingers old
O'er the embers covered and cold
Of that most fiery spirit, when it fled;
What, Mother, do you laugh now he is dead?

'Who has known me of old,' replied
    Earth,
  'Or who has my story told?
It is thou who art over-bold.'
And the lightning of scorn laughed forth
As she sung, ' To my bosom I fold
All my sons when their knell is knolled,
And so with living motion all are fed,
And the quick spring like weeds out of the
    dead.

'Still alive and still bold,' shouted Earth,
  'I grow bolder, and still more bold.
  The dead fill me ten thousand-fold
Fuller of speed, and splendor, and mirth.
I was cloudy, and sullen, and cold,
Like a frozen chaos uprolled,
Till by the spirit of the mighty dead
My heart grew warm. I feed on whom I fed.

'Ay, alive and still bold,' muttered Earth,
  'Napoleon's fierce spirit rolled,
  In terror, and blood, and gold,
A torrent of ruin to death from his birth.
Leave the millions who follow to mould
  The metal before it be cold;
And weave into his shame, which like the
    dead
Shrouds me, the hopes that from his glory
    fled.'

SONNET

POLITICAL GREATNESS

Published by Mrs. Shelley, *Posthumous
Poems*, 1824.

NOR happiness, nor majesty, nor fame,
Nor peace, nor strength, nor skill in arms
    or arts,
Shepherd those herds whom tyranny makes
    tame;
Verse echoes not one beating of their hearts,
History is but the shadow of their shame,
Art veils her glass, or from the pageant
    starts
As to oblivion their blind millions fleet,
Staining that Heaven with obscene imagery
Of their own likeness. What are numbers
    knit
By force or custom? Man who man would be
Must rule the empire of himself; in it
Must be supreme, establishing his throne
On vanquished will, quelling the anarchy
Of hopes and fears, being himself alone.

A BRIDAL SONG

The poem was composed for insertion in a
projected play of Williams, *The Promise, or a
Year, a Month, and a Day.* Published by
Mrs. Shelley, *Posthumous Poems*, 1824.

I

THE golden gates of sleep unbar
  Where strength and beauty, met to-
    gether,
Kindle their image like a star
  In a sea of glassy weather !
Night, with all thy stars look down;
  Darkness, weep thy holiest dew;
Never smiled the inconstant moon
    On a pair so true.
Let eyes not see their own delight; —
Haste, swift hour, and thy flight
    Oft renew.

II

Fairies, sprites, and angels, keep her !
  Holy stars, permit no wrong !
And return to wake the sleeper,
    Dawn, — ere it be long.
O joy ! O fear! what will be done
  In the absence of the sun!
    Come along !

EPITHALAMIUM

Published by Medwin, *Life of Shelley*, 1847.

NIGHT, with all thine eyes look down !
  Darkness, shed its holiest dew !
When ever smiled the inconstant moon
  On a pair so true ?
Hence, coy hour ! and quench thy light,
Lest eyes see their own delight!
Hence, swift hour ! and thy loved flight
    Oft renew.

BOYS

O joy ! O fear ! what may be done
In the absence of the sun ?
                Come along !

The golden gates of sleep unbar !
  When strength and beauty meet together,
Kindles their image like a star
  In a sea of glassy weather.
Hence, coy hour ! and quench thy light,
Lest eyes see their own delight !
Hence, swift hour ! and thy loved flight
    Oft renew.

GIRLS

O joy ! O fear ! what may be done
In the absence of the sun ?

                Come along !
Fairies ! sprites ! and angels keep her !
  Holiest powers, permit no wrong !
And return, to wake the sleeper,
  Dawn, ere it be long.
Hence, swift hour ! and quench thy light,
Lest eyes see their own delight !
Hence, coy hour ! and thy loved flight
    Oft renew.

BOYS AND GIRLS

O joy ! O fear ! what will be done
In the absence of the sun ?
                Come along !

ANOTHER VERSION

Published by Rossetti, 1870.

BOYS SING

NIGHT ! with all thine eyes look down !
  Darkness ! weep thy holiest dew !
Never smiled the inconstant moon
  On a pair so true.

Haste, coy hour ! and quench all light,
Lest eyes see their own delight !
Haste, swift hour ! and thy loved flight
    Oft renew !

GIRLS SING

Fairies, sprites, and angels, keep her !
  Holy stars ! permit no wrong !
And return to wake the sleeper,
  Dawn, ere it be long !
O joy ! O fear ! there is not one
Of us can guess what may be done
    In the absence of the sun : —
      Come along !

BOYS

Oh, linger long, thou envious eastern lamp
    In the damp
      Caves of the deep !

GIRLS

Nay, return, Vesper ! urge thy lazy car !
  Swift unbar
    The gates of Sleep !

CHORUS

The golden gate of Sleep unbar,
  When Strength and Beauty, met to-
      gether,
Kindle their image, like a star
  In a sea of glassy weather.
May the purple mist of love
Round them rise, and with them move,
Nourishing each tender gem
Which, like flowers, will burst from them.
As the fruit is to the tree
May their children ever be !

EVENING

PONTE AL MARE, PISA

Published by Mrs. Shelley, *Posthumous Poems*, 1824.

I

THE sun is set; the swallows are asleep;
  The bats are flitting fast in the gray air ;
The slow soft toads out of damp corners
      creep,
  And evening's breath, wandering here
      and there
Over the quivering surface of the stream,
Wakes not one ripple from its summer
    dream.

II

There is no dew on the dry grass to-night,
  Nor damp within the shadow of the
    trees;
The wind is intermitting, dry, and light;
  And in the inconstant motion of the
    breeze
The dust and straws are driven up and
    down,
And whirled about the pavement of the
    town.

III

Within the surface of the fleeting river
  The wrinkled image of the city lay,
Immovably unquiet, and forever
  It trembles, but it never fades away;
Go to the
You, being changed, will find it then as
    now.

IV

The chasm in which the sun has sunk is
    shut
  By darkest barriers of enormous cloud,
Like mountain over mountain huddled —
    but
  Growing and moving upwards in a
    crowd,
And over it a space of watery blue,
Which the keen evening star is shining
    through.

THE AZIOLA

Published by Mrs. Shelley, *The Keepsake*,
1829.

I

'Do you not hear the Aziola cry ?
  Methinks she must be nigh,'
    Said Mary, as we sate
In dusk, ere stars were lit, or candles
    brought;
  And I, who thought
This Aziola was some tedious woman,
  Asked, 'Who is Aziola ? ' How elate
I felt to know that it was nothing human,
  No mockery of myself to fear or hate !
    And Mary saw my soul,
And laughed, and said, 'Disquiet yourself
    not,
  'T is nothing but a little downy owl.'

II

Sad Aziola ! many an eventide
  Thy music I had heard
By wood and stream, meadow and moun-
    tain-side,
  And fields and marshes wide, —
Such as nor voice, nor lute, nor wind, nor
    bird,
  The soul ever stirred;
Unlike and far sweeter than them all.
Sad Aziola ! from that moment I
  Loved thee and thy sad cry.

TO ——

Published by Mrs. Shelley, *Posthumous
Poems*, 1824.

I

ONE word is too often profaned
  For me to profane it,
One feeling too falsely disdained
  For thee to disdain it;
One hope is too like despair
  For prudence to smother,
And pity from thee more dear
  Than that from another.

II

I can give not what men call love,
  But wilt thou accept not
The worship the heart lifts above
  And the Heavens reject not, —
The desire of the moth for the star,
  Of the night for the morrow,
The devotion to something afar
  From the sphere of our sorrow ?

REMEMBRANCE

Shelley sent these lines enclosed in a letter
to Mrs. Williams : ' Dear Jane, — If this melancholy old song suits any of your tunes, or
any that humor of the moment may dictate,
you are welcome to it. Do not say it is mine
to any one, even if you think so ; indeed, it is
from the torn leaf of a book out of date. How
are you to-day, and how is Williams ? Tell
him that I dreamed of nothing but sailing
and fishing up coral. Your ever affectionate
P. B. S.' It was published by Mrs. Shelley,
Posthumous Poems, 1824.

I

Swifter far than summer's flight,
Swifter far than youth's delight,
Swifter far than happy night,
    Art thou come and gone.
As the wood when leaves are shed,
As the night when sleep is fled,
As the heart when joy is dead,
    I am left lone, alone.

II

The swallow summer comes again,
The owlet night resumes his reign,
But the wild swan youth is fain
    To fly with thee, false as thou.
My heart each day desires the morrow;
Sleep itself is turned to sorrow;
Vainly would my winter borrow
    Sunny leaves from any bough.

III

Lilies for a bridal bed,
Roses for a matron's head,
Violets for a maiden dead —
    Pansies let *my* flowers be;
On the living grave I bear,
Scatter them without a tear —
Let no friend, however dear,
    Waste one hope, one fear for me.

TO EDWARD WILLIAMS

Published by Ascham, 1834.

I

The serpent is shut out from paradise.
    The wounded deer must seek the herb
        no more
    In which its heart-cure lies;
    The widowed dove must cease to haunt
        a bower,
Like that from which its mate with
        feignèd sighs
        Fled in the April hour.
    I, too, must seldom seek again
Near happy friends a mitigated pain.

II

Of hatred I am proud, — with scorn con-
        tent;
    Indifference, that once hurt me, now is
        grown
        Itself indifferent;
    But, not to speak of love, pity alone

Can break a spirit already more than
        bent.
        The miserable one
    Turns the mind's poison into food, —
Its medicine is tears, — its evil good.

III

Therefore if now I see you seldomer,
    Dear friends, dear *friend !* know that I
        only fly
    Your looks, because they stir
    Griefs that should sleep, and hopes that
        cannot die.
The very comfort that they minister
        I scarce can bear; yet I,
    So deeply is the arrow gone,
Should quickly perish if it were with-
        drawn.

IV

When I return to my cold home, you
        ask
    Why I am not as I have ever been.
    You spoil me for the task
    Of acting a forced part in life's dull
        scene,
Of wearing on my brow the idle mask
        Of author, great or mean,
    In the world's carnival.   I sought
Peace thus, and but in you I found it
        not.

V

Full half an hour, to-day, I tried my lot
    With various flowers, and every one still
        said,
        ' She loves me — loves me not.'
    And if this meant a vision long since
        fled —
If it meant fortune, fame, or peace of
        thought —
        If it meant, — but I dread
    To speak what you may know too well:
Still there was truth in the sad oracle.

VI

The crane o'er seas and forests seeks her
        home;
    No bird so wild but has its quiet nest,
        When it no more would roam;
    The sleepless billows on the ocean's
        breast
Break like a bursting heart, and die in
        foam,
        And thus at length find rest:

Doubtless there is a place of peace
Where *my* weak heart and all its throbs
    will cease.

VII

I asked her, yesterday, if she believed
  That I had resolution. One who *had*
    Would ne'er have thus relieved
His heart with words, — but what his
    judgment bade
Would do, and leave the scorner unre-
    lieved.
    These verses are too sad
To send to you, but that I know,
Happy yourself, you feel another's woe.

TO-MORROW

Published by Mrs. Shelley, *Posthumous
Poems*, 1824.

WHERE art thou, belovèd To-morrow?
  When young and old, and strong and
    weak,
Rich and poor, through joy and sorrow,
  Thy sweet smiles we ever seek, —
In thy place — ah! well-a-day!
We find the thing we fled — To-day.

LINES

Published by Rossetti, 1870.

IF I walk in Autumn's even
  While the dead leaves pass,
If I look on Spring's soft heaven, —
  Something is not there which was.
Winter's wondrous frost and snow,
Summer's clouds, where are they now?

A LAMENT

Published by Mrs. Shelley, *Posthumous
Poems*, 1824.

I

O WORLD! O life! O time!
On whose last steps I climb,
  Trembling at that where I had stood
    before;
When will return the glory of your prime?
  No more — oh, never more!

II

Out of the day and night
A joy has taken flight;
  Fresh spring, and summer, and winter
    hoar,
Move my faint heart with grief, but with
    delight
  No more — oh, never more!

POEMS WRITTEN IN 1822

The last months of Shelley's life were passed at Pisa and Lerici. The incidents; and the general character of the household with its group of friends, are minutely recorded in Mrs. Shelley's long note, in Trelawny's *Records*, and in nearly all biographies of later date. A brief narrative is inadequate to tell the story.

LINES

Published by Mrs. Shelley, *Posthumous
Poems*, 1824.

I

WHEN the lamp is shattered,
  The light in the dust lies dead;
  When the cloud is scattered,
The rainbow's glory is shed;
  When the lute is broken,
Sweet tones are remembered not;
  When the lips have spoken,
Loved accents are soon forgot.

II

  As music and splendor
Survive not the lamp and the lute,
  The heart's echoes render
No song when the spirit is mute: —
  No song but sad dirges,
Like the wind through a ruined cell,
  Or the mournful surges
That ring the dead seaman's knell.

III

When hearts have once mingled,
Love first leaves the well-built nest;

The weak one is singled
To endure what it once possessed.
O Love ! who bewailest
The frailty of all things here,
    Why choose you the frailest
For your cradle, your home, and your
            bier ?

IV

Its passions will rock thee,
As the storms rock the ravens on high;
    Bright reason will mock thee,
Like the sun from a wintry sky.
    From thy nest every rafter
Will rot, and thine eagle home
    Leave thee naked to laughter,
When leaves fall and cold winds come.

THE MAGNETIC LADY TO HER PATIENT

Shelley wrote on this poem, ' For Jane and Williams only to see.' Medwin, who published it, *The Athenæum*, 1832, gives an account of the experiments out of which it grew, in his *Shelley Papers*: ' Shelley was a martyr to a most painful complaint, which constantly menaced to terminate fatally ; and was subject to violent paroxysms which, to his irritable nerves, were each a separate death. I had seen magnetism practised in India and at Paris, and at his earnest request consented to try its efficacy. Mesmer himself could not have hoped for more complete success. The imposition of my hand on his forehead instantaneously put a stop to the spasm, and threw him into a magnetic sleep, which for want of a better word is called somnambulism. Mrs. Shelley and another lady [Mrs. Williams] were present. The experiment was repeated more than once. During his trances I put some questions to him. He always pitched his voice in the same tone as mine. I enquired about his complaint, and its cure — the usual magnetic enquiries. His reply was, " What would cure me would kill me " . . . [Shelley answered in Italian.] He improvised also verses in Italian, in which language he was never known to write poetry.' Medwin adds, in his *Life of Shelley*: ' After my departure from Pisa he was magnetized by a lady, which gave rise to the beautiful stanzas entitled *The Magnetic Lady to her Patient*, and during which operation he made the same reply to an enquiry as to his disease and its cure as he had done to me, — " What would cure me would kill me." . . . Mrs. Shelley also magnetized him, but soon discontinued the practice, from finding that he got up in his sleep, and went one night to the window (fortunately barred), having taken to his old habit of sleep-walking, which I mentioned, in his boyhood and also in London.'

I

' SLEEP, sleep on ! forget thy pain;
    My hand is on thy brow,
My spirit on thy brain;
My pity on thy heart, poor friend;
    And from my fingers flow
The powers of life, and like a sign,
    Seal thee from thine hour of woe;
And brood on thee, but may not blend
            With thine.

II

' Sleep, sleep on ! I love thee not;
    But when I think that he
Who made and makes my lot
As full of flowers, as thine of weeds,
    Might have been lost like thee;
And that a hand which was not mine
    Might then have charmed his agony
As I another's — my heart bleeds
            For thine.

III

' Sleep, sleep, and with the slumber of
    The dead and the unborn
Forget thy life and love;
Forget that thou must wake forever;
    Forget the world's dull scorn;
Forget lost health, and the divine
    Feelings which died in youth's brief
            morn;
And forget me, for I can never'
            Be thine.

IV

' Like a cloud big with a May shower,
    My soul weeps healing rain
On thee, thou withered flower;
It breathes mute music on thy sleep;
    Its odor calms thy brain !
Its light within thy gloomy breast
    Spreads like a second youth again.
By mine thy being is to its deep
            Possessed.

V

' The spell is done.   How feel you now ? '
    ' Better — quite well,' replied
The sleeper, — ' What would do

You good when suffering and awake ?
    What cure your head and side ? '
' What would cure, that would kill me,
        Jane;
And as I must on earth abide
Awhile, yet tempt me not to break
        My chain.'

TO JANE

THE INVITATION

Williams, in his Journal, February 2, describes such an excursion : ' Fine warm day.
Jane accompanies Mary and S. to the sea-shore
through the Cascine.   They return about
three.'   The poem was published by Mrs.
Shelley, in an earlier form, in *Posthumous
Poems*, 1824, and, as here given, in her second
collected edition, 1839.

BEST and brightest, come away !
Fairer far than this fair Day,
Which, like thee to those in sorrow,
Comes to bid a sweet good-morrow
To the rough Year just awake
In its cradle on the brake.
The brightest hour of unborn Spring
Through the winter wandering,
Found it seems the halcyon Morn,
To hoar February born.   10
Bending from Heaven, in azure mirth,
It kissed the forehead of the Earth,
And smiled upon the silent sea,
And bade the frozen streams be free,
And waked to music all their fountains,
And breathed upon the frozen mountains,
And like a prophetess of May
Strewed flowers upon the barren way,
Making the wintry world appear
Like one on whom thou smilest, dear.   20

Away, away, from men and towns,
To the wild wood and the downs;
To the silent wilderness
Where the soul need not repress
Its music, lest it should not find
An echo in another's mind,
While the touch of Nature's art
Harmonizes heart to heart.
I leave this notice on my door
For each accustomed visitor : —   30
' I am gone into the fields
To take what this sweet hour yields.
Reflection, you may come to-morrow,
Sit by the fireside with Sorrow.

You with the unpaid bill, Despair, —
You, tiresome verse-reciter, Care, —
I will pay you in the grave, —
Death will listen to your stave.
Expectation too, be off !
To-day is for itself enough.   40
Hope, in pity mock not Woe
With smiles, nor follow where I go;
Long having lived on thy sweet food,
At length I find one moment's good
After long pain — with all your love,
This you never told me of.'

Radiant Sister of the Day,
Awake ! arise ! and come away !
To the wild woods and the plains,
And the pools where winter rains   50
Image all their roof of leaves,
Where the pine its garland weaves
Of sapless green, and ivy dun,
Round stems that never kiss the sun;
Where the lawns and pastures be
And the sand-hills of the sea;
Where the melting hoar-frost wets
The daisy-star that never sets,
And wind-flowers and violets,
Which yet join not scent to hue,   60
Crown the pale year weak and new:
When the night is left behind
In the deep east, dun and blind,
And the blue noon is over us,
And the multitudinous
Billows murmur at our feet,
Where the earth and ocean meet,
And all things seem only one,
In the universal sun.

THE RECOLLECTION

Shelley sent the lines to Mrs. Williams —
' not to be opened unless you are alone or with
Williams.'

I

Now the last day of many days,
    All beautiful and bright as thou,
    The loveliest and the last, is dead, —
Rise, Memory, and write its praise !
Up, — to thy wonted work ! come, trace
    The epitaph of glory fled,
For now the Earth has changed its face,
    A frown is on the Heaven's brow.

II

We wandered to the Pine Forest
    That skirts the Ocean's foam,

The lightest wind was in its nest,
  The tempest in its home.
The whispering waves were half asleep,
  The clouds were gone to play,
And on the bosom of the deep
  The smile of Heaven lay;
It seemed as if the hour were one
  Sent from beyond the skies,
Which scattered from above the sun
  A light of Paradise.

III

We paused amid the pines that stood
  The giants of the waste,
Tortured by storms to shapes as rude
  As serpents interlaced,
And soothed by every azure breath,
  That under heaven is blown,
To harmonies and hues beneath,
  As tender as its own;
Now all the treetops lay asleep,
  Like green waves on the sea,
As still as in the silent deep
  The ocean woods may be.

IV

How calm it was ! — the silence there
  By such a chain was bound
That even the busy woodpecker
  Made stiller by her sound
The inviolable quietness;
  The breath of peace we drew
With its soft motion made not less
  The calm that round us grew.
There seemed, from the remotest seat
  Of the white mountain waste
To the soft flower beneath our feet,
  A magic circle traced,
A spirit interfused around,
  A thrilling silent life, —
To momentary peace it bound
  Our mortal nature's strife;
And still I felt the centre of
  The magic circle there
Was one fair form that filled with love
  The lifeless atmosphere.

V

We paused beside the pools that lie
  Under the forest bough, —
Each seemed as 't were a little sky
  Gulfed in a world below;
A firmament of purple light,
  Which in the dark earth lay,

More boundless than the depth of night,
  And purer than the day, —
In which the lovely forests grew,
  As in the upper air,
More perfect both in shape and hue
  Than any spreading there.
There lay the glade and neighboring lawn,
  And through the dark green wood
The white sun twinkling like the dawn
  Out of a speckled cloud.
Sweet views which in our world above
  Can never well be seen,
Were imaged by the water's love
  Of that fair forest green.
And all was interfused beneath
  With an Elysian glow,
An atmosphere without a breath,
  A softer day below.
Like one beloved the scene had lent
  To the dark water's breast,
Its every leaf and lineament
  With more than truth expressed;
Until an envious wind crept by,
  Like an unwelcome thought,
Which from the mind's too faithful eye
  Blots one dear image out.
Though thou art ever fair and kind,
  The forests ever green,
Less oft is peace in Shelley's mind,
  Than calm in waters seen.

WITH A GUITAR: TO JANE

Shelley originally intended to give a harp to Mrs. Williams, and wrote to Horace Smith with regard to its purchase. The suggestion for the poem is found by Dr. Garnett in the fact that ' the front portion of the guitar is made of Swiss pine.' He continues : ' It is now clear how the poem took shape in Shelley's mind. The actual thought of the imprisonment of the Spirit of Music in the material of the instrument suggested Ariel's penance in the cloven pine ; the identification of himself with Ariel and of Jane Williams with Miranda was the easiest of feats to his brilliant imagination ; and hence an allegory of unequalled grace and charm, which could never have existed if the instrument had not been partly made of pine wood. The back, it should be added, is of mahogany, the finger board of ebony, and minor portions, chiefly ornamental, of some wood not identified. It was made by Ferdinando Bottari of Pisa in 1816. Having been religiously preserved since Shelley's death, it is in as perfect condition as when made. The strings, it is said, are better than those that are produced now.

'This guitar is also in a measure the subject of another of Shelley's most beautiful lyrics, "The keen stars were twinkling." In a letter dated June 18, 1822, speaking of his cruises "in the evening wind under the summer moon," he adds, "Jane brings her guitar." There is probably no other relic of a great poet so intimately associated with the arts of poetry and music, or ever will be, unless Milton's organ should turn up at a broker's or some excavating explorer should bring to light the lyre of Sappho.'

The guitar was given to the Bodleian Library by E. W. Silsbee, of Salem, Mass., who bought it of the grandson of Mrs. Williams on condition that it should be so disposed of. The composition of the poem is described by Trelawny: 'The strong light streamed through the opening of the trees. One of the pines, undermined by the water, had fallen into it. Under its lee, and nearly hidden, sat the Poet, gazing on the dark mirror beneath, so lost in his bardish reverie that he did not hear my approach. . . . The day I found Shelley in the pine-forest he was writing verses on a guitar. I picked up a fragment, but could only make out the first two lines. . . . It was a frightful scrawl; words smeared out with his finger, and one upon the other, over and over in tiers, and all run together "in most admired disorder;" it might have been taken for a sketch of a marsh overrun with bulrushes, and the blots for wild ducks; such a dashed-off daub as self-conceited artists mistake for a manifestation of genius.' The poem was published by Medwin, in two parts, *The Athenæum*, 1832, and *Fraser's*, 1833.

ARIEL to Miranda: — Take
This slave of Music, for the sake
Of him who is the slave of thee;
And teach it all the harmony
In which thou canst, and only thou,
Make the delighted spirit glow,
Till joy denies itself again,
And, too intense, is turned to pain.
For by permission and command
Of thine own Prince Ferdinand,   10
Poor Ariel sends this silent token
Of more than ever can be spoken;
Your guardian spirit, Ariel, who
From life to life must still pursue
Your happiness, — for thus alone
Can Ariel ever find his own.
From Prospero's enchanted cell,
As the mighty verses tell,

To the throne of Naples he
Lit you o'er the trackless sea,   20
Flitting on, your prow before,
Like a living meteor.
When you die, the silent Moon,
In her interlunar swoon,
Is not sadder in her cell
Than deserted Ariel.
When you live again on earth,
Like an unseen star of birth
Ariel guides you o'er the sea
Of life from your nativity.   30
Many changes have been run
Since Ferdinand and you begun
Your course of love, and Ariel still
Has tracked your steps and served your
    will;
Now in humbler, happier lot,
This is all remembered not;
And now, alas! the poor sprite is
Imprisoned, for some fault of his,
In a body like a grave.
From you, he only dares to crave,   40
For his service and his sorrow,
A smile to-day, a song to-morrow.

The artist who this idol wrought
To echo all harmonious thought,
Felled a tree, while on the steep
The woods were in their winter sleep,
Rocked in that repose divine
On the wind-swept Apennine;
And dreaming, some of Autumn past,
And some of Spring approaching fast,   50
And some of April buds and showers,
And some of songs in July bowers,
And all of love; and so this tree —
Oh, that such our death may be! —
Died in sleep, and felt no pain,
To live in happier form again:
From which, beneath Heaven's fairest
    star,
The artist wrought this loved guitar,
And taught it justly to reply,
To all who question skilfully,   60
In language gentle as thine own;
Whispering in enamoured tone
Sweet oracles of woods and dells,
And summer winds in sylvan cells;
For it had learned all harmonies
Of the plains and of the skies,
Of the forests and the mountains,
And the many-voicèd fountains;
The clearest echoes of the hills,
The softest notes of falling rills,   70

The melodies of birds and bees,
The murmuring of summer seas,
And pattering rain, and breathing dew,
And airs of evening; and it knew
That seldom-heard mysterious sound,
Which, driven on its diurnal round,
As it floats through boundless day,
Our world enkindles on its way.
All this it knows, but will not tell
To those who cannot question well   80
The spirit that inhabits it;
It talks according to the wit
Of its companions; and no more
Is heard than has been felt before
By those who tempt it to betray
These secrets of an elder day.
But, sweetly as its answers will
Flatter hands of perfect skill,
It keeps its highest, holiest tone
For our belovèd Jane alone.   90

TO JANE

Shelley sent the lines to Mrs. Williams with a note. 'I sat down to write some words for an ariette which might be profane; but it was in vain to struggle with the ruling spirit who compelled me to speak of things sacred to yours and to Wilhelm Meister's indulgence. I commit them to your secrecy and your mercy, and will try to do better another time.' The poem was published in part by Medwin, *The Athenæum*, 1832, and complete by Mrs. Shelley in her second collected edition, 1839.

I

THE keen stars were twinkling,
And the fair moon was rising among them,
     Dear Jane.
The guitar was tinkling,
But the notes were not sweet till you sung
     them
     Again.

II

As the moon's soft splendor
O'er the faint cold starlight of heaven
     Is thrown,
So your voice most tender
To the strings without soul had then given
     Its own.

III

The stars will awaken,
Though the moon sleep a full hour later
     To-night;
No leaf will be shaken

Whilst the dews of your melody scatter
     Delight.

IV

Though the sound overpowers,
Sing again, with your dear voice revealing
     A tone
Of some world far from ours,
Where music and moonlight and feeling
     Are one.

EPITAPH

Published by Mrs. Shelley, *Posthumous Poems*, 1824.

THESE are two friends whose lives were undivided;
So let their memory be, now they have glided
Under the grave; let not their bones be parted,
For their two hearts in life were single-hearted.

THE ISLE

Published by Mrs. Shelley, *Posthumous Poems*, 1824.

THERE was a little lawny islet
By anemone and violet,
     Like mosaic, paven;
And its roof was flowers and leaves
Which the summer's breath enweaves,
Where nor sun nor showers nor breeze
Pierce the pines and tallest trees,
     Each a gem engraven; —
Girt by many an azure wave
With which the clouds and mountains pave
     A lake's blue chasm.

A DIRGE

Published by Mrs. Shelley, *Posthumous Poems*, 1824.

ROUGH wind, that moanest loud
     Grief too sad for song;
     Wild wind, when sullen cloud
Knells all the night long;
Sad storm, whose tears are vain,
Bare woods whose branches strain,
Deep caves and dreary main, —
     Wail, for the world's wrong.

LINES WRITTEN IN THE BAY OF LERICI

Published by Garnett, *Macmillan's*, 1862.

SHE left me at the silent time
When the moon had ceased to climb
The azure path of Heaven's steep,
And like an albatross asleep,
Balanced on her wings of light,
Hovered in the purple night,
Ere she sought her ocean nest
In the chambers of the West.
She left me, and I stayed alone
Thinking over every tone   10
Which, though silent to the ear,
The enchanted heart could hear,
Like notes which die when born, but still
Haunt the echoes of the hill;
And feeling ever — oh, too much ! —
The soft vibration of her touch,
As if her gentle hand, even now,
Lightly trembled on my brow;
And thus, although she absent were,
Memory gave me all of her   20
That even Fancy dares to claim: —
Her presence had made weak and tame
All passions, and I lived alone
In the time which is our own;

The past and future were forgot,
As they had been, and would be, not.
But soon, the guardian angel gone,
The dæmon reassumed his throne
In my faint heart. I dare not speak
My thoughts, but thus disturbed and weak
I sat and saw the vessels glide   30
Over the ocean bright and wide,
Like spirit-wingèd chariots sent
O'er some serenest element
For ministrations strange and far;
As if to some Elysian star
They sailed for drink to medicine
Such sweet and bitter pain as mine.
And the wind that winged their flight
From the land came fresh and light,   40
And the scent of wingèd flowers,
And the coolness of the hours
Of dew, and sweet warmth left by day,
Were scattered o'er the twinkling bay.
And the fisher with his lamp
And spear about the low rocks damp
Crept, and struck the fish which came
To worship the delusive flame.
Too happy they, whose pleasure sought
Extinguishes all sense and thought   50
Of the regret that pleasure leaves,
Destroying life alone, not peace !

FRAGMENTS

Under FRAGMENTS are included, with a few exceptions, incomplete poems, sketches and cancelled passages, and those more inchoate passages which have been recovered from Shelley's notebooks. The exceptions are the *Prologue to Hellas*, which has been put with that drama, *A Vision of the Sea*, published by Shelley with the poems accompanying *Prometheus Unbound*, and five pieces, *To Mary Wollstonecraft Godwin*, 1814, *Death*, *An Allegory*, *On the Medusa of Leonardo da Vinci*, and *Evening, Pisa*, which, though lacking a word or a line, are in effect complete. The order of the FRAGMENTS is not strictly chronological in the first division, and is altogether arbitrary in the second. The dates assigned are those generally accepted, but, as a rule, they are conjectural and approximate only, not exact. The text is derived from the editions of Mrs. Shelley, the studies of Dr. Garnett in the Boscombe MSS., published by him mainly in *Relics of Shelley*, 1862, or by Rossetti, 1870, and Rossetti's own studies both in the same and other MSS. of which the results were given in his edition. A few pieces, originally published elsewhere, were also gathered by Rossetti and Forman in their editions, and Forman was enabled to add something more from independent MSS. The date and original publication of each piece are briefly indicated under each poem.

I

THE DÆMON OF THE WORLD

Nec tantum prodere vati,
Quantum scire licet. Venit ætas omnis in unam
Congeriem, miserumque premunt tot sæcula pectus.
LUCAN, PHARS. v. 176–178.

Shelley in his preface to *Alastor*, where this poem was published, says : ' The Fragment entitled *The Dæmon of the World* is a detached part of a poem which the author does not intend for publication. The metre in which it is composed is that of *Samson Agonistes* and the Italian pastoral drama, and may be considered as the natural measure into which poetical conceptions, expressed in harmonious language, necessarily fall.' The poem is part of a revision of *Queen Mab*.

I

How wonderful is Death,
Death and his brother Sleep!
One, pale as yonder wan and hornèd moon,
  With lips of lurid blue;
The other, glowing like the vital morn
  When throned on ocean's wave
  It breathes over the world;
Yet both so passing strange and wonderful!

Hath then the iron-sceptred Skeleton,
Whose reign is in the tainted sepulchres, 10
To the hell dogs that couch beneath his throne
Cast that fair prey? Must that divinest form,
Which love and admiration cannot view
Without a beating heart, whose azure veins
Steal like dark streams along a field of snow,
Whose outline is as fair as marble clothed
In light of some sublimest mind, decay?
  Nor putrefaction's breath
Leave aught of this pure spectacle
  But loathsomeness and ruin? 20
  Spare aught but a dark theme,
On which the lightest heart might moralize?
Or is it but that downy-wingèd slumbers
Have charmed their nurse, coy Silence, near her lids
  To watch their own repose?
  Will they, when morning's beam
  Flows through those wells of light,
Seek far from noise and day some western cave,
Where woods and streams with soft and pausing winds
  A lulling murmur weave? — 30

Ianthe doth not sleep
  The dreamless sleep of death;
Nor in her moonlight chamber silently
Doth Henry hear her regular pulses throb,
  Or mark her delicate cheek
With interchange of hues mock the broad moon,
  Outwatching weary night,
  Without assured reward.
  Her dewy eyes are closed;
On their translucent lids, whose texture fine 40
Scarce hides the dark blue orbs that burn below

With unapparent fire,
The baby Sleep is pillowed;
Her golden tresses shade
The bosom's stainless pride,
Twining like tendrils of the parasite
  Around a marble column.

Hark! whence that rushing sound?
'T is like a wondrous strain that sweeps
  Around a lonely ruin 50
When west winds sigh and evening waves respond
  In whispers from the shore:
'T is wilder than the unmeasured notes
Which from the unseen lyres of dells and groves
  The genii of the breezes sweep.

Floating on waves of music and of light
The chariot of the Dæmon of the World
  Descends in silent power.
Its shape reposed within; slight as some cloud
That catches but the palest tinge of day 60
  When evening yields to night;
Bright as that fibrous woof when stars endue
  Its transitory robe.
Four shapeless shadows bright and beautiful
Draw that strange car of glory; reins of light
Check their unearthly speed; they stop and fold
  Their wings of braided air.
The Dæmon, leaning from the ethereal car,
Gazed on the slumbering maid.
Human eye hath ne'er beheld 70
A shape so wild, so bright, so beautiful,
As that which o'er the maiden's charmèd sleep,
  Waving a starry wand,
  Hung like a mist of light.
Such sounds as breathed around like odorous winds
  Of wakening spring arose,
Filling the chamber and the moonlight sky.

'Maiden, the world's supremest spirit
  Beneath the shadow of her wings
Folds all thy memory doth inherit 80
  From ruin of divinest things, —
  Feelings that lure thee to betray,
  And light of thoughts that pass away.

'For thou hast earned a mighty boon;
　The truths, which wisest poets see
Dimly, thy mind may make its own,
　Rewarding its own majesty,
　　Entranced in some diviner mood
　　Of self-oblivious solitude.

'Custom and Faith and Power thou spurn-
　　est;　　　　　　　　　　　　　　　90
　From hate and awe thy heart is free;
Ardent and pure as day thou burnest,
　For dark and cold mortality
　　A living light, to cheer it long,
　　The watch-fires of the world among.

'Therefore from Nature's inner shrine,
　Where gods and fiends in worship bend,
Majestic spirit, be it thine
　The flame to seize, the veil to rend,
　　Where the vast snake Eternity　　100
　　In charmèd sleep doth ever lie.

'All that inspires thy voice of love,
　Or speaks in thy unclosing eyes,
Or through thy frame doth burn or move,
　Or think or feel, awake, arise !
　　Spirit, leave for mine and me
　　Earth's unsubstantial mimicry !'

It ceased, and from the mute and move-
　　less frame
　A radiant spirit arose,
All beautiful in naked purity.　　　　110
Robed in its human hues it did ascend,
Disparting as it went the silver clouds
It moved towards the car, and took its seat
　Beside the Dæmon shape.

Obedient to the sweep of aëry song,
　The mighty ministers
Unfurled their prismy wings.
　The magic car moved on.
The night was fair — innumerable stars
　Studded heaven's dark blue vault;　120
　The eastern wave grew pale
　With the first smile of morn.

　The magic car moved on.
　From the swift sweep of wings
The atmosphere in flaming sparkles flew;
　And where the burning wheels
Eddied above the mountain's loftiest peak
　Was traced a line of lightning.
Now far above a rock, the utmost verge
　Of the wide earth, it flew, —　　　130

The rival of the Andes, whose dark brow
　Frowned o'er the silver sea.

Far, far below the chariot's stormy path,
　Calm as a slumbering babe,
　Tremendous ocean lay.
Its broad and silent mirror gave to view
　The pale and waning stars,
　The chariot's fiery track,
　And the gray light of morn
　　Tingeing those fleecy clouds　　140
That cradled in their folds the infant
　　dawn.
　The chariot seemed to fly
Through the abyss of an immense concave,
Radiant with million constellations, tinged
　With shades of infinite color,
　And semicircled with a belt
　Flashing incessant meteors.

　As they approached their goal,　.
The wingèd shadows seemed to gather
　　speed.
The sea no longer was distinguished; earth
Appeared a vast and shadowy sphere, sus-
　　pended　　　　　　　　　　　　151
　In the black concave of heaven
　With the sun's cloudless orb,
　Whose rays of rapid light
Parted around the chariot's swifter course,
And fell like ocean's feathery spray
　Dashed from the boiling surge
　Before a vessel's prow.

　The magic car moved on.
　Earth's distant orb appeared　　160
The smallest light that twinkles in the
　　heavens,
　Whilst round the chariot's way
Innumerable systems widely rolled,
　And countless spheres diffused
　　An ever-varying glory.
It was a sight of wonder ! Some were
　　horned,
And like the moon's argentine crescent
　　hung
In the dark dome of heaven; some did shed
A clear mild beam like Hesperus, while the
　　sea
Yet glows with fading sunlight; others
　　dashed　　　　　　　　　　　　170
Athwart the night with trains of bickering
　　fire,
Like spherèd worlds to death and ruin
　　driven ;

Some shone like stars, and as the chariot
    passed
    Bedimmed all other light.

Spirit of Nature ! here,
In this interminable wilderness
Of worlds, at whose involved immensity
    Even soaring fancy staggers,
    Here is thy fitting temple !
    Yet not the lightest leaf   180
That quivers to the passing breeze
    Is less instinct with thee;
    Yet not the meanest worm,
That lurks in graves and fattens on the
    dead,
    Less shares thy eternal breath.
    Spirit of Nature ! thou,
Imperishable as this glorious scene,
    Here is thy fitting temple !

If solitude hath ever led thy steps
To the shore of the immeasurable sea,   190
    And thou hast lingered there
    Until the sun's broad orb
Seemed resting on the fiery line of ocean,
Thou must have marked the braided webs
    of gold
    That without motion hang
    Over the sinking sphere;
Thou must have marked the billowy moun-
    tain clouds,
    Edged with intolerable radiancy,
    Towering like rocks of jet
    Above the burning deep;   200
    And yet there is a moment,
    When the sun's highest point
Peers like a star o'er ocean's western edge,
When those far clouds of feathery purple
    gleam
Like fairy lands girt by some heavenly
    sea;
Then has thy rapt imagination soared
Where in the midst of all existing things
The temple of the mightiest Dæmon stands.

    Yet not the golden islands
That gleam amid yon flood of purple light,
    Nor the feathery curtains   211
That canopy the sun's resplendent couch,
    Nor the burnished ocean waves
    Paving that gorgeous dome,
    So fair, so wonderful a sight
As the eternal temple could afford.
The elements of all that human thought
Can frame of lovely or sublime did join

To rear the fabric of the fane, nor aught
Of earth may image forth its majesty.   220
Yet likest evening's vault that faëry hall;
As heaven low resting on the wave it
    spread
    Its floors of flashing light,
    Its vast and azure dome;
And on the verge of that obscure abyss,
Where crystal battlements o'erhang the
    gulf
Of the dark world, ten thousand spheres
    diffuse
Their lustre through its adamantine gates.

    The magic car no longer moved.
    The Dæmon and the Spirit   230
    Entered the eternal gates.
    Those clouds of aëry gold,
    That slept in glittering billows
    Beneath the azure canopy,
With the ethereal footsteps trembled not;
    While slight and odorous mists
Floated to strains of thrilling melody
Through the vast columns and the pearly
    shrines.

    The Dæmon and the Spirit
Approached the overhanging battlement.
Below lay stretched the boundless uni-
    verse !   241
    There, far as the remotest line
That limits swift imagination's flight,
Unending orbs mingled in mazy motion,
    Immutably fulfilling
    Eternal Nature's law.
    Above, below, around,
    The circling systems formed
    A wilderness of harmony —
    Each with undeviating aim   250
In eloquent silence through the depths of
    space
    Pursued its wondrous way.

Awhile the Spirit paused in ecstasy.
Yet soon she saw, as the vast spheres swept
    by,
Strange things within their belted orbs
    appear.
Like animated frenzies, dimly moved
Shadows, and skeletons, and fiendly shapes,
Thronging round human graves, and o'er
    the dead
Sculpturing records for each memory
In verse, such as malignant gods pro-
    nounce,   260

Blasting the hopes of men, when heaven
   and hell
Confounded burst in ruin o'er the world;
And they did build vast trophies, instru-
   ments
Of murder, human bones, barbaric gold,
Skins torn from living men, and towers of
   skulls
With sightless holes gazing on blinder
   heaven,
Mitres, and crowns, and brazen chariots
   stained
With blood, and scrolls of mystic wicked-
   ness,
The sanguine codes of venerable crime.
The likeness of a thronèd king came by,
When these had passed, bearing upon his
   brow   271
A threefold crown; his countenance was
   calm,
His eye severe and cold; but his right hand
Was charged with bloody coin, and he did
   gnaw
By fits, with secret smiles, a human heart
Concealed beneath his robe; and motley
   shapes,
A multitudinous throng, around him knelt,
With bosoms bare, and bowed heads, and
   false looks
Of true submission, as the sphere rolled by,
Brooking no eye to witness their foul
   shame,   280
Which human hearts must feel, while hu-
   man tongues
Tremble to speak ; they did rage horribly,
Breathing in self-contempt fierce blas-
   phemies
Against the Dæmon of the World, and
   high
Hurling their armèd hands where the pure
   Spirit,
Serene and inaccessibly secure,
Stood on an isolated pinnacle,
The flood of ages combating below,
The depth of the unbounded universe
   Above, and all around   290
Necessity's unchanging harmony.

THE DÆMON OF THE WORLD

This second part of the poem was published
by Forman, 1876, from a printed copy of
Queen Mab, on which Shelley had made MS.
revisions, with a view to republication under
the new title.

II

O HAPPY Earth ! reality of Heaven !
To which those restless powers that cease-
   lessly
Throng through the human universe
   aspire !
Thou consummation of all mortal hope !
Thou glorious prize of blindly-working
   will,
Whose rays, diffused throughout all space
   and time,
Verge to one point and blend forever there !
Of purest spirits thou pure dwelling-place,
Where care and sorrow, impotence and
   crime,
Languor, disease, and ignorance dare not
   come !   10
O happy Earth, reality of Heaven !

Genius has seen thee in her passionate
   dreams,
And dim forebodings of thy loveliness
Haunting the human heart have there en-
   twined
Those rooted hopes, that the proud Power
   of Evil
Shall not forever on this fairest world
Shake pestilence and war, or that his slaves
With blasphemy for prayer, and human
   blood
For sacrifice, before his shrine forever
In adoration bend, or Erebus   20
With all its banded fiends shall not uprise
To overwhelm in envy and revenge
The dauntless and the good, who dare to
   hurl
Defiance at his throne, girt though it be
With Death's omnipotence. Thou hast be-
   held
His empire, o'er the present and the past;
It was a desolate sight — now gaze on mine,
Futurity. Thou hoary giant Time,
Render thou up thy half-devoured babes,
And from the cradles of eternity,   30
Where millions lie lulled to their portioned
   sleep
By the deep murmuring stream of passing
   things,
Tear thou that gloomy shroud ! Spirit, be-
   hold
Thy glorious destiny !

                The Spirit saw
The vast frame of the renovated world
Smile in the lap of Chaos, and the sense

Of hope through her fine texture did suffuse
Such varying glow, as summer evening
    casts
On undulating clouds and deepening lakes.
Like the vague sighings of a wind at even,
That wakes the wavelets of the slumbering
    sea   41
And dies on the creation of its breath,
And sinks and rises, fails and swells by fits,
Was the sweet stream of thought that with
    mild motion
Flowed o'er the Spirit's human sympathies.
The mighty tide of thought had paused
    awhile,
Which from the Dæmon now like Ocean's
    stream
Again began to pour. —
                To me is given
The wonders of the human world to keep —
Space, matter, time and mind — let the
    sight   50
Renew and strengthen all thy failing hope.
All things are recreated, and the flame
Of consentaneous love inspires all life;
The fertile bosom of the earth gives suck
To myriads, who still grow beneath her care,
Rewarding her with their pure perfectness;
The balmy breathings of the wind inhale
Her virtues, and diffuse them all abroad;
Health floats amid the gentle atmosphere,
Glows in the fruits, and mantles on the
    stream;   60
No storms deform the beaming brow of
    heaven,
Nor scatter in the freshness of its pride
The foliage of the undecaying trees;
But fruits are ever ripe, flowers ever fair,
And Autumn proudly bears her matron
    grace,
Kindling a flush on the fair cheek of Spring,
Whose virgin bloom beneath the ruddy
    fruit
Reflects its tint and blushes into love.

The habitable earth is full of bliss;
Those wastes of frozen billows that were
    hurled   70
By everlasting snowstorms round the poles,
Where matter dared nor vegetate nor live,
But ceaseless frost round the vast solitude
Bound its broad zone of stillness, are un-
    loosed;
And fragrant zephyrs there from spicy isles
Ruffle the placid ocean-deep, that rolls
Its broad, bright surges to the sloping sand,

Whose roar is wakened into echoings sweet
To murmur through the heaven-breathing
    groves
And melodize with man's blest nature there.

The vast tract of the parched and sandy
    waste   81
Now teems with countless rills and shady
    woods,
Cornfields and pastures and white cottages;
And where the startled wilderness did hear
A savage conqueror stained in kindred blood
Hymning his victory, or the milder snake
Crushing the bones of some frail antelope
Within his brazen folds, the dewy lawn,
Offering sweet incense to the sunrise, smiles
To see a babe before his mother's door 90
Share with the green and golden basilisk,
That comes to lick his feet, his morning's
    meal.

Those trackless deeps, where many a
    weary sail
Has seen above the illimitable plain
Morning on night, and night on morning
    rise,
Whilst still no land to greet the wanderer
    spread
Its shadowy mountains on the sun-bright
    sea,
Where the loud roarings of the tempest-
    waves
So long have mingled with the gusty wind
In melancholy loneliness, and swept   100
The desert of those ocean solitudes
But vocal to the sea-bird's harrowing shriek,
The bellowing monster, and the rushing
    storm,
Now to the sweet and many-mingling
    sounds
Of kindliest human impulses respond;
Those lonely realms bright garden-isles
    begem,
With lightsome clouds and shining seas
    between,
And fertile valleys, resonant with bliss,
Whilst green woods overcanopy the wave,
Which like a toil-worn laborer leaps to
    shore   110
To meet the kisses of the flowerets there.

Man chief perceives the change; his
    being notes
The gradual renovation, and defines
Each movement of its progress on his mind.

Man, where the gloom of the long polar
   night
Lowered o'er the snow - clad rocks and
   frozen soil,
Where scarce the hardest herb that braves
   the frost
Basked in the moonlight's ineffectual glow,
Shrank with the plants, and darkened with
   the night;
Nor where the tropics bound the realms of
   day   120
With a broad belt of mingling cloud and
   flame,
Where blue mists through the unmoving
   atmosphere
Scattered the seeds of pestilence, and fed
Unnatural vegetation, where the land
Teemed with all earthquake, tempest and
   disease,
Was man a nobler being; slavery
Had crushed him to his country's blood-
   stained dust.

   Even where the milder zone afforded man
A seeming shelter, yet contagion there, 129
Blighting his being with unnumbered ills,
Spread like a quenchless fire; nor truth
   availed
Till late to arrest its progress, or create
That peace which first in bloodless victory
   waved
Her snowy standard o'er this favored
   clime;
There man was long the train-bearer of
   slaves,
The mimic of surrounding misery,
The jackal of ambition's lion-rage,
The bloodhound of religion's hungry zeal.

   Here now the human being stands adorn-
   ing
This loveliest earth with taintless body and
   mind;   140
Blest from his birth with all bland im-
   pulses,
Which gently in his noble bosom wake
All kindly passions and all pure desires.
Him, still from hope to hope the bliss pur-
   suing
Which from the exhaustless lore of human
   weal
Draws on the virtuous mind, the thoughts
   that rise
In time-destroying infiniteness gift
With self-enshrined eternity, that mocks

The unprevailing hoariness of age;
And man, once fleeting o'er the transient
   scene   150
Swift as an unremembered vision, stands
Immortal upon earth; no longer now
He slays the beast that sports around his
   dwelling,
And horribly devours its mangled flesh,
Or drinks its vital blood, which like a
   stream
Of poison through his fevered veins did
   flow
Feeding a plague that secretly consumed
His feeble frame, and kindling in his mind
Hatred, despair, and fear and vain belief,
The germs of misery, death, disease, and
   crime.   160
No longer now the wingèd habitants,
That in the woods their sweet lives sing
   away,
Flee from the form of man; but gather
   round,
And prune their sunny feathers on the
   hands
Which little children stretch in friendl
   sport
Towards these dreadless partners of their
   play.
All things are void of terror; man has lost
His desolating privilege, and stands
An equal amidst equals; happiness
And science dawn though late upon the
   earth;   170
Peace cheers the mind, health renovates the
   frame;
Disease and pleasure cease to mingle here,
Reason and passion cease to combat there;
Whilst mind unfettered o'er the earth ex-
   tends
Its all-subduing energies, and wields
The sceptre of a vast dominion there.

   Mild is the slow necessity of death.
The tranquil spirit fails beneath its grasp,
Without a groan, almost without a fear,
Resigned in peace to the necessity,   180
Calm as a voyager to some distant land,
And full of wonder, full of hope as he.
The deadly germs of languor and disease
Waste in the human frame, and Nature
   gifts
With choicest boons her human worship-
   pers.
How vigorous now the athletic form
   age !

How clear its open and unwrinkled brow !
Where neither avarice, cunning, pride, or
care,
Had stamped the zeal of gray deformity
On all the mingling lineaments of time. 190
How lovely the intrepid front of youth !
How sweet the smiles of taintless infancy.

Within the massy prison's mouldering
courts
Fearless and free the ruddy children play,
Weaving gay chaplets for their innocent
brows
With the green ivy and the red wall-flower,
That mock the dungeon's unavailing gloom;
The ponderous chains, and gratings of
strong iron,
There rust amid the accumulated ruins
Now mingling slowly with their native
earth; 200
There the broad beam of day, which feebly
once
Lighted the cheek of lean captivity
With a pale and sickly glare, now freely
shines
On the pure smiles of infant playfulness;
No more the shuddering voice of hoarse
despair
Peals through the echoing vaults, but
soothing notes
Of ivy-fingered winds and gladsome birds
And merriment are resonant around.

The fanes of Fear and Falsehood hear no
more
The voice that once waked multitudes to
war 210
Thundering through all their aisles, but
now respond
To the death dirge of the melancholy wind.
It were a sight of awfulness to see
The works of faith and slavery, so vast,
So sumptuous, yet withal so perishing,
Even as the corpse that rests beneath their
wall !
A thousand mourners deck the pomp of
death
To-day, the breathing marble glows above
To decorate its memory, and tongues
Are busy of its life; to-morrow, worms 220
In silence and in darkness seize their
prey.
These ruins soon leave not a wreck behind;
Their elements, wide scattered o'er the
globe,

To happier shapes are moulded, and be-
come
Ministrant to all blissful impulses;
Thus human things are perfected, and
earth,
Even as a child beneath its mother's love,
Is strengthened in all excellence, and
grows
Fairer and nobler with each passing year.

Now Time his dusky pennons o'er the
scene 230
Closes in steadfast darkness, and the past
Fades from our charmèd sight. My task
is done;
Thy lore is learned. Earth's wonders are
thine own,
With all the fear and all the hope they
bring.
My spells are past; the present now recurs.
Ah me ! a pathless wilderness remains
Yet unsubdued by man's reclaiming hand.

Yet, human Spirit, bravely hold thy
course.
Let virtue teach thee firmly to pursue 239
The gradual paths of an aspiring change.
For birth and life and death, and that
strange state
Before the naked powers, that through the
world
Wander like winds, have found a human
home;
All tend to perfect happiness, and urge
The restless wheels of being on their way,
Whose flashing spokes, instinct with infinite
life,
Bicker and burn to gain their destined
goal;
For birth but wakes the universal mind,
Whose mighty streams might else in silence
flow
Through the vast world, to individual sense
Of outward shows, whose unexperienced
shape 251
New modes of passion to its frame may
lend;
Life is its state of action, and the store
Of all events is aggregated there
That variegate the eternal universe;
Death is a gate of dreariness and gloom,
That leads to azure isles and beaming
skies
And happy regions of eternal hope.
Therefore, O Spirit ! fearlessly bear on.

Though storms may break the primrose on
     its stalk,   260
Though frosts may blight the freshness of
     its bloom,
Yet spring's awakening breath will woo
     the earth
To feed with kindliest dews its favorite
     flower,
That blooms in mossy banks and darksome
     glens,
Lighting the green wood with its sunny
     smile.

    Fear not then, Spirit, death's disrobing
     hand,
So welcome when the tyrant is awake,
So welcome when the bigot's hell-torch
     flares;
'T is but the voyage of a darksome hour,
The transient gulf-dream of a startling
     sleep.   270
For what thou art shall perish utterly,
But what is thine may never cease to be;
Death is no foe to virtue; earth has seen
Love's brightest roses on the scaffold
     bloom,
Mingling with freedom's fadeless laurels
     there,
And presaging the truth of visioned bliss.
Are there not hopes within thee, which this
     scene
Of linked and gradual being has confirmed ?
Hopes that not vainly thou, and living fires
Of mind, as radiant and as pure as thou
Have shone upon the paths of men — re-
     turn   281
Surpassing Spirit, to that world, where thou
Art destined an eternal war to wage
With tyranny and falsehood, and uproot
The germs of misery from the human heart.
Thine is the hand whose piety would soothe
The thorny pillow of unhappy crime,
Whose impotence an easy pardon gains,
Watching its wanderings as a friend's
     disease;
Thine is the brow whose mildness would
     defy   290
Its fiercest rage, and brave its sternest will,
When fenced by power and master of the
     world.
Thou art sincere and good; of resolute
     mind,
Free from heart-withering custom's cold
     control,
Of passion lofty, pure and unsubdued.

Earth's pride and meanness could not van-
     quish thee,
And therefore art thou worthy of the boon
Which thou hast now received; virtue shall
     keep
Thy footsteps in the path that thou hast
     trod,   299
And many days of beaming hope shall bless
Thy spotless life of sweet and sacred love.
Go, happy one, and give that bosom joy
    Whose sleepless spirit waits to catch
    Light, life and rapture from thy smile.

    The Dæmon called its wingèd ministers.
Speechless with bliss the Spirit mounts the
     car,
That rolled beside the crystal battlement,
Bending her beamy eyes in thankfulness.
    The burning wheels inflame
The steep descent of Heaven's untrodden
     way.   310
    Fast and far the chariot flew.
    The mighty globes that rolled
Around the gate of the Eternal Fane
Lessened by slow degrees, and soon ap-
     peared
Such tiny twinklers as the planet orbs,
That, ministering on the solar power,
With borrowed light, pursued their nar-
     rower way.
    Earth floated then below.
    The chariot paused a moment;
    The Spirit then descended;   320
    And from the earth departing
    The shadows with swift wings
Speeded like thought upon the light of
     Heaven.

    The Body and the Soul united then;
A gentle start convulsed Ianthe's frame;
Her veiny eyelids quietly unclosed;
Moveless awhile the dark blue orbs re-
     mained.
She looked around in wonder and beheld
Henry, who kneeled in silence by her couch,
Watching her sleep with looks of speech-
     less love,   330
    And the bright beaming stars
    That through the casement shone.

PRINCE ATHANASE

Shelley writes in a note : ' The Author was
pursuing a fuller development of the ideal
character of Athanase, when it struck him that

in an attempt at extreme refinement and analysis, his conceptions might be betrayed into the assuming a morbid character. The reader will judge whether he is a loser or gainer by the difference.'

Mrs. Shelley adds: 'The idea Shelley had formed of Prince Athanase was a good deal modelled on *Alastor*. In the first sketch of the poem, he named it *Pandemos and Urania*. Athanase seeks through the world the One whom he may love. He meets, in the ship in which he is embarked, a lady who appears to him to embody his ideal of love and beauty. But she proves to be Pandemos, or the earthly and unworthy Venus; who, after disappointing his cherished dreams and hopes, deserts him. Athanase, crushed by sorrow, pines and dies. "On his deathbed, the lady who can really reply to his soul comes and kisses·his lips." (*The Deathbed of Athanase.*) The poet describes her [ii. 155–160]. This slender note is all we have to aid our imagination in shaping out the form of the poem, such as its author imagined.' Date, 1817. Published, Mrs. Shelley, 1824.

PART I

THERE was a youth, who, as with toil and travel,
Had grown quite weak and gray before his time;
Nor any could the restless griefs unravel

Which burned within him, withering up his prime
And goading him, like fiends, from land to land.
Not his the load of any secret crime,

For nought of ill his heart could understand,
But pity and wild sorrow for the same;
Not his the thirst for glory or command,

Baffled with blast of hope-consuming shame;   10
Nor evil joys, which fire the vulgar breast
And quench in speedy smoke its feeble flame,

Had left within his soul their dark unrest;
Nor what religion fables of the grave
Feared he, — Philosophy's accepted guest.

For none than he a purer heart could have,
Or that loved good more for itself alone;
Of nought in heaven or earth was he the slave.

What sorrow strange, and shadowy, and unknown,
Sent him, a hopeless wanderer, through mankind? —   20
If with a human sadness he did groan,

He had a gentle yet aspiring mind;
Just, innocent, with varied learning fed;
And such a glorious consolation find

In others' joy, when all their own is dead.
He loved, and labored for his kind in grief,
And yet, unlike all others, it is said,

That from such toil he never found relief.
Although a child of fortune and of power,
Of an ancestral name the orphan chief,   30

His soul had wedded wisdom, and her dower
Is love and justice, clothed in which he sate
Apart from men, as in a lonely tower,

Pitying the tumult of their dark estate.
Yet even in youth did he not e'er abuse
The strength of wealth or thought to consecrate

Those false opinions which the harsh rich use
To blind the world they famish for their pride;
Nor did he hold from any man his dues,

But, like a steward in honest dealings tried
With those who toiled and wept, the poor and wise,   41
His riches and his cares he did divide.

Fearless he was, and scorning all disguise;
What he dared do or think, though men might start,
He spoke with mild yet unaverted eyes;

Liberal he was of soul, and frank of heart,
And to his many friends — all loved him well —
Whate'er he knew or felt he would impart,

If words he found those inmost thoughts to tell;
If not, he smiled or wept; and his weak foes   50
He neither spurned nor hated, though with fell

And mortal hate their thousand voices
  rose, —
They passed like aimless arrows from his
  ear;
Nor did his heart or mind its portal close

To those, or them, or any whom life's
  sphere
May comprehend within its wide array.
What sadness made that vernal spirit
  sere ? —

He knew not. Though his life, day after
  day,
Was failing like an unreplenished stream,
Though in his eyes a cloud and burden lay,

Through which his soul, like Vesper's serene beam   61
Piercing the chasms of ever rising clouds,
Shone, softly burning; though his lips did
  seem

Like reeds which quiver in impetuous
  floods;
And through his sleep, and o'er each waking hour,
Thoughts after thoughts, unresting multitudes,

Were driven within him by some secret
  power,
Which bade them blaze, and live, and roll
  afar,
Like lights and sounds from haunted tower
  to tower

O'er castled mountains borne, when tempest's war   70
Is levied by the night-contending winds
And the pale dalesmen watch with eager
  ear; —

Though such were in his spirit, as the
  fiends
Which wake and feed on ever living
  woe, —
What was this grief, which ne'er in other
  minds

A mirror found, he knew not — none could
  know;
But on whoe'er might question him he
  turned
The light of his frank eyes, as if to show

He knew not of the grief within that
  burned,
But asked forbearance with a mournful
  look;   80
Or spoke in words from which none ever
  learned

The cause of his disquietude; or shook
With spasms of silent passion; or turned
  pale:
So that his friends soon rarely undertook

To stir his secret pain without avail;
For all who knew and loved him then per-
  ceived
That there was drawn an adamantine veil

Between his heart and mind, — both unre-
  lieved
Wrought in his brain and bosom separate
  strife.
Some said that he was mad; others believed   90

That memories of an antenatal life
Made this, where now he dwelt, a penal
  hell;
And others said that such mysterious grief

From God's displeasure, like a darkness,
  fell
On souls like his which owned no higher law
Than love; love calm, steadfast, invincible

By mortal fear or supernatural awe;
And others, — ''Tis the shadow of a
  dream
Which the veiled eye of memory never saw,

'But through the soul's abyss, like some
  dark stream   100
Through shattered mines and caverns
  underground,
Rolls, shaking its foundations; and no
  beam

'Of joy may rise but it is quenched and
  drowned
In the dim whirlpools of this dream obscure;
Soon its exhausted waters will have found

' A lair of rest beneath thy spirit pure,
O Athanase ! — in one so good and great,
Evil or tumult cannot long endure.'   108

So spake they — idly of another's state
Babbling vain words and fond philosophy;
This was their consolation; such debate

Men held with one another; nor did he,
Like one who labors with a human woe,
Decline this talk; as if its theme might be

Another, not himself, he to and fro
Questioned and canvassed it with subtlest wit,
And none but those who loved him best could know

That which he knew not, how it galled and bit
His weary mind, this converse vain and cold;   119
For like an eyeless nightmare grief did sit

Upon his being; a snake which fold by fold
Pressed out the life of life, a clinging fiend
Which clenched him if he stirred with deadlier hold; —
And so his grief remained — let it remain — untold.

PART II

Prince Athanase had one belovèd friend,
An old, old man, with hair of silver white,
And lips where heavenly smiles would hang and blend

With his wise words, and eyes whose arrowy light
Shone like the reflex of a thousand minds.
He was the last whom superstition's blight

Had spared in Greece — the blight that cramps and blinds —
And in his olive bower at Œnoe
Had sate from earliest youth. Like one who finds

A fertile island in the barren sea,   10
One mariner who has survived his mates
Many a drear month in a great ship — so he

With soul-sustaining songs, and sweet debates
Of ancient lore there fed his lonely being.
'The mind becomes that which it contemplates,' —

And thus Zonoras, by forever seeing
Their bright creations, grew like wisest men;
And when he heard the crash of nations fleeing

A bloodier power than ruled thy ruins then,
O sacred Hellas ! many weary years   20
He wandered, till the path of Laian's glen

Was grass-grown, and the unremembered tears
Were dry in Laian for their honored chief,
Who fell in Byzant, pierced by Moslem spears;

And as the lady looked with faithful grief
From her high lattice o'er the rugged path,
Where she once saw that horseman toil, with brief,

And blighting hope, who with the news of death
Struck body and soul as with a mortal blight,
She saw beneath the chestnuts, far beneath,   30

An old man toiling up, a weary wight;
And soon within her hospitable hall
She saw his white hairs glittering in the light

Of the wood-fire, and round his shoulders fall;
And his wan visage and his withered mien
Yet calm and gentle and majestical.

And Athanase, her child, who must have been
Then three years old, sate opposite and gazed
In patient silence.
.   .   .   .
Such was Zonoras; and as daylight finds
One amaranth glittering on the path of frost,   41
When autumn nights have nipped all weaker kinds,

Thus through his age, dark, cold, and tempest-tossed,
Shone truth upon Zonoras; and he filled
From fountains pure, nigh overgrown and lost,

The spirit of Prince Athanase, a child,
With soul-sustaining songs of ancient lore
And philosophic wisdom, clear and mild.

And sweet and subtle talk they ever-
   more,
The pupil and the master, shared; until, 50
Sharing that undiminishable store,

The youth, as shadows on a grassy hill
Outrun the winds that chase them, soon
   outran
His teacher, and did teach with native
   skill

Strange truths and new to that experienced
   man;
Still they were friends, as few have ever
   been
Who mark the extremes of life's discordant span.

So in the caverns of the forest green,
Or by the rocks of echoing ocean hoar,
Zonoras and Prince Athanase were seen 60

By summer woodmen; and when winter's
   roar
Sounded o'er earth and sea its blast of
   war,
The Balearic fisher, driven from shore,

Hanging upon the peakèd wave afar,
Then saw their lamp from Laian's turret
   gleam,
Piercing the stormy darkness like a star

Which pours beyond the sea one steadfast
   beam,
Whilst all the constellations of the sky
Seemed reeling through the storm. They
   did but seem —

For, lo! the wintry clouds are all gone
   by,   70
And bright Arcturus through yon pines is
   glowing,
And far o'er southern waves, immovably

Belted Orion hangs — warm light is flowing
From the young moon into the sunset's
   chasm.
'O summer eve with power divine, bestowing

'On thine own bird the sweet enthusiasm
Which overflows in notes of liquid gladness,
Filling the sky like light! How many a
   spasm

'Of fevered brains, oppressed with grief
   and madness,
Were lulled by thee, delightful nightingale!   80
And these soft waves, murmuring a gentle
   sadness,

'And the far sighings of yon piny dale
Made vocal by some wind we feel not
   here, —
I bear alone what nothing may avail

'To lighten — a strange load!' — No human ear
Heard this lament; but o'er the visage
   wan
Of Athanase a ruffling atmosphere

Of dark emotion, a swift shadow, ran,
Like wind upon some forest-bosomed lake,
Glassy and dark. And that divine old
   man   90

Beheld his mystic friend's whole being
   shake,
Even where its inmost depths were gloomiest;
And with a calm and measured voice he
   spake,

And with a soft and equal pressure,
   pressed
That cold, lean hand: — 'Dost thou remember yet,
When the curvèd moon, then lingering in
   the west,

'Paused in yon waves her mighty horns to
   wet,
How in those beams we walked, half resting on the sea?
'T is just one year — sure thou dost not
   forget —

'Then Plato's words of light in thee and
   me   100
Lingered like moonlight in the moonless
   east;
For we had just then read — thy memory

' Is faithful now — the story of the feast;
And Agathon and Diotima seemed
From death and dark forgetfulness re-
leased.'

.   .   .   .

'T was at the season when the Earth upsprings
From slumber, as a spherèd angel's child,
Shadowing its eyes with green and golden
wings,

Stands up before its mother bright and
mild,
Of whose soft voice the air expectant
seems —   110
So stood before the sun, which shone and
smiled

To see it rise thus joyous from its dreams,
The fresh and radiant Earth. The hoary
grove
Waxed green, and flowers burst forth like
starry beams;

The grass in the warm sun did start and
move,
And sea-buds burst beneath the waves serene.
How many a one, though none be near to
love,

Loves then the shade of his own soul, half
seen
In any mirror, or the spring's young minions,
The wingèd leaves amid the copses green !

How many a spirit then puts on the pinions   121
Of fancy, and outstrips the lagging blast,
And his own steps, and over wide dominions

Sweeps in his dream-drawn chariot, far
and fast,
More fleet than storms — the wide world
shrinks below,
When winter and despondency are passed !

'T was at this season that Prince Athanase
Passed the white Alps; those eagle-baffling
mountains
Slept in their shrouds of snow; beside the
ways

The waterfalls were voiceless, for their
fountains   130
Were changed to mines of sunless crystal
now;
Or, by the curdling winds, like brazen
wings

Which clanged along the mountain's marble brow,
Warped into adamantine fretwork, hung,
And filled with frozen light the chasm below.

.   .   .   .

Thou art the wine whose drunkenness is
all
We can desire, O Love ! and happy
souls,
Ere from thy vine the leaves of autumn
fall,

Catch thee, and feed from their o'erflow-
ing bowls
Thousands who thirst for thy ambrosial
dew !   140
Thou art the radiance which where ocean
rolls

Investest it; and when the heavens are
blue
Thou fillest them; and when the earth is
fair
The shadow of thy moving wings imbue

Its deserts and its mountains, till they
wear
Beauty like some bright robe; thou ever
soarest
Among the towers of men, and as soft air

In spring, which moves the unawakened
forest,
Clothing with leaves its branches bare and
bleak,
Thou floatest among men, and aye im-
plorest   150

That which from thee they should implore;
the weak
Alone kneel to thee, offering up the
hearts
The strong have broken; yet where shall
any seek

A garment whom thou clothest not ?

.   .   .   .

Her hair was brown, her spherèd eyes were
    brown,
And in their dark and liquid moisture
    swam,
Like the dim orb of the eclipsèd moon;

Yet when the spirit flashed beneath, there
    came
The light from them, as when tears of de-
    light   159
Double the western planet's serene flame.

THE WOODMAN AND THE NIGHTINGALE

Date, 1818. Published in part by Mrs. Shelley, 1824, and the remainder by Garnett, 1862.

A WOODMAN, whose rough heart was out
    of tune
(I think such hearts yet never came to
    good),
Hated to hear, under the stars or moon,

One nightingale in an interfluous wood
Satiate the hungry dark with melody; —
And as a vale is watered by a flood,

Or as the moonlight fills the open sky
Struggling with darkness, as a tuberose
Peoples some Indian dell with scents which
    lie

Like clouds above the flower from which
    they rose,   10
The singing of that happy nightingale
In this sweet forest, from the golden close

Of evening till the star of dawn may fail,
Was interfused upon the silentness.
The folded roses and the violets pale

Heard her within their slumbers, the abyss
Of heaven with all its planets; the dull ear
Of the night-cradled earth; the loneliness

Of the circumfluous waters; every sphere
And every flower and beam and cloud and
    wave,   20
And every wind of the mute atmosphere,

And every beast stretched in its rugged
    cave,
And every bird lulled on its mossy bough,
And every silver moth fresh from the grave

Which is its cradle; — ever from below
Aspiring like one who loves too fair, too
    far,
To be consumed within the purest glow

Of one serene and unapproachèd star,
As if it were a lamp of earthly light,
Unconscious as some human lovers are   30

Itself how low, how high beyond all height
The heaven where it would perish ! — and
    every form
That worshipped in the temple of the
    night

Was awed into delight, and by the charm
Girt as with an interminable zone,
Whilst that sweet bird, whose music was a
    storm

Of sound, shook forth the dull oblivion
Out of their dreams; harmony became love
In every soul but one.

   .   .   .   .   .   .
And so this man returned with axe and
    saw   40
At evening close from killing the tall treen,
The soul of whom by nature's gentle law

Was each a wood-nymph, and kept ever
    green
The pavement and the roof of the wild
    copse,
Checkering the sunlight of the blue serene

With jagged leaves, and from the forest
    tops
Singing the winds to sleep, or weeping oft
Fast showers of aërial water drops

Into their mother's bosom, sweet and soft,
Nature's pure tears which have no bitter-
    ness; —   50
Around the cradles of the birds aloft

They spread themselves into the loveliness
Of fan-like leaves, and over pallid flow-
    ers
Hang like moist clouds; or, where high
    branches kiss,

Make a green space among the silent bow-
    ers,
Like a vast fane in a metropolis,
Surrounded by the columns and the towers

All overwrought with branch-like traceries
In which there is religion — and the mute
Persuasion of unkindled melodies,   60

Odors and gleams and murmurs, which the
        lute
Of the blind pilot-spirit of the blast
Stirs as it sails, now grave and now acute,

Wakening the leaves and waves ere it has
        passed
To such brief unison as on the brain
One tone, which never can recur, has cast,

One accent never to return again.

.   .   .   .

The world is full of Woodmen who expel
Love's gentle Dryads from the haunt of life,
And vex the nightingales in every dell.   70

OTHO

Date, 1817. Published, in part, by Mrs.
Shelley, 1839, first edition, and the remainder
by Garnett, 1862. Mrs. Shelley states that the
poem was suggested by Tacitus.

I

THOU wert not, Cassius, and thou couldst
        not be,
Last of the Romans, though thy memory
        claim
From Brutus his own glory, and on thee
Rests the full splendor of his sacred
        fame;
Nor he who dared make the foul tyrant
        quail
Amid his cowering senate with thy name,
Though thou and he were great; it will
        avail
To thine own fame that Otho's should not
        fail.

II

'T will wrong thee not — thou wouldst, if
        thou couldst feel,
Abjure such envious fame — great Otho
        died
Like thee — he sanctified his country's
        steel,
At once the tyrant and tyrannicide,
In his own blood. A deed it was to bring
Tears from all men — though full of
        gentle pride,

Such pride as from impetuous love may
        spring,
That will not be refused its offering.

III

Dark is the realm of grief: but human
        things
Those may not know who cannot weep
        for them.

.   .   .   .

TASSO

Date, 1818. Published by Garnett, 1862,
and the SONG by Mrs. Shelley, 1824. Shelley
writes to Peacock regarding the drama: ' I
have devoted this summer, and indeed the next
year, to the composition of a tragedy on the
subject of Tasso's madness; which, I find upon
inspection, is, if properly treated, admirably
dramatic and poetical. But you will say I
have no dramatic talent. Very true, in a certain sense; but I have taken the resolution to
see what kind of tragedy a person without
dramatic talent could write. It shall be better
morality than *Fazio*, and better poetry than
Bertram, at least.'

MADDALO, *a Courtier.*   PIGNA, *a Minister.*
MALPIGLIO, *a Poet.*   ALBANO, *an Usher.*

MADDALO

No access to the Duke! You have not
        said
That the Count Maddalo would speak with
        him?

PIGNA

Did you inform his Grace that Signor
        Pigna
Waits with state papers for his signature?

MALPIGLIO

The Lady Leonora cannot know
That I have written a sonnet to her fame,
In which I   Venus and Adonis.
You should not take my gold and serve me
        not.

ALBANO

In truth I told her, and she smiled and said,
' If I am Venus, thou, coy Poesy,
Art the Adonis whom I love, and he
The Erymanthian boar that wounded him.'
Oh, trust to me, Signor Malpiglio,
Those nods and smiles were favors worth
        the zechin.

MALPIGLIO

The words are twisted in some double
    sense
That I reach not; the smiles fell not on
    me.

PIGNA

How are the Duke and Duchess occupied?

ALBANO

Buried in some strange talk. The Duke
    was leaning,
His finger on his brow, his lips unclosed.
The Princess sate within the window-seat,
And so her face was hid; but on her knee
Her hands were clasped, veinèd, and pale
    as snow,
And quivering — young Tasso, too, was
    there.

MADDALO

Thou seest on whom from thine own wor-
    shipped heaven
Thou drawest down smiles — they did not
    rain on thee.

MALPIGLIO

Would they were parching lightnings for
    his sake
On whom they fell!

.   .   .   .

SONG

I

I loved — alas! our life is love;
But when we cease to breathe and move
I do suppose love ceases too.
I thought, but not as now I do,
Keen thoughts and bright of linkèd lore,
Of all that men had thought before,
And all that nature shows, and more.

II

And still I love and still I think,
But strangely, for my heart can drink
The dregs of such despair, and live,
And love;
And if I think, my thoughts come fast,
I mix the present with the past,
And each seems uglier than the last.

III

Sometimes I see before me flee
A silver spirit's form, like thee,

O Leonora, and I sit
    still watching it,
Till by the grated casement's ledge
It fades, with such a sigh, as sedge
Breathes o'er the breezy streamlet's edge.

MARENGHI

Date, 1818. Published in part by Mrs. Shelley, 1824, and the remainder by Rossetti, 1870. Mrs. Shelley gives as the source Sismondi, *Histoire des Républiques Italiennes*.

I

LET those who pine in pride or in revenge,
    Or think that ill for ill should be repaid,
Or barter wrong for wrong, until the ex-
    change
    Ruins the merchants of such thriftless
      trade,
Visit the tower of Vado, and unlearn
Such bitter faith beside Marenghi's urn.

II

A massy tower yet overhangs the town,
    A scattered group of ruined dwellings
      now.

.   .   .   .

III

Another scene ere wise Etruria knew
    Its second ruin through internal strife,
And tyrants through the breach of discord
      threw
    The chain which binds and kills. As
      death to life,
As winter to fair flowers (though some be
      poison)
So Monarchy succeeds to Freedom's foison.

IV

In Pisa's church a cup of sculptured gold
    Was brimming with the blood of feuds
      forsworn
At sacrament; more holy ne'er of old
    Etrurians mingled with the shades forlorn
Of moon-illumined forests.

.   .   .   .

V

And reconciling factions wet their lips
    With that dread wine, and swear to keep
      each spirit
Undarkened by their country's last eclipse.

.   .   .   .

VI

Was Florence the liberticide? that band
  Of free and glorious brothers who had
      planted,
Like a green isle 'mid Æthiopian sand,
  A nation amid slaveries, disenchanted
Of many impious faiths — wise, just — do
      they,
Does Florence, gorge the sated tyrants'
      prey?

VII

O foster-nurse of man's abandoned glory,
  Since Athens, its great mother, sunk in
      splendor;
Thou shadowest forth that mighty shape in
      story,
  As ocean its wrecked fanes, severe yet
      tender.
The light-invested angel Poesy
Was drawn from the dim world to welcome
      thee.

VIII

And thou in painting didst transcribe all
      taught
  By loftiest meditations; marble knew
The sculptor's fearless soul, and as he
      wrought,
  The grace of his own power and freedom
      grew.
And more than all, heroic, just, sublime,
Thou wert among the false — was this thy
      crime?

IX

Yes; and on Pisa's marble walls the twine
  Of direst weeds hangs garlanded; the
      snake
Inhabits its wrecked palaces; — in thine
  A beast of subtler venom now doth make
Its lair, and sits amid their glories over-
      thrown,
And thus thy victim's fate is as thine own.

X

The sweetest flowers are ever frail and rare,
  And love and freedom blossom but to
      wither;
And good and ill like vines entangled are,
  So that their grapes may oft be plucked
      together.
Divide the vintage ere thou drink, then
      make
Thy heart rejoice for dead Marenghi's sake.

XI

No record of his crime remains in story,
  But if the morning bright as evening
      shone,
It was some high and holy deed, by glory
  Pursued into forgetfulness, which won
From the blind crowd he made secure and
      free
The patriot's meed, toil, death, and infamy.

XII

For when by sound of trumpet was declared
  A price upon his life, and there was
      set
A penalty of blood on all who shared
  So much of water with him as might
      wet
His lips, which speech divided not, he
      went
Alone, as you may guess, to banishment.

XIII

Amid the mountains, like a hunted beast,
  He hid himself, and hunger, toil, and
      cold,
Month after month endured; it was a feast
  Whene'er he found those globes of deep-
      red gold
Which in the woods the strawberry-tree
      doth bear,
Suspended in their emerald atmosphere.

XIV

And in the roofless huts of vast morasses,
  Deserted by the fever-stricken serf,
All overgrown with reeds and long rank
      grasses,
  And hillocks heaped of moss-inwoven
      turf,
And where the huge and speckled aloe
      made,
Rooted in stones, a broad and pointed
      shade,

XV

He housed himself. There is a point of
      strand
  Near Vado's tower and town; and on
      one side
The treacherous marsh divides it from the
      land,
  Shadowed by pine and ilex forests wide,
And on the other creeps eternally,
Through muddy weeds, the shallow sullen
      sea.

XVI

Here the earth's breath is pestilence, and
    few
  But things whose nature is at war with
    life —
Snakes and ill worms — endure its mortal
    dew.
  The trophies of the clime's victorious
    strife —
White bones, and locks of dun and yellow
    hair,
And ringèd horns which buffaloes did
    wear —

  .   .   .   .

XVII

And at the utmost point   stood there
  The relics of a weed-inwoven cot,
Thatched with broad flags. An outlawed
    murderer
  Had lived seven days there; the pursuit
    was hot
When he was cold. The birds that were
    his grave
Fell dead upon their feast in Vado's wave.

XVIII

There must have lived within Marenghi's
    heart
  That fire, more warm and bright than
    life or hope,
(Which to the martyr makes his dun-
    geon . . .
  More joyous than the heaven's majestic
    cope
To his oppressor), warring with decay, —
Or he could ne'er have lived years, day by
    day.

XIX

Nor was his state so lone as you might
    think.
  He had tamed every newt and snake and
    toad,
And every seagull which sailed down to
    drink
  Those   ere the death-mist went
    abroad.
And each one, with peculiar talk and play,
Wiled, not untaught, his silent time away.

XX

And the marsh-meteors, like tame beasts,
    at night
  Came licking with blue tongues his
    veinèd feet;

And he would watch them, as, like spirits
    bright,
  In many entangled figures quaint and
    sweet
To some enchanted music they would
    dance —
Until they vanished at the first moon-
    glance.

XXI

He mocked the stars by grouping on each
    weed
  The summer dewdrops in the golden
    dawn;
And, ere the hoarfrost vanished, he could
    read
Its pictured footprints, as on spots of lawn
Its delicate brief touch in silence weaves
The likeness of the wood's remembered
    leaves.

XXII

And many a fresh Spring morn would he
    awaken,
  While yet the unrisen sun made glow,
    like iron
Quivering in crimson fire, the peaks un-
    shaken
  Of mountains and blue isles which did
    environ
With air-clad crags that plain of land and
    sea, —
And feel   liberty.

XXIII

And in the moonless nights, when the dim
    ocean
  Heaved underneath the heaven, . . .
Starting from dreams . . .
  Communed with the immeasurable
    world;
And felt his life beyond his limbs dilated,
Till his mind grew like that it contem-
    plated.

XXIV

His food was the wild fig and strawberry;
  The milky pine-nuts which the autumnal
    blast
Shakes into the tall grass; and such small fry
  As from the sea by winter-storms are
    cast;
And the coarse bulbs of iris flowers he
    found
Knotted in clumps under the spongy ground.

XXV

And so were kindled powers and thoughts
    which made
His solitude less dark. When memory
    came
(For years gone by leave each a deepening
    shade),
    His spirit basked in its internal flame, —
As, when the black storm hurries round at
    night
The fisher basks beside his red firelight.

XXVI

Yet human hopes and cares and faiths and
    errors,
    Like billows unawakened by the wind,
Slept in Marenghi still; but that all ter-
    rors,
    Weakness, and doubt, had withered in
    his mind.
His couch

. . . .

XXVII

And, when he saw beneath the sunset's
    planet
    A black ship walk over the crimson
    ocean, —
Its pennons streaming on the blasts that
    fan it,
    Its sails and ropes all tense and without
    motion,
Like the dark ghost of the unburied even
Striding across the orange-colored hea-
    ven, —

XXVIII

The thought of his own kind who made the
    soul
    Which sped that wingèd shape through
    night and day, —
The thought of his own country . . .

. . . .

LINES WRITTEN FOR JULIAN AND MADDALO

Published by Garnett, 1862, who conjectures
the title.

WHAT think you the dead are ?
                Why, dust and clay,
What should they be ?
                    'T is the last hour of day.

Look on the west, how beautiful it is
Vaulted with radiant vapors ! The deep
    bliss
Of that unutterable light has made
The edges of that cloud   fade
Into a hue, like some harmonious thought,
Wasting itself on that which it had
    wrought,
Till it dies   and between
The light hues of the tender, pure, serene,
And infinite tranquillity of heaven.
Ay, beautiful ! but when our . . .

. . . .

Perhaps the only comfort which remains
Is the unheeded clanking of my chains,
The which I make, and call it melody.

LINES WRITTEN FOR PROMETHEUS UNBOUND

Published by Mrs. Shelley, 1839, first edition.

    As a violet's gentle eye
    Gazes on the azure sky,
Until its hue grows like what it beholds;
    As a gray and empty mist
    Lies like solid amethyst
Over the western mountain it enfolds,
    When the sunset sleeps
      Upon its snow;
    As a strain of sweetest sound
    Wraps itself the wind around,
Until the voiceless wind be music too;
    As aught dark, vain and dull,
    Basking in what is beautiful,
    Is full of light and love.

LINES WRITTEN FOR MONT BLANC

Published by Garnett, 1862.

THERE is a voice, not understood by all,
Sent from these desert-caves. It is the roar
Of the rent ice-cliff which the sunbeams call,
Plunging into the vale — it is the blast
Descending on the pines — the torrents pour.

LINES WRITTEN FOR THE INDIAN SERENADE

Published by Rossetti, 1870, who conjectures
the title.

    O PILLOW cold and wet with tears !
    Thou breathest sleep no more !

LINES WRITTEN FOR THE ODE TO LIBERTY

Published by Garnett, 1862.

WITHIN a cavern of man's trackless spirit
Is throned an Image, so intensely fair
That the adventurous thoughts that wander
      near it
  Worship, and as they kneel tremble and
      wear
The splendor of its presence, and the light
  Penetrates their dreamlike frame
Till they become charged with the strength
      of flame.

STANZA WRITTEN FOR THE ODE WRITTEN OCTOBER, 1819

Published by Rossetti, The Times.

  GATHER, oh, gather,
Foeman and friend in love and peace !
  Waves sleep together
When the blasts that called them to
      battle cease.
For fangless Power, grown tame and mild,
Is at play with Freedom's fearless child —
The dove and the serpent reconciled !

LINES CONNECTED WITH EPI-PSYCHIDION

*Published in part by Mrs. Shelley, 1839, sec-
ond edition, and the remainder by Garnett, 1862.
From these lines, and also from other fragments, it is to be inferred that a poem, substantially Epipsychidion, was in Shelley's mind
before his meeting with Emilia Viviani, and
that she was less the inspiration of it than the
occasion of the form it took.*

HERE, my dear friend, is a new book for
      you;
I have already dedicated two
To other friends, one female and one
      male, —
What you are is a thing that I must veil;
What can this be to those who praise or
      rail ?
I never was attached to that great sect
Whose doctrine is that each one should se-
      lect
Out of the world a mistress or a friend,
And all the rest, though fair and wise,
      commend   9

To cold oblivion — though 't is in the code
Of modern morals, and the beaten road
Which those poor slaves with weary foot-
      steps tread
Who travel to their home among the dead
By the broad highway of the world — and so
With one sad friend, and many a jealous
      foe,
The dreariest and the longest journey go.

  Free love has this, different from gold
      and clay,
That to divide is not to take away.
Like ocean, which the general north wind
      breaks
Into ten thousand waves, and each one
      makes   20
A mirror of the moon — like some great
      glass,
Which did distort whatever form might
      pass,
Dashed into fragments by a playful child,
Which then reflects its eyes and forehead
      mild;
Giving for one, which it could ne'er ex-
      press,
A thousand images of loveliness.

  If I were one whom the loud world held
      wise,
I should disdain to quote authorities
In commendation of this kind of love.
Why there is first the God in heaven
      above,   30
Who wrote a book called Nature — 't is to
      be
Reviewed, I hear, in the next Quarterly;
And Socrates, the Jesus Christ of Greece,
And Jesus Christ himself did never cease
To urge all living things to love each
      other,
And to forgive their mutual faults, and
      smother
The Devil of disunion in their souls.
  .   .   .   .
  I love you ! — Listen, O embodied Ray
Of the great Brightness; I must pass away
While you remain, and these light words
      must be   40
Tokens by which you may remember me.
Start not — the thing you are is unbe-
      trayed,
If you are human, and if but the shade
Of some sublimer Spirit.
  .   .   .   .

And as to friend or mistress, 't is a form;
Perhaps I wish you were one. Some de-
clare
You a familiar spirit, as you are;
Others with a   more inhuman
Hint that, though not my wife, you are a
woman —
What is the color of your eyes and hair ? 50
Why, if you were a lady, it were fair
The world should know — but, as I am
afraid,
The Quarterly would bait you if betrayed;
And if, as it will be sport to see them
stumble
Over all sorts of scandals, hear them
mumble
Their litany of curses — some guess right,
And others swear you 're a Hermaphro-
dite;
Like that sweet marble monster of both
sexes,
With looks so sweet and gentle that it
vexes
The very soul that the soul is gone   60
Which lifted from her limbs the veil of
stone.

.   .   .   .

It is a sweet thing, friendship, a dear
balm,
A happy and auspicious bird of calm,
Which rides o'er life's ever tumultuous
Ocean;
A God that broods o'er chaos in commo-
tion;
A flower which fresh as Lapland roses are,
Lifts its bold head into the world's frore
air,
And blooms most radiantly when others
die,
Health, hope, and youth, and brief pros-
perity;   69
And with the light and odor of its bloom,
Shining within the dungeon and the tomb;
Whose coming is as light and music are
'Mid dissonance and gloom — a star
Which moves not 'mid the moving heavens
alone —
A smile among dark frowns — a gentle
tone
Among rude voices, a belovèd light,
A solitude, a refuge, a delight.
If I had but a friend ! Why, I have
three
Even by my own confession; there may be

Some more, for what I know, for 't is my
mind   80
To call my friends all who are wise and
kind, —
And these, Heaven knows, at best are very
few;
But none can ever be more dear than you.
Why should they be ? My muse has lost
her wings,
Or like a dying swan who soars and sings,
I should describe you in heroic style,
But as it is, are you not void of guile ?
A lovely soul, formed to be blessed and
bless;
A well of sealed and secret happiness;
A lute which those whom Love has taught
to play   90
Make music on to cheer the roughest day,
And enchant sadness till it sleeps ?

.   .   .   .

To the oblivion whither I and thou,
All loving and all lovely, hasten now
With steps, ah, too unequal ! may we meet
In one Elysium or one winding sheet !
If any should be curious to discover
Whether to you I am a friend or lover,
Let them read Shakespeare's sonnets, tak-
ing thence
A whetstone for their dull intelligence 100
That tears and will not cut, or let them
guess
How Diotima, the wise prophetess,
Instructed the instructor, and why he
Rebuked the infant spirit of melody
On Agathon's sweet lips, which as he spoke
Was as the lovely star when morn has
broke
The roof of darkness, in the golden dawn,
Half-hidden, and yet beautiful.

I 'll pawn
My hopes of Heaven — you know what
they are worth —
That the presumptuous pedagogues of
Earth,   110
If they could tell the riddle offered here
Would scorn to be, or, being, to appear
What now they seem and are — but let
them chide,
They have few pleasures in the world beside;
Perhaps we should be dull were we not
chidden;
Paradise fruits are sweetest when forbidden.
Folly can season Wisdom, Hatred Love.

.   .   .   .

Farewell, if it can be to say farewell
To those who —

I will not, as most dedicators do,   120
Assure myself and all the world and you,
That you are faultless — would to God they
   were
Who taunt me with your love! I then
   should wear
These heavy chains of life with a light
   spirit,
And would to God I were, or even as near
   it
As you, dear heart. Alas! what are we?
   Clouds
Driven by the wind in warring multi-
   tudes,
Which rain into the bosom of the earth,
And rise again, and in our death and birth,
And through our restless life, take as from
   heaven   130
Hues which are not our own, but which are
   given,
And then withdrawn, and with inconstant
   glance
Flash from the spirit to the countenance.
There is a Power, a Love, a Joy, a God,
Which makes in mortal hearts its brief
   abode,
A Pythian exhalation, which inspires
Love, only love — a wind which o'er the
   wires
Of the soul's giant harp —
There is a mood which language faints be-
   neath;
You feel it striding, as Almighty Death 140
His bloodless steed.

   .   .   .   .   .   .

And what is that most brief and bright de-
   light
Which rushes through the touch and
   through the sight,
And stands before the spirit's inmost throne,
A naked Seraph? None hath ever known.
Its birth is darkness, and its growth desire;
Untamable and fleet and fierce as fire,
Not to be touched but to be felt alone,
It fills the world with glory — and is gone.

   .   .   .   .   .   .

It floats with rainbow pinions o'er the
   stream   150
Of life, which flows, like a   dream
Into the light of morning, to the grave
As to an ocean.

   .   .   .   .   .   .

What is that joy which serene infancy
Perceives not, as the hours content them
   by,
Each in a chain of blossoms, yet enjoys
The shapes of this new world, in giant toys
Wrought by the busy   ever new?
Remembrance borrows Fancy's glass, to
   show
These forms more   sincere 160
Than now they are, than then, perhaps,
   they were.
When everything familiar seemed to be
Wonderful, and the immortality
Of this great world, which all things must
   inherit,
Was felt as one with the awakening spirit,
Unconscious of itself, and of the strange
Distinctions which in its proceeding change
It feels and knows, and mourns as if each
   were
A desolation.

   .   .   .   .   .   .

Were it not a sweet refuge, Emily,   170
For all those exiles from the dull insane
Who vex this pleasant world with pride
   and pain,
For all that band of sister-spirits known
To one another by a voiceless tone?

LINES WRITTEN FOR ADONAIS

Published by Garnett, 1862, who furnishes the
following note: 'Several cancelled passages of
the *Adonais* have been met with in Shelley's
notebooks. He appears to have originally
framed his conception on a larger scale than he
eventually found practicable. The passage in
which the contemporary minstrels are introduced, as mourning for Adonais, would have
been considerably extended, and the characteristics of each delineated at some length. It
must, however, have occurred to him that the
parenthesis would be too long, and would tend
to distract the reader's attention from the main
subject. Nothing, therefore, of the original
draft was allowed to subsist but the four incomparable stanzas descriptive of himself. A
fifth was cancelled, which ran as follows [first
fragment]. Several stanzas relating to Byron
and Moore are too imperfect for publication.
The following refers to the latter [second frag-
ment]. Leigh Hunt was thus described [third
fragment]. The following lines were also
written for the *Adonais* [remaining frag-
ments].' Forman conjectures that Coleridge
is described in the last fragment.

AND ever as he went he swept a lyre
Of unaccustomed shape, and   strings
Now like the   of impetuous fire,
Which shakes the forest with its mur-
    murings,
Now like the rush of the aërial wings
Of the enamoured wind among the treen,
Whispering unimaginable things,
And dying on the streams of dew serene,
Which feed the unmown meads with ever-
    during green.

.   .   .   .

And the green Paradise which western
    waves
Embosom in their ever wailing sweep,
Talking of freedom to their tongueless
    caves,
Or to the spirits which within them
    keep
A record of the wrongs which, though
    they sleep,
Die not, but dream of retribution, heard
His hymns, and echoing them from steep
    to steep,
Kept —

.   .   .   .

And then came one of sweet and earnest
    looks,
Whose soft smiles to his dark and night-
    like eyes
Were as the clear and ever living brooks
Are to the obscure fountains whence they
    rise,
Showing how pure they are: a Paradise
Of happy truth upon his forehead low
Lay, making wisdom lovely, in the guise
Of earth-awakening morn upon the brow
Of star-deserted heaven, while ocean
    gleams below.

His song, though very sweet, was low and
    faint,
A simple strain —

.   .   .   .

A mighty Phantasm, half concealed
In darkness of his own exceeding light,
Which clothed his awful presence unre-
    vealed,
Charioted on the   night
Of thunder-smoke, whose skirts were chrys-
    olite.

And like a sudden meteor, which outstrips
The splendor-wingèd chariot of the sun,
                                        eclipse

The armies of the golden stars, each one
Pavilioned in its tent of light — all strewn
Over the chasms of blue night —

LINES WRITTEN FOR HELLAS

Published by Garnett, 1862, who conjectures
the title.

I

FAIREST of the Destinies,
Disarray thy dazzling eyes:
Keener far thy lightnings are
    Than the wingèd [bolts] thou bear-
    est,
    And the smile thou wearest
Wraps thee as a star
    Is wrapped in light.

II

Could Arethuse to her forsaken urn
From Alpheus and the bitter Doris run,
    Or could the morning shafts of purest
    light
Again into the quivers of the Sun
    Be gathered — could one thought from
    its wild flight
Return into the temple of the brain
    Without a change, without a stain, —
    Could aught that is, ever again
    Be what it once has ceased to be,
        Greece might again be free !

III

A star has fallen upon the earth
'Mid the benighted nations,
    A quenchless atom of immortal light,
    A living spark of Night,
A cresset shaken from the constellations.
    Swifter than the thunder fell
    To the heart of Earth, the well
    Where its pulses flow and beat,
    And unextinct in that cold source
    Burns, and on   course
    Guides the sphere which is its prison,
    Like an angelic spirit pent
    In a form of mortal birth,
    Till, as a spirit half arisen
    Shatters its charnel, it has rent,
    In the rapture of its mirth,
The thin and painted garment of the
    Earth,
    Ruining its chaos — a fierce breath
Consuming all its forms of living death.

THE PINE FOREST OF THE CASCINE NEAR PISA

FIRST DRAFT OF 'TO JANE: THE INVI-
TATION, THE RECOLLECTION'

Date 1821. Published by Mrs. Shelley, 1824.

DEAREST, best and brightest,
    Come away,
To the woods and to the fields !
Dearer than this fairest day
Which, like thee to those in sorrow,
Comes to bid a sweet good-morrow
To the rough Year just awake
In its cradle in the brake.

The eldest of the hours of Spring,
Into the winter wandering,   10
Looks upon the leafless wood;
And the banks all bare and rude
Found, it seems, this halcyon Morn
In February's bosom born,
Bending from Heaven, in azure mirth,
Kissed the cold forehead of the Earth,
And smiled upon the silent sea,
And bade the frozen streams be free;
And waked to music all the fountains,
And breathed upon the rigid mountains, 20
And made the wintry world appear
Like one on whom thou smilest, dear.
Radiant Sister of the Day,
Awake ! arise ! and come away !
To the wild woods and the plains,
To the pools where winter rains
Image all the roof of leaves,
Where the pine its garland weaves
Sapless, gray, and ivy dun
Round stems that never kiss the sun — 30
To the sandhills of the sea,
Where the earliest violets be.

Now the last day of many days,
All beautiful and bright as thou,
The loveliest and the last, is dead,
Rise, Memory, and write its praise !
And do thy wonted work and trace
The epitaph of glory fled;
For now the Earth has changed its face,
A frown is on the Heaven's brow.   40

We wandered to the Pine Forest
    That skirts the Ocean's foam,
The lightest wind was in its nest,
    The tempest in its home.

The whispering waves were half asleep,
    The clouds were gone to play,
And on the woods, and on the deep,
    The smile of Heaven lay.

It seemed as if the day were one
    Sent from beyond the skies,   50
Which shed to earth above the sun
    A light of Paradise.

We paused amid the pines that stood
    The giants of the waste,
Tortured by storms to shapes as rude
    With stems like serpents interlaced.

How calm it was — the silence there
    By such a chain was bound
That even the busy woodpecker
    Made stiller by her sound   60

The inviolable quietness;
    The breath of peace we drew
With its soft motion made not less
    The calm that round us grew.

It seemed that from the remotest seat
    Of the white mountain's waste,
To the bright flower beneath our feet,
    A magic circle traced; —

A spirit interfused around,
    A thinking silent life,   70
To momentary peace it bound
    Our mortal nature's strife; —

And still it seemed the centre of
    The magic circle there,
Was one whose being filled with love
    The breathless atmosphere.

Were not the crocuses that grew
    Under that ilex-tree
As beautiful in scent and hue
    As ever fed the bee ?   80

We stood beside the pools that lie
    Under the forest bough,
And each seemed like a sky
    Gulfed in a world below;

A purple firmament of light,
    Which in the dark earth lay,
More boundless than the depth of night,
    And clearer than the day —

In which the massy forests grew
As in the upper air,   90
More perfect both in shape and hue
Than any waving there.

Like one beloved the scene had lent
To the dark water's breast
Its every leaf and lineament
With that clear truth expressed;

There lay far glades and neighboring lawn,
And through the dark green crowd
The white sun twinkling like the dawn
Under a speckled cloud.   100

Sweet views, which in our world above
Can never well be seen,
Were imaged by the water's love
Of that fair forest green.

And all was interfused beneath
Within an Elysium air
An atmosphere without a breath,
A silence sleeping there.

Until a wandering wind crept by,
Like an unwelcome thought,   110
Which from my mind's too faithful eye
Blots thy bright image out.

For thou art good and dear and kind,
The forest ever green,
But less of peace in S———'s mind,
Than calm in waters seen.

ORPHEUS

Date, 1820. Published by Garnett, 1862, and
revised and enlarged by Rossetti, 1870. Garnett adds the following note: 'No trace of
this poem appears in Shelley's notebooks; it
exists only in a transcript by Mrs. Shelley, who
has written, in playful allusion to her toils as
an amanuensis, "*Aspetto fin che il diluvio cala, ed
allora cerco di posare argine alle sue parole.*" "I
await the descent of the flood, and then I endeavor to embank the words." From this circumstance, as well as from the internal evidence of the piece, I should conjecture that it
was an attempt at improvisation. Shelley had
several times heard Sgricci, the renowned *im-
provvisatore*, in the winter of 1820, and this may
have inspired him with the idea of attempting
a similar feat. Assuredly this poem, though
containing many felicitous passages, hardly at-
tains his usual standard, either of thought or

expression. It *may* be a translation from the
Italian.'

A

Not far from hence. From yonder pointed
hill,
Crowned with a ring of oaks, you may be-
hold
A dark and barren field, through which
there flows,
Sluggish and black, a deep but narrow
stream,
Which the wind ripples not, and the fair
moon
Gazes in vain, and finds no mirror there.
Follow the herbless banks of that strange
brook
Until you pause beside a darksome pond,
The fountain of this rivulet, whose gush
Cannot be seen, hid by a rayless night   10
That lives beneath the overhanging rock
That shades the pool — an endless spring
of gloom,
Upon whose edge hovers the tender light,
Trembling to mingle with its paramour, —
But, as Syrinx fled Pan, so night flies day,
Or, with most sullen and regardless hate,
Refuses stern her heaven-born embrace.
On one side of this jagged and shapeless
hill
There is a cave, from which there eddies up
A pale mist, like aërial gossamer,   20
Whose breath destroys all life; awhile it
veils
The rock; then, scattered by the wind, it
flies
Along the stream, or lingers on the clefts,
Killing the sleepy worms, if aught bide
there.
Upon the beetling edge of that dark rock
There stands a group of cypresses; not such
As, with a graceful spire and stirring life,
Pierce the pure heaven of your native vale,
Whose branches the air plays among, but
not   29
Disturbs, fearing to spoil their solemn grace;
But blasted and all wearily they stand,
One to another clinging; their weak boughs
Sigh as the wind buffets them, and they
shake
Beneath its blasts — a weather-beaten crew!

CHORUS

What wondrous sound is that, mournful
and faint,

But more melodious than the murmuring
　　wind
Which through the columns of a temple
　　glides ?

A

It is the wandering voice of Orpheus' lyre,
Borne by the winds, who sigh that their
　　rude king
Hurries them fast from these air-feeding
　　notes;
But in their speed they bear along with　40
　　them
The waning sound, scattering it like dew
Upon the startled sense.

CHORUS

　　　　　　　　Does he still sing ?
Methought he rashly cast away his harp
When he had lost Eurydice.

A

　　　　　　　　　　Ah no !
Awhile he paused. — As a poor hunted
　　stag
A moment shudders on the fearful brink
Of a swift stream — the cruel hounds press
　　on
With deafening yell, the arrows glance and
　　wound, —
He plunges in: so Orpheus, seized and
　　torn　　　　　　　　　　　　50
By the sharp fangs of an insatiate grief,
Mænad-like waved his lyre in the bright
　　air,
And wildly shrieked, 'Where she is, it is
　　dark !'
And then he struck from forth the strings
　　a sound
Of deep and fearful melody.　Alas !
In times long past, when fair Eurydice
With her bright eyes sat listening by his
　　side,
He gently sang of high and heavenly
　　themes.
As in a brook, fretted with little waves,
By the light airs of spring, each riplet
　　makes　　　　　　　　　　　60
A many-sided mirror for the sun,
While it flows musically through green
　　banks,
Ceaseless and pauseless, ever clear and
　　fresh,
So flowed his song, reflecting the deep joy
And tender love that fed those sweetest
　　notes,

The heavenly offspring of ambrosial food.
But that is past.　Returning from drear
　　Hell,
He chose a lonely seat of unhewn stone,
Blackened with lichens, on a herbless plain.
Then from the deep and overflowing spring
Of his eternal, ever-moving grief　　　71
There rose to Heaven a sound of angry
　　song.
'T is as a mighty cataract that parts
Two sister rocks with waters swift and
　　strong,
And casts itself with horrid roar and din
Adown a steep; from a perennial source
It ever flows and falls, and breaks the air
With loud and fierce, but most harmonious
　　roar,
And as it falls casts up a vaporous spray 79
Which the sun clothes in hues of Iris light.
Thus the tempestuous torrent of his grief
Is clothed in sweetest sounds and varying
　　words
Of poesy.　Unlike all human works
It never slackens, and through every
　　change
Wisdom and beauty and the power divine
Of mighty poesy together dwell,
Mingling in sweet accord.　As I have seen
A fierce south blast tear through the dark-
　　ened sky,
Driving along a rack of wingèd clouds,　89
Which may not pause, but ever hurry on,
As their wild shepherd wills them, while
　　the stars,
Twinkling and dim, peep from between the
　　plumes.
Anon the sky is cleared, and the high dome
Of serene Heaven, starred with fiery flow-
　　ers,
Shuts in the shaken earth; or the still
　　moon
Swiftly, yet gracefully, begins her walk,
Rising all bright behind the eastern hills.
I talk of moon, and wind, and stars, and
　　not
Of song; but, would I echo his high song,
Nature must lend me words ne'er used be-
　　fore,　　　　　　　　　　　　100
Or I must borrow from her perfect works,
To picture forth his perfect attributes.
He does no longer sit upon his throne
Of rock upon a desert herbless plain,
For the evergreen and knotted ilexes,
And cypresses that seldom wave their
　　boughs,

And sea-green olives with their grateful
    fruit,
And elms dragging along the twisted vines,
Which drop their berries as they follow
    fast,
And blackthorn bushes with their infant
    race   110
Of blushing rose blooms; beeches, to lovers
    dear,
And weeping willow trees; all swift or slow,
As their huge boughs or lighter dress per-
    mit,
Have circled in his throne; and Earth her-
    self
Has sent from her maternal breast a growth
Of starlike flowers and herbs of odors
    sweet,
To pave the temple that his poesy
Has framed, while near his feet grim lions
    couch,
And kids, fearless from love, creep near
    his lair.
Even the blind worms seem to feel the
    sound.   120
The birds are silent, hanging down their
    heads,
Perched on the lowest branches of the
    trees;
Not even the nightingale intrudes a note
In rivalry, but all entranced she listens.

FIORDISPINA

Date, 1820. Published in part by Mrs.
Shelley, 1824, and the remainder by Garnett,
1862, who adds a note : ' *Fiordispina* and the
piece which I have ventured to entitle *To His
Genius* (using the latter word in the sense of
δαίμων) may be regarded as preliminary,
though unconscious studies, for this crowning
work [*Epipsychidion*]. This is indicated by
the general similarity among the three, as
well as by the fact that very many lines now
found in *Epipsychidion* have been transferred
to it from the others. Most of these have been
omitted from the poem as now published ; but
some instances will be observed in the second,
which was probably the earlier in point of date.
Fiordispina seems to have been written during
the first days of Shelley's acquaintance with
Emilia Viviani, who is also the *Ginevra* of the
poem thus entitled.'

THE season was the childhood of sweet
    June,
Whose sunny hours from morning until
    noon

Went creeping through the day with silent
    feet,
Each with its load of pleasure, slow yet
    sweet;
Like the long years of blest Eternity
Never to be developed. Joy to thee,
Fiordispina, and thy Cosimo,
For thou the wonders of the depth canst
    know
Of this unfathomable flood of hours,
Sparkling beneath the heaven which em-
    bowers —   10
.   .   .   .
They were two cousins, almost like two
    twins,
Except that from the catalogue of sins
Nature had rased their love — which could
    not be
But by dissevering their nativity.
And so they grew together like two flowers
Upon one stem, which the same beams and
    showers
Lull or awaken in their purple prime,
Which the same hand will gather, the same
    clime
Shake with decay. This fair day smiles to
    see
All those who love — and who e'er loved
    like thee,   20
Fiordispina ? Scarcely Cosimo,
Within whose bosom and whose brain now
    glow
The ardors of a vision which obscure
The very idol of its portraiture.
He faints, dissolved into a sea of love;
But thou art as a planet sphered above ;
But thou art Love itself — ruling the
    motion
Of his subjected spirit; such emotion
Must end in sin or sorrow, if sweet May
Had not brought forth this morn, your wed-
    ding-day.   30
.   .   .   .
' Lie there; sleep awhile in your own dew,
Ye faint-eyed children of the   Hours,'
Fiordispina said, and threw the flowers
Which she had from the breathing —
.   .   .   .
A table near of polished porphyry.
They seemed to wear a beauty from the
    eye
That looked on them, a fragrance from the
    touch
Whose warmth   checked their life; a
    light such

As sleepers wear, lulled by the voice they
   love,
             which did reprove   40
The childish pity that she felt for them,
And a   remorse that from their stem
She had divided such fair shapes   made
A feeling in the   which was a shade
Of gentle beauty on the flowers; there lay
All gems that make the earth's dark bosom
   gay.
     rods of myrtle-buds and lemon-blooms,
And that leaf tinted lightly which assumes
The livery of unremembered snow —
Violets whose eyes have drunk —   50
   .   .   .   .   .   .
Fiordispina and her nurse are now
Upon the steps of the high portico;
Under the withered arm of Media
She flings her glowing arm
   .   .   .   .   .   .
             step by step and stair by stair,
That withered woman, gray and white and
   brown —
More like a trunk by lichens overgrown
Than anything which once could have been
   human.
And ever as she goes the palsied woman
   .   .   .   .   .   .
'How slow and painfully you seem to
   walk,
                           60
Poor Media ! you tire yourself with talk.'
             ' And well it may,
Fiordispina, dearest — well-a-day !
You are hastening to a marriage-bed;
I to the grave ! ' — ' And if my love were
   dead,
Unless my heart deceives me, I would lie
Beside him in my shroud as willingly
As now in the gay night-dress Lilla
   wrought.'
'Fie, child ! Let that unseasonable thought
Not be remembered till it snows in June; 70
Such fancies are a music out of tune
With the sweet dance your heart must keep
   to-night.
What ! would you take all beauty and de-
   light
Back to the Paradise from which you
   sprung,
And leave to grosser mortals ? —
And say, sweet lamb, would you not learn
   the sweet
And subtle mystery by which spirits meet ?
Who knows whether the loving game is
   played,

When, once of mortal [venture] disarrayed,
The naked soul goes wandering here and
   there   80
Through the wide deserts of Elysian air ?
The violet dies not till it ' —

THE BIRTH OF PLEASURE

Date, 1819.   Published by Garnett, 1862.

At the creation of the Earth
Pleasure, that divinest birth,
From the soil of Heaven did rise,
Wrapped in sweet wild melodies —
Like an exhalation wreathing
To the sound of air low-breathing
Through Æolian pines, which make
A shade and shelter to the lake
Whence it rises soft and slow;
Her life-breathing [limbs] did flow
In the harmony divine
Of an ever-lengthening line
Which enwrapped her perfect form
With a beauty clear and warm.

LOVE, HOPE, DESIRE, AND FEAR

Date, 1821.   Published by Garnett, 1862.

   .   .   .   .   .   .
And many there were hurt by that strong
   boy;
   His name, they said, was Pleasure.
And near him stood, glorious beyond mea-
   sure,
Four Ladies who possess all empery
   In earth and air and sea;
Nothing that lives from their award is
   free.
   Their names will I declare to thee, —
   Love, Hope, Desire, and Fear;
   And they the regents are
Of the four elements that frame the
   heart, —   10
And each diversely exercised her art
   By force or circumstance or sleight
       To prove her dreadful might
       Upon that poor domain.
Desire presented her [false] glass, and then
       The spirit dwelling there
Was spellbound to embrace what seemed
   so fair
       Within that magic mirror;
       And, dazed by that bright error,

It would have scorned the [shafts] of the
    avenger, 20
And death, and penitence, and danger,
    Had not then silent Fear
      Touched with her palsying spear, —
So that, as if a frozen torrent,
    The blood was curdled in its current;
It dared not speak, even in look or motion,
But chained within itself its proud devo-
      tion.
    Between Desire and Fear thou wert
    A wretched thing, poor Heart!
Sad was his life who bore thee in his breast,
    Wild bird for that weak nest. 31
Till Love even from fierce Desire it bought,
And from the very wound of tender thought
Drew solace, and the pity of sweet eyes
Gave strength to bear those gentle agonies,
Surmount the loss, the terror, and the
      sorrow.
    Then Hope approached, she who can
      borrow
For poor to-day from rich to-morrow;
And Fear withdrew, as night when day
Descends upon the orient ray; 40
And after long and vain endurance
The poor heart woke to her assurance.

At one birth these four were born
With the world's forgotten morn,
And from Pleasure still they hold
All it circles, as of old.
When, as summer lures the swallow,
Pleasure lures the heart to follow —
O weak heart of little wit —
The fair hand that wounded it, 50
Seeking, like a panting hare,
Refuge in the lynx's lair, —
    Love, Desire, Hope, and Fear,
      Ever will be near.

A SATIRE ON SATIRE

Date, 1820. Published by Dowden, *Correspondence of Robert Southey and Caroline
Bowles*, 1880. Shelley writes to Hunt: ' I
began once a satire on satire, which I meant
to be very severe; it was full of *small knives*,
in the use of which practice would have soon
made me very expert.'

IF gibbets, axes, confiscations, chains,
And racks of subtle torture, if the pains
Of shame, of fiery Hell's tempestuous wave,
Seen through the caverns of the shadowy
    grave,

Hurling the damned into the murky air
While the meek blest sit smiling; if Despair
And Hate, the rapid bloodhounds with
    which Terror
Hunts through the world the homeless
    steps of Error,
Are the true secrets of the commonweal
To make men wise and just; . . . 10
And not the sophisms of revenge and fear,
Bloodier than is revenge . . .
Then send the priests to every hearth and
    home
To preach the burning wrath which is to
    come,
In words like flakes of sulphur, such as
    thaw
The frozen tears . . .
If Satire's scourge could wake the slum-
    bering hounds
Of Conscience, or erase the deeper wounds,
The leprous scars of callous infamy;
If it could make the present not to be, 20
Or charm the dark past never to have been,
Or turn regret to hope; who that has seen
What Southey is and was, would not ex-
    claim,
Lash on!   be the keen verse dipped
    in flame;
Follow his flight with wingèd words, and
    urge
The strokes of the inexorable scourge
Until the heart be naked, till his soul
See the contagion's spots   foul;
And from the mirror of Truth's sunlike
    shield,
From which his Parthian arrow . . . 30
Flash on his sight the spectres of the past,
Until his mind's eye paint thereon —
Let scorn like   yawn below,
And rain on him like flakes of fiery snow.
This cannot be, it ought not, evil still —
Suffering makes suffering, ill must follow
    ill.
Rough words beget sad thoughts,   and,
    beside,
Men take a sullen and a stupid pride
In being all they hate in others' shame,
By a perverse antipathy of fame. 40
'T is not worth while to prove, as I could,
    how
From the sweet fountains of our Nature
    flow
These bitter waters; I will only say,
If any friend would take Southey some
    day,

And tell him, in a country walk alone,
Softening harsh words with friendship's
    gentle tone,
How incorrect his public conduct is,
And what men think of it, 't were not
    amiss.
Far better than to make innocent ink —

GINEVRA

Date, 1821. Published by Mrs. Shelley,
1824, who gives the source of the story as
L'Osservatore Fiorentino.

WILD, pale, and wonder-stricken, even
    as one
Who staggers forth into the air and sun
From the dark chamber of a mortal fever,
Bewildered, and incapable, and ever
Fancying strange comments in her dizzy
    brain
Of usual shapes, till the familiar train
Of objects and of persons passed like things
Strange as a dreamer's mad imaginings,
Ginevra from the nuptial altar went;
The vows to which her lips had sworn as-
    sent   10
Rung in her brain still with a jarring din,
Deafening the lost intelligence within.

And so she moved under the bridal veil,
Which made the paleness of her cheek
    more pale,
And deepened the faint crimson of her
    mouth,
And darkened her dark locks, as moonlight
    doth, —
And of the gold and jewels glittering there
She scarce felt conscious, but the weary
    glare
Lay like a chaos of unwelcome light,
Vexing the sense with gorgeous undelight.
A moonbeam in the shadow of a cloud   21
Was less heavenly fair — her face was
    bowed,
And as she passed, the diamonds in her hair
Were mirrored in the polished marble stair
Which led from the cathedral to the street;
And even as she went her light fair feet
Erased these images.

The bride-maidens who round her
    thronging came,
Some with a sense of self-rebuke and
    shame,

Envying the unenviable; and others   30
Making the joy which should have been
    another's
Their own by gentle sympathy; and some
Sighing to think of a unhappy home;
Some few admiring what can ever lure
Maidens to leave the heaven serene and
    pure
Of parents' smiles for life's great cheat; a
    thing
Bitter to taste, sweet in imagining.

But they are all dispersed — and lo ! she
    stands
Looking in idle grief on her white hands,
Alone within the garden now her own;   40
And through the sunny air, with jangling
    tone,
The music of the merry marriage-bells,
Killing the azure silence, sinks and
    swells; —
Absorbed like one within a dream who
    dreams
That he is dreaming, until slumber seems
A mockery of itself — when suddenly
Antonio stood before her, pale as she.
With agony, with sorrow, and with pride,
He lifted his wan eyes upon the bride,
And said — 'Is this thy faith ? ' and then
    as one   50
Whose sleeping face is stricken by the
    sun
With light like a harsh voice, which bids
    him rise
And look upon his day of life with eyes
Which weep in vain that they can dream
    no more,
Ginevra saw her lover, and forbore
To shriek or faint, and checked the stifling
    blood
Rushing upon her heart, and unsubdued
Said — ' Friend, if earthly violence or ill,
Suspicion, doubt, or the tyrannic will
Of parents, chance, or custom, time, or
    change,   60
Or circumstance, or terror, or revenge,
Or wildered looks, or words, or evil speech,
With all their stings and venom, can im-
    peach
Our love, — we love not. If the grave,
    which hides
The victim from the tyrant, and divides
The cheek that whitens from the eyes that
    dart
Imperious inquisition to the heart

That is another's, could dissever ours,
We love not.' — ' What ! do not the silent
  hours
Beckon thee to Gherardi's bridal bed ?   70
Is not that ring ' — a pledge, he would have
  said,
Of broken vows, but she with patient look
The golden circle from her finger took,
And said — ' Accept this token of my faith,
The pledge of vows to be absolved by
  death;
And I am dead or shall be soon — my
  knell
Will mix its music with that merry bell;
Does it not sound as if they sweetly said,
" We toll a corpse out of the marriage-
  bed " ?
The flowers upon my bridal chamber
  strewn   80
Will serve unfaded for my bier — so soon
That even the dying violet will not die
Before Ginevra.'   The strong fantasy
Had made her accents weaker and more
  weak,
And quenched the crimson life upon her
  cheek,
And glazed her eyes, and spread an atmo-
  sphere
Round her, which chilled the burning noon
  with fear,
Making her but an image of the thought,
Which, like a prophet or a shadow, brought
News of the terrors of the coming time. 90
Like an accuser branded with the crime
He would have cast on a belovèd friend,
Whose dying eyes reproach not to the end
The pale betrayer — he then with vain re-
  pentance
Would share, he cannot now avert, the
  sentence —
Antonio stood and would have spoken,
  when
The compound voice of women and of
  men
Was heard approaching; he retired, while
  she
Was led amid the admiring company
Back to the palace, — and her maidens
  soon   100
Changed her attire for the afternoon,
And left her at her own request to keep
An hour of quiet and rest. Like one
  asleep
With open eyes and folded hands she lay,
Pale in the light of the declining day.

Meanwhile the day sinks fast, the sun is
  set,
And in the lighted hall the guests are met;
The beautiful looked lovelier in the light
Of love, and admiration, and delight,
Reflected from a thousand hearts and
  eyes   110
Kindling a momentary Paradise.
This crowd is safer than the silent wood,
Where love's own doubts disturb the soli-
  tude;
On frozen hearts the fiery rain of wine
Falls, and the dew of music more divine
Tempers the deep emotions of the time
To spirits cradled in a sunny clime.
How many meet, who never yet have
  met,
To part too soon, but never to forget ?
How many saw the beauty, power, and
  wit   120
Of looks and words which ne'er enchanted
  yet !
But life's familiar veil was now withdrawn.
As the world leaps before an earthquake's
  dawn,
And unprophetic of the coming hours
The matin winds from the expanded flow-
  ers
Scatter their hoarded incense, and awaken
The earth, until the dewy sleep is shaken
From every living heart which it possesses,
Through seas and winds, cities and wilder-
  nesses,
As if the future and the past were all   130
Treasured i' the instant; so Gherardi's hall
Laughed in the mirth of its lord's festi-
  val, —
Till some one asked, ' Where is the Bride ? '
  And then
A bridesmaid went, and ere she came again
A silence fell upon the guests — a pause
Of expectation, as when beauty awes
All hearts with its approach, though unbe-
  held;
Then wonder, and then fear that wonder
  quelled; —
For whispers passed from mouth to ear
  which drew
The color from the hearer's cheeks, and
  flew   140
Louder and swifter round the company;
And then Gherardi entered with an eye
Of ostentatious trouble, and a crowd
Surrounded him, and some were weeping
  loud.

They found Ginevra dead ! if it be death
To lie without motion, or pulse, or breath,
With waxen cheeks, and limbs cold, stiff,
    and white,
And open eyes, whose fixed and glassy
    light
Mocked at the speculation they had owned;
If it be death, when there is felt around 150
A smell of clay, a pale and icy glare,
And silence, and a sense that lifts the hair
From the scalp to the ankles, as it were
Corruption from the spirit passing forth,
And giving all it shrouded to the earth,
And leaving as swift lightning in its flight
Ashes, and smoke, and darkness: in our
    night
Of thought we know thus much of death,
    — no more
Than the unborn dream of our life before
Their barks are wrecked on its inhospitable
    shore. 160

The marriage feast and its solemnity
Was turned to funeral pomp; the company,
With heavy hearts and looks, broke up;
    nor they
Who loved the dead went weeping on their
    way
Alone, but sorrow mixed with sad surprise
Loosened the strings of pity in all eyes,
On which that form, whose fate they weep
    in vain,
Will never, thought they, kindle smiles
    again.
The lamps which, half-extinguished in their
    haste
Gleamed few and faint o'er the abandoned
    feast, 170
Showed as it were within the vaulted room
A cloud of sorrow hanging, as if gloom
Had passed out of men's minds into the
    air.
Some few yet stood around Gherardi there,
Friends and relations of the dead, — and
    he,
A loveless man, accepted torpidly
The consolation that he wanted not;
Awe in the place of grief within him
    wrought.
Their whispers made the solemn silence
    seem
More still — some wept, 180
Some melted into tears without a sob,
And some with hearts that might be heard
    to throb

Leaned on the table, and at intervals
Shuddered to hear through the deserted
    halls
And corridors the thrilling shrieks which
    came
Upon the breeze of night, that shook the
    flame
Of every torch and taper, as it swept
From out the chamber where the women
    kept; —
Their tears fell on the dear companion
    cold
Of pleasures now departed; then was
    knolled 190
The bell of death, and soon the priests ar-
    rived,
And finding death their penitent had
    shrived,
Returned like ravens from a corpse whereon
A vulture has just feasted to the bone.
And then the mourning-women came. —

.   .   .   .

THE DIRGE

Old winter was gone
In his weakness back to the mountains
    hoar,
    And the spring came down
From the planet that hovers upon the shore
    Where the sea of sunlight encroaches 200
On the limits of wintry night; —
If the land, and the air, and the sea,
    Rejoice not when spring approaches,
We did not rejoice in thee,
    Ginevra !

She is still, she is cold
    On the bridal couch.
One step to the white death-bed,
    And one to the bier,
And one to the charnel — and one, oh
    where ? 210
    The dark arrow fled
    In the noon.

Ere the sun through heaven once more has
    rolled,
    The rats in her heart
    Will have made their nest,
And the worms be alive in her golden hair;
While the spirit that guides the sun
Sits throned in his flaming chair,
    She shall sleep.

THE BOAT ON THE SERCHIO

Date, 1821. Published in part by Mrs. Shelley, 1824, and the remainder by Rossetti, 1870. Medwin furnishes the note: 'I have heard Shelley often speak with rapture of the excursions they [Shelley and Williams] made together. The canal fed by the Serchio, of the clearest water, is so rapid that they were obliged to tow the boat up against the current; but the swift descent, through green banks enamelled with flowers and overhung with trees that mirrored themselves on its glassy surface, gave him a wonderful delight. He has left a record of these trips in a poem entitled *The Boat on the Serchio*, and calls Williams and himself *Melchior* and *Lionel*.'

OUR boat is asleep on Serchio's stream,
Its sails are folded like thoughts in a
    dream,
The helm sways idly, hither and thither;
    Dominic, the boatman, has brought the
        mast,
    And the oars, and the sails; but 't is
        sleeping fast
Like a beast, unconscious of its tether.

The stars burned out in the pale blue air,
And the thin white moon lay withering
    there;
To tower, and cavern, and rift, and tree,
The owl and the bat fled drowsily.   10
Day had kindled the dewy woods,
    And the rocks above and the stream be-
        low,
And the vapors in their multitudes,
    And the Apennine's shroud of summer
        snow,
And clothed with light of aëry gold
The mists in their eastern caves uprolled.

Day had awakened all things that be, —
The lark and the thrush and the swallow
    free,
    And the milkmaid's song and mower's
        scythe,   19
And the matin-bell and the mountain bee.
Fire-flies were quenched on the dewy corn;
    Glow-worms went out on the river's
        brim,
    Like lamps which a student forgets to
        trim;
The beetle forgot to wind his horn;
    The crickets were still in the meadow
        and hill;

Like a flock of rooks at a farmer's gun,
Night's dreams and terrors, every one,
Fled from the brains which are their prey
From the lamp's death to the morning ray.

All rose to do the task He set to each, 30
    Who shaped us to his ends and not our
        own;
The million rose to learn, and one to teach
    What none yet ever knew or can be
        known.
        And many rose
    Whose woe was such that fear became
        desire;
Melchior and Lionel were not among those;
They from the throng of men had stepped
    aside,
And made their home under the green
    hillside.
It was that hill, whose intervening brow
    Screens Lucca from the Pisan's envious
        eye,   40
Which the circumfluous plain waving be-
    low,
    Like a wide lake of green fertility,
With streams and fields and marshes bare,
    Divides from the far Apennines, which
        lie
Islanded in the immeasurable air.

'What think you, as she lies in her green
    cove,
Our little sleeping boat is dreaming of?
If morning dreams are true, why I should
    guess
That she was dreaming of our idleness,
And of the miles of watery way   50
We should have led her by this time of
    day.'
                'Never mind,' said Lionel,
'Give care to the winds, they can bear it
    well
About yon poplar tops; and see!
The white clouds are driving merrily,
And the stars we miss this morn will light
More willingly our return to-night.
How it whistles, "Dominic's long black
    hair!
List, my dear fellow, the breeze blows fair;
    Hear how it sings into the air."   60
    — of us and of our lazy motions,'
    Impatiently said Melchior,
'If I can guess a boat's emotions;
    And how we ought, two hours before,
To have been the devil knows where.'

And then, in such transalpine Tuscan
As would have killed a Della-Cruscan,

. . . .

So, Lionel according to his art
  Weaving his idle words, Melchior said:
' She dreams that we are not yet out of
    bed ;   70
We 'll put a soul into her, and a heart
Which like a dove chased by a dove shall
    beat.'

. . . .

  ' Ay, heave the ballast overboard,
  And stow the eatables in the aft locker.'
' Would not this keg be best a little low-
    ered ? '
' No, now all 's right.' ' Those bottles of
    warm tea —
(Give me some straw) — must be stowed
    tenderly ;
Such as we used, in summer after six,
To cram in great-coat pockets, and to
    mix
Hard eggs and radishes and rolls at Eton, 80
And, couched on stolen hay in those green
    harbors
Farmers called gaps, and we schoolboys
    called arbors,
Would feast till eight.'

. . . .

  With a bottle in one hand,
  As if his very soul were at a stand,
Lionel stood, when Melchior brought him
    steady, —
' Sit at the helm — fasten this sheet — all
    ready ! '

The chain is loosed, the sails are spread,
  The living breath is fresh behind,
As with dews and sunrise fed   90
  Comes the laughing morning wind.
The sails are full, the boat makes head
Against the Serchio's torrent fierce,
Then flags with intermitting course,
  And hangs upon the wave, and stems
  The tempest of the
Which fervid from its mountain source
Shallow, smooth, and strong, doth come, —
Swift as fire, tempestuously
It sweeps into the affrighted sea ;   100
  In morning's smile its eddies coil,
  Its billows sparkle, toss, and boil,
  Torturing all its quiet light
  Into columns fierce and bright.

              The Serchio, twisting forth
Between the marble barriers which it clove
  At Ripafratta, leads through the dread
    chasm
The wave that died the death which lovers
    love,
  Living in what it sought ; as if this spasm
Had not yet passed, the toppling mountains
    cling,   110
But the clear stream in full enthusiasm
Pours itself on the plain, then wandering,
  Down one clear path of effluence crystal-
    line
Sends its superfluous waves, that they may
    fling
At Arno's feet tribute of corn and wine ;
Then, through the pestilential deserts wild
  Of tangled marsh and woods of stunted
    pine,
It rushes to the Ocean.

THE ZUCCA

Date, January, 1822. Published by Mrs.
Shelley, 1824.

I

SUMMER was dead and Autumn was expir-
    ing,
  And infant Winter laughed upon the land
All cloudlessly and cold ; when I, desiring
  More in this world than any understand,
Wept o'er the beauty, which, like sea re-
    tiring,
  Had left the earth bare as the wave-worn
    sand
Of my lorn heart, and o'er the grass and
    flowers
Pale for the falsehood of the flattering hours.

II

Summer was dead, but I yet lived to weep
  The instability of all but weeping ;
And on the earth lulled in her winter sleep
  I woke, and envied her as she was sleep-
    ing.
Too happy Earth ! over thy face shall creep
  The wakening vernal airs, until thou,
    leaping
From unremembered dreams shalt   see
No death divide thy immortality.

III

I loved — oh, no, I mean not one of ye,
  Or any earthly one, though ye are dear

As human heart to human heart may be;
  I loved I know not what — but this low
    sphere,
And all that it contains, contains not thee,
  Thou, whom, seen nowhere, I feel every-
    where.
From heaven and earth, and all that in
    them are
Veiled art thou like a   star.

IV

By Heaven and Earth, from all whose
    shapes thou flowest,
  Neither to be contained, delayed, nor
    hidden;
Making divine the loftiest and the lowest,
  When for a moment thou art not for-
    bidden
To live within the life which thou bestow-
    est;
  And leaving noblest things vacant and
    chidden,
Cold as a corpse after the spirit's flight,
Blank as the sun after the birth of night.

V

In winds, and trees, and streams, and all
    things common,
  In music, and the sweet unconscious
    tone
Of animals, and voices which are human,
  Meant to express some feelings of their
    own;
In the soft motions and rare smile of wo-
    man,
  In flowers and leaves, and in the grass
    fresh shown
Or dying in the autumn, — I the most
Adore thee present, or lament thee lost.

VI

And thus I went lamenting, when I saw
  A plant upon the river's margin lie,
Like one who loved beyond his nature's
    law,
  And in despair had cast him down to
    die;
Its leaves which had outlived the frost, the
    thaw
  Had blighted, like a heart which hatred's
    eye
Can blast not, but which pity kills; the
    dew
Lay on its spotted leaves like tears too
    true.

VII

The Heavens had wept upon it, but the
    Earth
  Had crushed it on her unmaternal breast.
. . . .

VIII

I bore it to my chamber and I planted
  It in a vase full of the lightest mould;
The winter beams which out of Heaven
    slanted
  Fell through the window panes, disrobed
    of cold,
Upon its leaves and flowers; the star which
    panted
  In evening for the Day, whose car has
    rolled
Over the horizon's wave, with looks of light
Smiled on it from the threshold of the
    night.

IX

The mitigated influences of air
  And light revived the plant, and from it
    grew
Strong leaves and tendrils, and its flowers
    fair,
  Full as a cup with the vine's burning dew,
O'erflowed with golden colors; an atmo-
    sphere
  Of vital warmth enfolded it anew,
And every impulse sent to every part
The unbeheld pulsations of its heart.

X

Well might the plant grow beautiful and
    strong,
  Even if the air and sun had smiled not
    on it;
For one wept o'er it all the winter long
  Tears pure as Heaven's rain, which fell
    upon it
Hour after hour; for sounds of softest
    song,
  Mixed with the stringèd melodies that
    won it
To leave the gentle lips on which it slept,
Had loosed the heart of him who sat and
    wept.

XI

Had loosed his heart, and shook the leaves
    and flowers
  On which he wept, the while the savage
    storm

Waked by the darkest of December's hours
　　Was raving round the chamber hushed
　　　　and warm;
The birds were shivering in their leafless
　　　　bowers,
　　The fish were frozen in the pools, the
　　　　form
Of every summer plant was dead
Whilst this

LINES

Date, 1822. Published by Garnett, 1862.

I

WE meet not as we parted,
　　We feel more than all may see;
My bosom is heavy-hearted,
　　And thine full of doubt for me.
　　One moment has bound the free.

II

That moment is gone forever,
　　Like lightning that flashed and died,
Like a snowflake upon the river,
　　Like a sunbeam upon the tide,
　　Which the dark shadows hide.

III

That moment from time was singled
　　As the first of a life of pain;
The cup of its joy was mingled —
　　Delusion too sweet though vain !
　　Too sweet to be mine again.

IV

Sweet lips, could my heart have hidden
　　That its life was crushed by you,
Ye would not have then forbidden
　　The death which a heart so true
　　Sought in your briny dew.

V

Methinks too little cost
For a moment so found, so lost !

CHARLES THE FIRST

Shelley had the subject of Charles the First
in mind for a tragedy as early as 1818, and desired Mrs. Shelley to attempt it. He had begun to think of it for himself in the summer of
1820 and wrote to Medwin : ' What think you
of my boldness ? I mean to write a play, in
the spirit of human nature, without prejudice
or passion, entitled *Charles the First*. So vanity intoxicates people ; but let those few who
praise my verses, and in whose approbation I
take so much delight, answer for the sin.'

Later, he wrote to Ollier : ' I doubt about
Charles the First ; but, if I do write it, it shall
be the birth of severe and high feelings. You
are very welcome to it, on the terms you mention, and, when once I see and feel that I can
write it, it is already written. My thoughts
aspire to a production of a far higher character ; but the execution of it will require
some years. I write what I write chiefly to
enquire, by the reception which my writings
meet with, how far I am fit for so great a task,
or not.'

By the summer of 1821 he had done some
shaping-out thought on it, and in September
wrote again to Ollier : ' *Charles the First* is
conceived, but not born. Unless I am sure of
making something good, the play will not
be written. Pride, that ruined Satan, will kill
Charles the First, for his midwife would be
only *less than him whom thunder has made
greater*. I am full of great plans ; and if I
should tell you them, I should add to the list
of these riddles.'

He began seriously upon it about January 1,
1822, and wrote to Ollier it would be ready by
spring, saying that it ' promises to be good, as
tragedies go,' and that it ' is not colored by
the party-spirit of the author ; ' to Hunt he
confided his hope that it would ' hold a higher
rank than *The Cenci* as a work of art.' He
apparently soon discontinued the work, and in
answer to Hunt wrote, in March : ' So you
think I can make nothing of Charles the First.
Tanto peggio. Indeed, I have written nothing
for this last two months : a slight circumstance
gave a new train to my ideas, and shattered
the fragile edifice when half built. What
motives have I to write ? I *had* motives, and
I thank the God of my own heart they were
totally different from those of the other apes of
humanity who make mouths in the glass of the
time. But what are *those* motives now ? The
only inspiration of an ordinary kind I could descend to acknowledge would be the earning
£100 for you ; and that it seems I cannot.' In
the same strain he wrote in April to Gisborne :
' I have done some of *Charles the First ;* but although the poetry succeeded very well, I cannot seize on the conception of the subject as a
whole, and seldom now touch the canvas ; ' and
again, in June : ' I write little now. It is impossible to compose except under the strong
excitement of an assurance of finding sympathy
in what you write. Imagine Demosthenes re-
citing a Philippic to the waves of the Atlantic.
Lord Byron is in this respect fortunate. He
touched the chord to which a million hearts

responded, and the coarse music which he produced to please them, disciplined him to the perfection to which he now approaches. I do not go on with *Charles the First.* I feel too little certainty of the future, and too little satisfaction with regard to the past to undertake any subject seriously and deeply. I stand, as it were, upon a precipice, which I have ascended with great, and cannot descend without greater peril, and I am content if the heaven above me is calm for the passing moment.'

Medwin adds some details: 'I must now speak of his *Charles the First.* He had designed to write a tragedy on this ungrateful subject as far back as 1818, and had begun it at the end of the following year, when he asked me to obtain for him that well-known pamphlet, which was in my father's library — *Killing no Murder.* He was, however, *in limine,* diverted at that time to more attractive subjects, and now resumed his abandoned labors, of which he has left a very unsatisfactory, though valuable, *bozzo.* The task seemed to him an irksome one. His progress was slow; one day he expunged what he had written the day before. He occasionally showed and read to me his MS., which was lined and interlined and interworded, so as to render it almost illegible. The scenes were disconnected, and intended to be interwoven in the tissue of the drama. He did not thus compose *The Cenci.* He seemed tangled in an inextricable web of difficulties, as to the treatment of his subject; and it was clear that he had formed no definite plan in his own mind, how to connect the links of the complicated yarn of events that led to that frightful catastrophe, or to justify it. . . . Shelley meant to have made the last of King's fools, Archy, a more than subordinate among his *dramatis personæ,* as Calderon had done in his *Cisma de l'Inglaterra,* a fool *sui generis,* who talks in fable, "weaving a world of mirth out of the wreck of all around." . . . Other causes, besides doubt as to the manner of treating the subject, operated to impede its progress. The ever-growing fastidiousness of his taste had, I have often thought, begun to cramp his genius. The opinion of the world, too, at times shook his confidence in himself. I have often been shown the scenes of this tragedy in which he was engaged; like the MSS. of Tasso's *Gerusalemme Liberata,* in the library at Ferrara, his were larded with word on word, till they were scarcely decipherable.'

Mrs. Shelley writes: 'Whether the subject proved more difficult than he anticipated, or whether in fact he could not bend his mind away from the broodings and wanderings of thought divested from human interest, which

he best loved, I cannot tell; but he proceeded slowly, and threw it aside for one of the most mystical of his poems, *The Triumph of Life,* on which he was employed at the last.'

The fragment was published in part by Mrs. Shelley, 1824, and the remainder by Rossetti, 1870.

CHARLES THE FIRST

DRAMATIS PERSONÆ

KING CHARLES I.
QUEEN HENRIETTA.
LAUD, Archbishop of Canterbury.
WENTWORTH, Earl of Strafford.
LORD COTTINGTON.
LORD WESTON.
LORD COVENTRY.
WILLIAMS, Bishop of Lincoln.
Secretary LYTTELTON.

JUXON.
ST. JOHN.
ARCHY, the Court Fool.
HAMPDEN.
PYM.
CROMWELL.
CROMWELL'S DAUGHTER.
SIR HARRY VANE the younger.
LEIGHTON.
BASTWICK.
PRYNNE.

Gentlemen of the Inns of Court, Citizens, Pursuivants, Marshalsmen, Law Students, Judges, Clerk.

SCENE I. — *The Masque of the Inns of Court.*

A PURSUIVANT

PLACE for the Marshal of the Masque!

FIRST CITIZEN

What thinkest thou of this quaint masque which turns,
Like morning from the shadow of the night,
The night to day, and London to a place
Of peace and joy?

SECOND CITIZEN

And Hell to Heaven.
Eight years are gone,
And they seem hours, since in this populous street
I trod on grass made green by summer's rain;
For the red plague kept state within that palace
Where now that vanity reigns. In nine years more   10
The roots will be refreshed with civil blood;
And thank the mercy of insulted Heaven
That sin and wrongs wound, as an orphan's cry,
The patience of the great Avenger's ear.

A YOUTH

Yet, father, 't is a happy sight to see,
Beautiful, innocent, and unforbidden

By God or man. 'T is like the bright pro-
cession
Of skyey visions in a solemn dream
From which men wake as from a paradise,
And draw new strength to tread the thorns
of life.   20
If God be good, wherefore should this be
evil ?
And if this be not evil, dost thou not draw
Unseasonable poison from the flowers
Which bloom so rarely in this barren
world ?
Oh, kill these bitter thoughts which make
the present
Dark as the future ! —

.   .   .   .

When Avarice and Tyranny, vigilant Fear
And open-eyed Conspiracy, lie sleeping
As on Hell's threshold; and all gentle
thoughts
Waken to worship Him who giveth joys 30
With his own gift.

SECOND CITIZEN

How young art thou in this old age of
time !
How green in this gray world ! Canst thou
discern
The signs of seasons, yet perceive no hint
Of change in that stage-scene in which
thou art
Not a spectator but an actor ? or
Art thou a puppet moved by [enginery ?]
The day that dawns in fire will die in
storms,
Even though the noon be calm. My
travel 's done, —
Before the whirlwind wakes I shall have
found   40
My inn of lasting rest; but thou must
still
Be journeying on in this inclement air.
Wrap thy old cloak about thy back;
Nor leave the broad and plain and beaten
road,
Although no flowers smile on the trodden
dust,
For the violet paths of pleasure. This
Charles the First
Rose like the equinoctial sun, . . .
By vapors, through whose threatening omi-
nous veil
Darting his altered influence he has gained
This height of noon — from which he must
decline   50

Amid the darkness of conflicting storms,
To dank extinction and to latest night . . .
                        There goes
The apostate Strafford; he whose titles . . .
                whispered aphorisms
From Machiavel and Bacon; and, if Judas
Had been as brazen and as bold as he . . .

FIRST CITIZEN
                                    That
Is the Archbishop.

SECOND CITIZEN
                Rather say the Pope:
London will be soon his Rome. He walks
As if he trod upon the heads of men.   61
He looks elate, drunken with blood and
gold.
Beside him moves the Babylonian woman
Invisibly, and with her as with his shadow,
Mitred adulterer ! he is joined in sin,
Which turns Heaven's milk of mercy to
revenge.

THIRD CITIZEN (*lifting up his eyes*)
Good Lord ! rain it down upon him ! . . .
Amid her ladies walks the papist queen,
As if her nice feet scorned our English
earth.
The Canaanitish Jezebel ! I would be 70
A dog if I might tear her with my teeth !
There 's old Sir Henry Vane, the Earl of
Pembroke,
Lord Essex, and Lord Keeper Coventry,
And others who made base their English
breed
By vile participation of their honors
With papists, atheists, tyrants, and apos-
tates.
When lawyers masque 't is time for honest
men
To strip the vizor from their purposes.
A seasonable time for masquers this !
When Englishmen and Protestants should
sit   80
        dust on their dishonored heads,
To avert the wrath of Him whose scourge
is felt
For the great sins which have drawn down
from Heaven
                and foreign overthrow.
The remnant of the martyred saints in
Rochefort
Have been abandoned by their faithless
allies

To that idolatrous and adulterous torturer
Lewis of France, — the Palatinate is
lost. . . .

Enter LEIGHTON (*who has been branded in the
face*) *and* BASTWICK

Canst thou be — art thou . . . ?

LEIGHTON
I *was* Leighton: what
I *am* thou seest. And yet turn thine eyes,
And with thy memory look on thy friend's
mind,   91
Which is unchanged, and where is written
deep
The sentence of my judge.

THIRD CITIZEN
Are these the marks with which
Laud thinks to improve the image of his
Maker
Stamped on the face of man ?   Curses
upon him,
The impious tyrant !

SECOND CITIZEN
It is said besides
That lewd and papist drunkards may pro-
fane
The Sabbath with their
And has permitted that most heathenish
custom
Of dancing round a pole dressed up with
wreaths   100
On May-day.
A man who thus twice crucifies his God
May well   his brother. In my mind,
friend,
The root of all this ill is prelacy.
I would cut up the root.

THIRD CITIZEN
And by what means ?

SECOND CITIZEN
Smiting each Bishop under the fifth rib.

THIRD CITIZEN
You seem to know the vulnerable place
Of these same crocodiles.

SECOND CITIZEN
I learned it in
Egyptian bondages, sir. Your worm of
Nile

Betrays not with its flattering tears like
they;   110
For, when they cannot kill, they whine and
weep.
Nor is it half so greedy of men's bodies
As they of soul and all; nor does it wallow
In slime as they in simony and lies
And close lusts of the flesh.

A MARSHALSMAN
Give place, give place !
You torch-bearers, advance to the great
gate,
And then attend the Marshal of the Masque
Into the royal presence.

A LAW STUDENT
What thinkest thou
Of this quaint show of ours, my agèd
friend ?
Even now we see the redness of the torches
Inflame the night to the eastward, and the
clarions   121
[Gasp ?] to us on the wind's wave. It
comes !
And their sounds, floating hither round the
pageant,
Rouse up the astonished air.

FIRST CITIZEN
I will not think but that our country's
wounds
May yet be healed. The king is just and
gracious,
Though wicked counsels now pervert his
will.
These once cast off —

SECOND CITIZEN
As adders cast their skins
And keep their venom, so kings often
change;
Counsels and counsellors hang on one
another,   130
Hiding the loathsome . . .
Like the base patchwork of a leper's rags.

THE YOUTH
Oh, still those dissonant thoughts ! — List
how the music
Grows on the enchanted air ! And see, the
torches
Restlessly flashing, and the crowd divided
Like waves before an admiral's prow !

.   .   .   .

A MARSHALSMAN

Give place

To the Marshal of the Masque !

A PURSUIVANT

Room for the King !

THE YOUTH

How glorious ! See those thronging char-
iots
Rolling, like painted clouds before the wind,
Behind their solemn steeds: how some are
shaped   140
Like curved sea-shells dyed by the azure
depths
Of Indian seas; some like the new-born
moon;
And some like cars in which the Romans
climbed
(Canopied by Victory's eagle-wings out-
spread)
The Capitolian ! See how gloriously
The mettled horses in the torchlight stir
Their gallant riders, while they check their
pride,
Like shapes of some diviner element
Than English air, and beings nobler than
The envious and admiring multitude. 150

SECOND CITIZEN

Ay, there they are —
Nobles, and sons of nobles, patentees,
Monopolists, and stewards of this poor
farm,
On whose lean sheep sit the prophetic
crows.
Here is the pomp that strips the houseless
orphan,
Here is the pride that breaks the desolate
heart.
These are the lilies glorious as Solomon,
Who toil not, neither do they spin — unless
It be the webs they catch poor rogues
withal.
Here is the surfeit which to them who
earn   160
The niggard wages of the earth scarce
leaves
The tithe that will support them till they
crawl
Back to her cold, hard bosom. Here is
health
Followed by grim disease, glory by shame,
Waste by lame famine, wealth by squalid
want,

And England's sin by England's punish-
ment.
And, as the effect pursues the cause fore-
gone,
Lo, giving substance to my words, behold
At once the sign and the thing signified —
A troop of cripples, beggars, and lean out-
casts,   170
Horsed upon stumbling jades, carted with
dung,
Dragged for a day from cellars and low
cabins
And rotten hiding-holes, to point the moral
Of this presentment, and bring up the rear
Of painted pomp with misery !

THE YOUTH

'T is but
The anti-masque, and serves as discords do
In sweetest music. Who would love May
flowers
If they succeeded not to Winter's flaw;
Or day unchanged by night; or joy itself
Without the touch of sorrow ?

SECOND CITIZEN

I and thou . . .

A MARSHALSMAN

Place, give place !   181

SCENE II. — *A Chamber in Whitehall.*

Enter the KING, QUEEN, LAUD, LORD
STRAFFORD, LORD COTTINGTON, *and other
Lords ;* ARCHY ; *also* ST. JOHN, *with some
Gentlemen of the Inns of Court.*

KING

Thanks, gentlemen. I heartily accept
This token of your service; your gay
masque
Was performed gallantly. And it shows
well
When subjects twine such flowers of [ob-
servance ?]
With the sharp thorns that deck the Eng-
lish crown.
A gentle heart enjoys what it confers,
Even as it suffers that which it inflicts,
Though Justice guides the stroke.
Accept my hearty thanks.

QUEEN

And, gentlemen,
Call your poor Queen your debtor. Your
quaint pageant   10

Rose on me like the figures of past years,
Treading their still path back to infancy,
More beautiful and mild as they draw
     nearer
The quiet cradle. I could have almost wept
To think I was in Paris, where these shows
Are well devised — such as I was ere yet
My young heart shared a portion of the
     burden,
The careful weight, of this great monarchy.
There, gentlemen, between the sovereign's
     pleasure
And that which it regards, no clamor lifts
Its proud interposition.   21
In Paris ribald censurers dare not move
Their poisonous tongues against these sin-
     less sports;
And *his* smile
Warms those who bask in it, as ours would
     do
If . . . Take my heart's thanks; add them,
     gentlemen,
To those good words which, were he King
     of France,
My royal lord would turn to golden deeds.

ST. JOHN

Madam, the love of Englishmen can make
The lightest favor of their lawful king   30
Outweigh a despot's. We humbly take our
     leaves,
Enriched by smiles which France can never
     buy.

[*Exeunt* ST. JOHN *and the Gentlemen of the
     Inns of Court.*

KING

My Lord Archbishop.
Mark you what spirit sits in St. John's
     eyes?
Methinks it is too saucy for this presence.

ARCHY

Yes, pray your Grace look : for, like an
unsophisticated [eye] sees everything upside
down, you who are wise will discern the
shadow of an idiot in lawn sleeves and a
rochet setting springes to catch woodcocks
in haymaking time. Poor Archy, whose
owl-eyes are tempered to the error of his
age, and because he is a fool, and by special ordinance of God forbidden ever to see
himself as he is, sees now in that deep eye
a blindfold devil sitting on the ball, and
weighing words out between king and sub-

jects. One scale is full of promises, and
the other full of protestations; and then
another devil creeps behind the first out
of the dark windings [of a] pregnant lawyer's brain, and takes the bandage from
the other's eyes, and throws a sword into
the left-hand scale, for all the world like
my Lord Essex's there.

STRAFFORD

A rod in pickle for the Fool's back !

ARCHY

Ay, and some are now smiling whose
tears will make the brine; for Fool sees . . .

STRAFFORD

Insolent ! You shall have your coat
turned and be whipped out of the palace
for this.

ARCHY

When all the fools are whipped, and all
the protestant writers, while the knaves
are whipping the fools ever since a thief
was set to catch a thief. If all turncoats
were whipped out of palaces, poor Archy
would be disgraced in good company. Let
the knaves whip the fools, and all the fools
laugh at it. [Let the] wise and godly slit
each other's noses and ears (having no need
of any sense of discernment in their craft);
and the knaves, to marshal them, join in a
procession to Bedlam, to entreat the madmen to omit their sublime Platonic contemplations, and manage the state of England.
Let all the honest men who lie penned up
at the prisons or the pillories, in custody
of the pursuivants of the High-Commission
Court, marshal them.

Enter Secretary LYTTELTON, *with papers*

KING (*looking over the papers*)
                         These stiff Scots 80
His Grace of Canterbury must take order
To force under the Church's yoke. — You,
     Wentworth,
Shall be myself in Ireland, and shall add
Your wisdom, gentleness, and energy,
To what in me were wanting. — My Lord
     Weston,
Look that those merchants draw not with-
     out loss
Their bullion from the Tower; and, on the
     payment

Of ship-money, take fullest compensation
For violation of our royal forests,
Whose limits, from neglect, have been o'er-
    grown   90
With cottages and cornfields. The utter-
    most
Farthing exact from those who claim ex-
    emption
From knighthood; that which once was a
    reward
Shall thus be made a punishment, that sub-
    jects
May know how majesty can wear at will
The rugged mood. — My Lord of Coven-
    try,
Lay my command upon the Courts below
That bail be not accepted for the prisoners
Under the warrant of the Star Chamber.
The people shall not find the stubbornness
Of Parliament a cheap or easy method 101
Of dealing with their rightful sovereign;
And doubt not this, my Lord of Coventry,
We will find time and place for fit re-
    buke. —
My Lord of Canterbury.

ARCHY

              The fool is here.

LAUD

I crave permission of your Majesty
To order that this insolent fellow be
Chastised; he mocks the sacred character,
Scoffs at the state, and —

KING

             What, my Archy?
He mocks and mimics all he sees and hears,
Yet with a quaint and graceful license.
    Prithee   111
For this once do not as Prynne would, were
    he
Primate of England. With your Grace's
    leave,
He lives in his own world; and, like a
    parrot
Hung in his gilded prison from the win-
    dow
Of a queen's bower over the public way,
Blasphemes with a bird's mind; his words,
    like arrows
Which know no aim beyond the archer's
    wit,
Strike sometimes what eludes philosophy.
             (To ARCHY)

Go, sirrah, and repent of your offence 120
Ten minutes in the rain; be it your pen-
    ance
To bring news how the world goes there. —
    Poor Archy !
               [Exit ARCHY.
He weaves about himself a world of mirth
Out of the wreck of ours.

LAUD

I take with patience, as my Master did,
All scoffs permitted from above.

KING

                 My lord,
Pray overlook these papers. Archy's
    words
Had wings, but these have talons.

QUEEN

              And the lion
That wears them must be tamed. My
    dearest lord,   129
I see the new-born courage in thine eye
Armed to strike dead the spirit of the time,
Which spurs to rage the many-headed
    beast.
Do thou persist; for, faint but in resolve,
And it were better thou hadst still re-
    mained
The slave of thine own slaves, who tear
    like curs
The fugitive, and flee from the pursuer;
And Opportunity, that empty wolf,
Flies at his throat who falls. Subdue thy
    actions
Even to the disposition of thy purpose, 139
And be that tempered as the Ebro's steel;
And banish weak-eyed Mercy to the weak,
Whence she will greet thee with a gift of
    peace,
And not betray thee with a traitor's kiss,
As when she keeps the company of rebels,
Who think that she is Fear. This do, lest
    we
Should fall as from a glorious pinnacle
In a bright dream, and wake, as from a
    dream,
Out of our worshipped state.

KING

              Belovèd friend,
God is my witness that this weight of
    power,
Which he sets me my earthly task to wield

Under his law, is my delight and pride   151
Only because thou lovest that and me.
For a king bears the office of a God
To all the under world; and to his God
Alone he must deliver up his trust,
Unshorn of its permitted attributes.
[It seems] now as the baser elements
Had mutinied against the golden sun
That kindles them to harmony, and quells
Their self-destroying rapine.   The wild
    million   160
Strike at the eye that guides them; like as
    humors
Of the distempered body that conspire
Against the spirit of life throned in the
    heart, —
And thus become the prey of one another,
And last of death. . . .

STRAFFORD

That which would be ambition in a subject
Is duty in a sovereign; for on him,
As on a keystone, hangs the arch of life,
Whose safety is its strength.   Degree and
    form,
And all that makes the age of reasoning
    man   170
More memorable than a beast's, depend on
    this —
That Right should fence itself inviolably
With power; in which respect the state of
    England
From usurpation by the insolent commons
Cries for reform.
Get treason, and spare treasure.   Fee with
    coin
The loudest murmurers; feed with jealous-
    ies
Opposing factions, — be thyself of none;
And borrow gold of many, for those who
    lend
Will serve thee till thou payest them; and
    thus   180
Keep the fierce spirit of the hour at bay,
Till time, and its coming generations
Of nights and days unborn, bring some one
    chance,
.   .   .   .
Or war or pestilence or Nature's self,
By some distemperature or terrible sign,
Be as an arbiter betwixt themselves.
                        Nor let your Majesty
Doubt here the peril of the unseen event.
How did your brother kings, coheritors
In your high interest in the subject earth,

Rise past such troubles to that height of
    power   191
Where now they sit, and awfully serene
Smile on the trembling world?   Such
    popular storms
Philip the Second of Spain, this Lewis of
    France,
And late the German head of many bodies,
And every petty lord of Italy,
Quelled or by arts or arms.   Is England
    poorer
Or feebler? or art thou who wield'st her
    power
Tamer than they? or shall this island be —
[Girdled] by its inviolable waters —   200
To the world present and the world to come
Sole pattern of extinguished monarchy?
Not if thou dost as I would have thee do.

KING

Your words shall be my deeds;
You speak the image of my thought.   My
    friend
(If kings can have a friend, I call thee
    so),
Beyond the large commission which [be-
    longs?]
Under the great seal of the realm, take
    this:
And, for some obvious reasons, let there be
No seal on it, except my kingly word   210
And honor as I am a gentleman.
Be — as thou art within my heart and
    mind —
Another self, here and in Ireland:
Do what thou judgest well, take amplest
    license,
And stick not even at questionable means.
Hear me, Wentworth.   My word is as a
    wall
Between thee and this world thine enemy —
That hates thee, for thou lovest me.

STRAFFORD
                                I own
No friend but thee, no enemies but thine;
Thy lightest thought is my eternal law.   220
How weak, how short, is life to pay —

KING
                        Peace, peace!
Thou ow'st me nothing yet. —
                        (To LAUD)
                        My lord, what say
Those papers?

LAUD

Your Majesty has ever interposed,
In lenity towards your native soil,
Between the heavy vengeance of the
    Church
And Scotland. Mark the consequence of
    warming
This brood of northern vipers in your
    bosom.
The rabble, instructed no doubt
By Loudon, Lindsay, Hume, and false
    Argyll,   230
(For the waves never menace heaven until
Scourged by the wind's invisible tyranny)
Have in the very temple of the Lord
Done outrage to his chosen ministers.
They scorn the liturgy of the Holy Church,
Refuse to obey her canons, and deny
The apostolic power with which the Spirit
Has filled its elect vessels, even from him
Who held the keys with power to loose
    and bind
To him who now pleads in this royal pre-
    sence. —   240
Let ampler powers and new instructions be
Sent to the High Commissioners in Scot-
    land.
To death, imprisonment, and confiscation,
Add torture, add the ruin of the kindred
Of the offender, add the brand of infamy,
Add mutilation: and if this suffice not,
Unleash the sword and fire, that in their
    thirst
They may lick up that scum of schismatics.
I laugh at those weak rebels who, desiring
What we possess, still prate of Christian
    peace;   250
As if those dreadful arbitrating messengers
Which play the part of God 'twixt right
    and wrong,
Should be let loose against the innocent
    sleep
Of templed cities and the smiling fields,
For some poor argument of policy
Which touches our own profit or our pride,
(Where it indeed were Christian charity
To turn the cheek even to the smiter's
    hand);
And, when our great Redeemer, when our
    God,
When he who gave, accepted, and retained,
Himself in propitiation of our sins,   261
Is scorned in his immediate ministry,
With hazard of the inestimable loss
Of all the truth and discipline which is

Salvation to the extremest generation
Of men innumerable, they talk of peace !
Such peace as Canaan found, let Scotland
    now !
For, by that Christ who came to bring a
    sword,
Not peace, upon the earth, and gave com-
    mand
To his disciples at the passover   270
That each should sell his robe and buy a
    sword, —
Once strip that minister of naked wrath,
And it shall never sleep in peace again
Till Scotland bend or break.

KING

              My Lord Archbishop,
Do what thou wilt and what thou canst in
    this.
Thy earthly even as thy heavenly King
Gives thee large power in his unquiet
    realm.
But we want money, and my mind mis-
    gives me
That for so great an enterprise, as yet,
We are unfurnished.

STRAFFORD

              Yet it may not long
Rest on our wills.

COTTINGTON

              The expenses   281
Of gathering ship-money, and of distraining
For every petty rate (for we encounter
A desperate opposition inch by inch
In every warehouse and on every farm),
Have swallowed up the gross sum of the
    imposts;
So that, though felt as a most grievous
    scourge
Upon the land, they stand us in small stead
As touches the receipt.

STRAFFORD

             'T is a conclusion
Most arithmetical: and thence you infer
Perhaps the assembling of a parliament.
Now, if a man should call his dearest
    enemies   292
To sit in licensed judgment on his life,
His Majesty might wisely take that course.
            (*Aside to* COTTINGTON)
It is enough to expect from these lean im-
    posts

That they perform the office of a scourge,
Without more profit.

(*Aloud*)
Fines and confiscations,
And a forced loan from the refractory
city,
Will fill our coffers; and the golden love
Of loyal gentlemen and noble friends   300
For the worshipped father of our common
country,
With contributions from the Catholics,
Will make Rebellion pale in our excess.
Be these the expedients until time and
wisdom
Shall frame a settled state of government.

LAUD

And weak expedients they ! Have we not
drained
All, till the   which seemed
A mine exhaustless ?

STRAFFORD

And the love which *is*,
If loyal hearts could turn their blood to
gold.   309

LAUD

Both now grow barren; and I speak it not
As loving parliaments, which, as they have
been
In the right hand of bold, bad, mighty
kings
The scourges of the bleeding Church, I
hate.
Methinks they scarcely can deserve our
fear.

STRAFFORD

Oh, my dear liege, take back the wealth
thou gavest;
With that, take all I held, but as in trust
For thee, of mine inheritance; leave me but
This unprovided body for thy service,
And a mind dedicated to no care
Except thy safety; but assemble not   320
A parliament. Hundreds will bring, like
me,
Their fortunes, as they would their blood,
before —

KING

No ! thou who judgest them art but one.
Alas !
We should be too much out of love with
heaven,

Did this vile world show many such as
thee,
Thou perfect just and honorable man !
Never shall it be said that Charles of Eng-
land
Stripped those he loved for fear of those
he scorns;
Nor will he so much misbecome his throne
As to impoverish those who most adorn
And best defend it. That you urge, dear
Strafford,   331
Inclines me rather —

QUEEN

To a parliament ?
Is this thy firmness ? and thou wilt preside
Over a knot of   censurers,
To the unswearing of thy best resolves,
And choose the worst, when the worst
comes too soon ?
Plight not the worst before the worst must
come.
Oh, wilt thou smile whilst our ribald foes,
Dressed in their own usurped authority,
Sharpen their tongues on Henrietta's fame ?
It is enough ! Thou lovest me no more !
(*Weeps*)

KING

Oh, Henrietta !

(*They talk apart*)

COTTINGTON [*to* LAUD]
Money we have none;
And all the expedients of my Lord of
Strafford   343
Will scarcely meet the arrears.

LAUD

Without delay
An army must be sent into the north;
Followed by a Commission of the Church,
With amplest power to quench in fire and
blood,
And tears and terror, and the pity of hell,
The intenser wrath of Heresy. God will
give
Victory; and victory over Scotland give 350
The lion England tamed into our hands.
That will lend power, and power bring gold.

COTTINGTON

Meanwhile
We must begin first where your Grace
leaves off.
Gold must give power, or —

LAUD

I am not averse
From the assembling of a parliament.
Strong actions and smooth words might
        teach them soon
The lesson to obey. And are they not
A bubble fashioned by the monarch's mouth,
The birth of one light breath? If they
        serve no purpose,   360
A word dissolves them.

STRAFFORD

                    The engine of parliaments
Might be deferred until I can bring over
The Irish regiments; they will serve to
        assure
The issue of the war against the Scots.
And, this game won — which if lost, all is
        lost —
Gather these chosen leaders of the rebels,
And call them, if you will, a parliament.

KING

Oh, be our feet still tardy to shed blood,
Guilty though it may be ! I would still
        spare   369
The stubborn country of my birth, and ward
From countenances which I loved in youth
The wrathful Church's lacerating hand.
                          (To LAUD)
Have you o'erlooked the other articles ?

Reënter ARCHY

LAUD

Hazlerig, Hampden, Pym, young Harry
        Vane,
Cromwell, and other rebels of less note,
Intend to sail with the next favoring wind
For the Plantations.

ARCHY

                    Where they think to found
A commonwealth like Gonzalo's in the play,
Gynæcocœnic and pantisocratic.

KING

What 's that, sirrah ?

ARCHY

                    New devil's politics.
Hell is the pattern of all commonwealths;
Lucifer was the first republican.   382
Will you hear Merlin's prophecy, how three
        [posts ?]

' In one brainless skull, when the white-
        thorn is full,
Shall sail round the world, and come back
        again:
Shall sail round the world in a brainless
        skull,
And come back again when the moon is at
        full: ' —
When, in spite of the Church,
They will hear homilies of whatever length
Or form they please.   390

[COTTINGTON ?]

So please your Majesty to sign this order
For their detention.

ARCHY

If your Majesty were tormented night
and day by fever, gout, rheumatism, and
stone, and asthma, etc., and you found these
diseases had secretly entered into a conspiracy to abandon you, should you think it
necessary to lay an embargo on the port by
which they meant to dispeople your unquiet kingdom of man ?

KING

If fear were made for kings, the Fool
        mocks wisely ;   401
But in this case — (*writing*) Here, my lord,
        take the warrant,
And see it duly executed forthwith. —
That imp of malice and mockery shall be
        punished.
        [*Exeunt all but* KING, QUEEN, *and* ARCHY.

ARCHY

Ay, I am the physician of whom Plato
prophesied, who was to be accused by the
confectioner before a jury of children, who
found him guilty without waiting for the
summing-up, and hanged him without benefit of clergy. Thus Baby Charles, and the
Twelfth-night Queen of Hearts, and the
overgrown schoolboy Cottington, and that
little urchin Laud — who would reduce a
verdict of 'guilty, death,' by famine, if it
were impregnable by composition — all im-
panelled against poor Archy for presenting
them bitter physic the last day of the holi-
days.

QUEEN

Is the rain over, sirrah ?

KING

When it rains
And the sun shines, 't will rain again to-
   morrow; 420
And therefore never smile till you 've done
   crying.

ARCHY

But 't is all over now; like the April
anger of woman, the gentle sky has wept
itself serene.

QUEEN

What news abroad? how looks the world
this morning?

ARCHY

Gloriously as a grave covered with virgin
flowers. There 's a rainbow in the sky.
Let your Majesty look at it, for 429

> ' A rainbow in the morning
> Is the shepherd's warning ; '

and the flocks of which you are the pastor
are scattered among the mountain-tops,
where every drop of water is a flake of
snow, and the breath of May pierces like a
January blast.

KING

The sheep have mistaken the wolf for
their shepherd, my poor boy; and the shepherd, the wolves for the watchdogs. 439

QUEEN

But the rainbow was a good sign, Archy;
it says that the waters of the deluge are
gone, and can return no more.

ARCHY

Ay, the salt-water one; but that of tears
and blood must yet come down, and that of
fire follow, if there be any truth in lies. —
The rainbow hung over the city with all its
shops, . . . and churches, from north to
south, like a bridge of congregated lightning pieced by the masonry of heaven —
like a balance in which the angel that dis-
tributes the coming hour was weighing that
heavy one whose poise is now felt in the
lightest hearts, before it bows the proudest
heads under the meanest feet.

QUEEN

Who taught you this trash, sirrah?

ARCHY

A torn leaf out of an old book trampled
in the dirt. — But for the rainbow. It
moved as the sun moved, and . . . until
the top of the Tower . . . of a cloud
through its left-hand tip, and Lambeth
Palace look as dark as a rock before the
other. Methought I saw a crown figured
upon one tip, and a mitre on the other. So,
as I had heard treasures were found where
the rainbow quenches its points upon the
earth, I set off, and at the Tower —— But
I shall not tell your Majesty what I found
close to the closet-window on which the
rainbow had glimmered.

KING

Speak: I will make my Fool my conscience.

ARCHY

Then conscience is a fool. — I saw there
a cat caught in a rat-trap. I heard the
rats squeak behind the wainscots; it seemed
to me that the very mice were consulting
on the manner of her death.

QUEEN

Archy is shrewd and bitter.

ARCHY

Like the season,
so blow the winds. — But at the other end
of the rainbow, where the gray rain was
tempered along the grass and leaves by a
tender interfusion of violet and gold in the
meadows beyond Lambeth, what think you
that I found instead of a mitre?

KING

Vane's wits perhaps.

ARCHY

Something as vain. I saw
a gross vapor hovering in a stinking ditch
over the carcass of a dead ass, some rotten
rags, and broken dishes — the wrecks of
what once administered to the stuffing-out
and the ornament of a worm of worms.
His Grace of Canterbury expects to enter
the New Jerusalem some Palm Sunday in
triumph on the ghost of this ass.

QUEEN

Enough, enough! Go desire Lady Jane
She place my lute, together with the music

Mari received last week from Italy,
In my boudoir, and —

[*Exit* ARCHY.

KING

I 'll go in.

QUEEN

My belovèd lord,
Have you not noted that the Fool of late
Has lost his careless mirth, and that his words
Sound like the echoes of our saddest fears ?
What can it mean ?   I should be loath to think   500
Some factious slave had tutored him.

KING

Oh, no !
He is but Occasion's pupil.   Partly 't is
That our minds piece the vacant intervals
Of his wild words with their own fashioning;
As in the imagery of summer clouds,
Or coals of the winter fire, idlers find
The perfect shadows of their teeming thoughts;
And, partly, that the terrors of the time
Are sown by wandering Rumor in all spirits,
And in the lightest and the least may best
Be seen the current of the coming wind. 511

QUEEN

Your brain is overwrought with these deep thoughts.
Come, I will sing to you; let us go try
These airs from Italy; and, as we pass
The gallery, we 'll decide where that Correggio
Shall hang — the Virgin Mother
With her child, born the King of heaven and earth,
Whose reign is men's salvation.   And you shall see
A cradled miniature of yourself asleep, 519
Stamped on the heart by never-erring love;
Liker than any Vandyke ever made,
A pattern to the unborn age of thee,
Over whose sweet beauty I have wept for joy
A thousand times, and now should weep for sorrow,
Did I not think that after we were dead
Our fortunes would spring high in him, and that

The cares we waste upon our heavy crown
Would make it light and glorious as a wreath
Of heaven's beams for his dear innocent brow.

KING

Dear Henrietta !   530

SCENE III. — *The Star Chamber.* LAUD,
JUXON, STRAFFORD, *and others, as Judges.*
PRYNNE, *as a Prisoner, and then* BASTWICK.

LAUD

Bring forth the prisoner Bastwick; let the clerk
Recite his sentence.

CLERK

' That he pay five thousand
Pounds to the king, lose both his ears, be branded
With red-hot iron on the cheek and forehead,
And be imprisoned within Lancaster Castle
During the pleasure of the Court.'

LAUD

Prisoner,
If you have aught to say wherefore this sentence
Should not be put into effect, now speak.

JUXON

If you have aught to plead in mitigation,
Speak.

BASTWICK

Thus, my lords.   If, like the prelates, I
Were an invader of the royal power,   11
A public scorner of the word of God,
Profane, idolatrous, popish, superstitious,
Impious in heart and in tyrannic act,
Void of wit, honesty and temperance;
If Satan were my lord, as theirs, — our God
Pattern of all I should avoid to do;
Were I an enemy of my God and King
And of good men, as ye are; — I should merit
Your fearful state and gilt prosperity,   20
Which, when ye wake from the last sleep, shall turn
To cowls and robes of everlasting fire.
But, as I am, I bid ye grudge me not
The only earthly favor ye can yield,

Or I think worth acceptance at your
hands, —
Scorn, mutilation and imprisonment.
             Even as my Master did,
Until Heaven's kingdom shall descend on
earth,
Or earth be like a shadow in the light
Of Heaven absorbed. Some few tumultu-
ous years   30
Will pass, and leave no wreck of what op-
poses
His will whose will is power.

LAUD

Officer, take the prisoner from the bar,
And be his tongue slit for his insolence.

BASTWICK

While this hand holds a pen —

LAUD
               Be his hands —

JUXON
                  Stop !
Forbear, my lord ! The tongue, which
now can speak
No terror, would interpret, being dumb,
Heaven's thunder to our harm; . . .
And hands, which now write only their own
shame
With bleeding stumps might sign our blood
away.   40

LAUD

Much more such 'mercy' among men
would be,
Did all the ministers of Heaven's revenge
Flinch thus from earthly retribution. I
Could suffer what I would inflict.
          [*Exit* BASTWICK *guarded*.
                  Bring up
The Lord Bishop of Lincoln. —
            (*To* STRAFFORD)
            Know you not
That, in distraining for ten thousand pounds
Upon his books and furniture at Lincoln,
Were found these scandalous and seditious
letters   48
Sent from one Osbaldistone, who is fled ?
I speak it not as touching this poor person;
But of the office which should make it holy,
Were it as vile as it was ever spotless.
Mark too, my lord, that this expression
strikes
His Majesty, if I misinterpret not.

Enter BISHOP WILLIAMS *guarded*

STRAFFORD

'T were politic and just that Williams taste
The bitter fruit of his connection with
The schismatics. But you, my Lord Arch-
bishop,
Who owed your first promotion to his favor,
Who grew beneath his smile —

LAUD
            Would therefore beg
The office of his judge from this High
Court, —   60
That it shall seem, even as it is, that I,
In my assumption of this sacred robe,
Have put aside all worldly preference,
All sense of all distinction of all persons,
All thoughts but of the service of the
Church. —
Bishop of Lincoln !

WILLIAMS
          Peace, proud hierarch !
I know my sentence, and I own it just.
Thou wilt repay me less than I deserve
In stretching to the utmost
.   .   .   .

SCENE IV. — HAMPDEN, PYM, CROMWELL, *his
Daughter, and young* SIR HARRY VANE.

HAMPDEN

England, farewell ! Thou, who hast been
my cradle,
Shalt never be my dungeon or my grave !
I held what I inherited in thee
As pawn for that inheritance of freedom
Which thou hast sold for thy despoiler's
smile.
How can I call thee England, or my coun-
try ? —
Does the wind hold ?

VANE
          The vanes sit steady
Upon the Abbey towers. The silver light-
nings
Of the evening star, spite of the city's
smoke,
Tell that the north wind reigns in the upper
air.   10
Mark too that fleet of fleecy-wingèd clouds
Sailing athwart St. Margaret's.

HAMPDEN

Hail, fleet herald
Of tempest ! that rude pilot who shall
guide
Hearts free as his, to realms as pure as
thee,
Beyond the shot of tyranny,
Beyond the webs of that swoln spider . . .
Beyond the curses, calumnies, and [lies ?]
Of atheist priests !   And thou
Fair star, whose beam lies on the wide At-
lantic,   19
Athwart its zones of tempest and of calm,
Bright as the path to a belovèd home,
Oh, light us to the isles of the evening
land !
Like floating Edens cradled in the glimmer
Of sunset, through the distant mist of years
Touched by departing hope, they gleam !
lone regions,
Where power's poor dupes and victims yet
have never
Propitiated the savage fear of kings
With purest blood of noblest hearts; whose
dew
Is yet unstained with tears of those who
wake
To weep each day the wrongs on which it
dawns;   30
Whose sacred silent air owns yet no echo
Of formal blasphemies; nor impious rites
Wrest man's free worship, from the God
who loves,
To the poor worm who envies us his love !
Receive, thou young   of Paradise,
These exiles from the old and sinful world !

.   .   .   .

This glorious clime, this firmament, whose
lights
Dart mitigated influence through their
veil
Of pale blue atmosphere; whose tears keep
green
The pavement of this moist all-feeding
earth;   40
This vaporous horizon, whose dim round
Is bastioned by the circumfluous sea,
Repelling invasion from the sacred
towers, —
Presses upon me like a dungeon's grate,
A low dark roof, a damp and narrow wall.
The boundless universe
Becomes a cell too narrow for the soul
That owns no master; while the loathliest
ward

Of this wide prison, England, is a nest
Of cradling peace built on the mountain
tops, —   50
To which the eagle spirits of the free,
Which range through heaven and earth,
and scorn the storm
Of time, and gaze upon the light of truth,
Return to brood on thoughts that cannot
die
And cannot be repelled.
Like eaglets floating in the heaven of time,
They soar above their quarry, and shall
stoop
Through palaces and temples thunder-
proof.

SCENE V

ARCHY

I 'll go live under the ivy that overgrows
the terrace, and count the tears shed on its
old [roots ?] as the [wind ?] plays the song
of

'A widow bird sate mourning
Upon a wintry bough.'

(Sings)

Heigho ! the lark and the owl !
One flies the morning, and one lulls
the night;
Only the nightingale, poor fond soul,
Sings like the fool through darkness
and light.

'A widow bird sate mourning for her
love   10
Upon a wintry bough;
The frozen wind crept on above,
The freezing stream below.

'There was no leaf upon the forest bare,
No flower upon the ground,
And little motion in the air
Except the mill-wheel's sound.'

FRAGMENTS OF AN UNFIN-
ISHED DRAMA

Date 1821–22. Published in part by Mrs.
Shelley, 1824, and the remainder by Garnett,
1862, and Rossetti, 1870. Mrs. Shelley writes :
'The following fragments are part of a drama,
undertaken for the amusement of the individuals who composed our intimate society, but

left unfinished. I have preserved a sketch of the story, so far as it had been shadowed out in the poet's mind.' It is possibly connected with the project of a play on Trelawny's career. Garnett gives a note on the portion which he called *The Magic Plant*. ' A close scrutiny, however, of one of Shelley's MS. books has revealed the existence of much more of this piece than has hitherto been suspected to exist. By far the larger portion of this, forming an episode complete in itself, is here made public, under the title of *The Magic Plant*. . . . The little drama of which this charming sport of fancy forms a portion was written at Pisa during the late winter or early spring of 1822. The episode of *The Magic Plant* was obviously suggested by the pleasure Shelley received from the plants grown indoors in his Pisan dwelling, which he says in a letter written in January, 1822, " turn the sunny winter into spring." See also the poem of *The Zucca*, composed about the same time.'

[An Enchantress, living in one of the islands of the Indian Archipelago, saves the life of a Pirate, a man of savage but noble nature. She becomes enamoured of him ; and he, inconstant to his mortal love, for a while returns her passion : but at length, recalling the memory of her whom he left, and who laments his loss, he escapes from the enchanted island, and returns to his lady. His mode of life makes him again go to sea, and the Enchantress seizes the opportunity to bring him, by a spirit-brewed tempest, back to her island.]

SCENE — *Before the Cavern of the Indian Enchantress. The* ENCHANTRESS *comes forth.*

ENCHANTRESS

HE came like a dream in the dawn of life,
  He fled like a shadow before its noon;
He is gone, and my peace is turned to
    strife,
  And I wander and wane like the weary
    moon.
    O sweet Echo, wake,
    And for my sake
Make answer the while my heart shall
    break !

But my heart has a music which Echo's
    lips,
  Though tender and true, yet can answer
    not,
And the shadow that moves in the soul's
    eclipse   10
  Can return not the kiss by his now for-
    got;

Sweet lips ! he who hath
  On my desolate path
Cast the darkness of absence, worse than
    death !
(*The* ENCHANTRESS *makes her spell : she is answered by a Spirit*)

SPIRIT

Within the silent centre of the earth
My mansion is; where I have lived in-
    sphered
From the beginning, and around my sleep
Have woven all the wondrous imagery
Of this dim spot, which mortals call the
    world;
Infinite depths of unknown elements   20
Massed into one impenetrable mask;
Sheets of immeasurable fire, and veins
Of gold and stone, and adamantine iron.
And as a veil in which I walk through
    Heaven
I have wrought mountains, seas, and waves,
    and clouds,
And lastly light, whose interfusion dawns
In the dark space of interstellar air.

   .   .   .   .   .   .

[A good Spirit, who watches over the Pirate's fate, leads, in a mysterious manner, the lady of his love to the Enchanted Isle. She is accompanied by a youth, who loves the lady, but whose passion she returns only with a sisterly affection. The ensuing scene takes place between them on their arrival at the Isle.]

INDIAN YOUTH *and* LADY

INDIAN

And, if my grief should still be dearer to me
Than all the pleasures in the world beside,
Why would you lighten it ? —

LADY

             I offer only
That which I seek, some human sympathy
In this mysterious island.

INDIAN

           Oh, my friend,
My sister, my belovèd ! — What do I say ?
My brain is dizzy, and I scarce know
    whether
I speak to thee or her.

LADY

         Peace, perturbed heart !
I am to thee only as thou to mine,

The passing wind which heals the brow at
      noon,
And may strike cold into the breast at night,
Yet cannot linger where it soothes the most,
Or long soothe could it linger.

INDIAN

                              But you said
You also loved ?

LADY

            Loved ! Oh, I love.   Methinks
This word of love is fit for all the world, 42
And that for gentle hearts another name
Would speak of gentler thoughts than the
      world owns.
I have loved.

INDIAN

                  And thou lovest not ? if so
Young as thou art thou canst afford to weep.

LADY

Oh, would that I could claim exemption
From all the bitterness of that sweet name.
I loved, I love, and when I love no more
Let joys and grief perish, and leave de-
      spair   50
To ring the knell of youth.   He stood be-
      side me,
The embodied vision of the brightest dream,
Which like a dawn heralds the day of life;
The shadow of his presence made my world
A paradise.   All familiar things he touched,
All common words he spoke, became to me
Like forms and sounds of a diviner world.
He was as is the sun in his fierce youth,
As terrible and lovely as a tempest;   59
He came, and went, and left me what I am.
Alas !   Why must I think how oft we two
Have sate together near the river springs,
Under the green pavilion which the willow
Spreads on the floor of the unbroken foun-
      tain,
Strewn, by the nurslings that linger there,
Over that islet paved with flowers and
      moss, —
While the musk-rose leaves, like flakes of
      crimson snow,
Showered on us, and the dove mourned in
      the pine,
Sad prophetess of sorrows not her own ? 69
The crane returned to her unfrozen haunt,
And the false cuckoo bade the spray good
      morn;
And on a wintry bough the widowed bird,

Hid in the deepest night of ivy-leaves,
Renewed the vigils of a sleepless sorrow.
I, left like her, and leaving one like her,
Alike abandoned and abandoning
(Oh ! unlike her in this !) the gentlest
      youth,
Whose love had made my sorrows dear to
      him,
Even as my sorrow made his love to me !

INDIAN

One curse of Nature stamps in the same
      mould   80
The features of the wretched; and they are
As like as violet to violet,
When memory, the ghost, their odors keeps
Mid the cold relics of abandoned joy. —
Proceed.

LADY

            He was a simple innocent boy.
I loved him well, but not as he desired;
Yet even thus he was content to be: —
A short content, for I was . . .

INDIAN (aside)

                        God of heaven !
From such an islet, such a river-spring . . . !
I dare not ask her if there stood upon it 90
A pleasure-dome, surmounted by a cres-
      cent,
With steps to the blue water. (Aloud) It
      may be
That Nature masks in life several copies
Of the same lot, so that the sufferers
May feel another's sorrow as their own
And find in friendship what they lost in
      love.
That cannot be: yet it is strange that we,
From the same scene, by the same path to
      this
Realm of abandonment . . . But speak !
      your breath —
Your breath is like soft music, your words
      are   100
The echoes of a voice which on my heart
Sleeps like a melody of early days.
But as you said —

LADY

                  He was so awful, yet
So beautiful in mystery and terror,
Calming me as the loveliness of heaven
Soothes the unquiet sea: — and yet not so,
For he seemed stormy, and would often
      seem

A quenchless sun masked in portentous
  clouds;
For such his thoughts, and even his actions
  were;   109
But he was not of them, nor they of him,
But as they hid his splendor from the
  earth.
Some said he was a man of blood and peril,
And steeped in bitter infamy to the lips.
More need was there I should be innocent,
More need that I should be most true and
  kind,
And much more need that there should be
  found one
To share remorse, and scorn and solitude,
And all the ills that wait on those who do
The tasks of ruin in the world of life.
He fled, and I have followed him.

INDIAN

                              Such a one
Is he who was the winter of my peace.   121
But, fairest stranger, when didst thou de-
  part
From the far hills where rise the springs of
  India ?
How didst thou pass the intervening sea ?

LADY

If I be sure I am not dreaming now,
I should not doubt to say it was a dream.
Methought a star came down from heaven,
And rested mid the plants of India,
Which I had given a shelter from the frost
Within my chamber. There the meteor
  lay,   130
Panting forth light among the leaves and
  flowers,
As if it lived, and was outworn with speed;
Or that it loved, and passion made the
  pulse
Of its bright life throb like an anxious
  . heart,
Till it diffused itself, and all the chamber
And walls seemed melted into emerald fire
That burned not ; in the midst of which
  appeared
A spirit like a child, and laughed aloud
A thrilling peal of such sweet merriment
As made the blood tingle in my warm
  feet;   140
Then bent over a vase, and murmuring
Low, unintelligible melodies,
Placed something in the mould like melon-
  seeds,

And slowy faded, and in place of it
A soft hand issued from the veil of fire,
Holding a cup like a magnolia flower,
And poured upon the earth within the vase
The element with which it overflowed,
Brighter than morning light and purer
  than
The water of the springs of Himalah.   150

INDIAN

You waked not ?

LADY

                    Not until my dream became
Like a child's legend on the tideless sand,
Which the first foam erases half, and half
Leaves legible. At length I rose, and went,
Visiting my flowers from pot to pot, and
  thought
To set new cuttings in the empty urns,
And when I came to that beside the lat-
  tice,
I saw two little dark-green leaves
Lifting the light mould at their birth, and
  then   159
I half-remembered my forgotten dream.
And day by day, green as a gourd in June,
The plant grew fresh and thick, yet no one
  knew
What plant it was; its stem and tendrils
  seemed
Like emerald snakes, mottled and dia-
  monded
With azure mail and streaks of woven
  silver;
And all the sheaths that folded the dark
  buds
Rose like the crest of cobra-di-capel,
Until the golden eye of the bright flower
Through the dark lashes of those veinèd
  lids,
Disencumbered of their silent sleep,   170
Gazed like a star into the morning light.
Its leaves were delicate, you almost saw
The pulses
With which the purple velvet flower was
  fed
To overflow, and, like a poet's heart
Changing bright fancy to sweet sentiment,
Changed half the light to fragrance. It
  soon fell,
And to a green and dewy embryo-fruit
Left all its treasured beauty. Day by day
I nursed the plant, and on the double flute
Played to it on the sunny winter days   181

Soft melodies, as sweet as April rain
On silent leaves, and sang those words in
   which
Passion makes Echo taunt the sleeping
   strings;
And I would send tales of forgotten love
Late into the lone night, and sing wild songs
Of maids deserted in the olden time,
And weep like a soft cloud in April's bosom
Upon the sleeping eyelids of the plant,
So that perhaps it dreamed that Spring was
   come,   190
And crept abroad into the moonlight air,
And loosened all its limbs, as, noon by noon,
The sun averted less his oblique beam.

INDIAN

And the plant died not in the frost?

LADY

                 It grew;
And went out of the lattice which I left
Half open for it, trailing its quaint spires
Along the garden and across the lawn,
And down the slope of moss and through
   the tufts
Of wild-flower roots, and stumps of trees
   o'ergrown   199
With simple lichens, and old hoary stones,
On to the margin of the glassy pool,
Even to a nook of unblown violets
And lilies-of-the-valley yet unborn,
Under a pine with ivy overgrown.
And there its fruit lay like a sleeping lizard
Under the shadows; but when Spring in-
   deed
Came to unswathe her infants, and the
   lilies
Peeped from their bright green masks to
   wonder at
This shape of autumn couched in their re-
   cess,
Then it dilated, and it grew until   210
One half lay floating on the fountain wave,
Whose pulse, elapsed in unlike sympathies,
Kept time
Among the snowy water-lily buds.
Its shape was such as summer melody
Of the south wind in spicy vales might
   give
To some light cloud bound from the golden
   dawn
To fairy isles of evening, and it seemed
In hue and form that it had been a mirror
Of all the hues and forms around it and

Upon it pictured by the sunny beams   221
Which, from the bright vibrations of the
   pool,
Were thrown upon the rafters and the roof
Of boughs and leaves, and on the pillared
   stems
Of the dark sylvan temple, and reflections
Of every infant flower and star of moss
And veined leaf in the azure odorous air.
And thus it lay in the Elysian calm
Of its own beauty, floating on the line
Which, like a film in purest space, divided
The heaven beneath the water from the
   heaven   231
Above the clouds; and every day I went
Watching its growth and wondering;
And as the day grew hot, methought I saw
A glassy vapor dancing on the pool,
And on it little quaint and filmy shapes,
With dizzy motion, wheel and rise and fall,
Like clouds of gnats with perfect linea-
   ments.

.   .   .   .

O friend, sleep was a veil uplift from
   heaven —
As if heaven dawned upon the world of
   dream —   240
When darkness rose on the extinguished
   day
Out of the eastern wilderness.

INDIAN

                 I too
Have found a moment's paradise in sleep
Half compensate a hell of waking sorrow.

II

MINOR FRAGMENTS

   These minor fragments have been recovered,
often with great difficulty, principally from
the Shelley MSS., by successive editors. Their
general character is described by Mrs. Shelley :
'In addition to such poems as have an intelligible aim and shape, many a stray idea and
transitory emotion found imperfect and abrupt
expression, and then again lost themselves in
silence. As he never wandered without a book
and without implements of writing, I find
many such in his manuscript books, that
scarcely bear record; while some of them,
broken and vague as they are, will appear
valuable to those who love Shelley's mind, and
desire to trace its workings.' The titles are,
as a rule, those given in previous editions.
The dates of composition, often conjectural,
and of publication, are affixed.

HOME

DEAR home, thou scene of earliest hopes
and joys,
The least of which wronged Memory ever
makes
Bitterer than all thine unremembered tears.
1816. Garnett, 1862.

FRAGMENT OF A GHOST STORY

A SHOVEL of his ashes took
From the hearth's obscurest nook,
Muttering mysteries as she went.
Helen and Henry knew that Granny
Was as much afraid of ghosts as any,
    And so they followed hard —
But Helen clung to her brother's arm,
And her own spasm made her shake.
1816. Garnett, 1862.

TO MARY

O MARY dear, that you were here!
With your brown eyes bright and clear,
    And your sweet voice, like a bird
Singing love to its lone mate
In the ivy bower disconsolate;
Voice the sweetest ever heard!
And your brow more
Than the   sky
Of this azure Italy.
Mary dear, come to me soon,
I am not well whilst thou art far;
As sunset to the spherèd moon,
As twilight to the western star,
Thou, belovèd, art to me.

O Mary dear, that you were here!
The Castle echo whispers ' Here !'
    Este, 1818. Mrs. Shelley, 1824.

TO MARY

This, and the following, probably refer to
Mrs. Shelley's grief for the death of their child,
William.

    THE world is dreary,
    And I am weary
Of wandering on without thee, Mary;

A joy was erewhile
In thy voice and thy smile,
And 't is gone, when I should be gone too,
Mary.
1819. Mrs. Shelley, 1839, 2d ed.

TO MARY

MY dearest Mary, wherefore hast thou
gone,
And left me in this dreary world alone !
Thy form is here indeed — a lovely one —
But thou art fled, gone down the dreary
road,
That leads to Sorrow's most obscure abode;
Thou sittest on the hearth of pale despair,
where
For thine own sake I cannot follow thee.
1819. Mrs. Shelley, 1839, 2d ed.

TO WILLIAM SHELLEY

With what truth may I say —
Roma, Roma, Roma,
Non è più come era prima !

Mrs. Shelley describes Shelley's grief for
the death of this child : ' Shelley had suffered
severely from the death of our son during this
summer. His heart, attuned to every kindly
affection, was full of burning love for his offspring. No words can express the anguish he
felt when his elder children were torn from
him. . . . When afterwards this child [Wil-
liam] died at Rome, he wrote, apropos of the
English burying ground in that city: " This
spot is the repository of a sacred loss, of which
the yearnings of a parent's heart are now prophetic ; he is rendered immortal by love, as his
memory is by death. My beloved child is buried here. I envy death the body far less than
the oppressors the minds of those whom they
have torn from me. The one can only kill the
body, the other crushes the affections." '

I

MY lost William, thou in whom
    Some bright spirit lived, and did
That decaying robe consume
    Which its lustre faintly hid, —
Here its ashes find a tomb;
    But beneath this pyramid
Thou art not — if a thing divine
Like thee can die, thy funeral shrine
Is thy mother's grief and mine.

II

Where art thou, my gentle child?
  Let me think thy spirit feeds,
With its life intense and mild,
The love of living leaves and weeds
Among these tombs and ruins wild;
  Let me think that through low seeds
Of sweet flowers and sunny grass
Into their hues and scents may pass
A portion ——

June, 1819. Mrs. Shelley, 1824.

LINES WRITTEN FOR THE POEM TO WILLIAM SHELLEY

I

THE world is now our dwelling-place;
Where'er the earth one fading trace
  Of what was great and free does keep,
That is our home!
Mild thoughts of man's ungentle race
  Shall our contented exile reap;
For who that in some happy place
His own free thoughts can freely chase
By woods and waves can clothe his face
  In cynic smiles? Child! we shall weep.

II

          This lament,
  The memory of thy grievous wrong
Will fade
But genius is Omnipotent
To hallow

1818. Garnett, 1862.

TO WILLIAM SHELLEY

THY little footsteps on the sands
  Of a remote and lonely shore;
The twinkling of thine infant hands
  Where now the worm will feed no more;
  Thy mingled look of love and glee
  When we returned to gaze on thee —

1819. Mrs. Shelley, 1839, 1st ed.

TO CONSTANTIA

I

THE rose that drinks the fountain dew
  In the pleasant air of noon,
Grows pale and blue with altered hue
In the gaze of the nightly moon;
For the planet of frost, so cold and bright,
Makes it wan with her borrowed light.

II

Such is my heart — roses are fair,
  And that at best a withered blossom;
But thy false care did idly wear
  Its withered leaves in a faithless bosom;
And fed with love, like air and dew,
Its growth

1817. Mrs. Shelley, 1839, 1st ed.

TO EMILIA VIVIANI

Medwin writes: ' Shelley felt deeply the fate of poor Emilia, frequently wrote to her, and received from her in reply bouquets of flowers, in return for one of which he sent her the following exquisite madrigal.'

I

MADONNA, wherefore hast thou sent to me
  Sweet-basil and mignonette?
Embleming love and health, which never
    yet
In the same wreath might be.
  Alas, and they are wet!
Is it with thy kisses or thy tears?
  For never rain or dew
  Such fragrance drew
From plant or flower — the very doubt en-
    dears
  My sadness ever new,
The sighs I breathe, the tears I shed for
    thee.

II

Send the stars light, but send not love to
    me,
  In whom love ever made
Health like a heap of embers soon to fade.

March, 1821. Mrs. Shelley, 1824, completed by Garnett, 1862, Forman, 1876.

TO ——

Rossetti conjectures that Byron is addressed.

O MIGHTY mind, in whose deep stream
    this age
Shakes like a reed in the unheeding storm,
Why dost thou curb not thine own sacred
    rage?

1818. Garnett, 1862.

SONNET TO BYRON

Medwin writes: ' What his real opinion of Byron's powers was may be collected from a sonnet he once showed me, and which the subject of it never saw. The sentiments accord well with that diffidence of his own powers, that innate modesty which always distinguished him. It begins thus '

[I am afraid these verses will not please you, but]

IF I esteemed you less, Envy would kill
   Pleasure, and leave to Wonder and Despair
   The ministration of the thoughts that fill
   The mind which, like a worm whose life may share
A portion of the unapproachable,
   Marks your creations rise as fast and fair
As perfect worlds at the Creator's will.
   But such is my regard that nor your power
To soar above the heights where others [climb],
   Nor fame, that shadow of the unborn hour
   Cast from the envious future on the time,
Move one regret for his unhonored name
   Who dares these words: — the worm beneath the sod
   May lift itself in homage of the God.
1821. Medwin, 1832, 1847, revised by Rossetti, 1870.

A LOST LEADER

MY head is wild with weeping for a grief
   Which is the shadow of a gentle mind.
I walk into the air (but no relief
To seek, — or haply, if I sought, to find;
It came unsought); — to wonder that a chief
   Among men's spirits should be cold and blind.
1818. Rossetti, 1870.

ON KEATS

WHO DESIRED THAT ON HIS TOMB
SHOULD BE INSCRIBED —

' HERE lieth One whose name was writ on
   water ! '
But ere the breath that could erase it blew,

Death, in remorse for that fell slaughter, —
Death, the immortalizing winter, flew
Athwart the stream, and time's printless
   torrent grew
A scroll of crystal, blazoning the name
Of Adonais !
1821. Mrs. Shelley, 1839, 1st ed.

TO ——

Rossetti conjectures that the lines are addressed to Leigh Hunt; Forman, that they may be a cancelled passage of *Rosalind and Helen*.

FOR me, my friend, if not that tears did
   tremble
   In my faint eyes, and that my heart beat
   fast
With feelings which make rapture pain
   resemble,
   Yet, from thy voice that falsehood starts
   aghast,
I thank thee — let the tyrant keep
His chains and tears, yea let him weep
With rage to see thee freshly risen,
Like strength from slumber, from the
   prison,
In which he vainly hoped the soul to bind
Which on the chains must prey that fetter
   humankind.
1817. Garnett, 1862.

MILTON'S SPIRIT

I DREAMED that Milton's spirit rose, and
   took
From life's green tree his Uranian lute;
And from his touch sweet thunder flowed,
   and shook
All human things built in contempt of
   man, —
And sanguine thrones and impious altars
   quaked,
Prisons and citadels.
1820. Rossetti, 1870.

'MIGHTY EAGLE'

MIGHTY eagle ! thou that soarest
O'er the misty mountain forest,
   And amid the light of morning
Like a cloud of glory hiest,
And when night descends defiest
   The embattled tempests' warning !
1817. Forman, 1882.

LAUREL

'WHAT art thou, presumptuous, who pro-
 fanest
The wreath to mighty poets only due,
Even whilst like a forgotten moon thou
 wanest ?
Touch not those leaves which for the
 eternal few
Who wander o'er the paradise of fame,
 In sacred dedication ever grew:
One of the crowd thou art without a name,'
' Ah, friend, 't is the false laurel that I wear.
Bright though it seem, it is not the same
As that which bound Milton's immortal
 hair:
Its dew is poison; and the hopes that
 quicken
Under its chilling shade, though seeming
 fair,
Are flowers which die almost before they
 sicken.'
 1821. Mrs. Shelley, 1839, 1st ed.

'ONCE MORE DESCEND'

Forman conjectures this and the following to
be fragments of *Otho*.

    ONCE more descend
The shadows of my soul upon mankind;
For, to those hearts with which they never
 blend,
Thoughts are but shadows which the
 flashing mind
From the swift clouds, which track its
 flight of fire,
Casts on the gloomy world it leaves behind.
 1817. Garnett, 1862.

INSPIRATION

THOSE whom nor power, nor lying faith,
 nor toil,
 Nor custom, queen of many slaves,
  makes blind,
Have ever grieved that man should be the
 spoil
 Of his own weakness, and with earnest
  mind
Fed hopes of its redemption; these recur
 Chastened by deathful victory now, and
  find
Foundations in this foulest age, and stir
Me whom they cheer to be their minister.
 1817. Garnett, 1862.

TO THE PEOPLE OF ENGLAND

PEOPLE of England, ye who toil and
 groan,
Who reap the harvests which are not your
 own,
Who weave the clothes which your oppressors wear,
And for your own take the inclement
 air;
Who build warm houses . . .
And are like gods who give them all they
 have,
And nurse them from the cradle to the
 grave . . .
 1819. Garnett, 1862.

'WHAT MEN GAIN FAIRLY'

Forman joins this with the preceding.

WHAT men gain fairly, that they should
 possess;
And children may inherit idleness,
From him who earns it — this is under-
 stood;
Private injustice may be general good.
But he who gains by base and armèd
 wrong,
Or guilty fraud, or base compliances,
May be despoiled; even as a stolen dress
Is stripped from a convicted thief, and he
Left in the nakedness of infamy.
 1819. Mrs. Shelley, 1839, 2d ed.

ROME

ROME has fallen; ye see it lying
 Heaped in undistinguished ruin:
Nature is alone undying.
 1819. Mrs. Shelley, 1839, 2d ed.

TO ITALY

As the sunrise to the night,
 As the north wind to the clouds,
As the earthquake's fiery flight,
 Ruining mountain solitudes,
Everlasting Italy,
Be those hopes and fears on thee.
 1819. Garnett, 1862.

'UNRISEN SPLENDOR'

UNRISEN splendor of the brightest sun,
To rise upon our darkness, if the star
Now beckoning thee out of thy misty throne
Could thaw the clouds which wage an ob-
    scure war
With thy young brightness !
  1820. Garnett, 1862.

TO ZEPHYR

COME, thou awakener of the spirit's ocean,
    Zephyr, whom to thy cloud or cave
No thought can trace ! speed with thy
    gentle motion !
  1821. Rossetti, 1870.

'FOLLOW'

FOLLOW to the deep wood's weeds,
Follow to the wild briar dingle,
Where we seek to intermingle,
And the violet tells her tale
To the odor-scented gale,
For they two have enough to do
Of such work as I and you.
  1819. Garnett, 1862.

THE RAIN-WIND

THE gentleness of rain was in the wind.
  1821. Rossetti, 1870.

RAIN

THE fitful alternations of the rain,
When the chill wind, languid as with pain
Of its own heavy moisture, here and there
Drives through the gray and beamless at-
    mosphere.
  1819. Mrs. Shelley, 1839, 2d ed.

'WHEN SOFT WINDS'

WHEN soft winds and sunny skies
With the green earth harmonize,
And the young and dewy dawn,
Bold as an unhunted fawn,
Up the windless heaven is gone, —
Laugh — for, ambushed in the day,
Clouds and whirlwinds watch their prey.
  1821. Mrs. Shelley, 1839, 2d ed.

THE VINE

FLOURISHING vine, whose kindling clusters
    glow
  Beneath the autumnal sun, none taste of
    thee;
For thou dost shroud a ruin, and below
  The rotting bones of dead antiquity.
  1818. Rossetti, 1870.

THE WANING MOON

AND like a dying lady, lean and pale,
Who totters forth, wrapped in a gauzy
    veil,
Out of her chamber, led by the insane
And feeble wanderings of her fading brain,
The mood arose up in the murky East,
A white and shapeless mass.
  1820. Mrs. Shelley, 1824.

TO THE MOON

BRIGHT wanderer, fair coquette of heaven,
To whom alone it has been given
To change and be adored forever,
Envy not this dim world, for never
But once within its shadow grew
One fair as ——
  1822. Garnett, 1862.

TO THE MOON

I

ART thou pale for weariness
Of climbing heaven and gazing on the
    earth,
Wandering companionless
Among the stars that have a different
    birth, —
And ever changing, like a joyless eye
That finds no object worth its constancy ?

II

Thou chosen sister of the spirit,
That gazes on thee till in thee it pities . . .
  1820. Mrs. Shelley, 1824, completed by
Rossetti, 1870.

POETRY AND MUSIC

How sweet it is to sit and read the tales
Of mighty poets, and to hear the while

Sweet music, which when the attention
    fails
Fills the dim pause !
    1819. Mrs. Shelley, 1839, 2d ed.

'A GENTLE STORY'

A GENTLE story of two lovers young,
    Who met in innocence and died in sor-
        row,
And of one selfish heart, whose rancor
    clung
    Like curses on them; are ye slow to
      borrow
    The lore of truth from such a tale ?
    Or in this world's deserted vale,
    Do ye not see a star of gladness
    Pierce the shadows of its sadness, —
When ye are cold, that love is a light sent
From heaven, which none shall quench, to
    cheer the innocent ?
    1819. Mrs. Shelley, 1839, 2d ed.

THE LADY OF THE SOUTH

FAINT with love, the Lady of the South
    Lay in the paradise of Lebanon
Under a heaven of cedar boughs; the
    drouth
    Of love was on her lips; the light was
      gone
Out of her eyes.
    1821. Rossetti, 1870.

THE TALE UNTOLD

ONE sung of thee who left the tale untold,
    Like the false dawns which perish in the
      bursting;
Like empty cups of wrought and dædal
    gold,
    Which mock the lips with air, when they
    are thirsting.
    1819. Mrs. Shelley, 1839, 2d ed.

WINE OF EGLANTINE

I AM drunk with the honey wine
Of the moon-unfolded eglantine,
Which fairies catch in hyacinth bowls.
The bats, the dormice, and the moles

Sleep in the walls or under the sward
Of the desolate Castle yard;
And when 't is spilt on the summer earth
Or its fumes arise among the dew,
Their jocund dreams are full of mirth,
They gibber their joy in sleep; for few
Of the fairies bear those bowls so new !
    1819. Mrs. Shelley, 1839, 1st ed.

A ROMAN'S CHAMBER

I

IN the cave which wild weeds cover
Wait for thine ethereal lover;
For the pallid moon is waning,
O'er the spiral cypress hanging,
And the moon no cloud is staining.

II

It was once a Roman's chamber, —
And the wild weeds twine and clamber,
Where he kept his darkest revels;
It was then a chasm for devils.
    1819. Mrs. Shelley, 1839, 2d ed.

SONG OF THE FURIES

WHEN a lover clasps his fairest,
Then be our dread sport the rarest.
Their caresses were like the chaff
In the tempest, and be our laugh
His despair — her epitaph !

When a mother clasps a child,
Watch till dusty Death has piled
His cold ashes on the clay;
She has loved it many a day —
She remains, — it fades away.
    1819. Mrs. Shelley, 1839, 2d ed.

'THE RUDE WIND IS SINGING'

THE rude wind is singing
    The dirge of the music dead;
The cold worms are clinging
    Where kisses were lately fed.
    1821. Mrs. Shelley, 1839, 1st ed.

BEFORE AND AFTER

THE babe is at peace within the womb;
The corpse is at rest within the tomb:
We begin in what we end.
    1821. Mrs. Shelley, 1839, 2d ed.

THE SHADOW OF HELL

A GOLDEN-WINGÈD Angel stood
  Before the Eternal Judgment-seat:
His looks were wild, and Devils' blood
  Stained his dainty hands and feet.
The Father and the Son
Knew that strife was now begun.
They knew that Satan had broken his
    chain,
And with millions of demons in his train,
Was ranging over the world again.
Before the Angel had told his tale,
  A sweet and a creeping sound
Like the rushing of wings was heard
    around;
And suddenly the lamps grew pale —
The lamps, before the Archangels seven —
That burn continually in heaven.
  1817. Rossetti, 1870.

CONSEQUENCE

THE viewless and invisible Consequence
Watches thy goings-out, and comings-in,
And . . . hovers o'er thy guilty sleep,
Unveiling every new-born deed, and
    thoughts
More ghastly than those deeds.
  1820. Rossetti, 1870.

A HATE-SONG

Rossetti gives the source of this : ' Mr.
Browning has furnished me with this amusing
absurdity, retailed to him by Leigh Hunt.
It seems that Hunt and Shelley were talking
one day (probably in or about 1817) concerning
Love-Songs ; and Shelley said that he did n't
see why Hate-Songs also should not be written,
and that he could do them ; and on the spot
he improvised these lines of doggerel.'

A HATER he came and sat by a ditch,
  And he took an old cracked lute;
And he sang a song which was more of a
    screech
'Gainst a woman that was a brute.
  1817. Rossetti, 1870.

A FACE

HIS face was like a snake's — wrinkled and
    loose
And withered.
  1820. Rossetti, 1870.

THE POET'S LOVER

I AM as a spirit who has dwelt
Within his heart of hearts, and I have felt
His feelings, and have thought his thoughts,
    and known
The inmost converse of his soul, the tone
Unheard but in the silence of his blood,
When all the pulses in their multitude
Image the trembling calm of summer seas.
I have unlocked the golden melodies
Of his deep soul, as with a master-key,
And loosened them and bathed myself
    therein —
Even as an eagle in a thunder-mist
Clothing his wings with lightning.
  1819. Garnett, 1862.

'I WOULD NOT BE A KING'

I WOULD not be a king — enough
  Of woe it is to love;
The path to power is steep and rough,
  And tempests reign above.
I would not climb the imperial throne;
  'T is built on ice which fortune's sun
Thaws in the height of noon.
Then farewell, king, yet were I one,
  Care would not come so soon.
Would he and I were far away
Keeping flocks on Himalay !
  1821. Mrs. Shelley, 1839, 2d ed.

'IS IT THAT IN SOME BRIGHTER SPHERE'

Is it that in some brighter sphere
We part from friends we meet with here ?
Or do we see the Future pass
Over the Present's dusky glass ?
Or what is that that makes us seem
To patch up fragments of a dream,
Part of which comes true, and part
Beats and trembles in the heart ?
  1819. Garnett, 1862.

TO-DAY

AND who feels discord now or sorrow ?
  Love is the universe to-day;
These are the slaves of dim to-morrow,
  Darkening Life's labyrinthine way.
  1819. Mrs. Shelley, 1839, 1st ed.

LOVE'S ATMOSPHERE

THERE is a warm and gentle atmosphere
About the form of one we love, and thus
As in a tender mist our spirits are
Wrapped in the　　　　　of that which is to us
The health of life's own life.
　　1819.　Mrs. Shelley, 1839, 2d ed.

TORPOR

MY head is heavy, my limbs are weary,
And it is not life that makes me move.
　　1820.　Garnett, 1862.

'WAKE THE SERPENT NOT'

WAKE the serpent not — lest he
Should not know the way to go;
Let him crawl which yet lies sleeping
Through the deep grass of the meadow !
Not a bee shall hear him creeping,
Not a May-fly shall awaken,
From its cradling blue-bell shaken,
Not the starlight as he 's sliding
Through the grass with silent gliding.
　　1819.　Mrs. Shelley, 1839, 2d ed.

'IS NOT TO-DAY ENOUGH?'

Is not to-day enough ?　Why do I peer
　　Into the darkness of the day to come ?
Is not to-morrow even as yesterday ?
　　And will the day that follows change thy
　　　　doom ?
Few flowers grow upon thy wintry way;
　　And who waits for thee in that cheerless
　　　　home
Whence thou hast fled, whither thou must
　　　　return
Charged with the load that makes thee faint
　　　and mourn ?
　　1819.　Garnett, 1862.

'TO THIRST AND FIND NO FILL'

　　Mrs. Shelley introduces the fragment thus :
' And then again this melancholy trace of the
sad thronging thoughts, which were the well
whence he drew the idea of *Athanase*, and

express the restless, passion-fraught emotions of
one whose sensibility, kindled to too intense
a life, perpetually preyed upon itself.'　Forman conjectures that it is a cancelled passage
of *Julian and Maddalo*.

To thirst and find no fill — to wail and wan-
　　　der
With short uneasy steps — to pause and
　　　ponder —
To feel the blood run through the veins
　　　and tingle
Where busy thought and blind sensation
　　　mingle;
To nurse the image of unfelt caresses
Till dim imagination just possesses
The half-created shadow.
　　1817.　Mrs. Shelley, 1839, 1st ed.

LOVE

　　Mrs. Shelley introduces the fragment thus :
' In the next page I find a calmer sentiment,
better fitted to sustain one whose whole being
was love.'

WEALTH and dominion fade into the mass
　　Of the great sea of human right and
　　　wrong,
When once from our possession they must
　　　pass;
　　But love, though misdirected, is among
The things which are immortal, and sur-
　　　pass
All that frail stuff which will be — or which
　　　was.
　　1817.　Mrs. Shelley, 1839, 1st ed.

MUSIC

I

I PANT for the music which is divine,
　　My heart in its thirst is a dying flower ;
Pour forth the sound like enchanted wine,
　　Loosen the notes in a silver shower;
Like a herbless plain for the gentle rain,
I gasp, I faint, till they wake again.

II

Let me drink of the spirit of that sweet
　　　sound,
　　More, oh, more, — I am thirsting yet;
It loosens the serpent which care has bound
　　Upon my heart to stifle it;

The dissolving strain through every vein
Passes into my heart and brain.

III

As the scent of a violet withered up,
  Which grew by the brink of a silver lake,
When the hot noon has drained its dewy
    cup,
  And mist there was none its thirst to
    slake —
And the violet lay dead while the odor flew
On the wings of the wind o'er the waters
  blue —

IV

As one who drinks from a charmèd cup
  Of foaming, and sparkling, and murmur-
    ing wine,
Whom, a mighty enchantress filling up,
  Invites to love with her kiss divine —

.   .   .   .

1821. Mrs. Shelley, 1824.

TO ONE SINGING

My spirit like a charmèd bark doth swim
  Upon the liquid waves of thy sweet sing-
    ing
Far away into the regions dim
  Of rapture — as a boat, with swift sails
    winging
Its way adown some many-winding river.
1817. Mrs. Shelley, 1839, 1st ed.

TO MUSIC

Silver key of the fountain of tears,
  Where the spirit drinks till the brain is
    wild;
Softest grave of a thousand fears,
  Where their mother, Care, like a drowsy
    child,
Is laid asleep in flowers.
1817. Mrs. Shelley, 1839, 1st ed.

TO MUSIC

No, Music, thou art not the 'food of Love,'
Unless Love feeds upon its own sweet self,
Till it becomes all Music murmurs of.
1817. Mrs. Shelley, 1839, 1st ed.

'I FAINT, I PERISH WITH MY LOVE!'

I faint, I perish with my love! I grow
  Frail as a cloud whose [splendors] pale
Under the evening's ever-changing glow ;
  I die like mist upon the gale,
And like a wave under the calm I fail.
1821. Rossetti, 1870.

TO SILENCE

Silence ! Oh, well are Death and Sleep
  and Thou
Three brethren named, the guardians
  gloomy-winged
Of one abyss, where life, and truth, and
  joy
Are swallowed up — yet spare me, Spirit,
  pity me,
Until the sounds I hear become my soul,
And it has left these faint and weary limbs,
To track along the lapses of the air
This wandering melody until it rests
Among lone mountains in some . . .
1818. Garnett, 1862.

'OH, THAT A CHARIOT OF CLOUD WERE MINE!'

Oh, that a chariot of cloud were mine !
  Of cloud which the wild tempest weaves
    in air,
When the moon over the ocean's line
  Is spreading the locks of her bright gray
    hair.
Oh, that a chariot of cloud were mine !
  I would sail on the waves of the billowy
    wind
To the mountain peak and the rocky lake,
And the . . .
1817. Garnett, 1862.

'THE FIERCE BEASTS'

The fierce beasts of the woods and wildernesses
Track not the steps of him who drinks of
  it;
For the light breezes, which forever fleet
Around its margin, heap the sand thereon.
1818. Rossetti, 1817.

HE WANDERS

HE wanders, like a day-appearing dream,
  Through the dim wildernesses of the
    mind;
Through desert woods and tracts, which
    seem
  Like ocean, homeless, boundless, uncon-
    fined.
    1821. Mrs. Shelley, 1839, 1st ed.

THE DESERTS OF SLEEP

I WENT into the deserts of dim sleep —
  That world which, like an unknown wil-
    derness,
Bounds this with its recesses wide and
  deep.
    1820. Rossetti, 1870.

A DREAM

METHOUGHT I was a billow in the crowd
  Of common men, that stream without a
    shore,
That ocean which at once is deaf and loud;
  That I, a man, stood amid many more
  By a wayside   which the aspect
    bore
Of some imperial metropolis,
  Where mighty shapes — pyramid, dome,
    and tower —
  Gleamed like a pile of crags.
    1821. Rossetti, 1870.

THE HEART'S TOMB

AND where is truth? On tombs? for such
    to thee
Has been my heart — and thy dead memory
Has lain from childhood, many a change-
    ful year,
Unchangingly preserved and buried there.
    1819. Mrs. Shelley, 1839, 1st ed.

HOPE, FEAR, AND DOUBT

SUCH hope, as is the sick despair of good,
Such fear, as is the certainty of ill,
Such doubt, as is pale Expectation's food
Turned while she tastes to poison, when
    the will
Is powerless, and the spirit . . .
    1820. Garnett, 1862.

'ALAS! THIS IS NOT WHAT I THOUGHT LIFE WAS'

Mrs. Shelley introduces the fragment thus:
'That he felt these things [public neglect and
calumny] deeply cannot be doubted, though
he armed himself with the consciousness of
acting from a lofty and heroic sense of right.
The truth burst from his heart sometimes in
solitude, and he would write a few unfinished
verses that showed he felt the sting. Among
such I find the following.'

ALAS! this is not what I thought life was.
I knew that there were crimes and evil
    men,
Misery and hate; nor did I hope to pass
Untouched by suffering, through the rugged
    glen.
In mine own heart I saw as in a glass
The hearts of others   And
    when
I went among my kind, with triple brass
Of calm endurance my weak breast I
    armed,
To bear scorn, fear, and hate, a woful
    mass!
    1820. Mrs. Shelley, 1839, 1st ed.

CROWNED

Originally published as the conclusion of
'When soft winds and sunny skies.' Rossetti
joins it with Laurel at the end.

AND that I walked thus proudly crowned
    withal
Is that 't is my distinction; if I fall,
I shall not weep out of the vital day,
To-morrow dust, nor wear a dull decay.
    1821. Mrs. Shelley, 1839, 2d ed.

'GREAT SPIRIT'

Forman conjectures that this and the following are addressed to Liberty.

GREAT Spirit whom the sea of boundless
    thought
  Nurtures within its unimagined caves,
In which thou sittest sole, as in my mind,
  Giving a voice to its mysterious waves.
    1821. Rossetti, 1870.

'O THOU IMMORTAL DEITY'

O THOU immortal deity
Whose throne is in the depth of human
    thought,
  I do adjure thy power and thee
By all that man may be, by all that he is
    not,
  By all that he has been and yet must be!
1821.   Mrs. Shelley, 1839, 2d ed.

'YE GENTLE VISITATIONS'

YE gentle visitations of calm thought,
  Moods like the memories of happier
    earth,
  Which come arrayed in thoughts of little
    worth,
Like stars in clouds by the weak winds
    enwrought, —
  But that the clouds depart and stars
    remain,
  While they remain, and ye, alas, depart!
1819.   Mrs. Shelley, 1839, 1st ed.

'MY THOUGHTS'

MY thoughts arise and fade in solitude,
  The verse that would invest them melts
    away
  Like moonlight in the heaven of spread-
    ing day:
How beautiful they were, how firm they
    stood,
Flecking the starry sky like woven pearl!
  1817.   Mrs. Shelley, 1839, 1st ed.

TRANSLATIONS

The *Translations* were published partly by Shelley, with other poems, partly by Mrs. Shelley, and partly by Medwin, Garnett, Rossetti and Forman from MSS. They were written from 1818 to 1822. Two pieces, hypothetically ascribed to Shelley by Forman, *The Dinner Party Anticipated*, a paraphrase of Horace III. xix., and *The Magic Horn* from Bronzino, are excluded from the text, there being no substantial evidence that Shelley wrote them.

HYMN TO MERCURY

FROM THE GREEK OF HOMER

This remarkable piece of facile rendering from the Homeric Hymn was composed in the summer of 1820. Shelley mentions it in a letter to Peacock, July 20: 'I am translating, in *ottava rima*, the *Hymn to Mercury* of Homer. Of course my stanza precludes a literal translation. My next effort will be that it should be legible — a quality much to be desired in translations.' It was published by Mrs. Shelley, *Posthumous Poems*, 1824.

I

SING, Muse, the son of Maia and of Jove,
  The Herald-child, king of Arcadia
And all its pastoral hills, whom, in sweet love
  Having been interwoven, modest May
Bore Heaven's dread Supreme. An antique grove
  Shadowed the cavern where the lovers lay
In the deep night, unseen by Gods or Men,
And white-armed Juno slumbered sweetly then.

II

Now, when the joy of Jove had its fulfilling,
  And Heaven's tenth moon chronicled her relief,
She gave to light a babe all babes excelling,
  A schemer subtle beyond all belief,
A shepherd of thin dreams, a cow-stealing,
  A night-watching, and door-waylaying thief,
Who 'mongst the Gods was soon about to thieve,
And other glorious actions to achieve.

III

The babe was born at the first peep of day;
  He began playing on the lyre at noon,
And the same evening did he steal away
  Apollo's herds. The fourth day of the moon,
On which him bore the venerable May,
  From her immortal limbs he leaped full soon,
Nor long could in the sacred cradle keep,
But out to seek Apollo's herds would creep.

IV

Out of the lofty cavern wandering
  He found a tortoise, and cried out — 'A treasure!'
(For Mercury first made the tortoise sing)
  The beast before the portal at his leisure
The flowery herbage was depasturing,
  Moving his feet in a deliberate measure
Over the turf. Jove's profitable son
Eying him laughed, and laughing thus begun: —

V

'A useful godsend are you to me now,
  King of the dance, companion of the feast,
Lovely in all your nature! Welcome, you
  Excellent plaything! Where, sweet mountain beast,
Got you that speckled shell? Thus much I know,
  You must come home with me and be my guest;
You will give joy to me, and I will do
All that is in my power to honor you.

VI

'Better to be at home than out of door,
  So come with me; and though it has been said
That you alive defend from magic power,
  I know you will sing sweetly when you 're dead.'
Thus having spoken, the quaint infant bore,
  Lifting it from the grass on which it fed
And grasping it in his delighted hold,
His treasured prize into the cavern old.

VII

Then, scooping with a chisel of gray steel,
  He bored the life and soul out of the
    beast.
Not swifter a swift thought of woe or
  weal
  Darts through the tumult of a human
    breast
Which thronging cares annoy — not swifter
  wheel
The flashes of its torture and unrest
Out of the dizzy eyes — than Maia's son
All that he did devise hath featly done.

VIII

And through the tortoise's hard stony
  skin
At proper distances small holes he made,
  And fastened the cut stems of reeds
    within,
And with a piece of leather overlaid
  The open space and fixed the cubits in,
Fitting the bridge to both, and stretched
  o'er all
Symphonious cords of sheep-gut rhythmi-
  cal.

IX

When he had wrought the lovely instru-
  ment,
  He tried the chords, and made division
    meet,
Preluding with the plectrum, and there
  went
  Up from beneath his hand a tumult sweet
Of mighty sounds, and from his lips he
  sent
  A strain of unpremeditated wit
Joyous and wild and wanton — such you
  may
Hear among revellers on a holiday.

X

He sung how Jove and May of the bright
  sandal
  Dallied in love not quite legitimate;
And his own birth, still scoffing at the
  scandal
  And naming his own name, did celebrate;
His mother's cave and servant maids he
  planned all
  In plastic verse, her household stuff and
    state,
Perennial pot, trippet, and brazen pan, —
But singing, he conceived another plan.

XI

Seized with a sudden fancy for fresh
  meat,
He in his sacred crib deposited
  The hollow lyre, and from the cavern
    sweet
Rushed with great leaps up to the moun-
  tain's head,
  Revolving in his mind some subtle feat
Of thievish craft, such as a swindler might
Devise in the lone season of dun night.

XII

Lo ! the great Sun under the ocean's bed
  has
  Driven steeds and chariot. The child
    meanwhile strode
O'er the Pierian mountains clothed in
  shadows,
  Where the immortal oxen of the God
Are pastured in the flowering unmown
  meadows
  And safely stalled in a remote abode.
The archer Argicide, elate and proud,
Drove fifty from the herd, lowing aloud.

XIII

He drove them wandering o'er the sandy
  way,
  But, being ever mindful of his craft,
Backward and forward drove he them
  astray,
  So that the tracks which seemed before,
    were aft;
His sandals then he threw to the ocean
  spray,
  And for each foot he wrought a kind of
    raft
Of tamarisk and tamarisk-like sprigs,
And bound them in a lump with withy
  twigs.

XIV

And on his feet he tied these sandals
  light,
The trail of whose wide leaves might not
  betray
  His track; and then, a self-sufficing
    wight,
Like a man hastening on some distant way,
  He from Pieria's mountain bent his
    flight;
But an old man perceived the infant pass
Down green Onchestus heaped like beds
  with grass.

XV

The old man stood dressing his sunny vine.
  'Halloo! old fellow with the crookèd
    shoulder!
You grub those stumps? before they will
    bear wine
  Methinks even you must grow a little
    older.
Attend, I pray, to this advice of mine,
  As you would 'scape what might appall a
    bolder:
Seeing, see not — and hearing, hear not —
    and —
If you have understanding, understand.'

XVI

So saying, Hermes roused the oxen vast;
  O'er shadowy mountain and resounding
    dell
And flower-paven plains great Hermes
    passed;
  Till the black night divine, which favor-
    ing fell
Around his steps, grew gray, and morning
    fast
  Wakened the world to work, and from
    her cell
Sea-strewn the Pallantean Moon sublime
Into her watch-tower just began to climb.

XVII

Now to Alpheus he had driven all
  The broad-foreheaded oxen of the Sun;
They came unwearied to the lofty stall
  And to the water troughs which ever run
Through the fresh fields; and when with
    rushgrass tall,
  Lotos and all sweet herbage, every one
Had pastured been, the great God made
    them move
Towards the stall in a collected drove.

XVIII

A mighty pile of wood the God then
    heaped,
  And, having soon conceived the mystery
Of fire, from two smooth laurel branches
    stripped
  The bark, and rubbed them in his palms;
    on high
Suddenly forth the burning vapor leaped,
  And the divine child saw delightedly.
Mercury first found out for human weal
Tinder-box, matches, fire-irons, flint and
    steel.

XIX

And fine dry logs and roots innumerous
  He gathered in a delve upon the
    ground —
And kindled them — and instantaneous
  The strength of the fierce flame was
    breathed around;
And, whilst the might of glorions Vulcan
    thus
  Wrapped the great pile with glare and
    roaring sound,
Hermes dragged forth two heifers, lowing
    loud,
Close to the fire — such might was in the
    God.

XX

And on the earth upon their backs he
    threw
  The panting beasts, and rolled them o'er
    and o'er,
And bored their lives out. Without more
    ado
  He cut up fat and flesh, and down be-
    fore
The fire on spits of wood he placed the
    two,
  Toasting their flesh and ribs, and all the
    gore
Pursed in the bowels; and while this was
    done
He stretched their hides over a craggy
    stone.

XXI

We mortals let an ox grow old, and then
  Cut it up after long consideration, —
But joyous-minded Hermes from the glen
  Drew the fat spoils to the more open
    station
Of a flat smooth space, and portioned them;
    and when
  He had by lot assigned to each a ration
Of the twelve Gods, his mind became
    aware
Of all the joys which in religion are.

XXII

For the sweet savor of the roasted meat
  Tempted him though immortal. Nathe-
    less
He checked his haughty will and did not
    eat,
  Though what it cost him words can
    scarce express,

And every wish to put such morsels sweet
  Down his most sacred throat he did re-
    press;
But soon within the lofty portaled stall
He placed the fat and flesh and bones and
  all.

XXIII

And every trace of the fresh butchery
  And cooking the God soon made disap-
    pear,
As if it all had vanished through the
    sky;
  He burned the hoofs and horns and head
    and hair, —
The insatiate fire devoured them hungrily;
  And, when he saw that everything was
    clear,
He quenched the coals, and trampled the
    black dust,
And in the stream his bloody sandals
    tossed.

XXIV

All night he worked in the serene moon-
    shine.
  But when the light of day was spread
    abroad
He sought his natal mountain-peaks divine.
  On his long wandering neither man nor
    god
Had met him, since he killed Apollo's
    kine,
  Nor house-dog had barked at him on his
    road;
Now he obliquely through the key-hole
    passed,
Like a thin mist or an autumnal blast.

XXV

Right through the temple of the spacious
    cave
  He went with soft light feet, as if his
    tread
Fell not on earth; no sound their falling
    gave;
  Then to his cradle he crept quick, and
    spread
The swaddling-clothes about him; and the
    knave
  Lay playing with the covering of the
    bed
With his left hand about his knees — the
    right
Held his belovèd tortoise-lyre tight.

XXVI

There he lay innocent as a new-born child,
  As gossips say; but though he was a god,
The goddess, his fair mother, unbeguiled
  Knew all that he had done being abroad.
'Whence come you, and from what ad-
    venture wild,
  You cunning rogue, and where have you
    abode
All the long night, clothed in your impu-
    dence?
What have you done since you departed
    hence?

XXVII

'Apollo soon will pass within this gate
  And bind your tender body in a chain
Inextricably tight, and fast as fate,
  Unless you can delude the God again,
Even when within his arms. Ah, runa-
    gate!
  A pretty torment both for gods and men
Your father made when he made you!'—
  'Dear mother,'
Replied sly Hermes, 'wherefore scold and
    bother?

XXVIII

'As if I were like other babes as old,
  And understood nothing of what is what,
And cared at all to hear my mother scold.
  I in my subtle brain a scheme have
    got,
Which whilst the sacred stars round
    Heaven are rolled
  Will profit you and me; nor shall our
    lot
Be as you counsel, without gifts or food,
To spend our lives in this obscure abode.

XXIX

'But we will leave this shadow-peopled
    cave
  And live among the Gods, and pass each
    day
In high communion, sharing what they
    have
  Of profuse wealth and unexhausted prey;
And from the portion which my father
    gave
  To Phœbus, I will snatch my share
    away;
Which if my father will not, natheless I,
Who am the king of robbers, can but
    try.

XXX

' And, if Latona's son should find me out,
  I 'll countermine him by a deeper plan;
I 'll pierce the Pythian temple-walls, though
    stout,
  And sack the fane of everything I can —
Caldrons and tripods of great worth no
    doubt,
  Each golden cup and polished brazen
    pan,
All the wrought tapestries and garments
    gay.'
So they together talked. Meanwhile the
    Day,

XXXI

Ethereal born, arose out of the flood
  Of flowing Ocean, bearing light to men.
Apollo passed toward the sacred wood,
  Which from the inmost depths of its
    green glen
Echoes the voice of Neptune; and there
    stood,
  On the same spot in green Onchestus
    then,
That same old animal, the vine-dresser,
Who was employed hedging his vineyard
    there.

XXXII

Latona's glorious Son began: — ' I pray
  Tell, ancient hedger of Onchestus green,
Whether a drove of kine has passed this
    way,
  All heifers with crooked horns ? for they
    have been
Stolen from the herd in high Pieria,
  Where a black bull was fed apart, be-
    tween
Two woody mountains in a neighboring
    glen,
And four fierce dogs watched there, unani-
    mous as men.

XXXIII

' And what is strange, the author of this
    theft
  Has stolen the fatted heifers every one,
But the four dogs and the black bull are
    left.
  Stolen they were last night at set of sun,
Of their soft beds and their sweet food be-
    reft.
  Now tell me, man born ere the world
    begun,

Have you seen any one pass with the
    cows ? '
To whom the man of overhanging brows:

XXXIV

' My friend, it would require no common
    skill
  Justly to speak of everything I see;
On various purposes of good or ill
  Many pass by my vineyard, — and to
    me
'T is difficult to know the invisible
  Thoughts, which in all those many minds
    may be.
Thus much alone I certainly can say,
I tilled these vines till the decline of day,

XXXV

' And then I thought I saw, but dare not
    speak
  With certainty of such a wondrous thing,
A child, who could not have been born a
    week,
  Those fair-horned cattle closely follow-
    ing,
And in his hand he held a polished stick;
  And, as on purpose, he walked wavering
From one side to the other of the road,
And with his face opposed the steps he
    trod.'

XXXVI

Apollo hearing this, passed quickly on —
  No wingèd omen could have shown more
    clear
That the deceiver was his father's son.
  So the God wraps a purple atmosphere
Around his shoulders, and like fire is gone
  To famous Pylos, seeking his kine there,
And found their track and his, yet hardly
    cold,
And cried — ' What wonder do mine eyes
    behold !

XXXVII

' Here are the footsteps of the hornèd herd
  Turned back towards their fields of as-
    phodel;
But these are not the tracks of beast or
    bird,
  Gray wolf, or bear, or lion of the dell,
Or manèd Centaur — sand was never stirred
  By man or woman thus ! Inexplicable !
Who with unwearied feet could e'er impress
The sand with such enormous vestiges ?

XXXVIII

'That was most strange — but this is
  stranger still !'
Thus having said, Phœbus impetuously
Sought high Cyllene's forest-cintured hill,
  And the deep cavern where dark shad-
  ows lie,
And where the ambrosial nymph with
  happy will
Bore the Saturnian's love-child, Mercury;
And a delightful odor from the dew
Of the hill pastures, at his coming, flew.

XXXIX

And Phœbus stooped under the craggy
  roof
  Arched over the dark cavern. Maia's
  child
Perceived that he came angry, far aloof,
  About the cows of which he had been
  beguiled;
And over him the fine and fragrant woof
  Of his ambrosial swaddling clothes he
  piled,
As among firebrands lies a burning spark
Covered, beneath the ashes cold and dark.

XL

There, like an infant who had sucked his
  fill
  And now was newly washed, and put to
  bed,
Awake, but courting sleep with weary
  will,
  And gathered in a lump, hands, feet, and
  head,
He lay, and his belovèd tortoise still
  He grasped, and held under his shoulder-
  blade.
Phœbus the lovely mountain-goddess knew,
Not less her subtle, swindling baby, who

XLI

Lay swathed in his sly wiles. Round every
  crook
Of the ample cavern for his kine Apollo
Looked sharp; and when he saw them not,
  he took
  The glittering key, and opened three
  great hollow
Recesses in the rock, where many a nook
  Was filled with the sweet food immortals
  swallow;
And mighty heaps of silver and of gold
Were piled within — a wonder to behold !

XLII

And white and silver robes, all overwrought
  With cunning workmanship of tracery
  sweet;
Except among the Gods there can be nought
  In the wide world to be compared with it.
Latona's offspring, after having sought
  His herds in every corner, thus did greet
Great Hermes : — 'Little cradled rogue,
  declare
Of my illustrious heifers, where they are !

XLIII

'Speak quickly ! or a quarrel between us
  Must rise, and the event will be that I
Shall hurl you into dismal Tartarus,
  In fiery gloom to dwell eternally;
Nor shall your father nor your mother loose
  The bars of that black dungeon; utterly
You shall be cast out from the light of day,
To rule the ghosts of men, unblessed as
  they.'

XLIV

To whom thus Hermes slyly answered: —
  'Son
Of great Latona, what a speech is this !
Why come you here to ask me what is done
  With the wild oxen which it seems you
  miss ?
I have not seen them, nor from any one
  Have heard a word of the whole business;
If you should promise an immense reward,
I could not tell more than you now have
  heard.

XLV

'An ox-stealer should be both tall and
  strong,
  And I am but a little new-born thing,
Who, yet at least, can think of nothing
  wrong.
  My business is to suck, and sleep, and
  fling
The cradle-clothes about me all day long, —
  Or half asleep, hear my sweet mother
  sing,
And to be washed in water clean and warm,
And hushed and kissed and kept secure
  from harm.

XLVI

'Oh, let not e'er this quarrel be averred !
  The astounded Gods would laugh at you,
  if e'er

You should allege a story so absurd
  As that a new-born infant forth could
    fare
Out of his home after a savage herd.
  I was born yesterday — my small feet
    are
Too tender for the roads so hard and rough.
And if you think that this is not enough,

XLVII

' I swear a great oath, by my father's head,
  That I stole not your cows, and that I
    know
Of no one else, who might, or could, or did.
  Whatever things cows are I do not know,
For I have only heard the name.' This said,
  He winked as fast as could be, and his
    brow
Was wrinkled, and a whistle loud gave he,
Like one who hears some strange absurdity.

XLVIII

Apollo gently smiled and said: — ' Aye,
  aye, —
  You cunning little rascal, you will bore
Many a rich man's house, and your array
  Of thieves will lay their siege before his
    door,
Silent as night, in night; and many a day
  In the wild glens rough shepherds will
    deplore
That you or yours, having an appetite,
Met with their cattle, comrade of the night !

XLIX

' And this among the Gods shall be your
  gift,
  To be considered as the lord of those
Who swindle, house-break, sheep-steal, and
  shop-lift.
  But now if you would not your last sleep
    doze,
Crawl out !' — Thus saying, Phœbus did
  uplift
The subtle infant in his swaddling clothes,
And in his arms, according to his wont,
A scheme devised the illustrious Argiphont.

L

.   .   .   .   .   .

And sneezed and shuddered. Phœbus on
  the grass
  Him threw ; and whilst all that he had
    designed

He did perform — eager although to pass,
  Apollo darted from his mighty mind
Towards the subtle babe the following scoff:
' Do not imagine this will get you off,

LI

' You little swaddled child of Jove and
  May ! '
  And seized him : — ' By this omen I shall
    trace
My noble herds, and you shall lead the
  way.'
Cyllenian Hermes from the grassy place,
Like one in earnest haste to get away,
  Rose, and with hands lifted towards his
    face,
Round both his ears up from his shoulders
  drew
His swaddling clothes, and — ' What mean
  you to do

LII

' With me, you unkind God ? ' — said Mer-
  cury:
  ' Is it about these cows you tease me
    so ?
I wish the race of cows were perished ! — I
  Stole not your cows — I do not even know
What things cows are.   Alas ! I well may
  sigh
That since I came into this world of woe
I should have ever heard the name of one —
But I appeal to the Saturnian's throne.'

LIII

Thus Phœbus and the vagrant Mercury
  Talked without coming to an explanation,
With adverse purpose. As for Phœbus, he
  Sought not revenge, but only informa-
    tion,
And Hermes tried with lies and roguery
  To cheat Apollo.   But when no evasion
Served — for the cunning one his match
  had found —
He paced on first over the sandy ground.

LIV

He of the Silver Bow the child of Jove
Followed behind, till to their heavenly Sire
  Came both his children, beautiful as Love,
And from his equal balance did require
  A judgment in the cause wherein they
    strove.
O'er odorous Olympus and its snows
A murmuring tumult as they came arose, —

LV

And from the folded depths of the great
Hill,
While Hermes and Apollo reverent stood
Before Jove's throne, the indestructible
Immortals rushed in mighty multitude;
And whilst their seats in order due they fill,
The lofty Thunderer in a careless mood
To Phœbus said : — 'Whence drive you this
sweet prey,
This herald-baby, born but yesterday ? —

LVI

'A most important subject, trifler, this
To lay before the Gods !' — 'Nay, fa-
ther, nay,
When you have understood the business,
Say not that I alone am fond of prey,
I found this little boy in a recess
Under Cyllene's mountains far away —
A manifest and most apparent thief,
A scandal-monger beyond all belief.

LVII

'I never saw his like either in heaven
Or upon earth for knavery or craft.
Out of the field my cattle yester-even,
By the low shore on which the loud sea
laughed,
He right down to the river-ford had driven;
And mere astonishment would make you
daft
To see the double kind of footsteps strange
He has impressed wherever he did range.

LVIII

'The cattle's track on the black dust full
well
Is evident, as if they went towards
The place from which they came — that
asphodel
Meadow, in which I feed my many herds;
His steps were most incomprehensible.
I know not how I can describe in words
Those tracks; he could have gone along
the sands
Neither upon his feet nor on his hands;

LIX

'He must have had some other stranger
mode
Of moving on. Those vestiges immense,
Far as I traced them on the sandy road,
Seemed like the trail of oak-toppings;
but thence

No mark or track denoting where they
trod
The hard ground gave. But, working at
his fence,
A mortal hedger saw him as he passed
To Pylos, with the cows, in fiery haste.

LX

'I found that in the dark he quietly
Had sacrificed some cows, and before
light
Had thrown the ashes all dispersedly
About the road; then, still as gloomy
night,
Had crept into his cradle, either eye
Rubbing, and cogitating some new
sleight.
No eagle could have seen him as he lay
Hid in his cavern from the peering day.

LXI

'I taxed him with the fact, when he averred
Most solemnly that he did neither see
Nor even had in any manner heard
Of my lost cows, whatever things cows
be;
Nor could he tell, though offered a reward
Not even who could tell of them to me.
So speaking, Phœbus sate; and Hermes
then
Addressed the Supreme Lord of Gods and
Men:

LXII

'Great Father, you know clearly before-
hand
That all which I shall say to you is
sooth;
I am a most veracious person, and
Totally unacquainted with untruth.
At sunrise Phœbus came, but with no band
Of Gods to bear him witness, in great
wrath,
To my abode, seeking his heifers there,
And saying that I must show him where
they are,

LXIII

'Or he would hurl me down the dark
abyss.
I know that every Apollonian limb
Is clothed with speed and might and man-
liness,
As a green bank with flowers — but, unlike him,

I was born yesterday, and you may guess
  He well knew this when he indulged the
    whim
Of bullying a poor little new-born thing
That slept, and never thought of cow-driv-
    ing.

LXIV

' Am I like a strong fellow who steals kine ?
  Believe me, dearest Father — such you
    are —
This driving of the herds is none of mine;
  Across my threshold did I wander ne'er,
So may I thrive ! I reverence the divine
  Sun and the Gods, and I love you, and
    care
Even for this hard accuser — who must
    know
I am as innocent as they or you.

LXV

' I swear by these most gloriously-wrought
    portals
  (It is, you will allow, an oath of might)
hrough which the multitude of the Im-
    mortals
  Pass and repass forever, day and night,
'evising schemes for the affairs of mor-
    tals —
That I am guiltless; and I will requite,
Although mine enemy be great and strong,
His cruel threat — do thou defend the
    young ! '

LXVI

So speaking, the Cyllenian Argiphont
  Winked, as if now his adversary was
    fitted;
And Jupiter according to his wont
  Laughed heartily to hear the subtle-
    witted
Infant give such a plausible account,
  And every word a lie. But he remitted
Judgment at present, and his exhortation
Was, to compose the affair by arbitration.

LXVII

And they by mighty Jupiter were bidden
  To go forth with a single purpose both,
Neither the other chiding nor yet chidden;
  And Mercury with innocence and truth
To lead the way, and show where he had
    hidden
  The mighty heifers. Hermes, nothing
    loath,

Obeyed the Ægis-bearer's will — for he
Is able to persuade all easily.

LXVIII

These lovely children of Heaven's highest
    Lord
  Hastened to Pylos and the pastures wide
And lofty stalls by the Alphean ford,
  Where wealth in the mute night is multi-
    plied
With silent growth. Whilst Hermes drove
    the herd
Out of the stony cavern, Phœbus spied
The hides of those the little babe had slain,
Stretched on the precipice above the plain.

LXIX

' How was it possible,' then Phœbus said,
  ' That you, a little child, born yesterday,
A thing on mother's milk and kisses fed,
  Could two prodigious heifers ever flay ?
Even I myself may well hereafter dread
  Your prowess, offspring of Cyllenian
    May,
When you grow strong and tall.' He
    spoke, and bound
Stiff withy bands the infant's wrists around.

LXX

He might as well have bound the oxen
    wild;
  The withy bands, though starkly inter-
    knit,
Fell at the feet of the immortal child,
  Loosened by some device of his quick
    wit.
Phœbus perceived himself again beguiled,
  And stared, while Hermes sought some
    hole or pit,
Looking askance and winking fast as
    thought
Where he might hide himself and not be
    caught.

LXXI

Sudden he changed his plan, and with
    strange skill
  Subdued the strong Latonian by the
    might
Of winning music to his mightier will;
  His left hand held the lyre, and in his
    right
The plectrum struck the chords; uncon-
    querable
  Up from beneath his hand in circling flight

The gathering music rose — and sweet as
    Love
The penetrating notes did live and move

LXXII

Within the heart of great Apollo. He
    Listened with all his soul, and laughed
    for pleasure.
Close to his side stood harping fearlessly
    The unabashèd boy; and to the measure
Of the sweet lyre there followed loud and
    free
    His joyous voice; for he unlocked the
    treasure
Of his deep song, illustrating the birth
Of the bright Gods and the dark desert
    Earth;

LXXIII

And how to the Immortals every one
    A portion was assigned of all that is ;
But chief Mnemosyne did Maia's son
    Clothe in the light of his loud melodies;
And, as each God was born or had begun,
    He in their order due and fit degrees
Sung of his birth and being — and did move
Apollo to unutterable love.

LXXIV

These words were wingèd with his swift
    delight:
    ' You heifer-stealing schemer, well do
    you
Deserve that fifty oxen should requite
    Such minstrelsies as I have heard even
    now.
Comrade of feasts, little contriving wight,
    One of your secrets I would gladly
    know,
Whether the glorious power you now show
    forth
Was folded up within you at your birth,

LXXV

' Or whether mortal taught or God inspired
    The power of unpremeditated song ?
Many divinest sounds have I admired,
    The Olympian Gods and mortal men
    among;
But such a strain of wondrous, strange,
    untired,
    And soul-awakening music, sweet and
    strong,
Yet did I never hear except from thee,
Offspring of May, impostor Mercury !

LXXVI

' What Muse, what skill, what unimagined
    use,
    What exercise of subtlest art, has given
Thy songs such power ? — for those who
    hear may choose
From three, the choicest of the gifts of
    Heaven,
Delight, and love, and sleep — sweet sleep
    whose dews
    Are sweeter than the balmy tears of even.
And I, who speak this praise, am that
    Apollo
Whom the Olympian Muses ever follow ;

LXXVII

' And their delight is dance, and the blithe
    noise
    Of song and overflowing poesy ;
And sweet, even as desire, the liquid voice
    Of pipes, that fills the clear air thrill-
    ingly ;
But never did my inmost soul rejoice
    In this dear work of youthful revelry,
As now. I wonder at thee, son of Jove;
Thy harpings and thy song are soft as love,

LXXVIII

' Now since thou hast, although so very
    small,
    Science of arts so glorious, thus I swear —
And let this cornel javelin, keen and tall,
    Witness between us what I promise
    here —
That I will lead thee to the Olympian Hall,
    Honored and mighty, with thy mother
    dear,
And many glorious gifts in joy will give
    thee,
And even at the end will ne'er deceive
    thee.'

LXXIX

To whom thus Mercury with prudent
    speech:
    ' Wisely hast thou inquired of my skill;
I envy thee no thing I know to teach
    Even this day; for both in word and
    will
I would be gentle with thee; thou canst
    reach
    All things in thy wise spirit, and thy sill
Is highest in heaven among the sons of
    Jove,
Who loves thee in the fulness of his love.

LXXX

'The Counsellor Supreme has given to
thee
Divinest gifts, out of the amplitude
Of his profuse, exhaustless treasury;
By thee, 't is said, the depths are under-
stood
Of his far voice; by thee the mystery
Of all oracular fates, — and the dread
mood
Of the diviner is breathed up; even I —
A child — perceive thy might and maj-
esty.

LXXXI

'Thou canst seek out and compass all that
wit
Can find or teach. Yet since thou wilt,
come take
The lyre — be mine the glory giving it —
Strike the sweet chords, and sing aloud,
and wake
Thy joyous pleasure out of many a fit
Of trancèd sound — and with fleet fin-
gers make
Thy liquid-voicèd comrade talk with
thee, —
It can talk measured music eloquently.

LXXXII

'Then bear it boldly to the revel loud,
Love-wakening dance, or feast of solemn
state,
A joy by night or day; for those endowed
With art and wisdom who interrogate
It teaches, babbling in delightful mood
All things which make the spirit most
elate,
Soothing the mind with sweet familiar
play,
Chasing the heavy shadows of dismay.

LXXXIII

'To those who are unskilled in its sweet
tongue,
Though they should question most im-
petuously
Its hidden soul, it gossips something
wrong —
Some senseless and impertinent reply.
But thou who art as wise as thou art
strong
Canst compass all that thou desirest. I
Present thee with this music-flowing shell,
Knowing thou canst interrogate it well.

LXXXIV

'And let us two henceforth together feed
On this green mountain slope and pas-
toral plain,
The herds in litigation. They will breed
Quickly enough to recompense our pain,
If to the bulls and cows we take good heed;
And thou, though somewhat over fond
of gain,
Grudge me not half the profit.' Having
spoke,
The shell he proffered, and Apollo took;

LXXXV

And gave him in return the glittering lash,
Installing him as herdsman; from the
look
Of Mercury then laughed a joyous flash.
And then Apollo with the plectrum
strook
The chords, and from beneath his hands a
crash
Of mighty sounds rushed up, whose
music shook
The soul with sweetness, and like an adept
His sweeter voice a just accordance kept.

LXXXVI

The herd went wandering o'er the divine
mead,
Whilst these most beautiful Sons of
Jupiter
Won their swift way up to the snowy head
Of white Olympus, with the joyous lyre
Soothing their journey; and their father
dread
Gathered them both into familiar
Affection sweet, — and then, and now,
and ever,
Hermes must love Him of the Golden
Quiver,

LXXXVII

To whom he gave the lyre that sweetly
sounded,
Which skilfully he held and played
thereon.
He piped the while, and far and wide re-
bounded
The echo of his pipings, — every one
Of the Olympians sat with joy astounded;
While he conceived another piece of fun,
One of his old tricks — which the God of Day
Perceiving, said: — 'I fear thee, Son of
May; —

LXXXVIII

' I fear thee and thy sly chameleon spirit,
  Lest thou shouldst steal my lyre and
    crookèd bow;
This glory and power thou dost from Jove
  inherit,
  To teach all craft upon the earth below;
Thieves love and worship thee — it is thy
  merit
To make all mortal business ebb and flow
By roguery. Now, Hermes, if you dare
By sacred Styx a mighty oath to swear

LXXXIX

'That you will never rob me, you will do
  A thing extremely pleasing to my heart.'
Then Mercury sware by the Stygian dew,
  That he would never steal his bow or
    dart,
Or lay his hands on what to him was due,
Or ever would employ his powerful art
Against his Pythian fane. Then Phœbus
  swore
There was no God or man whom he loved
  more.

XC

' And I will give thee as a good-will token,
  The beautiful wand of wealth and happi-
    ness;
A perfect three-leaved rod of gold un-
  broken,
  Whose magic will thy footsteps ever
    bless;
And whatsoever by Jove's voice is spoken
Of earthly or divine from its recess,
It, like a loving soul, to thee will speak, —
And more than this, do thou forbear to
  seek.

XCI

' For, dearest child, the divinations high
  Which thou requirest, 't is unlawful ever
That thou or any other deity
  Should understand — and vain were the
    endeavor;
For they are hidden in Jove's mind, and I
  In trust of them have sworn that I would
    never
Betray the counsels of Jove's inmost will
To any God — the oath was terrible.

XCII

' Then, golden-wanded brother, ask me not
  To speak the fates by Jupiter designed;

But be it mine to tell their various lot
  To the unnumbered tribes of human-
    kind.
Let good to these and ill to those be
  wrought
  As I dispense. But he, who comes con-
    signed
By voice and wings of perfect augury
To my great shrine, shall find avail in
  me.

XCIII

' Him will I not deceive, but will assist;
  But he who comes relying on such
    birds
As chatter vainly, who would strain and
  twist
  The purpose of the Gods with idle words,
And deems their knowledge light, he shall
  have missed
  His road — whilst I among my other
    hoards
His gifts deposit. Yet, O son of May,
I have another wondrous thing to say.

XCIV

' There are three Fates, three virgin Sisters,
  who,
  Rejoicing in their wind-outspeeding
    wings,
Their heads with flour snowed over white
  and new,
  Sit in a vale round which Parnassus
    flings
Its circling skirts; from these I have
  learned true
Vaticinations of remotest things.
My father cared not. Whilst they search
  out dooms,
They sit apart and feed on honeycombs.

XCV

' They, having eaten the fresh honey,
  grow
  Drunk with divine enthusiasm, and utter
With earnest willingness the truth they
  know;
  But if deprived of that sweet food, they
    mutter
All plausible delusions. These to you
  I give; if you inquire, they will not
    stutter.
Delight your own soul with them. Any
  man
You would instruct may profit if he can.

XCVI

'Take these and the fierce oxen, Maia's
　　child;
　O'er many a horse and toil-enduring
　　mule,
O'er jagged-jawèd lions, and the wild
　　White-tuskèd boars, o'er all, by field or
　　pool,
Of cattle which the mighty Mother mild
　Nourishes in her bosom, thou shalt rule;
Thou dost alone the veil from death uplift;
Thou givest not — yet this is a great gift.'

XCVII

Thus King Apollo loved the child of May
　In truth, and Jove covered their love
　　with joy.
Hermes with Gods and men even from that
　　day
　Mingled, and wrought the latter much
　　annoy,
And little profit, going far astray
　Through the dun night. Farewell, de-
　　lightful Boy,
Of Jove and Maia sprung, — never by me,
Nor thou, nor other songs, shall unremem-
　　bered be.

HOMER'S HYMN TO VENUS

This fragment was written in 1818, and published by Garnett, 1862.

[V. 1–55, with some omissions.]

MUSE, sing the deeds of golden Aphrodite,
Who wakens with her smile the lulled
　　delight
Of sweet desire, taming the eternal kings
Of Heaven, and men, and all the living
　　things
That fleet along the air, or whom the sea,
Or earth, with her maternal ministry,
Nourish innumerable, thy delight
All seek　　　　　O crownèd Aphrodite !
Three spirits canst thou not deceive or
　　quell,
Minerva, child of Jove, who loves too well
Fierce war and mingling combat, and the
　　fame
Of glorious deeds, to heed thy gentle flame.
Diana,　　　　　golden-shafted queen,
Is tamed not by thy smiles; the shadows
　　green
Of the wild woods, the bow, the

And piercing cries amid the swift pursuit
Of beasts among waste mountains, — such
　　delight
Is hers, and men who know and do the
　　right.
Nor Saturn's first-born daughter, Vesta
　　chaste,
Whom Neptune and Apollo wooed the last,
Such was the will of ægis-bearing Jove;
But sternly she refused the ills of Love,
And by her mighty father's head she swore
An oath not unperformed, that evermore
A virgin she would live 'mid deities
Divine; her father, for such gentle ties
Renounced, gave glorious gifts; thus in his
　　hall
She sits and feeds luxuriously. O'er all
In every fane, her honors first arise
From men — the eldest of Divinities.

These spirits she persuades not, nor de-
　　ceives,
But none beside escape, so well she weaves
Her unseen toils; nor mortal men, nor gods
Who live secure in their unseen abodes.
She won the soul of him whose fierce de-
　　light
Is thunder — first in glory and in might.
And, as she willed, his mighty mind deceiv-
　　ing,
With mortal limbs his deathless limbs in-
　　weaving,
Concealed him from his spouse and sister
　　fair,
Whom to wise Saturn ancient Rhea bare.

　　　　　　　　　　　　but in return,
In Venus Jove did soft desire awaken,
That, by her own enchantments overtaken,
She might, no more from human union
　　free,
Burn for a nursling of mortality.
For once, amid the assembled Deities,
The laughter-loving Venus from her eyes
Shot forth the light of a soft starlight
　　smile,
And boasting said, that she, secure the
　　while,
Could bring at will to the assembled gods
The mortal tenants of earth's dark abodes,
And mortal offspring from a deathless stem
She could produce in scorn and spite of
　　them.
Therefore he poured desire into her breast
Of young Anchises,

Feeding his herds among the mossy foun-
tains
Of the wide Ida's many-folded mountains,
Whom Venus saw, and loved, and the love
clung
Like wasting fire her senses wild among.

HOMER'S HYMN TO CASTOR AND POLLUX

This and the remaining Homeric Hymns
were written in 1818, and published by Mrs.
Shelley in her second collected edition, 1839.
She writes that they ' may be considered as
having received the author's ultimate corrections.'

YE wild-eyed Muses, sing the Twins of
Jove,
Whom the fair-ankled Leda, mixed in love
With mighty Saturn's heaven - obscuring
Child,
On Taygetus, that lofty mountain wild,
Brought forth in joy; mild Pollux void of
blame,
And steed-subduing Castor, heirs of fame.
These are the Powers who earth-born mor-
tals save
And ships, whose flight is swift along the
wave.
When wintry tempests o'er the savage sea
Are raging, and the sailors tremblingly
Call on the Twins of Jove with prayer and
vow,
Gathered in fear upon the lofty prow,
And sacrifice with snow-white lambs, — the
wind
And the huge billow bursting close behind
Even then beneath the weltering waters
bear
The staggering ship, — they suddenly ap-
pear,
On yellow wings rushing athwart the sky,
And lull the blasts in mute tranquillity,
And strew the waves on the white ocean's
bed,
Fair omen of the voyage; from toil and
dread,
The sailors rest, rejoicing in the sight,
And plough the quiet sea in safe delight.

HOMER'S HYMN TO MINERVA

I SING the glorious Power with azure eyes,
Athenian Pallas, tameless, chaste, and wise,
Tritogenia, town-preserving maid,
Revered and mighty; from his awful head
Whom Jove brought forth, in warlike
armor dressed,
Golden, all radiant ! wonder strange pos-
sessed
The everlasting Gods that shape to see,
Shaking a javelin keen, impetuously
Rush from the crest of Ægis-bearing Jove;
Fearfully Heaven was shaken, and did
move
Beneath the might of the Cerulean-eyed;
Earth dreadfully resounded, far and wide;
And, lifted from its depths, the sea swelled
high
In purple billows, the tide suddenly
Stood still, and great Hyperion's son long
time
Checked his swift steeds, till where she
stood sublime,
Pallas from her immortal shoulders threw
The arms divine; wise Jove rejoiced to
view.
Child of the Ægis-bearer, hail to thee,
Nor thine nor other's praise shall unre-
membered be.

HOMER'S HYMN TO THE SUN

OFFSPRING of Jove, Calliope, once more
To the bright Sun thy hymn of music pour,
Whom to the child of star-clad Heaven and
Earth
Euryphaëssa, large-eyed nymph, brought
forth;
Euryphaëssa, the famed sister fair
Of great Hyperion, who to him did bear
A race of loveliest children; the young
Morn,
Whose arms are like twin roses newly born,
The fair-haired Moon, and the immortal
Sun,
Who borne by heavenly steeds his race
doth run
Unconquerably, illuming the abodes
Of mortal men and the eternal Gods.

Fiercely look forth his awe-inspiring eyes
Beneath his golden helmet, whence arise
And are shot forth afar clear beams of light;
His countenance with radiant glory bright
Beneath his graceful locks far shines
around,
And the light vest with which his limbs
are bound,

Of woof ethereal delicately twined,
Glows in the stream of the uplifting wind.
His rapid steeds soon bear him to the west,
Where their steep flight his hands divine
　　　arrest,
And the fleet car with yoke of gold, which
　　　he
Sends from bright heaven beneath the
　　　shadowy sea.

HOMER'S HYMN TO THE MOON

DAUGHTERS of Jove, whose voice is melody,
Muses, who know and rule all minstrelsy,
Sing the wide-wingèd Moon !　Around the
　　　earth,
From her immortal head in Heaven shot
　　　forth,
Far light is scattered — boundless glory
　　　springs;
Where'er she spreads her many-beaming
　　　wings,
The lampless air glows round her golden
　　　crown.

　　But when the Moon divine from Heaven
　　　is gone
Under the sea, her beams within abide,
Till, bathing her bright limbs in Ocean's
　　　tide,
Clothing her form in garments glittering
　　　far,
And having yoked to her immortal car
The beam-invested steeds whose necks on
　　　high
Curve back, she drives to a remoter sky
A western Crescent, borne impetuously.
Then is made full the circle of her light,
And as she grows, her beams more bright
　　　and bright
Are poured from Heaven, where she is
　　　hovering then,
A wonder and a sign to mortal men.

　　The Son of Saturn with this glorious
　　　Power
Mingled in love and sleep, to whom she
　　　bore,
Pandeia, a bright maid of beauty rare
Among the Gods whose lives eternal are.

　　Hail Queen, great Moon, white-armed
　　　Divinity,
Fair-haired and favorable ! thus with thee,

My song beginning, by its music sweet
Shall make immortal many a glorious feat
Of demigods, — with lovely lips, so well
Which minstrels, servants of the Muses,
　　　tell.

HOMER'S HYMN TO THE EARTH,
　　　MOTHER OF ALL

O UNIVERSAL Mother, who dost keep
From everlasting thy foundations deep,
Eldest of things, Great Earth, I sing of
　　　thee !
All shapes that have their dwelling in the
　　　sea,
All things that fly, or on the ground divine
Live, move, and there are nourished —
　　　these are thine;
These from thy wealth thou dost sustain;
　　　from thee
Fair babes are born, and fruits on every
　　　tree
Hang ripe and large, revered Divinity !

　　The life of mortal men beneath thy sway
Is held; thy power both gives and takes
　　　away.
Happy are they whom thy mild favors
　　　nourish;
All things unstinted round them grow and
　　　flourish.
For them endures the life-sustaining field
Its load of harvest, and their cattle yield
Large increase, and their house with wealth
　　　is filled.
Such honored dwell in cities fair and free,
The homes of lovely women, prosperously;
Their sons exult in youth's new budding
　　　gladness,
And their fresh daughters, free from care
　　　or sadness,
With bloom-inwoven dance and happy song,
On the soft flowers the meadow-grass
　　　among,
Leap round them sporting; such delights
　　　by thee
Are given, rich Power, revered Divinity.

　　Mother of gods, thou wife of starry
　　　Heaven,
Farewell ! be thou propitious, and be given
A happy life for this brief melody,
Nor thou nor other songs shall unremem-
　　　bered be.

THE CYCLOPS;

A SATYRIC DRAMA

TRANSLATED FROM THE GREEK OF EURIPIDES

The Cyclops was translated in 1819, and published by Mrs. Shelley, *Posthumous Poems,* 1824. Shelley read it to Williams, November 5, 1821. He writes of it and the whole subject of translation to Hunt, November, 1819: ' With respect to translation, even *I* will not be seduced by it; although the Greek plays, and some of the ideal dramas of Calderon (with which I have lately, and with inexpressible wonder and delight, become acquainted), are perpetually tempting me to throw over their perfect and glowing forms the gray veil of my own words. And you know me too well to suspect that I refrain from a belief that what I could substitute for them would deserve the regret which yours would, if suppressed. I have confidence in my moral sense alone; but that is a kind of originality. I have only translated *The Cyclops* of Euripides, when I could absolutely do nothing else, and the *Symposium* of Plato, which is the delight and astonishment of all who read it, — I mean the original.'

SILENUS	CHORUS OF SATYRS
ULYSSES	THE CYCLOPS

SILENUS

O BACCHUS, what a world of toil, both now
And ere these limbs were overworn with age,
Have I endured for thee ! First, when thou fled'st
The mountain-nymphs who nursed thee, driven afar
By the strange madness Juno sent upon thee;
Then in the battle of the sons of Earth,
When I stood foot by foot close to thy side,
No unpropitious fellow-combatant,
And, driving through his shield my wingèd spear,
Slew vast Enceladus. Consider now,
Is it a dream of which I speak to thee ?
By Jove it is not, for you have the trophies !
And now I suffer more than all before.
For when I heard that Juno had devised
A tedious voyage for you, I put to sea
With all my children quaint in search of you,
And I myself stood on the beakèd prow
And fixed the naked mast; and all my boys
Leaning upon their oars, with splash and strain
Made white with foam the green and purple sea.
And so we sought you, king. We were sailing
Near Malea, when an eastern wind arose,
And drove us to this wild Ætnean rock;
The one-eyed children of the Ocean God,
The man-destroying Cyclopses inhabit,
On this wild shore, their soiltary caves,
And one of these, named Polypheme, has caught us
To be his slaves; and so, for all delight
Of Bacchic sports, sweet dance and melody,
We keep this lawless giant's wandering flocks.
My sons indeed, on far declivities,
Young things themselves, tend on the youngling sheep,
But I remain to fill the water casks,
Or sweeping the hard floor, or ministering
Some impious and abominable meal
To the fell Cyclops. I am wearied of it !
And now I must scrape up the littered floor
With this great iron rake, so to receive
My absent master and his evening sheep
In a cave neat and clean. Even now I see
My children tending the flocks hitherward.
Ha ! what is this ? are your Sicinnian measures
Even now the same as when with dance and song
You brought young Bacchus to Althæa's halls ?

CHORUS OF SATYRS

STROPHE

Where has he of race divine
Wandered in the winding rocks ?
Here the air is calm and fine
For the father of the flocks;
Here the grass is soft and sweet,
And the river-eddies meet
In the trough beside the cave,
Bright as in their fountain wave.
Neither here, nor on the dew
Of the lawny uplands feeding ?
Oh, you come ! — a stone at you
Will I throw to mend your breeding;
Get along, you hornèd thing,
Wild, seditious, rambling !

EPODE

An Iacchic melody
  To the golden Aphrodite
Will I lift, as erst did I
  Seeking her and her delight
With the Mænads whose white feet
To the music glance and fleet.
Bacchus, O belovèd, where,
Shaking wide thy yellow hair,
Wanderest thou alone, afar?
  To the one-eyed Cyclops, we,
Who by right thy servants are,
  Minister in misery,
In these wretched goat-skins clad,
  Far from thy delights and thee.

SILENUS

Be silent, sons; command the slaves to
  drive
The gathered flocks into the rock-roofed
  cave.

CHORUS

Go! But what needs this serious haste, O
  father?

SILENUS

I see a Grecian vessel on the coast,
And thence the rowers with some general
Approaching to this cave. About their necks
Hang empty vessels, as they wanted food,
And water-flasks. Oh, miserable strangers!
Whence come they that they know not
  what and who
My master is, approaching in ill hour
The inhospitable roof of Polypheme,
And the Cyclopian jaw-bone, man-destroy-
  ing?
Be silent, Satyrs, while I ask and hear
Whence coming they arrive the Ætnean
  hill.

ULYSSES

Friends, can you show me some clear water
  spring,
The remedy of our thirst? Will any one
Furnish with food seamen in want of it?
Ha! what is this? We seem to be ar-
  rived
At the blithe court of Bacchus. I observe
This sportive band of Satyrs near the caves.
First let me greet the elder. — Hail!

SILENUS

                              Hail thou
O Stranger! tell thy country and thy race.

ULYSSES

The Ithacan Ulysses and the king
Of Cephalonia.

SILENUS

              Oh! I know the man,
Wordy and shrewd, the son of Sisyphus.

ULYSSES

I am the same, but do not rail upon me.

SILENUS

Whence sailing do you come to Sicily?

ULYSSES

From Ilion, and from the Trojan toils.

SILENUS

How touched you not at your paternal
  shore?

ULYSSES

The strength of tempests bore me here by
  force.

SILENUS

The self-same accident occurred to me.

ULYSSES

Were you then driven here by stress of weather?

SILENUS

Following the Pirates who had kidnapped
  Bacchus.

ULYSSES

What land is this, and who inhabit it?

SILENUS

Ætna, the loftiest peak in Sicily.

ULYSSES

And are there walls, and tower-surrounded
  towns?

SILENUS

There are not. These lone rocks are bare
  of men.

ULYSSES

And who possess the land? the race of
  beasts?

SILENUS

Cyclops, who live in caverns, not in houses.

ULYSSES

Obeying whom ?   Or is the state popular ?

SILENUS

Shepherds; no one obeys any in aught.

ULYSSES

How live they ? do they sow the corn of
Ceres ?

SILENUS

On milk and cheese, and the flesh of sheep.

ULYSSES

Have they the Bromian drink from the
vine's stream ?

SILENUS

Ah, no; they live in an ungracious land.

ULYSSES

And are they just to strangers ? hospitable ?

SILENUS

They think the sweetest thing a stranger
brings
Is his own flesh.

ULYSSES

What ! do they eat man's flesh ?

SILENUS

No one comes here who is not eaten up.

ULYSSES

The Cyclops now — where is he ?   Not at
home ?

SILENUS

Absent on Ætna, hunting with his dogs.

ULYSSES

Know'st thou what thou must do to aid us
hence ?

SILENUS

I know not; we will help you all we can.

ULYSSES

Provide us food, of which we are in want.

SILENUS

Here is not anything, as I said, but meat.

ULYSSES

But meat is a sweet remedy for hunger.

SILENUS

Cow's milk there is, and store of curdled
cheese.

ULYSSES

Bring out.   I would see all before I bar-
gain.

SILENUS

But how much gold will you engage to give ?

ULYSSES

I bring no gold, but Bacchic juice.

SILENUS

Oh, joy !
'T is long since these dry lips were wet
with wine.

ULYSSES

Maron, the son of the God, gave it me.

SILENUS

Whom I have nursed a baby in my arms.

ULYSSES

The son of Bacchus, for your clearer knowledge.

SILENUS

Have you it now ? or is it in the ship ?

ULYSSES

Old man, this skin contains it, which you
see.

SILENUS

Why this would hardly be a mouthful for
me.

ULYSSES

Nay, twice as much as you can draw from
thence.

SILENUS

You speak of a fair fountain, sweet to me.

ULYSSES

Would you first taste of the unmingled
wine ?

SILENUS

'T is just; tasting invites the purchaser.

ULYSSES

Here is the cup, together with the skin.

SILENUS

Pour, that the draught may fillip my remembrance.

ULYSSES

See !

SILENUS

Papaiax ! what a sweet smell it has !

ULYSSES

You see it then ? —

SILENUS

By Jove, no ! but I smell it.

ULYSSES

Taste, that you may not praise it in words
only.

SILENUS

Babai ! Great Bacchus calls me forth to
dance !
Joy ! joy !.

ULYSSES

Did it flow sweetly down your throat ?

SILENUS

So that it tingled to my very nails.

ULYSSES

And in addition I will give you gold.

SILENUS

Let gold alone ! only unlock the cask.

ULYSSES

Bring out some cheeses now, or a young
goat.

SILENUS

That will I do, despising any master.
Yes, let me drink one cup, and I will give
All that the Cyclops feed upon their moun-
tains.

. . . .

CHORUS

Ye have taken Troy and laid your hands on
Helen ?

ULYSSES

And utterly destroyed the race of Priam.

. . . .

SILENUS

The wanton wretch ! she was bewitched to
see
The many-colored anklets and the chain
Of woven gold which girt the neck of
Paris,
And so she left that good man Menelaus.
There should be no more women in the
world
But such as are reserved for me alone.
See, here are sheep, and here are goats,
Ulysses,
Here are unsparing cheeses of pressed
milk;
Take them; depart with what good speed
ye may;
First leaving my reward, the Bacchic dew
Of joy-inspiring grapes.

ULYSSES

Ah·me ! Alas !
What shall we do ? the Cyclops is at hand !
Old man, we perish ! whither can we fly ?

SILENUS

Hide yourselves quick within that hollow
rock.

ULYSSES

'T were perilous to fly into the net.

SILENUS

The cavern has recesses numberless;
Hide yourselves quick.

ULYSSES

That will I never do !
The mighty Troy would be indeed dis-
graced
If I should fly one man. How many times
Have I withstood, with shield immovable,
Ten thousand Phrygians ! if I needs must
die,
Yet will I die with glory; if I live,
The praise which I have gained will yet
remain.

SILENUS

What, ho ! assistance, comrades, haste assistance !

The CYCLOPS, SILENUS, ULYSSES ; CHORUS.

CYCLOPS

What is this tumult ? Bacchus is not here,
Nor tympanies nor brazen castanets.

How are my young lambs in the cavern ?
  Milking
Their dams or playing by their sides ?
  And is
The new cheese pressed into the bulrush
  baskets ?
Speak ! I 'll beat some of you till you rain
  tears.
Look up, not downwards when I speak to
  you.

SILENUS

See ! I now gape at Jupiter himself;
I stare upon Orion and the stars.

CYCLOPS

Well, is the dinner fitly cooked and laid ?

SILENUS

All ready, if your throat is ready too.

CYCLOPS

Are the bowls full of milk besides ?

SILENUS

                          O'erbrimming;
So you may drink a tunful if you will.

CYCLOPS

Is it ewe's milk or cow's milk, or both
  mixed ?

SILENUS

Both, either; only pray don't swallow me.

CYCLOPS

By no means. —
 . . . .
What is this crowd I see beside the stalls ?
Outlaws or thieves ? for near my cavern-
  home,
I see my young lambs coupled two by
  two
With willow bands; mixed with my cheeses
  lie
Their implements; and this old fellow here
Has his bald head broken with stripes.

SILENUS

                              Ah me !
I have been beaten till I burn with fever.

CYCLOPS

By whom ? Who laid his fist upon your
  head ?

SILENUS

Those men, because I would not suffer
  them
To steal your goods.

CYCLOPS

                  Did not the rascals know
I am a God, sprung from the race of heaven ?

SILENUS

I told them so, but they bore off your
  things,
And ate the cheese in spite of all I said,
And carried out the lambs — and said,
  moreover,
They 'd pin you down with a three-cubit
  collar,
And pull your vitals out through your one
  eye,
Torture your back with stripes, then bind-
  ing you
Throw you as ballast into the ship's hold,
And then deliver you, a slave, to move
Enormous rocks, or found a vestibule.

CYCLOPS

In truth ? Nay, haste, and place in order
  quickly
The cooking knives, and heap upon the
  hearth,
And kindle it, a great faggot of wood.
As soon as they are slaughtered, they shall
  fill
My belly, broiling warm from the live
  coals,
Or boiled and seethed within the bubbling
  caldron.
I am quite sick of the wild mountain game;
Of stags and lions I have gorged enough,
And I grow hungry for the flesh of men.

SILENUS

Nay, master, something new is very pleasant
After one thing forever, and of late
Very few strangers have approached our
  cave.

ULYSSES

Hear, Cyclops, a plain tale on the other
  side.
We, wanting to buy food, came from our
  ship
Into the neighborhood of your cave, and
  here

This old Silenus gave us in exchange
These lambs for wine, the which he took
    and drank,
And all by mutual compact, without force.
There is no word of truth in what he says,
For slyly he was selling all your store.

SILENUS

I ? May you perish, wretch —

ULYSSES

                If I speak false !

SILENUS

Cyclops, I swear by Neptune who begot
    thee,
By mighty Triton and by Nereus old,
Calypso and the glaucous ocean nymphs,
The sacred waves and all the race of
    fishes —
Be these the witnesses, my dear sweet
    master,
My darling little Cyclops, that I never
Gave any of your stores to these false
    strangers.
If I speak false may those whom most I
    love,
My children, perish wretchedly !

CHORUS

              There stop !
I saw him giving these things to the stran-
    gers.
If I speak false, then may my father perish,
But do not thou wrong hospitality.

CYCLOPS

You lie ! I swear that he is juster far
Than Rhadamanthus. I trust more in him.
But let me ask, whence have ye sailed, O
    strangers ?
Who are you ? And what city nourished
    ye ?

ULYSSES

Our race is Ithacan; having destroyed
The town of Troy, the tempests of the sea
Have driven us on thy land, O Polypheme.

CYCLOPS

What, have ye shared in the unenvied spoil
Of the false Helen, near Scamander's
    stream ?

ULYSSES

The same, having endured a woful toil.

CYCLOPS

Oh, basest expedition ! sailed ye not
From Greece to Phrygia for one woman's
    sake ?

ULYSSES

'T was the Gods' work — no mortal was in
    fault.
But, O great offspring of the Ocean-king,
We pray thee and admonish thee with free-
    dom
That thou dost spare thy friends who visit
    thee,
And place no impious food within thy jaws.
For in the depths of Greece we have up-
    reared
Temples to thy great father, which are all
His homes. The sacred bay of Tænarus
Remains inviolate, and each dim recess
Scooped high on the Malean promontory,
And aëry Sunium's silver-veinèd crag
Which divine Pallas keeps unprofaned ever,
The Gerastian asylums, and whate'er
Within wide Greece our enterprise has kept
From Phrygian contumely; and in which
You have a common care, for you inhabit
The skirts of Grecian land, under the roots
Of Ætna and its crags, spotted with fire.
Turn then to converse under human laws.
Receive us shipwrecked suppliants, and
    provide
Food, clothes, and fire, and hospitable gifts;
Nor fixing upon oxen-piercing spits
Our limbs, so fill your belly and your jaws.
Priam's wide land has widowed Greece
    enough;
And weapon-wingèd murder heaped to-
    gether
Enough of dead, and wives are husbandless,
And ancient women and gray fathers wail
Their childless age. If you should roast
    the rest —
And 't is a bitter feast that you prepare —
Where then would any turn ? Yet be.
    persuaded;
Forego the lust of your jaw-bone; prefer
Pious humanity to wicked will.
Many have bought too dear their evil joys.

SILENUS

Let me advise you, do not spare a morsel
Of all his flesh. If you should eat his
    tongue
You would become most eloquent, O Cy-
    clops.

CYCLOPS

Wealth, my good fellow, is the wise man's
    God;
All other things are a pretence and boast.
What are my father's ocean promontories,
The sacred rocks whereon he dwells, to me ?
Stranger, I laugh to scorn Jove's thunder-
    bolt,
I know not that his strength is more than
    mine.
As to the rest I care not.   When he pours
Rain from above, I have a close pavilion
Under this rock, in which I lie supine,
Feasting on a roast calf or some wild beast,
And drinking pans of milk, and gloriously
Emulating the thunder of high heaven.
And when the Thracian wind pours down
    the snow,
I wrap my body in the skins of beasts,
Kindle a fire, and bid the snow whirl on.
The earth, by force, whether it will or no,
Bringing forth grass, fattens my flocks and
    herds,
Which, to what other God but to myself
And this great belly, first of deities,
Should I be bound to sacrifice ?   I well
    know
The wise man's only Jupiter is this,
To eat and drink during his little day,
And give himself no care.   And as for those
Who complicate with laws the life of man,
I freely give them tears for their reward.
I will not cheat my soul of its delight,
Or hesitate in dining upon you.
And that I may be quit of all demands,
These are my hospitable gifts; — fierce fire
And yon ancestral caldron, which o'erbub-
    bling
Shall finely cook your miserable flesh.
Creep in ! —

    .   .   .   .

ULYSSES

Ai ! ai ! I have escaped the Trojan toils,
I have escaped the sea, and now I fall
Under the cruel grasp of one impious man.
O Pallas, mistress, Goddess sprung from
    Jove,
Now, now, assist me !   Mightier toils than
    Troy
Are these.   I totter on the chasms of peril.
And thou who inhabitest the thrones
Of the bright stars, look, hospitable Jove,
Upon this outrage of thy deity,
Otherwise be considered as no God !

CHORUS (alone)

For your gaping gulf, and your gullet wide
The ravin is ready on every side,
The limbs of the strangers are cooked and
    done;
    There is boiled meat, and roast meat,
        and meat from the coal,
You may chop it, and tear it, and gnash it
        for fun,
    An hairy goat's-skin contains the whole.
Let me but escape, and ferry me o'er
The stream of your wrath to a safer shore.
The Cyclops Ætnean is cruel and bold,
    He murders the strangers
        That sit on his hearth,
    And dreads no avengers
        To rise from the earth.
He roasts the men before they are cold,
He snatches them broiling from the coal,
And from the caldron pulls them whole,
And minces their flesh, and gnaws their
    bone
With his cursèd teeth, till all be gone.
    Farewell, foul pavilion:
        Farewell, rites of dread !
    The Cyclops vermilion,
        With slaughter uncloying,
        Now feasts on the dead,
        In the flesh of strangers joying !

ULYSSES

O Jupiter !   I saw within the cave
Horrible things; deeds to be feigned in
    words,
But not to be believed as being done.

CHORUS

What ! sawest thou the impious Polypheme
Feasting upon your loved companions now ?

ULYSSES

Selecting two, the plumpest of the crowd,
He grasped them in his hands. —

CHORUS

                        Unhappy man !

    .   .   .   .

ULYSSES

Soon as we came into this craggy place,
Kindling a fire, he cast on the broad hearth
The knotty limbs of an enormous oak,
Three wagon-loads at least, and then he
    strewed
Upon the ground, beside the red firelight,

His couch of pine leaves; and he milked
 the cows,
And, pouring forth the white milk, filled a
 bowl
Three cubits wide and four in depth, as
 much
As would contain ten amphoræ, and bound
 it
With ivy wreaths; then placed upon the
 fire
A brazen pot to boil, and made red hot
The points of spits, not sharpened with the
 sickle,
But with a fruit tree bough, and with the
 jaws
Of axes for Ætnean slaughterings.
And when this God-abandoned cook of
 hell
Had made all ready, he seized two of us
And killed them in a kind of measured
 manner;
For he flung one against the brazen rivets
Of the huge caldron, and seized the other
By the foot's tendon, and knocked out his
 brains
Upon the sharp edge of the craggy stone;
Then peeled his flesh with a great cooking-
 knife
And put him down to roast. The other's
 limbs
He chopped into the caldron to be boiled.
And I, with the tears raining from my
 eyes,
Stood near the Cyclops, ministering to
 him;
The rest, in the recesses of the cave,
Clung to the rock like bats, bloodless with
 fear.
When he was filled with my companions'
 flesh,
He threw himself upon the ground and
 sent
A loathsome exhalation from his maw.
Then a divine thought came to me. I
 filled
The cup of Maron, and I offered him
To taste, and said: — 'Child of the Ocean
 God,
Behold what drink the vines of Greece pro-
 duce,
The exultation and the joy of Bacchus.'
He, satiated with his unnatural food,
Received it, and at one draught drank it off,
And, taking my hand, praised me: — 'Thou
 hast given

A sweet draught after a sweet meal, dear
 guest.'
And I perceiving that it pleased him, filled
Another cup, well knowing that the wine
Would wound him soon and take a sure
 revenge.
And the charm fascinated him, and I
Plied him cup after cup, until the drink
Had warmed his entrails, and he sang aloud
In concert with my wailing fellow-seamen
A hideous discord — and the cavern rung.
I have stolen out, so that if you will
You may achieve my safety and your own.
But say, do you desire, or not, to fly
This uncompanionable man, and dwell
As was your wont among the Grecian
 Nymphs
Within the fanes of your belovèd God?
Your father there within agrees to it,
But he is weak and overcome with wine,
And, caught as if with bird-lime by the
 cup,
He claps his wings and crows in doting joy.
You who are young, escape with me, and find
Bacchus your ancient friend; unsuited he
To this rude Cyclops.

CHORUS

      Oh, my dearest friend,
That I could see that day, and leave for-
 ever
The impious Cyclops.

. . . .

ULYSSES

Listen then what a punishment I have
For this fell monster, how secure a flight
From your hard servitude.

CHORUS

       Oh, sweeter far
Than is the music of an Asian lyre
Would be the news of Polypheme de-
 stroyed.

ULYSSES

Delighted with the Bacchic drink he goes
To call his brother Cyclops, who inhabit
A village upon Ætna not far off.

CHORUS

I understand, catching him when alone
You think by some measure to dispatch
 him,
Or thrust him from the precipice.

ULYSSES

Oh, no;
Nothing of that kind; my device is subtle.

CHORUS

How then ? I heard of old that thou wert
wise.

ULYSSES

I will dissuade him from this plan, by say-
ing
It were unwise to give the Cyclopses
This precious drink, which if enjoyed alone
Would make life sweeter for a longer
time.
When, vanquished by the Bacchic power,
he sleeps,
There is a trunk of olive wood within,
Whose point having made sharp with this
good sword
I will conceal in fire, and when I see
It is alight, will fix it, burning yet,
Within the socket of the Cyclops' eye
And melt it out with fire; as when a man
Turns by its handle a great auger round,
Fitting the framework of a ship with beams,
So will I in the Cyclops' fiery eye
Turn round the brand and dry the pupil
up.

CHORUS

Joy ! I am mad with joy at your device.

ULYSSES

And then with you, my friends, and the
old man,
We 'll load the hollow depth of our black
ship,
And row with double strokes from this
dread shore.

CHORUS

May I, as in libations to a God,
Share in the blinding him with the red
brand ?
I would have some communion in his
death.

ULYSSES

Doubtless; the brand is a great brand to
hold.

CHORUS

Oh ! I would lift an hundred wagon-loads,
If like a wasp's nest I could scoop the eye
out
Of the detested Cyclops.

ULYSSES

Silence now !
Ye know the close device; and when I call,
Look ye obey the masters of the craft.
I will not save myself and leave behind
My comrades in the cave; I might escape,
Having got clear from that obscure recess,
But 't were unjust to leave in jeopardy
The dear companions who sailed here with
me.

CHORUS

Come ! who is first, that with his hand
Will urge down the burning brand
Through the lids, and quench and pierce
The Cyclops' eye so fiery fierce ?

SEMICHORUS I

(*Song within*)

Listen ! listen ! he is coming,
A most hideous discord humming.
Drunken, museless, awkward, yelling,
Far along his rocky dwelling;
Let us with some comic spell
Teach the yet unteachable.
By all means he must be blinded,
If my counsel be but minded.

SEMICHORUS II

Happy those made odorous
    With the dew which sweet grapes
        weep,
To the village hastening thus,
    Seek the vines that soothe to sleep,
Having first embraced thy friend,
There in luxury without end,
With the strings of yellow hair,
Of thy voluptuous leman fair,
Shalt sit playing on a bed ! —
Speak what door is openèd ?

CYCLOPS

Ha ! ha ! ha ! I 'm full of wine,
Heavy with the joy divine,
With the young feast oversated;
Like a merchant's vessel freighted
To the water's edge, my crop
Is laden to the gullet's top.
The fresh meadow grass of spring
Tempts me forth thus wandering
    To my brothers on the mountains,
    Who shall share the wine's sweet
        fountains.
Bring the cask, O stranger, bring !

CHORUS

One with eyes the fairest
    Cometh from his dwelling;
Some one loves thee, rarest,
    Bright beyond my telling.
In thy grace thou shinest
Like some nymph divinest,
In her caverns dewy;
All delights pursue thee,
Soon pied flowers, sweet-breathing,
Shall thy head be wreathing.

ULYSSES

Listen, O Cyclops, for I am well skilled
In Bacchus, whom I gave thee of to drink.

CYCLOPS

What sort of God is Bacchus then accounted?

ULYSSES

The greatest among men for joy of life.

CYCLOPS

I gulped him down with very great delight.

ULYSSES

This is a God who never injures men.

CYCLOPS

How does the God like living in a skin?

ULYSSES

He is content wherever he is put.

CYCLOPS

Gods should not have their body in a skin.

ULYSSES

If he gives joy, what is his skin to you?

CYCLOPS

I hate the skin, but love the wine within.

ULYSSES

Stay here, now drink, and make your spirit glad.

CYCLOPS

Should I not share this liquor with my brothers?

ULYSSES

Keep it yourself, and be more honored so.

CYCLOPS

I were more useful, giving to my friends.

ULYSSES

But village mirth breeds contests, broils, and blows.

CYCLOPS

When I am drunk none shall lay hands on me.

ULYSSES

A drunken man is better within doors.

CYCLOPS

He is a fool, who, drinking, loves not mirth.

ULYSSES

But he is wise, who drunk remains at home.

CYCLOPS

What shall I do, Silenus? Shall I stay?

SILENUS

Stay — for what need have you of pot companions?

CYCLOPS

Indeed this place is closely carpeted
With flowers and grass.

SILENUS

                      And in the sun-warm noon
'T is sweet to drink. Lie down beside me now,
Placing your mighty sides upon the ground.

CYCLOPS

What do you put the cup behind me for?

SILENUS

That no one here may touch it.

CYCLOPS

                            Thievish one!
You want to drink. Here place it in the midst.
And thou, O stranger, tell how art thou called?

ULYSSES

My name is Nobody. What favor now
Shall I receive to praise you at your hands?

CYCLOPS

I 'll feast on you the last of your companions.

ULYSSES

You grant your guest a fair reward, O Cyclops.

CYCLOPS

Ha! what is this? Stealing the wine, you
rogue!

SILENUS

It was this stranger kissing me because
I looked so beautiful.

CYCLOPS

You shall repent
For kissing the coy wine that loves you not.

SILENUS

By Jupiter! you said that I am fair.

CYCLOPS

Pour out, and only give me the cup full.

SILENUS

How is it mixed? let me observe.

CYCLOPS

Curse you!
Give it me so.

SILENUS

Not till I see you wear
That coronal, and taste the cup to you.

CYCLOPS

Thou wily traitor!

SILENUS

But the wine is sweet.
Ay, you will roar if you are caught in
drinking.

CYCLOPS

See now, my lip is clean and all my beard.

SILENUS

Now put your elbow right and drink again.
As you see me drink — . . .

CYCLOPS

How now?

SILENUS

Ye Gods, what a delicious gulp!

CYCLOPS

Guest, take it. You pour out the wine for
me.

ULYSSES

The wine is well accustomed to my hand.

CYCLOPS

Pour out the wine!

ULYSSES

I pour; only be silent.

CYCLOPS

Silence is a hard task to him who drinks.

ULYSSES

Take it and drink it off; leave not a dreg.
Oh, that the drinker died with his own
draught!

CYCLOPS

Papai! the vine must be a sapient plant.

ULYSSES

If you drink much after a mighty feast,
Moistening your thirsty maw, you will sleep
well;
If you leave aught, Bacchus will dry you
up.

CYCLOPS

Ho! ho! I can scarce rise. What pure
delight!
The heavens and earth appear to whirl
about
Confusedly. I see the throne of Jove
And the clear congregation of the Gods.
Now if the Graces tempted me to kiss
I would not, for the loveliest of them all
I would not leave this Ganymede.

SILENUS

Polypheme,
I am the Ganymede of Jupiter.

CYCLOPS

By Jove you are; I bore you off from Dar-
danus.

. . . .

ULYSSES *and the* CHORUS

ULYSSES

Come, boys of Bacchus, children of high
race,
This man within is folded up in sleep,
And soon will vomit flesh from his fell maw;
The brand under the shed thrusts out its
smoke;
No preparation needs, but to burn out
The monster's eye; — but bear yourselves
like men.

CHORUS

We will have courage like the adamant
    rock.
All things are ready for you here; go in
Before our father shall perceive the noise.

ULYSSES

Vulcan, Ætnean king ! burn out with fire
The shining eye of this thy neighboring
    monster !
And thou, O sleep, nursling of gloomy
    night,
Descend unmixed on this God-hated beast,
And suffer not Ulysses and his comrades,
Returning from their famous Trojan toils,
To perish by this man, who cares not either
For God or mortal; or I needs must
    think
That Chance is a supreme divinity,
And things divine are subject to her power.

CHORUS

  Soon a crab the throat will seize
    Of him who feeds upon his guest;
  Fire will burn his lamp-like eyes
    In revenge of such a feast !
  A great oak stump now is lying
  In the ashes yet undying.
    Come, Maron, come !
  Raging let him fix the doom,
  Let him tear the eyelid up
  Of the Cyclops — that his cup
    May be evil !
Oh, I long to dance and revel
With sweet Bromian, long desired,
In loved ivy wreaths attired;
Leaving this abandoned home —
Will the moment ever come ?

ULYSSES

Be silent, ye wild things ! Nay, hold your
    peace,
And keep your lips quite close; dare not to
    breathe,
Or spit, or e'en wink, lest ye wake the mon-
    ster, —
Until his eye be tortured out with fire.

CHORUS

Nay, we are silent, and we chaw the air.

ULYSSES

Come now, and lend a hand to the great
    stake
Within — it is delightfully red hot.

CHORUS

You then command who first should seize
    the stake
To burn the Cyclops' eye, that all may share
In the great enterprise.

SEMICHORUS I

            We are too far;
We cannot at this distance from the door
Thrust fire into his eye.

SEMICHORUS II

            And we just now
Have become lame; cannot move hand or
    foot.

CHORUS

The same thing has occurred to us; our
    ankles
Are sprained with standing here, I know
    not how.

ULYSSES

What, sprained with standing still ?

CHORUS

           And there is dust
Or ashes in our eyes, I know not whence.

ULYSSES

Cowardly dogs ! ye will not aid me then ?

CHORUS

With pitying my own back and my back-
    bone,
And with not wishing all my teeth knocked
    out,
This cowardice comes of itself. But stay,
I know a famous Orphic incantation
To make the brand stick of its own accord
Into the skull of this one-eyed son of Earth.

ULYSSES

Of old I knew ye thus by nature; now
I know ye better. I will use the aid
Of my own comrades. Yet though weak
    of hand
Speak cheerfully, that so ye may awaken
The courage of my friends with your blithe
    words.

CHORUS

This I will do with peril of my life,
And blind you with my exhortations, Cy-
    clops.
    Hasten and thrust,
    And parch up to dust,

The eye of the beast,
Who feeds on his guest !
Burn and blind
The Ætnean hind !
Scoop and draw,
But beware lest he claw
Your limbs near his maw.

CYCLOPS

Ah me ! my eyesight is parched up to cinders.

CHORUS

What a sweet pæan ! sing me that again !

CYCLOPS

Ah me ! indeed, what woe has fallen upon me !
But wretched nothings, think ye not to flee
Out of this rock; I, standing at the outlet,
Will bar the way and catch you as you pass.

CHORUS

What are you roaring out, Cyclops ?

CYCLOPS

I perish !

CHORUS

For you are wicked.

CYCLOPS

And besides miserable.

CHORUS

What, did you fall into the fire when drunk ?

CYCLOPS

'T was Nobody destroyed me.

CHORUS

Why, then no one
Can be to blame.

CYCLOPS

I say 't was Nobody
Who blinded me.

CHORUS

Why, then you are not blind.

CYCLOPS

I wish you were as blind as I am.

CHORUS

Nay,
It cannot be that no one made you blind.

CYCLOPS

You jeer me; where, I ask, is Nobody ?

CHORUS

Nowhere, O Cyclops.

CYCLOPS

It was that stranger ruined me. The wretch
First gave me wine and then burned out my eye,
For wine is strong and hard to struggle with.
Have they escaped, or are they yet within ?

CHORUS

They stand under the darkness of the rock
And cling to it.

CYCLOPS

At my right hand or left ?

CHORUS

Close on your right.

CYCLOPS

Where ?

CHORUS

Near the rock itself.
You have them.

CYCLOPS

Oh, misfortune on misfortune !
I 've cracked my skull.

CHORUS

Now they escape you there.

CYCLOPS

Not there, although you say so.

CHORUS

Not on that side.

CYCLOPS

Where then ?

CHORUS

They creep about you on your left.

CYCLOPS

Ah ! I am mocked ! They jeer me in my ills.

CHORUS

Not there ! he is a little there beyond you.

CYCLOPS

Detested wretch ! where are you ?

ULYSSES

Far from you
I keep with care this body of Ulysses.

CYCLOPS

What do you say? You proffer a new
name.

ULYSSES

My father named me so; and I have taken
A full revenge for your unnatural feast;
I should have done ill to have burned down
Troy
And not revenged the murder of my com-
rades.

CYCLOPS

Ai ! ai ! the ancient oracle is accomplished;
It said that I should have my eyesight
blinded
By you coming from Troy, yet it foretold
That you should pay the penalty for this
By wandering long over the homeless sea.

ULYSSES

I bid thee weep — consider what I say;
I go towards the shore to drive my ship
To mine own land, o'er the Sicilian wave.

CYCLOPS

Not so, if, whelming you with this huge
stone,
I can crush you and all your men together.
I will descend upon the shore, though
blind,
Groping my way adown the steep ravine.

CHORUS

And we, the shipmates of Ulysses now,
Will serve our Bacchus all our happy
lives.

EPIGRAMS FROM THE GREEK

I

SPIRIT OF PLATO

EAGLE ! why soarest thou above that
tomb ?
To what sublime and star-y-paven home
Floatest thou ? —

I am the image of swift Plato's spirit,
Ascending heaven; Athens doth inherit
His corpse below.

Undated. Mrs. Shelley, 1839, 1st ed.

II

CIRCUMSTANCE

A MAN who was about to hang himself,
Finding a purse, then threw away his
rope;
The owner, coming to reclaim his pelf,
The halter found, and used it. So is
Hope
Changed for Despair; one laid upon the
shelf,
We take the other. Under heaven's
high cope
Fortune is God; all you endure and do
Depends on circumstance as much as you.

Undated. Mrs. Shelley, 1839, 1st ed.

III

TO STELLA

FROM PLATO

Medwin describes the composition of this
stanza: 'Plato's epigram on *Aster*, which
Shelley had applied to Keats, happened to be
mentioned, and I asked Shelley if he could
render it. He took up the pen and improvised.'

It was published by Mrs. Shelley in her first
collected edition, 1839, as was also the following.

THOU wert the morning star among the
living,
Ere thy fair light had fled;
Now, having died, thou art as Hesperus,
giving
New splendor to the dead.

IV

KISSING HELENA

FROM PLATO

KISSING Helena, together
With my kiss, my soul beside it
Came to my lips, and there I kept it, —

For the poor thing had wandered thither,
  To follow where the kiss should guide it,
  Oh, cruel I, to intercept it !

FROM MOSCHUS

I

Τὰν ἅλα τὰν γλαυκὰν ὅταν ὤνεμος ἀτρέμα βάλλῃ

WHEN winds that move not its calm sur-
    face sweep
The azure sea, I love the land no more;
The smiles of the serene and tranquil deep
Tempt my unquiet mind. But when the
    roar
Of ocean's gray abyss resounds, and foam
Gathers upon the sea, and vast waves burst,
I turn from the drear aspect to the home
Of earth and its deep woods, where, inter-
    spersed,
When winds blow loud, pines make sweet
    melody.
Whose house is some lone bark, whose toil
    the sea,
Whose prey the wandering fish, an evil
    lot
Has chosen. But I my languid limbs will
    fling
Beneath the plane, where the brook's mur-
    muring
Moves the calm spirit, but disturbs it
    not.

Undated. Published with *Alastor*, 1816.

II

PAN, ECHO, AND THE SATYR

PAN loved his neighbor Echo, but that
    child
  Of Earth and Air pined for the Satyr
    leaping;
The Satyr loved with wasting madness
    wild
  The bright nymph Lyda; and so three
    went weeping.
As Pan loved Echo, Echo loved the Satyr,
  The Satyr, Lyda; and so love consumed
    them.
And thus to each — which was a woful
    matter —
  To bear what they inflicted Justice
    doomed them;

For, inasmuch as each might hate the
    lover,
  Each, loving, so was hated. — Ye that
    love not
Be warned — in thought turn this example
    over,
  That when ye love, the like return ye
    prove not.

Undated. Published by Mrs. Shelley, *Posthumous Poems*, 1824.

III

FRAGMENT OF THE ELEGY ON THE DEATH OF BION

YE Dorian woods and waves lament
    aloud, —
Augment your tide, O streams, with fruit-
    less tears,
For the belovèd Bion is no more.
Let every tender herb and plant and flower,
From each dejected bud and drooping
    bloom,
Shed dews of liquid sorrow, and with
    breath
Of melancholy sweetness on the wind
Diffuse its languid love; let roses blush,
Anemones grow paler for the loss
Their dells have known; and thou, O hya-
    cinth,
Utter thy legend now — yet more, dumb
    flower,
Than 'ah ! alas !' — thine is no common
    grief —
Bion the [sweetest singer] is no more.

Undated. Published by Forman, 1876.

FROM BION

FRAGMENT OF THE ELEGY ON THE DEATH OF ADONIS

I MOURN Adonis dead — loveliest Adonis —
Dead, dead Adonis — and the Loves la-
    ment.
Sleep no more, Venus, wrapped in purple
    woof.
Wake, violet-stolèd queen, and weave the
    crown
Of Death — 't is Misery calls — for he is
    dead !

The lovely one lies wounded in the mountains,
His white thigh struck with the white tooth; he scarce
Yet breathes; and Venus hangs in agony there.
The dark blood wanders o'er his snowy limbs,
His eyes beneath their lids are lustreless,
The rose has fled from his wan lips, and there
That kiss is dead, which Venus gathers yet.

A deep, deep wound Adonis . . .
A deeper Venus bears upon her heart.
See, his belovèd dogs are gathering round —
The Oread nymphs are weeping. Aphrodite
With hair unbound is wandering through the woods,
Wildered, ungirt, unsandalled — the thorns pierce
Her hastening feet and drink her sacred blood.
Bitterly screaming out she is driven on
Through the long vales; and her Assyrian boy,
Her love, her husband calls. The purple blood
From his struck thigh stains her white navel now,
Her bosom, and her neck before like snow.

Alas for Cytherea ! the Loves mourn —
The lovely, the beloved is gone ! — And now
Her sacred beauty vanishes away.
For Venus whilst Adonis lived was fair —
Alas ! her loveliness is dead with him.
The oaks and mountains cry, Ai ! ai ! Adonis !
The springs their waters change to tears and weep —
The flowers are withered up with grief . . .

Ai ! ai !   Adonis is dead
Echo resounds   Adonis dead.
Who will weep not thy dreadful woe, O Venus ?
Soon as she saw and knew the mortal wound
Of her Adonis — saw the life blood flow
From his fair thigh, now wasting, wailing loud

She clasped him, and cried   'Stay Adonis !
Stay, dearest one, —
         and mix my lips with thine !
Wake yet a while Adonis — oh, but once !
That I may kiss thee now for the last time —
But for as long as one short kiss may live !
Oh, let thy breath flow from thy dying soul
Even to my mouth and heart, that I may suck
That

Undated. Published by Forman, 1876.

FROM VIRGIL

THE TENTH ECLOGUE

[V. 1-26]

MELODIOUS Arethusa, o'er my verse
  Shed thou once more the spirit of thy stream.
Who denies verse to Gallus ? So, when thou
  Glidest beneath the green and purple gleam
Of Syracusan waters, mayst thou flow
  Unmingled with the bitter Doric dew !
Begin, and, whilst the goats are browsing now
  The soft leaves, in our way let us pursue
The melancholy loves of Gallus. List !
  We sing not to the dead; the wild woods knew
His sufferings, and their echoes . . .
  Young Naiads,   in what far woodlands wild
Wandered ye when unworthy love possessed
  Your Gallus ? Not where Pindus is uppiled,
Nor where Parnassus' sacred mount, nor where
Aonian Aganippe expands
  The laurels and the myrtle-copses dim.
The pine-encircled mountain, Mænalus,
  The cold crags of Lycæus, weep for him;
And Sylvan, crowned with rustic coronals,
Came shaking in his speed the budding wands
And heavy lilies which he bore; we knew
Pan the Arcadian.

.   .   .   .

What madness is this, Gallus? Thy
    heart's care
With willing steps pursues another there.
    Undated. Published by Rossetti, 1870.

FROM DANTE

I

ADAPTED FROM A SONNET IN THE VITA NUOVA

Forman who published the lines, 1876,
vouches for them thus: ' These lines . . . are
said to have been scratched by Shelley on a
window-pane at a house wherein he lodged
while staying in London. I have them on the
authority of a gentleman whose mother was
the proprietress of the house.'

WHAT Mary is when she a little smiles
I cannot even tell or call to mind,
It is a miracle so new, so rare.

II

SONNET

DANTE ALIGHIERI *to* GUIDO CAVALCANTI

GUIDO, I would that Lappo, thou, and I,
Led by some strong enchantment, might
    ascend
A magic ship, whose charmèd sails should
    fly
With winds at will where'er our thoughts
    might wend,
So that no change, nor any evil chance
Should mar our joyous voyage, but it
    might be
That even satiety should still enhance
Between our hearts their strict community;
And that the bounteous wizard then would
    place
Vanna and Bice and my gentle love,
Companions of our wandering, and would
    grace
With passionate talk wherever we might
    rove
Our time, and each were as content and
    free
As I believe that thou and I should be.
    Undated. Published with *Alastor*, 1816.

III

THE FIRST CANZONE OF THE CONVITO

I

YE who intelligent the Third Heaven move,
Hear the discourse which is within my
    heart,
    Which cannot be declared, it seems so
    new.
The Heaven whose course follows your
    power and art,
    O gentle creatures that ye are ! me drew,
    And therefore may I dare to speak to
    you,
Even of the life which now I live, — and
    yet
    I pray that ye will hear me when I cry,
    And tell of mine own Heart this novelty;
How the lamenting Spirit moans in it,
And how a voice there murmurs against her
Who came on the refulgence of your
    sphere.

II

A sweet Thought, which was once the life
    within
This heavy Heart, many a time and oft
    Went up before our Father's feet, and
    there
    It saw a glorious Lady throned aloft;
And its sweet talk of her my soul did win,
    So that I said, ' Thither I too will fare.'
    That Thought is fled, and one doth
    now appear
Which tyrannizes me with such fierce stress
    That my heart trembles — ye may see it
    leap —
    And on another Lady bids me keep
Mine eyes, and says: ' Who would have
    blessedness
Let him but look upon that Lady's eyes;
Let him not fear the agony of sighs.'

III

This lowly Thought, which once would talk
    with me
Of a bright Seraph sitting crowned on high,
    Found such a cruel foe it died; and so
    My Spirit wept — the grief is hot even
    now —
And said, ' Alas for me ! now swift could
    flee

That piteous Thought which did my life
    console ! '
And the afflicted one   question-
    ing
  Mine eyes, if such a Lady saw they
    never,
And why they would . . .
    I said: ' Beneath those eyes might
    stand forever
He whom   regards must kill with . . .
To have known their power stood me in
    little stead;
Those eyes have looked on me, and I am
    dead.'

IV

' Thou art not dead, but thou hast wan-
    derèd,
  Thou Soul of ours, who thyself dost
    fret,'
A Spirit gentle Love beside me said:
  ' For that fair Lady, whom thou dost re-
    gret,
Hath so transformed the life which thou
    hast led,
Thou scornest it, so worthless art thou
    made.
And see how meek, how pitiful, how staid,
Yet courteous, in her majesty she is.
  And still call thou her " Woman " in thy
    thought;
  Her whom, if thou thyself deceivest not,
Thou wilt behold decked with such loveli-
    ness,
That thou wilt cry: " [Love] only Lord, lo
    here
Thy handmaiden, do what thou wilt with
    her." '

V

My song, I fear that thou wilt find but few
  Who fitly shall conceive thy reasoning,
    Of such hard matter dost thou enter-
    tain.
  Whence, if by misadventure chance
    should bring
Thee to base company, as chance may do,
  Quite unaware of what thou dost con-
    tain,
  I prithee comfort thy sweet self again,
My last delight; tell them that they are
    dull,
And bid them own that thou art beautiful.

  Published (i–iv) by Garnett, 1862, with date,
1820; v with *Epipsychidion*, 1821.

IV

MATILDA GATHERING FLOW-ERS

PURGATORIO, xxviii. 1-51

  Published by Medwin, *The Angler in Wales*,
1834, and *Life of Shelley*, 1847, and completed
by Garnett, 1862. Medwin describes how he
obtained the copy : ' I had also the advantage
of reading Dante with him ; he lamented that
no adequate translation existed of the *Divina
Commedia*, and though he thought highly of
Carey's work, — with which he said he had for
the first time studied the original, praising the
fidelity of the version, — it by no means satisfied him. What he meant by an adequate
translation was one in *terza rima ;* for, in Shelley's own words, he held it an essential justice
to an author to render him in the same form.
I asked him if he had never attempted this, and,
looking among his papers, he showed, and gave
me to copy, the following fragment from the
Purgatorio, which leaves on the mind an inextinguishable regret that he had not completed
— nay, more, that he did not employ himself
in rendering other of the finest passages.'

AND earnest to explore within — around —
That divine wood whose thick green living
    woof
Tempered the young day to the sight, I
    wound

Up the green slope, beneath the forest's
    roof,
With slow soft steps leaving the mountain's
    steep;
And sought those inmost labyrinths' motion-
    proof

Against the air, that, in that stillness
    deep
And solemn, struck upon my forehead bare
The slow, soft stroke of a continuous . . .

In which the   leaves tremblingly
    were
All bent towards that part where earliest
The sacred hill obscures the morning air.

Yet were they not so shaken from the
    rest,
But that the birds, perched on the utmost
    spray,
Incessantly renewing their blithe quest,

With perfect joy received the early day,
Singing within the glancing leaves, whose
sound
Kept a low burden to their roundelay,

Such as from bough to bough gathers
around
The pine forest on bleak Chiassi's shore,
When Æolus Sirocco has unbound.

My slow steps had already borne me o'er
Such space within the antique wood that I
Perceived not where I entered any more,

When, lo ! a stream whose little waves
went by,
Bending towards the left through grass that
grew
Upon its bank, impeded suddenly

My going on. Water of purest hue
On earth would appear turbid and impure
Compared with this, whose unconcealing
dew,

Dark, dark, yet clear, moved under the
obscure
Eternal shades, whose interwoven looms
No ray of moon or sunshine would endure.

I moved not with my feet, but mid the
glooms
Pierced with my charmèd eye, contemplating
The mighty multitude of fresh May blooms

That starred that night; when, even as a
thing
That suddenly, for blank astonishment,
Charms every sense, and makes all thought
take wing, —

A solitary woman ! and she went
Singing, and gathering flower after flower,
With which her way was painted and be-
sprent.

' Bright lady, who, if looks had ever power
To bear true witness of the heart within,
Dost bask under the beams of love, come
lower

' Towards this bank. I prithee let me win
This much of thee, to come, that I may hear
Thy song. Like Proserpine, in Enna's glen,

' Thou seemest to my fancy, singing here
And gathering flowers, as that fair maiden
when
She lost the spring, and Ceres her, more
dear.'

V

UGOLINO

INFERNO xxxiii. 22–75

TRANSLATED BY MEDWIN AND COR-
RECTED BY SHELLEY

Medwin describes this joint composition:
' At Shelley's request and with his assistance,
I attempted to give the *Ugolino*, which is
valuable to the admirers of Shelley, on account of his numerous corrections, which almost indeed make it his own.'
The piece was first published in Medwin's
Sketches in Hindoostan with other poems, 1821,
and revised in the present form, with Shelley's
part in italics, in *Life of Shelley*, 1847. Forman conjectures that he ascribes less to Shelley
than was due. Shelley is said to have com-
plained to Mrs. Shelley that Medwin had carried off some of his translations.

Now had the loophole of that dungeon, still
Which bears the name of Famine's Tower
from me,
And where 't is fit that many another will

Be doomed to linger in captivity,
Shown through its narrow opening in my
cell
Moon after moon slow waning, when a sleep,

That of the future burst the veil, in dream
Visited me. It was a slumber deep
And evil ; for I saw, or I did seem

To see *that* tyrant Lord his revels keep,
The leader of the cruel hunt to them,
Chasing the wolf and wolf-cubs up the
steep

Ascent, that from *the Pisan is the screen*
Of *Lucca ;* with him Gualandi came,
Sismondi, and Lanfranchi, *bloodhounds lean,*

Trained to the sport and eager for the game,
Wide ranging in his front ; but soon were
seen,
Though by so short a course, with *spirits*
tame,

The father and *his whelps* to flag at once,
And then the sharp fangs gored their
   bosoms deep.
Ere morn I roused myself, and heard my
   sons,

For they were with me, moaning in their
   sleep,
And begging bread. Ah for those darling
   ones !
Right cruel art thou, if thou dost not weep

In thinking of my soul's sad augury;
And if thou weepest not now, weep never
   more !
They were already waked, as wont drew
   nigh

The allotted hour for food, and in that hour
Each drew a presage from his dream.
   When I
*Heard locked beneath me of that horrible
   tower*

The outlet ; then into their eyes alone
I looked to read myself, without a sign
Or word. I wept not — turned within to
   stone.

They wept aloud, and little Anselm mine,
Said, — 't was my youngest, dearest little
   one, —
' What ails thee, father ! why look so at
   thine ? '

In all that day, and all the following night,
I wept not, nor replied; but when to shine
Upon the world, not us, came forth the
   light

Of the new sun, and thwart my prison
   thrown
Gleamed through its narrow chink, a dole-
   ful sight,
Three faces, each the reflex of my own,

Were imaged by its faint and ghastly ray ;
Then I, of either hand unto the bone,
Gnawed, in my agony; and thinking they

'T was done from hunger pangs, in their
   excess,
All of a sudden raise themselves, and say,
' Father ! our woes, so great, were yet the
   less

Would you but eat of us, — 't was *you who
   clad*
*Our bodies in these weeds of wretchedness,
Despoil them.'* Not to make their hearts
   more sad,

I *hushed* myself. That day is at its
   close, —
Another — still we were all mute. Oh, had
The obdurate earth opened to end our
   woes !

The fourth day dawned, and when the new
   sun shone,
Outstretched himself before me as it rose
My Gaddo, saying, ' Help, father ! hast
   thou none

' For thine own child — is there no help
   from thee ? '
He died — there at my feet — and one by
   one,
I saw them fall, plainly as you see me.

Between the fifth and sixth day; ere 't was
   dawn,
I found *myself blind-groping o'er the three.*
Three days I called them after they were
   gone.

Famine of grief can get the mastery.

SONNET

TRANSLATED   FROM   THE   ITALIAN   OF
CAVALCANTI

GUIDO CAVALCANTI *to* DANTE ALIGHIERI

Published by Forman, 1876, and dated by
him 1815.

RETURNING from its daily quest, my Spirit
Changed thoughts and vile in thee doth
   weep to find.
It grieves me that thy mild and gentle
   mind
Those ample virtues which it did inherit
Has lost. Once thou didst loathe the mul-
   titude
Of blind and madding men; I then loved
   thee —
I loved thy lofty songs and that sweet
   mood
When thou wert faithful to thyself and me.

I dare not now through thy degraded state
Own the delight thy strains inspire — in
     vain
I seek what once thou wert — we cannot
     meet
As we were wont. Again, and yet again,
Ponder my words: so the false Spirit shall
     fly
And leave to thee thy true integrity.

SCENES FROM THE MAGICO PRODIGIOSO

TRANSLATED FROM THE SPANISH OF
CALDERON

Shelley's acquaintance with Spanish began
apparently with reading Calderon in company
with Mrs. Gisborne in August, 1819, and under
Charles Clairmont's friendly tutoring in September of the same year. He wrote to Peacock in the former month:

Shelley (from Leghorn) to Peacock, August
22 (?), 1819: 'I have been reading Calderon
in Spanish [with Mrs. Gisborne]. A kind of
Shakespeare is this Calderon; and I have some
thoughts, if I find that I cannot do anything
better, of translating some of his plays;' and
again in September: 'Charles Clairmont is
now with us on his way to Vienna. He has
spent a year or more in Spain, where he has
learned Spanish, and I make him read Spanish
all day long. It is a most powerful and expressive language, and I have already learned
sufficient to read with great ease their poet
Calderon. I have read about twelve of his
plays. Some of them certainly deserve to be
ranked amongst the grandest and most perfect
productions of the human mind. He exceeds
all modern dramatists, with the exception of
Shakespeare, whom he resembles, however, in
the depth of thought and subtlety of imagination of his writings, and in the rare power
of interweaving delicate and powerful comic
traits with the most tragical situations, without
diminishing their interest. I rate him far above
Beaumont and Fletcher.' Shelley translated
these scenes in March, 1822, and they had not
received his final correction. They were published by Mrs. Shelley, *Posthumous Poems*,
1824.

SCENE I. — *Enter* CYPRIAN, *dressed as a Student;* CLARIN *and* MOSCON *as poor Scholars,
with books.*

CYPRIAN

IN the sweet solitude of this calm place,
This intricate wild wilderness of trees
And flowers and undergrowth of odorous
     plants,
Leave me; the books you brought out of
     the house
To me are ever best society.
And while with glorious festival and song,
Antioch now celebrates the consecration
Of a proud temple to great Jupiter,
And bears his image in loud jubilee
To its new shrine, I would consume what
     still
Lives of the dying day in studious thought,
Far from the throng and turmoil. You,
     my friends,
Go, and enjoy the festival; it will
Be worth your pains. You may return for
     me
When the sun seeks its grave among the
     billows,
Which among dim gray clouds on the hori-
     zon,
Dance like white plumes upon a hearse; —
     and here
I shall expect you.

MOSCON
                    I cannot bring my mind,
Great as my haste to see the festival
Certainly is, to leave you, Sir, without
Just saying some three or four thousand
     words.
How is it possible that on a day
Of such festivity you can be content
To come forth to a solitary country
With three or four old books, and turn
     your back
On all this mirth?

CLARIN
                    My master's in the right;
There is not anything more tiresome
Than a procession day, with troops, and
     priests,
And dances, and all that.

MOSCON
                    From first to last,
Clarin, you are a temporizing flatterer;
You praise not what you feel but what he
     does.
Toadeater!

CLARIN
                    You lie — under a mistake —
For this is the most civil sort of lie

That can be given to a man's face. I now
Say what I think.

CYPRIAN

Enough, you foolish fellows !
Puffed up with your own doting ignorance,
You always take the two sides of one ques-
tion.
Now go; and as I said, return for me
When night falls, veiling in its shadows
wide
This glorious fabric of the universe.

MOSCON

How happens it, although you can main-
tain
The folly of enjoying festivals,
That yet you go there ?

CLARIN

Nay, the consequence
Is clear. Who ever did what he advises
Others to do ? —

MOSCON

Would that my feet were wings,
So would I fly to Livia.
[Exit.

CLARIN

To speak truth,
Livia is she who has surprised my heart;
But he is more than half way there. — Soho !
Livia, I come; good sport, Livia, Soho !
[Exit.

CYPRIAN

Now, since I am alone, let me examine
The question which has long disturbed my
mind
With doubt, since first I read in Plinius
The words of mystic import and deep sense
In which he defines God. My intellect
Can find no God with whom these marks
and signs
Fitly agree. It is a hidden truth
Which I must fathom.

(CYPRIAN reads; the DEMON, dressed in a
Court dress, enters)

DEMON

Search even as thou wilt,
But thou shalt never find what I can hide.

CYPRIAN

What noise is that among the boughs ?
Who moves ?
What art thou ? —

DEMON

'T is a foreign gentleman.
Even from this morning I have lost my way
In this wild place; and my poor horse at
last,
Quite overcome, has stretched himself upon
The enamelled tapestry of this mossy moun-
tain,
And feeds and rests at the same time. I
was
Upon my way to Antioch upon business
Of some importance, but wrapped up in
cares
(Who is exempt from this inheritance ?)
I parted from my company, and lost
My way, and lost my servants and my com-
rades.

CYPRIAN

'T is singular that even within the sight
Of the high towers of Antioch you could lose
Your way. Of all the avenues and green
paths
Of this wild wood there is not one but leads,
As to its centre, to the walls of Antioch;
Take which you will you cannot miss your
road.

DEMON

And such is ignorance ! Even in the sight
Of knowledge, it can draw no profit from it.
But as it still is early, and as I
Have no acquaintances in Antioch,
Being a stranger there, I will even wait
The few surviving hours of the day,
Until the night shall conquer it. I see,
Both by your dress and by the books in
which
You find delight and company, that you
Are a great student ; for my part, I feel
Much sympathy with such pursuits.

CYPRIAN

Have you
Studied much ?

DEMON

No, — and yet I know enough
Not to be wholly ignorant.

CYPRIAN

Pray, Sir,
What science may you know ?

DEMON

Many.

CYPRIAN

Alas!
Much pains must we expend on one alone,
And even then attain it not; but you
Have the presumption to assert that you
Know many without study.

DEMON

And with truth.
For in the country whence I come the sciences·
Require no learning, — they are known.

CYPRIAN

Oh, would
I were of that bright country! for in this
The more we study, we the more discover
Our ignorance.

DEMON

It is so true, that I
Had so much arrogance as to oppose
The chair of the most high Professorship,
And obtained many votes, and, though I lost,
The attempt was still more glorious than the failure
Could be dishonorable. If you believe not,
Let us refer it to dispute respecting
That which you know the best, and although I
Know not the opinion you maintain, and though
It be the true one, I will take the contrary.

CYPRIAN

The offer gives me pleasure. I am now
Debating with myself upon a passage
Of Plinius, and my mind is racked with doubt
To understand and know who is the God
Of whom he speaks.

DEMON

It is a passage, if
I recollect it right, couched in these words:
'God is one supreme goodness, one pure essence,
One substance, and one sense, all sight, all hands.'

CYPRIAN

'T is true.

DEMON

What difficulty find you here?

CYPRIAN

I do not recognize among the Gods
The God defined by Plinius; if he must
Be supreme goodness, even Jupiter
Is not supremely good; because we see
His deeds are evil, and his attributes
Tainted with mortal weakness. In what manner
Can supreme goodness be consistent with
The passions of humanity?

DEMON

The wisdom
Of the old world masked with the names of Gods
The attributes of Nature and of Man;
A sort of popular philosophy.

CYPRIAN

This reply will not satisfy me, for
Such awe is due tò the high name of God
That ill should never be imputed. Then,
Examining the question with more care,
It follows that the Gods would always will
That which is best, were they supremely good.
How then does one will one thing, one another?
And that you may not say that I allege
Poetical or philosophic learning,
Consider the ambiguous responses
Of their oracular statues; from two shrines
Two armies shall obtain the assurance of
One victory. Is it not indisputable
That two contending wills can never lead
To the same end? And, being opposite,
If one be good is not the other evil?
Evil in God is inconceivable;
But supreme goodness fails among the Gods
Without their union.

DEMON

I deny your major.
These responses are means towards some end
Unfathomed by our intellectual beam.
They are the work of providence, and more
The battle's loss may profit those who lose
Than victory advantage those who win.

CYPRIAN

That I admit; and yet that God should not
(Falsehood is incompatible with deity)
Assure the victory; it would be enough

To have permitted the defeat. If God
Be all sight, — God, who had beheld the
    truth,
Would not have given assurance of an end
Never to be accomplished; thus, although
The Deity may according to his attributes
Be well distinguished into persons, yet
Even in the minutest circumstance
His essence must be one.

DEMON

                    To attain the end
The affections of the actors in the scene
Must have been thus influenced by his voice.

CYPRIAN

But for a purpose thus subordinate
He might have employed Genii, good or
    evil, —
A sort of spirits called so by the learned,
Who roam about inspiring good or evil,
And from whose influence and existence we
May well infer our immortality.
Thus God might easily, without descent
To a gross falsehood in his proper person,
Have moved the affections by this media-
    tion
To the just point.

DEMON

                These trifling contradictions
Do not suffice to impugn the unity
Of the high Gods; in things of great im-
    portance
They still appear unanimous; consider
That glorious fabric, man, — his workman-
    ship
Is stamped with one conception.

CYPRIAN

                        Who made man
Must have, methinks, the advantage of the
    others.
If they are equal, might they not have risen
In opposition to the work, and being
All hands, according to our author here,
Have still destroyed even as the other
    made?
If equal in their power, unequal only
In opportunity, which of the two
Will remain conqueror?

DEMON

                    On impossible
And false hypothesis there can be built

No argument. Say, what do you infer
From this?

CYPRIAN

        That there must be a mighty God
Of supreme goodness and of highest grace,
All sight, all hands, all truth, infallible,
Without an equal and without a rival,
The cause of all things and the effect of
    nothing,
One power, one will, one substance, and
    one essence,
And in whatever persons, one or two,
His attributes may be distinguished, one
Sovereign power, one solitary essence,
One cause of all cause.

                        (*They rise*)

DEMON

                    How can I impugn
So clear a consequence?

CYPRIAN

                    Do you regret
My victory?

DEMON

                Who but regrets a check
In rivalry of wit? I could reply
And urge new difficulties, but will now
Depart, for I hear steps of men approach-
    ing,
And it is time that I should now pursue
My journey to the city.

CYPRIAN

                    Go in peace!

DEMON

Remain in peace! — Since thus it profits
    him
To study, I will wrap his senses up
In sweet oblivion of all thought but of
A piece of excellent beauty; and, as I
Have power given me to wage enmity
Against Justina's soul, I will extract
From one effect two vengeances.
                        [*Aside and exit.*

CYPRIAN

                            I never
Met a more learnèd person. Let me now
Revolve this doubt again with careful
    mind.
                            [*He reads.*

FLORO *and* LELIO *enter*

LELIO

Here stop. These toppling rocks and tan-
gled boughs,
Impenetrable by the noonday beam,
Shall be sole witnesses of what we —

FLORO

Draw !
If there were words, here is the place for
deeds.

LELIO

Thou needest not instruct me; well I
know
That in the field the silent tongue of steel
Speaks thus, —
[*They fight*

CYPRIAN

Ha ! what is this ? Lelio, — Floro, —
Be it enough that Cyprian stands between
you,
Although unarmed.

LELIO

Whence comest thou to stand
Between me and my vengeance ?

FLORO

From what rocks
And desert cells ?

Enter MOSCON *and* CLARIN

MOSCON

Run ! run ! for where we left
My master, I now hear the clash of swords.

CLARIN

I never run to approach things of this
sort,
But only to avoid them.   Sir ! Cyprian !
sir !

CYPRIAN

Be silent, fellows ! What ! two friends
who are
In blood and fame the eyes and hope of
Antioch,
One of the noble race of the Colalti,
The other son o' the Governor, adventure
And cast away, on some slight cause no
doubt,
Two lives, the honor of their country ?

LELIO

Cyprian !
Although my high respect towards your
person
Holds now my sword suspended, thou canst
not
Restore it to the slumber of the scabbard:
Thou knowest more of science than the duel;
For when two men of honor take the field,
No counsel nor respect can make them
friends
But one must die in the dispute.

FLORO

I pray
That you depart hence with your people,
and
Leave us to finish what we have begun
Without advantage.

CYPRIAN

Though you may imagine
That I know little of the laws of duel,
Which vanity and valor instituted,
You are in error.   By my birth I am
Held no less than yourselves to know the
limits
Of honor and of infamy, nor has study
Quenched the free spirit which first ordered
them;
And thus to me, as one well experienced
In the false quicksands of the sea of honor,
You may refer the merits of the case;
And if I should perceive in your relation
That either has the right to satisfaction
From the other, I give you my word of
honor
To leave you.

LELIO

Under this condition then
I will relate the cause, and you will cede
And must confess the impossibility
Of compromise; for the same lady is
Beloved by Floro and myself.

FLORO

It seems
Much to me that the light of day should
look
Upon that idol of my heart — but he —
Leave us to fight, according to thy word.

CYPRIAN

Permit one question further: is the lady
Impossible to hope or not ? .

LELIO

She is
So excellent that if the light of day
Should excite Floro's jealousy, it were
Without just cause, for even the light of
  day
Trembles to gaze on her.

CYPRIAN

Would you for your
Part, marry her?

FLORO

Such is my confidence.

CYPRIAN

And you?

LELIO

Oh! would that I could lift my hope
So high, for though she is extremely poor,
Her virtue is her dowry.

CYPRIAN

And if you both
Would marry her, is it not weak and vain,
Culpable and unworthy, thus beforehand
To slur her honor? What would the
  world say
If one should slay the other, and if she
Should afterwards espouse the murderer?

[*The rivals agree to refer their quarrel to* CY-
PRIAN; *who in consequence visits* JUSTINA,
*and becomes enamoured of her: she disdains
him, and he retires to a solitary seashore.*

SCENE II

CYPRIAN

O memory! permit it not
That the tyrant of my thought
Be another soul that still
Holds dominion o'er the will,
That would refuse, but can no more,
To bend, to tremble, and adore.
Vain idolatry!—I saw,
And gazing, became blind with error;
Weak ambition, which the awe
Of her presence bound to terror!
So beautiful she was—and I,
Between my love and jealousy,
Am so convulsed with hope and fear,
Unworthy as it may appear.
So bitter is the life I live,
That, hear me, Hell! I now would give

To thy most detested spirit
My soul, forever to inherit,
To suffer punishment and pine,
So this woman may be mine.
Hear'st thou, Hell! dost thou reject it?
My soul is offered!

DEMON (*unseen*)

I accept it.
[*Tempest, with thunder and lightning.*

CYPRIAN

What is this? ye heavens forever pure,
 At once intensely radiant and obscure!
  Athwart the ethereal halls
The lightning's arrow and the thunder-
  balls
  The day affright,
  As from the horizon round
  Burst with earthquake sound
In mighty torrents the electric fountains;
Clouds quench the sun, and thunder smoke
 Strangles the air, and fire eclipses heaven.
Philosophy, thou canst not even
Compel their causes underneath thy yoke;
 From yonder clouds even to the waves
  below
The fragments of a single ruin choke
 Imagination's flight;
For, on flakes of surge, like feathers light,
The ashes of the desolation, cast
  Upon the gloomy blast,
Tell of the footsteps of the storm;
And nearer, see, the melancholy form
Of a great ship, the outcast of the sea,
 Drives miserably!
And it must fly the pity of the port,
Or perish, and its last and sole resort
Is its own raging enemy.
The terror of the thrilling cry
 Was a fatal prophecy
Of coming death, who hovers now
 Upon that shattered prow,
That they who die not may be dying still.
 And not alone the insane elements
 Are populous with wide portents,
But that sad ship is as a miracle
 Of sudden ruin, for it drives so fast
It seems as if it had arrayed its form
With the headlong storm.
It strikes—I almost feel the shock—
It stumbles on a jagged rock,—
 Sparkles of blood on the white foam are
  cast.
[*A Tempest.*

All exclaim (within)

We are all lost !

DEMON (*within*)
                Now from this plank will I
Pass to the land and thus fulfil my scheme.

CYPRIAN

As in contempt of the elemental rage
    A man comes forth in safety, while the
        ship's
    Great form is in a watery eclipse
Obliterated from the Ocean's page,
And round its wreck the huge sea-monsters
        sit,
A horrid conclave, and the whistling wave
Is heaped over its carcass, like a grave.

The DEMON *enters, as escaped from the sea*

DEMON (*aside*)

It was essential to my purposes
To wake a tumult on the sapphire ocean,
That in this unknown form I might at
        length
Wipe out the blot of the discomfiture
Sustained upon the mountain, and assail
With a new war the soul of Cyprian,
Forging the instruments of his destruction
Even from his love and from his wis-
        dom. — O
Belovèd earth, dear Mother, in thy bosom
I seek a refuge from the monster who
Precipitates itself upon me.

CYPRIAN
                        Friend,
Collect thyself; and be the memory
Of thy late suffering, and thy greatest sor-
        row
But as a shadow of the past, — for nothing
Beneath the circle of the moon but flows
And changes, and can never know repose.

DEMON

And who art thou, before whose feet my
        fate
Has prostrated me ?

CYPRIAN
            One who, moved with pity,
Would soothe its stings.

DEMON
            Oh ! that can never be !
No solace can my lasting sorrows find.

CYPRIAN

Wherefore ?

DEMON
            Because my happiness is lost.
Yet I lament what has long ceased to be
The object of desire or memory,
And my life is not life.

CYPRIAN
                Now, since the fury
Of this earthquaking hurricane is still,
And the crystalline heaven has reassumed
Its windless calm so quickly that it seems
As if its heavy wrath had been awakened
Only to overwhelm that vessel, — speak,
Who art thou, and whence comest thou ?

DEMON
                        Far more
My coming hither cost than thou hast seen
Or I can tell.   Among my misadventures
This shipwreck is the least.   Wilt thou
        hear ?

CYPRIAN
                        Speak.

DEMON

Since thou desirest, I will then unveil
Myself to thee; for in myself I am
A world of happiness and misery;
This I have lost, and that I must lament
Forever.   In my attributes I stood
So high and so heroically great,
In lineage so supreme, and with a genius
Which penetrated with a glance the world
Beneath my feet, that, won by my high
        merit,
A king — whom I may call the King of
        kings,
Because all others tremble in their pride
Before the terrors of his countenance,
In his high palace roofed with brightest
        gems
Of living light — call them the stars of
        Heaven —
Named me his counsellor.   But the high
        praise
Stung me with pride and envy, and I rose
In mighty competition to ascend
His seat, and place my foot triumphantly
Upon his subject thrones.   Chastised, I
        know
The depth to which ambition falls; too mad
Was the attempt, and yet more mad were
        now

Repentance of the irrevocable deed.
Therefore I chose this ruin, with the glory
Of not to be subdued, before the shame
Of reconciling me with him who reigns
By coward cession. Nor was I alone,
Nor am I now, nor shall I be alone;
And there was hope, and there may still be
  hope,
For many suffrages among his vassals
Hailed me their lord and king, and many
  still
Are mine, and many more perchance shall
  be.
Thus vanquished, though in fact victorious,
I left his seat of empire, from mine eye
Shooting forth poisonous lightning, while
  my words
With inauspicious thunderings shook Hea-
  ven,
Proclaiming vengeance public as my wrong,
And imprecating on his prostrate slaves
Rapine, and death, and outrage. Then I
  sailed
Over the mighty fabric of the world, —
A pirate ambushed in its pathless sands,
A lynx crouched watchfully among its caves
And craggy shores; and I have wandered
  over
The expanse of these wide wildernesses
In this great ship, whose bulk is now dis-
  solved
In the light breathings of the invisible
  wind,
And which the sea has made a dustless
  ruin,
Seeking ever a mountain, through whose
  forests
I seek a man, whom I must now compel
To keep his word with me. I came ar-
  rayed
In tempest, and, although my power could
  well
Bridle the forest winds in their career,
For other causes I forbore to soothe
Their fury to Favonian gentleness;
I could and would not; (thus I wake in
  him   [*Aside.*
A love of magic art). Let not this tem-
  pest,
Nor the succeeding calm excite thy wonder;
For by my art the sun would turn as pale
As his weak sister with unwonted fear;
And in my wisdom are the orbs of Hea-
  ven
Written as in a record; I have pierced

The flaming circles of their wondrous
  spheres
And know them as thou knowest every
  corner
Of this dim spot. Let it not seem to thee
That I boast vainly; wouldst thou that I
  work
A charm over this waste and savage wood,
This Babylon of crags and aged trees,
Filling its leafy coverts with a horror
Thrilling and strange ? I am the friend-
  less guest
Of these wild oaks and pines; and as from
  thee
I have received the hospitality
Of this rude place, I offer thee the fruit
Of years of toil in recompense; whate'er
Thy wildest dream presented to thy
  thought
As object of desire, that shall be thine.

.   .   .   .

And thenceforth shall so firm an amity
'Twixt thee and me be, that neither for-
  tune,
The monstrous phantom which pursues
  success,
That careful miser, that free prodigal,
Who ever alternates with changeful hand
Evil and good, reproach and fame; nor
  Time,
That lodestar of the ages, to whose beam
The wingèd years speed o'er the intervals
Of their unequal revolutions; nor
Heaven itself, whose beautiful bright stars
Rule and adorn the world, can ever make
The least division between thee and me,
Since now I find a refuge in thy favor.

SCENE III. — *The* DEMON *tempts* JUSTINA, *who
  is a Christian.*

DEMON

Abyss of Hell ! I call on thee,
Thou wild misrule of thine own anarchy !
From thy prison-house set free
The spirits of voluptuous death
That with their mighty breath
They may destroy a world of virgin
  thoughts;
Let her chaste mind with fancies thick as
  motes
Be peopled from thy shadowy deep,
Till her guiltless fantasy
Full to overflowing be !

And with sweetest harmony,
Let birds, and flowers, and leaves, and all
 things move
  To love, only to love.
Let nothing meet her eyes
But signs of Love's soft victories;
Let nothing meet her ear
But sounds of Love's sweet sorrow,
So that from faith no succor she may bor-
  row,
But, guided by my spirit blind
And in a magic snare entwined,
 She may now seek Cyprian.
Begin, while I in silence bind
 My voice, when thy sweet song thou hast
  began.

A VOICE (*within*)

What is the glory far above
All else in human life ?

ALL

    Love ! love !

[*While these words are sung, the* DEMON *goes out
at one door, and* JUSTINA *enters at another.*]

THE FIRST VOICE

There is no form in which the fire
 Of love its traces has impressed not.
Man lives far more in love's desire
 Than by life's breath, soon possessed
  not.
If all that lives must love or die,
All shapes on earth, or sea, or sky,
With one consent to Heaven cry
⸒That the glory far above
All else in life is —

ALL

    Love ! O, love !

JUSTINA

Thou melancholy thought which art
 So flattering and so sweet, to thee
When did I give the liberty
Thus to afflict my heart ?
What is the cause of this new power
 Which doth my fevered being move,
Momently raging more and more ?
 What subtle pain is kindled now
 Which from my heart doth overflow
Into my senses ? —

ALL

    Love, O, love !

JUSTINA

'T is that enamoured nightingale
 Who gives me the reply;
He ever tells the same soft tale
 Of passion and of constancy
To his mate, who, rapt and fond,
Listening sits, a bough beyond.

Be silent, Nightingale — no more
 Make me think, in hearing thee
Thus tenderly thy love deplore,
 If a bird can feel his so,
 What a man would feel for me.
 And, voluptuous Vine, O thou
Who seekest most when least pursuing, —
 To the trunk thou interlacest
 Art the verdure which embracest,
And the weight which is its ruin, —
No more, with green embraces, Vine,
 Make me think on what thou lovest, —
For whilst thus thy boughs entwine,
 I fear lest thou shouldst teach me,
  sophist,
How arms might be entangled too.

Light-enchanted Sunflower, thou
Who gazest ever true and tender
On the sun's revolving splendor !
Follow not his faithless glance
With thy faded countenance,
Nor teach my beating heart to fear,
If leaves can mourn without a tear,
How eyes must weep ! O Nightingale,
Cease from thy enamoured tale, —
Leafy Vine, unwreathe thy bower,
Restless Sunflower, cease to move, —
Or tell me all, what poisonous power
Ye use against me —

ALL

   Love ! love ! love !

JUSTINA

It cannot be ! — Whom have I ever loved ?
Trophies of my oblivion and disdain,
Floro and Lelio did I not reject ?
And Cyprian ? —

(*She becomes troubled at the name of Cyprian.*)

    Did I not requite him
With such severity that he has fled
Where none has ever heard of him again ? —
Alas ! I now begin to fear that this
May be the occasion whence desire grows
 bold,

As if there were no danger. From the
   moment
That I pronounced to my own listening
   heart
Cyprian is absent, — oh, me miserable !
I know not what I feel !
                [*More calmly.*
            It must be pity
To think that such a man whom all the
   world
Admired should be forgot by all the world,
And I the cause.
        [*She again becomes troubled.*
       And yet if it were pity,
Floro and Lelio might have equal share,
For they are both imprisoned for my sake.
                [*Calmly.*
Alas ! what reasonings are these ? it is
Enough I pity him, and that, in vain,
Without this ceremonious subtlety.
And, woe is me ! I know not where to find
   him now,
Even should I seek him through this wide
   world.

        Enter DEMON

DEMON

Follow, and I will lead thee where he is.

JUSTINA

And who art thou who hast found entrance
   hither
Into my chamber through the doors and
   locks ?
Art thou a monstrous shadow which my
   madness
Has formed in the idle air ?

DEMON

             No. I am one
Called by the thought which tyrannizes thee
From his eternal dwelling; who this day
Is pledged to bear thee unto Cyprian.

JUSTINA

So shall thy promise fail. This agony
Of passion which afflicts my heart and soul
May sweep imagination in its storm;
The will is firm.

DEMON

          Already half is done
In the imagination of an act.
The sin incurred, the pleasure then remains;
Let not the will stop half-way on the road.

JUSTINA

I will not be discouraged, nor despair,
Although I thought it, and although 't is
   true
That thought is but a prelude to the deed.
Thought is not in my power, but action is.
I will not move my foot to follow thee.

DEMON

But a far mightier wisdom than thine own
Exerts itself within thee, with such power
Compelling thee to that which it inclines
That it shall force thy step; how wilt thou
   then
Resist, Justina ?

JUSTINA

          By my free-will.

DEMON

Must force thy will.

JUSTINA

          It is invincible;
It were not free if thou hadst power upon it.
       [*He draws, but cannot move her.*

DEMON

Come, where a pleasure waits thee.

JUSTINA

             It were bought
Too dear.

DEMON

  'T will soothe thy heart to softest peace.

JUSTINA

'T is dread captivity.

DEMON

         'T is joy, 't is glory.

JUSTINA

'T is shame, 't is torment, 't is despair.

DEMON

             But how
Canst thou defend thyself from that or me,
If my power drags thee onward ?

JUSTINA

             My defence
Consists in God.
[*He vainly endeavors to force her, and at last re-
   leases her.*

DEMON

        Woman, thou hast subdued me
Only by not owning thyself subdued.
But since thou thus findest defence in God,
I will assume a feignèd form, and thus
Make thee a victim of my baffled rage.
For I will mask a spirit in thy form
Who will betray thy name to infamy,
And doubly shall I triumph in thy loss,
First by dishonoring thee, and then by
    turning
False pleasure to true ignominy.

                        [*Exit.*

JUSTINA

                  I

Appeal to Heaven against thee; so that
    Heaven
May scatter thy delusions, and the blot
Upon my fame vanish in idle thought,
Even as flame dies in the envious air,
And as the floweret wanes at morning frost,
And thou shouldst never — But, alas ! to
    whom
Do I still speak ? — Did not a man but
    now
Stand here before me ? — No, I am alone,
And yet I saw him. Is he gone so quickly ?
Or can the heated mind engender shapes
From its own fear? Some terrible and
    strange
Peril is near. Lisander ! father ! lord !
Livia ! —

Enter LISANDER *and* LIVIA

LISANDER

Oh, my daughter ! What ?

LIVIA

                        What ?

JUSTINA

                        Saw you
A man go forth from my apartment now ?—
I scarce contain myself !

LISANDER

                  A man here !

JUSTINA

Have you not seen him ?

LIVIA

                  No, Lady.

JUSTINA

I saw him.

LISANDER

          'T is impossible; the doors
Which led to this apartment were all
    locked.

LIVIA (*aside*)

I dare say it was Moscon whom she saw,
For he was locked up in my room.

LISANDER

                        It must
Have been some image of thy fantasy.
Such melancholy as thou feedest is
Skilful in forming such in the vain air
Out of the motes and atoms of the day.

LIVIA

My master's in the right.

JUSTINA

              Oh, would it were
Delusion; but I fear some greater ill.
I feel as if out of my bleeding bosom
My heart was torn in fragments; ay,
Some mortal spell is wrought against my
    frame;
So potent was the charm that, had not God
Shielded my humble innocence from wrong,
I should have sought my sorrow and my
    shame
With willing steps. — Livia, quick, bring
    my cloak,
For I must seek refuge from these extremes
Even in the temple of the highest God
Where secretly the faithful worship.

LIVIA

                        Here.

JUSTINA (*putting on her cloak*)

In this, as in a shroud of snow, may I
Quench the consuming fire in which I burn,
Wasting away !

LISANDER

        And I will go with thee.

LIVIA

When I once see them safe out of the house
I shall breathe freely.

JUSTINA

              So do I confide
In thy just favor, Heaven !

LISANDER

                  Let us go.

JUSTINA

Thine is the cause, great God ! turn for my sake,
And for thine own, mercifully to me !

STANZAS FROM CALDERON'S CISMA DE INGLATERRA

TRANSLATED BY MEDWIN AND CORRECTED BY SHELLEY

Medwin published these stanzas, with Shelley's corrections in italics, in his *Life of Shelley*, 1847, with the following note : ' But we also read a tragedy of Calderon's which, though it cannot compete with Shakespeare's *Henry the VIII.* contains more poetry — the *Cisma d'Inglaterra*. Shelley was much struck with the characteristic Fool who plays a part in it, and deals in fables, but more so with the octave stanzas (a strange metre in a drama, to choose) spoken by Carlos, enamorado di Anna Bolena, whom he had met at Paris, during her father's embassy. So much did Shelley admire these stanzas that he copied them out into one of his letters to Mrs. Gisborne, of the two last of which I append a translation marking in italics the lines corrected by Shelley.' He had previously published these stanzas with nine others in *Sketches in Hindoostan, with Other Poems*, 1821. Forman conjectures that Shelley coöperated with Medwin in the other stanzas, where no credit has been given.

Shelley's letter to Mrs. Gisborne was of the date November 16, 1819 : ' *I have been reading Calderon without you.* I have read the *Cisma de Inglaterra*, the *Cabellos de Absalom*, and three or four others. These pieces, inferior to those we read, at least to the *Principe Constante*, in the splendor of particular passages, are perhaps superior in their satisfying completeness. . . . I transcribe you a passage from the *Cisma de Inglaterra* — spoken by " Carlos, Embaxador de Francia, enamorado de Ana Bolena." Is there anything in Petrarch finer than the second stanza ? '

I

HAST thou not seen, officious with delight,
    Move through the illumined air about the flower
The Bee, that fears to drink its purple light,
    Lest danger lurk within that Rose's bower ?
Hast thou not marked the moth's enamoured flight
    About the Taper's flame at evening hour,

Till kindle in that monumental fire
His sunflower wings their own funereal pyre ?

II

My heart, its wishes trembling to unfold,
    Thus round the Rose and Taper hovering came,
And Passion's slave, Distrust, in ashes cold,
    Smothered awhile, but could not quench the flame,
Till Love, that grows by disappointment bold,
    And Opportunity, had conquered Shame,
And like the Bee and Moth, in act to close,
I burned my wings, and settled on the Rose.'

SCENES FROM THE FAUST OF GOETHE

These scenes were translated in the spring of 1822, and published, in part, by Hunt, *The Liberal*, 1822, and entire by Mrs. Shelley, *Posthumous Poems*, 1824. The admiration of Shelley for *Faust*, and his feeling with regard to the translation, are fully shown in two letters to Mr. Gisborne, one in January, 1822 : ' We have just got the etchings of *Faust*, the painter is worthy of Goethe. The meeting of him and Margaret is wonderful. It makes all the pulses of my head beat — those of my heart have been quiet long ago. The translations, both these and in *Blackwood*, are miserable. Ask Coleridge if their stupid misintelligence of the deep wisdom and harmony of the author does not spur him to action ; ' the second, April 10, 1822 : ' I have been reading over and over again *Faust*, and always with sensations which no other composition excites. It deepens the gloom and augments the rapidity of ideas, and would therefore seem to me an unfit study for any person who is a prey to the reproaches of memory, and the delusions of an imagination not to be restrained. And yet the pleasure of sympathizing with emotions known only to few, although they derive their sole charm from despair, and the scorn of the narrow good we can attain in our present state, seems more than to ease the pain which belongs to them. . . .

' Have you read Calderon's *Magico Prodigioso ?* I find a striking similarity between *Faust* and this drama, and if I were to acknowledge Coleridge's distinction, should say Goethe was the *greatest* philosopher, and Calderon the *greatest* poet. Cyprian evidently furnished the *germ* of Faust, as Faust may furnish the germ of other poems ; although it is as different from it in structure and plan as the acorn from the oak. I have — imagine my presumption — translated several scenes from both, as the basis of a paper for our journal. I am well content with those from Calderon, which in fact gave me very little trouble ; but those from Faust — I feel how imperfect a representation, even with all the license I assume to figure to myself how Goethe would have written in English, my words convey. No one but Coleridge is capable of this work.

' We have seen here a translation of some scenes, and indeed the most remarkable ones, accompanying those astonishing etchings which have been published in England from a German master. It is not bad — and faithful enough — but how weak ! how incompetent to represent *Faust !* I have only attempted the scenes omitted in this translation, and would send you that of the *Walpurgisnacht*, if I thought Ollier would place the postage to my account. What etchings those are ! I am never satiated with looking at them ; and, I fear, it is the only sort of translation of which *Faust* is susceptible. I never perfectly understood the Hartz Mountain scene, until I saw the etching ; and then, Margaret in the summer-house with Faust ! The artist makes one envy his happiness that he can sketch such things with calmness, which I only dared look upon once, and which made my brain swim round only to touch the leaf on the opposite side of which I knew that it was figured. Whether it is that the artist has surpassed *Faust*, or that the pencil surpasses language in some subjects, I know not, or that I am more affected by a visible image, but the etching certainly excited me far more than the poem it illustrated. Do you remember the fifty-fourth letter of the first part of the *Nouvelle Héloïse ?* Goethe, in a subsequent scene, evidently had that letter in his mind, and this etching is an idealism of it. So much for the world of shadows !'

SCENE I. — PROLOGUE IN HEAVEN.

The Lord and the Host of Heaven.   Enter three Archangels.

RAPHAEL

THE sun makes music as of old
  Amid the rival spheres of Heaven,
On its predestined circle rolled
  With thunder speed: the Angels even
Draw strength from gazing on its glance,
  Though none its meaning fathom may;
The world's unwithered countenance
  Is bright as at creation's day.

GABRIEL

And swift and swift, with rapid lightness,
  The adornèd Earth spins silently,
Alternating Elysian brightness
  With deep and dreadful night; the sea
Foams in broad billows from the deep
Up to the rocks, and rocks and ocean,
Onward, with spheres which never sleep,
  Are hurried in eternal motion.

MICHAEL

And tempests in contention roar
  From land to sea, from sea to land;
And, raging, weave a chain of power,
  Which girds the earth, as with a band.
A flashing desolation there
  Flames before the thunder's way;
But thy servants, Lord, revere
  The gentle changes of thy day.

CHORUS OF THE THREE

The Angels draw strength from thy glance,
  Though no one comprehend thee may;
Thy world's unwithered countenance
  Is bright as on creation's day.

Enter MEPHISTOPHELES

MEPHISTOPHELES

As thou, O Lord, once more art kind enough
To interest thyself in our affairs,
And ask, ' How goes it with you there below ? '
And as indulgently at other times
Thou tookest not my visits in ill part,
Thou seest me here once more among thy household.
Though I should scandalize this company,
You will excuse me if I do not talk
In the high style which they think fashionable;
My pathos certainly would make you laugh too,
Had you not long since given over laughing.
Nothing know I to say of suns and worlds;
I observe only how men plague themselves.
The little god o' the world keeps the same stamp,
As wonderful as on creation's day.
A little better would he live, hadst thou
Not given him a glimpse of Heaven's light,
Which he calls reason, and employs it only

To live more beastlily than any beast.
With reverence to your Lordship be it spoken,
He's like one of those long-legged grasshoppers,
Who flits and jumps about, and sings forever
The same old song i' the grass.   There let him lie,
Burying his nose in every heap of dung.

THE LORD

Have you no more to say ?   Do you come here
Always to scold, and cavil, and complain ?
Seems nothing ever right to you on earth ?

MEPHISTOPHELES

No, Lord ! I find all there, as ever, bad at best.
Even I am sorry for man's days of sorrow;
I could myself almost give up the pleasure
Of plaguing the poor things.

THE LORD

Knowest thou Faust ?

MEPHISTOPHELES

The Doctor ?

THE LORD

Ay; my servant Faust.

MEPHISTOPHELES

In truth
He serves you in a fashion quite his own;
And the fool's meat and drink are not of earth.
His aspirations bear him on so far
That he is half aware of his own folly,
For he demands from Heaven its fairest star,
And from the earth the highest joy it bears,
Yet all things far, and all things near, are vain
To calm the deep emotions of his breast.

THE LORD

Though he now serves me in a cloud of error,
I will soon lead him forth to the clear day.
When trees look green, full well the gardener knows
That fruits and blooms will deck the coming year.

MEPHISTOPHELES

What will you bet ? — now I am sure of winning —
Only, observe you give me full permission
To lead him softly on my path.

THE LORD

As long
As he shall live upon the earth, so long
Is nothing unto thee forbidden.   Man
Must err till he has ceased to struggle.

MEPHISTOPHELES

Thanks.
And that is all I ask; for willingly
I never make acquaintance with the dead.
The full fresh cheeks of youth are food for me,
And if a corpse knocks, I am not at home.
For I am like a cat — I like to play
A little with the mouse before I eat it.

THE LORD

Well, well ! it is permitted thee.   Draw thou
His spirit from its springs; as thou find'st power,
Seize him and lead him on thy downward path;
And stand ashamed when failure teaches thee
That a good man, even in his darkest longings,
Is well aware of the right way.

MEPHISTOPHELES

Well and good.
I am not in much doubt about my bet,
And if I lose, then 't is your turn to crow;
Enjoy your triumph then with a full breast.
Ay; dust shall he devour, and that with pleasure,
Like my old paramour, the famous Snake.

THE LORD

Pray come here when it suits you; for I never
Had much dislike for people of your sort.
And, among all the Spirits who rebelled,
The knave was ever the least tedious to me.
The active spirit of man soon sleeps, and soon
He seeks unbroken quiet; therefore I
Have given him the Devil for a companion,

Who may provoke him to some sort of work,
And must create forever. — But ye, pure
Children of God, enjoy eternal beauty.
Let that which ever operates and lives
Clasp you within the limits of its love;
And seize with sweet and melancholy thoughts
The floating phantoms of its loveliness.
[*Heaven closes; the Archangels exeunt.*]

MEPHISTOPHELES

From time to time I visit the old fellow,
And I take care to keep on good terms with him.
Civil enough is this same God Almighty,
To talk so freely with the Devil himself.

SCENE II

MAY-DAY NIGHT

SCENE — *The Hartz Mountain, a desolate Country*

FAUST, MEPHISTOPHELES

MEPHISTOPHELES

Would you not like a broomstick? As for me
I wish I had a good stout ram to ride;
For we are still far from the appointed place.

FAUST

This knotted staff is help enough for me,
Whilst I feel fresh upon my legs. What good
Is there in making short a pleasant way?
To creep along the labyrinths of the vales,
And climb those rocks, where ever-babbling springs
Precipitate themselves in waterfalls,
Is the true sport that seasons such a path.
Already Spring kindles the birchen spray,
And the hoar pines already feel her breath.
Shall she not work also within our limbs?

MEPHISTOPHELES

Nothing of such an influence do I feel.
My body is all wintry, and I wish
The flowers upon our path were frost and snow.
But see how melancholy rises now,
Dimly uplifting her belated beam,

The blank unwelcome round of the red moon,
And gives so bad a light that every step
One stumbles 'gainst some crag. With your permission,
I 'll call an Ignis-fatuus to our aid.
I see one yonder burning jollily.
Halloo, my friend! may I request that you
Would favor us with your bright company?
Why should you blaze away there to no purpose?
Pray be so good as light us up this way.

IGNIS-FATUUS

With reverence be it spoken, I will try
To overcome the lightness of my nature;
Our course, you know, is generally zigzag.

MEPHISTOPHELES

Ha, ha! your worship thinks you have to deal
With men. Go straight on, in the Devil's name,
Or I shall puff your flickering life out.

IGNIS-FATUUS

        Well,
I see you are the master of the house;
I will accommodate myself to you.
Only consider that to-night this mountain
Is all enchanted, and if Jack-a-lantern
Shows you his way, though you should miss your own,
You ought not to be too exact with him.

FAUST, MEPHISTOPHELES, *and* IGNIS-FATUUS, *in alternate Chorus*

The limits of the sphere of dream,
 The bounds of true and false, are passed.
Lead us on, thou wandering Gleam,
Lead us onward, far and fast,
To the wide, the desert waste.

But see, how swift advance and shift
 Trees behind trees, row by row;
How, clift by clift, rocks bend and lift
 Their frowning foreheads as we go.
The giant-snouted crags, ho! ho!
How they snort, and how they blow!

Through the mossy sods and stones,
 Stream and streamlet hurry down —
 A rushing throng! A sound of song
Beneath the vault of Heaven is blown!

Sweet notes of love, the speaking tones
Of this bright day, sent down to say
  That Paradise on Earth is known,
Resound around, beneath, above.
All we hope and all we love
Finds a voice in this blithe strain,
  Which wakens hill and wood and rill,
    And vibrates far o'er field and vale,
    And which Echo, like the tale
Of old times, repeats again.

To-whoo! to-whoo! near, nearer now
The sound of song, the rushing throng!
Are the screech, the lapwing, and the
  jay,
All awake as if 't were day?
See, with long legs and belly wide,
  A salamander in the brake!
  Every root is like a snake!
And along the loose hillside,
With strange contortions through the
  night,
Curls, to seize or to affright;
And, animated, strong, and many,
They dart forth polypus-antennæ,
To blister with their poison spume
The wanderer. Through the dazzling
  gloom
The many-colored mice, that thread
The dewy turf beneath our tread,
In troops each other's motions cross,
Through the heath and through the moss;
And, in legions intertangled,
  The fireflies flit, and swarm, and throng,
Till all the mountain depths are spangled.

  Tell me, shall we go or stay?
Shall we onward? Come along!
Everything around is swept
  Forward, onward, far away!
Trees and masses intercept
The sight, and wisps on every side
Are puffed up and multiplied.

MEPHISTOPHELES

Now vigorously seize my skirt, and gain
This pinnacle of isolated crag.
One may observe with wonder from this
  point,
How Mammon glows among the mountains.

FAUST

                  Ay —
And strangely through the solid depth below

A melancholy light, like the red dawn,
Shoots from the lowest gorge of the abyss
Of mountains, lightning hitherward; there
  rise
Pillars of smoke, here clouds float gently by;
Here the light burns soft as the enkindled
  air,
Or the illumined dust of golden flowers;
And now it glides like tender colors spread-
  ing;
And now bursts forth in fountains from the
  earth;
And now it winds, one torrent of broad
  light,
Through the far valley, with a hundred
  veins;
And now once more within that narrow
  corner
Masses itself into intensest splendor.
And near us, see, sparks spring out of the
  ground,
Like golden sand scattered upon the dark-
  ness;
The pinnacles of that black wall of moun-
  tains
That hems us in are kindled.

MEPHISTOPHELES

                Rare, in faith!
Does not Sir Mammon gloriously illumi-
  nate
His palace for this festival — it is
A pleasure which you had not known be-
  fore.
I spy the boisterous guests already.

FAUST

                      How
The children of the wind rage in the air!
With what fierce strokes they fall upon my
  neck!

MEPHISTOPHELES

Cling tightly to the old ribs of the crag.
  Beware! for if with them thou warrest
  In their fierce flight towards the wil-
    derness,
Their breath will sweep thee into dust, and
  drag
  Thy body to a grave in the abyss.
  A cloud thickens the night.
Hark! how the tempest crashes through
  the forest!
  The owls fly out in strange affright;
The columns of the evergreen palaces

Are split and shattered;
  The roots creak, and stretch, and
    groan;
  And ruinously overthrown,
The trunks are crushed and shattered
By the fierce blast's unconquerable stress.
Over each other crack and crash they all
In terrible and intertangled fall ;
And through the ruins of the shaken moun-
    tain
  The airs hiss and howl.
It is not the voice of the fountain,
  Nor the wolf in his midnight prowl.
    Dost thou not hear ?
    Strange accents are ringing
    Aloft, afar, anear;
    The witches are singing !
The torrent of a raging wizard song
Streams the whole mountain along.

CHORUS OF WITCHES

The stubble is yellow, the corn is green,
  Now to the Brocken the witches go;
The mighty multitude here may be seen
  Gathering, wizard and witch, below.
Sir Urian is sitting aloft in the air;
  Hey over stock ! and hey over stone !
  'Twixt witches and incubi, what shall be
    done ?
Tell it who dare ! tell it who dare !

A VOICE

Upon a sow-swine, whose farrows were
    nine,
  Old Baubo rideth alone.

CHORUS

Honor her, to whom honor is due,
Old mother Baubo, honor to you !
An able sow, with old Baubo upon her,
Is worthy of glory, and worthy of honor !
The legion of witches is coming behind,
Darkening the night, and outspeeding the
    wind —

A VOICE

Which way comest thou !

A VOICE.

            Over Ilsenstein;
The owl was awake in the white moon-
    shine;
  I saw her at rest in her downy nest,
And she stared at me with her broad, bright
    eyne.

VOICES

And you may now as well take your course
    on to Hell,
Since you ride by so fast on the headlong
    blast.

A VOICE

She dropped poison upon me as I passed.
Here are the wounds —

CHORUS OF WITCHES

            Come away ! come along !
The way is wide, the way is long,
But what is that for a Bedlam throng ?
Stick with the prong, and scratch with the
    broom.
The child in the cradle lies strangled at
    home,
And the mother is clapping her hands. —

SEMICHORUS I OF WIZARDS

            We glide in
Like snails when the women are all
    away;
And from a house once given over to sin
  Woman has a thousand steps to stray.

SEMICHORUS II

A thousand steps must a woman take,
Where a man but a single spring will
    make.

VOICES ABOVE

Come with us, come with us, from Felsen-
    see.

VOICES BELOW

With what joy would we fly through the
    upper sky !
We are washed, we are 'nointed, stark
    naked are we;
  But our toil and our pain are forever in
    vain.

BOTH CHORUSES

The wind is still, the stars are fled,
The melancholy moon is dead;
The magic notes, like spark on spark,
Drizzle, whistling through the dark.
  Come away !

VOICES BELOW

            Stay, oh, stay !

VOICES ABOVE

Out of the crannies of the rocks,
Who calls ?

VOICES BELOW

　　　Oh, let me join your flocks !
I three hundred years have striven
To catch your skirt and mount to Hea-
　　ven, —
And still in vain.　Oh, might I be
With company akin to me !

BOTH CHORUSES

Some on a ram and some on a prong,
On poles and on broomsticks we flutter
　　along;
Forlorn is the wight who can rise not to-
　　night.

A HALF-WITCH BELOW

I have been tripping this many an hour:
Are the others already so far before ?
No quiet at home, and no peace abroad !
And less methinks is found by the road.

CHORUS OF WITCHES

Come onward, away ! aroint thee, aroint !
A witch to be strong must anoint —
　　anoint —
Then every trough will be boat enough;
With a rag for a sail we can sweep through
　　the sky, —
Who flies not to-night, when means he to
　　fly ?

BOTH CHORUSES

We cling to the skirt, and we strike on the
　　ground;
Witch-legions thicken around and around;
Wizard-swarms cover the heath all over.
　　　　　　　　　[*They descend.*

MEPHISTOPHELES

What thronging, dashing, raging, rustling;
What whispering, babbling, hissing, bus-
　　tling;
What glimmering, spurting, stinking, burn-
　　ing,
As Heaven and Earth were overturning.
There is a true witch element about us;
Take hold on me, or we shall be divided: —
Where are you ?

FAUST (*from a distance*)
　　　Here !

MEPHISTOPHELES
　　　　　　　What !
I must exert my authority in the house.
Place for young Voland ! pray make way,
　　good people.

Take hold on me, doctor, and with one
　　step
Let us escape from this unpleasant crowd.
They are too mad for people of my sort.
Just there shines a peculiar kind of light;
Something attracts me in those bushes.
　　Come
This way; we shall slip down there in a
　　minute.

FAUST

Spirit of Contradiction !　Well, lead on —
'T were a wise feat indeed to wander out
Into the Brocken upon May-day night,
And then to isolate one's self in scorn,
Disgusted with the humors of the time.

MEPHISTOPHELES

See yonder, round a many-colored flame
A merry club is huddled altogether:
Even with such little people as sit there
One would not be alone.

FAUST
　　　　　　Would that I were
Up yonder in the glow and whirling smoke,
Where the blind million rush impetuously
To meet the evil ones; there might I solve
Many a riddle that torments me !

MEPHISTOPHELES
　　　　　　　　　Yet
Many a riddle there is tied anew
Inextricably.　Let the great world rage !
We will stay here safe in the quiet dwell-
　　ings.
'T is an old custom.　Men have ever built
Their own small world in the great world
　　of all.
I see young witches naked there, and old
　　ones
Wisely attired with greater decency.
Be guided now by me, and you shall buy
A pound of pleasure with a dram of
　　trouble.
I hear them tune their instruments — one
　　must
Get used to this damned scraping.　Come,
　　I 'll lead you
Among them; and what there you do and
　　see,
As a fresh compact 'twixt us two shall be.
How say you now ? this space is wide
　　enough —
Look forth, you cannot see the end of it, —

An hundred bonfires burn in rows, and they
Who throng around them seem innumer-
    able:
Dancing and drinking, jabbering, making
    love,
And cooking, are at work. Now tell me,
    friend,
What is there better in the world than this ?

FAUST

In introducing us, do you assume
The character of wizard or of devil ?

MEPHISTOPHELES

In truth, I generally go about
In strict incognito; and yet one likes
To wear one's orders upon gala days.
I have no ribbon at my knee; but here
At home, the cloven foot is honorable.
See you that snail there ? — she comes
    creeping up,
And with her feeling eyes hath smelt out
    something.
I could not, if I would, mask myself here.
Come now, we 'll go about from fire to
    fire:
I 'll be the pimp, and you shall be the lover.

(*To some Old Women, who are sitting round a
heap of glimmering coals*)

Old gentlewomen, what do you do out
    here ?
You ought to be with the young rioters
Right in the thickest of the revelry —
But every one is best content at home.

GENERAL

Who dare confide in right or a just claim ?
So much as I had done for them ! and
    now —
With women and the people 't is the same,
Youth will stand foremost ever, — age
    may go
To the dark grave unhonored.

MINISTER
                Nowadays
People assert their rights; they go too
    far;
But as for me, the good old times I praise;
    Then we were all in all, 't was some-
        thing worth
    One's while to be in place and wear a
        star;
        That was indeed the golden age on
        earth.

PARVENU

We too are active, and we did and do
What we ought not, perhaps; and yet we
    now
Will seize, whilst all things are whirled
    round and round,
A spoke of Fortune's wheel, and keep our
    ground.

AUTHOR

Who now can taste a treatise of deep sense
And ponderous volume ? 't is impertinence
To write what none will read, therefore
    will I
To please the young and thoughtless people
    try.

MEPHISTOPHELES (*who at once appears to have
grown very old*)

I find the people ripe for the last day,
Since I last came up to the wizard moun-
    tain;
And as my little cask runs turbid now,
So is the world drained to the dregs.

PEDLAR-WITCH
                Look here,
Gentlemen; do not hurry on so fast
And lose the chance of a good pennyworth.
I have a pack full of the choicest wares
Of every sort, and yet in all my bundle
Is nothing like what may be found on earth;
Nothing that in a moment will make rich
Men and the world with fine malicious
    mischief.
There is no dagger drunk with blood; no
    bowl
From which consuming poison may be
    drained
By innocent and healthy lips; no jewel,
The price of an abandoned maiden's shame;
No sword which cuts the bond it cannot
    loose,
Or stabs the wearer's enemy in the back;
No —

MEPHISTOPHELES
    Gossip, you know little of these times.
What has been, has been; what is done, is
    past.
They shape themselves into the innovations
They breed, and innovation drags us with
    it.
The torrent of the crowd sweeps over us:
You think to impel, and are yourself im-
    pelled.

FAUST

Who is that yonder ?

MEPHISTOPHELES

Mark her well.   It is Lilith.

FAUST

Who ?

MEPHISTOPHELES

Lilith, the first wife of Adam.
Beware of her fair hair, for she excels
All women in the magic of her locks;
And when she winds them round a young
    man's neck,
She will not ever set him free again.

FAUST

There sit a girl and an old woman — they
Seem to be tired with pleasure and with
    play.

MEPHISTOPHELES

There is no rest to-night for any one:
When one dance ends another is begun;
Come, let us to it.   We shall have rare
    fun.

(FAUST *dances and sings with a Girl, and*
MEPHISTOPHELES *with an old Woman*)

FAUST

I had once a lovely dream
  In which I saw an apple-tree,
Where two fair apples with their gleam
  To climb and taste attracted me.

THE GIRL

She with apples you desired
  From Paradise came long ago;
With joy I feel that, if required,
  Such still within my garden grow.

· · · · · · ·

PROCTO-PHANTASMIST

What is this cursèd multitude about ?
Have we not long since proved to demon-
    stration
That ghosts move not on ordinary feet ?
But these are dancing just like men and
    women.

THE GIRL

What does he want then at our ball ?

FAUST

Oh ! he
Is far above us all in his conceit:
Whilst we enjoy, he reasons of enjoyment ;
And any step which in our dance we
    tread,
If it be left out of his reckoning,
Is not to be considered as a step.
There are few things that scandalize him
    not:
And when you whirl round in the circle
    now,
As he went round the wheel in his old
    mill,
He says that you go wrong in all respects,
Especially if you congratulate him
Upon the strength of the resemblance.

PROCTO-PHANTASMIST

Fly !
Vanish !   Unheard of impudence !   What,
    still there !
In this enlightened age, too, since you have
    been
Proved not to exist ! — But this infernal
    brood
Will hear no reason and endure no rule.
Are we so wise, and is the *pond* still
    haunted ?
How long have I been sweeping out this
    rubbish
Of superstition, and the world will not
Come clean with all my pains ! — it is a
    case
Unheard of !

THE GIRL

Then leave off teasing us so.

PROCTO-PHANTASMIST

I tell you, spirits, to your faces now,
That I should not regret this despotism
Of spirits, but that mine can wield it not.
To-night I shall make poor work of it,
Yet I will take a round with you, and
    hope
Before my last step in the living dance
To beat the poet and the devil together.

MEPHISTOPHELES

At last he will sit down in some foul pud-
    dle;
That in his way of solacing himself;
Until some leech, diverted with his gravity,
Cures him of spirits and the spirit together.

[*To* FAUST, *who has seceded from the dance.*
Why do you let that fair girl pass from
you,
Who sung so sweetly to you in the dance?

FAUST

A red mouse in the middle of her singing
Sprung from her mouth.

MEPHISTOPHELES

That was all right, my friend:
Be it enough that the mouse was not
gray.
Do not disturb your hour of happiness
With close consideration of such trifles.

FAUST

Then saw I —

MEPHISTOPHELES

What?

FAUST

Seest thou not a pale,
Fair girl, standing alone, far, far away?
She drags herself now forward with slow
steps,
And seems as if she moved with shackled
feet.
I cannot overcome the thought that she
Is like poor Margaret.

MEPHISTOPHELES

Let it be — pass on —
No good can come of it — it is not well
To meet it — it is an enchanted phantom,
A lifeless idol; with its numbing look,
It freezes up the blood of man; and they
Who meet its ghastly stare are turned to
stone,
Like those who saw Medusa.

FAUST

Oh, too true!
Her eyes are like the eyes of a fresh corpse
Which no belovèd hand has closed, alas!
That is the breast which Margaret yielded
to me —
Those are the lovely limbs which I en-
joyed!

MEPHISTOPHELES

It is all magic, poor deluded fool!
She looks to every one like his first love.

FAUST

Oh, what delight! what woe! I cannot
turn
My looks from her sweet piteous counte-
nance.
How strangely does a single blood-red line,
Not broader than the sharp edge of a
knife,
Adorn her lovely neck!

MEPHISTOPHELES

Ay, she can carry
Her head under her arm upon occasion;
Perseus has cut it off for her. These plea-
sures
End in delusion. — Gain this rising ground,
It is as airy here as in a . . .
And if I am not mightily deceived,
I see a theatre. — What may this mean?

ATTENDANT

Quite a new piece, the last of seven, for
't is
The custom now to represent that number.
'T is written by a Dilettante, and
The actors who perform are Dilettanti;
Excuse me, gentlemen; but I must vanish.
I am a Dilettante curtain-lifter.

JUVENILIA

The *Juvenilia* were published in part by
Shelley, but mainly by Medwin, Rossetti, and
Dowden. In this division all verse earlier than

Queen Mab is included, except what is placed
under DOUBTFUL, LOST, AND UNPUBLISHED
POEMS.

VERSES ON A CAT

Published by Hogg, *Life of Shelley*, 1858,
and dated, 1800. Miss Helen Shelley furnished
the verses to Mrs. Hogg, with the following
note: 'I have just found the lines which I
mentioned; a child's effusion about some cat,

which evidently *had* a story, but it must have
been before I can remember. It is in Elizabeth's handwriting, copied probably later than
the composition of the lines, though the handwriting is unformed. It seems to be a tabby
cat, for it has an indistinct brownish-gray coat
[there was a painting of a cat on the copy].

... That *last* expression is, I imagine, still classical at boys' schools, and it was a favorite one of Bysshe's, which I remember from a painful fact, that one of my sisters ventured to make use of it, and was punished in some old-fashioned way, which impressed the sentence on my memory.'

I

A CAT in distress,
Nothing more, nor less;
Good folks, I must faithfully tell ye,
As I am a sinner,
It waits for some dinner
To stuff out its own little belly.

II

You would not easily guess
All the modes of distress
Which torture the tenants of earth;
And the various evils,
Which like so many devils,
Attend the poor souls from their birth.

III

Some a living require,
And others desire
An old fellow out of the way;
And which is the best
I leave to be guessed,
For I cannot pretend to say.

IV

One wants society,
Another variety,
Others a tranquil life;
Some want food,
Others, as good,
Only want a wife.

V

But this poor little cat
Only wanted a rat,
To stuff out its own little maw;
And it were as good
Some people had such food,
To make them *hold their jaw!*

OMENS

Published by Medwin, *Shelley Papers*, 1833, and dated 1807. He gives it from memory: 'I remember well the first of his effusions, a very German-like fragment, beginning with ... I think he was then about fifteen.' In

his *Life of Shelley*, 1847, he ascribes it to Shelley's love of Chatterton: 'Chatterton was then one of his great favorites; he enjoyed very much the literary forgery and successful mystification of Horace Walpole and his contemporaries; and the Immortal Child's melancholy and early fate often suggested his own. One of his earliest effusions was a fragment beginning — it was indeed almost taken from the pseudo Rowley.'

HARK! the owlet flaps his wings
In the pathless dell beneath;
Hark! 't is the night-raven sings
Tidings of approaching death.

EPITAPHIUM

LATIN VERSION OF THE EPITAPH IN
GRAY'S ELEGY

Published by Medwin, *Life of Shelley*, 1847, and dated 1808–9, with this note: 'That he had certainly arrived at great skill in the art of versification, I think I shall be able to prove by the following specimens I kept among my treasures, which he gave me in 1808 or 9. The first is the Epitaph on Gray's *Elegy in a Country Churchyard*, probably a school task.'

I

HIC sinu fessum caput hospitali
Cespitis dormit juvenis ; nec illi
Fata ridebant, popularis ille
      Nescius auræ.

II

Musa non vultu genus arroganti
Rusticâ natum grege despicata;
Et suum tristis puerum notavit
      Sollicitudo.

III

Indoles illi bene larga; pectus
Veritas sedem sibi vindicavit;
Et pari tantis meritis beavit
      Munere cœlum.

IV

Omne quod mœstis habuit miserto
Corde largivit, lacrymam; recepit
Omne quod cœlo voluit, fidelis
      Pectus amici.

V

Longius sed tu fuge curiosus
Cæteras laudes fuge suspicari;

Cæteras culpas fuge velle tractas
Sede tremendâ.

VI

Spe tremescentes recubant in illâ
Sede virtutes pariterque culpæ,
In sui Patris gremio, tremendâ
Sede Deique.

IN HOROLOGIUM

Medwin adds, continuing the preceding note : ' The second specimen of his versification is of a totally different character, and shows a considerable precocity.'

MacCarthy, *Shelley's Early Life*, affords further light : ' Something of the precocity is explained, however, and all of the originality removed, by a reference to *The Oxford Herald* of Saturday, September 16, 1809, where the following English Epigram appears : —

ON SEEING A FRENCH WATCH ROUND THE NECK OF A BEAUTIFUL YOUNG WOMAN.

" Mark what we gain from foreign lands,
    Time cannot now be said to linger, —
Allowed to lay his two rude hands
    Where others *dare* not lay a finger."

' It is plain that Shelley's Latin lines are simply a translation of this epigram, which he most probably saw in *The Oxford Herald*, but may have read in some other paper of the time as I distinctly recollect having met with it elsewhere when making my researches among the journals of the period.'

INTER marmoreas Leonoræ pendula colles
Fortunata nimis Machina dicit horas.
Quas *manibus* premit illa duas insensa papillas
Cur mihi sit *digito* tangere, amata, nefas ?

A DIALOGUE

Published by Hogg, *Life of Shelley*, 1858, and composed 1809.

DEATH

FOR my dagger is bathed in the blood of the brave,
I come, careworn tenant of life, from the grave,
Where Innocence sleeps 'neath the peace-giving sod,
And the good cease to tremble at Tyranny's nod;

I offer a calm habitation to thee,
Say, victim of grief, wilt thou slumber with me ?
My mansion is damp, cold silence is there,
But it lulls in oblivion the fiends of despair;
Not a groan of regret, not a sigh, not a breath,
Dares dispute with grim Silence the empire of Death.
I offer a calm habitation to thee,
Say, victim of grief, wilt thou slumber with me ?

MORTAL

Mine eyelids are heavy; my soul seeks repose;
It longs in thy cells to embosom its woes;
It longs in thy cells to deposit its load,
Where no longer the scorpions of Perfidy goad,
Where the phantoms of Prejudice vanish away,
And Bigotry's bloodhounds lose scent of their prey.
Yet tell me, dark Death, when thine empire is o'er,
What awaits on Futurity's mist-covered shore ?

DEATH

Cease, cease, wayward Mortal ! I dare not unveil
The shadows that float o'er Eternity's vale;
Nought waits for the good but a spirit of Love
That will hail their blessed advent to regions above.
For Love, Mortal, gleams through the gloom of my sway,
And the shades which surround me fly fast at its ray.
Hast thou loved ? — Then depart from these regions of hate,
And in slumber with me blunt the arrows of fate.
I offer a calm habitation to thee,
Say, victim of grief, wilt thou slumber with me ?

MORTAL

Oh ! sweet is thy slumber ! oh ! sweet is the ray
Which after thy night introduces the day;

How concealed, how persuasive, self-in-
　　terest's breath,
Though it floats to mine ear from the bosom
　　of Death !
I hoped that I quite was forgotten by all,
Yet a lingering friend might be grieved at
　　my fall,
And duty forbids, though I languish to die,
When departure might heave Virtue's
　　breast with a sigh.
Oh, Death ! oh, my friend ! snatch this
　　form to thy shrine,
And I fear, dear destroyer, I shall not re-
　　pine.

TO THE MOONBEAM

Composed September 23, 1809, and published by Hogg, *Life of Shelley*, 1858. He
gives a letter from Shelley: 'There is rhap-
sody! Now, I think, after this you ought to
send me some poetry.'

I

Moonbeam, leave the shadowy vale,
　　To bathe this burning brow.
Moonbeam, why art thou so pale,
As thou walkest o'er the dewy dale,
　　Where humble wild flowers grow ?
　　　　Is it to mimic me ?
　　　　But that can never be;
　　　　For thine orb is bright,
　　　　And the clouds are light,
That at intervals shadow the star-studded
　　night.

II

Now all is deathy still on earth;
　　Nature's tired frame reposes;
And, ere the golden morning's birth
　　Its radiant hues discloses,
　　　　Flies forth its balmy breath.
　　　　But mine is the midnight of Death,
　　　　And Nature's morn
　　　　To my bosom forlorn
Brings but a gloomier night, implants a
　　deadlier thorn.

III

Wretch ! Suppress the glare of mad-
　　ness
　　Struggling in thine haggard eye,
For the keenest throb of sadness,
　　Pale Despair's most sickening sigh,

Is but to mimic me;
And this must ever be,
　　When the twilight of care,
　　And the night of despair,
Seem in my breast but joys to the pangs
　　that rankle there.

THE SOLITARY

Published by Rossetti, 1870, and dated 1810.

I

Dar'st thou amid the varied multitude
　　To live alone, an isolated thing ?
　　To see the busy beings round thee spring,
And care for none; in thy calm solitude,
A flower that scarce breathes in the desert
　　rude
　　　　To Zephyr's passing wing ?

II

Not the swart Pariah in some Indian grove,
　　Lone, lean, and hunted by his brother's
　　　　hate,
　　Hath drunk so deep the cup of bitter
　　　　fate
As that poor wretch who cannot, cannot
　　love.
He bears a load which nothing can re-
　　move,
　　　　A killing, withering weight.

III

He smiles — 't is sorrow's deadliest mock-
　　ery;
　　He speaks — the cold words flow not
　　　　from his soul;
　　He acts like others, drains the genial
　　　　bowl, —
Yet, yet he longs — although he fears — to
　　die;
He pants to reach what yet he seems to
　　fly,
　　　　Dull life's extremest goal.

TO DEATH

Composed at Oxford, 1810, and published by
Hogg, *Life of Shelley*, 1858.

　　　　Death ! where is thy victory ?
　　　　To triumph whilst I die,
　　To triumph whilst thine ebon wing
　　　　Enfolds my shuddering soul ?

O Death ! where is thy sting ?
  Not when the tides of murder roll,
When nations groan that kings may bask
    in bliss,
  Death ! canst thou boast a victory such
    as this —
  When in his hour of pomp and power
  His blow the mightiest murderer
    gave,
  Mid Nature's cries the sacrifice
  Of millions to glut the grave —
When sunk the tyrant desolation's
    slave,
Or Freedom's life-blood streamed upon
    thy shrine, —
Stern Tyrant, couldst thou boast a victory
  such as mine ?

  To know in dissolution's void
    That mortals' baubles sunk decay;
  That everything, but Love, destroyed
    Must perish with its kindred clay, —
      Perish Ambition's crown,
      Perish her sceptred sway;
From Death's pale front fades Pride's
    fastidious frown;
In Death's damp vault the lurid fires de-
    cay,
That Envy lights at heaven-born Virtue's
    beam;
      That all the cares subside,
      Which lurk beneath the tide
      Of life's unquiet stream; —
      Yes ! this is victory !
And on yon rock, whose dark form glooms
    the sky,
  To stretch these pale limbs, when the
    soul is fled;
To baffle the lean passions of their prey;
  To sleep within the palace of the dead !
Oh ! not the King, around whose dazzling
    throne
His countless courtiers mock the words
    they say,
Triumphs amid the bud of glory blown,
As I in this cold bed, and faint expiring
  groan !

Tremble, ye proud, whose grandeur mocks
    the woe
  Which props the column of unnatural
    state !
  You the plainings faint and low,
  From misery's tortured soul that flow,
    Shall usher to your fate.

Tremble, ye conquerors, at whose fell com-
    mand
The war-fiend riots o'er a peaceful land !
  You desolation's gory throng
  Shall bear from victory along
    To that mysterious strand.

.   .   .   .

LOVE'S ROSE

Sent by Shelley to Hogg, in a letter : ' I
transcribe for you a strange medley of maddened stuff, which I wrote by the midnight
moon last night. [Here follow *To a Star* and
Love's Rose.] *Ohe ! jam satis dementiæ !* I
hear you exclaim.' Composed in 1810 or 1811,
and published by Hogg, *Life of Shelley,* 1858.

I

Hopes, that swell in youthful breasts,
  Live not through the waste of time ?
Love's rose a host of thorns invests;
  Cold, ungenial is the clime,
  Where its honors blow.
Youth says, ' The purple flowers are mine,'
  Which die the while they glow.

II

Dear the boon to Fancy given,
  Retracted whilst it 's granted:
Sweet the rose which lives in heaven,
  Although on earth 't is planted,
  Where its honors blow,
While by earth's slaves the leaves are
    riven
  Which die the while they glow.

III

Age cannot Love destroy,
  But perfidy can blast the flower,
  Even when in most unwary hour
  It blooms in Fancy's bower.
Age cannot Love destroy,
But perfidy can rend the shrine
In which its vermeil splendors shine.

EYES

Published by Rossetti, 1870, and dated 1810.

  How eloquent are eyes !
Not the rapt poet's frenzied lay
When the soul's wildest feelings stray
  Can speak so well as they.
  How eloquent are eyes !

Not music's most impassioned note
On which love's warmest fervors float
   Like them bids rapture rise.

   Love, look thus again, —
That your look may light a waste of years,
Darting the beam that conquers cares
   Through the cold shower of tears.
   Love, look thus again !

POEMS FROM ST. IRVYNE, OR THE ROSICRUCIAN

Shelley's romance, *St. Irvyne, or the Rosicrucian*, was in MS. by April 1, 1810, and published about December 18, of that year. Medwin writes : ' This work contains several poems, some of which were written a year or two before the date of the Romance. . . . Three of them are in the metre of Walter Scott's *Helvellyn*, a poem he greatly admired.' Rossetti ascribes I, III, V, and VI to the year 1808, and II and IV to 1809.

I

VICTORIA

I

'T WAS dead of the night, when I sat in my
   dwelling;
  One glimmering lamp was expiring and
   low;
Around, the dark tide of the tempest was
   swelling,
Along the wild mountains night-ravens
   were yelling, —
  They bodingly presaged destruction and
   woe.

II

'T was then that I started ! — the wild
   storm was howling,
  Nought was seen save the lightning
   which danced in the sky;
Above me the crash of the thunder was
   rolling,
  And low, chilling murmurs the blast
   wafted by.

III

My heart sank within me — unheeded the
   war
  Of the battling clouds on the mountain-
   tops broke;

Unheeded the thunder-peal crashed in mine
   ear —
This heart, hard as iron, is stranger to
   fear;
  But conscience in low, noiseless whispering spoke.

IV

'T was then that, her form on the whirlwind
   upholding,
  The ghost of the murdered Victoria
   strode;
In her right hand a shadowy shroud she
   was holding;
  She swiftly advanced to my lonesome
   abode.

V

I wildly then called on the tempest to bear
   me —

. . . .

II

'ON THE DARK HEIGHT OF JURA'

I

GHOSTS of the dead ! have I not heard
   your yelling
  Rise on the night-rolling breath of the
   blast,
When o'er the dark ether the tempest is
   swelling,
  And on eddying whirlwind the thunder-
   peal passed ?

II

For oft have I stood on the dark height of
   Jura,
  Which frowns on the valley that opens
   beneath;
Oft have I braved the chill night-tempest's
   fury,
  Whilst around me, I thought, echoed
   murmurs of death.

III

And now, whilst the winds of the mountain
   are howling,
  O father ! thy voice seems to strike on
   mine ear;
In air whilst the tide of the night-storm is
   rolling,
  It breaks on the pause of the elements'
   jar.

IV

On the wing of the whirlwind which roars
    o'er the mountain
  Perhaps rides the ghost of my sire who
    is dead, —
On the mist of the tempest which hangs
    o'er the fountain,
  Whilst a wreath of dark vapor encircles
    his head.

III

SISTER ROSA: A BALLAD

I

The death-bell beats ! —
The mountain repeats
The echoing sound of the knell;
  And the dark monk now
  Wraps the cowl round his brow,
As he sits in his lonely cell.

II

And the cold hand of death
Chills his shuddering breath,
As he lists to the fearful lay,
  Which the ghosts of the sky,
  As they sweep wildly by,
Sing to departed day.
  And they sing of the hour
  When the stern fates had power
To resolve Rosa's form to its clay.

III

But that hour is past;
And that hour was the last
Of peace to the dark monk's brain;
  Bitter tears from his eyes gushed silent
    and fast;
And he strove to suppress them in vain.

IV

Then his fair cross of gold he dashed on
  the floor,
When the death-knell struck on his ear, —
  ' Delight is in store
  For her evermore;
But for me is fate, horror, and fear.'

V

Then his eyes wildly rolled,
When the death-bell tolled,
And he raged in terrific woe;

And he stamped on the ground, —
But, when ceased the sound,
Tears again began to flow.

VI

And the ice of despair
Chilled the wild throb of care,
And he sate in mute agony still;
  Till the night-stars shone through the
    cloudless air,
And the pale moonbeam slept on the hill.

VII

Then he knelt in his cell, —
And the horrors of hell
Were delights to his agonized pain;
  And he prayed to God to dissolve the
    spell,
Which else must forever remain.

VIII

And in ·fervent prayer he knelt on the
  ground,
  Till the abbey bell struck one;
His feverish blood ran chill at the sound;
A voice hollow and horrible murmured
  around, —
  ' The term of thy penance is done !'

IX

Grew dark the night;
The moonbeam bright
Waxed faint on the mountain high;
  And from the black hill
  Went a voice cold and still, —
' Monk ! thou art free to die.'

X

Then he rose on his feet,
And his heart loud did beat,
And his limbs they were palsied with
  dread;
  Whilst the grave's clammy dew
  O'er his pale forehead grew;
And he shuddered to sleep with the
  dead.

XI

And the wild midnight storm
Raved around his tall form,
As he sought the chapel's gloom:
  And the sunk grass did sigh
  To the wind, bleak and high,
As he searched for the new-made tomb.

XII

And forms, dark and high,
Seemed around him to fly,
And mingle their yells with the blast, —
And on the dark wall
Half-seen shadows did fall,
As, enhorrored, he onward passed.

XIII

And the storm-fiends wild rave
O'er the new-made grave,
And dread shadows linger around; —
The Monk called on God his soul to save,
And, in horror, sank on the ground.

XIV

Then despair nerved his arm
To dispel the charm,
And he burst Rosa's coffin asunder;
And the fierce storm did swell
More terrific and fell
And louder pealed the thunder.

XV

And laughed in joy the fiendish throng,
Mixed with ghosts of the mouldering
dead;
And their grisly wings, as they floated
along,
Whistled in murmurs dread.

XVI

And her skeleton form the dead Nun reared,
Which dripped with the chill dew of hell;
In her half-eaten eyeballs two pale flames
appeared,
And triumphant their gleam on the dark
monk glared,
As he stood within the cell.

XVII

And her lank hand lay on his shuddering
brain,
But each power was nerved by fear, —
'I never, henceforth, may breathe again;
Death now ends mine anguished pain.
The grave yawns, — we meet there.'

XVIII

And her skeleton lungs did utter the sound,
So deadly, so lone and so fell
That in long vibrations shuddered the
ground;
And, as the stern notes floated around,
A deep groan was answered from hell.

IV

ST. IRVYNE'S TOWER

I

How swiftly through heaven's wide ex-
panse
Bright day's resplendent colors fade !
How sweetly does the moonbeam's glance
With silver tint St. Irvyne's glade !

II

No cloud along the spangled air,
Is borne upon the evening breeze;
How solemn is the scene ! how fair
The moonbeams rest upon the trees !

III

Yon dark gray turret glimmers white,
Upon it sits the mournful owl;
Along the stillness of the night
Her melancholy shriekings roll.

IV

But not alone on Irvyne's tower
The silver moonbeam pours her rays;
It gleams upon the ivied bower,
It dances in the cascade's spray.

V

' Ah ! why do darkening shades conceal
The hour when man must cease to be ?
Why may not human minds unveil
The dim mists of futurity ?

VI

' The keenness of the world hath torn
The heart which opens to its blast;
Despised, neglected, and forlorn,
Sinks the wretch in death at last.'

V

BEREAVEMENT

I

How stern are the woes of the desolate
mourner,
As he bends in still grief o'er the hal-
lowed bier,
As enanguished he turns from the laugh of
the scorner,
And drops to perfection's remembrance a
tear;

When floods of despair down his pale cheek
   are streaming,
When no blissful hope on his bosom is
   beaming,
Or, if lulled for a while, soon he starts
   from his dreaming,
And finds torn the soft ties to affection
   so dear.

II

Ah! when shall day dawn on the night of
   the grave,
   Or summer succeed to the winter of
   death?
Rest awhile, hapless victim, and Heaven
   will save
   The spirit that faded away with the
   breath.
Eternity points in its amaranth bower,
Where no clouds of fate o'er the sweet prospect lower,
Unspeakable pleasure, of goodness the
   dower,
   When woe fades away like the mist of
   the heath.

VI

THE DROWNED LOVER

Ah! faint are her limbs, and her footstep
   is weary,
   Yet far must the desolate wanderer
   roam;
Though the tempest is stern, and the moun-
   tain is dreary,
   She must quit at deep midnight her
   pitiless home.
I see her swift foot dash the dew from the
   whortle,
As she rapidly hastes to the green grove of
   myrtle;
And I hear, as she wraps round her figure
   the kirtle,
   'Stay thy boat on the lake, — dearest
   Henry, I come.'

II

High swelled in her bosom the throb of
   affection,
   As lightly her form bounded over the
   lea,

And arose in her mind every dear recollection;
   'I come, dearest Henry, and wait but for
   thee.'
How sad, when dear hope every sorrow is
   soothing,
When sympathy's swell the soft bosom is
   moving,
And the mind the mild joys of affection is
   proving,
   Is the stern voice of fate that bids happiness flee!

III

Oh! dark lowered the clouds on that horrible eve,
   And the moon dimly gleamed through
   the tempested air;
Oh! how could fond visions such softness
   deceive?
   Oh! how could false hope rend a bosom
   so fair?
Thy love's pallid corse the wild surges are
   laving,
O'er his form the fierce swell of the tempest is raving;
But fear not, parting spirit; thy goodness
   is saving,
   In eternity's bowers, a seat for thee there.

POSTHUMOUS FRAGMENTS

OF

MARGARET NICHOLSON;

BEING POEMS FOUND AMONGST THE PAPERS
OF THAT NOTED FEMALE WHO ATTEMPTED
THE LIFE OF THE KING IN 1786.

EDITED BY JOHN FITZVICTOR

The *Posthumous Fragments of Margaret
Nicholson* was published in November, 1810,
at Oxford, probably as a pamphlet. Hogg
narrates the origin and history of this volume
at length. The material points of his account
are that he found Shelley reading the proofs
of some poems which were meant to be published, and advised him to burlesque them and
issue them as a joke; that this plan was
adopted, and the poems, revised by the two
friends and ascribed on·Hogg's suggestion to
Peg Nicholson, a mad woman, then still living,
who had attempted the life of George III.,
were printed at the publishers' expense and
eagerly taken up by the Oxford collegians. He

adds that the first poem was not Shelley's, but was the production of a 'rhymester of the day' and had been confided to him. This account is discredited by Dowden and others; the intentionally burlesque portion is thought to be confined to the *Epithalamium* in the lines referred to by Shelley below; 'the rhymester' is presumed to be Hogg, and his work not the first poem, but the aforesaid passage of the *Epithalamium*.

Shelley throws a dubious light on the matter in a letter to Graham, November 30, 1810: 'The part of the *Epithalamium* which you mention (*i. e.* from the end of Satan's triumph) is the production of a friend's *mistress;* it had been concluded there, but she thought it abrupt and added this; it is omitted in numbers of the copies — that which I sent to my Mother of course did not contain it. I shall possibly send you the abuse to-day, but I am afraid that they will not insert it. But you mistake; the *Epithalamium* will make it sell like wildfire, and as the *Nephew* is kept a profound secret, there can arise no danger from the indelicacy of the Aunt. It sells wonderfully here, and is become the fashionable subject of discussion. . . . Of course to my Father Peg is a profound secret.'

The composition of the verses is described by an eye-witness, whose account is given in Montgomery's *Oxford*, quoted by Dowden: 'The ease with which Shelley composed many of the stanzas therein contained is truly astonishing. When surprised with a proof from the printers on the morning he would frequently start off his sofa exclaiming that that had been his only bed; and on being informed that the men were waiting for more copy, he would sit down and write off a few stanzas, and send them to the press without even revising or reading them.'

ADVERTISEMENT

The energy and native genius of these Fragments must be the only apology which the Editor can make for thus intruding them on the Public Notice. The first I found with no title, and have left it so. It is intimately connected with the dearest interests of universal happiness; and much as we may deplore the fatal and enthusiastic tendency which the ideas of this poor female had acquired, we cannot fail to pay the tribute of unequivocal regret to the departed memory of genius, which, had it been rightly organized, would have made that intellect, which has since become the victim of frenzy and despair, a most brilliant ornament to society.

In case the sale of these Fragments evinces that the Public have any curiosity to be presented with a more copious collection of my unfortunate Aunt's Poems, I have other papers in my possession, which shall, in that case, be subjected to their notice. It may be supposed they require much arrangement; but I send the following to the press in the same state in which they came into my possession.

J. F.

WAR

AMBITION, power, and avarice, now have hurled
Death, fate, and ruin, on a bleeding world.
See! on yon heath what countless victims lie!
Hark! what loud shrieks ascend through yonder sky!
Tell then the cause, 't is sure the avenger's rage
Has swept these myriads from life's crowded stage.
Hark to that groan — an anguished hero dies,
He shudders in death's latest agonies;
Yet does a fleeting hectic flush his cheek,
Yet does his parting breath essay to speak: —

'O God! my wife, my children! Monarch, thou
For whose support this fainting frame lies low,
For whose support in distant lands I bleed,
Let his friends' welfare be the warrior's meed.
He hears me not — ah! no — kings cannot hear,
For passion's voice has dulled their listless ear.
To thee, then, mighty God, I lift my moan;
Thou wilt not scorn a suppliant's anguished groan.
Oh! now I die — but still is death's fierce pain —
God hears my prayer — we meet, we meet again.'
He spake, reclined him on death's bloody bed,
And with a parting groan his spirit fled.

Oppressors of mankind, to *you* we owe
The baleful streams from whence these miseries flow;

For you how many a mother weeps her
son,
Snatched from life's course ere half his
race was run !
For you how many a widow drops a tear,
In silent anguish, on her husband's bier !

   ' Is it then thine, Almighty Power,' she
cries,
' Whence tears of endless sorrow dim these
eyes ?
Is this the system which thy powerful sway,
Which else in shapeless chaos sleeping lay,
Formed and approved ? — it cannot be —
but oh !
Forgive me Heaven, my brain is warped by
woe.'

'T is not — he never bade the war-note
swell,
He never triumphed in the work of hell.
Monarchs of earth ! thine is the baleful
deed,
Thine are the crimes for which thy subjects
bleed.
Ah ! when will come the sacred fated time,
When man unsullied by his leaders' crime,
Despising wealth, ambition, pomp, and
pride,
Will stretch him fearless by his foemen's
side ?
Ah ! when will come the time, when o'er
the plain
No more shall death and desolation reign ?
When will the sun smile on the bloodless
field,
And the stern warrior's arm the sickle
wield ?
Not whilst some King, in cold ambition's
dreams,
Plans for the field of death his plodding
schemes;
Not whilst for private pique the public fall,
And one frail mortal's mandate governs
all, —
Swelled with command and mad with diz-
zying sway;
Who sees unmoved his myriads fade away,
Careless who lives or dies — so that he
gains
Some trivial point for which he took the
pains.
What then are Kings ? — I see the trem-
bling crowd,
I hear their fulsome clamors echoed loud;

Their stern oppressor pleased appears
awhile,
But April's sunshine is a Monarch's smile.
Kings are but dust — the last eventful
day
Will level all and make them lose their
sway;
Will dash the sceptre from the Monarch's
hand,
And from the warrior's grasp wrest the
ensanguined brand.

   O Peace, soft Peace, art thou forever
gone ?
Is thy fair form indeed forever flown ?
And love and concord hast thou swept
away,
As if incongruous with thy parted sway ?
Alas I fear thou hast, for none appear.
Now o'er the palsied earth stalks giant
Fear,
With War and Woe and Terror in his
train;
List'ning he pauses on the embattled plain,
Then, speeding swiftly o'er the ensanguined
heath,
Has left the frightful work to hell and
death.
See ! gory Ruin yokes his blood-stained
car;
He scents the battle's carnage from afar;
Hell and destruction mark his mad ca-
reer;
He tracks the rapid step of hurrying Fear;
Whilst ruined towns and smoking cities
tell,
That thy work, Monarch, is the work of
hell.
' It is thy work !' I hear a voice repeat,
' Shakes the broad basis of thy blood-
stained seat;
And at the orphan's sigh, the widow's
moan,
Totters the fabric of thy guilt-stained
throne —
It is thy work, O Monarch.' Now the
sound
Fainter and fainter yet is borne around;
Yet to enthusiast ears the murmurs tell
That heaven, indignant at the work of
hell,
Will soon the cause, the hated cause re-
move,
Which tears from earth peace, innocence
and love.

FRAGMENT

SUPPOSED TO BE AN EPITHALAMIUM OF
FRANCIS RAVAILLAC AND CHARLOTTE
CORDAY

'T is midnight now — athwart the murky
    air
Dank lurid meteors shoot a livid gleam;
From the dark storm-clouds flashes a fear-
    ful glare,
    It shows the bending oak, the roaring
      stream.
I pondered on the woes of lost mankind,
    I pondered on the ceaseless rage of
      kings;
My rapt soul dwelt upon the ties that bind
    The mazy volume of commingling things,
When fell and wild misrule to man stern
    sorrow brings.

I heard a yell — it was not the knell,
    When the blasts on the wild lake sleep,
That floats on the pause of the summer
    gale's swell
    O'er the breast of the waveless deep.

I thought it had been death's accents cold
    That bade me recline on the shore;
I laid mine hot head on the surge-beaten
    mould,
    And thought to breathe no more.

    But a heavenly sleep
    That did suddenly steep
      In balm my bosom's pain,
    Pervaded my soul,
    And free from control
      Did mine intellect range again.

Methought enthroned upon a silvery cloud,
    Which floated mid a strange and bril-
      liant light,
My form upborne by viewless ether rode,
    And spurned the lessening realms of
      earthly night.
What heavenly notes burst on my ravished
    ears,
    What beauteous spirits met my dazzled
      eye!
Hark! louder swells the music of the
    spheres,
    More clear the forms of speechless bliss
      float by,
And heavenly gestures suit ethereal melody.

But fairer than the spirits of the air,
    More graceful than the Sylph of symme-
      try,
Than the enthusiast's fancied love more
    fair,
    Were the bright forms that swept the
      azure sky.
Enthroned in roseate light, a heavenly
    band
    Strewed flowers of bliss that never fade
      away;
They welcome virtue to its native land,
    And songs of triumph greet the joyous
      day
When endless bliss the woes of fleeting life
    repay.

Congenial minds will seek their kindred
    soul,
    E'en though the tide of time has rolled
      between;
They mock weak matter's impotent control,
    And seek of endless life the eternal
      scene.
At death's vain summons *this* will never
    die,
    In Nature's chaos *this* will not decay.
These are the bands which closely, warmly,
    tie
    Thy soul, O Charlotte, 'yond this chain
      of clay,
To him who thine must be till time shall
    fade away.

Yes, Francis! thine was the dear knife
    that tore
    A tyrant's heartstrings from his guilty
      breast;
Thine was the daring at a tyrant's gore
    To smile in triumph, to contemn the
      rest;
And thine, loved glory of thy sex! to
    tear
    From its base shrine a despot's haughty
      soul,
To laugh at sorrow in secure despair,
    To mock, with smiles, life's lingering
      control,
And triumph mid the griefs that round thy
    fate did roll.

Yes! the fierce spirits of the avenging
    deep
    With endless tortures goad their guilty
      shades.

I see the lank and ghastly spectres sweep
  Along the burning length of yon arcades;
And I see Satan stalk athwart the plain —
  He hastes along the burning soil of hell;
' Welcome, thou despots, to my dark do-
    main !
With maddening joy mine anguished senses
    swell
To welcome to their home the friends I
    love so well.'

. . . .

Hark ! to those notes, how sweet, how thrill-
    ing sweet
They echo to the sound of angels' feet.

. . . .

Oh, haste to the bower where roses are
    spread,
For there is prepared thy nuptial bed.
Oh, haste — hark ! hark ! — they 're gone.

. . . .

CHORUS OF SPIRITS

Stay, ye days of contentment and joy,
  Whilst love every care is erasing;
Stay, ye pleasures that never can cloy,
  And ye spirits that can never cease
    pleasing !

And if any soft passion be near,
  Which mortals, frail mortals, can
    know,
Let love shed on the bosom a tear,
  And dissolve the chill ice-drop of woe.

SYMPHONY

FRANCIS

Soft, my dearest angel stay,
Oh ! you suck my soul away;
Suck on, suck on, I glow, I glow !
Tides of maddening passion roll,
And streams of rapture drown my
    soul.
Now give me one more billing kiss,
Let your lips now repeat the bliss,
Endless kisses steal my breath,
No life can equal such a death.

CHARLOTTE

Oh ! yes, I will kiss thine eyes so fair,
  And I will clasp thy form;
Serene is the breath of the balmy air,
  But I think, love, thou feelest me
    warm.

And I will recline on thy marble neck
  Till I mingle into thee;
And I will kiss the rose on thy cheek,
  And thou shalt give kisses to me;
For here is no morn to flout our delight,
  Oh ! dost thou not joy at this ?
And here we may lie an endless night,
  A long, long night of bliss.

Spirits ! when raptures move,
Say what it is to love,
When passion's tear stands on the cheek,
  When bursts the unconscious sigh;
And the tremulous lips dare not speak
  What is told by the soul-felt eye.
But what is sweeter to revenge's ear
  Than the fell tyrant's last expiring yell ?
Yes ! than love's sweetest blisses 't is more
    dear
  To drink the floatings of a despot's
    knell.
I wake — 't is done — 't is o'er.

DESPAIR

AND canst thou mock mine agony, thus
    calm
  In cloudless radiance, Queen of silver
    night ?
Can you, ye flowerets, spread your perfumed
    balm
  Mid pearly gems of dew that shine so
    bright ?
And you wild winds, thus can you sleep so
    still
  Whilst throbs the tempest of my breast
    so high ?
Can the fierce night-fiends rest on yonder
    hill,
  And, in the eternal mansions of the sky,
Can the directors of the storm in powerless
    silence lie ?

Hark ! I hear music on the zephyr's
    wing —
  Louder it floats along the unruffled sky;
Some fairy sure has touched the viewless
    string —
  Now faint in distant air the murmurs
    die.
Awhile it stills the tide of agony;
  Now — now it loftier swells — again
    stern woe

Arises with the awakening melody;
  Again fierce torments, such as demons
    know,
In bitterer, feller tide, on this torn bosom
  flow.

Arise, ye sightless spirits of the storm,
  Ye unseen minstrels of the aërial song,
Pour the fierce tide around this lonely
    form,
  And roll the tempest's wildest swell
    along.
Dart the red lightning, wing the forkèd
    flash,
  Pour from thy cloud-formed hills the
    thunder's roar;
Arouse the whirlwind — and let ocean dash
  In fiercest tumult on the rocking
    shore, —
Destroy this life or let earth's fabric be no
  more !

Yes ! every tie that links me here is dead;
  Mysterious fate, thy mandate I obey !
Since hope and peace, and joy, for aye are
    fled,
  I come, terrific power, I come away.
Then o'er this ruined soul let spirits of hell,
  In triumph, laughing wildly, mock its
    pain;
And, though with direst pangs mine heart-
    strings swell,
  I 'll echo back their deadly yells again,
Cursing the power that ne'er made aught
  in vain.

FRAGMENT

Yes ! all is past — swift time has fled
    away,
  Yet its swell pauses on my sickening
    mind.
How long will horror nerve this frame of
    clay ?
  I 'm dead, and lingers yet my soul be-
    hind.
Oh ! powerful fate, revoke thy deadly
    spell,
  And yet that may not ever, ever be,
Heaven will not smile upon the work of
    hell;
  Ah ! no, for heaven cannot smile on me;
Fate, envious fate, has sealed my wayward
  destiny.

I sought the cold brink of the midnight
    surge;
  I sighed beneath its wave to hide my
    woes;
The rising tempest sung a funeral dirge,
  And on the blast a frightful yell arose.
Wild flew the meteors o'er the maddened
    main,
  Wilder did grief athwart my bosom
    glare;
Stilled was the unearthly howling, and a
    strain
  Swelled 'mid the tumult of the battling
    air,
'T was like a spirit's song, but yet more
  soft and fair.

I met a maniac — like he was to me;
  I said — ' Poor victim, wherefore dost
    thou roam ?
And canst thou not contend with agony,
  That thus at midnight thou dost quit
    thine home ? '
' Ah, there she sleeps: cold is her bloodless
    form,
  And I will go to slumber in her grave;
And then our ghosts, whilst raves the mad-
    dened storm,
  Will sweep at midnight o'er the wildered
    wave;
Wilt thou our lowly beds with tears of pity
  lave ? '

' Ah ! no, I cannot shed the pitying tear,
  This breast is cold, this heart can feel no
    more;
But I can rest me on thy chilling bier,
  Can shriek in horror to the tempest's
    roar.'

.   .   .   .

THE SPECTRAL HORSEMAN

What was the shriek that struck fancy's
    ear
As it sate on the ruins of time that is past ?
Hark ! it floats on the fitful blast of the
    wind,
And breathes to the pale moon a funeral
    sigh.
It is the Benshie's moan on the storm,
Or a shivering fiend that, thirsting for
    sin,
Seeks murder and guilt when virtue sleeps,

Winged with the power of some ruthless
    king,
And sweeps o'er the breast of the prostrate
    plain.
It was not a fiend from the regions of hell
That poured its low moan on the stillness
    of night;
It was not a ghost of the guilty dead,
Nor a yelling vampire reeking with gore;
But aye at the close of seven years' end
That voice is mixed with the swell of the
    storm,
And aye at the close of seven years' end,
A shapeless shadow that sleeps on the hill
Awakens and floats on the mist of the
    heath.
It is not the shade of a murdered man,
Who has rushed uncalled to the throne of
    his God,
And howls in the pause of the eddying
    storm.
This voice is low, cold, hollow, and chill;
'T is not heard by the ear, but is felt in the
    soul.
'T is more frightful far than the death-
    demon's scream,
Or the laughter of fiends when they howl
    o'er the corpse
Of a man who has sold his soul to hell.
It tells the approach of a mystic form,
A white courser bears the shadowy sprite;
More thin they are than the mists of the
    mountain,
When the clear moonlight sleeps on the
    waveless lake.
More pale *his* cheek than the snows of
    Nithona
When winter rides on the northern blast,
And howls in the midst of the leafless
    wood.
Yet when the fierce swell of the tempest is
    raving,
And the whirlwinds howl in the caves of
    Inisfallen,
Still secure 'mid the wildest war of the
    sky,
The phantom courser scours the waste,
And his rider howls in the thunder's roar.
O'er him the fierce bolts of avenging
    heaven
Pause, as in fear, to strike his head,
The meteors of midnight recoil from his
    figure;
Yet the wildered peasant, that oft passes
    by,

With wonder beholds the blue flash through
    his form;
And his voice, though faint as the sighs of
    the dead,
The startled passenger shudders to hear,
More distinct than the thunder's wildest
    roar.
Then does the dragon, who, chained in the
    caverns
To eternity, curses the champion of Erin,
Moan and yell loud at the lone hour of
    midnight,
And twine his vast wreaths round the forms
    of the demons;
Then in agony roll his death-swimming
    eyeballs,
Though wildered by death, yet never to
    die !
Then he shakes from his skeleton folds the
    nightmares,
Who, shrieking in agony, seek the couch
Of some fevered wretch who courts sleep
    in vain;
Then the tombless ghosts of the guilty
    dead
In horror pause on the fitful gale.
They float on the swell of the eddying
    tempest,
And scared seek the caves of gigantic . . .
Where their thin forms pour unearthly
    sounds
On the blast that sweeps the breast of the
    lake,
And mingles its swell with the moonlight
    air.

MELODY TO A SCENE OF
FORMER TIMES

ART thou indeed forever gone,
    Forever, ever, lost to me ?
Must this poor bosom beat alone,
    Or beat at all, if not for thee ?
Ah, why was love to mortals given,
To lift them to the height of heaven,
Or dash them to the depths of hell ?
    Yet I do not reproach thee, dear !
Ah ! no, the agonies that swell
    This panting breast, this frenzied brain,
    Might wake my ——'s slumbering tear.
Oh ! heaven is witness I did love,
And heaven does know I love thee still, —
Does know the fruitless sickening thrill,
    When reason's judgment vainly strove

To blot thee from my memory;
But which might never, never be.
Oh! I appeal to that blest day
When passion's wildest ecstasy
Was coldness to the joys I knew,
When every sorrow sunk away.
Oh! I had never lived before,
But now those blisses are no more.
  And now I cease to live again,
I do not blame thee, love; ah no!
The breast that feels this anguished woe
Throbs for thy happiness alone.
Two years of speechless bliss are gone, —
I thank thee, dearest, for the dream.
'T is night — what faint and distant scream
Comes on the wild and fitful blast?·
It moans for pleasures that are past,
It moans for days that are gone by,
Oh! lagging hours, how slow you fly!
  I see a dark and lengthened vale,
The black view closes with the tomb;
But darker is the lowering gloom
  That shades the intervening dale.
In visioned slumber for awhile
I seem again to share thy smile,
I seem to hang upon thy tone.
  Again you say, 'confide in me,
For I am thine, and thine alone.
  And thine must ever, ever be.'
But oh! awakening still anew,
Athwart my enanguished senses flew
  A fiercer, deadlier agony!

STANZA

FROM A TRANSLATION OF THE MAR-
SEILLAISE HYMN

Sent by Shelley in a letter to Graham.
Published by Forman, 1876, and dated 1810.

TREMBLE Kings despised of man!
Ye traitors to your Country
Tremble! Your parricidal plan
  At length shall meet its destiny . . .
We all are soldiers fit to fight
But if we sink in glory's night
Our mother Earth will give ye new
The brilliant pathway to pursue
  Which leads to Death or Victory . . .

BIGOTRY'S VICTIM

Published by Hogg, *Life of Shelley*, 1858.
Dated in the Esdaile MS. 1809.

I

DARES the lama, most fleet of the sons of
  the wind,
  The lion to rouse from his skull-covered
    lair?
When the tiger approaches can the fast-
  fleeting hind
  Repose trust in his footsteps of air?
No! Abandoned he sinks in a trance of
  despair,
  The monster transfixes his prey,
  On the sand flows his life-blood away;
Whilst India's rocks to his death-yells reply,
Protracting the horrible harmony.

II

Yet the fowl of the desert, when danger
  encroaches,
  Dares fearless to perish defending her
    brood,
Though the fiercest of cloud-piercing ty-
  rants approaches,
  Thirsting — ay, thirsting for blood;
And demands, like mankind, his brother
  for food;
  Yet more lenient, more gentle than
    they;
  For hunger, not glory, the prey
Must perish. Revenge does not howl in
  the dead,
Nor ambition with fame crown the mur-
  derer's head.

III

Though weak as the lama that bounds on
  the mountains,
  And endued not with fast-fleeting foot-
    steps of air,
Yet, yet will I draw from the purest of
  fountains,
  Though a fiercer than tiger is there.
Though more dreadful than death, it scat-
  ters despair,
  Though its shadow eclipses the day,
  And the darkness of deepest dismay
Spreads the influence of soul-chilling terror
  around,
And lowers on the corpses, that rot on the
  ground.

IV

They came to the fountain to draw from
  its stream,
  Waves too pure, too celestial, for mortals
    to see;

They bathed for a while in its silvery beam,
  Then perished, and perished like me.
For in vain from the grasp of the Bigot I
    flee;
  The most tenderly loved of my soul
  Are slaves to his hated control.
He pursues me, he blasts me! 'T is in
    vain that I fly; —
What remains, but to curse him, — to curse
    him and die ?

ON AN ICICLE THAT CLUNG TO THE GRASS OF A GRAVE

Sent in a letter to Hogg, January 6, 1811,
and published by him, *Life of Shelley*, 1858.
Dated in the Esdaile MS. 1809.

I

Oh ! take the pure gem to where southerly
    breezes
  Waft repose to some bosom as faithful
    as fair,
In which the warm current of love never
    freezes,
  As it rises unmingled with selfishness
    there,
  Which, untainted with pride, unpolluted
    by care,
Might dissolve the dim ice-drop, might bid
    it arise,
Too pure for these regions, to gleam in the
    skies.

II

Or where the stern warrior, his country
    defending,
  Dares fearless the dark-rolling battle to
    pour,
Or o'er the fell corpse of a dread tyrant
    bending,
  Where patriotism red with his guilt-
    reeking gore
  Plants liberty's flag on the slave-peopled
    shore,
With victory's cry, with the shout of the
    free,
Let it fly, taintless spirit, to mingle with
    thee.

III

For I found the pure gem, when the day-
    beam returning
  Ineffectual gleams on the snow-covered
    plain,

When to others the wished-for arrival of
    morning
  Brings relief to long visions of soul-
    racking pain;
  But regret is an insult — to grieve is in
    vain:
And why should we grieve that a spirit so
    fair
Seeks Heaven to mix with its own kindred
    there ?

IV

But still 't was some spirit of kindness
    descending
  To share in the load of mortality's woe,
Who over thy lowly-built sepulchre bending
  Bade sympathy's tenderest tear-drop to
    flow.
  Not for *thee* soft compassion celestials
    did know,
But if *angels* can weep, sure *man* may re-
    pine,
May weep in mute grief o'er thy low-laid
    shrine.

V

And did I then say, for the altar of glory,
  That the earliest, the loveliest of flowers
    I 'd entwine,
Though with millions of blood-reeking
    victims 't was gory,
  Though the tears of the widow polluted
    its shrine,
  Though around it the orphans, the father-
    less pine ?
O Fame, all thy glories I 'd yield for a tear
To shed on the grave of a heart so sincere.

LOVE

Sent by Shelley to Hogg in a letter, May 2,
1811, and published by him, *Life of Shelley*,
1858.

Why is it said thou canst not live
  In a youthful breast and fair,
Since thou eternal life canst give,
  Canst bloom forever there ?
Since withering pain no power possessed,
  Nor age, to blanch thy vermeil hue,
Nor time's dread victor, death, confessed,
  Though bathèd with his poison dew ?
Still thou retainest unchanging bloom,
Fixed, tranquil, even in the tomb.

And oh! when on the blest, reviving,
  The day-star dawns of love,
Each energy of soul surviving
  More vivid soars above,
Hast thou ne'er felt a rapturous thrill,
  Like June's warm breath, athwart thee
    fly,
O'er each idea then to steal,
  When other passions die?
Felt it in some wild noonday dream,
When sitting by the lonely stream,
Where Silence says, Mine is the dell;
  And not a murmur from the plain,
And not an echo from the fell,
  Disputes her silent reign.

ON A FÊTE AT CARLTON HOUSE

FRAGMENT

Repeated from memory by Rev. Mr. Grove
to Garnett. Published by Rossetti, 1870, and
dated 1811.

  . . . By the mossy brink,
With me the Prince shall sit and think;
Shall muse in visioned Regency,
Rapt in bright dreams of dawning Royalty.
. . . .

TO A STAR

Sent by Shelley to Hogg in a letter, and
published by him, *Life of Shelley*, 1858, and
dated 1811.

SWEET star, which gleaming o'er the dark-
    some scene
Through fleecy clouds of silvery radiance
    flyest,
Spanglet of light on evening's shadowy
    veil,
Which shrouds the day-beam from the
    waveless lake,
Lighting the hour of sacred love; more
    sweet
Than the expiring morn-star's paly fires.
Sweet star! When wearied Nature sinks
    to sleep,
And all is hushed, — all, save the voice of
    Love,
Whose broken murmurings swell the balmy
    blast
Of soft Favonius, which at intervals
Sighs in the ear of stillness, art thou aught
    but

Lulling the slaves of interest to repose
With that mild, pitying gaze! Oh, I
    would look
In thy dear beam till every bond of sense
Became enamoured —

TO MARY, WHO DIED IN THIS OPINION

One of several poems suggested by a story
told Shelley by Hogg. Shelley sent it to Miss
Hitchener, in a letter, November 23, 1811: 'I
transcribe a little poem I found this morning.
It was written some time ago; but, as it appears to show what I then thought of eternal
life, I send it.' Published by Rossetti, 1870.

I

MAIDEN, quench the glare of sorrow
  Struggling in thine haggard eye;
    Firmness dare to borrow
From the wreck of destiny;
For the ray morn's bloom revealing
Can never boast so bright an hue
    As that which mocks concealing,
And sheds its loveliest light on you.

II

  Yet is the tie departed
Which bound thy lovely soul to bliss?
  Has it left thee broken-hearted
In a world so cold as this!
    Yet, though, fainting fair one,
Sorrow's self thy cup has given,
    Dream thou 'lt meet thy dear one,
Never more to part, in heaven.

III

  Existence would I barter
For a dream so dear as thine,
  And smile to die a martyr
On affection's bloodless shrine.
  Nor would I change for pleasure
That withered hand and ashy cheek,
  If my heart enshrined a treasure
Such as forces thine to break.

A TALE OF SOCIETY AS IT IS

FROM FACTS, 1811

Sent by Shelley (from Keswick) to Miss
Hitchener, in a letter, January 7, 1812: 'I
now send you some poetry; the subject is not

fictitious. It is the overflowings of the mind this morning. . . . The facts are real; that recorded in the last fragment of a stanza is literally true. The poor man said: "None of my family ever came *to parish*, and I would starve first. I am a poor man; but I could never hold my head up after that." ' Published by Rossetti, 1870.

I

SHE was an agèd woman; and the years
　　Which she had numbered on her toil-
　　　some way
　　Had bowed her natural powers to de-
　　　cay.
She was an agèd woman; yet the ray
Which faintly glimmered through her
　　starting tears,
Pressed into light by silent misery,
Hath soul's imperishable energy.
She was a cripple, and incapable
To add one mite to gold-fed luxury;
　　And therefore did her spirit dimly feel
That poverty, the crime of tainting stain,
Would merge her in its depths, never to
　　rise again.

II

One only son's love had supported her.
　　She long had struggled with infirmity,
　　Lingering to human life-scenes; for to
　　　die,
　　When fate has spared to rend some
　　　mental tie,
Would many wish, and surely fewer dare.
But, when the tyrant's bloodhounds
　　forced the child
For his cursed power unhallowed arms
　　to wield —
　　Bend to another's will — become a
　　　thing
More senseless than the sword of battle-
　　field —
　　Then did she feel keen sorrow's keen-
　　　est sting;
And many years had passed ere comfort
　　they would bring.

III

For seven years did this poor woman live
In unparticipated solitude.
　　Thou mightst have seen her in the for-
　　　est rude
　　Picking the scattered remnants of its
　　　wood.

If human, thou mightst then have learned
　　to grieve.
The gleanings of precarious charity
Her scantiness of food did scarce sup-
　　ply.
　　The proofs of an unspeaking sorrow
　　　dwelt
Within her ghastly hollowness of eye:
　　Each arrow of the season's change she
　　　felt.
Yet still she groans, ere yet her race
　　were run,
One only hope: it was — once more to see
　　her son.

IV

It was an eve of June, when every star
　　Spoke peace from heaven to those on
　　　earth that live.
　　She rested on the moor. 'T was such
　　　an eve
　　When first her soul began indeed to
　　　grieve;
Then he was there; now he is very far.
The sweetness of the balmy evening
A sorrow o'er her agèd soul did fling,
　　Yet not devoid of rapture's mingled
　　　tear;
A balm was in the poison of the sting.
This agèd sufferer for many a year
Had never felt such comfort. She sup-
　　pressed
A sigh — and, turning round, clasped Wil-
　　liam to her breast!

V

And, though his form was wasted by the
　　woe
　　Which tyrants on their victims love to
　　　wreak,
　　Though his sunk eyeballs and his
　　　faded cheek
　　Of slavery's violence and scorn did
　　　speak,
Yet did the agèd woman's bosom glow.
The vital fire seemed reillumed within
By this sweet unexpected welcoming.
　　Oh, consummation of the fondest hope
That ever soared on fancy's wildest wing!
　　Oh, tenderness that found'st so sweet
　　　a scope!
Prince who dost pride thee on thy mighty
　　sway,
When *thou* canst feel such love, thou shalt
　　be great as they!

VI

Her son, compelled, the country's foes
    had fought,
    Had bled in battle; and the stern con-
    trol
    Which ruled his sinews and coerced
    his soul
Utterly poisoned life's unmingled bowl,
And unsubduable evils on him brought.
He was the shadow of the lusty child
Who, when the time of summer season
    smiled,
    Did earn for her a meal of honesty,
And with affectionate discourse beguiled
    The keen attacks of pain and poverty;
Till Power, as envying her this only joy,
From her maternal bosom tore the un-
    happy boy.

VII

And now cold charity's unwelcome dole
    Was insufficient to support the pair;
    And they would perish rather than
    would bear
    The law's stern slavery, and the insolent
    stare
With which law loves to rend the poor
    man's soul —
The bitter scorn, the spirit-sinking noise
Of heartless mirth which women, men
    and boys
Wake in this scene of legal misery.

.   .   .   .

TO THE REPUBLICANS OF NORTH AMERICA

Sent by Shelley to Miss Hitchener in a letter February 14, 1812: 'Have you heard a
new republic is set up in Mexico? I have just
written the following short tribute to its success. These are merely sent as lineaments in
the picture of my mind. On these two topics
[Mexico and Ireland] I find that I can sometimes write poetry when I feel, such as it is.'
Published by Rossetti, 1870.

I

BROTHERS ! between you and me
    Whirlwinds sweep and billows roar:
Yet in spirit oft I see
    On thy wild and winding shore
Freedom's bloodless banners wave, —
Feel the pulses of the brave

Unextinguished in the grave, —
    See them drenched in sacred gore, —
Catch the warrior's gasping breath
Murmuring ' Liberty or death ! '

II

Shout aloud ! Let every slave,
    Crouching at Corruption's throne,
Start into a man, and brave
    Racks and chains without a groan;
And the castle's heartless glow,
And the hovel's vice and woe,
Fade like gaudy flowers that blow —
    Weeds that peep, and then are gone;
Whilst, from misery's ashes risen,
Love shall burst the captive's prison.

III

Cotopaxi ! bid the sound
    Through thy sister mountains ring,
Till each valley smile around
    At the blissful welcoming !
And, O thou stern Ocean deep,
Thou whose foamy billows sweep
Shores where thousands wake to weep
    Whilst they curse a villain king,
On the winds that fan thy breast
Bear thou news of Freedom's rest !

IV

Can the daystar dawn of love,
    Where the flag of war unfurled
Floats with crimson stain above
    The fabric of a ruined world ?
Never but to vengeance driven
When the patriot's spirit shriven
Seeks in death its native heaven !
    There, to desolation hurled,
Widowed love may watch thy bier,
Balm thee with its dying tear.

TO IRELAND

Sent by Shelley to Miss Hitchener in the
same letter as above, and published in part by
Rossetti, 1870, and completed by Dowden,
Life of Shelley, 1887, and Kingsland, Poet-
Lore, 1892.

I

BEAR witness, Erin ! when thine injured isle
Sees summer on its verdant pastures smile,
Its cornfields waving in the winds that
    sweep
The billowy surface of thy circling deep !

Thou tree whose shadow o'er the Atlantic
    gave
Peace, wealth and beauty, to its friendly
    wave,
                    its blossoms fade,
And blighted are the leaves that cast its
    shade;
Whilst the cold hand gathers its scanty
    fruit,
Whose chillness struck a canker to its root.

II

                I could stand
Upon thy shores, O Erin, and could count
The billows that, in their unceasing swell,
Dash on thy beach, and every wave might
    seem
An instrument in Time, the giant's grasp,
To burst the barriers of Eternity.
Proceed, thou giant, conquering and to con-
    quer;
March on thy lonely way! The nations fall
Beneath thy noiseless footstep; pyramids
That for millenniums have defied the blast,
And laughed at lightnings, thou dost crush
    to nought.
Yon monarch, in his solitary pomp,
Is but the fungus of a winter day
That thy light footstep presses into dust.
Thou art a conqueror, Time; all things give
    way
Before thee but the 'fixed and virtuous
    will;'
The sacred sympathy of soul which was
When thou wert not, which shall be when
    thou perishest.

  .   .   .   .   .   .

ON ROBERT EMMET'S GRAVE

Published by Dowden, *Life of Shelley*, 1887,
and dated 1812. Shelley mentions the poem
in a letter to Miss Hitchener, April 18, 1812:
'I have written some verses on Robert Emmet
which you shall see, and which I will insert in
my book of poems.'

  .   .   .   .   .   .

VI

No trump tells thy virtues — the grave
    where they rest
  With thy dust shall remain unpolluted by
    fame,

Till thy foes, by the world and by fortune
    caressed,
  Shall pass like a mist from the light of
    thy name.

VII

When the storm-cloud that lowers o'er
    the daybeam is gone,
  Unchanged, unextinguished its life-spring
    will shine;
When Erin has ceased with their memory
    to groan,
  She will smile through the tears of re-
    vival on thine.

THE RETROSPECT: CWM ELAN, 1812

Published by Dowden, *Life of Shelley*, 1887.
Peacock mentions the place: 'Cwm Elan House
was the seat of Mr. Grove, whom Shelley
had visited there before his marriage in 1811.
. . . At a subsequent period I stayed a day at
Rhayader, for the sake of seeing this spot.
It is a scene of singular beauty.'

A scene, which wildered fancy viewed
In the soul's coldest solitude,
With that same scene when peaceful love
Flings rapture's color o'er the grove,
When mountain, meadow, wood and stream
With unalloying glory gleam,
And to the spirit's ear and eye
Are unison and harmony.
The moonlight was my dearer day;
Then would I wander far away,
And, lingering on the wild brook's shore
To hear its unremitting roar,
Would lose in the ideal flow
All sense of overwhelming woe;
Or at the noiseless noon of night
Would climb some heathy mountain's height,
And listen to the mystic sound
That stole in fitful gasps around.
I joyed to see the streaks of day
Above the purple peaks decay,
And watch the latest line of light
Just mingling with the shades of night;
For day with me was time of woe
When even tears refused to flow;
Then would I stretch my languid frame
Beneath the wild woods' gloomiest shade,
And try to quench the ceaseless flame
That on my withered vitals preyed;

Would close mine eyes and dream I were
On some remote and friendless plain,
And long to leave existence there,
If with it I might leave the pain
That with a finger cold and lean
Wrote madness on my withering mien.

It was not unrequited love
That bade my 'wildered spirit rove;
'T was not the pride disdaining life,
That with this mortal world at strife
Would yield to the soul's inward sense,
Then groan in human impotence,
And weep because it is not given
To taste on Earth the peace of Heaven.
'T was not that in the narrow sphere
Where nature fixed my wayward fate
There was no friend or kindred dear
Formed to become that spirit's mate,
Which, searching on tired pinion, found
Barren and cold repulse around;
Oh, no! yet each one sorrow gave
New graces to the narrow grave.

For broken vows had early quelled
The stainless spirit's vestal flame;
Yes! whilst the faithful bosom swelled,
Then the envenomed arrow came,
And apathy's unaltering eye
Beamed coldness on the misery;
And early I had learned to scorn
The chains of clay that bound a soul
Panting to seize the wings of morn,
And where its vital fires were born
To soar, and spurn the cold control
Which the vile slaves of earthly night
Would twine around its struggling flight.

Oh, many were the friends whom fame
Had linked with the unmeaning name,
Whose magic marked among mankind
The casket of my unknown mind,
Which hidden from the vulgar glare
Imbibed no fleeting radiance there.
My darksome spirit sought — it found
A friendless solitude around.
For who that might undaunted stand,
The savior of a sinking land,
Would crawl, its ruthless tyrant's slave,
And fatten upon Freedom's grave,
Though doomed with her to perish, where
The captive clasps abhorred despair.

They could not share the bosom's feeling,
Which, passion's every throb revealing,

Dared force on the world's notice cold
Thoughts of unprofitable mould,
Who bask in Custom's fickle ray,
Fit sunshine of such wintry day!
They could not in a twilight walk
Weave an impassioned web of talk,
Till mysteries the spirits press
In wild yet tender awfulness,
Then feel within our narrow sphere
How little yet how great we are!
But they might shine in courtly glare,
Attract the rabble's cheapest stare,
And might command where'er they move
A thing that bears the name of love;
They might be learned, witty, gay,
Foremost in fashion's gilt array,
On Fame's emblazoned pages shine,
Be princes' friends, but never mine!

Ye jagged peaks that frown sublime,
Mocking the blunted scythe of Time,
Whence I would watch its lustre pale
Steal from the moon o'er yonder vale:

Thou rock, whose bosom black and vast,
Bared to the stream's unceasing flow,
Ever its giant shade doth cast
On the tumultuous surge below:

Woods, to whose depths retires to die
The wounded echo's melody,
And whither this lone spirit bent
The footstep of a wild intent:

Meadows! whose green and spangled
  breast
These fevered limbs have often pressed,
Until the watchful fiend Despair
Slept in the soothing coolness there!
Have not your varied beauties seen
The sunken eye, the withering mien,
Sad traces of the unuttered pain
That froze my heart and burned my
  brain?
How changed since Nature's summer form
Had last the power my grief to charm,
Since last ye soothed my spirit's sadness,
Strange chaos of a mingled madness!
Changed! — not the loathsome worm that
  fed
In the dark mansions of the dead
Now soaring through the fields of air,
And gathering purest nectar there,
A butterfly, whose million hues
The dazzled eye of wonder views,

Long lingering on a work so strange,
Has undergone so bright a change.

How do I feel my happiness ?
I cannot tell, but they may guess
Whose every gloomy feeling gone,
Friendship and passion feel alone;
Who see mortality's dull clouds
Before affection's murmur fly,
Whilst the mild glances of her eye
Pierce the thin veil of flesh that shrouds
The spirit's inmost sanctuary.

O thou ! whose virtues latest known,
First in this heart yet claim'st a throne;
Whose downy sceptre still shall share
The gentle sway with virtue there;
Thou fair in form, and pure in mind,
Whose ardent friendship rivets fast
The flowery band our fates that bind,
Which incorruptible shall last
When duty's hard and cold control
Had thawed around the burning soul, —
The gloomiest retrospects that bind
With crowns of thorn the bleeding mind,
The prospects of most doubtful hue
That rise on Fancy's shuddering view, —
Are gilt by the reviving ray
Which thou hast flung upon my day.

FRAGMENT OF A SONNET

TO HARRIET

Published by Dowden, *Life of Shelley*, 1887,
and dated August 1, 1812.

EVER as now with Love and Virtue's glow
May thy unwithering soul not cease to
    burn,
Still may thine heart with those pure
    thoughts o'erflow
Which force from mine such quick and
    warm return.

TO HARRIET

Published in part with *Notes to Queen Mab*,
1813, and completed by Forman, 1876, and
Dowden, *Life of Shelley*, 1887 ; dated 1812.

IT is not blasphemy to hope that Heaven
More perfectly will give those nameless
    joys

Which throb within the pulses of the blood
And sweeten all that bitterness which
    Earth
Infuses in the heaven-born soul.   O thou
Whose dear love gleamed upon the gloomy
    path
Which this lone spirit travelled, drear and
    cold,
Yet swiftly leading to those awful limits
Which mark the bounds of time and of the
    space
When Time shall be no more; wilt thou
    not turn
Those spirit-beaming eyes and look on me,
Until I be assured that Earth is Heaven,
And Heaven is Earth ? — will not thy
    glowing cheek,
Glowing with soft suffusion, rest on mine,
And breathe magnetic sweetness through
    the frame
Of my corporeal nature, through the soul
Now knit with these fine fibres ?   I would
    give
The longest and the happiest day that fate
Has marked on my existence but to feel
One soul-reviving kiss. . . . O thou most
    dear,
'Tis an assurance that this Earth is Hea-
    ven,
And Heaven the flower of that untainted
    seed
Which springeth here beneath such love as
    ours.
Harriet ! let death all mortal ties dissolve,
But ours shall not be mortal !   The cold
    hand
Of Time may chill the love of earthly
    minds
Half frozen now; the frigid intercourse
Of common souls lives but a summer's day;
It dies, where it arose, upon this earth.
But ours ! oh, 't is the stretch of fancy's
    hope
To portray its continuance as now,
Warm, tranquil, spirit-healing; nor when
    age
Has tempered these wild ecstasies, and
    given
A soberer tinge to the luxurious glow
Which blazing on devotion's pinnacle
Makes virtuous passion supersede the power
Of reason; nor when life's æstival sun
To deeper manhood shall have ripened me;
Nor when some years have added judg-
    ment's store

To all thy woman sweetness, all the fire
Which throbs in thine enthusiast heart;
    not then
Shall holy friendship (for what other name
May love like ours assume ?), not even
    then
Shall custom so corrupt, or the cold forms
Of this desolate world so harden us,
As when we think of the dear love that
    binds
Our souls in soft communion, while we
    know
Each other's thoughts and feelings, can we
    say
Unblushingly a heartless compliment,
Praise, hate, or love with the unthinking
    world,
Or dare to cut the unrelaxing nerve
That knits our love to virtue. Can those
    eyes,
Beaming with mildest radiance on my heart
To purify its purity, e'er bend
To soothe its vice or consecrate its fears ?
Never, thou second self ! Is confidence
So vain in virtue that I learn to doubt
The mirror even of Truth ? Dark flood of
    Time,
Roll as it listeth thee; I measure not
By month or moments thy ambiguous
    course.
Another may stand by me on thy brink,
And watch the bubble whirled beyond his
    ken,
Which pauses at my feet. The sense of
    love,
The thirst for action, and the impassioned
    thought
Prolong my being; if I wake no more,
My life more actual living will contain
Than some gray veterans of the world's
    cold school,
Whose listless hours unprofitably roll
By one enthusiast feeling unredeemed,
Virtue and Love ! unbending Fortitude,
Freedom, Devotedness and Purity !
That life my spirit consecrates to you.

SONNET

TO A BALLOON LADEN WITH KNOW-LEDGE

In August, 1812, at Lynmouth, Shelley
amused himself with sending off fire-balloons
by air, and boxes and green bottles by water,
containing his *Declaration of Rights*, and
Devil's Walk. Both this and the next poem
were published by Dowden, *Life of Shelley*,
1887, and dated 1812.

BRIGHT ball of flame that through the
    gloom of even
    Silently takest thine ethereal way,
    And with surpassing glory dimm'st each
      ray
Twinkling amid the dark blue depths of
    Heaven, —
Unlike the fire thou bearest, soon shalt thou
    Fade like a meteor in surrounding gloom,
Whilst that unquenchable is doomed to
    glow
    A watch-light by the patriot's lonely
      tomb;
A ray of courage to the oppressed and
    poor;
    A spark, though gleaming on the hovel's
      hearth,
Which through the tyrant's gilded domes
    shall roar;
A beacon in the darkness of the Earth;
A sun which, o'er the renovated scene,
Shall dart like Truth where Falsehood yet
    has been.

SONNET

ON LAUNCHING SOME BOTTLES FILLED WITH KNOWLEDGE INTO THE BRISTOL CHANNEL

VESSELS of heavenly medicine ! may the
    breeze
    Auspicious waft your dark green forms
    to shore;
    Safe may ye stem the wide surrounding
      roar
Of the wild whirlwinds and the raging seas;
And oh ! if Liberty e'er deigned to stoop
    From yonder lowly throne her crownless
      brow,
Sure she will breathe around your emerald
    group
    The fairest breezes of her west that blow.
Yes ! she will waft ye to some freeborn
    soul
    Whose eye-beam, kindling as it meets
      your freight,
    Her heaven-born flame in suffering
    Earth will light,

Until its radiance gleams from pole to
   pole,
And tyrant-hearts with powerless envy
   burst
To see their night of ignorance dispersed.

THE DEVIL'S WALK

A BALLAD

Composed at Dublin, 1812, and printed as a
broadside. It was unknown until 1871, when
Rossetti recovered it from the copy in the
Public Record Office where it had been sent
with the *Declaration of Rights* and other property of Shelley's supposed by government
agents to be treasonable. For circulating it,
Shelley's servant, Daniel Healey, was imprisoned for six months. Shelley sent an earlier
draft to Miss Hitchener, January 20, 1812.

I

ONCE, early in the morning,
   Beelzebub arose,
With care his sweet person adorning,
   He put on his Sunday clothes.

II

He drew on a boot to hide his hoof,
   He drew on a glove to hide his claw,
His horns were concealed by a *Bras Cha-
      peau*,
And the Devil went forth as natty a
      Beau
   As Bond-street ever saw.

III

He sate him down, in London town,
   Before earth's morning ray;
With a favorite imp he began to chat,
On religion, and scandal, this and that,
   Until the dawn of day.

IV

And then to St. James's court he went,
   And St. Paul's Church he took on his
      way;
He was mighty thick with every Saint,
   Though they were formal and he was
      gay.

V

The Devil was an agriculturist,
   And as bad weeds quickly grow,
In looking over his farm, I wist,
   He would n't find cause for woe.

VI

He peeped in each hole, to each chamber
      stole,
   His promising live-stock to view;
Grinning applause, he just showed them
      his claws,
And they shrunk with affright from his
      ugly sight,
   Whose work they delighted to do.

VII

Satan poked his red nose into crannies so
      small
   One would think that the innocents
      fair,
Poor lambkins! were just doing nothing at
      all
But settling some dress or arranging some
      ball,
   But the Devil saw deeper there.

VIII

A Priest, at whose elbow the Devil during
      prayer
   Sate familiarly, side by side,
Declared that, if the tempter were there,
   His presence he would not abide.
Ah! ah! thought Old Nick, that's a very
      stale trick,
For without the Devil, O favorite of evil,
   In your carriage you would not ride.

IX

Satan next saw a brainless King,
   Whose house was as hot as his own;
Many imps in attendance were there on the
      wing,
They flapped the pennon and twisted the
      sting,
   Close by the very Throne.

X

Ah, ha! thought Satan, the pasture is
      good,
   My Cattle will here thrive better than
      others;
They dine on news of human blood,
They sup on the groans of the dying and
      dead,
And supperless never will go to bed;
   Which will make them fat as their
      brothers.

XI

Fat as the fiends that feed on blood,
  Fresh and warm from the fields of Spain,
    Where ruin ploughs her gory way,
Where the shoots of earth are nipped in
    the bud,
    Where Hell is the Victor's prey,
  Its glory the meed of the slain.

XII

Fat — as the death-birds on Erin's shore,
That glutted themselves in her dearest
    gore,
  And flitted round Castlereagh,
When they snatched the Patriot's heart,
    that *his* grasp
Had torn from its widow's maniac clasp,
  And fled at the dawn of day.

XIII

Fat — as the reptiles of the tomb,
  That riot in corruption's spoil,
That fret their little hour in gloom,
  And creep, and live the while.

XIV

Fat as that Prince's maudlin brain,
  Which, addled by some gilded toy,
Tired, gives his sweetmeat, and again
  Cries for it, like a humored boy.

XV

For he is fat, — his waistcoat gay,
When strained upon a levee day,
  Scarce meets across his princely paunch;
And pantaloons are like half moons
  Upon each brawny haunch.

XVI

How vast his stock of calf ! when plenty
  Had filled his empty head and heart,
Enough to satiate foplings twenty,
  Could make his pantaloon seams start.

XVII

The Devil (who sometimes is called nature),
  For men of power provides thus well,
Whilst every change and every feature,
  Their great original can tell.

XVIII

Satan saw a lawyer a viper slay,
  That crawled up the leg of his table,
It reminded him most marvellously
  Of the story of Cain and Abel.

XIX

The wealthy yeoman, as he wanders
  His fertile fields among,
And on his thriving cattle ponders,
  Counts his sure gains, and hums a song;
Thus did the Devil, through earth walk-
    ing,
  Hum low a hellish song.

XX

For they thrive well whose garb of gore
  Is Satan's choicest livery,
And they thrive well who from the poor
  Have snatched the bread of penury,
And heap the houseless wanderer's store,
  On the rank pile of luxury.

XXI

The Bishops thrive, though they are big;
  The Lawyers thrive, though they are
    thin;
For every gown, and every wig,
  Hides the safe thrift of Hell within.

XXII

Thus pigs were never counted clean,
  Although they dine on finest corn;
And cormorants are sin-like lean,
  Although they eat from night to morn.

XXIII

Oh ! why is the Father of Hell in such
    glee,
  As he grins from ear to ear ?
Why does he doff his clothes joyfully,
  As he skips, and prances, and flaps his
    wing,
  As he sidles, leers, and twirls his sting,
    And dares, as he is, to appear ?

XXIV

A statesman passed — alone to him,
  The Devil dare his whole shape uncover,
To show each feature, every limb,
  Secure of an unchanging lover.

XXV

At this known sign, a welcome sight,
  The watchful demons sought their King,
And every fiend of the Stygian night,
  Was in an instant on the wing.

XXVI

Pale Loyalty, his guilt-steeled brow,
  With wreaths of gory laurel crowned :

The hell-hounds, Murder, Want and Woe,
  Forever hungering flocked around;
From Spain had Satan sought their food,
'T was human woe and human blood !

XXVII

Hark ! the earthquake's crash I hear, —
  Kings turn pale, and Conquerors start,
Ruffians tremble in their fear,
  For their Satan doth depart.

XXVIII

This day fiends give to revelry
  To celebrate their King's return,
And with delight its sire to see
  Hell's adamantine limits burn.

XXIX

But were the Devil's sight as keen
  As Reason's penetrating eye,
His sulphurous Majesty I ween,
  Would find but little cause for joy.

XXX

For the sons of Reason see
  That, ere fate consume the Pole,
The false Tyrant's cheek shall be
  Bloodless as his coward soul.

FRAGMENT OF A SONNET

FAREWELL TO NORTH DEVON

Published by Dowden, *Life of Shelley*, 1887,
and dated August, 1812.

. . . .

Where man's profane and tainting hand
Nature's primeval loveliness has marred,
And some few souls of the high bliss de-
    barred
·Which else obey her powerful command;
            . . . mountain piles
That load in grandeur Cambria's emerald
  vales.

ON LEAVING LONDON FOR WALES

Published by Dowden, *Life of Shelley*, 1887,
and dated November, 1812.

HAIL to thee, Cambria ! for the unfet-
    tered wind
Which from thy wilds even now methinks
    I feel,

Chasing the clouds that roll in wrath be-
    hind,
And tightening the soul's laxest nerves
    to steel;
True mountain Liberty alone may heal
The pain which Custom's obduracies bring,
And he who dares in fancy even to steal
One draught from Snowdon's ever sacred
    spring
Blots out the unholiest rede of worldly
    witnessing.

And shall that soul, to selfish peace re-
    signed,
So soon forget the woe its fellows share ?
Can Snowdon's Lethe from the freeborn
    mind
So soon the page of injured penury
    tear ?
Does this fine mass of human passion
    dare
To sleep, unhonoring the patriot's fall,
Or life's sweet load in quietude to bear
While millions famish even in Luxury's
    hall,
And Tyranny high raised stern lowers on
    all ?

No, Cambria ! never may thy matchless
    vales
A heart so false to hope and virtue
    shield;
Nor ever may thy spirit-breathing gales
Waft freshness to the slaves who dare to
    yield.
For me ! . . . the weapon that I burn to
    wield
I seek amid thy rocks to ruin hurled,
That Reason's flag may over Freedom's
    field,
Symbol of bloodless victory, wave un-
    furled,
A meteor-sign of love effulgent o'er the
    world.

. . . .

Do thou, wild Cambria, calm each strug-
    gling thought;
Cast thy sweet veil of rocks and woods
    between,
That by the soul to indignation wrought
Mountains and dells be mingled with the
    scene;
Let me forever be what I have been,
But not forever at my needy door

Let Misery linger speechless, pale and
    lean;
I am the friend of the unfriended poor, —
Let me not madly stain their righteous
    cause in gore.

THE WANDERING JEW'S SOLILOQUY

Published by Dobell, 1887.

Is it the Eternal Triune, is it He
Who dares arrest the wheels of destiny
And plunge me in the lowest Hell of Hells?
Will not the lightning's blast destroy my
    frame?
Will not steel drink the blood-life where it
    swells?
No — let me hie where dark Destruction
    dwells,
To rouse her from her deeply caverned
    lair,
And taunting her cursed sluggishness to
    ire
Light long Oblivion's death torch at its
    flame
And calmly mount Annihilation's pyre.

Tyrant of Earth! pale misery's jackal thou!
Are there no stores of vengeful violent fate
Within the magazines of thy fierce hate?
No poison in the clouds to bathe a brow
That lowers on thee with desperate con-
    tempt?
Where is the noonday pestilence that slew
The myriad sons of Israel's favored nation?
Where the destroying minister that flew
Pouring the fiery tide of desolation
Upon the leagued Assyrian's attempt?
Where the dark Earthquake demon who
    ingorged
At the dread word Korah's unconscious
    crew?
Or the Angel's two-edged sword of fire
    that urged
Our primal parents from their bower of
    bliss
(Reared by thine hand) for errors not their
    own
By Thine omniscient mind foredoomed,
    foreknown?
Yes! I would court a ruin such as this,
Almighty Tyrant! and give thanks to
    Thee —
Drink deeply — drain the cup of hate —
    remit this I may die.

DOUBTFUL, LOST AND UNPUBLISHED POEMS
VICTOR AND CAZIRE

DOUBTFUL POEMS

THE WANDERING JEW

A poem in MS., entitled *The Wandering Jew*, was offered by Shelley to Ballantyne & Co. of Edinburgh in the early summer of 1810, and declined by them September 24. It was immediately afterward, on September 28, offered by him to Stockdale of London, to whom he ordered Ballantyne & Co. to send the MS.; but, as they delayed or failed to do so, he sent to Stockdale a second MS. which he had retained. A poem, thus entitled, was published, as by Shelley, in *The Edinburgh Literary Journal*, June 27 and July 4, 1829. The editor stated that the MS. was in Shelley's handwriting, and had remained for the preceding twenty years in the custody of a literary gentleman of Edinburgh, to whom Shelley in person had offered it for publication while on a visit to that city. A second version of the same

poem was published, as by Shelley, and with Mrs. Shelley's consent, but without mention of the former publication, in *Fraser's*, July, 1831. Lines 435, 443–451, were quoted by Shelley as a motto for chapter viii., and lines 780, 782–790 for chapter x. of *St. Irvyne*, 1811. These last lines, and lines 1401–1408, were quoted by Medwin (*Life*, i. 56, 58), who ascribes them to Shelley, and are given among the *Juvenilia* by Rossetti, Forman and Dowden. The poem, as it appeared in *Fraser's*, appears to have been edited, by omission or alteration or both, and Mrs. Shelley's statement made below refers exclusively to such editing. Three lines are quoted in the *Introduction to Fraser's* version, as follows, — 'There is a pretty, affecting passage at the end of the fourth canto, which we dare say bore reference to the cloud of family misfortune in which he [Shelley] was then enveloped: —

' "'T is mournful when the deadliest hate
    Of friends, of fortune, and of fate,
    Is levelled at one fated head."'

These lines are also quoted by Medwin (*Life*, i. 364) as written 'in his seventeenth year,' but he does not mention independent authority for them. They do not, however, appear in the poem as given in either version. Such are the facts making for Shelley's authorship.

On the other hand Medwin claims to have written the poem, with aid from Shelley, and ascribes to him a concluding portion, embodying speculative opinions, which has never come to light. It is plain that the poem was not printed from Medwin's MS., which he does not himself seem to have consulted. His memory of the past was at best a confused one, as is shown by the inaccuracy of his *Life* of the poet; and, when the matter related to his literary partnership with Shelley, as in his translations at Pisa, his recollection of the share of each in their joint work was, one is compelled to think, very feeble indeed. It may, at least, be fairly surmised that more of Shelley's work goes under Medwin's name than has ever been affirmed. In the present instance Medwin's assertion of authorship, in which several blunders are obvious, is of no more value than other unsupported and loose statements by him, which would certainly be accepted only provisionally and with doubt. In view of the facts above, that Shelley twice offered the poem as his own and that it was twice printed from different MSS. without Medwin's interposition, the claim of a far more trustworthy writer would be much impaired. If the internal evidence of the poem be appealed to, the opinion that it is substantially Shelley's work is as much strengthened. The most plausible hypothesis is that Shelley worked with Medwin upon the subject in prose and in the first versification made of the prose; that he then rewrote the whole, confined the poem to the story, and reserved the speculative part, which has never appeared, among those early materials out of which *Queen Mab* was made and to which, both prose and verse, he referred in saying, that *Queen Mab* was written in his eighteenth and nineteenth year, or 1809–10; but that *The Wandering Jew*, as we have it, is substantially the poem offered by him for publication in 1810, and that it was Shelley's work and not Medwin's, are statements as well supported by external and internal evidence as can be looked for in such cases. Forman and, though with less decision, Dowden reject the poem, and therefore it is here placed in this division.

The following documentary account of it is condensed from the Introduction to the reprint in the Shelley Society Publications by Mr. Bertram Dobell, who discovered the Edinburgh 1829 version.

Messrs. Ballantyne & Co. (from Edinburgh) to Shelley, September 24, 1810 : 'Sir, — The delay which occurred in our reply to you, respecting the poem you have obligingly offered us for publication, has arisen from our literary friends and advisers (at least such as we have confidence in) being in the country at this season, as is usual, and the time they have bestowed on its perusal.

'We are extremely sorry at length, after the most mature deliberation, to be under the necessity of declining the honor of being the publishers of the present poem; not that we doubt its success, but that it is perhaps better suited to the character and liberal feelings of the English, than the bigoted spirit which yet pervades many cultivated minds in this country. Even Walter Scott is assailed on all hands, at present, by our Scotch spiritual and evangelical magazines and instructors, for having promulgated atheistical doctrines in *The Lady of the Lake*.

'We beg you will have the goodness to advise us how it should be returned, and we think its being consigned to some person in London would be more likely to ensure its safety than addressing it to Horsham.' *Stockdale's Budget*, 1827. (Hotten's *Shelley*, i. 41.)

Shelley (from Field Place) to Stockdale, September 28, 1810 : 'Sir, — I sent, before I had the pleasure of knowing you, the MS. of a poem to Messrs. Ballantyne & Co., Edinburgh ; they have declined publishing it, with the enclosed letter. I now offer it to you, and depend upon your honor as a gentleman for a fair price for the copyright. It will be sent to you from Edinburgh. The subject is *The Wandering Jew*. As to its containing atheistical principles, I assure you I was wholly unaware of the fact hinted at. Your good sense will point out the impossibility of inculcating pernicious doctrines in a poem which, as you will see, is so totally abstract from any circumstances which occur under the possible view of mankind.' *Stockdale's Budget*, 1827. (Hotten, i. 140.)

Shelley (from University College) to Stockdale, November 14, 1810: 'I am surprised that you have not received *The Wandering Jew*, and in consequence write to Mr. Ballantyne to mention it; you will, doubtlessly, therefore receive it soon.' *Stockdale's Budget*, 1827. (Hotten, i. 44.)

Shelley (from University College) to Stockdale, November 19, 1810: 'If you have not got *The Wandering Jew* from Mr. B., I will send you a MS. copy which I possess.' (Hotten, i. 44.)

Shelley (from Oxford) to Stockdale, December 2, 1810 : 'Will you, if you have got two copies of *The Wandering Jew*, send one of them to me, as I have thought of some corrections which I wish to make ; your opinion on it will likewise much oblige me.' *Stockdale's Budget*, 1827. (Hotten, i. 45.) *The Edinburgh Literary Journal*, No. 32, June 20, 1829 : —

'THE POET SHELLEY

' There has recently been put into our hands a manuscript volume, which we look upon as one of the most remarkable literary curiosities extant. *It is a poem in four cantos, by the late poet Shelley, and entirely written in his own hand.* It is entitled *The Wandering Jew*, and contains many passages of great power and beauty. It was composed upwards of twenty years ago, and brought by the poet to Edinburgh, which he visited about that period. It has since lain in the custody of a literary gentleman of this town, to whom it was then offered for publication. We have received permission to give our readers a further account of its contents, with some extracts, next Saturday ; and it affords us much pleasure to have it in our power to be thus instrumental in rescuing, through the medium of the *Literary Journal*, from the obscurity to which it might otherwise have been consigned, one of the earliest and most striking of this gifted poet's productions, the very existence of which has never hitherto been surmised.' [The poem was published, Nos. 33, 34 (June 27, July 4, 1829), with the following remarks] : —
' It may possibly have been offered to one or two booksellers, both in London and Edinburgh, without success, and this may account for the neglect into which the author allowed it to fall, when new cares crowded upon him, and new prospects opened round him. Certain it is, that it has been carefully kept by the literary gentleman to whom he entrusted its perusal when he visited Edinburgh in 1811, and would have been willingly surrendered by him at any subsequent [period, had any application to that effect been made. . . .
' Mr. Shelley appears to have some doubts whether to call his poem *The Wandering Jew* or *The Victim of the Eternal Avenger*. Both names occur in the manuscript ; but had the work been published, it is to be hoped that he would finally have fixed on the former, the more especially as the poem itself contains very little calculated to give offence to the religious reader. The motto on the title-page is from the 22d chapter of St. John : " If I will that he tarry till I come, what is that to thee ? — follow thou me." Turning over the leaf, we meet with the following Dedication : " To Sir Francis Burdett, Bart., M. P., in consideration of the active virtues by which both his public and private life is so eminently distin-guished, the following poem is inscribed by the Author." Again turning the leaf, we meet with the —

' " PREFACE

' " " The subject of the following Poem is an imaginary personage, noted for the various and contradictory traditions which have prevailed concerning him — the Wandering Jew. Many sage monkish writers have supported the au-thenticity of this fact, the reality of his exist-ence. But as the quoting them would have led me to annotations perfectly uninteresting, although very fashionable, I decline presenting anything to the public but the bare poem, which they will agree with me not to be of sufficient consequence to authorize deep anti-quarian researches on its subject. I might, indeed, have introduced, by anticipating future events, the no less grand, although equally groundless, superstitions of the battle of Ar-mageddon, the personal reign of J—— C——, etc. ; but I preferred, improbable as the fol-lowing tale may appear, retaining the old method of describing past events : it is cer-tainly more consistent with reason, more inter-esting, even in works of imagination. With respect to the omission of elucidatory notes, I have followed the well-known maxim of ' Do unto others as thou wouldest they should do unto thee.' — *January*, 1811." '

' The poem introduced by the above Preface is in four cantos ; and though the octosyllabic verse is the most prominent, it contains a vari-ety of measures, like Sir Walter Scott's poeti-cal romances. The incidents are simple, and refer rather to an episode in the life of the Wandering Jew, than to any attempt at a full delineation of all his adventures. We shall give an analysis of the plot, and intersperse, as we proceed, some of the most interesting pas-sages of the poem.'
Medwin, *Shelley Papers*, pp. 7–9 : ' Shortly afterwards we wrote, in conjunction, six or seven cantos on the subject of the Wandering Jew, of which the first four, with the exception of a very few lines, were exclusively mine. It was a thing such as boys usually write, a *cento* from different favorite authors ; the crucifixion scene altogether a plagiary from a volume of Cambridge Prize Poems. The part which I contributed I have still, and was surprised to find *totidem verbis* in *Fraser's Magazine*. . . . As might be shown by the last cantos of that poem, which *Fraser* did not think worth pub-lishing, his [Shelley's] ideas were, at that time, strange and incomprehensible, mere ele-ments of thought — images wild, vast and Titanic.'

Medwin, *Life*, i. 54–57 : ' Shelley, having abandoned prose for poetry, now formed a *grand* design, a metrical romance on the subject of the Wandering Jew, of which the first three cantos were, with a few additions and alterations, almost entirely mine. It was a sort of thing such as boys usually write, a *cento* from different favorite authors ; the vision in the third canto taken from Lewis's *Monk*, of which, in common with Byron, he was a great admirer ; and the crucifixion scene altogether a plagiarism from a volume of Cambridge Prize Poems. The part which I supplied is still in my possession. After seven or eight cantos were *perpetrated*, Shelley sent them to Campbell for his opinion on their merits, with a view to publication. The author of the *Pleasures of Hope* returned the MS. with the remark that there were only two good lines in it : —

' " It seemed as if an angel's sigh
  Had breathed the plaintive symphony."

Lines, by the way, savoring strongly of Walter Scott. This criticism of Campbell's gave a death-blow to our hopes of immortality, and so little regard did Shelley entertain for the production, that he left it at his lodgings in Edinburgh, where it was disinterred by some correspondent of *Fraser's*, and in whose magazine, in 1831, four of the cantos appeared. The others he very wisely did not think worth publishing.

' It must be confessed that Shelley's contributions to this juvenile attempt were far the best, and those, with my MS. before me, I could, were it worth while, point out, though the contrast in the style, and the inconsequence of the opinions on religion, particularly in the last canto, are sufficiently obvious to mark two different hands, and show which passages were his. . . . The finale of *The Wandering Jew* is also Shelley's, and proves that thus early he had imbibed opinions which were often the subject of our controversies. We differed also as to the conduct of the poem. It was my wish to follow the German fragment, and put an end to the Wandering Jew — a consummation Shelley would by no means consent to.' [Mr. Dobell examines the inconsistencies and the precise statements of Medwin at length.]

Fraser's, July, 1831 : ' An obscure contemporary has accused us of announcing for publication Shelley's poem without proper authority. We beg to assure him that we have the sanction of Mrs. Shelley. O[liver] Y[orke].'

The same : ' The important literary curiosity which the liberality of the gentleman into whose hands it has fallen, enables us now to lay before the public for the first time, *in a complete state*, was offered for publication by Mr. Shelley when quite a boy.'

Mrs. Shelley, Note on *Queen Mab*, 1839, i. 102 : ' He wrote also a poem on the subject of Ahasuerus — being led to it by a German Fragment he picked up, dirty and torn, in Lincoln's Inn Fields. This fell afterwards into other hands — and was considerably altered before it was printed.'

THE WANDERING JEW

[The passages in italics are from the Edinburgh version.]

CANTO I

' Me miserable, which way shall I fly ?
Infinite wrath and infinite despair —
Which way I fly is hell — myself am hell ;
And in this lowest deep a lower deep,
To which the hell I suffer seems a heaven.'
                                Paradise Lost.

THE brilliant orb of parting day
Diffused a rich and mellow ray
Above the mountain's brow ;
It tinged the hills with lustrous light,
It tinged the promontory's height,
Still sparkling with the snow ;
And, as aslant it threw its beam,
Tipped with gold the mountain stream
That laved the vale below ;
Long hung the eye of glory there,
And lingered as if loth to leave
A scene so lovely and so fair.

'T were luxury even, there to grieve.
*So soft the clime, so balm the air,
So pure and genial were the skies,
In sooth 't was almost Paradise,
For ne'er did the sun's splendor close
On such a picture of repose.*
All, all was tranquil, all was still,
Save when the music of the rill,
Or distant waterfall,
At intervals broke on the ear,
Which Echo's self was charmed to hear,
And ceased her babbling call.
*With every charm the landscape glowed
Which partial Nature's hand bestowed ;
Nor could the mimic hand of art
Such beauties or such hues impart.*

Light clouds in fleeting livery gay
Hung, painted in grotesque array,
Upon the western sky ;
Forgetful of the approaching dawn,
The peasants danced upon the lawn,
For the vintage time was nigh.
How jocund to the tabor's sound
O'er the smooth, trembling turf they bound,
In every measure light and free,
The very soul of harmony !

Grace in each attitude, they move,
They thrill to amorous ecstasy,
Light as the dewdrops of the morn,
That hang upon the blossomed thorn,
Subdued by the power of resistless Love.
Ah! days of innocence, of joy,
Of rapture that knows no alloy,
Haste on, — ye roseate hours,
Free from the world's tumultuous cares,
From pale distrust, from hopes and fears,
Baneful concomitants of time, —
'T is yours, beneath this favored clime,
Your pathway strewn with flowers,
Upborne on pleasure's downy wing,
To quaff a long unfading spring,
And beat with light and careless step the ground ;
The fairest flowers too soon grow sere,
Too soon shall tempests blast the year,
And sin's eternal winter reign around.

But see, what forms are those,
Scarce seen by glimpse of dim twilight,
Wandering o'er the mountain's height?
They swiftly haste to the vale below.
One wraps his mantle around his brow,
As if to hide his woes ;
And as his steed impetuous flies,
What strange fire flashes from his eyes !
The far-off city's murmuring sound
Was borne on the breeze which floated around ;
Noble Padua's lofty spire
Scarce glowed with the sunbeam's latest fire,
Yet dashed the travellers on ;
Ere night o'er the earth was spread,
Full many a mile they must have sped,
Ere their destined course was run.
Welcome was the moonbeam's ray,
Which slept upon the towers so gray.
But, hark ! a convent's vesper bell —
It seemed to be a very spell !
The stranger checked his courser's rein,
And listened to the mournful sound ;
Listened — and paused — and paused again ;
A thrill of pity and of pain
Through his inmost soul had passed,
While gushed the tear-drops silently and fast.

A crowd was at the convent gate,
The gate was opened wide ;
No longer on his steed he sate,
But mingled with the tide.
He felt a solemn awe and dread,
As he the chapel enterèd
Dim was the light from the pale moon beaming,
As it fell on the saint-cyphered panes,
Or, from the western window streaming,
Tinged the pillars with varied stains.
To the eye of enthusiasm strange forms were gliding
In each dusky recess of the aisle ;
And indefined shades in succession were striding
O'er the coignes [1] of the Gothic pile.
The pillars to the vaulted roof
In airy lightness rose ;

[1] Buttress or coign of vantage. *Macbeth.*

Now they mount to the rich Gothic ceiling aloof
And exquisite tracery disclose.

The altar illumined now darts its bright rays,
The train passed in brilliant array ;
On the shrine Saint Pietro's rich ornaments blaze,
And rival the brilliance of day.
Hark ! — now the loud organ swells full on the ear —
So sweetly mellow, chaste, and clear ;
Melting, kindling, raising, firing,
Delighting now, and now inspiring,
Peal upon peal the music floats ;
Now they list still as death to the dying notes ;
Whilst the soft voices of the choir,
Exalt the soul from base desire,
Till it mounts on unearthly pinions free,
Dissolved in heavenly ecstasy.

Now a dead stillness reigned around,
Uninterrupted by a sound ;
Save when in deadened response ran
The last faint echoes down the aisle,
Reverberated through the pile,
As within the pale the holy man,
With voice devout and saintly look,
Slow chanted from the sacred book,
Or pious prayers were duly said
For spirits of departed dead.
With beads and crucifix and hood,
Close by his side the abbess stood ;
Now her dark penetrating eyes
Were raised in suppliance to heaven,
And now her bosom heaved with sighs,
As if to human weakness given.
Her stern, severe, yet beauteous brow
Frowned on all who stood below ;
And the fire which flashed from her steady gaze,
As it turned on the listening crowd its rays,
Superior virtue told, —
Virtue as pure as heaven's own dew,
But which, untainted, never knew
To pardon weaker mould.
The heart though chaste and cold as snow —
'T were faulty to be virtuous so.

Not a whisper now breathed in the pillared aisle.
The stranger advanced to the altar high —
Convulsive was heard a smothered sigh !
Lo ! four fair nuns to the altar draw near,
With solemn footstep, as the while
A fainting novice they bear ;
The roses from her cheek are fled
But there the lily reigns instead ;
Light as a sylph's, her form confessed
Beneath the drapery of her vest,
A perfect grace and symmetry ;
Her eyes, with rapture formed to move,
To melt with tenderness and love,
Or beam with sensibility,
To Heaven were raised in pious prayer,
A silent eloquence of woe ;
Now hung the pearly tear-drop there ;

Sate on her cheek a fixed despair ;
And now she beat her bosom bare,
As pure as driven snow.

Nine graceful novices around
Fresh roses strew upon the ground ;
In purest white arrayed,
Nine spotless vestal virgins shed
Sabæan incense o'er the head
Of the devoted maid.

They dragged her to the altar's pale,
The traveller leant against the rail,
And gazed with eager eye, —
His cheek was flushed with sudden glow,
On his brow sate a darker shade of woe,
As a transient expression fled by.

The sympathetic feeling flew
Through every breast, from man to man ;
Confused and open clamors ran —
Louder and louder still they grew ;
When the abbess waved her hand,
A stern resolve was in her eye,
And every wild tumultuous cry
Was stilled at her command.

The abbess made the well-known sign —
The novice reached the fatal shrine,
And mercy implored from the power divine ;
At length she shrieked aloud,
She dashed from the supporting nun,
Ere the fatal rite was done,
And plunged amid the crowd.
Confusion reigned throughout the throng —
Still the novice fled along,
Impelled by frantic fear,
When the maddened traveller's eager grasp
In firmest yet in wildest clasp
Arrested her career.
As fainting from terror she sank on the ground,
Her loosened locks floated her fine form around ;
The zone which confined her shadowy vest
No longer her throbbing bosom pressed,
Its animation dead ;
No more her feverish pulse beat high,
Expression dwelt not in her eye,
Her wildered senses fled.

. . . .

Hark ! Hark ! the demon of the storm !
I see his vast expanding form
Blend with the strange and sulphurous glare
Of comets through the turbid air.
Yes, 't was his voice, I heard its roar,
The wild waves lashed the caverned shore
In angry murmurs hoarse and loud, —
Higher and higher still they rise ;
Red lightnings gleam from every cloud
And paint wild shapes upon the skies ;
The echoing thunder rolls around,
Convulsed with earthquake rocks the ground.

The traveller yet undaunted stood,
He heeded not the roaring flood ;
Yet Rosa slept, her bosom bare,
Her cheek was deadly pale,

The ringlets of her auburn hair
Streamed in a lengthened trail,
And motionless her seraph form ;
Unheard, unheeded raved the storm ;
Whilst, borne on the wing of the gale,
The harrowing shriek of the white sea-mew
As o'er the midnight surge she flew, —
The howlings of the squally blast,
As o'er the beetling cliffs it passed,
Mingled with the peals on high,
That, swelling louder, echoed by, —
Assailed the traveller's ear.
He heeded not the maddened storm
As it pelted against his lofty form ;
He felt no awe, no fear ;
In contrast, like the courser pale [1]
That stalks along Death's pitchy vale
With silent, with gigantic tread,
Trampling the dying and the dead.

Rising from her deathlike trance,
Fair Rosa met the stranger's glance ;
She started from his chilling gaze, —
Wild was it as the tempest's blaze,
It shot a lurid gleam of light,
A secret spell of sudden dread,
A mystic, strange, and harrowing fear,
As when the spirits of the dead,
Dressed in ideal shapes appear,
And hideous glance on human sight ;
Scarce could Rosa's frame sustain
The chill that pressed upon her brain.

Anon, that transient spell was o'er ;
Dark clouds deform his brow no more,
But rapid fled away ;
Sweet fascination dwelt around,
Mixed with a soft, a silver sound,
As soothing to the ravished ear,
As what enthusiast lovers hear ;
Which seems to steal along the sky,
When mountain mists are seen to fly
Before the approach of day.
He seized on wondering Rosa's hand,
'And, ah ! ' cried he, ' be this the band
Shall join us, till this earthly frame
Sinks convulsed in bickering flame —
When around the demons yell,
And drag the sinful wretch to hell,
Then, Rosa, will we part —
Then fate, and only fate's decree,
Shall tear thy lovely soul from me,
And rend thee from my heart.
Long has Paulo sought in vain
A friend to share his grief ;
Never will he seek again,
For the wretch has found relief,
Till the Prince of Darkness bursts his chain,
Till death and desolation reign.
Rosa, wilt thou then be mine ?
Ever fairest, I am thine ! '
He ceased, and on the howling blast,
Which wildly round the mountain passed,

[1] ' Behold a pale horse, and his name that sate upon him was Death, and Hell followed with him.' — *Revelation*, vi. 8.

Died his accents low ;
Yet fiercely howled the midnight storm,
As Paulo bent his awful form,
And leaned his lofty brow.

ROSA

'Stranger, mystic stranger, rise ;
Whence do these tumults fill the skies ?
Who conveyed me, say, this night,
To this wild and cloud-capped height ?
Who art thou ? and why am I
Beneath Heaven's pitiless canopy ?
For the wild winds roar around my head ;
Lightnings redden the wave ;
Was it the power of the mighty dead,
Who live beneath the grave ?
Or did the Abbess drag me here
To make yon swelling surge my bier ? '

PAULO

' Ah, lovely Rosa ! cease thy fear,
It was thy friend who bore thee here —
I, thy friend, till this fabric of earth
Sinks in the chaos that gave it birth ;
Till the meteor-bolt of the God above
Shall tear its victim from his love, —
That love which must unbroken last,
Till the hour of envious fate is past,
Till the mighty basements of the sky
In bickering hell-flames heated fly.
E'en then will I sit on some rocky height,
Whilst around lower clouds of eternal night ;
E'en then will I loved·Rosa save
From the yawning abyss of the grave ;
Or, into the gulf impetuous hurled
If sinks with its latest tenants the world,
Then will our souls in union fly
Throughout the wide and boundless sky ;
Then, free from the ills that envious fate
Has heaped upon our mortal state,
We 'll taste ethereal pleasure ;
Such as none but thou canst give,
Such as none but I receive, —
And rapture without measure.'

As thus he spoke, a sudden blaze
Of pleasure mingled in his gaze.
Illumined by the dazzling light,
He glows with radiant lustre bright ;
His features with new glory shine,
And sparkle as with beams divine.
'Strange, awful being,' Rosa said,
' Whence is this superhuman dread,
That harrows up my inmost frame ?
Whence does this unknown tingling flame
Consume and penetrate my soul ?
By turns with fear and love possessed,
Tumultuous thoughts swell high my breast ;
A thousand wild emotions roll,
And mingle their resistless tide ;
O'er thee some magic arts preside ;
As by the influence of a charm,
Lulled into rest, my griefs subside,
And, safe in thy protecting arm,
I feel no power can do me harm.
But the storm raves wildly o'er the sea, —
Bear me away ! I confide in thee ! '

CANTO II

' I could a tale unfold, whose slightest word
Would harrow up thy soul, freeze thy young blood,
Make thy two eyes, like stars, start from their spheres ;
Thy knotted and combinèd locks to part,
And each particular hair to stand on end,
Like quills upon the fretful porcupine.'
Hamlet.

THE horrors of the mighty blast,
The lowering tempest clouds, were passed —
Had sunk beneath the main ;
Light baseless mists were all that fled
Above the weary traveller's head,
As he left the spacious plain.

Fled were the vapors of the night,
Faint streaks of rosy tinted light
Were painted on the matin gray ;
And as the sun began to rise
To pour his animating ray,
Glowed with his fire the eastern skies,
The distant rocks, the far-off bay,
The ocean's sweet and lovely blue,
The mountain's variegated breast,
Blushing with tender tints of dawn,
Or with fantastic shadows dressed ;
The waving wood, the opening lawn,
Rose to existence, waked anew,
In colors·exquisite of hue ;
Their mingled charms Victorio viewed,
And lost in admiration stood.

From yesternight how changed the scene,
When howled the blast o'er the dark cliff's side,
And mingled with the maddened roar
Of the wild surge that lashed the shore.
To-day — scarce heard the whispering breeze,
And still and motionless the seas,
Scarce heard the murmuring of their tide ;
All, all is peaceful and serene ;
Serenely on Victorio's breast
It breathed a soft and tranquil rest,
Which bade each wild emotion cease,
And hushed the passions into peace.

Along the winding Po he went ;
His footsteps to the spot were bent
Where Paulo dwelt, his wandered friend,
For thither did his wishes tend.
Noble Victorio's race was proud,
From Cosmo's blood he came ;
To him a wild untutored crowd
Of vassals in allegiance bowed,
Illustrious was his name ;
Yet vassals and wealth he scorned to go
Unnoticed with a man of woe ;
Gay hope and expectation sate
Throned in his eager eye,
And, ere he reached the castle gate,
The sun had mounted high.

Wild was the spot where the castle stood,
Its towers embosomed deep in wood ;
Gigantic cliffs, with craggy steeps,
Reared their proud heads on high, —

Their bases were washed by the foaming deeps,
Their summits were hid in the sky;
From the valley below they excluded the day,
That valley ne'er cheered by the sunbeam's ray;
Nought broke on the silence drear,
Save the hungry vultures darting by,
Or eagles yelling fearfully,
As they bore to the rocks their prey;
Or when the fell wolf ravening prowled,
Or the gaunt wild boar fiercely howled
His hideous screams on the night's dull ear.
Borne on pleasure's downy wing,
Downy as the breath of spring,
Not thus fled Paulo's hours away,
Though brightened by the cheerful day.
Friendship or wine, or softer love,
The sparkling eye, the foaming bowl,
Could with no lasting rapture move,
Nor still the tumults of his soul.
And yet there was in Rosa's kiss
A momentary thrill of bliss;
Oft the dark clouds of grief would fly
Beneath the beams of sympathy;
And love and converse sweet bestow,
A transient requiem from woe. —

Strange business, and of import vast,
On things which long ago were past
Drew Paulo oft from home;
Then would a darker, deeper shade,
By sorrow traced, his brow o'erspread
And o'er his features roam.
Oft as they spent the midnight hour,
And heard the wintry wild winds rave
Midst the roar and spray of the dashing wave,
Was Paulo's dark brow seen to lower.
Then, as the lamp's uncertain blaze
Shed o'er the hall its partial rays,
And shadows strange were seen to fall,
And glide upon the dusky wall,
Would Paulo start with sudden fear.
Why then unbidden gushed the tear,
As he muttered strange words to the ear?
Why frequent heaved the smothered sigh?
Why did he gaze on vacancy,
As if some strange form was near?
Then would the fillet of his brow
Fierce as a fiery furnace glow,
As it burned with red and lambent flame;
Then would cold shuddering seize his frame,
As gasping he labored for breath.
The strange light of his gorgon eye,
As, frenzied and rolling dreadfully,
It glared with terrific gleam,
Would chill like the spectre gaze of death,
As, conjured by feverish dream,
He seems o'er the sick man's couch to stand,
And shakes the dread lance in his skeleton
    hand.

But when the paroxysm was o'er,
And clouds deformed his brow no more,
Would Rosa soothe his tumults dire,
Would bid him calm his grief,
Would quench reflection's rising fire,
And give his soul relief.
As on his form with pitying eye

The ministering angel hung,
And wiped the drops of agony,
The music of her siren tongue
Lulled forcibly his griefs to rest;
Like fleeting visions of the dead,
Or midnight dreams, his sorrows fled;
Waked to new life, through all his soul
A soft delicious languor stole,
And lapped in heavenly ecstasy
He sank and fainted on her breast.

'T was on an eve, the leaf was sere,
Howled the blast round the castle drear,
The boding night-bird's hideous cry
Was mingled with the warning sky;
Heard was the distant torrent's dash,
Seen was the lightning's dark red flash,
As it gleamed on the stormy cloud;
Heard was the troubled ocean's roar,
As its wild waves lashed the rocky shore;
The thunder muttered loud,
As wilder still the lightnings flew;
Wilder as the tempest blew,
More wildly strange their converse grew.

They talked of the ghosts of the mighty
    dead, —
If, when the spark of life were fled,
They visited this world of woe?
Or, were it but a fantasy,
Deceptive to the feverish eye,
When strange forms flashed upon the sight,
And stalked along at the dead of night?
Or if, in the realms above,
They still, for mortals left below,
Retained the same affection's glow,
In friendship or in love? —
Debating thus, a pensive train,
Thought upon thought began to rise;
Her thrilling wild harp Rosa took;
What sounds in softest murmurs broke
From the seraphic strings!
Celestials borne on odorous wings
Caught the dulcet melodies;
The life-blood ebbed in every vein,
As Paulo listen'd to the strain.

SONG

What sounds are those that float upon the air,
As if to bid the fading day farewell, —
What form is that so shadowy, yet so fair,
Which glides along the rough and pathless
    dell?

Nightly those sounds swell full upon the breeze,
Which seems to sigh as if in sympathy;
They hang amid yon cliff-embosomed trees,
Or float in dying cadence through the sky.

Now rests that form upon the moonbeam pale,
In piteous strains of woe its vesper sings;
Now — now it traverses the silent vale,
Borne on transparent ether's viewless wings.

Oft will it rest beside yon abbey's tower,
Which lifts its ivy-mantled mass so high;

Rears its dark head to meet the storms that
    lower,
And braves the trackless tempests of the
    sky.

That form, the embodied spirit of a maid,
Forced by a perjured lover to the grave ;
A desperate fate the maddened girl obeyed,
And from the dark cliffs plunged into the
    wave.

There the deep murmurs of the restless surge,
The mournful shriekings of the white sea-
    mew,
The warring waves, the wild winds, sang her
    dirge,
And o'er her bones the dark red coral grew.

Yet though that form be sunk beneath the
    main,
Still rests her spirit where its vows were
    given;
Still fondly visits each loved spot again,
And pours its sorrows on the ear of Heaven.

That spectre wanders through the abbey dale,
And suffers pangs which such a fate must
    share ;
Early her soul sank in death's darkened vale,
And ere long all of us must meet her there.

She ceased, and on the listening ear
Her pensive accents died ;
So sad they were, so softly clear,
It seemed as if some angel's sigh
Had breathed the plaintive symphony ;
So ravishingly sweet their close,
The tones awakened Paulo's woes ;
Oppressive recollections rose,
And poured their bitter tide.
Absorbed awhile in grief he stood ;
At length he seemed as one inspired,
His burning fillet blazed with blood —
A lambent flame his features fired.
' The hour is come, the fated hour ;
Whence is this new, this unfelt power ? —
Yes, I 've a secret to unfold,
And such a tale as ne'er was told,
A dreadful, dreadful mystery !
Scenes, at whose retrospect e'en now,
Cold drops of anguish on my brow,
The icy chill of death I feel :
Wrap, Rosa, bride, thy breast in steel,
Thy soul with nerves of iron brace,
As to your eyes I darkly trace
My sad, my cruel destiny.

' Victorio, lend your ears, arise,
Let us seek the battling skies,
Wild o'er our heads the thunder crashing,
And at our feet the wild waves dashing,
As tempest, clouds, and billows roll,
In gloomy concert with my soul.
Rosa, follow me —
For my soul is joined to thine,
And thy being 's linked to mine —
Rosa, list to me.'

CANTO III

' His form had not yet lost
All its original brightness, nor appeared
Less than archangel ruined, and the excess
Of glory obscured ; but his face
Deep scars of thunder had intrenched, and care
Sate on his faded cheek.'
                                    Paradise Lost.

PAULO

'T is sixteen hundred years ago,
Since I came from Israel's land ;
Sixteen hundred years of woe ! —
With deep and furrowing hand
God's mark is painted on my head ;
Must there remain until the dead
Hear the last trump, and leave the tomb,
And earth spouts fire from her riven womb.

How can I paint that dreadful day,
That time of terror and dismay,
When, for our sins, a Saviour died,
And the meek Lamb was crucified !
As dread that day, when, borne along
To slaughter by the insulting throng,
Infuriate for Deicide,
I mocked our Saviour, and I cried,
' Go, go,' ' Ah ! I will go,' said he,
' Where scenes of endless bliss invite ;
To the blest regions of the light
I go, but thou shalt here remain —
Thou diest not till I come again.' —
E'en now, by horror traced, I see
His perforated feet and hands ;
The maddened crowd around him stands ;
Pierces his side the ruffian spear,
Big rolls the bitter anguished tear.
Hark, that deep groan ! — he dies — he
    dies, —
And breathes, in death's last agonies,
Forgiveness to his enemies.
Then was the noonday glory clouded,
The sun in pitchy darkness shrouded.
Then were strange forms through the darkness
    gleaming,
And the red orb of night on Jerusalem beam-
    ing ;
Which faintly, with ensanguined light,
Dispersed the thickening shades of night.

Convulsed, all nature shook with fear,
As if the very end was near ;
Earth to her centre trembled ;
Rent in twain was the temple's veil ;
The graves gave up their dead ;
Whilst ghosts and spirits, ghastly pale,
Glared hideous on the sight.
Seen through the dark and lurid air,
As fiends arrayed in light
Threw on the scene a frightful glare,
And, howling, shrieked with hideous yell —
They shrieked in joy, for a Saviour fell !
'T was then I felt the Almighty's ire ;
Then full on my remembrance came
Those words despised, alas ! too late !
The horrors of my endless fate

Flashed on my soul and shook my frame;
They scorched my breast as with a flame
Of unextinguishable fire;
An exquisitely torturing pain
Of frenzying anguish fired my brain.
By keen remorse and anguish driven,
I called for vengeance down from Heaven.
But, ah! the all-wasting hand of Time
Might never wear away my crime!
I scarce could draw my fluttering breath —
Was it the appalling grasp of death?
I lay entranced, and deemed he shed
His dews of poppy o'er my head;
But, though the kindly warmth was dead,
The self-inflicted torturing pangs
Of conscience lent their scorpion fangs,
Still life prolonging after life was fled.

Methought what glories met my sight,
As burst a sudden blaze of light
Illumining the azure skies, —
I saw the blessed Saviour rise.
But how unlike to him who bled!
Where then his thorn-encircled head?
Where the big drops of agony
Which dimmed the lustre of his eye?
Or deathlike hue that overspread
The features of that heavenly face?
Gone now was every mortal trace;
His eyes with radiant lustre beamed —
His form confessed celestial grace,
And with a blaze of glory streamed.
Innumerable hosts around,
Their brows with wreaths immortal crowned,
With amaranthine chaplets bound,
As on their wings the cross they bore,
Deep dyed in the Redeemer's gore,
Attune their golden harps, and sing
Loud hallelujahs to their King.

But in an instant from my sight
Fled were the visions of delight.
Darkness had spread her raven pall;
Dank, lurid darkness covered all.
All was as silent as the dead;
I felt a petrifying dread,
Which harrowed up my frame;
When suddenly a lurid stream
Of dark red light, with hideous gleam,
Shot like a meteor through the night,
And painted Hell upon the skies —
The Hell from whence it came.
What clouds of sulphur seemed to rise!
What sounds were borne upon the air!
The breathings of intense despair —
The piteous shrieks — the wails of woe —
The screams of torment and of pain —
The red-hot rack — the clanking chain!
I gazed upon the gulf below,
Till, fainting from excess of fear,
My tottering knees refused to bear
My odious weight. I sink — I sink!
Already had I reached the brink.
The fiery waves disparted wide
To plunge me in their sulphurous tide;
When, racked by agonizing pain,
I started into life again.

Yet still the impression left behind
Was deeply graven on my mind
In characters whose inward trace
No change or time could ere deface;
A burning cross illumed my brow,
I hid it with a fillet gray,
But could not hide the wasting woe
That wore my wildered soul away,
And ate my heart with living fire.
I knew it was the avenger's sway,
I felt it was the avenger's ire!

A burden on the face of earth,
I cursed the mother who gave me birth;
I cursed myself — my native land.
Polluted by repeated crimes,
I sought in distant foreign climes
If change of country could bestow
A transient respite from my woe.
Vain from myself the attempt to fly,
Sole cause of my own misery.

Since when, in deathlike trance I lay,
Passed, slowly passed, the years away
That poured a bitter stream on me;
When once I fondly longed to see
Jerusalem, alas! my native place,
Jerusalem — alas! no more in name —
No portion of her former fame
Had left behind a single trace.
Her pomp, her splendor, was no more.
Her towers no longer seem to rise
To lift their proud heads to the skies, —
Fane and monumental bust
Long levelled even with the dust.
The holy pavements were stained with gore,
The place where the sacred temple stood
Was crimson-dyed with Jewish blood.
Long since my parents had been dead,
All my posterity had bled
Beneath the dark Crusader's spear,
No friend was left my path to cheer,
To shed a few last setting rays
Of sunshine on my evening days!

Racked by the tortures of the mind,
How have I longed to plunge beneath
The mansions of repelling death!
And strove that resting place to find
Where earthly sorrows cease!
Oft, when the tempest-fiends engaged,
And the warring winds tumultuous raged,
Confounding skies with seas,
Then would I rush to the towering height
Of the gigantic Teneriffe,
Or some precipitous cliff,
All in the dead of the silent night.

I have cast myself from the mountain's height,
Above was day — below was night;
The substantial clouds that lowered beneath
Bore my detested form;
They whirled it above the volcanic breath
And the meteors of the storm;
The torrents of electric flame
Scorched to a cinder my fated frame.

Hark to the thunder's awful crash—
Hark to the midnight lightning's hiss!
At length was heard a sullen dash,
Which made the hollow rocks around
Rebellow to the awful sound ;
The yawning ocean opening wide
Received me in its vast abyss,
And whelmed me in its foaming tide.
Though my astounded senses fled,
Yet did the spark of life remain;
Then the wild surges of the main
Dashed and left me on the rocky shore.
Oh! would that I had waked no more!
Vain wish! I lived again to feel
Torments more fierce than those of hell!
A tide of keener pain to roll,
And the bruises to enter my inmost soul!

I cast myself in Etna's womb,[1]
If haply I might meet my doom
In torrents of electric flame ;
Thrice happy had I found a grave
'Mid fierce combustion's tumults dire,
'Mid oceans of volcanic fire
Which whirled me in their sulphurous wave,
And scorched to a cinder my hated frame,
Parched up the blood within my veins,
And racked my breast with damning pains, —
Then hurled me from the mountain's entrails
    dread.
With what unutterable woe
Even now I feel this bosom glow —
I burn — I melt with fervent heat —
Again life's pulses wildly beat —
What endless throbbing pains I live to feel!
The elements respect their Maker's seal, —
That seal deep printed on my fated head.
Still like the scathèd pine-tree's height,
Braving the tempests of the night,
Have I 'scaped the bickering fire.
Like the scathèd pine which a monument
    stands
Of faded grandeur, which the brands
Of the tempest-shaken air
Have riven on the desolate heath,
Yet it stands majestic even in death,
And rears its wild form there.
Thus have I 'scaped the ocean's roar
The red-hot bolt from God's right hand,
The flaming midnight meteor brand,
And Etna's flames of bickering fire.
Thus am I doomed by fate to stand,

---

[1] 'I cast myself from the overhanging summit of the gigantic Teneriffe into the wide weltering ocean. The clouds which hung upon its base below, bore up my odious weight ; the foaming billows, swoln by the fury of the northern blast, opened to receive me. and, burying in a vast abyss, at length dashed my almost inanimate frame against the crags. The bruises entered into my soul, but I awoke to life and all its torments. I precipitated myself into the crater of Vesuvius ; the bickering flames and melted lava vomited me up again, and though I felt the tortures of the damned, though the sulphureous bitumen scorched the blood within my veins, parched up my flesh and burnt it to a cinder, still did I live to drag the galling chain of existence on. Repeatedly have I exposed myself to the tempestuous battling of the elements ; the clouds which burst upon my head in crash terrific and exterminating, and

A monument of the Eternal's ire ;
Nor can this being pass away,
Till time shall be no more.

I pierce with intellectual eye,
Into each hidden mystery ;
I penetrate the fertile womb
Of nature ; I produce to light
The secrets of the teeming earth,
And give air's unseen embryos birth ;
The past, the present, and to come,
Float in review before my sight ;
To me is known the magic spell,
To summon e'en the Prince of Hell ;
Awed by the Cross upon my head,
His fiends would obey my mandates dread,
To twilight change the blaze of noon
And stain with spots of blood the moon —
But that an interposing hand
Restrains my potent arts, my else supreme
    command. —

He raised his passion-quivering hand,
He loosed the gray encircling band,
A burning Cross was there ;
Its color was like to recent blood,
Deep marked upon his brow it stood,
And spread a lambent glare.
Dimmer grew the taper's blaze,
Dazzled by the brighter rays,
Whilst Paulo spoke — 't was dead of night —
Fair Rosa shuddered with affright ;
Victorio, fearless, had braved death
Upon the blood-besprinkled heath ;
Had heard, unmoved, the cannon's roar,
Echoing along the Wolga's shore.
When the thunder of battle was swelling,
When the birds for their dead prey were yelling,
When the ensigns of slaughter were stream-
    ing,
And falchions and bayonets were gleaming,
And almost felt death's chilling hand,
Stretched on ensanguined Wolga's strand,
And, careless, scorned for life to cry,
Yet now he turned aside his eye,
Scarce could his death-like terror bear,
And owned now what it was to fear.

[PAULO]

Once a funeral met my aching sight,
It blasted my eyes at the dead of night,

the flaming thunderbolt, hurled headlong on me its victim, stunned but not destroyed me. The lightning, in bickering coruscation, blasted me ; and like the scattered [? shattered] oak, which remains a monument of faded grandeur, and outlives the other monarchs of the forest, doomed me to live forever. Nine times did this dagger enter into my heart — the ensanguined tide of existence followed the repeated plunge ; at each stroke, unutterable anguish seized my frame, and every limb was convulsed by the pangs of approaching dissolution. The wounds still closed, and still I breathe the hated breath of life.'

I have endeavored to deviate as little as possible from the extreme sublimity of idea which the *style* of the German author, of which this is a translation, so forcibly impresses.

When the sightless fiends of the tempests rave,
And hell-birds howl o'er the storm-blackened
    wave.
Nought was seen, save at fits, but the meteor's
    glare
And the lightnings of God painting hell on the
    air ;
Nought was heard save the thunder's wild voice
    in the sky,
And strange birds who, shrieking, fled dismally
    by.
'T was then from my head my drenched hair
    that I tore,
And bade my vain dagger's point drink my
    life's gore ;
'T was then I fell on the ensanguined earth,
And cursed the mother who gave me birth !
My maddened brain could bear no more —
Hark ! the chilling whirlwind's roar ;
The spirits of the tombless dead
Flit around my fated head, —
Howl horror and destruction round,
As they quaff my blood that stains the ground,
And shriek amid their deadly stave, —
' Never shalt thou find the grave !
Ever shall thy fated soul
In life's protracted torments roll,
Till, in latest ruin hurled,
And fate's destruction, sinks the world !
Till the dead arise from the yawning ground,
To meet their Maker's last decree,
Till angels of vengeance flit around,
And loud yelling demons seize on thee ! '
Ah ! would were come that fated hour,
When the clouds of chaos around shall lower ;
When this globe calcined by the fury of God
Shall sink beneath his wrathful nod ! —

As thus he spake, a wilder gaze
Of fiend-like horror lit his eye
With a most unearthly blaze,
As if some phantom-form passed by.
At last he stilled the maddening wail
Of grief, and thus pursued his tale : —

Oft I invoke the fiends of hell,
And summon each in dire array —
I know they dare not disobey
My stern, my powerful spell.
Once on a night, when not a breeze
Ruffled the surface of the seas,
The elements were lulled to rest,
And all was calm save my sad breast, —
On death resolved — intent,
I marked a circle round my form ;
About me sacred relics spread,
The relics of magicians dead,
And potent incantations read —
I waited their event.

All at once grew dark the night,
Mists of swarthiness hung o'er the pale moon-
    light.
Strange yells were heard, the boding cry
Of the night raven that flitted by,
Whilst the silver-wingèd mew,
Startled with screams, o'er the dark wave flew.

'T was then I seized a magic wand,
The wand by an enchanter given,
And deep dyed in his heart's red blood.
The crashing thunder pealed aloud ;
I saw the portentous meteor's glare
And the lightnings gleam o'er the lurid air ;
I raised the wand in my trembling hand,
And pointed Hell's mark at the zenith of Hea-
    ven.

A superhuman sound
Broke faintly on the listening air ;
Like to a silver harp the notes,
And yet they were more soft and clear.
I wildly strained my eyes around —
Again the unknown music floats.
Still stood Hell's mark above my head —
In wildest accents I summoned the dead —
And through the unsubstantial night
It diffused a strange and fiendish light ;
Spread its rays to the charnel-house air,
And marked mystic forms on the dark vapors
    there.
The winds had ceased — a thick dark smoke
From beneath the pavement broke ;
Around ambrosial perfumes breathe
A fragrance, grateful to the sense,
And bliss, past utterance, dispense.

The heavy mists, encircling, wreathe,
Disperse, and gradually unfold
A youthful female form ; — she rode
Upon a rosy-tinted cloud ;
Bright streamed her flowing locks of gold;
She shone with radiant lustre bright,
And blazed with strange and dazzling light ;
A diamond coronet decked her brow,
Bloomed on her cheek a vermeil glow ;
The terrors of her fiery eye
Poured forth insufferable day,
And shed a wildly lurid ray.
A smile upon her features played,
But there, too, sate portrayed
The inventive malice of a soul
Where wild demoniac passions roll ;
Despair and torment on her brow,
Had marked a melancholy woe
In dark and deepened shade.
Under these hypocritic smiles,
Deceitful as the serpent's wiles,
Her hate and malice were concealed ;
Whilst on her guilt-confessing face,
Conscience the strongly printed trace
Of agony betrayed,
And all the fallen angel stood revealed.
She held a poniard in her hand,
The point was tinged by the lightning's
    brand ;
In her left a scroll she bore,
Crimsoned deep with human gore ;
And, as above my head she stood,
Bade me smear it with my blood.
She said that when it was my doom
That every earthly pang should cease,
The evening of my mortal woe
Would close beneath the yawning tomb,
And, lulled into the arms of death,

I should resign my laboring breath,
And in the sightless realms below
Enjoy an endless reign of peace.
She ceased — O, God, I thank thy grace,
Which bade me spurn the deadly scroll ;
Uncertain for a while I stood —
The dagger's point was in my blood.
Even now I bleed ! — I bleed !
When suddenly what horrors flew,
Quick as the lightnings, through my frame ;
Flashed on my mind the infernal deed,
The deed which would condemn my soul
To torments of eternal flame.
Drops colder than the cavern dew
Quick coursed each other down my face,
I labored for my breath ;
At length I cried, ' Avaunt ! thou fiend of Hell,
Avaunt ! thou minister of death ! '
I cast the volume on the ground,
Loud shrieked the fiend with piercing yell,
And more than mortal laughter pealed around.
The scattered fragments of the storm
Floated along the Demon's form,
Dilating till it touched the sky ;
The clouds that rolled athwart his eye,
Revealed by its terrific ray,
Brilliant as the noontide day,
Gleamed with a lurid fire ;
Red lightnings darted around his head,
Thunders hoarse as the groans of the dead
Pronounced their Maker's ire ;
A whirlwind rushed impetuous by,
Chaos of horror filled the sky ;
I sunk convulsed with awe and dread.
When I waked the storm was fled.
But sounds unholy met my ear,
And fiends of hell were flitting near.

Here let me pause — here end my tale,
My mental powers begin to fail ;
At this short retrospect I faint ;
Scarce beats my pulse — I lose my breath,
I sicken even unto death.
Oh ! hard would be the task to paint
And gift with life past scenes again ;
To knit a long and linkless chain,
Or strive minutely to relate
The varied horrors of my fate.
Rosa ! I could a tale disclose,
So full of horror — full of woes,
Such as might blast a demon's ear,
Such as a fiend might shrink to hear —
But, no —

Here ceased the tale. Convulsed with fear,
The tale yet lived in Rosa's ear —
She felt a strange mysterious dread,
A chilling awe as of the dead ;
Gleamed on her sight the Demon's form ?
Heard she the fury of the storm ?
The cries and hideous yells of death ?
Tottered the ground her feet beneath ?
Was it the fiend before her stood ?
Saw she the poniard drop with blood ?
All seemed to her distempered eye
A true and sad reality.

. . . .

CANTO IV

Οὔτοι, γυναῖκας, ἀλλὰ Γοργόνας λέγω·
ὐδ αὖτε Γοργείοισιν εἰκάσω τύποις·
—— μέλαιναι δ' ἐς τὸ πᾶν βδελύκτροποι·
ῥέγκουσι δ' οὐ πλατοῖσι φυσιάμασιν·
ἐκ δ' ὀμμάτων λείβουσι δυσφιλῆ βίαν.
ÆSCHYLUS, *Eumenides*, v. 48.

' What are ye
So withered and so wild in your attire,
That look not like th' inhabitants of earth,
And yet are on't ? — Live you, or are you aught
That man may question ? '
Macbeth.

Ah ! why does man, whom God has sent
As the Creation's ornament,
Who stands amid his works confessed
The first — the noblest — and the best,
Whose vast — whose comprehensive eye,
Is bounded only by the sky,
O'erlook the charms which Nature yields,
The garniture of woods and fields,
The sun's all vivifying light,
The glory of the moon by night,
And to himself alone a foe,
Forget from whom these blessings flow ?
And is there not in friendship's eye,
Beaming with tender sympathy,
An antidote to every woe ?
And cannot woman's love bestow
An heavenly paradise below ?
Such joys as these to man are given,
And yet you dare to rail at Heaven ;
Vainly oppose the Almighty Cause,
Transgress His universal laws ;
Forfeit the pleasures that await
The virtuous in this mortal state ;
Question the goodness of the Power on high,
In misery live, despairing die.
What then is man, how few his days,
And heightened by what transient rays ;
Made up of plans of happiness,
Of visionary schemes of bliss ;
The varying passions of his mind
Inconstant, varying as the wind ;
Now hushed to apathetic rest,
Now tempested with storms his breast ;
Now with the fluctuating tide
Sunk low in meanness, swoln with pride ;
Thoughtless, or overwhelmed with care,
Hoping, or tortured by despair !

The sun had sunk beneath the hill,
Soft fell the dew, the scene was still ;
All nature hailed the evening's close.
Far more did lovely Rosa bless
The twilight of her happiness.
Even Paulo blessed the tranquil hour
As in the aromatic bower,
Or wandering through the olive grove,
He told his plaintive tale of love ;
But welcome to Victorio's soul
Did the dark clouds of evening roll !
But, ah ! what means his hurried pace,
Those gestures strange, that varying face ;
Now pale with mingled rage and ire,
Now burning with intense desire ;

That brow where brood the imps of care,
That fixed expression of despair,
That haste, that laboring for breath —
His soul is madly bent on death.
A dark resolve is in his eye,
Victorio raves — I hear him cry,
' Rosa is Paulo's eternally.'

But whence is that soul-harrowing moan,
Deep drawn and half suppressed —
A low and melancholy tone,
That rose upon the wind ?
Victorio wildly gazed around,
He cast his eyes upon the ground,
He raised them to the spangled air,
But all was still — was quiet there.
Hence, hence, this superstitious fear ;
'T was but the fever of his mind
That conjured the ideal sound,
To his distempered ear.

With rapid step, with frantic haste,
He scoured the long and dreary waste ;
And now the gloomy cypress spread
Its darkened umbrage o'er his head ;
The stately pines above him high
Lifted their tall heads to the sky ;
Whilst o'er his form, the poisonous yew
And melancholy nightshade threw
Their baleful deadly dew.
At intervals the moon shone clear ;
Yet, passing o'er her disk, a cloud
Would now her silver beauty shroud.
The autumnal leaf was parched and sere ;
It rustled like a step to fear.
The precipice's battled height
Was dimly seen through the mists of night,
As Victorio moved along.
At length he reached its summit dread,
The night-wind whistled round his head
A wild funeral song.
A dying cadence swept around
Upon the waste of air ;
It scarcely might be called a sound,
For stillness yet was there,
Save when the roar of the waters below
Was wafted by fits to the mountain's brow.
Here for a while Victorio stood
Suspended o'er the yawning flood,
And gazed upon the gulf beneath.
No apprehension paled his cheek,
No sighs from his torn bosom break,
No terror dimmed his eye.
' Welcome, thrice welcome, friendly death,'
In desperate harrowing tone he cried,
' Receive me, ocean, to your breast,
Hush this ungovernable tide.
This troubled sea to rest.
Thus do I bury all my grief —
This plunge shall give my soul relief,
This plunge into eternity !'
I see him now about to spring
Into the watery grave :
Hark ! the death angel flaps his wing
O'er the blackened wave.
Hark ! the night-raven shrieks on high
To the breeze which passes on ;

Clouds o'ershade the moonlight sky —
The deadly work is almost done —
When a soft and silver sound,
Softer than the fairy song
Which floats at midnight hour along
The daisy-spangled ground,
Was borne upon the wind's soft swell.
Victorio started — 't was the knell
Of some departed soul ;
Now on the pinion of the blast,
Which o'er the craggy mountain passed,
The lengthened murmurs roll —
Till, lost in ether, dies away
The plaintive, melancholy lay.
'T is said congenial sounds have power,
To dissipate the mists that lower
Upon the wretch's brow —
To still the maddening passions' war —
To calm the mind's impetuous jar —
To turn the tide of woe.
Victorio shuddered with affright,
Swam o'er his eyes thick mists of night ;
Even now he was about to sink
Into the ocean's yawning womb,
But that the branches of an oak,
Which, riven by the lightning's stroke,
O'erhung the precipice's brink,
Preserved him from the billowy tomb ;
Quick throbbed his pulse with feverish heat,
He wildly started on his feet,
And rushed from the mountain's height.

The moon was down, but through the air
Wild meteors spread a transient glare ;
Borne on the wing of the swelling gale,
Above the dark and woody dale,
Thick clouds obscured the sky.
All was now wrapped in silence drear,
Not a whisper broke on the listening ear,
Not a murmur floated by.

In thought's perplexing labyrinth lost
The trackless heath he swiftly crossed.
Ah ! why did terror blanch his cheek ?
Why did his tongue attempt to speak,
And fail in the essay ?
Through the dark midnight mists an eye,
Flashing with crimson brilliancy,
Poured on his face its ray.
' What sighs pollute the midnight air ?
What mean those breathings of despair ? '
Thus asked a voice, whose hollow tone
Might seem but one funereal moan.
Victorio groaned, with faltering breath,
' I burn with love, I pant for death !'

Suddenly a meteor's glare,
With brilliant flash illumed the air ;
Bursting through clouds of sulphurous smoke,
As on a Witch's form it broke,
Of herculean bulk her frame
Seemed blasted by the lightning's flame ;
Her eyes that flared with lurid light,
Were now with bloodshot lustre filled.
They blazed like comets through the night,
And now thick rheumy gore distilled ;

Black as the raven's plume, her locks
Loose streamed upon the pointed rocks;
Wild floated on the hollow gale,
Or swept the ground in matted trail;
Vile loathsome weeds, whose pitchy fold
Were blackened by the fire of Hell,
Her shapeless limbs of giant mould
Scarce served to hide — as she the while
'Grinned horribly a ghastly smile,'
And shrieked with demon yell.

Terror unmanned Victorio's mind,
His limbs, like lime leaves in the wind,
Shook, and his brain in wild dismay
Swam — vainly he strove to turn away.
'Follow me to the mansions of rest,'
The weird female cried;
The life-blood rushed through Victorio's breast
In full and swelling tide.
Attractive as the eagle's gaze,
And bright as the meridian blaze,
Led by a sanguine stream of light,
He followed through the shades of night —
Before him his conductress fled,
As swift as the ghosts of the dead,
When on some dreadful errand they fly,
In a thunderblast sweeping the sky.

They reached a rock whose beetling height
Was dimly seen through the clouds of night;
Illumined by the meteor's blaze,
Its wild crags caught the reddened rays
And their refracted brilliance threw
Around a solitary yew,
Which stretched its blasted form on high,
Braving the tempests of the sky.
As glared the flame, a caverned cell,
More pitchy than the shades of hell,
Lay open to Victorio's view.
Lost for an instant was his guide;
He rushed into the mountain's side.
At length with deep and harrowing yell
She bade him quickly speed,
For that ere again had risen the moon
'T was fated that there must be done
A strange — a deadly deed.

Swift as the wind Victorio sped;
Beneath him lay the mangled dead;
Around dank putrefaction's power
Had caused a dim blue mist to lower.
Yet an unfixed, a wandering light
Dispersed the thickening shades of night;
Yet the weird female's features dire
Gleamed through the lurid yellow air,
With a deadly livid fire,
Whose wild, inconstant, dazzling light
Dispelled the tenfold shades of night,
Whilst her hideous fiendlike eye,
Fixed on her victim with horrid stare,
Flamed with more kindled radiancy;
More frightful far than that of Death,
When exulting he stalks o'er the battle heath;
Or of the dread prophetic form,
Who rides the curled clouds in the storm,
And borne upon the tempest's wings,
Death, despair, and horror brings.

Strange voices then and shrieks of death
Were borne along the trackless heath;
Tottered the ground his steps beneath;
Rustled the blast o'er the dark cliff's side,
And their works unhallowed spirits plied,
As they shed their baneful breath.
Yet Victorio hastened on —
Soon the dire deed will be done.
'Mortal,' the female cried, 'this night
Shall dissipate thy woe;
And, ere return of morning light,
The clouds that shade thy brow
Like fleeting summer mists shall fly
Before the sun that mounts on high.
I know the wishes of thy heart —
A soothing balm I could impart:
Rosa is Paulo's — can be thine,
For the secret power is mine.'

VICTORIO

Give me that secret power — Oh! give
To me fair Rosa — I will live
To bow to thy command.
Rosa but mine — and I will fly
E'en to the regions of the sky,
Will traverse every land.

WITCH

Calm then those transports and attend,
Mortal, to one, who is thy friend —
The charm begins. —

An ancient book
Of mystic characters she took;
Her loose locks floated on the air;
Her eyes were fixed in lifeless stare;
She traced a circle on the floor,
Around dank chilling vapors lower;
A golden cross on the pavement she threw,
'T was tinged with a flame of lambent blue,
From which bright scintillations flew;
By it she cursed her Saviour's soul;
Around strange fiendish laughs did roll,
A hollow, wild, and frightful sound,
At fits was heard to float around.
She uttered then, in accents dread,
Some maddening rhyme that wakes the dead,
And forces every shivering fiend
To her their demon-forms to bend;
At length a wild and piercing shriek,
As the dark mists disperse and break,
Announced the coming Prince of Hell —
His horrid form obscured the cell.
Victorio shrunk, unused to shrink,
E'en at extremest danger's brink;
The witch then pointed to the ground,
Infernal shadows flitted around
And with their Prince were seen to rise;
The cavern bellows with their cries,
Which, echoing through a thousand caves,
Sound like as many tempest waves.

Inspired and wrapped in bickering flame,
The strange, the awful being stood.
Words unpremeditated came
In unintelligible flood

From her black tumid lips, arrayed
In livid fiendish smiles of joy ;
Lips, which now dropped with deadly dew
And now, extending wide, displayed
Projecting teeth of mouldy hue,
As with a loud and piercing cry
A mystic, harrowing lay she sang ;
Along the rocks a death-peal rang ;
In accents hollow, deep and drear,
They struck upon Victorio's ear.
As ceased the soul-appalling verse,
Obedient to its power grew still
The hellish shrieks ; the mists disperse ;
Satan — a shadeless, hideous beast —
In all his horrors stood confessed !
And as his vast proportions fill
The lofty cave, his features dire
Gleam with a pale and sulphurous fire ;
From his fixed glance of deadly hate
Even she *shrunk back, appalled with dread —*
For there contempt and malice sate,
And from his basiliskine eye
Sparks of living fury fly,
Which wanted but a being to strike dead.
A wilder, a more awful spell
Now echoed through the long-drawn cell ;
The demon bowed to its mandates dread.
' Receive this potent drug,' he cried,
' Whoever quaffs its fatal tide,
Is mingled with the dead.'
Swept by a rushing sulphurous blast,
Which wildly through the cavern passed,
The fatal word was borne.
The cavern trembled with the sound,[1]
Trembled beneath his feet the ground ;
With strong convulsions torn,
Victorio, shuddering, fell ;
But soon awakening from his trance,
He cast around a fearful glance,
Yet gloomy was the cell,
Save where a lamp's uncertain flare
Cast a flickering, dying glare.

WITCH

Receive this dear-earned drug — its power
Thou, mortal, soon shalt know :
This drug shall be thy nuptial dower,
This drug shall seal thy woe.
Mingle it with Rosa's wine,
Victorio — Rosa then is thine.

She spake, and, to confirm the spell,
A strange and subterranean sound
Reverberated long around
In dismal echoes — the dark cell
Rocked as in terror — through the sky
Hoarse thunders murmured awfully,
And, winged with horror, darkness spread
Her mantle o'er Victorio's head.
He gazed around with dizzy fear,
No fiend, no witch, no cave, was near ;
But the blasts of the forest were heard to roar,
The wild ocean's billows to dash on the shore.

[1] ' Death !
Hell trembled at the hideous name and sighed
From all its caves, and back resounded death.'
Paradise Lost.

The cold winds of Heaven struck chill on his
        frame ;
For the cave had been heated by hell's black-
        ening flame,
And his hand grasped a casket — the philtre
        was there !

. . . .

Sweet is the whispering of the breeze
Which scarcely sways yon summer trees ;
Sweet is the pale moon's pearly beam,
Which sleeps upon the silver stream,
In slumber cold and still ;
Sweet those wild notes of harmony,
Are wafted from yon hill ;
Which on the blast that passes by,
So low, so thrilling, yet so clear,
Which strike enthusiast fancy's ear, —
Which sweep along the moonlight sky,
Like notes of heavenly symphony.

SONG

See yon opening flower
Spreads its fragrance to the blast ;
It fades within an hour,
Its decay is pale, is fast.
Paler is yon maiden ;
Faster is her heart's decay ;
Deep with sorrow laden,
She sinks in death away.

. . . .

'T is the silent dead of night —
Hark ! hark ! what shriek so low yet clear,
Breaks on calm rapture's pensive ear
From Lara's castled height ?
'T was Rosa's death-shriek fell !
What sound is that which rides the blast,
As onward its fainter murmurs passed ?
'T is Rosa's funeral knell !
What step is that the ground which shakes ?
'T is the step of a wretch, Nature shrinks from
        his tread ;
And beneath their tombs tremble the shudder-
        ing dead ;
And while he speaks the churchyard quakes.

PAULO

Lies she there for the worm to devour,
Lies she there till the judgment hour,
Is then my Rosa dead !
False fiend ! I curse thy futile power !
O'er her form will lightnings flash,
O'er her form will thunders crash,
But harmless from my head
Will the fierce tempest's fury fly,
Rebounding to its native sky, —
Who is the God of Mercy ? — where
Enthroned the power to save ?
Reigns he above the viewless air ?
Lives he beneath the grave ?
To him would I lift my suppliant moan,
That power should hear my harrowing groan ; —
Is it then Christ's terrific Sire ?
Ah ! I have felt his burning ire,
I feel, — I feel it now, —
His flaming mark is fixed on my head,
And must there remain in traces dread ;

Wild anguish glooms my brow;
Oh! Griefs like mine that fiercely burn
Where is the balm can heal!
Where is the monumental urn
Can bid to dust this frame return,
Or quench the pangs I feel!

As thus he spoke grew dark the sky,
Hoarse thunders murmured awfully,
' O Demon! I am thine!' he cried.
A hollow fiendish voice replied,
' Come! for thy doom is misery.'

**THE DINNER PARTY ANTICIPATED: A PARA-
PHRASE OF HORACE III. 19**

This poem was found by Forman among the
Hunt MSS. in Mrs. Shelley's handwriting. It
was printed in Hunt's *Companion*, March 26,
1828, without the name of the translator. There
is no other evidence that it was written by
Shelley, and it is rejected by Dowden.

**THE MAGIC HORSE: TRANSLATED FROM THE
ITALIAN OF CRISTOFANO BRONZINO**

This poem forms a continuous manuscript
with that of the preceding, and is also rejected
by Dowden.

TO THE QUEEN OF MY HEART

Published by Medwin, the *Shelley Papers*,
1833, and by Mrs. Shelley, 1839, 1st ed., and
also by Forman and Dowden. Mrs. Shelley
omitted it in her second edition, with the following note: ' It was suggested that the poem
To the Queen of My Heart was falsely attributed
to Shelley; and certainly I find no trace of it
among his papers; and, as those of his intimate
friends whom I have consulted never heard of
it, I omit it.' The story of the hoax is told in
the *Eclectic Review*, 1851 (ii.), 66 : ' It is curious
to observe the wisdom and penetration of those
who have at all mingled in literary society.
They read an author, study his peculiarities and
style, and imagine they perfectly understand
his whole system of thought, and could detect
one mistake instantly. But to show that even
authors themselves are not always infallible
judges, we will relate an anecdote which has
never yet been made public, though, having
received it from an undoubted source, we venture to vouch for its veracity. Shelley, whose
poems many years ago were so much read and
admired, necessarily excited much discussion in
literary circles. A party of literary men were
one evening engaged in canvassing his merits,
when one of them declared that he knew the
turns of Shelley's mind so well that amongst a
thousand anonymous pieces he would detect his,
no matter when published. Mr. James Au-
gustus St. John, who was present, not liking
the blustering tone of the speaker, remarked
that he thought he was mistaken, and that it
would, amongst so many, be difficult to trace

the style of Shelley. Every one present, however, sided with his opponent, and agreed that
it was perfectly impossible that any one could
imitate his style. A few days after, a poem,
entitled *To the Queen of My Heart*, appeared
in the *London Weekly Review*, with Shelley's
signature, but written by Mr. St. John himself.
The same coterie met and discussed the poem
brought to their notice, and prided themselves
much upon their discrimination : said they at
once recognized the " style of Shelley, could not
be mistaken, his soul breathed through it — it
was himself." And so *The Queen of My Heart*
was settled to be Shelley's! and to this day it
is numbered with his poems (see Shelley's
Works, edited by Mrs. Shelley, vol. iv. p. 166.
It deceived even his wife), and very few are in
the secret that it is not actually his. The imitation was perfect, and completely deceived
every one, much to the discomfiture of all concerned.'

LOST POEMS

*Horsham Publication. Reminiscences of a
Newspaper Editor*, *Fraser's*, June, 1841 : ' It
was his [Sir Bysshe Shelley] purse which supplied young Bysshe with the means of printing
many of his fugitive pieces. These issued from
the press of a printer at Horsham named Phil-
lips; and although they were not got up in good
style, the expense was much greater than Shelley could have afforded, if he had not received
assistance from his grandfather.' No examples
are known.

An Essay on Love. Shelley (from Keswick)
to Godwin, January 16, 1812 : ' I have desired
the publications of my early youth to be sent to
you. You will perceive that *Zastrozzi* and *St.
Irvyne* were written prior to my acquaintance
with your writings — the *Essay on Love*, a little
poem, since.' Hogg, ii. 62. No copy is known.

*A Poetical Essay on the Existing State of
Things.* The *Oxford Herald*, March 9, 1811 :
' Literature. Just published, Price Two Shil-
lings, A Poetical Essay on the Existing State of
Things.

And Famine at her bidding wasted wide
  The Wretched Land, till in the Public way,
Promiscuous where the dead and dying lay,
  Dogs fed on human bones in the open light of day.
                              CURSE OF KEHAMA.

By a Gentleman of the University of Oxford.
For assisting to maintain in prison Mr. Peter
Finnerty, imprisoned for a libel. London: sold
by B. Crosby & Co., and all other book-sellers.
1811.' No copy is known. The following are
all the contemporary notices of it.

The Weekly Messenger, Dublin, March 7,
1812 : ' Mr. Shelley, commiserating the sufferings of our distinguished countryman, Mr. Finnerty, whose exertions in the cause of political
freedom he much admired, wrote a very beautiful poem, the profits of which we understand,
from *undoubted* authority, Mr. Shelley remitted

to Mr. Finnerty: we have heard they amounted to nearly one hundred pounds.' MacCarthy, *Shelley's Early Life*, p. 255.

A Diary, Illustrative of the Times of George the Fourth. C. Kirkpatrick Sharpe (from Christ Church, Oxford) to —— March 15, 1811 : —

' Talking of books, we have lately had a literary Sun shine forth upon us here, before whom our former luminaries must hide their diminished heads — a Mr. Shelley, of University College, who lives upon arsenic, aqua-fortis, half-an-hour's sleep in the night, and is desperately in love with the memory of Margaret Nicholson. He hath published what he terms the Posthumous Poems, printed for the benefit of Mr. Peter Finnerty, which, I am grieved to say, though stuffed full of treason, is extremely dull, but the Author is a great genius, and if he be not clapped up in Bedlam or hanged, will certainly prove one of the sweetest swans in the tuneful margin of the Charwell. . . . Our Apollo next came out with a prose pamphlet in praise of atheism . . . and there appeared a monstrous romance in one volume, called *St. Ircoyne [sic], or the Rosicrucian.* Shelley's last exhibition is a *Poem on the State of Public Affairs.*' Forman, *Shelley Library*, pp. 21, 22.

From these conflicting statements it appears certain that Shelley printed some poem for the benefit of Finnerty. The profits (£100) may refer to the public subscription made for Finnerty to which Shelley was a contributor. See *The Satire of* 1811, below.

Lines on a Fête at Carlton House. C. H. Grove to Miss Helen Shelley, February 25, 1857 : ' I forgot to mention before, that during the early part of the summer which Bysshe spent in town after leaving Oxford the Prince Regent gave a splendid fête at Carlton House, in which the novelty was introduced of a stream of water, in imitation of a river, meandering down the middle of a very long table in a temporary tent erected in Carlton Gardens. This was much commented upon in the papers, and laughed at by the Opposition. Bysshe also was of the number of those who disapproved of the fête and its accompaniments. He wrote a poem on the subject of about fifty lines, which he published immediately, wherein he apostrophized the Prince as sitting on the bank of his tiny river : and he amused himself with throwing copies into the carriages of persons going to Carlton House after the fête.' Hogg, ii. 556, 557.

No copy of this poem is known, but some lines from it will be found in JUVENILIA. A burlesque letter from Shelley to Graham, no date, is connected with this poem by Forman, *Shelley Library*, p. 24, and by Dowden, i. 136, 137, but it seems doubtful whether the Ode, there mentioned, is not the translation of the Marseillaise Hymn, of which one stanza is there given.

Satire: 1811. Shelley (from Field Place) to Hogg, December 20, 1810: ' I am composing a *satirical* poem : I shall print it at Oxford, unless

I find on visiting him that R[obinson] is ripe for printing whatever will sell. In case of that he is my man.' Hogg, i. 143.

Thornton Hunt: note on *The Autobiography of Leigh Hunt*, ii. 21: ' Mr. Rowland Hunter, who first brought Leigh Hunt and his most valued friend personally together. Shelley had brought a manuscript poem, which proved by no means suited to the publishing house in St. Paul's Churchyard. But Mr. Hunter sent the young reformer to seek the counsel of Leigh Hunt.'

Forman suggests that the manuscript poem offered to Hunter was the same mentioned in the letter to Hogg : and he conjectures, that a poem entitled '*Lines addressed to His Royal Highness, the Prince of Wales, on his being appointed Regent,*' by Philopatria, Jr., and printed in London by Sherwood, Neely & Jones (later connected with the publication of *Laon and Cythna*) 1811, is the missing satire. Dowden rejects the conjecture.

MacCarthy (*Shelley's Early Life*, 102–106) conjectures that the *Poetical Essay on the Existing State of Things* is the missing satire.

The Creator. Shelley (from the Baths of San Giuliano) to Mr. and Mrs. Gisborne June 5, 1821: ' My unfortunate box ! . . . If the idea of *The Creator* had been packed up with them it would have shared the same fate ; and that, I am afraid, has undergone another sort of shipwreck.' Mrs. Shelley, *Essays and Letters*, ii. 294.

Mrs. Shelley to Mr. and Mrs. Gisborne, June 30, 1821 : ' *The Creator* has not yet made himself heard.' Dowden, ii. 413.

Possibly connected with the plans of this summer, vaguely alluded to in letters to Ollier, or with the drama on the Book of Job, and hardly begun. There is no other reference to it, but a familiar quotation of Shelley's from Tasso, — ' non c' è in mondo chi merita nome di creatore che Dio ed il Poeta,' — (Shelley to Peacock, August 16, 1818), may be connected with the title.

UNPUBLISHED POEMS

Shelley to Graham. A poetical epistle described by Forman (Aldine edition i. xix.), who gives from it the following lines, referring to Shelley's younger brother John.

> ' I have been
> With little Jack upon the green —
> A dear delightful red-faced brute,
> And setting up a parachute.'

Esdaile Manuscript. A manuscript book containing poems, which Shelley intended to publish simultaneously with *Queen Mab*, in the possession of his grandson, Mr. Esdaile, is partly described by Dowden. Shelley's references to this volume are as follows : —

Shelley (from Tanyrallt) to Hookham, January 2, 1813 : ' My poems will, I fear, little stand the criticism even of friendship: some of the later ones have the merit of conveying, a meaning in every word, and all are faithful pictures of my feelings at the time of writing them. But they are in a great measure abrupt and obscure — all breathing hatred to government and religion, but I think not too openly for publication. One fault they are indisputably exempt from, that of being a volume of *fashionable literature*. I doubt not but that your friendly hand will clip the wings of my Pegasus considerably.' Dowden, i. 344. [*Shelley Memorials*, pp. 50, 51, omits some parts.]

Shelley (from Tanyrallt) to Hookham, February 19, 1813: ' You will receive it [*Queen Mab*] with the other poems. I think that the whole should form one volume.' *Shelley Memorials*, p. 52. [Hogg, ii. 183, modifies the text.]

Shelley (from Tanyrallt) to Hookham, December 17, 1812: 'I am also preparing a volume of minor poems, respecting whose publication I shall expect your judgment, both as publisher and friend. A very obvious question would be — Will they sell or not ? ' *Shelley Memorials*, p. 48.

Shelley (from Tanyrallt) to Hookham, January 26, 1813: ' *Queen Mab* . . . will contain about twenty-eight hundred lines ; the other poems contain probably as much more.' Hogg, ii. 182.

Shelley (from Keswick) to Miss Hitchener, January 26, 1812: 'I have been busily engaged in the Address to the Irish people, which will be printed as Paine's works were, and posted on the walls of Dublin. My poems will be printed there.' MacCarthy, *Shelley's Early Life*, p. 133.

The contents of this volume are described by Dowden, i. 345–349. The poems appear to be as follows : —

Dedication : *To Harriet.* Printed, revised, as the Dedication of *Queen Mab.*

Falsehood and Vice: A Dialogue. Printed in Shelley's notes to *Queen Mab.*

On Death (' The pale, the cold and the moony smile '). Printed, revised, with *Alastor.*

The Tombs. Dowden quotes the following lines : —

> 'Courage and charity and truth
> And high devotedness.'

On Robert Emmet's Grave. Seven stanzas, of which Dowden prints vi., vii.

The Retrospect: Cwm Elan, 1812. A poem contrasting the landscape as it appeared then with the same scene the year before. Dowden prints the greater portion.

Sonnet : To Harriet, August 1, 1812. Dowden prints four lines.

To Harriet. Partly printed (58–69) by Shelley, notes to *Queen Mab* ; partly (5–13) by Garnett from the Boscombe manuscript, and entire by Dowden.

Sonnet : To a Balloon Laden with Knowledge. Printed by Dowden.

Sonnet : on Launching some Bottles filled with Knowledge into the Bristol Channel. Printed by Dowden.

Sonnet : Farewell to North Devon. Dowden prints six lines.

On Leaving London for Wales. Eight stanzas, of which Dowden prints four.

A Tale of Society as it is from Facts, 1811. Published, except three stanzas, by Rossetti from the Hitchener MS.

Marseillaise Hymn, translated. Forman prints the second stanza from Locker-Lampson MS.

Henry and Louisa. Dowden, i. 347. A narrative poem in two parts, the scene changing from England in the first part to Egypt in the second. Dowden describes the catastrophe as follows: 'Henry, borne from his lover's arms by the insane lust of conquest and of glory, is pursued by Louisa, who finds him dying on the bloody sands, and, like Shakespeare's Juliet, is swift to pursue her beloved through the portals of the grave.' Shelley notes on this poem : ' The stanza of this poem is radically that of Spenser, although I suffered myself at the time of writing it to be led into occasional deviations.'

Zeinab and Kathema. A tragedy in six-line stanzas, possibly suggested by Miss Owenson's novel, *The Missionary.* Dowden, i. 347–368, describes as follows : ' From this may have come the suggestion to choose as the heroine of his poem the maiden of Cashmire, borne away from her native home by Christian guile and rapine. Kathema follows his betrothed Zeinab to England.

" Meanwhile through calm and storm, through night and
day,
Unvarying in her aim the vessel went,
As if some inward spirit ruled her way,
And her tense sails were conscious of intent,
Till Albion's cliffs gleamed o'er her plunging bow,
And Albion's river floods bright sparkled round her
prow."

But Zeinab had been flung to perish upon the streets by her betrayers, had risen in crime against those who caused her ruin, and had suffered death by the vengeance of indiscriminating and pitiless laws. It is a bitter December evening when Kathema, weary with vain search for his beloved, sinks wearily upon the heath. At the moment of his awaking, the winter moonbeams fall upon a dead and naked female form, swinging in chains from a gibbet, while her dark hair tosses in the wind, and ravenous birds of prey cry in the ear of night. The lover recognizes his Zeinab and is seized with madness ; he scales the gibbet, and, twining the chains about his neck, leaps forward " to meet the life to come." Here is romantic ghastliness, as imagined by a boy, in extravagant profusion ; but at heart, each of the two poems is designed less as a piece of romantic art than as an indictment of widespread evils — the one, a setting forth of the criminal love of glory and conquest ; the other, a setting forth of the cruelty of sensual passion and the injustice of formerly administered laws.'

The Voyage. Dowden, i. 284 : ' A fragment of some three hundred lines . . . It tells, in the irregular unrhymed verse which Shelley adopted from *Thalaba* and employed in *Queen Mab*, of a ship returning across the summer sea from her voyage ; and of her company of voyagers, with their various passions and imaginings — two ardent youths who have braved all dangers side by side ; the landsman mean and crafty, who bears across the stainless ocean all the base thoughts and selfish greeds of the city ; the sailor returning to his cottage home and wife and babes, but seized at the moment of his dearest hope by minions of the press-gang and hurried away reluctant.'

A Retrospect of Times of Old. Dowden, i. 285 : ' A rhymed piece having much in common with those earlier pages of *Queen Mab*, which picture the fall of empires, and celebrate the oblivion that has overtaken the old rulers of men and lords of the earth.'

Soliloquy of the Wandering Jew. Printed by Dobell.

Dowden, i. 348, further describes the contents: — ' The collection . . . opens with a series of poems in unrhymed stanzas, the use of which Shelley had learned from Southey's early volumes. Such lines as those to Liberty : —

" And the spirits of the brave
Shall start from every grave,
Whilst from her Atlantic throne
Freedom sanctifies the groan
That fans the glorious fires of its change — "

are a direct reminiscence,' etc.

Of other poems unentitled, Dowden prints the following fragments : —

I

' Consigned to thoughts of holiness
And deeds of living love.'

II

' Then may we hope the consummating hour,
Dreadfully, swiftly, sweetly is arriving,
When light from darkness, peace from desolation,
Bursts unresisted.'

Dowden, i. 346: ' Having copied his best short pieces, Shelley falls back on [four of] the Oxford poems suggested by the story of Hogg's friend Mary and on the pieces written in the winter of 1810, 1811, which are strikingly inferior both in form and feeling to the poems of a later date.'

Dowden, *Shelley's Poems*, p. 695: ' Mr. Esdaile's MS. contains three poems, *To Mary*, with an advertisement prefixed, and one *To the Lover of Mary*. The date of these is November, 1810. They are selected, Shelley says, from many written during three weeks of an entrancement caused on hearing Mary's story.' [See note on *To Mary, who died in this Opinion*.]

Dowden, i. 107: ' The piteous story of a certain Mary — a real person, — known in her distress to Hogg, had been related by his friend to Shelley ; it had thrown him into a three weeks' " entrancement," and formed the occasion of a series of poems, rapidly produced.'

February 28, 1805. To St. Irvyne. Dowden, i. 48: ' I have seen an unpublished poem — six stanzas — of Shelley's, in Harriet Shelley's handwriting, headed " February 28, 1805. To St. Irvyne " — St. Irvyne the name of a place where the writer often sat on " the mouldering height " with " his Harriet " — and having the words " To H. Grove " subscribed, also in Harriet Shelley's handwriting. The poem can hardly have been written in 1805, but the title may refer to some incident of February in that year, which might be viewed as a starting-point in the course of their love. A reference in this poem to Strood, the property of John Commerell, Esq., hard by Field Place, leads one to suppose that " St. Irvyne " may have been formed from the name of the proprietor of Hills Place, also close to Field Place, — Lady Irvine.'

The poems, otherwise undefined, which are mentioned by Dowden as existing in MS., presumably the Esdaile, are, *A Dialogue*, 1809 ; *To the Moonbeam*, 1809 ; *The Solitary*, 1810 ; *To Death*, 1810 (twenty unpublished lines) ; *Love's Rose*, 1810 ; *Eyes*, 1810 (four unpublished eight-line stanzas) ; *On an Icicle that Clung to the Grass of a Grave*, 1809 ; *To the Republicans of North America* (one unpublished stanza), 1812 ; *To Ianthe*, 1813. These have all been published, except as here noted, and further information regarding them will be found under their titles in the NOTES or JUVENILIA.

All the poems printed by Dowden from these sources, except such fragments as are quoted above, are placed in this edition under JUVENILIA.

Ballad. Young Parson Richards; twenty-one four-line stanzas, except the first, which has five lines, in the Harvard MS.

To Constantia Singing, an early draft, in which the first stanza of the poem as now printed stands last. Not further described.

—— A poem sent to Peacock from Italy, 1818, in a rough state, and relating to Wordsworth. Not further described.

ORIGINAL POETRY BY VICTOR AND CAZIRE

sm. 8vo, pp. 64

A copy of this volume, previously known only by title, some contemporary notices and the account of it in *Stockdale's Budget*, was found by the grandson of Charles Henry Grove, the brother of Harriet Grove, Shelley's cousin, among the family books, and was reprinted under the editorship of Dr. Garnett, London, 1898. The book was printed, in 1810, at Worthing, apparently in an edition of 1500 copies, and taken up by Stockdale, at Shelley's request, September 17, of that year. It was noticed by the *Poetical Register*, 1810–11, and the *British Critic*, April, 1811. It was written by Shelley (Victor) and his sister Elizabeth (Cazire), and contains seventeen pieces, of which Dr. Garnett ascribes two certainly and one other probably to Elizabeth, ten certainly and two others (if not plagiarisms) to Shelley, and he leaves two unassigned. The last poem was reprinted as VICTORIA in St. Irvyne. He classifies the contents as follows : '1. Familiar poems in the style of Anstey's "Bath Guide," the first two in the volume, already mentioned as by Elizabeth Shelley. 2. A cycle of little poems evidently addressed by Shelley to Harriet Grove in the summer of 1810 (Nos. 3–7, 12, 13). 3. Tales of terror and wonder in the style of Monk Lewis (Nos. 14–17). 4. A few miscellaneous pieces (Nos. 8–11).' Stockdale states that he recognized one of the pieces as by Monk Lewis, and that on his communicating the fact to Shelley the latter 'with all the ardor natural to his character expressed the warmest resentment at the imposition practised upon him by his coadjutor, and entreated me to destroy all the copies, of which about one hundred had been put in circulation.' Dr. Garnett is unable to identify any poem as by Monk Lewis, and suggests that the plagiarized poem may be a song on Laura (No. 11). GHASTA (No. 16) is the poem mentioned by Medwin as containing a plagiarism from Chatterton. Of the value of the volume as a whole, Dr. Garnett says : 'It shows, at all events, that the youthful Shelley could write better verse than can be found in his novels, and that he even then possessed the feeling for melody that is rarely dissociated from more or less of endowment with the poetical faculty. Biographically, it contributes something to illustrate an obscure period of his life, and strengthens the belief that his attachment for his fair cousin was more than a passing fancy.'

SELECTIONS FROM SHELLEY'S PROSE

NOTE ON THE SELECTIONS

Except for *The Necessity of Atheism*, none of the following essays was published during Shelley's lifetime. *The Necessity of Atheism*, which led to Shelley's expulsion from Oxford during his first year of residence and to the summary burning of all copies at the booksellers, was published anonymously in 1811. Shelley sent copies to professors, heads of colleges, and bishops in an evidently sincere desire to elicit intelligent, temperate discussion. Contrary to assumptions based on the title of *The Necessity of Atheism* and on a few references in the juvenile *Queen Mab*, Shelley's view of Christ was generally sympathetic. The unfinished "Essay on Christianity" (1815? 1816–1817?), like *Prometheus Unbound* (1818–1819) and *Hellas* (1821), presents Christ as a human idealist and liberator with godlike character — benign, gentle, loving, and possessing extraordinary genius.

The fragment "On Love" (1815? 1818?) defines Shelley's yearning commitment to a quasi-Platonic ideal of disinterested, all-embracing love. Love between the sexes is but one of its manifestations. As Mary Shelley wrote, it "reveals the secrets of the most impassioned, and yet the purest and softest heart that ever yearned for sympathy." From "Alastor" in 1815 and the "Hymn" in 1816 to *Prometheus* (1818–1819) and "Epipsychidion" and *Adonais* in 1821, this selfless love aspiring to the ideal offers a key to the subtle and richly symbolical visions, quests, prayers, and adorations of these and many other poems. The same may be said for "Una Favola" (1820), Shelley's fable composed in Italian, presented here in Richard Garnett's translation. It is a parable of a youth's vision guided by Love and occurring within a labyrinthine and forested valley (symbol of the error, suffering, and partial knowledge that beset mortality), of three alluring women, each of whom enchants him in turn and leads him forth in an ardent pilgrimage. The two principal women are sisters: Life, and Death. Each seeks to possess him. Only Life unveils herself to him, but she appears to be full of deceit. The third woman is a mortal embodiment of the youth's ideal of love, so glorious that he wonders whether she is more than human. The pair are alternately beckoned and threatened by Life and Death. 'I love thee, and wish so well to thee and thy bride," says Death, "that in my kingdom, which thou mayest call Paradise, I have set apart a chosen spot, where ye may securely fulfill your happy loves." From "Alastor" and the "Hymn" to "Ode to the West Wind," "To a Skylark," "The Witch of Atlas," "The Sensitive Plant," "Epipsychidion," *Adonais*, and "The Triumph of Life" there is scarcely a poem that does not turn upon the veiled hints, enigmatic questions, and covert ironies of this parable of life and love, mortality and eternity.

"A Defence of Poetry" was written in 1821, in answer to Peacock's attack ("The Four Ages of Poetry," 1820) on the poetry of the age as a reversion to second childhood and semibarbarism in an age of advancing knowledge and scientific accomplishment. One could scarcely miss the tongue-in-cheek irony of Peacock's clever and witty essay, but Shelley feared it might do damage to the cause of poetry in general, and especially to the signal achievements of his poetic contemporaries. "Your anathemas against poetry . . . excited me to a sacred rage," wrote Shelley to Peacock. "I had the greatest possible desire to break a lance with you, . . . in honour of my mistress Urania . . . Besides, I was at that moment reading Plato's *Ion*, which I recommend you to reconsider." Shelley's "Defence" did not appear, unfortunately, until 1840, eighteen years after his death. The magazine that published Peacock's "Four Ages" in its first issue and to which Shelley sent his reply did not survive to a second issue.

Typically Shelley's "Defence" became almost an Exaltation — of the creative imagination, of the efficacy of poetry on both the ethical and esthetic level, of the correlation of distinguished poetic output with a marked advance in enlightenment, in political and social liberation, in charity and toleration and fraternity. Had the "Defence" been published in the year of its composition (1821), Byron, Wordsworth, Coleridge, Scott, and possibly Keats himself, who was mortally ill in Rome at the time, would have been moved by Shelley's high tribute to the poetry of his contemporaries: "For the literature of England . . . has arisen as it were from a new birth . . . our own will be a memorable age in intellectual achievements, and we live among such philosophers and poets as surpass beyond comparison any who have appeared since the last national struggle for civil and religious liberty." Time has vindicated Shelley's high claim, and not a few readers in the twentieth century can verify his fur-

ther contention: "It is impossible to read the compositions of the most celebrated writers of the present day without being startled with the electric life which burns within their words."

N. F. F.

NOTE ON THE TEXT

The basis for the text of these few samplings of Shelley's prose is the Julian Edition, *The Complete Works* . . . , edited by Roger Ingpen and W. E. Peck, 1926–1930, recently reprinted. In this ten-volume edition Shelley's prose fills three volumes, exclusive of the three volumes devoted to his letters. The letters are now available in a more recent edition of two volumes prepared by F. L. Jones. The most convenient and inexpensive collection of Shelley's prose is the one-volume text edited and annotated by David L. Clark. The student should be warned, however, that the editor's dating of many of these pieces is probably too early, and that his commentary is valuable on Shelley's legacy from eighteenth-century empiricism and scepticism but shows little interest in his Platonic inheritance or leanings. Shelley's translations of Plato may be found in Volume 7 of the Julian Edition and in Notopoulos' definitive study, *Shelley's Platonism*. His translation of the *Ion* appears also in the inexpensive Everyman text, Plato, *Five Dialogues*.

N. F. F.

THE NECESSITY OF ATHEISM

ADVERTISEMENT

As a love of truth is the only motive which actuates the Author of this little tract, he earnestly entreats that those of his readers who may discover any deficiency in his reasoning, or may be in possession of proofs which his mind could never obtain, would offer them, together with their objections to the Public, as briefly, as methodically, as plainly as he has taken the liberty of doing. Thro' deficiency of proof,

AN ATHEIST.

A close examination of the validity of the proofs adduced to support any proposition, has ever been allowed to be the only sure way of attaining truth, upon the advantages of

which it is unnecessary to descant; our knowledge of the existence of a Deity is a subject of such importance that it cannot be too minutely investigated; in consequence of this conviction, we proceed briefly and impartially to examine the proofs which have been adduced. It is necessary first to consider the nature of Belief.

When a proposition is offered to the mind, it perceives the agreement or disagreement of the ideas of which it is composed. A perception of their agreement is termed belief, many obstacles frequently prevent this perception from being immediate, these the mind attempts to remove in order that the perception may be distinct. The mind is active in the investigation, in order to perfect the state of perception which is passive; the investigation being confused with the perception has induced many falsely to imagine that the mind is active in belief, that belief is an act of volition, in consequence of which it may be regulated by the mind; pursuing, continuing this mistake they have attached a degree of criminality to disbelief of which in its nature it is incapable; it is equally so of merit.

The strength of belief like that of every other passion is in proportion to the degrees of excitement.

The degrees of excitement are three.

The senses are the sources of all knowledge to the mind, consequently their evidence claims the strongest assent.

The decision of the mind founded upon our own experience derived from these sources, claims the next degree.

The experience of others which addresses itself to the former one, occupies the lowest degree. —

Consequently no testimony can be admitted which is contrary to reason, reason is founded on the evidence of our senses.

Every proof may be referred to one of these three divisions; we are naturally led to consider what arguments we receive from each of them to convince us of the existence of a Deity.

1st. The evidence of the senses. — If the Deity should appear to us, if he should convince our senses of his existence; this revelation would necessarily command belief; — Those to whom the Deity has thus appeared, have the strongest possible conviction of his existence.

Reason claims the 2nd. place, it is urged that man knows that whatever is, must either have had a beginning or existed from all eternity, he also knows that whatever is not eternal must have had a cause. — Where this is applied to the existence of the universe, it is necessary to prove that it was created, until that is clearly demonstrated, we may reasonably suppose that it has endured from all eternity. — In a case where two propositions are diametrically opposite, the mind believes that which is less incomprehensible, it is easier to suppose that the Universe has existed from all eternity, than to conceive a being capable of creating it; if the mind sinks beneath the weight of one, is it an alleviation to increase the intolerability of the burden? — The other argument which is founded upon a man's knowledge of his own existence, stands thus. . . . A man knows not only he now is, but that there was a time when he did not exist, consequently there must have been a cause. . . . But what does this prove? we can only infer from effects causes exactly adequate to those

effects; . . . But there certainly is a generative power which is effected by particular instruments; we cannot prove that it is inherent in these instruments, nor is the contrary hypothesis capable of demonstration; we admit that the generative power is incomprehensible, but to suppose that the same effect is produced by an eternal, omniscient, Almighty Being, leaves the cause in the obscurity, but renders it more incomprehensible.

The 3rd. and last degree of assent is claimed by Testimony . . . it is required that it should not be contrary to reason. . . . The testimony that the Deity convinces the senses of men of his existence can only be admitted by us, if our mind considers it less probable that these men should have been deceived, than that the Deity should have appeared to them . . . our reason can never admit the testimony of men, who not only declare that they were eye-witnesses of miracles but that the Deity was irrational, for he commanded that he should be believed, he proposed the highest rewards for faith, eternal punishments for disbelief . . . we can only command voluntary actions, belief is not an act of volition, the mind is even passive, from this it is evident that we have not sufficient testimony, or rather that testimony is insufficient to prove the being of a God, we have before shewn that it cannot be deduced from reason, . . . they who have been convinced by the evidence of the senses, they only can believe it.

From this it is evident that having no proofs from any of the three sources of conviction: the mind *cannot* believe the existence of a God, it is also evident that as belief is a passion of the mind, no degree of criminality can be attached to disbelief, they only are reprehensible who willingly neglect to remove the false medium thro' which their mind views the subject.

It is almost unnecessary to observe, that the general knowledge of the deficiency of such proof, cannot be prejudicial to society: Truth has always been found to promote the best interests of mankind. . . . Every reflecting mind must allow that there is no proof of the existence of a Deity. — Q.E.D.

ESSAY ON CHRISTIANITY

[IN PART]

The Being who has influenced in the most memorable manner the opinions and the fortunes of the human species, is Jesus Christ. At this day, his name is connected with the devotional feelings of two hundred millions of the race of man. The institutions of the most civilized portion of the globe derive their authority from the sanction of his doctrines. He is the God of our popular religion. His extraordinary genius, the wide and rapid effect of his unexampled doctrines, his invincible gentleness and benignity, the devoted love borne to him by his adherents suggested a persuasion to them that he was something divine. The supernatural events which the historians of this wonderful man subsequently asserted to have been connected with every gradation of his career, established the opinion. His death is said to have been accompanied by an accumulation of tremendous prodigies. Utter darkness fell upon the earth, blotting the noonday sun, dead bodies, arising from their graves walked thro the public streets, and an earthquake shook the astonished city, rending the rocks of the surrounding mountains. The philosopher may attribute the application of these events *to* the death of a reformer or the events themselves to a visitation of that Universal Pan who may be a God or man. It is the profound wisdom and the comprehensive morality of his doctrines which essentially distinguished him from the crowd of martyrs and of patriots who have exulted to devote themselves for what they conceived would contribute to the benefit of their fellow men. —

. . . .

GOD

The thoughts which the word, God, suggests to the human mind are susceptible of as many variations as human minds themselves. The Stoic the Platonist and the Epicurean, the Polytheist the Dualist and the Trinitarian, differ infinitely in their conceptions of its meaning. They agree only in considering it the most awful and most venerable of names, as a common term devised to express all of mystery or majesty or power which the invisible world contains. And not only has every sect distinct conceptions of the application of this name, but scarcely two individuals of the same sect, who exercise in any degree the freedom of their judgement, or yield themselves with any candour of feeling to the influencings of the visible world, find perfect coincidence of opinion to exist between them. It is interes[ting] to enquire in what acceptation Jesus Christ employed this term.

We may conceive his mind to have been predisposed on this subject to adopt the opinions of his countrymen. Every human being is indebted for a multitude of his sentiments to the religion of his early years. Jesus Christ probably studied the historians of his country with the ardour of a spirit seeking after truth. They were undoubtedly the companions of his childish years the food and nutriment and materials of his youthful meditations. The sublime dramatic poem entitled Job had familiarized his imagination with the boldest imagery afforded by the human mind and the material world. Ecclesiastes had diffused a seriousness and solemnity over the frame of his spirit glowing with youthful hope, and made audible to his listening heart

> The still, sad music of humanity
> Not harsh or grating but of ample power
> To chasten and subdue.

He had contemplated this name as having been prophanely perverted to the sanctioning of the most enormous and abominable crimes. We can distinctly trace in the tissue of his doctrines the persuasion that God is some universal being, differing both from man and from the mind of man. — According to Jesus Christ, God is neither the Jupiter who sends rain upon the earth, nor the Venus thro whom all living things are produced, nor the Vulcan who presides over the terrestrial element of fire, nor the Vesta that preserves the light which is inshrined in the sun and moon and stars. He is neither the Proteus or the Pan of the material world. But the word God, according to the acceptation of Jesus Christ, unites all the attributes which these denominations contain, and is the interfused and overruling Spirit of all the energy and wisdom included within the circle of existing things. It is important to observe that the author of the Christian system had a conception widely differing from the gross imaginations of the vulgar relatively to the ruling Power of the universe. He every where represents this power as something mysteriously and illimitably pervading the frame of things.

. . . . . .

Blessed are the pure in heart, for they shall see God — blessed are those who have preserved internal sanctity of soul, who are conscious of no secret deceit, who are the same in act as they are in desire, who conceal no thought no tendencies of thought from their own conscience, who are faithful and sincere witnesses before the tribunal of their own judgement of all that passes within their mind. Such as these shall see God. What! after death, shall their awakened eyes behold the King of Heaven? shall they stand in awe before the golden throne on which he sits, and gaze upon the venerable countenance of the paternal Monarch?. Is this the reward of the virtuous and the pure? These are the idle dreams of the visionary, or the pernicious representations of impostors, who have fabricated from the very materials of wisdom a cloak for their own dwarfish or imbecile conceptions. Jesus Christ has said no more than the most excellent philosophers have felt and expressed — that virtue is its own reward. It is true that such an expression as he has used was prompted by the energy of genius, it was the overflowing enthusiasm of a   poet, but it is the less literally true, clearly repugnant to the mistaken conceptions of the multitude. God, it has been asserted, was contemplated by Jesus Christ as every poet and every philosopher must have contemplated that mysterious principle. He considered that venerable word to express the overruling Spirit of the collective energy of the moral and material world. He affirms therefore no more than that a simple and sincere mind is an indispensable requisite of true science and true happiness. He affirms that a being of pure and gentle habits will not fail in every thought, in every object of every thought, to be aware of benignant visitings from the invisible energies by which he is surrounded. Whosoever is free from the contamination of luxury and licence may go forth to the fields and to the woods, inhaling joyous renovation from the breath of Spring, or catching from the odours and the sounds of Autumn some diviner mood of sweetest sadness, which improves the [solitary] heart. Whosoever is no deceiver or destroyer of his fellowmen, no liar, no flatterer, no murderer, may walk among his species, deriving from the communion with all which they contain of beautiful or of majestic, some intercourse with the Universal God. Whoever has maintained with his own heart the strictest correspondence of confidence, who dares to examine and to estimate every imagination which suggests itself to his mind, who is that which he designs to become, and only aspires to that which the divinity of his own nature shall consider and approve — he, has already seen God. We live and move and think, but we are not the creators of our own origin and existence, we are not the arbiters of every motion of our own complicated nature; we are not the masters of our own imaginations

and moods of mental being. There is a Power by which we are surrounded, like the atmosphere in which some motionless lyre is suspended, which visits with its breath our silent chords, at will. Our most imperial and stupendous qualities — those on which the majesty and the power of humanity is erected — are, relatively to the inferior portion of its mechanism, indeed active and imperial; but they are the passive slaves of some higher and more omnipresent Power. This Power is God. And those who have seen God, have, in the period of their purer and more perfect nature, been harmonized by their own will to so exquisite [a] consentaneity of powers as to give forth divinest melody when the breath of universal being sweeps over their frame.

That those who are pure in heart shall see God, and that virtue is its own reward, may be considered as equivalent assertions. The former of these propositions is a metaphorical repetition of the latter. The advocates of literal interpretation have been the most efficacious enemies of those doctrines whose institutor they profess to venerate.

. . . . . .

The doctrine of what some fanatics have termed a peculiar Providence, that is of some power beyond and superior to that which ordinarily guides the operations of the Universe, interfering to punish the vicious and reward the virtuous — is explicitly denied by Jesus Christ. The absurd and execrable doctrine of vengeance seems to have been contemplated in all its shapes by this great moralist with the profoundest disapprobation. Nor would he permit the most venerable of names to be perverted into a sanction for the meanest and most contemptible propensities incident to the nature of man. 'Love your enemies bless those who curse you that ye may be the sons of your Heavenly Father who makes the sun to shine on the good and on the evil, and the rain to fall on the just and the unjust.' How monstrous a calumny have not impostors dared to advance against the mild and gentle author of this just sentiment, and against the whole tenor of his doctrines and his life overflowing with benevolence and forbearance and compassion! They have represented him asserting that the Omnipotent God, that merciful and benignant power who scatters equally upon the beautiful earth all the elements of security and happiness, whose influencings are distributed to all whose natures admit of a participation in them, who sends to the weak and vicious creatures of his will all the benefits which they are capable of sharing, that this God has devised a scheme whereby the body shall live after its apparent dissolution, and be rendered capable of indefinite torture. He is said to have compared the agonies which the vicious shall then endure, to the excruciations of a living body bound among the flames and being consumed sinew by sinew and bone by bone. And this is to be done, not because it is supposed (and the supposition would be sufficiently detestable) that the moral nature of the sufferer would be emproved by his tortures. It is done because it *is just* to be done. My neighbour or my servant or my child has done me an injury, and it is just that he should suffer an injury in return. Such is the doctrine which Jesus Christ summoned his whole resources of persuasion to oppose. 'Love your enemy, bless those who curse you

. . . .

We die, says Jesus Christ, and when we awaken from the lang[uo]r of disease the glories and the happiness of Paradise are around us. All evil and pain have ceased for ever. Our happiness also corresponds [with,] and is adapted to, the nature of what is most excellent in our being. We see God, and we see that he is good. How delightful a picture even if it be not true! How magnificent & illustrious is the conception which this bold theory suggests to the contemplation, even if it be no more than the imagination of some sublimest and most holy poet, who impressed with the loveliness and majesty of his own nature, is impatient and discontented, with the narrow limits which this imperfect life and the dark grave have assigned for ever as his melancholy portion.

It is not to be believed that Hell or punishment was the conception of this daring mind. It is not to be believed that the most prominent group of this picture which it framed so heart-moving and lovely, the accomplishment of all human hope the extinction of all mortal fear and anguish, would consist of millions of sensitive beings enduring in every variety of torture which omniscient vengeance could invent, immortal agony.

Jesus Christ opposed with earnest eloquence the panic fears and hateful superstitions which have enslaved mankind for ages. Nations had risen against nations employing the subtilest devices of mechanism and mind to waste and excruciate and overthrow. The great community of mankind had been subdivided into ten thousand communities each organized for the ruin of the other. Wheel within wheel the vast machine was instinct with the restless spirit of desolation. Pain has been inflicted, therefore pain should be inflicted in return. Retaliation is the only remedy which can be applied to violence, because it teaches the injurer the true nature of his own conduct, and operates as a warning against its repetition.

. . . .

Every nation of the East was united to ruin the Græcian States. Athens was burned to the ground the whole territory laid waste, and every living thing which it [was] containing. After suffering and inflicting incalculable mischiefs they desisted from their purpose only when they became impotent to effect it. The desire of revenge for the aggression of Persia outlived among the Greeks that love of liberty which had been their most glorious distinction among the nations of mankind, and Alexander became the instrument of its completion. The mischiefs attendant on this consummation of fruitless ruin are too manifold and too tremendous to be related. If all the thought which had been expended on the construction of engines of agony and death, the modes of aggression and defence, the raising of armies, and the acquirement of those arts of tyranny and falsehood without which mixed multitudes deluded and goaded to mutual ruin could neither be led nor governed, had been employed to promote the true welfare, and extend the real empire of man how different would have been the present situation of human society! How different the state of knowledge on physical and moral science, on which the power and happiness of mankind essentially depend! What nation has the example of the desolation of Attica by Mardonius and Xerxes, or the extinction of the Persian empire by Alexander of Macedon restrained from outrage? Was not the pretext of this latter system of spoliation derived immediately from the former? Had revenge in this instance any other effect than to increase instead of diminishing the mass of malice and evil already existing in the world?

The emptiness and folly of retaliation is apparent from every example which can be brought forward. Not only Jesus Christ, but the most eminent professors of every sect of philosophy have reasoned against this futile superstition.

. . . .

Jesus Christ instructed his disciples to be

perfect as their father in Heaven is perfect, declaring at the same time his belief that human perfection requires the refraining from revenge or retribution in any of its various shapes. The perfection of the human and the divine character is thus asserted to be the same: man by resembling God fulfils most accurately the tendencies of his nature, and God comprehends within itself all that constitutes human perfection. Thus God is a model thro which the excellence of man is to be estimated, whilst the *abstract* perfection of the human character is the type of the *actual* perfection of the divine. It is not to [be] believed that a person of such comprehensive views as Jesus Christ could have fallen into so manifest a contradiction as to assert that men would be tortured after death by that being whose character is held up as a model to human kind because he is incapable of malevolence or revenge.

. . . . . .

The system of equality was attempted, after Jesus Christ's death to be carried into effect by his followers. 'They that believed had all things common: they sold their possessions and goods and parted them to all men as every man had need, and they continued daily with one accord in the temple and breaking bread from house to house did eat their meat with gladness and singleness of heart.' *Acts chap.* 2, *v.* 44 etc. The practical application of the doctrines of strict justice to a state of society established in its contempt was such as might have been expected. After the transitory glow of enthusiasm had faded from the minds of men precedent and habit resumed their empire, broke like a universal deluge on one shrinking and solitary island.

. . . . . .

Meanwhile some benefit has not failed to flow from the imperfect attempts which have been made to erect a system of equal rights to property and power upon the basis of arbitrary institutions. They have undoubtedly in every case from the very instability of their foundation failed. Still they constitute a record of those epochs at which a true sense of justice suggested itself to the understandings of men, so that they consented to forego all the cherished delights of luxury all the habitual gratifications arising out of the possession or the expectations of power, all the superstitions which the accumulated authority of ages had made dear and venerable to them. They are so many trophies erected in the enemies land, to mark the limits of the victorious progress of truth and justice.

ON LOVE

What is love? Ask him who lives, what is life? ask him who adores, what is God?

I know not the internal constitution of other men, nor even thine, whom I now address. I see that in some external attributes they resemble me, but when, misled by that appearance, I have thought to appeal to something in common, and unburthen my inmost soul to them, I have found my language misunderstood, like one in a distant and savage land. The more opportunities they have afforded me for experience, the wider has appeared the interval between us, and to a greater distance have the points of sympathy been withdrawn. With a spirit ill fitted to sustain such proof, trembling and feeble through its tenderness, I have everywhere sought sympathy, and have found only repulse and disappointment.

Thou demandest what is love? It is that powerful attraction towards all that we conceive, or fear, or hope beyond ourselves, when we find within our own thoughts the chasm of an insufficient void, and seek to awaken in all things that are, a community with what we experience within ourselves. If we reason, we would be understood; if we imagine, we would that the airy children of our brain were born anew within another's; if we feel, we would that another's nerves should vibrate to our own, that the beams of their eyes should kindle at once and mix and melt into our own, that lips of motionless ice should not reply to lips quivering and burning with the heart's best blood. This is Love. This is the bond and the sanction which connects not only man with man, but with every thing which exists. We are born into the world, and there is something within us which, from the instant that we live, more and more thirsts after its likeness. It is probably in correspondence with this law that the infant drains milk from the bosom of its mother; this propensity develops itself with the development of our nature. We dimly see within our intellectual nature a miniature as it were of our entire self, yet deprived of all that we condemn or despise, the ideal prototype of every thing excellent or lovely that we are capable of conceiving as belonging to the nature of man. Not only the portrait of our external being, but an assemblage of the minutest particles of which our nature is composed [1]; a mirror whose surface reflects only the forms of purity and brightness; a soul within our soul that describes a circle around its proper paradise, which pain, and sorrow, and evil dare not overleap. To this we eagerly refer all sensations, thirsting that they should resemble or correspond with it. The discovery of its antitype; the meeting with an understanding capable of clearly estimating our own; an imagination which should enter into and seize upon the subtle and delicate peculiarities which we have delighted to cherish and unfold in secret; with a frame whose nerves, like the chords of two exquisite lyres, strung to the accompaniment of one delightful voice, vibrate with the vibrations of our own; and of a combination of all these in such proportion as the type within demands; this is the invisible and unattainable point to which Love tends; and to attain which, it urges forth the powers of man to arrest the faintest shadow of that, without the possession of which there is no rest nor respite to the heart over which it rules. Hence in solitude, or in that deserted state when we are surrounded by human beings, and yet they sympathise not with us, we love the flowers, the grass, and the waters, and the sky. In the motion of the very leaves of spring, in the blue air, there is then found a secret correspondence with our heart. There is eloquence in the tongueless wind, and a melody in the flowing brooks and the rustling of the reeds beside them, which by their inconceivable relation to something within the soul, awaken the spirits to a dance of breathless rapture, and bring tears of mysterious tenderness to the eyes, like the enthusiasm of patriotic success, or the voice of one beloved singing to you alone. Sterne says that, if he were in a desert, he would love some cypress. So soon as this want or power is dead, man becomes the living sepulchre of himself, and what yet survives is the mere husk of what once he was.

[1] These words are ineffectual and metaphorical. Most words are so — No help! [Shelley's Note.]

UNA FAVOLA

A FABLE

(Translated by Richard Garnett)

There was a youth who travelled through distant lands, seeking throughout the world a lady of whom he was enamoured. And who this lady was, and how this youth became enamoured of her, and how and why the great love he bore her forsook him, are things worthy to be known by every gentle heart.

At the dawn of the fifteenth spring of his life, a certain one calling himself Love awoke him, saying that one whom he had ofttimes beheld in his dreams abode awaiting him. This Love was accompanied by a great troop of female forms, all veiled in white, and crowned with laurel, ivy, and myrtle, garlanded and interwreathed with violets, roses, and lilies. They sang with such sweetness that perhaps the harmony of the spheres, to which the stars dance, is not so sweet. And their manners and words were so alluring, that the youth was enticed, and, arising from his couch, made himself ready to do all the pleasure of him who called himself Love; at whose behest he followed him by lonely ways and deserts and caverns, until the whole troop arrived at a solitary wood, in a gloomy valley between two most lofty mountains, which valley was planted in the manner of a labyrinth, with pines, cypresses, cedars, and yews, whose shadows begot a mixture of delight and sadness. And in this wood the youth for a whole year followed the uncertain footsteps of this his companion and guide, as the moon follows the earth, save that there was no change in him, and nourished by the fruit of a certain tree which grew in the midst of the labyrinth — a food sweet and bitter at once, which being cold as ice to the lips, appeared fire in the veins. The veiled figures were continually around him, ministers and attendants obedient to his least gesture, and messengers between him and Love, when Love might leave him for a little on his other errands. But these figures, albeit executing his every other command with swiftness, never would unveil themselves to him, although he anxiously besought them; one only excepted, whose name was Life, and who had the fame of a potent enchantress. She was tall of person and beautiful, cheerful and easy in her manners, and richly adorned, and, as it seemed from her ready unveiling of herself, she wished well to this youth. But he soon perceived that she was more false than any Siren, for by her counsel Love abandoned him in this savage place, with only the company of these shrouded figures, who, by their obstinately remaining veiled, had always wrought him dread. And none can expound whether these figures were the spectres of his own dead thoughts, or the shadows of the living thoughts of Love. Then Life, haply ashamed of her deceit, concealed herself within the cavern of a certain sister of hers dwelling there; and Love, sighing, returned to his third heaven.

Scarcely had Love departed, when the masked forms, released from his government, unveiled themselves before the astonished youth. And for many days these figures danced around him whithersoever he went, alternately mocking and threatening him; and in the night while he reposed they defiled in long and slow procession before his couch, each more hideous and terrible than the other. Their horrible aspect and loathsome figure so overcame his heart with sadness that the fair heaven, covered with that shadow, clothed itself in clouds before his eyes; and he wept so much that the herbs upon his path, fed with tears instead of dew, became pale and bowed like himself. Weary at length of this suffering, he came to the grot of the Sister of Life, herself also an enchantress, and found her sitting before a pale fire of perfumed wood, singing laments sweet in their melancholy, and weaving a white shroud, upon which his name was half wrought, with the obscure and imperfect beginning of a certain other name; and he besought her to tell him her own, and she said, with a faint but sweet voice, "Death." And the youth said "O lovely Death, I pray thee to aid me against these hateful phantoms, companions of thy sister, which cease not to torment me." And Death comforted him, and took his hand with a smile, and kissed his brow and cheek, so that every vein thrilled with joy and fear, and made him abide with her in a chamber of her cavern, whither, she said, it was against Destiny that the wicked companions of Life should ever come. The youth continually conversing with Death, and she, like-minded to a sister, caressing him and showing him every courtesy both in deed and word, he quickly became enamoured of her, and Life herself, far less any of her troop, seemed fair to him no longer: and his passion so overcame him, that upon his knees he prayed Death to love him as he loved her, and consent to do his pleasure. But Death said, "Audacious that thou art, with whose desire has Death ever complied? If thou lovedst me not, perchance I might love thee — beloved by thee, I hate thee and I fly thee." Thus saying, she went forth from the cavern, and her dusky and etherial form was soon lost amid the interwoven boughs of the forest.

From that moment the youth pursued the track of Death; and so mighty was the love that led him, that he had encircled the world and searched through all its regions, and many years were already spent, but sorrows rather than years had blanched his locks and withered the flower of his beauty, when he found himself upon the confines of the very forest from which his wretched wanderings had begun. He cast himself upon the grass and wept for many hours, so blinded by his tears that for much time he did not perceive that not all that bathed his face and his bosom were his own, but that a lady bowed behind him wept for pity of his weeping. And lifting up his eyes he saw her, and it seemed to him never to have beheld so glorious a vision, and he doubted much whether she were a human creature. And his love of Death was suddenly changed into hate and suspicion, for this new love was so potent that it overcame every other thought. This compassionate lady at first loved him for mere pity; but love grew up swiftly with compassion, and she loved for Love's own sake, no one beloved by her having need of pity any more. This was the lady in whose quest Love had led the youth through that gloomy labyrinth of error and suffering, haply for that he esteemed him unworthy of so much glory, and perceived him too weak to support such exceeding joy. After having somewhat dried their tears, the twain walked together in that same forest, until Death stood before them, and said, "Whilst, O youth, thou didst love me, I hated thee, and now that thou hatest me, I love thee, and wish so well to thee and thy bride that in my kingdom, which thou mayest call Paradise, I have set apart a chosen spot, where ye may securely fulfil your happy loves." And the lady, offended, and perchance somewhat jealous by reason of the past love of her spouse, turned her back upon Death, saying within herself, "What would this lover of my husband who comes here to trouble us?" and cried, "Life! Life!" and Life came, with a gay visage, crowned with a rainbow, and clad in a various mantle of chameleon skin; and Death went away weeping, and departing said with a sweet voice, "Ye mistrust me, but I forgive ye, and await ye where ye needs must come, for I dwell with Love and Eternity, with whom the souls whose love is everlasting must hold communion; then will ye perceive whether I have deserved your distrust. Meanwhile I commend ye to Life; and, sister mine, I beseech thee, by the love of that Death with whom thou wert twin born, not to employ thy customary arts against these lovers, but content thee with the tribute thou hast already received of sighs and tears, which are thy wealth." The youth, mindful of how great evil she had wrought him in that wood, mistrusted Life; but the lady, although she doubted, yet being jealous of Death. . . .

A DEFENCE OF POETRY

[IN PART]

PART I

According to one mode of regarding those two classes of mental action, which are called reason and imagination, the former may be considered as mind contemplating the relations borne by one thought to another, however produced; and the latter, as mind acting upon those thoughts so as to colour them with its own light, and composing from them, as from elements, other thoughts, each containing within itself the principle of its own integrity. The one is the τὸ ποιεῖν, or the principle of synthesis, and has for its objects those forms which are common to universal nature and existence itself; the other is the τὸ λογίζειν, or principle of analysis, and its action regards the relations of things, simply as relations; considering thoughts, not in their integral unity, but as the algebraical representations which conduct to certain general results. Reason is the enumeration of quantities already known; imagination is the perception of the value of those quantities, both separately and as a whole. Reason respects the differences, and imagination the similitudes of things. Reason is to imagination as the instrument to the agent, as the body to the spirit, as the shadow to the substance.

Poetry, in a general sense, may be defined to be "the expression of the imagination": and poetry is connate with the origin of man. Man is an instrument over which a series of external and internal impressions are driven, like the alternations of an ever-changing wind over an Æolian lyre, which move it by their motion to ever-changing melody. But there is a principle within the human being, and perhaps within all sentient beings, which acts otherwise than in the lyre, and produces not melody, alone, but harmony, by an internal adjustment of the sounds or motions thus excited to the impressions which excite them. It is as if the lyre could accommodate its chords to the motions of that which strikes them, in a determined proportion of sound; even as the musician can accommodate his voice to the sound of the lyre. A child at play by itself will express its delight by its voice and motions; and every inflexion of tone and every gesture will bear exact rela-

tion to a corresponding antitype in the pleasurable impressions which awakened it; it will be the reflected image of that impression; and as the lyre trembles and sounds after the wind has died away, so the child seeks, by prolonging in its voice and motions the duration of the effect, to prolong also a consciousness of the cause. In relation to the objects which delight a child, these expressions are, what poetry is to higher objects. The savage (for the savage is to ages what the child is to years) expresses the emotions produced in him by surrounding objects in a similar manner; and language and gesture, together with plastic or pictorial imitation, become the image of the combined effect of those objects, and of his apprehension of them. Man in society, with all his passions and his pleasures, next becomes the object of the passions and pleasures of man; an additional class of emotions produces an augmented treasure of expressions; and language, gesture, and the imitative arts, become at once the representation and the medium, the pencil and the picture, the chisel and the statue, the chord and the harmony.

. . . .

In the youth of the world, men dance and sing and imitate natural objects, observing in these actions, as in all others, a certain rhythm or order.

. . . .

Those in whom it exists in excess are poets, in the most universal sense of the word; and the pleasure resulting from the manner in which they express the influence of society or nature upon their own minds, communicates itself to others, and gathers a sort of reduplication from that community. Their language is vitally metaphorical; that is, it marks the before unapprehended relations of things and perpetuates their apprehension, until the words which represent them, become, through time, signs for portions or classes of thoughts instead of pictures of integral thoughts; and then if no new poets should arise to create afresh the associations which have been thus disorganised, language will be dead to all the nobler purposes of human intercourse. These similitudes or relations are finitely said by Lord Bacon to be "the same footsteps of nature impressed upon the various subjects of the world [1]" — and he considers the faculty which perceives them as the storehouse of axioms common to all

---

[1] *De Augment. Scient.*, cap. 1, lib. iii.

knowledge. In the infancy of society every author is necessarily a poet, because language itself is poetry; and to be a poet is to apprehend the true and the beautiful, in a word, the good which exists in the relation, subsisting, first between existence and perception, and secondly between perception and expression. Every original language near to its source is in itself the chaos of a cyclic poem: the copiousness of lexicography and the distinctions of grammar are the works of a later age, and are merely the catalogue and the form of the creations of poetry.

But poets, or those who imagine and express this indestructible order, are not only the authors of language and of music, of the dance and architecture, and statuary, and painting; they are the institutors of laws, and the founders of civil society, and the inventors of the arts of life, and the teachers, who draw into a certain propinquity with the beautiful and the true, that partial apprehension of the agencies of the invisible world which is called religion. Hence all original religions are allegorical, or susceptible of allegory, and, like Janus, have a double face of false and true. Poets, according to the circumstances of the age and nation in which they appeared, were called, in the earlier epochs of the world, legislators, or prophets: a poet essentially comprises and unites both these characters.

.   .   .   .

Language, colour, form, and religious and civil habits of action, are all the instruments and materials of poetry; they may be called poetry by that figure of speech which considers the effect as a synonyme of the cause. But poetry in a more restricted sense expresses those arrangements of language, and especially metrical language, which are created by that imperial faculty, whose throne is curtained within the invisible nature of man. And this springs from the nature itself of language, which is a more direct representation of the actions and passions of our internal being, and is susceptible of more various and delicate combinations, than colour, form, or motion, and is more plastic and obedient to the control of that faculty of which it is the creation. For language is arbitrarily produced by the imagination, and has relation to thoughts alone; but all other materials, instruments, and conditions of art, have relations among each other, which limit and interpose between conception and expression. The former is as a mirror which reflects, the latter as a cloud which enfeebles,

the light of which both are mediums of communication. Hence the fame of sculptors, painters, and musicians, although the intrinsic powers of the great masters of these arts may yield in no degree to that of those who have employed language as the hieroglyphic of their thoughts, has never equalled that of poets in the restricted sense of the term; as two performers of equal skill will produce unequal effects from a guitar and a harp. The fame of legislators and founders of religions, so long as their institutions last, alone seems to exceed that of poets in the restricted sense; but it can scarcely be a question, whether, if we deduct the celebrity which their flattery of the gross opinions of the vulgar usually conciliates, together with that which belonged to them in their higher character of poets, any excess will remain.

We have thus circumscribed the meaning of the word Poetry within the limits of that art which is the most familiar and the most perfect expression of the faculty itself. It is necessary, however, to make the circle still narrower, and to determine the distinction between measured and unmeasured language; for the popular division into prose and verse is inadmissible in accurate philosophy.

Sounds as well as thoughts have relation both between each other and towards that which they represent, and a perception of the order of those relations has always been found connected with a perception of the order of those relations of thoughts. Hence the language of poets has ever affected a certain uniform and harmonious recurrence of sound, without which it were not poetry, and which is scarcely less indispensable to the communication of its action, than the words themselves, without reference to that peculiar order. Hence the vanity of translation; it were as wise to cast a violet into a crucible that you might discover the formal principle of its colour and odour, as seek to transfuse from one language into another the creations of a poet. The plant must spring again from its seed, or it will bear no flower — and this is the burthen of the curse of Babel.

An observation of the regular mode of the recurrence of this harmony in the language of poetical minds, together with its relation to music, produced metre, or a certain system of traditional forms of harmony of language. Yet it is by no means essential that a poet should accommodate his language to this traditional form, so that the harmony, which is its spirit, be observed. The practice is indeed convenient and popular, and to be preferred, especially in such composition as includes much form and action: but every great poet must inevitably innovate upon the example of his predecessors in the exact structure of his peculiar versification. The distinction between poets and prose writers is a vulgar error. The distinction between philosophers and poets has been anticipated. Plato was essentially a poet — the truth and splendour of his imagery, and the melody of his language, is the most intense that it is possible to conceive. He rejected the measure of the epic, dramatic, and lyrical forms, because he sought to kindle a harmony in thoughts divested of shape and action, and he forbore to invent any regular plan of rhythm which should include, under determinate forms, the varied pauses of his style. Cicero sought to imitate the cadence of his periods, but with little success. Lord Bacon was a poet.[1] His language has a sweet and majestic rhythm, which satisfies the sense, no less than the almost superhuman wisdom of his philosophy satisfies the intellect; it is a strain which distends, and then bursts the circumference of the hearer's mind, and pours itself forth together with it into the universal element with which it has perpetual sympathy. All the authors of revolutions in opinion are not only necessarily poets as they are inventors, nor even as their words unveil the permanent analogy of things by images which participate in the life of truth; but as their periods are harmonious and rhythmical, and contain in themselves the elements of verse; being the echo of the eternal music. Nor are those supreme poets, who have employed traditional forms of rhythm on account of the form and action of their subjects, less capable of perceiving and teaching the truth of things, than those who have omitted that form. Shakespeare, Dante, and Milton (to confine ourselves to modern writers) are philosophers of the very loftiest power.

. . . .

Having determined what is poetry, and who are poets, let us proceed to estimate its effects upon society.

Poetry is ever accompanied with pleasure: all spirits on which it falls open themselves to receive the wisdom which is mingled with its delight. In the infancy of the world, neither poets themselves nor their auditors are fully aware of the excellence of poetry: for it acts in a divine and unapprehended manner, beyond and above consciousness; and it is reserved for future generations to

[1] See the *Filum Labyrinthi* and the *Essay on Death* particularly.

contemplate and measure the mighty cause and effect in all the strength and splendour of their union. Even in modern times, no living poet ever arrived at the fulness of his fame; the jury which sits in judgment upon a poet, belonging as he does to all time, must be composed of his peers: it must be impanneled by Time from the selectest of the wise of many generations. A Poet is a nightingale, who sits in darkness and sings to cheer its own solitude with sweet sounds; his auditors are as men entranced by the melody of an unseen musician, who feel that they are moved and softened, yet know not whence or why. The poems of Homer and his contemporaries were the delight of infant Greece; they were the elements of that social system which is the column upon which all succeeding civilization has reposed. Homer embodied the ideal perfection of his age in human character; nor can we doubt that those who read his verses were awakened to an ambition of becoming like to Achilles, Hector, and Ulysses: the truth and beauty of friendship, patriotism, and persevering devotion to an object, were unveiled to the depths in these immortal creations: the sentiments of the auditors must have been refined and enlarged by a sympathy with such great and lovely impersonations, until from admiring they imitated, and from imitation they identified themselves with the objects of their admiration.

. . . .

The whole objection, however, of the immorality of poetry rests upon a misconception of the manner in which poetry acts to produce the moral improvement of man. Ethical science arranges the elements which poetry has created, and propounds schemes and proposes examples of civil and domestic life: nor is it for want of admirable doctrines that men hate, and despise, and censure, and deceive, and subjugate one another. But Poetry acts in another and diviner manner. It awakens and enlarges the mind itself by rendering it the receptacle of a thousand unapprehended combinations of thought. Poetry lifts the veil from the hidden beauty of the world, and makes familiar objects be as if they were not familiar; it reproduces all that it represents, and the impersonations clothed in its Elysian light stand thenceforward in the minds of those who have once contemplated them, as memorials of that gentle and exalted content which extends itself over all thoughts and actions with which it coexists. The great secret of morals is love; or a going out of our own nature, and an identification of ourselves with the beautiful which exists in thought, action, or person, not our own. A man, to be greatly good, must imagine intensely and comprehensively; he must put himself in the place of another and of many others; the pains and pleasures of his species must become his own. The great instrument of moral good is the imagination; and poetry administers to the effect by acting upon the cause. Poetry enlarges the circumference of the imagination by replenishing it with thoughts of ever new delight, which have the power of attracting and assimilating to their own nature all other thoughts, and which form new intervals and interstices whose void for ever craves fresh food. Poetry strengthens that faculty which is the organ of the moral nature of man, in the same manner as exercise strengthens a limb. A Poet therefore would do ill to embody his own conceptions of right and wrong, which are usually those of his place and time, in his poetical creations, which participate in neither. By this assumption of the inferior office of interpreting the effect, in which perhaps after all he might acquit himself but imperfectly, he would resign the glory in a participation in the cause. There was little danger that Homer, or any of the eternal Poets, should have so far misunderstood themselves as to have abdicated this throne of their widest dominion. Those in whom the poetical faculty, though great, is less intense, as Euripides, Lucan, Tasso, Spenser, have frequently affected a moral aim, and the effect of their poetry is diminished in exact proportion to the degree in which they compel us to advert to this purpose.

Homer and the cyclic poets were followed at a certain interval by the dramatic and lyrical Poets of Athens, who flourished contemporaneously with all that is most perfect in the kindred expressions of the poetical faculty; architecture, painting, music, the dance, sculpture, philosophy, and we may add, the forms of civil life. For although the scheme of Athenian society was deformed by many imperfections which the poetry existing in Chivalry and Christianity have erased from the habits and institutions of modern Europe; yet never at any other period has so much energy, beauty, and virtue, been developed; never was blind strength and stubborn form so disciplined and rendered subject to the will of man, or that will less repugnant to the dictates of the beautiful and the true, as during the century which preceded the death of Socrates. Of no other epoch in the history of our species have we records and fragments stamped so visibly with the image of the divinity in man. But it is Poetry alone, in form, in action, or in language, which has rendered this epoch memorable above all others, and the storehouse of examples to everlasting time.

.   .   .   .   .

It was at the period here adverted to, that the Drama had its birth; and however a succeeding writer may have equalled or surpassed those few great specimens of the Athenian drama which have been preserved to us, it is indisputable that the art itself never was understood or practised according to the true philosophy of it, as at Athens. For the Athenians employed language, action, music, painting, the dance, and religious institutions, to produce a common effect in the representation of the loftiest idealisms of passion and of power; each division in the art was made perfect in its kind by artists of the most consummate skill, and was disciplined into a beautiful proportion and unity one towards another. On the modern stage a few only of the elements capable of expressing the image of the poet's conception are employed at once. We have tragedy without music and dancing; and music and dancing without the high impersonations of which they are the fit accompaniment, and both without religion and solemnity; religious institution has indeed been usually banished from the stage.

.   .   .   .   .

The modern practice of blending comedy with tragedy, though liable to great abuse in point of practice, is undoubtedly an extension of the dramatic circle; but the comedy should be as in King Lear, universal, ideal, and sublime. It is perhaps the intervention of this principle which determines the balance in favour of King Lear against the Œdipus Tyrannus or the Agamemnon, or, if you will the trilogies with which they are connected; unless the intense power of the choral poetry, especially that of the latter, should be considered as restoring the equilibrium. King Lear, if it can sustain this comparison, may be judged to be the most perfect specimen of the dramatic art existing in the world;

.   .   .   .   .

The drama at Athens, or wheresoever else it may have approached to its perfection, coexisted with the moral and intellectual greatness of the age. The tragedies of the Athenian poets are as mirrors in which the spectator beholds himself, under a thin disguise of circumstance, stript of all but that ideal perfection and energy which every one feels to be the internal type of all that he loves, admires, and would become. The imagination is enlarged by a sympathy with pains and passions so mighty, that they distend in their conception the capacity of that by which they are conceived; the good affections are strengthened by pity, indignation, terror and sorrow; and an exalted calm is prolonged from the satiety of this high exercise of them into the tumult of familiar life: even crime is disarmed of half its horror and all its contagion by being represented as the fatal consequence of the unfathomable agencies of nature.

. . . . . .

Lucretius is in the highest, and Virgil in a very high sense, a creator. The chosen delicacy of the expressions of the latter, are as a mist of light which conceal from us the intense and exceeding truth of his conceptions of nature. Livy is instinct with poetry. Yet Horace, Catullus, Ovid, and generally the other great writers of the Virgilian age, saw man and nature in the mirror of Greece. The institutions also, and the religion of Rome, were less poetical than those of Greece, as the shadow is less vivid than the substance. Hence poetry in Rome, seemed to follow, rather than accompany, the perfection of political and domestic society. The true poetry of Rome lived in its institutions; for whatever of beautiful, true, and majestic, they contained, could have sprung only from the faculty which creates the order in which they consist.

. . . . . .

At length the antient system of religion and manners had fulfilled the circle of its revolution. And the world would have fallen into utter anarchy and darkness, but that there were found poets among the authors of the Christian and Chivalric systems of manners and religion, who created forms of opinion and action never before conceived; which, copied into the imaginations of men, became as generals to the bewildered armies of their thoughts. It is foreign to the present purpose to touch upon the evil produced by these systems: except that we protest, on the ground of the principles already established, that no portion of it can be imputed to the poetry they contain.

It is probable that the astonishing poetry of Moses, Job, David, Solomon, and Isaiah, had produced a great effect upon the mind of Jesus and his disciples. The scattered fragments preserved to us by the biographers of this extraordinary person, are all instinct with the most vivid poetry. But his doctrines seem to have been quickly distorted.

. . . . . .

It was not until the eleventh century that the effects of the poetry of the Christian and Chivalric systems began to manifest themselves. The principle of equality had been discovered and applied by Plato in his Republic, as the theoretical rule of the mode in which the materials of pleasure and of power produced by the common skill and labour of human beings ought to be distributed among them. The limitations of this rule were asserted by him to be determined only by the sensibility of each, or the utility to result to all. Plato, following the doctrines of Timæus and Pythagoras, taught also a moral and intellectual system of doctrine, comprehending at once the past, the present, and the future condition of man. Jesus Christ divulged the sacred and eternal truths contained in these views to mankind, and Christianity, in its abstract purity, became the exoteric expression of the esoteric doctrines of the poetry and wisdom of antiquity.

. . . . . .

The abolition of personal and domestic slavery, and the emancipation of women from a great part of the degrading restraints of antiquity, were among the consequences of these events.

The abolition of personal slavery is the basis of the highest political hope that it can enter into the mind of man to conceive. The freedom of women produced the poetry of sexual love. Love became a religion, the idols of whose worship were ever present. It was as if the statues of Apollo and the Muses had been endowed with life and motion, and had walked forth among their worshippers; so that earth became peopled by the inhabitants of a diviner world. The familiar appearance and proceedings of life became wonderful and heavenly; and a paradise was created as out of the wrecks of Eden. And as this creation itself is poetry, so its creators were poets; and language was the instrument of their art: "Galeotto fù il libro, e chi lo scrisse." The Provençal Trouveurs, or inventors, preceded Petrarch, whose verses are as spells, which unseal the inmost enchanted fountains of the delight which is in the grief of love. It is impossible to feel them without becoming a portion of that beauty which we contemplate: it were superfluous to explain how the gentleness and the elevation of mind connected with these sacred emotions can render men more amiable, and generous and wise, and lift them out of the dull vapours of the little world of self. Dante understood the secret things of love even more than Petrarch. His *Vita Nuova* is an inexhaustible fountain of purity of sentiment and language: it is the idealised history of that period, and those intervals of his life which were dedicated to love. His apotheosis of Beatrice in Paradise, and the gradations of his own love and her loveliness, by which as by steps he feigns himself to have ascended to the throne of the Supreme Cause, is the most glorious imagination of modern poetry. The acutest critics have justly reversed the judgment of the vulgar, and the order of the great acts of the "Divine Drama," in the measure of the admiration which they accord to the Hell, Purgatory, and Paradise. The latter is a perpetual hymn of everlasting Love. Love, which found a worthy poet in Plato alone of all the antients, has been celebrated by a chorus of the greatest writers of the renovated world; and the music has penetrated the caverns of society, and its echoes still drown the dissonance of arms and superstition. At successive intervals, Ariosto, Tasso, Shakspeare, Spenser, Calderon, Rousseau, and the great writers of our own age, have celebrated the dominion of love, planting as it were trophies in the human mind of that sublimest victory over sensuality and force. The true relation borne to each other by the sexes into which human kind is distributed, has become less misunderstood; and if the error which confounded diversity with inequality of the powers of the two sexes has become partially recognised in the opinions and institutions of modern Europe, we owe this great benefit to the worship of which Chivalry was the law, and poets the prophets.

The poetry of Dante may be considered as the bridge thrown over the stream of time, which unites the modern and antient World. The distorted notions of invisible things which Dante and his rival Milton have idealised, are merely the mask and the mantle in which these great poets walk through eternity enveloped and disguised.

.   .   .   .   .   .

And Milton's poem contains within itself a philosophical refutation of that system, of which, by a strange and natural antithesis, it has been a chief popular support. Nothing can exceed the energy and magnificence of the character of Satan as expressed in "Paradise Lost." It is a mistake to suppose that he could ever have been intended for the popular personification of evil. Implacable hate, patient cunning and a sleepless refinement of device to inflict the extremest anguish on an enemy, these things are evil; and, although venial in a slave, are not to be forgiven in a tyrant; although redeemed by much that ennobles his defeat in one subdued, are marked by all that dishonours his conquest in the victor. Milton's Devil as a moral being is as far superior to his God, as One who perseveres in some purpose which he has conceived to be excellent in spite of adversity and torture, is to One who in the cold security of undoubted triumph inflicts the most horrible revenge upon his enemy, not from any mistaken notion of inducing him to repent of a perseverance in enmity, but with the alleged design of exasperating him to deserve new torments. Milton has so far violated the popular creed (if this shall be judged to be a violation) as to have alleged no superiority of moral virtue to his God over his Devil. And this bold neglect of a direct moral purpose is the most decisive proof of the supremacy of Milton's genius. He mingled as it were the elements of human nature as colours upon a single pallet, and arranged them in the composition of his great picture according to the laws of epic truth; that is, according to the laws of that principle by which a series of actions of the external universe and of intelligent and ethical beings is calculated to excite the sympathy of succeeding generations of mankind. The Divina Commedia and Paradise Lost have conferred upon modern mythology a systematic form; and when change and time shall have added one more superstition to the mass of those which have arisen and decayed upon the earth, commentators will be learnedly employed in elucidating the religion of ancestral Europe, only not utterly forgotten because it will have been stamped with the eternity of genius.

.   .   .   .   .   .

Dante was the first religious reformer, and Luther surpassed him rather in the rudeness and acrimony, than in the boldness of his censures of papal usurpation. Dante was the first awakener of entranced Europe; he created a language, in itself music and persuasion, out of a chaos of inharmonious barbarisms. He was the congregator of those great spirits who presided over the resurrection of learning; the Lucifer of that starry flock which in the thirteenth century shone forth from republican Italy, as from a heaven, into the darkness of the benighted world. His very words are instinct with spirit; each is as a spark, a burning atom of inextinguishable thought; and many yet lie covered in the ashes of their birth, and pregnant with a lightning which has yet found no conductor. All high poetry is infinite; it is as the first acorn, which contained all oaks potentially. Veil after veil may be undrawn, and the inmost naked beauty of the meaning never exposed. A great poem is a fountain for ever overflowing with the waters of wisdom and delight; and after one person and one age has exhausted all its divine effluence which their peculiar relations enable them to share, another and yet another succeeds, and new relations are ever developed, the source of an unforeseen and an unconceived delight.

.   .   .   .

The exertions of Locke, Hume, Gibbon, Voltaire, Rousseau,[1] and their disciples, in favour of oppressed and deluded humanity, are entitled to the gratitude of mankind. Yet it is easy to calculate the degree of moral and intellectual improvement which the world would have exhibited, had they never lived. A little more nonsense would have been talked for a century or two; and perhaps a few more men, women, and children, burnt as heretics. We might not at this moment have been congratulating each other on the abolition of the Inquisition in Spain. But it exceeds all imagination to conceive what would have been the moral condition of the world if neither Dante, Petrarch, Boccaccio, Chaucer, Shakspeare, Calderon, Lord Bacon, nor Milton, had ever existed; if Raphael and Michael Angelo had never been born; if the Hebrew poetry had never been translated; if a revival of the study of Greek literature had never taken place; if no monuments of antient sculpture had been handed down to us; and if the poetry of the religion of the antient world had been extinguished together with its be-

[1] I follow the classification adopted by the Author of the Four Ages of Poetry; but he was essentially a Poet. The others, even Voltaire, were mere reasoners. [Shelley's note.]

lief. The human mind could never, except by the intervention of these excitements, have been awakened to the invention of the grosser sciences, and that application of analytical reasoning to the aberrations of society, which it is now attempted to exalt over the direct expression of the inventive and creative faculty itself.

We have more moral, political and historical wisdom, than we know how to reduce into practice; we have more scientific and economical knowledge than can be accommodated to the just distribution of the produce which it multiplies. The poetry in these systems of thought, is concealed by the accumulation of facts and calculating processes. There is no want of knowledge respecting what is wisest and best in morals, government, and political economy, or at least, what is wiser and better than what men now practise and endure. But we let "*I dare not* wait upon *I would*, like the poor cat i' the adage." We want the creative faculty to imagine that which we know; we want the generous impulse to act that which we imagine; we want the poetry of life: our calculations have outrun conception; we have eaten more than we can digest. The cultivation of those sciences which have enlarged the limits of the empire of man over the external world, has, for want of the poetical faculty, proportionally circumscribed those of the internal world; and man, having enslaved the elements, remains himself a slave. To what but a cultivation of the mechanical arts in a degree disproportioned to the presence of the creative faculty, which is the basis of all knowledge, is to be attributed the abuse of all invention for abridging and combining labour, to the exasperation of the inequality of mankind? From what other cause has it arisen that these inventions which should have lightened, have added a weight to the curse imposed on Adam? Thus Poetry, and the principle of Self, of which Money is the visible incarnation, are the God and Mammon of the world.

The functions of the poetical faculty are twofold; by one it creates new materials for knowledge, and power and pleasure; by the other it engenders in the mind a desire to reproduce and arrange them according to a certain rhythm and order which may be called the beautiful and the good. The cultivation of poetry is never more to be desired than at periods when, from an excess of the selfish and calculating principle, the accumulation of the materials of external life exceed the quantity of the power of assimilating them to the internal laws of human nature. The body has then become too unwieldy for that which animates it.

Poetry is indeed something divine. It is at once the centre and circumference of knowledge; it is that which comprehends all science, and that to which all science must be referred. It is at the same time the root and blossom of all other systems of thought; it is that from which all spring, and that which adorns all; and that which, if blighted, denies the fruit and the seed, and withholds from the barren world the nourishment and the succession of the scions of the tree of life. It is the perfect and consummate surface and bloom of things; it is as the odour and the colour of the rose to the texture of the elements which compose it, as the form and the splendour of unfaded beauty to the secrets of anatomy and corruption. What were Virtue, Love, Patriotism, Friendship — what were the scenery of this beautiful Universe which we inhabit; what were our consolations on this side of the grave, and what were our aspirations beyond it, if Poetry did not ascend to bring light and fire from those eternal regions where the owl-winged faculty of calculation dare not ever soar? Poetry is not like reasoning, a power to be exerted according to the determination of the will. A man cannot say, "I will compose poetry." The greatest poet even cannot say it: for the mind in creation is as a fading coal, which some invisible influence, like an inconstant wind, awakens to transitory brightness: this power arises from within, like the colour of a flower which fades and changes as it is developed, and the conscious portions of our natures are unprophetic either of its approach or its departure. Could this influence be durable in its original purity and force, it is impossible to predict the greatness of the results; but when composition begins, inspiration is already on the decline, and the most glorious poetry that has ever been communicated to the world is probably a feeble shadow of the original conception of the Poet. I appeal to the great poets of the present day, whether it be not an error to assert that the finest passages of poetry are produced by labour and study. The toil and the delay recommended by critics, can be justly interpreted to mean no more than a careful observation of the inspired moments, and an artificial connexion of the spaces between their suggestions by the intertexture of conventional expressions; a necessity only imposed by the limitedness of the poetical

faculty itself. For Milton conceived the Paradise Lost as a whole before he executed it in portions. We have his own authority also for the Muse having "dictated" to him the "unpremediated song," and let this be an answer to those who would allege the fifty-six various readings of the first line of the Orlando Furioso. Compositions so produced are to poetry what mosaic is to painting. This instinct and intuition of the poetical faculty is still more observable in the plastic and pictorial arts; a great statue or picture grows under the power of the artist as a child in the mother's womb; and the very mind which directs the hands in formation is incapable of accounting to itself for the origin, the gradations, or the media of the process.

Poetry is the record of the best and happiest moments of the happiest and best minds. We are aware of evanescent visitations of thought and feeling sometimes associated with place or person, sometimes regarding our own mind alone, and always arising unforeseen and departing unbidden, but elevating and delightful beyond all expression: so that even in the desire and the regret they leave, there cannot but be pleasure, participating as it does in the nature of its object. It is as it were the interpenetration of a diviner nature through our own; but its footsteps are like those of a wind over a sea, which the coming calm erases, and whose traces remain only, as on the wrinkled sand which paves it. These and corresponding conditions of being are experienced principally by those of the most delicate sensibility and the most enlarged imagination; and the state of mind produced by them is at war with every base desire. The enthusiasm of virtue, love, patriotism, and friendship, is essentially linked with these emotions; and whilst they last, self appears as what it is, an atom to a Universe. Poets are not only subject to these experiences as spirits of the most refined organisation, but they can colour all that they combine with the evanescent hues of this ethereal world; a word, or a trait in the representation of a scene or a passion, will touch the enchanted chord, and reanimate, in those who have ever experienced these emotions, the sleeping, the cold, the buried image of the past. Poetry thus makes immortal all that is best and most beautiful in the world; it arrests the vanishing apparitions which haunt the interlunations of life, and veiling them, or in language or in form, sends them forth among mankind, bearing sweet news of kindred joy to those with whom their sisters abide — abide, because there is no portal of expression from the caverns of the spirit which they inhabit into the universe of things. Poetry redeems from decay the visitations of the divinity in Man.

Poetry turns all things to loveliness; it exalts the beauty of that which is most beautiful, and it adds beauty to that which is most deformed; it marries exultation and horror, grief and pleasure, eternity and change; it subdues to union under its light yoke, all irreconcilable things. It transmutes all that it touches, and every form moving within the radiance of its presence is changed by wondrous sympathy to an incarnation of the spirit which it breathes; its secret alchemy turns to potable gold the poisonous waters which flow from death through life; it strips the veil of familiarity from the world, and lays bare the naked and sleeping beauty, which is the spirit of its forms.

All things exist as they are perceived; at least in relation to the percipient. "The mind is its own place, and of itself can make a Heaven of Hell, a Hell of Heaven." But poetry defeats the curse which binds us to be subjected to the accident of surrounding impressions. And whether it spreads its own figured curtain, or withdraws life's dark veil from before the scene of things, it equally creates for us a being within our being. It makes us the inhabitants of a world to which the familiar world is a chaos. It reproduces the common Universe of which we are portions and percipients, and it purges from our inward sight the film of familiarity which obscures from us the wonder of our being. It compels us to feel that which we perceive, and to imagine that which we know. It creates anew the universe, after it has been annihilated in our minds by the recurrence of impressions blunted by reiteration. It justifies that bold and true word of Tasso: *Non merita nome di creatore, se non Iddio ed il Poeta.*

. . . .

I have thought it most favourable to the cause of truth to set down these remarks according to the order in which they were suggested to my mind, by a consideration of the subject itself, instead of following that of the treatise that excited me to make them public. Thus although devoid of the formality of a polemical reply; if the view they con-

tain be just, they will be found to involve a refutation of the doctrines of the Four Ages of Poetry, so far at least as regards the first division of the subject.

. . . .

The first part of these remarks has related to Poetry in its elements and principles; and it has been shewn, as well as the narrow limits assigned them would permit, that what is called poetry, in a restricted sense, has a common source with all other forms of order and of beauty, according to which the materials of human life are susceptible of being arranged, and which is Poetry in an universal sense.

The second part will have for its object an application of these principles to the present state of the cultivation of Poetry, and a defence of the attempt to idealize the modern forms of manners and opinions, and compel them into a subordination to the imaginative and creative faculty. For the literature of England, an energetic development of which has ever preceded or accompanied a great and free development of the national will, has arisen as it were from a new birth. In spite of the low-thoughted envy which would undervalue contemporary merit, our own will be a memorable age in intellectual achievements, and we live among such philosophers and poets as surpass beyond comparison any who have appeared since the last national struggle for civil and religious liberty. The most unfailing herald, companion, and follower of the awakening of a great people to work a beneficial change in opinion or institution, is Poetry. At such periods there is an accumulation of the power of communicating and receiving intense and impassioned conceptions respecting man and nature. The persons in whom this power resides, may often as far as regards many portions of their nature, have little apparent correspondence with that spirit of good of which they are the ministers. But even whilst they deny and abjure, they are yet compelled to serve, the Power which is seated upon the throne of their own soul. It is impossible to read the compositions of the most celebrated writers of the present day without being startled with the electric life which burns within their words. They measure the circumference and sound the depths of human nature with a comprehensive and all-penetrating spirit, and they are themselves perhaps the most sincerely astonished at its manifestations; for it is less their spirit than the spirit of the age. Poets are the hierophants of an unapprehended inspiration; the mirrors of the gigantic shadows which futurity casts upon the present; the words which express what they understand not; the trumpets which sing to battle, and feel not what they inspire; the influence which is moved not, but moves. Poets are the unacknowledged legislators of the world.

NOTES AND ILLUSTRATIONS

Page 1. QUEEN MAB.

The unusual metrical form in which the poem is cast is described by Shelley in a letter to Hogg, February 7, 1813: 'I have not been able to bring myself to rhyme. The didactic is in blank heroic verse, and the description in blank lyrical measure. If an authority is of any weight in support of this singularity, Milton's *Samson Agonistes*, the Greek choruses, and (you will laugh) Southey's *Thalaba* may be adduced.' The model of the lyrical portion is, in fact, *Thalaba*, the cadences of which are closely reproduced in general. The motive of the poem, as is shown by the motto prefixed, is Lucretian; Shelley imagined that in attacking religion he was performing a service to humanity similar to that of the Latin poet in attacking superstition, and also that in his philosophy of nature and necessity he was following in the footsteps of the most illustrious poet who has embodied scientific conceptions in verse. The form of the tale he took from Volney, *Les Ruines*. The sources of his thought, both with respect to his view of the system of nature and to his reflections on human institutions and their operation on society, are developed with sufficient fulness in his own NOTES, which have attracted perhaps more attention than the poem they illustrate. These, with a few exceptions noted in the place of omission, are given below, the text being revised so as not to reproduce obvious errors; Shelley's references and extracts, except when he may have meant to paraphrase, have also been corrected; that is to say, the original editions which he himself probably used have been consulted, and *the passages printed as they there occur literally;* thus in the extracts from the *Système de la Nature par M. Mirabaud*, for example, there are many errors, but the text that Shelley had before him has been faithfully transcribed, in all cases. Much of these NOTES had been previously published by Shelley. The note, ' There is no God,' embodies Shelley's Oxford tract, *The Necessity of Atheism*, published at Worthing in 1811 ; the note, 'I will beget a Son,' embodies portions of the *Letter to Lord Ellenborough*, printed at Barnstable, 1812, and the note, 'No longer now he slays,' etc., was published slightly revised as *A Vindication of Natural Diet*, London, 1813. The fragment of *Ahasuerus*, referred to in the note, ' Ahasuerus, rise,' was picked up by Medwin (*Life*, i. 57), and is a modified translation of Schubart's *Der Ewige Jude*, which appeared in *The German Museum*, vol. iii. 1802.

SHELLEY'S NOTES TO QUEEN MAB.

I. 242, 243 : —

> The sun's unclouded orb
> Rolled through the black concave.

Beyond our atmosphere the sun would appear a rayless orb of fire in the midst of a black concave. The equal diffusion of its light on earth is owing to the refraction of the rays by the atmosphere and their reflection from other bodies. Light consists either of vibrations propagated through a subtle medium or of numerous minute particles repelled in all directions from the luminous body. Its velocity greatly exceeds that of any substance with which we are acquainted. Observations on the eclipses of Jupiter's satellites have demonstrated that light takes up no more than 8′ 7″ in passing from the sun to the earth, a distance of 95,000,-000 miles. Some idea may be gained of the immense distance of the fixed stars when it is computed that many years would elapse before light could reach this earth from the nearest of them ; yet in one year light travels 5,422,400,-000,000 miles, which is a distance 5,707,600 times greater than that of the sun from the earth.

I. 252, 253 : —

> Whilst round the chariot's way
> Innumerable systems rolled.

The plurality of worlds — the indefinite immensity of the Universe — is a most awful subject of contemplation. He who rightly feels its mystery and grandeur is in no danger of seduction from the falsehoods of religious systems, or of deifying the principle of the universe. It is impossible to believe that the Spirit that pervades this infinite machine begat a son upon the body of a Jewish woman ; or is angered at the consequences of that necessity which is a synonym of itself. All that miserable tale of the Devil and Eve and an Intercessor, with the childish mummeries of the God of the Jews, is irreconcilable with the knowledge of the stars. The works of his fingers have borne witness against him.

The nearest of the fixed stars is inconceivably distant from the earth, and they are probably proportionally distant from each other. By a calculation of the velocity of light Sirius is supposed to be at least 54,224,000,000,000 miles from the earth.[1] That which appears only like a thin and silvery cloud streaking the heaven is in effect composed of innumerable clusters of suns, each shining with its own light and illuminating numbers of planets that revolve around them. Millions and millions of suns are ranged around us, all attended by innumerable worlds, yet calm, regular and harmonious, all keeping the paths of immutable necessity.

IV. 178, 179: —

> These are the hired bravos who defend
> The tyrant's throne.

To employ murder as a means of justice is an idea which a man of an enlightened mind will not dwell upon with pleasure. To march forth in rank and file, and all the pomp of streamers and trumpets, for the purpose of shooting at our fellowmen as a mark ; to inflict upon them all the variety of wound and anguish ; to leave them weltering in their blood ; to wander over the field of desolation, and count the number of the dying and the dead, — are employments which in thesis we may maintain to be necessary, but which no good man will contemplate with gratulation and delight. A battle we suppose is won : — thus truth is established, thus the cause of justice is confirmed ! It surely requires no common sagacity to discern the connection between this immense heap of calamities and the assertion of truth or the maintenance of justice.

'Kings and ministers of state, the real authors of the calamity, sit unmolested in their cabinet, while those against whom the fury of the storm is directed are, for the most part, persons who have been trepanned into the service, or who are dragged unwillingly from their peaceful homes into the field of battle. A soldier is a man whose business it is to kill those who never offended him, and who are the innocent martyrs of other men's iniquities. Whatever may become of the abstract question of the justifiableness of war, it seems impossible that the soldier should not be a depraved and unnatural being.

'To these more serious and momentous considerations it may be proper to add a recollection of the ridiculousness of the military character. Its first constituent is obedience : a soldier is, of all descriptions of men, the most completely a machine ; yet his profession inevitably teaches him something of dogmatism, swaggering and self-consequence ; he is like the puppet of a showman, who, at the very time he is made to strut and swell and display the most farcical airs, we perfectly know cannot assume the most insignificant gesture, advance either to the right or the left, but as he is moved by his exhibitor.' — Godwin's *Enquirer*, Essay V.

I will here subjoin a little poem, so strongly expressive of my abhorrence of despotism and falsehood that I fear lest it never again may be depictured so vividly. This opportunity is perhaps the only one that ever will occur of rescuing it from oblivion.

[1] See Nicholson's *Encyclopedia*, art. 'Light.'

FALSEHOOD AND VICE

A DIALOGUE

WHILST monarchs laughed upon their thrones
To hear a famished nation's groans,
And hugged the wealth wrung from the woe
That makes its eyes and veins o'erflow, —
Those thrones, high built upon the heaps
Of bones where frenzied Famine sleeps,
Where Slavery wields her scourge of iron,
Red with mankind's unheeded gore,
And War's mad fiends the scene environ,
Mingling with shrieks a drunken roar, —
There Vice and Falsehood took their stand,
High raised above the unhappy land.

FALSEHOOD

Brother ! arise from the dainty fare,
Which thousands have toiled and bled to bestow ;
A finer feast for thy hungry ear
Is the news that I bring of human woe.

VICE

And, secret one, what hast thou done,
To compare, in thy tumid pride, with me ?
I, whose career through the blasted year
Has been tracked by despair and agony.

FALSEHOOD

What have I done ! — I have torn the robe
From baby Truth's unsheltered form,
And round the desolated globe
Borne safely the bewildering charm ;
My tyrant-slaves to a dungeon-floor
Have bound the fearless innocent,
And streams of fertilizing gore
Flow from her bosom's hideous rent,
Which this unfailing dagger gave —
I dread that blood ! — no more — this day
Is ours, though her eternal ray
    Must shine upon our grave.
Yet know, proud Vice, had I not given
To thee the robe I stole from heaven,
Thy shape of ugliness and fear
Had never gained admission here.

VICE

And know that had I disdained to toil,
But sate in my loathsome cave the while,
And ne'er to these hateful sons of heaven,
GOLD, MONARCHY and MURDER, given ;
Hadst thou with all thine art essayed
One of thy games then to have played,
With all thine overweening boast,
Falsehood ! I tell thee thou hadst lost ! —
Yet wherefore this dispute ? — we tend,
Fraternal, to one common end ;
In this cold grave beneath my feet
Will our hopes, our fears and our labors meet.

FALSEHOOD

I brought my daughter, RELIGION, on earth ;
She smothered Reason's babes in their birth,
But dreaded their mother's eye severe, —
So the crocodile slunk off slyly in fear,
And loosed her bloodhounds from the den.
They started from dreams of slaughtered men,
And, by the light of her poison eye,
Did her work o'er the wide earth frightfully.
The dreadful stench of her torches' flare,
Fed with human fat, polluted the air.
The curses, the shrieks, the ceaseless cries
Of the many-mingling miseries,

As on she trod, ascended high
And trumpeted my victory ! —
Brother, tell what thou hast done.

VICE

I have extinguished the noonday sun
In the carnage-smoke of battles won.
Famine, murder, hell and power
Were glutted in that glorious hour
Which searchless fate had stamped for me
With the seal of her security ;
For the bloated wretch on yonder throne
Commanded the bloody fray to rise ;
Like me he joyed at the stifled moan
Wrung from a nation's miseries ;
While the snakes, whose slime even him *defiled*,
In ecstasies of malice smiled.
They thought 't was theirs, — but mine the deed !
Theirs is the toil, but mine the meed —
Ten thousand victims madly bleed.
They dream that tyrants goad them there
With poisonous war to taint the air.
These tyrants, on their beds of thorn,
Swell with the thoughts of murderous fame,
And with their gains to lift my name
Restless they plan from night to morn ;
I — I do all ; without my aid
Thy daughter, that relentless maid,
Could never o'er a death-bed urge
The fury of her venomed scourge.

FALSEHOOD

Brother, well : — the world is ours ;
And whether thou or I have won,
The pestilence expectant lours
On all beneath yon blasted sun.
Our joys, our toils, our honors meet
In the milk-white and wormy winding-sheet.
A short-lived hope, unceasing care,
Some heartless scraps of godly prayer,
A moody curse, and a frenzied sleep
Ere gapes the grave's unclosing deep,
A tyrant's dream, a coward's start,
The ice that clings to a priestly heart,
A judge's frown, a courtier's smile,
Make the great whole for which we toil.
And, brother, whether thou or I
Have done the work of misery,
It little boots. Thy toil and pain,
Without my aid, were more than vain ;
And but for thee I ne'er had sate
The guardian of heaven's palace gate.

V. 1, 2 : —

Thus do the generations of the earth
Go to the grave and issue from the womb.

'One generation passeth away, and another
generation cometh : but the earth abideth for
ever. The sun also ariseth, and the sun goeth
down, and hasteth to his place where he arose.
The wind goeth toward the south, and turneth
about unto the north ; it whirleth about continually, and the wind returneth again according
to his circuits. All the rivers run into the sea ;
yet the sea is not full ; unto the place from
whence the rivers come, thither they return
again.'

Ecclesiastes, i. 4–7.

V. 4–6 : —

Even as the leaves
Which the keen frost-wind of the waning year
Has scattered on the forest soil.

Οἴη περ φύλλων γενεή, τοιήδε καὶ ἀνδρῶν.
Φύλλα τὰ μέν τ' ἄνεμος χαμάδις χέει, ἄλλα δέ θ' ὕλη
Τηλεθόωσα φύει, ἔαρος δ' ἐπιγίνεται ὥρη·
Ὣς ἀνδρῶν γενεὴ ἣ μὲν φύει ἣ δ' ἀπολήγει.

ΙΛΙΑΔ. Ζʹ. 146.

V. 58 : —

The mob of peasants, nobles, priests and kings.

Suave, mari magno turbantibus æquora ventis,
E terra magnum alterius spectare laborem ;
Non quia vexari quemquam 'st jucunda voluptas,
Sed quibus ipse malis careas quia cernere suave est.
Suave etiam belli certamina magna tueri
Per campos instructa tua sine parte pericli.
Sed nil dulcius est, bene quam munita tenere
Edita doctrina sapientum templa serena,
Despicere unde queas alios passimque videre
Errare atque viam palantis quærere vitæ,
Certare ingenio, contendere nobilitate,
Noctes atque dies niti præstante labore
Ad summas emergere opes rerumque potiri.
O miseras hominum mentes ! O pectora cæca !

Lucretius, ii. 1–14.

V. 93, 94 : —

And statesmen boast
Of wealth !

There is no real wealth but the labor of man.
Were the mountains of gold and the valleys of
silver, the world would not be one grain of corn
the richer ; no one comfort would be added to
the human race. In consequence of our consideration for the precious metals one man is
enabled to heap to himself luxuries at the expense of the necessaries of his neighbor ; a system admirably fitted to produce all the varieties
of disease and crime which never fail to characterize the two extremes of opulence and penury.
A speculator takes pride to himself, as the pro-
moter of his country's prosperity, who employs
a number of hands in the manufacture of articles avowedly destitute of use or subservient
only to the unhallowed cravings of luxury and
ostentation. The nobleman who employs the
peasants of his neighborhood in building his
palaces, until '*jam pauca aratro jugera regiæ
moles relinquent*,' flatters himself that he has
gained the title of a patriot by yielding to the
impulses of vanity. The show and pomp of
courts adduce the same apology for its continuance ; and many a fête has been given, many a
woman has eclipsed her beauty by her dress, to
benefit the laboring poor and to encourage
trade. Who does not see that this is a remedy
which aggravates whilst it palliates the countless diseases of society ? The poor are set to
labor, — for what ? Not the food for which
they famish ; not the blankets for want of
which their babes are frozen by the cold of
their miserable hovels ; not those comforts of
civilization without which civilized man is far
more miserable than the meanest savage, oppressed as he is by all its insidious evils, within
the daily and taunting prospect of its innumerable benefits assiduously exhibited before him :
— no ; for the pride of power, for the miserable
isolation of pride, for the false pleasures of the
hundredth part of society. No greater evidence is afforded of the wide extended and
radical mistakes of civilized man than this

fact: those arts which are essential to his very being are held in the greatest contempt; employments are lucrative in an inverse ratio to their usefulness; [1] the jeweller, the toyman, the actor gains fame and wealth by the exercise of his useless and ridiculous art; whilst the cultivator of the earth, he without whom society must cease to subsist, struggles through contempt and penury, and perishes by that famine which, but for his unceasing exertions, would annihilate the rest of mankind.

I will not insult common sense by insisting on the doctrine of the natural equality of man. The question is not concerning its desirableness, but its practicability; so far as it is practicable, it is desirable. That state of human society which approaches nearer to an equal partition of its benefits and evils should, *cæteris paribus*, be preferred; but so long as we conceive that a wanton expenditure of human labor, not for the necessities, not even for the luxuries of the mass of society, but for the egotism and ostentation of a few of its members, is defensible on the ground of public justice, so long we neglect to approximate to the redemption of the human race.

Labor is required for physical, and leisure for moral improvement; from the former of these advantages the rich, and from the latter the poor, by the inevitable conditions of their respective situations, are precluded. A state which should combine the advantages of both would be subjected to the evils of neither. He that is deficient in firm health or vigorous intellect is but half a man. Hence it follows that to subject the laboring classes to unnecessary labor is wantonly depriving them of any opportunities of intellectual improvement; and that the rich are heaping up for their own mischief the disease, lassitude and ennui by which their existence is rendered an intolerable burden.

English reformers exclaim against sinecures, but the true pension list is the rent-roll of the landed proprietors. Wealth is a power usurped by the few, to compel the many to labor for their benefit. The laws which support this system derive their force from the ignorance and credulity of its victims; they are the result of a conspiracy of the few against the many who are themselves obliged to purchase this pre-eminence by the loss of all real comfort.

☞

'The commodities that substantially contribute to the subsistence of the human species form a very short catalogue; they demand from us but a slender portion of industry. If these only were produced, and sufficiently produced, the species of man would be continued. If the labor necessarily required to produce them were equitably divided among the poor, and, still more, if it were equitably divided among all, each man's share of labor would be light, and his portion of leisure would be ample. There was a time when this leisure would have been

[1] See Rousseau, *De l'Inégalité parmi les Hommes*, note 7.

of small comparative value: it is to be hoped that the time will come when it will be applied to the most important purposes. Those hours which are not required for the production of the necessaries of life may be devoted to the cultivation of the understanding, the enlarging our stock of knowledge, the refining our taste, and thus opening to us new and more exquisite sources of enjoyment.

. . . .

'It was perhaps necessary that a period of monopoly and oppression should subsist before a period of cultivated equality could subsist. Savages perhaps would never have been excited to the discovery of truth and the invention of art but by the narrow motives which such a period affords. But surely, after the savage state has ceased and men have set out in the glorious career of discovery and invention, monopoly and oppression cannot be necessary to prevent them from returning to a state of barbarism.' — Godwin's *Enquirer*, Essay II. See also *Political Justice*, book VIII., chap. ii.

It is a calculation of this admirable author that all the conveniences of civilized life might be produced, if society would divide the labor equally among its members, by each individual being employed in labor two hours during the day.

V. 112, 113 : —

or religion
Drives his wife raving mad.

I am acquainted with a lady of considerable accomplishments and the mother of a numerous family, whom the Christian religion has goaded to incurable insanity. A parallel case is, I believe, within the experience of every physician.

Nam jam sæpe homines patriam carosque parentis
Prodiderunt, vitare Acherusia templa petentes.
Lucretius, iii. 85.

V. 189 : —

Even love is sold.

Not even the intercourse of the sexes is exempt from the despotism of positive institution. Law pretends even to govern the indisciplinable wanderings of passion, to put fetters on the clearest deductions of reason, and, by appeals to the will, to subdue the involuntary affections of our nature. Love is inevitably consequent upon the perception of loveliness. Love withers under constraint; its very essence is liberty; it is compatible neither with obedience, jealousy nor fear; it is there most pure, perfect and unlimited, where its votaries live in confidence, equality and unreserve.

How long then ought the sexual connection to last? what law ought to specify the extent of the grievances which should limit its duration? A husband and wife ought to continue so long united as they love each other; any law which should bind them to cohabitation for one moment after the decay of their affection would be a most intolerable tyranny and the most unworthy of toleration. How odious an usurpation of the right of private judgment should that law be considered which should make the ties of friendship indissoluble, in spite of the caprices, the inconstancy, the fallibility and capacity for improvement of the human mind! And by so much would the fetters of love be heavier and more unendurable than those of friendship as love is more vehement and capricious, more dependent on those delicate peculiarities of imagination, and less capable of reduction to the ostensible merits of the object. The state of society in which we exist is a mixture of feudal savageness and imperfect civilization. The narrow and unenlightened morality of the Christian religion is an aggravation of these evils. It is not even until lately that mankind have admitted that happiness is the sole end of the science of ethics as of all other sciences ; and that the fanatical idea of mortifying the flesh for the love of God has been discarded. I have heard, indeed, an ignorant collegian adduce, in favor of Christianity, its hostility to every worldly feeling ![1]

But if happiness be the object of morality, of all human unions and disunions ; if the worthiness of every action is to be estimated by the quantity of pleasurable sensation it is calculated to produce ; then the connection of the sexes is so long sacred as it contributes to the comfort of the parties, and is naturally dissolved when its evils are greater than its benefits. There is nothing immoral in this separation. Constancy has nothing virtuous in itself, independently of the pleasure it confers, and partakes of the temporizing spirit of vice in proportion as it endures tamely moral defects of magnitude in the object of its indiscreet choice. Love is free ; to promise forever to love the same woman is not less absurd than to promise to believe the same creed ; such a vow, in both cases, excludes us from all inquiry ; The language of the votarist is this. 'The woman I now love may be infinitely inferior to many others ; the creed I now profess may be a mass of errors and absurdities ; but I exclude myself from all future information as to the amiability of the one and the truth of the other, resolving blindly, and in spite of conviction, to adhere to them.' Is this the language of delicacy and reason ? Is the love of such a frigid heart of more worth than its belief?

The present system of constraint does no more, in the majority of instances, than make hypocrites or open enemies. Persons of delicacy and virtue, unhappily united to one whom they find it impossible to love, spend the loveliest season of their life in unproductive efforts to appear otherwise than they are, for the sake of the feelings of their partner or the welfare of their mutual offspring ; those of less generosity and refinement openly avow their disappointment, and linger out the remnant of that union, which only death can dissolve, in a state

of incurable bickering and hostility. The early education of their children takes its color from the squabbles of the parents ; they are nursed in a systematic school of ill humor, violence, and falsehood. Had they been suffered to part at the moment when indifference rendered their union irksome, they would have been spared many years of misery ; they would have connected themselves more suitably and would have found that happiness in the society of more congenial partners which is forever denied them by the despotism of marriage. They would have been separately useful and happy members of society, who, whilst united, were miserable, and rendered misanthropical by misery. The conviction that wedlock is indissoluble holds out the strongest of all temptations to the perverse ; they indulge without restraint in acrimony, and all the little tyrannies of domestic life, when they know that their victim is without appeal. If this connection were put on a rational basis, each would be assured that habitual ill temper would terminate in separation, and would check this vicious and dangerous propensity.

Prostitution is the legitimate offspring of marriage and its accompanying errors. Women, for no other crime than having followed the dictates of a natural appetite, are driven with fury from the comforts and sympathies of society. It is less venial than murder ; and the punishment which is inflicted on her who destroys her child to escape reproach is lighter than the life of agony and disease to which the prostitute is irrecoverably doomed. Has a woman obeyed the impulse of unerring Nature ? society declares war against her, pitiless and eternal war ; she must be the tame slave, she must make no reprisals ; theirs is the right of persecution, hers the duty of endurance. She lives a life of infamy ; the loud and bitter laugh of scorn scares her from all return. She dies of long and lingering disease ; yet *she* is in fault, *she* is the criminal, *she* the froward and untamable child, — and society, forsooth, the pure and virtuous matron, who casts her as an abortion from her undefiled bosom ! Society avenges herself on the criminals of her own creation ; she is employed in anathematizing the vice today which yesterday she was the most zealous to teach. Thus is formed one tenth of the population of London. Meanwhile the evil is twofold. Young men, excluded by the fanatical idea of chastity from the society of modest and accomplished women, associate with these vicious and miserable beings, destroying thereby all those exquisite and delicate sensibilities whose existence cold-hearted worldlings have denied ; annihilating all genuine passion, and debasing that to a selfish feeling which is the excess of generosity and devotedness. Their

[1] The first Christian emperor made a law by which seduction was punished with death : if the female pleaded her own consent, she also was punished with death ; if the parents endeavored to screen the criminals, they were banished and their estates were confiscated ; the slaves who might be accessory were burned alive, or forced to swallow melted lead. The very offspring of an illegal love were involved in the consequences of the sentence. — Gibbon's *Decline and Fall*, vol. ii. p. 210. See also, for the hatred of the primitive Christians to love and even marriage, p. 269.

body and mind alike crumble into a hideous wreck of humanity ; idiocy and disease become perpetuated in their miserable offspring, and distant generations suffer for the bigoted morality of their forefathers. Chastity is a monkish and evangelical superstition, a greater foe to natural temperance even than unintellectual sensuality ; it strikes at the root of all domestic happiness, and consigns more than half of the human race to misery that some few may monopolize according to law. A system could not well have been devised more studiously hostile to human happiness than marriage.

I conceive that from the abolition of marriage the fit and natural arrangement of sexual connection would result. I by no means assert that the intercourse would be promiscuous ; on the contrary it appears from the relation of parent to child that this union is generally of long duration, and marked above all others with generosity and self-devotion. But this is a subject which it is perhaps premature to discuss. That which will result from the abolition of marriage will be natural and right, because choice and change will be exempted from restraint.

In fact, religion and morality, as they now stand, compose a practical code of misery and servitude ; the genius of human happiness must tear every leaf from the accursed book of God ere man can read the inscription on his heart. How would Morality, dressed up in stiff stays and finery, start from her own disgusting image, should she look in the mirror of Nature ! ☞

VI. 45, 46 : —

> To the red and baleful sun
> That faintly twinkles there.

The north polar star to which the axis of the earth in its present state of obliquity points. It is exceedingly probable from many considerations that this obliquity will gradually diminish until the equator coincides with the ecliptic ; the nights and days will then become equal on the earth throughout the year, and probably the seasons also. There is no great extravagance in presuming that the progress of the perpendicularity of the poles may be as rapid as the progress of intellect ; or that there should be a perfect identity between the moral and physical improvement of the human species. It is certain that wisdom is not compatible with disease, and that, in the present state of the climates of the earth, health, in the true and comprehensive sense of the word, is out of the reach of civilized man. Astronomy teaches us that the earth is now in its progress, and that the poles are every year becoming more and more perpendicular to the ecliptic. The strong evidence afforded by the history of mythology and geological researches that some event of this nature has taken place already affords a strong presumption that this progress is not merely an oscillation, as has been surmised by some late astronomers.[1] Bones of animals peculiar to

[1] Laplace, *Système du Monde.*

the torrid zone have been found in the north of Siberia and on the banks of the river Ohio. Plants have been found in the fossil state in the interior of Germany, which demand the present climate of Hindostan for their production.[2] The researches of M. Bailly [3] establish the existence of a people who inhabited a tract in Tartary 49° north latitude, of greater antiquity than either the Indians, the Chinese, or the Chaldeans, from whom these nations derived their sciences and theology. We find from the testimony of ancient writers that Britain, Germany, and France were much colder than at present, and that their great rivers were annually frozen over. Astronomy teaches us also that since this period the obliquity of the earth's position has been considerably diminished.

VI. 171–173 : —

> No atom of this turbulence fulfils
> A vague and unnecessitated task,
> Or acts but as it must and ought to act.

Deux exemples serviront à nous rendre plus sensible le principe qui vient d'être posé ; nous emprunterons l'une du physique et l'autre du moral. Dans un tourbillon de poussière qu'élève un vent impétueux, quelque confus qu'il paraisse à nos yeux ; dans la plus affreuse tempête excitée par des vents opposés qui soulèvent les flots, il n'y a pas une seule molécule de poussière ou d'eau qui soit placée au *hazard*, qui n'ait sa cause suffisante pour occuper le lieu où elle se trouve, et qui n'agisse rigoureusement de la manière dont elle doit agir. Une géomètre qui connaîtrait exactement les différentes forces qui agissent dans ces deux cas, et les propriétés des molécules qui sont mues, demontrerait que d'après des causes données, chaque molécule agit précisément comme elle doit agir, et ne peut agir autrement qu'elle ne fait.

Dans les convulsions terribles qui agitent quelquefois les sociétés politiques, et qui produisent souvent le renversement d'un empire, il n'y a pas une seule action, une seule parole, une seule pensée, une seule volonté, une seule passion dans les agens qui concourent à la révolution comme destructeurs ou comme victimes, qui ne soit nécessaire, qui n'agisse comme elle doit agir, qui n'opère infailliblement les effets qu'elle doit opérer, suivant la place qu'occupent ces agens dans ce tourbillon moral. Cela paraîtrait évident pour une intelligence qui serait en état de saisir et d'apprécier toutes les actions et réactions des esprits et des corps de ceux qui contribuent à cette révolution.

> *Système de la Nature*, vol. i. p. 44.

VI. 198° : —

> Necessity, thou mother of the world !

He who asserts the doctrine of Necessity means that, contemplating the events which compose the moral and material universe, he beholds only an immense and uninterrupted

[2] Cabanis, *Rapports du Physique et du Moral de l'Homme*, vol. ii. p. 406.

[3] Bailly, *Lettres sur les Sciences, à Voltaire.*

chain of causes and effects, no one of which could occupy any other place than it does occupy, or act in any other place than it does act. The idea of Necessity is obtained by our experience of the connection between objects, the uniformity of the operations of Nature, the constant conjunction of similar events, and the consequent inference of one from the other. Mankind are therefore agreed in the admission of Necessity if they admit that these two circumstances take place in voluntary action. Motive is to voluntary action in the human mind what cause is to effect in the material universe. The word liberty, as applied to mind, is analogous to the word chance as applied to matter; they spring from an ignorance of the certainty of the conjunction of antecedents and consequents.

Every human being is irresistibly impelled to act precisely as he does act; in the eternity which preceded his birth a chain of causes was generated, which, operating under the name of motives, make it impossible that any thought of his mind or any action of his life should be otherwise than it is. Were the doctrine of Necessity false, the human mind would no longer be a legitimate object of science; from like causes it would be in vain that we should expect like effects; the strongest motive would no longer be paramount over the conduct; all knowledge would be vague and undeterminate; we could not predict with any certainty that we might not meet as an enemy to-morrow him with whom we have parted in friendship to-night; the most probable inducements and the clearest reasonings would lose the invariable influence they possess. The contrary of this is demonstrably the fact. Similar circumstances produce the same unvariable effects. The precise character and motives of any man on any occasion being given, the moral philosopher could predict his actions with as much certainty as the natural philosopher could predict the effects of the mixture of any particular chemical substances. Why is the aged husbandman more experienced than the young beginner? Because there is a uniform, undeniable Necessity in the operations of the material universe. Why is the old statesman more skilful than the raw politician? Because relying on the necessary conjunction of motive and action, he proceeds to produce moral effects by the application of those moral causes which experience has shown to be effectual. Some actions may be found to which we can attach no motives, but these are the effects of causes with which we are unacquainted. Hence the relation which motive bears to voluntary action is that of cause to effect; nor, placed in this point of view, is it, or ever has it been, the subject of popular or philosophical dispute. None but the few fanatics who are engaged in the herculean task of reconciling the justice of their God with the misery of man will longer outrage common sense by the supposition of an event without a cause, a voluntary action without a motive. History, politics, morals, criticisms, all grounds of reasonings, all principles of science, alike assume the truth of the doctrine of Necessity. No farmer carrying his corn to market doubts the sale of it at the market price. The master of a manufactory no more doubts that he can purchase the human labor necessary for his purposes than that his machinery will act as they have been accustomed to act.

But, whilst none have scrupled to admit Necessity as influencing matter, many have disputed its dominion over mind. Independently of its militating with the received ideas of the justice of God, it is by no means obvious to a superficial inquiry. When the mind observes its own operations, it feels no connection of motive and action; but as we know 'nothing more of causation than the constant conjunction of objects and the consequent inference of one from the other, as we find that these two circumstances are universally allowed to have place in voluntary action, we may be easily led to own that they are subjected to the necessity common to all causes.' The actions of the will have a regular conjunction with circumstances and characters; motive is to voluntary action what cause is to effect. But the only idea we can form of causation is a constant conjunction of similar objects, and the consequent inference of one from the other; wherever this is the case Necessity is clearly established.

The idea of liberty, applied metaphorically to the will, has sprung from a misconception of the meaning of the word power. What is power? — id quod potest, that which can produce any given effect. To deny power is to say that nothing can or has the power to be or act. In the only true sense of the word power it applies with equal force to the lodestone as to the human will. Do you think these motives, which I shall present, are powerful enough to rouse him? is a question just as common as, Do you think this lever has the power of raising this weight? The advocates of free-will assert that the will has the power of refusing to be determined by the strongest motive; but the strongest motive is that which, overcoming all others, ultimately prevails; this assertion therefore amounts to a denial of the will being ultimately determined by that motive which does determine it, which is absurd. But it is equally certain that a man cannot resist the strongest motive as that he cannot overcome a physical impossibility.

The doctrine of Necessity tends to introduce a great change into the established notions of morality and utterly to destroy religion. Reward and punishment must be considered by the Necessarian merely as motives which he would employ in order to procure the adoption or abandonment of any given line of conduct. Desert, in the present sense of the word, would no longer have any meaning; and he who should inflict pain upon another for no better reason than that he deserved it would only gratify his revenge under pretence of satisfying justice. It is not enough, says the advocate of free-will, that a criminal should be prevented from a repetition of his crime; he should feel pain, and his torments, when justly inflicted, ought precisely to be proportioned to his fault. But utility is morality; that which is incapable of producing happiness is useless; and though the crime of Damiens must be condemned, yet the frightful torments which revenge, under the name of justice, inflicted on this unhappy man, cannot be supposed to have augmented, even at the long run, the stock of pleasurable sensation in the world. At the same time the doctrine of Necessity does not in the least diminish our disapprobation of vice. The conviction which all feel that a viper is a poisonous animal, and that a tiger is constrained by the inevitable condition of his existence to devour men, does not induce us to avoid them less sedulously, or, even more, to hesitate in destroying them; but he would surely be of a hard heart, who, meeting with a serpent on a desert island or in a situation where it was incapable of injury, should wantonly deprive it of existence. A Necessarian is inconsequent to his own principles if he indulges in hatred or contempt; the compassion which he feels for the criminal is unmixed with a desire of injuring him; he looks with an elevated and dreadless composure upon the links of the universal chain as they pass before his eyes; whilst cowardice, curiosity and inconsistency only assail him in proportion to the feebleness and indistinctness with which he has perceived and rejected the delusions of free-will.

Religion is the perception of the relation in which we stand to the principle of the universe. But if the principle of the universe be not an organic being, the model and prototype of man, the relation between it and human beings is absolutely none. Without some insight into its will respecting our actions religion is nugatory and vain. But will is only a mode of animal mind; moral qualities also are such as only a human being can possess; to attribute them to the principle of the universe is to annex to it properties incompatible with any possible definition of its nature. It is probable that the word God was originally only an expression denoting the unknown cause of the known events which men perceived in the universe. By the vulgar mistake of a metaphor for a real being, of a word for a thing, it became a man endowed with human qualities and governing the universe as an earthly monarch governs his kingdom. Their addresses to this imaginary being, indeed, are much in the same style as those of subjects to a king. They acknowledge his benevolence, deprecate his anger and supplicate his favor.

But the doctrine of Necessity teaches us that in no case could any event have happened otherwise than it did happen, and that, if God is the author of good, he is also the author of evil; that, if he is entitled to our gratitude for the one, he is entitled to our hatred for the other; that, admitting the existence of this hypothetic being, he is also subjected to the dominion of an immutable Necessity. It is plain that the same arguments which prove that God is the author of food, light and life, prove him also to be the author of poison, darkness and death. The wide-wasting earthquake, the storm, the battle and the tyranny are attributable to this hypothetic being in the same degree as the fairest forms of Nature, sunshine, liberty and peace.

But we are taught by the doctrine of Necessity that there is neither good nor evil in the universe otherwise than as the events to which we apply these epithets have relation to our own peculiar mode of being. Still less than with the hypothesis of a God will the doctrine of Necessity accord with the belief of a future state of punishment. God made man such as he is and then damned him for being so; for to say that God was the author of all good, and man the author of all evil, is to say that one man made a straight line and a crooked one, and another man made the incongruity.

A Mahometan story, much to the present purpose, is recorded, wherein Adam and Moses are introduced disputing before God in the following manner. 'Thou,' says Moses, 'art Adam, whom God created and animated with the breath of life and caused to be worshipped by the angels, and placed in Paradise, from whence mankind have been expelled for thy fault.' Whereto Adam answered, 'Thou art Moses, whom God chose for his apostle and entrusted with his word by giving thee the tables of the law and whom he vouchsafed to admit to discourse with himself. How many years dost thou find the law was written before I was created?' Says Moses, 'Forty.' 'And dost thou not find,' replied Adam, 'these words therein,—"And Adam rebelled against his Lord and transgressed"?' Which Moses confessing, 'Dost thou therefore blame me,' continued he, 'for doing that which God wrote of me that I should do, forty years before I was created, nay, for what was decreed concerning me fifty thousand years before the creation of heaven and earth?'—Sale's *Preliminary Discourse to the Koran*, p. 164.

VII. 13:—

There is no God!

This negation must be understood solely to affect a creative Deity. The hypothesis of a pervading Spirit, coeternal with the universe, remains unshaken.

A close examination of the validity of the proofs adduced to suppport any proposition is the only secure way of attaining truth, on the advantages of which it is unnecessary to descant; our knowledge of the existence of a Diety is a subject of such importance that it cannot be too minutely investigated; in consequence of this conviction we proceed briefly and impartially to examine the proofs which have been adduced. It is necessary first to consider the nature of belief.

When a proposition is offered to the mind, it perceives the agreement or disagreement of the ideas of which it is composed. A perception of their agreement is termed *belief*. Many obstacles frequently prevent this perception from being immediate; these the mind attempts to remove in order that the perception may be distinct. The mind is active in the investigation in order to perfect the state of perception of the relation which the component ideas of the proposition bear to each, which is passive; the investigation being confused with the perception has induced many falsely to imagine that the mind is active in belief, — that belief is an act of volition, — in consequence of which it may be regulated by the mind. Pursuing, continuing this mistake, they have attached a degree of criminality to disbelief, of which in its nature it is incapable; it is equally incapable of merit.

Belief, then, is a passion, the strength of which, like every other passion, is in precise proportion to the degrees of excitement.

The degrees of excitement are three.

The senses are the sources of all knowledge to the mind; consequently their evidence claims the strongest assent.

The decision of the mind, founded upon our own experience, derived from these sources, claims the next degree.

The experience of others, which addresses itself to the former one, occupies the lowest degree.

(A graduated scale, on which should be marked the capabilities of propositions to approach to the test of the senses, would be a just barometer of the belief which ought to be attached to them.)

Consequently no testimony can be admitted which is contrary to reason; reason is founded on the evidence of our senses.

Every proof may be referred to one of these three divisions. It is to be considered what arguments we receive from each of them, which should convince us of the existence of a Deity.

1st. The evidence of the senses. If the Deity should appear to us, if he should convince our senses of his existence, this revelation would necessarily command belief. Those to whom the Deity has thus appeared have the strongest possible conviction of his existence. But the God of theologians is incapable of local visibility.

2nd. Reason. It is urged that man knows that whatever is must either have had a beginning, or have existed from all eternity; he also knows that whatever is not eternal must have had a cause. When this reasoning is applied to the universe, it is necessary to prove that it was created; until that is clearly demonstrated, we may reasonably suppose that it has endured from all eternity. We must prove design before we can infer a designer. The only idea which we can form of causation is derivable from the constant conjunction of objects, and the consequent inference of one from the other. In a case where two propositions are diametrically opposite, the mind believes that which is least incomprehensible: it is easier to suppose that the universe has existed from all eternity than to conceive a being beyond its limits capable of creating it; if the mind sinks beneath the weight of one, is it an alleviation to increase the intolerability of the burden?

The other argument, which is founded on a man's knowledge of his own existence, stands thus. A man knows not only that he now is, but that once he was not; consequently there must have been a cause. But our idea of causation is alone derivable from the constant conjunction of objects and the consequent inference of one from the other; and, reasoning experimentally, we can only infer from effects causes exactly adequate to those effects. But there certainly is a generative power which is effected by certain instruments; we cannot prove that it is inherent in these instruments; nor is the contrary hypothesis capable of demonstration. We admit that the generative power is incomprehensible; but to suppose that the same effect is produced by an eternal, omniscient, omnipotent being leaves the cause in the same obscurity, but renders it more incomprehensible.

3rd. Testimony. It is required that testimony should not be contrary to reason. The testimony that the Deity convinces the senses of men of his existence can only be admitted by us, if our mind considers it less probable that these men should have been deceived than that the Deity should have appeared to them. Our reason can never admit the testimony of men who not only declare that they were eye-witnesses of miracles, but that the Deity was irrational; for he commanded that he should be believed, he proposed the highest rewards for faith, eternal punishments for disbelief. We can only command voluntary actions; belief is not an act of volition; the mind is even passive, or involuntarily active; from this it is evident that we have no sufficient testimony, or rather that testimony is insufficient to prove the being of a God. It has been before shown that it cannot be deduced from reason. They alone, then, who have been convinced by the evidence of the senses, can believe it.

Hence it is evident that, having no proofs from either of the three sources of conviction, the mind *cannot* believe the existence of a creative God; it is also evident that, as belief is a passion of the mind, no degree of criminality is attachable to disbelief; and that they only are reprehensible who neglect to remove the false medium through which their mind views any subject of discussion. Every reflecting mind must acknowledge that there is no proof of the existence of a Deity.

God is an hypothesis, and, as such, stands in need of proof; the *onus probandi* rests on the theist. Sir Isaac Newton says: ' Hypotheses non fingo, quicquid enim ex phænomenis non deducitur hypothesis vocanda est, et hypothesis vel metaphysicæ, vel physicæ, vel qualitatum occultarum, seu mechanicæ, in philosophiâ locum non habent.' To all proofs of the existence of a creative God apply this valuable rule. We see a variety of bodies possessing a variety of powers; we merely know their effects; we are in a state of ignorance with respect to their essences and causes. These Newton calls the phenomena of things; but the pride of philosophy is unwilling to admit its ignorance of their causes. From the phenomena, which are the objects of our senses, we attempt to infer a cause, which we call God, and gratuitously endow it with all negative and contradictory qualities. From this hypothesis we invent this general name to conceal our ignorance of causes and essences. The being, called God, by no means answers with the conditions prescribed by Newton; it bears every mark of a veil woven by philosophical conceit to hide the ignorance of philosophers even from themselves. They borrow the threads of its texture from the anthropomorphism of the vulgar. Words have been used by sophists for the same purposes, from the 'occult qualities' of the Peripatetics to the *effluvium* of Boyle and the *crinities* or *nebulæ* of Herschel. God is represented as infinite, eternal, incomprehensible; he is contained under every *prædicate in non* that the logic of ignorance could fabricate. Even his worshippers allow that it is impossible to form any idea of him; they exclaim with the French poet,

Pour dire ce qu'il est, il faut être lui-même.

☞

Lord Bacon says, that 'atheism leaves to man reason, philosophy, natural piety, laws, reputation, and everything that can serve to conduct him to virtue; but superstition destroys all these, and erects itself into a tyranny over the understandings of men: hence atheism never disturbs the government, but renders man more clear-sighted, since he sees nothing beyond the boundaries of the present life.'

Bacon's *Moral Essays.*

[Here a long passage from *Système de la Nature par M. Mirabaud* (Baron d'Holbach), London, 1781, is omitted by the advice of the general editor.]

The enlightened and benevolent Pliny thus publicly professes himself an atheist: 'Quapropter effigiem Dei formamque quærere imbecillitatis humanæ reor. Quisquis est Deus (si modo est alius) et quacunque in parte, totus est sensus, totus est visus, totus auditus, totus animæ, totus animi, totus sui. . . . Imperfectæ vero in homine naturæ præcipua solatia ne deum quidem posse omnia. Namque nec sibi potest mortem consciscere, si velit, quod homini dedit optimum in tantis vitæ pœnis: nec mortales æternitate donare, aut revocare defunctos; nec facere ut qui vixit non vixerit, qui honores gessit non gesserit, nullumque habere in præterita jus præterquam oblivionis, atque (ut facetis quoque argumentis societas hæc cum deo copuletur) ut bis dena viginta non sint aut multa similiter efficere non posse, per quæ declaratur haud dubie naturæ potentia idque esse quod Deum vocemus.' — Plin. *Nat. Hist.* ii. cap. 7.

The consistent Newtonian is necessarily an atheist. See Sir W. Drummond's *Academical Questions*, chap. iii. — Sir W. seems to consider

the atheism to which it leads, as a sufficient presumption of the falsehood of the system of gravitation; but surely it is more consistent with the good faith of philosophy to admit a deduction from facts than an hypothesis incapable of proof, although it might militate with the obstinate preconceptions of the mob. Had this author, instead of inveighing against the guilt and absurdity of atheism, demonstrated its falsehood, his conduct would have been more suited to the modesty of the sceptic and the toleration of the philosopher.

☞

Omnia enim per Dei potentiam facta sunt. Imo quia Naturæ potentia nulla est nisi ipsa Dei potentia, certum est nos eatenus Dei potentiam non intelligere, quatenus causas naturales ignoramus; adeoque stulte ad eandem Dei potentiam recurritur, quando rei alicujus causam naturalem, hoc est ipsam Dei potentiam, ignoramus.

Spinoza, *Tract. Theologico-Pol.* cap. i. p. 14. VII. 67: —

Ahasuerus, rise!

'Ahasuerus the Jew crept forth from the dark cave of Mount Carmel. Near two thousand years have elapsed since he was first goaded by never-ending restlessness to rove the globe from pole to pole. When our Lord was wearied with the burden of his ponderous cross and wanted to rest before the door of Ahasuerus, the unfeeling wretch drove him away with brutality. The Saviour of mankind staggered, sinking under the heavy load, but uttered no complaint. An angel of death appeared before Ahasuerus, and exclaimed indignantly, "Barbarian! thou hast denied rest to the Son of Man; be it denied thee also, until he comes to judge the world."

'A black demon, let loose from hell upon Ahasuerus, goads him now from country to country; he is denied the consolation which death affords and precluded from the rest of the peaceful grave.

'Ahasuerus crept forth from the dark cave of Mount Carmel; he shook the dust from his beard, and taking up one of the skulls heaped there hurled it down the eminence; it rebounded from the earth in shivered atoms. "This was my father!" roared Ahasuerus. Seven more skulls rolled down from rock to rock, while the infuriate Jew, following them with ghastly looks, exclaimed — "And these were my wives!" He still continued to hurl down skull after skull, roaring in dreadful accents — "And these, and these, and these, were my children! They *could die*, but I, reprobate wretch, alas! I cannot die! Dreadful beyond conception is the judgment that hangs over me. Jerusalem fell — I crushed the sucking babe, and precipitated myself into the destructive flames. I cursed the Romans — but, alas! alas! the restless curse held me by the hair, — and I could not die!

'"Rome, the giantess, fell; I placed myself before the fallen statue; she fell, and did not crush me. Nations sprung up and disappeared before me ; but I remained and did not die. From cloud-encircled cliffs did I precipitate myself into the ocean ; but the foaming billows cast me upon the shore, and the burning arrow of existence pierced my cold heart again. I leaped into Etna's flaming abyss, and roared with the giants for ten long months, polluting with my groans the Mount's sulphureous mouth — ah ! ten long months ! The volcano fermented, and in a fiery stream of lava cast me up. I lay torn by the torture-snakes of hell amid the glowing cinders, and yet continued to exist. A forest was on fire ; I darted on wings of fury and despair into the crackling wood. Fire dropped upon me from the trees, but the flames only singed my limbs ; alas ! it could not consume them. I now mixed with the butchers of mankind and plunged in the tempest of the raging battle. I roared defiance to the infuriate Gaul, defiance to the victorious German ; but arrows and spears rebounded in shivers from my body. The Saracen's flaming sword broke upon my skull ; balls in vain hissed upon me ; the lightnings of battle glared harmless around my loins ; in vain did the elephant trample on me, in vain the iron hoof of the wrathful steed ! The mine, big with destructive power, burst under me, and hurled me high in the air. I fell on heaps of smoking limbs, but was only singed. The giant's steel club rebounded from my body, the executioner's hand could not strangle me, the tiger's tooth could not pierce me, nor would the hungry lion in the circus devour me. I cohabited with poisonous snakes, and pinched the red crest of the dragon. The serpent stung, but could not destroy me. The dragon tormented, but dared not to devour me. I now provoked the fury of tyrants. I said to Nero, ' Thou art a bloodhound ! ' I said to Christiern, ' Thou art a bloodhound ! ' I said to Muley Ismael, ' Thou art a bloodhound ! ' The tyrants invented cruel torments, but did not kill me. — Ha ! not to be able to die — not to be able to die — not to be permitted to rest after the toils of life — to be doomed to be imprisoned forever in the clay-formed dungeon — to be forever clogged with this worthless body, its load of diseases and infirmities — to be condemned to hold for millenniums that yawning monster Sameness, and Time, that hungry hyena, ever bearing children and ever devouring again her offspring ! — Ha ! not to be permitted to die ! Awful avenger in heaven, hast thou in thine armory of wrath a punishment more dreadful ? then let it thunder upon me ; command a hurricane to sweep me down to the foot of Carmel that I there may lie extended ; may pant, and writhe, and die ! ' ' '

This fragment is the translation of part of some German work, whose title I have vainly endeavored to discover. I picked it up, dirty and torn, some years ago, in Lincoln's-Inn Fields.

VII. 135, 136 : —

> I will beget a Son, and he shall bear
> The sins of all the world.

A book is put into our hands when children, called the Bible, the purport of whose history is briefly this. That God made the earth in six days, and there planted a delightful garden, in which he placed the first pair of human beings. In the midst of the garden he planted a tree, whose fruit, although within their reach, they were forbidden to touch. That the Devil, in the shape of a snake, persuaded them to eat of this fruit; in consequence of which God condemned both them and their posterity yet unborn to satisfy his justice by their eternal misery. That four thousand years after these events (the human race in the meanwhile having gone unredeemed to perdition) God engendered with the betrothed wife of a carpenter in Judea (whose virginity was nevertheless uninjured), and begat a Son, whose name was Jesus Christ ; and who was crucified and died, in order that no more men might be devoted to hell-fire, he bearing the burden of his Father's displeasure by proxy. The book states, in addition, that the soul of whoever disbelieves this sacrifice will be burned with everlasting fire.

During many ages of misery and darkness this story gained implicit belief ; but at length men arose who suspected that it was a fable and imposture, and that Jesus Christ, so far from being a God, was only a man like themselves. But a numerous set of men, who derived and still derive immense emoluments from this opinion in the shape of a popular belief, told the vulgar that if they did not believe in the Bible, they would be damned to all eternity ; and burned, imprisoned and poisoned all the unbiassed and unconnected inquirers who occasionally arose. They still oppress them, so far as the people, now become more enlightened, will allow.

The belief in all that the Bible contains is called Christianity. A Roman governor of Judea, at the instance of a priest-led mob, crucified a man called Jesus eighteen centuries ago. He was a man of pure life, who desired to rescue his countrymen from the tyranny of their barbarous and degrading superstitions. The common fate of all who desire to benefit mankind awaited him. The rabble at the instigation of the priests demanded his death, although his very judge made public acknowledgment of his innocence. Jesus was sacrificed to the honor of that God with whom he was afterwards confounded. It is of importance, therefore, to distinguish between the pretended character of this being as the Son of God and the Saviour of the world, and his real character as a man, who for a vain attempt to reform the world paid the forfeit of his life to that overbearing tyranny which has since so long desolated the universe in his name. Whilst the one is a hypocritical demon, who announces himself as the God of compassion and peace even whilst he stretches forth his blood-red hand with the sword of discord to waste the earth, having confessedly devised this scheme of desolation from eternity ; the other stands in the foremost list of those true heroes who have died in the glorious martyrdom of liberty and have braved torture, contempt and poverty in the cause of suffering humanity.[1]

The vulgar, ever in extremes, became persuaded that the crucifixion of Jesus was a supernatural event. Testimonies of miracles, so frequent in unenlightened ages, were not wanting to prove that he was something divine. This belief, rolling through the lapse of ages, met with the reveries of Plato and the reasonings of Aristotle, and acquired force and extent, until the divinity of Jesus became a dogma, which to dispute was death, which to doubt was infamy.

Christianity is now the established religion. He who attempts to impugn it must be contented to behold murderers and traitors take precedence of him in public opinion; though, if his genius be equal to his courage and assisted by a peculiar coalition of circumstances, future ages may exalt him to a divinity and persecute others in his name, as he was persecuted in the name of his predecessor in the homage of the world.

The same means that have supported every other popular belief have supported Christianity. War, imprisonment, assassination and falsehood, deeds of unexampled and incomparable atrocity, have made it what it is. The blood, shed by the votaries of the God of mercy and peace since the establishment of his religion, would probably suffice to drown all other sectaries now on the habitable globe. We derive from our ancestors a faith thus fostered and supported; we quarrel, persecute and hate for its maintenance. Even under a government which, whilst it infringes the very right of thought and speech, boasts of permitting the liberty of the press, a man is pilloried and imprisoned because he is a deist, and no one raises his voice in the indignation of outraged humanity. But it is ever a proof that the falsehood of a proposition is felt by those who use coercion, not reasoning, to procure its admission; and a dispassionate observer would feel himself more powerfully interested in favor of a man who, depending on the truth of his opinions, simply stated his reasons for entertaining them, than in that of his aggressor who, daringly avowing his unwillingness or incapacity to answer them by argument, proceeded to repress the energies and break the spirit of their promulgator by that torture and imprisonment whose infliction he could command.

Analogy seems to favor the opinion that, as like other systems, Christianity has arisen and augmented, so like them it will decay and perish; that, as violence, darkness and deceit, not reasoning and persuasion, have procured its admission among mankind, so, when enthusiasm has subsided, and time, that infallible controverter of false opinions, has involved its pretended evidences in the darkness of antiquity, it will become obsolete; that Milton's poem alone will give permanency to the remembrance

[1] Since writing this note I have seen reason to suspect that Jesus was an ambitious man who aspired to the throne of Judea.

of its absurdities; and that men will laugh as heartily at grace, faith, redemption and original sin, as they now do at the metamorphoses of Jupiter, the miracles of Romish saints, the efficacy of witchcraft, and the appearance of departed spirits.

Had the Christian religion commenced and continued by the mere force of reasoning and persuasion, the preceding analogy would be inadmissible. We should never speculate on the future obsoleteness of a system perfectly conformable to Nature and reason; it would endure so long as they endured; it would be a truth as indisputable as the light of the sun, the criminality of murder, and other facts whose evidence, depending on our organization and relative situations, must remain acknowledged as satisfactory so long as man is man. It is an incontrovertible fact, the consideration of which ought to repress the hasty conclusions of credulity or moderate its obstinacy in maintaining them, that, had the Jews not been a fanatical race of men, had even the resolution of Pontius Pilate been equal to his candor, the Christian religion never could have prevailed, it could not even have existed; on so feeble a thread hangs the most cherished opinion of a sixth of the human race! When will the vulgar learn humility? When will the pride of ignorance blush at having believed before it could comprehend?

Either the Christian religion is true, or it is false; if true, it comes from God and its authenticity can admit of doubt and dispute no further than its omnipotent author is willing to allow. Either the power or the goodness of God is called in question if he leaves those doctrines most essential to the well being of man in doubt and dispute; the only ones which, since their promulgation, have been the subject of unceasing cavil, the cause of irreconcilable hatred. '*If God has spoken, why is the universe not convinced?*'

There is this passage in the Christian Scriptures: 'Those who obey not God and believe not the Gospel of his Son, shall be punished with everlasting destruction.' This is the pivot upon which all religions turn; they all assume that it is in our power to believe or not to believe; whereas the mind can only believe that which it thinks true. A human being can only be supposed accountable for those actions which are influenced by his will. But belief is utterly distinct from and unconnected with volition; it is the apprehension of the agreement or disagreement of the ideas that compose any proposition. Belief is a passion, or involuntary operation of the mind, and, like other passions, its intensity is precisely proportionate to the degrees of excitement. Volition is essential to merit or demerit. But the Christian religion attaches the highest possible degrees of merit and demerit to that which is worthy of neither and which is totally unconnected with the peculiar faculty of the mind whose presence is essential to their being.

Christianity was intended to reform the

world. Had an all-wise Being planned it, nothing is more improbable than that it should have failed ; omniscience would infallibly have foreseen the inutility of a scheme which experience demonstrates, to this age, to have been utterly unsuccessful.

Christianity inculcates the necessity of supplicating the Deity. Prayer may be considered under two points of view ; — as an endeavor to change the intentions of God, or as a formal testimony of our obedience. But the former case supposes that the caprices of a limited intelligence can occasionally instruct the Creator of the world how to regulate the universe ; and the latter, a certain degree of servility analogous to the loyalty demanded by earthly tyrants. Obedience indeed is only the pitiful and cowardly egotism of him who thinks that he can do something better than reason.

Christianity, like all other religions, rests upon miracles, prophecies and martyrdoms. No religion ever existed which had not its prophets, its attested miracles, and, above all, crowds of devotees who would bear patiently the most horrible tortures to prove its authenticity. It should appear that in no case can a discriminating mind subscribe to the genuineness of a miracle. A miracle is an infraction of Nature's law by a supernatural cause ; by a cause acting beyond that eternal circle within which all things are included. God breaks through the law of Nature that he may convince mankind of the truth of that revelation which, in spite of his precautions, has been since its introduction the subject of unceasing schism and cavil.

Miracles resolve themselves into the following question : [1] — Whether it is more probable the laws of Nature, hitherto so immutably harmonious, should have undergone violation, or that a man should have told a lie ? Whether it is more probable that we are ignorant of the natural cause of an event or that we know the supernatural one ? That, in old times, when the powers of Nature were less known than at present, a certain set of men were themselves deceived or had some hidden motive for deceiving others ; or that God began a son who in his legislation, measuring merit by belief, evidenced himself to be totally ignorant of the powers of the human mind — of what is voluntary, and what is the contrary ?

We have many instances of men telling lies ; none of an infraction of Nature's laws, those laws of whose government alone we have any knowledge or experience. The records of all nations afford innumerable instances of men deceiving others either from vanity or interest, or themselves being deceived by the limitedness of their views and their ignorance of natural causes ; but where is the accredited case of God having come upon earth, to give the lie to his own creations ? There would be something truly wonderful in the appearance of a ghost ; but the assertion of a child that he saw one as he passed through the churchyard is universally admitted to be less miraculous.

But even supposing that a man should raise a dead body to life before our eyes, and on this fact rest his claim to being considered the son of God ; — the Humane Society restores drowned persons, and because it makes no mystery of the method it employs its members are not mistaken for the sons of God. All that we have a right to infer from our ignorance of the cause of any event is that we do not know it. Had the Mexicans attended to this simple rule when they heard the cannon of the Spaniards, they would not have considered them as gods. The experiments of modern chemistry would have defied the wisest philosophers of ancient Greece and Rome to have accounted for them on natural principles. An author of strong common sense has observed that ' a miracle is no miracle at second-hand ; ' he might have added that a miracle is no miracle in any case ; for until we are acquainted with all natural causes we have no reason to imagine others.

There remains to be considered another proof of Christianity — Prophecy. A book is written before a certain event, in which this event is foretold ; how could the prophet have foreknown it without inspiration ? how could he have been inspired without God ? The greatest stress is laid on the prophecies of Moses and Hosea on the dispersion of the Jews, and that of Isaiah concerning the coming of the Messiah. The prophecy of Moses is a collection of every possible cursing and blessing ; and it is so far from being marvellous that the one of dispersion should have been fulfilled that it would have been more surprising if, out of all these, none should have taken effect. In *Deuteronomy*, chap. xxviii. v. 64, where Moses explicitly foretells the dispersion, he states that they shall there serve gods of wood and stone : ' And the Lord shall scatter thee among all people, from the one end of the earth even unto the other, *and there thou shalt serve other gods, which neither thou nor thy fathers have known, even gods of wood and stone.*' The Jews are at this day remarkably tenacious of their religion. Moses also declares that they shall be subjected to these curses for disobedience to his ritual : ' And it shall come to pass if thou wilt not hearken unto the voice of the Lord thy God, to observe to do all the commandments and statutes which I command you this day, that all these curses shall come upon thee and overtake thee.' Is this the real reason ? The third, fourth and fifth chapters of Hosea are a piece of immodest confession. The indelicate type might apply in a hundred senses to a hundred things. The fifty-third chapter of Isaiah is more explicit, yet it does not exceed in clearness the oracles of Delphos. The historical proof that Moses, Isaiah and Hosea did write when they are said to have written, is far from being clear and circumstantial.

But prophecy requires proof in its character as a miracle ; we have no right to suppose that a man foreknew future events from God, until

[1] See Hume's *Essays*, vol. ii. p. 121.

it is demonstrated that he neither could know them by his own exertions, nor that the writings which contain the prediction could possibly have been fabricated after the event pretended to be foretold. It is more probable that writings, pretending to divine inspiration, should have been fabricated after the fulfilment of their pretended prediction, than that they should have really been divinely inspired, when we consider that the latter supposition makes God at once the creator of the human mind and ignorant of its primary powers, particularly as we have numberless instances of false religions and forged prophecies of things long past, and no accredited case of God having conversed with men directly or indirectly. It is also possible that the description of an event might have foregone its occurrence : but this is far from being a legitimate proof of a divine revelation, as many men, not pretending to the character of a prophet, have nevertheless, in this sense, prophesied.

Lord Chesterfield was never yet taken for a prophet, even by a bishop, yet he uttered this remarkable prediction : 'The despotic government of France is screwed up to the highest pitch ; a revolution is fast approaching; that revolution, I am convinced, will be radical and sanguinary.' This appeared in the letters of the prophet long before the accomplishment of this wonderful prediction. Now, have these particulars come to pass, or have they not ? If they have, how could the Earl have foreknown them without inspiration ? If we admit the truth of the Christian religion on testimony such as this, we must admit, on the same strength of evidence, that God has affixed the highest rewards to belief and the eternal tortures of the never-dying worm to disbelief ; both of which have been demonstrated to be involuntary.

The last proof of the Christian religion depends on the influence of the Holy Ghost. Theologians divide the influence of the Holy Ghost into its ordinary and extraordinary modes of operation. The latter is supposed to be that which inspired the Prophets and Apostles ; and the former to be the grace of God, which summarily makes known the truth of his revelation to those whose mind is fitted for its reception by a submissive perusal of his word. Persons convinced in this manner can do anything but account for their conviction, describe the time at which it happened or the manner in which it came upon them. It is supposed to enter the mind by other channels than those of the senses, and therefore professes to be superior to reason founded on their experience.

Admitting, however, the usefulness or possibility of a divine revelation, unless we demolish the foundations of all human knowledge, it is requisite that our reason should previously demonstrate its genuineness ; for, before we extinguish the steady ray of reason and common sense, it is fit that we should discover whether we cannot do without their assistance, whether or no there be any other which may suffice to guide us through the labyrinth of life : [1] for, if a man is to be inspired upon all occasions, if he is to be sure of a thing because he is sure, if the ordinary operations of the Spirit are not to be considered very extraordinary modes of demonstration, if enthusiasm is to usurp the place of proof, and madness that of sanity, all reasoning is superfluous. The Mahometan dies fighting for his prophet, the Indian immolates himself at the chariot-wheels of Brahma, the Hottentot worships an insect, the Negro a bunch of feathers, the Mexican sacrifices human victims ! Their degree of conviction must certainly be very strong ; it cannot arise from reasoning, it must from feelings, the reward of their prayers. If each of these should affirm, in opposition to the strongest possible arguments, that inspiration carried internal evidence, I fear their inspired brethren, the orthodox missionaries, would be so uncharitable as to pronounce them obstinate.

Miracles cannot be received as testimonies of a disputed fact, because all human testimony has ever been insufficient to establish the possibility of miracles. That which is incapable of proof itself is no proof of anything else. Prophecy has also been rejected by the test of reason. Those, then, who have been actually inspired, are the only true believers in the Christian religion.

> Mox numine viso
> Virginei tumuere sinus, innuptaque mater
> Arcano stupuit compleri viscera partu
> Auctorem paritura suum. Mortalia corda
> Artificem texere poli, . . .
> . . . latuitque sub uno
> Pectore, qui totum late complectitur orbem.
> Claudian, *Carmen Paschali.*

Does not so monstrous and disgusting an absurdity carry its own infamy and refutation with itself ?

VIII. 203–207 : —

> Him, still from hope to hope the bliss pursuing
> Which from the exhaustless store of human weal
> Draws on the virtuous mind the thoughts that rise
> In time-destroying infiniteness gift
> With self-enshrined eternity, &c.

Time is our consciousness of the succession of ideas in our mind. Vivid sensation of either pain or pleasure makes the time seem long, as the common phrase is, because it renders us more acutely conscious of our ideas. If a mind be conscious of an hundred ideas during one minute by the clock, and of two hundred during another, the latter of these spaces would actually occupy so much greater extent in the mind as two exceed one in quantity. If, therefore, the human mind by any future improvement of its sensibility should become conscious of an infinite number of ideas in a minute, that minute would be eternity. I do not hence infer that the actual space between the birth and death of a man will ever be prolonged ; but that his sensibility is perfectible, and that the number of ideas

[1] See Locke's *Essay on the Human Understanding,* book iv. chap. xix., on Enthusiasm.

which his mind is capable of receiving is indefinite. One man is stretched on the rack during twelve hours, another sleeps soundly in his bed; the difference of time perceived by these two persons is immense; one hardly will believe that half an hour has elapsed, the other could credit that centuries had flown during his agony. Thus the life of a man of virtue and talent, who should die in his thirtieth year, is with regard to his own feelings longer than that of a miserable priest-ridden slave who dreams out a century of dulness. The one has perpetually cultivated his mental faculties, has rendered himself master of his thoughts, can abstract and generalize amid the lethargy of every-day business; the other can slumber over the brightest moments of his being and is unable to remember the happiest hour of his life. Perhaps the perishing ephemeron enjoys a longer life than the tortoise.

> Dark flood of time!
> Roll as it listeth thee — I measure not
> By months or moments thy ambiguous course.
> Another may stand by me on the brink
> And watch the bubble whirled beyond his ken
> That pauses at my feet. The sense of love,
> The thirst for action, and the impassioned thought,
> Prolong my being; if I wake no more,
> My life more actual living will contain
> Than some grey veteran's of the world's cold school,
> Whose listless hours unprofitably roll,
> By one enthusiast feeling unredeemed.

See Godwin's *Pol. Jus.* vol. i. p. 411; — and Condorcet, *Esquisse d'un Tableau Historique des Progrès de l'Esprit Humain*, Epoque ix.

VIII. 211, 212: —

> No longer now
> He slays the lamb that looks him in the face.

I hold that the depravity of the physical and moral nature of man originated in his unnatural habits of life. The origin of man, like that of the universe of which he is a part, is enveloped in impenetrable mystery. His generations either had a beginning or they had not. The weight of evidence in favor of each of these suppositions seems tolerably equal; and it is perfectly unimportant to the present argument which is assumed. The language spoken, however, by the mythology of nearly all religions seems to prove that at some distant period man forsook the path of Nature and sacrificed the purity and happiness of his being to unnatural appetites. The date of this event seems to have also been that of some great change in the climates of the earth, with which it has an obvious correspondence. The allegory of Adam and Eve eating of the tree of evil and entailing upon their posterity the wrath of God and the loss of everlasting life, admits of no other explanation than the disease and crime that have flowed from unnatural diet. Milton was so well aware of this that he makes Raphael thus exhibit to Adam the consequence of his disobedience: —

> 'Immediately a place
> Before his eyes appeared, sad, noisome, dark;
> A lazar-house it seem'd, wherein were laid
> Numbers of all diseased — all maladies
> Of ghastly spasm, or racking torture, qualms
> Of heart-sick agony, all feverous kinds,
> Convulsions, epilepsies, fierce catarrhs,
> Intestine stone and ulcer, colic pangs,
> Dæmoniac frenzy, moping melancholy,
> And moon-struck madness, pining atrophy,
> Marasmus, and wide-wasting pestilence,
> Dropsies and asthmas, and joint-racking rheums.

And how many thousands more might not be added to this frightful catalogue!

The story of Prometheus is one likewise which, although universally admitted to be allegorical, has never been satisfactorily explained. Prometheus stole fire from heaven and was chained for this crime to Mount Caucasus, where a vulture continually devoured his liver, that grew to meet its hunger. Hesiod says that before the time of Prometheus mankind were exempt from suffering; that they enjoyed a vigorous youth, and that death, when at length it came, approached like sleep and gently closed their eyes. Again, so general was this opinion, that Horace, a poet of the Augustan age, writes: —

> Audax omnia perpeti,
> Gens humana ruit per vetitum nefas;
> Audax Iapeti genus
> Ignem fraude mala gentibus intulit:
> Post ignem ætheria domo
> Subductum, macies et nova febrium
> Terris incubuit cohors,
> Semotique prius tarda necessitas
> Lethi corripuit gradum.

How plain a language is spoken by all this! Prometheus (who represents the human race) effected some great change in the condition of his nature, and applied fire to culinary purposes; thus inventing an expedient for screening from his disgust the horrors of the shambles. From this moment his vitals were devoured by the vulture of disease. It consumed his being in every shape of its loathsome and infinite variety, inducing the soul-quelling sinkings of premature and violent death. All vice arose from the ruin of healthful innocence. Tyranny, superstition, commerce and inequality were then first known when reason vainly attempted to guide the wanderings of exacerbated passion. I conclude this part of the subject with an extract from Mr. Newton's *Defence of Vegetable Regimen*, from whom I have borrowed this interpretation of the fable of Prometheus.

'Making allowance for such transposition of the events of the allegory as time might produce after the important truths were forgotten which this portion of the ancient mythology was intended to transmit, the drift of the fable appears to be this: — Man at his creation was endowed with the gift of perpetual youth; that is, he was not' formed to be a sickly suffering creature as now we see him, but to enjoy health, and to sink by slow degrees into the bosom of his parent earth without disease or pain. Prometheus first taught the use of animal food' (*primus bovem occidit Prometheus* [1]) ' and of fire, with which to render it more digestible and

[1] Plin. *Nat. Hist.* lib. vii. sect. 57.

pleasing to the taste. Jupiter, and the rest of the gods, foreseeing the consequences of these inventions, were amused or irritated at the short-sighted devices of the newly formed creature, and left him to experience the sad effects of them. Thirst, the necessary concomitant of a flesh diet,' (perhaps of all diet vitiated by culinary preparation) 'ensued; water was resorted to, and man forfeited the inestimable gift of health which he had received from heaven: he became diseased, the partaker of a precarious existence, and no longer descended slowly to his grave.'[1]

> ' But just disease to luxury succeeds,
> And every death its own avenger breeds;
> The fury passions from that blood began,
> And turned on man a fiercer savage — man.'

Man and the animals whom he has infected with his society or depraved by his dominion are alone diseased. The wild hog, the mouflon, the bison and the wolf are perfectly exempt from malady and invariably die either from external violence or natural old age. But the domestic hog, the sheep, the cow and the dog are subject to an incredible variety of distempers; and, like the corrupters of their nature, have physicians who thrive upon their miseries. The supereminence of man is like Satan's, a supereminence of pain; and the majority of his species, doomed to penury, disease and crime, have reason to curse the untoward event that by enabling him to communicate his sensations raised him above the level of his fellow animals. But the steps that have been taken are irrevocable. The whole of human science is comprised in one question: How can the advantages of intellect and civilization be reconciled with the liberty and pure pleasures of natural life? How can we take the benefits and reject the evils of the system which is now interwoven with all the fibres of our being? — I believe that abstinence from animal food and spirituous liquors would in a great measure capacitate us for the solution of this important question.

It is true that mental and bodily derangement is attributable in part to other deviations from rectitude and Nature than those which concern diet. The mistakes cherished by society respecting the connection of the sexes, whence the misery and diseases of unsatisfied celibacy, unenjoying prostitution, and the premature arrival of puberty, necessarily spring; the putrid atmosphere of crowded cities; the exhalations of chemical processes; the muffling of our bodies in superfluous apparel; the absurd treatment of infants; — all these, and innumerable other causes, contribute their mite to the mass of human evil.

Comparative anatomy teaches us that man resembles frugivorous animals in everything and carnivorous in nothing; he has neither claws wherewith to seize his prey, nor distinct and pointed teeth to tear the living fibre. A Mandarin of the first class, with nails two inches long, would probably find them alone inefficient to hold even a hare. After every

[1] *Return to Nature.* Cadell, 1811.

subterfuge of gluttony the bull must be degraded into the ox, and the ram into the wether, by an unnatural and inhuman operation, that the flaccid fibre may offer a fainter resistance to rebellious nature. It is only by softening and disguising dead flesh by culinary preparation that it is rendered susceptible of mastication or digestion, and that the sight of its bloody juices and raw horror does not excite intolerable loathing and disgust. Let the advocate of animal food force himself to a decisive experiment on its fitness, and, as Plutarch recommends, tear a living lamb with his teeth, and, plunging his head into its vitals, slake his thirst with the steaming blood; when fresh from the deed of horror, let him revert to the irresistible instincts of Nature that would rise in judgment against it, and say, 'Nature formed me for such work as this.' Then, and then only, would he be consistent.

Man resembles no carnivorous animal. There is no exception, unless man be one, to the rule of herbivorous animals having cellulated colons.

The orang-outang perfectly resembles man both in the order and number of his teeth. The orang-outang is the most anthropomorphous of the ape tribe, all of which are strictly frugivorous. There is no other species of animals, which live on different food, in which this analogy exists.[2] In many frugivorous animals, the canine teeth are more perfect and distinct than those of man. The resemblance also of the human stomach to that of the orang-outang is greater than to that of any other animal.

The intestines are also identical with those of herbivorous animals, which present a larger surface for absorption and have ample and cellulated colons. The cæcum also, though short, is larger than that of carnivorous animals; and even here the orang-outang retains its accustomed similarity.

The structure of the human frame, then, is that of one fitted to a pure vegetable diet, in every essential particular. It is true that the reluctance to abstain from animal food, in those who have been long accustomed to its stimulus, is so great in some persons of weak minds as to be scarcely overcome; but this is far from bringing any argument in its favor. A lamb, which was fed for some time on flesh by a ship's crew, refused its natural diet at the end of the voyage. There are numerous instances of horses, sheep, oxen and even wood-pigeons having been taught to live upon flesh until they have loathed their natural aliment. Young children evidently prefer pastry, oranges, apples and other fruit to the flesh of animals, until by the gradual depravation of the digestive organs the free use of vegetables has for a time produced serious inconveniences; *for a time*, I say, since there never was an instance wherein a change from spirituous liquors and animal food to vegetables and pure water has

[2] Cuvier, *Leçons d'Anat. Comp.* tom. iii. pp. 169, 373, 448, 465, 480. Rees's *Cyclopædia*, article ' Man.'

failed ultimately to invigorate the body by rendering its juices bland and consentaneous, and to restore to the mind that cheerfulness and elasticity which not one in fifty possesses on the present system. A love of strong liquors is also with difficulty taught to infants. Almost every one remembers the wry faces which the first glass of port produced. Unsophisticated instinct is invariably unerring; but to decide on the fitness of animal food from the perverted appetites which its constrained adoption produces is to make the criminal a judge in his own cause; it is even worse, it is appealing to the infatuated drunkard in a question of the salubrity of brandy.

What is the cause of morbid action in the animal system? Not the air we breathe, for our fellow denizens of Nature breathe the same uninjured; not the water we drink (if remote from the pollutions of man and his inventions [1]) for the animals drink it too; not the earth we tread upon; not the unobscured sight of glorious Nature, in the wood, the field or the expanse of sky and ocean; nothing that we are or do in common with the undiseased inhabitants of the forest. Something then wherein we differ from them: our habit of altering our food by fire so that our appetite is no longer a just criterion for the fitness of its gratification. Except in children there remain no traces of that instinct which determines, in all other animals, what aliment is natural or otherwise; and so perfectly obliterated are they in the reasoning adults of our species that it has become necessary to urge considerations drawn from comparative anatomy to prove that we are naturally frugivorous.

Crime is madness. Madness is disease. Whenever the cause of disease shall be discovered, the root, from which all vice and misery have so long overshadowed the globe, will lie bare to the axe. All the exertions of man from that moment may be considered as tending to the clear profit of his species. No sane mind in a sane body resolves upon a real crime. It is a man of violent passions, blood-shot eyes and swollen veins, that alone can grasp the knife of murder. The system of a simple diet promises no Utopian advantages. It is no mere reform of legislation, whilst the furious passions and evil propensities of the human heart, in which it had its origin, are still unassuaged. It strikes at the root of all evil and is an experiment which may be tried with success, not alone by nations, but by small societies, families, and even individuals. In no cases has a return to vegetable diet produced the slightest injury; in most it has been attended with changes undeniably beneficial. Should ever a physician be born with the genius of Locke, I am persuaded that he might trace all bodily and mental derangements to our unnatural habits as clearly as that philosopher has traced

all knowledge to sensation. What prolific sources of disease are not those mineral and vegetable poisons that have been introduced for its extirpation! How many thousands have become murderers and robbers, bigots and domestic tyrants, dissolute and abandoned adventurers, from the use of fermented liquors, who, had they slaked their thirst only with pure water, would have lived but to diffuse the happiness of their own unperverted feelings! How many groundless opinions and absurd institutions have not received a general sanction from the sottishness and intemperance of individuals! Who will assert that, had the populace of Paris satisfied their hunger at the ever-furnished table of vegetable nature, they would have lent their brutal suffrage to the proscription-list of Robespierre? Could a set of men, whose passions were not perverted by unnatural stimuli, look with coolness on an *auto da fé*? Is it to be believed that a being of gentle feelings, rising from his meal of roots, would take delight in sports of blood? Was Nero a man of temperate life? could you read calm health in his cheek, flushed with ungovernable propensities of hatred for the human race? Did Muley Ismael's pulse beat evenly, was his skin transparent, did his eyes beam with healthfulness and its invariable concomitants, cheerfulness and benignity? Though history has decided none of these questions, a child could not hesitate to answer in the negative. Surely the bile-suffused cheek of Buonaparte, his wrinkled brow and yellow eye, the ceaseless inquietude of his nervous system, speak no less plainly the character of his unresting ambition than his murders and his victories. It is impossible, had Buonaparte descended from a race of vegetable feeders, that he could have had either the inclination or the power to ascend the throne of the Bourbons. The desire of tyranny could scarcely be excited in the individual, the power to tyrannize would certainly not be delegated by a society neither frenzied by inebriation nor rendered impotent and irrational by disease. Pregnant indeed with inexhaustible calamity is the renunciation of instinct, as it concerns our physical nature; arithmetic cannot enumerate, nor reason perhaps suspect, the multitudinous sources of disease in civilized life. Even common water, that apparently innoxious pabulum, when corrupted by the filth of populous cities, is a deadly and insidious destroyer.[2] Who can wonder that all the inducements held out by God himself in the Bible to virtue should have been vainer than a nurse's tale, and that those dogmas, by which he has there excited and justified the most ferocious propensities, should have alone been deemed essential, whilst Christians are in the daily practice of all those habits which have infected with disease and crime, not only the reprobate sons, but these favored children

---

[1] The necessity of resorting to some means of purifying water, and the disease which arises from its adulteration in civilized countries, is sufficiently apparent. ... See Dr. Lambe's *Reports on Cancer*. I do not

assert that the use of water is in itself unnatural, but that the unperverted palate would swallow no liquid capable of occasioning disease.

[2] Lambe's *Reports on Cancer*.

of the common Father's love! Omnipotence itself could not save them from the consequences of this original and universal sin.

There is no disease, bodily or mental, which adoption of vegetable diet and pure water has not infallibly mitigated, wherever the experiment has been fairly tried. Debility is gradually converted into strength, disease into healthfulness; madness, in all its hideous variety, from the ravings of the fettered maniac to the unaccountable irrationalities of ill temper that make a hell of domestic life, into a calm and considerate evenness of temper that alone might offer a certain pledge of the future moral reformation of society. On a natural system of diet old age would be our last and our only malady; the term of our existence would be protracted; we should enjoy life and no longer preclude others from the enjoyment of it; all sensational delights would be infinitely more exquisite and perfect; the very sense of being would then be a continued pleasure, such as we now feel it in some few and favored moments of our youth. By all that is sacred in our hopes for the human race I conjure those who love happiness and truth to give a fair trial to the vegetable system. Reasoning is surely superfluous on a subject whose merits an experience of six months would set forever at rest. But it is only among the enlightened and benevolent that so great a sacrifice of appetite and prejudice can be expected, even though its ultimate excellence should not admit of dispute. It is found easier by the short-sighted victims of disease to palliate their torments by medicine than to prevent them by regimen. The vulgar of all ranks are invariably sensual and indocile; yet I cannot but feel myself persuaded that when the benefits of vegetable diet are mathematically proved, when it is as clear that those who live naturally are exempt from premature death as that nine is not one, the most sottish of mankind will feel a preference towards a long and tranquil, contrasted with a short and painful life. On the average out of sixty persons four die in three years. Hopes are entertained that, in April, 1814, a statement will be given that sixty persons, all having lived more than three years on vegetables and pure water, are then *in perfect health.* More than two years have now elapsed; *not one of them has died;* no such example will be found in any sixty persons taken at random. Seventeen persons of all ages (the families of Dr. Lambe and Mr. Newton) have lived for seven years on this diet without a death and almost without the slightest illness. Surely, when we consider that some of these were infants and one a martyr to asthma now nearly subdued, we may challenge any seventeen persons taken at random in this city to exhibit a parallel case. Those who may have been excited to question the rectitude of established habits of diet by these loose remarks should consult Mr. Newton's luminous and eloquent essay.[1]

[1] *Return to Nature, or Defence of Vegetable Regimen.* Cadell, 1811.

When these proofs come fairly before the world and are clearly seen by all who understand arithmetic, it is scarcely possible that abstinence from aliments demonstrably pernicious should not become universal. In proportion to the number of proselytes, so will be the weight of evidence; and when a thousand persons can be produced, living on vegetables and distilled water, who have to dread no disease but old age, the world will be compelled to regard animal flesh and fermented liquors as slow but certain poisons. The change which would be produced by simpler habits on political economy is sufficiently remarkable. The monopolizing eater of animal flesh would no longer destroy his constitution by devouring an acre at a meal, and many loaves of bread would cease to contribute to gout, madness and apoplexy, in the shape of a pint of porter or a dram of gin, when appeasing the long-protracted famine of the hard-working peasant's hungry babes. The quantity of nutritious vegetable matter consumed in fattening the carcase of an ox would afford ten times the sustenance, undepraving indeed, and incapable of generating disease, if gathered immediately from the bosom of the earth. The most fertile districts of the habitable globe are now actually cultivated by men for animals at a delay and waste of aliment absolutely incapable of calculation. It is only the wealthy that can, to any great degree, even now, indulge the unnatural craving for dead flesh, and they pay for the greater license of the privilege by subjection to supernumerary diseases. Again, the spirit of the nation that should take the lead in this great reform, would insensibly become agricultural; commerce, with all its vice, selfishness and corruption, would gradually decline; more natural habits would produce gentler manners, and the excessive complication of political relations would be so far simplified that every individual might feel and understand why he loved his country and took a personal interest in its welfare. How would England, for example, depend on the caprices of foreign rulers, if she contained within herself all the necessaries and despised whatever they possessed of the luxuries of life? How could they starve her into compliance with their views? Of what consequence would it be that they refused to take her woollen manufactures, when large and fertile tracts of the island ceased to be allotted to the waste of pasturage? On a natural system of diet, we should require no spices from India; no wines from Portugal, Spain, France or Madeira; none of those multitudinous articles of luxury, for which every corner of the globe is rifled, and which are the causes of so much individual rivalship, such calamitous and sanguinary national disputes. In the history of modern times the avarice of commercial monopoly, no less than the ambition of weak and wicked chiefs, seems to have fomented the universal discord, to have added stubbornness to the mistakes of cabinets and indocility to the infatuation of the people. Let it ever be remembered that it is the direct influence of commerce to make the interval between the richest and the poorest man wider and more unconquerable. Let it be remembered that it is a foe to everything of real worth and excellence in the human character. The odious and disgusting aristocracy of wealth is built upon the ruins of all that is good in chivalry or republicanism, and luxury is the forerunner of a barbarism scarce capable of cure. Is it impossible to realize a state of society, where all the energies of man shall be directed to the production of his solid happiness? Certainly, if this advantage (the object of all political speculation) be in any degree attainable, it is attainable only by a community, which holds out no factitious incentives to the avarice and ambition of the few and which is internally organized for the liberty, security and comfort of the many. None must be entrusted with power (and money is the completest species of power) who do not stand pledged to use it exclusively for the general benefit. But the use of animal flesh and fermented liquors directly militates with this equality of the rights of man. The peasant cannot gratify these fashionable cravings without leaving his family to starve. Without disease and war, those sweeping curtailers of population, pasturage would include a waste too great to be afforded. The labor requisite to support a family is far lighter[1] than is usually supposed. The peasantry work, not only for themselves, but for the aristocracy, the army and the manufacturers.

The advantage of a reform in diet is obviously greater than that of any other. It strikes at the root of the evil. To remedy the abuses of legislation, before we annihilate the propensities by which they are produced, is to suppose that by taking away the effect the cause will cease to operate. But the efficacy of this system depends entirely on the proselytism of individuals, and grounds its merits, as a benefit to the community, upon the total change of the dietetic habits in its members. It proceeds securely from a number of particular cases to one that is universal, and has this advantage over the contrary mode, that one error does not invalidate all that has gone before.

Let not too much, however, be expected from this system. The healthiest among us is not exempt from hereditary disease. The most symmetrical, athletic, and long-lived is a being inexpressibly inferior to what he would have been, had not the unnatural habits of his ancestors accumulated for him a certain portion of malady and deformity. In the most perfect specimen of civilized man something is still found wanting by the physiological critic. Can a return to Nature, then, instantaneously eradicate

predispositions that have been slowly taking root in the silence of innumerable ages? Indubitably not. All that I contend for is, that from the moment of the relinquishing all unnatural habits no new disease is generated; and that the predisposition to hereditary maladies gradually perishes for want of its accustomed supply. In cases of consumption, cancer, gout, asthma, and scrofula, such is the invariable tendency of a diet of vegetables and pure water.

Those who may be induced by these remarks to give the vegetable system a fair trial, should, in the first place, date the commencement of their practice from the moment of their conviction. All depends upon breaking through a pernicious habit resolutely and at once. Dr. Trotter[2] asserts that no drunkard was ever reformed by gradually relinquishing his dram. Animal flesh in its effects on the human stomach is analogous to a dram. It is similar in the kind, though differing in the degree, of its operation. The proselyte to a pure diet must be warned to expect a temporary diminution of muscular strength. The subtraction of a powerful stimulus will suffice to account for this event. But it is only temporary and is succeeded by an equable capability for exertion far surpassing his former various and fluctuating strength. Above all, he will acquire an easiness of breathing, by which such exertion is performed, with a remarkable exemption from that painful and difficult panting now felt by almost every one after hastily climbing an ordinary mountain. He will be equally capable of bodily exertion or mental application after as before his simple meal. He will feel none of the narcotic effects of ordinary diet. Irritability, the direct consequence of exhausting stimuli, would yield to the power of natural and tranquil impulses. He will no longer pine under the lethargy of ennui, that unconquerable weariness of life, more to be dreaded than death itself. He will escape the epidemic madness which broods over its own injurious notions of the Deity and 'realizes the hell that priests and beldams feign.' Every man forms as it were his god from his own character; to the divinity of one of simple habits no offering would be more acceptable than the happiness of his creatures. He would be incapable of hating or persecuting others for the love of God. He will find, moreover, a system of simple diet to be a system of perfect epicurism. He will no longer be incessantly occupied in blunting and destroying those organs from which he expects his gratification. The pleasures of taste to be derived from a dinner of potatoes, beans, peas, turnips, lettuces, with a dessert of apples, gooseberries, strawberries, currants, raspberries, and, in winter, oranges, apples, and pears, is far

---

[1] It has come under the author's experience, that some of the workmen on an embankment in North Wales, who, in consequence of the inability of the proprietor to pay them, seldom received their wages, have supported large families by cultivating small spots of sterile ground by moonlight. In the notes to Pratt's

Poem, *Bread or the Poor*, is an account of an industrious laborer who by working in a small garden before and after his day's task attained to an enviable state of independence.

[2] See Trotter on *The Nervous Temperament*.

greater than is supposed. Those who wait until they can eat this plain fare with the sauce of appetite will scarcely join with the hypocritical sensualist at a lord-mayor's feast, who declaims against the pleasures of the table. Solomon kept a thousand concubines, and owned in despair that all was vanity. The man whose happiness is constituted by the society of one amiable woman would find some difficulty in sympathizing with the disappointment of this venerable debauchee.

I address myself not only to the young enthusiast, the ardent devotee of truth and virtue, the pure and passionate moralist yet unvitiated by the contagion of the world. He will embrace a pure system, from its abstract truth, its beauty, its simplicity and its promise of wide-extended benefit; unless custom has turned poison into food, he will hate the brutal pleasures of the chase by instinct; it will be a contemplation full of horror and disappointment to his mind that beings capable of the gentlest and most admirable sympathies should take delight in the death-pangs and last convulsions of dying animals. The elderly man, whose youth has been poisoned by intemperance, or who has lived with apparent moderation and is afflicted with a variety of painful maladies, would find his account in a beneficial change produced without the risk of poisonous medicines. The mother, to whom the perpetual restlessness of disease and unaccountable deaths incident to her children are the causes of incurable unhappiness, would on this diet experience the satisfaction of beholding their perpetual healths and natural playfulness.[1] The most valuable lives are daily destroyed by diseases that it is dangerous to palliate and impossible to cure by medicine. How much longer will man continue to pimp for the gluttony of death, his most insidious, implacable and eternal foe?

[Four brief extracts from Plutarch, περὶ σαρκοφαγίας, are here omitted, by advice of the general editor.]

Notes and Illustrations

For the sources of QUEEN MAB, beyond those indicated in Shelley's notes, the student should consult the Latin authors; Volney's *Ruins* suggested the framework. The text presents few difficulties. Mrs. Shelley made a few changes in the interest of grammar, and Rossetti increased their number and added other changes in the interest of what he conceived to be Shelley's sense. Some of these grammatical corrections are unnecessary, and those in the sense are usually arbitrary. The most important points are the following:

[1] See Mr. Newton's book. His children are the most beautiful and healthy creatures it is possible to conceive; the girls are perfect models for a sculptor; their dispositions are also the most gentle and conciliating; the judicious treatment, which they experience in other points, may be a correlative cause of this. In the first five years of their life, of 18,000 children that are born 7500 die of various diseases; and how many more of those that survive are not rendered miserable by

Page 10. Line 151. Rossetti reads *As* for *Who*.

Page 13. Line 115. Rossetti reads *sanctify*.

Line 140. Dowden accepts Tutin's conjecture in punctuation, reading a colon after *element* and deleting the period after *remained* in the next line.

Page 14. Line 176. All editors follow Mrs. Shelley in reading *secure*.

Page 15. Line 9. The reading of the text is Rossetti's, the original having a period after *promise*.

Page 18. Line 219. Rossetti reads *his* for *its*.

Page 25. Line 56. Rossetti reads *Shows*.

Page 27. Line 182. Rossetti reads *his* for *their*.

Page 28. Line 205. Shelley in quoting the line in his NOTES reads *Dawns* for *Draws*, which Rossetti adopts.

Page 30. Line 139. Rossetti reads *future* for *past*.

Page 31. ALASTOR.

This poem has been examined in a more scholarly way than any other of Shelley's longer works, Dr. Richard Ackermann having made it in part the subject of an inaugural dissertation, *Quellen, Vorbilder, Stoffe zu Shelley's Poetischen Werken*, I. *Alastor*, etc. (Erlangen & Leipzig, 1890), and Prof. Al. Beljame having translated and edited it, with elaborate notes, *Alastor, ou le génie de la solitude* (Paris, 1895). Dr. Ackermann traces the influence of Wordsworth and Coleridge in the special romantic features of the nature-handling, vision element, and what might be called the psychology of the poem; and also that of Southey and Landor in some of the Oriental coloring and detail of the narrative; but, like Brandl in his *Life of Coleridge*, he pushes the theory of direct obligation too far, inasmuch as what is common in subject-matter and spontaneous to the method of any poetic period or group cannot fairly be regarded as peculiar to the originality of even its earliest members. Professor Beljame does not fall into this error, and gives illustrative parallelisms of phrase and image merely as such unless the borrowing is clear. The versification and diction recall Coleridge and Wordsworth in their most musical blank verse, but except in a few passages (lines 46–49, 482–485, 718–720) the rhythm has distinctly Shelley's rapid and peculiar modulation. The substance of the poem, however, is variously embedded in Shelley's literary studies and in his actual observation of nature, while the feeling of the whole is a personal mood. It is customary to regard Shelley's landscape as unreal; but, though it is imaginative, it contains elements of actuality, transcripts of scenes as witnessed by him, to a far

maladies not immediately mortal? The quality and quantity of a woman's milk are materially injured by the use of dead flesh. In an island near Iceland, where no vegetables are to be got, the children invariably die of tetanus before they are three weeks old, and the population is supplied from the mainland. — Sir G. Mackenzie's *History of Iceland*. See, also, *Emile*, chap. i. pp. 53, 54, 56.

greater extent than has ever been acknowledged ; in the present poem, his own river-navigation, his life in Wales and travels abroad, as well as the forest at Windsor, have left direct traces, as Dr. Ackermann especially remarks. Shelley himself mentions his opportunities for observation as among his qualifications for poetry, in the preface to THE REVOLT OF ISLAM. The notes that follow ascribe to each commentator what seems to be his own. The meaning of the title and its source are given in the head-notes. The motto is from the first chapter of the third book of St. Augustine's *Confessions*, and the full text is given by Beljame : Veni Carthaginem ; et circumstrepebat me undique sartago flagitiosorum amorum. Nondum amabam, et amare amabam, et secretiore indigentia oderam me minus indigentem. Quærebam quod amarem, amans amare, et oderam securitatem et viam sine muscipulis.

Line 1. Beljame happily compares the invocation in Ben Jonson's *Cynthia's Revels*, V. 2, which is identical in structure. The substance, or feeling for nature, is Wordsworthian ; compare, for example, *Influence of natural objects*, *Lines composed a few miles above Tintern Abbey*, and *Lines left upon a Seat in a Yew-Tree*.

3. *Natural piety*, an example of Shelley's direct borrowings of phrase from Wordsworth (*My heart leaps up*), of which others occur below, — *obstinate questionings*, line 26 (*Ode on Intimations of Immortality*, IX. 13, and *too deep for tears*, line 713 (the same, XI. 17).

13. Ackermann compares Wordsworth, *The Excursion*, II. 41-47, but the humanitarian feeling toward animal life belongs to the period, and is a fundamental source of Shelley's inspiration.

20-29. Compare HYMN TO INTELLECTUAL BEAUTY, V.

30. Brandl (*Life of Coleridge*, 190) compares the situation with Coleridge's *Frost at Midnight*, but I can see in the two only a parallelism of the romantic temperament and method.

38. Beljame cites the inscription of the veiled Isis from Volney, *Les Ruines*: Je suis tout ce qui a été, tout ce qui est, tout ce qui sera, et nul mortel n'a levé mon voile.

54. *Waste wilderness*. Forman quotes Blake for the phrase, and Beljame follows him, but in this as in other instances the attempt to tie Shelley to Blake fails. Had he known Blake's works he would have shown clearer evidences of it. The present phrase is, of course, Milton's, *Paradise Regained*, I. 7.

'And Eden raised in the waste wilderness.'

83. *Volcano*, Ætna.

85. *Bitumen lakes*. Beljame identifies these with the Dead Sea, and notes Southey's description of *Ait's bitumen-lake*, *Thalaba*, V. 22. It seems as likely that Shelley's sole source is Southey, and that he had no particular local reference.

87-94. Beljame supposes that Shelley here blends in one description the marvels of the two isles Antiparos and Milo, one for its stalactite

grotto, the other for its sulphurous exhalations. The grotto had been recently described by Leake, *Travels in Northern Greece*, 1806, and Clarke, *Travels in Various Countries*, etc., 1814. From some such source Shelley may have derived the idea, but his poetic description is heightened to the point of fantasy and retains very little of mere geography. Compare Coleridge, *A Tombless Epitaph*, 28-32 ; also line 400, note.

100-106. Ackermann compares Landor, *Gebir*, II. 108:

'And as he passes on, the little hinds
That shake for bristly herds the foodful bough
Wonder, stand still, gaze, and trip satisfied ;
Pleased more if chestnut, out of prickly husk,
Shot from the sandal, roll along the glade.'

108. The background of the following passage appears to be, as Beljame suggests, Volney's *Les Ruines*, from the first four chapters of which he quotes to show a general sympathy, and also analogies of detail. The pilgrim literature, which both Volney and Chateaubriand (*René*, also cited, but inconclusively) illustrate, may well include ALASTOR as among its kindred.

119. *The Zodiac's brazen mystery*, the Zodiac of the temple of Denderah in Upper Egypt. Beljame refers to Volney, *Les Ruines*, XXII., note. It is now in the Bibliothèque Nationale at Paris.

120. *Mute*, written just before Champollion's labors, as Beljame notes.

129. *Arab maiden*. Ackermann derives the character from *Thalaba's* Oneiza, as also the *veiled maid* below (line 151), and compares the description of the latter from point to point with that in *Thalaba*, III. 24, 25. The parallel is somewhat forced, as becomes more evident on examination. The lines 161-162 have as the corresponding passage in *Thalaba*:

'Oh ! even with such a look as fables say
The Mother Ostrich fixes on her egg,
Till that *intense affection*
Kindle its light of life, —
Even in *such deep and breathless tenderness*
Oneiza's soul is centred on the youth.'

So, too, in the alleged parallelism for lines 167,168, and 175, 176, we find in *Thalaba*

' for a brother's eye
Were her long fingers tinged,
As when she trimmed the lamp,
And through the veins and delicate skin
The light shone rosy ; '

that is, as a long note shows, being 'tinged with henna' so as to make the fingers seem in some instances 'branches of transparent red coral.' Shelley's meaning is far different, and is unlikely to be in any way connected in its origin with a recollection of Southey, in either of these two passages, though in introducing the *Arab maiden* he would naturally recall *Oneiza*. The *veiled maid* is, however, not an Arabian, but the spirit of the ideal.

140-144. The background of the Poet's wandering seems to be found in Arrian's *Expedition of Alexander*, and possibly similar passages in Quintus Curtius and Dion Cassius. The *wild Carmanian waste* is the Desert of Kerman ; the *aërial mountains* are the Hindoo Koosh, or Indian Caucasus, where Arrian wrongly places the sources of the *Indus and Oxus.*

145. *The vale of Cashmire,* the earthly paradise of that name, often mentioned in poetry. The particular descriptions given by Shelley, both here in the place of the vision, and later in the glen of the Caspian Caucasus, seem to me to recall the scenery and atmosphere of Miss Owenson's (Lady Morgan) *The Missionary,* a romance which Shelley read in 1811. See note on line 400.

161. Rossetti reads *Himself* for *Herself* in his first edition, and was defended by James Thomson, but no other editor has adopted the conjecture, and Rossetti himself has restored the original reading not without some apologetic protest.

177. *Woven wind,* the *ventum textilem* of the ancients, and also perhaps with a recollection of the transparent veils of *Thalaba,* VI. 26, note. For the development of the structure of the whole vision here given (lines 149–191) compare the passage in the preface where Shelley states the elements of his conception in prose.

204. See note on line 129. This *vision* is the ALASTOR or evil genius, the spirit of solitude, the embodiment of all the responses to his own nature which the Poet lacked through his separation from society, and was sent by 'the spirit of sweet human love' who had spurned her choicest gifts' by his self-isolation ; it was sent, as an Avenger, and leads or drives him on in search of its own phantasm till he dies. The folly of devotion to the idealizing faculty apart from human life seems to be the moral of the allegory, which most critics have found a dark one ; but the treatment of the Poet is so sympathetic, notwithstanding the latter's error, and the presentation of the Destroyer in the shape of the visionary maid is so alluring, that the reader forgets the didactic intent of the fable, and sees only an adumbration of the life of Shelley as seen by himself in the clairvoyance of genius, and consciously seen by him as a fate which he would avoid by mingling sympathetically with the life of men. If, as Dowden says, the poem be 'in its inmost sense a pleading on behalf of human love,' shown by the fate of those who reject it, it is also not without a tragic sense of the pity of that fate in those in whose life such a rejection is rather the isolation of a noble nature and the result less of choice than of temperament and circumstance. Compare Shelley's comment in the preface.

210. Compare Æschylus, *Agamemnon,* 415.

211–219. The union of Sleep and Death in Shelley's poetry is a fixed idea ; compare in this poem lines 293, 368. The use of water-reflections as a detail is also constant, and is repeated below no less than five times, lines 385, 408, 459, 470, 501. The tenacity with which Shelley's mind clings to its images is characteristic, and shows intensity of application

rather than poverty of material, in a young writer ; not only in ALASTOR are there some of his images permanent in his verse, such as Ahasuerus, the *serpent,* and the *boat,* but instances of pure repetition frequently occur, as above ; compare, below, the *alchemist,* 31, 682, the *bird and snake,* 227, 325, the *lyre,* 42, 667, the *cloud,* 663, 687.

219. *Conducts,* Rossetti thus corrects the original reading, *conduct,* which is, however, retained by all other editors. Shelley doubtless wrote *conduct,* the verb being attracted into the plural by the number of details mentioned in connection with *vault ;* other explanations, on the ground of *does* understood, in one or another way, are only ingenious excuses ; the structure of the group of questions is so continuous that it seems best to make the change.

227. Compare THE REVOLT OF ISLAM, I. viii.–xiv.

240. *Aornos,* 'identified by General Abbott in 1854 as Mount Mahabunn near the right bank of the Indus about sixty miles above its confluence with the Cabul,' Chinnock, *Arrian's Anabasis,* 237, note. *Petra,* identified as the Sogdian rock (Arrian, IV. 18) ; for the name Beljame quotes Quintus Curtius, VIII. 11 ; *Una erat Petra.*

242. *Balk,* Bactria was the ancient name.

242–244. It was Caracallus who violated the Parthian royal tombs and scattered the dust of the kings to the four winds. Beljame gives the reference Dion Cassius, LXXVIII. 1.

262–267. Ackermann and Beljame trace the detail to *Thalaba,* VIII. 1 and IX. 17, Shelley having united the two in one image.

272. *Chorasmian shore,* properly the Aral Sea, but Shelley apparently intends the Caspian Sea.

299. *Shallop,* the detail is from *Thalaba,* XI. 31, as Ackermann remarks, as is the general conception of the voyage on the underground river. The opening passage is as follows :

> ' A little boat there lay,
> Without an oar, without a sail,
> One only seat it had, one seat.'

Compare also the boat of THE WITCH OF ATLAS.

337–339. Beljame compares the same image in A SUMMER EVENING CHURCHYARD, but it is used most memorably in TO NIGHT :

> 'Bind with thy hair the eyes of Day,
> Kiss her till she be wearied out.'

349. Other editors retain the original reading of a period after *ocean ;* but Rossetti changed this to a semicolon and dash, which seems justifiable where no pretence is made of reproducing Shelley's punctuation.

353. *Caucasus,* the Caspian Caucasus.

376. The cascade, like the underground voyage, is from *Thalaba,* VII. 6, quoted by Ackermann :

> ' And lo ! where raving o'er a hollow course
> The ever flowing flood
> Foams in a thousand whirlpools ! Then adown
> The perforated rock

Plunge the whole waters : so precipitous,
So fathomless a fall,
That their earth-shaking roar came deadened up
Like subterranean thunder.'

Ackermann also recalls the river in *Kubla Khan*.

400. The following extracts, from Miss Owenson's *The Missionary*, seem apposite here :

'Surrounded by those mighty mountains whose summits appear tranquil and luminous above the regions of cloud which float on their brow, whose grotesque forms are brightened by innumerable rills, and dashed by foaming torrents, the valley of Cashmire presented to the wandering eye scenes of picturesque and glowing beauty, whose character varied with each succeeding hour. . . . It was evening when the missionary reached the base of a lofty mountain, which seemed a monument of the first day of creation. It was a solemn and sequestered spot, where an eternal spring seemed to reign, and which looked like the cradle of infant Nature, when she first awoke in all her primæval bloom of beauty. It was a glen screened by a mighty mass of rocks, over whose bold fantastic forms and variegated hues dashed the silvery foam of the mountain torrent, flinging its dewy sprays around. . . . He proceeded through a path which from the long cusa-grass matted over it and the entangled creepers of the parasite plants, seemed to have been rarely if ever explored. The trees, thick and umbrageous, were wedded in their towering branches above his head, and knitted in their spreading roots beneath his feet. The sound of a cascade became his sole guide through the leafy labyrinth. He at last reached the pile of rocks whence the torrent flowed, pouring its tributary flood into a broad river. . . . Before the altar appeared a human form, if human it might be called, which stood so bright and so ethereal in its look that it seemed but a transient incorporation of the brilliant mists of the morning ; so light and so aspiring in its attitude that it appeared already ascending from the earth it scarcely touched to mingle with its kindred air. The resplendent locks of the seeming sprite were enwreathed with beams, and sparkled with the waters of the holy stream whence it appeared recently to have emerged.' (Chap. VI.)

'Not a sound disturbed the mystic silence, save the low murmurs of a gushing spring, which fell with more than mortal music from a mossy cliff, sparkling among the matted roots of overhanging trees, and gliding, like liquid silver, beneath the network of the parasite plants. The flowers of the mangosteen gave to the fresh air a balmy fragrance. The mighty rocks of the Pagoda, which rose behind in endless perspective, scaling the heavens, which seemed to repose upon their summits, lent the strong relief of their deep shadows to the softened twilight of the foreground.' (Chap. XII.)

The landscape of the vale of Cashmire as here described is, in effect, the same as that of the glen in ALASTOR, and in the figure of Luxima

there is something sympathetic, at least, with the *veilèd maid* of the vision. In Hilarion (the missionary) there is also something sympathetic with the *Poet* of the poem, as he has rejected love, and now suffers the penalty of a great passion, doomed necessarily to a tragic conclusion, under influences of solitude and nature. (See chap. IX., where his psychological character is developed : ' he resembled the enthusiast of experimental philosophy who shuts out the light and breath of heaven to inhale an artificial atmosphere and enjoy an ideal existence.') It is interesting to observe also the description of the subterranean cave, with stalactite formation, lit by blue subterraneous fire, — the temple ' most ancient and celebrated in India, after that of Elephanta ' (chap. XII.). See, also, for other traces of this romance in Shelley's work, the notes on THE REVOLT OF ISLAM, XII., and THE INDIAN SERENADE.

421, 422. Beljame quotes from Mrs. Shelley's Journal, August, 1814, in Dowden's *Life of Shelley*, ' At Noè [Nouaille ?] — in a noontide of intense heat — whilst our postilion waited, we walked into the forest of pines ; it was a scene of enchantment, where every sound and sight contributed to charm. Our mossy seat in the deepest recesses of the wood was inclosed from the world by an impenetrable veil.'

431-438. Ackermann compares Scott, *Rokeby*, IV. 3 ; but there are many forest descriptions in English verse as similar, the original of all in this style being Milton's *Paradise Lost*, IV.

451-454. Ackermann here again seeks the original detail in *Thalaba*, VI. 22 :

' And oh ! what *odours the voluptuous vale*
Scatters from *jasmine bowers,*
From *yon rose wilderness,*
From clustered henna, and from orange groves
That with *such perfumes* fill the breeze.'

So definite an origin for general properties seems to me most unlikely.

454-456. Beljame compares A SUMMER EVENING CHURCHYARD, V. 5, 6.

479. *Spirit*, apparently an embodiment of Nature evoked by and reflecting the mood of death-melancholy in the Poet ; not the spirit of the vision which he seeks, which is ' the light that shone within his soul ' (lines 492, 493), but it may also be regarded as a later incarnation of the latter.

502-514. Ackermann compares the very similar though more diffuse passage in Wordsworth, *The Excursion*, III. 967-991.

543-548. Editors and commentators have struggled to extract the precise meaning from these lines, but without establishing any likely emendation. Miss Blind proposes *inclosed* for *disclosed ;* Forman suggests *amidst precipices* for *its precipice ;* Madox Brown guesses *Hid* for *Mid ;* ' E. S.' would read *their precipice* for *its ;* Swinburne thinks a verse has been dropped, and an anonymous writer conjectures that the lost verse may be represented by inserting after 547

' A cataract descending with wild roar.'

Rossetti, after some ineffectual wanderings,

returned to the original text, which Dowden also
sustains. The interpretation, however, remains
different, Rossetti taking *precipice* as the subject of *disclosed* used for *disclosed itself*, and
Dowden taking *which* as the subject of *disclosed* with *gulfs and caves* as its object, and *its
precipice obscuring the ravine* as parenthetical.
Brooke also retains the text, and takes *its* as
equivalent to *its own*. The simplest explanation where all are awkward is to consider the
clause beginning *and its precipice* as parallel
with the earlier half beginning *now rose rocks*,
and the sense briefly would be : the rocks rose
in the evening light, and also the precipice rose
(shadowing the ravine below), disclosed above
in the same light. I take *precipice* as subject
to *rose* understood and *disclosed* as a participle ;
its is the same as in 542, 543, *i. e., the loud
streams* in 550. If this is rejected I should prefer to take *which* as the subject of *disclosed* and
precipice as its object. To take *precipice* as the
subject of *disclosed* with *gulfs and caves* as its
object, involves a construction of line 548 so
forced as to amount in my mind to impossibility.

602–605. Ackermann quotes from Mrs. Shelley's Journal (Dowden's *Life of Shelley*) : ' The
evening was most beautiful ; the horned moon
hung in the light of sunset, which threw a glow
of unusual depth of redness above the piny
mountains and the dark deep valleys. . . . The
moon becomes yellow, and hangs close to the
woody horizon.'

668–671. The passage has been somewhat
discussed, but Brooke's note settles the meaning easily : ' It is quite in Shelley's manner . . .
to go back and bring together his illustrations.
Here the poet's frame is a lute, a bright stream,
a dream of youth. The lute is still, the stream is
dark and dry, the dream is unremembered.' The
practice is common to English poetry from the
early days. Compare EPIPSYCHIDION, 73–75.

677. The reference is to Ahasuerus, the wandering Jew. Compare QUEEN MAB, VI. and
Shelley's NOTES on the passage. The character again appears in HELLAS.

Page 43. THE REVOLT OF ISLAM.
The text was made from the sheets of *Laon
and Cythna* by the insertion of 26 cancel-leaves.
The copy upon which Shelley worked in recom-
posing is described at length by Forman, *The
Shelley Library*, 83–86. The cancelled passages
are as follows :

Canto II. xxi. 1
I had a little sister whose fair eyes

xxv. 2
To love in human life, this sister sweet

Canto III. i. 1
What thoughts had sway over my sister's slumber

i. 3
As if they did ten thousand years outnumber

Canto IV. xxx. 6
And left it vacant — 't was her brother's face —

Canto V. xlvii. 5
I had a brother once, but he is dead ! —

Canto VI. xxiv. 8
My own sweet sister looked, with joy did quail,

xxxi. 6
The common blood which ran within our frames,

xxxix. 6–9
With such close sympathies, for to each other
Had high and solemn hopes, the gentle might
Of earliest love, and all the thoughts which smother
Cold Evil's power, now linked a sister and a brother.

xl. 1
And such is Nature's modesty, that those

Canto VIII. iv. 9
Dream ye that God thus builds for man in solitude ?

v. 1.
What then is God ? Ye mock yourselves and give

vi. 1
What then is God ? Some moonstruck sophist stood

vi. 8, 9
And that men say God has appointed Death
On all who scorn his will to wreak immortal wrath.

vii. 1–4
Men say they have seen God, and heard from God,
Or known from others who have known such things,
And that his will is all our law, a rod
To scourge us into slaves — that Priests and Kings

viii. 1
And it is said, that God will punish wrong ;

viii. 3, 4
And his red hell's undying snakes among
Will bind the wretch on whom he fixed a stain

xiii. 3, 4
For it is said God rules both high and low,
And man is made the captive of his brother ;

Canto IX. xiii. 8
To curse the rebels. To their God did they

xiv. 6
By God, and Nature, and Necessity.

xv. 4–7
There was one teacher, and must ever be,
They said, even God, who, the necessity
Of rule and wrong had armed against mankind,
His slave and his avenger there to be ;

xviii. 3–6
And Hell and Awe, which in the heart of man
Is God itself ; the Priests its downfall knew,
As day by day their altars lovelier grew,
Till they were left alone within the fane;

Canto X. xxii. 9
On fire ! Almighty God his hell on earth has spread !

xxvi. 7, 8
Of their Almighty God, the armies wind
In sad procession : each among the train.

xxviii. 1
O God Almighty ! thou alone hast power.

xxxi. 1
And Oromaze, and Christ, and Mahomet.

xxxii. 1
He was a Christian Priest from whom it came

xxxii. 4
To quell the rebel Atheists; a dire guest

xxxii. 9
To wreak his fear of God on vengeance on mankind

xxxiv. 5, 6

His cradled Idol, and the sacrifice
Of God to God's own wrath — that Islam's creed

xxxv. 9

And thrones, which rest on faith in God, nigh over-
turned.

xxxix. 4

Of God may be appeased.' He ceased, and they

xl. 5

With storms and shadows girt, sate God, alone,

xliv. 9

As 'hush! hark! Come they yet? God,
God, thine hour is near!'

xlv. 8

Men brought their atheist kindred to appease

xlvii. 6

The threshold of God's throne, and it was she!

Canto XI. xvi. 1

Ye turn to God for aid in your distress;

xxv. 7

Swear by your dreadful God.' — 'We swear, we
swear!'

Canto XII. x. 9

Truly for self, thus thought that Christian Priest
indeed,

xi. 9

A woman? God has sent his other victim here.

xii. 6–8

Will I stand up before God's golden throne,
And cry, O Lord, to thee did I betray
An Atheist; but for me she would have known

xxix. 4

In torment and in fire have Atheists gone;

xxx. 4

How Atheists and Republicans can die.

In THE REVOLT OF ISLAM, Shelley unites
the landscape and sentiment of ALASTOR with
the didactic teaching of QUEEN MAB. In political and social philosophy he shows no intellectual advance, though it is noticeable that in
the preface he disclaims responsibility for the
views which have 'a dramatic propriety in
reference to the character they are designed to
elucidate' and are 'injurious to the character'
of the 'benevolences' of the Deity, and which he
says are 'widely different' from his own; and
it should be remarked that his expressions with
respect to the immortality of the spirit are per-
ceptibly more strong and favorable. It is rather
on the poetic side that he shows development;
but here, too, the didactic element seems to me
less evenly eloquent than in QUEEN MAB, and
the imaginative element less pervaded with
charm than in ALASTOR. Medwin says that
Shelley told him that Keats and he agreed to
attempt a long poem, and that ENDYMION and
THE REVOLT OF ISLAM were the fruit of this
friendly rivalry. It can hardly be doubted that
the deliberate ambition to compose a long work
entered into the motive which prompted the
poem.

The new element which distinguishes THE
REVOLT OF ISLAM from its predecessors is the
fable, or story, which is made the vehicle of
revolutionary doctrine. Shelley asserted that
it was free from the intervention of the supernatural, except at the beginning and end; but
the machinery and incidents are of the romantic school, in the 'Gothic' taste, in which his
interest in fiction began, though here oriental-
ized in sympathy with the literary taste of a
time later than Monk Lewis and the young
Scott. The tower-prison, the hermit's retreat,
the cave of Laone with its underground entrance, the 'Tartarean steed,' are all in the
region of romance; the human conduct of the
characters — the yielding of the gaolers to the
hermit's voice and looks, the protest of Laon in
behalf of his foes and of the tyrant, the devotion of the child to the latter, the final surrender of Laon — are all in the vein of pure moral
sentimentality; and though there are few such
puerilities as the 'small knife' and the eagle
who could not be taught to 'bring ropes' (and
I should regard the original scheme by which
Laon and Laone were made brother and sister
merely as a puerility), yet the hold on reality,
both in human nature at large and in the sense
of the action of life, is of the feeble and tenuous
sort that belongs to the fiction of the opening
of the century, which gave to Shelley his idea
of how and from what materials to construct a
tale. Though he uses the Spenserian stanza,
and read Spenser continuously while composing, it is only the land of pseudo-romance and
not Faëryland that he enters; and, as he is
dealing with political and social actualities, one
cannot but be aware of an unreality in the
movement of the poem, which Spenser himself
did not escape when he touched historic ground.
Not only the first Canto, in fact, is allegorical;
the whole tale is essentially allegory, and the
sole realities in it are moral realities, of which
the invincible power of love, its rightful sovereignty and final victory, is the chief, shown also
in reverse as the futility of force in all its forms,
tyranny, law, custom, fraud, or crime. The
characters are not much more vital than the
fable is real, with the exception of Laon, who is
a reincarnation of the youth in ALASTOR (or
Shelley's spirit) touched more with mortal passion and involved in human events; Laone is
the double of Laon, set forth somewhat as the
spirit of the vision in ALASTOR, but made more
actual through the facts of living; the hermit
is the wise old man; the tyrant is the *King* of
QUEEN MAB (a stage tyrant if ever there was
one), and the child is merely a property and has
no value except for sentimental effect.

There are *longueurs* in the poem, and some of
the causes of them are contained in these considerations. A moral allegory with but one
lesson, and that a lesson in revolution-mak-
ing, would require great powers of verisimili-
tude, of invention and of attraction, to maintain interest through twelve Cantos, and these
qualities THE REVOLT OF ISLAM does not possess. The analysis of its construction, in story,

incident and character, brings out its least favorable points; it has, taken in the mass, great excellences, especially power of description (both of scene and action) which in the best portions can only be described as splendor of description; it has also moral elevation, and enthusiasm inexhaustible in spontaneity and glow; and in several of the episodes there is a noble dignity of style. It is, it seems to me, the most uneven, the least completely one, of Shelley's works; but if on the one hand it has affinities with the crudity of his prose fiction, it also approaches on the other the visions of the PROMETHEUS UNBOUND; and it contains the moral truth that burnt in his own heart.

Page 47. *An alexandrine.* Rossetti points out three: IV. xxvii. 5; VIII. xxvii. 3; IX. xxxvi. 5.

48. Dedication. The motto is from Chapman's *Byron's Conspiracy*, III. i. (end).

49. *To Mary.* Mary Wollstonecraft Godwin, Shelley's second wife.

Stanza ii. 2. See Head-note for the circumstances here put into verse.

iii. 3 *hour*, the passage is regarded as autobiographical, and faithfully represents the atmosphere of Shelley's school-days, and his own attitude toward the 'tyranny' he then encountered. Cf. HYMN TO INTELLECTUAL BEAUTY, V.

v. 9 *thirst*, the mood depicted in ALASTOR.

vi. 3 *despair*, referring to the year before he met with Mary.

vii. 5 *burst*, referring to the elopement of Mary with him, in disregard of his marriage with Harriet.

x. 4 referring to his fears of approaching death.

9 Cf. THE SUNSET, 4.

xii. 3 *One*, Mary Wollstonecraft, the author of *A Vindication of the Rights of Woman*, and many other works, marked by independence and strength of mind, while her *Letters to Imlay* show deep feeling. A knowledge of her life is indispensable to a true understanding of Mary's union with Shelley.

9 *Sire*, William Godwin, author of *Political Justice* and many other radical works and novels, from whom Shelley derived in youth much of his revolutionary principles and social views.

xiii. 1 *One voice*, the voice of Truth.

xiv. 4 *his pure name*, Shelley means any philanthropist.

Page 52. Canto I. vi. 8. The image may be from *The Ancient Mariner*, pt. iii.: but effects of sunset on the sea are frequent in the early poems and are reminiscences of Shelley's life on the west coast. Cf. below I. xv. 2 and QUEEN MAB, ii. 4; also, of the moon, PRINCE ATHANASE, II. 96.

I. xxiii. 1. Cf. ALASTOR, 299, note.

I. xxv. 5. The myth here invented by Shelley to typify the conflict of the principles of Good and Evil as shown in man's social progress is the most imaginative and elaborate presentation

of this ancient idea in modern literature. The identification of the Morning Star, changed into the snake, with the Spirit of Good, and of the Ruling Power with Evil, a not unparalleled reversal of Christian symbolism, anticipates the conception of the relation of Good and Evil in PROMETHEUS UNBOUND.

I. xxxvii. 7. Cf. ALASTOR, 129. The moods of ALASTOR frequently recur in the poem: e. g., below, xliii., xlv., lvii.; II. x., xi.; IV. xxx.; VI. xxviii.

I. lii. Cf. QUEEN MAB, ii. 22 *et seq.*

Canto II. The opening stanzas of the Second Canto are characteristic of Shelley's autobiographical idealizations of his youth. Cf. the Dedicatory Stanzas above and the HYMN TO INTELLECTUAL BEAUTY.

II. xxxvi. 4 *half of humankind*, women.

III. xxvii. 7 *old man*, the idealized figure of Dr. Lind, who also appears in PRINCE ATHANASE.

V. xlix. 5 *three shapes*, the 'Giant' is Equality, the 'Woman' is Love, the 'third Image' is Wisdom. Cf. below, stanza iii. 1, 2. The following Hymn is to be regarded as the earliest of Shelley's greater odes, and is the highest lyrical expression that his political and social theories by themselves ever reached.

VII. xxxi. 6. The reference is to Pythagoras.

VIII. v. *et seq.* The speech of Laone is the most compact and full statement of Shelley's moral ideas in the time intermediate between QUEEN MAB and PROMETHEUS UNBOUND, with both of which poems it may be closely compared; especially the opening passage with QUEEN MAB, VII.; stanzas xi.-xii. with PROMETHEUS UNBOUND, IV. 554-578; and the whole with the same, III. iii. 130-204.

IX. xxi.-xxv. An anticipation of the ODE TO THE WEST WIND.

IX. xxxvi. 5. A translation of the famous epigram of Plato.

X. xviii. 5 *creaked*. Cf. Coleridge, *This Lime-Tree Bower my Prison*, 74 *Flew creeking*, with note: 'Some months after I had written this line, it gave me pleasure to observe that Bartram had observed the same circumstance of the Savanna crane. "When these birds move their wings in flight, their strokes are slow, moderate and regular, and even when at a considerable distance or high above us, we plainly hear the quill feathers: their shafts and webs upon one another creek as the joints or working of a vessel in a tempestuous sea."'

XII. ix. 1. The situation is parallel to that in Miss Owenson's *Missionary* (see ALASTOR, 400, note). Hilarion, the priest-lover of Luxima, has been condemned by the Inquisition at Goa and stands at the pile to be burnt. The story continues: 'In this awful interval, while the presiding officers of death were preparing to bind their victim to the stake, a form scarcely human, darting with the velocity of lightning through the multitude, reached the foot of the pile, and stood before it in a grand and aspiring attitude; the deep red flame of the slowly kindling fire shone through a transparent drapery which flowed in loose folds from the bosom of the seeming vision, and tinged with golden hues those long dishevelled tresses, which streamed like the rays of a meteor on the air; thus bright and aërial as it stood, it looked like a spirit sent from heaven in the awful moment of dissolution to cheer and to convey to the regions of the blessed, the soul which would soon arise pure from the ordeal of earthly suffering.

'The sudden appearance of the singular phantom struck the imagination of the credulous and awed multitude with superstitious wonder. . . . Luxima, whose eyes and hands had been hitherto raised to heaven, while she murmured the *Gayatra*, pronounced by the Indian women before their voluntary immolation, now looked wildly round her, and catching a glimpse of the Missionary's figure, through the waving of the flames, behind which he struggled in the hands of his guards, she shrieked, and in a voice scarcely human, exclaimed, "My beloved, I come! *Brahma* receive and eternally unite our spirits!"' She sprang upon the pile.' *The Missionary*, ch. xvii. pp. 259, 260. The scene closes with a rising of the people, and the escape of the lovers.

Page 136. ROSALIND AND HELEN. This, the least significant of Shelley's longer poems, was little valued by himself. It is intended as a plea in behalf of natural love against conventions, and shows how experience of life might reconcile two friends who had been parted because one of them had sinned against convention. It contains Shelley's characteristic prepossessions, such as the story of Fenici, the incident of brother and sister parted at the altar, and the cruelty of the husband's last will, and also his characteristic idealizations in the two stages of Lionel's life, the first in health another Laon, and the second in illness with traces of the ALASTOR type; the moral sentimentality of Lionel's power over the base and wicked and the delineations of febrile passion in one whose spirit only seems vital, are familiar from preceding work; in the nature description there is nothing novel.

Line 229. Rossetti points out the inconsistency of this with line 488.

Line 272. Rossetti points out the inconsistency of this with line 406.

Lines 405-410. The passage is defective, and unintelligible. Forman suggests *while* for *which* and *had* for *and*. Rossetti refers to Peacock's MS. letter to Ollier noting the imperfection in the proof.

Line 764. The poem appears to be a personal lyric of Shelley's.

Line 894. Cf. To WILLIAM SHELLEY, 1818.

Line 1208. Forman conjectures *which* for *whilst* and omits *had* in the next line. The meaning is obvious, and its plainness is little helped by the change.

Page 151. JULIAN AND MADDALO. The poem is the first in this style of verse, which Shelley made his own by the singular felicity of its combination of metrical beauty with familiar diction and tone, and it stands by itself by virtue of the fact that his other work of this sort is fragmentary. The monologue of the madman gives evidence of dramatic power, and the power of description is matured. For the rest, the poem is most remarkable for the deeply felt pathetic sentiment, the bitterness of suffering in the wounded feelings, which pervades the madman's words. Mrs. Shelley's account of where the poem was written is interesting:

'I Capuccini was a villa built on the site of a Capuchin convent, demolished when the French suppressed religious houses; it was situated on the very overhanging brow of a low hill at the foot of a range of higher ones. The house was cheerful and pleasant; a vine-trellised walk, a *pergola* as it is called in Italian, led from the hall door to a summer-house at the end of the garden, which Shelley made his study, and in which he began the PROMETHEUS; and here also, as he mentions in a letter, he wrote JULIAN AND MADDALO; a slight ravine, with a road in its depth, divided the garden from the hill, on which stood the ruins of the ancient castle of Este, whose dark massive wall gave forth an echo, and from whose ruined crevices owls and bats flitted forth at night, as the crescent moon sunk behind the black and heavy battlements. We looked from the garden over the wide plain of Lombardy, bounded to the west by the far Apennines, while to the east the horizon was lost in misty distance. After the picturesque but limited view of mountain, ravine, and chestnut wood at the Baths of Lucca, there was something infinitely gratifying to the eye in the wide range of prospect commanded by our new abode.'

Line 1. Shelley describes his rides with Byron in a letter to Mrs. Shelley, August 23, 1818: 'He [Byron] took me in his gondola across the laguna to a long sandy island, which defends Venice from the Adriatic. When we disembarked, we found his horses waiting for us, and we rode along the sands of the sea, talking. Our conversation consisted in histories of his wounded feelings, and questions as to my affairs, and great professions of friendship and regard for me. He said that if he had been in England at the time of the Chancery affair, he would have moved heaven and earth to have prevented such a decision. We talked of literary matters, his Fourth Canto [Childe Harold], which he says is very good, and indeed he repeated some stanzas of great energy to me.'

Line 40 *poets*, Milton, *Paradise Lost*, ii. 559.

Line 99. The madhouse is on San Servolo, but Rossetti quotes Browning to the effect that the building described by Shelley was the penitentiary on San Clemente. Rossetti declines to decide the point.

Line 143 *child*, Allegra.

Page 160. PROMETHEUS UNBOUND. This poem, as a lyrical drama dealing with the myth of Prometheus, has for its principal poetic source the *Prometheus* of Æschylus. Shelley wrote, 'It has no resemblance to the Greek drama. It is original;' and essentially the statement is true. The relation of Prometheus to Jupiter, as a sufferer under tyranny because of his love of mankind, the scene of his torture on the mountain side over the sea, the attendance of sea nymphs in the chorus, the herald Mercury, the vulture, and the insistence on the violent elements of nature, earthquake, lightning and whirlwind, in the imagery, are common to both poems; but Shelley by his treatment has so modified all these as to recreate them. The ethical motive of Shelley, his allegorical meanings, his metaphysical suggestions, the development of the old and introduction of new characters, the conduct of the action, the interludes of pastoral, music and landscape, the use of new imaginary beings neither human nor divine, and the conception of universal nature, totally transform the primitive Æschylean myth; and in its place arises the most modern poem of the century by virtue of its being the climax of the Revolution, in imaginative literature, devoted to the ideal of democracy as a moral force. The crude Æschylean matter may be easily traced in the following notes in detail. The interpretation of the modern poem is more difficult, and may be studied in the essays of Rossetti in the *Shelley Society Publications*, Todhunter's *A Study of Shelley*, Thomson's *Notes*, in the *Athenœum*, 1881, and Miss Scudder's *Shelley's Prometheus Unbound*, as well as in numerous biographies and essays. I am unable to follow these commentators in giving more precise meaning to the characters and the plot than is contained in Shelley's and Mrs. Shelley's exposition already cited in the Head-note to the poem, and the preface, supplemented by the statements of the text itself. Prometheus may be the 'Human Mind,' Ione 'Hope' and Panthea 'Faith,' and the Semichoruses of Act II. sc. ii. may represent respectively the passage of 'Love and Faith [Asia and Panthea] through the sphere of the Senses . . . of the Emotions . . . of the Reason and Will,' and so on; but that Shelley had any conscious logic of this sort in his poem seems too uncertain to be asserted. The drama is an emanation of his imagination, working out his deepest sentiments and convictions in a form nearer to the power of music than language ever before achieved; it is haunted by the presence of the inexpressible in the heart of its most transcendent imagery; and in all its moods and motions is far from the domain in which the prose of articulated thought is discerned through a veil of figured phrase. The intellectual skeleton, in any case, even were it discoverable, is not the soul of the poem. Certain theories of Shelley, as to philosophical problems, are present in the verse; but they control only instinctively, and not by deliberate thought, the structure of character, scene, event, and act. They are noted below.

Page 165. *Dramatis Personæ*. Prometheus, the Titan, bound to the icy precipice, suffers this punishment from Jupiter as a consequence of the gift of fire and other benefits to mankind. Jupiter is the 'supreme of living things,' of whom Prometheus says, 'I gave all he has,'

and 'O'er all things but thyself I gave thee power, and my own will.' Prometheus possesses the secret 'which may transfer the sceptre of wide heaven' from Jupiter, and refuses to divulge it. The knowledge that the reign of Jupiter will end sustains him in his torture, which has now lasted for many centuries. Asia, a sea nymph, daughter of Oceanus, is the beloved of Prometheus, and separated from him in India. Panthea is the messenger between the two; Ione is her companion; both are sisters of Asia. Demogorgon is the child of Jupiter who overthrows his father, at the appointed time, as Jupiter had dethroned Saturn; the foreknowledge of this is the secret of Prometheus. The other persons of the drama have little or no part in the action, and are easily comprehended. The obvious allegorical meaning of these greater characters can be briefly stated. Prometheus is a type of mankind suffering under the oppression of the evil of the world. Jupiter is this incarnate tyranny conceived primarily in a broadly political rather than in any moral sense, the 'one name of many shapes' already described in THE REVOLT OF ISLAM. Asia is, in Mrs. Shelley's words, 'the same as Venus and Nature,' or essentially the Aphrodite of Lucretius humanized by Shelley's imagination and recreated as the life of nature animated by the spirit of love. The separation of Prometheus from Asia during the reign of Jupiter typifies the discordance between man and nature due to the tyranny of convention, custom, institutions, laws, and all the arbitrary organization of society, — one of the cardinal ideas inherited by Shelley from eighteenth century thought. The fall of Jupiter, which is the abolition of human law, is followed by the triumph of love, in which man and nature are once more in accord; this accord is presented doubly in the drama as the marriage of Prometheus, and the regeneration of the world in millennial happiness. For the interpretation of Demogorgon, Panthea, and the various spirits, see below. The references to Æschylus are to Paley's third edition, London, 1870.

Page 165. Act I. *Scene* i. The landscape setting of the Act is Æschylean, and borrows some details from the Greek, but as mountain scenery it is Alpine and directly studied from nature. Shelley's Journal, March 26, 1818, gives a special instance of it, describing Les Echelles: 'The rocks, which cannot be less than a thousand feet in perpendicular height, sometimes overhang the road on each side, and almost shut out the sky. The scene is like that described in the *Prometheus* of Æschylus: vast rifts and caverns in the granite precipices; wintry mountains with ice and snow above; the loud sounds of unseen waters within the caverns, and walls of toppling rocks, only to be scaled as he describes, by the winged chariot of the ocean nymphs.'

I. 2 *One*, Prometheus.
I. 12. Cf. Æschylus, 32, 94.
I. 22. Cf. Æschylus, 21.

I. 23. Cf. Æschylus, 98–100.
I. 25–29. Cf. Æschylus, 88–92.
I. 34. Cf. Æschylus, 1043.
I. 45, 46. Cf. Æschylus, 24, 25.
I. 58. The pity of Prometheus for Jupiter and his wish to recall the curse formerly pronounced mark the moral transformation of the character from that conceived by Æschylus. This is the point of departure from the ancient myth, which is here left behind. Shelley thus clothes Prometheus with the same ideal previously depicted in Laon, — the spiritual power of high-minded and forgiving endurance of wrong, the opposition of love to force, the victory of the higher nature of man in its own occult and inherent right. It appears to me that this perfecting of Prometheus through suffering, so that he lays aside his hate of Jupiter for pity, shown in his repentance for the curse and his withdrawal of it, is the initial point of the action of the drama and marks the appointed time for the overthrow of the tyrant. The fulfilment of the moral ideal in Prometheus is the true cause of the end of the reign of evil, though this is dramatically brought about by the instrumentality of Demogorgon.

In this opening speech, and in the remainder of the drama, it is unnecessary to point out the echoes of English poets. It is enough to observe generally, once for all, that Milton and Shakespeare have displaced Wordsworth and Coleridge as sources of phrase and tone, though they have not entirely excluded them, especially the latter; just as Plato has displaced Godwin and the eighteenth century philosophers in the intellectual sphere, though here again without entirely excluding them.

I. 74. The dramatic choruses constructed of responding voices, both in Shelley and in Byron, go back to the witch choruses of *Macbeth*; but they may be more immediately derived from Coleridge's *Fire, Famine, and Slaughter.*

I. 132 *whisper*, the 'inorganic voice' of the earth.

I. 137 *And love*, i. e., dost love (Swinburne). Forman conjectures *I love*; Rossetti, *and Jove.*

I. 140. Cf. Æschylus, 321.

I. 150 *tongue*, the earth has apparently two voices, that of the dialogue and the 'inorganic voice' above, which is the same as 'the language of the dead' above (cf. I. 183) and the tongue 'known only to those who die' in this line.

I. 165 *et seq.* Cf. Æschylus, 1064–1070, for parallel imagery; but the passage recalls especially the sorrow of Demeter after the rape of Persephone and the woes then visited on the earth in the classic myth.

I. 192 *et seq.* Zoroaster. The story is not known to Zoroastrian literature. The conception of the double world of shades and forms, with the reunion of the two after death, seems original with Shelley, suggested by the notion of Plato's world of ideas.

I. 262 *et seq.* Cf. Æschylus, 1010–1017.

I. 289 *robe*. The reference is to the shirt of Nessus.

I. 296. Cf. Æschylus, 936–940.

I. 328. The detail is borrowed from the action of Apollo in Æschylus, *Eumenides,* 170. The character of Mercury is developed by including in his mood the pity shown by Hyphæstos in the PROMETHEUS. The Furies are in character, description, and language, Shelley's creation.

I. 345. The reference is to Dante, *Inferno,* ix.

I. 354. Cf. Æschylus, 19, 20, 66.

I. 376. Cf. Æschylus, 382.

I. 386. Cf. Æschylus, 1014.

I. 399. The sword of Damocles.

I. 402. Cf. Æschylus, 958–960.

I. 408. Cf. Æschylus, 52, 53.

I. 416. Cf. Æschylus, 774–779.

I. 451. The idea is Platonic, and frequent in Shelley. Cf., below, II. iv. 83 and PRINCE ATHANASE, II. 2.

I. 458. Cf. Æschylus, 218; THE REVOLT OF ISLAM, VIII. ix.-x., xxi.

I. 471. The ethical doctrine that each sin brings its own penalty of necessity, and essentially is its own punishment, is involved in the image that the Furies are shapeless in themselves.

I. 484. The intimacy of remorse in the soul is partly indicated by the expressions used. The nature of the suffering brought by sin is most truly conceived and presented in what the Furies say of themselves throughout the scene. The idea, however, is confused by the addition of the element of the evil nature active within the soul and assailing it. The two notions are not incompatible, but the second has little pertinence to Prometheus here.

I. 490. The case illustrated, for example, in Tennyson's *Lucretius.*

I. 547. The torture of Prometheus, as was indicated by the speeches of the Furies, ceases to be physically rendered, and becomes mental. He is shown two visions of the defeat of good, first the Crucifixion, second, the French Revolution; the lesson the Furies draw is the folly of Prometheus in having opened the higher life for man, since it entails the greater misery the more he aspires, and is doomed at each supreme effort to increase rather than alleviate the state of man (cf. I. 595–597). The torture inflicted by the Furies, as well as the description of their methods in the abstract just commented on, gives an ethical reality to them which takes them out of the morals of the ancient world and transforms them into true shapes of modern imagination.

I. 592. Cf. Æschylus, 710–712.

I. 618. Cf. Æschylus, 759–760.

I. 619–632. The state of mankind, as Shelley saw it, described in cold, blunt, hard terms, is the climax and summary of the torture Prometheus suffers at the last moment; but his preference to feel such pain rather than be dull to it, and his continuance in faith that it shall end, combined with his lack of hatred or desire for vengeance, signalizes his perfection of soul under experience.

I. 641. Cf. Æschylus, 772.

I. 660. Cf. Æschylus, 288, 289.

I. 673. The torture-scene (with which, in the physical sense, the drama of Æschylus closes) being now over, the modern drama goes on to develop the regeneration of man, and first introduces this counter scene of the consolation of Prometheus by the spirits of the human mind, which inhabit thought; the voices are severally those of Revolution, Self-Sacrifice, Wisdom, and Poetry.

I. 712 *Between*, between arch and sea.

I. 766 *Shape*, Love.

I. 772. Cf. Plato, *Symposium*, 195 : ' For Homer says that the Goddess Calamity is delicate, and that her feet are tender. " Her feet are soft," he says, " for she treads not upon the ground, but makes her path upon the heads of men." ' (Shelley's translation.) The two spirits who sing the passage of Love followed by Ruin, present in poetical and intense imagery the one comprehensive and symbolic sorrow of the state of man : love is not denied, but its fruits are misery to mankind. The prophecy that ' begins and ends ' in Prometheus is that he shall destroy this death that follows in Love's track, of which the Crucifixion and the Revolution have been taken as the great symbols, but similar ruin pervades all life acted on by love.

I. 832. There is here the hint of philosophical idealism which makes nature's life dependent on man's consciousness ; nature lives in his apprehension of and union with it.

Page 178. Act II. i. Scene. The question of the time of the drama has been much commented upon, but to little effect. The scheme which regards the time as twelve hours, from midnight to high noon, is perhaps most satisfactory. The inconsistencies which conflict with such a theory are no greater than are usually to be found in Shelley's work ; and it is not probable that he considered the matter carefully. ' Morning ' at the beginning of this Act is the same as the dawn at the end of the preceding Act ; and the journey of Asia and Panthea to the cave of Demogorgon is timeless ; it is dawn when they arrive. The phrase, II. v. 10, ' The sun will rise not until noon ' is not to be taken literally, but only as an image of the amazement in heaven at the fall of Jupiter. Beyond that point the drama has no relation with time whatsoever.

The character of Panthea is wholly developed in this Act. She has no being of her own, but is the mystical medium of communication between Prometheus and Asia ; to each she is the other. In Act I. 824, she tells Prometheus that she never sleeps ' but when the shadow of thy spirit falls on her ' [i. e., herself]. She is addressed by Asia, II. i. 31, as wearing ' the shadow of that soul [Prometheus] by which I live ; ' she describes how that shadow falls upon her, and is made her being, in the dream, II. i. 71-82 ; and in her eyes, rather than through her words, Asia would read Prometheus' ' soul,' II. i. 110, and does behold him as if present, II. i. 119-126. On the other hand Prometheus in the dream describes her as the shadow of

Asia, II. i. 71, ' Whose shadow thou art,' and Panthea asks of Asia, II. i. 113, what she can see in her eyes except ' thine own fairest shadow imaged there.' Panthea describes the double relation in saying, II. i. 50, that she is ' made the wind which fails beneath the music that I bear of thy most wordless converse,' and, II. i. 52, as ' dissolved into the sense with which love talks ; ' and Asia describes Panthea's words, II. iv. 39, as ' echoes ' of Prometheus. It has been suggested that Panthea, in these relations, is Faith in the Ideal, but it does not seem to me that there is any so precise meaning ; her function is purely emotional, bringing into apparent conjunction the disunited lovers.

The character of Demogorgon, also, is sufficiently developed in this Act for comment. The name has been traced to Lactantius, and occurs in English in Spenser, *Faerie Queene*, I. v. 22, IV. ii. 47, and in Milton, *Paradise Lost*, II. 965. Shelley clothes it with a new personality. In Act III. i. 52, he describes himself as ' eternity.' His dwelling-place, before his ascent and after it, is in the Cave, which is what Shelley was accustomed to write of as the ' caves of unimagined being.' From it, II. iii. 4, ' the oracular vapor is hurled up ' which is the nurture of enthusiastic genius, — ' truth, virtue, love, genius, or joy, that maddening wine of life.' The spirit that abides there is, in its negative phase, II. iv. 5, ' ungazed upon and shapeless ; ' it can answer all questions, as in the colloquy with Asia, but a voice is wanting to express the things of eternity, II. iv. 116, ' the deep truth is imageless,' and II. iv. 123, ' of such truths each to itself must be the oracle.' The conception has points of contact with that of the soul of being in the HYMN TO INTELLECTUAL BEAUTY, and with numerous other apprehensions of the divine element in Shelley's poetry. It is more abstract and gray, in this shape of the genius presiding even over Jupiter's fate, than usual, because a part of the cosmic idea it embodies is transferred to Asia in this drama, as the being in whom love kindles and through whom creation becomes beautiful ; Demogorgon is thus elemental in the highest degree, lying in a region back even of the great poetic conceptions of Love and Beauty, as well as of apparently Omnipotent Power, in the world of celestial time. To him, as the ultimate of being conceivable by man's imagination, the concluding chorus of the drama is fitly given.

II. i. 71-87. Cf. ROSALIND AND HELEN, 1028–1046.

II. i. 117. Cf. v. 53, note.

II. i. 140, *written grief*, the Ai, Ai, which the Greeks fancied they discerned in the color markings of the hyacinth. Cf. ADONAIS, xvi. 5, note.

II. i. 142. It is noticeable that the first dream belongs to Prometheus, and the second appears to be that of Asia. She recollects the dream, as her own. The double character of Panthea, as the mirror of both lovers, is thus preserved.

II. i. 166. The Echo songs are of course Ariel songs.

II. ii. 1. The commentators who describe this chorus as the journey of love and faith through experience, in sense, emotion, will, etc. (see Miss Scudder's *Prometheus Unbound*, p. 151), seem to me over-subtle. The sequence from nature to emotion and impassioned thought belongs to many of Shelley's poems, and is his natural lyrical form; in each of these acts, especially I., II., and IV., it is exhibited on the grand scale, but in his minor poems it is usual. The significant part of the chorus is lines 41–63, where the stream of sound, an image so repeated as to be cardinal in the drama, is introduced, here as a symbol of the force impelling will (perhaps conceived as desire in love), controlling it. The manner of it, II. ii. 48–50, is after Plato, as in the *Symposium* and *Phædrus;* the imagery of the boat and the stream is a strange and subtle development of the voyage images in ALASTOR and THE REVOLT OF ISLAM.

II. ii. 62 *fatal mountain.* that at which Asia and Panthea arrive in II. iii. 1.

II. ii. 64. The Fauns are after the character of the *Attendant Spirit* in Milton's *Comus.*

II. ii. 91 *songs,* cf. Virgil, *Eclogues,* VI. 31–42. Such Virgilian echoes are found, though rarely, in Shelley.

II. iii. 40. The image is one of the few sublime images in English poetry.

II. iii. 54. The first and third stanzas describe the Cave of Demogorgon as the place of increate eternity or absolute being; it is set forth necessarily by negatives, except in the attributes of universality and unity in II. iii. 80.

II. iii. 94 *meekness,* i. e., the meekness of Prometheus in his mood toward Jupiter, as shown in Act I., and in his whole moral character as developed at the end of that Act. It is because of this change in Prometheus, as noted above, that now 'the Eternal, the Immortal' (Demogorgon) 'must unloose through life's portal that Snake-like Doom' (the Spirit of the Hour of Jupiter's overthrow), 'by that alone,' i. e., the inherent moral power of Prometheus' spiritual state. It should be recalled that Prometheus is mankind, to get the full force of the lesson enunciated.

II. iv. 12. Rossetti and Swinburne conjecture that a line is missing. The former corrects *when* into *at;* but this only avoids the difficulty. The sense is plain, and the text must be accepted as corrupt.

II. iv. 48. Cf. Æschylus, 232, 233.

II. iv. 49 *et seq.* The speech is based on Æschylus, 205–262, 444–514, but is highly developed, possibly with some obligation to Lucretius, Bk. v.

II. iv. 83. Cf. I. 451, note.

II. iv. 146. Cf. I. 471, note.

II. v. 20. The story of the birth of Venus. The irradiation of Asia, as the spirit of love filling the world with created beauty (into which complex conception enter so many mythological and metaphysical strands from Lu-

cretius, Plato, and antique legend) is the highest point reached by Shelley in rendering the character dramatically, as the lyrics immediately following are the highest point reached in its lyrical expression. The lines II. iv. 40–47 are the antithesis of I. 619–632. They are the abstract statement of love, as the former of hatred. The lyrics following are a highly imaginative statement of love and parallel with I. 764–780.

II. v. 48. The lyric is an invocation of Asia as 'the light of life, shadow of beauty unbeheld' (III. iii. 6) — the spirit presiding in creation, the divine *vivida vis,* the invisible power making for beauty, through love, in the world of sensible experience. In the first two stanzas, Shelley presents the supernal brightness as half revealed in the breath and smile of life, but insupportable, and again as burning through the beauty of nature, which is an atmosphere about it; but in the third and fourth stanzas he returns to its invisibility, as a thing heard like music, as the source of all beauty of shape and all joy of soul, — but insupportable in these modes of knowledge and experience as in its half-visible forms.

II. v. 53. Forman aptly quotes Shelley to Peacock, April 6, 1819: 'The only inferior part [in the Roman beauties] are the eyes, which, though good and gentle, want the mazy depth of color behind color with which the intellectual women of England and Germany entangle the heart in soul-inspiring labyrinths.' Cf. i. 117; THE REVOLT OF ISLAM, XII. v. 2.

II. v. 72. The following lyric takes up the image of the boat and the stream from II. ii. 41–63 (cf. note), and elaborates it, the boat being the soul of Asia, driven on the song of the Singer; the Singer and Asia are thus united spiritually in the song and guided musically on the mystic voyage backward through the forms of human life to the soul's preëxistent eternity (reversing Wordsworth's *Ode on the Intimations of Immortality*). Cf. To CONSTANTIA, SINGING, and To ONE SINGING, p. 488.

Page 189. Act III. i. 40. Cf. Lucan, *Pharsalia,* ix. 723.

III. i. 69. Jupiter acknowledges the real supremacy of the moral nature.

III. i. 72. Cf. THE REVOLT OF ISLAM, I. vi. *et seq.*

III. ii. The scene is idyllic, not only by virtue of the calm classical figures of Apollo and Oceanus, but as containing the first of the millennial descriptions which now recur to the end of the drama.

III. ii. 46. Cf. THE REVOLT OF ISLAM, II. xxix. 1.

III. iii. 10 *Cave,* the first of the caves which Shelley delighted to depict as refuges from the world. It is to be taken as an Italian element in his verse.

III. iii. 15. The stalactite formations met with in ALASTOR.

III. iii. 25 *mutability,* a constant and characteristic word and thought of Shelley.

III. iii. 49–60. This æsthetic theory is purely

Platonic. Cf. Plato, especially *Symposium* and *Phædrus*. Cf. ODE TO LIBERTY, xvii. 9.

III. iii 70 *shell*. Salt quotes from Hogg : 'Sir Guyon de Shelley, one of the most famous of the Paladins, carried about with him three conches. . . . When he made the third conch, the golden one, vocal, the law of God was immediately exalted, and the law of the devil annulled and abrogated wherever the potent sound reached. Was Shelley thinking of this golden conch when he described, in his great poem, that mystic shell from which is sounded the trumpet-blast of universal freedom ? '

III. iii. 91–93. The sympathy of Shelley with life in its humblest forms was almost Buddhistic in solicitude. Cf. below, III. iv. 36, or THE SENSITIVE PLANT, II. 41.

III. iii. 111. Cf. I. 150.

III. iii. 113. Cf. SONNET, 'Lift not the painted veil.'

III. iii. 124. The cavern where Prometheus was born, seemingly the same as in III. iii. 10, more developed in the description.

III. iii. 171. This line, in connection with 108–110, intimates a greater faith in immortality than any previous passage of Shelley, but it is a shadowy intimation. Cf. IV. 536. The dead, throughout the drama, are described in the pagan spirit, and the lot of man, not exempt even in this millennium from ' chance and death and mutability,' is opposed to the lot of the immortals as at a pagan distance below them — the fate that Lucretius described.

III. iv. The Spirit of the Earth now takes the place of the Earth in the drama. The form it wears is a characteristic Shelleyan conception, belonging to his most unshared originality in creation. Cf. PRINCE ATHANASE, II. 106, note.

III. iv. 54 *sound*, the shell.

III. iv. 76, 77. The ease with which all things ' put their evil nature off,' and the ' little change ' the action involved, are both characteristic of Shelley's ethical scheme. Evil was conceived as something that could be laid aside, like a garment, by the will of man. Cf. III. iv. 199, note.

III. iv. 104, 105. Through the power of love. III. iv. 128 *change*. Cf. III. iv. 104, 105.

III. iv. 172. Rossetti conjectures a comma after *conquerors* and a period after *round*. The text of Shelley seems plain without the change. The emblems of Power and Faith stand in the new world unregarded and mouldering memorials of a dead past, just as the Egyptian monuments imaged to a later time than their own a vanished monarchy and religion ; the fact that these monuments survived the new race and last into our still later time is an unnecessary and subordinate incident inserted because it appealed to Shelley's imagination. Cf. Swinburne, *Notes on the Text of Shelley*.

III. iv. 193, 197. The ideal here described is anarchistic, but it is also the ultimate of the ideas of freedom, fraternity, and equality, and of the supremacy of that inward moral order which would dispense with those functions of government in which Shelley believed wrong necessarily resides.

III. iv. 199. The supremacy of the ' will ' of man, though less dwelt on in this drama, is conceived in the same way as in THE REVOLT OF ISLAM, VIII. xvi., the ODE TO LIBERTY, V. 10, SONNET, POLITICAL GREATNESS, 11. It is fundamental in Shelley's beliefs.

Page 197. Act IV. This act was, as the Head-note states, an afterthought. It is to be observed that Prometheus, after his release, ceases to be of importance, owing to the fact that his symbolic character as mankind is dropped, and liberated and regenerated society is directly described in the millennial passages. In this Act he does not appear at all, though the true significance of his deed closes the drama. Similarly, Asia disappears. Panthea and Ione are the spectators and act as the chorus, in the Greek sense, to the other participants. The part of the chorus has from the beginning of the drama threatened to overwhelm the part of the actors ; here it does so to such an extent that the Act presents the anomaly (in form) of lyrical passages as the main interest, with the chorus, properly speaking, in blank verse. The Act has three movements : the pæan of the Hours, the antiphony of the Earth and the Moon, the Invocation of the Universe by Demogorgon.

IV. 34 *One*, Prometheus.

IV. 65–67. These three lines might be taken severally as a summary of the theme of Acts I., II., and III.

IV. 82. A singularly felicitous expression to describe the double aspect of language as sound and color.

IV. 186. The harmony of the sphere.

IV. 203. The image of the stream of sound is here again introduced. Cf. II. v. 72, note.

IV. 210. The image is of ' the new moon with the old moon in her arms.' Cf. THE TRIUMPH OF LIFE, 79–85.

IV. 213 *regard*, appear.

IV. 217. The sunset image accounts for the phrase ' ebbing ' in 208. Cf. REVOLT OF ISLAM, I. vi. 8, note.

IV. 238 *sphere*, the earth.

IV. 247. The intention seems to be to suggest the incessant operation of manifold natural forces and processes in the sphere, each in its own realm.

IV. 265. This is the same spirit as in III. iii. 148.

IV. 272. The reference is to Harmodius and Aristogeiton.

IV. 281 *valueless*, above all value. The speech reveals the history of the earth as the previous speech reveals its physical structure. Shelley does not consider the chronology of the spectacle, but merely presents, first, the antique ruins of humanity, and, second, the fossil primeval world.

IV. 314 *blue globe*, the world of waters.

IV. 376. The construction of this and the following stanzas is unusually involved. *It* (Love), from the preceding stanza, is the subject of *has arisen* ; *sea* is in apposition with *world* (384) ; *which* (385) refers to *love ; Leave* (388) repeating *Leave* in 382, takes up the dropped construction ; and *Man* (394) similarly repeating *Man* from 388, introduces a new train of thought.

IV. 400, 401. The most compact statement of Shelley's social ideal, with its spontaneous ethical order of love.

IV. 404. The fact that Shelley did not exclude toil and suffering from his millennium of society is a cardinal point. Cf. III. iii. 171 note, and III. iii. 201.

IV. 406. Cf. III. iii. 199 note.

IV. 414. Cf. II. iv. 83 note.

IV. 423. The prophecy of scientific progress is apocalyptic in visionary energy.

IV. 444. A singular instance of precise scientific imagination in poetry. Cf. ÉPIPSYCHIDION, 227, HELLAS, I. 943.

IV. 493, 494. The lines are given by Rossetti to the preceding speech, but without probability. Cf. LINES, p. 435.

IV. 503. The development of the image of the stream of sound could not go further than in this and the following lines.

IV. 536. Cf. III. iii. 171 note.

IV. 554 *Demogorgon.* The sudden and complete subordination of all the beings of the universe to the idea of the Eternal Principle is accomplished with sublime effect. The drama is thus brought to an end, after its lyrical jubilee, by its highest intellectual conception giving utterance to its highest moral command,— Demogorgon, the voice of Eternity, phrasing, in the presence of the listening Universe of all being, the encomium of Prometheus as the type of the soul's wisdom in action in an evil world leading to the achievement of such regeneration on earth as is possible to a mortal race.

IV. 555 *Earth-born's*, Prometheus.

IV. 557. Love is here identified with Prometheus, in whom it reigned and suffered.

IV. 565 *Eternity.* Demogorgon is properly Eternity, but here speaks of Eternity under another conception.

IV. 568. The use of the serpent image for the principle of evil is contrary to Shelley's practice.

IV. 570. Cf. THE REVOLT OF ISLAM, VIII. xi., xii., xxii., where Laone's speech contains these maxims in a weaker and diffused form ; they constitute Shelley's persistent ideal, and of them he made Prometheus the type; he here identifies this ideal, which is one of suffering under wrong, with all forms of the good and of power, thereby affirming the supremacy of spiritual moral order at all times and under all circumstances. Neither Platonic nor Christian faith is more absolute.

Page 206. THE CENCI. The narrative of the events upon which THE CENCI is founded is reprinted in the Centenary Edition, ii. 447-463, with notes of other accounts. The Shaksperian echoes, mainly from *Lear, Macbeth*, and *Othello*, are easily recognizable. The simile from Calderon, mentioned in the Preface, is in

Act III. i. 247. The passage in Act II. ii. 141, recalls the FRAGMENT, page 487, TO THIRST AND FIND NO FILL. The text offers no difficulty. Criticism of the play has been uniformly appreciative, though it did not succeed when privately acted, May 7, 1886, in London. The action, owing to the difficulty of displaying the story, is weak; the characterization of Cenci and Beatrice is vigorous, and that of Orsino and Giacomo is studied with attention and ingenuity ; the other persons only serve to carry on the scenes. The dignity of the diction, the elevation of the sentiments, and the adherence to Italian contemporary habits of mind as understood by Shelley, are admirable. The total effect is of intense and awful gloom, and the play is more powerful as a whole than in any detail, scene, or act. In it culminates that fascination of horror in Shelley which was as characteristic as his worship of beauty and love, though it is less omnipresent in his poetry.

Page 252. THE MASK OF ANARCHY. Salt refers, for the events giving occasion for this poem, to Martineau, *History of the Peace*, I. chaps. xvi., xvii. A MS. facsimile of the text in Shelley's hand was published by the Shelley Society, 1887.

Stanzas iv., v. Cf. TO THE LORD CHANCELLOR, xiii. ; and ŒDIPUS TYRANNUS, I. 334.

Stanza xxviii. 1 *Shape.* Salt identifies the figure as that of Liberty.

Stanza xxx. Cf. PROMETHEUS UNBOUND, I. 772 note.

Stanza xxxv. The doctrine of PROMETHEUS UNBOUND and THE REVOLT OF ISLAM.

Stanza xlv. Cf. ŒDIPUS TYRANNUS, I. 196 note.

Page 258. PETER BELL THE THIRD. The poem satirizes Wordsworth on the ground of his conservatism in politics and the dulness of much of his poetry.

Page 259 *Thomas Brown, Esq., the Younger,* H. F. The pseudonym under which Moore published *The Fudge Family.* H. F. is interpreted by Dr. Garnett as 'Historian of the Fudges ;' Rossetti suggests *Hiberniæ Filius.*

The world of all of us, Wordsworth, *Prelude,* XI. 142.

Page 260 '*to occupy a permanent station.*' Rossetti compares Wordsworth's preface to *Peter Bell.*

SHELLEY'S NOTES on the poem are as follows :

Prologue 36. The oldest scholiasts read —

    A *dodecagamic* Potter.

This is at once more descriptive and more megalophonous, — but the alliteration of the text had captivated the vulgar ear of the herd of later commentators.

I. ii. 3. To those who have not duly appreciated the distinction between *Whale* and *Russia* oil, this attribute might rather seem to belong to the Dandy than the Evangelic. The effect, when to the windward, is indeed so similar, that it requires a subtle naturalist to discriminate the animals. They belong, however, to distinct genera.

III. viii. 2. One of the attributes in Linnæus's description of the Cat. To a similar cause the caterwauling of more than one species of this genus is to be referred ; — except, indeed, that the poor quadruped is compelled to quarrel with its own pleasures, whilst the biped is supposed only to quarrel with those of others.

viii. 5. What would this husk and excuse for a virtue be without its kernel prostitution, or the kernel prostitution without this husk of a virtue ? I wonder the women of the town do not form an association, like the Society for the Suppression of Vice, for the support of what may be called the 'King, Church, and Constitution' of their order. But this subject is almost too horrible for a joke.

xvi. 1. This libel on our national oath, and this accusation of all our countrymen of being in the daily practice of solemnly asseverating the most enormous falsehood, I fear deserves the notice of a more active Attorney-General than that here alluded to.

VI. xi. 5 *Vox populi, vox dei.* As Mr. Godwin truly observes of a more famous saying, *of some merit as a popular maxim, but totally destitute of philosophical accuracy.*

xvi. 2. Quasi, *Qui valet verba : —* i. e. all the words which have been, are, or may be expended by, for, against, with, or on him. A sufficient proof of the utility of this history. Peter's progenitor who selected this name seems to have possessed *a pure anticipated cognition* of the nature and modesty of this ornament of his posterity.

xxv. 5. A famous river in the New Atlantis of the Dynastophylic Pantisocratists.

xxvi. 5. See the description of the beautiful colors produced during the agonizing death of a number of trout, in the fourth part of a long poem in blank verse [*The Excursion,* Book VIII. 559–572] published within a few years. That poem contains curious evidence of the gradual hardening of a strong but circumscribed sensibility, of the perversion of a penetrating but panic-stricken understanding. The author might have derived a lesson which he had probably forgotten from these sweet and sublime verses.

This lesson, Shepherd, let us two divide,
Taught both by what she [nature] shows and what conceals,
Never to blend our pleasure or our pride
With sorrow of the meanest thing that feels.
[Wordsworth, *Hartleap Well,* II. xxi.]

xxxviii. 6. It is curious to observe how often extremes meet. Cobbett and Peter use the same language for a different purpose: Peter is indeed a sort of metrical Cobbett. Cobbett is, however, more mischievous than Peter, because he pollutes a holy and now unconquerable cause with the principles of legitimate murder ; whilst the other only makes a bad one ridiculous and odious. If either Peter

or Cobbett should see this note, each will feel more indignation at being compared to the other than at any censure implied in the moral perversion laid to their charge.

Page 260, PROLOGUE, line 3. Reynolds's poem.
Line 16. Wordsworth's poem.
Line 22. Shelley's poem. The three are said to present Peter in the state before, during, and after life.
III. ii. 1 *Castles,* identified by Rossetti as a Government spy.
III. xiii. 4 *Alemannic,* German.
IV. ix. The stanza, a striking critical statement of the originality of a creator in literature, seems sincerely meant. Cf. also the praise hidden in the satire of V. vii.–xv. ; THE WITCH OF ATLAS, iv.–vi. ; the sonnet To WORDSWORTH ; AN EXHORTATION.
IV. xiv. 1–2. 'A mouth kissed loses not charm but renews as does the moon.' Rossetti quotes Shelley to Hunt, 27 September 1819, where Boccaccio is praised and these words referred to.
V. i. 3 *man,* Coleridge. The characterization is remarkable for one who did not know the poet ; it is discriminating and vivid, and not unjust, allowing for the satirical tone. Cf. LETTER TO MARIA GISBORNE, 202.
VI. xii. The reference is to Wordsworth's prefaces.
VI. xv. The reference is to Drummond's *Academical Questions,* a favorite book of Shelley's.
VI. xxix. 4. Sheridan.
VI. xxxvi. 2. Wordsworth, *Thanksgiving Ode on the Battle of Waterloo,* first version (see Knight's ed. *Poetical Works,* Second Ode, iv. 20).
VII. iv. 4 *Oliver,* identified by Forman as a Government spy ' prominent in the case of Brandreth, Turner, and Ludlam, whose execution in 1817 inspired Shelley to write *The Address to the People on the Death of the Princess Charlotte.*'
xiv. 4 *Guatimozin,* son-in-law of Montezuma, whom he succeeded as the last Aztec prince. He was tortured by Cortez.
Page 271. THE WITCH OF ATLAS. This poem derives its tone from Homer's *Hymn to Mercury,* which Shelley had recently translated in the same measure and literary manner. To search for its meaning is like plucking the rose apart ; for once, it seems to me, though without losing the rich suggestiveness inherent in the workings of his mind, Shelley allowed his genius to play with its habitual images and tendencies without definite intention, in pure self-enjoyment of its own beauty and sweetness. No poem of his is so happy, so free from the mortal strain of life and effort, so disengaged from the wretchedness of men. In the earlier stages one might find analogies with the HYMN TO INTELLECTUAL BEAUTY and guess that Shelley was weaving round the spirit of universal life the robe of illusion that should render it visible in

transparency of human form and activity; but as the verse flows on, with the familiar imagery of the boat and its voyage through subterranean caverns and among mountains, and develops the wanderings of the Witch among cities and in the solitudes of far-off nature, it appears to me that Shelley interprets half-consciously the functions of genius, imagination, and poetry conceived almost as interdependent existences with only a remote and dreamy relation to human life. The Witch, who cannot die, is in the world of Prometheus and Urania, a semi-divine world separated from the miserable fate of men, though not detached from the knowledge of their life. I associate the Hermaphrodite of the poem with the undefined figure of the LINES CONNECTED WITH EPIPSYCHIDION. Shelley uses the word 'Witch' in a similar connection twice: 'In the still cave of the witch Poesy,' MONT BLANC, ii. 33, and 'the quaint witch, Memory,' LETTER TO MARIA GISBORNE, 132. The poem most analogous with THE WITCH OF ATLAS is THE SENSITIVE PLANT; the figure of the Witch, while not less touched with mystery than the Lady of the garden, is more definite; and the ideality of the landscape, nowhere in Shelley's verse so great as here, is superior in the same proportion as the expanse of the globe exceeds the limits of the garden.

Page 272 *To Mary*, his wife.

Stanza iii. 1 *winged Vision*, THE REVOLT OF ISLAM.

Stanza iv. 2. Cf. PETER BELL, IV. ix. note.

Page 273, stanza ii. Cf. Homer's *Hymn to Memory*, i. and Spenser's *Faërie Queene*, III. vi. 7.

vi. Here, and in the following stanzas, there appear to be reminiscences of Spenser's Una.

ix. 5. A variant of the idea of Demogorgon in PROMETHEUS UNBOUND.

xi. 2 *pastoral Garamant*, Fezzan.

xi. 8 *bosom-eyed*, a suggestion associated with Coleridge's Witch in *Christabel*.

xviii. 2. *Archimage*, Spenser's magician in the *Faërie Queene*, I. i.

xxv. 7. Cf. stanza i.; the reference is to the belief that the old divinities passed away at the birth of Christ. Cf. HELLAS, 225-238; Milton, *Ode on the Nativity*, xix.-xxi.

xxxii., xxxiii. Cf. THE ZUCCA and FRAGMENTS OF AN UNFINISHED DRAMA, 127.

xlvii. 8 *Thamandocana*, Timbuctoo.

lvii. 4 *Axumé*, Abyssinia.

lix. 1-4. A favorite and oft-repeated image of Shelley's. Cf. ODE TO LIBERTY, vi. 1 note.

lxiii. The contrast between the lot of men and that of the immortals is the same as in PROMETHEUS UNBOUND.

lxvii. 8 *The Heliad*, the lady-witch.

Page 283. ŒDIPUS TYRANNUS. Salt refers, for the historical basis of this grotesque drama, to Martineau's *History of the Peace*, II. ch. ii. He suggests, besides the identifications mentioned in the Head-note, that the *Leech* is taxes, the *Gadfly*, slander; the *Rat*, espionage. The Minotaur is, of course, John Bull; *Adiposa* (I.

290), Rossetti says, was an easily identified titled lady of the time, whose name he allows 'to sleep.' The example is rare enough to merit imitation.

SHELLEY'S NOTES on the drama are as follows:

I. 8. See *Universal History* for an account of the number of people who died, and the immense consumption of garlic by the wretched Egyptians, who made a sepulchre for the name as well as the bodies of their tyrants.

I. 153. And the Lord whistled for the gadfly out of Æthiopia, and for the bee of Egypt, etc. — *Ezekiel*. [The proper reference is to Isaiah vii. 18: 'And it shall come to pass in that day that the Lord shall hiss for the fly that is in the uttermost part of the rivers of Egypt, and for the bee that is in the land of Assyria.']

I. 204. If one should marry a gallows, and beget young gibbets, I never saw one so prone. — *Cymbeline*.

II. 173. Rich and rare were the gems she wore. — See *Moore's Irish Melodies*.

Page 286, I. 77 *arch-priest*, perhaps Malthus is meant.

I. 101. Rossetti notes that this line was a '*de facto* utterance of Lord Castlereagh.'

I. 196 *Chrysaor*. Rossetti notes the allusion to 'paper-money discussions.' Cf. THE MASK OF ANARCHY, xlv.

I. 334. Cf. THE MASK OF ANARCHY, iv. note.

II. 60-66. Shelley writes to Peacock, November 8, 1818: 'Every here and there one sees people employed in agricultural labors, and the plough, the harrow, or the cart, drawn by long teams of milk-white or dove-colored oxen of immense size and exquisite beauty. This, indeed, might be the country of Pasiphaes.' Cf. LINES WRITTEN AMONG THE EUGANEAN HILLS, 220.

Page 297. EPIPSYCHIDION. This poem has been edited, with a careful study of it, by Rev. Stopford A. Brooke, in the Shelley Society's Publications (Second Series, No. 7), 1887, and its sources have been examined by Dr. Richard Ackermann in his *Quellen, Vorbilder, Stoffe zu Shelley's Poetischen Werken*, 1890. It represents the final outcome of conceptions which had been present, in a half-formed state, in Shelley's mind from the beginning of his true poetic career in 1816. They constituted, as it were, the elements of an unwritten poem in a fluid state, and were suddenly precipitated by the accident of his meeting with Emilia Viviani under circumstances that made a romantic appeal to his genius. It is easy to enumerate these elements. The conception of a Spiritual Power which is felt in the loveliness of nature and in the thought of man is set forth in the HYMN TO INTELLECTUAL BEAUTY (cf. THE REVOLT OF ISLAM, VI. xxxviii. 1), and to it Shelley dedicates his powers; the pursuit of this spirit, typified under the form of woman and seen only in vision, is the substance of ALASTOR, and the end is represented as the lonely death of the poet. The conception of a youth in whom 'genius and death contended' — a variant of the youth in ALASTOR — occurs in THE SUNSET, 4, and in the Dedication to THE REVOLT OF ISLAM, x. 9, and it is noticeable that the figure is repeated as late as ADONAIS, xliv., in nearly identical terms. In THE SUNSET, as in ALASTOR, the youth dies. A new poem, PRINCE ATHANASE, was partly written, in which apparently the same pursuit of the ideal was to be represented ; but the conduct of the poem was to be complicated by the error of Athanase in mistaking the earthly love for the heavenly love, in consequence of which Shelley first named the poem PANDEMOS AND URANIA. The figure of Urania would have appeared at the deathbed of Athanase. The pursuit of the ideal was given a metaphysical form in the prose fragment ON LOVE. He there describes the ideal self as 'a miniature as it were of our entire self, yet deprived of all that we condemn or despise ; the ideal prototype of everything excellent or lovely that we are capable of conceiving as belonging to the nature of man.' He calls it 'a soul within our soul ;' and he adds, 'the discovery of its antitype [the responding being] is the invisible and unattainable point to which Love tends.' In the absence of this beloved one, nature solaces us (cf. THE ZUCCA). Shelley had thus conceived of the ideal, both in its universal and in a particular form, — the latter under the form of woman. In the PROMETHEUS UNBOUND he blended the two in Asia, but not so as to humanize her ; she remains elemental, Titanic, and divine. He returned to the conception of PRINCE ATHANASE in UNA FAVOLA, in which he presents the same subject much Italianized in imagery and tone, and essentially as an autobiography. The ideas of the pursuit, of the contest for the youth, of his error and recovery, are all present. In the LINES CONNECTED WITH EPIPSYCHIDION, beside rejected passages of that poem, there is a dedication (possibly meant for FIORDISPINA) in which Shelley addresses an imaginary and uncertain figure, aptly named 'his Genius,' by Dr. Garnett, and in this he develops a statement of free love after Plato's *Symposium*, in which all objects of beauty are to be loved in an ascending series as varying and incomplete embodiments of the infinite and eternal beauty.

EPIPSYCHIDION resumes these elements and combines them into one poem. The 'soul within the soul' of the prose fragment ON LOVE is figured to have left the poet, and he pursues it and finds it, as if it were 'the antitype' of the same fragment, in Emily. The Spirit of Beauty and Love, also, the eternal soul of the world, is represented as veiling itself in this form of woman, one of its incarnations ; and communion with it is sought in her. Thus under the form of Emily, Shelley unites these cognate and separable conceptions. The pursuit of the ideal after the manner of both ALASTOR and PRINCE ATHANASE is easily recognizable, and the part of Pandemos in the forest of error of UNA FAVOLA is plain. The autobiographical element of the latter is much more defined and more violently stated, with novel imagery of winter and of the planetary system ; but it remains essentially the conflict, variously stated by Shelley as between 'genius and death,' 'love and death,' and 'life and love,' over the lost youth. The passage relating to free love is an episode, and stands by itself. The description of the paradise is a late rendering of that bower of bliss which is a constant element in Shelley's verse. A poem made up of such various thoughts and subjects, not naturally consistent, could not fail to present much difficulty to the reader, as they are incapable of being reduced to intellectual unity, though, as has been said, they are cognate and intimately related matters.

If Shelley had in mind the *Vita Nuova* of Dante (cf. also Shelley's translation of THE FIRST CANZONE OF THE CONVITO) and would have placed Emily in a relation to his doctrine of love and beauty in a way similar to that which Dante attempted, his intention was infelicitous ; for the lack of reality is felt too strongly. Emily is, at best, a fiction of thought, and her human personality, where felt, detracts from the power of the poem. It appears to me that a similar unreality, as to fact, belongs to the autobiographical passages. The spiritual history of Shelley's pursuit of the ideal (the 'idealized history of my life and feelings') is clearly set forth in the poem, and can be verified by the succession of his previous works as above. On the other hand, the personal history of Shelley is obscurely told, at best, and except for the representation of Mary and Emily as the moon and the sun, is incapable of verification. How little essential truth there was in the part ascribed to Emily is well known. The other passages, which have been interpreted as personal, may be similarly touched with tenuity as matters of fact, though correctly representing in allegory the moods of Shelley's inner life as he remembered them. The memory of a poet, especially if it be touched with pain and remorse, when he allows his eloquence to work in images of sorrow and despair to express what would otherwise remain forever unutterable by his lips, is an entirely untrustworthy witness of fact. Shelley's self-description has the truth of his poetic consciousness at the time, and its moods are sadly sustained by many passages of his verse ; but to seek precise fact and named individuals as meant by his words is, I believe, futile, and may be misleading. It is only as a poem of the inner life that EPIPSYCHIDION has its high imaginative interest. In the last movement of the poem, the voyage, the isle, and the passion are a mystical symbol of the soul communing with the ideal object of its pursuit under images of mortal beauty and love ; the possession of the ideal, so far as living man can in any way attain to such consciousness of it, is pictured. The suggestion of Prospero's isle is very strongly felt, 457, and the mysticism of the intention is plain, as in 410 and 477-479. It appears to me that the realm of poetry may be the specific underlying thought in the allegory, poetry being to Shelley what the isle of the *Tempest* was to Prospero, his kingdom of enchantment and also the medium through which he had communion with the Eternal Spirit. I associate the imagery, so far as it is descriptive of nature and contains veiled meanings, with the similar passages of THE WITCH OF ATLAS, where to my mind the ways and delights of Genius, Imagination, and Poetry, are the subject of the verse. At all events, the poem, in this section, is entirely disengaged from the personality of Emily, and of the others, and belongs with such delineations of supersensual being as THE WITCH OF ATLAS and THE SENSITIVE PLANT.

Page 297. EPIPSYCHIDION. *L'anima*, the soul that loves, projects itself beyond creation, and creates for itself in the infinite a world all its own, very different from this obscure and fearful gulf.

Page 298. ADVERTISEMENT, *gran vergogna* the passage, not quite accurately quoted, is from Dante's *Vita Nuova*, xxv.: 'It would be a great disgrace to him who should rhyme anything under the garb of a figure or of rhetorical coloring, if afterward, being asked, he should not be able to denude his words of this garb, in such wise that they should have a true meaning.' (Norton's trans.)

DEDICATION. Cf. LINES CONNECTED WITH EPIPSYCHIDION, p. 436, line 1.

Voi, Dante, *Convito, Trattato Secondo* (cf. Shelley's trans., p. 522). 'Ye who intelligent the third heaven move,' i.e., the angelic beings who guide the sphere of Venus, or love. The lines translated below, *My Song*, are lines 53–61 of the Canzone.

Page 298, line 1 *spirit*, Emilia; *orphan one*, Mary.

Line 2 *name*, Shelley.

Line 4 *withered memory*. The reference is to the autobiographical character of the poem.

Line 5 *captive bird*. The suggestion is given by the confinement of Emilia in the convent; but the poem, wherever it touches the fact of life and the person of Emilia, tends immediately to escape into the free world of poetry, as here the idea of the *captive bird* leads at once to Shelley's imaging his relation as that of the rose to the nightingale, but a rose without mortal life or passion, a dead and thornless rose; and, directly, in lines 13–18, the image of the bird and the cage loses touch with Emilia and becomes the metaphor for the spirit in the body.

Line 21 *Seraph*. In this invocation, through its succession of characteristic images that Shelley uses to symbolize the eternal Loveliness, nothing is present in the verse except the general symbolization of the Ideal under the form of woman, as in Dante's Beatrice. Emilia's personality does not color the conceptions, but rather the conceptions give life to her. Shelley's source is his lifelong idea of the Eternal Loveliness, not now new-found in Plato or Dante, though possibly quickened by his recent reading of the latter, and touched in some details by

reminiscences of it. Ackermann compares with lines 21–24 *Vita Nuova*, xix. 43–44 (Norton's trans.):

'Love saith concerning her: "How can it be
That mortal thing be thus adorned and pure?"'

xlii. 7, 8:

'Who so doth shine that through her splendid light
The pilgrim spirit upon her doth gaze,'

Convito, ii. 59–60: Her aspect overcomes our intelligence as the sun's ray weak vision.

Such parallelism is slight, and less than that with Shelley's earlier expression of the same conception in the image of Asia, whom line 26 especially recalls.

Lines 30–32. Ackermann compares *Vita Nuova*, xxi. 1, 2 (Norton's trans.),

'Within her eyes my lady beareth Love,
So that whom she regards is gentle made.'

Line 35. The verse returns momentarily to Emilia as a weeping and sympathetic figure, life-like through the description of her eyes, in line 38, and, except for the second series of images, 56, 69, remains near her in thought to line 72.

Line 42 *Youth's vision*, the vision of ALASTOR.

Line 44 *its unvalued shame*. The contempt that Shelley is indifferent to.

Line 46 *name*, spouse, cf. 130.

Line 49 *one*, the second; *other*, the wish expressed in line 45.

Line 50 *names*, sister and spouse.

Line 57. The second series of images deals rather with human aspects of ideal love as the first dealt rather with the visible aspects of ideal beauty.

Line 68, *wingless*, i.e., without the power to fly away, and hence lasting.

Line 71. The *infirmity* lies in the fact that Shelley has a double subject, mortal and eternal, Emily and the ideal vision, and nowhere in the poem does he really fuse them into one as Dante did in Beatrice.

Line 72 *She*, the figure here ideally described is the type given in lines 25–32, more particularized in vision. At the beginning of the passage, there is a similar absence of personality, and the imagery and idea are reminiscent of the vision of ALASTOR and the description of Asia; and only in line 112 does the verse suggest the living figure of Emily, and then only momentarily, the imagery immediately soaring away from her.

Line 75 *light, life, peace*, refer severally to *Day, Spring, Sorrow*, by a usage common to English verse.

Lines 78, 79. Cf. for the gradual development and illustration of the image, constant in Shelley, ALASTOR, 161–177, THE REVOLT OF ISLAM, I. lvii., PROMETHEUS UNBOUND, II. i. 70–79, II. v. 26.

Lines 83–85. Ackermann compares *Vita Nuova*, xxi. 9, 10; xxvi. 12–14; *Convito*, iii. 5–8, 41–43.

The parallelism is slight, that of the second passage being nighest:

'And from her countenance there seems to move
A spirit sweet and in Love's very guise,
Who to the soul, in going, sayeth: Sigh!'
(Norton's trans.)

It is true that the word translated *countenance* is *labbia*, used (says the comment) for *faccia*, *volto*.

Lines 87–90. Cf. PROMETHEUS UNBOUND, II. v. 53, note.

Lines 91–100. An expansion of line 78. The description attempts too great subtlety. The 'glory' issues from the eyes under an aspect of light and motion, blended yet separately perceived, and diffuses itself (as it were) over and through the countenance and form, seen in flowing outlines that pass into the blood-warmed cheeks and fingers, and finally lose the eye that follows in the vision of that supreme beauty which is hardly to be supported by mortal sight. The passage is built up of three elements, apparently: the function of the eye (as in the older Italian poets) as the gateway of the soul; the function of the physical loveliness of the body as the revelation of the soul that animates it; the function of all particular beauty, whether of soul or body, or as here inextricably blended, to lead the mind back to the Eternal Beauty.

Line 105. The description here becomes more purely human, preparing for line 112, which must be taken as a direct recurrence to Emily, the 'mortal shape;' but as the intervening images of lines 109–111 exceed true human description, so the series of images that follow, lines 115–123, apply to the idealized presence of beauty rather than to any 'mortal shape.'

Line 117 *the third sphere*, that of Venus. Cf., above, p. 298, *Voi*, note.

Line 130. Cf. line 50. The interval from this point to line 189 is of the nature of an interruption or *excursus*, in which Shelley presents and defends his doctrine of freedom in love as it had come to take on a form of Platonic philosophy in his mind. Emily is directly addressed, as one loved by him.

Line 137 *substance*, her spirit.

Line 148 *Beacon*, place a warning light upon.

Line 149. Cf. LINES CONNECTED WITH EPIPSYCHIDION, p. 436.

Line 169. Cf. Plato, *Symposium*, 210–211.

Line 190. The poem here makes a new beginning, and from here to line 344 is 'the idealized history' of Shelley's life and feelings, *Being*, the vision of ALASTOR, and also the 'awful shadow of some unseen power,' of the HYMN TO INTELLECTUAL BEAUTY.

Lines 211, 212. In whatever outlives death, and is immortal in the works of art.

Line 228 *cone*, cf. PROMETHEUS UNBOUND, IV. 444.

Line 236. Cf. prose fragment ON LOVE.

Line 238 *this soul out of my soul*, Shelley's translation of the title of the poem, cf. line 455. It goes back to the fragment ON LOVE, where

are the phrases, 'a miniature, as it were, of our entire self,' 'a soul within our own soul,' the 'antitype,' etc.

Lines 239, 240. Cf. HYMN TO INTELLECTUAL BEAUTY, V.

Line 249. Cf. UNA FAVOLA.

Line 256. Venus Pandemos. I incline to this interpretation because PANDEMOS AND URANIA was one of the titles of PRINCE ATHANASE, which was one of Shelley's early treatments of the generic theme of this poem.

Line 267, i.e., he sought the realization of the ideal in living persons. The identification of such persons in the three lines following has been attempted by Ackermann and others but unsatisfactorily.

Line 272. Cf. ADONAIS, xxxi. 8–9.

Line 277 *One*, Mary Shelley.

Line 301. Cf. UNA FAVOLA.

Line 308–320. The elucidation of the passage as autobiography is futile. The character of the Maniac in JULIAN AND MADDALO, and the mysterious lady of Naples in the life of Shelley (cf. INVOCATION TO MISERY, note), have been referred to by commentators; but what reality there was in either is unknown.

Line 345 *Twin Spheres*, i.e., Mary and Emily, as the Moon and Sun, Shelley being the Earth.

Line 368 *Comet*, the third person, who is to be made the Evening Star, after the analogy of the Sun, Moon, and Earth, is not to be identified.

Line 388. The last movement of the poem here begins. Cf. LINES WRITTEN AMONG THE EUGANEAN HILLS, 335–373, and PROMETHEUS UNBOUND, III. iii.

Line 592. Cf. Dante, *Vita Nuova*, XII, *Ballata*, 35–40.

Line 595. Cf. Dante, *Vita Nuova*, XXXII, *Canzone*, 71–74.

Line 601. Cf. Dante, *Sonetto*, II. 9 (Shelley's trans. p. 522). *Marina* is Mary, *Vanna*, Jane Williams, *Primus*, Edward Williams.

Page 307. ADONAIS. This poem has been edited, with elaborate notes and other matter, by Rossetti (Clarendon Press, 1891), and its sources have been studied by Dr. Richard Ackermann, *Quellen, Vorbilder, Stoffe zu Shelley's Poetischen Werken*, 1890. Rossetti refers also to Lt.-Col. Hime's *Greek Materials of Shelley's Adonais*, 1888, a volume I have never seen. ADONAIS is based upon Bion's *Lament for Adonais* and Moschus' *Lament for Bion*, very much as PROMETHEUS UNBOUND is based upon Æschylus' *Prometheus*: that is to say, the Greek material, while recognizable in many details, is so modified by Shelley's treatment as to be recreated. The result is an original modern poem. The obligation is, as in the PROMETHEUS UNBOUND, most felt in the earlier part of the work, and finally the poem takes leave of the Greek imagery and spirit, and in the manner of Spenser and Milton ends in the affirmation of the eternal blessedness of the spirit lost in the radiance of heavenly being. From Bion the picture of Aphrodite's mourning, accompanied by the weeping Loves, is transformed into Urania's mourning, accompanied by the Dreams; from Moschus the picture of the lamenting Satyrs, Priapi, Fanes, Fairies, Echo, nightingales, sea-birds, and others, is transformed into the sorrow of the Desires, Adorations, Persuasions, the elements, Echo, the season, the flowers, the nightingale and the eagle. From Moschus, also, the contrast of the life of the year with that of man, and the ascribing of the death to poison, and from Bion, the suffering of Urania on her journey, the kiss and the ascribing of the death to the 'dragon in his den' are derived, though these elements are originally treated, expanded, and varied. In Stanza xxviii., with the introduction of the circumstances and persons of the time, the contemporary element begins; the mourning of the idealized figures of the poets continues it; the curse upon the destroyer follows; and the final movement of the poem, its pæan of immortality, commencing at Stanza xxxix., is in the purely modern spirit, an overflow of Shelley's eloquence in his most characteristic phrases and ideas, — the best sustained, the most condensed, the most charged with purely spiritual passion in personal form, of any of his poems of hunger for eternity. The development of the poem, beginning with the poignancy of human grief rendered through images of beauty and the saddening of the things of earthly life however lovely, and then changing by subtle interpretations of the spirit evoking its own eternal nature in brooding over the dead form of what it loved, and ending at last in the triumphant reversion of its initial grief into joy in the presence of the eternal life foretasted in fixed faith and enduring love even here, — this is the classic form of Christian elegy. ADONAIS, as a work of art, effects this evolution of life out of death, with more unconsciousness, greater unity and steadfast tendency, with passion more spontaneous and irresistible, with melody more plaintive, eloquence more sweet and springing, imagination more comprehensive and sublime, than any other English elegy. It is artificial only to those whose minds are not yet familiarized with the language of imagery, — those to whom the gods of Greece speak an unknown tongue; it is cold only to those who confound personal grief with that universal sorrow for youthful death which has been the burden of elegy from the first; it is dark with metaphysics only to those who have not yet caught a single ray from the spirit of Plato. What particular mode of being Shelley had in mind as the lot of mankind hereafter is a matter of small concern. He used, here, the imagery of both the theory of pantheism and of personal immortality, apparently with indifference, though with a natural poetic clinging to the latter, as a thing of the concrete. The essential interest he felt was rather in the fact than the mode. Further statements, as to this, are given below; but it would, I think, be wrong to interpret ADONAIS as a pantheistic poem in any narrow, definite, or dogmatic sense. To my mind individuality survives in Shelley's conception of the eternal life here, as it does in

the other illustrations he has given of his faith, — say, for example, in the EPIPSYCHIDION.

Page 307. MOTTO, *Plato.* Cf. Shelley's translation TO STELLA, p. 519.

PREFACE, *Moschus*, 111–114. 'Poison came, Bion, to thy mouth — thou didst know poison. To such lips as thine did it come and was not sweetened? What mortal was so cruel that could mix poison for thee, or who could give thee the venom that heard thy voice? Surely, he had no music in his soul' (Lang's trans.).

Twenty-fourth year. Keats was twenty-five at his death, which occurred February 23, 1821.

Quarterly Review, April, 1818. The rupture of the blood vessel described below was in no way due to the effect of this criticism on Keats' spirits.

Calumniator. Shelley refers to Milman, but he was mistaken in thinking him his unknown assailant.

Lavished his fortune. The reference is to the family relations of Keats, and is apparently undeserved.

[The references to Bion and Moschus are to Meineke's edition, Berlin, 1856.]

Page 308. Stanza i. 1. Cf. Bion, 1.

ii. 1. Cf. Milton, *Lycidas*, 50.

ii. 3 *Urania.* Aphrodite Urania, though borrowing some elements from the conception of the Muse Urania.

ii. 7. Cf. Moschus, 53.

iii. 6, 7. Cf. Bion, 55, 96.

iv. 1. Cf. Moschus, 70.

iv. 2 *He*, Milton.

iv. 9. 'Homer was the first and Dante the second epic poet. . . . Milton was the third epic poet.' DEFENSE OF POETRY.

v. 3. The humbler poets.

vi. 3. The reference is to Keats' *Isabella.*

vii. 1 *Capital.* Rome.

vii. 7. Cf. Bion, 71.

viii. 5 *His extreme way to her dim dwelling-place.* The dissolution of the body.

viii. 6 *Hunger.* Corruption.

ix. 1 *Dreams.* Poems.

x. 1, 2. Cf. Bion, 85.

xi. 1, 2. Cf. Bion, 83, 84.

xi. 3–8. Cf. Bion, 80–82.

xii. 5 *death*, the dampness of death upon his lips.

xiii. Cf. Moschus, 26–29.

xiv. 3–6. The image is of a clouded dawn. Cf. xli. 6, 7.

xv. 6–9. Cf. Moschus, 30, 31.

xvi. 1–3. Cf. Moschus, 31, 32.

xvi. 5–6. Cf. Moschus, 6, 7, 32.

xvii. 1. Cf. Moschus, 38–48, 87–93. *Sister*, the reference is to Keats' *Ode to the Nightingale.*

xvii. 5. A reminiscence of Milton's *Areopagitica.*

xviii. Cf. Moschus, 101–106.

xxi. 6 *lends what life must borrow.* Reality is beyond the grave, the eternal substance, and mortal life derives its apparent reality from it, and is its shadow only.

xxii. 2. Cf. Shelley's translation of Bion, p. 520, where he introduces this phrase from his own invention.

xxii. 8. A thought of pain roused by memory.

xxiv. Cf. Bion, 21, 22, 65, and Plato, *Symposium*, 195; the stanza is blended of the three sources.

xxv. 3–5. Death ceased and life came back to the body, or with less vital imagery in line 9, 'Death rose and smiled' — the reanimation of the body being only a phantom of life.

xxvi. Cf. Bion, 43–53. In line 9 the turn given to the thought of Bion is singular, and in fact the words sound like an anticipation of the closing mood of the poem, and a direct expression of Shelley's own sadness.

xxvii. 1. Cf. Bion, 60, 61.

xxvii. 6 *shield*, the reference is to Perseus.

xxviii. 7 *Pythian*, Byron. The reference is to his *English Bards and Scotch Reviewers*.

xxix. The inferior contemporaries of genius share its mortal day of life, but being ephemeral, they are forgotten in death, as insects cease at sunset, while genius lives on as a star of immortal fame. The imagery is mixed.

xxx. 2 *magic mantles*, the reference is to Prospero.

xxx. 3 *Pilgrim*, Byron.

xxx. 8 *lyrist*, Moore.

xxxi. 1 *one*, Shelley.

xxxiii. Cf. REMEMBRANCE, iii. 4.

xxxiv. 4 *unknown land*, England.

xxxiv. 8, 9. Branded like Cain's and ensanguined like Christ's.

xxxv. 6 *He*, Leigh Hunt.

xxxvi. 1–9. Cf. Moschus, 111–114.

xxxvi. 6 *prelude*, i. e., what Keats had sung was but the prelude to the real song that death silenced.

xxxviii. 4. A reminiscence of Milton's *Paradise Lost*, iv. 829. With this stanza the poem begins the pæan of immortality which closes it, in harmony with the tradition of Milton and Spenser. Shelley resumes again the mood which had received such repeated and various illustration in his verse, and finally in EPIPSYCHIDION, and presents the opposition of Life to Death as the shadow to the substance, the night to the day, and declares the absorption of the soul of Keats into the Spiritual Power whose manifestations in our knowledge are Life, Beauty, and Love. Of the state of the dead, as individuals, he refrains from speaking, as he had refrained from the time of THE SUNSET, leaving it in uncertainty; of the permanence of the spirit in the eternal world he once more and for the last time speaks with passionate conviction, both as the infinite of being in original creative activity and as the hope, faith, and home of the human soul.

xl. Ackermann compares Spenser, *The Shepheardes Calendar*, xi. The resemblance is great; and so, in the case of other passages from this lament, the parallelism is clear; but I do not believe that the poem of Spenser was in Shelley's mind except secondarily through Milton's echoes of it in *Lycidas*.

xlii. The pantheistic suggestion in this and the following stanzas is strong; but it cannot be held that Shelley commits himself definitely to the theory of pantheism here any more than to the theory of individual immortality in xlv. and elsewhere. In xlii. 1–5 Shelley appears to have in mind the immortality of Keats through his poetry, which in interpreting Nature has mingled with it, and become in a sense a part of it (cf. Coleridge, *The Nightingale*, 30–33) to the apprehension of the mind that has been fed upon his music and imagination; and from this conception the passage is easy for Shelley to restate the idea in the higher and abstract terms of a union of Keats with the operant might of that power 'which has withdrawn his being to its own,' the same, of couse, with 'the burning fountain' of xxxviii.

xliii. The stanza is a repetition of the preceding; lines 1, 2 being identical with lines 1–5 in the former stanza, and lines 2–9 being identical with lines 6–9 of the former. The process of the operation of the 'One Spirit' is explained, — namely, that it reveals itself according to the nature of its medium. The union of the soul of Keats primarily with the Eternal Spirit, and secondarily with Nature, through which that Spirit is revealed, is clearly affirmed; but the loss of individuality is not affirmed, but on the contrary the suggestion of it remains in xlii. 2, xliv. 8, and is at once developed, with no sense of inconsistency, in xlv., xlvi. and is still felt as an element of the verse to the last line of the poem. The fact seems to be, as stated above, that Shelley used the imagery of pantheism and of personal immortality indifferently to express his faith in the continuance of the soul under unknown conditions of existence.

xliv. 7. The conflict of 'life and love' for the youth is familiar to Shelley's thought from the first. Cf. EPIPSYCHIDION, note.

xlv. 1. Those whom early death overtook before the accomplishment of their genius, of whom the three named are types.

xlvi. 3. Cf. LINES ON THE EUGANEAN HILLS, 269.

xlvi. 9. The reference is to Plato's epigram. Cf. Shelley's trans. p. 519.

xlvii. The germ of this stanza may, perhaps, be found in Coleridge's *Ode to France*, V. 18–20:

'Yet while I stood and gazed, my temples bare,
And shot my being through earth, sea and air,
Possessing all things with intensest love.'

The idea of the stanza seems to lie in the opposition between the insignificance of the individual and the infinity of his powers of comprehension and sympathy, which is, perhaps, the more obvious interpretation. It may be, however, that Shelley here indicates a way of approaching before death the mystical union which is in his thoughts; the idea would then be, — shoot thy being through the universe, and *then*, still comprehending all things in thy spirit, gather the universe back into thy individuality as a mortal in time, and standing thus at the utmost limit of earthly being, on the brink of eternity, fear lest at the moment of such exaltation thou shouldst sink in despair with a heavy heart, as Shelley so often represents such failure at the climax of emotion, in the EPIPSYCHIDION, the PROMETHEUS UNBOUND, the ODE TO LIBERTY, and elsewhere.

xlviii. 8–9. Cf. EPIPSYCHIDION, 209–212.

xlix. 7 *slope*, the Roman cemetery. Cf. PREFACE, pp. 307, 308. Shelley also describes it in a letter to Peacock, December 22, 1818: 'The English burying-place is a green slope near the walls, under the pyramidal tomb of Cestius, and is, I think, the most beautiful and solemn cemetery I ever beheld. To see the sun shining on its bright grass, fresh, when we visited it, with the autumnal dews, and hear the whispering of the wind among the leaves of the trees which have overgrown the tomb of Cestius, and the soil which is stirring in the sun-warm earth, and to mark the tombs, mostly of women and young people who were buried there, one might, if one were to die, desire the sleep they seem to sleep. Such is the human mind, and so it peoples with its wishes vacancy and oblivion.'

l. 3. The tomb of Cestius.

li. 3–5. Inquire not into another's grief. There may be an obscure reference to the fact that Shelley's child, William, was buried there.

lii. The opposition of the permanent to the transitory, of the ever shining light to the shadows of earthly life, of the 'white radiance of Eternity' to the prismatic colors of its 'portions' in time; Death as the Liberator and Restorer of the soul to true being, whose glory transcends its revelation in nature and the forms of art, — over these cardinal convictions of his poetry, long familiarized to his imagination, Shelley throws for the last time, the veil of words.

liii. The poem here becomes purely personal, and after the self-portraiture of this stanza, rises with vital lyric passion to its outburst of mingled worship, prophecy, and aspiration driving through the gulf of death on the verge of eternal life.

liv. The clearest, most comprehensive and most condensed expression of Shelley's conception of the infinite and its presence and operation in this life.

liv. 5–7. Cf. xliii. 5–8.

lv. 1 *breath*, the Infinite.

lv. 4. The reference to his own troubled career is clear.

lv. 9 *Beacons*, lights homeward.

Page 317. HELLAS. The sources of this drama have been studied by Dr. Richard Ackermann in his *Quellen, Vorbilder, Stoffe zu Shelley's Poetischen Werken*, 1890. HELLAS is based on Æschylus' *Persæ*, so far as its structure is concerned, and is indebted to that drama for some details. As in his other borrowings from the Greek, however, Shelley recreated the material into an original modern poem. In this instance, owing perhaps to the historical character of its main matter, he departs less from

his model, and does not develop the work at its close into 'something new and strange,' as in the PROMETHEUS UNBOUND and ADONAIS. He introduces, on the lips of the Wandering Jew, a metaphysical theory of existence, but does not evolve it to further issues of thought or imagination, and at the end he takes leave of the actual Greece and sings a hymn of the millennial land after the famous eclogue of Virgil. These are the two principal points in which he varies from the Æschylean model, unless the opening after Calderon be also included.

In the first instance Shelley apparently returned to his projected drama on the Book of Job, and adapting this idea to the situation of Greece attempted to blend the two subjects. The Prologue, rescued from his note-books by Dr. Garnett, represents this scheme. In it Christ appears as the genius presiding over the better fate of mankind, concentrating under his power as the incarnating spirit of civilization all those ideas of Freedom, Love, and social good which were dearest to Shelley; Satan similarly presides over their opposites, slavery, hatred, wrong in all its forms; and these two 'mighty opposites' are conceived, seemingly, after the analogy of the angelic intelligences animating and guiding the spheres, as each the spirit of his own orb of energy. Dr. Garnett cites, appositely, a passage from Johnson on Dryden, dealing with a similar idea; but it is not shown, nor does it seem to me at all likely, that Shelley knew the passage. Very little of the drama in this form was written, and Shelley abandoned it for the less ambitious shape in which HELLAS was created. The majesty of the persons, the grandeur of the conception, opening fresh avenues for poetic originality untried in any literature, and the loftiness of the execution in the few score lines he wrote, convince me that, had Shelley been equal to the task, this work would have far surpassed all his other poetry, including the PROMETHEUS UNBOUND, in sublime and novel power. And after long familiarity with his works I may perhaps be pardoned for owning that his faculty of creative imagination seems to me to exceed immeasurably his ability to execute conception. The weakness under which he so often describes himself as sinking was the weight of power, — of a rapid and intense creative faculty, as intellectual as it was imaginative, as concrete in operation as it was universal in intention, as rich in multitude as in unity, and constituting a power of genius beyond his mortal strength to sustain, both physically and artistically. He, for some reason, did not go on to this new task; and in the HELLAS he wrote, which derives its strength from his enthusiasm for freedom in practical struggle and his unfailing dream of good for man, there are, I think, signs of the lassitude of his power in the unusual way in which he leans not only on Æschylus, but on Shakespeare, Virgil, and others; in the repetition beyond his wont of ideas and images of his own former works, and in the use of accustomed phrases in his diction. The drama is, it is true, an improvisation, and as such, rapidly done, and naturally it is studded in these ways with reminiscences of others and of himself in style and matter; but, charged as it is with the love of liberty, the adoration of ancient Greece, and the hope of peace, and instinct as its choruses are with haunting melody of that strange sort where music seems to outvalue the words as a means of expression of the mood, yet one feels in it a wearied pulse, though the pulse still of one of 'the sons of light.'

SHELLEY'S NOTES ON HELLAS.

Line 60. Milan was the centre of the resistance of the Lombard league against the Austrian tyrant. Frederic Barbarossa burned the city to the ground, but liberty lived in its ashes, and it rose like an exhalation from its ruin. See Sismondi's *Histoire des Républiques Italiennes,* a book which has done much towards awakening the Italians to an imitation of their great ancestors.

Line 197. The popular notions of Christianity are represented in this chorus as true in their relation to the worship they superseded, and that which in all probability they will supersede, without considering their merits in a relation more universal. The first stanza contrasts the immortality of the living and thinking beings which inhabit the planets, and to use a common and inadequate phrase, *clothe themselves in matter,* with the transience of the noblest manifestations of the external world.

The concluding verses indicate a progressive state of more or less exalted existence, according to the degree of perfection which every distinct intelligence may have attained. Let it not be supposed that I mean to dogmatize upon a subject concerning which all men are equally ignorant, or that I think the Gordian knot of the origin of evil can be disentangled by that or any similar assertions. The received hypothesis of a Being, resembling men in the moral attributes of his nature, having called us out of non-existence, and after inflicting on us the misery of the commission of error, should superadd that of the punishment and the privations consequent upon it, still would remain inexplicable and incredible. That there is a true solution of the riddle, and that in our present state that solution is unattainable by us, are propositions which may be regarded as equally certain: meanwhile, as it is the province of the poet to attach himself to those ideas which exalt and ennoble humanity, let him be permitted to have conjectured the condition of that futurity towards which we are all impelled by an inextinguishable thirst for immortality. Until better arguments can be produced than sophisms which disgrace the cause, this desire itself must remain the strongest and the only presumption that eternity is the inheritance of every thinking being.

Line 245. The Greek Patriarch, after having been compelled to fulminate an anathema against the insurgents, was put to death by the Turks.

Fortunately the Greeks have been taught that they cannot buy security by degradation, and the Turks, though equally cruel, are less cunning than the smooth-faced tyrants of Europe. As to the anathema, his Holiness might as well have thrown his mitre at Mount Athos for any effect that it produced. The chiefs of the Greeks are almost all men of comprehension and enlightened views on religion and politics.

Line 563. A Greek who had been Lord Byron's servant commands the insurgents in Attica. This Greek, Lord Byron informs me, though a poet and an enthusiastic patriot, gave him rather the idea of a timid and unenterprising person. It appears that circumstances make men what they are, and that we all contain the germ of a degree of degradation or of greatness whose connection with our character is determined by events.

Line 598. It is reported that this Messiah had arrived at a seaport near Lacedæmon in an American brig. The association of names and ideas is irresistibly ludicrous, but the prevalence of such a rumor strongly marks the state of popular enthusiasm in Greece.

Line 815. For the vision of Mahmud of the taking of Constantinople in 1453, see Gibbon's *Decline and Fall of the Roman Empire,* vol. xii. p. 223.

The manner of the invocation of the spirit of Mahomet the Second will be censured as over subtle. I could easily have made the Jew a regular conjurer, and the Phantom an ordinary ghost. I have preferred to represent the Jew as disclaiming all pretension, or even belief, in supernatural agency, and as tempting Mahmud to that state of mind in which ideas may be supposed to assume the force of sensations through the confusion of thought with the objects of thought, and the excess of passion animating the creations of imagination.

It is a sort of natural magic, susceptible of being exercised in a degree by any one who should have made himself master of the secret associations of another's thoughts.

Line 1060. The final chorus is indistinct and obscure, as the event of the living drama whose arrival it foretells. Prophecies of wars, and rumors of wars, etc., may safely be made by poet or prophet in any age, but to anticipate, however darkly, a period of regeneration and happiness is a more hazardous exercise of the faculty which bards possess or feign. It will remind the reader 'magno *nec* proximo intervallo' of Isaiah and Virgil, whose ardent spirits, overleaping the actual reign of evil which we endure and bewail, already saw the possible and perhaps approaching state of society in which the '*lion shall lie down with the lamb,*' and 'omnis feret omnia tellus.' Let these great names be my authority and my excuse.

Line 1090. Saturn and Love were among the deities of a real or imaginary state of innocence and happiness. *All* those *who fell,* or the Gods of Greece, Asia, and Egypt; the *One who rose,* or Jesus Christ, at whose appearance the idols of the Pagan World were amerced of their worship; and *the many unsubdued,* or the monstrous objects of the idolatry of China, India, the Antarctic islands, and the native tribes of America, certainly have reigned over the understandings of men in conjunction or in succession, during periods in which all we know of evil has been in a state of portentous, and, until the revival of learning and the arts, perpetually increasing activity. The Grecian gods seem indeed to have been personally more innocent, although it cannot be said, that as far as temperance and chastity are concerned, they gave so edifying an example as their successor. The sublime human character of Jesus Christ was deformed by an imputed identification with a power who tempted, betrayed, and punished the innocent beings who were called into existence by his sole will; and for the period of a thousand years, the spirit of this most just, wise, and benevolent of men has been propitiated with myriads of hecatombs of those who approached the nearest to his innocence and wisdom, sacrificed under every aggravation of atrocity and variety of torture. The horrors of the Mexican, the Peruvian, and the Indian superstitions are well known.

Page 317. HELLAS. The motto is the one which Shelley asked Peacock to have placed on two seals, 'one smaller and the other handsomer; the device a dove with outspread wings, and this motto round it.'

Page 318. DEDICATION. *Mavrocordato*, a member of Shelley's Pisan circle of friends, of whom Shelley repeatedly wrote with enthusiam. He read *Antigone* with Mary, and the *Agamemnon* and *Paradise Lost* with Shelley.

PREFACE. *Goat-song*, THE CENCI.

Page 320. PROLOGUE. Dr. Garnett's note, on first publishing this fragment, gives all needed information about it. 'Mrs. Shelley informs us, in her Note on the *Prometheus Unbound*, that at the time of her husband's arrival in Italy, he meditated the production of three dramas. One of these was the *Prometheus* itself; the second, a drama on the subject of Tasso's madness; the third, one founded on the Book of Job; "of which," she adds, "he never abandoned the idea." That this was the case will be apparent from the following newly-discovered fragment, which may have been, as I have on the whole preferred to describe it, an unfinished Prologue to *Hellas*, or perhaps the original sketch of that work, discarded for the existing more dramatic, but less ambitious version, for which the *Persæ* of Æschylus evidently supplied the model. It is written in the same book as the original MS. of *Hellas*, and so blended with this as to be only separable after a very minute examination. Few even of Shelley's rough drafts have proved more difficult to decipher or connect; numerous chasms will be observed which, with every diligence, it has proved impossible to fill up; the correct reading of many printed lines is far from certain; and the imperfection of some passages is such as to have occasioned their entire omission. Nevertheless, I am confident that the unpolished and mutilated remnant will be accepted as a worthy emanation of one of Shelley's sublimest moods, and a noble earnest of what he might have accomplished, could he have executed his original design of founding a drama on the Book of Job. Weak health, variable spirits, and, above all, the absence of encouragement, must be enumerated as chief among the causes which have deprived our literature of so magnificent a work.

'Besides the evident imitation of the Book of Job, the resemblance of the first draft of *Hellas* to the machinery of Dryden's intended epic is to be noted. "He gives," says Johnson, summarizing Dryden's preface to his translation of Juvenal, "an account of the design which he had once formed to write an epic poem on the actions either of Arthur or the Black Prince. He considered the epic as necessarily involving some kind of supernatural agency, and had imagined a new kind of contest between the guardian angels of kingdoms, of which he conceived that each might be represented zealous for his charge without any intended opposition to the purposes of the Supreme Being, of which all created minds must in part be ignorant.

' "This is the most reasonable scheme of celestial interposition that ever was formed." '

[The references to Æschylus below are to Paley's third edition, London, 1870.]

Page 320. PROLOGUE.

Line 69 *giant Powers*, cf. Dr. Garnett's note above.

Line 87 *Aurora*, Greece.

Line 99. Cf. EPIPSYCHIDION, note.

Line 107. The familiar image of THE REVOLT OF ISLAM, I.

Line 139. The doctrine of the Furies in PROMETHEUS UNBOUND.

Line 146. A reminiscence of Lucretius, I. 64.

Page 322. *Chorus*. Cf. Calderon, *El Principe Constante*, I.

Line 46. Cf. ADONAIS, xix. 4.

Line 56. Cf. Æschylus, *Agamemnon*, 272.

Line 70 *Atlantis*, America.

Line 95 *thy*, Freedom's.

Line 128. Cf. Æschylus, *Persæ*, 178.

Line 133. Ahasuerus, the Wandering Jew.

Line 177. Cf. PROMETHEUS UNBOUND, II. i. 156.

Line 189. A reminiscence of PROMETHEUS UNBOUND, III. i.

Line 192. Cf. Plato, *Republic*, VI.

Line 195. Cf. Bacon, *Essays, Of Empire*.

Line 209. The theory here stated is the ordinary belief of transmigration.

Line 211. *A power*, Christ.

Line 224. The reference is to the Cross of Constantine.

Line 230. Cf. Milton, *Ode on the Nativity*, xix.–xxi.

Line 266. Cf. PROLOGUE, 172.

Line 303. *Queen*, England.

Line 307. Cf. Æschylus, *Persæ*, 207–212.

Line 373. Cf. Æschylus, *Persæ*, 449 *et seq.*

Line 447. Cf. PROLOGUE, 101.

Line 476. Cf. Æschylus, *Persæ*, 355–432, especially line 486 with 410, 494 with 408, 503 with 393, 505 with 420.

Line 587. Cf. ODE TO LIBERTY, xiii. 3–7.

Line 591. *Santons*, a sect of enthusiasts inspired by divine love and regarded as saints.

Line 696. The main metaphysical idea of the poem, the primacy of thought and its sole reality, begins here.

Line 701. Cf. PROLOGUE, 9.

Line 711. Cf. PROLOGUE, 121.

Line 729. Cf. Æschylus, *Agamemnon*, 734–735. Shelley quotes the passage in a letter to his wife, August 10, 1821.

Lines 767–806. The speech develops the philosophical theory alluded to above, line 696, and is variously reminiscent of Shakespeare (as are other passages of the drama) in style and diction.

Line 771. Cf. PROLOGUE, 19.

Lines 814–841. Cf. Gibbon, *Decline and Fall of the Roman Empire*, ch. 68.

Line 852–854. Cf. PROLOGUE, 161.

Line 860. The Phantom is possibly suggested by the figure of Darius in the *Persæ*. The passage has analogies with PROMETHEUS UNBOUND, I.

Line 906. The familiar image from Plato, *Symposium*, 195.

Line 925. Cf. THE CENCI, III. i. 247, and note.

Line 943. Cf. PROMETHEUS UNBOUND, IV. 444.

Line 985. The reference is to the Shield of Arthur, Spenser, *Faërie Queene*, Bk. I. *passim*.

Line 989. The Retreat of the Ten Thousand under Xenophon, told in the *Anabasis*.

Line 1030 *Evening land*. Here and in the following lines, America appears to furnish the elements of the idealized new age, which soon changes imaginatively into a glorification of a newly arisen ideal Greece.

Line 1060 *Chorus*. Cf. Virgil, *Eclogues*, iv. and Byron's *Isles of Greece*.

Page 340. THE TRIUMPH OF LIFE. This poem, the last work of Shelley, is obviously Italian in suggestion and manner, and is obscure to the ordinary reader. It is a pure and mystical allegory, in which Shelley has blended many elements of his intellectual culture under an imaginative artistic form of the Renaissance rarely modernized. The meaning, however, is not obscure to one who will let his mind dwell on and penetrate the imagery, after becoming familiarized with Shelley's previous works. A few notes only, and those of an obvious kind, can be given here.

Line 103. *that*, the charioteer.

Line 133. The sense is broken.

Line 190 *grim Feature*. Cf. Milton, *Paradise Lost*, x. 279.

Line 255. Socrates: because he did not love.

Line 261. Alexander and Aristotle.

Line 283. The Roman Emperors.

Line 290. The Papacy.

Line 352. The last and most mystical of the eternal beings of Shelley's phantasy.

Line 422. Mrs. Shelley's note: 'The favorite song, *Stanco di pascolar le ecorelli*, is a Brescian national air.'

Line 472 *him*, Dante.

Page 350. To ——. Cf. PETER BELL THE THIRD, V. i. note.

352. To MARY WOLLSTONECRAFT GODWIN, i.e. 3 *fear*, Rossetti suggests *yearn* to amend a plainly corrupt passage.

354. To WORDSWORTH, cf. PETER BELL THE THIRD, IV. ix. note.

355. Lines. If the poem refers to Harriet it is dated a year too early.

355. THE SUNSET, line 4. Cf. EPIPSYCHIDION, note.

Line 22. Forman conjectures *I never saw the sunrise? we will wake*, substituting a melodramatic for a natural effect.

356. HYMN TO INTELLECTUAL BEAUTY, cf. EPIPSYCHIDION, note. Mrs. Shelley's note is as follows: 'He spent the summer on the shores of the Lake of Geneva. *The Hymn to Intellectual Beauty* was conceived during his voyage round the Lake with Lord Byron. He occupied himself during this voyage by reading the *Nouvelle Héloïse* for the first time. The reading it on the very spot where the scenes are laid, added to the interest; and he was at once surprised and charmed by the passionate eloquence and earnest enthralling interest that pervades this work. There was something in the character of Saint-Preux, in his abnegation of self, and in the worship he paid to Love, that coincided with Shelley's own disposition; and, though differing in many of the views, and shocked by others, yet the effect of the whole was fascinating and delightful.' Ackermann refers to Spenser's *Hymns* as a source, but without plausibility. Cf. THE ZUCCA.

Stanza i. 1. Cf. THE REVOLT OF ISLAM, VI. xxxviii. 1.

Stanza iv. 1. *Self-esteem*, the use of *Self-esteem* and *Self-contempt* as measures of happiness and misery is constant from the earliest verse to ADONAIS, and is characteristic of his moral ideal. Cf. PROMETHEUS UNBOUND, *passim*.

Stanza v. Cf. THE REVOLT OF ISLAM, DEDICATION, iii.–v.

Stanza vii. 12. The line is, perhaps, the simplest and noblest statement of Shelley's ideal of his own life.

Page 357. MONT BLANC, i. The metaphysical intention of the symbol should be remembered as a part of the entire poem and as differentiating its scope from that of Coleridge on the same subject.

Line 79. *But for such faith*, the Boscombe MS. reads *In such a faith*, which yields the only intelligible meaning. The faith of Shelley's poetic age in the power of nature over human life could hardly find more startling statement than in the next two lines.

Line 96. This is an anticipation of the conception imaginatively defined in Demogorgon (cf. lines 139–141 below). This poem and the preceding HYMN are forerunners of the main lines of thought in the PROMETHEUS UNBOUND.

Page 362. To CONSTANTIA. The poem, as a whole, is a forerunner of PROMETHEUS UNBOUND, in its imagery of music as a power of motion in stanza iv., and in its diction (e. g. iii. 2) as well as in its lyrical rapture. The reminiscences of Plato and Lucretius in stanza ii. 7 and 11 are obvious. In the Harvard MS. the last stanza is first, but this may represent rather the order of composition than of true arrangement; certainly it belongs last, as it is the climax of emotion.

Page 363. To THE LORD CHANCELLOR, i. 4. The star-chamber.

iv. 3 cowl, cf. Dante, *Inferno*, XXIII.

xvi. 1. The close of the curse is characteristic of Shelley's moral ideal. In a similar way he brings his political odes, several of which are odes of agitation, such as ODE WRITTEN OCTOBER, 1819, and the ODE TO NAPLES to an end in counsels of love, forgiveness, and brotherhood after the storm of execration or of incitement had been exhausted in the earlier part.

Page 364. To WILLIAM SHELLEY. Mrs. Shelley adds to her note: 'When afterward this child died at Rome, he wrote, apropos of the English burying-ground in that city, "This spot is the repository of a sacred loss, of which the yearnings of a parent's heart are now prophetic; he is rendered immortal by love as his memory is by death. My beloved child lies buried here. I envy death the body far less than the oppressors the minds of those whom they have torn from me. The one can kill only the body, the other crushes the affections." '

Stanza iv. Cf. ROSALIND AND HELEN, 894–901.

Page 360. ON A FADED VIOLET. Cf. To SOPHIA, *Head-note*.

Stanza i. In the later edition of Mrs. Shelley this stanza reads:

The colour from the flower is gone
  Which like thy sweet eyes smiled on me:
The odour from the flower is flown
  Which breathed of thee and only thee.

In the next stanza she also reads *withered* for *shrivelled*. Her version is sustained by the Oxford MS. described by Zupitza. The text given is that of Hunt, 1821, Mrs. Shelley, 1824, and of the MS. as described by Rossetti.

Page 360. LINES WRITTEN AMONG THE EUGANEAN HILLS.

Line 175 *songs*. Forman conjectures *sons*, which destroys the highly imaginative unity of the figure and substitutes a mere mixed metaphor therefor. Byron is referred to.

Line 220. Cf. ŒDIPUS TYRANNUS, II. 60.

Line 319. Cf. THE REVOLT OF ISLAM, II. xxx. 2.

Line 344. Cf. EPIPSYCHIDION, note.

Page 372. INVOCATION TO MISERY. The story referred to in the Head-note was first told by Medwin. He writes, 'Had she [Mrs. Shelley] been able to disentangle the threads of the mystery, she would have attributed his feelings to more than purely physical causes. Among the verses which she had probably never seen till they appeared in print was the *Invocation to Misery*, an idea taken from Shakespeare — making love to Misery, betokening his soul lacerated to rawness by the tragic event above

detailed — the death of his unknown adorer.' *Life*, i. 330, 331. He refers to a story, previously told by him in *The Angler in Wales*, ii. 194, related by Shelley to him and Byron, that 'the night before his departure from London in 1814 [1816], he received a visit from a married lady, young, handsome, and of noble connections, and whose disappearance from the world of fashion, in which she moved, may furnish to those curious in such inquires a clue to her identity;' and he goes on to describe how, in spite of Shelley's entreaty and unknown to him, this lady followed him to the continent, kept near him, and at Naples, in this year, met him, told her wandering devotion, and there died (*Life*, i. 324–329). Medwin ascribes to this incident the next poem, and also the lines ON A FADED VIOLET. Rossetti (i. 90) says he is 'assured on good authority' that Medwin's connecting MISERY with these events is 'not correct.' Lady Shelley says: 'Of this strange narrative it will be sufficient to say here that not the slightest allusion to it is to be found in any of the family documents' (*Shelley Memorials*, p. 92). Rossetti connects with the story Shelley's letter to Peacock, May, 1820, in which he refers to his health as affected 'by certain moral causes,' and also his letter to Ollier, December 15, 1819, in which he expresses his intention to 'write three other poems [besides JULIAN AND MADDALO] the scenes of which will be laid at Rome, Florence, and Naples, but the subjects of which will be all drawn from dreadful or beautiful realities, as that of this was.' Miss Clairmont asserted that she knew the lady's name and had seen her. At Naples there died a little girl who was to some extent in Shelley's charge, and of whom he wrote with feeling. Dowden (ii. 252, 253) suggests some connection between the two incidents.

Page 377. ODE TO THE WEST WIND. Cf. THE REVOLT OF ISLAM, IX. xxi.–xxv.

379. AN ODE. Cf. STANZA, p. 436, and To THE LORD CHANCELLOR, xvi. 1, note.

380. THE INDIAN SERENADE. The most important variations of the text are ii. 3, *and the champak's*, iii. 7, *press it to thine own again;* and iii. 8, *must break*, from the Browning MS.

ii. 3. 'The buchampaca, the flower of the dawn, whose vestal buds blow with the sun's first ray, and fade and die beneath his meridian beam, leaving only their odour to survive their transient blooms.' Miss Owenson, *The Missionary*, ch. vi. p. 59; cf. also ch. vii. pp. 75, 76, and ALASTOR, 400, note.

Page 381. LOVE'S PHILOSOPHY. A MS. sent to Miss Stacey December 29, 1820, gives two interesting variations: i. 7, *In one spirit meet and;* ii. 7, *What is all this sweet work worth.* These readings are adopted by Forman and Dowden. Other variations exist.

Page 386. THE SENSITIVE PLANT, III. 66. The first edition, 1820, inserts the following:

Their moss rotted off them, flake by flake,
Till the thick stalk stuck like a murderer's stake,
Where rags of loose flesh yet tremble on high,
Infecting the winds that wander by.

The stanza is cancelled in the Harvard MS. and omitted by Mrs. Shelley, 1839. It is included by Rossetti and Forman.

Page 391. To a Skylark. The interesting Harvard MS. of this poem may be found in facsimile in the Harvard University Library Bibliographical Contributions, No. 35. Two emendations have been suggested; the transference of the semicolon, line 8, to the end of the previous line; and *embodied* for *unbodied*, line 15. Neither has been adopted by editors.

Page 392. Ode to Liberty. The poem is in the mood of Prometheus Unbound, of which it is reminiscent.

iii. 6. Cf. Prometheus Unbound, II. iv. 49.

v. 10. Cf. Prometheus Unbound, III. iv. 199, note.

vi. 1–4. Cf. Evening: Ponte al Mare, Pisa, iii. 1–4.

vii. 2. Shelley's note: 'See the *Bacchæ* of Euripides.'

viii. 14. *The Galilean serpent*, Christianity in its mediæval forms.

xii. 10. *Anarch*, Napoleon.

xiii. 3–7. Cf. Hellas, I. 587.

xiii. 12–15 *Twins*, England and Spain; *West*, America; *Impress . . . conceal*, the sense may be, impress us with your past which time cannot conceal. The passage is variously explained by Swinburne, Forman, and Rossetti. The suggested emendation of *as* for *us*, is not of itself sufficient to clarify the construction or meaning, but is possibly correct. Any explanation of the text appears unsatisfactory.

xvii. 9 *intercessor*. Cf. Prometheus Unbound, III. iii. 49–60; Ode to Naples, 69. The idea is suggested by Plato's theories in the *Phædrus* and *Symposium*; and is much developed by Shelley. Cf. Prince Athanase, II. 106–113, note.

Page 397. Arethusa. This and the following poem were written to be inserted in a drama entitled *Proserpine*, as the Hymns to Apollo and Pan were similarly written for a drama called *Midas*. Both dramas were the work of Williams. Zupitza describes the MSS. of these at length, with extracts, in *Archiv für das Studium der neuren Sprachen und Literaturen*, Band, xciv. Heft 1.

II. 8. The reading *unsealed* for *concealed* is given by Zupitza as that of the Oxford MS.; he interprets the passage 'the wind unsealed in the rear the urns of the snow,' *it* being pleonastic, and the *urns* meaning *the snow-springs*.

Page 398. Song of Proserpine, cf. Arethusa, note.

Page 398. Hymn of Apollo, cf. Arethusa, note.

Stanza vi. 6 *its* for *their* is given by Zupitza as the reading of the Oxford MS.

Page 399. Hymn of Pan, cf. Arethusa, note.

Stanza i. 5, 12. Zupitza gives *listening my* for *listening to my*, as the reading of the Oxford MS.

Stanzas ii., iii. Cf. Virgil, *Eclogues*, vi.

Page 399. The Question, ii. 7, cf. Coleridge, *To a Young Friend*, 37, 'the rock's collected tears.' The reading *heaven-collected*, Mrs. Shelley, 1824, adopted by Forman, is improbable in view of the citation, while the text is supported by the first issue of Hunt and the Harvard and Ollier MSS.

Page 400. Letter to Maria Gisborne.

Line 75. The *boat* and the *hollow screw* are the same.

Line 77 *Henry*, Mr. Reveley, Mrs. Gisborne's son.

Line 130. 'The Libecchio here howls like a chorus of fiends all day.' Shelley to Peacock, July 12, 1820.

Line 185. Mrs. Gisborne read Calderon with him.

Line 195. Cf. Time, 7.

Line 202. Cf. Peter Bell the Third, V. i. 3, note.

Line 226 *Hogg*, Thomas Jefferson Hogg, Shelley's friend, and biographer of his Oxford days.

Line 233 *Peacock*, Thomas Love Peacock, the novelist. The play on the name in the next line is obvious.

Line 250 *Horace Smith*, perhaps the wisest and best friend Shelley had.

Line 313. Shelley's note: '"Ιμερος, from which the river Himera was named, is, with some slight shade of difference, a synonym of Love.'

Page 405. Ode to Naples. The Oxford MS. is fully described by Zupitza.

Shelley's Notes:

Line 1. Pompeii.

Line 39. Homer and Virgil.

Line 104. Ææa, the island of Circe.

Line 112. The viper was the armorial device of the Visconti, tyrants of Milan.

Line 45. Zupitza gives *sunbright* for *sunlit* as the reading of the Oxford MS.

Line 69. Cf. Ode to Liberty, xvii. 9, note.

Line 109. Cf. Hellas, Shelley's notes, line 60.

Page 411. Good-night. A version known as the Stacey MS. is followed by Rossetti. It varies from the text as follows:

i. 1, Good-night? no, love! the night is ill

ii. 1, How were the night without thee good

iii. 1, The hearts that on each other beat

3, Have nights as good as they are sweet

4, But never *say* good-night

This version is poetically inferior, and may or may not represent Shelley's final choice for publication. The matter being uncertain, it seems best to retain the better form, especially as it is the one that has grown familiar, and is well supported by the authority of the Harvard MS. as well as by the first editors, Hunt and Mrs. Shelley.

Page 413. From the Arabic. Medwin gives Hamilton's *Antar* as the source of these lines, but the passage has not been identified.

Page 413. To Night, i. 1 *o'er*, the reading is from the Harvard MS.

ii. 3. The image is familiar in Shelley's verse. Cf. Alastor, 337, note.

Page 416. SONNET. Entitled in the Harvard MS., SONNET TO THE REPUBLIC OF BENEVENTO.

Page 417. ANOTHER VERSION. From the Trelawny MS., of Williams's play.

Page 417. EVENING: PONTE AL MARE, PISA, iv. 2. The Boscombe MS. reads *cinereous* for *enormous*, and is followed by Rossetti, Forman, and Dowden.

Page 418. REMEMBRANCE. Another version, known as the Trelawny MS., gives the following variations:

i. 2, 3, transpose.
5–7, As the earth when leaves are dead,
    As the night when sleep is sped,
    As the heart when joy is fled
8, alone, alone.
ii. 2, her.
5, My heart to-day desires to-morrow.
iii. 4, Sadder flowers find for me.
8, a hope, a fear.

The text follows the Houghton MS., a copy written on a fly-leaf of ADONAIS by Shelley.

Page 419. TO EDWARD WILLIAMS. Rossetti gives the following letter from Shelley to Williams:

'My dear Williams: Looking over the portfolio in which my friend used to keep his verses, and in which those I sent you the other day were found, I have lit upon these; which, as they are too dismal for *me* to keep, I send you. If any of the stanzas should please you, you may read them to Jane, but to no one else. And yet, on second thoughts, I had rather you would not. Yours ever affectionately, P. B. S.' Williams notes in his journal, Saturday, January 26, 1822: 'S. sent us some beautiful but too melancholy lines ("The Serpent is shut out from Paradise").' Byron named Shelley the Serpent.

Page 425. THE ISLE. Garnett conjectures that this poem was intended for the FRAGMENTS OF AN UNFINISHED DRAMA.

Page 425. A DIRGE, 6 *strain*, Rossetti's emendation for *stain*, given by all editors.

Page 426. LINES WRITTEN IN THE BAY OF LERICI. The lines were written during the last weeks of Shelley's life, perhaps, as Garnett conjectures, about May 1, the last time that Shelley was at Lerci at the time of the full moon.

Page 434. PRINCE ATHANASE. Cf. EPIPSYCHIDION, note.

II. 2. Cf. THE REVOLT OF ISLAM, II. xxvii. 7, note.

II. 15. Cf. PROMETHEUS UNBOUND, I. 451, note.

II. 103, *story of the feast*, the *Symposium*.

II. 106–113. This is the original germ of the *Spirit of the Earth* in PROMETHEUS UNBOUND, not perhaps without some indebtedness to Coleridge, *Ode on the Departing Year*, iv. The same passage may also have been not without influence on Shelley's idea of the 'intercessors' (cf. PROMETHEUS UNBOUND, III. iii. 49–60; ODE TO NAPLES, 69; ODE TO LIBERTY, xvii. 9, note), and of the guardian angels of the PROLOGUE TO

HELLAS. Shelley, however, entirely recreates the image in these several instances, and shows his highest original power in so doing.

II. 118. Cf. Shelley, ON LOVE, under EPIPSYCHIDION, note.

Page 441. TASSO. Garnett gives from the Boscombe MS. Shelley's notes for intended scenes of this drama: 'Scene when he reads the sonnet which he wrote to Leonora to herself as composed at the request of another. His disguising himself in the habit of a shepherd, and questioning his sister in that disguise concerning himself, and then unveiling himself.' Rossetti identifies the passage in Sismondi (Paris, 1826), viii. 142–143.

Page 445. LINES WRITTEN FOR PROMETHEUS UNBOUND. Cf. PROMETHUS UNBOUND, IV. iv. 493.

Page 446. LINES WRITTEN FOR EPIPSYCHIDION. Cf. EPIPSYCHIDION, note.

Page 448. LINES WRITTEN FOR ADONAIS. Rossetti suggests, rightly, I think, that the first fragment refers to Moore, the lyre being the Irish harp, and he transposes the first and second fragments. In the latter *green Paradise* is Ireland. In the last fragment Rossetti is unable to find any human figure, and in this he also appears to be right.

Page 456. GINEVRA. Garnett identified the source as *L'Osservatore Fiorentino sugli edifizi della sua Patria*, 1821, p. 119. In the story Ginevra revives. Cf. Hunt, *A Legend of Florence*.

Page 459. THE BOAT ON THE SERCHIO, line 30. Cf. THE TRIUMPH OF LIFE, 18.

Line 40. Cf. TRANSLATIONS FROM DANTE, V. 13.

Page 460. THE ZUCCA. Cf. EPIPSYCHIDION, note, and FRAGMENTS OF AN UNFINISHED DRAMA, 127.

Page 462. CHARLES THE FIRST. The Headnotes contain the history of the fragment.

Page 476. FRAGMENTS OF AN UNFINISHED DRAMA. This poem is the most characteristic example of the last manner of Shelley in verse. It is shot through with reminiscences of his own work and with those of the poets he had long used as familiar masters and guides; the sentiment is as before; the material is not different; but over all, and pervading all, is a new charm, original, pure, and delicate, which makes the verse a new kind in English.

Page 480. MINOR FRAGMENTS. The available information regarding these poems is given in the Head-notes.

Page 491. TRANSLATIONS. The Head-notes contain the records of these compositions. The text of THE CYCLOPS has been examined by Swinburne, *Essays and Studies*, 201–211. In SCENES FROM THE FAUST OF GOETHE, a slight correction, *joy* for *you*, ii. 333 (p. 545), is made in accordance with Zupitza's suggestion.

Page 547. JUVENILIA. The Head-notes include all that is known of the history of these pieces.

INDEX OF FIRST LINES

[Including the first lines of independent songs contained in the longer poems and dramas.]

INDEX OF TITLES